Child Psychology

Child Psychology

A Handbook of Contemporary Issues

Second Edition

Edited by

Lawrence Balter
Catherine S. Tamis-LeMonda

Psychology Press
New York • Hove

Published in 2006 by
Psychology Press
Taylor & Francis Group
270 Madison Avenue
New York, NY 10016

Published in Great Britain by
Psychology Press
Taylor & Francis Group
27 Church Road
Hove, East Sussex BN3 2FA

Printed in the United States of America on acid-free paper
10 9 8 7 6 5 4 3 2 1

International Standard Book Number-10: 1-84169-415-0 (Hardcover)
International Standard Book Number-13: 978-1-84169-415-3 (Hardcover)
Library of Congress Card Number 2005002646

Library of Congress Cataloging-in-Publication Data

Child psychology : a handbook of contemporary issues / edited by Lawrence Balter,
    Catherine S. Tamis-LeMonda.-- 2nd ed.
        p. cm.
    Includes bibliographical references.
    ISBN 1-84169-415-0 (hardcover : alk. paper)
    1. Child psychology. I. Balter, Lawrence. II. Tamis-LeMonda, Catherine S. (Catherine Susan), 1958-

BF721.C5155 2005
155.4--dc22
                                                                                2005002646

Taylor & Francis Group
is the Academic Division of Informa plc.

Visit the Taylor & Francis Web site at
http://www.taylorandfrancis.com

and the Psychology Press Web site at
http://www.psypress.com

To Karen, for her endless dedication and support.
—LB

For Brittany, Christopher, and Michael, who taught
me many truths about child development.
—CTL

Contents

Part III: Childhood

Part IV: Adolescence

Part V: Ecological Influences

Contributors

J. Lawrence Aber
New York University

Jeffrey Jensen Arnett
Journal of Adolescent Research

Meredith A. Bachman

Lawrence Balter
New York University

Bronwyn E. Becker
New York University

Jay Belsky
University of London

Marc H. Bornstein
National Institute for Child Health and Human Development

Robert H. Bradley
University of Arkansas, Little Rock

Jeanne Brooks-Gunn
Columbia University

Tonia N. Cristofaro
New York University

Robert F. Corwyn
University of Arkansas, Little Rock

Judy S. DeLoache
University of Virginia

Joanne Agayoff Deocampo
Rutgers University

Laura M. DeRose
Columbia University

Jacquelynne S. Eccles
University of Michigan

Nancy Eisenberg
Arizona State University

Richard A. Fabes
Arizona State University

Jennifer Fredricks

Andrew Fuligni

Mikal Galperin
University of Texas, Dallas

Elizabeth T. Gershoff
University of Michigan

Melissa L. Greene
Cornell University

Wendy S. Grolnick
Clark University

Lowry Hemphill
Harvard University

Carollee Howes
University of California, Los Angeles

Judith A. Hudson
Rutgers University

Diane Hughes
New York University

Aletha C. Huston
University of Texas, Austin

Robert D. Kavanaugh
Williams College

Carolyn O. Kurowski
Clark University

Linda Lee
University of California, Los Angeles

Michelle D. Leichtman
University of New Hampshire

Jacqueline V. Lerner
Boston College

Richard M. Lerner
Tufts University

Lynn S. Liben
The Pennsylvania State University

L. Oriana Linares
New York University

Linda L. Liu
University of Michigan

Lara Mayeux
University of Oklahoma

Jannette M. McMenamy
Clark University

Cindy Faith Miller
New York University

Nicole A. Morin
New York University

Barbara Alexander Pan
Harvard University

Paul C. Quinn
University of Delaware

Marika N. Ripke
University of Hawaii, Manoa

Eileen T. Rodriguez
New York University

Robert Roeser
Stanford University

Diane N. Ruble
New York University

Ellyn G. Sheffield
Rutgers University

Catherine Snow
Harvard University

Catherine S. Tamis-LeMonda
New York University

Hanns Martin Trautner
New York University

Paola Uccelli
Harvard University

Marion K. Underwood
University of Texas, Dallas

David H. Uttal
Northwestern University

Mira Vida

Theodore D. Wachs
Purdue University

Niobe Way
New York University

Allan Wigfield
University of Maryland, College Park

Preface

Since the first edition of the book, the field of developmental psychology has continued to grow at an extraordinary pace. Increasingly sophisticated and varied research methods now make it possible to examine the highly complex interactions among the many interrelated factors that contribute to children's cognitive, emotional, and social development. It is with these considerations in mind that we undertook our second edition.

The second edition of *Child Psychology: A Handbook of Contemporary Issues* is a new book in many ways. Although we retained a similar overall structure, and many of the contributors from the previous edition appear in this volume, there are significant changes from the earlier edition. To begin, chapters that appeared in the previous edition have been updated. Second, contributions from a number of outstanding researchers who did not appear in the previous edition have been introduced in various sections of this book. Third, a new section on adolescence has been introduced, which constitutes a major change that increases this volume's value as a comprehensive and practical course-related resource. Fourth, the section on ecological influences offers enhanced and extended coverage on contextual factors in development.

This edition builds on the four cornerstones that formed the basis of the chapters appearing in the earlier edition: (1) describing the nature of development and individual variation in developmental trajectories across multiple domains (social, emotional, cognitive, and language development); (2) attending to the multiple contexts or settings within which development unfolds—including family, school, neighborhood, and culture; (3) identifying the processes/mechanisms that underlie developmental and contextual change; and (4) applying cutting-edge research designs, methodologies, and analytic approaches to models of development and contextual change. These are covered in five sections: Infancy, Preschool Years, Childhood, Adolescence, and Ecological Influences.

Chapters in this handbook emphasize the nature of development and change. What is changing over the course of development and how might individual variation in patterns and trajectories of change be characterized? On the one hand, developmental researchers continue to make great strides in documenting what are referred to as "species-typical progressions" or "universal developmental processes." Chapters throughout this book present rigorous studies on developmental progressions that are *common* across the majority of infants, children, and youth in the domains of cognition, language, and social and emotional development. The authors complement these findings with equal consideration of intra- and interindividual variation across stages of reorganization. Why do different infants/children/youths display *different* patterns of developmental change? Differences among individuals are regarded as central to the generation and testing of developmental theories, rather than as random noise in the system.

Authors highlight the multiple, nested settings in which individuals develop. Families, schools, communities, and the overarching beliefs, ideologies, and practices of cultures and subcultures synergistically shape children's development. When the unique characteristics of individual children are added to the equation, the challenge of understanding human development increases exponentially. Contexts are continually changing as well, at both "micro" and "macro" levels. For example, family interactions, the structuring of the home environment, and teachers' engagements change in response to characteristics of individual children from moment-to-moment, day-to-day, and over lengthier time frames. At a more "macro" level, institutions, schools, and neighborhoods change in response to social, political, and historical pressures. A task for developmental researchers is to document and understand these contextual changes in relation to social, cognitive, and emotional developments in children and youth. In response to this challenge, this second edition of the handbook contains a new section that emphasizes multiple contexts of development.

The field of developmental psychology has shifted away from an emphasis on describing the chronology of specific milestones, to a focus on theory and process, and this newer emphasis is evident throughout the chapters of this handbook. It is insufficient to describe a particular pattern or direction of change across successive ages in the absence of theories about how and why such changes occur. Identifying the start and end points of a specific developmental achievement is only the first step. How and why do children transition from point 1 to point 2? What mechanisms or processes underlie development? At a more concrete, empirical level, the challenge is to identify variables that are responsible for observed changes in specific constructs. The laws that govern change, the mechanisms underlying change, and the rules by which changes occur are central to developmental science.

The chapters of this volume present a plethora of rigorous research designs, methodologies, and analytic approaches that are commonly used in the study of development. This handbook, as its predecessor, contains original research by prominent investigators who address various issues in contemporary developmental research within their individual areas of expertise. These investigators each showcase their original research, and the product is a book that is replete with examples drawn from the full array of developmental methodologies. The diversity of research methods that are presented span laboratory experiments with infants; naturalistic observations of infants, children, and youth in homes and schools; surveys, qualitative interviews, and narratives with children, youth, parents, and teachers; and large-scale national studies on policies, neighborhood and poverty contexts, and preventive interventions.

The four developmental themes—the nature of change, the mechanisms/processes of change, developmental contexts, and multiple-methodological approaches—lie at the core of the contemporary research that is presented in this book. The book is divided into five sections.

The first section, Infancy, spans the period from birth to approximately age 3. This section highlights critical early achievements across the domains of development, including emotional self regulation (Grolnick, McMenamy, and Kurowski), temperament (Wachs), attachment (Belsky), language development (Tamis-LeMonda, Cristofaro, Rodriguez, and Bornstein), and perceptual organization and categorization (Quinn). These chapters demonstrate approaches to studying the competencies of babies and toddlers and the multiple factors that affect the earliest foundations of learning and development.

The section on the Preschool Years delves into the emerging cognitive, linguistic, and social-emotional competencies of this important period. As children bridge the period between infancy and childhood, their world widens to include new ways of engaging with peers, representing and acting upon their worlds, and reflecting on and talking about past and current experiences. These themes are captured in the five chapters of the section, which cover the topics of peer relations (Howes and Lee), pretend play and theory of mind (Kavanaugh), symbolic development (Uttal, Liu, and DeLoache), children recollections of the past (Hudson, Sheffield, and Deocampo), and narratives and story telling (Uccelli, Hemphill, Pan, and Snow).

The section on Childhood highlights developments that coincide with children's entry into school and their experiences across the middle school years. During this period of development, peer relationships become increasingly central to the formation of identity, and social comparisons permeate social constructions and interactions. Children's views about gender, self, and others shape psychological and behavioral patterns. Socioemotional competencies, newly emerging cognitive skills, and motivational factors are paramount in children's well-being and school success. These themes are reflected in the five chapters in this section, which cover peer relationships (Underwood, Mayeux, and Galperin), spatial and graphic representation (Liben), gender development (Miller, Trautner, and Ruble), academics and motivation (Eccles, Roeser, and Wigfield), and socioemotional functioning (Eisenberg and Fabes).

Section four represents a major addition to this volume. It focuses on issues that lie at the core of adolescence. Adolescence represents a period of major physical, cognitive, and social-emotional change.

As individuals set upon the path that leads them from the world of childhood to the responsibilities of emerging adulthood, they navigate a multitude of challenges and tasks that lay the foundation for the later years. These are captured in the four chapters that address issues such as pubertal changes (DeRose and Brooks-Gunn), the deeper meanings and qualities of friendships (Way, Becker, and Greene), the development of positive behavioral characteristics and outlooks (Lerner, Lerner, and colleagues), and conceptions of what it means to be an adult (Arnett).

The fifth section, Ecological Influences, reflects increasing appreciation of the ways in which various contexts interact to affect developmental trajectories. Here the focus is on the settings that are inextricably linked to children's cognitive, linguistic, and social-emotional capacities. The chapters highlight the roles of parents (Bradley and Corwyn), poverty (Ripke and Huston), family and community violence (Linares and Morin), culture (Leichtman), racial socialization (Hughes, Bachman, Ruble, and Fuligni), and neighborhoods and schools (Gershoff and Aber).

In summary, this edition of *Child Psychology: A Handbook of Contemporary Issues* brings to the reader a substantially updated and significantly expanded assortment of contributions. The topics are wide-ranging, the methodologies are varied, and the contexts are diverse. The programmatic research that has been prepared by an exceptional group of experts and is presented in these pages reflects the latest advances in the field of developmental psychology. The handbook provides professionals and advanced students with material that is comprehensive, cutting edge, and creative.

—Lawrence Balter and Catherine S. Tamis-LeMonda
New York University

ACKNOWLEDGMENT

Catherine S. Tamis-LeMonda wishes to acknowledge funding from NSF #0218159 to support NYU's Center for Research on Culture, Development, and Education.

Part I

Infancy

Emotional Self-Regulation in Infancy and Toddlerhood

Wendy S. Grolnick
Jannette M. McMenamy
Carolyn O. Kurowski

INTRODUCTION

How do young children calm themselves when they are upset? What factors contribute to children's abilities to modulate distress and to "rev up" when it is playtime? What are the consequences for adaptive behavior of being facile at managing distress? These questions fall under the broad rubric of emotion regulation, and, more particularly, the development of emotional self-regulation. This topic cuts across traditionally separate areas in psychology such as temperament, neurophysiology, motivation, and personality. One of the reasons the area has become popular in the field of child development is that it is a broad rubric that can account for how and why emotions organize and facilitate various psychological processes such as attention and problem solving, or, alternatively disrupt such processes (Cole, Martin, & Dennis, 2004). In addition, emotion regulation applies to the life span (Cicchetti, Ganiban, & Barnett, 1991): While clearly the capacity to regulate emotion changes with age, even newborns have rudimentary strategies for dealing with emotions.

The past few years have seen increasing interest in the development of emotion regulation. Several volumes have been devoted to the topic (e.g., *Infancy*, Vol. 3(2), 2002) and comment and debate about conceptual and methodological issues in the field have received journal space (e.g., Bridges, Denham, & Ganiban, 2004; Cole, Martin, & Dennis, 2004). Some of our recent progress in understanding the development of emotion regulation has been the result of advances in related areas such as the development of attention (e.g., Posner & Rothbart, 2000) and the neurophysiological bases of reactivity (e.g., Fox & Calkins, 2003). Further, methodological additions such as the use of temporal analysis (e.g., Buss & Goldsmith, 1998) have allowed us to increasingly take a process view of emotion regulation. All of these advances contribute to a reaffirmation that emotion regulation is a construct that allows us to better understand children's developmental pathways.

The area of emotional self-regulation highlights the changing role of the self in the development of emotion regulation. In our work, we have been interested in the processes by which children develop the internal mechanisms to "self-regulate" emotion; that is, to be the origin of such capacities. Using self-determination theory (Deci & Ryan, 1985), we conceptualize the development of emotional self-regulation as a movement from reliance on outside sources or control-related processes to a growing capacity for autonomous, flexible, smooth, and adaptive regulation. We see this movement as an active process, part of the organism's innate propensity to master and become autonomous with respect to both his or her internal and external environments. Self-determination theory provides a way for us to understand the processes through which the development of emotion regulation takes place, including its energization and the factors which facilitate or forestall it.

In this chapter, we present a theory of the development of emotional self-regulation, focusing in particular on the toddler and early preschool years. We begin by describing the functionalist approach to emotions which underlies our work. We then tie this view of emotions to the concept of emotion regulation. Next, we describe self-determination theory, the lens through which we view the development of emotional self-regulation. Given the varied use of terminology in the literature, we include a section on key distinctions such as those between emotion control and emotion regulation and emotion management versus emotional integration. Following this, we provide an in-depth discussion of our framework for understanding the development of emotional self-regulation that includes a review of empirical support for our theory. Drawing on our own work and that of others (e.g., Calkins, 1994; Kopp, 1989), we also present a model of factors that contribute to emotional self-regulation, including those within the child (temperament) and aspects of the social environment (caregiver practices). We conclude by discussing some of the conceptual and methodological issues facing emotion regulation researchers, the implications of emotion regulation for adaptation, and the directions for future research.

TOWARD A DEFINITION OF EMOTIONAL SELF-REGULATION

To provide an understanding of our view of emotional self-regulation first entails placing our work within a general framework of emotion. Underlying our conceptualization is a functionalist view of emotions (e.g., Campos, Campos, & Barrett, 1989). This view suggests that emotions are evolutionarily adapted responses that have motivating and organizing functions which help individuals in the pursuit of their goals (Campos, Campos, & Barrett, 1989). Emotions, which register the significance of a mental or physical event (Campos, Frankel, & Camras, 2004), allow rapid appraisals of experience and prepare the individual for action. Stressing the goal-directed nature of emotion, Barrett and Campos (1987) described the functions, both intra- and interpersonal, of emotions in individuals' goal-oriented behavior. According to their theory, anger, for example, could be viewed as the result of a person trying to overcome an obstacle. It signals to the self to mobilize energy to try and overcome the obstacle as well as to others that they should submit to the individual. Joy has the function of maintaining the individual's behavior and of signaling to others to keep the interaction going (Emde, 1988). If emotions are viewed in this way, the goal of emotion regulation processes would not necessarily be to diminish or suppress emotions but, rather, to facilitate the adaptive use of emotions. Thus, there is no good or bad way of experiencing or expressing emotion—the context determines its usefulness (Campos, Frankel, & Camras, 2004).

Definitions of emotion regulation generally focus on changes in emotions. Campos, Mumme, Kermoian, and Campos (1994) described emotion regulation as the process of maintaining or changing an emotional stance. Fox (1994) described emotion regulation as the ability to modulate affect in terms of socially and culturally defined norms and Cole, Martin, and Dennis (2004) define it as a change in activated emotion. In his comprehensive definition, Thompson (1994) defined emotion regulation as "the extrinsic and intrinsic processes responsible for monitoring, evaluating, and modifying emotional reactions, especially their intensive and temporal features, to accomplish one's goals" (pp. 27–28). Inherent in this definition is the notion of modulation or management of emotion—the common thread across most definitions—as well as the functionalist idea that the way one expresses and experiences emotion may affect behavior in the individual's pursuit of various ends.

Recent work has questioned the notion of change in emotion as the definition of emotion regulation (e.g., Campos, Frankel, & Camras, 2004; Eisenberg & Spinrad, 2004). Theorists, for example, have suggested that emotion regulation can precede an emotion, such as when a person avoids a situation that he or she sees as potentially distressing. Thus, definitional issues remain a controversial topic in the field.

We have defined emotional self-regulation broadly as the set of processes involved in initiating, maintaining, and modulating emotional responsiveness, both positive and negative (Grolnick, Bridges, & Connell, 1996). We include positive and negative emotions because, consistent with a functionalist perspective, we recognize that both types of emotion serve adaptive functions for the child. In addition, we include not only the modulation and termination of emotional responsiveness but also its initiation and maintenance. While most research on emotion regulation has focused on the dampening of negative emotions, the goals of children and adults might well be served by the enhancement and maintenance of emotional arousal, both negative and positive (Thompson, 1994). For example, initiating positive emotions may involve caretakers in play and other positive exchanges. Intensification of anger might help to mobilize action, such as enabling oneself to stand up for one's rights or state one's needs. The inclusion of the initiation and maintenance of emotional states allows for a more comprehensive account of the function of emotion regulation in goal-directed behavior.

A SELF-DETERMINATION PERSPECTIVE

Our developmental view of emotional self-regulation centers around the construct of autonomy and is based on self-determination theory. This theory stresses the key roles of three psychological needs—autonomy, competence, and relatedness—for motivated action. Self-determination theory can be characterized as an organismic theory stressing that development is a motivated process which emanates from the organism (Deci & Ryan, 1985). According to this viewpoint, individuals are born with innate tendencies to operate on their inner and outer environments in attempts to master them. Underlying this tendency to master, organize, and overtake oneself is the energy source referred to as *intrinsic motivation*. Intrinsic motivation, then, fuels the seeking out of novelty, pursuit of challenges, and other growth-promoting experiences. In short, intrinsic motivation is the fuel for development.

The theory further postulates three psychological needs underlying intrinsic motivation. The first need is to feel autonomous or to feel that one's actions emanate from oneself. A second is to feel competent in dealing with the environment, including both the internal and external environments. A third need is for relatedness or connectedness with important others. These needs are complementary. For example, one can fulfill needs for autonomy and relatedness by being choicefully connected to another person.

From this viewpoint, children will naturally move toward autonomy, competence, and relatedness, as long as the environment does not thwart this movement. Applying this concept to emotional development, movement toward more active, self-initiated regulation is an expression of children's natural tendencies toward growth and development more generally in the direction of autonomy, competence, and relatedness. Children fulfill needs for autonomy as they experience a greater sense of agency in the expression of emotion as well as a greater capacity to use the information contained in their emotional experiences to serve their goals. Autonomous regulation is the converse of being other-reliant in one's emotion regulation or of being overwhelmed by emotional experiences, both of which lack a sense of self as an active regulator of one's experience. Also, as children take more responsibility for regulating emotion, they obtain a sense of competence as they master impulses and emotions rather than being overtaken by them. Finally, as children move toward greater self-regulation of emotion, they are able to fulfill the goals that others have for them, such as expressing emotions in a socially acceptable manner (Kopp, 1989). In addition, they are more likely to be able to initiate and maintain positive interactions with others. Both of these tendencies bring them closer to others and increase their sense of relatedness to them. In these ways, autonomy and relatedness work together and enhance one another.

While children will naturally move toward greater autonomy, competence, and relatedness with respect to emotional processes, there are aspects of development in relation to emotion regulation that are not natural or spontaneous. For example, modulating the expression of strong negative emotions is not something that children are intrinsically motivated to do but, rather, it represents the social expectations of children's caregivers and social groups. Such regulation first must be accomplished through caregiver prompts and interventions. The taking on of initially externally regulated behaviors or strategies falls under the rubric of internalization (Grolnick, Ryan, & Deci, 1997; Ryan, Connell, & Deci, 1985). *Internalization* is the means through which regulatory processes that originally are external in origin become transformed into part of the personal repertoire of the child. Intrinsically motivated activities as well as the internalization of extrinsically afforded regulations are the two major strands of development. As such, they both are fueled by intrinsic motivation and the underlying needs for autonomy, competence, and relatedness.

Another relevant aspect of this theory is the specification of environments that facilitate or inhibit intrinsically motivated activity and the internalization of externally afforded regulations. A corollary of the theory is that environments which support the child's needs for autonomy, competence, and relatedness will facilitate the two processes of intrinsic motivation and internalization, and those undermining these needs will forestall them. In particular, we have suggested that environments characterized by support for autonomy, structure, and involvement facilitate the development of behavioral self-regulation (Grolnick & Ryan, 1989), and we have now expanded this theory to the emotional realm (Ryan, Deci, & Grolnick, 1995). We will return to this social-contextual aspect of the theory in the Caregiver Contributions section.

DISENTANGLING CONCEPTS

Emotional Control Versus Regulation

Consistent with a functionalist perspective, emotion regulation is a flexible process that allows the individual to use emotional responses to pursue his or her goals. Consequently emotion regulation is not just a matter of controlling or stifling internal responses. In managing their arousal, some children will exert great effort, forcing themselves to push emotions out of awareness. The experience of such regulation is one of feeling pressured or controlled. Controlling emotions in this way requires energy and attention and diminishes the child's capacity to engage with the environment. It also does not allow one to adaptively use the information inherent in the emotional experience. The chronic stifling or controlling of emotions may play a role in problem behavior or psychopathology (Buck, 1984). Other children may regulate emotions, even relatively strong distress, by engaging in alternative activities or by talking about their disappointment. They may be able to more flexibly choose strategies to manage emotions that allow them to solve the problem presented by the particular situation. Such emotion management has more of the quality of autonomous emotion regulation.

Others, theorists, notably Kopp (1982) and Block and Block (1980), have made distinctions between emotion control and emotion regulation. Kopp (1982), for example, discussed self-control and self-regulation as stages in the child's development of behavior regulation. In the stage of self-control, the child has the ability to comply with the caregiver's demands and directives in the absence of the caregiver. Though emitted by the child, the behavior is rigid, conforming to the original directive. In contrast, the stage of self-regulation involves the flexible guiding of behavior. The child's behavior at this point is actively and flexibly adjusted to meet the demands of new situations. We concur with this distinction between control and regulation; however, we do not see these as developmental stages but, rather, as a continuum of regulation which is a function both of development and individual differences among children. While for Kopp (1982) the stage of self-control is not considered to begin until the second year, our emotional self-regulatory continuum is relevant from birth. As children develop, they move toward greater autonomy. In addition, within any age, children can be characterized as being at a more or less self-regulated point on the continuum.

Block and Block (1980) described the concepts of ego resiliency and ego control. *Ego control* involves the expression or inhibition of feelings, desires, and impulses. *Ego overcontrol* involves the suppression of action and expression across contexts regardless of the appropriateness of such actions and expressions. *Ego undercontrol* involves the expression of impulses regardless of context. *Ego resiliency*, on the other hand, is the extent to which ego control is modifiable based on contextual input. It is the extent to which the individual can meet contextual demands by altering the expression or containment of impulses and behavior. Similar to the concept of ego resiliency, the goal of emotional self-regulation is not to inhibit emotion, but to flexibly modulate the expression and containment of emotional arousal and to adaptively use the information provided by one's emotional arousal.

Finally, Mischel's (1974) concept of delay of gratification is also relevant to the issue of emotional control versus emotion regulation. Research on delay of gratification focuses on children's abilities to restrict behavior in tempting situations (Mischel, 1974). The typical paradigm involves placing a desired object near the child and asking the child to refrain from touching the object until a certain time. The dependent variable in such experiments is time to delay behavior. Though informative in terms of assessing children's inhibition of impulses, the paradigm does not allow one to determine the nature of the regulatory processes through which children are able to delay. For example, delay behavior can be accomplished through self-imposed pressure which results in the experience of tension and discomfort and the suppression of other adaptive behaviors. Alternately, individuals can delay smoothly through the use of attention deployment and diversion which allows for engagement in other adaptive behaviors. Our experimental paradigms are designed to examine behavior during mildly stressful periods so that the specific processes through which distress is regulated can be examined.

EMOTION MANAGEMENT VERSUS EMOTIONAL INTEGRATION

In discussing the issue of emotion regulation, we distinguish between emotion management per se, which involves the face of expression to the outside world, and emotional integration. When autonomously regulating emotions, individuals use emotions as guides to behavior, choicefully integrating the information inherent in them. The goal of emotional integration not only is to comply with social norms or act in opposition to one's experiences, but also to use one's inner experiences in acting flexibly. Sometimes individuals may choose to act counter to the urge or emotion and, at other times, to act consistently with it. For example, having a toy taken away often elicits anger in children. A child who is capable of emotion management without integration might respond to the situation in a socially appropriate manner (e.g., by walking away from the situation). However, this child will be unable to actively resolve his or her present anger or find ways to prevent himself or herself from becoming angry in the future. In contrast, a second child who is also capable of emotion integration may respond in the same way, but also may be able to recognize his or her feelings of anger and use that information adaptively (e.g., by seeking the assistance of an adult or by not playing with the offending child again). The key point is that whether or not an emotion is integrated cannot be judged on the basis of socially appropriate behavior alone. A child's ability to recognize his or her emotions and use them adaptively is equally as important. Thus, the concept of emotional self-regulation includes two aspects: (a) emotion management, whereby emotional arousal can be modulated appropriately; and (b) emotional integration, whereby emotions are assimilated and utilized.

Independent Versus Autonomous Self-Regulation

Our theory that children move toward more autonomous regulation does not imply that they increasingly manage their emotions apart from others. Autonomous self-regulation of emotion is not synonymous with regulation that is independent from others or is accomplished alone. Autonomous regulation may actively involve others. In fact, emotion regulation can be conceptualized as a mutual process in which caretakers and children influence each other in ongoing ways. Such mutual regulation is a quality of close relationships and is the context within which children develop regulatory strategies (Cole, Teti, & Zahn-Waxler, 2003).

Consistent with this view, strategies can be characterized as in-relation to others without being other-reliant. For example, in a waiting situation, self-regulating emotion may involve engaging the mother in a game, a strategy that clearly is in-relation. This is strikingly different from a child who waits for the mother to intervene and allows her to take responsibility for providing distracting activities. Such a strategy would be considered other-reliant. While, in the first situation, the child is active and self-initiating in his or her regulatory attempts, the second situation involves passivity and dependence. Therefore, in our work examining the emotion regulation strategies that parents and children use, we note who is initiating the strategy as well as who is maintaining it.

The adaptiveness of engaging others in one's regulatory attempts and, thus, its status as in-relation versus other-reliant, also depends on the context. For example, when others are unavailable or temporarily unresponsive, it is not particularly adaptive to try to involve them (Grolnick, Bridges, & Connell, 1996). However, when they are available and willing to be involved, such strategies may be most helpful. We return to this issue later in the chapter in the Conceptual and Methodological Issues section.

Emotional Responsiveness and Self-Regulatory Strategies

We posit that the capacity for emotional self-regulation is composed of two interrelated processes: emotional responsiveness and emotional self-regulation strategies (Grolnick, Bridges, & Connell, 1996). *Emotional responsiveness* represents the degree to which an individual responds both expressively and experientially to arousing events. This process is evident in characteristics of an individual's emotional expressions, such as intensity, latency to respond, and duration. Emotional self-regulation strategies are the various behaviors that can be used to modify or alter emotional responses. Certainly these two processes are intertwined and empirically are extremely difficult to untangle. For example, the emotional expression we see in a child represents both the emotion and the regulation of the emotion. Though we recognize its difficulties, in our work we have elected to operationally separate emotion expressiveness from strategy use so that we can explore the links of particular strategies to emotional expressiveness within and across contexts (Grolnick, Bridges, & DeCourcey, 2004).

Consistent with the self-determination framework outlined above, we conceptualize the development of these processes as involving movement from more passive, stimulus-bound, and other-reliant strategies to more active, autonomous forms of regulation. In our work, we have identified strategies that young children use to regulate distress in mildly stressful situations. These strategies are viewed as lying along a continuum from passive, reactive, and stimulus-bound to more active, proactive, and reorienting strategies. Below, we describe three sets of strategies from which six specific strategy codes are derived.

Our first set of strategies involves shifts in attention away from arousing stimuli. Attentional processes play an important role in modulating arousal from infancy onward (Rothbart & Posner, 1985). Voluntary or executive attention, its neurophysiological bases, and developmental progression has received much recent attention (e.g., Posner & Rothbart, 1998). The newborn is equipped with rudimentary mechanisms for disengaging from stimuli (Kessen & Mandler, 1961) and overstimulating interactions (Gianino & Tronick, 1988), although the more voluntary shifting of attention begins to occur between 3 and 6 months (Rothbart, Posner, & Boylan, 1990). Further shifts in voluntary attention occur between 9 and 12 months—for example, in studies of reaching along the line of sight in order to retrieve an object from a box, at 9 months the line of sight dominates attention, with children reaching according to what they see. By 12 months, infants can look at a closed side but reach through an open end, showing their capacity for cognitive control (Diamond, 1991). Posner and Rothbart (2000) used the Stroop procedure to study further developments in attention in the 2nd and 3rd years of life. Children were presented pictures of objects and a key to press that either matched or did not match the stimulus. The key could be on the same side of the stimulus or the opposite side. The child was to press the key that matched the object regardless of location. Performance at 2 years was perseverative and much better on compatible (i.e., object and key on the same side) than incompatible trials. By the second half of the 3rd year and first half of the 4th year, children performed with high accuracy on both compatible and incompatible trials. Redirection of attention away from a distressing stimulus and toward another object, person, or event is a strategy used frequently by older infants, toddlers, and their parents (Grolnick, Kurowski, McMenamy, Rivkin, & Bridges, 1998).

While particular strategies can be seen as ranging from those that are more passive and stimulus bound to those that are more active and autonomous, it is important to note that any type of strategy can be more or less active and sustained. Redirection of attention can be conceptualized in this way. It can range from brief looks away in the newborn period (Fox, 1989) to sustained toy play in toddlers. Thus, one can conceptualize attentional deployment strategies as being more or less active. We have tried to capture this distinction in our categorization by coding two strategies: active engagement with objects and passive exploration and object use.

The usefulness of attentional distraction, and, particularly, more active kinds of attention deployment including abilities to shift and maintain attention, has been demonstrated by several researchers. Rothbart and her colleagues (e.g., Rothbart, Ziaie, & O'Boyle, 1992) demonstrated that the ability to control attention was associated with low levels of negative emotion in infants. Mischel (1974) found that children who are most able to delay obtaining an object are those who use a variety of self-distraction techniques. Braungart and Stifter (1991) differentiated between toy play (engaged and sustained behavior) and looking at objects and people (less sustained behavior). These authors examined the use of these strategies and their relations with distress in separation episodes. Their findings indicated that higher levels of distress were associated with less toy play. Finally, children characterized as "easily frustrated" at 6 months were less attentive in attention tasks, and used less distraction in challenge situations than those less easily frustrated (Calkins et al., 2002).

A second set of behaviors used by children to regulate their emotions are those for comfort or reassurance. We include three types of comforting strategies: physical comforting, other-directed comforting, and symbolic self-soothing. Comfort behaviors can be self-directed, including physical self-soothing behaviors such as thumb sucking or using familiar or special objects to obtain comfort (Klackenberg, 1949; Passman & Weisberg, 1975). Stifter (1993) described the prevalence of physical self-soothing strategies in 5- through 10-month-olds and noted their effectiveness in decreasing distress levels in children of this age. Interestingly, self-soothing behaviors have also been found to be positively correlated with distress in older (12–13 months) children (Diener, Mangelsdorf, McHale, & Frosch, 2002).

Comfort behaviors can be directed toward a caregiver, such as in attempts to attain proximity and contact (e.g., Ainsworth & Wittig, 1969). Children who orient to their mothers during frustrating situations tend to show greater distress (Calkins et al., 2002).

Comforting behaviors also can be symbolic in nature. Piaget (1954) noted that the use of the symbolic function, such as in play or imitation, helps children to master a difficult situation. The child may evoke a representation of an object or situation causing distress and develop game-like activity in the service of emotion regulation. For example, a child may pretend that he or she has obtained a desired object. Such behaviors differ from engagement in alternative activities since the child remains focused on the distressing object. Yet, by using his or her representational capacities, the child transforms the situation into one that is manageable and, thus, is comforted. The child's repertoire of symbolic self-soothing strategies is expanded by the acquisition of language. Linguistic abilities can help children to state their feelings, to obtain verbal feedback about appropriate regulation, and to hear about and think about ways to manage emotions (Kopp, 1989). Self-directed speech also may facilitate the child's ability to bring action and emotion under control. Flavell (1966) used the term *private speech* to describe this self-directed speech, and noted that the function of such speech was self-guidance. Berk (1986) demonstrated that private speech helped children to inhibit off-task behavior in a task situation, and Bivens and Berk (1990) demonstrated greater use of private speech in older versus younger elementary children.

Finally, the distressed child can maintain or increase focus on the distressing stimulus and attempt to alter a temporarily unresponsive environment. For example, during a separation, the child can search for his or her mother or, while in a delay situation, he or she can focus on the desired object. We thus include focus on the desired object/search for mother as a final strategy. Supporting the less adaptive nature of this type of strategy, Bridges and Connell (1991) found that, during a brief separation, the child's search for his or her mother was positively correlated with distress. Putnam, Spritz, and Stifter (2002) demonstrated with toddlers and Mischel (1974) demonstrated with older children that, when a child's attention was directed toward the goal, voluntary delay was diminished.

We have conducted several studies examining these six strategies (see Figure 1.1), their relations to emotional expressiveness, and the effects of context on their use. Context may have many meanings, including the type of stimulus presented, who is present, and whether those present are available to assist the child. We have examined each of these issues in our work. The first study (Grolnick, Bridges, & Connell, 1996) examined emotional expressiveness and strategy use in thirty-seven 24-month-old children. We observed the children in two paradigms: a separation paradigm and a delay paradigm, each with two variants. In one of the two delay situations, children had to wait to receive a present and, in the other, they had to wait to eat some goldfish crackers and raisins. Further, the delays were conducted under one of two conditions: under one condition, the mother was free to do anything she wanted while her child waited (parent-active); under the other, she was asked to read a magazine and remain relatively passive, though she could respond to her child (parent-passive) during the waiting period. In the separation paradigm, children participated in a modified stranger situation. Our focus was on the portion of the session when the mother left the room and the child was with an experimenter (experimenter-present) and the portion when the child was alone (child-alone).

For each of the four situations (two delay and two separation), we rated the children's affect in 5-second intervals using Thompson's facial and vocal scales which range from positive to negative. Also coded in the same intervals was children's use of the six strategies: active engagement with substitute objects, passive use of objects and exploration, symbolic self-soothing, physical self-soothing, other-directed comforting, and focus on the desired object/search for mother (see Figure 1.1).

Among these 2-year-olds, active engagement with substitute objects was the most frequently used strategy, followed by focus on the desired object/search for mother. These results indicate that children of this age are able to use active distraction during mildly stressful situations, though their attention is also vulnerable to pulls by the stimulus. We also examined the relations between children's use of the various strategies and their levels of distress. These results appear in Table 1.1. Use of active engagement was highly negatively associated with children's distress while, as expected, focus on desired object/search for mother was positively related to distress in all situations. Relations between other strategies and distress levels varied by situation, but generally supported the continuum model, whereby those strategies defined as more active and reorienting were most negatively correlated with distress while those defined as more passive, other-directed, and stimulus-bound were most positively correlated with distress.

In general, our findings supported the continuum of autonomy in which active, autonomous strategies are more adaptive than passive, other-reliant ones.

Our results also strongly showed that the context affected children's strategy use. Children more actively engaged in toy play when an adult was present and participatory than when an adult was not present or passive. Conversely, when an adult was unavailable, children tended to be more focused on the desired object. This finding was replicated in a longitudinal study of 12- and 14-month-olds (Bridges, Grolnick, & Connell, 1997). This finding was similar to that of Diener and Mangelsdorf (2000) who found that children showed more positive affect during anger and fear eliciting situations when their mothers were involved versus constrained in their behavior. These studies each illustrate that children were able to use the most active and adaptive strategies and to show the least distress when regulating in relation to their caregivers. These findings illustrate the relative dependence of children on caretakers for regulatory assistance during the first 2 years.

Another part of our theory suggests that emotional self-regulation should change with age—both in decreased emotional expressiveness and in the use of more autonomous strategies to regulate emotion. Other investigators have provided data relevant to this issue and we have extended our own work with 2-year-olds to 12-, 18-, and 32-month-olds. While not specifically categorizing their strategies along an active to passive continuum, Mangelsdorf, Shapiro, and Marzolf (1995) found that, relative to 6- and 12-month-olds, 18-month-olds were more likely to attempt to direct interactions with strangers during separations. They also found that 12-month-olds were more likely to self-soothe than 18-month-olds. Parritz (1996) found that, in "challenging situations" (e.g., presentation of a mechanical toy), 18-month-olds were more likely to attempt to control the situation with various

Children's Self-Regulatory Strategies

Active Engagement

Passive Use of Objects

Symbolic Self-Soothing

Physical Self-Soothing

Other-Directed Comfort Seeking

Focus on Desired Object/ Search for Mother

Figure 1.1   Self-regulatory strategies displayed by children in delay and separation situations.

behavioral strategies than 12-month-olds. These findings support the notion that older children are more able to utilize active strategies than their younger counterparts.

Building upon our earlier work, a recent study (Grolnick, Bridges, & DeCourcey, 2004), examined children's use of seven strategies (active engagement was divided into that with mother and independent play) in a cross-sectional study of 137 12-, 18-, 24-, and 32-month-olds using the delay and separation paradigms described above. Supporting the developmental model, there were differences between younger (12 and 18 months) and older (24 and 32 months) children in their level of emotional expressiveness and five of the seven strategies. Younger children expressed more distress than older children. Further, younger children were less likely to use the more active strategies of active engagement, independent play, and symbolic self-soothing. Younger children were more likely to use passive engagement and other-directed strategies, such as comfort seeking, relative to older children.

TABLE 1.1
Within Situation Correlations Between Strategy Use and Emotional Expressiveness

	Separation		Delay	
	Experimenter Absent	Experimenter Present	Parent Active	Parent Passive
Active engagement with substitute objects	−.56*	−.84*	−.54*	−.27
Passive use of objects and exploration	−.49**	−.35***	−.09	−.39***
Symbolic self-soothing	−.10	−.19	−.02	−.22
Physical self-soothing	−.004	.48**	.25	.30***
Other-directed comforting	—	.31*	.00	.15
Focus on the desired object/search for mother	.63*	.63*	.47**	.02

*p < .001. **p < .01. ***p < .05.

Interestingly, there was some evidence that age differences were more apparent when children were in a context that did not include the support of adults; there were no differences in the independent play strategy when children were in the situation in which the parent was active. However, in the situation in which the parent was passive, younger children were less likely to engage in this strategy. The results of our study support the expected developmental progression toward increasingly autonomous forms of regulation outlined above and illustrates the younger toddler's greater reliance on caretakers for supporting regulatory attempts.

A second set of findings of the study involved age-related differences in associations between strategy use and emotional distress. Correlations between particular strategies (e.g., the negative relations between focus on the desired object and distress) were stronger in the older relative to the younger children. This suggests a greater coherence of the emotional regulatory system as children move through the toddler period.

The findings from the Grolnick, Bridges, and DeCourcey (2004) study highlight the developmental nature of emotional self-regulation. The results are consistent with the view that development is characterized by increasing autonomy and systemic coherence. In general, these results, and those from our earlier studies support a self-determination model of the development of emotional self-regulation.

As indicated earlier, dampening down negative affect is only one aspect of emotional self-regulation, increasing positive affect is another type of regulation that can facilitate goal pursuit. Thus, in another study, Grolnick, Cosgrove, and Bridges (1996) focused on the initiation of positive affect during free play in 140 toddlers. First, all expressions of positive affect by children were identified. Next, we coded whether these affective displays were child-initiated (i.e., spontaneous), prompted (i.e., following some maternal verbal or nonverbal behavior that did not involve the expression of positive affect), or mother-initiated (i.e., following a maternal affective display). Results indicated that the proportion of prompted episodes increased with age, particularly between 12 and 18 months, and then leveled off. Thus, by 18 months, children were able to respond with positive affect to neutral actions and verbalizations by their mothers at a rate comparable to older children. The proportion of child-initiated displays also increased with age, particularly between 24 and 32 months. Finally, mother-initiated episodes decreased with age. The results support our thesis that, as they become older, children take greater responsibility for regulating affective exchanges with others. We speculate that the transition between 12 and 18 months in prompted episodes may be due to children's emerging representational capacities. Such capacities, including recall memory, enable the child to evoke representations of earlier positive exchanges and enact them in the present (Kopp, 1989). However, children still require concrete prompts to exercise these capacities. By 24 months, children have developed their representational capacities to the point that they are able to initiate positive exchanges in an unsupported manner.

UNDERSTANDING INDIVIDUAL DIFFERENCES IN EMOTIONAL SELF-REGULATION

Within any age group, children differ greatly in both their level of emotional responsiveness and in the types of strategies they have available to regulate emotion. We now turn to a discussion of some of the factors that contribute to these individual differences in children's emotional self-regulatory abilities. In our model (see Figure 1.2) we focus on the role of child factors, especially temperament, that children might bring to the task of emotion regulation. We also examine the role of the social context, and in particular caregiver styles, in explaining individual differences in children's emotional expressiveness and strategy use.

Temperament

While there are many different conceptualizations of temperament, there is relative agreement that *temperament* describes a collection of behavioral tendencies thought to have some biological basis as well as a certain degree of continuity over the life span (Goldsmith et al., 1987). These tendencies or

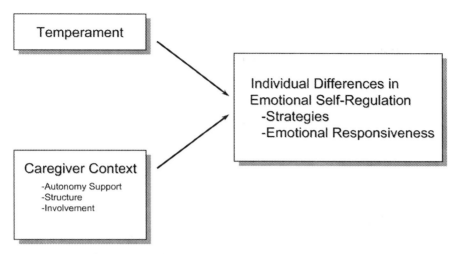

Figure 1.2   Factors influencing children's emotional self-regulation.

styles of responding are thought to be distinct from specific behaviors, but are believed to influence how different individuals act and feel about similar circumstances and events.

Several recent conceptualizations of temperament focus on individuals' dispositions to express emotions, including the intensity of emotional experiences, emotional reactivity, or both, constructs with obvious relevance to emotion regulation. For example, Goldsmith and Campos (1982) defined temperament as individual differences in the expression of basic emotions such as anger and sadness, fear, pleasure, and interest. In an approach that perhaps is most relevant to our work, Rothbart and her colleagues (e.g., Rothbart & Derryberry, 1981; Rothbart & Bates, 1998) defined temperament as constitutionally based individual differences in reactivity and self-regulation. According to this theory, reactivity is the quality of individuals' responses to changes in the environment. A key aspect of reactivity is susceptibility to distress (i.e., how much stimulation is needed to generate arousal). The second component of temperament, self-regulation, encompasses children's capacities for dealing with various levels of arousal. Conceptualized in this way, it is clear that temperament affects both the extent to which regulation is required as well as the ways in which children might acquire regulatory strategies.

Fox (1989) used this conceptualization of temperament to account for differences in the types of strategies that children need to regulate their emotions. He argued that children's reactivity levels shape the sort of emotion regulation strategies they need to acquire. For example, a child who is highly reactive, but possesses few regulatory skills, may become aroused too quickly and may be prevented from exercising existing strategies. He or she thus may be forced to rely on the assistance of caregivers more often than another, less reactive child. Under such circumstances, highly reactive children would have fewer opportunities to elaborate or expand their repertoire of regulatory strategies compared to less reactive children or those who possess some self-regulatory skills. Fox also claimed that temperamental factors, such as mood lability and domination by only one or a couple of emotions, can be linked to less adaptive emotion regulatory processes, such as lack of access to the full range of emotions and inability to make fluid shifts between affective states (Fox, 1997).

Eisenberg and Fabes (1992) similarly conceptualized the importance of the dimensions of reactivity and regulation in their work with preschoolers. They postulated that individuals high in emotional intensity and low in regulatory ability would be prone to emotional regulatory problems. Thus, those children whose extreme emotional responses most require regulation would be least capable of providing it. Supporting their view, they found that such children tended to have less constructive anger reactions (Fabes & Eisenberg, 1992). Again, their work supports the idea that temperament may be an important contributor to individual differences in emotion regulation processes.

Researchers also have linked temperament to individual differences in the types of strategies that children employ when experiencing stressful circumstances. Mangelsdorf et al. (1995) found that wary 12-month-olds tended to engage in more passive types of strategies, such as self-soothing and proximity seeking with their mothers, when placed in the company of strangers. Less wary children, on the other hand, tended to use more active strategies, like self-distraction, when placed in the same situation. Similarly, Parritz (1996) found that infants described as wary by their mothers engaged in more self-soothing as well as whining and proximity seeking with their mothers than less wary infants. Perhaps the emotional responses of more wary and reactive infants are too overwhelming, causing such infants to rely on others to assist them in regulating their emotions or reverting to less active and adaptive strategies when such assistance is unavailable. This research suggests that temperamental characteristics may play a role in determining where children's strategies for regulating distress may fall on the continuum of autonomy.

Work by Morales and Bridges (1996) further supports the notion that temperament is associated with the types of strategies children use. In their work, they used a research paradigm similar to our own and focused on the relations between mothers' perceptions of their children's temperament and children's strategy use during delay episodes. More specifically, they asked the mothers to report on aspects of their children's emotional responses in various situations. Children who were seen as experiencing more negative emotionality focused more on the desired object and engaged in more other-directed comfort seeking and low level play in the laboratory delay. Children who were seen as exhibiting less negative emotionality engaged in more active play with the parent. At the same time, children who were seen as more positive and responsive by their mothers were found to engage less in passive forms of regulation, including physical self-soothing, focusing on the desired object, and other-directed comfort seeking.

A temperamental variable related to the development of attention that is important for self-regulation is effortful control. This construct represents the ability to inhibit a dominant response and to perform a subdominant one. Supporting its status as a temperamental dimension, effortful control tends to be consistent across tasks and across time (Kochanska, Murray, & Harlan, 2000). Further, it is negatively related to negative affectivity and aggression (Rothbart, Ahadi, & Hershey, 1994). Effortful control may moderate the experience of negative affect, making children able to use cognitive mechanisms in arousing situations.

Finally, a number of researchers have identified physiological mechanisms underlying temperamental dimensions of reactivity, self-regulation, and effortful control. Recent advances in the study of the biological and physiological aspects of temperament indicate that these factors may contribute to individual differences in children's capacities for emotion regulation. Calkins, Fox, and Marshall (1996) found that different patterns of activation in the frontal regions of the brain were associated with differences in arousal thresholds and affective expressions. Autonomic activity, as indexed by heart rate and vagal tone, has been related to temperamental characteristics (Stifter & Fox, 1990). Specifically, infants with high vagal tone exhibit greater sociability and outgoingness, while infants with low vagal tone appear more inhibited. Research by Gunnar and her colleagues (e.g., Gunnar, 1980) on the adrenocortical system indicated that adrenocortical stress reactivity predicts temperamental characteristics such as proneness to distress. Research such as this promises to increase our understanding of the biological mechanisms through which children come to acquire regulation and through which they carry out regulatory strategies.

Caregiver Differences

A number of researchers have conceptualized emotion regulation as developing within the context of the parent–child relationship (e.g., Gianino & Tronick, 1988). Parent–child interaction involves mutual regulation in which caregiver and child each modulate the affect of the other (e.g., Tronick, 1989). The parent–child context may be characterized as more unresponsive and poorly coordinated; in which case, the parent fails to recognize the child's emotional needs or ignores the child's existing capabilities or smoothly coordinated with matching of parent and child affect (Field, 1994).

Theoretical work in the psychoanalytic tradition describes the importance of parents as early regulators of children's affect. For example, Winnicott (1960) described the "holding environment" as one in which the infant's impulses, affects, and frustrations are satisfied by the parent before they become overwhelming. He further claimed that these experiences of having been soothed in the presence of the caretaker lead the child to be able to soothe himself or herself. In contrast, when infants are not responded to and are left with strong unsatisfied urges, the child may respond either by suppressing these urges or being overwhelmed by them, thus not making steps toward self-regulation.

Greenspan (1981) similarly discussed the growth-promoting early environment as one that balances the child's need for stimulation with his or her need to experience homeostasis or self-regulation. According to his view, the parent initially provides soothing or comforting to supplement the child's emerging capacities. As the child becomes older, the parent helps the child integrate affective polarities into organized interpersonal responses. Without such availability, whereby comfort and a sense of security in the manageability of emotions are offered, the infant cannot stabilize emerging cycles and patterns and build on his or her own capacities for comforting. These theoretical works highlight the importance of caregivers' responses to their children in children's emotion regulation development.

We have been interested in whether and how parents adapt the strategies they use to help their toddlers modulate mild distress. We assume that parents, at least in part, mold the strategies they use with their infants and toddlers in response to changes in children's capacities to modulate distress. During the infant and toddler periods, numerous neurophysiological and cognitive changes occur which most certainly impact children's emotion regulation capacities. Neurophysiological development allows for more modulated reactions to stress (Stansbury & Gunnar, 1994), and increased control over arousal (Fox, 1994). The cognitive advances that, at least in part, stem from these neural maturations (including increased planfulness, voluntary attention, self-awareness, and understanding of causality) certainly contribute to developmental changes in the use of the emotion regulatory strategies described above (Kopp, 1989). Parents are able to capitalize on these changes in their attempts to regulate their children's distress. For example, very young infants primarily are able to vary arousal by shifting visual control (Tronick & Weinberg, 1990), thus allowing caregivers to use visual distraction as a soothing strategy (Thompson, 1994). Children's developing linguistic abilities during the second year (Ridgeway, Waters, & Kuczaj, 1985) provide caregivers with more opportunities to engage in language-based regulation strategies. Increases in motor capabilities and the fact that attention mechanisms become more flexible and object oriented during toddlerhood (Gunnar, Mangelsdorf, Larson, & Hertsgaard, 1989) allow caregivers to engage children in more active, sustained play with toys.

Although changes in caregiver strategies are likely to be linked to children's changing capacities, we assume that caregivers, in tailoring their strategies to their children, are doing more than simply responding to their children's existing abilities. We speculate that caregivers also are striving to create environments in which their children are challenged to engage in strategies that are just above their current abilities. This perspective, consistent with the Vygotskian notion of the zone of proximal development (Vygotsky, 1962), emphasizes that, through such challenging interactions with others, children increasingly internalize or take on the strategies they practice with those others. We have suggested that, as children become older, there will be a transition in the source of the initiation of strategies from the mothers to the children themselves. We argue that these shifts in the initiation of strategies will provide evidence that children are internalizing the strategies initially introduced to them by their parents.

In one study (Grolnick, Kurowski, McMenamy, Rivkin, & Bridges, 1998), we investigated the strategies that mothers used to assist their 12-, 18-, 24-, and 32-month-old children during the delay situation in which mothers were free to be active. We developed a coding system for rating mothers' behavior that paralleled our child strategy coding system (see Figure 1.3). Categories were placed along a continuum from those that were more reorienting for the child to those that were more stimulus-focused. In particular, we coded six maternal strategies in 5-second intervals. The strategies were active game-like engagement (mother engages the child in game-like activity), redirection of attention (mother distracts child), reassurance (mother assures child that he or she will obtain the desired object), following (mother reflects, extends, or elaborates on the child's distress or preoccupation with

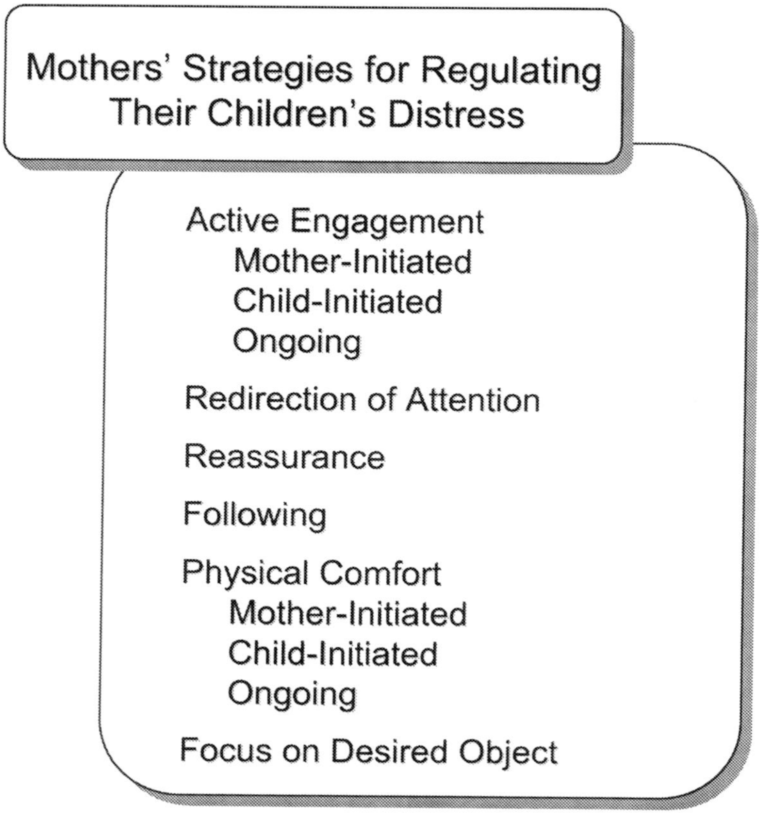

Mothers' Strategies for Regulating
Their Children's Distress

Active Engagement
Mother-Initiated
Child-Initiated
Ongoing

Redirection of Attention

Reassurance

Following

Physical Comfort
Mother-Initiated
Child-Initiated
Ongoing

Focus on Desired Object

Figure 1.3 Strategies mothers use to help their children regulate distress during the parent-active delay situation.

the frustrating object), physical comforting, and focus on the desired object. When active engagement or comforting was coded, raters noted whether the mother or the child initiated the activity or whether the behavior was continued from a previous interval.

Across all ages, active engagement was the strategy most used by mothers. Mothers' use of several strategies, including active engagement, distraction, and reassurance, occurred more often when their children were more distressed. We also found age differences in mothers' use of various strategies (see Table 1.2). As expected, mother-initiated active engagement showed a linear decrease with age while child-initiated and ongoing episodes of active engagement increased. These results support the idea that mothers take less responsibility, and children take more responsibility, for children's affect regulation with children's increasing ages. We believe that this shift occurs both because of children's developing abilities and because mothers are scaffolding their children's skills. There also were changes in the use of verbal strategies, such as reassurance, redirection, and following, with increases between 12 and 18 months and decreases thereafter. This finding provides support for our claim that mothers tailor their strategies to children's changing capacities. As children become more verbal between 12 and 18 months, mothers are more able to use linguistic strategies. The explanation for the decreases in the use of such strategies after 18 months is less obvious. It could be that children are increasingly employing their own self-directed speech to self-regulate and may require less of such intervention. Future research might examine these transitions and explore whether children do, in fact, take over these verbal functions.

Finally, also of interest were differences in the strategies that mothers used with their sons and with their daughters. In particular, mothers used more active emotion regulation strategies, such as

TABLE 1.2
**Analyses of Covariance Illustrating Effects of Age
(and Linear Trends) on Maternal Strategies**

Strategy	Age	Linear Trend
	F	*t*
Active engagement		
Mother-initiated	8.30*	−4.80*
Child-initiated	4.55**	2.62**
Ongoing	7.16*	3.25**
Redirecting attention	7.02*	−.22
Reassurance	11.65*	.38
Following	4.36**	1.32
Physical comfort		
Mother-initiated	1.71	−1.08
Child-initiated	.65	−1.01
Ongoing	1.00	−.94
Focus on object	2.31	.17
Other behavior	7.96*	1.77
Passive	5.31**	−2.32***

Note. Sex and Age X Sex interactions also were included in these analyses.
Distress was included as a covariant.
*$p < .001$. **$p < .01$. ***$p < .05$.

redirection of attention and reassurance, with their daughters while remaining more passive with their sons. This pattern suggests that mothers may facilitate independent emotion regulation more with their sons than with their daughters by providing their sons with more opportunities to independently regulate emotions. This finding links up with work on older children which has suggested that boys show different patterns of problem solving and expressing emotion than girls (Zahn-Waxler et al., 1994). Whether these differences in problem solving are linked to different emotion regulation socialization strategies used by mothers remains a question for future research.

The work described above focused on developmental changes in mothers' use of various strategies. Also of interest in our work, as well as in that of others (e.g., Calkins, 1997b), are the effects of individual differences in caregiver styles and strategies on children's emotion regulation. In order to organize research in this area, we return to the self-determination model presented above. Our model suggests that characteristics of the context provided by caretakers will determine whether children actively internalize strategies presented in their environments (Grolnick & Ryan, 1989; Ryan, Connell, & Grolnick, 1992). In particular, in order to move along the autonomy continuum, the context that the caregivers create must support the child's activity and initiation, provide the structures that can be internalized, and include the proximal support that children need to be successful in their regulatory attempts. The environment thus must provide structure, involvement, and autonomy support. First, the context must provide adequate structures to be internalized. Included in the provision of such structures are that caregivers set up conditions which are optimal, make sure that regulatory tasks are not overwhelming, and provide strategies which are not too complex to be used and incorporated into children's repertoires. Second, parents must be involved and available for assistance. Children thus can be supported in their attempts and supplemented by adults' interventions before experiences become overwhelming. Third, caregivers must provide structures and be involved in an autonomy supportive manner (i.e., they must allow the child to take increasing responsibility for initiating and maintaining emerging strategies). If strategies are provided in a controlling manner without opportunities for self-regulation, the child's activity and internalization may be undermined.

While no studies to date have specifically examined the three dimensions of the environment in relation to children's emotional self-regulation, much work is relevant to these dimensions. With regard to parents' involvement and availability, research in the domain of social referencing has described the powerful effects of mothers' availability as a resource for children in their attempts to regulate affect (Walden & Ogan, 1988). The assumption in much of this work is that regulation involves an appraisal process in which primary emotional reactions are modulated by the meaning ascribed to the situation. Caregivers' facial and vocal expressions are important sources of meaning in ambiguous situations.

The effects of mothers' availability as referencing resources have been demonstrated in several studies. For example, Sorce and Emde (1981) presented a robot toy to children under one of two conditions: Either the mother was asked to read a newspaper or to be available for referencing. Infants whose mothers were available (not reading) showed more positive affect, more smiling, and more vocalization. In addition, they were more positive in relation to a stranger also in the room and touched the toy more. Diener, Mangelsdorf, Fosnot, and Kienstra (1997) examined children's self-regulatory behaviors (mother-related, self-soothing, engaging the stimulus) during a fear-inducing situation under conditions in which either the mother was available or unavailable. Children exhibited more self-soothing when the mother was unavailable and more engagement of the stimulus in the mother-available condition. These studies are consistent with our claim that caregiver involvement is crucial for children's attempts to regulate emotion, and suggest that systematic differences in availability might influence the types of strategies children acquire, use, or both.

With regard to structure, the kinds of strategies parents use with their children are related to the degree of regulation children exhibit. For example, children whose mothers use distraction with them spent more time orienting to alternative objects and less to a forbidden object than those using nondistracting strategies (Putnam, Spritz, & Stifter, 2002). With older children, Holden (1983) showed that mothers who preempted opportunities for distress by actively distracting children were less distressed than those of mothers who waited until children were distressed.

While the aforementioned studies examined parents and children together, it is important to also examine the effects of parents' behaviors on children's capacities to regulate emotion on their own. Here, the level of parents' autonomy supportiveness versus controllingness in their interactions with their children becomes especially relevant. While not proposing such a model, several studies have examined parent behaviors that can be related to an autonomy support to control continuum. Silverman and Ragusa (1990) found that mothers who were more active in a parent–child compliance task had children who performed more poorly on an independent delay task, even controlling for performance on the compliance tasks. Nachmias, Gunnar, Manglesdorf, Parritz, and Buss (1996) examined the strategies that mothers used to help their wary children deal with a mildly fear-inducing stimulus. Mothers who forced their children to focus on a novel event had children with higher postsession cortisol levels, indicating less effective regulation and possible interference with the children's own attempts to regulate proximity and contact with an arousing stimulus. Calkins (1997a) examined mothers' styles of interacting with their children and their children's tendencies to become distressed when frustrated as well as the behaviors children used to manage that distress. Maternal preemptive action (i.e., mothers doing activities for the child rather than allowing the child to do them for himself or herself) was related to tendencies to display distress. Conversely, toddlers whose mothers used more positive feedback and guidance when interacting with their children tended to use distraction and constructive coping. Thus, it appears that whether mothers are involved in an autonomy-supportive or a controlling manner may be related to children's developing abilities to utilize effective regulatory strategies.

In our study, we were interested in whether mothers' use of certain strategies would be related to children's distress when required to regulate alone. We thus examined relations between mothers' use of the six strategies in the parent-active situation and children's distress in the parent-passive situation. To do so, we computed both zero-order correlations between strategies used in the parent-active delay and distress in the parent-passive delay as well as partial correlations between these two variables controlling for both children's ages and distress in the parent-active delay. Therefore, in our analyses, we focused on the relations between strategies mothers used in the parent-active situation and children's distress in the parent-passive situation beyond what would be expected by children's levels of distress in the parent-active situation. Notably, levels of distress tended to be consistent across the two situations.

TABLE 1.3
Zero-Order and Partial Correlations (Controlling for Children's Distress in Parent-Active Delay and Age) Between Maternal Strategies and Children's Distress in Parent-Passive Delay

Strategy	Zero-Order	Partial
Active engagement		
Mother-initiated	.28**	.13
Child-initiated	−.17	.01
Ongoing	−.06	.24**
Redirecting attention	.28**	.01
Reassurance	.29*	.06
Following	.10	.12
Physical comfort		
Mother-initiated	.17***	.13
Child-initiated	.03	.05
Ongoing	.17***	.10
Focus on object	.00	−.06
Other behavior	−.32*	−.22***
Passive	−.20***	−.26**

$^*p < .001.$ $^{**}p < .01.$ $^{***}p < .05.$

Our results (see Table 1.3) showed that mothers who used more ongoing active engagement in the parent-active situation had children who were more distressed in the parent-passive situation (controlling for distress in the parent-active situation). Interestingly, this finding did not occur for mother-initiated active engagement, indicating that it is not mothers' responses per se (which tend to be reactions to child distress) but, rather, the maintenance of engagement despite decreases in distress that appears to undermine children's self-regulation. Mothers who were more passive in the parent-active situation had children who were less distressed when required to regulate with relative independence.

These results suggest that mothers who behave in a controlling manner with regard to their children's emotion regulation, either by maintaining strategies beyond what the child needs to decrease distress or by not allowing opportunities for children to practice more self-regulating strategies, may undermine their children's capacities to develop more autonomous self-regulatory capacities. On the other hand, mothers who provide their children with opportunities to actively regulate, while being available to provide assistance when needed, encourage the internalization of emotion regulation strategies.

Conceptual and Methodological Issues

Despite the popularity of the area of emotion regulation, the field has a number of challenges ahead. Tackling these conceptual and methodological challenges will help to increase our understanding of emotion regulation processes and their potential for predicting behavioral and emotional outcomes.

A first methodological challenge is disentangling emotion and emotion regulation. For example, when one observes a child engaging in toy play in a delay situation, is the child successfully regulating distress by using a distraction strategy or simply not upset at that moment? A methodological advance has been to measure distress and strategy use independently. Yet finding relations between the use of certain strategies and distress does not assure us that the strategies *are responsible* for decreases in upset. Strategies may coincide with distress, or lack thereof, for several reasons. The strategy may reduce distress, a lack of distress may afford the use of the strategy, or another variable may account for this relation.

One recent methodological advance to address emotion/regulation connections has been to examine temporal relations between distress and strategy use using contingency analyses. These techniques allow the researcher to ask whether certain strategies are followed by increases or decreases in distress. For example, in young infants, self-soothing and orienting were more likely to occur in intervals of decreasing negativity than stable or increasing negativity (Stifter & Braungart, 1995). In one study using a delay paradigm, focus on the desired object was followed by increases in anger while information gathering was followed by decreases in anger (Gilliom et al., 2002). While not fully disentangling emotions and regulatory strategies (Bridges, Denham, & Ganiban, 2004), such techniques provide promise in helping to understand how component processes of the self-regulation system interact to facilitate emotion regulation.

Another set of challenges concerns the generality versus specificity of the adaptiveness of emotion regulation processes. As discussed above, the adaptiveness of various strategies depends on the context within which they are occurring. For example, the functionality of the use of caregivers depends on their availability and other situational constraints. If this is so, a taxonomy of adaptive strategies and developmentally appropriate emotion regulation is highly dependent on the situation. This issue is paralleled in the coping literature in which researchers stress that the same coping strategy may be adaptive or nonadaptive, depending on the situation (Lazarus & Folkman, 1984). For example, denial and avoidance-like processes may be constructive in situations in which no direct action can overcome the harm or threat. Conversely, problem-focused strategies are presumed to be more useful with potentially controllable stressors (Lazarus & Folkman, 1984).

A final challenge is that emotion regulation, including its developmental progression and the significance of its components, is likely to be dependent on the affect involved. Different affects appear to have different hormonal response patterns (Mason, 1975) and are likely to have different developmental progressions and features. The development of specific affects will be determined, at least somewhat, by cultural variability in the meaning of these emotions and expectations for the expression of these emotions. For example, in Japan, the goal in socialization attempts is to facilitate harmony and avoid conflict. Thus, Japanese parents attempt to shield their children from frustration and anger expressions (Miyake, Campos, Kagan, & Bradshaw, 1986). The developmental progression of the regulation of anger is likely to be quite different in such a culture relative to one in which anger is more readily tolerated.

Emotion Regulation and Later Adaptation

In this section, we explore some implications of our model of emotional self-regulation for later adaptation. Included are possible links between early emotion regulation processes and later social competence, coping, and psychopathology.

The attainment of a reasonable level of emotional self-regulation can be considered a major developmental task of toddlerhood and early childhood (Kopp, 1989). Consistent with the developmental psychopathology perspective, effective negotiation of this issue should predict competence on developmentally salient tasks in later stages. Such continuity can be explained by the need for self-regulatory capacities for other processes such as task engagement, concentration, and maintaining interchanges with others (Shields, Cicchetti, & Ryan, 1994). Thus, emotion regulation may serve as a foundation for maintaining the homeostasis that allows individuals to engage with their environments and with others. Children who do not develop these abilities therefore would be more likely to develop intra- and interpersonal problems (Calkins, 1997b; Eisenberg & Fabes, 1992).

One of the key developmental tasks of the early childhood years is the engagement with peers in cooperative, mutual play. In line with a recent focus on intersystem connections (Cicchetti, Ackerman, & Izard, 1995), studies have examined relations between emotion regulation abilities and children's social competence. Calkins (1997a) looked at patterns of emotion regulation in preschoolers indexed physiologically through vagal tone. She also rated children's play patterns in the preschool including solitary, social/active, and reticent behavior. The results of her study indicated that children who engaged in high levels of solitary play were more regulated in their affect as indexed by greater vagal suppression (decrease in vagal tone from baseline to affect-eliciting episodes) relative to those who engaged in more social/active (including aggressive) or reticent behavior. This author concluded that physiological regulation makes possible immersement in solitary activity and the negotiation of one-on-one interactions with peers. Fabes and Eisenberg (1992) found that frequent displays of anger were related to lower levels of social competence in children, and Raver (1997) found that toddlers' emotion regulation strategies were related to social competence above and beyond measures of attentional control.

Further evidence connects early self-regulation with behavior problems. Emotion dysregulation has been described as the common dimension of most categories of psychopathology (Cole, Michel, & Teti, 1994). Cole, Michel, and Teti (1994) described emotional dysregulation as emotional patterns that disrupt other processes such as attention and social relations. Similarly, Cicchetti et al. (1995) defined emotional dysregulation as existing control structures that operate in a maladaptive manner and direct emotion toward inappropriate sources. Researchers have described pathological consequences of both overcontrol (e.g., internalizing behavior, depression) and undercontrol (e.g., externalizing behavior, aggression). Children with undercontrolled behavior problems tend to show difficulty with emotion regulation in the laboratory (Calkins & Dedmon, 2000) and children's emotion regulation has been linked to externalizing behavior in school (Eisenberg et al., 2001; Chang, Schwartz, Dodge, & McBride-Chang, 2003). Preschoolers with behavior problems have intense and prolonged distress and protest during separations (Speltz, Greenberg, & DeKlyen, 1990). Cole, Teti, and Bohnert (1997) examined 4- and 5-year-olds in emotionally challenging situations and coded facial expressions as inexpressive, modulated, or full blown. Inexpressive children reported more symptoms of anxiety and depression.

While these studies provide links between emotion regulation processes and social competence, measures taken in these studies were concurrent. Thus, it is difficult to know whether behavior problems or difficulties in interacting with others were apparent before affect regulation problems or whether they were a consequence or concomitant of them. Longitudinal studies addressing whether early emotion regulation is related to later social outcomes are beginning to examine cross-time links. For example, emotion regulation in preschool predicts symptoms in the school years (Cole, Teti, & Zahn-Waxler, 2002)

Beyond finding links between emotion regulation and later adjustment, some studies have begun to delineate the processes through which relations between emotion regulation and social difficulties might occur. For example, Kobak and Cole (1994) conducted such a process-oriented study with adolescents in which they argued that links can be found between social withdrawal and the dampening down of undesired emotions. Specifically, they claimed that deactivating attachment strategies divert attention from attachment needs and cues. These strategies are used by the adolescent to dampen undesired emotions. This dampening is then linked to social withdrawal. Such process-oriented studies help us to understand how emotion regulation relates to social outcomes.

Possibly more direct are potential links between emotional self-regulation and coping in children and adults. Coping has been defined as strategies directed at managing or altering problems causing distress or emotional responses to problems (Lazarus & Folkman, 1984). Coping strategies, such as avoidance or denial, can be directly linked to attentional emotion regulation strategies described above. Altshuler and Ruble (1989) examined age-related (ages 5 through 11) changes in children's suggested coping strategies. Children were given scenarios involving a child having to wait (e.g., to receive a large candy bar) and asked to suggest strategies that the child might use. The results of their study showed that avoidance/distraction type strategies were most frequently named by children of all ages. At the same time, there was an increase with age in cognitive types of distraction (i.e., thinking about something else) and a decrease in escape strategies. The developmental component of these coping strategies provides a potential link between emotional self-regulation and this coping work, and several questions regarding the origins of coping strategies and emotion dysregulation in early emotion regulation processes become relevant. For example, are children who are able early to use attention deployment strategies more able to use cognitive strategies as they become older? What sorts of caregiver influences impact on individual differences in the use of coping strategies? When does the use of less autonomous strategies become emotional dysregulation? What roles do temperament and caregiver styles play in extreme forms of dysregulation? How early are these difficulties evident? In addressing these and other questions, the study of emotion regulation promises to provide important insight into the development of problem behaviors and clinical disorders.

Conclusion and Future Directions

In this chapter, we have presented a model of the development of emotional self-regulation in infancy and toddlerhood that is organized around the construct of autonomy. In our framework, we focus on children's emotional responsiveness as well as the strategies children use to modulate that responsiveness. We argue that movement along a continuum of autonomy toward more active, flexible strategies for regulating affect is a natural phenomenon fueled by children's innate propensities to master their environments and to take on or internalize regulatory structures provided by caregivers. We provide evidence that emotional self-regulation is a developmental phenomenon, with more autonomous strategies evident with increasing age, as well as an individual difference phenomenon, influenced by both temperamental characteristics and caregiver influences. The complex nature of emotional self-regulation is illustrated by the contextual and situational nature of adaptive strategies, specificity to particular emotions, and the key influence of cultural factors.

While a complex phenomenon, emotional self-regulation may provide important links with later coping, peer relations, and psychopathology. A challenge for the field is to specify the processes through which emotional self-regulation might impact these key developmental outcomes.

In this last section, we delineate future directions for our own and others' research. First, the field would benefit from research addressing the conceptual and methodological challenges outlined in the previous section. This includes research targeted toward disentangling emotion–emotion regulation processes, that specifying the domains in which emotional regulatory processes are adaptive and maladaptive, and that addressing the regulation of specific emotions such as anger and sadness. Beyond these specific areas, we will need to develop models and provide data on the interplay between factors in the child and factors in the context (including the caregiver environment) that predict emotional self-regulation. For instance, how do different temperamental characteristics and caregiver styles interact to create specific patterns of emotional responsiveness and strategy use? Do temperamental factors have more of an influence in certain domains relative to others? The answers to these and other questions will provide us with a more complete understanding of the development of emotional self-regulation.

Another future area of research concerns the origins of caregiver reactions and strategies. For example, parents' attitudes toward and comfort with the expression versus the containment of strong emotions may determine the types of strategies that they use to help their children regulate distress. The ways in which emotions were handled in parents' families of origin may be crucial factors in determining such attitudes.

Finally, the roles of various caregivers (e.g., mothers, fathers, siblings, peers) in children's development of emotion regulation is an area for future research. Research on emotion regulation has tended to focus on the contributions of mothers to children's developing emotion regulation. Fathers and siblings therefore represent an interesting and potentially distinct source of influence on children's self-regulation. It also has been found that, as children become older, peers play an increasingly important role in their social and emotional lives (Parker & Gottman, 1989). This role may be particularly important as children begin to face the emotional experiences and concerns associated with early adolescence and to look for ways to deal with these new feelings. Attention to these issues will expand our understanding of early emotion regulation and extend research into middle childhood and adolescence.

REFERENCES

Ainsworth, M. D. S., & Wittig, B. (1969). Attachment and exploratory behavior of one-year-olds in a strange situation. In B. Foss (Ed.), *Determinants of Infant Behavior* (Vol. 4, pp. 111–136). London: Methuen.

Altshuler, J. L., & Ruble, D. N. (1989). Developmental changes in children's awareness of strategies for coping with uncontrollable stress. *Child Development, 60,* 1337–1349.

Barrett, K., & Campos, J. J. (1987). Perspectives on emotional development: II. A functionalist approach to emotions. In J. D. Osofsky (Ed.), *Handbook of infant development* (2nd ed., pp. 555–578). New York: Wiley.

Berk, L. E. (1986). Children's private speech: An overview of theory and the status of research. In R. M. Diaz & L. E. Berk (Eds.), *Private speech: From social interaction to self-regulation.* Hillsdale, NJ: Erlbaum.

Bivens, J. A., & Berk, L. E. (1990). A longitudinal study of the development of elementary school children's private speech. *Merrill-Palmer Quarterly, 36,* 443–467.

Block, J. H., & Block, J. (1980). The role of ego-resiliency in the organization of behavior. In W. A. Collins (Ed.), *Minnesota Symposia on Child Psychology* (Vol. 13, pp. 39–101). Hillsdale, NJ: Erlbaum.

Braungart, J. M., & Stifter, C. A. (1991). Regulation of negative reactivity during the strange situation: Temperament and attachment in 12-month-old infants. *Infant Behavior and Development, 14,* 349–364.

Bridges, L. J., & Connell, J. P. (1991). Consistency and inconsistency in infant emotional and social interactive behavior across contexts and caregivers. *Infant Behavior and Development, 14,* 471–487.

Bridges, L.J., Denham, S.A., & Ganiban, J.M. (2004). Definitional issues in emotion regulation research. *Child Development, 75,* 340–345.

Bridges, L. J., Grolnick, W. S., & Connell, J. P. (1997). Infant emotion regulation with mothers and fathers. *Infant Behavior and Development, 20,* 47–57.

Buck, R. (1984). *The communication of emotion.* New York: Guilford.

Buss, K. A., & Goldsmith, H. H. (1998). Fear and anger regulation in infancy: Effects on the temporal dynamics of affective expression. *Child Development, 69,* 359–374.

Calkins, S. D. (1994). Origins and outcomes of individual differences in emotion regulation. In N. Fox (Ed.), *The development of emotion regulation: Biological and behavioral considerations. Monographs of the Society for Research in Child Development, 59* (2–3, Serial No. 240), 53–72.

Calkins, S. D. (1997a). *Physiological regulations and the control of emotion during toddlerhood.* Paper presented at the biennial meeting of the Society for Research in Child Development, Washington, DC.

Calkins, S. D. (1997b). *Maternal interactive style and emotional, behavioral, and physiological regulation in toddlerhood.* Paper presented at the biennial meeting of the Society for Research in Child Development, Washington, DC.

Calkins, S. D., & Dedmon, S. E. (2000). Physiological and behavioral regulation in two-year-old children with aggressive/destructive behavior problems. *Journal of Abnormal Child Psychology, 28,* 103–118.

Calkins, S. D., Dedmon, S. E., Gill, K. L., Lomax, L. E., & Johnson, L. M. (2002). Frustration in infancy: Implications for emotion regulation, physiological processes, and temperament. *Infancy, 3,* 175–197.

Calkins, S. D., Fox, N. A., & Marshall, T. R. (1996). Behavioral and physiological antecedents of inhibition in infancy. *Child Development, 67,* 523–540.

Campos, J. J., Campos, R., & Barrett, K. C. (1989). Emergent themes in the study of emotional development and emotion regulation. *Developmental Psychology, 25,* 394–402.

Campos, J. J., Frankel, C. B., & Camras, L. (2004). On the nature of emotion regulation. *Child Development, 75,* 377–394.

Campos, J. J., Mumme, D. L., Kermoian, R., & Campos, R. G. (1994). A functionalist perspective on the nature of emotion. In N. Fox (Ed.), *The development of emotion regulation: Biological and behavioral considerations; Monographs of the Society for Research in Child Development, 59* (2–3, Serial No. 240), 284–303.

Chang, L., Schwartz, D., Dodge, K. A., & McBride-Chang, D. (2003). Harsh parenting in relation to child emotion regulation and aggression. Journal of Family Psychology, 17, 598–606.

Cicchetti, D., Ackerman, B., & Izard, C. (1995). Emotions and emotion regulation in developmental psychopathology. *Development and Psychopathology, 7,* 1–10.

Cicchetti, D., Ganiban, J., & Barnett, D. (1991). Contributions from the studies of high-risk populations to understanding the development of emotion regulation. In J. Garber & K. A. Dodge (Eds.), *The development of emotion regulation and dysregulation* (pp. 15–48). Cambridge: Cambridge University Press.

Cole, P. M., Martin, S. E., & Dennis, T. A. (2004). Emotion regulation as a scientific construct: Methodological challenges and directions for child development research. *Child Development, 75,* 317–333.

Cole, P. M., Michel, M. K., & Teti, C. O. (1994). The development of emotion regulation and dysregulation: A clinical perspective. In N. Fox (Ed.), *The development of emotion regulation: Biological and behavioral considerations. Monographs of the Society for Research in Child Development, 59* (2–3, Serial No. 240), 73–100.

Cole, P. M., Teti, L. O., & Bohnert, A. M. (1997). *Challenges for the study of the development of emotion regulation.* Paper presented at the biennial meeting of the Society for Research in Child Development, Washington, DC.

Cole, P. M., Teti, L. O., & Zahn-Waxler, C. (2003). Mutual emotion regulation and the stability of conduct problems between preschool and school age. *Development and Psychopathology, 15,* 1–18.

Cole, P. M., Zahn-Waxler, C., & Smith, K. D. (1994). Expressive control during a disappointment: Variations related to preschoolers' behavior problems. Developmental Psychology, 30, 835–846.

Deci, E. L., & Ryan, R. M. (1985). *Intrinsic motivation and self-determination in human behavior.* New York: Plenum.

Derryberry, D., & Rothbart, M.K. (1988). Arousal, affect and attention as components of temperament. *Journal of Personality and Social Psychology, 55,* 958–966.

Diamond, A. (1991). Neuropsychological insights into the meaning of object concept development. In S. Carey and R. Gelman (Eds.), *The epigenesis of mind: Essays on biology and cognition* (pp. 67–110). Hillsdale, NJ: Lawrence Erlbaum Associates.

Diener, M., Mangelsdorf, S. C., Fosnot, K., & Kienstra, M. (1997). *Effects of maternal involvement on toddlers' emotion regulation strategies.* Paper presented at the biennial meeting of the Society for Research in Child Development, Washington, DC.

Diener, M. L., Mangelsdorf, S. C., McHale, J. L., & Frosch, C. A. (2002). Infants' behavioral strategies for emotion regulation with fathers and mothers: Associations with emotional expressions and attachment quality. *Infancy, 3,* 153–174.

Eisenberg, N., Cumberland, A., Spinrad, T. L., (2001). The relations of regulation and emotionality to children's externalizing and internalizing problems. *Journal of Family Psychology, 15,* 183–295.

Eisenberg, N., & Fabes, R. A. (1992). *Emotion and its regulation in early development. New directions for child development* (Vol. 55). San Francisco: Jossey-Bass.

Eisenberg, N., & Spinrad, T. (2004). Emotion-related regulation: Sharpening the definition. *Child Development, 75,* 334–339.

Emde, R. (1988). Development terminable and interminable: I. Innate and motivational factors from infancy. *International Journal of Psychoanalysis, 69,* 23–42.

Fabes, R., & Eisenberg, N. (1992). Young children's coping with interpersonal anger. *Child Development, 63,* 116–128.

Field, T. (1994). The effects of mother's physical and emotional unavailability on emotion regulation. In N. A. Fox (Ed.), Monographs of the Society for Research in Child Development: Vol. 59 (2–3). *The development of emotion regulation: Biological and behavioral considerations* (pp. 208–227, 250–283). Chicago: University of Chicago Press.

Flavell, J. (1966). Le langage prive [private language]. *Bulletin de Psychologie, 19,* 698–701.

Fox, N. A. (1989). Psychophysiological correlates of emotional reactivity in the first year of life. *Developmental Psychology, 19,* 815–831.

Fox, N. A. (1994). Dynamic cerebral processes underlying emotion regulation. In N. A. Fox (Ed.), *The development of emotion regulation: Biological and behavioral considerations, Monographs of the Society for Research in Child Development, 59* (2–3, Serial No. 240), 152–166.

Fox, N. A. (1997). *The role of anterior cortical brain systems in the development of the regulation of emotions.* Paper presented at the biennial meeting of the Society for Research in Child Development, Washington, DC.

Fox, N. A., & Calkins, S. C. (2003). The development of self-control of emotion: Intrinsic and extrinsic influences. *Motivation and Emotion, 27,* 7–26.

Gianino, A., & Tronick, E. Z. (1988). The mutual regulation model: The infant's self and interactive regulation and coping and defensive capacities. In T. M. Field, P. M. McCabe, & N. Schneiderman (Eds.), *Stress and coping across development* (pp. 47–68). Hillsdale, NJ: Erlbaum.

Gilliom, M., Shaw, D. S., Beck, J. E., Schonberg, M. A., & Lukon, J. L. (2002). Anger regulation in disadvantaged preschool boys: Strategies, antecedents, and the development of self-control. *Developmental Psychology, 38,* 222–235.

Goldsmith, H. H., Buss, A. H., Plomin, R., Rothbart, M. K., Thomas, A., Chess, S., Hinde, R. A., & McCall, R. B. (1987). Roundtable: What Is temperament? Four approaches. *Child Development, 58,* 505–529.

Goldsmith, H. H., & Campos, J. J. (1982). Toward a theory of infant temperament. In R. N. Emde & R. J. Harman (Eds.), *The development of attachment and affiliative systems: Psychobiological aspects* (pp. 161–193). New York: Plenum.

Greenspan, S. I. (1981). *Psychopathology and adaptation in infancy and early childhood: Principles of clinical diagnosis and early intervention.* New York: International Universities Press.

Grolnick, W. S., Bridges, L. J., & Connell, J. P. (1996). Emotion regulation in two-year-olds: Strategies and emotional expression in four contexts. *Child Development, 67,* 928–941.

Grolnick, W. S., Bridges, L.J., & DeCourcey, W. M.. (2004). The development of self-regulatory strategies in infancy and toddlerhood. Unpublished manuscript, Clark University.

Grolnick, W. S., Cosgrove, T. J., & Bridges, L. J. (1996). Age-graded change in the initiation of positive affect. *Infant Behavior and Development, 19,* 153–157.

Grolnick, W. S., Kurowski, C. O., McMenamy, J. M., Rivkin, I., & Bridges, L. J. (1998). Mothers' strategies for regulating their toddlers' distress: Developmental changes and outcomes. *Infant Behavior and Development.*

Grolnick, W. S., & Ryan, R. M. (1989). Parent styles associated with children's self-regulation and competence in school. *Journal of Educational Psychology, 81,* 143–154.

Grolnick, W. S., Ryan, R. M., & Deci, E. L. (1997). Internalization within the family; the self-determination perspective. In J. E. Grusec and L. Kuczynski, L (Eds.), *Parenting and the internalization of children's values* (pp. 135–161). New York: Wiley.

Gunnar, M. R. (1980). Control, warning signals and distress in infancy. *Developmental Psychology, 16,* 281–289.

Gunnar, M. R., Mangelsdorf, S. C., Larson, M., & Hertsgaard, L. (1989). Attachment, temperament and adrenocortical activity in infancy: A study of psychoendocrine regulation. *Developmental Psychology, 25,* 355–363.

Holden, G. W. (1983). Avoiding conflict: Mothers as tacticians in the supermarket. *Child Development, 54,* 233–240.

Kessen, W., & Mandler, G. (1961). Anxiety, pain and the inhibition of distress. *Psychological Review, 68,* 396–404.

Klackenberg, G. (1949). Thumbsucking: Frequency & etiology. *Pediatrics, 4,* 418–424.

Kobak, R., & Cole, H. (1994). Attachment and meta-monitoring: Implications for adolescent autonomy and psychopathology. In D. Cicchetti & S. L. Toth (Eds.), *Rochester Symposium on Developmental Psychopathology: Vol. 5. Disorders and dysfunctions of the self* (pp. 267–298). Rochester, NY: University of Rochester Press.

Kochanska, G., Murray, K., & Harlan, E. (2000). Effortful control in early childhood: Continuity and change, antecedents, and implications for social development. *Developmental Psychology, 36,* 220–232.

Kopp, C. B. (1982). Antecedents of self-regulation: A developmental perspective. *Developmental Psychology, 18,* 199–214.

Kopp, C. B. (1989). Regulation of distress and negative emotions: A developmental view. *Developmental Psychology, 25,* 343–354.

Lazarus, R. S., & Folkman, S. (1984). *Stress, appraisal, and coping.* New York: Springer-Verlag.

Mangelsdorf, S. C., Shapiro, J. R., & Marzolf, D. (1995). Developmental and temperamental differences in emotion regulation in infancy. *Child Development, 66,* 1817–1828.

Mason, J. (1975). Emotion as reflected in patterns of endocrine integration. In L. Levi (Ed.), *Emotions: Their parameters and measurement* (pp. 143–181). New York: Raven Press.

Mischel, W. (1974). Processes in delay of gratification. In L. Berkowitz (Ed.), *Progress in experimental personality research* (Vol. 3, pp. 249–292). New York: Academic Press.

Miyake, K., Campos, J., Kagan, J., & Bradshaw, D. (1986). Issues in socioemotional development in Japan. In H. Azuma, I. Hakuta, & H. Stevenson (Eds.), *Kodomo: Child development and education in Japan* (pp. 239–261). San Francisco: Freeman.

Morales, M., & Bridges, L. J. (1996). Associations between nonparental care experience and preschoolers' emotion regulation in the presence of the mother. *Journal of Applied Developmental Psychology, 17,* 577–596.

Nachmias, M., Gunnar, M., Mangelsdorf, S., Parritz, R. H., & Buss, K. (1996). Behavioral inhibition and stress reactivity: The moderating role of attachment security. *Child Development, 67,* 508–522.

Parker, J. G., & Gottman, J. M. (1989). Social and emotional development in a relational context. In T. J. Berndt & G. W. Ladd (Eds.), *Peer relationships in child development* (pp. 95–131). New York: Wiley.

Parritz, R. H. (1996). A descriptive analysis of toddler coping in challenging circumstances. *Infant Behavior and Development, 19,* 171–180.

Passman, R. H., & Weisberg, P. (1975). Mothers and blankets as agents for promoting play and exploration by young children in a novel environment: The effects of social and non-social attachment objects. *Developmental Psychology, 11,* 170–177.

Piaget, J. (1954). *The origins of intelligence in children.* New York: International Universities Press.

Posner, M.I., & Rothbart, M.K. 91998). Attention, self-regulation, and consciousness. *Philosophical Transactions of the Royal Society of London B, 353,* 1915–1927.

Posner, M.I., & Rothbart, M.K. (2000). Developing mechanisms of self-regulation. *Development and Psychopathology, 12,* 427–441.

Putnam, S. P., Spritz, B. L., & Stifter, C. A. (2002). Mother-child coregulation during delay of gratification at 30 months. *Infancy, 3,* 209–225.

Raver, C. C. (1997). *Relations between effective emotional self-regulation and low-income preschoolers' social competence.* Paper presented at the biennial meeting of the Society for Research in Child Development, Washington, DC.

Ridgeway, D., Waters, E., & Kuczaj, C. A., II. (1985). Acquisition of emotion-descriptive language: Receptive and productive vocabulary norms for ages 18 months to 6 years. *Developmental Psychology, 21,* 901–908.

Rothbart, M. K., Ahadi, S. A., & Hershey, K. L. (1994). Temperament and social behavior in childhood. Merrill-Palmer Quarterly, 40, 21–39.

Rothbart, M. K., & Bates, J. E. (1998). Temperament. In W. Damon & N. Eisenberg (Eds.), *Handbook of child psychology. Vol.3. Social, emotional, and personality development* (5th ed., pp. 105–176). New York: Wiley.

Rothbart, M. K., & Derryberry, D. (1981). Development of individual differences in temperament. In M. E. Lamb and A. L. Brown (Eds.), *Advances in developmental psychology, Vol I.* (pp. 37–86). Hillsdale, NJ: Erlbaum.

Rothbart, M. K., & Posner, M. I. (1985). Temperament and the development of self-regulation. In L. C. Hartlage & C. F. Telzrow (Eds.), *The neuropsychology of individual differences* (pp. 93–123). New York: Plenum.

Rothbart, M. K., Posner, M., & Boylan, A. (1990). Regulatory mechanisms in infant development. In J. T. Enns (Ed.), *The development of attention: Research and theory* (pp. 47–66). New York: Elsevier Science.

Rothbart, M. K., Ziaie, H., & O'Boyle, C. G. (1992). Self-regulation and emotion in infancy. In N. Eisenberg & R. A. Fabes (Eds.), *Emotion and its regulation in early development, new directions in child development* (Vol. 55). San Francisco: Jossey-Bass.

Ryan, R. M., Connell, J. P., & Deci, E. L. (1985). A motivational analysis of self-determination and self-regulation in education. In C. Ames & R. E. Ames (Eds.), *Research on motivation in education: The classroom milieu* (pp. 13–51). New York: Academic Press.

Ryan, R. M., Connell, J. P., & Grolnick, W. S. (1992). When achievement is not intrinsically motivated: A theory of self-regulation in school. In A. K. Boggiano & T. S. Pittman (Eds.), *Achievement and motivation: A social-developmental perspective* (pp. 167–188). New York: Cambridge University Press.

Ryan, R. M., Deci, E. L., & Grolnick, W. S. (1995). Autonomy, relatedness and the self: Their relation to development and psychopathology. In D. Cicchetti & D. J. Cohen (Eds.), *Developmental Psychopathology* (Vol. 1, pp. 618–655). New York: Wiley.

Shields, A., Cicchetti, D., & Ryan, R. M. (1994). The development of emotional and behavioral self-regulation and social competence among maltreated school-age children. *Development and Psychopathology, 6,* 57–75.

Silverman, I. W., & Ragusa, D. M. (1990). Child and maternal correlates of impulse control in 24-month-old children. Genetic, Social and General Psychology Monographs, 116, 435–473.

Sorce, J., & Emde, R. (1981). Mothers' presence is not enough: The effects of emotional availability on infant exploration and play. *Developmental Psychology, 17,* 737–745.

Speltz, M. J., Greenberg, M. T., & DeKlyen, M. (1990). Attachment in preschoolers with disruptive behavior: A comparison of clinic-referred and non problem children. *Development and Psychopathology, 2,* 31–46

Stansbury, K., & Gunnar, M. R. (1994). Adrenocortical activity and emotion regulation. In N. Fox (Ed.), *The development of emotion regulation: Biological and behavioral considerations. Monographs of the Society for Research in Child Development,* 59 (2–3, Serial No. 240), 108–134.

Stifter, C. A. (1993). *Infant emotion regulation: The effectiveness of certain behaviors to modulate negative arousal.* Paper presented at the biennial meeting of the Society for Research in Child Development, New Orleans, LA.

Stifter, C. A., & Braungart, J. M. (1995). The regulation of negative reactivity in infancy: Function and development. *Developmental Psychology, 31,* 448–455.

Stifter, C. A., & Fox, N. A. (1990). Infant reactivity: Physiological correlates of newborn and 5-month temperament. *Developmental Psychology, 26,* 582–588.

Thompson, R. A. (1994). Emotional regulation: A theme in search of definition. In N. A. Fox (Ed.), *The development of emotion regulation: Biological and behavioral aspects. Monographs of the Society for Research in Child Development, 59,* (2–3, Serial No. 240), 25–52.

Tronick, E. Z. (1989). Emotions and emotional communication in infants. *American Psychologist, 44,* 112–119.

Tronick, E. Z., & Weinberg, M. K. (1990, April). *The stability of regulation behaviors.* Paper presented at the biennial meeting of the International Conference on Infant Studies, Montreal.

Vygotsky, L. S. (1962). *Thought and language.* Cambridge: MIT Press.

Walden, T., & Ogan, T. (1988). Development of social referencing. *Child Development, 59,* 1230–1240.

Winnicott, D. W. (1960). The theory of the parent-infant relationship. *International Journal of Psychoanalysis, 41,* 585–595.

Zahn-Waxler, C., Cole, P., Richardson, D., Friedman, R., Michel, M., & Beloud, F. (1994). Social problem solving in disruptive preschool children: Reactions to hypothetical situations of conflict and distress. *Merrill-Palmer Quarterly, 40,* 98–119.

The Nature, Etiology, and Consequences of Individual Differences in Temperament

Theodore D. Wachs

INTRODUCTION

Over the past 10 years the increasing importance of temperament as both a critical developmental outcome and as a moderator and predictor of other developmental outcomes is mirrored by the increasing number of books and major review chapters devoted to this domain (e.g., Guerin, Gottfried, Oliver, & Thomas, 2003; Halverson, Kohnstamm & Martin, 1994; Molfese & Molfese, 2000; Rothbart & Bates, 1998; Wachs & Kohnstamm, 2002). Given this wealth of information, a very obvious question is: Does the world really need another chapter on temperament? Answering this question in the affirmative is based on what appears to be a shift in our understanding of the nature and consequences of individual differences in temperament. Historically, with some notable exceptions, conceptualization of and research on the nature and consequences of individual differences in temperament have focused on temperament as a main effect predictor and outcome. A fundamental thesis of this chapter is that, by focusing just on temperament as a single main effect predictor or outcome, we severely limit our ability to deal with critical issues such as the delineation of the domains of temperament, discordance between parent reports of their child's temperament, the modest stability of temperament traits over time, the etiology of individual differences in temperament, and the consequences of individual differences in temperament. Rather than viewing temperament in isolation, I will argue it is essential that we view temperament as one part of a system of linked multiple influences and outcomes. Other parts of this system include:

1. Other developmental domains like cognition and motivation;
2. Nontemperament child characteristics like age, gender, and biomedical or nutritional status;
3. Changes in the structure and functioning of the central nervous system or gene action patterns;
4. Different levels of the individual's context including:
   a. proximal environmental characteristics such as parental sensitivity, involvement, and responsivity, as well as environmental "chaos" in the home;
   b. quality of parental marital relationship;

c. distal environmental characteristics such as cultural values and beliefs about the desirability of various child characteristics, or the availability of environmental "niches" that are open to the individual.

As will be discussed, by viewing temperament as part of a system rather than in isolation, we are far better able to understand the nature and changes in different dimensions of temperament, how best to measure temperament, and the role temperament plays in various aspects of individual development.

The seeds for both the mainstream approach to temperament in isolation and the alternative view of temperament as part of a system were sown in the pioneering work of Thomas and Chess (Thomas & Chess, 1977; Thomas, Chess, & Birch, 1968). A major rationale underlying the New York Longitudinal Study of Thomas and Chess was to document how the prevailing view of the etiology of behavior disorders—inadequate or inappropriate parenting—was insufficient given the potential importance of biologically based individual differences in children's behavioral styles (temperament). By contrasting temperament as etiology versus parenting as etiology, Thomas and Chess laid the groundwork for later researchers who focused on temperament as an isolated influence. One result has been the increasing number of studies which have focused on two variable questions, with temperament serving as either the predictor or the outcome. Questions addressed by these types of two variable studies include whether specific temperament dimensions are heritable, whether individual differences in attachment reflect individual differences in temperament, whether differences in child temperament produce differences in parent behavior, whether parent reports of children's temperament primarily reflect parent characteristics, the link between early temperament and later personality and how well children with certain temperaments perform in school or test situations (for a review of evidence on these questions see Molfese & Molfese, 2000 or Rothbart & Bates, 1998). For example, there have been multiple studies using point-to-point correlations which have focused on the stability of specific dimensions of temperament or on the degree of linkage between temperament and Big Five personality dimensions. In much of this research, little consideration has been given to nontemperament influences which could act to moderate or mediate observed correlations (Wachs, 1994).

While Thomas and Chess may have sparked our focus on temperament in isolation, in their research and conceptualization they have always been careful to emphasize that the developmental consequences of individual characteristics like temperament cannot be understood without detailed consideration of the context within which an individual with specific temperament characteristics functions—their well-known concept of "goodness of fit." By focusing on the match between temperament and context as the major contributor to individual differences in adjustment Thomas and Chess also laid the groundwork for an alternative viewpoint; namely, that we cannot understand the impact of temperament on behavior without also understanding the nature of the context within which individuals with different temperaments function. This alternative viewpoint is best reflected in studies that have looked at the joint contributions of temperament and contextual characteristics to a variety of developmental outcomes including behavior disorders (Bates, 2001; Eisenberg et al., 2001), infant cognitive performance (Halpern et al., 2001), attachment (Kochanska & Coy, 2002), and children's development of an internalized conscience (Kochanska, 1993, 1995).

There seems to be no doubt that the study of temperament in isolation was a necessary and critical step in terms of helping researchers understand the nature of temperament, the development of specific dimensions of temperament, and the contributions of temperament to development. However, I argue that the extent of our database on temperament is more than sufficient to allow us to take the next necessary step; namely, moving from the artificial world of temperament in isolation to the real world of temperament as part of a system. For purposes of the present discussion, I will use a simplified structural definition of a system; namely, a set of organized multiple elements, with each element linked to and interacting with at least some of the other elements in the set (Wachs, 2000a). As I illustrate in the following sections, viewing temperament as part of a system has two advantages. First, it allows us to deal better with certain perennial problems involving the conceptualization and measurement of temperament which have not been satisfactorily resolved by looking at temperament in isolation. Second, viewing temperament as part of a larger system allows us to develop a more comprehensive picture, both about the etiology and development of individual differences in temperament, as well as about the extent and nature of the contributions of temperament to individual variability in behavior and development. The advantages of viewing temperament as part of a larger system will be illustrated below through use of questions involving what, why, and how. Specifically, the following questions will be addressed: (a) What are the domains of temperament? (b) Why are levels of interparent agreement on child temperament characteristics and stability of temperament so modest? (c) What accounts for individual variability in the development of temperament? (d) How does temperament influence context? (e) How does individual variability in temperament translate into variability in individual developmental patterns?

WHAT ARE THE DOMAINS OF TEMPERAMENT?

At present, there is neither a single agreed on definition of temperament nor agreement on what constitutes the domains of temperament (Belsky, Hsieh, & Crnic, 1996). This problem is not unique to temperament; similar problems are also found in other areas studied by psychologists, such as intelligence. Given the social nature of science (Kuhn, 1970), the existence of multiple definitions and domains has not proven to be a major hindrance to progress as long as there is general consensus among researchers as to the major definitional features of a given construct and the domains that fit under this construct (McCall, 1986). While there are multiple definitions of *temperament*, for all intents and purposes the majority of researchers in the field would accept as a "working definition": "Biologically rooted individual differences in behavior tendencies that are present early in life and are relatively stable across various kinds of situations and over the course of time" (Bates, 1989, p. 4). There also appears to be agreement that the individual differences referred to in the working definition should bear some resemblance to later appearing personality traits (Halverson et al., 1994; Strelau, 1987).

While a variety of individual characteristics have been listed under the rubric of temperament, from the relatively restricted focus on emotionality by Goldsmith and Campos (1982) to the Big Nine of Thomas and Chess (1977), there does appear to be general agreement that the following list defines the major dimensions of temperament (Bates, 1989):

1. Negative emotionality (e.g., fear, anger),
2. Difficultness (e.g., high intense, easily evoked negative moods),
3. Adaptability to new situations or people (e.g., inhibition),
4. Activity level,
5. Self-regulation (e.g., soothability),
6. Reactivity (e.g., how intense a stimulus is needed to invoke a response),
7. Sociability-positive emotionality (e.g., pleasure in social interactions).

Going beyond individual dimensions there also is increasing agreement that the various temperament dimensions listed above fall into one of two overall domains: reactivity and self-regulation (Rothbart & Bates, 1998).[1] Reactivity encompasses those dimensions of temperament involved in the onset, duration, and intensity of response to social and object stimulation, and can be further divided into positive and negative reactivity, with negative reactivity in turn being subdivided into anger (e.g., distress to limits) and fear (e.g., distress to novelty) (Rothbart & Derryberry, 1981; Rothbart, Derryberry, & Hershey, 2000). Self regulation refers to those processes that act to attenuate or accentuate the individual's reactivity to stimulation (Rothbart et al., 2000). Like reactivity, self-regulation can also be subdivided. The earliest appearing form of self-regulation is reactive control, which involves involuntary tendencies to avoid or inhibit responding to negative stimulation and to approach positive stimuli. Active control, which involves voluntary attentional regulation and the ability to inhibit ongoing behavior, appears later in development and can supersede the influence of reactive control tendencies (Eisenberg, 2002; Derryberry & Rothbart, 1997). Within this two domain framework it is the interaction between different levels of reactivity and self-regulation that acts to guide the course of temperament driven behavior (Belsky, Friedman, & Hsieh, 2001; Eisenberg et al., 2001). For example, 5-month-old infants who were high in reactivity showed different degrees of defiant behavior at 30 months, depending upon their level of self-regulation at 5 months (Stifter, Spinrad, & Braungart-Rieker, 1999).

Regardless of whether temperament is viewed at the dimension or the domain level, a continuing problem has been the difficulty in defining what distinguishes the behaviors that we call temperament from similar behaviors in other domains. Certainly, if we look at the major features of the working definition of temperament (early appearing, relatively stable, biologically rooted), these criteria easily could be applied to a variety of behaviors from distinctly different domains, such as intelligence or motivation. At the dimensional level, in Strelau's (1989) theory of temperament, activity level is linked to goal-directed behavior, with individual differences appearing in the difficulty and complexity of activities in which the individual engages. However, goal directed persistence and preference for challenging tasks have been claimed as fundamental aspects of mastery motivation (Barrett & Morgan, 1995). Similarly, the potential overlap between negative emotionality as a dimension of temperament versus negative emotionality as an index of internalizing behavior disorders has long been noted (Lemery, Essex, & Smider, 2002). At the domain level individual differences in self-regulation are viewed as due to the operation of inhibitory control processes, which are linked to attentional mechanisms such as selective attention (Rothbart, 1991). However, inhibitory control has also been labeled as a cognitive phenomenon (Williams et al., 1999), while both attentional flexibility and attentional control (e.g., vigilance) also have been claimed as domains of information processing by cognitive theorists (Kinchla, 1992). Similarly, self-regulation itself is viewed by many cognitive theorists as the "hallmark" of cognition and cognitive processing (Borkowski & Dukewich, 1996).

It could be argued that the question of what field of study a given construct "truly" belongs to could be viewed as a form of semantic nit-picking. However, I see this problem as potentially much more fundamental. One of the major criticisms of social science theories is their lack of preciseness (Dar, 1987). I would argue that such imprecision is more likely to occur when theories that are designed to explain the nature of a particular domain (e.g., temperament) simply assimilate constructs from other domains as an essential part of the theory, without due regard for the origins of such constructs. For example, individual differences in activity level may reflect disorganized behavior as in the case of attention deficit hyperactivity disorder, in which case activity would serve as a risk influence upon subsequent development. Alternatively, individual differences in activity level may reflect temperament driven goal directed surgency, in which case activity could serve as a protective influence upon subsequent development (Wills et al., 2001). As seen in the case of classic psychoanalysis, theories that are definitionally imprecise ultimately become overelastic: being able to explain everything while truly explaining nothing. While current theories of temperament cannot be considered as overelastic, I believe there is a danger of these theories evolving in this direction, unless they attempt to deal with perennial questions such as what criteria can be used to define the realm into which a particular individual characteristic best fits. This problem is further compounded when researchers do not distinguish between different aspects of temperament dimensions (e.g., focused attention versus distractibility versus attention shifting) and lump them together as a composite index (Belsky et al., 2001). When this is done, specific predictive relations may be lost, as in the case where different dimensions of inhibition have been shown to be related to the ability to sustain ongoing behavior versus the ability to inhibit ongoing behavior (Kochanska, Coy, & Murray, 2001). To deal with such issues I would argue that it is essential to go beyond studying temperament in isolation and look at how and how much the various domains of temperament noted above overlap with similarly named constructs from other nontemperament domains.

There are two ways to deal with the question of potential overlap between similarly named constructs from different domains. As exemplified in our working definition, the first way is to acknowledge that we do have a construct definition problem. Among other things, this means not assuming that, because a trait fits our working definition of temperament, the trait is uniquely temperament in nature. Particularly for individual characteristics involving early personality traits, some individual traits do appear to fit better within the domain of temperament than in other domains. Traits fitting into this category would include emotionality, reactivity, difficultness, and activity. For other individual traits, such as attention or task orientation, where nontemperament domains appear to have equivalent claims, I would argue for viewing these as a separate "hybrid" class. Hybrid traits, while sharing some features with more classic temperament characteristics, also share features with characteristics from nontemperament domains. This situation is illustrated in Figure 2.1.

Viewing individual characteristics such as attention or task orientation as a hybrid class is not a semantic "sleight of hand" device. There are conceptual and analytic tools available that are designed to deal with situations where the boundaries that determine classification of a trait are unclear. Particularly for hybrid individual traits whose characteristics allow them to be assigned to any one of a number of domains, one potential approach is to apply what has been called "fuzzy logic" (Ohayon, 1999). Fuzzy logic involves both a theory and a method that can be used in situations where there are multiple, nondichotomous linguistic constructs that have overlapping boundaries (e.g., the boundaries of attention as temperament may well overlap with the boundaries of attention as cognition). Using fuzzy logic, it is possible to assess the degree of resemblance of a specific characteristic to the characteristics of a larger class, with the degree of resemblance ranging from zero (no overlap) to 1.0 (total overlap). For what appear to be nonhybrid traits, like emotionality or reactivity, we would expect the degree of resemblance between characteristics of these traits and characteristics of traits drawn from cognition or motivation to be essentially zero order. For what appear to be hybrid traits, like attention or persistence, we would expect the degree of resemblance to characteristics drawn from cognition or motivation to be more than zero order, but less than perfect in magnitude.

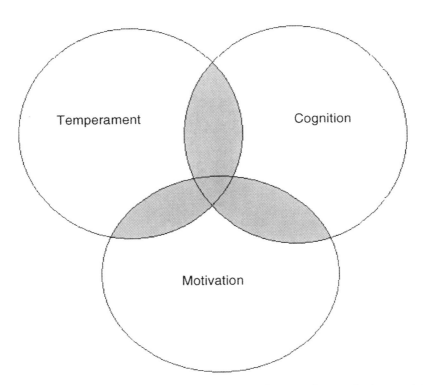

Figure 2.1   Example of a hybrid grouping of traits. Unshaded areas refer to trait characteristics that are unique to a specific domain. Shaded areas refer to aspects of trait characteristics that overlap multiple domains.

Use of fuzzy logic approaches would make it possible not only to determine to what degree a trait fits the criteria for membership in the domain of temperament versus the degree to which it is a hybrid trait, but also to determine what characteristics of the trait are more likely to fall under the membership criteria for each class. For example, for the hybrid dimension of attention, experts in cognition and temperament could be given lists of characteristics defining attention and their task would be to rate such characteristics as more likely to reflect attention as cognition or attention as temperament. Using fuzzy logic analytic procedures similar to those applied to understanding how individuals categorize objects or make social judgments (Massaro, 1987), such ratings could be used to determine which characteristics are most salient in defining the temperament components of attention versus those that are more applicable to attention as cognition. The former class of characteristics would be those we would want to emphasize when designing temperament assessment procedures that include attention as a salient dimension. Obviously, this is a very different line of research from what temperament researchers have done in the past. However, the use of alternative strategies, such as fuzzy logic, would seem to be a potentially important future line of inquiry if we are to truly understand what temperament means, and what defines those individual characteristics that uniquely or primarily fall within the domain of temperament.

WHY IS THERE ONLY MODEST INTERPARENT AGREEMENT AND STABILITY OF TEMPERAMENT?

Parent Agreement

As noted, one of our major assumptions underlying the construct of temperament is that temperament is a stable individual characteristic. Stability of temperament is assumed to occur both across situations and across time. Given the possibility of different contexts influencing children's expression of temperament at home and at school (Goldsmith, Rieser-Danner, & Briggs, 1991), it is perhaps not surprising to find only modest relations between parent and preschool teachers temperament ratings of individual children (Eisenberg et al., 2001; Lemery et al., 2002). However, contextual influences should be less likely to occur with mother-father ratings of their child's temperament, given that parent ratings presumably are based on observing the child in the same environmental context—the home. Thus, it is extremely troubling to find only moderate agreement by parents on the nature of their child's temperament (Mangelsdorf, Schoppe, & Buur, 2000; Slabach, Morrow, & Wachs, 1991), with mean correlations between mothers' and fathers' ratings of infants and toddlers (Goldsmith, 1996), preschool children (Lemery et al., 2002) or school age children (Rothbart et al., 2001) typically in the $r = .3$ to $r = .4$ range. The modest levels of interparent agreement shown for ratings of children's temperament are problematical, if for no other reason than their implications for the stability of temperament across time. How can we propose individual stability of a child's inhibition or activity level across time when there is disagreement at the initial measurement point about how temperamentally inhibited or active a child actually is?

What might be the reasons for the moderate level of parental agreement about the characteristics of their child's temperament? The hypothesis that fathers' ratings are less accurate because fathers spend less time with their children has not received strong empirical support (Slabach et al., 1991). There is some evidence indicating that level of agreement between parents varies as a function of the temperament dimension being considered. Higher interparent agreement has been found to occur for scales assessing negative emotionality (e.g., fear, fussy, difficultness), activity or shyness than for scales assessing positive emotionality, attention, perceptual sensitivity or persistence (Goldsmith, 1996; Goldsmith & Campos, 1990; Mebert, 1989; Rothbart et al., 2001). These data suggest that parents may be more attuned to those aspects of their child's temperament, such as high activity, negative emotionality or shyness, that call for more active parental involvement (Bell & Chapman, 1986). However, even for these domains, the level of parental agreement rarely goes beyond the $r = .5$ range, suggesting that other factors are operating besides just some temperament dimensions being more salient for parents (Rothbart et al., 2001). With regard to the possibility that the structure of temperament may differ for mothers and fathers (e.g., mothers and fathers may be using different behaviors to represent the same temperament dimension for their child), the evidence is mixed. When subscales from temperament questionnaires are the basis of analysis some studies show different factor structures underlying mothers' and fathers' ratings of their child's temperament (Goldsmith & Campos, 1990). In contrast, other studies suggest little difference in the types of behaviors used by mothers and fathers to rate specific temperament characteristics of their child (Hubert, 1989). The extent to which such differences reflect methodological differences among studies in regard to what parents are rating remains unclear.

It is possible that the moderate level of interparent agreement is a narrow methodological issue that is unique to questionnaire measures of temperament, perhaps reflecting the possibility that parental temperament ratings primarily reflect subjective aspects of parental rather then child characteristics (Mangelsdorf et al., 2000). Differences in mothers' and fathers' ratings of their child's temperament have been associated with levels of parental anxiety or depression (Mebert, 1991). However, such a conclusion is problematical given evidence that parental report measures of their child's temperament are not purely subjective, but also assess real existing differences in those domains of individual child characteristics which we call temperament (Bates, 1994). For example, if parental report measures of their infant's temperament were purely subjective, we would not expect to see the significant levels of relation between parent report measures and objective laboratory assessments of temperament that repeatedly have been documented in the literature (Rothbart & Bates, 1998; Slabach et al., 1991).

If the moderate levels of interparent agreement documented above cannot be understood solely by reference to issues involving the measurement of temperament per se, what other possibilities are there? Continuing the overall theme of this chapter I would argue that we need to go beyond temperament in isolation if we are to more fully understand the sources of moderate levels of reliability of parent temperament ratings. One possibility is that nontemperament individual child characteristics may play a role in explaining the modest level of interparent agreement. Some evidence has suggested that mothers' ratings are influenced more by the age of their child while fathers' ratings tend to be influenced more by their child's gender and parity (Slabach et al., 1991). Another potential explanation is based on the possibility that while parents share the same overall home context with their children there may be differences in the types of behaviors that mothers and fathers use when interacting with their children, and that these differences may be reflected in different temperament related behavioral patterns displayed by the child to their mother and father (Mangelsdorf et al., 2000; Rothbart et al., 2001). Unfortunately, at present all too little evidence is available relating differences in parental ratings of child temperament to differences in child characteristics or to differences in parent-specific interactions with their children.

Reviews focusing on biological contributions to temperament have offered another potential explanation for the modest levels of interparent agreement. Both Nelson (1994) and Rothbart, Derryberry, and Posner (1994) have noted two fundamental points about central nervous system contributions to the development and expression of temperament. First, there are multiple central nervous system areas involved in the development and expression of temperament. For example, behavioral inhibition appears to develop as a function of coordinated interaction between the hippocampus, prefrontal cortex, and portions of the motor system. Second, the different central nervous system areas which underlie the development of specific dimensions of temperament reach functional maturity at different times. For example, the hippocampal region matures earlier than does the prefrontal cortex (Nelson, 1994). What are the implications of these biological foundations for understanding levels of interparent agreement? As pointed out by Nelson (1994), while young infants have the capacity for short-term reactivity to stimulation, they may not have the capacity during the first year of life to store emotional memories associated with such reactivity. What this means is that the developing central nervous system structure of young infants may not permit consistency across different situations, until the relevant central nervous system structures that allow emotional memory storage have reached functional maturity (sometime between 12 and 24 months). As a result, mothers and fathers may be seeing fairly inconsistent reactions from their young child to particular stimuli, making it difficult for them to come up with a coherent and agreed on characterization of their infant, particularly if mothers and fathers treat their infant differently (Wachs & King, 1994). This does not mean that the young infant is deliberately tailoring different reactivity patterns to their mothers and their fathers, but rather that the nature of the early central nervous system may not permit infants to display consistent emotional reactivity patterns. Indirect support for this hypothesis is seen in the increase in parental agreement across the first two years of life (Mangelsdorf et al., 2000) with little change in level of agreement between the preschool and early school years (Rothbart et al., 2001). Such differences could reflect the faster rate of brain development earlier in life, as compared to the slower developmental rate after preschool. Again, this neurobiological approach to the question of moderate interparent agreement is one that could not have been developed by focusing on the measurement of temperament in isolation.

Stability of Temperament[2]

As long as temperament was regarded as primarily biologically-genetically driven, the logical assumption was that individual differences in temperament should be stable over time (Wilson & Matheny, 1986). However, with the increasing evidence on the role played by contextual factors on the expression of individual differences in temperament (Wachs & Kohnstamm, (2002), it is now more logical to expect only modest stability of temperament over time.[3] Further, given changes in both the expression and measurement of temperament at different ages, it is also likely that what stability there is will take the form of heterotypic continuity, with stability occurring for the underlying structure of temperament even as the behavioral form of temperament changes (Fox et al., 2001). For the most part these predictions appear to have been confirmed. Based on parent report measures moderate stability of individual temperament dimensions appears to be the norm (Guerin et al., 2003; Kerr, Lambert, Stattin, & Larson, 1994; Rothbart, Derryberry, & Hershey, 2000), with increasing stability after 2 years of age (Lemery et al., 1999; Pfeifer et al., 2002). For example, mean stability of parent ratings of their children between 18 and 48 months on five temperament dimensions assessed by the Toddler Behavior Assessment Questionnaire was $r = .35$, with a range from $r = .06$ to $r = .54$ (Goldsmith, 1996). When dimensional analysis is used, based on stability of the factor structure of temperament over time, a similar pattern of moderate stability again emerges (Pedlow, Sanson, Prior, & Oberklaid, 1993; Rothbart et al., 2001).

One concern about the research literature on stability of parent reports of child temperament is the issue of whether the findings reflect stability of child temperament or parent perceptions (Lemery et al., 1999). One way of dealing with this question is to look at the stability of objective, laboratory based temperament assessments. The evidence from this body of literature is quite consistent with the evidence from the parent report literature, again indicating moderate stability of laboratory assessments of child temperament (Matheny & Phillips, 2002; Rothbart et al., 2000). For example, a measure of preschoolers' reticence in a novel laboratory situation was moderately correlated with their scores on laboratory based assessments of general inhibition ($r = .24$) and social inhibition ($r = .23$) obtained two years earlier. Again, stability of laboratory assessments of temperament is found to be greater after 24 months of age (Kochanska, 2001). For both parent report and laboratory measures degree of stability depends in part on what dimension of temperament is assessed. For example, data taken from parent report measures indicate generally higher stability for activity level (Guerin et al., 2003), while studies using laboratory assessments report higher stability for indices of positive affect (Rothbart et al., 2000).

A similar pattern is seen when a person centered typological approach is utilized, where laboratory assessments are used to classify individual children as extremely inhibited or uninhibited. In these types of studies stability is assessed by determining which children maintain their extreme rankings over time. The results from these indicate that while the majority of those children who are extremely inhibited or uninhibited in infancy are not at the extremes later in life, there is a subset of children who do remain at the extremes across time (Fox et al., 2001; Kagan, Snidman, & Arcus, 1998). For example, Pfiefer et al. (2002) report that 74% of children who had been classified as extremely inhibited as toddlers were not in the extreme inhibition group at 7 years of age; similarly, 83% of toddlers who were classified as extremely uninhibited were no longer classified in this way at 7 years. While the results from these studies indicate a shift away from early extreme classifications, the pattern of findings across studies indicates that toddlers at one extreme rarely fall into the other extreme group later in life. Rather, the shift is from extreme toward less extreme temperament patterns.

As previously noted, a shift in our conceptualization of the nature of influences on temperament has led to an increasing appreciation of the potential plasticity in temperament. Temperament is a moderately stable individual characteristic, but it is not fixed in time. A critical question is what factors lead to continuity or discontinuity in individual patterns of temperament over time. Within the framework of this chapter the focus is on contextual factors that can influence the stability of temperament. However, context is not the whole story. Besides context, other influences that can impact on the stability of temperament include neonatal biomedical status (Garcia-Coll, Halpern, Vohr, Seifer, & Oh, 1992; Riese, 1987) and individual differences in intelligence (Asendorpf, 1994).

CONTEXTUAL CONTRIBUTIONS TO THE ETIOLOGY, DEVELOPMENT, AND CONSEQUENCES OF INDIVIDUAL DIFFERENCES IN TEMPERAMENT

In the accepted working definition presented at the start of this chapter, traditionally temperament has been defined and conceptualized as a phenomenon with strong biological roots. In delineating the biological roots of temperament there has been a strong and continuing emphasis on the contribution of genetics to individual differences in temperament (Goldsmith, 1989; DiLalla & Jones, 2000; Plomin & Saudino, 1994). Particularly in recent years there also has been an increasing amount of evidence documenting central nervous system (Calkins & Fox, 1994; Fox et al., 2001; Kagan et al., 1989; Strelau, 1994), subcortical (Woodward et al., 2001) and autonomic nervous system contributions to individual differences in temperament (Boyce et al., 2002; Stifter et al., 1999). The possibility that individual variability in temperament may be related to nutritional influences has also been recently raised as well (Wachs, 2000b). However, even among temperament theorists who have a strong biological orientation, there is agreement that temperament is not just a biological phenomenon (Goldsmith et al., 2002; Strelau, 2002). Indeed, one of the surprising conclusions drawn from an earlier review of biological contributions to temperament was that contextual influences, such as the nature of the child's psychosocial environment, or environmental processes such as learning, cannot be ignored in the study of temperament (Bates & Wachs, 1994). What is the role that context plays in the study of temperament? I would argue that temperament-contextual linkages can be seen in five areas.

1. Context can act to change the nature of the individual's temperament, certainly on the behavioral level and possibly on the biological level.
2. The expression of temperament, in terms of issues like stability, can be influenced by the overall cultural context within which the individual develops.
3. Temperament can act to influence the nature of the individual's microcontext. Once we understand the issues involved in areas 1–3, we are in a position to look at the developmental consequences of individual variability in temperament.
4. In understanding linkings between temperament and environment, it is essential to remember that such findings are bidirectional and not unidirectional in nature.
5. Temperament and environment may interact in a nonlinear fashion to produce developmental outcomes that could be predicted neither by temperament or environment acting in isolation, nor by linear combinations of temperament and environment.

My choice of evidence to address the first area listed above is based on methodological considerations. As Crockenberg (1986) has noted, in studies that concurrently measure temperament and context it often is difficult to establish whether it is the child's temperament influencing their caregiver's rearing style, or the caregiver's rearing style that is influencing the child's level of temperament. Given this potential confound my conclusions on temperament and context will be based on: (a) longitudinal investigations in which the measurement of temperament precedes the measurement of context or vice versa; (b) studies assessing nonparental aspects of the environment that are less likely to be influenced by the child's temperament, thus allowing inferences to be made about directionality when relations between temperament and environment are found; and (c) intervention studies that allow causal inferences to be made. Obviously, there still will be interpretive problems, even with these types of designs. Longitudinal predictive relations may be carried by the auto-correlation of either temperament or environment over time, while the absence of intervention effects may not mean that environment does not influence temperament but only that the wrong aspects of environment were chosen as the focus of intervention. However, even with these limitations, these types of studies serve to advance our understanding of the nature of links between temperament and context.

CONTEXTUAL INFLUENCES ON TEMPERAMENT

While not in any way negating the essential biological roots of individual differences in temperament, evidence also has shown that the level and course of temperament can be influenced by environmental characteristics. Three lines of evidence are of particular relevance.

Longitudinal Studies

Initial evidence showing how changes in individual temperament are associated with the nature of the child's environment typically involved assessment of negative emotionality during the first year of life. Specifically, Belsky, Fish, and Isabella (1991) have shown that infants who shifted from low to high negative emotionality during the first year of life had fathers who were both less involved with them early in infancy and who had greater feelings of marital dissatisfaction, as compared to infants whose level of negative emotionality remained low during this time period. In contrast, infants whose level of high negative emotionality declined over the first year of life had parents who had better marital relations and whose mothers displayed greater sensitivity, as compared to infants whose level of negative emotionality remained high during this time period. Similarly, Fish (1997) has reported that infants whose level of negative emotionality declined over the first year of life had mothers who received higher levels of social support, whereas infants whose levels of negative emotionality remained low had parents who were in a more harmonious marital relationship. Interestingly, relations between environment and positive emotionality in these studies were generally either nonsignificant or inconsistent. Going beyond the first year of life, Engfer (1986) has reported that children who switched from easy to difficult temperament between 4 and 18 months were in families with more marital problems, as compared to children who continued to display easy temperaments; children who switched from difficult to easy temperament had mothers who were higher in sensitiveness than mothers of children who continued to display difficult temperaments. The generalizability of findings relating context to negative emotionality also has been shown for older infants living in non-Western, developing countries. In my own research we attempted to determine if we could replicate the results found for North American infants that parental nonresponse to infant distress leads to even more negative infant emotionality (Bell & Ainsworth, 1972; Crockenberg & Smith, 1982). Using a sample of rural Egyptian toddlers studied between 18 and 30 months, based on repeated naturalistic observations of both toddler behavior and parents' reactions to these behaviors our results did show that lower parental responsivity to toddler distress was related to higher levels of toddler distress from 24 to 29 months, even after statistically controlling for level of toddler distress from 18 to 23 months (Wachs et al., 1993). The importance of family characteristics noted above has also been shown with regard to other dimensions of temperament besides negative emotionality. For example, Halverson & Deal (2001) have reported that changes in the level of persistence during the preschool years was systematically related to more family cohesion and better quality of marital relationships.

Other recent evidence also has related contextual characteristics to variability in self-regulation of older infants. Specifically, higher levels of self-regulation during the second year of life have been found to be related to greater mother–infant synchrony during the first year of life (Feldman, Greenbaum, & Yirmiya, 1999) and to higher maternal responsiveness at 22 months (Kochanska et al., 2000), even after controlling for initial levels of reactivity and self-regulation. Going well past the infancy period Feldman and Weinberger (1994) have reported that boys who demonstrated increasing levels of self-regulation between 12 and 16 years of age were more likely to come from cohesive families, even after controlling for initial levels of self-regulation.

Recent studies also have focused on changes in inhibition as a function of parental rearing styles. Arcus (2001) has reported that infants who were over-reactive to stimuli in the first year of life exhibited less inhibited behavior during the second year of life if their mothers set firm limits, did not reinforce infant distress signals by extra attention, and made age appropriate demands of their infants. Similar findings also have been reported by Park et al. (1997) who found lower inhibition at 3 years of age related to higher levels of parental instrusiveness and lower levels of sensitivity. The possibility that parental overattention and sensitivity to infant distress may act to stabilize early inhibition, also is seen in the results reported by Rubin et al. (2002), indicating that toddlers who were highly inhibited in interaction with peers at 2 years of age were more likely to continue to be highly inhibited two years later if their mother's rearing styles were characteristically overprotective and negative/intrusive.

Nonparental Contextual Characteristics

In distinguishing contextual influences on child temperament from influences of child temperament on context, one approach would be to look at aspects of the environment which are potentially less sensitive to the influence of child temperament. One such aspect is the physical environment the stage or setting on which social transactions between child and caregiver take place (Wohlwill & Heft, 1987). The extent to which a child's temperamental characteristics can act to influence dimensions of the physical environment, such as number of wall decorations or rooms to people ratio, is both less likely and less intuitively obvious. Rather, it is more likely that specified dimensions of the physical environment can act to influence child temperament characteristics. One such dimension is environmental chaos, which involves factors such as crowding (e.g., rooms to people ratio), and levels of nonhuman noise in the home. Several studies provide converging evidence of the importance of environmental chaos as an influence on child temperament. Matheny, Wilson, and Thoben (1987) have reported that higher levels of environmental noise and confusion in the homes of 18-month-old toddlers were related to behavior indicating less tractable temperaments. In my own research, direct observations of home physical environments were used to assess noise level, crowding, and home traffic pattern (number of people coming and going in the home), while parent responses to the Toddler Temperament Questionnaire were used to assess temperament characteristics of the infant (Wachs, 1988). Results indicated that higher levels of home crowding were related to 12-month-old infants being characterized as lower in approach, less adaptive, and having more intense negative moods. These results held even after statistically partialling out the potential influence of parent temperament, based on parent self-report scores on the revised Dimensions of Temperament Scale. More recent evidence (Matheny & Phillips, 2001) has indicated that increases in negative emotionality during the first year of life were related to higher levels of home chaos while increases in negative emotionality during the second year were related to higher levels of home crowding. Consistent with earlier research, the Matheny & Phillips data also suggest that boys may be particularly sensitive to the negative influences of home chaos.

Another aspect of context that may be less sensitive to child temperament involves the child's out of home experiences. Fox et al. (2001) have reported that 75% of children who exhibited stable high inhibition over the first 4 years of life had exclusive parental care during the first 2 years of life; in contrast 69% of children who shifted from high inhibition to less extreme inhibition over the first 4 years were in nonparental care with at least one other nonsib peer during their first 2 years. Consistent with the findings on inhibition described earlier, Fox et al. suggest that increased exposure to other experiences outside the home and reduced attention by nonparental caregivers may act to reduce initial levels of inhibition.

Intervention Studies

Perhaps the strongest evidence for contextual environmental influences on child temperament comes from studies where specific aspects of the child's environment are manipulated to determine whether such manipulation can influence later temperament. While such intervention studies are relatively scarce, they do provide converging evidence on the role of environment in the development of early temperament. In terms of global interventions, MacPhee, Burchinal, and Ramey (1997) compared the temperament patterns of disadvantaged infants who were enrolled in a special day care program designed to remediate cognitive deficits. While not all dimensions of temperament were influenced by day care intervention, infants in the special day care did show significantly greater increases in measures of task orientation over a 2-year period, as compared either to control infants who did not receive intervention or to infants who were in routine family care situations. These results may, in part, reflect the hybrid nature of task orientation, as discussed earlier in this chapter. Evidence which is more relevant to temperament per se comes from research by Van den Boom (1994) using a sample of highly irritable 6-month-old infants, whose mothers were enrolled in a special 3-month program designed to increase maternal sensitivity and appropriate responsivity. As compared to infants whose mothers did not receive this special intervention, infants in the intervention group were rated by observers as being more sociable, more self-soothing, and displaying lower levels of negative emotionality at 9 months of age.

Summary: Influence of Context Upon Temperament

Taken together, the evidence from these three lines of research clearly converges in the conclusion that at least some aspects of temperament are sensitive to contextual influences. This pattern of findings does not contradict conclusions about the essential biological nature of temperament, but does underline the fact that an understanding of individual variability in the development of temperament will require focusing on both the biology and the context of the child. This may be particularly true for those aspects of temperament that are likely to prove problematic for parents, such as negative emotionality or inhibition. Whether this reflects a greater sensitivity of these domains to contextual influences, or a greater effort by parents to change aspects of infant temperament that they regard as problematical, remains an unanswered question.

Given that environment can act to influence the characteristics and course of individual temperament, a fundamental question is the level at which environmental influences on temperament operate. Bates (1989) has proposed a conceptual scheme wherein temperament can be viewed as operating simultaneously on three levels: the behavioral, the neural, and the constitutional (e.g., genetics, hormones). While it would be easy to assume that environmental influences on temperament operate only on the behavioral level, such a conclusion is not necessarily warranted (Calkins & Fox, 1994).

Environmental factors have been shown to influence central nervous system development at the human level (Nelson & Bloom, 1997). Both human and infrahuman research have also extensively documented the impact of stress exposure to the operation of temperament-related neural–hormonal systems linked to individual differences in reactivity (Gunnar, 2000). In addition, environmental influences also can act to turn on or turn off specific regulator genes that determine which structural genetic influences actually are operating (Plomin et al., 1997). This evidence suggests that it may be premature to conclude that environmental influences on temperament operate only at the behavioral level.

CULTURAL INFLUENCES ON THE EXPRESSION OF INDIVIDUAL DIFFERENCES IN TEMPERAMENT

Differences in the level and pattern of temperament have been observed across different population or cultural groups (Gartstein, Slobodskaya, & Kinsht, 2003; Kohnstamm et al., 1998; Russell et al., 2003). For example, school age children in China are rated by their parents as being lower in conscientiousness (a measure encompassing distractibility and task persistence) then are same age children from western European countries (Kohnstamm et al., 1998). In addition, results from factor analytic based studies indicate that while the major dimensions of temperament such as emotionality appear across different cultures, secondary differences in the structure of temperament do vary between cultures (Gartstein et al., 2003; Rothbart et al., 2001). For example, Ahadi, Rothbart, & Ye (1993) have noted that while positive affect loaded on both the effortful control and extraversion factors in a U.S. sample, positive affect loaded only on the extraversion factor in a Chinese sample. What accounts for such differences is an open question. We cannot necessarily assume that population or group differences are due purely to cultural influences. Population groups also differ in biological characteristics, such as diet during pregnancy, which have the potential to influence infant physiology and, thereby, subsequent individual differences in temperament (Chisholm, 1981). For example, rural Egyptian populations typically have diets low in animal protein, which is a major source for vitamin B6. Egyptian neonates, whose mothers had low vitamin B6 status as measured in breast milk, were far more likely to demonstrate poor self-regulation when assessed with the Brazelton scale (McCullough et al., 1990). In addition, measurement issues also may be critical. As noted by Lewis, Ramsey, and Kawakami (1993), the belief that Japanese infants are less stress reactive than American infants holds only at the behavioral level; physiologically, Japanese infants appear to be more stress reactive than American infants.

These cautions notwithstanding, it is important to recognize that we cannot fully understand the expression of individual differences in temperament without taking into account cultural context. Kagan, Arcus, and Snidman (1993) have speculated that population differences in temperament can influence the nature of cultures within which individuals reside. Specifically, Kagan et al. (1993) have suggested that cultures are less likely to develop philosophies that contradict the temperamental characteristics of the majority of individuals within the culture. For example, in cultures where the majority of individuals are highly reactive, philosophies based on calmness and placidity (e.g., Buddhism) are less likely to be accepted as valid. While clearly speculative, this argument does raise the question of direct linkages from temperament to culture.

While there is little direct evidence for the position taken by Kagan et al. (1993), some evidence does exist for the operation of a reverse process; namely, that the meaning, expression, and consequences of temperament can be moderated by cultural characteristics. Perhaps the most dramatic example of this phenomena is seen in evidence indicating that fussy difficult infants living in developing countries are more likely to survive during drought conditions (DeVries, 1984), or where there are high levels of infant mortality (Scheper-Hughes, 1987). Differential survival rates appear to be based, in part, on culturally driven beliefs about the desirability of certain infant characteristics. Less dramatic but equally valid, Thomas and Chess (1986) have noted how concepts like difficult temperament may have very different meanings in different cultural contexts. Characteristics that are viewed as difficult in one culture may not be viewed in the same way in other cultures. For example, in cultures like Kenya where caregiving by multiple siblings is the norm, infants who are less soothable or who are less able to adapt to multiple caregivers are more likely to be considered as difficult than in cultures where multiple caregiving is not utilized (Super & Harkness, 1986). Similarly, the infant's ability to get on a regular schedule (regularity) is a far more meaningful temperament trait for caregivers in time-driven Western cultures (Super & Harkness, 1999) than for parents in non-Western cultures, such as India, where time demands are not central (Malhotra, 1989).

We also see the importance of cultural context in regard to the consequences associated with different temperament traits. In the traditional goodness-of-fit model described by Thomas and Chess (1986), adjustment is a function of the degree to which the individual's characteristics match or fit the characteristics of the microcontext within which the individual lives (e.g., the home environment). We also can extend the concept of goodness of fit to culture, given evidence indicating that children whose temperamental characteristics provide a better fit to culturally based values and preferences are more likely to show better adjustment (Ballantine & Klein, 1990; Korn & Gannon, 1983). For example, the long-term negative consequences found for inhibited males in the United States are less likely to be seen in Sweden, where inhibited behavior by males is not necessarily viewed as a negative trait (Kerr, 1996).

A similar role for culture can also be seen in regard to developmental issues like the stability of temperament. Differential stability of temperament may be seen for individuals whose trait characteristics either fit or do not fit cultural beliefs about the value of such characteristics. For example, in cultures where inhibition is valued females who were inhibited as toddlers were far more likely to be inhibited as adolescents, whereas females who were uninhibited as toddlers were far less likely to be uninhibited as adolescents (Kerr et al., 1994).

At this point, there are far more studies based on simple cross-cultural comparisons of group differences in temperament than there are studies looking at specific cultural contributions to the nature, consequences, and development of temperament. However, it does seem clear from available evidence that we cannot understand the expression of individual differences in temperament in isolation from the cultural context in which the individual resides.

HOW DOES TEMPERAMENT INFLUENCE THE NATURE OF THE INDIVIDUAL'S CONTEXT?

A fundamental assumption in the pioneering work of the New York Longitudinal Study was that children with specific temperaments elicit specific patterns of reactivity from their parents (Thomas et al., 1968). Viewed in this way, temperament can be seen as an influence on the subsequent environment of the child. The process whereby children with specific temperaments are more likely to elicit certain types of reactions from others is an example either of *reactive covariance* (Plomin, DeFries, & Loehlin, 1977) or *control system theory* (Bell & Chapman, 1986). Thus, when children's behavior becomes overly intense (e.g., fussy difficult temperament, high activity level), caregivers are more likely to react by attempting to lower the level or the intensity of the child's behavior. In contrast, when children's behavior is overly passive (e.g., inhibited temperament), caregivers are more likely to react by attempting to raise the level or intensity of their child's behavioral style through techniques such as reward or prompting.

Though not deriving directly from the New York Longitudinal Study, a related concept is that of *active covariance* (Plomin et al., 1977), wherein individuals with different temperaments attempt to seek out niches in the environment that best fit the characteristics of their specific temperament. For example, evidence derived from Strelau's psychobiological model suggested that individuals with a low threshold for arousal would be less likely to prefer being in highly stimulating situations (e.g., heavy metal concerts) or occupations (e.g., air traffic controller), whereas individuals with a relatively high threshold for arousal would be more likely to prefer such contexts (Strelau, 1983). While active covariance processes do not necessarily change the nature of the individual's environment, they do change the likelihood of individuals with different temperaments encountering certain types of environmental settings.

In understanding how active and reactive covariance processes relate to the influence of temperament on context, two points are essential. First, as noted, the meaning of different dimensions of temperament and the nature of reactivity of others to children with different types of temperament may well vary as a function of cultural context (Chess & Thomas, 1991). Second, for both active and reactive covariance, relations between temperament and context are probabilistic and not deterministic in nature. Having a specific temperament increases the probability of certain reactions from others, or the probability that one will prefer to be in certain environments, but does not guarantee either differential reactivity or differential exposure. Probabilistic and not deterministic linkages occur because a variety of nontemperament factors can serve to accentuate or attenuate the degree to which individual temperament characteristics influence the nature of the individual's subsequent environment. Potential moderators of temperament-environment covariance include, but are not limited to, nontemperament child characteristics such as age or gender, individual parental characteristics such as preference for certain types of child behavior patterns, child and parent nutritional status, and contextual characteristics like the level of chaos or flexibility in the environment (Slabach et al., 1991; Wachs, 1992). For example, experienced mothers and mothers who believe they have the ability to deal effectively with their infant's behavior appear to be less reactive to temperamentally fussy and difficult behavior by their infants than are less experienced mothers or mothers who have doubts about their ability to cope (Cutrona & Troutman, 1986; Lounsbury & Bates, 1982).

Reactive Covariance

Keeping these constraints in mind, what is the nature of evidence linking variability in individual temperament to the characteristics of the individual's environment? In regard to the question of reactive covariance, particularly during the first 2 years of life, some individual longitudinal studies have recorded evidence suggesting that variability in infant temperament influences subsequent parenting behavior. For example, Van den Boom and Hoeksma (1994) have found that over time mothers of irritable infants show less visual and physical contact, less effective stimulation, less involvement, and less responsivity to positive signals from their infants as compared to mothers of nonirritable infants. Similarly, in a controlled laboratory study, Lounsbury and Bates (1982) have reported that adult raters expressed more irritation at the cries of difficult temperament infants than they did to the cries of easy temperament infants. Going beyond parenting per se, Guerin et al. (2003) have reported that higher levels of fussy difficult temperament in infancy are related to higher levels of family conflict through adolescence. However, other well-designed, large sample studies have reported few significant relations between early infant temperament and later caregiver interaction patterns (Pettit & Bates, 1984; Worobey & Blajda, 1989). These complex and inconsistent patterns of findings have led reviewers to conclude that there is a gap between the level of theoretical attention given to processes like reactive covariance and the degree of empirical validation of the operation of these processes, at least for the first several years of life (Crockenberg, 1986; Slabach et al., 1991).

There are a number of reasons why links between infant temperament and subsequent caregiver behavior patterns have not been consistently demonstrated. Some researchers have questioned whether parent report measures of infant temperament are the best approach for dealing with this question (Seifer, Schiller, Sameroff, Resnick, & Riordan, 1996). There is also the possibility that existing methodological practices may limit our ability to detect existing links between infant temperament and caregiver behavior. Methodological factors may be particularly important for the many studies in this area that use single short-term observations of caregiver–infant interaction. Average within week stability of single short term observations of mother–infant interactions is $r = .35$, a value which clearly raises doubts about the representativeness of measurements of caregiver behavior patterns toward infants which are based on single short-term observations (Wachs, 1987a). Going beyond only measurement issues, there also is the issue of whether or not reactive covariance between infant and temperament and later caregiver behavior is best assessed by point to point correlations over two time periods. If we look at trajectories of caregiver behavior over time across such dimensions as soothing (Van den Boom & Hoeksma, 1994) or teaching efforts (Maccoby, Snow, & Jacklin, 1984), results suggest a pattern of declining involvement by parents toward their more fussy difficult infants. Thus, depending on the time point chosen, we could see either differences or no differences in parent reaction to fussy difficult infants.

However, measurement and methodological issues are not the whole story, given evidence suggesting that, for some caregiver dimensions like physical contact stimulation or responsivity to fussing, there is little difference in maternal behavior toward irritable versus nonirritable infants, even when maternal behaviors are looked at across time (Van den Boom & Hoeksma, 1994). One hypothesized possibility is that reactive covariance is more likely to be found for infants with extreme temperament traits, who are viewed as being more likely to have an influence over their environment than are infants with less extreme temperament traits (Clarke & Clarke, 1988). Unfortunately, evidence on this hypothesis is sorely lacking. In one of the few studies in this area Sullivan and McGrath (1995) have found that correlations between infant and caregiver behaviors shown for extreme temperament infants are not found when a full sample is studied, including both extreme and nonextreme temperament infants. Unfortunately, since the correlations were taken concurrently, it is difficult to determine if the pattern of results reflects extreme temperament infants being more likely to influence their environment or environment being more likely to influence the behavior of extreme temperament infants. Support for the extreme temperament hypothesis is seen in the results of a study by Fox et al. (2001), who reported that infants who showed very high levels of negative reactivity at 4 months of age were significantly less likely to be placed in out of home daycare during their first two years than infants with initial high levels of positive reactivity or infants who were low in reactivity. The latter two groups did not differ, suggesting the possibility that the likelihood that reactive covariance will occur may depend not only on the intensity of the temperament trait but also on the characteristics of the trait.

More probable as an explanatory framework is evidence documenting how reactive covariance patterns between infant temperament and subsequent caregiver behavior patterns can be moderated by a variety of nontemperamental infant and adult characteristics (Slabach et al., 1991). For example, trajectories of caregiver response patterns toward their difficult infant have been shown to be moderated by factors such as infant gender (Maccoby et al., 1984), maternal substance abuse (Schuler, Black, & Starr, 1995), and maternal attitudes about how responsive they should be toward their infant (Crockenberg & McCluskey, 1986). Similarly, level of environmental chaos in the home has been shown to moderate the relation between infant difficult temperament and lower parental self-efficacy beliefs, with this relation occurring significantly more often in low chaos as opposed to highly chaotic homes (Corapci & Wachs, 2002). The overall pattern of findings supports a hypothesis that infant temperament is a necessary but not sufficient condition for producing variability in subsequent caregiver behavior patterns. This means that if we are to understand the processes underlying reactive covariance between infant temperament and caregiver behavior it is essential to go beyond temperament per se, and look at temperament as part of a larger system involving linked contributions between other aspects of the system such as nontemperamental child characteristics, home characteristics, and caregiver preferences and attitudes.

Active Covariance

While the concept of active covariance (niche picking) has been the focus of much theoretical speculation (e.g., Plomin, 1994; Scarr & McCartney, 1983), remarkably little research exists that actually documents how individuals with different temperaments act in ways that result in their inhabiting different types of contexts. One of the few examples we have of the process of active temperament-context covariance is seen in the work of Matheny (1986), showing how more active children, or children with less tractable temperaments, have a higher probability of putting themselves in dangerous situations that result in a greater frequency of physical injuries. Based on an underlying model where low arousability promotes high sensation seeking (Strelau, 1994), individual differences in sensation seeking have been linked to a variety of contextually relevant behavioral characteristics, such as substance abuse, sexual patterns, and reckless behavior, that could act to increase the individual's level of exposure to physical danger (Zuckerman, 1994). Alternatively, Gunnar (1994) has provided an elegant documentation of how, even in the same classroom, highly inhibited or uninhibited children experience different microenvironments, with inhibited children being more likely to be involved in familiar low peer contact activities while uninhibited children are more likely to be engaged in unfamiliar activities and have higher levels of peer social interactions and peer conflict.

Unfortunately, in terms of understanding the extent and impact of active temperament-context covariance currently we are restricted to these few examples. There are a variety of reasons why our database is so limited. One obvious reason involves the effort required to document such covariance. Obviously, we need highly accurate measures of individual temperament. Perhaps even more critically, we need detailed measures of the physical and social contextual characteristics that individuals with different temperaments inhabit. Such contextual measures are time consuming to obtain and cannot be derived from global, social address context assessments. However, even if we had such detailed assessments, I predict that we would not find the strong relations between individual temperament and subsequent contexts predicted by some theories (e.g., Scarr & McCartney, 1983). In good part, this is because active covariance processes will be moderated by, or will act in concert with, a variety of nontemperament characteristics. The operation of such nontemperament moderators is seen in some of the examples presented above. Thus, Matheny (1991) has reported that, in addition to child temperament, risk of child injury is also influenced by aspects of the child's context that are not likely to be influenced by the child's temperament, such as home chaos. Gunnar (1994) has noted that the degree to which inhibited children engage in unfamiliar classroom activities will depend on nontemperament aspects of classroom characteristics, such as organization level in the classroom and degree of teacher sensitivity and support.

The fact that links between an individual's temperament and an individual's context can be attenuated by a variety of influences other than temperament illustrates a larger issue directly related to the active covariance process itself. In general, the assumption underlying both theory (Scarr & McCartney, 1983) and research in this area (Schulenberg, Wadsworth, O'Malley, Bachman, & Johnston, 1996) is that individuals have a high degree of freedom to self-select into a variety of different contextual niches. In contrast, I would argue that there will be multiple limitations on one's ability to self-select into different types of contexts. Specifically, a variety of biological (e.g., malnutrition, chronic illness), caregiver belief (e.g., tolerance of child independence, authoritarian rearing styles), cultural (e.g., racism), and nontemperament individual characteristics (e.g., attachment, cognitive ability) can act both to influence the individual's exposure to different environmental contexts as well as the individual's ability to self-select into different contexts (Wachs, 2000a). For example, over time children with an extremely difficult temperament may be more likely to find themselves limited not only in terms of the types of peer groups available to them (Cairns, Cairns, Neckerman, Crest, & Gariety, 1988), but also in terms of educational and employment opportunities (Caspi, Elder, & Bem, 1987). Thus, even in a situation where there are ongoing active temperament-context covariance processes occurring, it will be essential to go beyond only temperament per se when attempting to understand how individuals with specific temperament characteristics have a higher probability of encountering and staying in different types of contexts.

THE NATURE OF TEMPERAMENT-CONTEXT LINKAGES

In previous sections, I have documented temperament influences on environment and environmental influences on temperament. However, it also is important to consider the possibility that transactional processes (Sameroff & Fiese, 1990), involving mutual bi-directional influences between temperament and environment operating over time, may be a better way of understanding relations between environment and temperament. One such example of mutual influences is seen in the work of Maccoby et al. (1984), who assessed both level of child difficultness and degree of maternal involvement during task situations at 12 and 18 months. Maccoby et al. reported that, while boys whose mothers were highly involved in teaching activities became less difficult between 12 and 18 months (environment → temperament), mothers with more difficult boys became less involved in teaching activities over the same time period (temperament → environment). A similar pattern of bidirectional reactivity was shown by Engfer (1986), who measured maternal sensitivity and child emotionality from the neonatal period through 18 months of age. Engfer's results indicated that, while maternal sensitivity in the neonatal period related to lower child difficultness at 4 months of age, child difficultness at 4 months of age related to lower maternal sensitivity at 8 months of age which, in turn, predicted lower child difficultness at 18 months of age (environment → temperament → environment). Bidirectional relations between infant sociability and maternal responsivity (Thoman, 1990), between infants' negative emotionality and maternal responsivity and sensitivity (Crockenberg & McCluskey, 1986), between infants soothability and degree of maternal soothing (Lewis & Ramsay, 1999) and between children's emotional self-regulation capacity and patterns of peer interaction also have been reported (Eisenberg & Fabes, 1992). Such bi-directional influences between temperament and context reinforce the basic hypothesis of this chapter; namely, that one cannot understand the nature or development of temperament in isolation from context. However, such findings also support the hypothesis that one cannot understand the nature or impact of context without also considering the temperamental characteristics of individuals in specific contexts.

HOW DO TEMPERAMENT AND CONTEXT INTERACT?

Relations between temperament and subsequent development can be either conceptualized in main effect terms (temperament → development) or in terms of multiple main effects (additive coaction: temperament + environment → development). However, main effects and additive coaction are not the only means by which temperament can influence development. As noted earlier, there also is the possibility of interactions among different temperament dimensions, as seen in evidence showing that linkages between negative emotionality and subsequent behavior problems will vary depending on the individual's level of self-regulation (Eisenberg et al., 1996). In addition, evidence has further suggested the possibility of nonlinear interactions between temperament and context.

By temperament-context interactions, I refer to the same environments having a different influence on individuals with different temperament characteristics, or the same temperament characteristics having a different influence on individuals living in different environments. In looking for temperament-context interactions, it is essential to keep in mind the multiple methodological and statistical problems that limit our ability to detect existing interactions. Such problems include but are not limited to the insensitivity of traditional analytic designs to interaction effects, the likelihood that interactions will appear in only certain segments of a given population group, and the need for highly sensitive measures to detect interaction effects (McClelland & Judd, 1993; Wachs & Plomin, 1991).

Given the multiple methodological and statistical problems that limit our ability to detect interactions, it is remarkable that there is a consistent body of evidence showing context by temperament interactions. One set of findings has shown how the impact of the environment can be moderated by individual differences in temperament (Wachs, 1992). An excellent example of this type of interaction is seen in studies indicating that the impact on development of *environmental stressors*, such as home chaos (Wachs, 1987b; Wachs & Gandour, 1883), maternal anger (Crockenberg, 1987), maternal unavailability (Lumley, Ables, Melamed, Pistone, & Johnson, 1990), disorganized attachment (as a marker for problematical parent–child relations; Stams, Juffer, & van Ijsendoorn, 2002), or divorce (Hetherington, 1989), is significantly greater for difficult temperament children than for children with easy temperaments. For example, relations between adolescents' level of substance abuse and environmental risk factors such as parent–child conflict or peer or parental substance abuse were significantly stronger for adolescents with a difficult temperament (Wills et al., 2001). Interestingly, the fact that having a difficult temperament is likely to increase the child's sensitivity to environmental risk factors does not negate the possibility that difficult temperament children may also be more sensitive to environmental protective factors as well. Evidence supporting this latter hypothesis is found in several studies. Feldman et al. (1999) have reported stronger relations between mother–infant synchrony in infancy and child compliance and ability to tolerate delay at two years of age for more difficult than for less difficult infants.

The other major temperament dimension that has been shown to interact with contextual characteristics is activity level. Results from several studies have indicated that higher levels of stimulation were needed to facilitate the development of low active infants but that the same levels of stimulation either were unrelated to or even inhibited the development of infants with higher activity levels (Gandour, 1989; Schaffer, 1966). For example, higher levels of parent object mediation (e.g., naming objects) were associated with higher levels of object mastery motivation in low active 12-month-old infants, but tended to inhibit mastery motivation in more active 12-month-olds (Wachs, 1987b).

Another aspect of context–temperament interaction occurs when the developmental consequences of individual differences in temperament are moderated by characteristics of the individual's psychosocial environment. One example of this second type of interaction is seen in the data presented by Guerin et al. (2003), showing how the link between difficult temperament in infancy and externalizing problems during the school years was significantly attenuated when difficult temperament infants were reared in a low conflict family environment (Guerin et al., 2003).

A further example of this type of interaction is seen in a series of studies by Kochanska (1993, 1995, 1997) showing how inhibited children are more likely to develop internal regulation mechanisms if their parents use gentle discipline than if they use more arousing forms of discipline. A similar set of findings has documented how relations between children's early resistance to parental control and later externalizing problems will vary as a function of the level of maternal control, with highly resistant children being less likely to show later externalizing problems when their mothers were high in control (Bates, Pettit, Dodge, & Ridge, 1997).

The pattern of findings presented in this final section shows how the contributions of temperament to development do not necessarily reflect the operation of temperament in isolation but, rather, can vary as a function of contributions from another domain; namely, characteristics of the child's environment. Obviously the converse also holds; namely, that we should not necessarily assume environmental main effects without also considering the temperamental characteristics of the individual on whom the environment impinges.

CONCLUSIONS: PERENNIAL PROBLEMS AND FUTURE DIRECTIONS

Our understanding of both the nature of children's development and the factors influencing variability in children's development has benefited greatly from research and theorizing on the role played by individual differences in temperament. As a result of this research and theorizing, we have gained a greater understanding of the contributions that the individual makes to his or her own development as well as the dimensions of temperament, such as self-regulation and reactivity that are fundamental to understanding these individual contributions. Of necessity, much of our past and present research in this area has focused primarily on temperament as a single, main effect predictor or outcome variable. This narrow focus is not unique to studies of temperament. Early studies in behavioral genetics focused essentially on demonstrating that genetic influences were relevant for an understanding of behavioral developmental variability; it is only recently that behavior genetic researchers have focused on process questions such as how genetic and nongenetic influences combine to impact on behavioral developmental variability (e.g., Plomin, 1994). It seems clear that we have reached a similar point in regard to temperament. We have established beyond doubt the relevance of temperament, both as an independent field of study and as a major contributor to individual behavioral and developmental variability. The time is now ripe to broaden the range of both our research and theorizing by looking at how temperament fits into a larger system of multiple influences on development and how temperament, in combination with other developmental influences, relates to individual differences in behavior and development. Focusing on temperament as part of a larger system of multiple developmental influences will allow us to go beyond temperament, while not losing our understanding of the unique role that temperament plays in development.

An example of such a system is shown in Figure 2.2, which illustrates patterns of bi-directional influences between temperament and nontemperament factors. One of the major implications to be drawn from Figure 2.2 is that in order to understand how temperament relates to development, we need to understand how temperament is related to biological, bio-social, and contextual influences on behavioral development. Viewing temperament as part of a larger system of multiple linked influences increases the likelihood of being able both to resolve longstanding issues in this field, as well as identifying important future research directions.

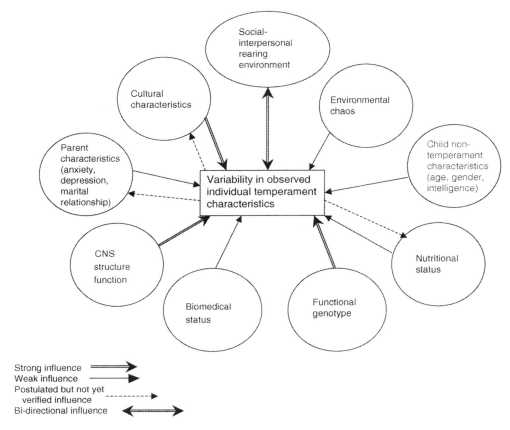

Figure 2.2 Temperament as part of a system of developmental influences. It is important to keep in mind that many of the nontemperament influences pictured in this figure are themselves linked. For example, the social interpersonal rearing environment covaries with genotype, nutritional status, culture, and environmental chaos; central nervous system (CNS) structure covaries with both biomedical and nutritional status which, in turn, covary with each other.

Within the systems framework described above three longstanding issues seem to be of particular salience. First, the increasing emphasis on self-regulation as a major domain of temperament increases the need to identify the nature of links between the construct of temperament and constructs such as attentional control, which traditionally have been viewed in cognitive terms but are now being viewed as an important component of self-regulation (Rothbart et al., 2000). Are there certain aspects of attentional control that are uniquely temperament-like in nature and different from attentional control as described by cognitive theorists, or is attentional control a cognitive process that has links with and influences individual differences in temperament? Within a systems framework, one way to deal with this question is further study on the neural underpinnings of temperament constructs such as self-regulation and cognitive constructs such as attentional control. Unique neural substrates would support the former explanation while distinct but linked substrates would support the latter explanation. Answers to this question are becoming increasingly likely, given advances in neural measurement techniques of both cognitive and temperament functions (Posner et al., 2001). A second longstanding problem is the issue of the modest levels of interparent agreement on characteristics of their child's temperament. Within a systems framework one way of approaching this question is to do detailed studies of parent–child interactions to determine if differential treatment of infants by mothers and fathers leads to the child displaying somewhat different temperament patterns for each parent. This question is directly linked to a third longstanding issue, namely that of reactive covariance. To what degree do individual differences in child temperament translate into individual differences in patterns of parent–child relations, and under what conditions is reactive covariance between child temperament and parent–child relationship patterns attenuated or accentuated. Satisfactory resolution of these issues will be illuminated in part by a more detailed focus on both child temperament (extreme versus nonextreme for a given dimension) and adult temperament (the degree of "fit" between child and parent temperament characteristics. However, illumination will also require not only a more detailed analysis of the family microenvironment (parent and child behavior patterns), but also an analysis of the role played by larger aspects of the context that can impact upon parent–child relationships, such as outside stresses and supports that impact upon the family.

Similar conclusions can also be made with regard to future directions in temperament research. Given both methodological advances and increasing knowledge it is clear that studies linking individual differences in temperament to neural processes will be an important future direction. However, with increasing knowledge on the nature of brain plasticity (e.g., Nelson, 1999) it becomes increasingly important to ask what and how extrinsic factors influence those neural and biochemical brain processes that underlie individual differences in temperament. If there are experience driven changes in neural structure or brain chemistry that result in differential temperament patterns, what are these experiences? Some studies have begun to deal with this issue (e.g., Gunnar, 2000), but far more needs to be known. Further, if we look at the child's context as encompassing both a psychosocial component and a biological component (Wachs, 2003), it also becomes important to focus on the links between brain processes, temperament, and elements of the biological context such as the child's nutritional status and biomedical history.

In addition to investigations of links between context, brain, and temperament, two other important research directions emerge when we view temperament within a systems framework. While both active covariance and temperament–environment interactions have been noted earlier in this chapter as important topics, remarkably little has been done in either area. We know far too little about the degree of influence individual differences in temperament have upon niche selection, what other factors besides temperament moderate links between individual temperament and niche selection or the consequences for the subsequent development of temperament of a child with a certain temperament selecting into a specific niche. Similarly, while we have begun to identify replicable temperament–context interactions, we know all too little about critical questions such as whether difficult children are equally sensitive to protective and risk factors in the environment or are primarily sensitive to environmental risk factors. Our ability to answer such questions within a systems framework will illuminate not only the nature and developmental contributions of individual differences in temperament, but also the nature of the developmental process itself.

NOTES

1. Following Rothbart & Bates (1998) I am assuming that differences among individuals in the specific dimensions and domains of temperament are quantitative in nature, with individuals being distributed along a continuum. However, it is important to note that there continues to be controversy on the issue of whether individual differences in temperament are best viewed as qualitative or quantitative in nature. For those espousing a qualitative viewpoint, individuals with different temperament patterns are best conceived as falling into different categorical groupings (Woodward et al., 2000).

2. A critical distinction is between stability (maintenance of rank order on a trait for a population of individuals, traditionally assessed by trait correlations over time) versus continuity (change in the level of the trait traditionally assessed by mean changes in a trait over time) (McCall, 1986). Clearly, the level of temperament traits changes over time (Eaton, 1994; Worobey & Blajda, 1989). However, it is

entirely possible for there to be changes in a trait over time (discontinuity), while stability (rank order of individuals) is still maintained. For the present discussion, I will be focusing on stability.

3. The prediction of only modest stability is further reinforced by changes in our knowledge of gene action. While we traditionally think of gene systems as being switched on prenatally and continuing to operate unchanged throughout the life span, this traditional picture clearly is oversimplified. More recent models of gene action have illustrated how different gene systems can turn on or turn off at different points of development (Plomin, DeFries, McClearn, & Rutter, 1997). If gene systems underlying specific dimensions of temperament change across the life span, again we would not necessarily expect a high degree of stability for those dimensions of temperament that are coded by such a gene system.

REFERENCES

Ahadi, S., Rothbart, M., & Ye, R (1993). Children's temperament in the US & China: Similarities and differences. *European Journal of Personality, 7,* 359–377.

Arcus, D. (2001). Inhibited and uninhibited children: Biology in the social context. In T. D. Wachs & G. Kohnstamm (Eds.), *Temperament in context* (pp. 43–60). Mahwah NJ: Erlbaum.

Asendorpf, J. (1994). The malleability of behavior inhibition. *Developmental Psychology, 30,* 912–919.

Ballantine, J., & Klein, H. (1990). The relationship of temperament and adjustment in Japanese schools. *Journal of Psychology, 124,* 299–309.

Barrett, K., & Morgan, G. (1995). Continuities and discontinuities in mastery motivation during infancy and toddlerhood. In R. MacTurk & G. Morgan (Eds.), *Mastery motivation: Origins, conceptualizations and applications* (pp. 57–94). Norwood, NJ: Ablex.

Bates, J. (1989). Concepts and measures of temperament. In G. Kohnstamm, J. Bates, & M. Rothbart (Eds.), *Temperament in childhood* (pp. 3–27). New York: Wiley.

Bates, J. (1994). Parents as scientific observers of their children's development. In S. Friedman & C. Haywood (Eds.), *Developmental follow-up* (pp. 197–216). San Diego, CA: Academic Press.

Bates, J (2001). Adjustment style in childhood as a product of parenting and temperament. In T. D. Wachs & G. Kohnstamm (Eds.), *Temperament in context* (pp. 173–200). Mahwah NJ: Erlbaum.

Bates, J., Pettit, G., Dodge, K., & Ridge, B. (1997, April). *The interaction of temperamental resistance to control and restrictive parenting in the development of externalizing behavior.* Symposium presentation at the Society of Research and Child Development, Washington, DC.

Bates, J., & Wachs, T. D. (1994). *Temperament: Individual differences at the interface of biology and behavior.* Washington, DC: American Psychological Association.

Bell, R., & Chapman, M. (1986). Child effects and studies using experimental or brief longitudinal approaches to socialization. *Developmental Psychology, 22,* 595–603.

Bell, S., & Ainsworth, M. (1972). Infant crying and maternal responsiveness. *Child Development, 43,* 1171–1190.

Belsky, J., Fish, M., & Isabella, R. (1991). Continuity and discontinuity in infant negative and positive emotionality. *Developmental Psychology, 27,* 421–431.

Belsky, J., Friedman, S., & Hsieh, K (2001). Testing a core emotion-regulation prediction: Does early attentional persistence moderate the effect of infant negative emotionality on later development. *Child Development, 72,* 123–133.

Belsky, J., Hsieh, K., & Crnic, K. (1996). Infant positive and negative emotionality. *Developmental Psychology, 32,* 289–298.

Borkowski, J., & Dukewich, T. (1996). Environment covariations and intelligence. In D. Detterman (Ed.), *Current topics in human intelligence: The environment* (Vol. 5, pp. 3–16). Norwood, NJ: Ablex.

Boyce, W., Essex, M., Alkon, A., Smider, N., Pickrell, T., & Kagan, J (2002). Temperament, tympanum and temperature: Four provisional studies of the biobehavioral correlates of tympanic membrane temperature asymmetries. *Child Development, 73,* 718–733.

Cairns, R., Cairns, B., Neckerman, H., Gest, S., & Gariety, J. (1988). Social networks and aggressive behavior. *Developmental Psychology, 24,* 815–823.

Calkins, S., & Fox, N. (1994). Individual differences in the biological aspects of temperament. In J. Bates & T. D. Wachs (Eds.), *Temperament: Individual differences at the interface of biology and behavior* (pp. 199–218). Washington, DC: American Psychological Association.

Caspi, A., Elder, G., & Bem, B. (1987). Moving against the world: Life course patterns of explosive children. *Developmental Psychology, 23,* 308–313.

Chess, S., & Thomas, A. (1991). Temperament and the concept of goodness of fit. In J. Strelau & A. Angleitner (Eds.), *Exploration in temperament* (pp. 15–28). New York: Plenum.

Chisholm, J. (1981). Prenatal influences on Aboriginal-White Australian differences in neonatal irritability. *Ethnology and Sociobiology, 2,* 67–73.

Clarke, A., & Clarke, A. (1988). The adult outcome of early behavioral abnormalities. *International Journal of Behavioral Development, 11,* 3–19.

Corapci, F., & Wachs, T. D (2002). Does parental mood or efficacy mediate the influence of environmental chaos upon parenting behavior? *Merrill-Palmer Quarterly, 48,* 182–201.

Crockenberg, S. (1986). Are temperamental differences in babies associated with predictable differences in caregiving? In J. Lerner & R. Lerner (Eds.), *Temperament and interaction in infancy and childhood* (pp. 53–73). San Francisco: Jossey-Bass.

Crockenberg, S. (1987). Predictors and correlates of anger toward and punitive control of toddlers by adolescent mothers. *Child Development, 58,* 964–975.

Crockenberg, S., & McCluskey, K. (1986). Change in maternal behavior during the baby's first years of life. *Child Development, 57,* 746–753.

Crockenberg, S., & Smith, P. (1982). Antecedents of mother infant interaction and infant irritability in the first three months of life. *Infant Behavior and Development, 5,* 105–120.

Cutrona, C., & Troutman, B. (1986). Social support, infant temperament and parenting self-efficacy. *Child Development, 57,* 1507–1518.

Dar, R. (1987). Another look at Meehl, Lakatos and the scientific practice of psychology. *American Psychologist, 42,* 145–151.

Derryberry, D., & Rothbart, M (1997). Reactive and effortful processes in the organization of temperament. *Development and Psychopathology, 9,* 633–652.

DeVries, M. (1984). Temperament and infant mortality among the Masai of East Africa. *American Journal of Psychiatry, 141,* 1189–1194.

DiLalla, L., & Jones, S (2000). Genetic and environmental influences on temperament in preschoolers. In V. Molfese & D. Molfese (Eds.), *Temperament and personality development across the life span* (pp. 33–56). Mahwah NJ: Erlbaum.

Eaton, W. (1994). Methodological implications of the impending engagement of temperament and biology. In J. Bates & T. D. Wachs (Eds.), *Temperament: Individual differences at the interface of biology and behavior* (pp. 259–274). Washington, DC: American Psychological Association.

Eisenberg, N. (2002). Emotion-related regulation and its relation to quality of social functioning. In W. Hartup & R. Weinberg (Eds.), *Minnesota symposium of child psychology vol 32: Child psychology in retrospect and prospect* (pp. 133–171). Mahwah, NJ: Erlbaum.

Eisenberg, N., Cumberland, A., Spinrad, T., Fabes, R., Shepard, S., Reiser, M., Murphy, B., Losoya, S., & Guthrie, I. (2001). The relations of regulation and emotionality to children's externalizing and internalizing problem behavior. *Child Development, 72,* 1112–1134.

Eisenberg, N., & Fabes, R. (1992). Emotion, regulation and the development of social competence. In M. Clark (Ed.), *Review of personality and social psychology* (Vol. 14, pp. 119–150). Newbury Park, CA: Sage.

Eisenberg, N., Fabes, R., Murphy, B., Karbon, M., Smith, M., & Maszk, P. (1996). The relations of children's dispositional empathy-related responding to their emotionality, regulation and social functioning. *Developmental Psychology, 32,* 195–209.

Engfer, A. (1986). Antecedents of perceived behavior problems in infancy. In G. Kohnstamm (Ed.), *Temperament discussed* (pp. 165–180). Lisse, the Netherlands: Swets & Zeitlinger.

Feldman, R., Greenbaum, C., & Yirmiya, N. (1999). Mother-infant affect synchrony as an antecedent of the emergence of self-control. *Developmental Psychology, 35,* 223–231.

Feldman, S., & Weinberger, D. (1994). Self-restraint as a mediator of family influences on boys' delinquent behavior. *Child Development, 65,* 195–211.

Fish, M. (1997, April). *Stability and change in infant temperament.* Paper presented at the Society for Research in Child Development, Washington, DC.

Fox, N., Henderson, H., Rubin, K., Calkins, S., & Schmidt, L (2001). Continuity and discontinuity of behavioral inhibition and exuberance: psychophysiological and behavioral influences across the first four years of life. *Child Development, 72,* 1–21.

Gandour, M. (1989). Activity level as a dimension of temperament in toddlers. *Child Development, 60,* 1092–1098.

Garcia-Coll, C., Halpern, L., Vohr, B., Seifer, R., & Oh, W. (1992). Stability and correlates of change in early temperament in preterm and full term infants. *Infant Behavior and Development, 15,* 137–153.

Gartstein, M., Slobodskaya, H., & Kinsht, I. (2003). Cross-cultural differences in temperament in the first year of life: United States of America (US) and Russia. *International Journal of Behavioral Development, 27,* 316–328.

Goldsmith, H. (1989). Behavior genetic approaches to temperament. In G. Kohnstamm, J. Bates, & M. Rothbart (Eds.), *Temperament and childhood* (pp. 111–132). New York: Wiley.

Goldsmith, H. (1996). Studying temperament via construction of the Toddler Behavior Assessment Questionnaire. *Child Development, 67,* 218–235.

Goldsmith, H., Aksan, N., Essex, N., Smider, N., & Vandell, D. (year). Temperamenrt and socioemotional adjustment to kindergarten: A multi-informant perspective. In T. D. Wachs & G. Kohnstamm (Eds.), *Temperament in context* (pp. 103–138). Mahwah NJ: Erlbaum.

Goldsmith, H., & Campos, J. (1982). Toward a theory of infant temperament. In R. Emde & R. Harmon (Eds.), *The development of attachment and affiliative systems* (pp. 161–193). New York: Plenum.

Goldsmith, H., & Campos, J. (1990). The structure of temperamental fear and pleasure in infants. *Child Development, 61,* 1944–1964.

Goldsmith, H., Rieser-Danner, L., & Briggs, S. (1991). Evaluating convergent and discriminant validity of temperament questionnaires for preschoolers, toddlers and infants. Developmental Psychology, 27, 566–579.

Guerin, D., Gottfried, A., Oliver, P., & Thomas, C (2003). *Temperament: Infancy through adolescence.* New York: Kluwer Academic.

Gunnar, M. (2000). Early adversity and the development of stress reactivity and regulation. In C. Nelson (Eds.), *Effects of early adversity on neurobehavioral development: The Minnesota Symposium on Child Psychology, Vol. 31* (pp. 163–200). Mahwah NJ: Erlbaum.

Halpern, L., Garcia-Coll, C., Meyer, E., & Bendersky, K (2001). The contributions of temperament and maternal responsiveness to the mental development of small-for-gestational age and appropriate-for-gestational-age infants. *Journal of Applied Developmental Psychology, 22,* 199–224.

Halverson, C., & Deal, J. (2001). Temperamental change, parenting and the family context. In T. D. Wachs & G. Kohnstamm (Eds.), *Temperament in context* (pp. 61–80). Mahwah NJ: Erlbaum.

Halverson, C., Kohnstamm, G., & Martin, R. (1994). *The developing structure of temperament and personality from infancy to adulthood.* Hillsdale, NJ: Erlbaum.

Hetherington, E. (1989). Coping with family transitions. *Child Development, 60,* 1–14.

Hubert, N. (1989). Parental reactions to perceived temperament behaviors in their six and twenty-four month old children. *Infant Behavior and Development, 12,* 185–198.

Kagan, J., Snidman, N., & Arcus, D (1998). Childhood derivatives of high and low reactivity in infancy. *Child Development, 69,* 1483–1493.

Kagan, J., Arcus, D., & Snidman, N. (1993). The idea of temperament: Where do we go from here? In R. Plomin & G. McClearn (Eds.), *Nature nurture & psychology* (pp. 197–212). Washington, DC: American Psychological Association.

Kagan, J., Reznick, J., & Snidman, N. (1989). Issues in the study of temperament. In G. Kohnstamm, J. Bates, & N. Rothbart (Eds.), *Temperament in childhood* (pp. 133–144). New York: Wiley.

Kerr, M. (1996, June). *Temperament and culture.* Paper presented at the Netherlands Institute for Advanced Studies Conference on Temperament in Context, Wassenaer, the Netherlands.

Kerr, M., Lambert, W., Stattin, H., & Larson, I. (1994). Stability of inhibition in a Swedish longitudinal sample. *Child Development, 65,* 138–146.

Kinchla, R. (1992). Attention. *Annual Review of Psychology, 43,* 711–742.

Kochanska, G. (1993). Toward a synthesis of parental socialization and child temperament in early development of conscience. *Child Development, 64,* 325–347.

Kochanska, G. (1995). Children's temperament, mother's discipline and security of attachment. *Child Development, 66,* 597–615.

Kochanska, G. (1997). Multiple pathways to conscience for children with different temperaments. *Developmental Psychology, 33,* 228–240.

Kochanska, G. (2001). Emotional development in children with different attachment histories: The first three years. *Child Development, 72,* 474–490.

Kochanska, G., & Coy, K. (2002). Child emotionality and maternal responsiveness as predictors of reunion behaviors in the strange situation. *Child Development, 73,* 228–240.

Kochanska, G., Coy, K., & Murray, K. (2001). The development of self-regulation in the first four years of life. *Child Development, 72,* 1091–1111.

Kochanska, G., Murray, K., & Harlan, E. (2000). Effortful control in early childhood: continuity and change, antecedents, and implications for social development. *Developmental Psychology, 36,* 220–232.

Kohnstamm, G., Zhang, Y., Slotboom, A., & Elphick, E. (1998). A developmental integration of conscientiousness from childhood to adulthood. In G. Kohnstamm, C. Halverson, I. Mervielde, & V. Hacill (Eds.), *Parental descriptions of child personality* (pp. 65–84). Mahwah NJ: Erlbaum.

Korn, S., & Gannon, S. (1983). Temperament, cultural variation and behavior disorders in preschool children. *Child Psychiatry and Human Behavior, 13,* 203–212.

Kuhn, T. (1970). *The structure of scientific revolutions* (2nd ed.). Chicago: University of Chicago Press.

Lemery, K., Essex, M., & Smider, N (2002). Revealing the relation between temperament and behavior problem symptoms by eliminating measurement confounding. *Child Development, 73,* 867–882.

Lemery, K., Goldsmith, H., Klinnert, M., & Mrazek, D. (1999). Developmental models of infant and childhood temperament. *Developmental Psychology, 35,* 189–204.

Lewis, M., & Ramsay, D (1999). Effect of maternal soothing on infant stress response. *Child Development, 70,* 11–20.

Lewis, M., Ramsey, D., & Kawakami, K. (1993). Differences between Japanese infants and Caucasian American infants in the behavioral and cortisol response to inoculation. *Child Development, 64,* 1722–1731.

Lounsbury, M., & Bates, J. (1982). The cries of infants of differing levels of perceived temperamental difficulties. *Child Development, 53,* 677–686.

Lumley, N., Ables, L., Melamed, B., Pistone, L., & Johnson, J. (1990). Coping outcome in children undergoing stressful medical procedures. *Behavioral Assessment, 12,* 223–238.

Maccoby, E., Snow, M., & Jacklin, C. (1984). Children's disposition and mother child interactions at 12 and 18 months. *Developmental Psychology, 20,* 459–472.

MacPhee, D., Burchinal, M., & Ramey, C. (1997, April). *Individual differences in response to interventions.* Paper presented at the Society for Research in Child Development, Washington, DC.

Malhotra, S. (1989). Varying risk factors in outcomes: An Indian perspective. In W. Carey & S. McDevit (Eds.), *Clinical and educational applications of temperament research.* Amsterdam: Swets & Zeitlinger.

Mangelsdorf, S., Schoppe, S., & Buur, H (2000). The meaning of parental reports: A contextual approach to the study of temperament and behavior problems in childhood. In V. Molfese & D. Molfese (Eds.), *Temperament and personality development across the life span* (pp. 121–140). Mahwah NJ: Erlbaum.

Massaro, D. (1987). *Speech perception by ear and eye.* Hillsdale, NJ: Erlbaum.

Matheny, A. (1986). Injuries among toddlers. *Journal of Pediatric Psychology, 11,* 163–176.

Matheny, A. (1991). Play assessment of infant temperament. In C. Schaefer, K. Gitling, & A Sandgrund (Eds.), *Play diagnosis and assessment.* New York: Wiley.

Matheny, A., & Phillips, K (2001). Temperament and context: Correlates of home environment with temperament continuity and change. In T. D. Wachs & G. Kohnstamm (Eds.), *Temperament in context* (pp. 81–102). Mahwah, NJ: Erlbaum.

Matheny, A., Wilson, R., & Thoben, A. (1987). Home and mother: Relations with infant temperament. *Developmental Psychology, 23,* 323–331.

McCall, R. (1986). Issues of stability and continuity in temperament research. In R. Plomin & J. Dunn (Eds.), *The study of temperament* (pp. 13–26). Hillsdale: NJ: Erlbaum.

McClelland, G., & Judd, C. (1993). Statistical difficulties of detecting interactions and moderator effects. *Psychological Bulletin, 114,* 376–390.

McCullough, A., Kirksey, A., Wachs, T. D., McCabe, G., Bassily, N., Bishry, Z., Galal, D., Harrison, G., & Jerome, N. (1990). Vitamin B6 status of Egyptian mothers. *American Journal of Clinical Nutrition, 51,* 1067–1074.

Mebert, C. (1989). Stability and change in parents' perceptions of infant temperament. *Infant Behavior and Development, 12,* 237–244.

Mebert, C. (1991). Dimensions of subjectivity in parents' ratings of infant temperament. *Child Development, 62,* 352–361.

Molfese, V., & Molfese, D. (2000). *Temperament and personality development across the life span.* Mahwah NJ: Erlbaum.

Nelson, C. (1994). Neural basis of infant temperament. In J. Bates & T. D. Wachs (Eds.), *Temperament: Individual differences at the interface of biology and behavior* (pp. 47–82). Washington, DC: American Psychological Association.

Nelson, C (1999). Neural plasticity and human development. *Current directions in Psychological Science, 8,* 42–45.

Nelson, C., & Bloom, F (1997). Child development and neuroscience. *Child Development, 68,* 970–987.

Ohayon, M (1999). Improving decisionmaking processes with the fuzzy logic approach in the epidemiology of sleep disorders. *Journal of Psychosomatic Research, 47,* 297–311.

Park, S., Belsky, J., Putnam, S., & Crnic, K (1997). Infant emotionality, parenting and 3 year inhibition. *Developmental Psychology, 33,* 218–227.

Pedlow, R., Sanson, A., Prior, M., & Oberklaid, F. (1993). Stability of maternally reported temperament from infancy to 8 years. *Developmental Psychology, 29,* 998–1007.

Pettit, G., & Bates, J. (1984). Continuity of individual differences in the mother infant relationship from six to thirteen months. *Child Development, 55,* 729–739.

Pfeifer, M., Goldsmith, H., Davidson, R., & Rickman, M (2002). Continuity and change in inhibited and uninhibited children. *Child Development, 73,* 1474–1485.

Plomin, R. (1994). *Genetics and experience.* Thousand Oaks, CA: Sage.

Plomin, R., DeFries, J., & Loehlin, J. (1977). Genotype environment interaction and correlation in the analysis of human development. *Psychological Bulletin, 84,* 309–322.

Plomin, R., DeFries, J., McClearn, G., & Rutter, M. (1997). *Behavioral genetics* (3rd ed.). New York: Freeman.

Plomin, R., & Saudino, K. (1994). Quantitative genetics and molecular genetics. In J. Bates & T. D. Wachs (Eds.), *Temperament: Individual differences at the interface of biology and behavior* (pp. 143–174). Washington, DC: American Psychological Association.

Posner, M., Rothbart, M., Farah, M., & Bruer, J (2001). The developing human brain. *Developmental Science, 4,* 253–387.

Riese, M. (1987). Longitudinal assessment of temperament from birth to two years. *Infant Behavior and Development, 10,* 347–363.

Rothbart, M. (1991). Temperament: A developmental framework. In J. Strelau & A. Angleitner (Eds.), *Exploration in temperament* (pp. 61–74). New York: Plenum.

Rothbart, M., Ahadi, S., Hershey, K., & Fisher, P (2001). Investigations of temperament at three to seven years: The children's behavior questionnaire. *Child Development, 72,* 1394–1408.

Rothbart, M., & Bates, J. (1998). Temperament. In N. Eisenberg (Ed.), *Handbook of child psychology* (Vol. 3, pp. 105–176). New York: Wiley.

Rothbart, M., & Derryberry, D. (1981). Development of individual differences in temperament. In M. Lamb & A. Brown (Eds.), *Advances in developmental psychology* (Vol. 1, pp. 37–86). Hillsdale, NJ: Erlbaum.

Rothbart, M., Derryberry, D., & Hershey, K. (2000). Stability of temperament in childhood: Laboratory infant assessment to parent report at seven years. In V. Molfese & D. Molfese (Eds.), *Temperament and personality development across the life span* (pp. 85–120). Mahwah NJ: Erlbaum.

Rothbart, M., Derryberry, D., & Posner, M. (1994). A psychobiological approach to the development of temperament. In J. Bates & T. D. Wachs (Eds.), *Temperament: Individual differences at the interface of biology and behavior* (pp. 82–116). Washington, DC: American Psychological Association.

Rubin, K., Burgess, K., & Hastings, P (2002). Stability and social-behavioral consequences of toddlers inhibited temperament and parenting behaviors. *Child Development, 73,* 483–495.

Russell, A., Hart, C., Robinson, C., & Olsen, S (2003). Children's sociable and aggressive behavior with peers: A comparison of the US and Australia and contributions of temperament and parenting style. *International Journal of Behavioral Development, 27,* 74–86.

Sameroff, A., & Fiese, B. (1990). Transactional regulation and early intervention. In S. Meisels & J. Shonkoff (Eds.), *Handbook of early childhood intervention* (pp. 119–149). Cambridge: Cambridge University Press.

Scarr, S., & McCartney, K. (1983). How people make their own environments. *Child Development, 54,* 424–435.

Schaffer, H. (1966). Activity level as a constitutional determinant of infantile reaction to deprivation. *Child Development, 37,* 595–602.

Scheper-Hughes, N. (1987). Maternal estrangement and infant death. In C. Super (Ed.), *The role of culture in developmental disorder.* San Diego, CA: Academic Press.

Schulenberg, J., Wadsworth, K., O'Malley, P., Bachman, J., & Johnston, L. (1996). Adolescent risk factors for binge drinking during the transition to young adulthood. *Developmental Psychology, 32,* 659–674.

Schuler, M., Black, M., & Starr, R. (1995). Determinants of mother infant interaction. *Journal of Clinical Child Psychology, 24,* 397–405.

Seifer, R., Schiller, M., Sameroff, A., Resnick, S., & Riordan, K. (1996). Attachment, maternal sensitivity and infant temperament during the first year of life. *Developmental Psychology, 32,* 12–35.

Slabach, E., Morrow, J., & Wachs, T. D. (1991). Questionnaire measurement of infant and child temperament. In J. Strelau & A. Angleitner (Eds.), *Exploration in temperament* (pp. 205–234). New York: Plenum.

Stams, G., Juffer, F., & van Ijzendoorn, M. (2002). Maternal sensitivity, infant attachment and temperament in early childhood predict adjustment in middle childhood: The case of adopted children and their biologically unrelated parents. *Developmental Psychology, 38,* 806–821.

Stifter, C., Spinrad, T., & Braungart-Ricker, J (1999). Toward a developmental model of child compliance: The role of emotion regulation in infancy. *Child Development, 70,* 21–32.

Strelau, J. (1983). *Temperament, personality and activity.* New York: Academic Press.

Strelau, J. (1987). Concepts of temperament in personality research. *European Journal of Personality, 1,* 107–117.

Strelau, J. (1989). The regulative theory of temperament as a result of East-West influences. In G. Kohnstamm, J. Bates, & M. Rothbart (Eds.), *Temperament in childhood* (pp. 35–48). New York: Wiley.

Strelau, J. (1994). The concepts of arousal and arousability as used in temperament studies. In J. Bates & T. D. Wachs (Eds.), *Temperament: Individual differences at the interface of biology and behavior* (pp. 117–142). Washington, DC: American Psychological Association.

Strelau, J (2002). The role of temperament as a moderator of stress. In T. D. Wachs & G. Kohnstamm (Eds.), *Temperament in context* (pp. 153–172). Mahwah NJ: Erlbaum.

Sullivan, M., & McGrath, M. (1995, April). *The linkage between dimensions of maternal interaction and child temperament.* Paper presented at the Society for Research in Child Development, Indianapolis, IN.

Super, C., & Harkness, S. (1986). Temperament, development and culture. In R. Plomin & J. Dunn (Eds.), *The study of temperament* (pp. 131–150). Hillsdale, NJ: Erlbaum.

Super, C., & Harkness, S. (1999). The environment in cultural and developmental research. In S. Friedman & T. D. Wachs (Eds.), *Conceptualization and measurement of the environment across the lifespan* (pp. 279–326). Washington, DC: American Psychological Association.

Thoman, E. (1990). Sleeping and waking states of infants. *Neuroscience and Biobehavioral Reviews, 14,* 93–107.

Thomas, A., & Chess, S. (1977). *Temperament and development.* New York: Brunner-Mazel.

Thomas, A., & Chess, S. (1986). The New York Longitudinal Study: From infancy to early adult life. In R. Plomin & J. Dunn (Eds.), *The study of temperament* (pp. 39–52). Hillsdale, NJ: Erlbaum.

Thomas, A., Chess, S., & Birch, H. (1968). *Temperament and behavior disorder in children.* New York: New York University Press.

Van den Boom, D. (1994). The influence of temperament and mothering on attachment and exploration. *Child Development, 65,* 1457–1477.

Van den Boom, D., & Hoeksma, J. (1994). The effect of infant irritability on mother-infant interaction: A growth curve analysis. *Developmental Psychology, 30,* 581–590.

Wachs, T. D. (1987a). Short term stability of aggregated and nonaggregated measures of parent behavior. *Child Development, 58,* 796–797.

Wachs, T. D. (1987b). Specificity of environmental action as manifest in environmental correlates of infants' mastery motivation. *Developmental Psychology, 23,* 782–790.

Wachs, T. D. (1988). Relevance of physical environmental influences for toddler temperament. *Infant Behavior and Development, 11,* 431–445.

Wachs, T. D. (1992). *The nature of nurture.* Newbury Park, CA: Sage.

Wachs, T. D. (1994). Fit, context and the transition between temperament and personality. In C. Halverson, G. Kohnstamm, & R. Martin (Eds.), *The developing structure of personality from infancy to adulthood* (pp. 209–222). Hillsdale, NJ: Erlbaum.

Wachs, T. D. (2000a). *Necessary but not sufficient: The respective roles of single and multiple influences on individual development.* Washington DC: American Psychological Association.

Wachs, T. D. (2000b). Linking nutrition and temperament. In V. Molfese & D. Molfese (Eds.), *Temperament and personality development across the life span* (pp. 57–84). Mahway NJ: Erlbaum.

Wachs, T. D. (2003). Expanding our view of context: The bioecological environment and development. In R. Kail (Ed),

Advances in Child Development and Behavior (vol. 31, pp. 363–409). Boston: Academic/Elsevier Press.

Wachs, T. D., Bishry, Z., Sobhy, A., McCabe, G., Galal, O., & Shaheen, F. (1993). Relation of rearing environment to adaptive behavior of Egyptian toddlers. *Child Development, 64*, 586–604.

Wachs, T. D., & Gandour, M. (1983). Temperament, environment and six month cognitive-intellectual development. *International Journal of Behavioral Development, 6*, 135–152.

Wachs, T. D., & King, B. (1994). Behavioral research in the brave new world of neuroscience and temperament. In J. Bates & T. D. Wachs (Eds.), *Temperament: Individual differences at the interface of biology and behavior* (pp. 307–336). Washington, DC: American Psychological Association.

Wachs, T. D., & Kohnstamm, G. *Temperament in Context.* Mahwah NJ: Erlbaum.

Williams, B., Ponesse, J., Schachar, R., Logan, G., & Tannock, R (1999). Development of inhibitory control across the life span. *Developmental Psychology, 35*, 205–213.

Wills, T., Sandy, J., Yaeger, A., & Shinar, O (2001). Family risk factors and adolescent substance use: Moderation effects for temperament dimensions. *Developmental Psychology, 37*, 283–297.

Wilson, R., & Matheny, A. (1986). Behavior-genetics research in infant temperament. In R. Plomin & J. Dunn (Eds.), *The study of temperament: Changes, continuities and challenges* (pp. 81–98). Hillsdale NJ: Erlbaum.

Wohlwill, J., & Heft, H. (1987). The physical environment and the development of the child. In I. Altman & J. Stokols (Eds.), *Handbook of environmental psychology.* New York: Wiley.

Woodward. S., Lezenweger, M., Kagan. J., Snidman, N., & Arcus, D (2000). Taxonic structure of infant reactivity: Evidence from a taxometric perspective. *Psychological Science, 11*, 296–301.

Woodward, S., McManis, M., Kagan, J., Deldin, P., Snidman, N., Lewis, M., & Kahn, V (2001). Infant temperament and the brainstem auditory evoked response in later childhood. *Developmental Psychology, 37*, 533–538.

Worobey, J., & Blajda, V. (1989). Temperament ratings at two weeks, two months and one year. *Developmental Psychology, 25*, 257–263.

Zuckerman, M. (1994). Impulsive unsocialized sensation seeking. In J. Bates & T. D. Wachs (Eds.), *Temperament: Individual differences at the interface of biology and behavior* (pp. 219–258). Washington, DC: American Psychological Association.

3

Determinants and Consequences of Infant–Parent Attachment

Jay Belsky

INTRODUCTION

The topic of the infant's emotional tie to mother has been a focus of theorizing for hundreds if not thousands of years. Freud, however, is probably responsible for modern scientific interest in the topic, as he asserted that the relationship between mother and baby served as a "prototype" that would shape the remainder of the developing individual's life, especially his capacity to love and to work. But it is John Bowlby, the eminent British psychiatrist, who broke from the ranks of Freudian psychoanalysts to develop the prevailing theory of attachment that guides most developmental research on the topic today. Rather than considering the full scope of research and thinking about the infant–parent attachment relationship in this chapter, I focus upon results from several longitudinal studies that I have been involved in over the past 25 years in order to illuminate the antecedents and sequelae of individual differences in infant–parent attachment security. Thus, in this chapter, I report on findings pertaining to the origins or determinants of individual differences in infant–parent attachment security. In addition to considering the classical question of how the quality of maternal care affects the development of secure and insecure infant–mother attachment relationships, I address the role of temperament, individual differences in infant–father attachments, and broader contextual influences on infant–parent attachment security, including early child care, social support, marital quality, and work–family relations. Before describing this work and summarizing results, it is appropriate to review some core tenets of attachment theory that guided my research as well as that of many others.

JOHN BOWLBY'S THEORY OF ATTACHMENT AND ITS DERIVATIVES

Attachment theory can be viewed, in large part, as a theory of personality development, one which emphasizes the role of early experiences in shaping psychological and behavioral development. In contrast to the psychoanalytically trained psychiatrists whose ideas Bowlby came to reject, Bowlby regarded Freudians as inappropriately emphasizing the role of the individual's inner fantasies in shaping personality, at the expense of actual lived experiences. There were many possible aspects of early experience that could be considered developmentally important. Bowlby's clinical experience alerted him to the adverse effects of early separations from the mother on emotional well being, both in terms of the short-term distress it evoked and the longer-term consequences it appeared to have on children. In pondering such phenomena, Bowlby found himself dissatisfied with existing, secondary-drive explanations which suggested that because the mother satisfied the infant's primary need for nourishment, she became associated with feelings of satisfaction and, thereby, came to be regarded positively by the infant.

The Evolutionary Function of Attachment

Drawing upon a variety of theoretical perspectives, Bowlby fashioned an evolutionary theory of the child's tie to the mother: The child's intense affective tie to his mother, which was dramatically revealed by his behavior when away from her, was not the result of some associational learning process, but rather the direct consequence of a biologically-based desire for proximity and contact with adults that arose as a direct result of Darwinian natural selection. That is, infants and young children who protested separation, sought to maintain proximity to the caregiver, and engaged in other behaviors which are now considered attachment behaviors, were more likely than others not evincing them to be cared for well in ancestral human environments and were less likely to be consumed by predators or become lost. As a result, they were more likely to survive and to reproduce. In consequence, these genetically-determined proclivities of infants to become attached to their caregivers became part of the human behavioral repertoire, thereby promoting "the survival of the species" (Bowlby, 1969/1982, 1973, 1980). In the closing section of this chapter, questions are raised about Bowlby's original evolutionary theorizing and an effort is made to cast attachment theory in a more modern evolutionary perspective (Belsky, 1999).

Measuring Individual Differences in Attachment Security

Bowlby's foremost American collaborator and even co-constructor of attachment theory, Mary Ainsworth, used his original theoretical insights to develop a procedure for measuring individual differences in the security of the infant–mother attachment relationship that I adopted to address many of the same questions that interested Bowlby, Ainsworth, and an entire generation of attachment researchers (for review, see Belsky & Cassidy, 1994; Thompson, 1999). Noting the complementary activation and inhibition of two distinct behavioral systems, one which kept the child close to the mother and thereby promoted safety and survival (i.e., the attachment system) and another which fostered exploration and thus promoted learning (i.e., the exploratory system), Ainsworth (Ainsworth, Bell, & Stayton, 1971) came to refer to an "attachment-exploration balance" and the child's inclination to use the caregiver as a "secure base from which to explore" (Ainsworth, 1963). Most infants balance these two behavioral systems, responding flexibility to specific situation after assessing both the environment's characteristics and the caregiver's availability. For instance, when the attachment system is activated (perhaps by separation from the attachment figure, illness, fatigue, or by unfamiliar people and environments), infant exploration and play decline. Conversely, when the attachment system is not activated (e.g., when a healthy, well-rested infant is in a comfortable setting with an attachment figure nearby), exploration is enhanced.

Appreciating in Bowlby's theory the inherently stressful—and attachment-evoking—nature of being in an unfamiliar place, encountering unfamiliar people, and being separated from mother, Ainsworth purposefully designed all these features into a brief, 20-minute, 8-episode laboratory procedure in order to experimentally elicit infant attachment behavior (see Table 3.1). Just as important as the creative insight which led Ainsworth to invent such an experimental paradigm was the fact that she studied in the Strange Situation a small sample of 26 infants from middle-class homes whom she had been systematically observing throughout their first year of life, in their own homes. It was Ainsworth's goal to account for variation in infant attachment behavior in the Strange Situation by carefully considering the nature and course of mother–infant interaction during the first year of life, as it was her thesis that it was the quality of care that the child received at the hands of his caregiver during this developmental period that was principally responsible for individual differences in attachment security (Ainsworth, 1973).

TABLE 3.1
The Strange Situation

Episode	Persons present	Time
1	Experimenter, parent, infant	1 minute
2	Parent, infant	3 minutes
3	Parent, infant, stranger	3 minutes
4	Infant, stranger	3 minutes*
5	Parent, infant	3 minutes
6	Infant	3 minutes*
7	Stranger, infant	3 minutes*
8	Parent, infant	3 minutes

*Length of period reduced if infant is very distressed.

In light of the fact that one of the most dramatic differences between babies in how they react to separation from mother, especially when left with an unfamiliar individual in a strange place (even if only for a short period of time), involves the extent to which they become distressed, many believed initially that a focus upon crying would prove to be the window on individual differences in attachment security. As it turned out, Ainsworth's ground-breaking research revealed that it was reunion behavior with mother that was principally reflective of the quality of the infant's emotional tie to her mother, a discovery of no small proportion in the history of developmental psychology (Ainsworth et al., 1978).

Indeed, on the basis of variation in the attachment behavior of the 26 infants whom she studied, Ainsworth identified three distinct *patterns of attachment* that have guided research ever since (Ainsworth et al., 1978). Infants classified as securely attached (pattern B) use the mother as a secure base from which to explore, reduce their exploration and may be distressed in her absence, but greet her positively on her return, and then return to exploration. Secure infants classified into subcategories B1 and B2 are less distressed by separation than those subcategorized as B3 and B4 and greet mother following separation by vocalizing, smiling or waving across a distance rather than by immediately seeking physical contact and emotional comfort (see Figure 3.1).

Initially, two patterns of insecurity were identified using the Strange Situation. (A third, pattern D, has since been recognized but is not discussed here because it has not played a very significant role in

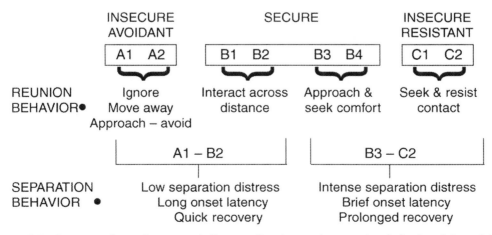

ATTACHMENT CLASSIFICATION SYSTEM

Figure 3.1 Patterns of attachment and distress: Reunion and separation behavior. Adapted from Ainsworth, Blehar, Waters, and Wall (1978).

my own research. See Lyons-Ruth & Jacobvitz, 1999, for recent analysis of the disorganized attachment pattern.) Infants classified as insecure-avoidant (pattern A) explore with little reference to the mother, are minimally distressed by her departure and seem to ignore or avoid her on return. Infants classified as insecure-resistant (pattern C) fail to move away from mother and explore minimally. These infants are highly distressed by separations and are often difficult to settle on reunions.

INITIAL EMPIRICAL SUPPORT
FOR CORE THEORETICAL PROPOSITIONS

Importantly, Ainsworth's contribution to our understanding of attachment went well beyond the development of an important method for measuring individual differences. Most significantly, it was she who first theorized in detail about why some infants would develop secure and others insecure attachments to their mothers and published data addressing this issue. Using highly detailed ratings of the quality of maternal behavior based upon repeated observations of her sample of 26 middle-class families, Ainsworth (1973) found that it was maternal sensitivity that accounted for why some infants behaved in a secure manner in the Strange Situation when one year of age whereas others behaved insecurely. Central to the notion of sensitivity was the mother's ability to read the infant's behavioral and especially emotional cues and respond in a timely and appropriate manner that served the infant's needs. Thus, mothers who reared secure infants responded in a timely manner to their infants' crying, were ready and able to physically handle the infant in a comforting manner, and were neither intrusive nor ignoring of the infant. In fact, it was Ainsworth's contention that insecure-avoidance developed in response to maternal rejection of the infant, especially when it came to the baby's desire for physical contact. Insecure-resistance, in contrast, was the result of inconsistent caregiving in which the mother was sometimes available and responsive but frequently not. Thus, the different patterns of insecurity were theorized—and found—to derive from different ways in which mothers were insensitive in their care of the infant.

Such findings which buttressed attachment theory led to a first round of investigations by Alan Sroufe and his colleagues at the University of Minnesota examining the sequelae of individual differences in attachment. This was of central importance because what might now be regarded as Bowlby-Ainsworth attachment theory was not only a theory of the nature of the infant's tie to the mother and of the determinants of individual differences in attachment security but, as noted at the outset, of personality development. Thus, there were theoretical grounds for expecting that infants securely and insecurely attached to their mothers would develop differently. Importantly, the work by Sroufe (1988) and his colleagues further buttressed the theory by providing evidence consistent with expectations. Specifically, preschoolers with secure attachment histories proved to be more sociable toward strangers than agemates with insecure histories (Pastor, 1981). These same children also were less emotionally dependent upon their teachers, yet more willing to call upon them for assistance when faced with a challenge they could not manage on their own (Sroufe, Fox, & Pancake, 1983). In addition, children with secure attachment histories evinced more empathy and positive affection toward peers (Sroufe, 1983), perhaps accounting for their greater popularity with classmates (Sroufe, Fox, & Pancake, 1983). These children also were less likely to be victimized by peers, or bully them (Troy & Sroufe, 1987). In fact, whereas insecure-avoidant attachment proved to be predictive of increased aggressiveness during the early-elementary school years, insecure-resistance forecast passive-withdrawn behavior (Renkin et al., 1989).

The developmental benefits of attachment security continued through the middle-childhood years and into adolescence. When 10-year-olds were studied at a summer camp established for research purposes (and enjoyment), ratings by camp counselors, as well as observational data, showed that children with insecure attachment histories of both the resistant and avoidant variety were more dependent on adults than were agemates with secure attachment histories (Urban, Carlson, Egeland, & Sroufe, 1991). Moreover, these differences in dependency continued to manifest themselves when the Minnesota children were studied as 15-year-olds (Sroufe, Carlson, & Shulman, 1993).

Children with secure histories also evinced greater social competence as they grew up. Not only was this evident in global ratings provided by school teachers (Weinfield, Sroufe, Egeland, & Carlson, 1999), but also when reciprocated friendships were measured using sociometric techniques, when camp counselors evaluated children, and when children's interactions with agemates were observed at camp (Elicker et al., 1992). In adolescence, teens with secure attachment histories were rated by camp counselors as more competent in general and more socially effective in mixed-gender crowds in particular (Englund, Levy, & Hyson, 1997). An interview study further revealed the girls with secure histories to be judged as more intimate in their interpersonal relationships (Ostoja, 1996). When considered in their entirety, these results from the groundbreaking Minnesota investigation demonstrate, indisputably, that a foundation of a secure attachment history appeared to be a developmental asset which the child carried at least through adolescence, whereas an insecure history was a risk factor or liability when it came to getting along well with others.

THE PENNSYLVANIA CHILD AND FAMILY DEVELOPMENT PROJECT

The Minnesota group's early research validating classifications of attachment security based on behavior in the Strange Situation proved to be extremely important in shaping my investigatory endeavors. Having received only minimal training in attachment theory as a graduate student at Cornell University in the mid-1970s, but a great deal on the role of family, community, cultural and historical context in shaping human development (Bronfenbrenner, 1978), I found the prospect of integrating these two distinct research traditions pregnant with opportunity. In fact, because my doctoral research had focused upon parenting and infant development, with a special concern for fathering as well as mothering and husband–wife as well as parent–child relationships (Belsky, 1979a,b), it proved rather easy to extend my research horizon to incorporate ideas from attachment theory into my ecologically-oriented program of research on early human experience in the family. What was principally required was the inclusion of Strange Situation assessments into what developed into a series of four short-term longitudinal studies focused upon the opening years of life that I have come to refer to collectively as the Pennsylvania Child and Family Development Project which I directed over the first two decades of my career while I was at Penn State University.

Inclusion of infant–mother and infant–father attachment assessments in these longitudinal studies enabled me to address a number of theoretically important questions. These concern the determinants of individual differences in infant–parent attachment security, including infant temperament, quality of parenting, early child care, and the social context in which the parent–child dyad is embedded. At the same time that this work was going on in central Pennsylvania, my collaboration with colleagues in a 10-site study of infant day care also enabled me to address issues of child care and attachment with greater precision than was possible in my more local investigations and to extend my basic empirical research on attachment to examine the developmental sequelae of individual differences in infant–mother attachment security. In what follows, I summarize many of the results of these inquiries. I consider first work pertaining to parenting and temperament influences on attachment security, before proceeding to consider the broader ecological context in which attachment relationships are embedded. Finally, before making some closing remarks intended to modernize the evolutionary basis of attachment theory, I review my research on nonmaternal child care and infant–parent attachment security, as well as on the developmental sequelae of infant–mother attachment security. It should be noted that no attempt will be made to extensively review related research on these and other topics pertinent to the study of attachment in infancy. For such reviews, see Belsky and Cassidy (1994), Colin (1996), and Cassidy and Shaver (1999).

MOTHERING AND ATTACHMENT SECURITY

Even though Ainsworth (1973) had theorized and found that the sensitivity of maternal care during the first year of life predicted attachment security when the child was one year of age, her work was limited in two important respects. First, her sample of 26 was quite small in size. Second, and more importantly, her evaluations of children's attachment security were informed by what she already knew about the quality of care that the children received at home. Thus, her assessment of maternal sensitivity and attachment security were not independent and this compromised the confidence that could be placed in the results of what, in some respects, had to be regarded as a (remarkable) "pilot" study (Lamb et al., 1984).

Like others, I was fascinated by Ainsworth's (1973) sensitivity hypothesis and used my first longitudinal study of marital change across the transition to parenthood to examine the relation between mothering observed on three occasions during the first year of the infant's life and infant–mother attachment security assessed at 12 months. In this study, 56 Caucasian mothers and their infants from working- and middle-class Caucasian families residing in and around the semi-rural central Pennsylvania community of State College where Penn State University is located were observed at home when infants were 1, 3, and 9 months of age. During each observation period, mothers were directed to go about their everyday household routine, trying as much as possible to disregard the presence of the observer. This naturalistic observational approach is one that I have used in all the research to be described. In order to record maternal and infant behavior, we noted the presence or absence every 15 seconds of an extensive series of maternal and infant behaviors, and one particular kind of dyadic exchange in which the infant or mother emits a behavior, the other responds to it, and the first then contingently responds to the other (i.e., three-step interchange).

Because we did not employ the same rating system as did Ainsworth, we needed a way of conceptualizing and parameterizing the frequency scores of particular behaviors that we generated into indices of sensitivity. Toward this end, we theorized that more was not inherently better and thus hypothesized that infants who established secure relationships with their mothers would have experienced neither the most frequent nor least frequent levels of reciprocal mother–infant interaction. In order to create an index of reciprocal interaction, we factor analyzed a set of 15 mother, child, and dyadic frequency scores. At each of three separate ages, the factor structure proved quite similar, with the principle factor reflecting reciprocal interaction. Loading highly on this factor were measures of maternal attention and care (e.g., undivided attention, vocalize to infant, vocally respond to infant, express positive affection, stimulate/arouse infant), infant behavior (e.g., look at mother, vocalize to mother), and dyadic exchange (i.e., three-step interaction).

We theorized that insecure-avoidance might develop in response to intrusive, overstimulating maternal care (which would force the child to turn away from mother) and that insecure-resistance might be the consequence of insufficiently responsive, unstimulating care. Thus we predicted—and found—that mothers of secure infants would score intermediate on the resulting composite index of reciprocal mother–infant interaction (see Figure 3.2). Moreover, as anticipated, we found that mothers of insecure-avoidant infants scored highest on this index, and that mothers of insecure-resistant infants scored lowest (Belsky, Rovine, & Taylor, 1984). In fact, when the reciprocal interaction composite variable was decomposed into indices of maternal involvement and infant behavior, it was clear that it was the former rather than the latter that distinguished attachment groups.

On the basis of these results, a graduate student at the time, Russ Isabella, extended this work in our second and third longitudinal studies by focusing not solely upon the raw, composited frequencies of maternal and infant behavior on which our original index of reciprocal interaction was based, but rather on the close-in-time co-occurrence of mother and infant behaviors which were theorized to reflect synchronous and asynchronous exchanges in the dyad. The subjects of this work were 153 working- and middle-class Caucasian families rearing firstborns drawn from the same community as our first study. Once again, mother–infant dyads had been observed for 45 minutes, this time at two distinct ages—6 and 9 months—using the same time-sampling methodology already described, and infants had been seen with their mothers in the university laboratory at 12 months to measure attachment security using the Strange Situation. For his dissertation Isabella pursued the hypothesis that dyads that fostered secure attachment would be characterized by interactions that appeared synchronous, whereas those that fostered insecurity would look asynchronous. And, based upon our

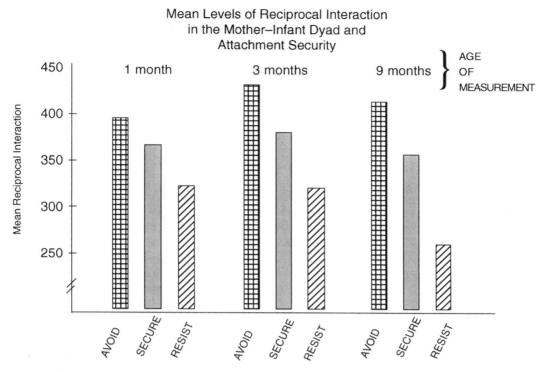

Figure 3.2 Reciprocal interaction at 1, 3, and 9 months as a function of one-year infant–mother attachment classification. (Adapted from Belsky, Rovine, & Taylor, 1984.)

earlier findings, it was predicted that insecure-avoidant dyads would be characterized by intrusive, overstimulating interactions and that insecure-avoidant dyads would be characterized by unresponsive-detached caregiving.

To generate indices of synchrony and asynchrony, it was necessary to inspect the behaviors checked off on our behavior checklist during each and every 15-second observation period, along with those checked off in each of the two adjacent 15-second sampling periods. This enabled Isabella to determine whether the infant and mother behaviors that were recorded within three adjacent periods reflected synchronous and asynchronous interactions. Then, relying upon a sophisticated point-prediction analytic technique, results again substantiated our hypotheses (Isabella, Belsky, & von Eye, 1989; Isabella & Belsky, 1991). Thus, findings from the first inquiry were replicated and extended. In fact, not only had interaction processes reflective of overstimulation been related to insecure-avoidance and those reflective of unresponsive-detachment proven predictive of insecure-resistance in three separate samples which relied on similar approaches to recording mother–infant interaction (i.e., time-sampled behaviors) but dramatically different approaches to parameterizing interaction processes, but in a number of other inquiries similar results obtained (e.g., Lewis & Feiring, 1989; Malatesta et al., 1989; Smith & Pedersen, 1988; Leyendecker et al.,1997). Significantly, all these findings were generally consistent with Ainsworth's (1973) original theorizing linking sensitive and appropriately responsive care with the establishment of a secure attachment to mother by baby (for meta-analysis, see De Wolff & van Ijzendoorn, 1997).

The same was true, it turned out, when the NICHD Early Child Care Research Network (1997), of which I was a part, examined the developmental antecedents of infant–mother attachment security, measured when infants were 15 months of age, as part of its effort to examine the effects of early child care on child development (see below). As expected, it was found that higher levels of observed maternal sensitivity when infants were 6 and 15 months of age predicted increased likelihood of a child establishing a secure attachment to mother—in a sample of over 1,000 children, the largest ever examined with respect to the determinants of attachment security. Especially interesting is that a meta-analysis of the results of 66 studies which did not include the findings from the just-cited NICHD Study of Early Child Care showed, as well, that a variety of indices of maternal sensitivity, interactional synchrony, and dyadic mutuality systematically related to attachment security in just the manner detected in my own work and that of the large child-care study (De Wolff & van IJzendoorn, 1997). Clearly, just as Ainsworth (1973) had theorized and found in her original very small sample investigation, the nature of the child's interactional experiences with mother contributed to determining whether an infant developed a secure or insecure attachment.

THE ROLE OF TEMPERAMENT

An alternative explanation of individual differences in attachment to that proposed by Ainsworth (1973) emphasizing the quality of maternal care draws attention to the infant's temperament, especially the dimension of negative emotionality or difficulty (e.g., Goldsmith & Alansky, 1987). In particular, it was argued that insecurity reflects distress in the Strange Situation, which itself is a function of temperament (Chess & Thomas, 1982; Kagan, 1982). A fundamental problem with this interpretation, of course, was that infants classified as both secure and insecure evince great variation in distress in the Strange Situation. Consideration of Figure 3.1 makes it clear that some secure infants typically evince a great deal of distress in the Strange Situation (i.e., those classified B3 and B4), whereas others do not (i.e., B1, B2), and that some insecure infants typically express a great deal of negativity in the Strange Situation (i.e., C1, C2), whereas others do not (i.e., A1, A2).

A possible way of bringing together competing perspectives on the role of temperament in the measurement of attachment security in the Strange Situation occurred to me upon considering results of findings generated by Thompson and Lamb (1984) and by Frodi and Thompson (1985). When it came to the expression and regulation of negative emotion in the Strange Situation, these investigators observed that secure infants receiving classifications of B1 and B2 looked more like insecure infants receiving classifications of A1 and A2 than like other secure infants (i.e., B3, B4); and that secure infants receiving classifications of B3 and B4 looked more like insecure infants classified C1 and C2 than like other secure infants (i.e., B1, B2). This observation raised the following question in my mind: Might temperament shape the way in which security or insecurity is manifested in the Strange Situation (A1, A2, B1, B2 vs. B3, B4, C1, C2), rather than directly determine whether or not a child was classified as secure? That is, might early temperament account for why some secure infants became highly distressed in the Strange Situation (i.e., those classified B3 or B4), whereas others did not (B1, B2), and why some insecure infants became highly distressed in the Strange Situation (C1, C2), whereas others did not (A1, A2). To address this question, we examined data available on 184 firstborn infants participating in our second and third longitudinal studies.

As theorized, we found that measures of temperament obtained during the newborn period, using the Brazelton Neonatal Behavior Exam, and when infants were 3 months of age, using maternal reports, discriminated infants classified as A1, A2, B1, and B2—that is, the ones who cried little in the Strange Situation—from those classified as B3, B4, C1, and C2 (i.e., those who tend to cry more). These measures did not distinguish infants classified secure (B1, B2, B3, B4) from those classified insecure (A1, A2, C1, C2), however (Belsky & Rovine, 1987). More specifically, although secure and insecure infants did not differ on any of the temperament measures in either of the two longitudinal samples, those most likely to express negative emotion in the Strange Situation at 12 months of age scored lower as newborns on orientation (i.e., visual following, alertness, attention) and evinced less autonomic stability (i.e., regulation of state) and scored higher at age 3 months on a cumulative difficulty index. Thus, consistent with my theorizing and the Thompson, Lamb, and Frodi analyses of emotion expression within the Strange Situation, early temperament appeared to affect the degree to which infants became overtly distressed in the Strange Situation but not how they regulated—with or without the assistance of their mother—their negative affect. In sum, early temperament was systematically related to how much distress infants evinced in the Strange Situation, but not whether they were secure or insecure.

In these first investigations, we, like all other investigators, focused solely upon temperament at a single point in time (i.e., during the newborn period or at 3 months of age). Such an approach was generally consistent with the then-prevailing view of temperament as an inborn, stable, constitutional trait not particularly subject to change. Because we had obtained identical temperament reports from mothers when infants were 3 and 9 months of age, we found ourselves in the enviable position of being able to reconceptualize temperament as a characteristic of the infant that was, in theory at least, subject to change. And when we examined change in temperament, as reported by mother, using data from our first longitudinal study, especially interesting results emerged: Infants who at 1 year of age were classified as secure became more predictable and adaptable from 3 to 6 months, whereas the exact opposite was true of infants who would develop insecure attachments to their mothers (Belsky & Isabella, 1988).

Such results raised the prospect that change in temperament may be what security of attachment, at least in some cases, is all about—a notion that Cassidy (1994) advanced in an effort to interpret attachment from an emotion-regulation perspective. That is, what security of attachment reflects is the child's ability to regulate on his own, or to co-regulate with the expected assistance of his mother, his emotions. Secure children, then, are ones who have developed, in the context of the mother–infant relationship, the ability to manage negative affect and share positive affect. Insecure children, in contrast, are inclined to suppress negativity, or lose control of it, and/or fail to share positive feelings. Theorizing, then, that change in the manifestation of emotion over time might reflect emotion-regulation processes and, thereby, be related to attachment security, we examined, using 148 firstborn infants participating in our second and third longitudinal studies, stability and change in two separate dimensions of temperament, positive and negative emotionality, each based upon composited observational and maternal-report measures obtained when infants were 3 and 6 months of age (Belsky, Fish, & Isabella, 1991). More specifically, at each age, we relied upon maternal reports of how often infants smiled and laughed, as well as cried and fussed, and frequencies of these same behaviors observed during the course of two separate observations, one when mother was home alone with the infant and another when mother and father were at home with the child.

To be noted is that it was consideration of the emotional expressions in the Strange Situation of insecure-avoidant and some secure infants, especially those classified B1 and B2, which led us to think about positive emotions as well as negative emotions with respect to temperament change and attachment security. Central to such thinking was the observation that one thing that distinguished these two groups of children (i.e., A1/A2 vs. B1/B2) was that the secure children classified as B1 or B2 in the Strange Situation *openly* greeted their mothers upon reunion—with smiles, gestures, and vocalizations—whereas insecure-avoidant infants classified A1 or A2 seemed to suppress any proclivity to greet and express positive sentiment. Also influencing our separate focus upon infant positive and negative emotionality was evidence from the literature on emotions and moods in adulthood highlighting the need to distinguish positive and negative emotionality (Belsky & Pensky, 1988).

Relying upon our repeatedly-measured (at 3 and 6 months) composites of infant positivity and negativity, we created four groups of infants with respect to each emotionality dimension: those scoring high on the dimension in question at both points in time, those scoring low at both points in time, those who changed from high to low, and those who changed from low to high. Figure 3.3 graphically illustrates the stability and change groups in the case of negativity. When we examined attachment security at 1 year of age as a function of these stability and change groups, several interesting findings emerged (Belsky, Fish, & Isabella, 1991). First, changes in negative emotionality were not as strongly related to later attachment as changes in positive emotionality. Consistent with the results of Malatesta et al. (1989), however, we discovered that it was infants who declined in the positivity they manifested between 3 and 9 months who were most likely to be classified as insecure in their attachment at 1 year of age. This suggested to us that change in the temperamental dimension of positive emotionality might reflect processes of emotion regulation and thus that emotion regulation and attachment were

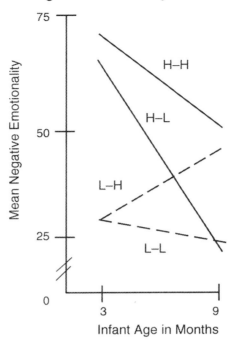

STABILITY AND CHANGE GROUPS:
Raw Negative Emotionality Mean Scores

Figure 3.3   Infant negativity change groups. (Adapted from Belsky, Fish, & Isabella, 1991.)

very much related (see Cassidy, 1994). Moreover, these data made intuitive sense in suggesting that children who ended up insecure at the end of the first year of life were the ones whose lives, at least while with their mothers, became less pleasurable over time.

Even though change in positive emotionality by itself, but not change in negative emotionality by itself, predicted attachment security, it was not the case that stability and change in negativity were not at all related to attachment security. This is because we discovered that certain combinations of stability and change in negative *and* positive emotionality predicted attachment security. Specifically, insecurity was most likely to be observed (i.e., 53% of the time) when (1) infant negativity remained high over time (i.e., high-high group) or increased (i.e., low-to-high group) *and* (2) infant positivity remained low over time (i.e., low-low group) or decreased (i.e., high-to-low group). In contrast, when none of these conditions obtained, insecurity was quite rare (i.e., 6%). To be noted is that in this work looking at change in positive and negative emotionality, we purposefully did not contrast effects of change against those of temperament or emotionality at a single point in time. And the reason for this was that we were explicitly pursuing a *developmental* approach which focused upon how specific emotional features of temperament change, not simply where they end up at some later time point or where they begin. Indeed, in our mind, one error often made in much temperament research, whether related to attachment or not, involves the assessment of dimensions of temperament at a single point in time. Such an approach fails to acknowledge that dimensions of temperament develop, or at least change; that is, they are not fixed.

When considered in their entirety, the findings summarized above regarding temperament and attachment dispel the notions that temperament determines attachment security in some simple, straightforward fashion or that there is no relation whatsoever between temperament and insecurity. Rather, they clearly and collectively suggest that the relation between these two constructs is complex. The fact, moreover, that stability and change in infant positive and negative emotionality between 3 and 9 months could be predicted using measures of the parent and family functioning obtained *before* the child was born and of parenting obtained when infants were 3 months of age strongly—with positive features of parents' personalities, their marriages and their parenting predicting improvements in temperament and the reverse being true of negative features of parents, marriages and parenting—suggests that it is a mistake to presume that emotional features of temperament reflect, exclusively, some inborn characteristic of the infant (Belsky et al., 1991). Because they can change, and because such change appears tied to experiences in the family, understanding of such change may tell us as much about the development of attachment security as it does about presumed constitutional features of the child.

Recent studies which take into account biological inheritance provide further evidence that attachment security is not a direct function of temperament. In perhaps the first test of the heritability of attachment security, Ricciuti (1992) combined data from three samples of twins and, after comparing concordance of attachment security across identical twins (who share 100% of the same genes) and fraternal twins (who share 50%), concluded that attachment security was not demonstrably heritable, at least in the case of 12- to 22-month-olds. More recently, O'Connor and Croft (2001) employed behavior genetic modeling of attachment data collected on 110 identical and fraternal twin pairs seen in the Strange Situation as preschoolers and detected only modest genetic influence, but substantial environmental influence—consistent with findings reviewed above linking maternal sensitivity and attachment security.

The largest and most comprehensive study of the heritability of attachment security conducted to date provides further evidence of the role of environmental factors rather than biological or temperamental ones in shaping attachment security. Indeed, when Bakermans-Kranenburg and Bokhorst (2003) subjected to analysis data on more than 200 pairs of twins, siblings, and unrelated children seen in the Strange Situation as infants, they discovered that biological inheritance did not play a role in determining whether children were classified as secure or insecure in their attachment to mother. More specifically, 48% of the variance in attachment security was explained by shared environmental influences and 52% by unique environmental influence and measurement error. Significantly, similar results highlighting the role of shared environment and yielding very little evidence of genetic effects emerged when the focus of attention was security of attachment to father. In contrast, indices of temperament, reflecting degree of distress in the Strange Situation, proved highly heritable. In sum, while security or insecurity does not appear to be a function of biological inheritance or of temperament per se, variation in emotionality seen in the Strange Situation, even if not the regulation of such emotion in the context of interacting with mother, does seem to be heritable.

THE BROADER ECOLOGY OF ATTACHMENT SECURITY

Through this point I have considered what might be referred to as "classical" determinants of attachment security, namely those considered in most developmental theorizing about the origins of secure and insecure attachment (Belsky, Rosenberger, & Crnic, 1995a). But an ecological perspective on human development, one that underscores the fact that the parent–child dyad is embedded in a family system (Belsky, 1981), which is itself embedded in a community, cultural, and even historical context (Bronfenbrenner, 1979), suggests that if one wants to account for why some infants develop secure and others insecure attachments to mother, father, or even child-care worker, then there is a need to look beyond the "proximate" determinants of mothering and temperament.

Toward this end, we undertook a series of inquires using data collected as part of our longitudinal studies based upon a contextual model of the determinants of parenting that I advanced more than a decade ago which highlights the role of parent, child, and social-contextual factors in shaping the parent–child relationship (Belsky, 1984; see Figure 3.4). As should be apparent from Figure 3.4, the model presumes that parenting and thus the parent–child relationship is multiply determined and that the contextual factors of work, social support, and marriage can affect parenting both directly and indirectly (through personality). Not explicit in the figure, however, but central to the conceptualization

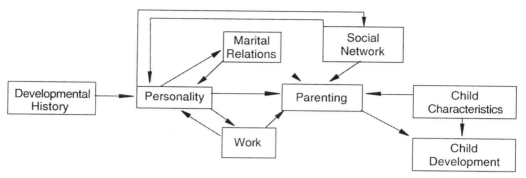

Figure 3.4 Determinants of parenting: A process model. Adapted from Belsky (1984).

on which the model is based, is the notion that parenting, and thus the parent–child relationship, is a well buffered system. This means that threats to its integrity stemming from limitations or vulnerabilities in any single source of influence (e.g., work) are likely to be compensated for by resources that derive from other sources of influence (e.g., marriage). Thus, parenting and the parent–child relationship are most likely to be adversely affected when *multiple* vulnerabilities exist (e.g., difficult temperament plus conflicted marriage) that accumulate and undermine the effectiveness of other sources of influence in promoting parental functioning. It is just such thinking that led us to examine the cumulative impact of multiple determinants of parenting in affecting attachment security, not just the impact of one or another source of influence.

In the first work of this kind that we carried out using data collected as part of our first longitudinal investigation, linkages were examined between attachment security measured at 1 year and (a) mother's own childrearing history reported during the prenatal period; (b) mother's personality assessed using questionnaires at the same point in time; (c) change in mother-reported infant temperament between 3 and 9 months (and already discussed above); (d) change in marital quality between the last trimester of pregnancy and 9 months postpartum (based upon self-reports obtained at both measurement occasions); and (e) prenatal reports by mothers of the friendliness and helpfulness of neighbors (i.e., social support). Results from univariate analyses revealed that mothers of secure infants scored higher than those of insecure infants on a personality measure of interpersonal affection, whereas mothers of avoidant infants scored lowest on a measure of ego strength; that the (mother-reported) temperaments of secure infants became, as indicated earlier, more predictable and adaptable over time, whereas the reverse was true of insecure infants; that insecure infants were living in families in which marriages were deteriorating in quality more precipitously than were secure infants; and that the neighbors of secure infants were perceived as more friendly and helpful than those of insecure infants (Belsky & Isabella, 1988). More important than these univariate findings, however, was evidence that emerged when maternal, infant, and contextual stressors and supports were considered collectively: The more that the family ecology could be described as well resourced (i.e., positive maternal personality, positive change in infant temperament, less marital deterioration), the more likely the child was to develop a secure attachment to mother.

This work was extended using data from our fourth longitudinal study, this one of a sample consisting exclusively of 125 firstborn sons whose families were enrolled when they were 10 months of age (rather than prenatally as in the first three investigations). These subjects were recruited from the same locale as those participating in the first three longitudinal investigations, though we relied upon birth announcements published in the local newspaper rather than names provided by local obstetricians to identify potential participants. Because of our interest in the multiple determinants of parent–child relations, extensive data were collected on a variety of sources of influence. At enrollment when infants were 10 months of age, mothers and fathers completed questionnaire-based personality assessments and self-reports pertaining to the social support available to them and their satisfaction with it, and whether work and family life interfered with each other or were mutually supportive. At 12 and 13 months, infants were seen in the laboratory to assess infant–mother and infant–father attachment, respectively. Following administration of the Strange Situation, parent and infant engaged in a short period of free play (in a separate lab room) and a number of procedures were implemented to evoke positive and negative emotions. For example, an experimenter tried to make the child laugh and smile using hand puppets; and the parent was directed to frustrate the child by taking a toy away from him while he was in a high chair. Videos of infant behavior following the Strange Situation were rated in terms of the extent to which the child expressed positive and negative emotion every 10 seconds; these ratings were then factor analyzed and combined with parent-report measures of temperament obtained at age 10 months in order to create composite indices of positive and negative emotionality.

Using these data, we again found that it is the cumulative vulnerabilities and resources of infants, parents and families that afford the best prediction of both infant–mother and infant–father attachment security, rather than any single variable or factor (Belsky, Rosenberger, & Crnic, 1995b; Belsky, 1996). Figure 3.5 depicts results pertaining to the cumulative effect of infant, parent and social-contextual factors in shaping infant–father attachment security (Belsky, 1996). In this research, three personality measures were composited (extraversion – neuroticism + agreeableness), as were two measures of infant temperament/emotionality (positivity-negativity), and four social-context measures ([social support satisfaction + number of people to provide support] + [work-family support-interference]). The measures derived from compositing each of these three sets of variables (i.e., personality, infant temperament, social context) were then split at its median; a high score on each composite measure was given a value of 1 to reflect conditions considered favorable for the development of a secure infant–father relationship, and a low score was given a value of 0 to reflect conditions presumed less conducive to the development of a secure relationship. These new values were then summed across sets of variables (i.e., parent, infant, social context), resulting in individual family scores ranging from a value of 0–3. As is apparent in the figure, the greater the family resources (i.e., cumulative resource score of 3), the more likely the infant–father relationship was classified as secure on the basis of the infant's behavior with father in the Strange Situation (Belsky, 1996). Similar results emerged in the case of the infant–mother attachment relationship (Belsky et al., 1995b).

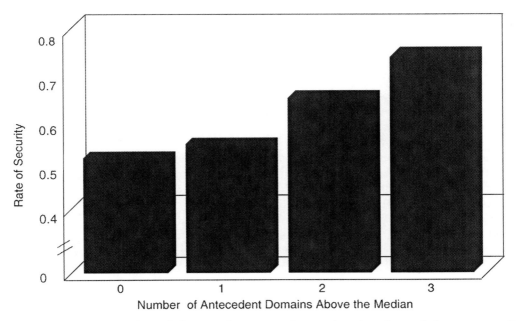

Figure 3.5 Probability of son–father attachment security as a function of cumulative resources (0 = low, 3 = high).

NONMATERNAL CARE

Because of the role that lengthy child–parent separations played in Bowlby's original formulations of attachment theory, concern has been raised often about the consequences of more routine, short-term separations of the kind experienced on a daily basis by children cared for by someone other than a parent when mother is employed. The initial work addressing this issue focused almost exclusively upon children being cared for in very-high-quality, university-based centers and generally failed to reveal any consistent association between day care and attachment insecurity (for reviews, see Belsky & Steinberg, 1978; Rutter, 1981). However, this first wave of attachment day care research used as an index of security the extent to which the child became upset upon separation from parent, even though it was never clear conceptually whether greater or lesser distress should be considered a marker of security (or insecurity).

When we examined the issue of relations between nonmaternal care and security of infant–parent attachment in our second and third longitudinal studies, using the Ainsworth et al. (1978) reunion-based Strange-Situation scoring system, two particularly interesting findings emerged. First, infants who experienced, on average, more than 20 hours per week of such care during their first year were more likely to develop insecure attachments than were children who experienced less nonmaternal care (Belsky & Rovine, 1988). In fact, when I compiled data from my own work and that from other studies of nonrisk samples that were published in the scientific literature , the same pattern emerged (Belsky, 1988). Subsequently, Clarke-Stewart (1989) and Lamb and colleagues (1990) undertook similar analyses, drawing upon both published and unpublished data. The results of these compilations of findings of research carried out in the United States across a variety of nonmaternal caregiving arrangements (e.g., centers, family day care homes, nanny care) all revealed a reliable association between more than 20 hours per week of such nonmaternal care in the first year of life and attachment insecurity. The magnitudes of association varied, however, with Belsky and Rovine (1988), Clarke-Stewart (1989) and Lamb et al. (1990) indicating, respectively, that the rate of infant–mother attachment insecurity was 65%, 24%, and 83% higher among infants with more than 20 hours per week of nonparental care in their first year relative to infants with less time (including none at all) in such care. Subsequent to the publication of this work, however, Roggmann et al. (1994) addressed the same issue using data from five studies they had carried out and failed to replicate these results.

The second noteworthy finding to emerge from our own work concerned infant–father attachment security. Like Chase-Lansdale and Owen (1987) before us, we found that sons with more than 35 or more hours per week of nonmaternal care (in the United States) were more likely to develop insecure attachments to their fathers and thus have two insecure attachments (one to mother and one to father) than were other boys (Belsky & Rovine, 1988). These findings seemed particularly significant as earlier work in our lab (Belsky, Garduque, & Hrncir, 1984) and by others (Easterbrooks & Goldberg, 1987; Howes et al., 1988; Main, Kaplan, & Cassidy, 1985; Main & Weston, 1981) indicated that children with two insecure attachment relationships functioned more poorly than did children with one or more secure attachments.

A variety of observations about and explanations of these findings linking extensive nonmaternal care in the first year of life with elevated rates of insecure attachment have been offered. Consider first the fact that more than half of the children who experience early and extensive infant day care were classified as secure; such variation in response to early day care suggests that separation per se is probably not the principal cause of the elevated rates of insecurity that have been repeatedly chronicled. Consider next that the quality of child care in the United States is known to be limited; thus, elevated rates of insecurity may have as much, or more, to do with the nature of the care infants receive when cared for by someone other than mother than by the fact that mother is not providing the care. Especially notable in this regard is the fact that toddlers are more likely to develop secure attachments to those who care for them in child care when these caregivers are more sensitive, responsive and available to them (Goosens & van IJzendoorn, 1990; Howes et al., 1988); and that security of attachment to caregiver is itself related to more competent social functioning, especially in concert with secure attachment to mother (Howes et al., 1988). These findings would again seem to implicate the quality of nonmaternal care which the child receives when it comes to understanding the developmental effects of early child care. Also to be considered is the quality of care which the child experiences at home when with his parents, especially since extensive time away from the parent may make it more difficult for the parent to provide the kind of care that fosters attachment security (i.e., sensitive care). Of course, the pressures that working parents experience when at home with the child may also make the provision of such care more difficult.

These varied and complex issues which remained unresolved in discussions of effects of day care led to the establishment of the NICHD Study of Early Child Care (NICHD Early Child Care Research Network, 1994), a research project in which exactly the same research protocol is being implemented at ten different research sites across the United States in order to illuminate the conditions under which early child care enhances or compromises children's development. More than 1,300 children and their families were recruited into this work when infants were 1 month of age, after identifying children and families at their local hospitals shortly after their births. The sample is quite varied demographically and ethnically, but does not include any families in which mother does not speak English fluently or in which the mother is under 18 years of age. A rather extensive research protocol has been implemented to study infant and family development, as well as child care, in this extensive project which is following the children from age 1 month through middle childhood (with pending prospects for further extension). Most importantly, the quality of child care received is measured in detail using observational methods that evaluate both the general child care setting, whether it be a private home or center, and the moment-to-moment experiences that the child has with caregiver(s) and other children when the child is 6, 15, 24, 36, and 54 months of age. At these same ages, multiple features of the family are measured; most important for purposes of this chapter are assessments of the sensitivity of mothering. Such assessments take the form of videotapes of mother–child interaction under free play conditions which are coded using Ainsworth-like rating scales and more naturalistic observations of maternal attentive responsiveness to the child while being interviewed. At all but 6 months of age, children are evaluated in the university laboratory using a variety of methodologies; Strange Situations were administered when children were 15 months of age (and again when children were 36 months old).

With respect to infant–mother attachment security and the effects of early child care, the NICHD Study of Early Child Care had two specific goals. The first was to assess the validity of Strange Situation measurements in the case of children with repeated experiences of being separated from mother due to concerns raised about this methodology with these particular children. The second goal concerned relations between early nonmaternal care and attachment security. Specifically, we sought to determine whether, or under what conditions, experience in child care increased or decreased the probability that a child would establish a secure attachment to his mother.

THE VALIDITY OF THE STRANGE SITUATION

Ever since linkages have been chronicled between nonmaternal care and attachment insecurity, questions have been raised about whether the infant's independent and exploratory behavior in the Strange Situation is mistakenly judged to be evidence of avoidance, especially in the case of infants who experience routine nonmaternal care. Clarke-Stewart (1989), Thompson (1988), and others have argued that these children's daily separation experiences may lead them to behave more independently in the Strange Situation because they are less stressed by the separations purposefully designed into the procedure. Such a methodological artifact could then cause them to be (erroneously) classified as insecure-avoidant more frequently than children without early and extensive infant day care experience. Not only is it the case that a comprehensive review of relevant studies by Clarke-Stewart and Fein (1983) showed that infant day care experience was not related to less (or more) stress in the Strange Situation (as indexed by distress), but when I carried out a small study using subjects from my second and third longitudinal investigations to directly address this proposition, I found no support whatsoever for it (Belsky & Braungart, 1991). More specifically, infants with extensive nonmaternal care experience who were classified insecure-avoidant did not evince less distress and more play than those similarly classified with limited or no nonmaternal care experience; in fact, the former actually played significantly less during reunions—exactly the opposite of what critics of the Strange Situation methodology had propositioned. Just as noteworthy as our findings are those of Berger, Levy, and Compaan (1995); these investigators found that classifications of children's attachment security based on their behavior during a standard pediatric exam (in which no separation of infant from parent occurred) are highly concordant with Strange Situation classifications for both infants with extensive child care experience in the first year (81.5% concordance) and those without such experience (76%). In others words, my own work as well as that of Berger et al. (1995) failed to find any evidence to suggest that the Strange Situation was an invalid methodology for studying one group of children in particular, namely those with repeated separation experiences due to routine nonmaternal care.

Because these evaluations of the validity of Strange Situation classifications in the case of infants with lots of experience being separated from their mothers involved small samples, the NICHD Study of Early Child Care provided an ideal opportunity to address this issue again. Comparisons were made between children who averaged more than 30 hours per week of care from 3–15 months of age with others who experienced less than 10 hours per week of nonmaternal care during the same developmental period on measures of distress when separated from mother. Not only was it the case that the two groups were not different in terms of how upset infants became when separated, but it was also true that coders' ratings of their confidence in classifying children in terms of the three primary attachment categories (i.e., avoidant, resistant, secure) did not vary as a function of nonmaternal care experience. Thus, it was concluded that there were no empirical grounds to question the internal validity of the Strange Situation in the large data set; therefore, classifications of children in this separation-based procedure could be regarded as valid even in the case of children with extensive experience with separation (NICHD Early Child Care Research Network, 1997).

Effects of Early Child Care

Having established empirically that one could have confidence in the Strange Situation classifications of children with extensive separation experience, the NICHD Early Child Care Research Network (1997) was now in a position to powerfully address a question that had stimulated much debate and controversy. Interestingly, results of this comprehensive investigation revealed that neither the quantity of nonmaternal care, the quality of such care, the stability of care, nor the child's age of entry (within the first 15 months of life), as isolated factors, accounted for variation in infant–mother attachment security. Even though maternal sensitivity when considered by itself did predict attachment security, yet features of child care, when considered individually, did not, it was not the case that features of early child care proved to be totally unrelated to attachment security. Consistent with Bronfenbrenner's (1979, p. 38) dictum that "in the ecology of human development the principal main effects are likely to be interactions," we found that even though most children with early care experience were not more (or less) likely to develop insecure attachments to their mothers, this was not the case when certain ecological conditions co-occurred. More specifically, rates of insecurity were higher than would otherwise have been expected (on the basis of maternal sensitivity alone) when infants received poorer quality (i.e., insensitive) care from their mothers and (a) low quality nonmaternal care, or (b) more than 10 hours per week of nonmaternal care, or (c) more than one nonmaternal care arrangement in their first 15 months of life. In other words, it was under conditions of "dual-risk" that early care was associated, for the most part, with attachment insecurity. These findings were not only consistent with a controversial risk-factor conclusion that I had drawn a decade earlier about the effects of infant day care as currently experienced in the United States (Belsky, 1986, 1988), but with the results summarized above linking parent, infant, and social-contextual conditions with the probability of an infant establishing a secure or insecure attachment relationship with mother or with father. That is, it is knowledge of multiple features of the caregiving ecology that provides the best prediction of attachment security. And, moreover, it is when sources of risk accumulate that the probability of insecurity is greatest (Belsky, 2001). Importantly, when infants were followed up at 3 years of age and seen again in the Strange Situation, only one of the dual-risk findings re-emerged, indicating that the combination of low levels of maternal sensitivity and lots of time in child care (irrespective of quality) was related to elevated rates of insecure attachment (NICHD Early Child Care Research Network, 2001).

THE DEVELOPMENTAL SEQUELAE OF INFANT–MOTHER ATTACHMENT SECURITY

In addition to affording an opportunity to evaluate the effects of early child care on infant–mother attachment security, data collected as part of the NICHD Study enabled me to explore individual differences in the future social and cognitive functioning of some 1,000 children studied in the course of investigating the long-term consequences of early child care experience. Drawing upon data gathered when children were 3, I examined two separate issues with respect to the developmental sequelae of early attachment security.

Are the Consequences of Attachment Security Dependent Upon Later Mothering?

Ever since the Minnesota investigators whose work was summarized earlier in this chapter started to chronicle the developmental consequences of attachment security and insecurity, demonstrating that early attachment predicted multiple aspects of later child development, there has been confusion about the developmental process by which early security comes to be related to later child functioning. Although some have mistakenly attributed to students of attachment theory the view that attachment security/insecurity has some automatic or inevitable impact on the course of children's future development (Breur, 1999; Kagan, 1982; Lewis, 1997), attachment theorists have been clear that this represents a fundamental misreading of the theory (Belsky & Cassidy, 1994). Indeed, Sroufe (1983, 1988) has asserted for years that development is a function of early and continuing experiences, such that what happens after infancy (or any other developmental period) can mitigate the otherwise anticipated consequences of experiences earlier in life. In fact, early work by the Minnesota team of investigators showed that the effects of attachment security on later development were, to a large extent, dependent upon the quality of maternal care that children experienced after attachment security was assessed at the end of the first year of life (Erikson, Egeland, & Sroufe, 1985).

Drawing upon this earlier work and theorizing, I set out to test the hypothesis that the developmental benefits of early security would be conditioned by the child's subsequent childrearing experiences, predicting that the most competent 3-year-olds participating in the NICHD Study of Early Child Care would be those who established secure attachments to their mothers by 15 months of age *and* whose mothers provided sensitive care to them when they were 24 months of age. Children who developed insecure attachments *and* experienced insensitive care subsequently were expected to function least competently, with all other children falling between these two extreme groups. And this is exactly what was found when data on socioemotional and cognitive-linguistic development gathered at 36 months of age was subjected to empirical assessment (Belsky & Fearon, 2002a). In other words, just as Sroufe (1983, 1988) had long argued, the developmental benefits of early security were dependent upon the continued experience of receiving emotionally supportive care and the developmental costs of insecurity were dependent upon the continued experience of receiving emotionally unsupportive care. Early security or insecurity did not inevitably have any developmental consequence—because development was a continuing process. The developmental sequelae of early attachment security/insecurity were determined, therefore, by whether experiences during the toddler years maintained earlier-established developmental trajectories, trajectories which, importantly, could be deflected by experiences which were inconsistent with earlier attachment security (i.e., insecure infants subsequently receiving sensitive care, secure infants subsequently experiencing insensitive care).

Do the Consequences of Attachment Security Vary by Contextual Risk?

In addition to addressing the question of whether the anticipated effects of early attachment security on later development were dependent upon the quality of maternal care experienced during toddlerhood, I drew upon the data collected as part of the NICHD Study of Early Child Care to see whether the effects of early attachment security varied as a function of the contextual conditions under which children grew up (Belsky & Fearon, 2002b). It seemed likely that the developmental benefits and costs of security/insecurity might vary as a function of whether children grew up under conditions expected to compromise their well being (e.g., low income, maternal depression, single-parent home) rather than under more developmentally supportive circumstances. To address this possibility, we created measures of cumulative contextual risk, classifying children as experiencing low, moderate, high, and very high levels of risk depending upon the circumstances in which they grew up across the first 3 years of life and then examined the extent to which early security (at 15 months) predicted later development (at 36 months) across ecological conditions.

Although we found that secure attachment proved to be a developmental benefit with regard to understanding spoken language (but not more general cognitive development or the ability to express oneself) irrespective of whether a child grew up under conditions of high or low contextual risk, in the case of expressive language and socioemotional outcomes, the predictive power of early attachment security varied as a function of contextual risk. Indeed, the expressive-language findings were consistent with what might be regarded as a simple risk-resilience model of attachment and later development in which security functions as a protective factor: Whereas the expressive language abilities of children with insecure attachment histories systematically declined as contextual risk increased, this was not the case for children with secure attachment histories (see Figure 3.6). Security, therefore, appeared to play a clear protective function when it came to children's ability to use spoken language.

In the case of problem behavior and social competence, it was the insecure-avoidant group that appeared to be most affected by contextual risk, evincing adverse effects of cumulative contextual risk at a level of risk lower than that at which all other attachment groups "succumbed" to contextual risk. In the case of behavior problems, whereas the attachment groups did not differ from each other at low levels of contextual risk (i.e., ≤ 1), and all groups were adversely affected by high levels of risk (i.e., ≥ 3), at moderate levels of risk (i.e., 2 risks) children with insecure-avoidant attachment histories showed the same level of poor functioning that the other attachment groups evinced only at high levels of risk (see Figure 3.7). A similar pattern emerged for social competence, with the avoidant

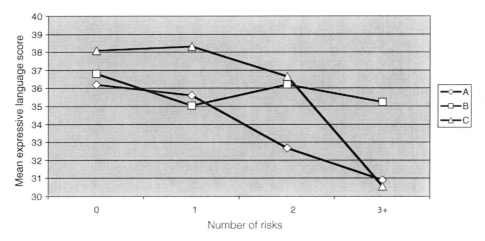

Figure 3.6 Mean expressive language scores as a function of attachment classification (A: Insecure-Avoidant, B: Secure, C: Insecure-Resistant) and degree of cumulative contextual risk (0: no risk, 1: low risk, 2: moderate risk, 3: high risk).

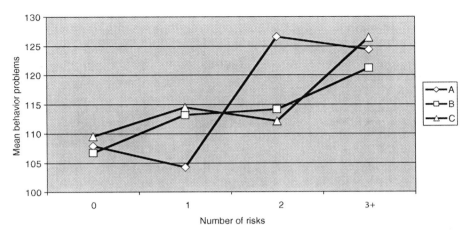

Figure 3.7 Mean problem behavior scores as a function of attachment classification (A: Insecure-Avoidant, B: Secure, C: Insecure-Resistant) and degree of cumulative contextual risk (0: no risk, 1: low risk, 2: moderate risk, 3: high risk).

group showing a marked decrease in performance under conditions of two risks (see Figure 3.8). In a sense, then, the avoidant group proved more vulnerable to contextual risk—at least at a lower level of risk—than children in all other groups. When levels of risk became especially high, however, even a history of attachment security failed to protect children from the adverse effects of growing up in a developmentally adverse environment, at least with respect to the development of social competence.

To summarize, then, it appears that security and insecurity afford children, respectively, developmental benefits and costs, but that in some cases these depend on (a) the type of insecurity the child manifests and (b) the ecological circumstances under which children grow up. Recall that when ecological circumstances were especially undermining of developmental well being, even secure attachment did not always function to protect the child's well being, and that it was a history of insecure-avoidant attachment that proved especially undermining of competent functioning, at least at 3 years of age. Exactly why a history of insecure-resistant attachment did not carry the same developmental costs as a history of insecure-avoidant attachment remains, for the time being, unclear.

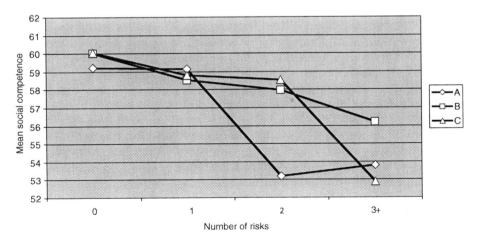

Figure 3.8 Mean social competence scores as a function of attachment classification (A: Insecure-Avoidant, B: Secure, C: Insecure-Resistant) and degree of cumulative contextual risk (0: no risk, 1: low risk, 2: moderate risk, 3: high risk).

One possibility, however, has to do with the developmental outcomes investigated (i.e., language ability, externalizing problems, social competence). It is conceivable that children with insecure-resistant attachment histories may prove more prone to behavior problems of the internalizing variety (i.e., anxiety, depression), but these are not only difficult to measure in 3-year-olds, but often do not clearly manifest themselves until children get older.

CONCLUSION: A MODERN EVOLUTIONARY PERSPECTIVE ON EARLY ATTACHMENT

Almost two decades of research on infant–parent attachment security, coupled with an emerging interest in evolutionary biology which figured so importantly in Bowlby's original formulation of attachment theory, has led me to rethink the meaning of what I have found in my work, as well as what others have found in their related inquiries. Moreover, it leads me to question some of the implicit assumptions that guide the interpretation of much work on attachment. Central to this rethinking is the evidence I have summarized from my own work showing that (a) cumulative stresses and supports affect the probability that an infant will develop a secure attachment; (b) as does the sensitivity of the care provided by the child's principal caregiver, typically his mother; (c) changes in the infants' behavioral development, especially his emotional functioning, across the first year, also predict attachment security; and that (d) the predictive power of attachment security often, though not always, varies as a function of the child's post-infancy childrearing circumstances (i.e., maternal sensitivity, contextual risk). When considered together, such findings raise the prospect of the following causal process: Contextual stresses and supports affect the sensitivity of maternal care, which affects emotional and temperamental development, which affects whether or not the child develops a secure attachment and whether, and how, attachment security comes to forecast later development.

Although it is clearly the case that the causal linkages just detailed between contextual circumstances and attachment security and between attachment security and later development are probabilistic rather than deterministic, and thus that contextual effects and resulting developmental trajectories are not fixed, a question must be asked that is rarely raised by developmental psychologists: *Why* do developmental processes operate the way they do? What developmentalists usually ask are not such questions about ultimate causation, but ones about proximate causation or processes of influence: *How* does development operate? Such questions lead most developmentalists, myself included, to examine what predicts the quality of maternal care or attachment security, or what security of attachment is related to in terms of the child's future functioning. But when we find answers to these psychological and developmental questions, as we clearly have, we rarely stop to ponder why the developmental processes we have discerned should be present in the first place. In other words, we tend to take them for granted. But should we? And what might we be missing by doing so? Might we be too close to the phenomena we are studying to recognize, in some sense, what they are *all* about? I am beginning to believe that this might indeed be the case.

When Bowlby first discussed the evolutionary basis of attachment behavior, he stressed the survival (i.e., adaptive) value of the infant maintaining proximity to his/her caregiver. And, when attachment researchers have written about the functioning of secure and insecure children, frequently they have spoken in terms of the adaptive functioning of the former and the maladaptive functioning of the latter. By using the same terminology to discuss evolutionary-biological and psychological-mental health phenomena, it is not surprising that some have come to equate the mental health benefits of a secure attachment with evolutionary benefits. Indeed, Ainsworth (1973, p. 45) herself seemed to imply as much when she argued "that 'securely attached' babies 'developed normally, i.e., along species-characteristic lines'" (Hinde, 1982, p. 69).

Yet, as Hinde (1982a; Hinde & Stevenson-Hinde, 1991) has made abundantly clear, and as Ainsworth (1984) herself came to acknowledge, levels of analysis need to be distinguished when terms like "adaptation" are employed. Although it may be beneficial in the contemporary psychological or mental health sense to develop a secure attachment, it is certainly mistaken to presume that from an evolutionary or phylogenetic perspective that a secure attachment is better or more adaptive than an insecure attachment—however much we value contextual supports and maternal sensitivity, that is, determinants of attachment security—and positive interpersonal relations, a presumed sequelae of security. As Hinde (1982, pp. 71–72) noted, "…there is no best mothering (or attachment) style, for different styles are better in different circumstances, and natural selection would act to favor individuals with a range of potential styles from which they select appropriately…mothers and babies will be programmed (by evolution) not simply to form one sort of relationship but a range of possible relationships according to circumstances…optimal mothering (and attachment) behavior will differ according to…the mother's social status, caregiving contributions from other family members, the state of physical resources, and so on…a mother–child relationship which produces successful adults in one situation may not do so in another." In other words, while it may be the case that securely attached children develop, in contemporary Western society (or perhaps just in middle-class American society), more competently and are more likely to grow up into happy, mentally healthy adults in this ecology, it is completely inaccurate to infer from such evidence or to otherwise presume that, on the basis of natural selection theory, one attachment or mothering style is necessarily best. This is so even as we find that under supportive and less stressful contextual conditions, and when care is more sensitive, that infants and young children are more likely to develop secure attachments.

Such evolutionary thinking has led me to reconceptualize secure and insecure attachment in terms of reproductive and life history strategies that are flexibly responsive to contextual and caregiving conditions and which evolved in the service of evolutionary goals, not mental health ones pertaining to happiness or psychological well being (Belsky, Steinberg, & Draper, 1991; Belsky, 1997, 1999; see also Chisholm, 1996). From the perspective of evolutionary biology, the goal of all life is the replication of genes in future generations. Not only do species vary in terms of how they accomplish this task, but so do individuals within some species. Moreover, in certain species, humans included perhaps, such variation can be determined by concurrent or developmentally antecedent experiences. Depending upon the circumstances that organisms find themselves in, if they have the flexibility to adjust their behavior and development according to these life conditions, it may make sense to bear few offspring and care for them intensively, a tactic our value system tends to regard favorably, or to bear many and care for them less devotedly, an approach which contemporary norms tend to frown upon and discourage.

This suggests to me that the developing attachment system evolved to provide a means through which the developing child could turn information acquired from parents about prevailing contextual conditions—via the caregiving experience—into knowledge and "awareness" of the kinds of future he is likely to face. More specifically, the capacity to develop different patterns of attachment in response to the quality of care received evolved to provide a kind of "navigational" device to direct development in one direction or another depending upon what would have optimized reproductive success in adulthood in the environments of evolutionary adaptation. Might it be the case, then, that security represents an evolved psychological mechanism that "informs" the child, based upon the sensitive care he has experienced, that others can be trusted; that close, affectional bonds are enduring; and that the world is a more rather than less caring place; and, as a result, that it makes reproductive sense to defer mating and reproduction until fully prepared to care well for one's young; to be selective in pair bonding; and to bear fewer rather than more children, but care for them intensively? In contrast, might insecure attachment represent a similarly evolved psychological mechanism, also responsive to caregiving conditions, that conveys to the child the developing understanding that others cannot be trusted; that close, affectional bonds are unlikely to be enduring; and that it makes more sense to participate in opportunistic, self-serving relationships rather than mutually beneficial ones? In consequence, does a child who develops such a psychological orientation, in response to the caregiving she/he has received, which itself has been fostered by the less rather than more supportive conditions that his/her parents have confronted, become inclined to mate earlier and more frequently, perhaps producing more offspring who are poorly cared for, because this approach to optimizing reproductive fitness makes more sense in the world as it is understood to be than by adopting the strategy more characteristic of those who have developed secure attachments? Or, even if this is no longer the case today, might these processes have operated in the environment of evolutionary adaptation, so that what we observe today are psychological mechanisms that have evolved and are still operative even if the reproductive "payoffs" that once were associated with them no longer obtain (Buss, 1995)?

While I would not want to argue definitively on behalf of these speculative propositions, I do want to suggest that the reason that our work (and that of others) linking antecedents of attachment security with attachment security generates the findings that it does may be because individual differences in attachment may be part of a complex developmental process that in human ancestral environments provided the means of directing development in particular ways that were reproductively strategic. To the extent that this was so, it suggests that findings linking contextual conditions and parenting processes to variation in attachment security, and variation in attachment security to variation in subsequent development, may be part of a developing system whose function was not originally understood or appreciated by Bowlby, Ainsworth or many current students of attachment theory.

Like many others of his time, when Bowlby (1962) initially conceptualized the evolutionary basis of attachment, he wrote in terms of survival of the species. What he eventually came to understand, however, was that it is not survival alone that natural selection rewards but differential reproduction, defined in terms of the dispersion of genes in future generations. Moreover, what he also came to appreciate was that natural selection worked at the level of individuals as well as genes, not species; so the evolutionary payoffs were to those individuals who survived to reproduce and thus whose genes came to be disproportionately represented in future generations.

In conclusion, consideration of the centrality of differential reproduction among individuals in the Darwinian process of evolution by natural selection raises the prospect that the reason that individual differences in attachment may be related to rearing conditions, as my research and that of others has shown, as well as to future social and emotional development, is because patterns of attachment evolved as strategic alternatives for promoting reproductive fitness under varying circumstances in the environment of evolutionary adaptation. What this suggests is that it may be useful to move beyond a mental health orientation toward attachment to one that focuses upon reproductive functioning (i.e., mating and parenting).

What is particularly intriguing about such reorientation is that it does not require the abandonment of much that has excited attachment researchers about the origins and especially sequelae of individual differences in attachment. This is because a reoriented focused-upon reproductive functioning involves many of the same processes that more mental-health-oriented thinking about attachment directs attention to, namely, social and emotional development, particularly in the context of interpersonal relatedness and parenting. Thus, it is not so much that a modern evolutionary perspective on attachment suggests that attachment researchers—myself included—have been misguided in examining the antecedents and consequences of attachment that they have over the past several decades, but rather that they may have not fully appreciated how great the significance of the early attachment system may be. Thus, by moving beyond traditional psychological and developmental questions pertaining to *how* development operates, to ones that focus upon why it operates the way it appears to, increased insight into the developmental phenomena under investigation may be realized. This might provide new directions for research, in the case of attachment, most notably toward issues of mating and parental investment. Unfortunately, at the present time, there is no good evidence that early attachments do indeed predict mating and parenting behavior, basically because the longitudinal samples that have been studied are not yet old enough to be rearing the next generation. This raises the possibility that in the not too distant future it will be possible to determine whether, in fact, attachment security forecasts reproductive behavior and parental investment.

REFERENCES

Ainsworth, M. (1963). The development of infant–mother interaction among the Ganda. In B. Foss (Ed.), *Determinants of Infant Behavior,* Vol. 2. New York: Wiley.

Ainsworth, M. D. (1967). *Infancy in Uganda: Infant care and the growth of attachment.* Baltimore: Johns Hopkins Press.

Ainsworth, M. D. (1973). The development of infant–mother attachment. In B. M. Caldwell & H. N. Ricciuti (Eds.), *Review of child development research* (Vol. 3, pp. 1–94). Chicago: University of Chicago Press.

Ainsworth, M. D. (1984, April). *Adaptation and attachment.* Paper presented to the International Conference on Infant Studies. New York City.

Ainsworth, M. D., Bell, S. M., & Stayton, D. J. (1971). Individual differences in strange situation behavior of one-year-olds. In H. R. Schaffer (Ed.), *The origins of human social relations.* London: Academic.

Ainsworth, M. D., Blehar, M. C., Waters, E., & Wall, S. (1978). *Patterns of attachment: A psychological study of the strange situation.* Hillsdale, NJ: Erlbaum.

Ainsworth, M. D., & Wittig, B. A. (1969). Attachment and exploratory behavior of one-year-olds in a strange situation. In B. M. Foss (Ed.), *Determinants of infant behavior* (Vol. 4, pp. 129–173). London: Metheum.

Bakermans-Kranenburg, M., & Bokhorst, C. (2003, April 26). *A large role for shared environment in infant attachment classifications.* Paper presented at the biennial meetings of the Society for Research in Child Development, Tampa, Florida.

Belsky, J. (1979a) Mother-father-infant interaction: A naturalistic observational study. *Developmental Psychology, 8,* 601–608.

Belsky, J. (1979b). The interrelation of parental and spousal behavior during infancy in traditional nuclear families. *Journal of Marriage and the Family, 41,* 62–68.

Belsky, J. (1981). Early human experience: A family perspective. *Developmental Psychology, 17,* 3–23.

Belsky, J. (1984). The determinants of parenting: A process model. *Child Development, 55,* 83–96.

Belsky, J. (1990). Developmetnal risks associated with infant day care: Attachment insecurity, noncompliance, and aggression? In S. Chehrazi (Ed.), *Psychosocial issues in day care* (pp. 37–68). New York: American Psychiatric Press.

Belsky, J. (1996). Parent, infant, and social-contextual antecedents of father-son attachment security. *Developmental Psychology, 32,* 905–913.

Belsky, J. (1997). Patterns of attachment mating and parenting: An evolutionary interpretation. *Human Nature, 8,* 361–381.

Belsky, J. (1999). Modern evolutionary theory and patterns of attachment. In J. Cassidy & P. Shaver (Eds.), *Handbook of attachment: Theory, research and clinical applications* (pp. 141–161). New York: Wiley.

Belsky, J., & Braungart, J. (1991). Are insecure-avoidant infants with extensive day care experience less stressed by and more independent in the Strange Situation? *Child Development, 62,* 567–571.

Belsky, J. & Cassidy, J. (1994). Attachment: theory and evidence. In M. Rutter & D. Hay (Eds.), *Developmental principles and clinical issues in psychology and psychiatry* (pp. 373–402). London: Blackwell.

Belsky, J., & Fearon, R. M. P. (2002a). Early attachment security, subsequent maternal sensitivity, and later child development: Does continuity in development depend upon continuity of Caregiving? *Attachment and Human Development, 3,* 361–387.

Belsky, J., & Fearon, R. M. P (2002b). Infant–mother Attachment Security, Contextual Risk and Early Development: A Moderational Analysis. *Development and Psychopathology, 14,* 293–310.

Belsky, J., Fish, M., & Isabella, R. (1991). Continuity and discontinuity in infant negative and positive emotionalisty: Family antecedents and attachment consequences.

Belsky, J., Garduque, L., & Hrncir, E. (1984). Assessing performance, competence, and executive capacity in infant play: Relations to home environment and security of attachment. *Developmental Psychology, 20,* 406–417.

Belsky, J., & Isabella, R. (1988). Maternal, infant, and social-contextual determinants of attachment security. In J. Belsky & T. Nezworski (Eds.), *Clinical implications of attachment* (pp. 41–94). Hillsdale, NJ: Erlbaum.

Belsky, J., & Pensky, E. (1988). Developmental history, personality and family relationshhips: Toward an emergent family system. In R. Hinde & J. Stevenson-Hinde (Eds.), *Relationships within families* (pp. 193–217). Oxford: Clarendon Press.

Belsky, J. Rosenberger, K., & Crnic, K. (1995a). The origins of attachment security: Classical and contextual determinants. In S. Goldberg, R. Muir, & J. Kerr (Eds.), *Attachment theory: Social, developmental and clinical perspectives* (pp. 153–184). Hillsdale, NJ: The Analytic Press.

Belsky, J., Rosenberger, K., & Crnic, K. (1995b). Maternal personality, marital quality, social support and infant temperament: their significance for infant–mother attachment in human families. In C. Pryce, R. Martin & D. Skuse (Eds.), *Motherhood in human and nonhuman primates: Biosocial determinants* (pp. 115–124). Basel, Switzerland: Karger.

Belsky, J., & Rovine, M. J. (1987). Temperament and attachment security in the strange situation: An empirical rapprochement. *Child Development, 58,* 787–795.

Belsky, J., & Rovine, M. J. (1988). Nonmaternal care in the first year of life and the security of infant–parent attachment. *Child Development, 59,* 157–167.

Belsky, J., Rovine, M., & Taylor, D. G. (1984). The Pennsylvania Infant and Family Development Project, III: The origins of individual differences in infant–mother attachment: Maternal and infant contributions. *Child Development, 55,* 718–728.

Belsky, J., & Steinberg, L. (1978). The effects of day care: A critical review. *Child Development, 49,* 929–949.

Belsky, J., Steinberg, L., & Draper, P. (1991). Childhood experience, interpersonal development and reproductive strategy: An evolutionary theory of socialization. *Child Development, 62,* 647–670.

Bender, L., & Yarnell, H. (1941). An observation nursery. American Journal of Psychiatry, 97, 1158–1174.

Berger, S., Levy, A., & Compaan, K. (1995, March). *Infant attachment outside the laboratory: New evidence in support of the Strange situation.* Paper presented at the biennial meetings of the Society for Research in Child Development, Indianapolis, IN.

Bowlby, J. (1969/1982). *Attachment and loss, Vol. 1: Attachment* (2nd ed.). New York: Basic Books.

Bowlby, J. (1973). *Attachment and loss, Vol, 2: Separation: Anxiety and anger.* New York: Basic Books.

Bowlby, J. (1980). *Attachment and loss, Vol. 3: Loss—sadness and depression.* New York: Basic Books.

Bowlby, J. (1989). Psychoanalysis as a natural science. In J. Sandler (Ed.), *Dimensions of psychoanalysis.* London: Karnac Books.

Breur, J. (1999). *The myth of the first three years.* New York: The Free Press.

Bronfenbrenner, U. (1979). *The ecology of human development.* Cambridge, MA: Harvard University Press.

Buss, D. (1995). Evolutionary psychology: A new paradigm for the psychological sciences. *Psychological Inquiry, 6,* 1–35.

Cassidy, J. (1994). Emotion regulation: Influences of attachment relationships. In N. Fox (Ed.), The development of emotion regulation (pp. 228–249). *Monographs of the Society for Research on Child Development, 59*, Nos. 2-3, Serial 240.

Cassidy, J., & Shaver, P. (Eds.) (1999), *Handbook of attachment: Theory, research and clinical applications.* New York: Wiley.

Chase-Lansdale, P. L., & Owen, M. T. (1987). Maternal employment in a family context: Effects on infant–mother and infant–father attachments. *Child Development, 58,* 1505–1512.

Chess, S., & Thomas, A. (1982). Infant bonding: Mystique and reality. *American Journal of Orthopsychiatry, 52,* 213–222.

Chisholm, J. (1996). The evolutionary ecology of attachment organization. *Human Nature, 7,* 1–38.

Clarke-Stewart, K. (1989). Infant day care: Maligned or malignant. *American Psychologist, 44,* 266–273.

Clarke-Stewart, K. A., & Fein, G. G. (1983). Early childhood programs. In P. H. Mussen (General ed.), *Handbook of child psychology,* Vol. 2, M. M. Haith & J. J. Campos (Vol. eds.), *Infancy and developmental psychobiology.* New York: Wiley.

Colin, V. (1996). Human attachment. NY: McGraw-Hill

Cosmides, L., & Tooby, J. (1987). From evolution to behavior: Evolutionary psychology as the missing link. In J. Dupre (Ed.), *The latest and the best: Essays on evolution and optimality* (pp. 277–306). Cambridge, MA: MIT Press.

De Wolff, M., & van IJzendoorn, M. (1997). Sensitivity and attachment: A meta-analysis on parental antecedents of infant attachment. *Child Development, 68,* 571–591.

Easterbrooks, M. A., & Goldberg, W. (1987, April). *Consequences of early family attachment patterns for later social-personality development.* Paper presented at the biennial meetings of the Society for Research in Child Development, Baltimore, MD.

Elicker, J., Englund, M., & Sroufe, L.A. (1992). Predicting peer competence and peer relationships in childhood from early parent–child relationships. In R. Parke & G. Ladd (Eds.), *Family-peer relationships: Modes of linkage* (pp. 77–106). Hillsdale, NJ: Erlbaum.

Englund, M., Levy, A., & Hyson, D. (1997, April). *Development of adolescent social competence: A prospective longitudinal study of family and peer contributions.* Poster session presented at the biennial meeting of the Society for Research in Child Development, Washington, DC.

Erickson, M., Egeland, B., & Sroufe, L. A. (1985). The relationship between quality of attachment and behavior problems in preschool in a high risk sample. In I. Bretherton & E. Waters (Eds.), *Growing points in attachment theory and research. Monographs of the Society for Research in Child Development, 50,* (Serial No. 209), 147–186.

Frodi, A., & Thompson, R. (1985). Infants' affective response in the Strange Situation: Effects of prematurity and of quality of attachment. *Child Development, 56,* 1280–1291.

Goldsmith, H. H., & Alansky, J. A. (1987). Maternal and infant temperamental predictors of attachment: A meta-analytic review. *Journal of Consulting and Clinical Psychology, 55,* 805–816.

Goosens, F., & van IJzendoorn, M. (1990). Quality of infants' attachment to professional caregivers. *Child Development, 61,* 832–837.

Hinde, R. A. (1982). Attachment: Some conceptual and biological issues. In C. Murray Parkes & J. Stevenson-Hinde (Eds.), *The place of attachment in human behavior.* New York: Basic Books.

Hinde, R., & Stevenson-Hinde, J. (1991). Perspectives on attachment. In C. M. Parkes, J. Stevenson-Hinde, & P. Morris (Eds.), *Attachment across the life cycle* (pp. 52–65). London: Routledge.

Howes, C., Rodning, C., Galluzzo, D. C., & Myers, L. (1988). Attachment and child care: Relationships with mother and caregiver. *Early Childhood Research Quarterly, 3,* 403–416.

Isabella, R., & Belsky, J. (1991). Interactional synchrony and the origins of infant–mother attachment: A replication study. *Child Development, 62,* 373–384.

Isabella, R. A., Belsky, J., & von Eye, A. (1989). Origins of infant–mother attachment: An examination of interactional synchrony during the infant's first year. *Developmental Psychology, 25,* 12–21.

Kagan, J. (1982). *Psychological research on the human infant: An evaluative summary.* New York: W. T. Grant Foundation.

Lamb. M. E., Thompson, R. A., Gardner, W. P., Charnov, E. L., & Estes, D. (1984). Security of infantile attachment as assessed in the "strange situation": Its study and biological interpretation. *The Behavioral and Brain Sciences, 7,* 127–172.

Lamb, M., Sternberg, K., & Prodromdis, M. (1990). Nonmaternal care and the security of infant–mother attachment: A reanalysis of the data. Unpublished manuscript. National Institute of Child Health and Human Development, Bethesda, MD.

Lewis, M. (1997). *Altering fate: Why the past does not predict the future.* New York: Guildford Press.

Lewis, M., & Feiring, C. (1989). Infant, mother, and mother-infant interaction behavior and subsequent attachment. *Child Development, 60,* 831–837.

Leyendecker, B., Lamb, M., Fracasso, M., Schjolmerich, A., & Larson, C. (1997). Playful interaction and the antecedents of attachment. *Merrill-Palmer Quarterly, 43,* 24–47.

Lyons-Ruth, K., & Jacobvitz, D. (1999). Attachment disorganization. In J. Cassidy & P. Shaver (Eds.), *Handbook of attachment: Theory, research, and clinical applications* (pp. 520–554). New York: Wiley.

Main, M., Kaplan, N., & Cassidy, J. (1985). Security in infancy, childhood, and adulthood: A move to the level of representation. In I. Bretherton & E. Waters (Eds.), *Monographs of the Society for Research in Child Development, 50,* 66–104.

Main, M., & Weston, D. (1981). The quality of the toddler's relationship to mother and father: Related to conflict behavior and readiness to establish new relationships. *Child Development, 52,* 932–940.

Malatesta, C. Z., Culver, C., Tesman, J., & Shepard, B. (1989). The development of emotion expression during the first two years of life: Normative trends and patterns of individual difference. *Monographs of the Society for Research in Child Development* (Serial No. 219).

NICHD Early Child Care Network. (1994). Child care and child development: The NICHD Study of Early child Care. In S. Friedman & H. Haywood (Eds.), *Developmental follow-up: Concepts, domains, and methods* (pp. 377–396). New York: Academic Press.

NICHD Early Child Care Research Network. (1997). The Effects of Infant Child Care on Infant–mother Attachment Security: Results of the NICHD Study of Early Child Care. *Child Development, 68,* 860–879.

NICHD Early Child Care Research Network. (2001). Child Care and Family Predictors of MacArthur Preschool Attachment and Stability from Infancy. *Developmental Psychology, 37,* 847–862.

O'Connor, T., & Croft, C. (2001). A twin study of attachment in preschool children. *Child Development, 72,* 1501–1511.

Ostoja, E. (1996). *Developmental antecedents of friendship competence in adolescence: The roles of early adapatational history and middle childhood peer competence.* Unpublsihed doctoral dissertation, University of Minnesota, Minneapolis, MN.

Pastor, D. L. (1981). The quality of mother-infant attachment and its relationship to toddlers initial sociability with peers. *Developmental Psychology, 17,* 326–335.

Renkin, B., Egeland, B., Marvinney, D., Sroufe, L. A., & Manglesforf, S. (1989). Early childhood antecedents of aggression and passive withdrawal in early elementary school. *Journal of Personality, 57,* 257–282.

Rheingold, H. L. (1969). The effect of a strange environment on the behavior of infants. In B. M. Foss (Ed.), *Determinants of infant behavior* (Vol. 4, pp. 137–166). London: Methuen.

Ricciuti, A. 1992. Child-mother attachment: A twin study. *Dissertation Abstracts International 54,* 3364–3364. (University Microfilms No. 9324873).

Roggman, L., Langlois, J., Hubbs-Tait, L., & Reiser-Danner, L. (1994). Infant day care, attachment, and the "file drawer problem." *Child Development, 65,* 1429–1443.

Rutter, M. (1981). Socioemotional consequences of day care for preschool children. *American Journal of Orthopsychiatry, 51,* 4–28.

Smith, P. B., & Pederson, D. R. (1988). Maternal sensitivity and patterns of infant–mother attachment. *Child Development, 59,* 1097–1101.

Sroufe, L. A. (1983). Infant-caregiver attachment and patterns of adaptation in preschool: The roots of maladaptation and competence. In M. Perlmutter (Ed.), *Minnesota Symposium in Child Psychology, 16,* 41–81.

Sroufe, L. A. (1988). The role of infant-caregiver attachment in development. In J. Belsky & T Nezworski (Eds.), *Clinical implications of attachment* (pp. 18–40). Hillsdale, NJ: Erlbaum.

Sroufe, L. A., Carlson, E., & Shulman, S. (1993). Individuals in relationships: Development from infancy through adolescence. In D. C. Funder, R. Parke, C. Tomlinson-Keesey, & K. Widaman (Eds.), *Studying lives through time: Approaches to personality and development* (pp. 315–342). Washington, DC: American Psychological Association.

Sroufe, L. A., Fox, N. E., & Pancake, V. R. (1983). Attachment and dependency in developmental perspective. *Child Development, 54,* 1615–1627.

Thompson, R. A. (1988). The effects of infant day care through the prism of attachment theory: A critical appraisal. *Early Childhood Research Quarterly, 3,* 273–282.

Thompson, R. A. (1999). Early attachment and later development. In J. Cassidy & P. Shaver (Eds.), *Handbook of attachment: Theory, research and clinical applications* (pp. 265–286). New York: Wiley.

Thompson, R. & Lamb, M. (1984). Assessing qualitative dimensions of emotional responsiveness in infants: Separation reactions in the strange situation. *Infant Behavior and Development, 7,* 423–445.

Troy, M., & Sroufe, L. A. (1987). Victimization of preschoolers: Role of attachment relationship history. *Journal of American Academy of Child and Adolescent Psychiatry, 26,* 166–172.

Urban, J., Carlson, E., Egeland, B., & Sroufe, L. A.. (1991). Patterns of individual adaptation across childhood. *Development and Psychopathology, 3,* 445–460.

Waters, E. (1978). The reliability and stability of individual differences in infant–mother attachment. *Child Development, 49,* 483–494.

Waters, E., Wippman, J., & Sroufe, L. A. (1979). Attachment, positive affect, and competence in the peer group: Two studies in construct validation. *Child Development, 50,* 821–829.

Weinfield, N., Sroufe, L. A., Egeland, B., & Carlson, E. (1999). The nature of individual differences in infant-caregiver attachment. In J. Cassidy & P. Shaver (Eds.), *Handbook of attachment: Theory, research and clinical applications* (pp. 68–88). New York: Wiley.

4

Early Language Development
Social Influences in the First Years of Life

Catherine S. Tamis-LeMonda
Tonia N. Cristofaro
Eileen T. Rodriguez
Marc H. Bornstein

INTRODUCTION

Children's understanding and production of their first words is undeniably one of the most heralded achievements in early development. The onset of language officially marks the transition from "infancy" (which derives from the Latin root *infans*, meaning "unable to speak") to early childhood, and radically alters the child's social world. Words enable children to share meanings with others and to participate in cultural learning in unprecedented ways. The fact that all normally developing children acquire language suggests that there exist universal properties that support children's language development, including the opportunity to communicate with others and direct and indirect access to analyzable language models (e.g., Meisel, 1995). Nonetheless, children vary enormously in the course of their language growth in terms of how quickly they achieve specific milestones, their receptive and productive vocabulary sizes, and in their eventual levels of competence in syntactic, semantic, and pragmatic aspects of language (Bloom, 1993; Hoff-Ginsberg, 1997; Tamis-LeMonda & Bornstein, 2002). For example, some children speak as early as 8 months while others express their first words several months later (e.g., Acredolo, Goodwyn, Horobin, & Emmons, 1999; Dapretto & Bjork, 2000). Bloom's (1993) research on the language achievements of 12 children illustrates the substantial variation in the age of onset of children's first words. Although children expressed their first conventional words (i.e., adult word forms) at the start of the second year on average, some children began to speak as early as 10 months while others did not achieve the first word milestone until 18 months.

Early differences in children's language are not transitory. Language achievements in the first years of life portend children's later abilities in literacy, school readiness, and cognitive development (e.g., Chall, Jacobs, & Baldwin, 1990; Bornstein & Haynes, 1998). In particular, children's oral language skills, which include spoken vocabulary and discourse, have been positively associated with reading and phonemic awareness (e.g., Beals, DeTemple, & Dickinson, 1994; Scarborough, 1989; Whitehurst & Lonigan, 2003), as well as with more developed abilities to construct meanings from conversations, reading, and writing (Beals et al., 1994). Research indicates strong associations between early vocabulary development and later reading comprehension (e.g., Anderson & Freebody, 1983). Moreover, parents' assessments of children's language skills between 3 and 4 years of age relate to teachers' assessments of vocabulary skills in second and fourth grades (e.g., Dickinson & DeTemple, 1998). Children with poor language skills are at a higher risk of literacy failure on school entry than are children with more developed oral language abilities (e.g., Snow, Burns, & Griffin, 1998). These effects are far reaching, such that children who exhibit delays at the onset of schooling are more likely to experience grade retention, special education placement, and failure to complete high school (Adams, 1990; McGill-Franzen, 1987).

The magnitude of associations from early child language to later school performance has incited decades of inquiry into the sources of early individual differences. Research on the social context of language development has underscored the role of more sophisticated language partners, most notably parents, in guiding novice toddlers toward understanding the meanings expressed in shared conversations (Bruner, 1974, 1983; Vygotsky, 1962). A cornerstone of this research has been the careful description of children's language environments in terms of the words and phrases that children hear and the ways that those words are presented to children. This literature has produced irrefutable evidence for the centrality of children's exposure to language for their receptive and productive language growth, literacy, and cognitive development (e.g., Bloom, 1993; Bornstein, 1985; Carpenter, Nagell, & Tomasello, 1998; Hart & Risley, 1995; Huttenlocher, Haight, Bryk, Seltzer, & Lyons, 1991; Landry, Smith, Miller-Loncar, & Swank, 1997; Nelson, 1973, 1988; Snow, 1986; Woodward & Markman, 1998).

In addition to studying the contributions that children themselves make to their language progress and learning (e.g., Bornstein et al., 2004), we have investigated the influence of parents' *verbal responsiveness* on children's early language development. Parents' verbal replies that are *prompt, contingent,* and *appropriate* to children's activities (i.e., responsiveness) predict children's language achievements within and across time. *Promptness* refers to the timing of parents' responses relative to children's behavior. Prompt responses facilitate children's processing of incoming verbal information due to the temporal contiguity between auditory and other perceptual experiences. *Contingency* refers to the dependence of parents' reactions on child behaviors. Contingent responses are those that evolve out of moments of shared attention and bear direct relevance to what the child is doing (e.g., "Look at the doll!" as the child looks to a doll). Contingency can be contrasted with asynchronous replies (e.g., "Look at the doll!" as a child reaches for a ball), which even if prompt, may actually interfere with the process of mapping words to referents, particularly during early stages of language (Tamis-LeMonda & Bornstein, 2002; Tomasello & Farrar, 1986). *Appropriateness* refers to maternal replies that are positively connected to the child's behavior. A mother who states, "You're feeding your bear!" as a child directs a spoon to the mouth of a toy bear is providing constructive information, whereas a mother who admonishes "Put that down!" is not.

In this chapter, we describe variation in children's language achievements across the first 3 years, and document findings on the significance of parents' responsiveness for children's early language. The chapter begins with a brief overview of the methods and measures that we have used to study children's language and parents' responsiveness, followed by a presentation of research findings across successive periods of language growth. Research is ordered chronologically, moving from infants' understanding of words (~9–10 months), to production of first words (~13 months), to the "vocabulary spurt" (~18 months), to first "sentences" and decontextualized uses of language (end of the second year). We end by describing our research on the language and cognitive development of 2- and 3-year-old children from low-income families, as children living in poverty are typically found to lag behind their more advantaged peers in their language abilities already in the toddler years. This recent work emphasizes the roles of both fathers and mothers in children's language development, and extends conceptualizations of responsive parenting to include the broader learning environments of young children.

METHODS FOR STUDYING CHILDREN'S LANGUAGE AND PARENTING

Over the past 15 years, we have conducted a series of longitudinal investigations on children's early language and communicative development in the context of parenting in both middle- and low-income populations. Middle-income families were recruited from private pediatric groups in New York City, and families from low-income backgrounds were recruited from community agencies as part of the Early Head Start National Evaluation Study (Love, Kisker, Ross, Schochet, Brooks-Gunn, Paulsell, et al., 2002). Samples ranged from 40 to over 1,000 children across studies. Families were visited in their homes every few months where children were assessed for their language gains and parents were coded on their verbal responsiveness. In the first year, visits occurred when infants were 5–6 months and/or 9 months, depending on the study. In the second year, families were revisited when children were 13–14, 17–18, and 22–24 months of age, and certain cohorts were seen again when children were 3 years of age.

Mother–child and sometimes father–child dyads were observed during free play at each assessment. Children and parents were provided with standard sets of toys and were videotaped for 10 to 20 minutes. Parents were instructed to remain with their children and to interact with them in whatever way was most natural. They were told they could use any or all of the toys provided, but not to introduce other toys into the play session.

Assessments of Children's Language

Measures of children's language and other forms of communication were based on maternal report and/or coding of children's language from verbatim transcriptions of the videotaped free-play sessions. Transcripts were coded for children's word types and tokens, semantic usage, and syntactic complexity (e.g., MLU) using the *Systematic Analysis of Language Transcripts* (SALT; Miller & Chapman, 1993) as well as special-purpose coding systems.

Maternal reports of children's language were based on the MacArthur Communicative Development Inventories (MCDI; Fenson et al., 1994), which were modified in various studies to access more detailed information about the situations in which children used specific words and phrases. In one longitudinal study of children's language growth from 9 to 21 months, which is later discussed in detail, data on children's language were obtained through biweekly interviews with mothers (Tamis-LeMonda, Bornstein, Kahana-Kalman, Baumwell, & Cyphers, 1998; Tamis-LeMonda, Bornstein, & Baumwell, 2001). To facilitate these interviews, we provided mothers with a packet of language inventories at the end of the 9-month home visit and scheduled weekly times to discuss children's language progress. Packets included versions of the Early Language Inventory (ELI; Bates, Bretherton, & Snyder, 1988) and MacArthur CDI (Fenson et al., 1994) as well as checklists exemplifying various semantic and syntactic uses of words and phrases (Tamis-LeMonda & Bornstein, 1994). At younger ages (i.e., from the start of the study to around 13 months), a subset of items from the MCDI was used (specifically, the ELI on which the MCDI was based), as children at these ages expressed few words and their receptive language was still limited. Early interviews lasted approximately 15 to 20 minutes, whereas interviews at later ages, which utilized the full MCDI, took up to 2 hours.

During telephone interviews, we asked the mother whether her child understood and/or expressed each word/phrase on the list, and in the case of an affirmative response, further probed as to whether the child's understanding and/or production of the word was context "restricted" (e.g., understanding "dog" only as referring to the child's dog; saying "dog" only in imitation or to the child's dog) or "flexible" (e.g., understanding and/or saying "dog" in reference to all dogs).

After probing for specific words/phrases, we asked about various other language milestones, including children's combination of words into simple sentences (e.g., see dog), and whether children used specific grammatical and semantic speech acts. From these interviews, children's receptive and productive vocabulary sizes were computed at each age, as was the timing of various language milestones (e.g., onset of understanding; first words in production; the timing of 50 flexible words in productive language; combinatorial speech).

In certain of these studies, children were also assessed using standardized tests of performance, including the Peabody Picture Vocabulary Test, Third Edition (PPVT-III; Dunn & Dunn, 1997) as well as the Mental Development Index (MDI) of the Bayley Scales of Infant Development—Second Edition (BSID-II; Bayley, 1993). The PPVT, a widely used measure of receptive vocabulary, assesses children's listening comprehension at various ages (for our purposes, focus was on children of 36 months). Children are presented with four pictures per testing plate and asked to point to the one that corresponds to the assessor's spoken word. Items are administered in sets of 12 and testing continues until children reach a ceiling, defined as 8 or more errors within a set of 12. Children in many of our studies were also administered the MDI at 14, 24, and 36 months of age as a measure of their mental status. The MDI assesses abilities in cognitive, language, and personal-social areas of development through items that code for children's vocalizations and language, memory, classification abilities, etc. Both the PPVT and MDI, although standardized tests, capture children's language abilities relative to normative samples.

Coding of Parents' Responsiveness

Parents' responsiveness was coded at either a macro-level (i.e., global ratings) or micro-level (i.e., coded for each parent and child behavioral turn). For macro-level coding systems, coders viewed videotaped free play sessions and coded maternal (or paternal) responsiveness on 5- or 7-point scales ranging from *never responsive* to *always responsive.*

For micro-level coding schemes, the play sessions were transcribed verbatim and included notes about target actions of the child and parent. From these transcripts (along with viewing of the videotapes), the frequencies of children's vocalizing, bidding toward mother, looking at objects, and playing were obtained. These child behaviors provided a starting point for coding whether or not the parent responded to each child behavior. Responsiveness to target behaviors was defined as a positive and meaningful change in the parent's behavior that was temporally contiguous (i.e., occurring within 5 seconds), contingent on a change in the child's behavior, and appropriate. We adopted a 5-second window for responsiveness based on research demonstrating the duration for various basic temporal events (e.g., lines of poetry, spoken sentences, breath cycles, and communicative movements) falls between 2 and 7 seconds (see Jaffe, Beebe, Feldstein, Crown, & Jasnow, 2001, for discussion; Rovee-Collier, 1995). As an example, if the child looked at a cup (target act = exploring) and the mother said, "cup," the mother was credited with being responsive; similarly, if the child said, "cup" (target act = vocalizing) and mother responded, "Yes, that's a cup," she would be credited with responding. For each instance of responsiveness, coders noted what the mother was responding to (response target) and the precise nature of her response (response type). The categories of child behaviors, as well as maternal responses to these individual behaviors, were mutually exclusive. From these data, frequency counts were obtained on infant target acts, mothers' responses to each target act, and various types of responses (e.g., descriptions, questions).

CHILDREN'S EARLY LANGUAGE ACHIEVEMENTS

In this section, findings from the various studies that we have conducted are presented in developmental order. Presentation begins with research on children's early understanding of words (receptive language), followed by children's first words in production, vocabulary spurt, and first sentences (combinatorial speech). Each of these subsections opens with a description of the target language achievement, followed by research on the role of parents in supporting the specific achievement.

Understanding Words: The Dawning of Language

The first months of life can be conceptualized as a protracted period of social-communicative "lessons." People have long been captivated by the rhythmic mutuality that characterizes the earliest infant-caregiver interactions (e.g., Bateson, 1975, 1979; Bloom, 1998a; Fogel, Messinger, Dickson, & Hsu, 1999). Caregivers and babies take turns gazing, vocalizing, pausing, smiling, and moving in exquisite synchrony, as though engaged in a communicative "dance" (Lock, 2001; Stern, 1985). Through their participation in these moment-to-moment exchanges, babies are socialized into the communication system (e.g., Hsu & Fogel, 2001). Already by 6 months of age, infants take an active lead in initiating interactions with familiar people, and they exhibit heightened responsiveness to their partners' cues (e.g., Lock, 2001). These early *protoconversations* (Bateson, 1975; Bloom, 1998a) lay the foundation for later conversations and verbal exchanges (e.g., Ginsburg & Kilbourne, 1988; Locke, 1995), which retain many of the temporal and affective qualities of earlier social communications, yet are marked by the infant's increasing appreciation of the meanings of the words that others use during social interactions.

It is somewhere around 9–10 months that the transition from prelinguistic to linguistic communications occurs, a milestone that is rooted in infants' growing social-cognitive understandings of others (Tamis-LeMonda & Adolph, in press). Through daily participation in reciprocal exchanges, infants acquire an understanding of agency and intentionality (e.g., Lock, 2001; Tomasello, 1995). By the end of the first year, infants are thought to appreciate that people can share attention toward objects and events in the outside world, an understanding that has been referred to as "secondary intersubjectivity" (Stern, 1985; Trevarthen, 1993). This recognition enables children to benefit from social interactions in new ways, and expands their opportunities for learning enormously (Baldwin & Moses, 1996; Tomasello, 1993). Children look where adults look, imitate adults' actions with novel objects, and reference adults in ambiguous situations. At this same time, infants begin to exhibit *deictic* gestures, such as pointing and showing, suggesting that they are engaged in purposeful communication and wish to convey their intentions or emotions to others (e.g., Bates, Benigni, Bretherton, Camaioni, & Volterra, 1979; Camaioni, Aureli, Bellagamba, & Fogel, 2003). These episodes of joint attention and shared understanding are central to children's social cognitive and language development (e.g., Baumwell, Tamis-LeMonda, & Bornstein, 1997; Bornstein & Tamis-LeMonda, 2001; Camaioni, 2001; Homer & Tamis-LeMonda, in press).

In light of these social-cognitive achievements, it is unsurprising that the 9-10 month period has also been referred to as the "dawning of language" as reflected in infants' rudimentary understanding of simple words and phrases (Bates et al., 1979; Volterra, Bates, Benigni, Bretherton, & Camaioni, 1979). These initial developments in language comprehension can be distinguished from the more sophisticated understanding of words and phrases that is exhibited by slightly older children. Specifically, infants' early understanding of words is routinized and depends on the contextual cues that accompany speech acts; infants appear to have a very rudimentary grasp of the meanings of words, and early word learning is often restricted to a specific context and specific actions (e.g., Barrett, 1995; Bloom, 1973; Camaioni, 2001; Camaioni et al., 2003; Tomasello, 1992; Snyder, Bates, & Bretherton, 1981).

We have documented the transition from restricted to flexible understanding over the period of 9 to 13 months based on data obtained from biweekly language interviews conducted with mothers (as described above). Virtually all infants displayed restricted understanding at the onset of language, with words becoming increasingly flexible with development. In the initial 2 months of interviews, the majority of infants demonstrated at least rudimentary understanding of their name and the names of familiar people (e.g., caregivers and siblings; mama, dada), basic foods (bottle, Cheerios), simple commands (e.g., "No!"), and performatives and games (e.g., "bye-bye," "clap hands," and "where's baby?"). Although mothers reported that their infants understood these simple words/phrases, further probing revealed that infants' understanding depended on the cues that accompanied these verbal expressions. For example, in several instances, infants responded to phrases such as "pattycake" or "clap hands" with the appropriate clapping behavior; however, their responses were cued by parents' own clapping, nodding of the head, smiles, and melodic chanting of "pattycake." Parents' facial expressions, vocal intonations and gestures cajoled infants to join in on the fun, and lent familiarity to the continued repetition of the words associated with "pattycake."

In other instances, infants responded to words/phrases in generalized, diffuse ways, again suggesting only a tenuous grasp of the word's true meaning. For example, several infants were reported to laugh, flail their arms, and kick their legs in response to hearing phrases that contained the word "out" or "outside" (e.g., "We're going out. Out? Out? Do you want to go out?"), as though anticipating an impending excursion. However, these verbal phrases were typically accompanied by the assemblage of a stroller, packing a bag, and walking towards the door. Again, infants' reactions appeared to be context-dependent, making it questionable whether their emotional reactions of enthusiasm signaled true understanding of the meaning of the word "out." (To illustrate this limited nature of early understanding, Table 4.1 presents a diary excerpt taken from the first language interview conducted with a mother of a girl who was 9.5 months at the time of the call.)

On the other hand, these early glimmers of understanding were meaningful precursors to more reliable forms of receptive and productive language, illustrating the ways in which infants' experiences with repeated and familiar events provide the structure for interpreting others' speech. Infants map words onto existing concepts or cognitive structures, which form the building blocks to language (e.g., Bloom, 1998a; Hoff-Ginsberg, 1997). By participating in familiar social and cultural routines, children develop scripts, or generalized event representations of their life experiences that are comprised of specific information about actors, actions, and the objects or recipients of their actions (e.g., Nelson, 1981, 1986).

Moreover, parents' reports about their infants' receptive vocabularies were neither arbitrary nor overly inclusive. Rather, mothers were very selective about the words they claimed their infants "understood." Each week mothers reported a select handful of words that elicited consistent behavioral responses from their infants. A typical pattern was for infants' restricted understanding of a specific word to shift to flexible understanding within 1 to 2 weeks, and many of the first words "understood" were those that appeared in children's productive language weeks or months later.

As expected, across the developmental period of 9 to 13 months, an increasing proportion of the words that children understood were flexible or independent of contextual cues. Thus, the word "pattycake" would eventually induce infant clapping in the absence of parents' clapping, and "Let's go out" would impel infants to toddle to the door before strollers appeared. Moreover, context-flexible words functioned to "bootstrap" the acquisition of new words. As children came to understand the meaning of specific verbs, for example, the nouns and noun phrases to those actions were more readily understood (e.g., "eat" facilitates mapping new food terms—"Eat your peas!", "Eat your Cheerios!", Eat your apple!").

TABLE 4.1
Infants' Restricted Understanding of Early Words: Example Diary Excerpt at 9 Months

Word/Phrase Reported to Be Understood	Infant's Response	Cues Necessary for Understanding
"No"	Stops and looks at speaker	Uses a raised tone of voice
"Good girl"	Smiles and gets happy	Claps or smiles
"Good job"	Smiles and gets happy	Claps or smiles
"Stop"	Hesitates	Uses a raised tone of voice
"Cheerios"	Smiles and/or bangs hands on table	Shows item
"Clap your hands"	Claps	Sings the phrase or claps first
"Peek-a-boo"	Laughs	Covers infant with blanket or appears from behind furniture

THE ROLE OF PARENTS IN EARLY UNDERSTANDING OF WORDS

What role do parents play in children's early understanding of words? At the most basic level, parents, as all humans, express words simultaneous with their actions. Indeed, the context-restricted nature of infants' early understanding reveals the universal dependencies that exist between language and action. Infants parse the action streams that they observe into meaningful units, and link those units to the words that are used to describe them (Baldwin, in press). Returning to the example of clapping, as infants view the motion of hand-repeatedly-meeting-hand and hear the chanting words of "clap hands," speech acts come to be associated with perceptual experiences. Parents, therefore, provide infants with gestures, actions, and emotions that support natural links between words and referents.

However, in addition to availing infants of these naturally occurring connections, parents differ in the ways they verbally communicate to their young children, in terms of the timing of their responses and the content of what they say, and these supports affect the course of children's receptive (and later productive) language. As noted earlier, parents' verbal responsiveness is thought to be especially supportive of children's understanding of words because responsive verbal information is offered at times of psychological salience. Adults who label objects and events that are the target of children's attention constrain interpretive possibilities, bolstering conceptual connections between words and referents (e.g., Baldwin & Markman, 1989; Bloom, 1993; Bloom, Margulis, Tinker, & Fujita, 1996; Carpenter et al., 1998; McCune, 1995; Rogoff, Mistry, Radziszewska, & Germond, 1992; Snow, 1986; Tomasello & Farrar, 1986). For example, a mother might gesture toward a novel object to elicit her child's attention and then name the object at precisely the point when her child shifts attention toward the object ("Ball. This is the ball. It's blue."). Or, she might wait for her child to demonstrate interest in an object, and use that interest as a springboard for providing verbal information (e.g., "Yes, that's a ball you have in your hand"). In both instances, the adult is being responsive by cueing into the child's interests such that the child need not "guess" the topic of conversation or rely solely on natural constraints (Nelson, 1988).

We offer empirical support for the role of parents' responsiveness in children's receptive language. In one investigation dyads were visited in their homes at 9 months of age and were visited again 4 months later (Baumwell et al., 1997). The question of interest was whether mothers who were responsive to their 9-month-olds would have toddlers who later exhibited larger receptive vocabularies.

From videotaped sessions of mother-infant play, the base rate frequencies of infant vocalizations, looks, and bids to mother, and play and exploration of toys were coded. Each maternal reaction to each infant behavior was classified into one of five categories: (1) verbal responses (mother replies promptly, contingently and appropriately within 5 seconds to a change in infant behavior—e.g., "doggie" as child shifts attention to a dog); (2) elaboration (mother builds on her prior response by providing additional information—e.g., "Furry dog!", after her first response to the child's interest in the dog); (3) focus shift (mother attempts to redirect her child's attention to something new—e.g., "Look at the bus!" as child looks at a dog); (4) prohibitions/reprimands (mother verbally restricts her child's actions—e.g., "Stop"); or (5) miss (mother ignores or shows no reaction to child's behavior). In addition, "refocus" was coded if a mother attempted to redirect her unfocused child's attention to the play materials (e.g., "Look at the dog!"—as child is not focused on anything in particular).

Analyses revealed two factors of maternal behaviors at each age (9 and 13 months): Sensitivity (a factor that loaded on mothers' verbal responsiveness, elaborations, and refocusing attempts) and Intrusiveness (a factor that loaded on focus shifts, prohibitions, and misses). Sensitivity predicted children's language comprehension at 13 months, but Intrusiveness did not. Specifically, maternal sensitivity to 9-month-olds uniquely accounted for a significant 15% of the variance in the size of infants' flexible language comprehension at 13 months after controlling for infants' 9-month language and mothers' later responsiveness. Together, infants' comprehension at 9 months and mothers' sensitivity at 9 and 13 months accounted for 37% of the variance in infants' 13-month language comprehension. In contrast, Intrusiveness accounted for a nonsignificant 1% variance in the size of children's receptive vocabularies. The fact that Intrusiveness contained verbal information (e.g., mothers' talking about objects/events outside of their children's focus and verbal prohibitions), but did not predict children's language, highlights the special significance of maternal responsiveness for children's early understanding of words and phrases.

PRODUCTION OF FIRST WORDS

Somewhere around the start of the second year children produce their first formal words. Prior to this point, children have been adding words to their receptive lexicons for several weeks or months; consequently, early in development children's production of words lags behind what they are able to comprehend (e.g., Bates et al., 1979; Childers & Tomasello, 2002). Nonetheless, children's first spoken words signal an important transition in language development and greatly affect their social environments. Parents enthusiastically welcome children's first words and are quick to respond to their children's new verbal achievements.

Similar to the patterns documented for receptive language, infants' productive language shifts from being context-restricted to context-flexible. In the early stage of word production, children often imitate the words of others. Rather than spontaneously generating words on their own, children parrot back words that they have just heard in their daily interactions (e.g., Mother: "Where's your ball Johnny?" Child: "Ball"; Mother: "Say bye-bye!" Child: "Bye-bye"). Additionally, children produce words in reference to a limited range of exemplars in narrow contexts. A child might say the word "dog," but only to indicate her own dog. Moreover, words are used sporadically, sometimes appearing and then seemingly disappearing from children's lexicons. Thus, the word "dog" might be used one week, not used for several weeks after that, and might "reenter" the lexicon with regularity weeks later. Consequently, early progress in productive language growth is gradual and effortful over the course of the first several weeks or even months of achievement (Bloom, 1998b).

Over the next few weeks and months, word production becomes more generative, regular, as well as more generalized. Words that were once only used in imitation are now produced spontaneously across a broad range of contexts. Children will now use the word "dog" to refer to dogs in general, pictures of dogs, the memory of dogs, and in anticipation of getting a new dog.

THE ROLE OF PARENTS IN EARLY WORD PRODUCTION

To what extent is children's early production influenced by parents' verbal responsiveness? We have used two approaches to study the role of parents' verbal responsiveness at the early stages of word production. In the first approach, parents' responsiveness was examined in relation to the size of infants' productive vocabularies at the start of the second year (i.e., 13 months), the point in development when most children are expressing their first words. In the second, parents' responsiveness was examined in relation to the developmental *timing* of specific language milestones in early productive language.

In several investigations, mothers' responsiveness related to children's productive vocabulary sizes concurrently and predictively. For example, in one study, mothers who responded more to their 5-month-old infants had babies who displayed larger flexible vocabularies at 13 months (Bornstein & Tamis-LeMonda, 1989). In other investigations, mothers' responsiveness to their 13-month-old toddlers' exploratory and communicative initiatives was concurrently related to children's productive vocabulary sizes (Tamis-LeMonda et al., 2001).

Perhaps more revealing than the predictive validity of responsiveness for vocabulary size at the start of the second year is the finding that mothers' responsiveness affects the timing of productive milestones in early language. In one study, we asked whether mothers' responsiveness would relate to the developmental onset of infants' first imitations and first words—that is, *when* in development children first imitated a word and when in development children first used words spontaneously and flexibly.

To address this question, we utilized the statistical technique of Events History Analysis (also referred to as Survival Analysis; Willett & Singer, 1991, 1993) which is suited to modeling whether and by how much specific predictors (here responsiveness) affect the timing of target events (here imitations and first words). Time is considered along its continuum, and the conditional as well as cumulative probabilities of an event occurring can be modeled and plotted across successive ages. As a hypothetical example, if a group of children were assessed on their ability to "walk" from 6 through 18 months, the cumulative probability of children walking independently might be .00 at 6 months (as no children have yet achieved the milestone), .10 by 9 months, .15 at 10 months, .50 at 12 months, and so forth, until all children have achieved the milestone of walking, at which point the cumulative probability reaches 1.00. The median lifetime represents the point when half of the population experiences the target event (i.e., when the cumulative probability reaches .50).

We assessed the contributions of maternal verbal responsiveness at 9 months (before children had begun producing conventional words) to the subsequent onset of children's first imitations and first words by comparing baseline conditional and cumulative probability functions (i.e., those in the absence of predictors) with "fitted" functions (i.e., those that included predictors) in nested, hierarchical chi-square analyses (Tamis-LeMonda et al., 2001). As anticipated, responsiveness was a robust predictor of the two milestones, as indicated by highly significant changes to chi-square statistics when responsiveness was added to models. To illustrate, when the language development of children at extremes of responsiveness were modeled (i.e., the top and bottom 10th percentiles), nearly all the children whose mothers demonstrated high levels of responding with descriptions at 9 months were estimated to imitate words by 13 months. In contrast, only 60% of the children with low responsive mothers were estimated to imitate words at 13 months (see Figure 4.1). Similarly, nearly all the children whose mothers displayed high levels of maternal responding with affirmations, descriptions, and play prompts at 9 months were estimated to produce their first words by 13 months, whereas only 20% of the children with low responsive mothers produced their first words at this age (see Figure 4.2).

THE VOCABULARY SPURT

The achievement of 50 words in children's production, which typically occurs midway through the second year, is often considered a benchmark in early language development (e.g., Bates, Dale, & Thal, 1995; Bloom, 1973, 1993, 1998a; Bloom, Tinker, & Margulis, 1993; Nelson, 1973). Around the time

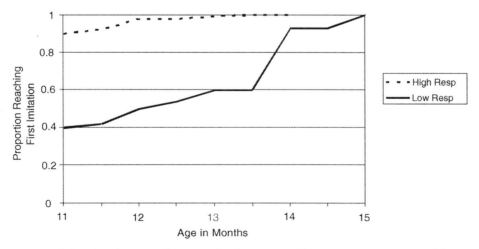

Figure 4.1 Modeling fitted survivor functions for the timing of first imitations: Estimated function for high levels of maternal responses with descriptions at 9 months (upper 10th percentile) and estimated function for low levels of maternal responses with descriptions at 9 months (lowest 10th percentile).

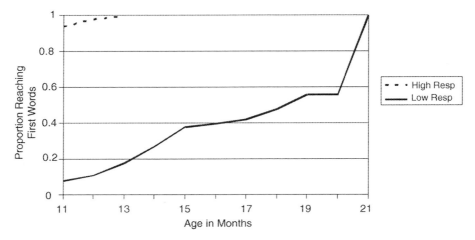

Figure 4.2 Modeling fitted survivor functions for the timing of first words: Estimated function for high levels of maternal responses with affirmations, descriptions, and play prompts at 9 months (upper 10th percentile) and estimated function for low levels of responding with affirmations, descriptions, and play prompts at 9 months (lowest 10th percentile).

children accumulate 50 words in their expressive vocabularies, they experience a sudden acceleration in production, referred to as the vocabulary "spurt" or vocabulary "explosion" (see Bates et al., 1988; Bloom, 1973, 1993, 1998a; Gershkoff-Stowe & Smith, 2004; Reznick & Goldfield, 1992). For example, Bloom (1993) showed that children averaged 51 different words in their productive vocabularies at the time of a vocabulary spurt and that all children in her research reached the 50-word vocabulary mark within 1 month of showing a substantial acceleration in their productive lexicons (Bloom et al., 1996).

In our research, we have also tracked children's language development from first words through the vocabulary spurt, and have documented a sharp incline in word growth around the 50-word mark. Specifically, children produced an average of 5.9 words per month prior to the 50-word mark, as

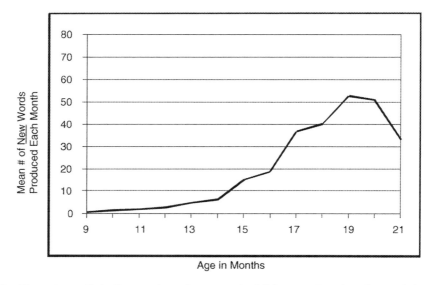

Figure 4.3 The net growth in the number of new words children produced each month between the ages of 9 and 21 months.

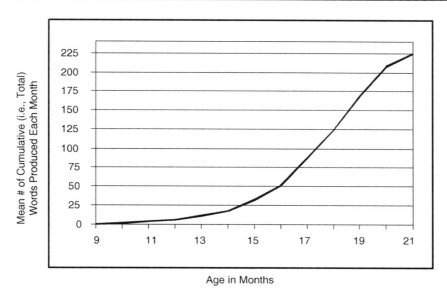

Figure 4.4 The cumulative growth of the number of total words in children's productive vocabularies at each month between the ages of 9 and 21 months.

compared to an average of 39.3 words per month subsequent to the 50-word mark (Tamis-LeMonda et al., 1998). Of course, children varied enormously in both when they achieved the 50-word milestone as well as in their growth rates both before and after this period. Therefore, our focus has been on both average gains across children as well as language growth at the individual level.

To illustrate the phenomenon of the vocabulary spurt, Figure 4.3 presents the *net growth* in children's language, which referred to the number of *new words* children produced each month between the ages of 9 and 21 months. Figure 4.4 presents the cumulative plot of the number of *total* words in children's productive vocabularies each month. As shown in Figure 4.3, there is an overall upward trend in word production across all children ($N = 107$). Prior to 15 months of age, children added fewer than 10 words to their vocabularies each month; by 18–19 months they added 40–50 words per month to their productive vocabularies on average. However, these average developmental functions (both in terms of net growth, Figure 4.3, and cumulative growth, Figure 4.4) obscure the rapid growth in word production that exists in individual children, and also mask the fact that some children showed little to no improvement in their language over this time frame.

Figures 4.5 through 4.10 present data on individual children to illustrate both the phenomenon of the growth spurt as well as the dramatic individual differences among children in growth over time. Certain children added over 100 words per month to their lexicons (with one acquiring over 200 new words in a month; see Figures 4.5–4.8). Other children hardly added any new words to their productive vocabularies, as illustrated in the individual plots in Figures 4.9 and 4.10. Children such as those depicted in Figures 4.9 and 4.10 had therefore failed to achieve the 50-word milestone by the end of the study (i.e., at 21 months), and showed no acceleration in their word growth.

In addition to children exhibiting quantitative change in language around the middle of the second year, as indexed by impressive gains in the absolute number of words in their productive vocabularies, word growth may be qualitatively different from the more effortful process of language acquisition observed at the start of the second year. At around the 50-word mark, word production is uniformly spontaneous, new words are acquired with greater facility, and words are no longer as transitory as they had been during earlier stages of production. Moreover, once children acquire a substantial number of nouns and verbs in their lexicons, they demonstrate a remarkable capacity to learn novel words from just a few exposures or even just one exposure (e.g., Clark, 1995); this phenomenon has been referred to as "fast mapping" (Carey, 1978), and is demonstrated by children as young as 2 years

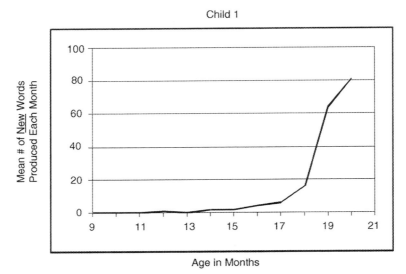

Figure 4.5 Individual plots of children's productive vocabulary growth spurts at different points in development between 9 and 21 months.

(e.g., Bloom, 2000; Heibeck & Markman, 1987). Children's acquisition of a relatively substantial large number of "count nouns" in production promotes comparisons across objects and increased attention to object shape, both of which further accelerate the rate of word learning (e.g., Gershkoff-Stowe & Smith, 2004; Namy & Gentner, 2002; Smith, 2003).

The expression of words around the vocabulary spurt appears to require fewer cognitive resources or less "effort" than the expression of words at the start of the second year (Bloom & Tinker, 2001). Support for this notion derives from Bloom's detailed, microgenetic tracking of the language of 12 children who were seen monthly from 9 months to 2½ years of age both in a laboratory playroom setting and in their families' homes (Bloom, 1993). The study consisted of hour-long videotaping of mother–child play sessions at each visit, and language diaries kept by mothers that chronicled the

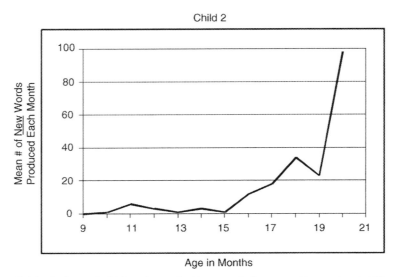

Figure 4.6 Individual plots of children's productive vocabulary growth spurts at different points in development between 9 and 21 months.

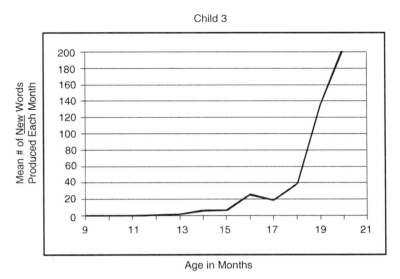

Figure 4.7 Individual plots of children's productive vocabulary growth spurts at different points in development between 9 and 21 months.

words their infants understood and produced during the 1-month intervals between visits. This enabled Bloom to document children's achievement of 50 words, and to examine the consequences of this milestone for children's abilities to express emotions and play acts simultaneous with the production of words. From videotapes, children's expressions of words, emotions, and play actions were documented in real-time through a frame-by-frame coding system; this detailed approach permitted analyses at time sampled units of less than 1 second. From these data, the overlap of word production with other forms of expression was documented. Bloom found that children were least likely to display positive or negative emotions simultaneous with talking if they were in the early stage of word production, but were adept at the simultaneous expression of words and emotions once they had achieved the 50-word mark. These findings suggest that the expression of words at the vocabulary spurt draws upon

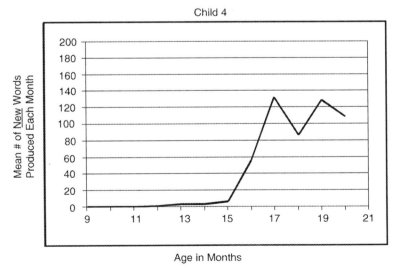

Figure 4.8 Individual plots of children's productive vocabulary growth spurts at different points in development between 9 and 21 months.

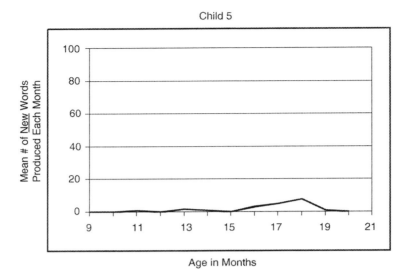

Figure 4.9 Individual plots of children's productive vocabulary between 9 and 21 months; trajectories of children who displayed little or no production of new words between 9 and 21 months..

fewer cognitive resources than the expression of words at the start of productive language. Similar findings have been extended to children's abilities to simultaneously produce words while engaged in play activities (Bloom & Tinker, 2001), and our research has revealed that children's production of words is inhibited when they are attending to toys at the start of the second year when word production is newly emerging (Tamis-LeMonda & Bornstein, 1990). In short, Bloom's finding that children are better able to simultaneously "talk" and "act" or "talk" and "emote" during the vocabulary spurt, but not at earlier stages of language production, suggests that the expression of words mid-way into the second year does not tax children's cognitive resources as much as early word use.

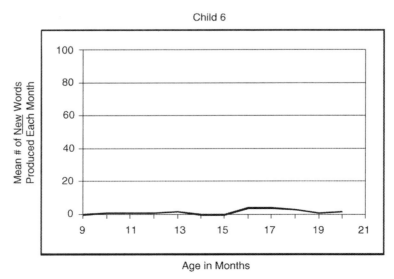

Figure 4.10 Individual plots of children's productive vocabulary between 9 and 21 months; trajectories of children who displayed little or no production of new words between 9 and 21 months..

FIRST SENTENCES: THE START OF GRAMMAR

Changes to the size of children's lexicon are paralleled by qualitative changes in the ways that words are used. We have found that even though most children were not yet combining words into sentences at the juncture of 50 words (and therefore are still in the "one-word-stage" of language), they used language to express a variety of functions and semantic categories. Children's earlier use of words to label objects (e.g., "ball"), participate in routinized exchanges (e.g., "bye-bye"), and label or request people (e.g., "mama," "dada") was replaced with word functions that referred to actors, actions, patients, objects of actions, locations, existence, possession, negation, objection and so forth (Tamis-LeMonda & Bornstein, 1994). For instance, younger infants most often said "mama" to label mother (nominal usage) or to plea for mother when distressed or upset (instrumental usage). In contrast, somewhat older toddlers used the word "mama" (or perhaps by this time, "mommy") to refer to mother as an actor, experiencer, recipient, patient, possessor, in anticipation, in memory, and so forth. By 18 months, for example, "mommy" might be used in mother's absence, while the child pointed at her shoes, thereby expressing the notion of possession (as in "those are mommy's shoes!"). This more flexible use of words at the vocabulary spurt suggests that words function as true "symbols" in that they are no longer integrally bound to the concrete here-and-now, but can be used in the service of different meanings across past, present, and future timeframes.

The expansion of children's vocabularies and growth in the functional use of words toward the middle of the second year closely precedes the combination of words into simple sentences. Children's first "sentences" express those categories of meaning that had already been in evidence in their vocabularies at the later one-word stage. Therefore, "mommy shoe" might be used to convey the notion of possession (as in "That's mommy's shoe.") or might alternatively be used to indicate actors and the objects of their actions (as in "Mommy's putting on her shoe."). Both constructions build on children's earlier ability to use the word "mommy" and "shoe" flexibly across different categories of meaning (e.g., to recognize that the symbolic word "mommy" can be used as a *possessor* as well as *actor* depending on context; and that "shoe" refers to objects owned and objects that can be acted upon). Consequently, the emergence of combinatorial speech reflects not only a child's ability to specify different symbolic categories of meaning *individually* (e.g., "actor", "object of action"), but to also encode the roles and relationships between these separate concepts by placing them into basic grammatical structures (Bloom, 1998; McCall, Eichorn, & Hogarty, 1977; Fenson et al., 1994).

THE ROLE OF PARENTS IN THE VOCABULARY SPURT AND EARLY GRAMMAR

What role does parents' responsiveness play in children's language development during the period of the vocabulary spurt and beyond? We speculated that verbal responsiveness would be associated with more rapid growth in children's productive language over the second year; would predict the *diversity* of meanings children use to express their verbal constructions; and would be associated with the developmental *timing* of both the vocabulary spurt and combinatorial speech (i.e., combining words into sentences). Empirical support has been obtained for each of these predictions.

In one study, we assessed the role of maternal responsiveness in two contexts, play and mealtime, for children's growing vocabularies across the second year (i.e., when toddlers were 13 and 20 months; Bornstein, Tamis-LeMonda, & Haynes, 1999). Here the focus was on changes to mothers' responsiveness over time in relation to changes to children's observed language production. In this investigation, measures of mothers' responsiveness and children's language at both ages and in both contexts derived from transcripts of their observed interactions.

Mothers who grew in their verbal responsiveness over time had children who demonstrated significant gains in their own vocabularies over the 7-month period, both in play as well as at mealtimes. These analyses covaried children's own 13-month contributions to language outcomes, which were also significant. Perhaps most notable was the finding that the absolute size of mothers' observed productive vocabulary did not predict children's language above verbal responsiveness, nor did children's language growth predict later maternal productive vocabulary size. In contrast, mothers' verbal responsiveness mattered above the amount of mothers' language.

In a second cohort, predictive associations between verbal responsiveness and the timing of the milestones 50 words in production and combinatorial speech were examined (Tamis-LeMonda et al., 1998), based on our biweekly interviews with mothers. Word counts on children's productive vocabularies offered data on when children reached 50 words in language production. During these same telephone surveys, each mother was asked whether her child was yet combining words into simple sentences, in order to document the date of this later milestone. Probing for combinatorial speech was highly specific and the crediting of achievement was conservative. For example, if a mother stated that her child was "putting two or more words together" she was asked to provide specific examples of the child's construction as well as information about the situation(s) in which her child expressed the phrase. The child was only credited with "combinatorial speech" if he or she (1) linked two or more words in a single phrase without pause; (2) each of the words in the phrase could be classified as independent words in the child's vocabulary; and (3) each of the words in the phrase could be classified into distinct categories of speech (e.g., actor, action, object of action, patient, possession; for additional details, see Tamis-LeMonda & Bornstein, 1994, Tamis-LeMonda et al., 1998).

For each outcome, the "date" when the child achieved each of the milestones was noted as the date of the telephone call, providing a window of error within 2 weeks. Again, using Events History Analyses, mothers' verbal responsiveness to their 13-month-olds (at the start of language production) was examined as a predictor of when in development children achieved the two milestones. Findings revealed that verbal responsiveness predicted the timing of the vocabulary spurt and combinatorial speech, and did so above the timing of children's first words in production, the timing of their achievement of 50 words in receptive language, and mothers' responsiveness at 9 months. Similarly, responsiveness at 13 months contributed unique variance to the timing of combinatorial speech over and above the timing of first words in production, children's earlier receptive language, and responsiveness at 9 months.

Moreover, specific forms of responsiveness related to specific targets of child behavior. In particular, children of mothers who responded contingently to children's *vocalizations* and *play* behaviors achieved 50 words in expressive language and engaged in combinatorial speech sooner than children of less responsive mothers. In addition, specific maternal responses at specific developmental periods facilitated the achievement of specific language milestones. For instance, mothers' affirmations and descriptions at 9 months, but not at 13 months, predicted children's language milestones. And, mothers' responses with vocal imitations and expansions at 13 months, but not at 9 months, influenced the timing of children's production of 50 words and combinatorial speech (Tamis-LeMonda et al., 2001).

To provide an example of these effects, Figures 4.11 and 4.12 illustrate the role of mothers' responsiveness in children's language spurt, as defined by 50 words in production. Specifically, Figure 4.11 contrasts the effects of high levels of maternal responsiveness to *children's play and vocalizations* at 13 months (upper 10th percentile) with low levels of maternal responsiveness to *children's play and vocalizations* at 13 months (lowest 10th percentile). Figure 4.12 contrasts the effects of high levels of maternal *responding with imitations* to children at 13 months (upper 10th percentile) with estimated functions for low levels of maternal *responding with imitations* at this age (lowest 10th percentile). When the language milestones of children at the extremes of these various forms of responsiveness were modeled (i.e., the top and bottom 10th percentiles), approximately half of all children whose mothers demonstrated high levels of responsiveness (either in terms of what they responded to—Figure 4.11—or how they responded—Figure 4.12) at 13 months were estimated to achieve 50 words in language production by 15 months of age. In contrast, only half of the children of low responsive mothers were estimated to achieve 50 words in production by 21 months of age, the end of the study. Not shown are the very similar patterns for the timing of combinatorial speech. Specifically, one-third

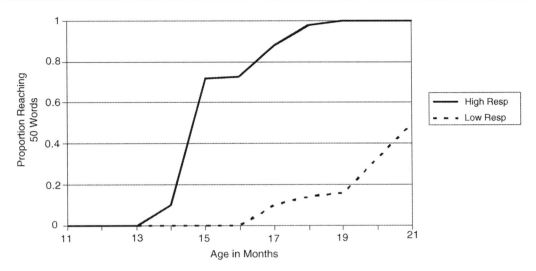

Figure 4.11 Modeling cumulative probability functions for the timing of 50 words in children's productive language: Estimated function for high levels of maternal responsiveness to children's play and vocalizations at 13 months (upper 10th percentile) and for low levels of maternal responsiveness to children's play and vocalization at 13 months (lowest 10th percentile).

of all children with highly responsive mothers were estimated to engage in combinatorial speech by 15 months, as compared to 21 months of age for children of low responsive mothers.

EARLY LANGUAGE AND COGNITIVE DEVELOPMENT IN LOW-INCOME FAMILIES

Thus far, emphasis has been on children's early achievements in receptive and productive language, and the facilitative role of parents' verbal responsiveness for these emerging abilities. In addition,

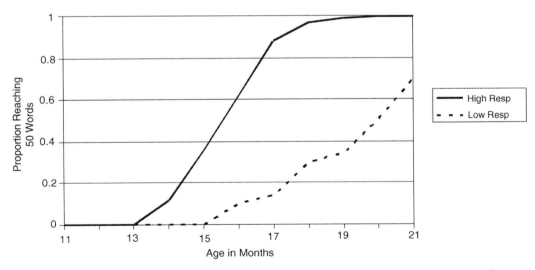

Figure 4.12 Modeling cumulative probability functions for the timing of 50 words: Estimated function for high levels of maternal responding with imitations to children at 13 months (upper 10th percentile) and estimated function for low levels of maternal responding with imitations to children at 4–13 months (lowest 10th percentile).

most of this work has been conducted with Anglo American children and mothers from middle- to high-socioeconomic status households (as determined by composite scores of parents' income and education). More recently, we have extended work on environmental correlates of children's language development to low-income, ethnically diverse families. Research on the language development of children from the low-income families is particularly important in light of studies that document the adverse consequences of poverty for children's cognitive and educational achievements (e.g., Burns, Griffin, & Snow, 1999; Brooks-Gunn & Duncan, 1997; Hoff, Laursen, & Tardif, 2002). In general, children living in economically disadvantaged households tend to have smaller vocabularies and less-than-optimal language competencies when compared to their more advantaged peers. As one example, children in poverty enter kindergarten with an average lexicon of about 5,000 words in comparison to vocabularies of approximately 20,000 words for children from higher-income families (e.g., Hart & Risley, 1995). These differences are thought to partly be explained by differences in the cognitive stimulation observed in low-income parents (e.g., Evans, 2004) and children's diminished participation in learning activities (e.g., bookreading; Anderson, Teale, & Estrada, 1980; Hart & Risley, 1995; Whitehurst, Arnold, Epstein, Angell, Smith, & Fischel et al., 1994).

Nonetheless there exists great variation in the language of children from low-income families. For example, 18-, 24-, and 36-month-old children living in poverty have MacArthur CDI scores that range from below the 10th to above the 90th percentile, even though their overall scores are lower than those of the normative population (Roberts, Burchinal, & Durham, 1999). Such findings challenge deficit models that emphasize group means at the expense of individual variation. Unsurprisingly, in light of this within-group variation, questions about the language environments of children living in poverty have been at the foreground of applied developmental research.

In response, and as an outgrowth of our earlier work, we have pursued two research directions on the language development of children from low-income families. First, we have begun to document children's language interactions with both their mothers and fathers. What is the role of fathers' language on children's language achievements in low-income households? Do patterns observed in mothers also extend to fathers? Second, we have extended inquiry on parent-child language engagements to incorporate children's broader learning experiences. This latter emphasis takes into consideration the various learning activities that children participate in with their parents (e.g., bookreading, storytelling) as well as the learning materials that are available to children (e.g., books and toys) (Tamis-LeMonda et al., 2004).

Language Engagements with Mothers and Fathers

There has been burgeoning attention to fathers' role in children's development over the past 20 years, and a number of large-scale national efforts have been designed to examine the nature, antecedents, and consequences of father involvement in low-income families more specifically (e.g., see Cabrera et al., 2002; Lamb, 2004; Tamis-LeMonda & Cabrera, 2002, for reviews). This heightened interest in father involvement stems from a number of social and demographic trends, including women's increased participation in the workforce, the prevalence of single-headed households in low-income families, and the adverse consequences of father absence for children's school readiness, academic performance, and social-emotional regulatory competencies (Tamis-LeMonda & Cabrera, 1999).

Limited resources, unstable employment, and inadequate education often make it difficult for fathers to establish and maintain positive and emotionally supportive relationships with their children (Black et al., 1999; Brophy-Herb et al., 1999; Cochran, 1997; Furstenberg & Harris, 1993; Garfinkel, McLanahan, & Hanson, 1998; Lerman, 1993; Marsiglio, 1987; McAdoo, 1986, 1988; McLoyd, 1989, 1990; Perloff & Buckner, 1996). These same obstacles also pose practical challenges to researchers who seek to understand the nature and meaning of fathering in economically disadvantaged, ethnically diverse groups (Cabrera et al., 2004; Tamis-LeMonda & Cabrera, 2002; Tamis-LeMonda, Shannon, Cabrera, & Lamb, 2004). While father "absence" is more prevalent in low-income households on average, over 80% of fathers from low-income households are involved in their young children's lives, seeing their children at least a few times per week if they do not reside with them (Cabrera et al., 2004).

However, relatively little is known about the ways in which present, involved low-income men interact with their young children, and how their engagements affect their children's early language and cognitive development. Merely a handful of studies has investigated fathers' influence in these areas of development (e.g., Black et al., 1999), and our current research addresses this gap.

In one study of 50 children and their mothers and fathers, we focused on children's observed vocabularies at 24 months (Cristofaro, Rodriguez, Baumwell, Tamis-LeMonda, & Nakae, 2004). As noted earlier, by 24 months, most children have experienced a vocabulary spurt and are using words to express a range of meanings. The majority of children are combining words into simple sentences that map to the grammatical structures of their native language. In light of children's language competencies at this age, focus was placed on children's communicative diversity (i.e., the range of meanings that children expressed during play) as well as their overall talkativeness, as indexed by the total number of utterances children expressed during the observation period.

As in past studies, child–mother and child–father dyads were videotaped separately in their residences for 10 minutes of play with standard sets of age-appropriate toys. These play interactions were transcribed and coded for various aspects of child and parent language. Children's speech was classified into 1 of 22 mutually exclusive functions, based on the meanings being expressed by the children (e.g., child labels an object; asks a question; refers to an action, etc.). These language functions could be classified into 3 broader categories: Referential Language (i.e., language in which the child used labels, descriptors, pronouns, or questions to indicate objects and people); Semantic Language (i.e., language in which the child used words that fit grammatical categories, such as "actors," "actions," "objects of action," "patients," "recipients," "locatives," and so forth; Brown, 1973); and Decontextualized Language (i.e., language that referred to nonpresent events or activities, such as using words to "pretend" or to refer to past or future events). In addition, a "Communicative Diversity" score, representing the number of *different* language functions the child expressed, was computed for each child.

Likewise, both fathers' and mothers' speech acts from the parent-child play sessions were each classified into 1 of 23 mutually exclusive language functions (e.g., labels, descriptions, questions) based on modifications of extant language coding systems that are reliable and valid (e.g., Longobardi, 1992; Camaioni & Longobardi, 1994; Roberts, 2001; Tamis-LeMonda et al., 2001). These language functions were collapsed into six broader categories, two of which were Referential Language (i.e., language in which the parent used labels, descriptors, pronouns, or questions to indicate objects and people) and Responsive Language (i.e., language that was in specific response to children's verbal overtures—such as imitations, expansions). As for children, each parent's Communicative Diversity was calculated as the number of different language functions that were expressed during the play session, and Total Language was based on parents' number of utterances.

Findings revealed that children expressed similar amounts of language and had equivalent Communicative Diversity scores during play with their fathers as with their mothers. Similarly, children expressed similar levels of Referential and Semantic language during play with both parents, indicating that they were no less likely to talk with their fathers than with their mothers.

Notably, measures of fathers' and mothers' language use yielded similar patterns of prediction to children's language use. First, both mothers' and fathers' Referential Language predicted children's Referential Language. Second, parents' Communicative Diversity was associated with children's Total Language and Communicative Diversity. Finally, both mothers' and fathers' Responsive Language was associated with virtually all measures of children's language. Specifically, Responsive Language predicted children's Total Language, Communicative Diversity, Referential Language, and Semantic Language. Moreover, mothers' and fathers' Responsive Language was associated with measures of children's language after covarying parents' Total Language, suggesting that these forms of language matter above sheer talk. Finally, mothers' and fathers' language each contributed unique variance to children's language above the language of one another, indicating a cumulative model of early language development, in which the contributions of different caregivers to children's language growth are additive. To illustrate the variation that existed in parents' language use, 1-minute excerpts of mothers' and fathers' language during play interactions with their toddlers are presented in Tables 4.2 and 4.3. These excerpts present conversations from two African American families of boys, one in which both parents' Total Language, Communicative Diversity, and Responsive language scores were high (Table 4.2), and the other in which both parents' scores were consistently low (Table 4.3). As indicated in the dialogues in Table 4.2, the mother and father expressed 37 and 38 total utterances, respectively, in the brief, 1-minute segment. The mother and the father each used 7 different language functions during this time. In contrast, Table 4.3 presents the relatively sparse language use by the second mother and father. This child's mother and father expressed 8 and 7 total utterances, respectively. The mother expressed 4 different language functions, and the father expressed a total of 3 different language functions. Thus, these two children, both from low-income backgrounds, experienced a fourfold difference in their sheer exposure to language and over a twofold difference in the range of language functions they heard.

These differences had implications for the children's own language use with their mothers and fathers (see Figures 4.13 and 4.14). Across the 10-minute interaction, the first child expressed a total of 92 utterances while interacting with his mother and 77 utterances while interacting with his father. In

TABLE 4.2
One-minute Excerpts of Parental Language High in Total Language and Diversity

Maternal Language	Paternal Language
Let's see what's in here.	Let's see what's in bag #2.
Look at this one.	Ah, okay, let's see what we have here.
What's that, (Child's name)?	Look, (unintelligible).
A surprise?	Look.
It's a present?	What's in here?
Take it out.	
Take it out.	
Ooh!	What's in here?
Take it out.	Ooh!
Take them all out.	Let's see what's in here.
Thank you.	Ooh!
Take the other one out.	What's in here?
Take it out.	Look, ooh!
What's this?	Ooh!
What's this?	Look look.
Ooh!	Here.
Ooh!	Can I have a piece?
Ooh what's this?	Can you give me a piece please?
What's this?	Can I have a piece?
Wait wait.	I'm hungry.
Right here.	I want food.
Ooh you cook on it.	Yeah.
You make food.	Give Daddy a piece.
You know like when Mommy makes food.	I don't want the whole thing.
We have to get you one of these.	Break me a piece off.
See?	Break it off.
It's hot.	Ooh!
You put the food on here and you cook.	Ooh ooh.
You see like Mommy cooks?	It's food.
Right?	See?
Here.	We cut it like this.
It's a bowl.	Look.
The top for the pot.	Ooh!
See?	Here.
The pot.	Uhhuh.
Cook.	Cut the food.
(Child's name), you cook.	Alright, let's put the (unintelligible).
	Where's the other piece?
	Let's put that in there.

TABLE 4.3
One-minute Excerpts of Parental Language Low in Total Language and Diversity

Maternal Language	Paternal Language
Put your food up here.	Here, (unintelligible), now you get to play
Like that.	with the next toy.
Put your food on the (unintelligible).	Huh look.
All right.	We're gonna cut some pie.
Hmm.	Gonna cut pizza.
Come on let's cook.	Hmm you get to cut the pizza.
Eggs.	Cut the pizza.
Here.	Uhhuh.

contrast, the second child produced 36 utterances while engaging with his mother and 20 utterances while engaging with his father. Moreover, the first child was beginning to combine words into simple sentences, whereas the second child did not express any combinatorial speech. Given the bidirectional nature of parent–child conversations, it is plausible that the second child was less talkative due to his parents' low language use, but this does not necessarily mean that the child was less capable in his language. However, further examination of children's Bayley MDI scores of children trends that paralleled these language differences. The child of high-language parents had a Bayley MDI score of 108 (above average), whereas the child of low-language parents received a score of 80 (delayed range), lending support to the idea that these excerpts capture differences in children's language abilities.

Fathers' influence on children's language, as evidenced at this "micro-level" coding of play conversations, also yields strong associations with children's cognitive development more broadly. Because language is fundamental to all virtually all forms of thinking and reasoning, it is unsurprising that fathers' verbal responsiveness relates to toddlers' scores on standardized mental tests such as the Bayley MDI and PPVT. For example, in another study of fathers at play with their 2-year-olds, the focus was on children's cognitive development as measured by their Bayley Mental DI (BSID-II; Bayley, 1993). We asked whether fathers' responsiveness would shift the odds of a child performing in the normal versus delayed range on this standardized test (Shannon, Tamis-LeMonda, London, & Cabrera, 2002). Toddlers and fathers were videotaped during play, and fathers were coded on their responsiveness to

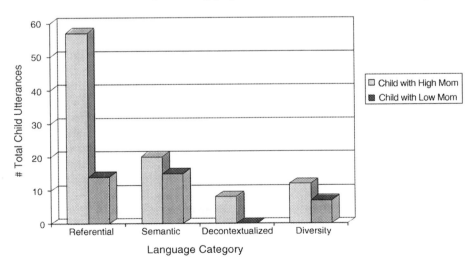

Figure 4.13 Two male children's total Referential, Semantic, and Decontextualized language and communicative Diversity with mothers high and low in language. Diversity refers to the different kinds of speech acts expressed, not the number of utterances.

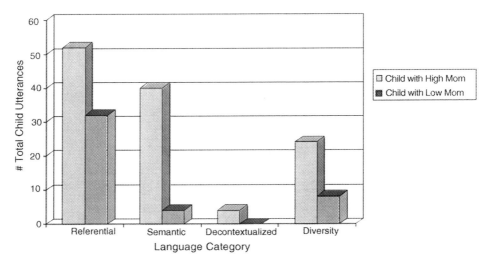

Figure 4.14 The total Referential, Semantic, and Decontextualized language and communicative Diversity of the same two male children in Figure 4.13 with fathers high and low in language. Diversity refers to the different kinds of speech acts expressed, not the number of utterances.

children's play and verbal initiatives. Children were independently tested on the Bayley MDI during a separate home visit. Fathers who were highly responsive during play were approximately 5 times more likely to have children who performed within the normal range on the MDI (i.e., as indexed by official cut-offs). In other words, the likelihood that a child would be in need of early intervention was 5 times as great if he/she had a low-responsive father versus a high-responsive father. Moreover, our work with a group of mothers and fathers of 2- and 3-year-olds shows that links from fathers' responsiveness to child Bayley outcomes maintain above the influence of mothers' responsiveness, fathers' education, and fathers' income (Tamis-LeMonda, Shannon, & Cabrera, in press).

CHILDREN'S BROADER LEARNING ENVIRONMENTS

The research presented to this point underscores the robust associations that exist between parents' language use (in terms of amount, diversity and responsiveness) and children's language milestones and cognitive development. However, parents' language is embedded in a larger learning context and represents only one of several parenting variables that support children's emerging language competencies. In this final section, we briefly discuss ongoing research that aims to elucidate how multiple aspects of children's early learning environments foster children's language and cognitive development, again with a specific focus on understanding patterns of prediction in children from low-income families.

To this end, we have longitudinally examined variation in children's language abilities at 14, 24, and 36 months in relation to three aspects of the learning environment: (1) children's direct engagements with responsive parents; (2) the frequency of children's participation in specific literacy activities (e.g., shared book reading, storytelling, being directly taught ABCs, counting, and so forth); and (3) children's access to age-appropriate learning materials (e.g., books and toys). Extant studies reveal that each of these aspects of the learning environment are foundational to children's language development, emergent literacy, and school readiness (e.g., Bryant & Bradley, 1987; Hart & Risley, 1995; Payne, Whitehurst, & Angell, 1994; Senechal & LeFevre, 2001; Tabors, Roach, & Snow, 2001; Tamis-LeMonda et al., 2001). However, no studies have explored the three aspects together, precluding a test of whether each explains unique variance in children's language and cognitive outcomes above the other two.

To address this question, we assessed mothers' responsiveness during interactions with their children, probed mothers about the frequency with which they engaged their children in specific learning activities, and asked them about their children's home access to age-appropriate learning materials. We tested whether a *specific aspect* of the early literacy environment was especially predictive of children's cognitive and language development, or alternatively, if each of the three aspects bore relevance for children's development. In addition, we investigated whether children's experiences at a *specific age* would be more predictive of outcomes than experiences at other periods in development.

Hierarchical regression analyses revealed that the three aspects of the literacy environment *uniquely* predicted children's cognitive and language development at 14, 24, and 36 months of age, over and above significant mother and child demographic characteristics. Although the three aspects covaried, they were only weakly to modestly associated with one another, and each related to child outcomes. Together, these experiences accounted for up to 19% of the variance in 14-month measures, 17% of the variance in 24-month measures, and 16% of the variance in 36-month measures. Moreover, literacy experiences at 14, 24, and 36 months each uniquely predicted Bayley MDI and PPVT scores at 36 months. Hence, literacy environments at each age mattered beyond experiences at the other two ages, suggesting a cumulative model of prediction.

To illustrate the magnitude of effects that the literacy environment had on children's language development, the language outcomes of 24- and 36-month-old children at the extremes of experience were compared (see Figures 4.15, 4.16, and 4.17). In these analyses, children were classified into one of two groups: those children who consistently received scores reflecting "insufficient" experiences across all three dimensions of the literacy environment, and those children who consistently received scores reflecting "enriched" experiences across the three dimensions of the literacy environment. As shown, the group of children with consistently insufficient experiences at 24 months produced 36 words on average, whereas those with consistently enriched experiences produced 67 words on average. Similarly, at 36 months, the literacy environment accounted for 15 points on a standardized measure of children's receptive language, such that children with consistently insufficient experiences averaged 78 on the PPVT, whereas those with consistently enriched experiences averaged 93. Finally, at 36 months, the average Bayley scores of children at the extremes of experience differed by nearly 20 points. Children who experienced insufficient literacy environments averaged 82.9 on the Bayley MDI, whereas those with enriched environments averaged 100.7, a difference of over one standard deviation.

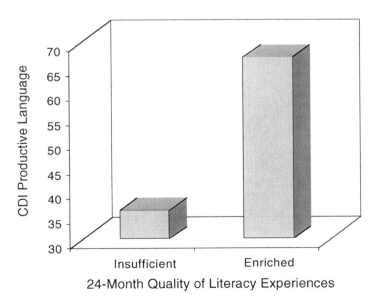

Figure 4.15 MacArthur CDI language production at 24 months for children at the extremes of literacy environments.

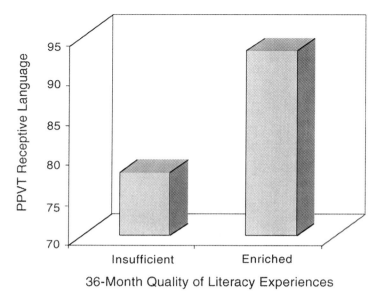

Figure 4.16   PPVT receptive language at 36 months for children at the extremes of literacy environments.

DISCUSSION

This chapter focused on children's early language development and the role of parents in supporting their children's language achievements. We documented the impressive variation that exists in children's early understanding and production of words, the developmental timing of specific language milestones, and children's cognitive performance more broadly. Longitudinal investigations in our laboratory consistently yield strong associations between children's emerging language competencies

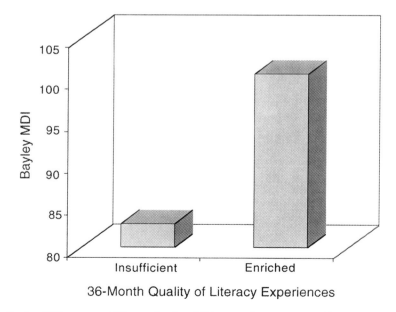

Figure 4.17   Bayley MDI scores at 36 months for children at the extremes of literacy environments.

and the quality of parent–child engagements, particularly verbal responsiveness, both within a given age and across the first 3 years of life.

Although infants are communicative partners from birth, the dawning of language is officially marked by infants' first understanding of conventional words. For many infants, this entry into "formal" language occurs around 9 months of age, and coincides with a number of important social-cognitive achievements, including infants' growing abilities to discern the attention and intentions of others during social exchanges. However, as we and others have shown, early understanding is fragile, and it is not for several weeks or even months that infants begin to display flexible understanding across different contexts. Language production, which is shifted up in time by about 3 months, shows a similar pattern, moving from the context-dependent and restricted use of words to flexible expression of words. At the start of production, words are "effortful" and bound to the concrete, here-and-now, not yet functioning as true symbols for the child. By around 18 months, children not only acquire words at an astonishingly impressive rate, but they can now use words flexibly across different contexts, categories of meaning and time frames. In short, a "word is not always a word," but instead varies with definitional criteria.

Notably, children vary enormously in these early language achievements, and our research has both documented this variation as well as sought to understand the parenting factors that predict these child differences. As we have shown, in both mothers and fathers and across middle- and low-income populations, parents' language use consistently predicted children's language and cognitive development. Moreover, the *quality* of parents' language, in terms of parents' verbal responsiveness to their children's initiatives and the diversity of meanings that parents express when talking with their children, predicted children's early language beyond the quantity of parents' language. Of course, mothers and fathers who frequently respond to their children's initiatives are likely to be talking more as well (Hoff, 2002), and the amount of language that children hear clearly has beneficial effects (Huttenlocher et al., 1991; Hart & Risley, 1992, 1995). However, when we contrasted quantitative measures of parental language, such as language amount or parents' total number of utterances, with qualitative indices of parental language, such as verbal responsiveness and language diversity, it was the quality of parental language that made a larger difference. This work attests to the importance of focusing research on both language amount and language quality.

A question that should be raised is *why* parents' responsiveness influences children's language development. We propose that verbal responsiveness supports children's language growth for many reasons, including its role in defining topics of communication. Responsive verbal information enhances children's opportunity to learn new words because the speaker's language is matched to children's current interests (Bloom, 1993, 1998a). Second, and relatedly, connections between words and their referents depend on psychological "salience." Children inform parents about what they deem to be worthy topics of communication through their facial expressions, eye gaze, gestures, and vocalizations, and other behaviors. During the early stages of language growth, children's own perspective and affective appraisals of situations dominate shared communications (Bloom, 1978, 2000). Consequently, the onus is largely placed on parents to match verbal input to what children consider to be salient.

Additionally, temporal contiguity or promptness is a key defining feature of responsiveness. *When* messages are communicated is important to consider together with *what* is communicated. Verbal information that coincides with changes in infant behavior (e.g., occurring as soon as a child shifts attention to a new object) exerts stronger influence on children's language gains than information that is not temporally connected with children's initiatives. We offer two explanations for the importance of timing (see Tamis-LeMonda & Bornstein, 2002). First, children are inclined toward identifying environmental contingencies early in development (Dunham & Dunham, 1995). Moreover, "dumb attentional mechanisms," such as those underlying learning more generally, have been posited to facilitate children's mapping words to objects and events (Plunkett, 1997; Smith, 1995). The likelihood that two events, such as a word/phrase and its external referent, will come to be associated increases if both events occur within a brief "time window" (Rovee-Collier, 1995). Conversely, new information that is encountered after a time window has "closed" is no longer associated with the initial event (Boller

& Rovee-Collier, 1992). The dependence on time windows is especially strong during infancy when a linguistic knowledge base is being established and associative networks are forming (Rovee-Collier, 1995). Accordingly, children should be more likely to connect words to experiences when the two are temporally connected and when the experience is salient to the child.

We also extended our research on the social contexts of early language development to children from low-income families, as well as to aspects of the broader home environment that extend beyond parents' responsive engagements. Although the developmental literature is characterized by continued controversy about whether parenting predicts child outcomes similarly across different ethnic/cultural and demographic groups, our research suggests that *certain features of parenting consistently predict positive child outcomes across diverse populations.* These include verbal responsiveness, language diversity, literacy activities, and the provision of learning activities to children. As an example, families from the Early Head Start National Evaluation study, which is comprised of substantial proportions of European American (45%), African American (30%), and Latin American (25%) families, were observed longitudinally when children were 14, 24, and 36 months. Children's home experiences were examined in relation to language and cognitive outcomes within and across the three ages. As described above, children from environments that were consistently high on parents' responsiveness, learning activities, and learning materials scored up to 20 points higher on standardized measures of cognitive status than did children who experienced consistently low environments. These patterns maintained across all three ethnic/racial groups. Therefore, although children from different groups might benefit from experiences that are *unique* to their cultural backgrounds, it is also the case that enriched language and learning environments are a common pathway to children's language development and school readiness.

A closing observation warrants discussion, and suggests important directions for modeling social influences on children's outcomes over time. Language development unfolds in a social context and should be considered from a transactional perspective (Sameroff, 1975). That is, parents affect children's emerging language abilities just as children's emerging abilities affect parenting. For example, by definition verbal responsiveness reflects the temporal sequence of "child act → parent respond," and therefore depends largely on children's own behavioral and verbal expressions. Mothers and fathers alike can only respond to their children's vocalizations, can only imitate or expand on their children's utterances, and can only remark on their children's play actions if their children emit a sound or word or act on objects. Therefore, children's language achievements are rooted in a dynamic history of behaviors in children, parents, and the dyad. Analytic models that capture both the micro-genetic unfolding of parent–child engagements in real-time, as well as models that test the transactional influences of child-to-parent and parent-to-child over developmental time, are warranted. Such models might reveal, for example, the specific characteristics and behaviors in children that evoke specific responses in parents, how those responses further affect children's development, and how developmental changes in children come to shape parenting over time.

ACKNOWLEDGMENT

CTL wishes to acknowledge NSF grant #021859 that has enabled researchers at New York University to establish a Center for Research on Culture, Development and Education.

REFERENCES

Acredolo, L. P., Goodwyn, S. W., Horobin, K. D., & Emmons, Y. D. (1999). The signs and sounds of early language development. In L. Balter & C. S. Tamis-LeMonda (Eds.), *Child psychology: A handbook of contemporary issues* (pp. 116–139). Philadelphia: Psychology Press.

Adams, M. J. (1990). *Beginning to read: Thinking and learning about print.* Cambridge, MA: MIT Press.

Anderson, A. B., Teale, W. H., & Estrada, E. (1980). Low-income preschool literacy experiences: Some naturalistic observations. *The Quarterly Newsletter of the Laboratory of Comparative Human Cognition, 2,* 59–65.

Anderson, R. C., & Freebody, P. (1983). Reading comprehension and the assessment and acquisition of word knowledge. In B. Hutson (Ed.), *Advances in reading/language research* (pp. 231–256). Greenwich, CT: JAI Press.

Baldwin (in press). Discerning intentions. In B. Homer & C. S. Tamis-LeMonda (Eds.), *The development of social cognition and communication.* Mahwah, NJ: Erlbaum.

Baldwin, D. A., & Moses, L. J. (1996). The ontogeny of social information-gathering. *Child Development, 67,* 1915–1939.

Baldwin, D. A., & Markman, E. M. (1989). Establishing word-object relations: A first step. *Child Development, 60,* 381–398.

Barrett, M. (1995). Early lexical development. In P. Fletcher & B. MacWhinney (Eds.), *The handbook of child language* (pp. 362–392). Oxford: Blackwell Publishers.

Bates, E., Benigni, L., Bretherton, I., Camaioni, L., & Volterra, V. (1979). *The emergence of symbols: Cognition and communication in infancy.* New York: Academic Press.

Bates, E., Bretherton, I., & Snyder, L. (1988). *From first words to grammar: Individual differences and dissociable mechanisms.* Cambridge: Cambridge University Press.

Bates, E., Dale, P., & Thal, D. (1995). Individual differences and their implications for theories of language development. In P. Fletcher & B. MacWhinney (Eds.), *The handbook of child language* (pp. 96–151). Oxford: Blackwell.

Bateson, C. (1975). Mother-infant exchanges: The epigenesis of conversational interaction. In D. Aronson & R. W. Rieber (Eds.), *Annals of the New York Academy of Sciences* (Vol. 263). *Development psycholinguistics and communication disorders* (pp. 101–113). New York: New York Academy of Sciences.

Bateson, C. M. (1979). The epigenesis of conversational interaction: A personal account of research development. In M. Bullowa (Ed.), *Before speech: The beginning of human communication* (pp. 63–77). New York: Cambridge University Press.

Baumwell, L., Tamis-LeMonda, C. S., & Bornstein, M. H. (1997). Maternal verbal sensitivity and child language comprehension. *Infant Behavior and Development, 20*(2), 247–258.

Bayley, N. (1993). *Manual for Bayley Scales of Infant Development* (2nd ed.). San Antonio, TX: Psychological Corporation.

Beals, D. E., DeTemple, J. M., & Dickinson, D. K. (1994). Talking and listening that support early literacy development of children from low-income families. In D. K. Dickinson (Ed.), *Bridges to literacy: Children, families, and schools* (pp. 19–40). Cambridge: Basil Blackwell Ltd.

Black, M. M., Dubowitz, H., & Starr R. H. (1999). African American fathers in low income, urban families: Development, behavior, and home environment of their three-year-old children. *Child Development, 70,* 967–978.

Bloom, K., Russell, A., & Wassenberg, K. (1987). Turn taking affects the quality of infant vocalizations. *Journal of Child Language, 14,* 211–227.

Bloom, L. (1973). *One word at a time: The use of single-word utterances before syntax.* The Hague: Mouton.

Bloom, L. (1978). The integration of form, content, and use in language development. In J. Kavanagh & W. Strange (Eds.), *Language and speech in the laboratory, school, and clinic* (pp. 210–246). Cambridge, MA: MIT Press.

Bloom, L. (1993). *The transition from infancy to language.* Cambridge: Cambridge University Press.

Bloom, L. (1998a). Language acquisition in its developmental context. In D. Kuhn & R. S. Siegler (Eds.), *Handbook of child psychology: Vol 2. Cognition, perception, and language* (5th ed., pp. 309–370). New York: Wiley.

Bloom, L. (1998b). Language development and emotional expression. *Pediatrics, 102*(5), 1272–1277.

Bloom, L. (2000). Commentary: Pushing the limits on theories of word learning. *Monographs of the Society for Research in Child Development, 65*(3) (serial no. 124–133).

Bloom, L., Margulis, C., Tinker, E., & Fujita, N. (1996). Early conversations and word learning: Contributions from child and adult. *Child Development, 67,* 3154–3157.

Bloom, L., & Tinker, E. (2001). The intentionality model and language acquisition: Engagement, effort, and the essential tension. *Monographs of the Society for Research in Child Development, 66*(4, serial no. 267).

Bloom, L., Tinker, E., & Margulis, C. (1993). The words children learn: Evidence against a noun bias in children's vocabularies. *Cognitive Development, 8,* 431–450.

Bloom, P. (2000). *How children learn the meanings of words.* Cambridge, MA: MIT Press.

Boller, K., & Rovee-Collier, C. (1992). Contextual coding and recoding of infant memory. *Journal of Experimental Child Psychology, 53,* 1–23.

Bornstein, M. H. (1985). How infant and mother jointly contribute to developing cognitive competence in the child. *Proceedings of the National Academy of Sciences, 82,* 7470–7473.

Bornstein, M., H., Cote, L. R., Maital, S., Painter, K., Park, S-Y., Pascual, L., et al. (2004). Cross-linguistic analysis of vocabulary in young children: Spanish, Dutch, French, Hebrew, Italian, Korean, and American English. *Child Development, 75,* 1115–1139.

Bornstein, M. H., & Haynes, O. M. (1998). Vocabulary competence in early childhood: Measurement, latent construct, and predictive validity. *Child Development, 69,* 654–671.

Bornstein, M. H., Miyake, K., Azuma, H., Tamis-LeMonda, C. S., & Toda, S. (1990). Responsiveness in Japanese mothers: Consequences and characteristics. *Annual Report of the Research and Clinical Center for Child Development* (pp. 15–26). Sapporo, Japan: University of Hokkaido.

Bornstein, M. H., & Tamis-LeMonda, C. S. (1989). Maternal responsiveness and cognitive development in children. In M. H. Bornstein (Ed.), *New directions for child development: No. 43. Maternal responsiveness: Characteristics and consequences* (pp. 49–61). San Francisco: Jossey-Bass.

Bornstein, M. H., & Tamis-LeMonda, C. S. (1997). Mother's Responsiveness in infancy and their toddlers' attention span, symbolic play, and language comprehension: Specific predictive relations. *Infant Behavior and Development, 20*(3), 283–296.

Bornstein, M. H., & Tamis-LeMonda, C. S. (2001). Mother-infant interaction. In G. Bremner & A. Fogel (Eds.), *Blackwell handbook of infant development* (pp. 269–295). Malden, MA: Blackwell.

Bornstein, M. H., Tamis-LeMonda, C. S., & Haynes, M. (1999). First words in the second year. Continuity, stability, and models of concurrent and lagged correspondence in vocabulary and verbal responsiveness across age and context. *Infant Behavior and Development, 22,* 67–87.

Brooks-Gunn, J., & Duncan, G. J. (1997). The effects of poverty on children. *The Future of Children, 7*(2), 55–71.

Brophy-Herb, H. E, Gibbons, C., Omar, M. A., & Schiffman, R. F. (1999). Low-income fathers and their infants: Interactions during teaching episodes. *Infant Mental Health Journal, 20,* 305–321.

Brown, R. (1973). *A first language: The early stages.* Cambridge: Harvard University Press.

Bruner, J. (1974). The ontogenesis of speech acts. *Journal of Child Language, 2,* 1–19.

Bruner, J. (1983). *Child's talk: Learning to use language.* New York: Norton.

Bryant, P., & Bradley, L. (1987). Rhymes, nursery rhymes, and reading in early childhood. *Merrill-Palmer Quarterly, 33,* 255–281.

Burns, M. S., Griffin, P., & Snow, C. E. (Eds.). (1999). *Starting out right: A guide to promoting children's reading success.* Washington, DC: National Academy Press.

Cabrera, N., Brooks-Gunn, J., Moore, K., West, J., Boller, K., & Tamis-LeMonda, C. S. (2002). Bridging research and policy: Including fathers of young children in national studies. In C. S. Tamis-LeMonda & N. Cabrera (Eds.), *Handbook of father involvement: Multidisciplinary perspectives* (pp. 489–523). New York: Erlbaum.

Cabrera, N., Ryan, R., Shannon, J., Brooks-Gunn, J., Vogel, C., Raikes, H., et al. (2004). Low-income biological fathers' involvement in their toddlers' lives: The Early Head Start National Research and Evaluation Study. *Fathering: A Journal of Theory, Research, and Practice about Men as Fathers, 2,* 5–30.

Camaioni, L. (2001). Early language. In G. Bremner & A. Fogel (Eds.), *Blackwell handbook of infant development* (pp. 404–426). Oxford: Blackwell.

Camaioni, L., Aureli, T., Bellagamba, F., & Fogel, A. (2003). A longitudinal examination of the transition to symbolic communication in the second year of life. *Infant and Child Development, 12,* 1–26.

Camaioni, L., & Longobardi, E. (1994). *A longitudinal examination of the relationship between maternal input and child language acquisition.* Paper presented at the First Lisbon Meeting on Child Language with Special Reference to Romance Languages, Lisbon.

Carey, S. (1978). The child as word-learner. In M. Halle, J. Bresnan, & G.A. Miller (Eds.), *Linguistic theory and psychological reality.* Cambridge, MA: MIT Press.

Carpenter, M., Nagell, K., & Tomasello, M. (1998). Social cognition, joint attention and communicative competence from 9 to 15 months of age. *Monographs of the Society for Research in Child Development, 63*(4, serial no. 255).

Chall, J. S., Jacobs, V. A., & Baldwin, L. E. (1990). *The reading crisis: Why poor children fall behind.* Cambridge: Harvard University Press.

Childers, J. B., & Tomasello, M. (2002). Two-year-olds learn novel nouns, verbs, and
conventional actions from massed or distributed exposures. *Developmental Psychology, 38,* 967–978.

Clark, E. V. (1995). Later lexical development and word formation. In P. Fletcher & B. MacWhinney (Eds.), *The handbook of child language* (pp. 393–412). Oxford, UK: Blackwell.

Cochran, E., & Cochran, M. (1997). *Child care that works: A parent's guide to finding quality care.* Boston, MA: Mariner Books.

Cristofaro, T. N., Rodriguez, E., Baumwell, L., Tamis-Le-Monda, C., & Nakae, M. (2004, May). *The specificity of parental language input and children's language competencies.* Poster session presented at the biennial meeting of the International Conference on Infant Studies, Chicago, Illinois.

Dapretto, M., & Bjork, E. L. (2000). The development of word retrieval abilities in the second year and its relation to early vocabulary growth. *Child Development, 71,* 635–648.

Dickinson, D. K., & DeTemple, J. (1998). Putting parents in the picture: Maternal reports of preschoolers' literacy as a predictor of early reading. *Early Childhood Research Quarterly, 13,* 241–261.

Dunham, P. J., & Dunham, F. (1995). Optimal Social Structures and Adaptive Infant Development. In C. Moore & P. J. Dunham (Eds.), *Joint attention: Its origins and role in development* (pp. 159–188). Hillsdale, NJ: Erlbaum.

Dunn, L. M., & Dunn, L. M. (1997). *Peabody Picture Vocabulary Test—Third Edition.* Circle Pines, MN: American Guidance Service.

Evans, G. W. (2004). The environment of childhood poverty. *American Psychologist, 59*(2), 77–92.

Fenson, L., Dale, P. S., Reznick, J. S., Bates, E., Thal, D., & Pethick, S. (1994). Variability in early communicative development. *Monographs of the Society for Research in Child Development, 59*(serial no. 242).

Fogel, A., Messinger, D. S., Dickson, K. L., & Hsu, H. (1999). Posture and gaze in early mother-infant communication: Synchronization of developmental trajectories. *Developmental Science, 2*(3), 325–332.

Furstenberg, F. F., & Harris, K. M. (1993). When fathers matter/why fathers matter: The impact of paternal involvement on the offspring of adolescent mothers. In A. Lawson & D. L. Rhode (Eds.), *The politics of pregnancy: Adolescent sexuality and public policy* (pp. 189–215). New Haven, CT: Yale University Press.

Garfinkel, I., McLanahan, S., & Hanson, T. (1998). A patchwork portrait of nonresident fathers. In I. Garfinkel, S. McLanahan, D. Meyer, & J. Seltzer (Eds.), *Fathers under fire: The revolution in child support enforcement.* New York: Russell Sage Foundation.

Gershkoff-Stowe, L., & Smith, L. B. (2004). Shape and the first hundred nouns. *Child Development, 75,* 1098–1114.

Ginsburg, G. P., & Kilbourne, B. K. (1988). Emergence of vocal alternation in mother-infant interchanges. *Journal of Child Language, 15,* 221–235.

Hart, B., & Risley, T. (1995). *Meaningful differences in the everyday experiences of young American children.* Baltimore, MD: Paul H. Brookes.

Hart, B., & Risley, T. R. (1992). American parenting of language-learning children: Persisting differences in family-child interactions observed in natural home environments. *Developmental Psychology, 28,* 1096–1105.

Heibeck, T. H., & Markman, E. M. (1987). Word learning in children: An examination of fast mapping. *Child Development, 58,* 1021–1034.

Hoff, E. (2002). Causes and consequences of SES-related differences in parent-to-child speech. In M. H. Bornstein & R. H. Bradley (Eds.), *Socioeconomic status, parenting, and child development* (pp. 231–252). Mahwah, NJ: Erlbaum.

Hoff, E., Laursen, B., & Tardif, T. (2002). Socioeconomic status and parenting. In M. H. Bornstein (Ed.), *Handbook of parenting: Vol. 2. Biology and ecology of parenting* (2nd ed., pp. 231–252). Mahwah, NJ: Erlbaum.

Hoff-Ginsberg, E. (1997). *Language development.* Pacific Grove, CA: Brooks/Cole.

Hollich, G., Hirsh-Pasek, K., & Golinkoff, R. M. (2000). Breaking the Language Barrier: An emergentist coalition model for the origins of word learning. *Monographs of the Society for Research in Child Development, 65*(3, serial no. 1–122).

Homer, B., & Tamis-LeMonda, C. S. (in press). *The development of social cognition and communication.* Mahwah, NJ: Erlbaum.

Hsu, H., & Fogel, A. (2001). Infant vocal development in a dynamic mother-infant communication system. *Infancy, 2*(1), 87–109.

Huttenlocher, J., Haight, W., Bryk, A., Seltzer, M., & Lyons, T. (1991). Early vocabulary growth: Relation to language input and gender. *Developmental Psychology, 27,* 236–248.

Jaffe, J., Beebe, B., Feldstein, S., Crown, C. L., & Jasnow, M. D. (2001). Rhythms of dialogue in infancy. *Monographs of the Society for Research in Child Development, 66*(2, serial no. 1–131).

Lamb, M. E. (Ed.). (2004). *The role of the father in child development* (4th ed.). Hoboken, NJ: Wiley.

Landry, S. H., Smith, K. E., Miller-Loncar, C. L., & Swank, P. R. (1997). Predicting cognitive-language and social growth curves from early maternal behaviors in children at varying degrees of biological risk. *Developmental Psychology, 33,* 1040–1053.

Lerman, R. (1993). A national profile of young unwed fathers. In R. I. Lerman & T. J. Ooms (Eds.), *Young unwed fathers: Changing roles and emerging policies* (pp. 27–51). Philadelphia: Temple University Press.

Lock, A. (2001). Preverbal communication. In G. Bremner &

A. Fogel (Eds.), *Blackwell handbook of infant development* (pp. 379–403). Oxford: Blackwell.

Locke, J. L. (1995). Development of the capacity for spoken language. In P. Fletcher & B. MacWhinney (Eds.), *The handbook of child language* (pp. 278–302). Oxford: Blackwell Publishers.

Longobardi, E. (1992). Funzione comunicativa del comportamento materno e sviluppo comunicativo-linguistico del bambino nel secondo anno di vita [Communicative functions of maternal behavior and the communicative-linguistic development of children in the second year of life]. *Giornale Italiano di Psicologia, 19,* 425–448.

Love, J. M., Kisker, E. E., Ross, C. M., Schochet, P. Z., Brooks-Gunn, J., Paulsell, D., et al. (2002). *Making a difference in the lives of infants and toddlers and their families: The impacts of Early Head Start.* Princeton, NJ: Mathematica Policy Research, Inc.

Marsiglio, W. (1987). Adolescent fathers in the United States: Their initial living arrangements, marital experience, and educational outcomes. *International Family Planning Perspectives, 19*(6), 240–251.

McAdoo, J. L. (1986). Black fathers' relationships with their preschool children and the children's ethnic identity. In R. A. Lewis & R. E. Salt (Eds.), *Men in families* (pp. 169–180). Newbury Park, CA: Sage.

McAdoo, J. L. (1988). Changing perspective on the role of the black father. In P. Bronstein & C. P. Cowan (Eds.), *Fatherhood today: Men's changing role in the family* (pp. 79–92). New York: Wiley.

McCall, R. B., Eichorn, D. H., & Hogarty, P. S. (1977). Transitions in early mental development. *Monographs of the Society for Research in Child Development, 42*(serial no. 108).

McCune, L. (1995). A normative study of representational play at the transition to language. *Developmental Psychology, 31,* 198–206.

McGill-Franzen, A. (1987). Failure to learn to read: Formulating a policy problem. *Reading Research Quarterly, 22,* 475–490.

McLoyd, V. C. (1989). Socialization and development in a changing economy: The effects of paternal job and income loss on children. *American Psychologist, 44,* 293–302.

McLoyd, V. C. (1990). The impact of economic hardship on black families and children: Psychological distress, parenting and socioemotional development. *Child Development, 61,* 311–346.

Meisel, J.M. (1995). Parameters in acquisition. In P. Fletcher & B. MacWhinney (Eds.), *The handbook of child language* (pp. 10–35). Oxford: Blackwell.

Miller, J. F., & Chapman, R. S. (1993). *SALT: Systematic analysis of language transcripts.* Madison, WI: Language Analysis Laboratory, Waisman Center, University of Wisconsin.

Namy, L. L., & Gentner, D. (2002). Making a silk purse out of two sow's ears: Young children's use of comparison in category learning. *Journal of Experimental Psychology: General, 131,* 5–15.

Nelson, K. (1973). Structure and strategy in learning to talk. *Monographs of the Society for Research in Child Development, 38*(1–2, serial no. 149).

Nelson, K. (1981). Social cognition in a script framework. In J. H. Flavell & L. Ross (Eds.), *Social cognitive development.* Cambridge: Cambridge University Press.

Nelson, K. (1986). *Event knowledge: Structure and function in development.* Hillsdale, NJ: Erlbaum.

Nelson, K. (1988). Constraints on word meaning? *Cognitive Development, 3,* 221–246.

Payne, A. C., Whitehurst, G. J., & Angell, A. L. (1994). The role of home literacy environment in the development of language ability in preschool children from low-income families. *Early Childhood Research Quarterly, 9,* 427–440.

Perloff, J. N., & Buckner, J. C. (1996). Fathers of children on welfare: Their impact on child well-being. *American Journal of Orthopsychiatry, 66,* 557–571.

Plunkett, K. (1997). Theories of early language acquisition. *Trends in Cognitive Sciences, 1*(4), 146–153.

Reznick, J. S., & Goldfield, B. (1992). Rapid change in lexical development in comprehension and production. *Developmental Psychology, 28,* 406–413.

Roberts, J. I. (2001). *Predictors of cognitive development in 14-month-old children from low-income families: The role of maternal language and play and support networks.* Unpublished doctoral dissertation, New York University.

Roberts, J. E., Burchinal, M., & Durham, M. (1999). Parents' report of vocabulary and grammatical development of African American preschoolers: Child and environmental associations. *Child Development, 70,* 92–106.

Rogoff, B., Mistry, J., Radziszewska, B., & Germond, J. (1992). Infants' instrumental social interaction with adults. In S. Feinman (Ed.), *Social referencing and the social construction of reality in infancy* (pp. 323–348). New York: Plenum.

Rovee-Collier, C. (1995). Time windows in cognitive development. *Developmental Psychology, 31*(2), 147–169.

Sameroff, A. J. (1975). Early influences on development: Fact or Fancy. *Merrill-Palmer Quarterly, 21,* 267–294.

Scarborough, H. (1989). Prediction of reading dysfunction from familial and individual differences. *Journal of Educational Psychology, 81,* 101–108.

Senechal, M., & LeFevre, J. A. (2001). Storybook reading and parent teaching: Links to language and literacy development. In P. R. Britto & J. Brooks-Gunn (Eds.), *The role of family literacy environments in promoting young children's emerging literacy skills: New directions for child and adolescent development* (pp. 39–52). San Francisco: Jossey-Bass Pfeiffer.

Shannon, J. D., Tamis-LeMonda, C. S., London, K., & Cabrera, N. (2002). Beyond rough and tumble: Low-income fathers' interactions and children's cognitive development at 24 months. *Parenting: Science and Practice, 2*(2), 77–104.

Smith, L. B. (1995). Self-organizing process in learning to learn words: Development is not induction. In C. A. Nelson (Ed.), *The Minnesota Symposia on Child Psychology* (Vol. 28). Mahwah, NJ: Erlbaum.

Smith, L. B. (2003). Learning to recognize objects. *Psychological Science, 14,* 244–250.

Snow, C. E. (1986). Conversations with children. In P. Fletcher & M. Garman (Eds.), *Language acquisition* (2nd ed., pp. 69–89). Cambridge: Cambridge University Press.

Snow, C. E., Burns, M.S., & Griffin, P. (Eds.). (1998). *Preventing reading difficulties in young children.* Washington, DC: National Academy Press.

Snyder, L., Bates, E., & Bretherton, I. (1981). Content and context in early lexical development. *Journal of Child Language, 5,* 565–582.

Stern, D. N. (1985). *The interpersonal world of the infant: A view from psychoanalysis and developmental psychology.* New York: Basic Books.

Tabors, P. O., Roach, K. A., & Snow, C. E. (2001). Home language and literacy environment: Final results. In D. K. Dickinson & P. O. Tabors (Eds.), *Beginning literacy with language: Young children learning at home and school* (pp. 111–138). Baltimore, MD: Paul H. Brookes.

Tamis-LeMonda, C. S., & Adolph, K. E. (in press). Social cognition in infant motor action. In B. Homer & C. S. Tamis-LeMonda (Eds.), *The development of social cognition and communication*. Mahwah, NJ: Erlbaum.

Tamis-LeMonda, C. S., & Bornstein, M. H. (1990). Language, play, and attention at one year. *Infant Behavior and Development, 13*, 85–98.

Tamis-LeMonda, C. S., & Bornstein, M. H. (1994). Specificity in mother-toddler language-play relations across the second year. *Developmental Psychology, 30*, 283–292.

Tamis-LeMonda, C. S., & Bornstein, M. H. (2002). Maternal responsiveness and early language acquisition. *Advances in Child Development, 29*, 89–127.

Tamis-LeMonda, C. S., Bornstein, M. H., & Baumwell, L. (2001). Maternal responsiveness and children's achievement of language milestones. *Child Development, 72*(3), 748–767.

Tamis-LeMonda, C. S., Bornstein, M. H., Kahana-Kalman, R., Baumwell, L., & Cyphers, L. (1998). Predicting variation in the timing of linguistic milestones in the second year: An events-history approach. *Journal of Child Language, 25*, 675–700.

Tamis-LeMonda, C. S., & Cabrera, N. (1999). Perspectives on father involvement: Research and Social policy. *Society for Research in Child Development, Social Policy Report, Vol. XIII*, No. 2.

Tamis-LeMonda, C. S., & Cabrera, N. (Eds.). (2002). *Handbook of father involvement: Multidisciplinary perspectives*. Mahwah, NJ: Erlbaum.

Tamis-LeMonda, C. S., Rodriguez, E. T., Spellmann, M., Raikes, H., Pan, B., & Luze, G. (2004, June). Children's early literacy experiences: Relations to language and cognitive outcomes at 14, 24, and 36 months of age. In H. Raikes (Chair), *Language and literacy environments of toddlers in low-income families: Relations to cognitive and language development*. Symposium conducted at Head Start's Seventh National Research Conference, Washington, DC.

Tamis-LeMonda, C. S., Shannon, J. D., Cabrera, N., & Lamb, M. (2004). Fathers and mothers at play with their 2- and 3-year-olds: Relations to children's language and cognitive development. *Child Development, 75*(6), 1806–1820.

Tomasello, M. (1992). *First verbs: A case study of early grammatical development*. Cambridge: Cambridge University Press.

Tomasello, M. (1993). On the interpersonal origins of self-concept. In U. Neisser (Ed.), *The perceived self: Ecological and interpersonal sources of self-knowledge* (pp. 174–184). Cambridge: Cambridge University Press.

Tomasello, M. (1995). Joint attention as a social cognition. In P. J. D. C. Moore (Ed.), *Joint attention: Its origin and role in development* (pp. 103–130). Hillsdale, NJ: Erlbaum.

Tomasello, M., & Farrar, M. J. (1986). Joint attention and early language. *Child Development, 57*, 1454–1463.

Trevarthen, C. (1993). The self born in intersubjectivity: The psychology of an infant communicating. In U. Neisser (Ed.), *The perceived self: Ecological and interpersonal sources of self-knowledge* (pp. 121–173). New York: Cambridge.

Volterra, V., Bates, E., Benigni, L., & Bretherton, I., & Camaioni, L. (1979). First words in language and action: A qualitative look. In E. Bates (Ed.), *The emergence of symbols: Cognition and communication in infancy* (pp. 141–222). New York: Academic Press.

Vygotsky, L. S. (1962). *Thought and language*. Cambridge, MA: MIT Press.

Whitehurst, G. J., Arnold, D. S., Epstein, J. N., Angell, A. L., Smith, M., & Fischel, J. (1994). A picture book reading intervention in day care and home for children from low-income families. *Developmental Psychology, 30*, 679–689.

Whitehurst, G. J., & Lonigan, C. J. (2003). Emergent literacy: Development from prereaders to readers. In S. B. Neuman & D. K. Dickinson (Eds.), *Handbook of early literacy research* (pp. 11–29). New York: Guilford Press.

Willett, J. B., & Singer, J. D. (1991). From whether to when: New methods for studying student dropout and teacher attrition. *Review of Educational Research, 61*, 407–450.

Willett, J. B., & Singer, J. D. (1993). Investigating onset, cessation, relapse and recovery: Why you should, and how you can, use discrete-time survival analysis to examine event occurrence. *Journal of Consulting and Clinical Psychology, 61*, 952–965.

Woodward, A. L., & Markman, E. M. (1998). Early word learning. In D. Kuhn & R. S. Siegler (Eds.), *Handbook of child psychology: Vol. 2. Cognition, perception, and language*. New York: Wiley.

5

On the Emergence of Perceptual Organization and Categorization in Young Infants
Roles for Perceptual Process and Knowledge Access

Paul C. Quinn

INTRODUCTION

This chapter will review what is known about the development of perceptual organization and categorization of objects in preverbal infants less than 1 year of age, with emphasis placed on research conducted in the author's laboratory. A number of difficult and related questions will guide the discussion. First, how does the infant begin to decompose a complex configuration of visual pattern information into elements that can be used as building blocks (i.e., units of processing) for purposes of representing objects? Second, how are the surface fragments (i.e., edge segments) of a visual scene spontaneously grouped into more complex structures (i.e., shapes) that serve as the basis for the representation of objects? Third, what visual properties of objects mediate a common categorization response? Fourth, what factors control infant visual attention during presentation of complex stimulus patterns that contain multiple visual features? Fifth, what is the contribution of previously acquired knowledge to on-line, within-task performance?

Before turning to a review of the relevant evidence, it needs to be acknowledged that there has been much recent debate over the appropriate "richness" of interpretation of the performance of infants participating in looking time studies (Aslin, 2000; Baillargeon, 1999; Haith, 1998; Smith, 1999). What kinds of skills and knowledge can be attributed to infants based on visual preference outcomes? In accord with traditional constructivist views of development, some theorists argue that infants may detect low-level stimulus variables, and gradually learn to organize them by means of maturation and experience into more complex mental structures that eventually attain the status of representations (e.g., Cohen, Chaput, & Cashon, 2002). From a more nativist perspective, other theorists propose that infants may be innately possessive of deep cognitive constraints that represent core knowledge, which in time take the form of theories that organize broad domains of experience (Carey, 2000;

Spelke, 2000). The question becomes whether one should characterize the infant as being primarily perceptual or intelligent.

The position taken in this chapter represents a third position about infants, which is to consider them both perceptual *and* intelligent (Kellman & Arterberry, 1998; Quinn & Bhatt, 2001; Quinn, 2002a). According to this view, in the extremes of the nativist versus empiricist debate, a point which may get lost is that basic processes when put into operation in the developing infant can begin to yield functional knowledge in a fairly short period of time. This view thus emphasizes core processes that quickly give rise to acquired knowledge which can in turn influence subsequent processing. For example, much of the experimental work reported in the present chapter was conducted with infants between 3 and 7 months of age. Infants in this age range may utilize sufficiently sensitive perceptual systems and a general learning mechanism to build up a set of representations for objects, their appearance, and their behavior. The representations may then be accessed to guide on-line performance occurring within experiments. The evidence that provides support for this position in the domains of perceptual organization and categorization will now be reviewed.

PERCEPTUAL ORGANIZATION

For purposes of this chapter, perceptual organization and categorization will be discussed in two sections: The first will consider a possible early stage of visual processing in which shapes and objects are extracted from a visual scene, and the second will consider a presumed later phase in which shapes and objects are categorized, that is, recognized as members of particular groups (see Farah, 1990, and Trick & Enns, 1997, for similar frameworks; but see Peterson, 1994, for an alternative view). A transitional section of the chapter will highlight the interaction of the processes of perceptual organization and categorization.

Historical Models of Parsing and Unit Formation

How are the connectedness, coherence, and outlines of objects in a visual scene established? How during development do humans come to know which edges and contours go together to form objects? Historically, different answers have been given to such questions. Gestalt psychologists argued that our nervous systems are constrained, even at birth, to follow certain principles (e.g., closure, common movement, good continuation, proximity, and similarity) that specify how small pieces of a visual scene should be organized to form larger perceptual units or perceptual wholes (Helson, 1933; Koffka, 1935; Kohler, 1929; Wertheimer, 1923/1958). Other theorists have emphasized that an extended period of perceptual learning of visual and motor associations may be needed to determine the spatial arrangement of features that comprise individual forms (Hebb, 1949; Piaget, 1952).

Newer Views

Modern theorists working in the tradition of cognitive science have suggested that some Gestalt-like biases (e.g., common movement, connected surface) combine with or are perhaps even derived from an innate representational structure for objects in general (i.e., an object concept) to initially perceive the coherence or unity of objects (Spelke, 1982). The amorphous but cohesive object "blobs" that are the outcomes of this primitive parsing process can then be tracked to determine their precise form, color, and surface texture. By this view, certain of the Gestalt principles, including good continuation and similarity, are learned rather than innate.

A different model regarding the development of object perception has been put forth by Kellman and colleagues (Kellman, 1996; Kellman & Arterberry, 1998; Kellman & Shipley, 1991). These researchers have argued for a two-process model of unit formation, inclusive of (1) a "primitive" edge insensitive process (EI) that is presumably available at birth and that responds to common motion information (but see Slater et al., 1990), and (2) a later "rich" edge sensitive process (ES) that becomes functional at around 7 months and that responds to good continuation information (but see Johnson & Aslin, 1996, for evidence of an earlier onset). By the Kellman account, the EI and ES processes reflect the workings of specialized perceptual input modules (Fodor, 1983) that have their own maturationally based time courses of operation. The Spelke and Kellman accounts of the development of object coherence share a view that older infants use information for unit formation that is not available to younger infants. They also have in common the idea that some kinds of information (e.g., movement) have priority because they are more essential (Spelke, 1982) or more ecologically valid (Kellman, 1993) than other sources of information (e.g., form) for individuating objects in a visual scene.

The most recent accounts of early object perception by infants have begun to suggest that we may need to revise our thinking about the sources of information that young infants can utilize to achieve unit formation (Johnson, 1998; Needham, 2001). For example, the experiments of Johnson and Aslin (1996) indicate that 4-month-old infants may rely on a variety of cues including common motion, depth, accretion and deletion of background texture, color similarity, and good continuation information to represent the unity of a partly occluded object. Based on their results, Johnson and Aslin have proposed a sensory-perceptual threshold model for describing infant performance. When multiple cues are detected from the same display, these cues sum together and become sufficient for unit formation. Failure to represent object unity may reflect lack of cues, lack of sensitivity to the cues, or both.

Needham and Baillargeon (1998) have also embraced the idea that there is a multiplicity of cues for object representation in young infants. These investigators have shown that 4.5-month-olds can use configural information (e.g., color, shape, and texture similarity) and experiential information (e.g., knowledge of object kinds and particular objects) to form segregated units from displays of adjacent objects (see also Needham, 1998). In addition, 8-month-olds were found to use physical information (e.g., knowledge of support and solidity relations) to supplement configural information to form individuated representations for adjacent objects (Needham & Baillargeon, 1997). Moreover, the physical information appeared to be weighted more heavily than the configural information when the two sources of information were in competition. These data have led to the formulation of a perceptual-cognitive information integration model of unit formation in infants (Needham & Kaufman, 1997). In this model, infants are believed to integrate different kinds of information into a coherent representation of a given stimulus display. The various kinds of information form a kind of checklist hierarchy with more "certain" physical information at the top and considered before more "probabilistic" configural information that is located at a lower level.

Lightness Similarity

Evidence from my own laboratory relevant to theoretical accounts of the development of object perception has focused on when and how humans become capable of grouping parts of a stimulus together to form a coherent whole. A study by Quinn, Burke, and Rush (1993) hints at answers to both questions. The stimuli are shown in the left half of Figure 5.1. As reported by Wertheimer (1923/1958), adult participants group together the elements of such stimuli on the basis of lightness similarity and represent the top pattern shown in Panel (a) as a set of columns, and the bottom pattern depicted in Panel (b) as a set of rows. Quinn et al. reasoned that if young infants, 3 months of age, organize the patterns shown in Panels (a) and (b) of Figure 5.1 into columns and rows based on lightness similarity, then they should respond differentially to the vertical- and horizontal-grating test stimuli shown in the right half of the figure. On the assumption that there is no spontaneous preference between the vertical and horizontal stripes, infants familiarized with columns should generalize to verticals and prefer horizontals, whereas infants familiarized with rows should generalize to horizontals and prefer verticals. This is precisely the result that was obtained—a finding indicating that young infants were able to use lightness similarity to represent the row- and column-like organization of the individual light and dark squares.

One could take issue with the grouping via lightness similarity interpretation proposed by Quinn et al. (1993) by claiming that the apparent perceptual grouping is actually a by-product of immature

FAMILIAR STIMULUS

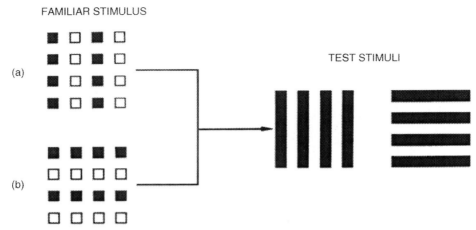

Figure 5.1 Familiarization and test stimuli used to test adherence to the lightness similarity Gestalt organizational principle in Quinn, Burke, and Rush (1993). The rationale is that if infants can organize familiar stimulus (a) into columns, then the vertical-column test stimulus should be perceived as familiar, and the horizontal-row test stimulus should be preferred. Similarly, if infants can organize the familiar stimulus (b) into rows, then the horizontal-row test stimulus should be perceived as familiar, and the vertical-column test stimulus should be preferred.

peripheral filtering by the infant's visual system (Banks & Ginsburg, 1985; Banks & Salapatek, 1981). That is, one could argue that immature resolution acuity and contrast sensitivity rendered the dark squares as indistinguishable from other dark squares and the light squares as indistinguishable from other light squares. The representation of familiar stimuli (a) and (b) resulting from such "low-pass" filtering would best be described as "two dark vertical (or horizontal) bars on a light background." Performance of the 3-month-olds could thus be explained by simple generalization from representations of this nature to the vertical (or horizontal bars) used as test stimuli, without invoking any grouping mechanism (cf. Ginsburg, 1986).

Quinn et al. (1993) attempted to choose between the Gestalt grouping and low-pass filtering explanations of the findings with both computer simulation and experimental evidence. First, the images of the familiar stimuli shown in Figure 5.1, and additional stimuli in which either the dark or light elements were changed from square to diamond, were fed into a low-pass spatial frequency filter that removed spatial frequencies above 4 cycles/degree, the cutoff spatial frequency for 3-month-olds as estimated by preferential looking techniques (e.g., Atkinson, Braddick, & Moar, 1977; Banks & Salapatek, 1978). Figure 5.2 shows the resulting patterns. It can be seen that the stimuli have lost some sharpness, but the individual elements comprising the patterns are clearly discernable. Figure 5.2 thus suggests that 3-month-olds have enough resolution acuity and contrast sensitivity to perceive the individual elements of the patterns, and that the initial preference results cannot be explained on the basis of peripheral immaturities in the young infant's visual system.

This suggestion was subsequently confirmed in a discrimination experiment utilizing the familiarization/novelty-preference methodology. Infants were familiarized with stimuli like those shown in the left half of Figure 5.1 and then presented with novel stimuli in which only the dark or light elements were changed from square to diamond. Preference for the novel stimuli was above chance in both cases, indicating that infants were able to process shape information for both the light and dark elements. The combined findings from the simulation and discrimination experiment thus provide strong evidence in favor of a Gestalt interpretation of the original preference results: infants had perceived the individual elements of the patterns and grouped these elements into alternating light and dark columns or rows on the basis of lightness similarity.

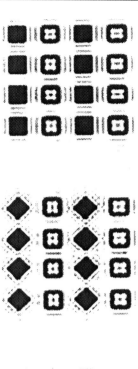

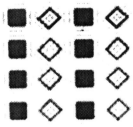

Figure 5.2 Patterns with spatial frequencies above 4 cycles/degree removed. While the individual elements of the patterns have lost some "sharpness," their shape (square or diamond) remains clearly discernable. (From Quinn, Burke, & Rush, 1993.)

Form Similarity

Lightness similarity may be the most robust form of grouping by similarity and possibly the earliest form of similarity that infants can use as a basis for perceptual grouping (Bremner, 1994). Indeed, the findings indicating that 3-month-olds can use lightness similarity to represent the column- versus row-like organization of the arrays of elements have since been extended to newborns (Farroni, Valenza, Simion, & Umilta, 2000), thereby suggesting an initial ability to group on the basis of luminance information. The question arises as to whether infants can also use other forms of similarity, such as shape, to organize visual pattern information. Evidence from the adult literature indicates that there may be distinct systems for grouping on the basis of luminance and edge information (Behrmann & Kimchi, 2003; Gilchrist, Humphreys, Riddoch, & Neumann, 1997). As noted earlier, Kellman (1996) has proposed a developmentally late functional onset for mechanisms sensitive to edge information. These issues motivated Quinn, Bhatt, Brush, Grimes, and Sharpnack (2002) to examine whether young infants could organize visual pattern information in accord with form similarity. Two groups of infants, 3- to 4-month-olds and 6- to 7-month-olds, were familiarized with arrays of elements consisting of alternating rows or columns of Xs and Os and then given a novelty preference test that paired horizontal versus vertical stripes. As can be seen in Figure 5.3, the stimuli were constructed so as to match those used by Quinn et al. (1993), except that the Xs and Os were used as individual elements.

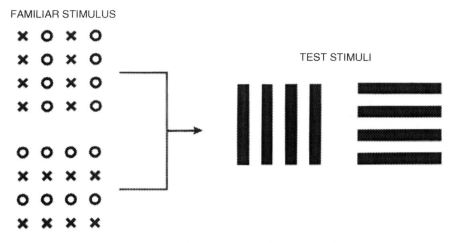

Figure 5.3   Familiarization and test stimuli used to test adherence to the form similarity Gestalt organizational principle in Quinn, Bhatt, Brush, Grimes, and Sharpnack (2002). The rationale is that if infants
can organize the familiar stimulus in the top panel into columns, then the vertical-column test stimulus
should be perceived as familiar, and the horizontal-row test stimulus should be preferred. Similarly, if
infants can organize the familiar stimulus in the bottom panel into rows, then the horizontal-row test
stimulus should be perceived as familiar, and the vertical-column test stimulus should be preferred.

The results were that only the older infants responded preferentially to the novel organization; the
younger infants divided their attention evenly between the two test stimuli. The failure of the young
infants to attend to the novel organization was also shown in control experiments not to be the result
of insufficient familiarization time or the inability to discriminate between the individual X and O
shapes.

The overall pattern of experimental results indicates that 6- to 7-month-olds, but not 3- to 4-month-
olds, used form similarity information to organize visual patterns. Bhatt, Quinn, Chia, and Bertin
(2001) have replicated this set of outcomes with stimuli in which the individual elements were arrows
and triangles, thereby suggesting a developmental trend of a general nature rather than an idiosyncratic response to a particular set of stimuli. In combination with the studies showing that newborns
and 3-month-olds can use lightness similarity (Farroni et al., 2000; Quinn et al., 1993), the present
findings indicating that only 6- to 7-month-olds can use form similarity are consistent with models
of the genesis of object perception which suggest that different Gestalt principles become functional
over different time courses of development.

Good Continuation

When considering the relevance of the Quinn et al. (1993, 2002) demonstrations of infant Gestalt-like
grouping via lightness and form similarity for understanding the early development of object recognition abilities more generally, two limitations become apparent. First, the stimuli used in the Quinn
et al. studies are more like surface textures than they are like objects (Spelke, Breinlinger, Jacobson,
& Phillips, 1993; Spelke, Gutheil, & Van de Walle, 1995). Second, in many natural scenes, numerous
objects appear simultaneously, and may be arranged so that their contours are partially overlapping,
rather than completely visible. Such scenes must be parsed into a set of primitive contours, and these
contours must be organized into coherent representations of whole shapes.

To examine how well infants parse and organize more complex visual configurations that only begin
to approximate the object processing demands of more natural scenes, Quinn et al. (1997) investigated
how young infants would represent the pattern shown in panel (a) of Figure 5.4. Adults tend to parse
and organize this pattern into the square and circle shapes shown in panel (b) of Figure 5.4, rather

STIMULUS   POSSIBLE ORGANIZATIONS

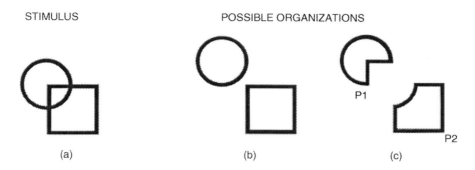

Figure 5.4 Intersecting circle-square stimulus in (a) and two possible organizations in (b) and (c). Adherence to the Gestalt principle of good continuation favors organization (b) over organization (c). (From Quinn, Brown, & Streppa, 1997.)

than the pacman shapes shown in panel (c). Presumably adults are following Gestalt organizational principles such as good continuation to represent the pattern information in this manner.

To determine whether 3- and 4-month-olds would parse and organize the pattern shown in Figure 5.4a into the square and circle shapes perceived by adults, a group of infants was familiarized in an experiment with the overlapping square–circle configuration and then preference tested with the circle versus P1 and the square versus P2. There are at least three ways in which infants may represent the familiar pattern information, each of which would produce a distinct pattern of looking among the test stimuli. First, if infants parse the pattern and organize its contours into the circle and square shapes in accord with the Gestalt principle of good continuation, then the circle and square shapes should be recognized as familiar in preference tests with P1 and P2, and P1 and P2 should be preferred. Second, if infants do not parse the unitary configuration, and the outcome is a representation of an unparsed whole, or if infants parse the configuration into more than one whole, but not the wholes predicted by adherence to good continuation, then one would not expect a consistent preference for P1 or P2 in either test. Third, infants may have spontaneous preferences for certain stimulus features (e.g., curvature, horizontal/vertical line elements) that could eventuate in parsing of the configuration and selective organization of the features into either the circle or square. In this case, one would expect a preference for the pacman shape (P1 or P2) in one or the other preference test, but not both. The results were that infants preferred the pacman shapes in both preference tests, a pattern of looking that is consistent with the idea that infants had organized the familiar configuration into the circle and square shapes in a manner predicted by adherence to the Gestalt principle of good continuation.

A potentially informative effect that was observed in Quinn et al. (1997) is that there was a spontaneous preference observed in a control group of infants who were assessed for possible a priori preferences among the test patterns. Specifically, without prior familiarization experience, the P2 shape was significantly preferred to the square. Although the novelty preference for P2 over the square in the experimental group occurred above and beyond that of the a priori preference for P2 in the control group, it is interesting to consider the possible significance of the spontaneous preference for P2.

The critical physical difference between P2 and the square is the presence of a curved contour in P2 and the absence of it in the square. In addition, there is evidence that infants have a spontaneous preference for curved over rectilinear contours (Fantz, Fagan, & Miranda, 1975). It is conceivable that the a priori preference for P2 is more than just a potential confound, a noise factor to be acknowledged, but then ruled out with appropriate statistical tests. The curvature-based preference for the P2 stimulus may help answer the question: How does the infant initially begin to break down a complex stimulus into a set of component contours? More specifically, where on the stimulus does the infant begin the complementary processes of parsing and organization? It may be that spontaneous preferences for some stimulus features over others could play an important "START HERE" role in initiating the parsing process for an unanalyzed configuration that contains a number of diverse features. A curvature preference, combined with a Gestalt principle like good continuation, may have allowed infants to first develop a representation for the circle shape. Once the circle was organized, infant attention may then have been free to explore other portions of the stimulus, thereby allowing for organization of the remaining contours into the square shape.

Summary

The evidence reviewed in the preceding sections indicates that young infants can group together the elements of a single visual pattern, presented in isolation from other patterns, so as to form a holistic representation of that pattern. Young infants may also be capable of parsing and organizing the more complex pattern information in a configuration of intersecting contours into two complete shapes. In achieving this degree of perceptual coherence infants may benefit from adherence to certain Gestalt principles such as lightness similarity and good continuation at 3 to 4 months, with form similarity beginning to exert a contribution to organization at 6 to 7 months. In addition, infants may rely on spontaneous preferences for particular features of contour information such as curvature to begin parsing and organizing global conglomerations of visual pattern information that contain multiple features.

The data contrasting the developmental onset of infants' use of lightness versus form similarity challenge the traditional Gestalt claim that all organizational principles are automatically and equivalently applied (Kohler, 1929). They are also consistent with recent studies from the adult literature suggesting that not all Gestalt principles are equally powerful or operational at the same time in the overall course of processing (Behrmann & Kimchi, 2003; Peterson, 2001). The findings suggest further that young infants are sensitive to more than just common movement and connected surface principles as organizers of visual pattern information (Kellman, 1996; Spelke, 1982). In particular, the findings of Quinn et al. (1993, 1997) indicate that lightness similarity and good continuation information are functional as organizational principles as early as 3 months of age (and possibly earlier in the case of lightness similarity; Farroni et al., 2000). These data are thus convergent with the work of Johnson (1997) and Needham (2001) in suggesting that a range of cues may be operational as sources for organization, although the difference in the developmental emergence of lightness similarity versus form similarity is consistent with the idea that some cues for organization may carry more weight than others at different points during development. As such, investigators may need to think in terms of how differentially weighted cues come together, in either a threshold or integration framework, to give rise to one or another percept.

AT THE INTERSECTION OF PERCEPTUAL ORGANIZATION AND CATEGORIZATION

Earlier in the chapter, an important distinction was made between the contributions of perceptual process and knowledge access toward explaining the performance of infants participating in looking time studies. A framework for thinking about the roles of perceptual process and knowledge access in perceptual organization has been offered by Schyns, Goldstone, and Thibaut (1998). Schyns et al. argue for a flexible system of perceptual unit formation, one in which the features that come to define objects are extracted during the task of concept learning. The idea is that an individual's history of concept formation (i.e., the concepts possessed by an individual at a specific point in time) will affect their subsequent perceptual organization processes.

Quinn and Schyns (2003) undertook a set of experiments to better understand the interplay between adherence to Gestalt organizational principles and flexible feature creation. The experiments were designed to answer the following question: Will features that are specified as functional by Gestalt principles be "overlooked" by young infants if alternative means of perceptual organization are "suggested" by presenting the infants with a category of objects in which the features uniting the objects are "nonnatural" in the Gestalt sense? In the first experiment, 3- and 4-month-olds were

Familiarization Trials

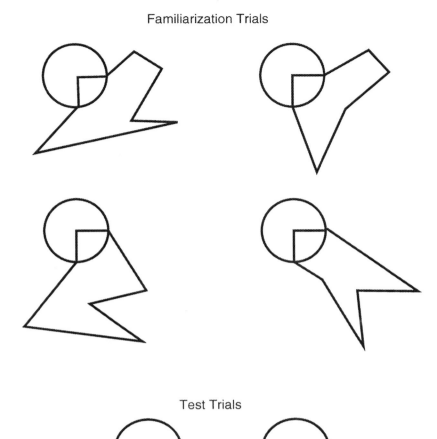

Test Trials

Figure 5.5 Examples of the familiarization stimuli and test stimuli used in Quinn and Schyns (2003). If the infants can parse the circle from the familiar patterns in accord with good continuation, then they should prefer the pacman shape over the circle shape during the test trials.

familiarized with a number of complex figures, examples of which are shown in the top portion of Figure 5.5. Subsequently, during a novelty preference test, the infants were presented with the pacman shape paired with the circle shown in the bottom portion of Figure 5.5. The infants were found to recognize the circle as familiar as evidenced by their preference for the pacman shape. This finding is consistent with the idea that the infants had parsed the circle from the complex figures in accord with good continuation.

In follow-up experiments, Quinn and Schyns (2003) asked whether an invariant part abstracted during category learning would interfere with perceptual organization achieved by adherence to good continuation. The experiments consisted of two parts. In Part 1, the infants were familiarized with multiple exemplars, each marked by an invariant pacman shape, and were subsequently administered a novelty preference test that paired the pacman shape with the circle shape. Examples of the stimuli are shown in Figure 5.6. The pacman shape was recognized as familiar, as evidenced by a preference for the circle shape. Part 2 of the procedure was then administered and it simply followed the design of Experiment 1. The expectation is that if the category learning from Part 1 of the procedure, in particular, the representation of the invariant pacman shape, can interfere with the Gestalt-based perceptual

Familiarization Trials

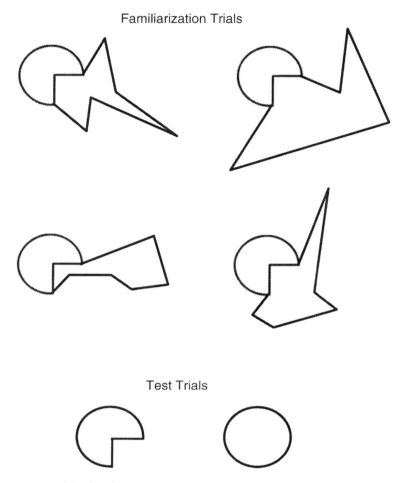

Test Trials

Figure 5.6 Examples of the familiarization stimuli and test stimuli used in Quinn and Schyns (2003). If the infants can extract the invariant pacman from the familiar patterns, then they should prefer the circle shape over the pacman shape during the test trials.

organization that was observed in Experiment 1, then the preference for the pacman shape that was observed in Experiment 1 should no longer be observed. In fact, if the representation of the pacman shape carries over from Part 1 to Part 2 of the procedure, one would expect the opposite result, that is, the infants should continue to prefer the circle. The latter result is what was observed and it suggests that perceptual units formed during category learning can be (1) entered into a perceptual system's working "featural" vocabulary, and (2) available to subsequent object recognition processes. The bias set by the Gestalt principle of good continuation is thus soft-wired and subject to interference. More generally, an individual's history of categorization will affect their subsequent object parsing abilities. In the following section of the chapter, the issue of how categorization emerges as a core process during the period of early infancy will be considered more fully.

PERCEPTUAL CATEGORIZATION

In addition to developing representations for coherent objects depicted in a single presentation of visual pattern information, members of the human species must at some point during development become capable of forming representations that are inclusive of numerous objects appearing over a more extended period of time. In compiling these representations inclusive of multiple items, individuals are apparently detecting some basis of equivalence among them. This basis could be perceptual, functional, conceptual, or some even more abstract combination of the attributes possessed by the items. Because representations of this nature are normally developed for categories of items (e.g., dogs, chairs), I have referred to them in past writings as *category representations* (Quinn, 2002b). Category representations of many common kinds of objects may be essential to (1) organizing memory, and (2) permitting us to respond to many novel objects with familiarity. The latter occurs because of the recognition of equivalence among certain attributes detected from the objects, and maintained in their category representations (Murphy, 2002).

Categorization is considered to be a critical cognitive ability because a system of mental representation that lacked category representations would be dominated by unrelated instance information and would face the problem of having to respond anew to each novel object encountered (Smith & Medin, 1981). Indeed, the importance of category representations to daily cognitive functioning has led Thelen and Smith (1994) to argue that categorization is the "primitive in all behavior and mental functioning" (p. 143).

Although there has been a historical tradition among scholars of cognitive development to consider the ability to form category representations to be an achievement of childhood (Bruner, Olver, & Greenfield, 1966; Vygotsky, 1962), more modern work has focused on the abilities of infants and toddlers to respond categorically to common object types (Cohen & Strauss, 1979; Mandler & McDonough, 1993; Mervis, 1987; Oakes, Madole, & Cohen, 1991; Quinn & Eimas, 1996b; Waxman & Markow, 1995; Xu & Carey, 1996; Younger, 1990). The chapter will now consider the evidence on categorization by these younger participants, with emphasis on studies of categorization of realistic photographic exemplars of animals and artifacts conducted with 3- to 4-month-olds in the author's laboratory. Particular issues of current contention include exemplar versus prototype storage of category information in memory, the perceptual versus conceptual basis for early object categories, and the relative roles of learning occurring within the laboratory versus knowledge acquired prior to arrival at the laboratory.

A Procedure for Assessing Categorization in Young Infants

In the familiarization/novelty-preference method of testing for categorization, infants are presented with a number of different instances from the same category during a familiarization period. Infants are then administered a paired presentation of a novel instance of the familiar category and a novel instance from a novel category. If infants generalize their familiarization to the novel exemplar of the familiar category, and display a preference for a novel exemplar from a novel category, and this pattern of looking cannot be attributed to an a priori preference or to an inability to discriminate among the familiar category exemplars, then it can be concluded that a representation of the familiar category exemplars has been formed. That is, one can infer that the familiar exemplars have in some manner been grouped together or categorized and that the representation of this category excludes the noninstance—the novel category exemplar. The procedure relies on the established preference that infants display for novel stimulation (Fantz, 1964; Slater, 1995).

Categorization of Animal Species and Artifacts

In a series of studies, young infants have been shown to form category representations for a variety of animal species and furniture artifacts (reviewed in Quinn, 2002c). In the experiments investigating young infants' category representations of various animal species, 3- and 4-month-olds familiarized with instances of 12 domestic cats, representing different breeds and depicted in a variety of stances, will generalize familiarization to novel instances of domestic cats, but show novel category preferences for birds, dogs, horses, tigers, and even female lions (Eimas & Quinn, 1994; Eimas, Quinn, & Cowan, 1994; Quinn, Eimas, & Rosenkrantz, 1993). Examples of the cats and dogs are shown in Figure 5.7.

Figure 5.7 Black and white examples of cat and dog stimuli used in the investigations of perceptual categorization of nonhuman animal species by young infants.

In addition, same-aged infants familiarized with 12 horses will generalize to novel horses, but display novel category preferences for cats, giraffes, and zebras (Eimas & Quinn, 1994). These findings indicate that young infants can form separate representations for cats and horses each of which excludes instances of the other along with exemplars from a number of basic-level categories from the same superordinate animal category.

Behl-Chadha (1996) extended the findings of early basic-level categorization among animal species to furniture. Three- and 4-month-olds familiarized with 12 pictorial instances of chairs (including arm chairs, desk chairs, kitchen chairs, rocking chairs, and stuffed chairs, depicted in a variety of colors and viewpoints) generalized their familiarization to novel chairs, but displayed novel category preferences for couches, beds, and tables. In addition, 3- and 4-month-olds presented with 12 couches generalized their familiarization to novel couches, but showed novel category preferences for chairs, beds, and tables. These results indicate that 3- and 4-month-olds can form individuated representations for chairs and couches, each of which excludes instances of the other as well as beds and tables. Overall, the findings provide evidence that young infants are capable of forming category representations for both natural kind animal species and artifactual items of furniture at a near basic-level of exclusiveness.

The findings of early categorization are significant because they suggest that young infants divide the world of objects appropriately into perceptual cluster representations that later come to have conceptual significance for adults. That is, the category distinctions made by quite young infants are often the same distinctions that later in life come to have a conceptual nature. As such, this early veridical parsing of the world should permit infants to begin to incorporate new "nonobvious" knowledge into category representations initially constructed on the basis of perceptual experience. For example, if young infants possess abilities to form a category representation for cats (e.g., one that is based on observable surface attributes including overall body shape, parts, markings, head and face information, communicative sounds, and motion), then more abstract information that is learned later (e.g., that cats have the verbal label or name "cat," are meat eaters, possess cat DNA, give birth to kittens, and like to play string games) can be used to enrich the early perceptually based category representation and allow for the development of a conceptually based representation (i.e., a concept) for cats. The conceptual representations found in children and adults can thus be viewed as informational enrichments of young infants' perceptual category representations (Quinn, 2002b; Quinn & Eimas, 1997, 2000). By this view, the abilities that young infants have to form perceptual category representations may form the primitive base from which adult conceptions of objects develop.

One clarification that may be helpful at this point in the discussion is to acknowledge that the infants who are presented with exemplars of nonhuman animals (e.g., cats) and form category representations in the laboratory are not necessarily leaving the laboratory with long-term representations for cats that will themselves represent the start-up structures into which subsequent experience and knowledge can be incorporated. The claim is more that the infants are demonstrating parsing skills in the laboratory that may be successfully deployed to form representations for classes of real objects when those objects are encountered in the natural environment. It is the latter group of representations that may serve as the actual supports for further knowledge acquisition.

Perceptual Cues for Category Representations of Nonhuman Animals

A question raised by the findings of categorization at the basic level by infants concerns the perceived attributes of the stimuli—the diagnostic cues—that allow streams of exemplars from multiple categories to be separated into different category representations. Are the infants using specific parts, the pattern of correlation among the parts, or perhaps overall shape as a basis for categorization? One study indicates that information from the head and face region may provide the means by which infants form a category representation for cats that excludes dogs (Quinn & Eimas, 1996a). Three- and 4-month-olds were randomly assigned to one of three experimental conditions: Whole Animal, Head Only, and Body Only. Infants in the Whole Animal group were presented with cats and tested with novel cat–novel dog pairings. The Head Only and Body Only groups were familiarized and tested with the same animals as the Whole Animal group, but with their bodies and heads occluded, respectively. The results were that the infants preferred the novel dog stimuli in the Whole Animal and Head Only groups, but not in the Body Only group. The findings suggest that information from the head and face region provides young infants with a sufficient basis to form a category representation for cats that excludes dogs (see also Quinn, Eimas, & Tarr, 2001; Spencer, Quinn, Johnson, & Karmiloff-Smith, 1997). The outcomes imply further that young infants categorically represent nonhuman animals on the basis of perceptual part or feature information.

Within-Task Learning versus Previously Acquired Knowledge

An important issue regarding the category representations of infants is whether they are constructed (presumably on the basis of real-life experience) *before* the experiment began or whether the category representations are formed on-line, during the course of an experiment (Mareschal & Quinn, 2001). The former view would argue that infants recognize the photographs as representations of objects in the world with which they are already familiar and for which they have previous category knowledge. By this view, the familiarization phase of the familiarization/novelty-preference procedure would serve to prime the knowledge that the infants have already acquired outside the laboratory.

The latter view would have it that the format of the familiarization/novelty-preference procedure better lends itself to an interpretation that can be understood in terms of category formation. Infants are presumed to construct the category representation as more and more exemplars from the familiar category are presented (Mareschal, French, & Quinn, 2000). Even by this reasoning, however, it is difficult to completely rule out the possibility that knowledge access does not facilitate the performance of the participating infants. Consider, for example, 3- to 4-month-olds presented with cats or horses and then tested with exemplars from contrasting animal categories such as birds, dogs, tigers, giraffes, and zebras. Given that young infants are not likely to have observed (at least directly) animals such as giraffes or zebras or the particular cat and horse exemplars to be presented in the task, one might be tempted to say that the participating infants rely exclusively on perceptual processing, and that they are forming the category representations during the course of the familiarization trials. However, parents are known to read to their infants from picture books that may contain pictorial exemplars of animals. In addition, even young infants may be able to recognize that animals like giraffes and zebras are more like other animals that they do know about (e.g., humans) than furniture items (Quinn & Eimas, 1998). Thus, even in an experiment that is designed as a study of concept formation, it is possible that young infants may recruit from a preexisting knowledge base that at least in part determines their preference behavior.

This issue of whether the experiments are investigations into category formation or possession has been addressed in two ways. First, because a number of studies conducted by Quinn and collaborators have investigated whether infants form separate category representations for cats and dogs, it is possible to compare the categorization performance of infants that have been exposed to pets at home with those that have not. A variety of analyses have been performed, and none have revealed a facilitative effect of a home pet on categorization performance. These null results thus fail to support the suggestion that infant categorization of nonhuman animals in the laboratory is assisted by real-world experience with nonhuman animals occurring prior to arrival at the laboratory.

Another way to think about perceptual process and knowledge access as contributors to infant categorization performance is to argue that if infants have preformed representations for nonhuman animal species that are simply tapped into as a basis for performance during an experiment conducted with the familiarization/novelty-preference procedure, then it should prove difficult to manipulate categorization performance via perceptual perturbations to the stimuli. That is, via knowledge access, cats should be recognized as cats and dogs should be recognized as dogs. However, a series of experiments has shown that infant categorization performance for classes of cats and dogs can be manipulated. This was possible because of an asymmetry in categorization performance that was detected in the initial investigation of Quinn et al. (1993). Although infants familiarized with cats displayed a novelty preference for dogs compared with novel cats, infants familiarized with dogs did not display a preference for cats over novel dogs. In other words, infants familiarized with cats formed a category representation for cats that included novel cats, but excluded dogs, whereas infants familiarized with dogs formed a category representation for dogs that included both novel dogs as well as cats.

In follow-up investigations, it was demonstrated that the cat versus dog category asymmetry could not be explained via a spontaneous preference for dogs: Infants presented with cats versus dogs without prior familiarization did not have an a priori preference for the dogs (Quinn et al., 1993). However, through a combination of typicality ratings obtained from adults, computational modeling, and further experimentation with infants, the initial asymmetry was shown to reflect the fact that the dogs were more variable than the cats, causing the cats to be subsumed under the broader class of dogs (Mareschal et al., 2000; Quinn et al., 1993). In one experiment conducted with 3- to 4-month-olds, when the variability of the dog class was reduced, presumably removing the inclusion relation of cats within dogs, the asymmetry was removed (Quinn et al., 1993). In another experiment carried out with same age group, the inclusivity relation of the categories was reversed through a combination of stimulus selection and image processing, and the asymmetry was reversed: the infants formed a category representation for cats that included dogs, and a category representation for dogs that excluded cats (French, Mermillod, Quinn, & Mareschal, 2001). These studies of categorization cats versus dogs by young infants make the important point that at least in the case of nonhuman animals, the infants are forming their category representations over the course of the familiarization trials, rather than tapping into preexisting concepts that had been formed prior to arriving at the laboratory.

Categorization of Humans

Any theory of knowledge acquisition about animals must account for how a category representation of humans arises. Given the evidence just reviewed demonstrating categorization of various nonhuman animal species as distinct from each other, it seemed reasonable to presuppose that young infants would form a category representation for humans that would exclude nonhuman animal species. However, Carey (1985) has argued that young children may develop a naive theory of biology by organizing their knowledge of animals around people; by this view, humans may function as a prototype for the category of animals, and nonhuman animals might actually be incorporated into a broadly inclusive category representation of humans.

To investigate whether young infants represent humans as a category that is differentiated from nonhuman animal species, Quinn and Eimas (1998) familiarized a group of 3- to 4-month-old infants with photographic exemplars of 12 humans, both men and women, depicted in a variety of standing, running, or walking poses, and in earth tone (i.e., nonpastel) clothing. Each infant was then tested with a novel human paired with a cat, and a different novel human paired with a horse. The expectation was that infants would in each case prefer the novel instance of the novel category (i.e., novel cat or horse) over the novel instance from the familiar human category. To the investigators' surprise, the infants did not prefer novel cats or horses to novel humans. It is possible that an a priori preference for humans could have interfered with novel category preferences for cats and horses, but a control experiment pairing humans with cats and humans with horses over a series of spontaneous preference trials indicated that this was not the case.

The results of the initial experiments with humans were consistent with the idea that infants had either not formed a category representation for humans or that they had formed a category representation for humans that was broadly inclusive of both cats and horses. In follow-up experiments, evidence was obtained that supported the latter explanation. Three- and 4-month-olds were familiarized with 12 humans or 12 horses, and then given novel category preference tests in which a different novel member of the familiar category was paired with a novel member of the nonfamiliar category (horses or humans, respectively), a novel fish, and a novel car. The results, when considered in conjunction with the results of tests assessing a priori preferences among the categories, indicated the following: infants familiarized with humans had formed a category representation for humans that included novel humans, horses, and fish, but excluded cars, whereas infants familiarized with horses formed a category representation for horses that included novel horses, but excluded humans, fish, and cars.

The findings from the horse familiarization condition are consistent with the previous evidence demonstrating a high level of categorization among nonhuman animal categories. By contrast, the outcome of broad inclusivity obtained in the human familiarization condition indicates that infants represent humans as a global category. A category representation of this nature could behave as an attractor or perceptual magnet (Kuhl, 1991; Thelen & Smith, 1994) that acts to pull in nonhuman animal stimuli with at least some attributes in common with humans, e.g., a generic animal form consisting of a head attached to an elongated body with skeletal appendages. The findings demonstrating an asymmetry in the exclusivity of the category representations for humans and horses are moreover suggestive that Carey's (1985) results showing that young children classify animals on the basis of their similarity to people may have an early perceptual basis.

Category Representations of Humans versus Nonhuman Animals: Exemplars versus Prototypes

An additional experiment conducted by Quinn and Eimas (1998) provided further evidence that infants represent humans differently from nonhuman animal species. Because 3- to 4-month-olds have greater exposure to human than to nonhuman animals, even if the set of humans is limited to parents or immediate family members, it is an arguable consequence that infants represent the highly familiar human exemplars individually. Also plausible is the view that the less frequently encountered animals are represented by means of a summary prototype (Quinn, 1987). To investigate these possibilities, one group of 3- to 4-month-olds was familiarized with 12 humans, and another with 12 cats. Both groups were administered two preference tests. A novel cat was paired with a novel human in one (the test of categorization), and a novel member of the familiar category was paired with a familiar member of the familiar category in the other (a test of exemplar memory). The results revealed a significant interaction: infants familiarized with cats preferred a novel human to a novel cat, but not a novel cat to a familiar one, whereas infants familiarized with humans did not prefer a novel cat over a novel human, but did prefer a novel over a familiar human. Thus, the category representation formed by infants for humans included novel cats and was based on exemplars, whereas the representation for cats excluded novel humans and was based on a summary representation.

It becomes interesting to speculate on what may be responsible for human infants coming to represent humans differently from nonhuman animals during the first few months of life. One possibility is that frequent encounters with several familiar humans may drive infants to become human "experts" (cf. Schyns, 1991; Tanaka & Taylor, 1991). The suggestion is that infants may develop an exemplar-based representation of humans, i.e., subordinate-like representations for individual humans clustered together in a representation of humans in general. This broad representation is in opposition to some form of relatively narrow summary representation for other species. For example, the exemplar nature of the human representation could be taken as a cluster of exemplar points defining a human region in psychological space, rather than a single summary (i.e., prototype) point defining nonhuman animal species (e.g., cats, horses).

One might then ask how an exemplar-based representation for humans comes to be "magnet-like" and attractive of nonhuman animals. Because of the size difference between the "human" region and the "cat" or "horse" point, the representation for humans would be more accepting of a range of values along relevant attributes, and thus more likely to incorporate nonhuman animals. The formation of a category representation for humans that incorporates nonhuman animals may be an important part of the process of infants' developing a category representation for animals in general. From this perspective, humans may be the "glue" that provides the coherence for a category representation of animals.

The data also correspond with recently proposed ideas regarding the representation of expertise that have emerged in the perceptual learning and categorization literatures in adults (Gauthier & Tarr, 1997). In particular, the possibility that humans may be represented at a more advanced stage of processing than nonhuman animals is consistent with a hypothesized representational shift from a summary structure to exemplar-based memory during the overall time-course of category learning (Smith & Minda, 1998).

In addition, it is important to mention that the simple computational model that could simulate the cat versus dog asymmetry (i.e., a model that embodies only a short-term memory for within-task learning) could not simulate the human versus nonhuman animal asymmetry. However, a model that incorporates a long-term memory structure along with previous training on humans can simulate the human versus nonhuman animal asymmetry (Mermillod, French, Quinn, & Mareschal, 2004). In particular, it was shown that a "dual-network" connectionist architecture that incorporates both bottom-up (i.e., short-term memory) and top-down (i.e., long-term memory) processing was sufficient to account for the empirical results on categorization of humans versus nonhuman animals obtained with the infants. The dual-network memory model was able to reproduce the results of Quinn and Eimas (1998) because the LTM network contained a representation of humans that influenced processing in the STM network. In particular, this LTM information had the effect of increasing the attractor basin for humans, causing it to largely include nonhuman animals (e.g., cats, horses), thereby giving rise to the asymmetry reported by Quinn and Eimas (1998). The computational data are thus consistent with the descriptive account of the human versus nonhuman animal asymmetry offered by Quinn and Eimas (1998).

Perceptual Cues for a Category Representation of Humans

One issue not yet discussed is the information used by infants to form a category representation for humans. A recent study investigated this question and specifically examined the perceptual information that was the basis for the human versus nonhuman animal asymmetry (Quinn, 2004). The experiment followed from the investigation of whether infants formed category representations for nonhuman animal species based on information from the whole animal, head, or body (Quinn & Eimas, 1996a). Three- and 4-month-old infants were familiarized with 12 exemplars of humans or 12 exemplars of cats, and tested with a novel human versus a novel cat. Within the human and cat conditions, the infants were randomly assigned to one of three experimental groups: Whole Animal, Head Only, and Body Only. In the Whole Animal Group, infants were familiarized and tested with entire, intact stimuli (head + body). In the Head Only group, only the heads of the stimuli were visible; the body information had been occluded. In the Body Only group, only the bodies of the stimuli were visible; the head information had been occluded. Examples of the stimuli are presented in Figure 5.8. The particular form of the asymmetry, a category representation for cats that excludes humans and a category representation for humans that includes cats, was observed only with the Whole Animal stimuli. Neither head nor body information alone were sufficient to produce the asymmetry. The results suggest that the incorporation of nonhuman animal species into a broadly inclusive category representation of humans may be based on the overall structure of the stimuli (e.g., a head region adjoining an elongated body axis with skeletal appendages). This finding, that the human representation is based on global Gestalt information, contrasts with the findings that representations for nonhuman animal species may be based on part or attribute (i.e., featural) information—heads in the case of cats versus dogs.

The data correspond well with the notion that young infants may be representing humans at an "expert" level and with recently proposed ideas regarding the representation of expertise that have emerged in the cognitive neuroscience literature (Gauthier & Nelson, 2001; Gauthier & Tarr, 2002). In particular, Gauthier and colleagues have argued that an area of the fusiform gyrus in the brains of adults, once believed to represent faces specifically, actually represents expert knowledge more generally. Moreover, these researchers have demonstrated that expert object recognition by this brain area is characterized by holistic-configural processing. The results described here are consistent with the idea that young infants may already possess an "expert" representation for humans that is based on holistic information.

Figure 5.8 Black and white examples of the nonhuman animals and human exemplars in the Whole Stimulus, Head Only, and Body Only depictions of Quinn (2004).

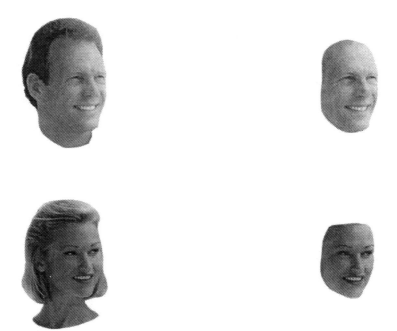

Figure 5.9 Black and white examples of the human face stimuli (with and without hair) used in Quinn, Yahr, Kuhn, Slater, and Pascalis (2002).

Within-Task Learning versus Previously Acquired Knowledge Revisited

Thus far in the chapter, it has been argued that the representation of humans by young infants is influenced by experience occurring prior to the experiment. In this section, direct evidence for this suggestion will be described. The experiments to be discussed investigate how infants categorize a human attribute, namely, the gender of human faces. In particular, Quinn, Yahr, Kuhn, Slater, and Pascalis (2002) used the familiarization/novelty-preference procedure to examine the representation of the gender of human faces by 3- to 4-month-olds. The faces were color photographs of female and male models. The female and male faces had neutral to slightly positive emotional expression, were judged to be of comparable attractiveness, and matched for direction of gaze. Examples are shown in the left half of Figure 5.9. In the first experiment, infants were administered familiarization trials with 8 male or female faces and then given test trials with a novel male face paired with a novel female face. The findings were that infants familiarized with males preferred females, but infants familiarized with females did not prefer males. Interestingly, this asymmetrical pattern of results had also been reported for older infants in the age range from 5 to 12 months by Leinbach and Fagot (1993).

In a second experiment, a possible explanation for the asymmetry, namely, that infants might spontaneously prefer female faces, was explored by presenting a group of 3- to 4-month-olds with a series of preference trials, each of which paired a different male face with a different female face. A mean preference for females was observed. The asymmetry reported in the categorization experiment thus appears to be the result of a spontaneous preference for female faces. This spontaneous preference could have facilitated a novel category preference for females after familiarization with males, and interfered with a novel category preference for males after familiarization with females.

In additional experiments, two lower-level sensory explanations for the spontaneous preference for female faces were assessed. The first inquiry was whether the spontaneous preference for female faces might be attributable to higher external contrast information resulting from a greater amount of hair surrounding the internal face region of the stimuli. The experiment assessing spontaneous preference was thus repeated, but in this instance with face stimuli without external hair cues. Examples are shown in the right half of Figure 5.9. Here, the infants still preferred the female faces, indicating that the preference for female faces is not the result of higher external contrast created by a greater amount of hair.

The second inquiry was whether the spontaneous preference for female faces was due to higher contrast of the internal features, possibly resulting from females' greater use of cosmetics. The first control experiment with faces without hair was thus repeated, but in this instance, the faces were inverted. The reasoning was that if the female preference was due to higher contrast of the internal features, then the preference should be preserved with the inversion manipulation, because the internal features are present in both upright and inverted faces. The result was that the infants no longer preferred the female faces, suggesting that the spontaneous preference depends on processing of the internal features in their upright orientation.

Given that the evidence did not support sensory explanations for the female face preference displayed by young infants, a cognitive explanation for the preference was investigated. This explanation rests on the idea that infants might prefer female over male faces because of greater familiarity with female faces. It is known that familiarity preferences can be observed in face comparisons as is evidenced by the finding that young infants will display a spontaneous preference for mother's face over a strange female face, even in the absence of external hair cues (Bartrip, Morton, & de Schonen, 2001). In addition, a majority of infants in the first 3 months of life are reared with female primary caregivers, and this was true for all the infants thus far described for the experiments of Quinn et al. (2002). These observations led to the hypothesis that infants might generalize their experiences with primary caregivers who are female to female faces more generally (at least when compared with male faces). The argument is that young infants reared with a female primary caregiver may possess an additional expertise-related advantage at processing female faces relative to processing male faces. Adult participants display an other-race effect in identification of human faces that may be the result of differential experience (O'Toole, Deffenbacher, Abdi, & Bartlett, 1991), and the hypothesis advanced here is that young infants may display an other-gender effect in the processing of human faces that results from early differential experience.

If young infants reared with female primary caregivers become "female experts," then it should be possible to reverse the gender preference in infants reared with male primary caregivers. Although far fewer infants are reared primarily by their fathers, Quinn et al. (2002) and Quinn (2003) tested 8 such infants, between 3 and 4 months of age. On the spontaneous preference test between upright male and female faces without hair, 7 of the 8 infants preferred the male faces. This outcome is consistent with the idea that infant attention to human stimuli may be biased toward the gender with which the infant has greater experience. More broadly, it provides evidence for the suggestion that representation of humans by infants as assessed in laboratory tasks is influenced by experiences occurring prior to participation in the tasks.

Summary

There are several important findings emerging from the studies examining young infants' abilities to form category representations for pictorial exemplars of nonhuman animals, furniture, and humans. First, infants can form both basic-level category representations for natural animal species and furniture artifacts. Second, representations for nonhuman animals are formed on-line during the course of an experiment, based on perceptual attribute or part information, and structured with summary-level information. Third, the representation for humans is observed to be global and magnet-like in attracting nonhuman animals, influenced by experience acquired prior to performing in the laboratory, structured by individual exemplars, and based on holistic, Gestalt information. As will be discussed in the concluding section of the chapter, the differences in the way that infants represent humans versus nonhuman animals may have implications for both the processes that infants deploy to organize experience and the developmental status of the resulting representations.

CONCLUDING COMMENTS

The question of "how to build a baby" has been a matter of debate among theorists of early cognitive development since the writings of Piaget (1952; see for example, Carey, 1985; Elman, Bates, Johnson, Karmiloff-Smith, Parisi, & Plunkett, 1996; Karmiloff-Smith, 1992; Keil, 1989; Mandler, 1988, 1992; Quinn & Eimas, 1996b, 1997, 2000; Spelke, 1994). What mechanisms and knowledge does one build into the infant? What structure is available in the environment? The approach taken in the present chapter has been to document the representations for objects that can emerge from a young infant's adherence to the fundamental grouping processes of organization and categorization.

We have observed that coherent representations for individual shapes may develop through the application of Gestalt principles such as lightness similarity, form similarity, and good continuation. The ability to use perceptual similarity to group individual elements of a single visual pattern may be extended to the formation of category representations for multiple stimulus patterns presented over time. Extraction of regularities from a set of exemplars by means of a summary representation may occur for stimulus classes such as basic-level categories of nonhuman animal species. Differential experience with humans versus other categories of stimulation may facilitate a kind of representational magnification for humans, with the consequence that the representation for humans becomes simultaneously exemplar-based and magnet-like.

It would seem that a considerable degree of coherence and order emerges in the application and reapplication of basic core processes that function to group elements of objects to form perceptual wholes and to group multiple objects into perceptual categories. Core processes may include (1) deployment of Gestalt organizational principles, (2) representation of within-category similarity and between-category dissimilarity, (3) registration of correlations among attributes, and (4) formation of summary representations (i.e., prototypes) from sets of exemplars. The explanatory framework proposed here for how infants begin to organize experience thus highlights the role of these core processes. It must also be recognized that the core processes allow infants to rapidly acquire functional knowledge that can in turn affect the subsequent utilization of the core processes. Support for this idea was observed in the Quinn and Schyns (2003) findings in which infant learning of a part characterized as nonnatural in the Gestalt sense in the context of category learning influenced the organization of later presented visual pattern information. Additional support for the theme that core processes yield functional knowledge comes with the recognition of the variety of differences that can be observed for the representation of humans versus nonhuman animals. Core processes that are applied to nonequivalently experienced inputs begin to yield representations that reflect more or less advanced levels of structuring. In the present case, young infants may represent humans at a more advanced stage of processing than nonhuman animals in a way that is consistent with the more generally recognized expert-novice difference in conceptual representation.

As investigations into the beginnings of knowledge acquisition continue, one question that remains for the theoretical account presented here is to determine more precisely how long-term experiential knowledge interacts with short-term experiential knowledge acquired during a series of familiarization trials to produce a particular pattern of looking on preference test trials. However this question is resolved, the proposed model of core processes that allow for the rapid build-up of a knowledge base about the world that can in turn influence subsequent responding can accommodate much of the data on organization and categorization by young infants, and may represent a viable framework for thinking about the early course of knowledge acquisition in general.

ACKNOWLEDGMENTS

Preparation of this chapter was supported by Grants HD-42451 and HD-46526 from the National Institute of Child Health and Human Development. The author thanks Lawrence Balter and Catherine S. Tamis-LeMonda for their comments on an earlier draft, and Jason E. Reiss for his assistance in creating the figures.

REFERENCES

Aslin, R. N. (2000). Why take the cog out of infant cognition? *Infancy, 1,* 463–470.

Atkinson, J., Braddick, O., & Moar, K. (1977). Development of contrast sensitivity over the first 3 months of life. *Vision Research, 17,* 1037–1044.

Baillargeon, R. (1999). Young infants' expectations about hidden objects: A reply to three challenges. *Developmental Science, 2*, 115–132.

Banks, M. S., & Ginsburg, M. S. (1985). Infant visual preferences: A review and new theoretical treatment. In H. W. Reese (Ed.), *Advances in child development and behavior* (vol. 19, pp. 207–246). New York: Academic Press.

Banks, M. S., & Salapatek, P. (1978). Acuity and contrast sensitivity in 1-, 2-, and 3-month-old human infants. *Investigative Ophthalmology and Visual Science, 17*, 361–365.

Banks, M. S., & Salapatek, P. (1981). Infant pattern vision: A new approach based on the contrast sensitivity function. *Journal of Experimental Child Psychology, 31*, 1–45.

Bartrip, J., Morton, J., & de Schonen, S. (2001). Responses to mother's face in 3-week to 5-month-old infants. *British Journal of Developmental Psychology, 19*, 219–232.

Behl-Chadha, G. (1996). Basic-level and superordinate-like categorical representations in early infancy. *Cognition, 60*, 105–141.

Behrmann, M., & Kimchi, R. (2003). What does visual agnosia tell us about perceptual organization and its relationship to object perception? *Journal of Experimental Psychology: Human Perception and Performance, 29*, 19–42.

Bhatt, R. S., Quinn, P. C., Chia, S., & Bertin, E. (2001, April). *The use of form similarity as a Gestalt organizing principle in infancy: Further evidence of a developmental change.* Presented at the meeting of the Society for Research in Child Development, Minneapolis, Minnesota.

Bremner, J. G. (1994). *Infancy.* Oxford: Blackwell.

Bruner, J. S., Olver, R. R., & Greenfield, P. M. (1966). *Studies in cognitive growth.* New York: Wiley.

Carey, S. (1985). *Conceptual change in childhood.* Cambridge, MA: MIT Press.

Carey, S. (2000). The origin of concepts. *Journal of Cognition and Development, 1*, 37–41.

Cohen, L. B., Chaput, H. H., & Cashon, C. H. (2002). A constructivist model of infant cognitive development. *Cognitive Development, 17*, 1323–1343.

Cohen, L. B., & Strauss, M. S. (1979). Concept acquisition in the human infant. *Child Development, 50*, 419–424.

Eimas, P. D., & Quinn, P. C. (1994). Studies on the formation of perceptually based basic-level categories in young infants. *Child Development, 65*, 903–917.

Eimas, P. D., Quinn, P. C., & Cowan, P. (1994). Development of exclusivity in perceptually-based categories of young infants. *Journal of Experimental Child Psychology, 58*, 418–431.

Elman, J. L., Bates, E. A., Johnson, M. H., Karmiloff-Smith, A., Parisi, D., & Plunkett, K. (1996). *Rethinking innateness: A connectionist perspective on development.* Cambridge, MA: MIT Press.

Fantz, R. L. (1964). Visual experience in infants: Decreased attention to familiar patterns relative to novel ones. *Science, 164*, 668–670.

Fantz, R. L., Fagan, J. F., III, & Miranda, S. B. (1975). Early visual selectivity as a function of pattern variables, previous experience, age from birth and conceptual and cognitive deficit. In L. B. Cohen & P. Salapatek (Eds.), *Infant perception: From sensation to cognition. Basic visual processes* (vol. 1, pp. 249–345). New York: Academic Press.

Farah, M. J. (1990). *Visual agnosia: Disorders of object recogni-*

tion and what they tell us about normal vision. Cambridge, MA: MIT Press.

Farroni, T., Valenza, E., Simion, F., & Umilta, C. (2000). Configural processing at birth: Evidence of perceptual organisation. *Perception, 29*, 355–372.

Fodor, J. A. (1983). *The modularity of mind: An essay on faculty psychology.* Cambridge, MA: MIT press.

French, R. M., Mermillod, M., Quinn, P. C., & Mareschal, D. (2001). Reversing category exclusivities in infant perceptual categorization: Simulations and data. In K. Stenning & J. Moore (Eds.), *Proceedings of the 23rd Annual Conference of the Cognitive Science Society* (pp. 307–312). Mahwah, NJ: Erlbaum.

Gauthier, I., & Nelson, C. A. (2001). The development of face expertise. *Current Opinion in Neurobiology, 11*, 219–224.

Gauthier, I., & Tarr, M. J. (1997). Becoming a "Greeble" expert: Exploring mechanisms for face recognition. *Vision Research, 37*, 1673–1681.

Gauthier, I., & Tarr, M. J. (2002). Unraveling mechanisms for expert object recognition: Bridging brain activity and behavior. *Journal of Experimental Psychology: Human Perception and Performance, 28*, 431–446.

Gilchrist, I. D., Humphreys, G. W., Riddoch, M. J., & Neumann, H. (1997). Luminance and edge information in grouping: A study using visual search. *Journal of Experimental Psychology: Human Perception and Performance, 23*, 464–480.

Ginsburg, A. P. (1986). Spatial filtering and visual form perception. In K. R. Boff, L. Kaufman, & J. P. Thomas (Eds.), *Handbook of perception and human performance* (Vol. 2, pp. 1–41). New York: Wiley.

Haith, M. M. (1998). Who put the cog in infant cognition? Is rich interpretation too costly? *Infant Behavior and Development, 21*, 167–179.

Hebb, D. O. (1949). *The organization of behavior.* New York: Wiley.

Helson, H. (1933). The fundamental propositions of Gestalt psychology. *Psychological Review, 40*, 13–32.

Johnson, S. P. (1997). Young infants' perception of object unity: Implications for the development of attentional and cognitive skills. *Current Directions in Psychological Science, 6*, 5–11.

Johnson, S. P. (1998). Object perception and object knowledge in young infants: A view from studies of visual development. In A. Slater (Ed.), *Perceptual development: Visual, auditory, and speech perception in infancy* (pp. 211–239). Hove, UK: Psychology Press.

Johnson, S. P., & Aslin, R. N. (1996). Perception of object unity in young infants: The roles of motion, depth, and orientation. *Cognitive Development, 11*, 161–180.

Karmiloff-Smith, A. (1992). *Beyond modularity.* Cambridge, MA: MIT Press.

Keil, F. C. (1989). *Concepts, kinds, and cognitive development.* Cambridge, MA: MIT Press.

Kellman, P. J. (1993). Kinematic foundations of infant visual perception. In C. Granrud (Ed.), *Carnegie Mellon symposia on cognition: Visual perception and cognition in infancy* (pp. 121–173). Hillsdale, NJ: Erlbaum.

Kellman, P. J. (1996). The origins of object perception. In R. Gelman & T. Kit-Fong Au (Eds.), *Perceptual and cognitive development* (pp. 3–48). San Diego: Academic Press.

Kellman, P. J., & Arterberry, M. E. (1998). *The cradle of knowledge: Development of perception in infancy.* Cambridge, MA: MIT Press.

Kellman, P. J., & Shipley, T. F. (1991). A theory of visual interpolation in object perception. *Cognitive Psychology, 23,* 141–221.

Koffka, K. (1935). *Principles of gestalt psychology.* New York: Harcourt, Brace & World.

Kohler, W. (1929). *Gestalt psychology.* New York: Horace Liveright.

Kuhl, P. K. (1991). Human adults and human infants show a "perceptual magnet effect" for the prototypes of speech categories, monkeys do not. *Perception & Psychophysics, 50,* 93–107.

Leinbach, M. D., & Fagot, B. I. (1993). Categorical habituation to male and female faces: Gender schematic processing in infancy. *Infant Behavior and Development, 16,* 317–332.

Mandler, J. M. (1988). How to build a baby: On the development of an accessible representational system. *Cognitive Development, 3,* 113–136.

Mandler, J. M. (1992). How to build a baby: II. Conceptual primitives. *Psychological Review, 99,* 587–604.

Mandler, J. M., & McDonough, L. (1993). Concept formation in infancy. *Cognitive Development, 8,* 291–318.

Mareschal, D., French, R. M., & Quinn, P. C. (2000). A connectionist account of asymmetric category learning in early infancy. *Developmental Psychology, 36,* 635–645.

Mermillod, M., French, R. M., Quinn, P. C., & Mareschal, D. (2004). The importance of long-term memory in infant perceptual categorization. In R. Alterman & D. Kirsh (Eds.), *Proceedings of the 25th annual conference of the Cognitive Science Society* (pp. 804–809). Mahwah, NJ: Erlbaum.

Mervis, C. B. (1987). Child-basic object categories and early development. In U. Neisser (Ed.), *Concepts and conceptual development* (pp. 201–233). Cambridge: Cambridge University Press.

Murphy, G. L. (2002). *The big book of concepts.* Cambridge, MA: MIT Press.

Needham, A. (1998). Infants' use of featural information in the segregation of stationary objects. *Infant Behavior and Development, 21,* 47–76.

Needham, A. (2001). Object recognition and object segregation in 4.5-month-old infants. *Journal of Experimental Child Psychology, 78,* 3–24.

Needham, A., & Baillargeon, R. (1997). Object segregation in 8-month-old infants. *Cognition, 62,* 121–149.

Needham, A., & Baillargeon, R. (1998). Effects of prior experience on 4.5-month-old infants' object segregation. *Infant Behavior and Development, 21,* 1–24.

Needham, A., Baillargeon, R., & Kaufman, L. (1997). Object segregation in infancy. In C. Rovee-Collier, & L. P. Lipsitt (Eds.), *Advances in Infancy Research* (vol. 11; pp. 1–44). Norwood, NJ: Ablex.

Needham, A., & Kaufman, J. (1997). Infants' integration of information from different sources in object segregation. *Early Development and Parenting, 6,* 137–147.

Oakes, L. M., Madole, K. L., & Cohen, L. B. (1991). Infants' object examining: Habituation and categorization. *Cognitive Development, 6,* 377–392.

O'Toole, A. J., Deffenbacher, K. A., Abdi, H., & Bartlett, J. C. (1991). Simulating the "other-race" effect as a problem in perceptual learning. *Connection Science, 3,* 163–178.

Peterson, M. A. (1994). Object recognition processes can and do operate before figure-ground organization. *Current Directions in Psychological Science, 3,* 105–111.

Peterson, M. A. (2001). Object perception. In E. B. Goldstein (Ed.), *Blackwell handbook of perception* (pp. 168–203). Malden, MA: Blackwell.

Piaget, J. (1952). *The origins of intelligence in children.* New York: Norton.

Quinn, P. C. (1987). The categorical representation of visual pattern information by young infants. *Cognition, 27,* 145–179.

Quinn, P. C. (2002a). Beyond prototypes: Asymmetries in infant categorization and what they teach us about the mechanisms guiding early knowledge acquisition. In R. Kail and H. Reese (Eds.), *Advances in child development and behavior* (vol. 29, pp. 161–193). San Diego: Academic Press.

Quinn, P. C. (2002b). Category representation in infants. *Current Directions in Psychological Science, 11,* 66–70.

Quinn, P. C. (2002c). Early categorization: A new synthesis. In U. Goswami (Ed.), *Blackwell Handbook of Childhood Cognitive Development* (pp. 84–101). Oxford: Blackwell.

Quinn, P. C. (2003, April). Why do young infants prefer female faces? In M. S. Strauss (Organizer), *Development of facial expertise in infancy.* Symposium conducted at the meeting of the Society for Research in Child Development, Tampa, FL.

Quinn, P. C. (2004). Is the asymmetry in young infants' categorization of humans versus nonhuman animals based on head, body, or global gestalt information? *Psychonomic Bulletin & Review, 11,* 92–97.

Quinn, P. C., & Bhatt, R. S. (2001). Object recognition and object segregation in infancy: Historical perspective, theoretical significance, "kinds" of knowledge, and relation to object categorization. *Journal of Experimental Child Psychology, 78,* 25–34.

Quinn, P. C., Bhatt, R. S., Brush, D., Grimes, A., & Sharpnack, H. (2002). Development of form similarity as a Gestalt grouping principle in infancy. *Psychological Science, 13,* 320–328.

Quinn, P. C., Brown, C. R., & Streppa, M. L. (1997). Perceptual organization of complex visual configurations by young infants. *Infant Behavior and Development, 20,* 35–46.

Quinn, P. C., Burke, S., & Rush, A. (1993). Part-whole perception in early infancy: Evidence for perceptual grouping produced by lightness similarity. *Infant Behavior and Development, 16,* 19–42.

Quinn, P. C., & Eimas, P. D. (1996a). Perceptual cues that permit categorical differentiation of animal species by infants. *Journal of Experimental Child Psychology, 63,* 189–211.

Quinn, P. C., & Eimas, P. D. (1996b). Perceptual organization and categorization in young infants. In C. Rovee-Collier & L. P. Lipsitt (Eds.), *Advances in infancy research* (vol. 10, pp. 1–36). Norwood, NJ: Ablex.

Quinn, P. C., & Eimas, P. D. (1997). A reexamination of the perceptual to conceptual shift in mental representations. *Review of General Psychology, 1,* 271–287.

Quinn, P. C., & Eimas, P. D. (1998). Evidence for a global categorical representation of humans by young infants. *Journal of Experimental Child Psychology, 69*, 151–174.

Quinn, P. C., & Eimas, P. D. (2000). The emergence of category representations during infancy: Are separate perceptual and conceptual processes required? *Journal of Cognition and Development, 1*, 55–61.

Quinn, P. C., Eimas, P. D., & Rosenkrantz, S. L. (1993). Evidence for representations of perceptually similar natural categories by 3- and 4-month-old infants. *Perception, 22*, 463–475.

Quinn, P. C., Eimas, P. D., & Tarr, M. J. (2001). Perceptual categorization of cat and dog silhouettes by 3- to 4-month-old infants. *Journal of Experimental Child Psychology, 79*, 78–94.

Quinn, P. C., & Schyns, P. G. (2003). What goes up may come down: Perceptual process and knowledge access in the organization of complex visual patterns by young infants. *Cognitive Science, 27*, 923–935.

Quinn, P. C., Yahr, J., Kuhn, A., Slater, A. M., & Pascalis, O. (2002). Representation of the gender of human faces by infants: A preference for female. *Perception, 31*, 1109–1121.

Schyns, P. G. (1991). A modular neural network model of concept acquisition. *Cognitive Science, 15*, 461–508.

Schyns, P. G., Goldstone, R. L., & Thibaut, J. P. (1998). The development of features in object concepts. *Behavioral and Brain Sciences, 21*, 1–54.

Slater, A. M. (1995). Visual perception and memory at birth. In C. Rovee-Collier & L. P. Lipsitt (Eds.), *Advances in infancy research* (vol. 9, pp. 107–162). Norwood, NJ: Ablex.

Smith, L. B. (1999). Do infants possess innate knowledge structures? The con side. *Developmental Science, 2*, 133–144.

Smith, E. E., & Medin, D. L. (1981). *Categories and concepts*. Cambridge: Harvard University Press.

Smith, J. D., & Minda, J. P. (1998). Prototypes in the mist: The early epochs of category learning. *Journal of Experimental Psychology: Learning, Memory, and Cognition, 24*, 1411–1436.

Spelke, E. S. (1982). Perceptual knowledge of objects in infancy. In J. Mehler, M. Garrett, & E. Walker (Eds.), *Perspectives on mental representation* (pp. 409–430). Hillsdale, NJ: Erlbaum.

Spelke, E. S. (1994). Initial knowledge: six suggestions. *Cognition, 50*, 431–445.

Spelke, E. S. (2000). Core knowledge. *American Psychologist, 55*, 1233–1243.

Spelke, E. S., Breinlinger, K., Jacobson, K., & Phillips, A. (1993). Gestalt relations and object perception: A developmental study. *Perception, 22*, 1483–1501.

Spelke, E. S., Gutheil, G., & Van de Walle, G. (1995). The development of object perception. In S. M. Kosslyn and D. N. Osherson (Eds.), *An invitation to cognitive science, 2nd ed.* (vol. 2, pp. 297–330). Cambridge, MA: MIT Press.

Spencer, J., Quinn, P. C., Johnson, M. H., & Karmiloff-Smith, A. (1997). Heads you win, tails you lose: Evidence for young infants categorizing mammals by head and facial attributes (Special Issue: Perceptual Development). *Early Development and Parenting, 6*, 113–126.

Tanaka, J. W., & Taylor, M. (1991). Object categorization and expertise: Is the basic level in the eye of the beholder? *Cognitive Psychology, 23*, 457–482.

Thelen, E., & Smith, L. B. (1994). *A dynamic systems approach to the development of cognition and action*. Cambridge, MA: MIT Press.

Trick, L. M., & Enns, J. T. (1997). Clusters precede shapes in perceptual organization. *Psychological Science, 8*, 124–129.

Vygotsky, L. S. (1962). *Thought and language* (E. Hanfmann & G. Vacar, Trans.). Cambridge, MA: MIT Press.

Waxman, S. R., & Markow, D. B. (1995). Words as invitations to form categories: Evidence from 12- to 13-month-old infants. *Cognitive Psychology, 29*, 257–302.

Wertheimer, M. (1923/1958). Principles of perceptual organization. In D. C. Beardslee & M. Wertheimer (Eds.), *Readings in perception* (pp. 115–135). Princeton, NJ: Van Nostrand. Translated from German by M. Wertheimer (originally published in 1923).

Xu, F., & Carey, S. (1996). Infants' metaphysics: The case of numerical identity. *Cognitive Psychology, 30*, 111–153.

Younger, B. A. (1990). Infants' detection of correlation among feature categories. *Child Development, 61*, 614–620.

Part II

Preschool Years

$\boxed{6}$

Peer Relations
in Young Children

Carollee Howes
Linda Lee

INTRODUCTION

A careful observer and listener can find young children exploring peer relations in all sorts of public spaces from playgrounds to grocery stores. Children barely able to toddle play peek-a-boo, run-and-chase, or simple pretend games like "I am pulling you in my wagon. We are going to the store." By 3 or 4 years of age, play becomes sophisticated with elaborate scripts and costumes. Children can say and act out. "We are going camping, and pretend that there is a bear, and you are the baby in your pajamas." "And I climb out of the tent and try to give the bear a cookie."

In this chapter we argue that, it is only within groups of peers that children develop both social interaction skills particular to peer interaction and construct social relationships particular to peers—friendships. The social interactions and relationships of the children within the group become the basis of that peer group's shared understandings and practices and a base for individual children's development. Through experiences within many different and at times overlapping in membership peer groups, children internalize representations of social relationships and of practices within peer groups that we assume influence their individual orientations to the social world as older children, adolescents, and adults.

Our approach to examining peer social interactions and relationships comes from a theoretical perspective best described as relationship development nested within socio-cultural contexts or cultural communities. In this framework a cultural community is defined as a grouping of people who participate in a shared set of practices and traditions (Rogoff, 2003). Peer groups are a kind of cultural community (Howes & Ritchie, 2002; Rogoff, 2003). As cultural communities peer groups construct shared understanding and meanings in forms that include shared scripts for pretend play, games, and conversations, knowledge of who hangs out with whom, who can and can not be trusted to gossip without hurting other people's feelings, and generally ways to behave within the group. These shared understandings and meanings are the practices of the peer community. Peer communities have shared histories as well as practices. Children within a peer group that lasts over time can remind each other of events that have meaning only within the context of the peer group, for example, "Remember when Sylvie was so mean to Nancy, and then they stopped being friends."

Much of the research on peer relations has been conducted as if all peer cultural communities were universally similar and thus developmental patterns were identical regardless of the characteristics of peer groups. We want to argue, in this chapter, that placing the development of peer interactions and friendships within cultural communities will help in resolving some of the contradictions that have persisted within the empirical literature on the topic. Take for example such a basic question of whether infants and toddlers engage in peer interaction. As we will discuss, research since the 1970s has documented that if 1-year-olds have regular playmates they engage in relatively sophisticated patterns of interactions (Lee, 1973; Rubenstein & Howes, 1976). However, if such young children are observed with unfamiliar peers they are fairly unskilled at interaction (Eckerman, Whatley, & Kutz, 1975). Many parents and teachers believe that infants and toddlers receive no benefit from peer interaction. Thus young children do not have regular playmates unless their families engage in practices that create baby peer groups such as enrolling the baby in child care, getting together regularly with friends who have same-age children, regularly attending a play group, or having regular extended family gatherings with age-mate children. Therefore in this example, the age of development of a particular social skill depends on belonging or not to a same-age regularly meeting peer group, and whether the child belongs to such a peer group depends on parent practices and values.

For another example, consider that children are in peer groups as diverse as those informally formed by living in a neighborhood, or by being part of a group of families that spends holidays or vacations together, or as formal as all the children in a child care arrangement, a school classroom, or a Scout Troop, or 4-H club, or religious club (Bryant, 1985; Ladd & Price, 1987; Medrich, Roizen, Rubin, & Buckley, 1982). The practices or ways to do things within each of these peer groups are particular to the peer group. For example, cross-gender or cross-age friendships may flourish in informal neighborhood peer groups and be actively discouraged within classroom based peer groups. Peer groups in school may facilitate cross-ethnic, cross-religious, or cross-class friendships forbidden within informal setting peer groups. Since children simultaneously hold membership in overlapping peer groups, they may have social practices that are competent in one peer group and incompetent in another. For example, ways to do things in one group (e.g., making in-group references and jokes), may be ways of not doing things in another group (e.g. the same references are not understood and are seen as denoting someone who does not belong). Such bridging of these different cultural communities may be tied to adaptive competence in children, a keen understanding and awareness of the significance of social context (Coll et al., 1996).

LEARNING TO INTERACT: INFANTS AND TODDLERS

So how do children become a group? How do they figure out how to engage with each other? How do they form friendships with some children and not others? When children only entered same-age peer groups as preschoolers the answer was that children first learned social skills from their parents or perhaps from older siblings and cousins and then applied them to peers at some later time. When children enter same-age peer groups as infants the answer is not as clear. From the 1920s and 1930s until the early 1970s, the study of peer relations in the United States was dominated by early descriptive research about the ways in which individuals' social skills developed. Pioneer researchers in the 1930s (Buhler, 1930; Maudry & Nekula, 1939), just as all researchers in all periods, based their conclusions on the cultural communities that were available to them to study. Because the earliest researchers studied naturally occurring peer groups of infants and toddlers (milk distribution centers in New York City's Central Park and orphanages), they concluded that infants and toddlers engage in games and other early forms of peer interaction (Buhler, 1930; Maudry & Nekula, 1939). Partens (1932, 1933), a researcher frequently cited in today's text books, studied children in nursery schools willing to enroll only those children who were 2 years 9 months of age *and* toilet trained. She argued that all children progressed through a set of social participation categories from solitary play, through parallel play, to true social participation in the form of cooperative play. The 2-, almost 3-year-olds were the solitary players, the 3-year-olds the parallel players, and the older children the truly social children.

In retrospect, we can see that the development captured in Partens' theory was closely linked to the context in which the observations typically took place: nursery schools. Nursery schools were part of a social movement that was based on a particular belief system. Within this belief system, it was assumed that the ideal child rearing environment for preschoolers consisted of a "stay-at-home mother" and, two or three mornings a week, a socialization experience with children of similar backgrounds. The ideal child rearing environment for younger children did not include peers. According to Reed (1950), "The nursery school is a place where young children learn as they play and as they share experiences with other children" (p. 3).

> Living with a group of equals is a significantly different experience for a child from that of being a member of a family group. As students in the nursery school laboratory we can add to our understanding of what relationships mean to people as we observe the children in their living group. (Reed, 1950, p. 332)

The first and most influential nursery schools were physically located in colleges and universities and served as laboratories for the study of child development and for training professional teachers. Because research in peer relations and teacher training was confounded with a particular social organization, for 50 years, early childhood teachers in training and parents seeking advice were told that 2- and 3-year-olds were solitary or parallel players, while 5-year-olds were cooperative players.

Current research and theory on peer interaction supports an alternative perspective. The forms of play identified by Partens (1932) are not an invariant sequence based on age but, instead, are categories of play which tend to be used by children of all ages as the play they engage in with peers gradually shows more signs of structure, cognitive ability, and communicative ability (Bakeman & Brownlee, 1980). When research begins with a different set of assumptions and takes place in a different context, children as young as 10 to 12 months of age can be seen engaging at least one peer in cooperative play, which is more social than expected based on early theories (Howes, 1988b).

This alternative perspective was established because of two sociocultural changes: (a) research on peer relations moved out of laboratory schools, and (b) a social movement changed our beliefs about appropriate child rearing environments. In the 1970s, the women's movement and changes in the structuring of the United States economy led to an influx of mothers of very young children into the workforce. Part-day nursery schools could not accommodate the child care needs of these women. There was a dramatic increase in full-day child care centers that served infants and toddlers, instead of just preschoolers. These social changes changed the social context for constructing peer interactions, peer relationships, and peer social networks. In the social context of child care, peer interactions and relationships developed within long periods of "everyday life events" rather than within relatively brief "socialization experiences." Children in child care centers were with their peers every day and stayed in child care from breakfast time, through nap time, until the end of the day. The nursery school experience might be compared to a date, while the child care experience is more like living together.

Beyond structural changes in the social context of peer encounters, the women's movement changed the context in which the researchers were formulating their questions. They began to ask questions about the function of peers and peer relationships. Rather than simply being part of enrichment experiences, peers potentially could function to provide the child with experiences of social support, trust, and intimacy in the absence of the child's mother. Children who grew up together sharing the common resources of the child care center might engage in close rather than conflictual interaction. Cross-sex or cross-ethnic peers who became friends in a different environment than a traditional nuclear family might form different kinds of relationships. In the context of these questions, research on developmental changes in the complexity of peer interaction structure began.

Casual observations of infants and toddlers within full day child care settings suggested that they were not behaving according to Partens' (1932) observations: Their play was more interesting and complex than that of an onlooker or parallel player. Faced with this discrepancy, the first author conducted a qualitative study of two sets of infants from their first encounters in child care through the end of their first year together. Based on detailed narrative observations, both sets of children appeared to form friendships (Howes, 1981). This led to a program of research designed to understand how infants and toddlers constructed their play encounters within peer groups within child care centers.

To answer these new questions about preverbal children engaged with each other, we needed new tools for looking at peer interaction. In 1972, Blurton-Jones (1972) published an influential collection of observational studies of peer behaviors using ethological methods, with careful attention to the description and functional meaning of behaviors. Ethology had its roots in biology and the study of animal behavior. It provided a method for close, detailed observations of behavior. Subsequently, a generation of researchers including Eckerman, Davis, and Didow (1989), Hay (1985), Howes (1988b), Ross and Goldman (1976), and Vandell, Wilson, and Buchanan (1980) applied ethological methods to the task of identifying and describing changing structures underlying peer interaction.

One descriptive system that emerged from this research was the Peer Play Scale (Howes, 1980, 1988b; Howes & Matheson, 1992). Because each of the points of the scale represent increases in the complexity of play, we will use the scale to frame our discussion of how young children participate in constructing social structures within peer groups. There are several assumptions underlying the peer play scale. One assumption is that a necessary condition for children to be considered friends is that adult observers can infer from their behavior that each child understood the other to be a social actor and that social actions between partners could be coordinated and communicated (Howes, 1983, 1996). Therefore, as a starting place, research had to establish that children behaved as if they had these understandings. A second assumption is that later development in social play could occur only as the child increasingly understood the role of the other, incorporated symbolic play, and communicated shared meaning (Howes, Unger, & Seidner, 1989). These assumptions are the bases for the behaviors that are captured in the Peer Play Scale. Initially, children are expected to show signs of each of these three components but, eventually, they are expected to use them fluidly and communicate negotiations with each other about their play.

There are two key aspects of early play that presuppose such social understanding: mutual social awareness and coordination of action. Together, these two markers represent the necessary components for what Howes (1980) called complementary and reciprocal play. Specifically, each play partner's actions reverse the actions of the other. A child chases his or her partner, then is chased. One child peeks at his or her partner, the partner says boo, and then peeks back. Research in cognitive and communicative development (Howes, 1988b) suggests that the representational underpinnings of these understandings are present in children as young as the toddler developmental period. Naturalistic observations (Howes, 1980, 1988b) established that toddler-age children constructing their peer interactions within full-time child care centers were indeed engaging in complementary and reciprocal play.

CONSTRUCTING SHARED MEANINGS: TODDLERS AND PRESCHOOLERS

The next developmental step is to incorporate symbols into shared play. Children in peer group settings first begin to use symbols or to play pretend alone or with a competent adult player (Howes, 1985b; Howes & Matheson, 1992; Howes, with Unger, & Matheson, 1992), but symbolic play soon enters the realm of peer play. Pretend play with a partner requires both that the child manipulate symbolic transformations and communicate the resulting symbolic meaning to a partner. We see the simplest form of social pretend play, called *cooperative social pretend play* in Peer Play Scale terminology, among toddlers in full-time child care centers. Note that once more we are placing a developmental event within a particular socio-cultural context. Central to this level of structure of interaction is that children enact nonliteral role exchanges (Howes, 1985b; Howes et al., 1989). Play partners integrate their pretend actions by using a familiar pretend theme or script such as a tea party. Similarly to complementary and reciprocal play, cooperative social pretend play requires that children reverse the actions of the other but, in this form of play, the actions are nonliteral or symbolic. The actions of the children presuppose that each partner understands that each player may engage in the symbolic behaviors. The children are able to share understanding about the symbolic meaning of their play, but this is communicated through the implicit script of the play rather than explicit talk about the play.

For example, when a toddler offers a cup to a partner who is holding a pitcher, the child is engaged in a very simple form of social pretend play compared to the preschool-age child who discusses the play script, sets the table, brings festively dressed toy bears to the table, and gives the bears a tea party. Nonetheless, toddler-age children are beginning to understand the role of the partner in constructing social sequences.

Despite the new skills incorporated into cooperative social pretend play, it remains a pale imitation of the well-developed fantasy play of older children that we label complex social pretend play. Toddlers have only just begun to transform symbols so their transformations are not fluid and may be only partially developed. By preschool age, children's symbolic, linguistic, and communicative development permits meta-communication about social pretend play. Children can plan and negotiate the sequences of symbolic actions with fluidity, modify the script as it progresses, and step out of the pretend frame to correct the actions or script. These behaviors, such as those seen in a tea party for the toy bears, indicate the most structurally complex play captured in the Peer Play Scale. This play form is labeled *complex social pretend play*.

The Peer Play Scale is based on a set of measurement assumptions: the play forms develop in the predicted sequence and children develop particular play forms before or during particular age intervals predicted by theories of cognitive and communicative development (Howes, 1987; Howes, with Unger et al., 1992). Longitudinal (Howes & Matheson, 1992) and cross-sectional studies (Howes, 1980, 1985b) which focused on validating the Peer Play Scale supported these two assumptions. For example, in a longitudinal study of 48 children all in full-time child care centers and observed at 6-month intervals, we calculated each child's highest level of the Peer Play Scale during each observation period (Howes & Matheson, 1992). More than half of the children had engaged in complementary and reciprocal peer play by 13 to 15 months and nearly all by 19 to 23 months. More than half of the children had engaged in cooperative social pretend play by 30 to 35 months, and nearly half of the children had engaged in complex social pretend by 42 to 47 months. Seventy-four percent of the children followed the predicted sequence for emergence of play forms: complementary and reciprocal play, cooperative social pretend play, and complex social pretend play. Furthermore, children who showed earlier emergence of complementary and reciprocal play also showed earlier emergence of cooperative and complex social pretend play.

As a measure of structural complexity, the Peer Play Scale makes no distinctions among positive, aggressive, or agonistic (instrumental aggression such as toy taking) social bids. A structurally complex interaction could reflect prosocial behavior, a conflict, or any number of social styles. As we discuss below, research examining associations between the structure and content of peer interaction appeared later in the 1980s and 1990s.

Perhaps because it captures structural complexity rather than the content of peer play, the Peer Play Scale has been successfully used in cultures other than the United States. Farver has used the Peer Play Scale to describe and examine peer interaction in such diverse cultures and ethnic groups as Mexican children (Farver, 1992), Latino and African American Head Start children in Los Angeles (Farver & Frosch, 1996; Farver, 1996), Indonesian children (Farver & Howes, 1988; Farver & Wimbarti, 1995), and Korean American children (Farver, 2000; Farver & Shin, 1997; Farver, Kim, & Lee, 1995). Across studies, children's play was represented at each structural play level and play forms emerged at similar ages. When differences emerged, they were in the frequency of play forms rather than in different play forms or a different sequence of play. Farver (1996) suggested that the sociocultural context influences the style or frequencies of peer play. In particular the types of themes in pretend play appear rooted within children's particular cultural communities (Goncu, 2002). Whether children play at wrapping the "babies" in shawls and placing them on their backs or enacting the latest TV superhero's antics is dependent on the practices of daily life within their cultural community.

Gender also appears to influence the style rather than the structure of peer play. There are well-established differences in the content of the play of boys and girls (Fabes, Hanish, & Martin, 2003; Maccoby, 1988, 1990; Martin & Fabes, 2001). However, consistent with the lack of cultural and ethnic differences in the structure of peer play, there appear to be few differences in the complexity of the structure of children's peer play (Howes, 1980, 1988b; Howes & Matheson, 1992; Howes & Wu, 1990). Girls and boys of the same age engage in structurally similar play when the content differs. For example, both a game of mother, sister, and baby among girls and a game of the day the tigers ate the village among boys are very likely to be rated as complex social pretend play.

However, consistent with a Vygotskian perspective, the complexity of the structure of play is influenced by the skill level of the play partner. If the sociocultural context of the peer group includes mixed age children such as in family child care homes, toddlers play more skillfully with their peers when their partner is somewhat older and presumably more skilled at play (Howes & Farver 1987a; Rothstein-Fisch & Howes, 1988). In contrast, when the mother is present as in parent cooperative preschools the presence of the child's mother appears to reduce the complexity of peer interaction (Smith & Howes, 1994). Similarly when adults engage with children in preschool settings, peer interaction is inhibited (Harper & McCluskey, 2003; Kontos & Keyes, 1999). Although adults are more skilled play partner than children, peer play in the presence of an adult may be less skillful because three partner interaction is more difficult than dyadic interaction or because adult-child play content is different from child–child play content (Howes, with Unger et al., 1992).

FORMING SOCIAL STRUCTURES WITHIN PEER GROUPS: I'LL BE YOUR FRIEND IF...

Young children's peer interaction is organized around networks of play partners (Howes, 1983, 1988b). Within any peer group, there are children who prefer to play with each other, and children who prefer not to play with each other. Some children have no problem finding and keeping play partners, while others have difficulty entering peer groups and sustaining play. Children as young as 3 years old who have experienced full time child care in stable peer groups can describe these patterns of peer acceptance within their classroom (Howes, 1988b). When shown pictures of all children in the classroom, they can identify by name each child in the classroom and reliably rate how much they would want that child as a friend. This picture sociometric procedure provides a description of social status.

In the late 1970s, a series of longitudinal studies were published suggesting that children's peer acceptance in middle childhood was associated with positive mental health outcomes in adulthood (Parker & Asher, 1987). These studies precipitated a period of intense research into children's sociometric status (e.g., Coie & Dodge, 1983; Ladd, 1983) and continues as an important area of research (Crick & Dodge, 1999; Stormshak et al., 1999). The term sociometric refers to ways of measuring peer acceptance and friendships. *Sociometric nominations* involve asking each child in a defined group to identify the children that he or she likes and the children that he or she dislikes as one means to determine peer acceptance. Children with reciprocated nominations of liking are usually considered friends. Children also can be assigned a *sociometric rating* based on the average of ratings provided by each of the children in the group. Social status groups (popular, rejected, neglected, and average) are formed using either nominations or ratings. Popular children have high liking and low disliking profiles. Rejected children have low liking and high disliking profiles. Neglected children have low liking and low disliking profiles. Average children fit none of the other profiles. Peer acceptance refers to high ratings or many positive and few negative nominations.

Studies of sociometric status found that children who were classified as popular or more socially accepted were more friendly and prosocial, and less likely than children who were not accepted to engage in aggressive behaviors with peers (Asher & Coie, 1990; Coie 1990). Although the original research was conducted in elementary school classrooms, similar findings have emerged in preschool settings (Walden, 1999). Furthermore, sociometric status tended to be stable over time (Asher & Coie, 1990). These findings based on sociometric measures raised two questions about the Peer Play Scale. First, if the Peer Play Scale represents socially competent behavior with peers, would children who engage in structurally complex play also have higher peer acceptance and engage in prosocial, nonaggressive interactions with peers? Second, is competent peer play stable over developmental periods? That is, does demonstrating marker behaviors of structurally complex peer interaction during an earlier developmental period predict engaging in marker behaviors of structurally complex peer interaction during a later developmental period?

Two longitudinal studies addressed the first question. In the first, 48 children were observed with their peers in their child care centers at 6-month intervals beginning at age 13 to 24 months (Howes & Matheson, 1992; Howes, Phillipsen, & Hamilton, 1993). Within developmental periods, independent observers rated children who engaged in more complex play as more prosocial and sociable, and less aggressive. Children tended to be stable over time in positive, gregarious, and aggressive behaviors. Children who engaged in more complex play at earlier developmental periods were observed and rated as more prosocial and sociable, and less aggressive and withdrawn, during subsequent periods.

Another longitudinal study followed 85 children from 12 months through adolescence. Children were observed with peers soon after entering group child care (Howes, Rodning, Galluzzo, & Myers, 1988) and again at 4 years of age (Howes, Hamilton, & Matheson, 1994). In addition, at these time period both preschool teachers and independent observers rated aggression and social withdrawal when the children were toddlers and, again, when they were preschoolers. When the children were 9 years of age, aggression, social withdrawal, and prosocial behaviors with peers were rated by elementary school teachers. Children who engaged in more complex play with peers as toddlers were more prosocial, engaged in more complex play, and were less withdrawn as preschoolers, and were less aggressive and withdrawn at age 9. Children who were either more aggressive or more withdrawn as preschoolers were more aggressive as 9-year-olds (Howes & Phillipsen, 1998). Children who were rated by teachers as having close friendships in preschool rated themselves as having a more positive friendship in middle childhood (Howes , Hamilton, & Phillipsen, 1998). Children who rated themselves as having a more positive friendship in middle childhood and who had a history of positive friendships as preschoolers rated themselves as having more positive friendships in early (Howes & Tonyan, 2000) and mid-adolescence (Howes & Aikins, 2002). The last two of these findings are important in that the peer relations literature has relatively few studies that follow children longitudinally from very early childhood into adolescence. They suggest that social competency in peer relations may be quite stable. Some of this stability may occur because once children develop early social skills with peers they continue to use them and become the type of older children who are comfortable and easy interacting with peers. On the other hand, the children who are shy or aggressive in early peer interactions have fewer and fewer opportunities to learn how to be comfortable and easy with peers as they become more isolated from positive peer interactions.

In a second more short term longitudinal study of stability in social skills with peers, 329 children between the ages of 12 and 53 months participated for 1, 2, or 3 years in a study of the development of social interaction with peers (Howes, 1988b). Naturalistic observations of peer play were conducted on a yearly basis. Complementary and reciprocal play in the early toddler period (13–23 months) predicted cooperative social pretend play in the late toddler period (24–35 months). Cooperative social pretend play predicted sociometric ratings in the preschool period. An extension of this longitudinal study, limited to 45 children who remained in the same school from prekindergarten through third grade, found that sociometric ratings in prekindergarten and kindergarten were associated with sociometric ratings in third grade (Howes, 1990). That is, children who more often engaged in complex social pretend play in their first year in the peer group were rated as more popular with the peers in this group 3 years later.

This last finding brings us full circle back to the idea first stated in the introduction that peer groups become a form of cultural community with its own particular practices and traditions. When the peers in their peer group accept children and the peer group socializes prosocial behavior this can be a wonderful context for individual development. The complement of this statement may also be true if the social status structure of a peer groups comes to be part of its practices and traditions, children who are not well accepted have a difficult time.

The natural variation in familiarity and stability of peer partners provides an opportunity to examine socio-cultural variations in children's experiences in peer groups. An example of this natural variation is found in study discussed above (Howes, 1988b). In the first year of the study, children were recruited from child care classrooms with peer groups that remained intact for 1 year. In each subsequent year of the study, investigators both returned to the original peer groups and followed children who moved to different child care centers. Thus, in the second year of the study, the sample included four distinct groups of children: (a) the children who had been in the toddler room of a particular child care center the previous year and who had moved "up" to the preschool room in the same center; (b) the children who had been newly enrolled in the original child care centers to fill in preschool classroom peer groups (generally, group size increases with age); (c) the children who were in the sample in year 1, but had changed child care centers; and (d) the children who were in the same child care center classrooms as the children from year 1 who had moved to different child care centers. The results of this study suggested that toddler and preschool peer interaction is more skillful when children enroll in group settings at earlier ages, and when they remain with the same peer group for longer periods of time (Howes, 1988b).

That is, it appears to be advantageous for children to enter peer groups as younger children and to maintain a familiar and stable peer network. Some children who moved between child care centers actually moved with a peer group, as opposed to moving to a child care center with an entirely new peer group. Those children who were able to move with a peer group, and who therefore did not have to reestablish relationships, were more competent in peer interaction (Howes, 1988b).

Of course, some peer groups might promote more social competence than others. In general children are more socially competent within a peer group if the peer group is within a child care program, center or family child care that is more supportive of positive relationships (Howes & Matheson, 1992; Howes, Phillips, & Whitebook, 1992; Howes & Stewart, 1987). These findings point to the importance of adults' structuring a child care environment which supports the construction of positive and skillful peer interaction (Howes, 2000). In a recent study the social-emotional climate of the child care environment as well as children's individual social competence and teacher-child relationships predicted social competence with peers five years after children were in child care.

A recent report of the NICHD early child care research study highlights these concerns (ECCRN, 2003). The NICHD study reported that at ages 2 and 3 children who had experienced positive and responsive caregivers and the opportunity to engage with other children in child care were observed to be more positive and skillful in their peer play in child care but not in play with a friend in a laboratory (ECCRN, 2001). When the children were 4-1/2 years old and in kindergarten, teachers, caregivers, and mothers rated children with more time in child care as having more problematic relationships and behaviors with others (ECCRN, 2003). While overall measures of child care quality did not mediate this relationship between time in child care and problematic behavior this study did not include specific measures of adult structuring of peer relationships. As one of the commentaries on this study suggests perhaps it was not the amount of child care but amount of time in a kind of child care that fosters individualistic rather than cooperative interactions with others (Maccoby & Lewis, 2003).

How do adults structure a child care environment that promotes positive peer relations? Not it turns out by coaching children in social skills. Inspired by the more traditional literature on the influence of adults on children's peer relations, Howes and colleagues conducted another 3-year longitudinal study of the development of peer relations that included a focus on a large number of adult behaviors that could be expected to enhance peer interaction (Howes & Galluzzo, 1994). These behaviors included teaching toddlers turn-taking games and structuring their peer interactions to support these games, intervening to redirect agonistic encounters, and so forth. Therefore, as well as coding the structure and content of children's interactions with peers, we also noted any simultaneously occurring adult behaviors. The findings of this study suggested that adults working with groups of children rarely engaged in such behaviors and whether or not they did so had no association with the development of toddlers' and preschoolers' social competence with their peers.

A more promising line of research examined relations between children's attachment relationship quality with the primary caregivers in the child care setting and the development of children's social competence with peers (Howes, 1999). Adult caregiving behaviors directly influence children's attachment relationships that, in turn, influence peer relations. More specifically, more securely attached children have caregivers who are rated as more sensitive and responsive to the children in their care (Howes, 1999). In turn, children who are more securely attached to their child care providers are more socially competent with their peers (Howes, 1997a, b; Howes et al., 1994; Howes, Matheson, & Hamilton, 1994). When children's attachment relationships with their child care provider are contrasted with their attachment relationships with their mothers, the child care attachment relationship is more powerful in predicting social competence with peers (Howes, Matheson, & Hamilton, 1994b). We suspect that this is because these adults are physically present with the children's earliest experiences within peer groups. The children can use the child care provider as a secure base as they explore interactions and relationships within the peer group.

Unfortunately, child care providers are not a stable presence in children's lives. In contrast, mothers usually remain constant. Changing child care providers appears to have implications for children's social competence with peers. In a 3-year longitudinal study, children who had the most changes in primary child care providers were most aggressive with peers (Howes & Hamilton, 1993). In this study, some of the caregiver changes had a positive effect in the short term: The child was able to construct a more secure relationship with the new provider than with the old and, simultaneously, became more skilled with peers. However, it appears that the cumulative effect of instability in child care caregivers is detrimental to the development of positive social competence with peers.

Broadening the study of peer relations to include a more careful examination of child–caregiver relationships has led to a particularly fruitful series of research studies. The evidence that children construct interactions and relationships with their peers from infancy onward highlights the importance of these early peer relationships. Likewise, the relationships that children form with the adults who supervise their encounters with peers influence social competence. It is noteworthy that both of these types of relationships, with peers as friends and with child care providers, are relationships outside of the family. While these results should in no way downplay the importance of family influences on child development, carefully examining alternative relationships underscores the value of social networks both inside and outside of the family.

Friendship As Affective Relationships

Up until this point in this chapter we have been discussing how children construct social skills and peer group social structure. We have been (almost) acting as if all dyadic relationships within the peer group were interchangeable. That is that dyads are created at random and that every possible dyad in the classroom interacts in a similar manner. And this is, of course, not true. Even the earliest of studies of the construction of peer interaction among infants (Lee, 1973) noted that babies seemed to form early preferences. And sociometric inquiry rests on the premise of differential preferences within the peer group. But are early friendships affective relationships or merely preferences? Friendships are relationships based on mutual support, affection, and companionship. School age children can articulate these qualities of friendship and tell an adult whether a friendship does or does not have these qualities. Infants and toddlers and even preschoolers do not have the verbal and cognitive capacities to articulate friendship characteristics. They simply say, "she is my friend." Are infants and toddlers able to form real friendship relationships based on mutual support, affection, and companionship or are all young friendships, including preschool friends, merely momentary playmates?

Again, both theoretical and sociocultural influences were important in shaping this emphasis on relationships. As intense research on social acceptance with peers and its correlates grew, so did a renewed interest in relationships as a context for development. In 1976, Hinde, an ethnologist, introduced the theoretical notion that relationships are more than a bidirectional effect of the influences of both partners. According to Hinde, a relationship is a new formation understood by examining not only the behaviors of both partners and their contingencies, but the pattern of relating unique to the two individuals (Hinde & Stevenson-Hinde, 1976).

Furthermore, the processes of relationship formation embedded in Bowlby's (1969, 1982) attachment theory began to be understood as also applicable to relationships other than the child–mother attachment (Howes, 1996). According to this reinterpretation of attachment theory, relationships (whether attachment or playmate relationships) develop through multiple and recursive interactive experiences. Recursive interactions are well-scripted social exchanges which are repeated many times with only slight variation (Bretherton, 1985). Examples include infant caregiver interaction around bedtime or repeated toddler-age peer run-and-chase games. From these experiences, the infant or young child internalizes a set of fundamental social expectations about the behavioral dispositions of the partner (Bowlby, 1969/1982). These expectations form the basis for an internal working model of relationships. Therefore, through repeated experiences of social and social pretend play with a particular peer, a child forms an internal representation of playmate relationships. Some playmate relationships become friendship relationships. It is important to note that both the structure and the content of experiences interacting with a partner are part of the child's representation of the partner. Children who engage in more complex interactions are more likely to recognize the partner as a social other and construct a relationship. Furthermore, the content of the interaction is likely to influence the quality of the resulting relationship.

Sociocultural influences also played a role in the research interest in friendships between very young children. When infants and toddlers had daily experiences within the stable peer groups of child care, parents and child care teachers began to notice that the children had preferences among their peers (Hartup, 1983; Rubenstein & Howes, 1976, 1979; Rubin, 1980). These preferential playmate relationships appeared to parents and teachers as friendships. Teachers and parents reported that these emerging friendships helped children separate from their parents at the beginning of the child care day. The children would greet the preferred peer and join in play with him or her as part of the ritual for parents saying good-bye. In the following sections, we will discuss the process of friendship formation in very young children and the functions of these early friendships.

The Process of Friendship Formation
When the Children Cannot (Yet) Talk About Friendships

We define an *affective relationship* as one that includes feelings of affection or what would be called "love" in adult–child relationships. Toddler affective relationships have attributes of friendship common to the 'best friendships' which provide older children with emotional security and closeness (Howes, 1996; Howes, with Unger et al., 1992). These early friendship relationships appear to be formed in a way similar to adult–child attachment relationships (Howes, 1996). In the following section, we will examine supports for these assumptions about early friendship formation.

In a similar manner to the research on structural complexity of peer interaction, the friendship studies began with the collection of observational data. Since toddler-age children cannot report on their friendships, we must use behaviors to distinguish friendship relationships from playmate relationships in prelinguistic children. This results in some discontinuity in research about friendships because later research relies heavily on a child's ability to talk about friendships. For example, reciprocity of friendship is an important dimension of later friendship research, but cannot be explored in early childhood. Because early friendships can be defined only based on observed behavior, the earliest identified friendships must be reciprocal, with both partners engaging in defining behaviors.

We assume, in this work a three-part criteria for *friendship*: preference, recognition of the other as a social partner, and enjoyment (Howes, 1983, 1988b, 1996). Within this definition, children must prefer the company of the friend over the company of others and must enjoy the time they spend together to be considered friends. To operationalize these constructs for observational research, the following criteria were developed: (a) proximity (being within 3 feet of each other at least 30% of the observational period), (b) at least one instance of complementary and reciprocal play to indicate recognition of the other as a social partner, and (c) shared positive affect (both children expressing positive affect while engaged in interactive social play).

This definition was first used in a year-long longitudinal study of five peer groups (Howes, 1983). The children ranged in age from 10 months to 5 years. Each peer group was composed of same-age children. Eight times over the course of the year, we observed each child's interaction with every potential partner in the group. These observations were used to identify friend pairs. To test the assertion that toddler friendships were indeed affective relationships, we compared the three components of the behavioral definition (preference, recognition of the partner, and shared affect) to determine which component would identify the fewest friend pairs. The most stringent component was assumed to be most essential to friendship. Using shared positive affect to define friends identified the fewest friendships and, thus, was the most stringent part of the definition (Howes, 1983). This supports the premise that early friendships are affective relationships based on mutual affection.

What remained to be explored, however, were the processes of friendship formation. The 1983 study included three groups of typically developing children in full time child care and two groups of children in therapeutic settings. The processes of friendship formation were somewhat different in the typical and atypical children, providing a glimpse of how this process occurs as well as the aspects that might be essential for typical social development.

Typical Children

As found in the first longitudinal descriptive study of infants and toddlers new to peer groups, the earliest friendships appeared when the children were 10 months old (Howes, 1983). Children in this early toddler period (10 to 24 months) tended to form only one or two friendship relationships. In three different longitudinal samples, these early toddler friendship relationships tended to be very stable, lasting a year in the first study (Howes, 1983). That is, once identified, friend pairs appeared at every subsequent observation period. In the two subsequent 3-year studies previously discussed, we again identified friend pairs at each observation period and found that friend pairs formed in the early toddler period reappeared for the 3 years of the longitudinal (Howes, 1988b; Howes & Phillipsen, 1992). That is, at each observation period, we identified friendship pairs within peer groups using observers blind to previous friendships. We then computed the probabilities of a particular friendship pair reappearing in more than one observation period. Friendship pairs formed when the children were toddlers were most likely to reappear in subsequent periods.

Of particular interest, given the prevalence of same-gender friendships in preschool and older children, friendships formed in the early toddler period are as likely to be same- as cross-gender in composition (Howes & Phillipsen, 1992). Further, cross- and same-gender friendships are equally likely to be maintained over time if formed in the toddler period (Howes & Phillipsen, 1992). This is in sharp contrast to the friendships of preschool- and school-age children who tend to form and maintain same-gender friendships.

Children in the late toddler period (24 to 36 months) had more friendship relationships than younger children, perhaps because they begin to differentiate between the different functions of friendship (Howes, 1987, 1988b). Some peers become friends, while others remain playmates. To be considered a playmate, but not a friend, a pair meets the criteria for preference and the recognition of the partner portions of the friendship definition but not the affective sharing component. In the late toddler period, friendships must still be identified by behaviors as children under 3 years of age cannot reliably complete a sociometric task. Again, the affective component of behaviorally defined friendship is critical in distinguishing friends from playmates (Howes, 1983).

By preschool age, children can play with children that they do not consider to be friends. Toddler-age children's social interactions are more fragile and more dependent on rituals and routines than the social interactions of preschoolers. Therefore, toddlers, more often than preschoolers, play only with their friends. We assume that this is because patterns of interaction between toddlers are highly ritualized.

Although behavior identification of friends is still a reliable measure in preschool (Howes, 1988b; Howes & Phillipsen, 1992), children also can reliably identify friends using sociometric ratings and nominations (Howes, 1988b). Beginning at age 3 and if they are enrolled in full-day child care and have a stable peer group, children select the same children in sociometric procedures as do observers (Howes, 1988b). This ability to communicate friendship status to another is a new skill. Perhaps this skill develops because preschoolers are now able to communicate the meaning of the construct of friendship. They use the language of friendship to control access to play ("I'll be your friend if you let me play").

While preschool age children are no longer dependent on rituals to sustain play, their play is still easily disrupted. For example, a pair of children may spend 10 minutes establishing the roles and scripts for a pretend play episode: "You be the lion and I'll be the little boy who finds you in the forest and then ... " "No, I want to be a baby ... " "OK, how about you be a baby lion and I'll be the little boy who finds you in the forest and ... " "OK, and then when you take me home, you feed me with a bottle ... " If a third child attempts to join, the play negotiations may have to start all over again and may not be successful. If the child attempting to enter the group is a friend, the other children appear more willing to undergo the negotiation process (Howes, 1988b). Children who are rejected by peers (using sociometric measures) but who have reciprocated friendships are more likely to be able to enter play groups because of having friends within the group (Howes, 1988b). Continuing the lion example, a child who is a friend might enter the play by saying, "Remember the time, I was the baby lion and then I got to be a great big lion and I roared but I didn't really hurt you. I'm going to be the daddy lion."

As discussed previously, just as there is stability in children's social interaction skills with peers (children who engage in complex play with peers in early developmental periods are the same children who are competent with peers in middle childhood), there is stability in children's friendship quality over developmental periods. This suggests an inter-relation between these two components of social competence—social interaction skills and friendship.

Atypical Children

Using observations rather than sociometric nominations to identify friends makes it possible to study friendship development in children who lack the social, cognitive, or linguistic skills to reliably complete sociometric interviews. We used the same behavioral identification of friends to study relationships among peers in two groups enrolled in outpatient programs for emotionally disturbed children directed by the child psychiatry unit of a mental hospital (Howes, 1983, 1984, 1985a). These children were diagnosed as severely emotionally disturbed with a predominance of nonorganic disorders. One group of children included toddlers, the other preschoolers. The children were observed eight times over the course of a year. Although the children in these groups formed fewer friendships than typical children, they did form friendships. That is, they demonstrated preference, recognition of the partner, and shared positive affect. However, unlike those of typical children, friendships among these atypical children were not sustained over time.

A second study examined friendship formation among abused toddlers who attended a daily child care program (Howes, 1984, 1988a; Howes & Eldredge, 1985; Howes & Espinosa, 1985). Again, these toddlers were found to form friendships as defined by preference, recognition of the partner, and shared positive affect. It is important to note that all of these children were enrolled in intervention programs which supported children's attempts to be prosocial and cooperative with peers. When abused children who were not enrolled in such programs were observed with their peers, a much different picture emerged. These children did not engage in shared positive affect, a necessary condition for friendship (Howes & Espinosa, 1985). These findings suggested that, in a context that supports positive relationships, very young children who have endured major disruptive life events can construct friendship relationships. Understanding which social contexts and which aspects of a particular social context can facilitate and enhance the development of trust and positive relationships among children who come from difficult life circumstances is an important area of future research.

The Functions of Friendships Between Very Young Children

Can peers provide other child experiences of social support, trust, and intimacy? Do children who grew up together sharing the common resources of the child care center have a different kind of social interaction than acquaintances? Do cross-sex peers and cross-ethnic peers who became friends in the context of child care form nontraditional relationships? Each of these questions describes a potential function of friendship: experiences of social support, trust, and intimacy; a context for mastering social interaction; and a context for engaging with children who are unlike the self. The first of these functions has received the most research attention; research on the third function is just emerging.

Friendships Provide Experiences of Social Support, Trust, and Intimacy

We expect that older children or adolescents derive feelings of social support, trust, and intimacy from their relationships with friends (Howes, 1996). It is difficult to directly apply these constructs to the friendships of very young children. There are, however, several pieces of evidence that support the idea that children who form friendships as preverbal children in child care do experience social support, trust, and intimacy within these relationships. The children who were used for the early case studies of friendship (Howes, 1981) are now young adults. Informal conversations with these children suggest that their toddler friend partner, although no longer a "best friend" remains a person of importance in their lives. And, as previously discussed, toddler friend pairs tend to remain stable friends. This suggests that toddler friendships function to provide affective support, rather than functioning merely as a context for play, when the child's life history allows for continuity of those friendships.

If toddler-age friend pairs are serving as sources of social support, we would expect them to respond to the distress of their friend. In one study of toddler-age children, we identified friends according to the behaviors identified above. We then used event coding to describe distress incidences in the classroom. The identity of the crier, the context of the distress, and the identity and behaviors of adults and peers who responded to the child were recorded. We found that children were most likely to respond to another child's crying if that child was a friend (Howes & Farver, 1987b).

Finally, we suggest that, once children become experts at social pretend play, friends use the context of play to explore issues of trust and intimacy (Howes, with Unger et al., 1992). In an exploratory study of these issues, we compared ratings of self-disclosure in the play of 4-year-old children who were asked to engage in pretend play with a particular partner (Howes, with Unger et al., 1992). One group of children had been in a longitudinal study, had been identified as friends as toddlers, and had kept these friendships. A second group of children were paired with short-term friends, developed within the prior 6 months. In the third group, children were paired with a child who was not an identified friend. Self-disclosure ratings were higher in the long-term friend group than in either the short-term or the nonfriend groups.

Child Care Friendships As a Way to Learn How to Engage With Peers

In this chapter and in general, the construction of social interaction has been treated as semi-independent of the construction of friendships (Howes, 1988b). The data suggest that more socially skilled children tend to have friends and children who have friends tend to be more socially skilled. In particular, children who engage in more complex play have less difficulty than less skilled children in entering play groups (Howes, 1988b). One reason that these socially skilled children can easily enter play groups is that they are likely to be friends with children within the play group.

Friendships appear to be a particularly important context for the construction of complex peer interactions during early developmental periods. In a year-long longitudinal study, infants and toddlers made the greatest increases in complexity of social play when they were engaged with stable friends, as opposed to acquaintances or playmates (Howes, 1983). Social pretend play, which involves the communication of symbolic meaning, also appears first within friendship dyads and then within playmate dyads (Howes, 1985b; Howes, with Unger et al., 1992). Likewise, preschoolers who had been friends for 3 years were better able to use communicative behaviors to extend and to clarify pretend play than preschoolers who had been friends for 6 months or less (Howes, Droege, & Matheson, 1994). Children who are friends do not have to simultaneously devise the game structure and integrate or communicate pretend meanings. Instead, they integrate new pretend meanings into well-developed and routine-like games. In a large landmark study within Head Start classrooms Vaughn and colleagues found similar relations between friendships formation and social competence (Vaughn et al., 2000; Vaughn, Colvin, Azria, Caya, & Krzysik, 2001)

The mastery of social skills within friendships is not limited to typical children. Friendships appear to facilitate conflict resolution and conflict avoidance in children enrolled in an intervention program for emotionally disturbed children (Howes, 1985a). Toddler-age friends were more likely than acquaintances to avoid conflict. Similarly, preschool friends were less likely than acquaintances to misinterpret prosocial bids and more likely to avoid conflict by decreasing their agonistic bids.

Friendships As a Context to Engage With Children Who Are Unlike the Self

To the extent that children of different genders and ethnic backgrounds have different social styles, friendships appear to give children access to these diverse social styles. As discussed, toddler-age children do not select their friends on the basis of gender (Howes, 1988c; Howes & Phillipsen, 1992). Instead, toddlers form and maintain cross-gender friendships into preschool. Likewise, in a study of young children in an ethnically diverse school, we found that children were able to form and maintain cross-ethnic friendships (Howes & Wu, 1990). As we discussed in the introduction, whether peer groups are diverse or homogeneous depends on the cultural context of the peer group. As child care institutions are segregated by income of parents, the resulting peer groups do not cross social class and in many instances race lines, and thus children loose opportunities to form friendships with children unlike themselves. As well, as pointed out in a review by Maccoby and Lewis, the cooperative versus competitive tone set in the child care arrangement may facilitate or inhibit social interaction and friendships among similar or dissimilar children (Maccoby & Lewis, 2003).

FUTURE DIRECTIONS

In this chapter we have examined how the study of peer relations, what we have chosen to study, and, to some extent, what we have concluded as we studied children forming relations with peers, has been influenced by the sociocultural influences of the historical period of the research as well as the theoretical lens through which we view peers. We suspect that these joint forces will continue to influence the study of the processes by which children construct and maintain their relationships with peers. One emerging sociocultural influence on research on peer relations is the changing demographics in both urban and increasingly rural areas of the United States. There is a large influx of families from societies that generally are considered more collectivist in their values than traditional U.S. families. Within collectivist societies, there is a greater emphasis placed on the individual within the group than on the individual self. These collectivist values are not dissimilar to the values of the visionaries that opened child care centers to infants and toddlers in the early 1970s. Those involved in the intersection of the women's movement and child care in the 1970s also dreamed of a society that valued the collective and helped children to be prosocial, altruistic members of a group.

These values on creating a group based on cooperation are somewhat different than the premise expressed in traditional early childhood education where the development of the individual child is paramount. It also differs from another prevailing force that emphasizes academics rather than social relationships in preschool. As more children and families from subcultures based on collectivist ideas enter child care settings, there may be renewed tension between constructing groups of children that support and help one another while simultaneously helping each child within the group to reach their individual potential. This tension emerges in the Maccoby and Lewis review (2003) and may influence the next set of studies of peer relations.

Attachment theory, once expanded beyond the study of early parent–child relationships, also is likely to continue be a powerful influence on the study of peer relationships. This work has suggested that attachments with alternative caregivers are influential to peer relations. Furthermore, descriptive studies have established that relationships between young children are stable affective bonds. These findings may lead researchers to move beyond the description of friendships towards the study of internal representations of friendships. The question of what internal representations are derived from early peer affective relationships and how these representations shape children's working models of relationships is far from answered. In this context, it is important that the earliest friendships appear to be based on some "chemistry" that leads toddlers to prefer each other rather than on matches between children of similar gender and ethnicity. As classrooms become filled with children who come from very different cultural communities, the study of peer relations will need to address the question of whether providing children with opportunities to form important relationships with persons unlike themselves at young ages will predict respectful relationships with others unlike themselves as older children and adults.

ACKNOWLEDGMENTS

Holli Tonyan was the second author on the first version of this revised chapter. We are grateful for her conceptual contributions to this version. The responsibility for the formulations in this version rests with the current authors.

REFERENCES

Asher, S. R., & Coie, J. (1990). *Peer rejection in childhood* (Vol.). Cambridge: Cambridge University Press.

Bakeman, R., & Brownlee. (1980). The strategic use of parallel play: A sequential analysis. *Child Development, 51*, 873–878.

Blurton-Jones, N. (1972). Categories of child-child interaction. In N. Blurton-Jones (Ed.), *Ethnological studies of child behavior*. Cambridge: Cambridge University Press.

Bowlby, J. (1969/1982). *Attachment and Loss: Vol. 1. Attachment*. London: Hogarth.

Bretherton, I. (1985). Attachment theory: Retrospect and prospect, Monographs of the Society for Research in Child Development (Vol. 50, pp. 3–35).

Bryant, B. (1985). The neighborhood walk sources of support in middle childhood. Monographs of the Society for Research in Child Development, 503 serial no. 210.

Buhler, C. (1930). *The first year of life*. New York: J. Day.

Coie, J., & Dodge, K. (1983). *Continuities and changes in children's social status a five year longitudinal study*. Merrill Palmer Quarterly, 29, 261–282.

Coie, J. D. (1990). Towards a theory of peer rejection. In S. R. Asher & J. D. Coie (Eds.), *Peer rejection in childhood* (pp. 17–59). New York: Cambridge University Press.

Coll, C. G., Lamberty, G., Jenkins, R., McAdoo, H. P., Cunic, K., Wasik, B., et al. (1996). An integrative model for the study of developmental competencies in minority children. *Child Development, 67*, 1891–1914.

Crick, N. R., & Dodge, K. A. (1999). 'Superiority' is in the eye of the beholder: A comment on Sutton, Smith, and Swettenham. *Social Development, 8*, 128–132.

ECCRN. (2001). Child Care and children's peer interaction at 24 and 36 months: The NICHD Study of Early Child Care. *Child Development, 72*, 1478–1500.

ECCRN. (2003). Does amount of spent in child care predict socioemotional adjustment during the transition to kindergarten? *Child Development, 74*, 976–1005.

Eckerman, C., Whatley, J., & Kutz, S. (1975). Growth of social play with peers during the second year of life. *Developmental Psychology, 11*, 42–49.

Eckerman, C. O., Davis, C. C., & Didow, S. M. (1989). Toddlers' emerging ways of achieving social coordination with a peers. *Child Development, 60*, 440–453.

Fabes, R. A., Hanish, L. D., & Martin, C. L. (2003). Children at play: The role of peers in understanding the effects of child care. *Child Development, 74*, 1039–1043.

Farver, J., & Howes, C. (1988). Cross-cultural differences in peer interaction A comparison of American and Indonesian Children. *Journal of Cross-Cultural Psychology, 19*, 203–215.

Farver, J. A., & Shin, Y. L. (1997). Social pretend play in Korean- and Anglo-American preschoolers. *Child Development, 68*, 544–556.

Farver, J. A. M. (1992). An analysis of young American and Mexican children's play dialogues. In C. Howes (Ed.), *The collaborative construction of pretend* (pp. 55–66). Albany. NY: SUNY Press.

Farver, J. A. M., & Frosch, D. (1996). L. A. Stories Aggression in preschool spontaneous narratives after the riots of 1992. *Child Development, 67*, 19–32.

Farver, J. A. M., Kim, Y. K., & Lee, Y. (1995). Cultural differences in Korean- and Anglo-American social interaction and play behaviors. *Child Development, 66*, 1088–1099.

Farver, J. A. M., Lee-Shin, Y. (2000). Acculturation and Korean-American children's social and play behavior. *Social Development, 9*, 316–336.

Farver, J. A. M., & Wimbarti, S. (1995). Indonesian children's play with their mothers and older siblings. *Child Development, 66*, 1493–1503.

Farver, J. M. (1996). Aggressive behavior in preschoolers' social networks Do birds of a feather flock together? *Early Childhood Research Quarterly, 11*, 333–350.

Goncu, A. (2002). Understanding young children's play in context. In P. S. C. Hart (Ed.), *Handbook of social development*. New York: Blackwell.

Harper, L. V., & McCluskey, K. S. (2003). Teacher-child and child-child interactions in inclusive preschool settings: Do adults inhibit peer interaction. *Early Childhood Research Quarterly, 18*, 163–184.

Hartup, W. (1983). The peer system. In M. P (Ed.), Carmichael's Manual of Child Psychology (Vol. In P. Mussen): peers.

Hay, D. (1985). Learning to form relationships in infancy: Parallel attainments with parents and peers. *Developmental Review, 5*, 122–161.

Hinde, R., & Stevenson-Hinde. (1976). Towards better understanding relationships. In P. Bateson & R. Hinde (Eds.), *Growing points in ethology*. New York: Cambridge University Press.

Howes, C. (1980). Peer play scale as an index of complexity of peer interaction. *Developmental Psychology, 16*, 371–372.

Howes, C. (1981). Danny and Robyn, Becca and Amy: Making friends at child care. (unpublished manuscript). Boston: Harvard University Press.

Howes, C. (1983). Patterns of friendship. *Child Development, 54*, 1041–1053.

Howes, C. (1984). Social interactions and patterns of friendship in normal and emotionally disturbed children. In T. Fields (Ed.), *Friendships between normal and handicapped children*. Norwalk NJ: Ablex.

Howes, C. (1985a). The patterning of agnostic behaviors among young friends and acquaintances in a program for emotionally disturbed children. *Journal of Applied Developmental Psychology, 6*, 303–331.

Howes, C. (1985b). Sharing fantasy Social pretend play in toddlers. *Child Development, 56*, 1253–1258.

Howes, C. (1987). Social competence with peers in young children Developmental sequences. *Developmental Review, 7*, 252–272.

Howes, C. (1988a). Abused and neglected children with their peers. In G. Hotaling (Ed.), *Research on violence* (pp. Vol. 2). Los Angeles: Sage.

Howes, C. (1988b). Peer interaction in young children. *Monograph of the Society for Research in Child Development, 217*(53, Serial No. 1).

Howes, C. (1988c). Same- and cross-sex friends Implications for interaction and social skills. *Early Childhood Research Quarterly, 3*, 21–37.

Howes, C. (1990). Social status and friendship from kindergarten to third grade. *Applied Developmental Psychology, 11*, 321–330.

Howes, C. (1996). The earliest friendships. In W. M. Bukowski, A. F. Newcomb & W. W. Hartup (Eds.), *The company they keep: Friendships in childhood and adolescence* (pp. 66–86). New York: Cambridge University Press.

Howes, C. (1997a). Continuity of care: The importance of infant toddler and caregiver relationships. *Zero to Three, 18*, 7–11.

Howes, C. (1997b). Teacher sensitivity children's attachment and play with peers. *Early Education and Development, 8*, 41–49.

Howes, C. (1999). Attachment Relationships in the Context of Multiple Caregivers. In J. Cassidy & P. R. Shaver (Eds.), *Handbook of attachment theory and research* (vol. , pp. 671–687). New York: Guilford Press.

Howes, C., & Aikins, J. W. (Eds.). (2002). *Peer relations in the transition to adolescence*. New York: Academic.

Howes, C., Droege, K., & Matheson, C. (1994). Play and communicative processes within long- and short-term friendship dyads. *Journal of Social and Personal Relationships, 11*, 401–410.

Howes, C., & Eldredge, R. (1985). Responses of abused neglected and non-maltreated children to the behavior of their peers. *Journal of Applied Developmental Psychology, 6*, 247–260.

Howes, C., & Espinosa, M. (1985). The consequences of child abuse for the formation of relationships with peers. *International Journal of Child Abuse and Neglect, 9*, 307–404.

Howes, C., & Farver , J. (1987a). Social pretend play in two-year-olds Effects of age of partner. *Early Childhood Research Quarterly, 2*, 305–334.

Howes, C., & Farver, J. (1987b). Toddler's responses to the distress of their peers. *Journal of Applied Developmental Psychology, 8*, 441–452.

Howes, C., & Galluzzo, D. C. (1994). Adult socialization of children's play in child care. In H. Goelman (Ed.), *Play and child care* (pp. 20–36). Albany, NY: SUNY Press.

Howes, C., & Hamilton, C. E. (1993). The changing experience of child care: Changes in teachers and in teacher-child relationships and children's social competence with peers. *Early Childhood Research Quarterly, 8*, 15–32.

Howes, C., Hamilton, C. E., & Matheson, C. C. (1994). Children's relationships with peers Differential associations with aspects of the teachers-child relationship. *Child Development, 65*, 253–263.

Howes, C., Hamilton, C. E., & Phillipsen, L. (1998). Stability and continuity of child-caregiver and child-peer relationships, 69, 418–426.

Howes, C., & Matheson, C. C. (1992). Sequences in the development of competent play with peers Social and social pretend play. *Developmental Psychology, 28*, 961–974.

Howes, C., Matheson, C. C., & Hamilton, C. E. (1994). Maternal teacher and child care history correlates of children's relationships with peers. *Child Development, 65*, 264.

Howes, C., Phillips, D. A., & Whitebook, M. (1992). Thresholds of quality in child care centers and children's social and emotional development. *Child Development, 63*, 449–460.

Howes, C., & Phillipsen, L. (1992). Gender and friendship: Relationships within peer groups of young children. *Social Development, 1*, 230–242.

Howes, C., Phillipsen, L., & Hamilton, C. E. (1993). Constructing social communication with peers Domains and sequences. In J. Nadel (Ed.), *Early Communication* (pp. 215–232). London: Routledge.

Howes, C., & Phillipsen, L. C. (1998). Continuity in children's relations with peers. *Social Development, 7*, 340–349.

Howes, C., & Ritchie, S. (2002). *A Matter of trust: Connecting teachers and learners in the early childhood classroom*. Teachers College Press.

Howes, C., Rodning, C., Galluzzo, D. C., & Myers, L. (1988). Attachment and child care Relationships with mother and caregiver. Special edition on infant day care. *Early Childhood Research Quarterly, 36*, 403–441.

Howes, C., & Stewart, P. (1987). Child's play with adults, toys, and peers: An examination of family and child-care influences. *Developmental Psychology, 23*, 423–430.

Howes, C., & Tonyan, H. (2000). Links between adult and peer relationship across four developmental periods. In K. A. Kerns & A. M. Neal-Barnett (Eds.), *Examining associations between parent-child and peer relationships* (pp. 85–114). NY: Greenwood/Praeger.

Howes, C., Unger, & Seidner, L. (1989). Social pretend play in toddlers Social pretend play forms and parallels with solitary pretense. *Child Development, 60*, 132.

Howes, C., with Unger, O. A., & Matheson, C. C. (1992). *The collaborative construction of pretend Social pretend play functions*. New York: SUNY Press.

Howes, C., & Wu, F. (1990). Peer interactions and friendships in an ethnically diverse school setting. *Child Development, 61*, 537–541.

Howes, C. R., Sharon. (2002). A matter of trust. New York: Teachers College Press.

Kontos, S., & Keyes, L. (1999). An ecobehavioral analysis of early childhood classrooms. *Early Childhood Research Quarterly, 14,* 35–50.

Ladd, G. (1983). Social networks of popular average and rejected children in school settings. *Merrill Palmer Quarterly, 29,* 283–307.

Ladd, G. W., & Price, J. M. (1987). Predicting children's social and school adjustment following the transition from preschool to kindergarten. Child Development.

Lee, L. (1973). Social encounters of infants the beginnings of popularity. Presented at International Society for Behavioral Development. Ann Arbor, MI August.

Maccoby, E., & Lewis, C. (2003). Less day care or different day care. *Child Development, 74,* 1069–1075.

Maccoby, E. E. (1988). Gender as a social category. *Developmental Psychology, 24,* 755–765.

Maccoby, E. E. (1990). Gender and relationships: A developmental account. *American Psychologist, 45,* 513–520.

Martin, C. L., & Fabes, R. A. (2001). The stability and consequences of young children's same-sex peer interaction. *Developmental Psychology, 37,* 431–446.

Maudry, M., & Nekula, M. (1939). Social relations between children of the same age during the first two years of life. *Journal of Genetic Psychology, 54,* 193–215.

Medrich, E. A., Roizen, J., Rubin, V., & Buckley, S. (1982). The serious business of growing up: A study of children's lives outside of school. Berkeley: University of California Press.

Parker, J. G., & Asher, S. R. (1987). Peer acceptance and later personal adjustment Are low-accepted children "at risk"? *Psychological Bulletin, 102,* 357–389.

Partens, M. (1932). Social participation among preschool children. *Journal of Abnormal and Social Psychology, 27,* 243–269.

Partens, M. (1933). Social play among preschool children. *Journal of Abnormal and Social Psychology, 28,* 136–147.

Reed, K. H. (1950). *The nursery school: A human relationships laboratory.* Philadelphia: W. B. Saunders

Rogoff, B. (2003). *The cultural nature of human development.* New York: Oxford University Press.

Ross, H., & Goldman, B. (1976). Establishing new social relations in infancy. In T. Alloway, L. Kramer & P. Pliner (Eds.), *Advances in communication and affect V4.* New York: Plenum.

Rothstein-Fisch, C., & Howes, C. (1988). Toddler peer interaction in mixed age groups. *Journal of Applied Developmental Psychology, 9,* 211–218.

Rubenstein, J., & Howes, C. (1976). The effects of peers on toddler's interactions with mother and toys. *Child Development, 47,* 597–605.

Rubenstein, J., & Howes, C. (1979). Caregiving and infant behavior in daycare and homes. *Developmental Psychology, 15,* 1–24.

Rubin, Z. (1980). *Children's friendships.* Cambridge: Harvard University Press.

Smith, E., & Howes, C. (1994). The effects of parent's presence on children's social interactions in preschool. *Early Childhood Research Quarterly, 9,* 45–59.

Stormshak, E. A., Bierman, K. L., Bruschi, C., Dodge, K. A., Coie, J. D., & group., C. P. P. R. (1999). The relation between behavior problems and peer preferences in different classroom contexts. *Child Development, 70,* 169–182.

Vandell, D. L., Wilson, K., & Buchanan, N. (1980). Peer interaction in the first year of life. *Child Development, 51,* 481–488.

Vaughn, B., Azria, M., Krzysik, L., Caya, L., Bost, K., Newell, W., et al. (2000). Friendship and social competence in a sample of preschool children attending Head Start. *Developmental Psychology, 36,* 326–338.

Vaughn, B. E., Colvin, T. N., Azria, M. R., Caya, L., & Krzysik, L. (2001). Dyadic analysis of friendship in a sample of preschool-age children attending Head Start: Correspondence between measures and implications for social competence. *Child Development, 72,* 862–878.

Walden, T., Lemerise, E. & Smith, M. C. (1999). Friendship and popularity in preschool classrooms. *Early Education and Development, 10,* 351–371.

7

Pretend Play and Theory of Mind

Robert D. Kavanaugh

INTRODUCTION

Research on pretend play and theory of mind has accumulated rapidly over the past 25 years and for much of that time psychologists and philosophers have debated the question of how the two topics are related. The debate began in earnest with Leslie's (1987) paper in which he outlined the case for pretend play as an early index of metarepresentational thought that assists the child in the later development of a theory of mind. Leslie's (1987) theoretical stance generated a good deal of interest in pretense, and together with recent revisions (Leslie, 2000; Scholl & Leslie, 1999), has played a prominent role in promoting important discussions about the precise nature of pretend play (Nichols & Stich, 2000), its relationship to children's understanding of mental states, particularly false beliefs (Harris, Lillard, & Perner, 1994; Lillard, 2001a), and its larger role in the development of imagination and reasoning (Harris, 2000; Taylor, 1999).

In this chapter, I review both theoretical and empirical work on the pretend play-theory-of-mind relationship. I begin with a brief discussion of the definition of key terms and a review of background literature.

PRETEND PLAY

In essence, to pretend is to engage in "acting as if"(Fein, 1981; Leslie, 1987), or what Garvey (1977, p. 72) referred to as the "voluntary transformation of the here and now, the you and me." Pretend actions are nonliteral and simulative (Fein, 1981) incorporating deliberate distortions that involve what McCune-Nicolich (1981) aptly referred to as "double knowledge"—knowledge of both the real and imagined properties of objects. Pretenders project an idea (e.g., serving tea) on to an actual situation (e.g., play partner's empty cup) (Lillard, 2001a) while clearly knowing the difference between the actual state of affairs and the nonactual situations they are enacting (Lillard, 2001b).

At least among North American and European children, there is reasonable consensus that pretend play begins during the early part of the second year often with brief "self-referenced" actions. Piaget's (1946/1962) classic observations of his own children illustrate this type of pretending, for example, Jacqueline (15 months) lying on her side and pretending to be asleep. Around this age children also begin to use props to assist their pretend action, for example, Jacqueline using the tail of a toy donkey as though it were a pillow (Piaget, 1946/1962). By 18 to 24 months, pretend play typically becomes more social in nature involving interactions with play partners, usually familiar adults or siblings/peers, as well as "replica" objects, such as dolls and toy animals. For example, a child might pretend to feed a doll, or to offer tea (an empty cup) to her mother. A further progression often observed in Western samples is that toward the middle of the third year (around age 2 1/2 years) children begin to ascribe make-believe states to replica objects. For example, a child might pretend that a baby doll placed on a bed is "sleeping". Attribution of an imagined animate state to an inanimate object has been called "passive" agency to distinguish it from "active" or independent agency in which children pretend that replica toys can carry out their own make-believe actions, e.g., the child uses a mother doll to pretend to give juice to a baby doll (Kavanaugh, Eizenman, & Harris, 1997).

Once children begin to incorporate independent agency into their pretend play the imagined scenarios they create become increasingly complex. By age 3 or 4 years, children assign make-believe emotions and simple moral judgments to dolls, stuffed animals, and other replica objects (e.g., a child proclaims that a "doll is bad to run away") followed by imagined cognitions (e.g., a child proclaims that a pirate figure "knows where to hide gold" so it won't be found) (Wolf, Rygh, & Altshuler, 1984, p. 202). In addition, by age 3 or 4 years, and even earlier among siblings and convivial peers (Dunn & Dale, 1984), children engage in shared pretend play that involves acting out complementary roles (e.g., doctor–patient or bus driver–passenger).

THEORY OF MIND

Theory of mind is an umbrella term that implies the capacity to make sense of (interpret, predict and explain) people's everyday behavior through the attribution of underlying mental states (Astington, 1988; Premack & Woodruff, 1978; Wellman, 1990). Theory of mind captures the critical idea that minds (mental states) represent how people understand the world, and that people act on the basis of their understandings regardless of the actual situation (Lillard, 2001a). Interestingly, Premack and Woodruff (1978) introduced the term theory of mind to the psychological literature by asking whether or not members of a nonhuman species (chimpanzees) could demonstrate mental state knowledge deserving of the characterization theory of mind. They showed an adult chimpanzee videotapes of a human actor struggling to solve a variety of problems, such as trying to reach food (e.g., banana) that was just beyond reach. After each videotape clip, the chimp could choose one of several photographs that depicted a solution to the problem (e.g., a stick to reach the inaccessible banana). Premack and Woodruff (1978) assumed that to choose the correct picture the chimp must impute mental states to the actor (e.g., desires out of reach object) and then identify an appropriate behavioral solution to resolve the difficulty (e.g., extend reach with a stick). However, as noted below, the commentary on this seminal paper generated considerable debate about the proper criteria for ascribing theory of mind (e.g., Dennett, 1978; Harman, 1978).

The notion of theory of mind entered the cognitive developmental literature through the work of Bretherton and her colleagues (Bretherton & Beeghly, 1982; Bretherton, McNew, & Beegly-Smith, 1981) and Wimmer and Perner (1983). Bretherton et al. (1981) argued that a rudimentary theory of mind, though not the capacity to reflect on mental states, emerges around 12 months with the onset of communicative intentions as demonstrated by shared attention and expressive language. By 28 months, Bretherton and Beeghly (1982) saw convincing evidence that children impute internal (mental) states to self and others in mothers' reports of children's spontaneous use of words denoting expressions of perceptions, feelings, knowledge, etc. They noted that children tended to speak first about their own internal states, and that references to perceptions and volitions (want, need) were far more common than references to cognition (think, remember), a developmental trajectory confirmed in subsequent research on children's mental state talk (Bartsch & Wellman, 1995).

Wimmer and Perner (1983), returning to the question of the proper assessment of theory of mind, followed Pylyshyn's (1978) assertion that to have a theory of mind an individual must be capable of metarepresentation. According to Wimmer and Perner (1983), the essence of Pylyshyn's (1978) claim is that a theory of mind implies the ability to represent explicitly how an individual stands in relationship to a particular situation, i.e., metarepresentation implies the capacity to represent (encode in some fashion) an individual's attitude toward a particular set of facts. Thus, I am capable of metarepresentation when I represent consciously that person A wants X or that person B believes Y. Although Wimmer and Perner (1983) acknowledged that children's talk about mental states demonstrated their capacity for metarepresentation, they suggested that a more difficult metarepresentational problem involves the ability to "represent the difference between one's own and somebody else's relation to the same propositional content" (Wimmer & Perner, 1983, p. 105). They proposed an experimental test of this claim—the unexpected change of location task—that has become one of the hallmarks of theory of mind research. In this task, a child observes a scene in which a doll places a favored object (e.g., piece of chocolate) in one location. Then, while the doll is away, the chocolate is moved to a new location. The doll then returns to the scene and the child is asked where the doll will search for the chocolate. Critically, the child and the doll now hold two different beliefs about the location of the chocolate. To answer the question correctly of where the doll will look, the child must recognize that the doll will be guided by its incorrect or false belief. Wimmer and Perner (1983) found that before age 4 children had great difficulty passing this test.

PRETEND PLAY AND THEORY OF MIND: THEORETICAL POSITIONS

There are three major conceptual approaches to the pretend play-theory of mind relationship: modularity, simulation, and a social-cognitive perspective. For each of these approaches, I have concentrated primarily on one theorist whose work represents the core principles of the theory under consideration.

Modularity

Modularity theorists assume that the brain has evolved to bring innate cognitive modules (discrete ways of understanding the world) on line at fixed points in development (Fodor, 1983; Leslie, 1994; Scholl & Leslie, 1999). Modules are thought to be domain specific, that is, highly specialized systems that process information rapidly in "mandatory" ways (Scholl & Leslie, 1999). The guiding principle of modularity theory is that specific "encapsulated" ways of knowing the world develop on schedule as part of the "cognitive architecture" of the mind (Scholl & Leslie, 1999, p. 131). For example, at roughly age 6 months infants acquire a module that permits a basic understanding of the physical properties of objects. By 9 months, a new module emerges allowing infants to make sense of people's goal-directed actions. By 18 months, a module permitting the representation of mental states, including pretense and beliefs, is in place (Leslie, 1994). Leslie (Scholl & Leslie, 1999) argues that by 18 months metarepresentations (below) are also possible, and he follows the nativist argument that the capacity for such complex thought could not be learned (Fodor, 1992). Leslie (1991) also argues that the well documented difficulty that children with autism experience on theory of mind tasks supports the claim that serious cognitive impairment arises from biological damage to the theory of mind module.

Leslie's (1987) influential paper on pretend play as metarepresentational thought foreshadowed his later work on modularity. Primary representations, he argued, are internal (mental) states that allow us to perceive and respond to the world "in an accurate, faithful, and literal way" (p. 414). Primary representations, then, are well designed "to represent situations seriously and literally" but ill suited to cope with pretense (p. 414). Accepting that pretend play involves "double knowledge" (McCune-Nicolich, 1981), the problem for a theory of pretense is to account for the fact that by the second year a child can deploy primary representations to categorize objects (e.g., a banana is a yellow concave edible object) but also pretend that an object is something else (e.g., banana is a telephone). However, the child's understanding of the real and pretend worlds would be overwhelmed and open to "representational abuse" if bananas became telephones and vice versa. To solve the problem, Leslie (1987) argued that when children engage in pretend play they create a second order "decoupled" copy (e.g. 'this banana is a telephone') of the primary representation. Decoupling solves the problem of representational abuse because the copy is "quarantined" from the primary representation thereby allowing the child to keep the actual and pretend worlds separate. Pretend representations, then, are "opaque" representations of representations or metarepresentations.

Although Leslie (1978) borrowed the term "metarepresentation" from Pylyshyn (1978) it is not clear that he used the term as Pylyshyn (1978) intended (Jarrold, Carruthers, Smith, & Boucher, 1994). In fact, Jarrold et al. (1994) argue convincingly that merely copying a primary representation, as Leslie (1987) described, is not sufficient to meet Pylyshyn's (1978) definition of metarepresentation as "the ability to represent the representation relationship itself." However, it is important to note that Leslie's position on metarepresentation has evolved since the publication of his original (1987) paper. In subsequent work (Leslie & Roth, 1993), he has used the term "M-representation" which seems to embody a richer notion that is closer both to Pylyshyn's (1978) definition and to the work of other prominent theories (Nichols & Stich, 2000). M-representations are not simply copies of primary representations but rather characterize agents who assume an epistemic stance, called an "informational relationship," toward both a primary representation and its decoupled secondary referent. Thus, to return to the example of the banana as a make-believe telephone, an M-representation would take the form, "mother pretends [of] the banana that 'it is a telephone'" (Leslie & Roth, 1993, p. 87).

Simulation

Simulation theory posits that young children can deploy mental states, particularly desires and beliefs, to explain why people behave as they do (Goldman, 1992; Gordon, 1992; Harris, 1991, 1992). Simulation theorists argue that during the early childhood years children become increasing adept at using their own mental states as an analogue for how other people think and feel (Harris, 2000). Effectively, through mental simulation children put themselves in the place of others and then act accordingly.[1] To engage in simulation children must be able to imagine a particular desire or belief and then imagine the ensuing outcome, i.e., the corresponding thoughts, actions, or emotions and, finally, attribute that outcome to other people (Harris, 1991).

Harris (1992) offers a developmental account of simulation by drawing on the known accomplishments of infants and young children (e.g., shared attention, visual perspective taking) that serve as precursors to understanding the mental states of others. He argues for a four step process, unfolding over the first 5 years, that involves (a) appreciating another person's "intentional stance" toward an object or event (e.g., shared attention between infant and parent); (b) regulating another person's intentional stance (e.g., changing the direction of a parent's gaze by pointing at a new object); (c) setting aside one's own intentional stance and recognizing the stance of others (e.g., recognizing that what other people see may be different from what you see); and (d) imagining an intentional stance toward counterfactual situations (e.g., the child imagines someone seeing/believing a situation that is opposite to her understanding of current reality).

Pretend role play is an obvious candidate to assist the process of simulation. Role play provides children with the opportunity "to imagine the world from the point of view of another person" (Harris, 2000, p. 48). The child who imagines she is a mother can tend to a crying baby just as an actual mother would; the child who pretends to be a pirate can plan a course of action to conceal a stolen treasure (Harris, 2000). Importantly for simulation theory, role play involves more than simply following well rehearsed scripts. In role play, children make their characters adapt to changing situations and to the responses (viewpoints, emotions) of their play partners (Harris, 2000).

A Social-Cognitive Perspective

Social-cognitive analyses of the pretend play-theory of mind relationship offer a broad conceptual framework that attempts to integrate relevant childhood experiences (e.g., role play) with the cognitive requirements (e.g., symbolic function) necessary for pretense and mental state knowledge. By definition a social-cognitive analysis is an inclusive approach that draws on the work of a variety of different researchers and theorists. To date, Lillard (2001a) has offered the most detailed social-cognitive analysis of the pretend play-theory of mind relationship. The center piece of her model is the decoupled world in which pretend play takes place. Lillard shares Leslie's (1987) concern about damage to the child's representational system if pretend acts are not "quarantined" from the real world, and she incorporates Leslie's decoupling notion into her model. However, unlike Lelsie (1987), and modularity theorists more generally, Lillard locates the emergence of pretense and theory of mind inside a strong developmental/experiential and, at times, bi-directional framework. She notes, for example, that social experiences (e.g., play with parents around 12–15 months) are crucial to the development of pretense. Pushing the developmental notion further, Lillard argues that play experiences themselves rest on earlier appearing social interactive skills that have implications for both pretense and theory of mind. Chief among these are joint attention and social referencing. Both are crucial, in Lillard's view, to unpacking the ambiguity that surrounds the child's first experiences with novel pretend acts, e.g., watching someone "sip" tea from an empty cup. Similarly, Lillard cites evidence that the emotional understanding involved in social referencing deserves consideration as a precursor to theory of mind.

The remaining components of Lillard's model continue her developmental theme. Children not only produce pretend acts but also understand the pretense of others (Harris & Kavanaugh, 1993). To do so, Lillard asserts, they must be adept at reading the intentions of others, a skill that is present by 18 months (Meltzoff, 1995). In addition, Lillard sees an intersection between pretense and symbolic thought. Thus, she argues that to make sense of the otherwise puzzling situations that arise during pretend play, such as someone appearing to talk to a banana, children must grasp the symbolic or *stands for* nature of pretense (e.g., banana represents a telephone). She draws empirical support for the notion of a symbolic substrate by noting evidence of strong positive relationship between pretense and early language development (Tamis-LeMonda & Bornstein, 1994) as well as the relative poverty of both pretense and language in children with autism (Baron-Cohen, 2001). Lillard notes that as pretend skills develop, children are likely to engage with each other in sociodramatic play in which they discuss desires and wishes, negotiate and enact roles, and work through imagined conflicts. A portion of her model highlights sociodramatic (role) play as an excellent vehicle for children to learn about other minds—how others think and feel and how thoughts and feelings change as new situations unfold. Although Lillard acknowledges a strong relationship between role play and theory of mind, in contrast to many others, she is agnostic about the direction of the relationship. She believes that role play may contribute to theory of mind understanding, but allows that the reverse relationship may hold as well (e.g., as mental state knowledge deepens children's role play improves). Moreover, other social experiences (e.g., number of older siblings) may serve as an underlying third variable that promotes both role play and theory of mind.

PRETEND PLAY AND THEORY OF MIND: EMPIRICAL FINDINGS

There is a substantial body of evidence pointing to a strong relationship between pretend play and theory of mind. The theory of mind tasks involved in these studies cover a wide range of abilities but the hallmark measure is the assessment of false belief that has two well known variants. One is Wimmer and Perner's (1983) change of location task described earlier. The other is a deceptive box task that involves showing preschool children a familiar container (e.g., a box of band-aids) that the experimenter has filled with unexpected contents (e.g., pencils). After revealing the actual contents of the container (e.g., pencils in the band-aid box), the experimenter asks the children what an unknowing friend will say about the contents when shown the container for the first time (e.g., does the box contain band-aids or pencils?). Children are credited with false belief understanding if they recognize that, in contrast to what they know, the friend will have a mistaken idea about the actual contents of the container (e.g., friend will say that it contains band-aids). In addition to these false belief tasks, another frequently used theory of mind measure involves appearance-reality tasks. Here children are shown visually deceptive objects (e.g., a sponge that looks like a rock) and then asked a series of questions to determine if they can distinguish between the appearance of the object (e.g., looks like a rock) and what it actually is (e.g., a sponge). Finally, there are a variety of tasks that assess the child's ability to engage in deception (e.g., provide false clues about the location of a hidden object).

Although there is evidence of a pretend play-theory of mind relationship, it is important to note at the outset that not all forms of pretend play appear to be implicated. Consistent with simulation theory, and to some extent with Lillard's (2001a) social-cognitive perspective, shared pretend play, and in particular role play, bears the strongest relationship to either contemporary or subsequent success on theory of mind tasks. As noted, Harris (2000) argues that role play involves imagining the world from another's perspective, an exercise that helps children understand the thought/emotions of others. This makes role play a potentially important vehicle for developing a theory of mind.

One body of work highlighting the importance of a role play-theory of mind relationship comes from the work of Dunn and her colleagues (Dunn & Cutting, 1999; Hughes & Dunn, 1997; Youngblade & Dunn, 1995). Dunn and Cutting (1999) videotaped pairs of 4-year-old friends playing together and also assessed them on a battery of theory of mind (false belief, deception) and emotion understanding tasks that required the children to identify both basic emotions (e.g., happiness, sadness) as well as emotions that differed from their own. They found that cooperative pretend play—discussing a joint pretend episode, assuming a pretend role, or following the pretend suggestion of a playmate—showed a strong positive relationship to the theory of mind and emotion understanding tasks, as well as to two other measures of language ability. Hughes and Dunn (1997) used a similar design videotaping pairs of 4-year-old in an area of a nursery school provisioned with props that encouraged pretend play (fireman's hat, cowboy hat, hand-puppets, cook sets). Pretend measures included role play (child specifically states a role) and role enactment (child acts out but does not specifically mention a role), as well as other forms of pretense (e.g., child asks play partner to pretend it's raining). One week later they assessed the children on false belief and deception tasks. Hughes and Dunn (1997) found that their pretend play measure correlated strongly with children's performance on theory of mind tasks, and that shared pretense facilitated mental state talk (e.g., speaker refers to his own or another's thoughts, "Do you think Captain Hook could be a policeman?"[2] Youngblade and Dunn's (1995) longitudinal study offers the strongest support for a role play-theory of mind relationship. At 33 months, they observed children interacting at home with their mothers and older siblings, and noted their involvement in pretend play. At 40 months, they assessed children's understanding of false belief. Only one pretend play measure, role enactment, correlated significantly with children's subsequent performance on false belief tasks.

Two independent studies (Astington & Jenkins, 1995; Schwebel, Rosen, & Singer, 1999) confirm the specificity of the role play-theory of mind relationship noting that among a variety of pretense measures only role play showed a positive relation to performance on theory of mind tasks. Astington and Jenkins (1995) observed children playing in small groups and found that discussions about make-believe games (e.g., who would be involved in the play) showed no relationship to performance on false belief tasks whereas actual engagement in role play did show a positive relationship. Schwebel et al. (1999) obtained a similar finding noting that role play, but not solitary pretend play, bore a strong relationship to 3- to 5-year olds' performance on theory of mind tasks. Importantly, in both studies the role play-false belief relationship held even after controlling for age and verbal abilities. Likewise, Lalonde and Chandler (1995) reported that another potential confounding variable, children's social abilities and play skills, showed no relationship to performance on a variety of false belief measures.

In addition to the traditional assessment of role play, Harris (2000) argues that having an imaginary companion, not uncommon among preschool children (Taylor, 1999), constitutes a sustained form of role play in which children become deeply absorbed with a make-believe identity that is stable over a relatively long period of time. Recent research has shown that children create several different types of imaginary companions. In addition to the classic invisible companion (Svendsen, 1934), children may project a distinct personality on to a doll/stuffed animal or spend long periods of time impersonating a particular character (Gleason, Sebanc, & Hartup, 2000; Taylor, 1999). Harris (2000) contends that all three types reveal the child's absorption in roles they have created. Two studies have confirmed a relationship between having an imaginary companion and theory of mind performance (Lalonde &

Chandler, 1995; Taylor & Carslon, 1997). Taylor and Carlson (1997) interviewed children between 3 1/2 and 4 1/2 years to identify those who had an imaginary companion of either the classical (invisible) type or of the impersonator variety. Compared to children who did not have an imaginary companion, those who had companions were better able to distinguish between their beliefs and the beliefs of others. LaLonde and Chandler (1995), using teachers' observations of 3-year-old preschoolers, also noted a positive relationship between having an imaginary companion (and other forms of make-believe play) and false belief understanding. Importantly, other teacher rated characteristics of the children, such as good social skills, that might be hypothesized to mediate such a relationship showed no important association with success on false belief tasks.

PRETEND PLAY–THEORY OF MIND: ALTERNATIVE POSSIBILITIES

There is an impressive body of evidence that supports a relationship between shared pretense, particularly role play, and theory of mind. Still, the data are correlational and fraught with all the attendant problems. Not only is the direction of the pretend play-theory of mind relationship uncertain (Lillard, 2001b), but it is also possible that other abilities (e.g., language skills) or social experiences (e.g., interactions with siblings) may either impact theory of mind directly or overlap with the mental processes involved in role play. In short, shared pretend (role) play might well promote theory of mind, but its contribution may not be as unique and powerful as it appears when we focus the lens sharply on childhood pretense. Below I briefly review possible qualifications and alternative explanations of the pretend play–theory of mind relationship.

Language

Although the effects of child language have been controlled for in a number of studies that support a pretend play–theory of mind relationship, language continues to play a pivotal role in discussions of theory of mind as a putative cause of advances in theory of mind (Astington, 2000), as a general pathway by which children join a "community of minds" (Nelson, 2005, p.28) and as a strong correlate of theory of mind performance (Happé, 1995). With respect to the latter point, measures of both expressive and receptive language show an impressive relationship to the full range of theory of mind tasks, with some indication of a causal role for language. For example, among a large sample of 4-year-olds, Cutting and Dunn (1999) found that both false belief and emotion understanding tasks correlated significantly with receptive language ability and narrative expressive language. Hughes and Dunn (1997) found a positive relationship between preschoolers' (MLU) and their performance on a battery of theory of mind (false belief and deception) tasks. Two other studies have corroborated and extended this result. Jenkins and Astington (1996) found a strong correlation between 3- to 5-year-olds' scores on false belief tasks and general language ability (syntactic and semantic skills) of the Test of Early Language Development (TELD), as well as a positive relationship between false belief and verbal memory (but not nonverbal memory) on the Stanford Binet. In a subsequent follow-up study, these same authors tested a group of 3-year-olds on three occasions over a 7 month period on the TELD and two different theory of mind measures (false belief and appearance-reality). TELD scores, particularly syntactic abilities, predicted later theory of mind performance, but the reverse relationship (early theory of mind predicting later TELD performance) did not hold true (Astington & Jenkins, 1999). With an even longer time delay, Watson, Painter, and Bornstein (2001) reported that an omnibus measure of child language (consisting of both maternal report and a structured language assessment) at 24 months accounted for a unique portion of the variance in false belief performance at 48 months.

Although Astington and Jenkins's (1999) analysis of the TELD found particular support for the relationship between syntactic abilities and theory of mind debate continues on the relative merits of syntax and semantics for theory of mind development. It is possible, of course, that both syntax and semantics make a unique contribution to theory of mind. This is precisely the conclusion that

Ruffman and colleagues (Ruffman, Slade, Rowlandson, & Garnham, 2003) drew from their study of language abilities in relationship to belief/desire and emotion understanding. Using measures from several standardized tests, these authors found it difficult to separate syntax and semantics. Ruffman et al. (2003) concluded that among normally developing children these two components of language are so interrelated that false belief understanding is associated with general language competence, or as they put it, "syntax plus semantics not syntax or semantics" (p. 154).

One additional possibility exists, however. There may be specialized linguistic structures of particular importance to theory of mind that are not readily observed through standardized tests. Of the candidate structures, object complementation has received the most attention because it permits a clear distinction between an actual state of affairs and the way a speaker represents those affairs (Tager-Flusberg, 2000). Object complements, also referred to as sentential complements, are the subordinate clauses formed from certain classes of verbs, particularly verbs conveying information about knowledge and beliefs (e.g., know, think) and communication (e.g., say, tell). For example, in "John thinks that Mary is upstairs" the subordinate clause, "that Mary is upstairs," is the object complement of what John thinks. One important feature of complementation is that it allows for the embedding of one proposition (e.g., what John thinks) under another (e.g., where Mary is). Crucial to the development of theory of mind, embedded complements can represent false propositions (e.g., Mary may not be upstairs) yet the statement about what John thinks remains true. Thus, object (sentential) complementation is a syntactic form that highlights the potential for people to hold contrary-to-fact propositions that can be viewed as "uniquely suited to the conceptual representation of false beliefs" (deVilliers and deVilliers, 2000, p. 193). The deVilliers have supported their position with longitudinal data showing that 3- and 4-year-olds' memory for sentential complements at an early point in time (e.g., "He thought that he found his ring, but it was really a bottle cap What did he think?") accounted for a substantial portion of the variance in false belief understanding at a later point in time while the reverse relationship (early false belief predicting later memory for complements) accounted for only a small portion of the variance (deVilliers & Pyers, 2002). Two recent lines of research support the importance of sentential complements for theory of mind development. In work with children with autism, Tager-Flusberg and Joseph (2005) found that understanding sentential complements made a unique contribution, beyond general language ability, to performance on theory of mind tasks while Lohmann, Tomasello, and Meyer (2005), using a training method that isolated sentential complements from other potential aids to theory of mind (e.g., perspective shifting), found significant posttest gains on false belief understanding among children trained to use sentential complements.

Social Experiences

From infancy onward, children have a range of experiences that might either assist or retard their understanding of the social world, including the mental life of others. I consider three different types of experience separately though it will be clear that they are not independent of one another.

Family Interaction

A potentially rich milieu to learn about what others think and feel is the give and take of social interactions within the family. Through discussions, arguments, and negotiations with parents and siblings, children confront a variety of perspectives, both intellectual and affective, that over time may help them discover that other people may view the world differently than they do.

One question of considerable interest is the potentially positive effects of siblings on theory of mind development (see, however, Cole & Mitchell, 2000, and Cutting and Dunn, 1999). There are really two possibilities here. One is that what matters is the total number of siblings with whom the child has the opportunity to interact. This hypothesis is affirmed by research showing a positive relationship between number of siblings and performance on false belief tasks (Perner, Ruffman, and Leekam, 1994) and between family size and false belief even after partialling out the effects of child age and language ability (Jenkins & Astington, 1996). Alternatively, it is possible to argue, perhaps from a Vygotskian perspective, that older siblings are particularly important because they guide the younger child toward an understanding of other minds. A number of studies have found that the greatest advantage on false beliefs tasks falls to children with older siblings (Lewis, Freeman, Kryiakidou, Maridaki-Kassotaki, & Berridge, 1996; Ruffman, Perner, Naito, Parkin, & Clements, 1998; Ruffman, Perner, & Parkman, 1999; Youngblade & Dunn, 1995). Consistent also with a Vygotskian perspective, Lewis et al. (1996), who examined both the number of siblings and the broader social context in which their sample lived (e.g., number of adult kin and older nonrelated children who interact regularly with the child), suggested that researchers will achieve their best predictions for success on theory of mind tasks by examining the full ecology of the child's environment.

Beyond the size and structure, what particular types of family social interaction are especially important to theory of mind. The work of Dunn and her colleagues (Dunn, 1991; Dunn, Brown, Slomkowski et al., 1991; Dunn, Brown, and Beardsall, 1991) suggests that "mind reading" is deeply rooted in children's social experiences emerging from contexts that are not "emotionally neutral" but rather from situations in which the child is "intensely involved." Pretend play with others is one such experience but so too are the "social exchanges" that involve humor, threats to self-interest, and discussions of causality (Dunn, 1991, p. 58). In a pioneering study supporting this view, Dunn, Brown, Slomkowski et al. (1991) conducted home observations of children at 33 months, interacting with their mothers and siblings, then tested the children at 40 months on false belief and affective labeling (identifying basic emotions—happiness, sadness) and perspective taking (recognition of emotions that differ from the child's). They found a positive relationship between family talk about emotions and causal talk (e.g., "Don't jump, you'll break that.") at 33 months, and all three measures taken at 40 months, leading them to conclude that involvement in discussion about the social world promotes advances in social cognition. In that world, children express their own emotions, explore conflicts with siblings, and hear parents sort out disagreements. Additionally, there is reason to believe that this emotional caldron may have relatively long term effects. For example, Dunn, Brown, and Beardsall (1991) showed that among 3-year-olds the frequency and diversity of emotional state talk with mothers and has a strong relationship to affective perspective taking at age 6 years.

Mental State Talk

In the past few years, researchers have focused attention on the relationship between parent's discussion of mental states and children's understanding of theory of mind, including knowledge of emotions (Garner, Jones, Gaddy, & Rennie, 1997; Peterson & Slaughter, 2003; Ruffman, Perner, & Parkman, 1999; Ruffman, Slade, & Crowe, 2002). In one study related to the family interaction style noted above, Ruffman et al. (1999) asked mothers of 3-year-olds to respond to questions about how they would discipline their children for selected transgression. They noted a positive relationship between the reported frequency of mothers asking their children to reflect on the feelings of others ("How would you feel if he did that to you?") and the children's performance on false belief tasks. Using a similar methodology, Peterson and Slaughter (2003) found a strong positive correlation between preschooler's performance on a false belief task and their mothers' tendency to select a mentally elaborated conversational style (frequent references to thoughts and feelings) in response to everyday problems portrayed in a series of hypothetical vignettes. Two other studies relied on mothers' responses to story books or pictures. Garner et al. (1997) asked a sample of low-income mothers to "read" a story book with no accompanying text to their young children who were also given a test of emotion understanding. Children whose mothers both referred to and explained the reasons for the emotional scenarios in the book scored higher on emotion understanding. Finally, in a study designed to address the direction of the relationship between mothers' mental state talk and children's theory of mind understanding, Ruffman et al (2002) asked mothers to describe pictures of people in everyday situations (e.g., mother bathing a baby) to their 3-year-old children at three different time points over roughly a 1-year period. At each time point, the authors also assessed the children's language ability and theory of mind understanding. Mothers' descriptions of the pictures were coded for mental state language, that is, descriptions that made reference to the depicted characters desires, emotions, and beliefs. The authors found that mothers' mental state utterances at the early time points (time 1 and time 2) predicted children's theory of mind performance at the later time points (time 2 and time 3), and, importantly, that the reverse relationship, (children's theory of mind predicting mother's mental state talk) did not hold. Additional analyses controlled for a number of possible mediating relationships, such as mothers educational level and children's age and language ability (including their use of mental terms), leading Ruffman et al. (2002) to propose a causal relationship between mother's mental state language and children's belief understanding.

Another important line of research on mental state talk comes from the work of Meins and her colleagues who have identified a maternal style emerging in infancy, known as mind mindedness, as a predictor of children's theory of mind (Meins, 1998; Meins & Fernyhough, 1999; Meins, Fernyhough, Wainwright, Das Gupta, Fradley, & Tuckey, 2002; Meins, Fernyhough, Wainwright, Clark-Carter, Das Gupta, Fradley, & Tuckey, 2003). Mind mindedness is the tendency to treat the child as an individual with a mind and not simply as an organism whose needs must be satisfied (Meins, 1998). Mothers who exhibit this characteristic tend to focus on the children's mental attributes rather than on their physical or behavioral attributes. Using maternal characterizations of children's language as well as general descriptions of children's behavior, Meins and Fernyhough (1999) demonstrated that mothers are consistent from 20 months to 3 years in their tendency toward mind mindedness and that mind mindedness relates positively to theory of mind performance at 5 years. Subsequent work showed that as early as 6 months mothers use mental state language in free play with their children and that appropriate use of such language predicts theory of mind performance at 45 and 48 months, with path analyses suggesting a direct link between appropriate maternal mind-related comments in infancy and theory of mind understanding at 48 months (Meins, Fernyhough, Wainwright, Das Gupta, Fradley, & Tuckey, 2002; Meins, Fernyhough, Wainwright, Clark-Carter, Das Gupta, Fradley, & Tuckey, 2003).

Attachment

Attachment theory offers a different though related perspective on mental state talk and one that elevates maternal sensitivity to the forefront. Mothers who talk to their children about thoughts and feelings adopt a parenting style that is both attuned to their children's emotional needs and one that is likely to promote mental state knowledge (Meins, 1998). Furthermore, because maternal sensitivity emerges in infancy, proponents of attachment theory predict that individual differences in the quality of infant–mother bonding will influence children's subsequent understanding of mental states (Fonagy & Target, 1997; Harris, 1999). Fonagy and Target (1997) elaborate this notion arguing that theory of mind is a key component of the "reflective function," a mental activity that "organizes the experience of one's own and others' behavior in terms of mental state constructs...that give rise to beliefs and emotions" (Fonagy & Target, 1997, p. 80). The reflective function is hypothesized to develop through early social experience that at core are influenced by the quality of the attachment relationship. In their empirical work, Fonagy and colleagues' support their claim using two different measures of attachment. In one, security of attachment at 1 year, as measured by the Strange situation, predicted comprehension of complex emotions at age 6 years (Steele, Steele, Croft, & Fonagy, 1999). In another, children rated as securely attached on the Separation Anxiety Test (pictures of parent–child separation scenes) were far more likely to pass a false belief emotion task than children rated as insecure (Fonagy, Redfern, & Charman, 1997). DeRosnay and Harris (2002) also found that attachment security, as measured by the Separation Anxiety Test, reliably predicted preschool children's performance on both a neutral emotion understanding task and a charged understanding task that invoked a separation theme.

In short, a mother's tendency to talk to her children about mental states, to be mind minded in Meins' terms, may be important to theory of mind primarily because it reveals psychological sensitivity toward her child (Harris, in press). Mothers of securely attached children develop ways of communicating that promote a sense of agency and independence in their children (DeRosnay & Harris,

2002). Proponents of attachment theory believe that there is stability to this communication style, and that over time it becomes consequential for children's understanding of beliefs and emotions. In this vein, Meins and colleagues report that at age 3 years children who were previously classified as securely attached in infancy had mothers who were more sensitive in tutoring them on difficult tasks than were the mothers of infants classified as insecurely attached, and that by age 4 years the securely attached children performed reliably better on false belief tasks than did the insecurely attached children (Meins, Fernyhough, C., Russell, J., & Clarke-Carter, 1998).

CONCLUSION

There is now a substantial body of research demonstrating that pretend play bears a plausible relationship to children's understanding of mental states. One possible reason for this relationship is that pretend play encourages children to appreciate the distinction between actual and represented events. However, as Harris (2000) notes, if this were true then most types of pretend play should be a stimulus for theory of mind development whereas to date there is convincing empirical support only for a relationship between role (sociodramatic) play and mental state understanding.

At the theoretical level, a role play-theory of mind relationship appears to offer support for simulation theory. One way to view role play is to think of it as a process by which children imagine themselves doing what others would do in a particular situation, and then adopting the cognitive-emotional disposition of the characters they portray (Harris, 2000). Over time, experienced role players find themselves involved in different play scenarios that call for simulation of how others would respond to a particular circumstance. Regularly imagining the world as another person sees it has the potential to become an important wedge in moving children toward the realization that mental states guide people's actions (Harris, 2000).

Lillard (2002) notes two allied features of role play that might also contribute to theory of mind development. One is that during role play children not only simulate the thoughts and emotions of the characters they enact but they also have the opportunity to observe their play partners doing much the same thing. In addition, role play often requires a good deal of "out of frame" work, such as first negotiating who will play what role or selecting the appropriate props. Effectively, out of frame work becomes a form of stage direction in which the children gain another opportunity to discuss mental states, e.g., the motivations and intentions of the characters they enact.

Although there is both theoretical and empirical support for a role play-theory of mind relationship two important caveats are worth noting. First, the data are correlational, and most studies simply show concurrent relationships between some form of role play and a variety of theory of mind measures.[3] Second, as noted previously, there are a number of alternative explanations for theory of mind development that might either covary with role play (e.g., family talk about thoughts and feelings) or arguably assume a more primary position (e.g., maternal sensitivity). These alternative explanations raise the question of the most productive way forward in pretend play-theory of mind research.

One possible strategy is to continue the *in situ* correlational studies, which offer the advantage of ecologically valid 'real world' observations, but to embrace the research designs adopted in a number of studies examining the relationship between theory of mind and either language or attachment. Two design features seem particularly promising. One involves the use of time-lagged analyses capable of examining bi-directional relationships. For example, Jenkins and Astington (1999) and Ruffman et al. (2002) used multiple data points to establish a relationship between a measure of either child or maternal language at any early time point and theory of mind at later time points, as well as analyses that ruled out the reverse explanations. Another promising design involves several variables entered as predictors in multiple regression to establish not only the presence of a relationship but also the amount of variance accounted for by each of the predictors. A number of studies have used multiple regression effectively in establishing relationships between theory of mind and language (Jenkins & Astington, 1999; Cutting & Dunn, 1999), parenting style (Ruffman et al., 1999), and attachment (Meins et al., 1998; Steele et al., 1999).

A second possible strategy is to use observational studies as the basis for training studies that have the best chance for establishing true causal relationships. For example, one can ask whether training on variables that emerge from correlational studies as possible predictors of theory of mind leads directly to improvement in mental state understanding. With respect to role play, there is an established literature on training studies that provides the outline of a way forward. Smilansky (1968) noted that infrequent and poorer quality role play was common among economically disadvantaged children, but that these children could be trained effectively to engage in robust role play. Smilansky's (1968) work inspired a number of subsequent studies which demonstrated that fantasy (role) play training led to improvements on intelligence, problem solving, and perspective taking (Rosen, 1974; Satz & Johnson, 1974). In a recent and more directly relevant study, Dockett (1998) found that during the course of a ten week preschool session, 4-year-olds who were given role play training showed significant improvement on both immediate and delayed theory of mind posttests in contrast to controls who participated in the standard curriculum and showed no posttest gains.

The potential benefit from the combination of correlational and training studies is substantial. We may well learn, however, that no single variable, including role play, is by itself a strong predictor of theory of mind. Lillard's (2001a) twin earth model predicts as much suggesting that there are multiple determinants of theory of mind. Harris (in press) makes a related point by suggesting that research on role play forms a natural bridge with research on the pragmatic functions of language, particularly the conversations that children have with caregivers. Certain parental/conversational styles, such as asking children to imagine how others feel, mirror the processes of imagining the perspective of others that unfold during role play. Together the two can form a "virtuous circle" that improves children's belief understanding as well as their appreciation of the feelings and emotions that make-up the social world they inhabit (Harris, in press). The search for multiple contributors to the development of theory of mind seems both warranted and consistent with the evidence we have to date on how children come to appreciate that minds matter.

NOTES

1. Gordon (1992) notes that even adults do not regularly put themselves (empathically) in the place of others and, in fact, often have to be instructed to do so. That point notwithstanding, children do appear capable of putting themselves in the place of others, via role play, in the sense that I am describing here.
2. Hughes and Dunn's (1997) used an omnibus pretend measure that appears to be weighted toward role play but does have other components that do not involve role play.
3. Youngblade and Dunn (1995) is an exception that shows a lagged correlation (play at 33 months related to belief understanding at 40 months) in the supporting direction.

REFERENCES

Astington, J. W. (1988). Theory of mind, Humpty Dumpty, and the ice box. *Human Development*, 41, 30–39.

Astington, J.W. (2000). Language and metalanguate in children's understanding of mind. In J. W. Astington (Ed.), *Minds in the making: Essays in honor of David R. Olson* (pp. 267–284). Oxford, UK: Blackkwell.

Astington, J. W., & Jenkins, J. J. (1995). Theory of mind development and social understanding. *Cognition and Emotion*, 9, 151–165.

Astington, J.W., & Jenkins, J.J. (1999). A longitudinal study of the relation between language and theory-of-mind development. *Developmental Psychology*, 35, 1311–1320.

Baron-Cohen, S. (2001). Theory of mind and autism: A review. *Special issue of the International Review of Mental Retardation*, 23(169), 3–35.

Bartsch, K., & Wellman, H. M. (1995). *Children's talk about the mind*. New York: Oxford University Press.

Bretherton, I., & Beeghly, M. (1982). Talking about internal states: The acquisition of an explicit theory of mind. *Developmental Psychology*, 18, 906–921.

Bretherton, I., McNew, S., & Beeghly-Smith, M. (1981). Early person knowledge as expressed in gestural and verbal communication: When do infants acquire a "theory of mind"? In M. E. Lamb & L. R. Sherod (Eds.), *Infant social cognition* (pp. 333–373). Hillsdale, NJ: Erlbaum.

Cole, K., & Mitchell, P. (2000). Siblings in the development of executive control and a theory of mind. *British journal of Developmental Psychology*, 18, 279–295.

Cutting, A. L., & Dunn, J. (1999). Theory of mind, emotion understanding, language, and family background: Individual differences and interrelations. *Child Development*, 70, 853–865.

Dennett, D. (1978). Beliefs about beliefs. *The Behavioral and Brain Sciences*, 1, 568–570.

DeRosnay, M., & Harris, P. L. (2002). Individual differences in children's understanding of emotion: The roles of attachment and language. *Attachment & Human Development*, 4, 39–54.

deVilliers, J. G., & deVilliers, P. A. (2000). Linguistic determinism and the understanding of false beliefs. In P. Mitchell & K. J. Riggs (Eds.), *Children's reasoning and the mind* (pp. 191–228). Hove, UK: Psychology Press.

deVilliers, J. G., & Pyers, J.E. (2002). Complements to cognition: A longitudinal study of the relationship between complex syntax and false-belief-understanding. *Cognition*, 17, 1037–1060

Dockett, S. (1998). Constructing understandings through play in the early years. *International Journal of Early Years Education*, 6, 105–116.

Dunn, J. (1991). Understanding others: Evidence from

naturalistic studies of children. In A. Whiten (Ed.), *Natural theories of mind: Evolution, development, and simulation in everyday mindreading* (pp. 51–61). Oxford: Blackwell.

Dunn, J. (1994). Changing minds and changing relationships. In C. Mitchell & P. Lewis (Eds.), *Origins of an understanding of mind* (pp. 297–310). Hillsdale, NJ: Erlbaum.

Dunn, J., & Dale, N. (1984). I a Daddy: 2-year-olds collaboration in joint pretend with sibling and mother. In I. Bretherton, *Symbolic play: The development of social understanding* (pp. 131–158). New York: Academic Press.

Dunn, J., Brown, J., & Beardsall, L. (1991). Family talk about feeling states and children's later understanding of emotions. *Developmental Psychology, 27,* 448–455.

Dunn, J., Brown, J., Slomkowski, C., Telsa, C., & Youngblade, L. (1991). Young children's understanding of other people's feelings and beliefs: Individual differences and their antecedents. *Child Development, 62,* 1352–1366.

Dunn, J., & Cutting, A. L. (1999). Understanding others, and individual differences in friendship interactions in young children. *Social Development, 8,* 201–219.

Fein, G. G. (1981). Pretend play: An integrative review. *Child Development, 52,* 1095–1118.

Fodor, J. A. (1992). A theory of the child's theory of mind. *Cognition, 44,* 283–296.

Fodor, J. A. (1983). *The modularity of mind.* Cambridge, MA: MIT Press.

Fonagy, P., & Target, M. (1997). Attachment and reflective function: Their role in self organization. *Development and Psychopathology, 9,* 679–700.

Fonagy, J. A., Redfern, S., & Charman, T. (1997). The relationship between belief-desire reasoning and a projective measure of attachment security (SAT). *British Journal of Developmental Psychology, 15,* 51–61.

Garner, P., Jones, D., Gaddy, D., & Rennie, K. (1997). Low income mothers' conversations about emotion and their children's emotional competence. *Social Development, 6,* 125–142.

Garvey, C. (1977). *Play.* Cambridge: Harvard University Press.

Gleason, T. R., Sebanc, A. M., & Hartup, W. W. (2000). Imaginary companions of preschool children. *Developmental Psychology, 36,* 419–428.

Goldman, A. I. (1992). In defense of simulation theory. *Mind & Language, 1,* 104–119.

Gordon, R. L. (1992). The simulation theory: Objections and misconceptions. *Mind and Language, 7,* 11–34.

Happé, F. G. E. (1995). The role of age and verbal ability in the theory of mind task performance of subjects with autism. *Child Development, 66,* 843–855.

Harman, G. (1978). Studying the chimpanzee's theory of mind. *The Behavioral and Brain Sciences, 1,* 515–526.

Harris, P. L. (1991). The work of the imagination. In A. Whiten (Ed.), *Natural theories of mind: Evolution, development, and simulation in everyday mindreading* (pp. 283–304). Oxford: Blackwell.

Harris, P. L. (1992). From simulation to folk psychology: The case for development. *Mind and Language, 7,* 120–144.

Harris, P. L. (1999). Individual differences in understanding emotions: The role of attachment status and emotional discourse. *Attachment and Human Development, 1,* 307–324.

Harris, P. L. (2000). *The work of the imagination.* Oxford: Blackwell.

Harris, P. L. (in press). Conversation, pretence and theory of mind. In J. W. Astington & J. Baird (Eds.), *Why language matters for theory of mind.*

Harris, P. L., & Kavanaugh, R. D. (1993). Young children's understanding of pretense. *Monographs of the Society for Research in Child Development, 58*(1, Serial No. 231).

Harris, P. L., Lillard, A., & Perner, J. (1994). Triangulating pretence and belief. In C. Lewis & P. Mitchell (Eds.), *Children's understanding of mind: Origins and development* (pp. 287–293). Hillsdale, NJ: Erlbaum.

Hughes, C., & Dunn, J. (1997). "pretend you didn't know": Young children's talk about mental states in pretend play. *Cognitive Development, 12,* 477–499.

Jenkins, J. M., & Astington, J. W. (1996). Cognitive factors and family structure associated with theory of mind development in young children. *Developmental Psychology, 32,* 70–78.

Jarrold, C., Carruthers, P., Smith, P. K., & Boucher, J. (1994). Pretend play: Is it metarepresentational? *Mind and Language, 9,* 445–468.

Kavanaugh, R. D., Eizenman, D. R., & Harris, P. L. (1997). Young children's understanding of pretense expressions of independent agency. *Developmental Psychology, 33,* 764–770.

Lalonde, C. E., & Chandler, M. J. (1995). False belief understanding goes to school: On the social-emotional consequences of coming early or late to a first theory of mind. *Cognition and Emotion, 9,* 167–185.

Leslie, A. M. (1987). Pretense and representation: The origins of "theory of mind." *Psychological Review, 94,* 412–426.

Leslie, A. M. (1991). The theory of mind impairment in autism: Evidence for a modular mechanism of development? In A. Whiten (Ed.), *Natural theories of mind: Evolution, development, and simulation in everyday mindreading* (pp. 63–78). Oxford: Blackwell.

Leslie, A. M. (1994). ToMM, ToBy, and agency: Core architecture and domain specificity. In L. A. Hirschfield & S. A. Gellman (Eds.), *Mapping the mind: Domain specificity and culture* (pp. 119–148). Cambridge: Cambridge University Press.

Leslie, A. M. (2000). "Theory of mind" as a mechanism of selective attention. In M. S. Gazzaniga (Ed.), *The new cognitive neurosciences* (pp. 1235–1247). Cambridge, MA: MIT Press.

Leslie, A. M., & Roth, D. (1993). What autism teaches us about metarepresentation. In S. Baron-Cohen, H. Tager-Flusberg, & D. Cohen (Eds.), *Understanding other minds: Perspectives from autism* (pp. 83–111). Oxford: Oxford University Press.

Lewis, C., Freeman, H. Kyriakidou, C. Maridaki-Kassotaki, K. M., & Berridge, D. M. (1996). Social influences on false belief access: Specific sibling influences or general apprenticeship? *Child Development, 67,* 2930–2947.

Lillard, A. S. (2001a). Pretend play as twin earth: A social-cognitive analysis. *Developmental Review, 21,* 495–531.

Lillard, A. S. (2001b). Pretending, understanding pretense, and understanding minds. In S. Reifel (Ed.), *Play and cultural studies* (Vol. 3, pp. 233–254). Westport, CT: Ablex.

Lillard, A. S. (2002). Pretend play and cognitive development. In U. Goswhami (Ed.), *Blackwell Handbook of Cognitive Development* (pp. 188–205). Oxford: Blackwell

Lohmann, H., Tomasello, M. & Meyer, S. (2005). Linguistic communication and social understanding. In J. W. Astington & J. A. Baird (Eds.), *Why language matters for theory of mind* (pp. 245–265). New York: Oxford University Press.

Meltzoff, A. N. (1995). Understanding the intentions of others: Re-enactment of intended acts by 18-month-old children. *Developmental Psychology, 31,* 838–850.

McCune-Nicolich, L. (1981). Toward symbolic functioning: Structure of early use of early pretend games and potential parallels with language. *Child Development, 52*, 785–797.

Meins, E. (1998). The effects of security of attachment and maternal attribution of meaning on children's linguistic acquisitional style. *Infant Behavior and Development, 21*, 237–252.

Meins, E., & Fernyhough, C. (1999). Linguistic acquisitional style and mentalising development: The role of maternal mind-mindedness. *Cognitive Development, 14*, 363–380.

Meins, E., Fernyhough, C., Russell, J., & Clark-Carter, D. (1998). *Social Development, 1*, 1–24.

Meins, E., Fernyhough, C., Wainwright, R., Das Gupta, M., Fradley, & Tuckey, M. (2002). Maternal mind mindedness and attachment security as predictors of theory of mind understanding. *Child Development, 73*, 1715–1726.

Meins, E., Fernyhough, C., Wainwright, R., Clark-Carter, D., Das Gupta, M., Fradley, & Tuckey, M. (2002). Pathways to understanding mind: Construct validity and predictive validity of maternal mind mindedness. *Child Development, 74*, 1194–1211.

Nelson, K. (2005). Language pathways into the community of minds. In J. W. Astington & J. A. Baird (Eds.), *Why language matters for theory of mind* (pp. 26–49). New York: Oxford University Press.

Nichols, S., & Stich, S. (2000). A cognitive theory of pretense. *Cognition, 74*, 115–147.

Piaget, J. (1946/1962). *Play, dreams and imitation in childhood.* New York: Norton (original publication, 1946).

Perner, J., Ruffman, T., & Leekam, S. R. (1994). Theory of mind is contagious: You catch it from your sibs. *Child Development, 65*, 1228–1238.

Peterson, C., & Siegal, M. (1999). Representing inner worlds: Theory of mind in autistic, deaf and normal hearing children. *Psychological Science, 10*, 126–129.

Peterson, C., & Slaughter, V. (2003). Opening windows into the mind: Mothers' preferences for mental state explanations and children's theory of mind. *Cognitive Development, 18*, 399–429.

Premack, D., & Woodruff, G. (1978). Does the chimpanzee have a theory of mind? *The Behavioral and Brain Sciences, 1*, 515–526.

Pylyshyn, Z. W. (1978). When is attribution of beliefs justified? *The Behavioral and Brain Sciences, 1*, 592–593.

Rosen, C. E. (1974). The effects of sociodramatic play on problem-solving behavior among culturally disadvantaged preschool children. *Child Development, 45*, 920–927.

Ruffman, T., Perner, J., & Parkin, L. (1999). How parenting style affects false belief understanding. *Social Development, 8*, 395–411.

Ruffman, T., Perner, J., Naito, M., Parkin, L., & Clements, W. (1998). Older (but not younger) siblings facilitate false belief understanding. *Developmental Psychology, 34*, 161–174.

Ruffman, T., Slade, L., & Crowe, E. (2002). The relation between children's and mothers' mental state language and theory of mind understanding. *Child Development, 73*, 734–751.

Ruffman, T., Slade, L., Rowlandson, K., & Garnham, A. (2003). How language relates to belief, desire, and emotion understanding. *Cognitive Development, 18*, 139–158.

Satz, E., & Johnson, J. (1974). Training for thematic-fantasy play in culturally disadvantage children: Preliminary results. *Child Development, 66*, 623–630.

Scholl, B. J. & Leslie, A. M. (1999). Modularity, development, and 'theory of mind'. *Mind and Language, 14*, 131–153.

Schwebel, D. C., Rosen, C. S., & Singer, J. L. (1999). Preschoolers' pretend play and theory of mind: The role of jointly constructed pretense. *British Journal of Psychology, 17*, 333–348.

Smilansky, S. (1968). *The effects of sociodramatic play on disadvantaged preschool children.* New York: Wiley.

Steele, H., Steele, M., Croft, C., & Fonagy, P. (1999). Infant-mother attachment at one year predicts children's understanding of mixed emotions at six years. *Social Development, 8*, 161–178.

Svendsen, M. (1934). Children's imaginary companions. *Archives of Neurology and Psychiatry, 2*, 985–989.

Tamis-LeMonda, C. S. & Bornstein, M. H. Specificity in mother-toddler language-play relations across the second year. *Developmental Psychology, 30*, 283–292.

Tager-Flusberg, H. (2000). Language and understanding minds: Connections in autism. In S. Baron-Cohen, H. Tager-Flusberg, & D. J. Cohen (Eds.), *Understanding other minds: Persepctives from developmental cognitive neuroscience* (pp. 124–149). New York: Oxford University Press.

Tager-Flusberg, H., & Joseph, R. M. (2005). How language facilitates the acquisition of fasle belief in children with autism. In J. W. Astington & J. A. Baird (Eds.), *Why language matters for theory of mind* (pp. 298–318). New York: Oxford University Press.

Taylor, M. (1999). *Imaginary companions and the children who create them.* New York: Oxford.

Watson, A. C., Painter, K. A., & Bornstein, M. H. (2001). Longitudinal relations between 2-year-olds' language and 4-year-old theory of mind. *Journal of Cognition and Development, 2*, 449–457.

Taylor, M., & Carlson, S. M. (1997). The relation between individual differences in fantasy and theory of mind. *Child Development, 68*, 436–455.

Wellman, H. W. (1990). *The child's theory of mind.* Cambridge, MA: MIT Press.

Wimmer, H., & Perner, J. (1983). Beliefs about beliefs: Representation and constraining function of wrong beliefs in young children's understanding of deception. *Cognition, 13*, 103–128.

Wolf, D. P., Rygh, J., & Altshuler, J. (1984). Agency and experience: Actions and states in play narratives. In I. Bretherton, *Symbolic play: The development of social understanding* (pp. 195–217). New York: Academic Press.

Youngblade, L. M., & Dunn, J. (1995). Individual differences in young children's pretend play with mother and sibling: Links to relationships and understanding of other people's feelings and beliefs. *Child Development, 66*, 1472–1492.

8

Concreteness and Symbolic Development

David H. Uttal
Linda L. Liu
Judy S. DeLoache

INTRODUCTION

The ability to understand and use symbols is one of the defining characteristics of being human. Symbols allow us to think about information that is not available to direct sensory experience. Symbol systems such as language also allow us to communicate with others and thus provide the foundation for learning. Similarly, numbers allow us to think about and mentally manipulate abstract representations rather than having to rely on the actual physical quantities. It is not surprising that the development of symbolic capacity is an important hallmark in almost all theories of cognitive development.

Much research on symbolic development is motivated by the assumption that young children's thinking is inherently concrete in nature, and that their thinking focuses only on immediately perceptible concepts (Bruner, 1966; Piaget, 1951; Vygotsky & Kozulin, 1986; Werner & Kaplan, 1963). In contrast, older children are more able to think about abstract concepts that are not tied to the concrete, perceptible properties of objects that they can see or feel. Put simply, the general notion that concrete thinking precedes abstract thinking is characteristic of most theories of development.

The general assumption that young children's thinking is inherently concrete in nature has had a tremendous effect on the development of educational curricula and materials. Many researchers and educators believe that the best way to help young children learn to understand the abstract properties of symbolic relations is to first make the symbols less abstract and more concrete (Ball, 1992; Clements & McMillen, 1996; Montessori, 1917). For example, Bruner (1966) suggested that the goal of early education should be to "empty the concept of specific sensory properties [in order to] grasp its abstract properties" (p. 65). This assumption has led to the development of a wide variety of educational materials that are specifically designed to appeal to young children's preference for concrete, tangible objects. Examples include letter blocks, number magnets, and formal manipulative systems, such as Dienes Blocks and Cuisenaire Rods. Many early childhood educators assume that these sorts of materials are the best, or even only, way for young children to learn. The assumption has been that "Concrete is inherently good; abstract is inherently not appropriate—at least at the beginning, at least for young learners" (Ball, 1992, p. 16).

The primary purpose of this chapter is to reexamine the focus on concreteness in cognitive development and early education. We will question both the theoretical background of the assumption as well as its educational implications. We will show that the characterization of development in terms of a shift from concrete to abstract is an oversimplification; there are situations in which very young children seem capable of abstract reasoning, and there are other situations in which older children's thinking is highly concrete. We also question the assumption that concrete objects should necessarily provide the foundation for young children's learning of symbolic relations. In some cases, the use of an attractive concrete object may actually have a negative effect because it may focus children's attention more on the object itself rather than on what the object is intended to represent. These claims are based on a review of both classic and current literature on the development of children's understanding of important symbols, including letters, numbers, mathematical symbols, and scale models. We begin by considering the historical and theoretical origins of the commonly accepted belief that young children's thinking is inherently concrete and that early childhood education therefore should focus on the use of concrete objects. We also review recent theoretical and empirical work that has demonstrated that these assumptions may not always be correct.

TRADITIONAL APPROACHES: THE CONCRETE-TO-ABSTRACT SHIFT

Development often has been characterized as children's struggle to transcend their shallow and shortsighted view of the world (Bruner, Goodnow, & Austin, 1956; Piaget, 1951; Werner & Kaplan, 1963). In classic developmental theories, the acquisition of symbolic competence is seen to proceed through a concrete-to-abstract shift: the progression from thinking that is rooted in concrete reality to thinking that is less constrained by context. Sigel (1993) described this developmental progression as the child's attempt to "separate him- or herself mentally from the ongoing here and now, and project him- or herself to some other temporal plane (past or future or the nonpalpable present), in turn transforming the received communication into some symbol or sign system" (p. 142). Eventually, children's mental representations are no longer directly linked, in an iconic fashion, to the information that they originally experienced. Instead, older children are able to represent information more abstractly, so that the information is now only distantly related to how it was experienced initially.

Almost all classic theories of cognitive development have appealed to the idea that young children's thinking is inherently concrete. For example, Piaget (Inhelder & Piaget, 1958; Piaget, 1951) suggested that the development of the ability to reason in terms of abstract, hypothetical propositions, without reference to more concrete information, was the end point or goal of cognitive development. Piaget found that concrete operational children had trouble reasoning about false propositions that involved relations that could not exist in the real world. For example, if concrete operational children are given the statements, "If mice are bigger than dogs and dogs are bigger than elephants," they typically cannot deduce "then mice are bigger than elephants." These sorts of problems require that children reason abstractly about the relations as given, rather than about the actual relations in the world (Werner & Kaplan, 1963). Concrete operational children fail because there is no concrete basis from which to reason about and solve the problem.

Other prominent theorists have also characterized development in terms of a shift from concrete to abstract. For example, in studies of early categorization, Bruner et al. (1956) described conceptual development as a perceptual-to-conceptual shift; children first think of objects only in terms of the properties directly available to their senses but eventually begin to consider abstract properties of objects. For example, children may think that birds and bats are in the same category because they look similar and because they both fly. With development, children become able to categorize objects and living things more on the basis of abstract and nonobservable information. Consequently, they now realize that bats and birds should be in separate categories, and that a creature that does not fly, such as a penguin, may nevertheless belong in the bird category. The developmental transition is thus from a reliance on concrete and perceptible properties to more abstract and less observable ones.

Some of Vygotsky's writings are reminiscent of the concrete-to-abstract shift. Specifically, Vygotsky (Vygotsky & Kozulin, 1986) conducted two lines of work that were motivated by this general assumption. First, he suggested that young children's classification is inherently thematic in nature. Thematic categories (e.g., rabbit and carrot) are based on highly concrete, salient properties that bind objects or living things together in a common setting, rather than on the underlying and abstract relations; they are developmentally primitive. The more developmentally advanced form of categorization (e.g., carrot and potato) is based on *taxonomic* properties. To think about objects in this way, children must learn to look beyond the concrete and perceptually similar characteristics in favor of deeper but less obvious similarities. Second, Vygotsky also pointed out the important role of concreteness in symbolic play. Young children's pretend play often involves the substitution of concrete objects for something else in the real world (e.g., a stick for a horse). He suggested that the use of concrete objects in this way was an early form of symbolization. In the context of the game, children are less bound to the properties of the objects and feel comfortable substituting the objects for something else. Pretend play thus serves the important function of helping children to see that the physical object can be thought of in a different way, as a representation of something else.

Werner and Kaplan (1963) provided what is perhaps the most specific articulation of the relation between concreteness and symbolic development. They argued that development involved a shift from holistic to analytic thinking. Young children initially focus on "physicochemical stimuli" from the environment. By this Werner and Kaplan meant that young children interpret stimuli in terms of their concrete, physical properties. Eventually, children transform stimuli and interpret them as "stimulus-signs or signals" (p. 9). For example, a young child might interpret the letter "A" as two diagonal lines and a crossbar. An older child instead interprets the letter as being related to language, even if he or she does not precisely know how this relation works (see Bialystok et al., 2000).

ALTERNATE PERSPECTIVES: DOES DEVELOPMENT ALWAYS PROCEED FROM CONCRETE TO ABSTRACT?

The notion that young children's thinking is inherently concrete in nature is not universally accepted. For example, researchers have recently presented evidence that even infants are capable of thinking about abstract concepts. Other researchers have challenged the notion that development proceeds from concrete to abstract, suggesting that in some cases the opposite could be true. In this section we briefly summarize these findings and theoretical perspectives.

Abstract Concepts in Infants

Recent research on cognitive development in infancy provides an important challenge to the idea that development proceeds from concrete to abstract. Several lines of research have revealed that infants can interpret movements or actions in terms of abstract concepts. For example, Quinn and colleagues (Quinn, 2003; Quinn, Adams, Kennedy, Shettler, & Wasnik, 2003) have found that infants interpret the position of objects in terms of abstract spatial concepts, such as above, below, and between. By 10 months of age, infants will notice if an object is moved from between two lines to above or below one of the lines, even if the object itself changes. Their judgments of spatial position therefore are not tied to the concrete properties of the objects themselves but are instead based on more abstract concepts such as "between." Likewise, young children are capable of interpreting another person's actions in terms of the goals or intentions that motivate those actions. For example, infants will interpret the hand motion of another person as related to the goal of opening a box to obtain a toy (Gergely, Nadasdy, Csibra, & Biro, 1995; Woodward, 2003; Woodward & Sommerville, 2000). After observing a person opening a box to obtain a toy, they are more surprised when the hand moves to a different box than when the hand moves in a different pattern to the same box. Moving to a different box indicates that the person has a different goal in mind. The infants appear to understand the association between where the hand moves and what the person's intent is. This sort of abstract knowledge allows infants to interpret an action, for example, "as getting a drink of milk rather than grasping a milk carton" (Woodward & Sommerville, 2000, p. 76).

Other research has demonstrated that preschoolers use abstracts concepts as a basis for reasoning, inference generation, and problem solving. For example, Gelman and colleagues (Gelman, 2000, 2003; Gelman & Wellman, 1991) have suggested that children understand that certain objects have an internal "essence" that is distinct from the outward appearance of the objects. Gelman has suggested that this understanding can exist in the absence of detailed scientific understanding of the essence. Gelman and Wellman (1991) tested children's understanding of this "inside-outside" distinction using a category induction task. Children 3 and 4 years of age were shown a target object and two choice objects. They were asked (1) to choose which of the two choice objects "looks most like" the target, and (2) to choose which of the two "has the same kinds of insides" as the target. For example, children were presented with triads of objects from which they could either choose the pair sharing the same outside (e.g., an orange and an orange balloon) or the pair sharing the same inside (e.g., an orange and a lemon). Counter to the idea that object concreteness exerts the primary influence on children's object categorization, they found that children as young as 3 years of age could correctly report both that oranges and orange balloons "look alike" and that oranges and lemons "share the same insides."

Thus, young children's understanding of objects is not inevitably bound to external appearances. Rather, children's understanding of the inside-outside distinction demonstrates that nonobvious and abstract object properties also are available to children (Gelman, 2003). These findings highlight the need to question the unqualified characterization of young children's thinking as being concrete. Children's performance on these sorts of tasks forms part of the basis for Gelman's (2003) claim that young children are *essentialists*. Even young children reason about animals and other entities in terms of abstract-like principles that define their essential characteristics. What matters most to young children, for example, is what is inside an animal, rather than its superficial appearance.

Simons and Keil (1995) presented the most radical reformulation to date of the developmental relation between abstract and concrete thinking. They suggest that the development of children's thinking may, in fact, proceed from abstract to concrete. They argued that very young children may first reason at an abstract level because they lack specific knowledge about objects and events. For example, a child explaining the function of a camera might initially discuss a camera's ability to capture a single point in time, such as its ability to record the moment when she blew out the candles on her birthday cake. Simons and Keil argued that this functional understanding of the camera can precede a more concrete and mechanistic understanding of how light enters the lens and how the various parts of the camera interact. In Simon and Keil's (1995) words, "Although ignorance of the physical components of a system may preclude a concrete explanation for the system's behavior, it is quite possible to generate a principled, abstract explanation without any knowledge of the physical components" (p. 131).

In summary, the notion that young children's thinking is inherently concrete in nature has been challenged in many ways. There is evidence that young children (perhaps even infants) can think in terms of abstract concepts, and there is also evidence that development may sometimes proceed in the opposite direction—from abstract to concrete. In the next section, we consider the relevance of these findings for research on symbolic development. The difficulties children have in using certain kinds of symbols shed light on the question of whether concrete objects do, in fact, facilitate children's learning of symbolic relations.

CONCRETENESS, SYMBOLIC DEVELOPMENT, AND CHILDREN'S USE OF SCALE MODELS

Much of our work on symbolic development has focused on children's understanding of a specific symbol system—scale models. Studying children's understanding of scale models has provided important windows onto the process of symbolic development and the effects of concreteness on symbolic understanding. The results of several studies clearly indicate that the relation between the concreteness of an intended symbol and its effect on children's comprehension of the symbolic relation is far more complex, and interesting, than has been assumed previously.

The Scale Model Task

Our task (DeLoache, 1987) for studying symbolic development is quite simple: We ask young children to use a scale model to find a hidden toy. Usually, the model and the room look very much alike except for size; the walls are the same colors, and the furniture in the model and the room are upholstered with the same fabric. Moreover, there is a high degree of spatial similarity as well. All of the objects in the model are usually placed in the same relative spatial positions as in the room.

We begin by explaining the task and by orienting children to the relation between the model and the room. First, the experimenter points out the two toys that will be hidden. One toy, a miniature dog, is labeled "Little Snoopy"; the second toy, a full-size stuffed dog, is labeled "Big Snoopy." The experimenter then demonstrates the correspondences between the model and the room. The experimenter says, "This is Big Snoopy's big room; Big Snoopy has lots of things in his room." The experimenter then names each of the furniture items. Next, the experimenter points to the model and says, "This is Little Snoopy's little room. He has all the same things in his room that Big Snoopy has." The experimenter then labels each of the furniture items again and highlights the correspondence between each item in the model and the corresponding item in the room. The experimenter carries each item from the model into the room. The miniature furniture item is held next to its counterpart in the room, and the experimenter says, for example, "Look—this is Big Snoopy's big couch, and this is Little Snoopy's little couch. They're just the same."

Next, the experimenter attempts to communicate that there is a relation between actions in the model and actions in the room. For example, the experimenter tells the child that "Big and Little Snoopy like to do the same things. When Big Snoopy sits on his chair, Little Snoopy likes to sit on his chair, too." The experimenter also illustrates the correspondence by placing the toys in the appropriate positions.

The test trials follow immediately after the orientation. On each of the test trials, the experimenter first hides the toy in one of the hiding locations in the model. The experimenter calls the child's attention to the act of hiding, but not to the specific hiding location, by saying, "Look, Little Snoopy is going to hide here." The child is told that an assistant is going to hide Big Snoopy in the same place in the big room.

The experimenter and child then enter the room, and the child is asked to find Big Snoopy. On each trial, the experimenter attempts to remind the child of the relation between the model and the room by saying, "Remember, Little Snoopy is hiding in the same place as Big Snoopy." If the child cannot find the toy, he or she is encouraged to continue searching at other locations, and the experimenter reminds the child again that the toy is in the "same place" as the other toy. Increasingly explicit hints are provided until the toy is found, but a search is counted as correct only if the child finds the toy in the first location that he or she searches.

After the child finds the toy on each trial, he or she is taken back to the model and is asked to find the miniature toy. This search provides a memory check that is critical to interpreting any difficulties that children may have in finding the toy in the room. If the children are able to locate the miniature toy in the model, then difficulties that they encounter finding the toy in the room cannot be attributed to simply forgetting where the toy is in the model. Instead, poor performance reflects a failure to appreciate that the location of the miniature toy in the model (the symbol) can be used to find the larger toy in the room (the referent).

Several aspects of this task and of our results are important in regard to the role of concreteness in children's insight into symbol-referent relations. First, and most importantly, the symbols involved in the task are highly concrete. The model itself, and the furniture in the model, are tangible, three-dimensional objects. Each one is both a real object and a symbolic representation of something other than itself.

Second, successful performance requires that the child comprehend and exploit a symbolic relation—the relation between the model and the room. To solve the task, the child must understand that the location of the toy in the model specifies the location in the room. The concreteness of the model is useful to children only if it helps them understand the abstract stands-for relation between the model and the room.

Third, children are required to solve a seemingly familiar task (searching for a hidden toy) in a novel way. Typically, when young children search for hidden objects, they rely exclusively on direct experience; like adults, they often search where they have last seen an object. To solve our task, however, children have to adopt a totally new strategy that involves relying exclusively on information from the symbol.

Two sets of results from our research on children's use of scale models are very relevant to understanding the effects of concreteness on cognitive development. First, young children's understanding of the model is quite fragile. Children have trouble initially understanding the relation between the model and the room, and even after they do, they can easily lose sight of this relation. Second, the concreteness of the model may actually contribute to the fragility of children's understanding of the model–room relation. The concrete nature of the model may even make it *more* difficult for young children to use it as a symbol than a less concrete object, such as a photograph. In the next two sections we review both aspects of children's understanding of scale models.

The Fragility of Children's Understanding of Scale Models

Despite the apparent simplicity of the model, very young children have great difficulty using it. These results are summarized in Figure 8.1. Children younger than 3 years of age usually perform very poorly (only about 20% correct retrievals). The difficulty that children encounter cannot be attributed to forgetting the location of the toy that they observed being hidden. Almost all children succeed on the memory-based search in which they return to the model to retrieve the miniature toy. Thus, 2½-year-olds can remember the location of the toy in the model, but they tend not to use this knowledge to find the toy in the room. Figure 8.1 also reveals that most 3-year-old children succeed in the standard model task (averaging over 85% correct searches).

The success of the 3-year-olds whose performance is shown in Figure 8.1 is not, however, the end of the developmental story. Although 3-year-olds can solve the standard model task, they have great difficulty even if seemingly minor changes are made in the procedures. For example, DeLoache, Kolstad, and Anderson (1991) found that young children's performance depends very much on the physical similarity between the model and the room. When the furniture in the model and the room are extremely similar in appearance, 3-year-olds are very successful. However, if the objects in

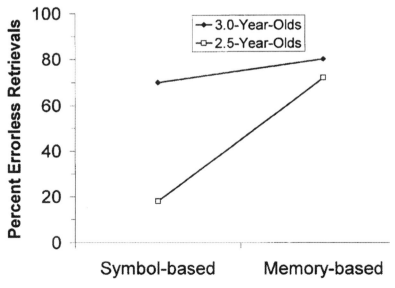

Figure 8.1 Children's performance in the original model study. Adapted from "Rapid Change in the Symbolic Functioning of Very Young Children," by J. S. DeLoache, 1987, *Science*, 238. For the symbol-based retrieval, children saw the miniature toy hidden in the model and then searched for the corresponding larger toy in the room. For the memory-based retrieval, children returned to the model and searched for the miniature toy. Note that only the symbol-based retrieval requires that children use the relation between the model and the room to find the toy.

the two spaces are dissimilar, the children perform at chance levels. Similarly, if the furniture in the model and in the room do not occupy the same relative spatial positions, performance deteriorates substantially (DeLoache, 1989).

Instructions are also critically important in children's comprehension and use of the model–scale relation (DeLoache, 1989). In the standard version of the task, we provide very specific and elaborate instructions about the correspondence between the model and the room. Providing less detailed instructions reduces 3- and even 3½-year-old children's performance to near-chance levels. It is not enough simply to tell the children that Little and Big Snoopy's rooms are alike and that the toys are hidden in the corresponding places in the two rooms. Instead, we must explicitly describe the relation and point out the correspondences between objects in the model and in the room (DeLoache, de Mendoza, & Anderson, 1999). Older children are less dependent on information from the experimenter. Four-year-olds can succeed with the less detailed instructions described above, although they still need explicit information about the general model–room relation. Older children are more able to detect the relation on their own. A group of 5- to 7-year-old children were shown the model, the room, and the two toys. They then observed a hiding event in the model and were asked to find the larger toy in the room (with no explanation of the relations between the spaces or the hiding events). Most of these older children inferred the "rules of the game" from this very minimal information and successfully retrieved the toy.

Even when children do initially grasp the relation between the model and the room, they may still have difficulty keeping track of the relevance of this relation for finding the toy. Uttal, Schreiber, and DeLoache (1995) showed that having to wait before using the information in the model to find the toy in the room caused 3-year-olds' performance to deteriorate dramatically. The task began as it usually does, with children watching us hide the toy in the model and then attempting to find the corresponding toy in the room. There was, however, one difference: We inserted delays between when the children saw the toy being hidden in the model and when they searched in the room. The delays were of three different lengths: 20 seconds, 2 minutes, and 5 minutes. Across the six search trials, all children experienced each of the delays twice. Different groups of children received the delays in one of three different orders. The groups were labeled in terms of the delay that they experienced first: the short-delay-first group had a 20-second delay first, the medium-delay-first group had a 2-minute delay first, and the long-delay-first group had a 5-minute delay first. After the initial trial, the children in each group received trials at the other delays, with delay length counterbalanced over trials.

As shown in Figure 8.2, the length of the initial delay greatly affected children's performance. The long-delay-first group performed poorly on all trials, but the short-delay-first group performed well on most of the trials. We can rule out one possible explanation for the poor performance of the long-delay first group: that children could not remember the location of the toy in the model during the initial delay. If this were true, then the children should perform much better on the shorter delay trials that followed the initial long delay. But this did not occur; the long-delay-first group performed generally poorly on all subsequent trials, even those trials with the short (20-second) delay that normally would give them little, if any, problem. Moreover, children could find the toy in the model even after the long delays. Thus they did not forget where the toy was hidden in the model; they instead forgot that the model could help them find the toy in the room. Uttal et al. (1995) concluded that, during the initial long delay, the children in the long-delay-first group lost track of the relation between the model and the room. Consequently, when they entered the room to search for the toy, they did not use the location of the toy in the model as a guide for searching in the room. The initial delay disrupted their tenuous grasp on the relation between the model and the room. Once the knowledge that the model could help was lost, the children continued to perform poorly, even on the subsequent, shorter delay trials.

Concreteness and the Dual Representation Hypothesis

What accounts for the fragility of young children's comprehension of the relation between the room and the model? In several studies we have demonstrated that the concreteness of the model is actually

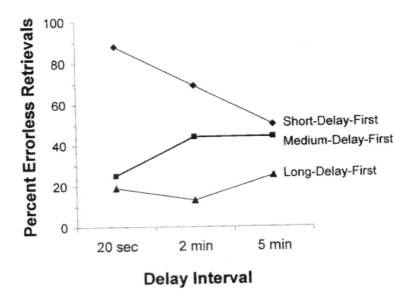

Figure 8.2 The effect of delay on children's use of a model. The initial delay led to much worse performance, even on the subsequent shorter days.

a cause of children's difficulty in using it as a symbol. Highly attractive and salient objects may be particularly difficult for children to think of as representations of something else—as symbols. This interpretation highlights the dual nature of the influence of concreteness on children's performance. Although concreteness may help children to perceive physical similarities between symbols and their referents, it also may make it more difficult for them to think about the abstract symbolic relation between the two.

A scale model such as the one used in our task has a dual nature; it is both a symbol and an object (or a set of objects) with a very high degree of physical salience. The very features that make it highly interesting and attractive to young children as a concrete object to play with, can obscure its role as a representation of something else. To use a model as a symbol, children must achieve *dual representation* (DeLoache, 1991, 1995, 2000; DeLoache & Burns, 1994; DeLoache, Miller, & Rosengren, 1997). They must mentally represent the model itself as an object and, at the same time, as a symbol for what it represents. In the model task, the child must form a meaningful mental representation of the model as a miniature room in which toys can be hidden and found, and he or she has to interact physically with it. At the same time, the child must represent the model as a term in an abstract, "stands for" relation, and he or she must use that relation as a basis for drawing inferences.

According to the dual representation hypothesis, the more salient a symbol is as a concrete object, the more difficult it is to appreciate its role as a symbol for something other than itself. Thus, the more young children are attracted to a model as an interesting object, the more difficult it will be for them to detect its relation to the room it stands for.

The dual representation hypothesis has generated several interesting predictions. For example, it suggests that factors that decrease children's attention to the model as an interesting object should increase their use of the model as a symbol. In one study, 2½-year-old children's access to the model was decreased by placing it behind a window (DeLoache, 2000). The children could still see the location of the toy in the model, but they could have no direct contact with the model. This manipulation led to better performance. Conversely, factors that increase children's attention to the model as an object should lead to a decrease in their use of the model as a representation of something else. This prediction also was confirmed. Allowing 3-year-old children to play with the model for 5 to 10 minutes led to a decrease in performance when children were asked to use it to find the toy in the room (DeLoache, 2000).

Another finding that supports the dual representation hypothesis concerns children's use of photographs, rather than the model, to find the toy. Two-and-one-half-year-olds, who typically perform very poorly in the standard model task, perform much better when a photograph is substituted for the model (DeLoache & Burns, 1993, 1994; DeLoache, Pierroutsakos, & Uttal, 2003). A photograph is less salient as an object and hence could be considered less concrete than a model is. Most obviously, the model is a three-dimensional representation, whereas the photograph is only two-dimensional. In support of the hypothesis, the 2½-year-olds performed much better with a photograph than their age-mates did with the model. In sum, the results indicate that a more concrete object, a model, may be more difficult to use than a less concrete object, a photograph.

DeLoache, Miller, and Rosengren (1997) have provided especially strong support for the dual representation hypothesis. In this research, 2½-year-old children were led to believe that a shrinking machine could shrink (and, subsequently, enlarge) a room. The idea was that if children believe that a scale model actually is a room that has been shrunk by a machine, then there is no symbolic relation between the two spaces; to the child, the model simply is the room. Hence, dual representation is not required, so children should have no trouble reasoning about the relation between the two spaces.

Each child was first given a demonstration in which a "shrinking machine" (an oscilloscope accompanied by computer-generated sounds described as the "sounds the machine makes while it's working") apparently caused a troll doll to turn into a miniature version of itself. The machine then supposedly "enlarged" the troll back to its original size. Next, the machine seemed to cause the "troll's room" (a tent-like room used in many previous model studies) to turn into a scale model identical to it except for size. It then enlarged the room.

The child then watched as the experimenter hid the larger troll somewhere in the portable room. After waiting while the machine "shrunk" the room, the child was asked to find the hidden toy. (The miniature troll was, of course, hidden in the same place in the model as the larger troll was in the room.) Thus, just as in the standard model task, the child had to use his or her knowledge of where the toy was hidden in one space to figure out where to search in the other. Unlike the standard task, there was no representational relation between the two spaces. As predicted on the basis of the dual representation hypothesis, performance was significantly better in this nonsymbolic task than in the standard model task. We know of no basis other than dual representation to explain this result.

The discussion thus far reveals that although the model is a highly salient concrete object, young children have difficulty using it as a symbol. Moreover, the concreteness of the model may be part of the problem, as children must look past the model's salient, concrete properties to understand that it is intended to be a representation of something else. These results have important implications for children's understanding of other symbol systems, such as letters and numbers. We explore these implications in the next section.

CONCRETENESS, DUAL REPRESENTATION, AND EDUCATIONAL SYMBOLS

In the preschool and early elementary school years, children are asked to master a variety of symbol systems, such as letters, numbers, maps, and musical notation. Symbolic reasoning is thus fundamentally important for educational achievement, and children who fail to become skilled in even one of the major symbol systems are at serious risk of being left behind.

The difficulty that children sometimes have in acquiring an understanding of these important symbol systems has led to a variety of materials that are designed to help children learn the relevant information. For example, teachers often use concrete objects as substitutes for abstract symbolic representations. These objects are often referred to as *manipulatives*. Examples of concrete, three-dimensional objects include Dienes Blocks, Base 10 blocks, Digi-Blocks, and Cuisenaire Rods. In addition, teachers use many household objects as informal manipulatives, including cereal, money, and paper clips (Stevenson & Stigler, 1992). Outside the classroom, parents can purchase a vast array of attractive objects of a symbolic nature in the hope that such objects will help their children acquire early literacy and number skills. Magnetic letters and numbers cover a large proportion of the refrigerators in the homes of young American children, stuck there to encourage early learning.

Manipulatives have been touted as solutions for children of a wide range of ages and ability levels; they have been offered as appropriate for all ability levels, ranging from the disabled to the gifted (Clements & McMillen, 1996; Sowell, 1989; Wearne & Hiebert, 1988). Indeed, faith in the value of manipulatives is almost a defining characteristic of modern approaches to early childhood education. Unfortunately, however, research on the effectiveness of manipulatives has not confirmed the anticipated benefits. Several studies have shown, at best, inconsistent or weak advantages for manipulatives in comparison to more traditional techniques for teaching mathematics to children (Ball, 1992; Clements, 1997; Clements & McMillen, 1996; Hughes, 1986). Longitudinal and intensive studies of the use of manipulatives in classrooms have shown that children often fail to establish connections between manipulatives and the information that the manipulatives are intended to communicate (Sarama & Clements, 2002, 2004; Sowell, 1989). Put simply, although manipulatives can facilitate thinking, they are not a panacea.

We suggest that part of the reason that manipulatives have not been shown to support symbol-based solutions involves challenges that are very similar to those that younger children encounter when using a scale model. There are at least two general similarities between what is required to succeed in our model task and what is required to effectively use a manipulative. The first is that the relation between a manipulative and what it is intended to represent may not be transparent to young children. In other words, the concreteness of a manipulative (or of our model) does not guarantee that children will understand that it is intended to represent something other than itself. To a teacher or parent, the relation between a manipulative-based solution and a more traditional written solution may seem obvious or even transparent. But the same may not be true in the minds of young children. As we discuss, the relation between manipulatives and other types of representations may be opaque to young children.

The second similarity between children's difficulties with our model and with manipulatives is that dual representation is relevant to both. As was true of our model, manipulatives have a dual nature; they are intended to be used as representations of something else, but they also are objects in their own right. In the next section, we review some difficulties that children encounter when using manipulatives, difficulties that parallel younger children's problems with our scale model and that are consistent with the dual representation perspective.

Children Often Fail to Grasp the Relation Between Manipulatives and Written Representations

From a teacher's point of view, the goal of using a manipulative is to provide support for learning more general mathematical concepts. However, this is no guarantee that children will see the manipulative in this way. Previous work on the use of manipulatives has documented numerous examples of mismatches between teachers' expectations and students' understandings. Even when young children do learn to perform mathematical operations using manipulatives, their knowledge of the two ways of solving the problems may remain encapsulated; that is, children often fail to see the relation between solving mathematics problems via manipulatives and solving the same or similar problems via abstract symbols (Uttal, Scudder, & DeLoache, 1997). For example, children may not see that the solutions to two-digit subtraction problems that they derive from manipulatives are also relevant to similar but written versions of the same problems. In the child's mind, the task of doing manipulatives-based arithmetic may be completely separate from doing written arithmetic.

An analogy to our scale model illustrates the differences between how students and teachers may view the relation between manipulatives and written representations of numbers. Our model is extremely concrete, and parents are amazed when the task proves difficult for intelligent, interested children. We believe that similar issues may arise when older children are asked to use manipulatives; to the teacher, the relation between the manipulative and a more abstract concept may be direct and obvious, but this relation may be, and may remain, obscure to young children, particularly if the relation is not pointed out explicitly.

Evidence that children often fail to draw connections between manipulatives and more traditional forms of mathematical symbols comes from Resnick and Omanson's (1987) intensive studies of children's use of manipulatives and their understanding of mathematical concepts. Resnick and Omanson systematically evaluated third-grade children's ability to solve problems both with and without manipulatives. Much of the work involved Dienes Blocks, which are a systematic set of manipulatives that are designed to help children acquire understanding of base 10 concepts. Most of the children understood what was asked of them and appeared to enjoy working with the blocks. Unfortunately, however, the children's ease with and knowledge of the blocks was not related to their understanding of similar kinds of problems expressed in more formal mathematical terms. The children did not relate approaches they had used to solve problems with manipulatives to the solution of similar problems involving written symbols. For example, children who were successful in using Dienes Blocks to solve subtraction problems involving two or three digits had trouble solving simpler written problems. Indeed, the child who performed best with the Dienes Blocks performed worst on the standard problems. Clearly, success with a manipulative did not guarantee success with written symbols; in fact, success with one form of mathematical expression was unrelated to success with the other.

Other researchers have provided additional evidence of the nonequivalence of concrete and more abstract forms of mathematical expressions. For example, Hughes (1986) investigated young elementary school children's ability to use simple blocks or bricks to solve addition and subtraction problems. What is most interesting about this study for the current discussion is that the children were explicitly asked to draw connections between solutions involving concrete objects and those involving more abstract, written problems. The children were asked to use the bricks to represent the underlying concepts that were expressed in the written problems. For example, the children were asked to use bricks to solve written problems, such as 1 + 7 = ?. The experimenter and the teachers expected that the children would use the bricks to show how the two numbers could be combined. For example, children might be expected to show 1 brick and a pile of 7 bricks. The process of addition could be represented by combining the single brick and the pile of 7 bricks to form one pile with 8 bricks. But this is not what happened. Overall, the children performed poorly. Regardless of whether they could solve the written problems, they had difficulty representing the problems with the bricks. Moreover, the children's errors demonstrated that they failed to appreciate that the bricks and written symbols were two alternate forms of mathematical expression. Many children took the instructions literally, using the bricks to physically spell out the written problems (Figure 8.3). For example, they

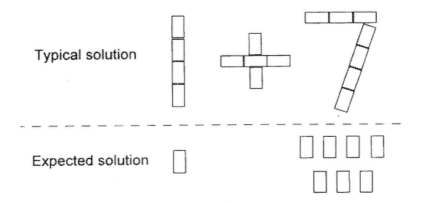

Figure 8.3   An example of how children use small bricks to represent the problem 1 + 7 = 8. The children often copied written problems with the bricks rather than using the bricks as an alternate representational system. From *Children and Numbers: Difficulties in Learning Mathematics*, by M. Hughes, 1986, pp. 99–103. Copyright 1986 by Basil Blackwell. Adapted with permission.

made a line of bricks to represent the "1" and two intersecting lines to represent the "+" and so on. These results again demonstrate that children may treat solutions involving manipulatives and those involving written mathematical symbols as cognitively distinct entities.

The research on children's understanding of manipulatives also highlights the conditions under which manipulatives are likely to be effective. Specifically, the results of several studies suggest that manipulatives are most effective when they are used to augment, rather than to substitute for, instructions involving written symbols. In successful cases of manipulative use, teachers have drawn specific connections between children's use of a manipulative and the related expression of the underlying concept in written form. For example, consider Wearne and Hiebert's (1988) program. It focuses on fractions, but the results are relevant to other mathematical concepts. At all stages of the program, the teacher draws specific links between manipulatives and written symbolic expressions. The manipulative is used as a bridge to the written expressions rather than as a substitute or precursor for written symbols. As a result, a scaffold is provided to assist children in learning written representations. The program gradually leads them away from a focus on concrete manipulatives and toward a focus on written representations. Thus, the focus of this and similar successful programs is on the relation between manipulatives and other forms of mathematical expression. Similarly, the *Building Blocks* curriculum (Sarama & Clements, 2002, 2004) uses manipulatives to help children gain insight into mathematical concepts, but it also includes activities to link manipulatives to other forms of representation. There is extensive use of concrete manipulatives, but the activities with the manipulatives are designed with the end goal of facilitating children's understanding of written representations. What makes this curriculum special, if not unique, is that there is, by design, a systematic formulation by which children grow out of using manipulatives. The materials are progressively layered, meaning that activities at earlier levels are designed to lay the foundation for later activities. In this way, the curriculum establishes linkages, both implicitly and explicitly, between manipulative-based solutions and written solutions.

Attractive Objects May Be Distracting Manipulatives

Another implication of the present analysis is that objects that are interesting in their own right may not make the best manipulatives. Observations of manipulative use in other countries have supported the idea that a good manipulative is not necessarily an inherently interesting object. For example, in Japan, children use the same set of manipulatives throughout the early elementary school years. Stevenson and Stigler (1992, pp. 186–187) who have conducted several cross-national comparisons of mathematics achievement in Asia and the United States, have observed the following:

> Japanese teachers … use the items in the math set repeatedly throughout the elementary school years. … American teachers seek variety. They may use Popsicle sticks in one lesson, and marbles, Cheerios, M&Ms, checkers, poker chips, or plastic animals in another. The American view is that objects should be varied in order to maintain children's interest. The Asian view is that using a variety of representational materials may confuse children, and thereby make it more difficult for them to use the objects for the representation and solution of mathematics problems. Multiplication is easier to understand when the same tiles are used as were used when the children learned to add.

In summary, one of the challenges of effective use of manipulatives is that children sometimes have difficulty linking manipulatives-based solutions to written solutions. In this regard, the concreteness of the manipulatives may contribute to the problem by focusing children's attention on the characteristics of the objects themselves rather than on what the objects are intended to represent. It is important to stress that this perspective does not mean that manipulatives are not useful or are harmful to children's learning. Using manipulatives can indeed help mathematical thinking in several ways (see, for example, Martin & Schwartz, in press). Thus we do not deny that manipulatives can serve an important role in preschool and early elementary school education. However, effective use of manipulatives requires that teachers consider both the advantages and disadvantages of using manipulatives. In this regard, we have identified a possible challenge of using manipulatives—children may have difficulty relating manipulatives-based solutions to written solutions.

Letters As a Symbol System

The questions raised in this chapter regarding children's acquisition of symbols also are relevant to the early development of reading. In learning to read, children must master the relation between an abstract symbol system and its referents. Given the importance of the alphabet and the problems children may have in learning it, parents often turn to other means of making letter learning more concrete. For example, concrete objects such as alphabet blocks or magnetic letters potentially can provide a tactile means of teaching reading in much the way that mathematics manipulatives allow hands-on learning of mathematics. Like mathematics manipulatives, concrete letters transform the abstractness of graphemes and phonemes into familiar, perceptually rich objects. Although the use of manipulatives for reading instruction has not been investigated as the use of manipulatives in math education has been, it seems likely that similar caution is appropriate. Simply putting the letters of the alphabet on magnets or on other toys does not guarantee that children will learn to use them for reading and writing rather than as building blocks. In this section we briefly review what children must learn to understand letter-sound correspondences and consider the possible influences of using concrete objects on this process.

Understanding letters is difficult because letters are noniconic symbols (Bialystok & Martin, 2003; Tolchinsky, 2003; Treiman, 2000). Unlike pictographs, there is nothing inherent in the structure of letters that reflects what they represent. In essence, understanding letters as notational symbols requires that children appreciate nonanalogous, noniconic symbolic relations (Bialystok, 1992; Munn, 1998).

Bialystok (Bialystok, 1992; Bialystok & Martin, 2003; Bialystok, Shenfield, & Codd, 2000) proposed that children must relinquish their hold on the specific perceptual properties of objects to understand them as symbols. Symbol acquisition emerges in three stages as children's initially fragile understanding of symbols becomes more flexible. Children first learn a set of symbols without understanding their relation to what they represent. For example, they may first be capable of verbally reproducing a sequence of symbols (e.g., counting in a series or reciting the alphabet). They may then begin to observe the relation of these objects to their referents. In this second stage, children tend to assume that the relations between symbols and referents are iconic and analogous. For example, they may believe that the word "ant" is shorter than the word "elephant" because ants are smaller than elephants. Similarly, Spanish and Italian children associate bigger words with bigger objects, in spite of the fact that this relationship is even less perfect in both of these languages. Both Spanish and Italian use suffixes to demarcate diminutives of root words, so that longer words actually denote smaller objects (Ferreiro, 1985). For example, the suffix "ita" in Spanish indicates the diminutive. When children finally acquire full symbolic competence in Bialystok's third stage, they are capable of understanding that symbols may be noniconic and nonanalogous (e.g., "car" is shorter than "banana," even though cars are larger than bananas). Thus, Bialystok has demonstrated that the acquisition of symbols such as letters and numbers occurs in a gradual three-step process, not as an abrupt concrete-to-abstract shift.

Once children know the correspondences between the written forms (graphemes) and auditory forms (phonemes), they have the requisite knowledge to read and write any word in the language (Ravid & Tolchinsky, 2002; Tolchinsky & Teberosky, 1998). Learning individual grapheme-phoneme correspondences, however, is neither easy nor a guarantee that children will learn to read. In fact, several studies (Landsmann & Karmiloff-Smith, 1992; Tolchinsky, 2003; Tolchinsky-Landsmann & Levin, 1985) have found that children's understanding of letters as part of a notational symbol system does not necessarily co-occur with their understanding of how the letters are used in referential communication. For example, Landsmann and Karmiloff-Smith (1992) asked children of ages 4 through 6 to invent nonletters, nonnumbers, and nonwords. Children in all age groups imposed different constraints on what qualified as nonletters and nonnumbers, demonstrating their understanding that letters and numbers were separate domains of symbols but also that they are not in the same domain as drawings. For example, one child produced "tttt" when asked to generate a nonword. Only the older children, however, understood that symbols serve a referential role as well as a notational role. Rather than simply using strings of repeated letters to create nonwords, 5- and 6-year-olds generated nonwords that were unpronounceable and, thus, could serve no referential function.

These results reveal some of the challenges that young children face in learning to understand the symbolic properties of letters. Will making letters concrete facilitate children's understanding? According to the dual representation hypothesis, attempts to make alphabet blocks colorful and engaging as objects might detract the child from seeing the letters on them as symbols. The physical features or concreteness of the blocks actually may obfuscate the symbol-referent relation. Alphabet blocks, for example, typically are constructed in different colors, which facilitate children's perceptual differentiation of different letters when they are learning the alphabet early on. The elaboration of individual letters is similarly evident in the topical organization of *Sesame Street*, which typically focuses on only two letters of the alphabet per episode (i.e., "This episode brought to you by the letter 'E'") and in different skits that are used to interest children in learning their letters (e.g., the letter beauty pageant). Such attempts to make individual letters interesting may distract from the collective function the letters serve within the notational system as a whole. Emphasizing letters as perceptually salient objects in their own right may, in fact, make it more difficult to see each letter as being a component of a word and as serving an equivalent notational role in the alphabet.

RESEARCH ON THE EFFECTS OF PLAYING WITH CONCRETE OBJECTS ON CHILDREN'S UNDERSTANDING OF THE SYMBOLIC PROPERTIES OF LETTERS AND NUMBERS.

The discussion thus far of the influences of playing with concrete objects on children's understanding of educational symbols has been theoretical. We have suggested that there are direct links between our earlier research on concrete models and the challenges that children face in coming to understand educational symbols. We are now putting these ideas to the test. In recent research supported by the U.S. Department of Education, we have specifically investigated how playing with concrete objects affects children's understanding of the symbolic properties of letters and numbers. This is the first study to address directly how interaction with concrete objects affects children's understanding of how letters and numbers can be used as symbolic representations.

Separate studies were conducted to investigate children's understanding of letters and numbers, and we therefore refer to the studies as the *letter* and *number* studies. In both studies, we tested children who were just turning 4 (M age = 47.4 months) and children approximately 6 months older (M age −53.5 months). The research took place in the children's homes. The researchers visited the children's homes three times to administer assessments or to demonstrate activities that children and parents could perform with traditional objects or concrete letters or numbers.

The first assessment provided baseline information regarding children's knowledge of letters or numbers and was based in part on subtests of the Woodcock-Johnson tests of preschool achievement or the Test of Early Mathematics Ability (TEMA) (Ginsburg & Baroody, 1990). We also included several measures of children's understanding of the symbolic properties of letters and numbers. The most important, the box labeling task, was adapted from Hughes (1986). It required that children use letters or numbers to keep track of the contents of three metal tins. In the letter study, we placed different toy animals (bear, duck, and frog) in the tin boxes; in the number study, we placed different quantities of paper "cookies" in the boxes. In both cases, the children were asked to "make something that will help [them] to remember what is in the box." This task gives children the opportunity to construct a symbolic representation to facilitate memory. The nature and quality of the representations that they construct can shed light on their conceptions of the process of representation and the symbolic properties of letters and numbers (see Deloache, Simcock, & Marzolf, 2004; Eskritt & Lee, 2002; Hughes, 1986; Marzolf & DeLoache, 1994; Munn, 1998).

Importantly, we asked children to complete the tasks twice, once with crayons and once with magnet letters or numbers. Half the children in both the letter and number studies completed the task with the magnets first; the remainder completed the task with the crayons first.

At the end of the first testing session, we left a set of toys for the children to play with in the days between the sessions, and we demonstrated the games that children and parents could play. Children in the control group were assigned randomly to play with traditional toys and objects. For example, they blew bubbles with a bubble wand, they made simple jewelry with beads, and they played a simple basketball game with a suction-cup hoop and a sponge ball. Children in the experimental group were asked to play similar games but to use toy letters or numbers as the toys. For example, these children blew bubbles with letters (e.g., o and e) or with numbers (e.g., 6, 8, or 9). Likewise, they played basketball with letters and numbers. The parents were asked to encourage their children to play the different games, to keep a log of how often they played, and to take photographs of what they made with the toys or symbols, such as jewelry, towers, etc.

Approximately 5 to 7 days later, the experimenters returned to the children's homes. They did not administer tests or assessments at this second visit. Instead, they demonstrated a second set of games that the children could play during the next week and left the appropriate materials for these new games with the parents. The demonstrations helped to ensure that the children understood the games that we were asking them to play.

The researchers returned to the homes a third and final time a week later, to administer the final assessments, which included most of the tests the children had taken at the first session. By administering the tests both before and after children played with the toys or the symbolic objects, we were able to assess the effects of treating symbolic objects as toys on children's understanding of the symbolic properties and basic knowledge of letters and numbers.

For the most part, children's performance was not affected by the play activities; the children performed comparably, regardless of whether they played with toys or, with letters or numbers. Thus playing with the concrete objects neither helped nor hurt children's performance, either on the tests of symbolic knowledge or on the basic achievement tests (e.g., the Woodcock-Johnson preliteracy tests).

There was, however, an interesting effect of the type of objects (crayons or magnets) with which the children performed the box labeling tasks. First, in both studies, children performed better with the magnets than with the crayons. More specifically, they often placed the correct magnet on the box to represent the stuffed animal or the quantity of cookies contained within. In contrast, when using the crayons, the children were less likely to produce symbolic representations. For example, some of the children made drawings that seemed to have little discernible relation to the contents of the boxes. There was, however, evidence of transfer from using the magnets to using the crayons. Children who performed the box labeling task with the magnets first were more likely to use the crayon in a symbolic manner, such as to write a letter or number. Thus using the magnets not only helped the children perform better with the magnets; it also facilitated their performance with the crayon.

We believe that using the magnets in a symbolic fashion provided a basis for transfer to the crayon task. The children who performed the task first with the magnets were now more likely to approach the same task with the crayon as a form of symbolic representation. In other words, the magnets provided a scaffold that allowed children to use their nascent knowledge of symbolic relations. Four-year-olds possess some knowledge of the relation between letters and text, but they are unlikely to use this knowledge spontaneously (Bialystok, 1992; Bialystok & Martin, 2003). The magnetic letters or numbers gave the children the opportunity to use their knowledge of letters or numbers. Using the magnets as symbols then provided a basis for transfer to the more challenging crayon task.

These results are consistent with our theoretical perspective on the development of symbolic reasoning, particularly the dual-representation hypothesis. Simply playing with the concrete objects was not helpful, but using concrete objects in a symbolic way did improve performance. Several lines of research have already established that performing a symbolic task successfully can promote symbolic thinking in a more difficult domain. For example, DeLoache and colleagues showed that experience in using a scale model helped children to use a symbol that they typically would not be able to use, a map (Deloache et al., 2004; Marzolf & DeLoache, 1994). We believe that the magnetic letters or numbers provided a similar basis for transfer and thus helped children use the crayon in a symbolic manner.

In summary, our results do provide evidence that using concrete objects can facilitate children's symbolic thinking. But it is very important to note that it is symbolic behavior with the concrete objects, and not simply playing with them, that provided the basis for the facilitative effect of the concrete objects. The concrete magnets facilitated children's symbolic thinking specifically because they helped the children to think about letters and numbers. Thus concrete objects can facilitate symbolic thinking; they are not a substitute for it.

IMPLICATIONS

The theoretical perspective that we have outlined above has important implications for the use of concrete objects in early childhood education. We have presented a theoretical perspective on the relation between concreteness and symbolic development that differs substantially from the traditional view. The ideas that we have developed in this chapter may prove useful in developing instructional strategies that maximize the effectiveness of manipulatives and other concrete objects.

Perhaps most importantly, our work reveals that *concreteness alone does not convey an inherent advantage*. Certainly there are circumstances in which working with concrete objects can in fact help children to acquire new knowledge or skills. However, this does not happen spontaneously simply because children work with a manipulative. For children to learn about symbolic relations from the use of concrete objects, the two forms of representation must be explicitly linked.

Importantly, our review also suggests that there are situations in which the *use of concrete objects may not be helpful and could even be harmful*. Like any learning technique or technology, concrete objects have both strengths and weaknesses. Highly attractive concrete objects may make it difficult for the child to think about using the concrete objects as representations of something else. Teachers and parents may want to reconsider the practice of providing children with highly attractive concrete symbols (e.g., letter magnets) and the expectation that this alone will facilitate symbolic development.

Finally, our review reveals that teachers must play a crucially important role in children's learning of symbolic relations. Whether a child draws a connection between a concrete object and a written representation depends critically on whether this relation is pointed out and reinforced by a teacher. Indeed, our review highlights specifically how teachers can integrate the use of concrete objects into instruction. Teachers can guide children's attention to the relation between manipulatives-based solutions and written representations of similar problems. The challenge for the teacher will be to decide specifically how and when such linkages should be made, but doing so should be an explicit goal of instruction.

CONCLUSIONS

Given the importance of learning symbol systems, it makes sense to try to help children in as many ways as possible. The use of concrete objects has been an important tool in this effort. Although we have raised serious questions about the use of concrete objects in early childhood education, we do not believe that the use of concrete objects should be eliminated or even reduced. Concrete objects such as letter blocks or number magnets can help children to discriminate one symbol from another and can awaken their interest in reading and mathematics. Moreover, our recent work has demonstrated that concrete objects can provide a scaffold on which an understanding of more abstract relations can be built.

Thus we would never endorse a proposal to eliminate the use of concrete objects in early childhood education. Our concern is not with the general use of such objects but rather with *how* they are used. The problems that we have cited only apply when the concrete objects are substituted for instruction or when the focus of children's activity is exclusively on highly attractive concrete objects. In such a situation, children's attention centers on the objects themselves rather than on what the symbols are intended to represent. The desire to help children learn and to engage their interest by making objects interesting in their own right may at times be counterproductive. We advocate a balanced view, in which the disadvantages of using concrete objects are considered along with the advantages. Concrete objects are most useful when they are used to support or augment the learning of abstract concepts. They should not be used as substitutes for abstract representations.

REFERENCES

Ball, D. L. (1992). Magical hopes: Manipulatives and the reform of math education. *American Educator, 16*, 14–18.

Bialystok, E. (1992). Symbolic representation of letters and numbers. *Cognitive Development, 7*, 301–316.

Bialystok, E., & Martin, M. M. (2003). Notation to symbol: Development in children's understanding of print. *Journal of Experimental Child Psychology, 86*, 223–243.

Bialystok, E., Shenfield, T., & Codd, J. (2000). Languages, scripts, and the environment: Factors in developing concepts of print. *Developmental Psychology, 36*, 66–76.

Bruner, J. S. (1966). *Toward a theory of instruction.* Cambridge Harvard University Press.

Bruner, J. S., Goodnow, J. J., & Austin, G. A. (1956). *A study of thinking.* New York: Wiley.

Clements, D. H. (1997). (Mis?)Constructing Constructivism. *Teaching Children Mathematics, 4*, 198–200.

Clements, D. H., & McMillen, S. (1996). Rethinking "Concrete" Manipulatives. *Teaching Children Mathematics, 2*, 270–279.

DeLoache, J. S. (1987). Rapid change in the symbolic functioning of very young children. *Science, 238*, 1556–1557.

DeLoache, J. S. (1989). Young children's understanding of the correspondence between a scale model and a larger space. *Cognitive Development, 4*, 121–139.

DeLoache, J. S. (1991). Symbolic functioning in very young children: Understanding of pictures and models. *Child Development, 62*, 736–752.

DeLoache, J. S. (1995). Early symbol understanding and use. In D. L. Medin (Ed.), *The psychology of learning and motivation: Advances in research and theory,* (Vol. 33, pp. 65–114). San Diego: Academic Press.

DeLoache, J. S. (2000). Dual representation and young children's use of scale models. *Child Development, 71*, 329–338.

DeLoache, J. S., & Burns, N. M. (1993). Symbolic development in young children: Understanding models and pictures. In C. Pratt & A. F. Garton (Eds.), *Systems of representation in children: Development and use* (pp. 91–107). Chichester, UK: Wiley.

DeLoache, J. S., & Burns, N. M. (1994). Symbolic functioning in preschool children. *Journal of Applied Developmental Psychology, 15*, 513–527.

DeLoache, J. S., de Mendoza, O. A., & Anderson, K. N. (1999). Multiple factors in early symbol use instructions, similarity, and age in understanding a symbol-referent relation. *Cognitive Development, 14*, 299–312.

DeLoache, J. S., Kolstad, V., & Anderson, K. N. (1991). Physical similarity and young children's understanding of scale models. *Child Development, 62*, 111–126.

DeLoache, J. S., Miller, K. F., & Rosengren, K. S. (1997). The credible shrinking room: Very young children's performance with symbolic and nonsymbolic relations. *Psychological Science, 8*, 308–313.

DeLoache, J. S., Pierroutsakos, S. L., & Uttal, D. H. (2003). The origins of pictorial competence. *Current Directions in Psychological Science, 12*, 114–118.

Deloache, J. S., Simcock, G., & Marzolf, D. P. (2004). Transfer by very young children in the symbolic retrieval task. *Child Development,75*, 1708 –1718

Eskritt, M., & Lee, K. (2002). "Remember where you last saw that card": Children's production of external symbols as a memory aid. *Developmental Psychology, 38*, 254–266.

Ferreiro, E. (1985). Literacy development: A psychogenetic perspective. In D. Olson, N. Torrance & A. Hildyard (Eds.), *Literacy, language and learning* (pp. 217–228). Cambridge: Cambridge University Press.

Gelman, S. A. (2000). The role of essentialism in children's concepts. In H. W. Reese (Ed.), *Advances in child development and behavior* (Vol. 27, pp. 55-98). San Diego, CA: Academic Press.

Gelman, S. A. (2003). *The essential child : Origins of essentialism in everyday thought.* New York: Oxford University Press.

Gelman, S. A., & Wellman, H. M. (1991). Insides and essence: Early understandings of the non-obvious. *Cognition, 38*, 213–44.

Gergely, G., Nadasdy, Z., Csibra, G., & Biro, S. (1995). Taking the intentional stance at 12 months of age. *Cognition, 56*, 165-193.

Ginsburg, H. P., & Baroody, A. J. (1990). *TEMA 2: Tests of Early Mathematics Achievement.* Austin, TX: Pro-Ed.

Hughes, M. (1986). *Children and number: Difficulties in learning mathematics.* Oxford, England: Basil Blackwell.

Inhelder, B., & Piaget, J. (1958). *The growth of logical thinking from childhood to adolescence: An essay on the construction of formal operational structures.*

Landsmann, L. T., & Karmiloff-Smith, A. (1992). Children's understanding of notations as domains of knowledge versus referential-communicative tools. *Cognitive Development, 7*, 287–300.

Martin, T., & Schwartz, D. (in press). Physically distributed learning: Adapting and reinterpreting physical environments in the development of fraction concepts. *Cognitive Science.*

Marzolf, D. P., & DeLoache, J. S. (1994). Transfer in young children's understanding of spatial representations. *Child Development, 65*, 1–15.

Montessori, M. (1917). *The advanced Montessori method.* New York: Frederick A. Stokes.

Munn, P. (1998). Symbolic function in pre-schoolers. In C. Donlan (Ed.), *The development of mathematical skills* (pp. 47–71). Hove, UK: Psychology Press.

Piaget, J. (1951). *Play, dreams and imitation in childhood* (C. Gattegno & F. M. Hodgson., Trans.). New York: Norton.

Quinn, P. C. (2003). Concepts are not just for objects: Categorization of spatial relation information by infants. In D. H. Rakison & L. M. Oakes (Eds.), *Early category and concept development: Making sense of the blooming, buzzing confusion* (pp. 50–76). London: Oxford University Press.

Quinn, P. C., Adams, A., Kennedy, E., Shettler, L., & Wasnik, A. (2003). Development of an abstract category representation for the spatial relation between in 6- to 10-month-old infants. *Developmental Psychology, 39*, 151–163.

Ravid, D., & Tolchinsky, L. (2002). Developing linguistic literacy: A comprehensive model. *Journal of Child Language, 29,* 417–447.

Resnick, L. B., & Omanson, S.F. (1987). Learning to understand arithmetic. *Advances in instructional psychology, 3,* 41–96.

Sarama, J., & Clements, D. H. (2002). Building Blocks for young children's mathematical development. *Journal of Educational Computing Research, 27,* 93–10.

Sarama, J., & Clements, D. H. (2004). Building Blocks for early childhood mathematics. *Early Childhood Research Quarterly, 19,* 181–189.

Sigel, I. E. (1993). The centrality of a distancing model for the development of representational competence. In R. R. Cocking & K. A. Renninger (Eds.), *The development and meaning of psychological distance* (pp. 141–158). Hillsdale, NJ: Erlbaum.

Simons, D. J., & Keil, F. C. (1995). An abstract to concrete shift in the development of biological thought: The insides story. *Cognition, 56,* 129–163.

Sowell, E. J. (1989). Effects of manipulative materials in mathematics instruction. *Journal for Research in Mathematics Education, 20,* 498–505.

Stevenson, H. W., & Stigler, J. W. (1992). *The learning gap: Why our schools are failing and what we can learn from Japanese and Chinese education.* New York: Summit Books.

Tolchinsky, L. (2003). *The cradle of culture and what children know about writing and numbers before being taught.* Mahwah, NJ: Erlbaum.

Tolchinsky, L., & Teberosky, A. (1998). The development of word segmentation and writing in two scripts. *Cognitive Development, 13,* 1–24.

Tolchinsky-Landsmann, L., & Levin, I. (1985). Writing in preschoolers: An age-related analysis. *Applied Psycholinguistics, 6,* 319–339.

Treiman, R. (2000). The foundations of literacy. *Current Directions in Psychological Science, 9,* 89–92.

Uttal, D. H., Schreiber, J. C., & DeLoache, J. S. (1995). Waiting to use a symbol: The effects of delay on children's use of models. *Child Development, 66,* 1875–1889.

Uttal, D. H., Scudder, K. V., & DeLoache, J. S. (1997). Manipulatives as symbols: A new perspective on the use of concrete objects to teach mathematics. *Journal of Applied Developmental Psychology, 18,* 37–54.

Vygotsky, L. S., & Kozulin, A. (1986). *Thought and language.* Cambridge, Mass.: MIT Press.

Wearne, D., & Hiebert, J. (1988). A cognitive approach to meaningful mathematics instruction: Testing a local theory using decimal numbers. *Journal for Research in Mathematics Education, 19,* 371–384.

Werner, H., & Kaplan, B. (1963). *Symbol formation; an organismic-developmental approach to language and the expression of thought.* New York: Wiley.

Woodward, A. L. (2003). Infants' developing understanding of the link between looker and object. *Developmental Science, 6,* 297–311.

Woodward, A. L., & Sommerville, J. A. (2000). Twelve-month-old infants interpret action in context. *Psychological Science, 11,* 73–77.

9

Effects of Representational Reminders on Young Children's Recall

Implications for Long-Term Memory Development

Judith A. Hudson
Ellyn G. Sheffield
Joanne Agayoff Deocampo

INTRODUCTION

In just the last decade, the study of memory development in young children has changed dramatically. Initial forays into this line of investigation tended to focus on the issue of whether or not preverbal children were capable of long-term memory and, if so, when it began. Important research documented impressive long-term retention in young, preverbal children and infants (e.g., Barr, Dowden, & Hayne, 1996; Bauer, 1995; Bauer, Hertsgaard, & Dow, 1994; Bauer & Shore, 1987; Greco, Rovee-Collier, Hayne, Griesler, & Earley, 1986; Hamond & Fivush, 1991; Hudson, 1990b; McDonough & Mandler, 1994; Meltzoff, 1995; Meltzoff & Moore, 1994; Rovee-Collier, Sullivan, Enright, Lucas, & Fagen, 1980). Although differences in methodology, and to some degree differences in criteria for what constitutes episodic memory, have segmented the literature on infant recall (largely based on response-contingency paradigms) and studies of toddlers and preschool children (using imitation and verbal recall tasks), in the last decade it has become evident that infants under 1 year were capable of long-term recall for several weeks, that 1-year-olds could remember episodes for several months, and that 2-year-olds can verbally recall unique experiences that took place when they were 13 to 30 months old (see Bauer, Burch, & Kleinknecht, 2002, and Rovee-Collier & Hayne, 2000 for reviews). Moreover, there is evidence that the temporal parameters of memory processing change dramatically during the first 3 years of life and continue to change throughout adulthood (Rovee-Collier & Hayne, 2000).

Thus, research on early memory has shifted from questions of whether and when young children demonstrate long-term memory and have focused on understanding the variables that influence long-term memory in very young children. For example, research has examined how the content and structure of an event affect long-term memory (Bauer, Wenner, Dropik, & Wewerka, 2000); whether infants and toddlers can remember actions they have seen, but not actually performed (Barr & Hayne,

1999; Collie & Hayne, 1999); how reexposure to event information can reinstate and extend event memories (the topic of this chapter), and how brain developments during the first 3 years of life contribute to the onset and development of long-term, verbally accessible recall (Bauer, 2002; Bauer, Wiebe, Carver, Waters, & Nelson, 2003).

In light of our newfound appreciation of infant memory ability, it seems even more puzzling that adults recall so little from this time period. Studies of adults' recollections of childhood have consistently found that adults report few, if any specific memories from the first 3 years of life, a phenomenon referred to as infantile amnesia (White & Pillemer, 1979). The lower frequency of memories for early childhood as compared to memories of middle childhood, adolescence, and adulthood are too great to be attributed to simple memory decay. Given that young children are capable of remembering over periods of days, weeks, months, and even years, it is important to understand what variables account for why some events are remembered while most are forgotten.

Several theories have been proposed to account for infantile amnesia. Originally, Freud (1935) proposed that memories from before the age of three are repressed. More recently, memory theories have focused on important cognitive, language, and social developments during the preschool years that contribute to the forging of explicit, self-conscious, and culturally embedded autobiographical memories (for reviews, see Howe & Courage, 1993; Nelson & Fivush, 2004; Pillemer & White, 1989). Social interactionist accounts of autobiographic memory development propose that children's emerging competence in verbally sharing event memories in conversations with adults allows young children to understand the social significance of autobiographical memories and provides a context for adults to assist children in retrieving memories and constructing personal memory narratives (Fivush, 1991; Hudson 1990b; Nelson, 1990, 1993; Nelson & Fivush, 2000, 2004). The ability to verbally report an event at the time of its occurrence appears to play a critical role in children's later ability to verbally recall and event (Bauer & Wewerka, 1997; Peterson & Rideout, 1998). However, there is some evidence that children can verbally recall events from a preverbal time (Bauer, Wenner, & Kroupina, 2002; Hudson, 1990b, 1993; Myers, Clifton, & Clarkson, 1987). Although events need not be encoded in a verbal form to be later recalled, the language used both during the experience and in later recall discussions helps children form a more coherent memory representation and improves verbal recall (Tessler & Nelson, 1994). Language may not be necessary for later verbal recall, but developments in both language comprehension and production clearly contribute to the consolidation and long-term accessibility of event memories during the preschool years. Other explanations for the offset of infantile amnesia have focused on the development of source monitoring (Leichtman, 1999) as well as the emergence of a cognitive sense of self (Howe & Courage, 1993) and theory of mind (Perner, 2000) as causal factors in the emergence of autobiographic memory. The ability to identify event memories as personally experienced events that happened to oneself at a particular place and time is critical to Tulving's (1983) definition of episodic memory and may depend, in part, on these cognitive developments.

It is most likely, however, that multiple and interacting cognitive and social developments occurring during the early childhood years contribute to the onset of durable autobiographic memories. Sharing memory narratives with others and an emerging understanding of self and others contribute to the construction of an internalized concept of one's own autobiography which is fundamental to autobiographic memory. The ability to identify the source of one's recollections and the ability to attribute memories to oneself are also important components of a concept of autobiography. At the same time, developments in long-term memory retention may allow for a larger pool of potentially retrievable event memories for children to think about and discuss with others. The critical role of memory reminders in sustaining event memories over increasingly longer periods of time so that they can become part of an emerging autobiography is the focus of our research.

The research discussed in this chapter examines effects of reexposure to event information on young children's long-term recall. Differential reexposure to events may account for why some events are remembered over long periods of time, even into adulthood, while others are soon forgotten. This is an important issue to investigate when studying the development of real-world event memory because there are numerous opportunities for children to reexperience parts of events or to encounter the same people, objects, or actions from a prior episode without repeating the entire event. To illustrate potential reminder effects for real-world as compared to laboratory-encountered events, consider the differences between a visit to a research laboratory playroom and a visit to the zoo with an out-of-town relative. Suppose 18-month-old children visited a laboratory playroom and were shown how to perform novel actions on novel sets of toys by an experimenter such as learning how to make a catapult by placing a ball on a lever and fulcrum apparatus and hitting one side (Sheffield & Hudson, 2004). After leaving the laboratory, it is unlikely that children will reencounter portions of this event outside of the laboratory setting. They will not run into the experimenter at home, at their day care center, or in their community and they will not see photographs of her in their homes. Their story books will not show pictures of the laboratory or the apparatus. They will not see the laboratory or the apparatus on television. There are no photographs or home videos of the event. Their parents have been instructed not to talk about the event so there will be no conversation about the experience. Perhaps, they will see balls similar to the one used in the laboratory, but they will not see the lever apparatus. In fact, the setting, the selection of actions and objects, and the instructions given to parents were all carefully orchestrated to prevent reexposure to any part of the event after children leave the laboratory.

Now consider a visit to the zoo with an aunt who has arrived from another state for a visit. After the event, children could encounter several types of reminders. Parents may talk about the visit or may simply talk about the aunt. Children could see pictures of zoo animals in story books and on wall posters. They may have plush animal replicas of zoo animals or small-scale zoo play sets that remind them of their zoo trip. They may have a souvenir item from the zoo such as a tee-shirt or toy. They may see zoo animals on television. They may view photographs taken during the trip or even a home video of the trip. Perhaps they encounter all of these potential reminders. It is possible that all of these experiences remind them or the trip or perhaps, only the photographs and home videos of the trip actually remind them of their visit. It is also possible that none of these remind them of the trip and they have no recall of the experience when questioned three months later.

These examples illustrate the ubiquitous nature of potential reminders for events in real-world contexts and how little we know about what kinds of reminders actually influence young children's memory. It is our contention that a full understanding of how children retain real-world event memories must consider the role of reminders. Laboratory controls that insure that children will not be reminded of events during the interval between encoding and recall are useful for assessing long-term memory without benefit of reminders, but we must also understand the degree to which reminders can both enhance and in some cases, distort recall if we are to understand the development of real-world event memory.

Examining the kinds of memory prompts and reminders that assist with the retrieval of event memories can also provide a greater understanding how children encode and store event informa-tion in memory. According to Tulving's (1983) encoding specificity principle, a retrieval cue (or a reminder) can only be effective if information in the cue was included in the original encoding of event information. For example, if a reminder such as viewing objects associated with an event is effective in improving children's recall for the actions performed on the objects as well, we can conclude that children encoded both object and action information when they experienced the event and that object and action information were encoded as separate but related elements so that recall of one component (objects) cues recall of the other (actions). This approach has also been used to examine context ef-fects on recall. If a reminder that includes event information without matching context information is effective in reminding children of a past event, then we can conclude that context information was encoded as a separate feature of the event. Similarly, if it can be shown that a reminder that provides information about one component of an action sequence enhances recall of other components in the sequence, we can conclude that both components are stored in memory as related components of an overall event. This type of semantic network for representing event information is evident in children from about 9 months as evidenced by their ability to recall multistep action sequences (Bauer et al., 2003). Research on reminder effects can provide more information on how different components of larger events are stored in memory

RESEARCH ON EVENT MEMORY AND REINSTATEMENT IN INFANTS AND YOUNG CHILDREN

Reinstatement in Infancy

The effect of reminders on long-term recall has received a great deal of attention in infant research due to the efforts of Rovee-Collier and her colleagues. In this research, reminders are defined as either reinstatements or reactivations, depending on the time the reminder is administered and the number of reminders children are exposed to. As originally defined by Campbell and Jaynes (1966), reinstatement is a process whereby an organism is reintroduced to a past activity by reexperiencing a portion of it, through a very brief exposure to a specific part of the original event, a small amount of practice with the task, or returning to the context in which the event took place. During reinstatement, original event information is activated and refreshed, and the retrievability of the memory is thereby strengthened (Howe et al., 1993; Rovee-Collier & Shyi, 1992). New information from the reinstating context may also be conjoined with old information, both strengthening and modifying information in long-term storage (Howe, 1991; Howe & Brainerd, 1989). In contrast, reactivation is a process whereby the organism is given a reminder treatment once after the organism no longer demonstrates active memory for the event (Spear & Parsons, 1976). Thus, reinstatements are intended to forestall forgetting and can occur any time during the retention interval (although effectiveness may vary at different intervals), whereas reactivations are administered at the end of the retention interval after forgetting has occurred and are thought to prime latent memories (Gallucio & Rovee-Collier, 1999).

Several experimental paradigms have examined effects of both reinstatement and reactivation on infants' and very young children's long-term recall. Although the procedures vary, they all involve exposing children to partial information about a past event. Passive exposure to a moving mobile can reactivate even 8-week-old infants' memory for a learned response (Rovee-Collier & Shyi, 1990; Rovee-Collier, Sullivan, Enright, Lucas, & Fagan, 1980). Using a conjugate reinforcement paradigm, infants learn to produce movement in a crib mobile by kicking (a ribbon tied to the infant's ankle is connected to the mobile to produce the movement). To measure recall, the mobile is reintroduced after a time delay, but the ribbon is not attached and infants' kicking response is used as a metric for the learned response contingency. Although 3-month-old infants do not demonstrate retention of training when tested for memory 14 days after training, their memories can be reinstated by a brief, noncontingent visual exposure to either a training cue or to the context in which training occurred (Rovee-Collier, Griesler, & Earley, 1985; Rovee-Collier et al., 1980). For example, viewing a moving mobile 13 days after training (the movement is produced by an experimenter and is unrelated to infants' movements), produces evidence of retention when tested at 14 days and infants continue to recognize the mobile for up to 28 days (Rovee-Collier et al., 1980). Although there is no difference in retention after short delays, older infants remember longer than younger infants, and the length of the retention interval increases linearly (Rovee-Collier, 1999). For example, 6-month-olds remember their training for 2 weeks without reinstatement, 9-month-olds remember for 6 weeks, 12-month-olds remember for 8 weeks, and 18-month-olds remember for 13 weeks (Rovee-Collier, 1999). The paradigm used for older infants is the same as the mobile-conjugate reinforcement paradigm, but it employs a task that is better suited for older children: pressing a lever to make a colorful train travel around a train track. As with the mobile task, children are trained to criterion on two consecutive days and later are tested for long-term retention.

The kind of information provided during the reminder session is critical to successful reinstatement in infants. For example, a study by Greco, Hayne, and Rovee-Collier (1990) demonstrated that reminders are only effective if they contain matching functional information. Infants were trained to kick to produce movement in several different mobiles and then exposed to different types of reminders including a stationary mobile identical to the training mobile and a different moving mobile. They found that functional information (movement) was critical for reinstatement; exposure to a different, moving mobile was effective in reinstating recall but exposure to the original, but stationary mobile was not effective. Additionally, for infants under 6 months, only the original training mobile acts as an effective retrieval cue if training and testing are separated by one day. A novel mobile will only cue young infants if training and cueing occur within a 24-hour period. However, for older infants between 9 and 12 months, a novel object can act to cue their memory for a learned task for up to 2 weeks, but not after longer delays (Rovee-Collier, 1999). Thus, with age infants become somewhat more flexible in that reinstatement can occur even when some of the information provided in the reminder session is slightly different from the original experience. Does this trend continue in the next couple of years? If so, then the range of effective reminders would increase with age. However, it may still be the case that some kinds of information such as functional information may be more salient than other types of information in reinstating event memories in toddlers and older children. In the zoo trip example discussed earlier, would viewing photographs of the zoo be sufficient to remind an 18-month-old of the trip or would the child require action information (such as in a home video) to remember the event?

Infant research has also shown that effects of reinstatement in vary depending on when the reminder is administered. Rovee-Collier (1995) has proposed that there is a recall "window" starting at the time of training and ending when training has been forgotten. Reminders are most effective for infants when presented just before the window closes, at the onset of forgetting. Does the same hold for older children? Research clearly indicates that with age, children can remember events over increasing time intervals in the absence of reminders. But do reminders continue to be more effective when administered toward the end of the recall window?

Finally, infant reinstatement research has shown that multiple reinstatements can be effective in sustaining infants' memories for periods of several weeks to over a year. Gallucio and Rovee-Collier (1999) demonstrated that 3-month-olds' memory for an event was extended when they received multiple reinstatements. Infants who would normally remember and event for less than 6 days exhibited retention after 6 weeks after three reinstatement treatments. Hartshorn (2002) showed that 6-month-olds who remembered an event for only 2 weeks exhibited retention for 1½ years when they were given five reinstatements. If this trend continues throughout the early childhood years, it would be possible to reinstate event memories so that they endure for several years. Moreover, children may require fewer reminders, perhaps three or four well-timed ones, to remember events even into adulthood. Until we know what kinds of reminders are effective for toddlers and preschool children, it is difficult to determine what kinds of timing are important. To complicate matters, it is possible that different types of reminders are more and less effective, so that an effective "timetable" for reminding over the very long term would vary depending on the type of reminder that is used.

Reinstatement in Toddlers and Preschool Children

To date, there has been scant investigation of effects of reexposure on toddlers and preschool children. In one study, Howe et al. (1993) investigated reinstatement of preschool children's memories using a hiding task. Children from 2 to 3 years visited a laboratory playroom and were shown the hiding places of 16 toys in the room. Half of the children returned 1 week later and were shown the toys again, but were not shown the hiding locations. Three weeks later, when all children were tested for recall, children who had participated in the reinstatement session recalled more locations than did children who received no reinstatement. This study showed that object information without action information was effective in reinstatement when the original context was also part of the reinstatement environment.

Our research examines effects of different types of reminders on children's recall from 14 to 36 months of age children including live modeling, videos, photographs, and scale model demonstrations. Our research goals are twofold. We want to understand the memory mechanisms involved in reinstatement during this age period and we also want to know how reinstatement can impact event recall in real-world contexts. Because it is likely that in real-world contexts children's reexposure to event information takes the form of viewing photographs or home videos, we have studied how these types of symbolic or representational reminders reinstate children's event memories. This, in turn, requires that we investigate how children understand the representational functions of these media. Our research therefore brings together literatures on memory development, memory reinstatement, and children's understanding of symbolic media. What follows is a discussion of our research program and how it relates to research on the development of event memory and children's understanding of symbolic media. We conclude with, a discussion of our views on the role of representational reminders in the development of children's long-term memory.

Young Children's Event Recall

Although very young children lack the verbal skills to describe their memory for past events, several paradigms using behavioral measures have yielded a wealth of data on infants' and toddlers' memory: (a) response-contingency tasks, (b) deferred imitation tasks, and (c) elicited imitation tasks. The results from these various lines of research provide compelling evidence that from infancy children are capable of retaining information from novel experiences over intervals from a few days (at 2 months of age) to several months (by 16 months of age).

As discussed earlier, in response-contingency tasks, infants learn to respond to a stimulus to produce a target behavior during one or more training sessions. To test for recall, the same or a highly similar stimulus is presented within a specific time interval. If infants recognize the stimulus and reproduce the target behavior, this is considered evidence of recall. Several studies using operant procedure in a response-contingency tasks, have shown that 2-month-old infants can remember a novel stimulus for 2 to 3 days (Davis & Rovee-Collier, 1983), by 6 months of age, infants remember training for up to 20 days (Boller, Rovee-Collier, Bovorsky, O'Conner, & Shyi, 1990), and by 12 months, infants can recall training experiences for up to 56 days (Hartshorn, Rovee-Collier, Gerhardstein, Bhatt, & Wondoloski, 1998)

Deferred and elicited imitation paradigms have capitalized on children's interest in and ability to imitate modeled actions. In deferred imitation experiments, an experimenter models a unique action or sequence of actions. Children are restricted from producing the action(s) during this initial training period. After a time delay, children are then encouraged to produce the target action(s). Because children only observe actions, but do not perform any actions themselves during the initial exposure to the event, their subsequent imitation of the actions is considered a form of explicit, declarative memory as opposed to implicit, procedural memory which is the result of practice (Bauer, 2002). Studies using the deferred imitation methodology have shown that infants as young as 6 months showed deferred imitation of actions after a 24-hour delay (Collie & Hayne, 1999) and those infants from 9 to 14 months can remember single actions and two-step action sequences for 1–2 days (Meltzoff, 1988a, 1988b; McDonough & Mandler, 1994). Nine-month-olds even show evidence of deferred imitation after 1 month if they have had a second demonstration with the stimuli one week into the retention interval (Bauer, Wiebe, Waters, & Bangston, 2001). However, consistent with other memory paradigms, the length of children's recall may be affected by the tasks they are required to remember and the amount of training they receive. In their deferred imitation task, Herbert and Hayne (2000) found that 18-month-olds forgot their training only after 2 weeks. At 24 months of age, children retained some of the information they learned after 3 months, but there was no evidence of recall after 6 months.

Elicited imitation research also takes advantage of toddlers' interest in imitating actions, but in this paradigm children are allowed to imitate multi-step sequences immediately after observing an experimenter's demonstration. As in deferred imitation, children return to the training context after a delay and are encouraged to reproduce the learned action sequences. The advantage of this procedure as compared to the deferred imitation method is that children's immediate imitation provides a measure of how well children attended to and encoded the event and how well they can produce the target actions. The disadvantage is that because children have had the opportunity to perform the action sequences, their recall may, in part, be based on procedural or implicit action memory (see Bauer, 2002, for a discussion). However, the single opportunity for reproduction after modeling is not equivalent to the prolonged training period required for infants to learn a contingent response. Studies using elicited imitation paradigms have found that children from 11 to 16 months of age at time of encoding can recall action sequences for intervals ranging from 1 week to 8 months (Bauer & Hertsgaard, 1993; Bauer et al., 1994, 2000; Bauer & Mandler, 1990; Bauer & Shore, 1987; Mandler & McDonough, 1995).

Although these various lines of research show that children are capable of long-term memory early in life, there is also considerable forgetting that takes place in infants and young children, even within minutes after an experience (Bauer, Cheatham, Cary, & Abbema, 2002). Even when event information is retained for several weeks or even months, it is not clear whether such memories can be sustained over very long intervals, even after multiple experiences. Although McDonough and Mandler (1994) found that 11-month-olds were able to recall action sequences over a 1-week interval, the same children only recalled one action sequence a year later. The single sequence that was recalled involved a highly familiar routine (feeding a teddy bear with a schematic bottle) and it is very likely that children produced this action without recalling the initial training session. A similar failure of long-term recall was reported by Boyer, Barran, and Farrar (1994). In this study, 20-month-olds learned how to enact a nine-step sequence of making play-dough over one or three training experiences. One week later, children in the three-visit condition performed more actions than children in the one-visit condition when tested for recall. However, after another delay of 12 to 22 months later, there was no indication of long-term recall of the event by children in either training condition.

Thus, children under the age of 3 are clearly able to remember events they observe for several days and if given a chance to enact events themselves, they can recall events for several weeks. However, the parameters of long-term memory in young children are still not fully charted. Evidence suggests that events that are experienced from 11 to 20 months are not retrievable after a year, but little is know about when forgetting begins or what variables can attenuate retention. In this chapter, we examine an important development that may allow 1- and 2-year-old children to remember events over increasingly long periods: the ability to use different types of reminders to assist recall.

EFFECTS OF PHYSICAL REMINDERS ON TODDLERS' LONG-TERM MEMORY

Reenactment

One way children are reminded of a past event is by physically repeating all or part of the event at another time. This procedure, reenactment, is similar to multiple training trials in that children physically reproduce some or all of the actions they learned in the past. We consider reenactment to be the most complete and concrete type of reminder. Not only do children actively participate in their retraining, but they interact directly with the experimenter, providing additional context for their experience. Our reenactment research began with an investigation of its effects on 18-month-olds' long-term memory (Hudson & Sheffield, 1998). The reenactment procedure was conducted in the following manner: During the *training session*, children visited our laboratory playroom and were shown how to perform eight novel, two-step activities using an elicited imitation procedure. The activities were designed to be interesting for 18-month-olds, but not to be things that they could discover on their own without training (such as finding a hidden box of fish food so that they can feed the goldfish or pressing a stuffed bear's paw to make it talk). Some time after training, children returned to the laboratory for *a reenactment session*. First, children were allowed 10 minutes of free play in the playroom to see if they would spontaneously produce the target actions. Next, the experimenter provided verbal prompts for any of the activities the child had not performed, such as "What could we do with this toy?" Finally, if children failed to produce the target actions after prompting, the experimenter demonstrated the action for the child and encouraged the child to imitate so that

TABLE 9.1
Schedule of Conditions, Reenactment Experiments

Condition	Training	Reenactment	Test	Long-term Test
Experiments 1 and 2: Effects of Timing				
Renactment conditions				
Immediate	Day 1	Day 1	8 weeks	8 months
2-week	Day 1	2 weeks	10 weeks	8 months
8-week	Day 1	8 weeks	16 weeks	10 months
Control conditions				
1 visit	—	—	8 weeks	
No reenactment	Day 1	—	8 weeks	
1 visit (26 mos.)	—	—	—	8 months
Experiment 3: Subset Reenactment				
Subset A	Day 1	2 weeks	8 weeks	
Subset B	Day 1	2 weeks	8 weeks	

Source: Hudson & Sheffield (1998).

all children reenacted all of the activities during the reenactment session. After another time delay, children returned to the laboratory for a *recall test session* when they were encouraged to reproduce the target actions in the same way as in the reenactment session.

Three reenactment conditions were included in this study (see Table 9.1). An *immediate* reenactment group re-enacted the activities on the same day as their training. After they were shown how to perform the activities, they left the playroom for 15 minutes before returning for an immediate (same day) reenactment session. They then returned to the laboratory 8 weeks later for a recall test session. Children in the *2-week* reenactment condition returned 2 weeks after training for reenactment and were also tested for recall 8 weeks later, 10 weeks after training. Children in the *8-week* reenactment condition returned 8 weeks after training for reenactment and were tested for recall 8 weeks later, 16 weeks after training. Thus, across reenactment conditions, the interval between training and reenactment varied but the interval between reenactment and testing was the same for all groups.

Two control groups were also included in this study. The *one visit* control group was not provided with training, but participated in a recall session just like the other groups. This group controlled for the potential for children to simply figure out what to do with the toys when given verbal prompts. Children in the *no reenactment* condition were trained to perform the activities and were tested for recall 8 weeks later, but did not participate in a reenactment session.

Results indicated that, regardless of when the reminder occurred, reenactment extended 18-month-olds' recall: As shown in Figure 9.1, all reenactment groups recalled more activities than the control groups. But equally important, the timing of reenactment strongly influenced children's recall. Reenactment was more effective after a significant time delay; children in the 8-week reenactment condition recalled significantly more actions in recall testing than children in the immediate and 2-week reenactment conditions. Similar to results from infant research, reminders may be more effective when presented after an experience has been stored in long-term memory. One reason for this may be that retrieval involves more reconstruction when the memory is almost forgotten then when memory traces are new and more coherent (Rovee-Collier, 1995).

In a follow-up investigation, we contacted participants from the reenactment conditions and asked them to return to the laboratory 6 months after their last visit. We were curious if children would show evidence of recall after such a long interval. We compared the performance of the returning participants to the performance of naive 26-month-olds to test whether the returning subjects were actually remembering their prior experiences and were not simply better able to infer how to use the props. Timing effects were even stronger in long-term recall. As shown in Figure 9.2, even 6 months later, children who had reenacted the activities after 8 weeks recalled more activities than children in the other two reenactment groups. In fact, children's performance in the immediate reenactment

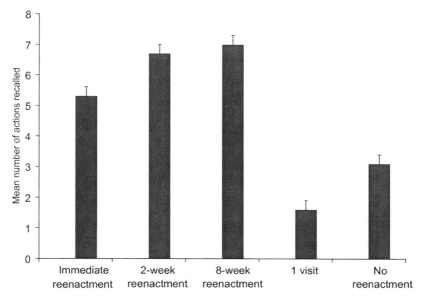

Figure 9.1   Mean number of actions recalled across experimental and control conditions with standard error bars, Reenactment Experiment 1. From Hudson & Sheffield (1998).

condition was not significantly better than that of children in the one visit control group at the 6-month test session. Thus, even for very young children, early memories may be retained for extremely long intervals if the children are given the opportunity to reenact events and if reenactment occurs at an opportune time.

Finally, we conducted another experiment to investigate whether reenacting a subset of the activities also enhances children's recall of the entire event. Two groups of 18-month-olds reenacted four of the original eight activities (either subset A or subset B) 2 weeks after training and were tested for memory of all activities 8 weeks later (see Table 9.1). The focus of this study was whether performing half of the activities (partial reenactment) could remind children of all the activities, including those that were not reenacted. We did not vary the timing of reenactment in this experiment and the 2-week

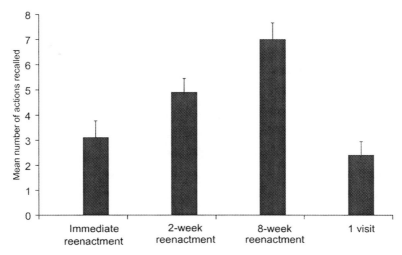

Figure 9.2   Mean number of actions recalled in long-term recall with standard error bars, Reenactment Experiment 2. From Hudson & Sheffield (1998).

point was selected as convenient point of comparison. Results showed that there were no significant differences in level of recall between the full reenactment and subset reenactment conditions, indicating that partial reenactment was as effective as full reenactment in reminding children of the original actions. This finding suggests that 18-month-olds encode and store event memories in an associative network linked in memory by the common temporal and spatial context of the event. Reinstatement of some of the event therefore activated memory for all of the event components. Our research on reinstatement provides further support for this interpretation.

Reinstatement

In addition to reenactment, children can also be reminded of the past activity by coming in contact with physical reminders, but without actually reproducing the actions. For example, children might observe someone else performing the activity, or they might see the props associated with activity. Are these types of experiences effective in reinstating young children's event memories? Reinstatement research in infants using the response-contingency paradigm reviewed above suggests that with increasing age, children may be reminded of past events by exposure to objects that are similar, but not identical to those encountered in initial training. Research using deferred imitation has also shown that between the first two years of life, children become more flexible in their use of retrieval cues (Hayne, MacDonald, & Barr, 1997) and more flexible in terms of the medium with which training is presented (Barr & Hayne, 1999). For example, Hayne et al. showed that 12-month-olds could not remember their training if at final test the original objects (i.e., puppets) were replaced with new objects differing in form or color, but 18-month-olds were successful if one of the two dimensions changed. By 21 months, children could accommodate both color and form change. Thus, with increased age throughout the second year of life, children were better able to retrieve information they learned during their initial session upon presentation of dissimilar stimuli at the test session.

It is also possible that this age-related increase in flexibility in use of retrieval cues is accompanied by a similar increase in the range of reminders that are effective for memory reinstatement. Developments in children's ability to use reminders to reinstate event memories may help to explain why memories for events occurring after the age of 3 are more likely to be retained in very long-term autobiographic memory as compared to memories from the infant and toddler years.

Reinstatement With Modeling

In our first reinstatement experiment (Sheffield & Hudson, 1994), we tested whether 14- and 18-month-olds could be reminded of a past event by viewing an experimenter perform some of the activities they had learned previously. We were interested in whether children could be reminded of a past event by passive exposure to a subset of activities from the original event. This study differed from the Hudson and Sheffield (1998) study in that children did not reenact any actions themselves during the reminder session, but merely watched an experiment reenact half of the activities. We selected children at different ages to see whether there were developmental differences in children's ability to use subset reminders.

Three conditions were used in this experiment (see Table 9.2). Children in the *train/remind* and *train only* (no reminder) conditions were trained to perform 6 novel activities similar to those used in the reenactment studies. Eight weeks after training, 14-month-olds in the *train/remind* condition participated in a reminder session while 10 weeks after training, 18-month-olds in the *train/remind* condition participated in a reminder session. Because pilot research had shown that the retention interval varied for children at different ages, different intervals were selected for each age group. In the reminder session, children viewed an experimenter model three of the six activities they had learned previously, but children did not perform the activities themselves. Both ages were tested for recall 24 hours later. Children in the *train/no remind* conditions did not participate in a reminder session and were tested for recall 8 or 10 weeks after training. Children in the *no train/remind* conditions were

TABLE 9.2
Schedule of Conditions, Modeling Reinstatement Experiment

Condition	Training	Reminder	Test
14-month-olds			
Train/Remind	Day 1	Week 8	Week 8
Train/No remind	Day 1	—	Week 8
No train/Remind	——	Week 8	Week 8
18-month-olds			
Train/Remind	Day 1	Week 10	Week 10
Train/No remind	Day 1	Week 10	Week 10
No train/Remind	Day 1	Week 10	Week 10

Source: Sheffield & Hudson (1994).

never trained to perform the activities, but viewed an experimenter perform three of the activities and then were tested on their ability to perform all of the activities 24 hours later. This condition provided a test of children's ability to perform the actions simply by imitating the experimenter.

We expected recall of modeled actions to be high for both the train/remind and no train/remind conditions. Results from deferred imitation research suggested that 14- and 18-month-olds would be able to remember actions seen the day before and reproduce them in a test session (Meltzoff, 1988a) which was equivalent to the experience of children in the *no train/remind* condition. However, the critical comparison was of children's recall of the unmodeled actions across conditions. If reinstatement occurred, recall should be high for unmodeled actions for children in the train/remind condition but not for children in the train/no remind condition.

Results showed clear evidence of reinstatement. As shown in Figure 9.3, recall of unmodeled activities was higher in the train/remind condition for both ages than in either of the other two conditions, indicating that a subset reminder effectively reinstated both 14- and 18-month-olds' memory for all of the activities. (As expected, recall of modeled activities was high for both the train/reminder and no train/remind conditions, indicating that children were capable of deferred imitation.). This indicated that partial reminders are effective in reinstating toddlers' memory for all of the event actions, even

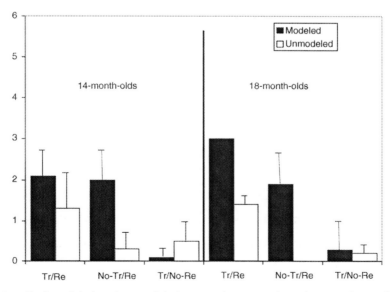

Figure 9.3   Recall of modeled and unmodeled actions by age and condition with standard error bars, Modeling Reinstatement Experiment. Includes recall scores from the Train/Remind (Tr/Re), No-Train/Remind (No-Tr/Re), and Train/No-Remind (Tr/No-Re) conditions. From Sheffield & Hudson (1994).

when children were not active participants. Interestingly, there were no developmental differences in reinstatement effects for 14- and 18-month-olds, indicating that partial reinstatement was equally effective across this age range.

These results led us to consider how other kinds of reminders could be effective in reinstating toddlers' event memories. In real-world situations, children may regularly encounter reminders that simulate or represent their experiences in different media such as watching videos or viewing photographs in a family album. The question remained; do these reminder situations actually reinstate children's memories?

REINSTATEMENT WITH REPRESENTATIONAL REMINDERS

Our recent research has focused on children's ability to use information presented in various media as reminders of past events. With a *video* simulation reminder, children watch a video tape of an event instead of a live model. With *photograph* reminders, children view photographs of past events with or without accompanying verbal narration. Finally, in a *model simulation* experiment, children view an experimenter perform the actions using a small-scale model replica of the room and props used in the original event. Each type of reminder provides different kinds of information about events using different symbolic systems. Videos can provide action information whereas photographs are only static images. Model simulations provide action information via live events, however, children view actions performed on small-scale replicas, not the original objects. The small-scale objects are used to symbolize the original objects.

By varying the type of reminder, we can examine the effects of different amounts of event information on reinstatement. As discussed above, videos, photographs and scale models provide varying amounts and types of event information. We can also use the media to manipulate the amount of information provided in different types of reminders. For example, a videotape may show children all of the actions they experienced in the past or only some of the actions. Reminders can therefore vary in terms of the medium of representation as well as the amount of information provided about a past event and each of these variables may affect their effectiveness in reinstating young children's memories.

By examining effects of these different types of reminders, we can also examine children's ability to use different types of representations to cue their memories. DeLoache and her colleagues (DeLoache, 1990; DeLoache & Burns, 1994; DeLoache, Pierroutsakos, & Troseth, 1996; Troseth & DeLoache, 1998) have found that children under 3 years of age often fail to appreciate how external representations such as scale models, photographs, and videos can be used to represent specific real-world contexts. They propose that young children lack representational insight, that is, the understanding of how external representations function as symbols of real-world referents. However, it is not clear that representational insight is necessary for a symbol to serve as a reminder of a past event. We (Deocampo & Hudson, 2003) have suggested that recall cueing may be a more implicit process (e.g., Brainerd, Reyna, Howe, & Kingma, 1990; Spear, 1978; Tulving, 1983) that requires matching retrieval cues to memory traces, but does not require explicit awareness of the symbol-referent relationship. Comparing children's performance on symbolic tasks that require representational insight to their use of symbolic reminders in reinstatement tasks can address this issue.

Development of Representational Insight: The Object Retrieval Task

Extensive research by DeLoache and her colleagues has examined young children's understanding of symbolic media using an object retrieval task.

Scale Models

In the scale model object retrieval task, young children are familiarized with a laboratory playroom and then shown a scale model of that room and its contents. Children's attention is drawn to the similarities between the room and the model of the room. Then, children watch as a toy is hidden in the scale model. They are subsequently told that the big toy is hiding in the same place in the big playroom and asked to go find it. DeLoache (1990) found that although 31- and 38-month-olds were both able to remember where the toy was hidden in the scale model, only 38-month-olds were able to use that knowledge to help them find the toy in the full-sized room. According to DeLoache, the younger children had difficulty using the placement of the toy in the model room to guide their searches for the large toy in the large playroom because they did not recognize the dual representational nature of the scale model. That is, they could not simultaneously recognize the model as a thing in and of itself *and* as a symbol of the larger room. Instead of using the scale model as a representation of the life-sized room, the salience of the model as a toy-like object caused the younger children to focus solely on the object status of the model. This is a particularly difficult representational task because the scale model's status as an object is so much more salient than its status as a representation of its referent.

Photographs

Experiments by DeLoache and Burns (1993) examined young children's performance in the object retrieval task when they were to find hidden objects after viewing photographs of the hiding location. They found that 30-month-olds were able to use photographs to help them find the hidden toy, but that younger children were not successful. Younger children's failure to find the hidden toys using photograph information was attributed to a lack of understanding of "representational specificity" of photographs. That is, children under 30 months failed to understand that that the photographs representations a specific room at the current moment in time and not a generic room or a generic time. Because young children's initial experience with photographs typically consists of viewing generic photographs of objects in picture books, they interpret photographs as representations of generic, not specific, realities. It is not until approximately 30 months of age that children come to understand that photographs have both generic and specific referential properties.

Video

Using the object retrieval task, Troseth and DeLoache (1998) found that 27-month-olds, but not 24-month-olds, were able to use location information represented on a video monitor to retrieve a hidden toy. The video monitor showed the experimenter hiding the toy in the adjacent room in real-time. As in the case of photographs, children's difficulty in this task can be attributed to their prior experience with the medium. Young children's initial experience with video is that of viewing videos and television programming for entertainment. They have very relatively little experience with viewing real-time television. Thus, they fail to realize the specific nature of the video representation, that is, that the information shown on the video monitor refers to a specific location in the adjacent room and that the information pertains to the present time. To support this view, one ingenious experiment tricked 24-month-olds into believing they were watching a live event through a window, when in fact, children shown a large video screen. When children believed that they were looking through a window (even though they were actually viewing a television monitor) their retrieval performance improved as compared to their performance when they knew they were looking at a video screen (DeLoache et al., 1996).

Thus, this line of research has uncovered important limitations in young children's understanding of symbolic media. DeLoache and her colleagues propose that children's experience with different media strongly influences the development of their understanding of the symbolic functions of media. Children's experience with model-like play sets makes it difficult for them to understand that models can also be used as symbols; experience with generic photographs makes it difficult to understand the use of photographs to depict specific referents; and experience with television as an entertainment media makes it difficult to for them to understand how it could provide information about real-world situations.

Children's Use of Video Representations in Imitation Tasks

Research showing that 2-year-olds are unable to take advantage of location information represented in photographs and video when searching for hidden objects suggests that they have limitations in understanding how symbolic media represent real-world, real-time events. This lack of understanding about the relationship between a representation and its real-world event referent could also impede 2-year-olds' ability to use symbolic representations as reminders of past events. However, children's ability to use representational information may vary in terms of the specific task at hand. Several studies have shown that very young children can imitate action sequences shown on video. Meltzoff (1988b) found that 14-month-olds were able to imitate action sequences they view on video monitor 1 day later and Barr and Hayne (1999) found that 18-month-olds could imitate tasks presented over video 24 hours later. These findings indicate that 1-year-old children can video encode and store information about actions viewed on a video monitor and retrieve that information to guide their own actions their own actions after a 24-hour delay. This ability may be sufficient for successful memory reinstatement using video information.

Video and Photograph Reinstatement in 18-Month-Olds

Children's ability to perform actions on three-dimensional objects after viewing a two-dimensional television representation suggests that video representations could also be used as reminders. It may not be necessary for children to understand the representational nature of video images for those images to act as reminders capable of cueing children's recall. Reinstatement may occur rather automatically if enough attributes on a two-dimensional display match the attributes contained in a child's original experience. Thus, the process of reinstatement may not require a child to understand the relationship between a representation and the physical world, as long as the attributes of the representational reminder are similar enough to the physical display.

A series of experiments tested whether toddlers could be reminded of a past event by watching a video simulation of their original experience (Sheffield & Hudson, 2004). Although video simulations provide as much information as viewing a live model, they are presented in a representational format and are not live events. Viewing a video simulation would only be effective in reinstating children's event memory if children were able to relate their internal memory representation of the event to the external, video representation of the event.

Effects of Video Reminders

This study was similar in design to our reenactment experiments. Eighteen-month-olds were trained to perform eight novel, two-step activities and returned to the laboratory for a reminder session 2 weeks later as in the original reenactment experiment. However, in this experiment, we tested effects of different kinds of reminders in the 2-week reinstatement session. Children in a *reenactment* condition physically reenacted all of the activities as in prior studies. For children in the *video reinstatement* condition, however, the reminder sessions consisted of returning to the laboratory to view a videotape depicting a preschool child performing the original activities with an experimenter similar to their initial training sessions. All the props associated with the original event were removed from the playroom during the video reminder session. Recall was assessed 8 weeks later (10 weeks after training) when children returned to the laboratory for testing (see Table 9.3). A third group of children in the *no reminder condition* were tested for recall 10 weeks after training, but did not receive any reminder. Although all props were removed from the playroom in the video reminder condition, it is still possible that simply returning to the laboratory context could reinstate children's memories. Boller et al. (1990) found that 3-month-old infants could be reminded of past training by exposure to the training context. To control for context effects, another group of children in the *video reinstatement control* condition were trained to perform the activities and also returned to the laboratory 2 weeks late and

TABLE 9.3
Schedule of Training, Reminder, and Recall Sessions for Reinstatement Experiments 1–5

Condition	Training	Reinstatement Type/Timing	Recall
Experiment 1: Effects of Video Reminders			
Live reenactment	Day 1	Reenact/2 weeks	12 weeks
Video reinstatement	Day 1	Video/2 weeks	12 weeks
No reminder	Day 1	—	12 weeks
Video reinstatement control	Day 1	Video/2 weeks	12 weeks
Video training control	—	Video/2 weeks	12 weeks
Experiment 2: Immediate Recall After Video Reinstatement			
Video reinstate 10-10	Day 1	Video/10 weeks	10 week
Video training 10-10	—	Video/10 weeks	10 weeks
Experiment 3: Delayed Recall After Video Reinstatement			
Video reinstate 10-12	Day 1	Video/10 weeks	12 weeks
Experiment 4: Effects of Video and Photograph Reminders			
Video reinstatement	Day 1	Video/10 weeks	10 weeks
Photo reinstatement	Day 1	Photo/10 weeks	10 weeks
Video training	—	Video/10 weeks	10 weeks
Photo training	—	Photo/10 weeks	10 weeks
No reminder	Day 1	—	10 weeks
Experiment 5: Objects Only Video Reminder			
Objects + actions	Day 1	Full video/10 weeks	10 weeks
Objects only	Day 1	Objects only video/10 weeks	10 weeks
No reminder	Day 1	—	10 weeks
Reminder only	—	Full video/10 weeks	10 weeks.

Source: Sheffield (in press), Sheffield & Hudson (2003).

viewed an unrelated video of a segment from *Sesame Street*. They also returned for testing 8 weeks later, 10 weeks after training.

A final group, the *video training control condition* provided a measure of children's ability to imitate the actions shown on the video when they had not been shown the activities in a live training session. These children did not participate in the training session, but simply watched the video reminder and were tested for recall 10 weeks later.

Results are displayed in Table 9.4. Both spontaneous production of target actions and cued production were analyzed separately. Cued production consisted of actions that were not performed by children in the first 5 minutes when they were allowed to interact with all props without any intervention., but were produced when the experimenter provided a nondirective verbal prompt ("What could we do with this toy?"). To show evidence of video reinstatement, children in the *video reinstatement* condition would have to show higher levels of recall than children in both all control conditions. As evident from Table 9.4, this was not the case. In both spontaneous and cued recall, children in the *video reinstatement* condition recalled no more activities than the children in the three control conditions. Children in the *live reenactment* condition showed higher levels of recall than all other groups, indicating once again, that reenactment was effective in sustaining children's recall.

Effects of Timing of Video Reminders

One explanation for why the video reminder was not effective was that it was administered relatively early in the recall time window. Reinstatement research with infants has found that reminders are most effective when administered late in the recall time window, close to the onset of forgetting. To examine timing effects, a second experiment examined the effects of a video reminder on 18-month-

TABLE 9.4
Mean Spontaneous and Cued Recall Scores, Reinstatement Experiment
1: Effects of Video Reminders

Condition	Spontaneous Production	SD	Cued Production	SD
Live reenactment	5.9*	2.68	3.9*	2.33
Video reinstatement	2.8	1.47	2.7	1.25
No reminder	2.6	1.42	2.0	1.63
Video reinstatement control	2.1	1.10	2.0	1.49
Video training control	.9	1.10	2.2	1.47

*Significantly different from all other conditions.
Source: Sheffield & Hudson (2003).

olds recall when it was administered immediately prior to recall testing (see Table 9.3). Children in an immediate recall condition, *the video reinstate 10-10 condition*, returned to the laboratory 10 weeks after training and viewed the video simulation. They then left the playroom and were occupied in other parts of the building while the props were replaced in the playroom. After this 15-minute break, children returned to the playroom for testing. Children in a control group *(video training control 10-10)* were not trained, but simply viewed the video and were allowed to play with the props 15 minutes later, controlling for the possibility that children might be able to imitate the activities after viewing the videotape without prior training.

Table 9.5 shows the mean number of actions produced in spontaneous and cued recall in the *video 10-10* immediate recall condition compared to recall of children in the 2-week video reminder condition, *video reinstatement 2-12*, from the previous experiment as well as that of children who watched the video without prior training (*video training control 10-10*) and were tested for recall 15 minutes later. Children in the *video reinstatement 10-10* condition performed significantly better than all other groups in both spontaneous and cued recall. This finding indicates that viewing a video reminder immediately before recall testing effectively reminded children of the past training event.

Children's performance in the video training control condition was relatively low, indicating that children were not able to reproduce the activities after seeing the video if they had not been given prior training. These findings are surprising in light of Meltzoff's (1988b) research showing that 14-month-olds were able to imitate actions demonstrated by a televised model. The difference in performance may be because the actions used in Meltzoff's study were very simple ones, repeated several times by the televised model. The activities used in our research were 2-step activities that often involved moving props from different locations in the playroom and the activities were presented only once in the video. A single exposure to several of these more complex events appeared to insufficient for children to remember the actions well enough to reproduce them after a short delay. However, the

TABLE 9.5
Mean Spontaneous Cued Recall Scores, Reinstatement Experiments 2 and 3

Condition	Spontaneous Production	SD	Cued Production	SD
Experiment 2: Immediate Recall After Video Reinstatement				
Video reinstatement 10-10	5.5*	2.27	4.6*	1.89
Video reinstatement 2-12	2.8	1.47	2.7	1.25
Video training control 10-10	1.4	1.07	2.7	1.94
Experiment 3: Delayed Recall After Video Reinstatement				
Video reinstatement 10-12	2.6	2.06	4.7*	1.63

*Significantly different from video reinstatement 2-12 and video training control 10-1.
Source: Sheffield & Hudson (2003).

video exposure was sufficient for children with prior training 10 weeks in the past to be reminded of how to perform the actions.

Effects of Video Reinstatement Over Time

After showing that video reminders were effective in reinstating 18-month-olds event memories, the next experiment examined the duration of video reinstatement effects. We had shown that video reinstatement could be effective when recall was assessed immediately after reinstatement, but would effects be evident after a longer delay between reinstatement and recall? In this experiment, 18-month-olds in a delayed recall condition viewed a video simulation in a reminder session 10 weeks after training, but the recall test was administered 2 weeks later, 12 weeks after training, the video reinstate 10-12 condition (see Table 9.3). Their performance was compared to that of subjects in the previous experiment who were tested for recall on the same day as the reminder session. As shown in Table 9.5, spontaneous recall in the *video reinstatement 10-12* condition was significantly less than that of children in the immediate, *video reinstatement 10-10* condition, and was not significantly different from spontaneous recall of children in the video training 10-10 control group. However, cued recall for children in the *video reinstatement 10-12* condition was as high as that of children in the video reinstatement 10-10 condition. Thus, reminder effects were found for children in the *video reinstatement 10-12* condition as evidenced by their significantly higher level of cued production. However, their total recall was significantly lower than children who were immediately tested. This finding suggests that the effects of the video reminder had diminished over the 2-week interval, but that the memory was not entirely gone.

This finding indicates that children can be reminded of an event if they watch a video of the event 10 weeks later and immediately reproduce the event. However, when tested 2 weeks after viewing the reminder, their recall had already decreased. When the reminder was viewed 2 weeks after the original event and recall was tested 8 weeks later, children did not demonstrate recall at all. In contrast, research by Hudson and Sheffield (1998) showed that reenacting activities 8 weeks after training significantly improved 18-month-olds recall when tested even up to 6 months after the reenactment session.

These findings indicate that information presented in a video was effective in reinstating 18-month-olds event memories, but the reinstated memories did not last for very long. Thus, watching a video of an event may be effective in reminding 18-month-olds of their past experience, but it is clearly not equivalent to actually reexperiencing the event.

Effects of Video versus Photograph Reminders

In the next experiment, we compared effects of video and photograph reminders at 18 months. Reminder sessions were held 10 weeks after training as in the previous experiments, and children in the *video reinstatement* condition viewed the same videos as used in previous experiment (see Table 9.3). Children in the *photograph reinstatement* conditions viewed two photographs of each activity in a photo album while an experimenter described each of the actions. Recall was tested 24 hours after the reminder sessions. Although photographs and videos are both symbolic media that provide visual information about events, there are several important differences between these types of representation that have implications for their use as reminders. The video representation of the action sequences used in our research is very similar to children's initial training. Entire action sequences are shown with accompanying narration by an experimenter in real time. The actors have changed, but the objects and actions children were shown in initial training are the same in the video representation. The photographs of the event differed in several ways from the video presentations. The same props were shown in the photographs, but photographs only provided static images without motion information. We provided a verbal narration of the action, but action information was not available from the photographs themselves. Photographs thus provided less information about the event and used a different representational medium.

Because photographs provide less event information and because research on children's use of photograph information in the object retrieval task showed that children under 30 months are unable to use photographs as symbolic representations of a large-scale space, we predicted that photograph reminders would be less effective than video reminders for 18-month-olds. Harris, Kavenaugh, and Dowson (1997) also found that children under 2 years of age were unable to use photographs to depict imaginary transformations in pretend play, providing further evidence of limitations in young children's understanding of photographs. These findings suggest that 18-month-olds would not be able to understand how photographs represent past events. Providing verbal narration about the event while viewing the photographs could provide children with more event information, but research on verbal recall with children less than 30 months suggests that conversations about past events do not facilitate subsequent verbal recall (Hudson, 1990b, 1993).

To rule out potential context effects, all reminder sessions took place in children's homes. One day later, children returned to the laboratory for their test session. Age-matched control subjects who were not trained to perform the activities were also shown either the video or the photographs in their homes one day before being tested for production of target actions in the laboratory (*video training* and *photo training* conditions) (see Table 9.3).

Results are displayed in Figure 9.4. As predicted, reinstatement occurred in the video reinstatement condition, but not in the photograph reinstatement condition; recall in the photo reinstatement condition was not significantly higher than recall in the control conditions. It is not clear from these findings whether photographs were ineffective in reinstating recall because they did not provide enough event information or because 18-month-olds failed to appreciate how photographs represent past events. To examine effects of diminished event information on reinstatement, Sheffield (in press) conducted two experiments using video reminders that included partial or altered event information. To examine effects of photograph reminders on older children's recall, Deocampo and Hudson (2003) tested effects of photograph reminders with 24- and 30-month-olds.

Effects of Partial Video Information

The previous study indicated that videos were more effective than photographs in reminding children of past events. This result is consistent with the hypothesis that children below the age of 24 months

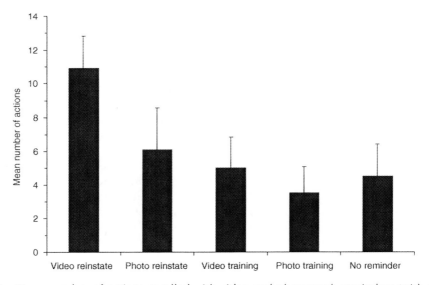

Figure 9.4 Mean number of actions recalled with video and photograph reminders (with standard error bars), Reinstatement Experiment 4. From Sheffield and Hudson (2003).

do not understand the representational nature of photographs to the degree necessary to use photographs as reminders of past events. The result also suggest that children are able to understand the representational nature of videos before they can appreciate photographs as representations of the past. However, because photographs include less event information than videos, it is not clear if the paucity in event information, particularly the absence of action information, can account for their ineffectiveness as reminders. To examine effects of partial event information, 18-month-olds in this experiment (Sheffield, 2004, Experiment 1) participated in a reminder session in which they viewed a video containing only object information about the activities they had learned 10 weeks prior (the *objects only video* condition). The video showed an experimenter displaying all of the props used in the activities and commenting on the props, for example, "Look, here's Mickey Mouse. He has a shirt on. And shoes, too. He's my friend." However, actions associated with the objects actions were not depicted or described. Research with infants indicates that they required functional information (e.g., a moving mobile) in order for reinstatement to occur (Greco et al., 1990), but a study with 2½-year-olds showed that their memory for location information was reinstated simply by viewing objects without actions (Howe et al., 1992). Would 18-month-olds' performance be more similar to infants' or to 2½-year-olds?

Performance of children viewing the *objects only* reminder was compared to that of children who viewed a complete *objects + actions video* of the actions performed on the objects. In the *objects + actions video*, an experimenter picked up each of the props and demonstrated each action while narrating, for example, "Let's see this toy. It's Mickey Mouse. All you have to do is pull his string and he'll talk to you. Listen. Isn't that fun?" Recall was tested one day after the reminder session that took place in the laboratory. Children in the *no reminder* condition were trained to perform the activities, returned to the laboratory 10 weeks later and viewed an unrelated video, and were tested for recall 10 weeks later. Children in the *reminder only* condition visited the laboratory and played with the props, but were not shown the target actions. Ten weeks later they returned to laboratory to view the complete objects + actions video and they were tested for recall one day later (see Table 9.3).

Results of this experiment are displayed in Table 9.6. It was apparent that both types of video reminders, *objects + actions* and *objects only*, were effective in reinstating children's memories; children in these conditions produced significantly more target actions than children in all control conditions. This finding indicates that unlike infants, 18-month-olds can be reminded of past events by viewing objects associated with the event without functional (action) information. Thus, the lack of reinstatement effects in 18-month-olds found in the previous experiment using photograph reminders cannot be explained merely by the fact that photographs did not include information about the target actions. Rather, these results suggest that there are several differences between video and photographs that may contribute to children's difference in performance. First, it is possible that despite the fact that the video contained no target actions, it still provided children with more action information matching their original experience than the photographs did. Although target actions were not performed, the experimenter still moved around, retrieved toys, held them up, and so on. Second, the size of the

TABLE 9.6
Mean Number of Actions Recalled in Experiment 5:
Objects Only Video Reinstatement

Condition	Recall Score	SD
Objects + actions	.59[*]	.22
Object-only	.46[*]	.18
No training	.14	.14
No reminder	.12	.11
Context-only	.25	.13

[*]There was no significant difference between objects + actions and object-levels of recall, but both are significantly different from no training, no reminder and context-only at $p < .01$.
Source: Sheffield (2004).

television monitor was larger than the photographs. Third, it is possible that 18-month-olds understand the relationship between a video and an event even when the video does not include action information, but they do not appreciate the relationship between a photograph and a physical event.

Concerning context reinstatement, children who returned to the laboratory to watch an unrelated video produced no more target actions than children who did not return to the laboratory for reinstatement. Although context may be an important component in reinstating memories for young infants (Rovee-Collier et al., 1985), these results support research which suggests that context plays a less salient role for older infants (Barnat, Klein, & Meltzoff, 1996).

Effects of New Information in Video Reinstatement

In the previous experiment, we showed children video reminders that did not include action information. What would the effects be if we showed them video reminders with different actions? This is another way of varying the amount of information presented in a reminder. By including new information, we examined the effects of modifications in event information on reinstatement. This is an important manipulation to investigate because it may be more similar to the types of reminders that are encountered in real-world contexts. In this experiment, we tested whether reminders that contained some new information could successfully reinstate toddlers' event memories and whether new object or new action information would differentially affect children.

Results from our experiments using subset reenactment, subset modeling, and partial (object only) information indicated that toddlers' memories could be reinstated by exposure to partial event information. The partial information (objects only) experiment presented a scenario in which action information was eliminated, but the opposite scenario of eliminating object information, (e.g., bouncing an invisible ball) was not tested, primarily because the condition does not exist in the real world. However, substituting objects and actions do occur frequently in children's lives. For example, children may drink from a cup on one occasion, from a glass on another, and from a mug on a third occasion. Here, the act of drinking is the same but the objects are interchangeable. Conversely, children may put their doll to sleep in a stroller, but dress the doll on another occasion. Would children's memory be reinstated by performing multiple actions on a single object, or by performing the same action on multiple objects? Experiment 2 systematically changed action and object information during a reminder session in order to compare the effect of different types of information on children's recall.

Children viewed video reminders of a past event that contained (a) all original information (*objects + actions*), (b) original object information but new action information (*new actions*), (c) original action information but new object information (*new objects*), or (d) new action and new object information (*new objects + new actions*). Four groups of 18-month-olds were trained to perform novel activities during an initial training session, returned for a reminder session 10 weeks later, and were tested for recall one day later (see Table 9.7). The videos containing all original information were the same *objects + actions* videos used in the complete video condition in the previous study and showed an experimenter performing the same actions children had learned to perform on the same objects they had used. The *new objects* videos showed the experimenter performing the same actions using

TABLE 9.7

Schedule of Conditions, Reinstatement Experiment 6: Effects of New Information

Condition	Training	Reminder	Video	Test
Objects + actions	Day 1	Week 10 — old objects + old actions		Week 10
New objects	Day 1	Week 10 — new objects + old actions		Week 10
New actions	Day 1	Week 10 — old objects + new actions		Week 10
New objects + new actions	Day 1	Week 10 — new objects + new actions		Week 10

Source: Sheffield (2004).

different objects, for example, pulling a string on a stuffed, Alvin the Chipmunk toy instead of Mickey Mouse. In the *new actions* videos, the experimenter performed new actions on the same objects that children had used during training, for example, removing Mickey Mouse's shoes instead of pulling a string to make him talk. In the *new objects + new actions* videos, the experimenter performed new actions on new objects, for example, taking the shoes off the stuffed Alvin toy if children had seen an experimenter pull Mickey Mouse's string. This condition controlled for the potential reinstatement effect of watching a video involving actions on objects. Because the previous study had shown that children who viewed a video of an experimenter performing actions on objects 24 hours prior to testing without prior training performed no more actions than children who had been trained to perform the actions but had not been reminded, reminder only control conditions were not included in this experiment.

Results from this experiment are shown in Table 9.8. Results indicated that children who viewed reminders that included changes in action information, either new actions on old objects or new actions on new objects, were not effective in reinstating recall. In contrast, videos that included original action information, either old actions on new objects or all original information, were effective reminders (the difference in recall between these conditions was not significant). Thus, reinstatement only occurred when the original action information was shown, regardless of whether objects were different. Action information was more important for reinstatement than object information. This finding is particularly interesting in light of the findings from the previous study indicating that reinstatement occurred even with the deletion of action information. Those findings indicated that 18-month-olds did not require action information to be specified in a reminder in order for reinstatement to occur; they were reminded of past actions by viewing associated objects without associated actions.

We may be able to account for this asymmetry by examining the nature of the task children were presented with. Recall that children were encouraged to complete activities that relied heavily on action information during these experiments. We believe that by at least 18 months, children are attending to information about how objects work, particularly when the information is crucial to successful completion of a task. In gleaning this information, children can begin to predict the way other, similar objects will act, particularly if the objects are perceptually similar and replaceable. In contrast, especially in these kinds of action-oriented tasks, young children may not see two actions performed on the same object as being the same event, and may maintain the two representations separately. However, there are different kinds of experiences, such as social interactions, which do not include specific actions taken upon specific objects. Under these circumstances, the asymmetric difference found in this experiment may be minimized.

Photograph Reinstatement in 24- and 30-Month-Olds

Our findings that changes in the information presented in a video reminder may reduce 18-month-olds' ability to be reminded by a video (Sheffield, 2004, Experiment 2) and that 18-month-olds were

TABLE 9.8
Children's Recall of Original Targets, Reinstatement Experiment 6:
Effects of New Information

Condition	Recall Score	SD
Old objects + old actions	.59*	.22
New objects	.43˙	.32
New actions	.30	.27
New actions + new objects	.17	.14
No reminder (taken from Exp. 5)	.12	.11

˙Significantly different from *No reminder* and *New action and object at reinstatement* conditions at $p < .05$.
Source: Sheffield (in press)

unable to use photographs as reminders (Sheffield & Hudson, 2004), could both be interpreted in terms of the amount of similarity between a reminder and the referent event. The first study (Sheffield, 2004, Experiment 2) suggests that deleting some information may not interfere with children's ability to notice a similarity between a reminder and their past experience, but changing information can prevent children from seeing the reminder as similar to their past experience. In the second investigation (Sheffield & Hudson, 2004), videos were effective as reminders for 18-month-olds, but photographs were not. Photographs may have been ineffective reminders for this age group because there was little event information provided in the photographs as compared to the video. However, results from Sheffield (2004) showing that videos that did not include action information but simply showed a person holding and describing target objects were effective as reminders suggests that differences in the media may also affect memory reinstatement.

Even if the medium of representation does influence children's use of reminders, research suggests that the timing and perhaps the sequence of development of representational understanding may be different for reminding tasks than for the object retrieval task used by DeLoache and her colleagues. Children as young as 18 months can use videos as reminders to reinstate event memories well before they are able to use video information to guide their search behavior (Troseth & DeLoache, 1998). However, it is not yet known when children are able to use photographs or scale models as reminders.

Because our previous investigation of toddlers' abilities to use photographs as reminders was inconclusive with regard to 24-month-olds, we designed a second study to test whether 24- and 30-month-olds could be reminded of an event by viewing unnarrated photographs (Deocampo & Hudson, 2003). Thirty-month-olds were included because that is the age at which DeLoache and Burns (1994) found that children first succeed at the object-retrieval task using photographs, showing evidence of understanding of the symbolic nature of photographs. A deferred imitation paradigm was used to test children's recall of activities learned in the laboratory. Twenty-four- and 30-month-olds watched an experimenter model three novel activities in a laboratory playroom, but children were not allowed to attempt to imitate those activities. After a delay of 2 weeks for 24-month-olds or 4 weeks for 30-month-olds, the children returned to the laboratory. These retention intervals were determined to be sufficiently long for forgetting to occur for each age group. After the delay, half of the children in each age group received a photograph reminder while the other half participated in an experience unrelated to the previously modeled activities. For each age group, the reminder consisted of a photo album containing 6 photographs: one photograph of each of the activities modeled during the training session (trained activities) as well one photograph of each of three new activities (untrained activities). The experimenter did not provide any verbal narration other than "Look at this." After the reminder or unrelated experience, the children were taken to the toys in the laboratory playroom and encouraged to try to perform all six of the activities, trained and untrained. For the reminder condition, the three tasks that each child did not observe but which were depicted in the photographs (untrained activities) served as a within-subject control to make sure that the children could not figure out how to perform the tasks by just looking at the photographs. For the no reminder condition, untrained activities served as a within-subject control to make sure that naive children could not spontaneously perform the experimental tasks.

Results showed that although 30-month-olds performed significantly more trained activities at the recall test than did 24-month-olds, children in the reminder condition at both ages performed equally more trained activities than did children in the no reminder condition. There were no age or condition differences in performance of untrained activities (see Figure 9.5). These results indicate that both 24- and 30-month-olds are capable of using photograph reminders to reinstate event memories. Thus, the symbolic medium of photographs is not itself a barrier to reinstatement for children as young as 24-month-olds. As discussed earlier, photographs are ineffective reminders for 18-month-olds (Sheffield & Hudson, 2004), so 24-month-olds' ability to be reminded by photographs represents a developmental achievement. This shows that as children age they are able to use more abstract representations as reminders of past experiences.

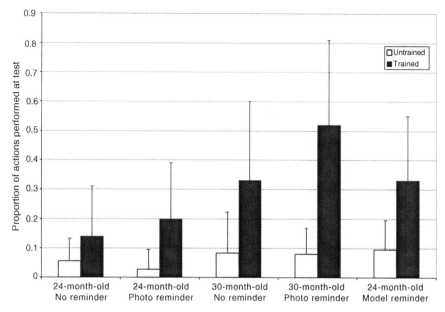

Figure 9.5   Mean trained and untrained recall proportion scores (actions performed at test) with standard error bars for 24- and 30-month-olds in photograph reminder and no reminder conditions (see Deocampo & Hudson, 2003, for full description of how proportions were calculated).

Scale Model Reinstatement in 24-Month-Olds

To further test children's ability to use representational reminders, in another experiment, we administered a reminder task to 24-month-olds using a scale model. The procedure for both the training and long-term retention test sessions was the same as for the 24-month-old reminder group described above (Deocampo & Hudson, 2003) except that the reminder treatment consisted of the children watching as an experimenter reenacted all of the previously trained and untrained activities inside a miniature model of the playroom using miniature replicas of the toys. DeLoache and colleagues' (e.g., DeLoache, 1990; DeLoache & Burns, 1994; DeLoache et al., 1996; Troseth & DeLoache, 1998) dual representation hypothesis would predict that understanding the symbolic nature of a scale model would be more difficult than understanding the symbolic nature of photographs because scale models are more salient as objects. However, we predicted that it might actually be easier for children to use a scale model than a photograph as a reminder because the scale model reminder provides more event information in that it is three-dimensional, it contains motion information, and it contains information about the beginning, end, and all in-between states of an activity rather than a static image of one state. As discussed earlier, the amount of information provided may be more important than representational understanding for the successful use of representational media as reminders. Thus, we hypothesized that although children are unable to succeed at the object retrieval task using a scale model until the age of 36 months, 24-month-olds might be able to use a scale model reenactment as a reminder.

Results showed that 24-month-olds who received a scale model reminder recalled significantly more than did 24-month-olds from the previous experiment who received either no reminder or a photograph reminder (see Figure 9.6). These findings are noteworthy in light of research on children's ability to use information from a scale model to retrieve hidden objects. In the object-retrieval task, children are unable to use information presented in a scale model to find a hidden toy until 36 months (DeLoache et al., 1996). These findings lend further support to the idea that the development of the

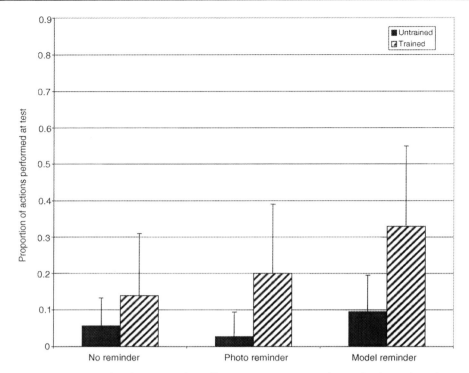

Figure 9.6 Mean trained and untrained recall proportion scores with standard error bars for 24-month-olds in photograph reminder, model reminder, and no reminder conditions (see Deocampo & Hudson, 2003, for full description of how proportions were calculated).

ability to use different representational media progresses in different sequences for reminding and object retrieval tasks. Further research is necessary to determine whether, perhaps, the ability to use scale models as reminders is in place even earlier than 24 months. If children are able to use scale models as reminders before 24 months, this would show that the ability to use particular representational reminders not only develops earlier than the ability to use the same representational medium in an object-retrieval task, but that the ability to use particular representational reminders develops in a different order than it does for the object-retrieval task. For memory reinstatement, the ability to use scale models as reminders may precede the ability to use photographs, but for object-retrieval tasks, the ability to use photographs as sources of location information precedes the ability to use scale models.

Although both photograph and scale model reminders were effective in reinstating 24-month-olds' recall, children recalled more activities with a scale model reminder than with a photograph reminder. This effect may be due to the fact that children who viewed a model reenactment were provided with more memory cues than children who viewed a single, static photograph. In addition, the scale model enactment may have seemed more similar to the stored memory than did the photograph reminder. However, recall of untrained activities was also higher in the model condition, suggesting that children may have been able to imitate some actions demonstrated by the experimenter during the scale model enactment. This interpretation would be consistent with imitation research by Barnat et al. (1996) showing that 14-month-olds were able to use full-sized props to imitate actions they had previously observed an experimenter perform using miniature objects in a different context. It is also consistent with research demonstrating that memory performance is best when older children participate in an event, better when they watch another person enact activities, and worse when they are merely told of the event (Muchaver, Pipe, Gordon, Owens, & Fivush, 1996).

REMINDERS, SYMBOLIC UNDERSTANDING AND MEMORY DEVELOPMENT

This line of research has shown that well-timed reminders are highly effective in extending young children's event memory. We have also shown that a variety of types of reminders are effective for children from 14 to 24 months of age. Children at 18 months can be reminded of an event they experienced 8 to 10 weeks in the past by reenacting a subset of the same actions, by viewing someone perform some of the same actions, by viewing a video of someone else performing the actions, viewing a videotape of someone showing the objects used, or viewing a videotape of the same actions performed on new objects. By 24 months of age, reinstatement occurs when children view photographs of an event or observe someone demonstrating the actions using a small-scale model.

The effectiveness of different kinds of reminders for young children, including the use of symbolic reminders such as videos and photographs indicates that 1- and 2-year-olds' are more flexible in the kinds of experiences that can reinstate past memories as compared to younger infants. If infants are trained on one exemplar, their memories will not be reinstated by partial reminders that do not contain functional information (Greco et al., 1990). In contrast, toddlers do not require action information in order for reinstatement to occur, but their recall is better when both object and action information is provided.

These findings suggest that at least by 18 months, children are encoding and storing more complete information about the individual components of events. Toddlers may be able to appreciate that activities are composed of various components (e.g., action and object information), and that some components may be interchangeable under certain circumstances. If children have encoded event information in terms of more specific event components, then partial event information can be effective in reinstating memories through a process of spreading activation. Even encountering information that is slightly different from the original experience can serve as a reminder if children can recognize the similarity between the reminder and the original event. In contrast, if events are encoded as single units, without parsing into event components, reinstatement may not occur unless a significant portion of the complete event is reencountered.

Children's developing understanding of the representational functions of symbolic media may also contribute to reminder effectiveness in young children. For example, photographs were not effective reminders for children at 18 months, but evidence of reinstatement with photographs was found at 24 months. Even greater memory enhancement with photograph reminders was evident at 30 months. The amount of information included in the photographs as compared to videos cannot wholly account for these findings; reinstatement occurred with 18-month-olds when they viewed videos of objects without action information which is similar to the kind of event information shown in photographs. Thus, with increasing age and experience, children may be reminded of events with increasingly more abstract reminders.

However, our research indicates that young children's ability to use video, photograph, and scale model reminders does not follow the same developmental progression as their ability to use information from video, photographs, and scale models to guide their search in an object-retrieval task. Children are able to use videos as reminders 18 months before they use video information to retrieve hidden objects; they use photographs as reminders 6 months earlier than they are able to use photographs as search guides; and they can use scale models as reminders 12 months earlier than they are able to use scale models as search guides. These ages must, of course, be considered as approximate. Both the reminding task and the object retrieval task can be made more or less difficult by varying the parameters of the task (e.g., DeLoache, 1995; Uttal, Schreiber, & DeLoache, 1995). For example, children's recall could be facilitated by providing them with fewer activities to remember, by shortening the retention interval, and perhaps, by providing additional memory cues. However, as summarized in Figure 9.7, the findings from this and the previous investigations add to the body of research on children's use of representational information indicating a different sequence of development across different tasks.

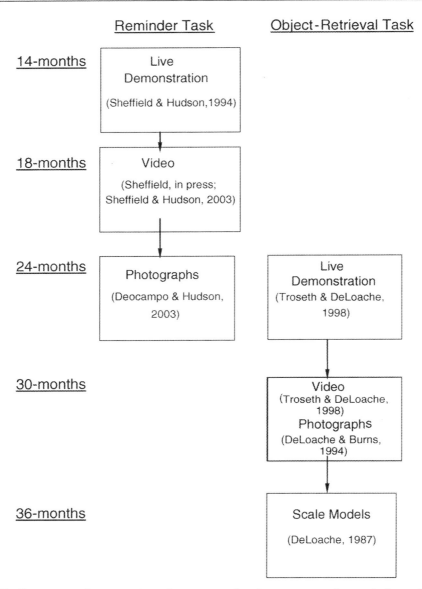

Figure 9.7 Sequences of progression of representational competence for reminder tasks and the object-retrieval task.

One explanation for these results may be that children do not need to understand the symbolic nature of representational media such as photographs, videos, and scale models for them to be effective reminders. It may be that to use a photograph, video, or a scale model effectively as a reminder, one must only recognize the similarity between the representational medium and the previously experienced event, and that is enough to activate the memory for the past event. This matching between the representational reminder and a child's memory of a previous event can take place at an implicit level that does not require conscious awareness (e.g., Tulving, 1983). Thus, an explicit understanding of the representation-referent relationship may not be necessary. Therefore, the amount of information and similarity of that information to a child's memory representation of a previous event may be the important factors in the development of children's understanding of representational reminders rather than the understanding of the symbolic nature of the representational medium.

Increased flexibility in both the type of reminders that are effective and in the amount of original event information that must be conveyed in a reminder for it to be effective may contribute to the emergence of durable autobiographic memories in the third year of life. Children's ability to use photographs as reminders, in particular, may allow young children to use family photograph collections as reminders of their own experiences. A corresponding increase in the retention period for episodic recall during this time period also impacts the frequency of reminding opportunities for young children. If 2- to 3-year-old children can remember events for several months without reminding, the window in which a reminder can reinstate memory for a past event becomes longer, increasing the likelihood of encountering an effective reminder within the retention interval (Bauer, 2002; Bauer et al., 2002; Howe & Courage, 1993). For example, in our study of photograph reminders with 24- and 30-month-olds, we had explored the possibility of using elicited imitation procedure instead of deferred imitation. However, we found that 24-month-olds were able to remember actions up to 16 weeks later without a reminder if they had the opportunity to enact them once during training. At 18 months, children showed evidence of forgetting the same action sequences after 10 weeks. Thus, from 18 to 24 months we found an increase in retention of 6 weeks for the action sequences used in our research after a single enactment. Assuming this trend would continue, by 3 years we would expect that children could recall events they experienced for at least 7 months without reminders. With an effective reminder, memory could be increased by several weeks or months.

A very significant development in reminding also occurs around 3 years of age which allows for even greater flexibility in memory reinstatement. In addition to physical and representational reminders, by three years of age children are engaging in verbal conversations about past events with their parents (Fivush, 1991; Hudson, 1990b; Nelson, 1993; Nelson & Fivush, 2000, 2004). Although children begin talking about the past sometime between 16 and 20 months (Eisenberg, 1985), children under three years of age show little evidence of being able to use language alone to reinstate event memories. When they engage in joint reminiscing between the ages of 2 to 3, however, conversations about past events provide an important reinstatement context for autobiographic memories. Several studies have shown that participation in parent–child conversations about past events enhances children's event recall, especially when parents provide complex and elaborate accounts of events (McCabe & Peterson, 1991; Reese, Haden, & Fivush, 1993; Haden, Haine, & Fivush, 1997). Through discussions about past events, children's event memories are .reinstated and event narratives are constructed. Conversations therefore assist children in recalling event details, but also help children develop a coherent account of events in an appropriate spatial-temporal context that includes evaluative information about events.

Toddlers, therefore, are in a transition phase in terms of their ability to used reminders to reinstate episodic memories. They are able to take advantage of a greater variety of reminder types as compared to infants including more abstract representations of events such as video displays. By 2 years, two-dimensional photographs of events are sufficient to remind them of past events. However, there is no evidence that 2-year-olds can use language alone to reinstate event memories. By age 3, verbally recalling an event, even with an experimenter, enhances later recall of the event (Hudson, 1990a). More research on the emergence of verbal reminders from 2 to 3 years of age is important for understanding this critical transition from visual to verbal reminders in memory reinstatement in young children.

To fully understand how reminders can extend children's memories over very long periods of time, some important questions regarding timing and reminder effectiveness also need to be addressed. One timing question concerns the time frame in which a reminder can be effective. We found that a video reminder provided 2 weeks after an event had no impact on 18-month-olds' recall 10 weeks later, but the same video reminder was effective if shown after 10 weeks and children were asked to recall the actions immediately after reinstatement (Sheffield & Hudson, 2004, Experiment 1). We also found reinstatement effects when the video reminder was provided in children's homes after 10 weeks and recall was assessed in the laboratory the next day (Sheffield & Hudson, 2004, Experiment 2). These findings indicate that a reminder is more effective when given closer to the point of forgetting. However, we have not yet tested points in time. For example, would a reminder shown after 8 or 9 weeks be effective if recall was tested 1 or 2 weeks later? Could a reminder be effective if it were administered 10 weeks later, after forgetting had occurred?

Another timing question concerns the long-term effects of reminders. Although viewing a video reminder after 10 weeks was effective in reinstating 18-month-olds' recall, the effects of the video reminder were almost gone 2 weeks later (Sheffield & Hudson, 2004, Experiment 3). Thus, watching a video of an event may be effective in reminding 18-month-olds of their past experience, but it is clearly not equivalent to actually reexperiencing the event. This may explain one reason why the vast majority of very young children's memories do not persist over long periods. If one of the key components to remembering an event is whether a reinstatement will endure, very young children may have multiple opportunities to be reinstated (e.g., by watching home videos or viewing family photograph albums), but without continual reminding, memories may not last even if reinstatement occurs.

This raises a third question regarding timing and reminders: What are the effects of multiple reinstatements over a very long time period? Infant research has shown that found that multiple reinstatement sessions can extend recall for up to 1½ years (Hartshorn, 2003; Hayne, 1990). If toddlers can already remember events for longer periods than infants, with multiple reinstatements they may be able to remember events for several years, perhaps into adulthood. Research is needed on the long-term effects of various kinds of reminders as well as on the effects of multiple reinstatements to understand how reinstatement can contribute to very long-term event memory.

Additional explorations of reminder effects in young children can address many of these important questions. As researchers seek to understand why the offset of infantile amnesia occurs around 3 years of age, explanations have focused largely on developments in fundamental memory mechanisms such as increases in retention duration, increased encoding specificity, and a waning of the context-dependent nature of early event encoding (e.g., Rovee-Collier & Hayne, 2000). Explanations have also emphasized the emergence of important developments around the age of 3 that contribute to the construction of an autobiographic memory system such as the formative role of parent–child talk about the past in providing children with a narrative framework for recalling the past (Nelson, 1993; Nelson & Fivush, 2004), the development of a sense of self (Howe & Courage, 1993), and improvements in source monitoring ability (Leichtman, 1999). However, the ability to be reminded of past events is a critical development with has received less attention. The few events from early childhood that adults can recall tend to be events that have been repeatedly discussed and therefore, have been repeatedly reinstated. Even as adults, not all experiences are recalled after long periods of time. Those that are remembered may be those that have been reinstated. Without a full understanding of how reminding contributes to children's event recall and how reminding parameters develop with age, we cannot fully understand the development of long-term event memory.

REFERENCES

Barnat, S. B., Klein, P., & Meltzoff, A. N. (1996). Deferred imitation across changes in context and object: memory and generalization in 14-month-old infants. *Infant Behavior and Development, 19*, 241–251.

Barr, R., & Hayne, H (1999). Developmental changes in imitation from television during infancy, *Child Development, 70*, 1067–1081.

Barr, R., Dowden, & Hayne, H. (1996). Developmental changes in deferred imitation by 6- to 24-month-old infants. *Infant Behavior and Development, 19*, 159–170.

Bauer, P. J. (1995). Recalling past events: From infancy to early childhood. *Annals of Child Development, 11*, 25–71.

Bauer, P. J. (2002). Long-term recall memory: Behavioral and neuro-developmental changes in the first 2 years of life. *Current Directions in Psychological Science, 11*, 137–141.

Bauer, P. J., Burch, M., & Kleinknecht, E. E. (2002). Developments in early recall memory: Normative trends and

individual differences. In R. V. Kail (Ed.), *Advances in child development and behavior* (Vol. 30, pp. 103–152). San Diego, CA: Academic Press.

Bauer, P. J., Cheatham, C. L., Cary, M. S., and Abbema, D. L. (2002). Short-term forgetting: Charting its course and implications for long-term remembering. In S. P. Shovhov (Ed.), *Advances in psychology research* (Vol. 9, pp. 53–74). Huntington, NY: Nova Science Publishers.

Bauer, P. J., & Hertsgaard, L. A. (1993). Increasing steps in recall of events: Factors facilitating immediate and long-term memory in 13.5- and 16.5-month-old children. *Child Development, 64*, 1204–1223.

Bauer, P. J., Hertsgaard, L. A., & Dow, A. (1994). After 8 months have passed: Long-term recall of events by 1- to 2-year-old children. *Memory, 2*, 353–382.

Bauer, P. J., & Mandler, J. M. (1990). Remembering what happened next: Very young children's recall of event sequences. In R. Fivush & J. A. Hudson (Eds.), *Knowing and remembering in young children* (pp. 9–29). New York: Cambridge University Press.

Bauer, P. J., & Shore, C. M. (1987). Making a memorable event: Effects of familiarity and organization on young children's recall of action sequences. *Cognitive Development, 2*, 237–338.

Bauer, P. J., Wenner, J. A., Dropik, P. L., & Wewerka, S. S. (2000). Parameters of remembering and forgetting in the transition from infancy to early childhood. *Monographs of the Society for Research in Child Development, 65*.

Bauer, P. J., Wenner, J. A., & Kroupina, M. G. (2002). Making the past present: Later verbal accessibility of early memories. *Journal of Cognition & Development, 3*, 21–47.

Bauer, P. J., & Wewerka, S. (1997). Saying is revealing: Verbal expression event memories in the transition from infancy to early childhood. In P. van den Broek, P. J. Bauer, & T. Bourg (Eds.), *Developmental spans in event comprehension and representation: Bridging fictional and actual events* (pp. 139–168). Hillsdale, NJ: Erlbaum.

Bauer, P. J., Wiebe, S. A., Carver, L. J., Waters, J. M., & Nelson, C. A. (2003). Developments in long-term explicit memory late in the first year of life: Behavioral and electrophysiological indices. *Psychological Science, 14*, 629–635.

Bauer, P. J., Wiebe, S. A., Waters, J. M., & Bangston, S. K. (2001). Reexposure breeds recall: Effects of experience on 9-month-olds' ordered recall. *Journal of Experimental Child Psychology, 80*, 174–200.

Boller, K., Rovee-Collier, C., Bovorsky, D., O'Conner, J., & Shyi, G. (1990). Developmental changes in the time-dependent nature of memory retrieval. *Developmental Psychology, 26*, 770–779.

Boyer, M., Barran, K. L., & Farrar, M. J. (1994). Three-year-olds remember a novel event from 20 months: Evidence for long-term memory in children? *Memory, 2*, 417–446.

Brainerd, C. J., Reyna, V. F., Howe, M. L., & Kingma, J. (1990). The development of forgetting and reminiscence. *Monographs of the Society for Research in Child Development, 55*.

Campbell, B. A., & Jaynes, J. (1966). Reinstatement. *Psychological Review, 73*, 478–480.

Collie, R., & Hayne, H. (1999). Deferred imitation by 6- and 9-month-old infants: More evidence for declarative memory. *Developmental Psychobiology, 35*, 83–90.

Davis, J., & Rovee-Collier, C. (1983). Alleviated forgetting of a learned contingency in 8-week-old infants. *Developmental Psychology, 19*, 353–365.

DeLoache, J. S. (1990). Young children's understanding of scale models. In R. Fivush & J. A. Hudson (Eds.), *Knowing and remembering in young children* (pp. 94–126). New York: Cambridge University Press.

DeLoache, J. S., & Burns, N. M. (1994). Early understanding of the representational function of pictures. *Cognition, 52*, 83–110.

DeLoache, J. S, Pierroutsakos, S. L., & Troseth, G. L. (1996). The three R's of pictorial competence. *Annals of Child Development, 12*, 1–48.

Deocampo, J. A., & Hudson, J. A. (2003). Reinstatement of 2-year-olds' event memory using photographs. *Memory, 11*, 13–25.

Eisenberg, A. (1985). Learning to describe past experience in conversation. *Discourse Processes, 8*, 177–204.

Fivush, R. (1991). The social construction of personal narratives. *Merrill-Palmer Quarterly, 37*, 59–81.

Freud (1935). *A general introduction to psychoanalysis.* New York: Clarion Books.

Galluccio, L., & Rovee-Collier, C. (1999). Reinstatement effects on retention at 3 months of age. *Learning and Motivation 30*, 296–316.

Greco, D., Rovee-Collier, C., Hayne, H., Griesler, P., & Earley, L. (1986). Ontogeny of early event memory: I. Forgetting and retrieval by 2- and 3-month-olds. *Infant Behavior and Development, 9*, 441–460.

Greco, C., Hayne, H., & Rovee-Collier, C. (1990). Roles of function, reminding and variability in categorization by 3-month-old infants. *Journal of Experimental Psychology: Learning, Memory & Cognition, 16*, 617–633.

Haden, C. A., Haine, R., & Fivush, R. (1997). Developing narrative structure in parent-child reminiscing across the preschool years. *Developmental Psychology, 33*, 295–307.

Hamond, N. R., & Fivush, R. (1991). Memories of Mickey Mouse: Young children recount their trip to Disneyland. *Cognitive Development, 6*, 433–448.

Harris, P. L., Kavenaugh, R. D., & Dowson, L. (1997). The depiction of imaginary transformations: Early comprehension of a symbolic function. *Cognitive Development, 12*, 1–19.

Hartshorn, K. (2003). Reinstatement maintains a memory in human infants for 1 ½ years. *Developmental Psychobiology, 42*, 269–282.

Hayne, H. (1990). The effect of multiple reminders on long-term retention in human infants. *Developmental Psychobiology, 23*, 453–477.

Hayne, H., MacDonald, S. & Barr, R. (1997) Age-related changes in the specificity of memory retrieval: Implications for cognitive development. *Infant Behavior and Development 20*, 233–245

Herbert, J. & Hayne, H. (2000). The ontogeny of long-term retention during the second year of life. *Developmental Science 3*, 50–56.

Howe, M. L. (1991). Misleading children's story recall: Forgetting and reminiscence of the facts. *Developmental Psychology, 27*, 746–462.

Howe, M. L., & Brainerd, C. J. (1989). Development of children's long-term retention. *Developmental Review, 9*, 301–340.

Howe, M. L., & Courage, M. L. (1993). On resolving the enigma of infantile amnesia. *Psychological Bulletin, 113*, 305–326.

Howe, M. L., Courage, M. L., & Bryant-Brown, L. (1993). Reinstating preschoolers' memories. *Developmental Psychology, 29*, 854–869.

Hudson, J. A. (1990a). Constructive processes in children's event memory. *Developmental Psychology, 26*, 180–187.

Hudson, J. A. (1990b). The emergence of autobiographic memory in mother-child conversation. In R. Fivush & J. A. Hudson (Eds.), *Knowing and remembering in young children* (pp. 166–196). New York: Cambridge University Press

Hudson, J. A. (1993). Reminiscing with mothers and others: Autobiographical memory in young two-year-olds. *Journal of Narrative and Life History, 3*(1), 1–32.

Hudson, J. A., & Sheffield, E. G. (1998). Deja vu all over again: Effects of re-enactment on one-year-olds' event memory. *Child Development, 69*(1), 51–67.

Mandler, J. M., & McDonough, L. (1995). Long-term recall of event sequences in infancy. *Journal of Experimental Psychology, 59*, 457–474.

McCabe, A., & Peterson, C. (1991). Getting the story: A longitudinal study of parental styles in eliciting narratives and development narrative skill. In A. McCabe & C. Peterson (Eds.), *Developing narrative structure* (pp. 217–253). Hillsdale, NJ: Erlbaum.

McDonough, L., & Mandler, J. M. (1994). Very long-term recall in infants: Infantile amnesia reconsidered. *Memory, 2*, 339–352.

Meltzoff, A. N. (1988a). Infant imitation after a 1-week delay: Long-term memory for novel acts and multiple stimuli. *Developmental Psychology, 24*, 470–476.

Meltzoff, A. N. (1988b). Infant imitation and memory: Nine-month-olds in immediate and deferred tests. *Child Development, 59*, 217–225.

Meltzoff, A. N. (1995). What infant memory tells us about infantile amnesia: Long-term recall and deferred imitation. *Journal of Experimental Child Psychology, 59*, 497–515.

Meltzoff, A. N., & Moore, M. K. (1994). Imitation, memory, and the representation of persons. *Infant Behavior and Development, 17*, 83–99.

Murachver, T., Pipe, M. E., Gorden, R., Owens, J. L., & Fivush, R. (1996). Do show and tell: Children's event memories acquired through direct experience, observation, and stories. *Child Development, 65*, 3029–3044.

Myers, N. A., Clifton, R. K., & Clarkson, M. G. (1987). When they were very young: Almost threes remember two years ago. *Infant Behavior and Development, 10*, 123–132.

Nelson, K. (1990). Remembering, forgetting, and childhood amnesia. In R. Fivush & J. A. Hudson (Eds.), *Knowing and remembering in young children* (pp. 301–316). New York: Cambridge University Press.

Nelson, K. (1993). The psychological and social origins of autobiographic memory. *Psychological Science, 4*, 1–8.

Nelson, K., & Fivush, R. (2000). Socialization of memory. In E. Tulving & F. I. M. Craik (Eds.), *The Oxford handbook of memory* (pp. 283–295). New York: Oxford University Press.

Nelson, K., & Fivush R. (2004). The emergence of autobiographical memory: A social cultural developmental theory. *Psychological Review, 111*, 486–511.

Perner, J. (2000). Memory and theory of mind. In E. Tulving and F. I. M. Craik (Eds.), *The Oxford handbook of memory* (pp. 297–312). New York: Oxford University Press.

Peterson, C., & Rideout, R. (1998). Memory for medical emergencies experienced by 1- and 2-year-olds. *Developmental Psychology, 34*, 1059–1072.

Pillemer, D., & White, S. (1989). Childhood events recalled by children and adults. In H. W. Reese (Ed.), *Advances in child development and behavior* (Vol. 21, pp. 297-340). New York: Academic Press.

Reese, E., Haden, C. A., & Fivush, R. (1993). Mother-child conversations about the past: Relationships of style and memory over time. *Cognitive Development, 8*, 403–430.

Rovee-Collier, C. (1995). Time windows in cognitive development. *Developmental Psychology, 31*, 147–169.

Rovee-Collier (1999). The development of infant memory. *Current Directions in Psychological Science, Vol. 8*(3), 80–85.

Rovee-Collier, C., Adler, S. A., & Borza, M. A. (1994). Substituting new details for old? Effects of delaying postevent memory on infant memory. *Memory and Cognition, 22*, 646–656.

Rovee-Collier, C., Borza, M. A., Adler, S. A., & Boller, K. (1993). Infants' eyewitness testimony: Effects of postevent information on a prior memory representation. *Memory & Cognition, 21*, 267–279.

Rovee-Collier, C., Griesler, P. C., & Earley, L. A. (1985). Contextual determinants of retrieval in three-month-old infants. *Learning and Motivation, 16*, 139–157.

Rovee-Collier, C., & Hayne, H. (2000). Memory in infancy and early childhood. In E. Tulving & F. I. M. Craik (Eds.), *The Oxford handbook of memory* (pp. 267–282). New York: Oxford University Press.

Rovee-Collier, C. K., & Shyi, G. (1992). A functional and cognitive analysis of infant long-term retention. In M. L. Howe, C. J. Brainerd, & V. F. Reyna (Eds.), *Development of long-term retention* (pp. 3–55). New York: Springer-Verlag.

Rovee-Collier, C. K., Sullivan, M. W., Enright, J., Lucas, D., & Fagan, J. W. (1980). Reactivation of infant memory. *Science, 208*, 1159–1161.

Sheffield, E. G. (2004). But I thought it was Mickey Mouse: Effects of postevent information on 18-month-olds' long-term memory for events. *Journal of Experimental Child Psychology, 87*(3), 221-238.

Sheffield, E. G., & Hudson, J. A. (1994). Reactivation of toddlers' event memories. *Memory, 2*, 447–465.

Sheffield, E. G., & Hudson, J. A. (in press). You must remember this: Effects of video reminders on toddlers' event memory. *Journal of Cognition and Development.*

Spear, N. E. (1978). *The processing of memories: Forgetting and retention.* Potomac, MD: Erlbaum.

Spear, N. E., & Parsons, P. J. (1976). Analysis of a reactivation treatment: Ontogenetic determinants of alleviated forgetting. In D. L. Medin, W. A. Roberts, & R. T. Davis (Eds), *Processes of Animal Memory* (pp. 135–165). Hillsdale, NJ: Erlbaum.

Tessler, M., & Nelson, K. (1994). Making memories: The influence of joint encoding on later recall by young children. *Consciousness and Cognition, 3*, 307–326.

Troseth, G. L., & DeLoache, J. (1998). The medium can obscure the message: Young children's understanding of video. *Child Development, 69*, 950–965.

Tulving, E. (1983). *Elements of episodic memory.* Oxford: Oxford University Press.

Uttal, D., Schreiber, J. C., & DeLoache, J. S. (1995). Waiting to use a symbol: The effects of delay on children's use of models. *Child Development, 66*, 1875–1889.

White, S. H., & Pillemer, D. B. (1979). Childhood amnesia and the development of a socially accessible memory system. In J. F. Kihlstrom & F. J. Evans (Eds.), *Functional disorders of memory* (pp. 29–74). Hillsdale, NJ: Erlbaum.

10

Conversing With Toddlers About the Nonpresent

Precursors to Narrative Development in Two Genres

Paola Uccelli
Lowry Hemphill
Barbara Alexander Pan
Catherine Snow

INTRODUCTION

Narratives are ubiquitous forms of oral discourse which represent shared cultural understandings of our human experience in the world (Bruner, 1986). Narratives provide an important means for translating experiences into language for purposes of communication (Berman & Slobin, 1994), for representing them in memory (Nelson, 1986), and for structuring and supplementing them with interpretations (Labov & Waletsky, 1967). Narratives emerge in parent–child conversations with children as young as 2 years of age (Eisenberg, 1985) but, as we will argue in this chapter, precursors to narrative development can be identified in the language exchanges of even younger children. Discussions of a joint focus of attention between 20-month-old children and their parents lead naturally into elaborations that introduce nonpresent elements—connections to the past, plans for the future, and memories of related objects or events. While these discussions are not narrative in the strict sense, they provide the child an opportunity to deal with some of the complexities of narrative. Another facilitative activity during early mother–child conversation is fantasy play, a context for learning about plot, character, and other narrative elements. Variability in children's opportunities for participation in discussions of joint focus and fantasy may help explain individual differences in later skills. In this chapter we explore how it is that children develop skills with two narrative genres, personal narrative and fantasy story, and why it is that some children excel at one or the other, some at both, and some at neither. We will argue that individual differences in narrative skills emerge at least in part from children's early capacities to engage in discussions of a joint focus of attention, typically a toy, a picture, or an ongoing activity, with adults. In the sections that follow, we describe a social interactionist theoretical framework for understanding narrative development. We then define and illustrate children's capacities with two important narrative genres at 5 years of age and present data about children's participation at 20 and

30 months in talk about the nonpresent and about fantasy. Finally, we turn to exploring relationships between children's early experiences with social interaction and their later narrative attainments.

The study of children's narratives encompasses a relatively recent but vast and varied body of research that illustrates the multifunctionality of narrative discourse in children's development. Narratives are ubiquitous forms of oral discourse found in a variety of contexts within and across cultures and seem to constitute a universal means of making sense of both the physical and social world. Following the narrative patterns of their specific communities and families, children produce narratives when they translate past experiences into language, retell tales previously told to them, or improvise fantasy stories. Narratives are also present in everyday life as they are told to children, told to others in the presence of children, and coconstructed in spontaneous adult-child conversations. Over time children are expected to produce increasingly autonomous narratives to achieve effective communication in situations with a passive audience, e.g., sharing time in classrooms or explaining the development of one's symptoms to a physician (Ochs & Capps, 2001). Progress toward becoming a skilled narrator relates to multiple aspects of a child's development, including the formation of self-concept, autobiographical memory, socio-emotional cognition, and literacy acquisition. Previous research has demonstrated that narratives communicate culturally shared values, beliefs and esthetic notions, and shape children's development toward particular ways of constructing identity, ways of remembering, ways of thinking and feeling, and ways of talking.

Drawing from theoretical conceptions that define the self as constructed in interaction with others (Gergen, 1994; Mead, 1934), from developmental theories that place language-mediated social practices at the core of children's social and cognitive advances (Vygotsky, 1934/1986), and from a view of language conceived as both the result of and the principal medium for transferring cultural practices (Gumperz & Hymes, 1972; Ochs & Schieffelin, 1984), developmental researchers have explored the prominent role of narratives in communicating cultural values that shape self-identity (Bruner, 1986; Miller, 1982; Miller, Potts, Fung, Hoogstra, & Mintz, 1990; Nelson, 1989, 2000, 2001; Stern, 1989). For instance, research has documented that in the United States, European-American mothers tend to highlight children's positive qualities in their stories, while Chinese mothers tend to portray the child as transgressor, thus utilizing narratives to emphasize moral lessons. A similar contrast is reported between Taiwanese and European-American families, with the additional finding that parents' past misdeeds are considered highly reportable by European-Americans because of their humor and potential to humanize parents, but are never narrated by Taiwanese parents, who view these situations as diminishing their authority (Miller, Sandel, Liang, & Fung, 2001). Children come to understand who they are in these narratives exchanges "by virtue of hearing how others portray and respond to them" (Miller, Mintz, Hoogstra, Fung, & Potts, 1992, p. 48). Children's exposure to and production of narratives are highlighted as providing a major source for the formation of an "enculturated self" (Nelson, 2000) and for the construction of a "continuing self" with a past and a future (Nelson, 2001). Children construct narratives, even in solitary contexts, to organize the flow of their own experiences in connection to others (Bruner, 1990; Nelson, 1989).

Narrative research has also contributed to our understanding of an area intimately linked to the study of self-formation: the development of autobiographical memory. Even though the idea that memory is related to language is not a new one (Bartlett, 1932), only recently has the social interaction model of autobiographical memory provided a theoretical framework in which the child's production of narratives is at the core of children's ability to retain experiences that are verbally accessible (Fivush & Hudson, 1990; Nelson, 1989, 1990, 1996; Pillemer & White, 1989). According to this theory, narratives offer children an external model of memory-cueing which they later internalize and reinstate. Snow (1990) illustrates how parents highlight—via narrative exchanges with children—which aspects of experience are reportable, and by inference, worth remembering. Different parental styles of talking about the past have been documented (Fivush, 1991; Hudson, 1990; Reese, Haden, & Fivush, 1993) and seem to have far-reaching effects on how children structure their own memories (Hudson, 1993). Studies show that children recall more information about events they have previously talked about with their parents (Hudson, 1993; Tessler & Nelson, 1994). Furthermore, increasing evidence supports the claim that memory is shaped in different ways according to the cultural practices of a child's community (Nelson & Fivush, 2000). Cultural differences among U.S., Korean, and Chinese children have been identified in the frequency of talk about the past and the age of earliest memories (Mullen, 1994; Mullen & Yi, 1995), as well as in the frequency with which specific components such as descriptions, internal state terms, and self-references are included in children's recollections (Han, Leichtman, & Wang, 1998). In narrating past experiences children learn not only how to structure narratives, but they also learn how to remember their own pasts.

Narratives are also relevant for children's emotional development and adaptation to their socio-cultural context. When telling a story, narrators report not only events, but also how they feel about events (Labov & Waletzky, 1967). Thus, parent–child coconstructions of narratives provide an avenue for discussing and learning about emotions (Fivush, 1991; Oppenheim, Emde, & Wamboldt, 1996). Indeed, the understanding of complex emotions has been linked to children's use of internal states in narrative discourse (Hughes & Dunn, 1998). Moreover, Oppenheim and his colleagues suggest that narratives contribute to the regulation of emotions, as children's emotionally coherent narratives are associated with fewer behavior problems (Oppenheim, Nir, Warren, & Emde, 1997).

School is a particular context in which the mastery of narrative discourse is of central importance in many communities. On the one hand, narrative mastery is positively associated with academic performance, in particular literacy (Bishop & Edmundson, 1987; Feagans & Applebaum, 1986; Roth, Speece, Cooper, & de la Paz, 1996; Snow, 1983). In learning to narrate, children learn the decontextual-ized features of language necessary to report real or fictional events removed from the "here and now." Many of these decontextualized linguistic features are shared with written discourse and therefore facilitate children's transition into literacy (Hemphill & Snow, 1996; Snow, 1983). Kindergartners who are skilled narrators of highly elaborated fictional stories show superior listening comprehension and print-awareness skills compared to kindergartners with less developed narrative abilities (Speece, Roth, Cooper, & de la Paz, 1999). Preschoolers' elaborative contributions to mother–child coconstruction of narratives predict story comprehension in kindergarten (Reese, 1995). On the other hand, narratives could also be a source of miscommunication. Assumptions about appropriate language use and patterns of structuring narrative differ even among people who speak what is officially considered the same language. An increasing body of literature documents culturally-specific characteristics of narrative structure and narrative practices (Blum-Kulka & Snow, 1992; Heath, 1983; Melzi, 2000; Michaels, 1981; Minami, 2001; Minami & McCabe, 1991; Peterson & McCabe, 1983). Adaptation to the school discourse style is a task faced by all children, but the transition is easier for children whose discourse style is closer to that of school (Cazden, 1988; Heath, 1983; Michaels, 1981).

Given narratives' ubiquity in casual face to face conversation as well as in more institutional forms of discourse (lessons, medical histories, interviews), it is not surprising that children typically can tell fairly autonomous fictional and personal stories by about age 5. While developmental profiles of children's narrative performance provide useful summaries of normative development (Botvin & Brian Sutton-Smith, 1977; Hudson & Shapiro, 1991; Peterson & McCabe, 1983), it is also important to highlight the enormous range of skill with which children as young as age 5 engage in these vari-ous narrative activities. Differences in children's narrative skill have been shown to be associated with cultural practices and parental discourse style (Blum-Kulka & Snow, 1992; Minami, 2001; Peterson & McCabe, 1992). In this study we explore children's early pragmatic abilities as another dimension contributing to distinct levels of narrative performance. The cognitive, social, emotional and academic correlates of narrative discourse further highlight the importance of this undertaking.

THEORETICAL FRAMEWORK: LANGUAGE DEVELOPMENT AS COMMUNICATIVE DEVELOPMENT

Language acquisition constitutes a process in which communication is always central (Ninio & Snow, 1996). Children clearly need to learn a great deal about the formal linguistic system and about con-ventional modes of expression in order to speak grammatically and correctly. While such learning is impressive, thinking of language acquisition as consisting entirely, or even primarily, of learning about the formal, conventionalized aspects of the language system omits the aspect of language development most crucial to understanding transitions from earlier to more sophisticated stages—the child's motive to communicate and capacity to respond to an ever widening array of communicative challenges.

Children's first words are typically not true lexical items that communicate information, but attempts to connect with their interlocutor. The earliest uses of conventional language can be analyzed as attempts to participate in social interaction through somewhat marginal linguistic forms that constitute turns in games (e.g., *peekaboo*) or formatted responses to adult utterances (*what does the kitty say?*) (Ninio, 1993). Parents recruit these semilinguistic forms for use in joint attention episodes (occasions when parents and children achieve shared attention to a real object, a toy, or a pictured object) and treat them as answers to questions about the joint focus of attention (Adult: *what's that?* Child: *meow*). Subsequently, of course, children start to learn real, conventional words in these exchanges, and eventually are able to initiate such exchanges themselves by naming objects to establish a joint focus of attention, or by asking *what's that?*

These early naming exchanges constitute the beginning of what, within the analytic system of communicative intents proposed by Ninio and Wheeler (1984), can be classified as "discussions". Although these earliest "discussions" are limited to the here and now, they soon are expanded to incorporate information that goes beyond what is visible. For example, often when children are still in the one-word stage, mothers name animals pictured in books and then model or request information about what sounds the animals make, where they typically live, or what their babies are called. Even later, joint attentional episodes trigger discussion of jointly remembered past events; this emergence of talk about objects, attributes, or events not observable in the here and now ("nonpresent talk") constitutes the first occurrence of narrative-like structures in the talk of young children.

While children typically can participate in discussions of information somewhat displaced from the here and now with parental help between the ages of 12—24 months, their ability to become full conversational partners in such exchanges depends on their newly developing capacities in the domain of communication. Beyond talking simply to participate socially, they discover that talk also provides the opportunity to exchange information—to request and to get new information verbally. Though we think of this as the basic function of language, in fact it is one which children are able to display only after some months of using language socially. The information-exchange based discussion is, we argue, a prerequisite to the emergence of proto-narrative discourse.

A further, enormous achievement in young children's communicative systems is represented by their emergent ability to take the listener's perspective. Young children provide information, but they often do so in ways that are poorly adapted to the needs of the listener. With growing cognitive and social sophistication, children become more adept at predicting what information listeners need, responding to listeners' cues, and anticipating and taking the listener's perspective. This capacity to take the listener's perspective becomes crucial to providing satisfactory narratives, which mark explicitly for the listener how one is expected to respond to the information being provided.

Paralleling the development of skills required for exchanging information about the real world of the here and now, as well as objects and events removed in time and space, are children's growing abilities to engage in conversation about fantasy worlds. While children can make moves into the symbolic, nonrepresentational, or fantasy domain by about the time of the first word (e.g., pushing a toy car along the table while saying *vroom-vroom),* organized fantasy play segments do not typically emerge until after the second birthday. It seems likely that opportunities to participate in fantasy talk interactions, in contexts supported by an adult, will lead to greater skill in the autonomous production of fantasy talk.

Our view, then, is that autonomous narrative skill depends on previous social and cognitive achievements, in particular achievements in the child's ability to engage in true (i.e., information-exchanging) conversation about topics in the here and now, in the real but nonpresent world, and in fantasy worlds. In the study reported here, we investigated whether participation in discussions of the nonpresent and participation in fantasy talk at ages 20 and 32 months are related to children's skill at producing more autonomous narratives at age 5. Specifically, we hypothesized that early experience talking about the nonpresent would allow children to practice skills necessary to later produce personal narratives, and that early experience engaging in fantasy talk with an adult would build the skills necessary for telling autonomous fantasy narratives at age 5.

DISTINGUISHING TWO TYPES OF NARRATIVE

Two common forms of narrative discourse during the preschool years are personal narratives and fantasy stories. In personal narratives children report their personal experiences in contexts like parent-child conversation and dinner-table talk (Aukrust & Snow, 1998; Blum-Kulka, 1997; Ochs, Taylor, Rudolph, & Smith, 1992; Peterson & McCabe, 1992). In fantasy stories children narrate fictional happenings in the context of everyday pretend play, initially with the support of mothers or other older family members, but with increasing autonomy as children get older (Haight & Miller, 1993; Sachs, Goldman, & Chaille, 1984). Competent renditions of these two forms of narrative generally share some important features: a focus on a protagonist or protagonists and a set of related actions that these actors carry out; the reporting of supportive details such as setting or character attributes; the use of a range of strategies for linking events together and tying actions to consequences; and the inclusion of the narrator's evaluative perspective on the reported events. Despite these structural similarities, stories of personal experience and fantasy narratives may show different developmental courses within individual children and may draw on a somewhat separate set of pragmatic and linguistic competencies. Factual narratives require that the child select a set of happenings from the flow of past experiences that cohere and together form a satisfying story. Successful factual narratives also require that the child take account of what information is shared and unshared with the listener, and use appropriate introducing, referring, and elaborating strategies for unshared information. Successful fantasy narratives, on the other hand, require skill at plot improvisation and the ability to create tension and interest through vivid action, reported speech, and sound effects. Joint attention to a play figure or object can substitute for the more elaborate referential strategies that are characteristic of other forms of narration. To illustrate both the similarities in these narrative types and their different development within individuals, consider the following narratives produced by two 5-year-old girls:

Margaret: Me and my sister went out for a snack.

Interviewer: Uh-huh.

Margaret: And Lizzie went over to the pond. And she saw a big snake. And she screamed.

Interviewer: Oh.

Margaret: And my mom didn't like it. So I went over and said, "What is it? Look, a big snake!" And then we stayed for a little while. And then, well we watched him go out of there.

Interviewer: Wow.

Margaret: Uh we ate some snack. And then we went home. And um we missed swimming lesson.

Margaret begins her narrative with a statement of the goal that initiated the events of the story (*Me and my sister went out for a snack*) and goes on to report an elaborated series of temporally linked happenings: going to the pond, seeing the snake, screaming, reacting, investigating, etc. Her narrative centers on a linguistically marked climax or high point (*Look, a big snake!*) and builds down from this high point with a final sequence of events that includes a practical consequence (*we missed swimming lesson*). Margaret's story makes use of a highly conventionalized narrative structure while situating its logic in the everyday world of snacks, sisters, moms, and swimming lessons. She uses orienting information to introduce the coparticipants, locate the story at a specific place, and situate the events in relation to each other with specific time markers (*then, for a little while*). These uses of orientation lend realism to the reported events and support Margaret's ability to tell the story to an audience unfamiliar with her experience. Finally, although Margaret's story is restrained in its depiction of a frightening experience, she uses a variety of types of evaluation (*screamed, didn't like it,* and the reported exclamation, *Look, a big snake!*) to construct a stance in relation to the narrated events.

Margaret's personal narrative is much clearer and more fully developed than a story told by another 5-year-old, Sarah.

Sarah: Well I swim pretty good and I like to do banzai!

Interviewer: Yeah? What is that? I don't know anything about it.

Sarah: Well first you have to run and then you dive in. And I was just practicing diving. And I also went off the life line in the deep end.

Interviewer: Wow.

Sarah: And I couldn't touch. But I swam over to my mom.

Sarah's story, like many personal narratives told at any age, begins in the context of general conversation, in this case Sarah's explanation of how to do her favorite dive, the banzai. She marks her move from explanation into narration with a shift in tense, *I was just practicing diving,* but she doesn't signal the initiation of the narrative with any other sort of framing. She reports a brief and unelaborated series of events (practicing, going off the life line, not touching, swimming to her mom), using simple *and* links to narrate the problematic situation and to set off the resolution. Her story isn't situated in a particular place, and the central coparticipant, her mom, only enters the story at the end. Sarah's story includes minimal evaluation; only the interviewer's interjected *wow* and Sarah's factual negative *I couldn't touch* elaborate on the stance she takes on the narrated events. However, while Sarah is not a particularly successful narrator of personal experience at age 5, she is much more skilled at fantasy narration:

Sarah: And the dragon said to all the other animals, "I don't like you. I'm gonna eat you all up." But they all hurried to get out of the way. But the dragon said, "I don't care cause I can eat you all up with my huge, I can burn you all up with my huge big breath of fire (*makes blowing sounds*)." He took a big breath and burned them all up. (*Points to dragon's mouth.*) That's fire. (*Noise from other room.*) That's just my sister.

Interviewer: Mmhm. And then what happened ?

Sarah: The trees fell over. But then something said, "Tum!" That was the fire drill because there was a fire getting closer and closer and closer. And so they all had to get out of the way of the fire. Even the dragon. Then they saw a fire. Cause it was burning up all the city. All everything. But that wasn't the dragon's breath. It was a match. So they all had to get out of the way. But then they tickled each other. I tickle my sister sometimes. She tickles me the most. I like to tickle her cause it makes her laugh.

Interviewer: What's happening in the story?

Sarah: The dragon had to go home. So he just went home to his cave. But then they all got back in place. Where they should be. In the jungle, of course. So that's the end.

With the help of an adult partner who provides a skeletal plot (a fierce dragon threatens a group of jungle animals), models narrative technique, and provides toy props to enact the fantasy, Sarah builds up a fantasy narrative. The focus of her storytelling is the elaboration of the compelling elements of the fantasy: the dragon's exaggerated threats, the menacing fire, and a satisfying resolution, they all got back in place, where they should be, in the jungle, of course. In the fantasy narrative, Sarah isn't burdened by the need to recapitulate a detailed real chronology of events; in fact, she can challenge typical story sequence with her side move into tickling. When reporting events would slow down the action or tax her skills of verbal improvisation, Sarah can enact events by manipulating the toys. Freed of most of the requirements of realism and with the basic characters and plot collaboratively constructed with the adult partner, she can focus her verbal art on evaluation, producing expressions like *the dragon's huge big breath of fire* and *the fire getting closer and closer and closer.*

Margaret, the skilled narrator of everyday happenings at age 5, is at a loss, however, when confronted with the demands of fantasy narrative:

> Interviewer: Boom-boom boom-boom. It was the dragon. Closer and closer he came. Splash! (*places dragon in pond*). And he sat right in the middle of the pond. Then what happened?
>
> Margaret: He blowed fire.
>
> Interviewer: Yeah? (*long pause*) Make more story happen.
>
> Margaret: Um (*long pause*). I don't know (*touches animals*).
>
> Interviewer: Here, make the elephant and dragon talk with each other (*hands elephant and dragon to Margaret*).
>
> Margaret: I don't know what to say.
>
> Interviewer: You can say anything.
>
> Margaret: There's nothing to say.
>
> Interviewer: What happened?
>
> Margaret: The dragon blowed fire on him. The elephant.
>
> Interviewer: Oh, then what happened?
>
> Margaret: The elephant told the other animals to hide.
>
> Interviewer: Oh. And then what happened?
>
> Margaret: They hided down (*puts animals in between cushions on the couch*).
>
> Interviewer: Oh? Even the elephant hid?
>
> Margaret: Uh-huh (*picks up dragon and turns it around*).
>
> Interviewer: What's happening?
>
> Margaret: I don't know (*drops dragon*).
>
> Interviewer: What's happening?
>
> Margaret: The dragon didn't find the other animals. The end.

In this fantasy narrative, 5-year-old Margaret resists making up events, perhaps because she feels she lacks authority for reporting things that she hasn't witnessed or experienced. With repeated prompts from her adult partner, she produces a logical but limited chronology of events: the dragon blows fire, the animals hide, the dragon is unsuccessful in finding them. This sketchy narrative meets minimal expectations of a story, but lacks all the elements of elaboration that make Sarah's narrative a compelling fantasy. Margaret's skills at introducing characters and situating events in real places are irrelevant to the demands of fantasy narration and her focus on logical ordering misses the elements that make fantasy satisfying. Thus two very common types of oral narrative appear to impose rather different demands on young narrators. Both personal experience stories and fantasy stories require the ability to set off the narrative from the surrounding talk, to report and link happenings, and to evaluate their meaning to the story participants or to the narrator, but each genre imposes different emphases on these narrative tasks. While assessing the listener's information status is crucial for a clear rendition of a personal narrative, skills at plot improvisation are at the core of effective fantasy stories. The contrasting characteristics of relatively mature, 5-year-old factual and fantasy narratives reflect both the different courses of development of these two genres in the preschool years and the possibly separate contributions of different types of early communicative experience to their success. What kinds of communicative experiences in the first three years of life might one expect to be relevant to the narrative skills children are developing at age 5? In the next section of this chapter, we investigate possible connections between children's conversational and narrative skills.

THE STUDY

The children and their parents described in this chapter are families from the New England sample (Pan, Imbens-Bailey, Winner, & Snow, 1996; Snow, Pan, Imbens-Bailey, & Herman, 1996) for whom longitudinal data were available at child ages 20 months, 32 months, and 5 years. There were 32 children (18 girls, 14 boys) for whom data were available at all three time points. Eighteen were first born children. Families were English-speaking, primarily middle-class families, with Hollingshead's Four Factor Index of Social Status (Hollingshead, 1975) scores ranging from 33–66 (mean = 55.34, sd = 10.29). Mean maternal age was 30.9 years.

At the 20- and 32-month observations, parent-child dyads were videotaped interacting in a laboratory playroom using age-appropriate toys and materials provided by the investigators. At age 5, children were asked to perform a number of tasks, including telling a personal narrative and telling a fantasy narrative using small toys and props. Resulting language samples at each observation were transcribed using the Child Language Data Exchange System (MacWhinney, 2000). Children's receptive and expressive vocabularies were measured at age 20 months using an early form of the MacArthur Communicative Development Inventories (CDI), a maternal checklist (Dale, Bates, Reznick, & Morisset, 1989). Children's morphosyntactic skills at 32 months were measured using Mean Length of Utterance (MLU) (Brown, 1973) and the Index of Productive Syntax (IPSyn), a measure of emergent morphosyntax (Scarborough, 1990). Summary statistics on these lexical and morphosyntactic measures for the present sample are presented in Table 10.1.

Nonpresent and Fantasy Talk at Ages 20 and 32 Months

Given our view of traditional measures of child language (e.g., MLU) as an incomplete reflection of children's developing communicative skills, we also examined children's expression of communicative intent. Parent–child talk at child ages 20 and 32 months was segmented into communicative acts, and each act was coded using the Inventory of Communicative Acts–Abridged (INCA-A), a shortened and modified version of the system developed by Ninio and Wheeler (1984) for coding the dyadic interaction of mothers and young children (see Ninio, Snow, Pan, & Rollins, 1994, and Snow, Pan, Imbens-Bailey, & Herman, 1996, for fuller discussions of the coding scheme). In this system, communicative intent is identified and coded at two different levels. The first is the level of interpersonally implicitly agreed-upon social interchange constructed across one or more rounds of talk. In the present study, social interchange categories of interest include discussions of nonpresent people and objects; discussions of nonobservable thoughts, feelings, likes and dislikes; discussions of

TABLE 10.1
Summary Statistics for the Sample (n = 32)

	Mean (SD)		Range
Measures of morphosyntax (32 months)			
MLU	2.68	(.72)	1.5–4.9
IPSyn	53.29	(11.33)	36–78
Measure of vocabulary (20 months)			
CDI-production	221.12	(164.21)	5–602
Measures of pragmatics			
Nonpresent talk (20 months)	.06	(.05)	0–.19
Fantasy talk (32 months)	.15	(.10)	.01–.34
Pragmatic flexibility (20 months)	13.84	(4.21)	4–23
Measures of narrative skill (5 years)			
Personal narrative (PN)	7.52	(4.38)	0–18.5
Fantasy narrative (FAN)	12.25	(6.42)	0–25
Fantasy: Genre specificity	2.94	(1.81)	0–8
Fantasy: Character voice	2.19	(1.45)	0–6

recent events and accomplishments; and discussions of attributes or events related to an object in the here and now ("related-to-present talk"). The second level at which communicative acts were coded is the specific speech act (e.g., whether the utterance serves the purpose of requesting, thanking, or questioning). The combination of these two levels (that is, the number of social interchange-speech act types produced) provides one measure of children's pragmatic sophistication. We refer to this measure as pragmatic flexibility (Snow, Pan, Imbens-Bailey, & Herman, 1996). Summary statistics for these pragmatic measures are also provided in Table 10.1.

The following examples illustrate the types of nonpresent talk observed in parent-child dyads at 20 and 32 months: Margaret and her mother talk about nonpresent people and objects; Elizabeth and her mother talk about an individual's nonobservable thoughts and feelings (in this case, Elizabeth's fondness for ice cream); and Sarah and her mother talk about events or accomplishments that have just occurred but are not ongoing, and thus are no longer observable.

Margaret: age 32 months
Margaret: Where's that lady? (*Investigator has left room*)
Mother: I don't know where she went.

Elizabeth: age 20 months
Mother: Mmm is that good? (*points to picture of ice cream*) You like that?
Elizabeth: Mmm. (*nods*)
Mother: Mmm that's ice cream, huh?
Elizabeth: I do like. (*points to picture of ice cream*)

Sarah: 32 months
Sarah: I can carry it. (*lifts box and carries it over to table*)
Sarah: I carried it.
Mother: You did. You put it right up.
Sarah: Yeah.

Children's engagement in nonpresent talk is often triggered by joint attentional episodes in which the conversation moves beyond the object of joint attention to comment on nonobservable attributes of the object, or to compare the observable object to a nonobservable one, as in the following exchange:

Elizabeth: age 20 months
Mother: What's that? (*points to picture in book*)
Elizabeth: Yeah. (*points to same picture*)
Mother: Do we have one of those?
(*Elizabeth nods*)
Mother: A gate, huh?
(*Mother and Elizabeth both nod*)
Mother: We've got one of those for Sheba and you, huh?
Elizabeth: Yeah.

As these examples illustrate, talk about the nonpresent between adults and very young children tends to be adult-initiated and rather brief. Children generally assume a minimal conversational role, and often rely heavily on nonverbal means to bolster their participation, as Elizabeth did in "talking" about the gate. Even very young children, however, are able to take a more active role when the topic is animal sounds:

Sarah: age 20 months
Mother: Oh, pigs! (*referring to picture in book*) What do the pigs say?
Sarah: Eek-eek.
Mother: Well, close.
Mother: He says oink-oink. Oink-oink.
Sarah: Oink.

Despite their rather routinized character, these interchanges tend to be interspersed with talk about the here-and-now in ways that require the child to repeatedly shift frames of reference, as in this conversation in which 20-month-old Sarah and her mother discuss a flattened rubber duck:

(*Sarah blows on rubber duck, then shows her mother*)
Mother: That's right, that's what we do with a beach ball isn't it? We blow it up.
(*Sarah fiddles with duck*)
Mother: Oh it came out by itself now. (*Mother squeezes the duck*) Peep-peep-peep-peep-peep.
  Sounds a little bit like a chick doesn't it? Peep-peep-peep-peep-peep.

Such shifts from the here-and-now to nonpresent frames of reference may preview shifts in genre (between personal narration and fantasy narration, for example) as well as shifts in narrative role that are demonstrated by 4- and 5-year-olds. In the earlier excerpt from Sarah's jungle story, for example, she shifts from direct narration (*The trees fell over*) to reported speech (*But then something said 'Turn!'*) to a side explanation (*That was the fire drill because...*).

Beginning about age 2, children engage in talk about the fantasy world, as well as talk about real but nonpresent objects and talk about nonobservable attributes of referents. While a child's active imagination can fashion fantasy talk around almost any object, some objects, materials, and contexts seem to be particularly inspirational in this regard. For that reason, it is difficult to estimate the frequency with which children engage in fantasy talk, either in private, with peers, or with adults. What is clear is that there are considerable individual differences in the conversational initiative and elaboration undertaken by children in these exchanges. Margaret, whom we saw struggling to produce a fantasy narrative autonomously at age 5, also produces rather sparse fantasy talk at 32 months, even with considerable scaffolding by her mother:

Mother: Who's this [*toy person*]?
Margaret: Annie.
Mother: That's Annie?
Margaret: That should be...
Mother: Who's that? (*points to toy*)
Margaret: Um... Annie.
Mother: That's Annie.
Margaret: That's a mother.
Mother: Mmhm!
Margaret: This is Mommy! (*places a toy next to the other toys on the floor*)
Mother: Oh.
Mother: What a nice family.
Mother: Now what are they going to do?
Margaret: [unintelligible] play music?

Thirty-two-month-old Sarah, on the other hand, already takes an active role in assigning roles and actions to characters in a similar fantasy context:

Sarah: There's papa (*picks up doll*).

Mother: Yep, there's a papa.

Sarah: [unintelligible] He can get in [the car (*puts doll in car*). He can drive.

Mother: Is he going to drive?

Mother: Where's he going to go?

Sarah: Go in hospital.

Mother: The hospital? Why's he going to the hospital?

Sarah: He's hurt.

Mother: He's hurt? Why is he hurt?

Sarah: He needs cast.

Mother: He needs a cast like papa does?

(*Sarah nods slightly.*)

Sarah: [unintelligible] papa has got cast.

The considerable skill at autonomous fantasy narration demonstrated by Sarah at age 5 may in part reflect her early participation in this type of adult-scaffolded fantasy world discussion. This episode begins with Sarah identifying the main character (papa) and proposing an appropriate action for him. With her mother's help, these basic ingredients are elaborated with information about goals and explanations (going to the hospital for a cast because he's hurt). Finally, Sarah's mother ties the negotiation of fantasy world back to Sarah's real experience, validating real-world experience as appropriate material for inclusion in fantasy narratives.

At ages 20 and 32 months, conversations about the nonpresent and about fantasy worlds are relatively rare events in parent–child discourse, and are not engaged in by all dyads. Although 94% of dyads in this sample engaged in some nonpresent talk at 20 months, most of this talk was what we have referred to as "related-to-present," that is, talk about nonobservable attributes of observable objects, or talk about nonpresent events tied to a present object or event. Related-to-present talk accounts for 5% of all talk at this age, while discussions of nonpresent people, objects, and events not tied to the here and now were quite rare (each accounting for less than 1% of all talk). At 32 months, nonpresent talk, though not more frequent overall, had begun to free itself from ties to the immediate context, with related-to-present talk accounting for only 2% of all talk, and discussions of objects and events not tied to an observable referent accounting for 1%–2%). Provided with toys to stimulate fantasy dialogue and discussion (i.e., puppets and a play house), nearly all the 32-month-old children and their mothers engaged in brief episodes of fantasy talk. However, such talk accounted for an average of less than 2% of all talk at this age, and children rarely produced initiatory moves in these conversations. Over the subsequent two and a half years, children made considerable strides in their ability to discuss nonpresent objects, events, and people, as well as their skills in initiating and participating in fantasy dialogue and discussion, as we shall see below as we examine children's production of two types of narrative genres: personal narratives and fantasy narratives.

PERSONAL NARRATIVES AT AGE 5

Children in the New England sample were videotaped again at age 5 participating in a range of discourse tasks, including telling a personal narrative to an experimenter about a recent experience and constructing a fantasy play narrative with the experimenter using small toy props (Hemphill, Feldman, Camp, & Griffin, 1994).

In the personal narratives they recounted, children turned real experiences into narrative accounts of events. Five-year-olds in this sample related an average of five events in their narratives (range of events per narrative 0–13), though coherent and successful narratives were sometimes produced with as few as three. Personal narratives, however, involve not only the structuring of events that advance the plot, but also require the child to provide relevant background information about space, time and actors, and to express his or her stance toward the narrated events through the use of evaluative devices. In this study, narratives were coded for the presence or absence of three features: structure, orientation and evaluation. Table 10.2 displays the sets of structural, orienting, and evaluative features found in these narratives and the proportion of children who included them in the narration of their personal experiences.

In the following paragraphs, we describe the broad range of variation present in this group of children by classifying their performances into better, average and poor productions of personal experiences.

The **better narrators** at 5 years of age produced conventional narratives that followed a sequential structure and were organized around a highpoint or climax. These narratives clearly convey the narrator's perspective through the use of sophisticated evaluative devices. Margaret's narrative, presented above, is one example of an excellent performance. Another example is this narrative told by Elizabeth at 5 years:

Elizabeth: Once upon a time I was in a shoe store and I had my pony with me. And I put him down. And then my mummy said: "Do you want to buy some shoes?" And I said: "Yes". And then I left him there for an hour. And then I came back to get him and he was gone.

Interviewer: Oh no.

Elizabeth: We had to search all over the store, we couldn't find him.

Interviewer: Oh no.

Elizabeth: A little girl must have took him home.

Interviewer: Ohhh. So what happened?

Elizabeth: My nanna bought me a new one.

TABLE 10.2
Types of Personal Narrative Elements and Proportion of Children Producing Each at Age 5

Narrative Element	Example	Proportion of Children Producing Element at Age 5
Structure		
Opening	*it all started when…*	.09
Highpoint	*and Sarah Clark's mother got squirted with the firehose, but she had the equipment on and she didn't even get wet!*	.22
Closing	*and that's it*	.19
Orientation		
Introduction of characters	*she let Julie who is my friend and me go*	.25
Location of action in a physical setting	*we went down to the Cape*	.31
Location of action in a specific time	*that night I put it under my pillow*	.25
Evaluation		
Intensifiers and delimiters	*we watched fireworks really late*	.53
Adjectives	*it was a pretty costume*	.47
Defeats of expectations	*I didn't go to the real top of the mountain*	.38
Causality	*it wasn't fun because there were too many mosquitoes*	.31
Intentions and purposes	*my mother and father were trying to get me to bed*	.31
Compulsions	*we had to sing a song*	.25
Reported speech	*I said yes*	.19
Internal states	*I believed her*	.19
Physical states	*it felt cold*	.16
Repetition for effect	*she did it again and again and again*	.13
Hypothetical situations	*there was no gate so she could have fallen right down the stairs*	.13
Comparisons	*I'm smarter than my mother and my father.*	.09

Interviewer: Oh that's good.

Elizabeth: He had twinkle eyes.

Elizabeth produces a highly conventional narrative: She introduces her anecdote with the appropriate background information and only after the setting is clear for the listener, she starts narrating the sequence of events that lead to the highpoint (the disappearance of the pony). At this point, she conveys the frustration elicited by the lost toy through a concentration of evaluative elements (*we had to search all over the store*; *we couldn't find him*) and finally closes the narrative with a resolution to the conflict described.

Narratives such as these by Margaret and Elizabeth combine both orientation, principally with reference to physical setting (*I was in a shoe store*) and sophisticated evaluation, which includes reported speech, hypothetical situations (*A little girl must have took it*), internal states (*Do you want to buy some shoes?*), and repetition for effect. Other evaluative elements more commonly used at this age, such as adjectives, defeats of expectations *(we couldn't find him),* intensifiers and delimiters (all over *the store*), compulsions (*We* had to *search…*) and intentions (*… to get him*) were also frequent in these narratives. These narrators had mastered a conventional pattern for telling personal anecdotes that was structured around a highpoint, often included conventional openers (*Once upon a time*) and closings, and that skillfully integrated both orientation information and different types of evaluation.

The **average performances** at 5 years of age can be characterized as displaying one of the following two patterns: (1) reportorial recasts, nonconventional narratives that report a list of events with little or no evaluation, or (2) evaluative accounts, nonconventional narratives that that are highly evaluated.

Interestingly and in line with previous research on gender differences in storytelling (Peterson & McCabe, 1983), there was a tendency for boys to fall in the first category and for girls to produce narratives of the second type. The following two examples illustrate these patterns:

John: age 5 years

Interviewer: Your mom told me that something very special just happened to your sister, what happened?

John: She had a graduation.

Interviewer: Did you go?

John: It was at this house.

Interviewer: Was it fun?

John: Yeah.

Interviewer: Tell me about it.

John: Well, all my cousins were there and moms and dads were there and I had lots of fun. And I went down and played some pool ball.

Interviewer: Yeah?

John: Yep. I went up and played up in the school yard.

Interviewer: You did?

John: Yep. And we had cake and lots of junk.

Corinna: 5 years

Interviewer: You went a long way away to visit your grandparents.

Corinna: Yeah. And I went swimming. And they didn't put the dock out yet, so I didn't go too far, because I didn't know like where it was over my head and stuff like that.

Interviewer: Mmhm.

Corinna: And so I didn't go too far. But I just swam back. And I did it slowly when I got up to here. (*Corinna points to midsection.*)

Interviewer: Uhhuh.

Corinna: Because I didn't want to go over my head by mistake. Because the dock wasn't there.

Neither of these narratives makes use of conventional narrative structure (e.g., the reporting of orienting information about setting and participants preceding an event that initiates a discrete sequence of actions) nor are they organized around a highpoint or climax, as Elizabeth's was. Nevertheless, some evaluative elements, especially intensifiers and delimiters (John: *I had lots of fun;* and Corinna: *I just swam back*) and compulsions (for example, *had to*) were frequently found in these performances. Despite these common features, there were differences in what narrators foregrounded in their texts. Narrators of reportorial recasts focused on conveying a list of events and occasionally, as John's narrative shows, added some orientation (*it was at this house; all my cousins were there*). Narrators of evaluated accounts, like Corinna, offered instead a concentration of evaluative devices, such as causality (*because the dock wasn't there*), defeats of expectations (*I didn't go too far*), internal states (*I didn't know...*) and intentions/purposes (*I didn't want to go over my head*), with the primary focus on conveying not only the events, but the narrator's interpretation of the experience, as well.

Poor narrators at age 5 conveyed unclear narratives with little evaluation and either a nonsequential structure or an obscure progression of events (as in Sarah's example). Even though these children remained on topic and within the boundaries of one anecdote, their narratives were often mixed with off-narrative talk. These least skilled narrators did not introduce actors nor offer general information to situate the action. The only evaluative elements, if any, present in their narratives were adjectives, physical states, intensifiers and delimiters. Andrew at age 5 illustrates this case:

Interviewer: Can you tell me about your chameleon?

Andrew: I got it for my birthday. And Greeney and Heidi died.

Interviewer: Yeah.

Andrew: So I got Spring and Cupcake left.

Interviewer: So you got more than one chameleon?

Andrew: Yeah. See when I had Heidi, um I had Spring. When Heidi died, I still had Spring. When Greeney died, I still had Heidi. And the lifespan is about ten days.

Interviewer: Their lifespan is ten days?

Andrew: I remember that my chameleons have been living for a long time (*shouting into microphone*).

FANTASY NARRATIVES AT AGE 5

In the fantasy narrative task, children were required to enter the terrain of pretense and symbolic talk. With the support of toys and a provided beginning for the plot, children had to construct a coherent story using talk in combination with enactment and sound effects. Because an adult partner also participated in this fantasy task, children could narrate relatively autonomously, or they could rely on their more competent partner to introduce and reintroduce play characters and to prompt for important structural and evaluative information.

The **most skilled fantasy storytellers** among our 5-year-olds used conventional narrative structure to frame and organize their fantasy performances. Structural elements present in the most successful fantasy narratives included orienting information about an imaginary setting, a build-up of events toward a narrative climax or highpoint, a resolution of the themes developed in the story, for example conflict between the animal participants, and a conventionalized closing, for example, *Everyone lived happily ever after.* The best storytellers elaborated on the conflict theme introduced by their adult partner, weaving in subplots around themes like a search for a magic mushroom. They made abundant use of a variety of types of evaluation, including in particular the reporting of character intentions (*then he...tried to attack him*) and internal states (*the mother saw the dragon and was terrified*). These fantasy storytellers built up a fully-realized story world (Wolf & Polanyi, 1990), achieving genre specificity through the explicit introduction of referents (*the lion saw the dragon sitting right in the middle of the pond*), rather than the use of deictic expressions (*sitting right there*), through the use of character delineation (*there was a bird that sang a sweet song*), and often through a focus on a particular story protagonist, around whose plans, actions, and reactions the story events were developed. They also represented character voice, displaying the perspectives of story characters through reported speech (*and then when the little lion heard that she said, "Here I am, mother"*), as well as through direct speech (*They went in a fight. "Arrrh!"*). These narrators used an anchor tense, typically the past tense, to hold together the diverse types of talk in the narrative, and employed strategies such as tense shifts and full nominal reintroduction of story characters to mark return to narration after stretches of nonnarrative talk. For example in Sarah's fantasy narrative, after she says, *So they all had to get out of the way, but then they tickled each other*, she digresses from the narrative to remark, *I tickle my sister sometimes. She tickles me the most. I like to tickle her cause it makes her laugh.* Then, she reintroduces the story character with *the dragon* to mark return to the narrative: *The dragon had to go home. So he just went home to his cave.* Table 10.3 summarizes the features included in successful fantasy narratives and the proportion of the children who produced each feature at 5 years of age.

Less successful 5-year-old fantasy narrators relied on their adult partner to provide the basic elements of story structure: information about the story setting, participants, and plot (*Adult: Annie, what do all the animals do? Annie: The lion can roar.*). They also relied on the adult partner to introduce story characters with full noun phrases, making ambiguous reference to the characters themselves with pronouns (*maybe he could push him*). The least successful fantasy storytellers relied on physical enactment, rather than narrative reporting, to represent events, used an undifferentiated present tense for both narrative and nonnarrative talk (*Pretend, pretend they're saying something. Now all the lions, now all the animals say bad things to them. You see?*), and often used inconsistent tense shifts. Rather

TABLE 10.3
Types of Fantasy Narrative Elements and Proportion of Children Producing Each at Age 5

Narrative Element	Example	Proportion of Children Producing Element at Age 5
Structure		
Setting	*there was a jungle and in the jungle they have dark trees and rocks*	.13
Highpoint	*and he went grr grr, and he knocked over all the trees cause he got so mad, and he knocked over this, and he knocked over everything!*	.41
Resolution	*then he kills the dragon and she kills the elephant and they live happily ever after*	.22
Closing	*the end*	.47
Genre Specificity		
Character delineation	*the father always gets mad at the little boy*	.44
Protagonist	*then he's [the dragon] gonna eat the elephant. Now he's gonna eat him. Now he's gonna throw him again. Now him. Now he's gonna throw the whole jungle and throw the tree*	.09
No deixis	*the elephant called the lioness on the telephone*	.25
Character Voice		
Direct speech	*get off me!*	.72
Reported speech	*and the duck said, Stop it!*	.13
Evaluation		
Intensifiers and delimiters	*the elephant almost stepped on the baby*	.41
Defeats of expectations	*the little one tried, but he couldn't do such a big jump*	.38
Intentions and purposes	*the dragon roared and tried to get him*	.41
Internal states	*the bird got mad at the lion*	.38
Repetition for effect	*it began to fire more and more*	.13
Complex temporal markers	*sometime, a lot later, the elephant died*	.31

than using reported speech, less successful narrators often held up an animal to indicate that a story character was talking, and instead of using verbal strategies of story character reidentification, simply turned back to the toy figures after engaging in side conversation with the adult partner. Narrative highpoints and plot resolutions were generally absent from these children's narratives. Most notably, the less successful narrators provided minimal evaluation of the story, reporting few character intentions or internal states.

Predictive Relationships Between Early Parent–Child Talk and Later Narrative Skill

The previous examples illustrate the wide range that characterizes children's likelihood of engaging in talk about the nonpresent and fantasy talk during the first three years of life. A similarly wide range of accomplishment is observable in children's capacities to produce narratives, whether personal or fantasy, at age 5. To summarize the variation displayed by children in each narrative task, two composite variables were formed: a personal narrative composite score (PN) representing the sum of scores for structure, orientation, and evaluation; and a fantasy narrative composite score (FAN), the sum of scores for structure, evaluation, genre specificity, and character voice. Table 10.1 shows children's measures on early pragmatic skills as well as means and ranges on the PN and FAN composite scores. In the assessments of relationships with early conversational participation, these composite scores are used as outcome measures.

We undertook this study to investigate whether participation in discussions of the nonpresent and of fantasy at the earlier ages was related to children's skill in producing autonomous narratives, both personal and fantasy, later on. In particular, we hypothesized that experience talking about the nonpresent constitutes opportunities to practice the language skills needed for personal narrative, and that experience engaging in fantasy talk with an adult builds skills needed to produce fantasy narratives. Alternatively, of course, participation in both of these forms of early talk might support the development of narrative competence in either genre, as might early experience with more diverse forms of conversational engagement, represented in our pragmatic flexibility measure.

While we are testing a set of precursors that would reflect social support for later narrative skills, another possibility is that various indices of the child's own language competence at earlier and later ages are all highly intercorrelated, each reflecting general underlying language competence. To test this alternative explanation, we first considered the simple correlations among the variables of interest. Table 10.4 shows the results of this correlational analysis. Because somewhat different narrative tendencies were identified for boys and girls, gender is also included.

TABLE 10.4
Correlations Between Narrative Outcome Measures and Potential Predictor Measures

	Personal Narrative (PN)	Fantasy Narrative (FAN)	Fantasy (Genre Specificity)	Fantasy (Character Voice)
MLU				
(32 months)	−.01	.04	.05	−.06
IPSyn				
(32 months)	.05	.13	.24	.02
CDI-production				
(20 months)	.05	.17	.28	.21
Nonpresent talk				
(20 months)	.48*	.36**	.28	.24
Fantasy talk				
(32 months)	.03	.14	.41**	.31***
Pragmatic flexibility				
(20 months)	.30***	.38**	.41**	.40**
Gender	.22	.45**	.43**	.03

*$p < .01$, **$p < .05$, ***$p < .10$

As displayed in Table 10.4, results showed that neither morphosyntactic skill (as measured by MLU and IPSyn), nor vocabulary skill (as measured by the CDI) at 20- and 32- months-old was associated with narrative performance at 5-years-old. Thus, these measures of general language ability do not appear to help explain variability in children's later narrative development. Most of the pragmatic measures, however, were positively correlated with PN and/or FAN and, thus, invited us to further explore their predictive power. Because gender was associated with FAN, we also decided to explore its effect more closely.

PERSONAL NARRATIVE

Two hypotheses were tested for personal narrative discourse. Our more specific hypothesis was that experience with past event talk would predict later skill at telling narratives of personal experience. Our more general hypotheses was that early experience with fantasy talk and pragmatic flexibility would also predict later skill in personal narrative. A series of regression models were constructed to test these hypotheses, including gender as another predictor. The models displayed in Table 10.5 indicate that the more children engage in nonpresent talk early in life, the better narrators of personal experience they tend to be at age 5. Indeed, 23% of the variance in personal narrative is explained by nonpresent talk alone, and even when we controlled for all the other predictors, nonpresent talk still contributed predictive power. As we can see from Model 6, pragmatic flexibility and gender, as well as nonpresent talk, each explain some of the variance in personal narrative performance. It is interesting, and somewhat puzzling, that the effect of pragmatic flexibility at higher levels varies by gender. Figure 10.1 shows personal narrative scores plotted against nonpresent talk for boys and girls with high and low pragmatic flexibility scores.

As the figure shows, girls with high pragmatic flexibility tended to be the best personal narrators, while boys with similarly high pragmatic flexibility scores performed at the lower extreme.

Fantasy Narrative

A similar series of regression models was constructed to predict skill in fantasy narrative at five, assessing both our more specific hypothesis, that early experience with fantasy talk would best support later competence in fantasy narration, and our more general hypotheses, that early experience with nonpresent talk and early pragmatic flexibility would also support fantasy talk at five. These models are displayed in Table 10.6. For fantasy narrative, even though nonpresent talk explains a portion of the variation ($R^2 = 13\%$), pragmatic flexibility and gender seem to play a more important role. Indeed, 41% of the variance in fantasy narrative is explained when these two variables are added to the regression model (see Model 5). Model 5 is illustrated in Figure 10.2, where fantasy scores are plotted against nonpresent talk for girls and boys at high and low levels of pragmatic flexibility. This

TABLE 10.5
Regression Models Explaining Variance in Personal Narrative (PN) at 5 Years of Age ($n = 32$)

Model	Nonpresent Talk β_i	se (β_i)	Fantasy Talk β_i	se (β_i)	Pragmatic Flexibility β_i	se (β_i)	Gender β_i	se (β_i)	Pragmatic Flexibility × Gender β_i	se (β_i)	df$_e$	R^2 (adj.)
M1	46.63*	15.36									1.30	.23 (.21)
M2			1.47	8.40							1.30	.00 (−.03)
M3	48.40*	15.71	5.23	7.52							2.29	.25 (.20)
M4	43.65**	17.60	3.24	8.25	.12	.20					3.28	.25 (.18)
M5	39.75**	18.06	2.12	8.33	.16	.20	1.43	1.46			4.27	.28 (.18)
M6	37.27**	16.97	1.20	7.82	−1.08***	.59	−8.99***	4.98	.75**	.34	5.26	.39 (.28)

* $p < .01$, ** $p < .05$, *** $p < .10$

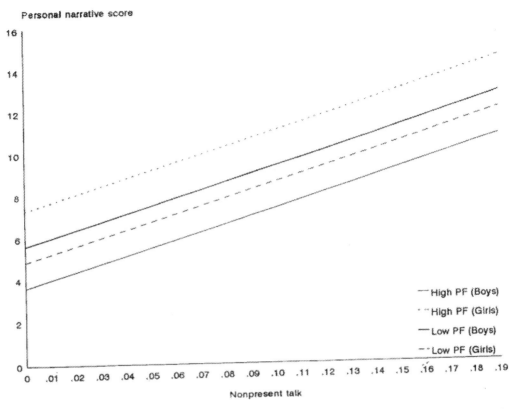

Figure 10.1   Predicted personal narrative score as a function of amount of Nonpresent talk for boys and girls at high (75th percentile) and low (25th percentile) levels of pragmatic flexibility.

figure demonstrates that the more nonpresent talk children produced at 20 months, the better fantasy narrators they tended to be at 5 years of age. In addition, the figure shows that girls tended to be better narrators of fantasy than boys, regardless of pragmatic flexibility. However, children with higher pragmatic flexibility produced better fantasy narratives than children of their same gender with lower pragmatic flexibility.

TABLE 10.6
Regression Models Explaining Variance in Fantasy Narrative (FAN) at 5 Years of Age (n = 32)

| Model | Nonpresent Talk | | Fantasy Talk | | Pragmatic Flexibility | | Gender | | Pragmatic Flexibility × Gender | | df$_e$ | R^2 (adj.) |
	β_1	se (β_1)	β_1	se (β_1)	β_1	se (β_1)	β_1	se (β_1)	β_1	se (β_1)		
M1	50.56**	24.04									1,30	.13 (.10)
M2			9.19	12.22							1,30	.02 (−.01)
M3	55.12**	24.22	13.47	11.60							2,29	.17 (.11)
M4	40.43	26.57	7.30	12.45	.38	.30					3,28	.21 (.13)
M5	24.67	24.09	2.79	11.12	.53***	.27	5.77*	1.95			4,27	.41 (.32)
M6	24.57	24.61	2.76	11.34	.48	.87	5.39	7.23	.03	.50	5,26	.41 (.29)

*p < .01, **p < .05, ***p < .10

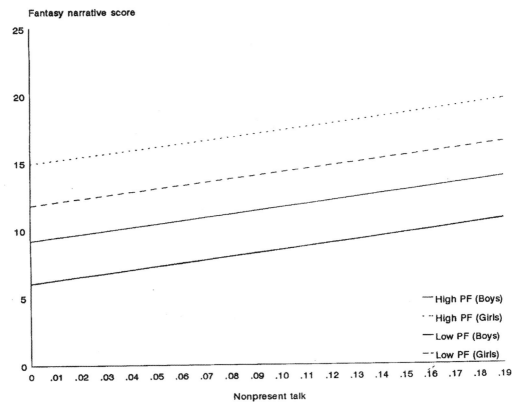

Figure 10.2 Predicted fantasy narrative score as a function of amount of Nonpresent talk for boys and girls at high (75th percentile) and low (25th percentile) levels of pragmatic flexibility.

The analyses up to this point, then, have confirmed our hypothesis that degree of participation in discussions of the nonpresent around age 2 affects the performance of more autonomous narratives at age 5. In addition, pragmatic flexibility and gender have been identified as contributing additional predictive power for both personal and fantasy narrative. We were surprised, though, at the lack of relationship between fantasy talk and the fantasy narrative composite score. Therefore, we decided to look more closely at two components of the FAN score that are distinctly characteristic of fantasy narrative: genre specificity, a category that comprises the maintenance of a protagonist, character delineation, anchor tense and lack of reliance on deixis; and character voice, which includes direct and reported speech, strategies that can function both for advancing the plot or for coloring the events of the story (see Table 10.3 for examples of features of each of these and Table 10.1 for means, ranges, and standard deviations for these fantasy components).

Two sets of regression models, analogous to those previously built for the composite scores, were constructed for these components of fantasy narrative. As Table 10.7 indicates, the strongest predictors for genre specificity were early fantasy talk and gender. That is, the more fantasy talk children produced early in life, the better they tended to perform in this particular dimension of fantasy narrative at age 5; in addition, girls once again tended to outperform boys at age 5. For character voice (see Table 10.7), nonpresent talk and fantasy talk combined accounted for 18% of the variance. For this dimension of fantasy narrative, there were not significant differences between boys and girls.

Summarizing, these findings indicate that participation in early discussions about the nonpresent positively influence overall performance in both personal and fantasy narration at age 5. We can also conclude that early participation in fantasy talk interactions stimulates development in specific areas of fantasy narrative: the achievement of genre specificity and the representation of character voice.

TABLE 10.7

Regression Models Explaining Variance in Fantasy Narrative Genre Specificity and Character Voice at 5 Years of Age ($n = 32$)

Model	Nonpresent Talk		Fantasy Talk		Pragmatic Flexibility		Gender		Pragmatic Flexibility × Gender		df$_e$	R² (adj.)
	β_1	se (β_1)	β_1	se (β_1)	β_1	se (β_1)	β_1	se (β_1)	β_1	se (β_1)		
Genre Specificity Models												
M1	11.14	6.98									1.30	.08 (.05)
M2			7.92**	3.12							1.30	.17 (.15)
M3	14.20**	6.29	9.02*	3.01							2.29	.30 (.25)
M4	11.90***	5.85	8.53*	2.78	.08	.07					3.28	.32 (.25)
M5	7.06	6.37	6.56**	2.94	.12	.07	1.47*	.52			4.27	.48 (.40)
M6	6.86	6.48	6.48**	2.99	.02	.23	.63	1.90	.06	.13	5.26	.48 (.38)
Character Voice Models												
M1	7.63	5.63									1.30	.06 (.03)
M2			4.69***	2.64							1.30	.10 (.06)
M3	9.47***	5.41	5.43**	2.59							2.29	.18 (.13)
M4	6.18	5.93	4.05	2.78	.08	.07					3.28	.23 (.14)
M5	6.12	6.20	4.03	2.86	.09	.07	.02	.50			4.27	.22 (.11)
M6	5.82	6.27	3.92	2.89	-.06	.22	-1.24	1.84	.09	.13	5.26	.24 (.10)

*$p < .01$, **$p < .05$, ***$p < .10$

These relationships are further affected by children's gender and their participation in a wide variety of social interchanges and speech acts, but are not dependent on children's early morphosyntactic skills or vocabulary.

DISCUSSION

In a broad sense, parents who habitually engage in more nonpresent and related-to-present talk with their young children provide more opportunities for children to learn to represent past events, to report intentions, feelings, and reactions, and to tie experiences in one context to those in another. All of these, we believe, are skills that are critical to later autonomous narrative production. As children become more capable of extended nonpresent talk, parents' topic extensions begin to include more specific prompts for information about narrative participants, setting, consequences, and resolutions, elements of narrative structure that our most successful children were able to produce independently at age 5. Thus, the relationships demonstrated between nonpresent talk at 20 and 32 months and the production of narrative structure and evaluation at 5 years of age, both in personal narrative and in fantasy play, reflect interactional histories that go beyond specific narrative exchanges. As Peterson and McCabe (1992, 1994) and Fivush and Hayden have argued (Fivush, 1994; Hayden & Fivush 1997), young children acquire understandings of culturally important elements of narrative structure through participation in joint conversation about past events with parents. The present study suggests that this interactional picture should be broadened to include other kinds of talk about the nonpresent (talk about nonobservable feelings and thoughts, for example), as well as talk about the related-to-present.

Pragmatic flexibility assesses another feature of extended parent–child talk, the ability to engage in a variety of communicative activities and to shift between here-and-now and nonpresent frames of reference. This aspect of interactional experience is only moderately associated with children's later ability to produce personal narrative, but shows stronger associations with the ability to participate successfully in fantasy play. Unlike personal narrative, fantasy play is a context that requires frequent shifts between talk with the adult partner in the immediate context of joint pretense (*Oops, the lion's tail fell off!*), relatively autonomous narration of story happenings (*Out jumped the lion cub's mommy*), and shifts into the voice of story characters. (*And the dragon said to all the other animals, "I don't like you. I'm gonna eat you all up."*) The ability to manage these shifts in narrative role may be facilitated by early practice in shifting frames of reference in conversation with parents.

Early morphosyntactic attainment as indexed by mean length of utterance and by IPSyn at 32 months shows little association with any of the areas of extended discourse competence at 5 years of age, though there is a hint of involvement in children's construction of a fantasy world. This may preview a larger role for morphosyntax as children begin to use more sophisticated anaphoric strategies for marking shifts in focus between central and peripheral story characters, and as they more consistently use anchor tense to bind together events in the story world.

The picture that emerges, then, as we consider continuity between early and later pragmatic skills is not simply one of homotypic continuity, with early experience in relating past events or engaging in fantasy narration with an adult partner predicting later personal narrative and fantasy narrative skills. Rather, it is also one of heterotypic continuity, in which experience in talking about the nonpresent, practice in negotiating shifts between talk about the here-and-now and talk about the nonpresent, and engagement in a broad range of communicative interchanges, may be crucial preparation for later autonomous narrative production.

FUTURE DIRECTIONS

The work described here is limited in a number of respects and only begins to scratch the surface of children's abilities to tell different kinds of stories. As is true of the vast bulk of spontaneous-language based research, the dyads studied here were primarily from white, English-speaking, middle-class families. Data on parent–child conversations in low-income and racial/ethnic minority families are woefully scarce, and for the most part have not been analyzed from a pragmatic perspective; we know little about the early language experiences of children in such families and how those experiences may be related to narrative and other discourse skills children bring to kindergarten. Greater depth of information is also needed about the naturally-occurring fantasy talk of children from all backgrounds in interaction with peers and siblings, and in small group as well as dyadic contexts. Mother–child verbal interaction, though indisputably important, is only one of many communicative participant structures most toddlers experience. Talk with fathers and other caregivers, siblings, and familiar peers undoubtedly each provides grist for the mill as toddlers and preschoolers come to understand and verbalize the physical (sometimes not present) world, multiple social worlds, and universe of fantasy worlds. Narrative offers a window on children's emerging understandings of such worlds and on the linguistic skills with which they navigate among them.

REFERENCES

Aukrust, V. G., & Snow, C. E. (1998). Narratives and explanations in Norwegian and American mealtime conversations. *Language in Society, 27*(2), 221–246.

Bartlett, F. (1932). *Remembering: A study in experimental and social psychology*. Cambridge: Cambridge University Press.

Berman, R. A., & Slobin, D. I. (1994). *Relating events in narrative: A crosslinguistic developmental study*. Hillsdale, NJ: Erlbaum.

Bishop, D. M., & Edmundson, A. (1987). Language impaired four year olds: Distinguishing transient from persistent impairment. *Journal of Speech and Hearing Disorders, 52*, 156–173.

Blum-Kulka, S. (1997). *Dinner talk: Cultural patterns of sociability and socialization in family discourse*. Mahwah, NJ: Erlbaum.

Blum-Kulka, S., & Snow, C. (1992). Developing autonomy for tellers, tales and telling in family narrative-events. *Journal of Narrative and Life History, 2*, 187–217.

Botvin, G., & Sutton-Smith, B. (1977). The development of structural complexity in children's fantasy narratives. *Developmental Psychology, 13*(4), 377–388.

Brown, R. (1973). *A first language: The early stages*. Cambridge: Harvard University Press.

Bruner, J. (1986). *Actual minds, possible worlds*. Cambridge: Harvard University Press.

Bruner, J. (1990). *Acts of meaning*. Cambridge: Harvard University Press.

Cazden, C. (1988). *Classroom discourse: The language of teaching and learning*. Portsmouth, NH: Heineman.

Dale, P., Bates, E., Reznick, J., & Morisset, C. (1989). The validity of a parent report instrument of child language at twenty months. *Journal of Child Language, 16*, 239–249.

Eisenberg, A. (1985). Learning to describe past experiences in conversation. *Discourse Processes, 8*, 177–204.

Feagans, L., & Applebaum, M. I. (1986). Validation of language subtypes in learning disabled children. *Journal of*

Educational Psychology, 78, 358–364.

Fivush, R. (1991). The social construction of personal narratives. *Merrill-Palmer Quarterly, 37,* 59–82.

Fivush, R., & Hudson, J. (1990). *Knowing and remembering in young children.* New York: Cambridge University Press.

Gergen, K. J. (1994). *Realities and Relationships: Soundings in Social Construction.* Cambridge, MA: Harvard Universtiy Press.

Gumperz, J. J. & Hymes, D. (1972). *Directions in sociolinguistics: The ethnography of communication.* New York: Holt, Reinhart, & Winston.

Haight, W., & Miller, P. (1993). *Pretending at home.* Albany: SUNY Press.

Han, J., Leichtman, M., & Wang, Q. (1998). Autobiographical memory in Korean, Chinese, and American children. *Developmental Psychology, 34,* 701–713.

Heath, S. B. (1983). *Ways with words: Language, life and work in communities and classrooms.* Cambridge: Cambridge University Press.

Hemphill, L., Feldman, H., Camp, L., & Griffin, T. (1994). Developmental changes in narrative and non-narrative discourse in children with and without brain injury. *Journal of Communication Disorders, 27,* 107–133.

Hemphill, L., & Snow, C. (1996). Language and literacy development: Discontinuities and differences. In D. Olson & N. Torrance (Eds.), *The handbook of education and human development: New models of learning, teaching and schooling* (pp. 173–201). Oxford:Blackwell Publishers.

Hollingshead, A. (1975). The four-factor index of social status. Unpublished manuscript. Yale University, Department of Sociology, New Haven, CT.

Hudson, J. (1990). The emergence of autobiographical memory in mother-child conversation. In R. Fivush & J. Hudson (Eds.), *Knowing and remembering in young children* (pp. 166–196). New York: Cambridge University Press.

Hudson, J. (1993). Reminiscing with mothers and others: Autobiographical memory in young two-year-olds. *Journal of Narrative and Life History, 3,* 1–32.

Hudson, J., & Shapiro, L. (1991). From knowing to telling: The development of children's scripts, stories, and personal narratives. In A. McCabe & C. Peterson (Eds.), *Developing narrative structure* (pp. 89–136). Hillsdale, NJ: Erlbaum.

Hughes, C., & Dunn, J. (1998). Understanding mind and emotion: Longitudinal associations with mental-state talk between young friends. *Developmental Psychology, 34*(5), 1026–1037.

Labov, W., & Waletzky, J. (1967). Narrative analysis: Oral versions of personal experience. In J. Helm (Ed.), *Essays on the verbal and visual arts* (pp. 12–44). Seattle: University of Washington Press.

MacWhinney, B. (2000). *The CHILDES Project: Tools for analyzing talk.* Mahwah, NJ: Erlbaum.

McCabe, A. (1996). *Chameleon readers: Teaching children how to appreciate all kinds of good stories.* New York: McGraw-Hill.

McCabe, A., & Peterson, C. (1991). *Developing narrative structure.* Hillsdale, NJ: Erlbaum.

Mead, G. (1934). *Mind, self, and society.* Chicago: Chicago University Press.

Melzi, G. (2000). Cultural variations in the construction of personal narratives: Central American and European American mothers' elicitation styles. *Discourse Processes, 30,* 153–177.

Michaels, S. (1981). Sharing time: Children's narrative styles and differential access to literacy. *Language and Society, 10,* 423–442.

Miller, P. J. (1982). *Amy, Wendy, and Beth: Learning Language in South Baltimore.* Austin, TX: University of Texas Press.

Miller, P. J., Potts, R., Fung, H., Hoogstra, L., & Mintz, J. (1990). Narrative practices and the social construction of self in childhood. *American Ethnologist, 17*(2), 292–311.

Miller, P. J., Mintz, J., Hoogstra, L., Fung, H., & Potts, R., (1992). The narrated self: Young children's construction of self in relations to others in conversational stories of personal experience. *Merrill-Palmer Quarterly, 38*(1), 45–67.

Miller, P., Sandel, T., Liang, C., & Fung, H. (2001). Narrating transgressions in Longwood: The discourses, meanings, and paradoxes of an American socializing practice. *Ethos, 29*(2), 159–186.

Minami, M. (2001). Maternal styles of narrative elicitation and the development of children's narrative skill: A study on parental scaffolding. *Narrative Inquiry, 11,* 55–80.

Minami, M., & McCabe, A. (1991). Haiku as a discourse regulation device: A stanza analysis of Japanese children's personal narratives. *Language in Society, 20,* 577–599.

Mullen, M. (1994). Earliest recollections of childhood: A demographic analysis. *Cognition, 52,* 55–79.

Mullen, M., & Yi, S. (1995). The cultural context of talk about the past: Implications for the development of autobiographical memory. *Cognitive Development, 40,* 407–419.

Nelson, K. (1986). *Event knowledge: Structure and function in development.* Hillsdale, NJ: Erlbaum.

Nelson, K. (1989). *Narratives from the crib.* Cambridge, MA: Harvard University Press.

Nelson, K. (1996). *Language in cognitive development: Emergence of the mediated mind.* Cambridge: Cambridge University Press.

Nelson, K. (2000). Narrative, time and the emergence of the encultured self. *Culture & Psychology, 6*(2), 183–196.

Nelson, K. (2001). Language and the self: From the "Experiencing I" to the "Continuing Me". In C. Moore, & K. Lemmon (Eds.), *The self in time: Developmental perspectives* (pp. 15–33). Hillsdale, NJ: Erlbaum.

Nelson, K., & Fivush, R. (2000). Socialization of memory. In E. Tulving & F. Craik (Eds.), *Handbook of memory* (pp. 283–295). New York: Oxford University Press.

Ninio, A. (1993). On the fringes of the system: Children's acquisition of syntactically isolated forms at the onset of speech. *First Language, 13,* 291–314.

Ninio, A., & Snow, C. E. (1996). *Pragmatic Development.* Boulder, CO: Westview Press.

Ninio, A., Snow, C. E., Pan, B. A., & Rollins, P. (1994). Classifying communicative acts in children's interactions. *Journal of Communications Disorders, 27,* 157–188.

Ninio, A., & Wheeler, P. (1984). A manual for classifying verbal communicative acts in mother-infant interaction. *Working Papers in Developmental Psychology, No. 1.* Jerusalem: The Martin and Vivian Levin Center, Hebrew University. Reprinted as *Transcript Analysis, 1986, 3,* 1–82.

Ochs, E., & Capps, L. (2001). *Living narrative: Creating lives in everyday storytelling.* Cambridge: Harvard University Press.

Ochs, E., & Schieffelin, B. (1984). Language acquisition and socialization: Three developmental stories and their application. In R. Shweder & R. A. Levine (Eds.), *Culture theory* (pp. 276–323). Cambridge: Cambridge University Press.

Ochs, E., Taylor, C., Rudolph, D., & Smith, R. (1992). Storytelling as a theory-building activity. *Discourse Processes, 15,* 37–72.

Oppenheim, D., Emde, R., & Wamboldt, F. (1996). Associations between 3-year-olds' narrative co-constructions with mothers and fathers and their story completions about affective themes. *Early Development & Parenting, 5*(3), 149–160.

Oppenheim, D., Nir, A., Warren, S., & Emde, R. N. (1997). Emotion regulation in mother-child narrative co-construction: Associations with children's narratives and adaptation. *Developmental Psychology, 33*, 284–294.

Pan, B. A., Imbens-Bailey, A., Winner, K., & Snow, C. E. (1996). Communicative intents expressed by parents in interaction with young children. *Merrill-Palmer Quarterly, 42*, 72–90.

Peterson, C., & McCabe, A. (1983). *Developmental psycholinguistics: Three ways of looking at a child's narrative.* New York: Plenum.

Peterson, C., & McCabe, A. (1992). Parental styles of narrative elicitation: Effect on children's narrative structure and content. *First Language, 12*, 299–321.

Peterson, C., & McCabe, A. (1994). A social interactionist account of developing decontextualized narrative skill. *Developmental Psychology, 30*, 937–948.

Pillemer, D., & White, S. (1989). Childhood events recalled by children and adults. In H. W. Reese (Ed.), Advances in child development and behavior (Vol. 21, pp. 297–340).

Reese, E. (1995). Predicting children's literacy from mother-child conversations. *Cognitive Development, 10*, 381–405.

Reese, E., Haden, C., & Fivush, R. (1993). Mother-child conversations about the past: Relationships of style and memory over time. *Cognitive Development, 8*, 403–430.

Roth, F., Speece, D. L., Cooper, D. H., & De La Paz, S. (1996). Unresolved mysteries: How do metalinguistic and narrative skills connect with early reading? *Journal of Special Education, 30*, 257–277.

Sachs, J., Goldman, J., & Chaille, C. (1984). Planning in pretend play: Using language to coordinate narrative development. In A. D. Pellegrini & T. D. Yawkey (Eds.), *Advances in discourse processes: Vol. 13. The development of oral and written language in social contexts* (pp. 119–128). Norwood, NJ: Ablex.

Scarborough, H. (1990). Index of productive syntax. *Applied Psycholinguistics, 11*, 1–22.

Snow, C. E. (1983). Literacy and language: Relationships during the preschool years. *Harvard Educational Review, 53*, 165–189.

Snow, C. E., Pan, B. A., Imbens-Bailey, A., & Herman, J. (1996). Learning how to say what one means: A longitudinal study of children's speech act use. *Social Development, 5*, 56–84.

Speece, D., Roth, F., Cooper, D. H., & de la Paz, S. (1999). The relevance of oral language skills to early literacy: A multivariate analysis. *Applied Psycholinguistics, 20*, 167–190.

Stern, D. (1989). Crib monologues from a psychoanalytic perspective. In K. Nelson (Ed.), *Narratives from the crib* (pp. 309–319). Cambridge: Harvard University Press.

Tessler, M., & Nelson, K. (1994). Making memories: The influence of joint encoding on later recall. *Consciousness and Cognition, 3*, 307–326

Vygotsky, L. (1934/1986). *Thought and Language* (A. Kozulin, Trans.). Cambridge, MA: The MIT Press.

Wolf, D., & Polanyi, L. (1990, October). *Walking into story: A five year old stumbles on the nature of semantic worlds.* Paper presented at the Conference on Language Development, Boston.

Part III

Childhood

11

Peer Relations During Middle Childhood
Gender, Emotions, and Aggression

Marion K. Underwood
Lara Mayeux
Mikal Galperin

INTRODUCTION

Most girls and boys care deeply about fitting in and getting along during the middle childhood years, especially with their same gender peers. Many desperately want to have someone to play with or to talk to at recess, to sit with at lunch, to choose them first for teams, and to support them when they feel left out or excluded. Forming and maintaining high quality peer relationships in middle childhood requires considerable skill in emotion regulation, particularly in coping with anger in peer interactions. Girls and boys may differ in the strategies they employ for managing anger in their peer interactions, both as a result of differential socialization by parents and authority figures, but also because girls and boys play predominantly with peers of the same gender, at least at school. Because girls and boys most often play in separate peer groups, some have argued that they grow up in different worlds and socialize one another in distinct ways (see Maccoby, 1998, for a powerful account of Two Worlds Theory).

For more than a decade, our research group has been fascinated with how girls and boys manage anger in their peer interactions during the age range of middle childhood. To set the context for our current empirical work, this introduction will describe how our approach emerges from studies within the peer relations tradition, but also from work on emotion regulation and research on gender development. The chapter will next discuss previous research on children's peer relations during middle childhood: children's friendships, networks, and the correlates and determinants of peer status. The majority of the chapter will present some of our current theoretical and empirical work on the following topics: the relation between peer status and children's choices for expressing and controlling emotions, observational research on anger and aggression, and important future directions for enhancing our understanding of girls' and boys' peer worlds.

Research in the area of peer relations has exploded since the 1980s; our knowledge of children's friendships, peer status, and social networks has become increasingly sophisticated (for a review of this massive body of work, see Rubin, Bukowski, & Parker, 1998). We now appreciate that friendships confer developmental advantages for children, but also that some children come to have enemies and that these mutual antipathies also influence children's development in important ways (Hartup & Abecassis, 2002). We continue to acknowledge the importance of understanding children's status in their peer groups at school, but we now know that being popular may not be the same as being well-liked (LaFontana & Cillessen, 1998, 2002; Parkhurst & Hopmeyer, 1998), and that there is heterogeneity among both popular (Rodkin, Farmer, Pearl, & Van Acker, 2000) and rejected children (French, 1988, 1990).

As exciting as these advances have been, it is striking that few of these studies have seriously considered how emotions and gender influence children's peer relationships. Especially given the current emphasis on the dark side of children's peer relationships, it seems important to consider further how girls and boys manage anger in their interactions with other children during the age range of middle childhood. This chapter will begin with a discussion of how peer relationships may be related to emotion regulation and to gender development, then move on to highlight our current empirical research on these questions. We will conclude with a substantial section on future directions that seem particularly important: gender and aggression, how parents contribute to children's peer relations, and the processes of peer social influence.

EMOTIONS, GENDER, AND PEERS: WHERE FEW HAVE DARED TO TREAD

Despite the massive numbers of peer relations studies conducted in the past few decades, the most recent large scale review included very little mention of emotions and concluded "…not much is known about the possibility that the peer culture can play different functions for boys and girls" (Rubin et al., 1998, p. 682). In commenting on research on gender and emotion, Deaux (2000) noted "…these two areas of study demand much of us" (p. 30). Research on emotions has long been fraught with conceptual and measurement problems (see Eisenberg & Fabes, 1999, and Saarni, 1999). Rational discussion of gender can be difficult in a culture so entranced with strong notions of differences that men and women are characterized as coming from different planets. Gender stereotypes pertaining to emotions are so broad, sweeping, and perhaps even misleading to the point of being deceptive because they ignore important factors such as emotional intensity, frequency, modality, and social context (Brody, 1997).

Still, despite these challenges, recent advances suggest that progress is possible in understanding children's peer relationships in light of emotion regulation and gender development. Increased attention to emotional development has resulted in refinements in models of emotion regulation, and a powerful, testable theoretical framework has emerged to guide research on gender and peer relations, called Two Cultures Theory.

Emotion Regulation

Emotion regulation is "the ability to manage one's subjective experience of emotion, especially its intensity and duration, and to manage strategically one's expression of emotion in communicative contexts" (Saarni, 1999, p. 200). Individual differences in emotional reactivity and emotion management relate to many dimensions of social functioning: empathic responding, prosocial behavior, shyness, and externalizing behavior problems (Eisenberg & Fabes, 1999). Children's capacity to control strong feelings in relationships with other children is particularly fascinating because these relationships are horizontal in that they require negotiation among individuals who are approximately similar in age and status (Hartup, 1989), authority figures are not present to provide structure, and children in close relationships frequently construct their own frameworks for social interaction (Laursen, Hartup, & Koplas, 1996).

Several theories and a small but growing body of research suggest that children's capacity to regulate emotions with peers may continue to develop during the middle childhood years. Comprehensive theories of development suggest that children might be particularly well prepared to learn to regulate emotions during middle childhood. Freud (1905) characterized middle childhood as the latency stage, during which children are relatively unperturbed by sexual impulses. During this period, children focus on learning skills and socializing primarily with children of the same gender. Piaget (1983) described these children as in the cognitive developmental stage of concrete operations, as being able to solve real world problems using logical mental procedures. Children may apply these logical principles to their emotional lives as they gain skills in negotiating rules and resolving conflicts. Erikson (1980) portrayed middle childhood as the conflict between industry and inferiority, a time when children work to gain competence in multiple domains, one of which might be emotion regulation in peer interactions. Sullivan (1953) proposed that individuals' personalities and relationships are formed around social needs, qualities we desire in our relationships with others, including warmth, companionship, acceptance, and intimacy (Buhrmester, 1996). These social needs expand with development. According to Sullivan's theory, children in the early elementary years desire a sense of belonging and acceptance with peers, and preadolescents additionally need intimate relationships with same-gender peers (called "chumships" by Sullivan).

In one of the few attempts to theorize more specifically about emotion regulation in older children, Gottman and Mettetal (1986) proposed a developmental account, based on careful observation of interactions between peers. They suggested that young children manage emotions in social interaction by maintaining a climate of agreement and discontinuing play if disagreements arise. Children in middle childhood regulate emotion by constructing elaborate rules for social interaction with same-sex peer groups to contain affective expression and avoid embarrassment. Adolescents regulate emotions by using their new skills in abstract reasoning to subject emotions to logical scrutiny in conversations with friends. The characterization of children in middle childhood as using rules to manage emotion expression fits with a large body of research demonstrating that these children value conformity, rules, and regulations (see Hartup, 1970). Gottman and Mettetal argued that the developmental function of this preoccupation with rules is to contain emotional intensity, that "the external structure is the vehicle for not being so controlled by the emotions" (p. 202).

Other research and theory suggests that not only are these children using explicit rules in their play to manage affect, they are starting to appreciate and obey the largely unspoken rules for expressing and controlling emotions. Children become masters of emotional dissemblance, as they try to cope with conflicting cultural messages about emotions in social interactions: be honest, but be careful about expressing negative feelings if you want to keep friends (Saarni & von Salisch, 1993). Although existing research largely supports this theoretical picture of elementary school-aged children becoming increasingly cool, calm, and collected as they deploy cultural rules for expressing emotions, much remains to be discovered about why some children become so competent in emotion regulation and whether and how girls and boys differ in their strategies for managing anger with peers.

Gender Development: Two Cultures Theory

Whereas peer relations researchers have been inconsistent at best in examining the role of gender, gender development scholars have proposed an elegant theoretical framework that could fruitfully guide research in this area, called Two Cultures or Two Worlds Theory (see Maccoby, 1998 for a comprehensive presentation of the theory, and Underwood, 2003, for a discussion of how this framework could inform research on children's peer relations). The most fundamental claim of Two Cultures Theory is "...the distinctive play styles of the two sexes manifest themselves in distinctive cultures that develop within girls' and boys' groups as the children grow older" (Maccoby, 1998, p. 78). Two Cultures Theory logically begins with the striking phenomenon of gender segregation, that girls and boys strongly prefer to interact with same-gender partners beginning in the third year of life (Serbin, Moller, Gulko, Powlishta, & Colbourne, 1994), and continuing until at least preadolescence (Gottman & Mettetal, 1986; Maccoby & Jacklin, 1987).

According to Two Cultures Theory, girls' and boys' groups differ on several dimensions: play styles and activity preferences, discourse, friendships, and the size and power of peer groups (Maccoby, 1998). Briefly, girls prefer activities involving turn-taking and cooperation, whereas boys engage in more competitive activities (Crombie & Desjardins, 1993). Although boys and girls' conversational styles are similar in many respects, girls are more likely than boys are to accede to others' wishes to avoid conflicts (Miller, Danaher, & Forbes, 1986), and boys are more likely than girls are to urge each other to take risks and to discuss risqué or antisocial topics (Thorne & Luria, 1986). Although Two Cultures theorists characterize girls' friendships as more intimate and exclusive than boys' are (Maccoby, 1998), peer relations evidence suggests that gender differences may be more complex and that social context may be a powerful determinate of whether boys and girls engage in intimate exchanges (Zarbatany, McDougal, & Hymel, 2000). Two Cultures Theory proposes that girls' social groups are smaller in size than boys' groups are and this may be the case for younger children, but evidence is more mixed for older children and girls' and boys' social networks appear to be similar in size in the middle childhood years (Bagwell, Coie, Terry, & Lochman, 2000; Cairns & Cairns, 1994).

Although there is some discrepancy in the details between the Two Cultures characterization of girls' and boys' peer groups and the findings of peer relations researchers (Underwood, 2003), this may be due to a focus on different age groups and to the fact the peer relations researchers have rarely been guided by Two Cultures Theory. In the remainder of this chapter, we will carefully consider gender differences and how Two Cultures Theory might inform work on peer relations during middle childhood.

PREVIOUS RESEARCH ON CHILDREN'S PEER RELATIONSHIPS

Developmental psychologists have focused on three aspects of children's peer relationships: friendships, social networks, and levels of social acceptance within the larger peer group. Friendship and peer social status seem to contribute to psychological adjustment in distinct ways (Parker & Asher, 1993). Because each of these relationship contexts demands different skills in emotion regulation, each will be considered separately here.

Friendships, Emotions, and Gender

For children to maintain close friendships, they have to be able to have fun getting excited together, know when to calm down, and know how to resolve disputes when they arise (Gottman & Mettetal, 1986). Little research has explicitly focused on emotion regulation processes between friends, but the literatures on children's expectations of friends and on conflict resolution are closely related.

Overall, research on friendships suggests that children expect to experience positive affect with peers, and to receive emotional support from friends when needed. In the middle childhood years, children report that same-sex friends provide them with more companionship and intimacy than parents, siblings, or teachers (Lempers & Clark-Lempers, 1992). In a diary study, children reported expecting that peers would provide a sense of sociability and belonging, concern for achievements and self-enhancement, and opportunities for learning (Zarbatany, Hartmann, & Rankin, 1990). When interacting with close friends, children expect inclusion and acceptance in noncompetitive activities, and support for self-evaluation in competitive contexts (Zarbatany, Ghesquierre, & Mohr, 1992). When asked to describe upsetting events, preadolescents often mention social situations, but report feeling better after talking with friends (Denton & Zarbatany, 1996). Interestingly, in this age range, friends seem to help each other cope with distress by distraction; Denton and Zarbatany found that preadolescents reported feeling better after receiving distracting social support from friends.

Although friends clearly expect and enjoy much positive interaction together, friends' interests inevitably collide and conflicts arise. A rich body of previous research has explored conflicts between friends and peers (see Laursen, et al., 1996, for a thoughtful review). Disagreements between friends may have both positive and negative functions; disputes can prompt children to make advances in their thinking, but disputes can also disrupt relationships and generate negative affect (Aboud, 1989). In a study of children's responses to discrepancies between their ratings of emotion judgments and the judgments of a friend, children tended to change their appraisals more when these were discrepant with the appraisals of a close friend than a "lukewarm" friend (Aboud, 1989).

Several previous investigations demonstrate that conflicts between friends are different than conflicts between children who are less closely affiliated. In one study, third- and fourth-grade friends and nonfriends were observed playing a board game designed to generate conflict, in a "closed field situation" (meaning that the children had little choice about what or with whom to play, Hartup, French, Laursen, Johnston, & Ogawa, 1993). Friends engaged in more conflicts than nonfriends (even when the total amount of interaction was statistically taken into account), and their disagreements lasted longer and tended to be less mild and polite than those between nonfriends. Other research suggests that with close friends, children respond more strongly to conflicts and also take care to protect the future of the relationship. In responding to hypothetical vignettes about anger with close friends and classmates, pre- and young adolescent children reported that with friends, they would feel a stronger sense of violation as a result of provocation, experience more complex emotions (anger and sadness, for example), be more likely to take partial responsibility for the dispute, and engage in more direct strategies to try to restore the relationship (Whitesell & Harter, 1996). Overall, research on conflict suggests that close friends resolve disagreements in ways that preserve the stability of the relationship, whereas nonfriends might resort to more hostile strategies in order to prevail in a particular dispute (Laursen et al., 1996).

Very few of these studies have found strong and consistent gender differences in how friends resolve conflicts during the age range of middle childhood. Although girls and boys cope with conflicts and provocation in largely similar ways, some evidence suggests that girls may be more distressed when angered by peers (Whitesell & Harter, 1996), and that girls' anger focuses more on social concerns (Murphy & Eisenberg, 1996).

Social Networks, Emotions, and Gender

In addition to studying dyadic friendships, researchers have also explored the structure and functions of children's larger social networks. With the possible exception of research showing that young adolescents who are aggressive tend to form networks with other aggressive youth (Cairns, Cairns, Neckerman, Gest, & Gariepy, 1988), little research has explored processes of emotion regulation among children's social networks. However, research and theory suggests that children might form networks based on similar styles of emotion management, and also socialize each other in how to manage strong feelings. For example, one study of the relation between children's naturally occurring social networks and their motivation in school found that children formed networks with others of similar academic motivation, but also that network members became more similar over time in their motivation for doing well in school (Kindermann, 1993). Given the centrality of emotion regulation in forming and maintaining relationships, it seems natural that similar processes might operate for strategies for emotion regulation. Children with similar emotion regulation styles might be attracted to form social groups, and in turn, the norms of the social network could shape individuals' styles of emotion management. Given that girls and boys are largely operating in separate social networks, it will be important to examine whether girls' and boys' groups develop different strategies for coping with anger and other negative emotions.

Peer Social Status and Emotion Regulation

In addition to having close friends and belonging to a group, children also value acceptance by larger peer groups such as their school classmates, neighborhood playmates, or members of their athletic teams. Sociometric status refers to the degree of a child's social acceptance by a group, as determined by nominations from other group members. Moreno (1934) pioneered the study of sociometry by visiting school classrooms and asking children to vote for those they would most like to sit beside. Moreno advocated sociometric testing as a way of understanding how individuals could preserve their autonomy and spontaneity but also participate in social groups. Moreno entitled his book *Who Shall Survive? The Problem of Human Interrelations*. Moreno's title hints at precisely the reason that contemporary psychologists have rediscovered sociometric testing, that is, that low acceptance by peers predicts later maladjustment (Kohlberg, LaCrosse, & Ricks, 1972; Kupersmidt & Coie, 1990; Parker & Asher, 1987).

In its modern form, sociometric testing is also conducted in school classrooms, but now researchers present children with rosters of all members of their grade at school and ask them to vote for peers for a variety of types of items. Children identify those peers whom they most like (positive sociometric nominations) and those whom they least like (negative nominations). In addition, researchers may also ask children to nominate peers for a variety of items to access specific behaviors, such as aggression ("Starts fights") and prosocial behavior ("Good leader" or "Is cooperative").

Researchers determine children's peer status by tabulating numbers of positive and negative nominations and assigning children to status groups based on one of several classification systems. In the most commonly used of these systems (Coie, Dodge, & Coppotelli, 1982), children are designated as having five types of peer status: average, popular, rejected, neglected, and controversial. Children in the average group have average numbers of like most and like least votes. Children in the popular group receive high numbers of positive nominations, and low numbers of negative nominations. Children classified as controversial receive high numbers of both positive and negative nominations. Children in the rejected group have a high number of like least nominations and very few nominations for like most. Neglected children receive very few of either positive or negative nominations. One strength of this classification system is that it discriminates between children who are actively disliked and children who are not well known because they are shy or do not interact much socially. Also, this system works well to identify children with extreme degrees of social acceptance or rejection. Using the Coie et al. (1982) system, by far the largest group of children is either not classified or classified as having average status (approximately 52%). Other peer status groups consist of much smaller proportions of children: popular (around 12%), rejected (about 13%), neglected (approximately 13%), and controversial (about 7%).

An extensive body of research has documented the behavioral correlates of these sociometric status groups. In a comprehensive meta-analysis of research on behaviors associated with these five social status groups, Newcomb, Bukowski, and Pattee (1993) documented that popular status is associated with sociability and low levels of aggression and withdrawal, and rejection is related to high levels of aggression and isolation and fewer positive interactions overall (but, as noted earlier, more recent research has reminded us that neither popular boys (French, 1988; Rodkin et al., 2000) nor popular girls (French, 1990) are homogeneous groups). Certainly these results suggest that the kind of extreme lack of emotional control that might be evident in aggressive behavior is associated with peer rejection (Coie & Kupersmidt, 1983). Much remains to be known about the relation between children's sociometric status and other more normative types of emotion regulation. Many of the behavioral correlates described in the Newcomb et al. meta-analysis relate to emotions, such as aggression and depression and loneliness, but because these broad categories of behavior are multiply determined, it is difficult to disentangle the role of emotion regulation. In their discussion, Newcomb et al. recommended that researchers broaden the types of question we ask about peer status, "especially the role of emotionality in children's peer relations" (p. 124).

In reviewing research on the relation between emotional responding and social competence, Hubbard and Coie (1994) suggested that positive peer status may be a reasonable criterion for social competence, at least in the peer domain. Although little empirical evidence exists, they argued that it is reasonable to expect that positive peer status would be associated with being able to recognize one's own emotions and the emotional displays of others, the ability to regulate emotional expressions, and the capacity to respond sympathetically to the emotional displays of others. To move forward in our understanding of the relation between peer relations and emotional competence, they suggested that researchers more thoroughly investigate differences between sociometric status groups on emotion variables.

Unfortunately, many studies to date have not examined gender differences in correlates of peer status (Newcomb et al., 1993), and whether peer status is related to different types of emotion regulation strategies for girls and for boys. We have sought to begin to examine these questions, by conducting questionnaire and observational studies to try to understand the relation between peer status and coping with angry provocation, for girls and for boys.

OUR RESEARCH ON PEER RELATIONS: GENDER, EMOTIONS, AND AGGRESSION

Our empirical research on peer relations and emotion regulation in middle childhood has been guided by several goals. We focus on interactions with peers because we think that children's capacity to regulate emotions might be most apparent in these contexts about which they care deeply, when authority figures are less in control. Although we acknowledge that positive emotions may also be regulated, we more carefully examine regulation of negative emotions such as anger because we believe that managing these is most challenging. We use combinations of questionnaire and observational methods; what children think and say about their emotional behaviors is interesting and important, but does not necessarily correspond to their actual behavior when provoked. We recognize that emotion regulation may well be specific to social context, and we try to study emotional behavior in contexts that make sense for both genders. Finally, we seek to understand how gender might influence children's expressions of anger and aggression, not only by examining gender differences in the frequency of key behaviors, but also by investigating gender differences in the relation between peer status and children's strategies for regulating strong emotions.

Peer Social Status and Children's Choices About the Expression and Control of Positive and Negative Emotions

In early studies, we used questionnaires to investigate the relation between peer social status and children's choices about the expression and control of positive and negative emotions (Underwood, 1997; Underwood, Coie, & Herbsman, 1992). Given that children who are actively disliked and children who behave aggressively can seem so emotionally dysregulated, we were interested in what they understand about social conventions for expression of emotions, called display rules.

In a study of children's understanding of display rules for anger, children in the third, fifth, and seventh grades watched videotaped vignettes of anger-provoking situations, and responded to questions about how they would feel, what kind of facial expression they would have, what they would say and do, and the reasons for any discrepancies between how they would feel and how they would behave (Underwood et al., 1992). Half of the vignettes depicted provocation by teachers (for example, a teacher falsely accusing a child of making a mess and scolding the child harshly); the other half of the vignettes portrayed provocation by peers (another child wrecking a tower of dominos). Children's responses were coded as display rules if they said they would feel angry, but that they would behave in a neutral or positive manner. Classroom sociometric data were available for all participants; thus we were also able to examine the relation between understanding of display rules for anger and peer rejection and peer nominations for aggression.

Overall, the results showed that children's understanding of display rules for anger is complex and related to context, gender, and age. Children reported masking anger more often with teachers than with peers. Boys' masking of anger increased with age, but girls' reported use of display rules decreased with age. Contrary to hypotheses, this study found that aggressive children did not differ consistently from nonaggressive peers in their understanding of display rules for anger; even highly aggressive children reported frequently that they would mask expressions of anger. Understanding of display rules may not account for individual differences in aggressive behavior, perhaps because aggressive children fight impulsively when they are furious and are unlikely to invoke display rules even if they know exactly what those rules are.

The relation between peer sociometric status and children's understanding of display rules for anger was much more complex than rejected children masking anger less often (Underwood, 1992). For the peer context, rejected girls reported display rules for anger less often than average status girls. For the peer context, there were not status group differences for boys on reporting of display rules. Expressing anger openly may not violate the norms of the peer culture for males.

In a subsequent study (Underwood, 1997), we sought to explore the relation between peer social status and several aspects of the pragmatics of emotion regulation with peers (Parke, 1994): children's choices to express and to control positive and negative emotions, and expectations of peer reactions to different emotional responses. Children in the second, fourth, and sixth grades responded to hypothetical vignettes read aloud, depicting situations provoking strong emotion in classroom situations: happiness at good fortune, pride in accomplishments, sadness, anger, disappointment, and embarrassment. For each hypothetical vignette, children were asked to imagine that they were in the situation, experiencing the designated strong emotion. For each situation, children responded to two types of questions. First, they chose one of four possible responses, arranged on a continuum from most expressive to most dissembling: expressing the emotion strongly, expressing the emotion but in a subdued fashion, masking the emotion by maintaining a neutral expression, and showing another more acceptable emotion. Next, for each of the four possible responses, children were asked to imagine enacting the particular emotional response in the presence of peers, and to rate each possible type of expression on how much it would make other children "want to be your friend." Last, children responded to a brief sociometric measure, including items for "like most" and "like least."

Overall, the findings suggested that children's choices to express or control emotions depended on both the type of emotion and individual difference variables such as gender, age, and peer status. As expected, all children reported that they would mask negative emotions more than positive feelings, although even for the positive emotions, children rarely endorsed strong open expression. There were not gender differences in children's choices of emotion expression.

Interestingly, the results provided only limited support for the hypothesis that, in general, older children would mask emotions more. Older children did report masking happiness more than younger children, but said that they would be more openly expressive of anger and disappointment. Contrary to predictions, there were no significant effects for peer social status on children's choices of emotional expressions. However, for expectations of peer reactions to emotional expressions, regardless of the type of emotional expression, rejected children thought that others would respond negatively to their behaviors. This finding confirms previous evidence that rejected children are perhaps painfully aware that others react negatively to them (see Asher, Parkhurst, Hymel, & Williams, 1990, for a review). Rejected children's uniformly negative expectations suggest that these children may be cognizant of possible reputation bias (Hymel, Wagner, & Butler, 1990) and believe that peers will dislike them no matter what they do. All children expected the most negative peer consequences for expressing anger, both strongly and moderately.

Observational Research on Peer Status and Coping with Angry Provocation

One serious limitation of the described research is that it relies heavily on children's responses to hypothetical vignettes, rather than on how children behave when actually confronted with angry provocation. To try to observe more directly how children behave when angry, we developed a laboratory method to provoke a mild degree of anger in participants in the age range of middle childhood (Underwood, Hurley, Johanson, & Mosley, 1999). Children in this study participated in a laboratory play session during which they played a competitive computer game for a desirable prize, with a same gender confederate thought to be another participant but in reality a child actor. During a 10-minute contest period, participant children were provoked in two ways: The computer game was rigged so that the participant child lost most of the rounds and the child actor was trained to make provoking comments as he or she won the game rounds. Data collection with over 500 children indicates that this experience is moderately provoking, but not harmful because we debrief children carefully and embed this 10-minute provoking period in a 1 hour-long play session that is predominantly positive.

The goals of this research included examining developmental and gender differences in anger expression, and also the relation between coping with peer provocation and peer social status at school and peer nominations for aggression. This summary will focus on the findings related to peer status and gender. Based on preliminary research, it was hypothesized that popular peer status would be associated with responding verbally to peer provocation for boys, but to keeping quiet for girls. Popular boys were predicted to respond to teasing with humorous or distracting comments. Popular children were expected to be more skillful in responding to provocation; they were predicted to assert their own needs appropriately but not to overreact in ways that would earn them scorn from their peers or disdain from their teachers. Rejected children were expected to be less skillful in responding to provocation; they would be less likely to assert their feelings verbally, and more likely to respond angrily or perhaps not to respond at all.

Method

Participants were 382 children (198 boys and 184 girls) who had just completed the second, fourth, and sixth grades (average ages 8, 10, and 12 years). The ethnic composition of the sample reflected that of an urban public school system in the northwestern United States (approximately 85% European-American and 15% other ethnic groups).

Sociometric data were collected and peer status was determined using the modified Coie, et al. (1982) method described by Terry and Coie (1991). For the peer status data reported here, the sample included true average ($n = 49$), popular ($n = 58$), and rejected children ($n = 66$), (unclassified children, those who do not meet criteria for any of the status groups, were eliminated from these analyses to make the average group more homogeneous, following the recommendation of Terry and Coie, 1991).

During a 1-hour laboratory play session, children were invited to play a computer game with an unfamiliar child of the same age and gender, who was a peer confederate. To increase participants' motivation to do well and care about the outcome of the game, they were told that a desirable prize would be given to the winner. After a brief practice session, the computer game was programmed to repeatedly (but not obviously) give an advantage to the actor so that the actor won approximately 75% of the rounds of the game. The child actors were trained to make a standard set of provoking remarks as they won rounds of the game. The remarks focused on the participant's competence at the game ("You're not very good at computer games, are you?", "Why don't you try a little harder?" and "That prize has my name on it.").

Play sessions were videotaped. Participants' facial and verbal responses to the provoking comments were reliably coded (kappa's for faces ranged from .4 to .8, kappa's for verbalizations ranged from .5 to .85). Facial responses immediately following provoking comments were coded as angry, sad, neutral, or happy. Verbal responses were coded into 39 categories of fairly specific statements related to the game and the actor. On conceptual grounds, these 39 categories were collapsed into 12 categories of verbal responses for the analyses: no immediate verbal response, negative, self-negative, game not working, distraction, game talk, humor, and positive.

Results and Discussion

Overall, children showed remarkable skill in maintaining poise in this provoking situation. Immediately following provoking comments by the actors, participants showed neutral facial expressions and gave no verbal response just over 50% of the time. The most common types of verbalizations were talking about the specifics of the game or the score, self-negative comments, or negative responses. In general, the pattern of participants' verbal reactions provides support for Gottman and Mettetal's

TABLE 11.1
Verbal Responses to Provocation by Gender

	Boys (n = 198)	Girls (n = 184)	F (1, 380)
No immediate verbal response	.48	.54	4.03, p < .05
Negative	.13	.10	8.60, p < .01
Self-negative	.06	.08	4.89, p < .05
Game not working	.01	.01	n.s.
Distraction	.03	.03	n.s.
Game talk	.09	.07	4.77, p < .05
Humor	.03	.03	n.s.
Positive	.04	.03	5.63, p < .05

Note. Values represent mean proportions of verbal responses to each type of provocation.

(1986) characterization of middle childhood as a time when children value containing emotional expression in order to avoid embarrassment.

Contrary to hypotheses, there were not significant interactions for gender and peer status, though there were significant main effects for both variables. Table 11.1 presents verbal responses to provocation by gender. Overall, girls expressed anger less openly than boys did during the provoking play session. As compared to boys, girls more often gave no immediate verbal response, responded with fewer negative remarks, and made more self-negative comments. However, it is important to note that most of these gender differences were not large, and many were evident during the practice portion of the experiment before the provocation began.

For peer status, there were no significant main effects of interactions for facial and verbal responses to provocation. However, for negative gestures in response to provocation, there was a significant effect for peer status. Table 11.2 presents mean sums of positive and negative gestures during the 10-minute provoking session.

Positive gestures included those that indicated success, winning, or feeling good (raising hands in victory, covering mouth with glee) and humorous body movements. Although the difference was not statistically significant, rejected children tended to make fewer of these positive gestures than popular or average children. Negative gestures were body movements that indicated loss, disbelief, or frustration, invading the actor's physical space, taking fake punches, bumping chairs, and banging on the keyboard. Rejected children made these gestures significantly more than popular and average children.

Interestingly, although rejected children seemed fully capable of controlling their verbal behavior so as to respond similarly to their average and popular peers, they were not as successful in regulating their negative gestures. Negative physical gestures had fairly low frequencies, but were extreme behaviors that are likely to be highly salient to peers. Rejected children made twice as many overt, physical expressions of negative affect as popular children. That rejected children seemed more successful in masking verbal expressions of emotion than gestures fits well with previous theory and research. Individual differences in children's understanding of emotions are likely to be subtle (Harris, 1993);

TABLE 11.2
Positive and Negative Physical Gestures by Peer Status

	Peer Status			F (2,155)
	Popular (n = 58)	Average (n = 49)	Rejected (n = 66)	
Positive gestures	.77	.82	.53	n.s.
Negative gestures	1.89 a	2.16 a	3.91 b	5.24, p < .01

Note. Within rows, means not sharing subscripts differ at p < .05.

this subtlety of individual differences seems even more likely for outward expressions of emotion which are probably heavily influenced by children's efforts to present themselves positively. Children master verbal display rules before facial display rules (Gnepp & Hess, 1986), suggesting that masking nonverbal expressions of emotion might be more challenging. That rejected children differed on overt physical expressions of emotion confirms that it may be important for intervention programs for improving the social relations of rejected children to focus more on helping children master their nonverbal expressions of emotion.

Other results suggested that the rejected children with the most extreme problems with anger regulation may not have been able to tolerate the play session and may have stopped participating because they were upset, and before they became very angry. Chi-square analyses indicated a significant difference between peer status groups in stopping the play session, and rejected children were far more likely to stop (12 of 66; 18%, $\chi^2 = 8.35$, $p < .05$) than popular (3 of 58; 5%) or average (6 of 87; 7%) children. Ethical considerations forced us to make it easy for children to stop the contest if they wanted, but this provision means we may have missed the opportunity to see the most dramatic angry expressions. Rejected children appeared to stop the sessions when they felt frustrated, which may have been their way of trying to regulate strong negative affect by extricating themselves from the situation. Had they been forced to continue the play sessions, we believe that we might have seen more of the extremely angry behavior that may contribute to rejected children being intensely disliked at school.

The results of this laboratory study may also have underestimated peer status group differences in coping with angry provocation because rejected children were provoked by peers whom they had never met. If rejected children had been interacting with particular types of familiar peers, status group differences might have been much more evident. Much aggressive behavior takes place within dyads of children, in which a relationship develops over time within which one or both children fight frequently (Coie et al., 1999). To fully understand the emotion regulation behaviors of children disliked by peers, it may be important to observe them in dyadic interactions with another child with whom they have a history of social difficulties.

To understand fully rejected children's capacity for emotion regulation, it may be important to observe them with known children in familiar environments. However, the methodological challenges of this would be considerable. Observing naturally occurring emotion-provoking episodes would require many hours, and older children might well be skillful in hiding the most important interactions from view. Creating a conflict between two known peers in the lab raises serious ethical questions, because researchers would be manipulating an ongoing relationship for a child with peer problems, in an age range during which peer interactions matter enormously.

Overall, the findings from this laboratory study suggest that in this particular context, rejected children seem as capable of controlling their verbal reactions to provocation as their popular and average peers, but perhaps less able to regulate their gestural responses. Regardless of peer status, girls tended to respond less negatively to provocation than boys did, though gender differences were not large in magnitude. This study focused entirely on coping with same-gender provocation. How do children respond when challenged or provoked by peers of the other gender?

Children's Responses to Provocation by Same- and Other-Gender Peers

Although the majority of children's peer interactions during middle childhood are with same-gender peers, "we must not fall into the error of assuming that spontaneous, cross-sex contact is absent in the school-age years" (Maccoby, 1994, p. 87). Children in the early elementary years play in mixed gender groups about 25% of the time (Crombie & DesJardins, 1993; Maccoby & Jacklin, 1987). In light of claims that boys and girls inhabit different cultures in middle childhood (Maccoby, 1990; Thorne & Luria, 1986) and that gender segregation may contribute to later difficulties in other-gender relationships in the home and in the workplace (Maccoby, 1998; Thorne & Luria, 1986), it is important to learn more about how children behave in these not infrequent other-gender encounters. How do boys and girls behave together in emotion-provoking situations, given their different play styles, preferences for different activities, and strong identities as part of their same-gender groups?

Using identical methods as in the study just described, we compared children's responses to provocation by same- and other-gender peers (Underwood, Schockner, & Hurley, 2001). Previous research suggests three possibilities for how children might respond to provocation by other gender peers as compared to same gender peers. The *both genders less interactive/more negative hypothesis* suggests that both girls and boys behave less positively when interacting with a peer of the other gender. This hypothesis is supported by research with preschool samples (Fagot, 1985; Jacklin & Maccoby, 1978; Serbin et al., 1994), and the fact that girls and boys have fairly strong same gender peer preferences during the middle childhood years (Serbin, Powlishta, & Gulko, 1993). The *girls and boys express emotions more similarly* hypothesis fits with studies with young children showing that in other gender encounters, girls' emotional expressions become more like those of boys, and vice versa (for example, Leaper, 1991). The *girls express emotions more like boys* hypothesis is supported by previous research showing that boys are more direct and competitive in resolving conflicts regardless of the gender of the partner, whereas girls become more forceful when they interact with boys than when they interact with other girls (Miller et al., 1986 ; Moely, Skarin, & Weil, 1979).

Method

Participants in this study were the same 382 dyads from the study described above, plus an additional 184 dyads in which children were provoked by other-gender partners. The same exact methods and procedures were used in this study to compare children's responses to provocation by same- and other-gender peers.

Results and Discussion

Overall, the results supported the hypothesis that responses to other-gender peers would be less interactive and more negative than to same-gender partners. Table 11.3 presents verbal responses to the provoking peer during the practice and contest sessions, by gender composition of the dyad. Children responded more negatively to other-gender peers during both the contest and the provoking periods of the play sessions. In addition, children interacting with other-gender peers showed fewer neutral and more negative facial expressions, and exhibited more negative gestures. Interestingly, in a short interview right after the provoking period of the experiment, children who experienced provocation by an other-gender peer reported feeling less bothered by the showing off than those provoked by a

TABLE 11.3
Verbal Responses During the Practice and Contest Sessions by Gender Composition of the Dyad

	Practice (Game fair, actor not provoking)			Contest (Game rigged, actor provoking)		
	Same Gender	Other Gender	F	Same Gender	Other Gender	F
No response	.51	.59	$6.98, p < .01$	.51	.51	n.s.
Negative	.09	.14	$17.83, p < .0001$	.11	.15	$10.91, p < .01$
Self-negative	.06	.04	$8.94, p < .01$	.07	.08	n.s.
Game not working	.003	.002	n.s.	.01	.01	n.s.
Distracting	.04	.008	$25.09, p < .0001$	.03	.03	n.s.
Game talk	.13	.07	$20.00, p < .0001$	.08	.05	$13.99, p < .001$
Humor	.06	.04	$3.82, p = .05$	.03	.03	n.s.
Positive	.02	.04	$5.77, p < .05$	.04	.05	$7.16, p < .01$

Note. Values represent mean proportions of verbal responses that were of each type. For the interaction of Time × Remark × Gender Composition, $F (6, 548) = 3.11, p < .05$.

same-gender peer. Interview responses also suggested that children pursued different social goals in interactions with other-gender than with same-gender peers. They tried less to speak up to make the teasing stop, they tried more to play better so that the other person would stop teasing them, and they worked less hard to get along with the other person.

Although there were consistent, significant differences showing that children responded more negatively to provocation by other-gender peers, it is important to acknowledge that many of these were evident even during the practice session, before the provocation began. Also, although children's responses to other-gender peers were more negative across all measures in the study, the magnitude of the differences between responses to same- and other-gender peers was often small. Understanding that children respond more negatively to provocation by an other-gender peer fits with the claims of Two Cultures Theory, but the small size of the differences suggests that these initial negative reactions may be amenable to change.

Observing More Subtle Forms of Anger Expression Among Children

One advantage of using a computer game context to provoke anger in children is that it is intense and involving; a disadvantage is that this competitive situation and playing computer games in general seems more relevant to boys' interests and concerns. Galen and Underwood (1997) developed a laboratory task that seems likely to elicit the more subtle ways that girls might express anger and contempt. In this study, dyads of female friends played the board game *Pictionary* with a third unfamiliar girl, who was an actor trained to be a difficult play partner. The task was less competitive and there was no prize for the winner. The outcome of the game was not rigged to reduce the focus on losing as part of the provoking experience and to highlight the interpersonal provocation; children participated with a best friend to elicit social referencing and exclusionary behavior.

We developed this laboratory task as a way to try to observe what we call "social aggression," the more subtle ways that children, perhaps girls in particular, might express anger and contempt toward one another (see Cairns, Cairns, Neckerman, Ferguson, & Gariepy, 1989). Social aggression consists of: disdainful facial expressions, negative evaluation gossip, exclusionary behavior, or friendship manipulation (Galen & Underwood, 1997). Social aggression is directed toward damaging another's friendships or social status, and may take direct forms such as verbal rejection, negative facial expressions or body movements, or more indirect forms such as slanderous rumors or social exclusion. We chose the term because it aptly describes a class of behaviors that belong together because they serve the same function in ongoing social interaction: to hurt another person by doing harm to her self-concept or social standing. Although many of the behaviors thought to be socially aggressive (such as relationship manipulation) cannot be observed in a single laboratory session, our goal was to directly observe some of the behaviors that may be elements of social aggression: disdainful facial expressions, social exclusion, and derisive remarks.

To date, we have used this method with a small sample of seventh grade girls (Galen & Underwood, 1997). We also have preliminary results from a study using this observational method with a large sample of boys and girls in the fourth, sixth, and eighth grades, to carefully observe gender and developmental differences in social aggression (Underwood, Scott, Galperin, Bjornstad, & Sexton, 2004).

Results and Discussion

In our first study in which we made every attempt to standardize behaviors by the provocateur, we chose to focus on the behaviors of individual girls as the unit of analysis. Participants' responses were variable, but several behaviors were evident in all sessions: staring ($M = 26.5$, $SD = 13.92$), glancing ($M = 5.36$, $SD = 2.66$), and ignoring ($M = 4.64$, $SD = 2.19$). Other frequently observed behaviors were using a snide tone of voice ($M = 3.14$, $SD = 3.75$), sarcastic comments ($M = 2.71$, $SD = 4.12$), and making a face ($M = 2.36$, $SD = 3.21$). Positive responses to the provocations (e.g. "Alright, you go first then") were relatively rare ($M = 1.36$, $SD = 1.73$), as were more direct behaviors such as verbal abuse ($M = 0.86$, $SD = 2.06$), threats of violence ($M = 0.36$, $SD = .95$) and physical responses ($M = 0.50$, $SD = 1.32$).

Girls' responses to the questionnaire they completed after the Pictionary game indicated that they viewed the confederate as mean, rude, and unpleasant. On a scale of 1 to 5, with 1 representing "not at all," participants reported that they did not like the confederate very much ($M = 2.29$, $SD = 1.70$, corresponding to "a little" on the scale), and that they did not think the confederate was nice ($M = 2.14$, $SD = .95$, corresponding to "a little" on the scale). Girls did think she was mean ($M = 3.21$, $SD = 1.19$, representing "pretty mean" on the scale) and reported that the confederate made them mad ($M = 3.14$, $SD = 1.70$, corresponding to "pretty mad"), and that they were not eager about the prospect of being friends with her ($M = 2.64$, $SD = 1.15$).

These findings indicate that this game task was successful in eliciting elements of social aggression. Reliable coding was possible even for subtle facial expressions. Although we recognize that not all types of socially aggressive behaviors could be observed in this setting (particularly aspects related to manipulating friendship patterns), some of the specific behaviors observed in response to an unpleasant stranger may be similar to those involved in social exclusion among friends, such as not responding to what a person says or does (ignoring) or exhibiting disdainful facial expressions (Olweus, 1991). Girls' responses to interview questions after the game indicated that the method was successful; the confederate was not well-liked by the participants. The participants found her to be mean rather than nice, and indicated that she made them moderately angry. Participants' descriptions of their overall impressions of the confederate were also predominantly negative.

To test further the ecological validity of this laboratory method and to explore children's perceptions of actual samples of social aggression, we showed a separate sample of children brief video clips from these play sessions, and asked them questions about how angry and hurt they would feel if they were the targets of these behaviors. We found that girls viewed actual samples of social aggression as indicating more anger than boys, and that older children viewed socially aggressive behavior as indicating more dislike.

An important strength of this method is that it allowed us to actually see socially aggressive behaviors among girls. With the slightly different construct of relational aggression, Crick and Grotpeter (1995) relied mostly on peer nominations to measure behaviors such as friendship manipulation. Although they sensibly argued that direct observation would be difficult because it would require prior knowledge about relationships among children, we worry about a construct that relies on only one method of measurement and that by definition is something that cannot really be seen. We suggest (tentatively, because of the small number of play sessions conducted here) that elements of social aggression can be elicited and reliably coded in carefully constructed laboratory situations.

To confirm this suggestion, it seems important to employ these methods with larger samples, and to include groups of boys as well as girls, and mixed-gender groups. Observational research is badly needed to confirm the suggestion from questionnaire and peer nomination data that social aggression is more common and more hurtful for girls. Answering this question requires observing boys in the same laboratory tasks used to elicit social aggression among girls. Preliminary results from our study using this same method with a larger sample of girls and boys shows that boys engaged in slightly more verbal social aggression, whereas girls showed more nonverbal social aggression than did boys (Underwood et al., 2004). Although it is important to understand gender differences in the frequency of social aggression, it is perhaps more important to know more about the processes by which girls' and boys' social aggression unfolds. Our preliminary findings show that girls' forms of social aggression are overall more surreptitious than boys are, which might contribute to girls feeling more hurt and more betrayed by social aggression (Galen & Underwood, 1997; Paquette & Underwood, 1999). In future studies, it will be important to observe children in more naturalistic settings to examine the social processes by which aggression unfolds in girls' and boys' groups. Also, by middle school, other-gender interaction is frequent enough that it seems important to observe how both boys and girls respond to this particular type of provocation by members of the opposite gender.

Summary

Overall, our research on children's peer relations in middle childhood confirms that both boys and girls care deeply about fitting and in and getting along with the same-gender peer group, and greatly value maintaining emotional control (Gottman & Mettetal, 1986). Our results fit with some of the claims of Two Cultures Theory of gender development, but also suggest some ways in which its claims may need to be refined.

Both genders seem to be masters of dissemblance in hiding negative emotions during middle childhood (Saarni, 1999); both girls and boys believe that when provoked to anger peers will respond negatively no matter how they respond (Underwood, 1997). Gender differences in peer relations, and in particular anger expression and aggression, are more complex than girls behaving less angrily than boys and girls manipulating and boys fighting (Bjorkqvist, Lagerspetz, & Kaukiainen, 1992). In some of our laboratory studies, girls do respond a bit more negatively to peer provocation than do boys, but these differences are not large (Underwood et al., 1999). Overall, there are not consistent relations between peer status and children's responses to provocation in our studies nor do these relations differ for boys and girls. Both girls and boys who are rejected by peers believe that any response to anger will be perceived negatively by peers (Underwood, 1997), and in our observational studies, both girls and boys who are actively disliked at school respond to provocation with more negative gestures. In support of Two Cultures Theory, both girls and boys responded more negatively to provocation by an other-gender peer than by a same-gender peer. Again, this difference was consistent but small, suggesting that girls' and boys' more negative responses to other-gender interactions may be amenable to change. Two Cultures Theory fits with the suggestion that boys and girls seek to hurt each other by different means, and though our observational work shows that both girls and boys engage in social aggression, they seem to do so in slightly different ways (boys may show more verbal social aggression, whereas girls use gestures more to convey social exclusion).

FUTURE DIRECTIONS

Research on peer relations in middle childhood continues to flourish and our understanding of children's friendships, social networks and peer social status is becoming increasingly sophisticated and complex. More and more, studies of peer relations are examining gender differences in the functions and social processes of children's peer groups, and these studies will benefit from being guided by Two Cultures Theory to test its claims with different age groups and using multiple methods (Underwood, 2003). Two Cultures theorists have emphasized differences in girls' and boys' peer cultures (see Maccoby, 1998, for an overview), mostly on the basis of laboratory studies with preschool children and ethnographic evidence with older samples. Peer relations researchers have found less dramatic gender differences, but this may be due to relying mostly on studies with larger samples of older children, using questionnaire and peer reports to measure friendships, networks, and peer status. Peer relations and gender scholars share an interest in testing the claims of Two Cultures Theory with diverse age groups and multiple measures, to understand whether and how girls and boys might grow up in different peer cultures, and what the developmental consequences of this might be.

Peer relations researchers are also paying increasing attention to the importance of emotions (see Lemerise & Arsenio, 2000, for a model of social information processing that integrates emotions) and using increasingly sophisticated methods to understand gender differences in how children experience and express emotions (Cole, Martin, & Dennis, 2004; Hubbard et al., 2002). Exploring how girls and boys regulate emotions in their same-gender interactions (and occasional other-gender encounters) may enrich Two Cultures Theory and help us understand why subtle differences may matter a great deal.

Our research group is pursuing three research directions that we believe will augment our understanding of peer relations in middle childhood. We seek to learn more about gender and aggression, developmental origins of social aggression, especially family relationships, and processes by which peers influence one another. In each of these areas of inquiry, we will be guided by Two Cultures Theory in that we seek to understand how social processes may unfold differently for girls and for boys (Maccoby, 2004).

Developmental Origins and Outcomes of Social Aggression

Although there has been a recent proliferation of research on gender and aggression much remains to be understood about the forms and functions of girls' and boys' aggression. Table 11.4 presents a list of the top ten pressing questions for the study of gender and childhood aggression (Underwood, Galen & Paquette, 2001).

As a first step toward answering some of these questions, we are beginning a large, longitudinal study of 300 children and their families beginning when the children are 9 years old. Our overarching goal is to understand developmental origins and outcomes related to social aggression. We are measuring children's social aggression in laboratory observational studies, and also using peer nominations, teacher reports, parent reports, friend reports and self-reports. We seek to refine definitions of social aggression, to understand which behaviors do and do not belong in this construct describing behaviors that harm friendships and social status by using multiple measures to assess social aggression in different social contexts. We acknowledge that most aggressive behaviors hurt in more than one way and serve multiple goals, and that children who behave aggressively likely hurt peers in multiple ways. We believe that at particular points in development, both social and physical aggression may be normative, but that at other points, frequently engaging in these behaviors may be related to psychological maladjustment. Perhaps most importantly, we are testing the possibility that different conceptual frameworks may be needed to understand social aggression, in addition to those that have been useful in illuminating physical aggression. An important part of our work in this area is investigating how parental relationships may contribute to children's propensity to engage in social aggression (we detail this direction below). We plan to move beyond studying gender differences in social aggression to investigating the social processes by which social aggression unfolds for girls and for boys. We also seek to understand how social aggression relates to social and emotional adjustment for each gender group as our sample enters adolescence, by investigating how frequency of engaging in and being victimized by social aggression relates to children's friendships, self-concept, academic adjustment, identity development, behavior problems, depression, anxiety, eating problems, and symptoms of emerging personality disorders.

TABLE 11.4
Top Ten Challenges for Understanding Gender and Aggression

1. Definitions perplex us, in part because aggression occurs in particular social contexts.
2. Most previous research has explored physical aggression among boys.
3. Subtypes abound.
4. Most aggressive behaviors hurt in more than one way, and serve multiple goals.
5. Are some forms of aggression developmentally normative, or personality traits indicating clinical problems?
6. Which children are identified as highly aggressive depends heavily on whether aggressive youth are selected within or across gender groups.
7. Children's gender role stereotypes may strongly influence their own aggressive behaviors and their perceptions of these behaviors in others.
8. Systematically observing aggressive behavior among children is difficult.
9. Conceiving of subtypes of aggression as personality traits may be difficult because aggressive children may engage in multiple forms of aggression.
10. The best understanding of aggression among girls might require different conceptual frameworks and research methods than those that have been used with boys.

Parental Relationships and Children's Peer Relations

A compelling direction for further research on social aggression is examining how parents, particularly mothers, may influence the development of children's social aggression. Mothers may play a unique role in children's peer relations due to the amount of time they spend as socializing agents. Existing research has indicated that mothers influence children's peer interactions in ways that may lead to difficulties. For example, when assessing hypothetical social dilemmas, children and mothers share similar attributions, both negative and positive, as well as anticipate the same consequences and goals (Burks & Parke, 1996). Mothers who display less prosocial and relationship-oriented strategies to settle conflicts have children who engage in more aggression, and who are rated lower in social acceptance (Pettit, Dodge, & Brown, 1988).

In addition to influencing social cognitions and providing instructive advice, other important ways mothers influence children's friendships in positive and negative ways include acting as managers of social opportunities and becoming involved in children's social lives (Hartup, 1979; Parke, 1978). For example, children with mothers who arrange opportunities for peer interaction are more likely to have larger peer networks, and to engage in more frequent play with friends than those having mothers with less involvement (Ladd & Golter, 1988). However, it is unclear from existing research what level of maternal involvement is optimal. We know some about the negative effects of mothers who are not involved in children's social lives, but much less about the effects of mothers becoming over-involved in peer relations. Could mothers who become enmeshed in children's peer relationships promote negative behaviors such as social aggression as a consequence of being overly invested in their children's social lives?

In addition, there is very little previous research investigating how mothers respond to their children's engaging in, or being victimized by social aggression. To date, we have no knowledge of any maternal behaviors related to children's social aggression. Presently, there is no systematic study examining how much mothers know of their child's involvement in social aggression, nor about specific maternal reactive or instructive behaviors related to social aggression. Investigating these variables may inform our understanding of why some children develop and utilize these behaviors more than others. An important next step in understanding the origins of social aggression is the comprehensive investigation of specific parenting characteristics and aspects of the family environment that may contribute to these behaviors in children.

Peer Social Influence

Although parents are without a doubt extremely powerful socialization agents, we believe that our understanding of peer relations in middle childhood can also be augmented by understanding more about peer social influence. Developmental researchers have long been aware of the importance of peer relationships for the socialization of children (e.g., Hartup, 1983; Kupersmidt & Dodge, 2004), and ample evidence exists that children who are successful in their peer relationships have better psychosocial adjustment and outcomes than do children who are rejected by peers (Rubin et al., 1998). Although research findings typically indicate that poor peer relations predict negative outcomes (Parker & Asher, 1987), more recent investigations have shown that positive peer relationships can predict antisocial behaviors as well (Rodkin et al., 2000). Along with the benefits of peer group membership, then, can come certain drawbacks. Peer pressure, for example, has for several decades been one focus of developmental researchers interested in group processes. Erikson (1968) addressed the issue of peer influence in his early writings, hypothesizing that it was the primary channel through which group norms and values are spread. Indeed, the cohesiveness and unity of the group as a whole can be strengthened when group members convince each other to conform to certain norms (Newman & Newman, 1976).

Problems arise, however, when the pressures children exert on each other encourage behaviors that are dangerous, unhealthy, or illegal. Much of children's and adolescents' antisocial behavior occurs in the presence of one or more peers. Peer influence is considered to be one of the most robust predictors of adolescent maladaptive behaviors (Dishion, McCord, & Poulin, 1999). As a result, research has been focused on the issues surrounding peer influence for negative behaviors, such as identifying peer-, self-, and parent-related variables that contribute to peer influence and children's decisions to succumb to it or to resist it.

One important recent advance in the study of peer influence is the change in emphasis from establishing that peer influence is important in the initiation or maintenance of negative behaviors to an emphasis on factors that actually mediate or moderate that influence. By maintaining a focus on the peer group as the context in which influence takes place, researchers have learned much about the factors that contribute (or not) to children's decisions to give in to peer pressure. For example, there are differential effects of peer smoking based on how close the friendship is: while the influence of a best friend's smoking has been shown to be a strong predictor of adolescent smoking, the influence of the social crowd to which adolescents belong is minimal (Urberg, 1992).

An important direction for future research is the extension of peer influence research to younger age groups. Most of this research has focused on adolescents, for good reasons. Behaviors investigated in "peer pressure" studies are typically health-risk-taking behaviors such as smoking, drinking alcohol, and drug use that are simply not as prevalent in childhood as they are in adolescence. Further, the importance of making friends as a way of finding a sense of belonging has been hypothesized to be a more salient developmental task in adolescence (Erikson, 1968). And although children do make attempts to influence the behavior of their peers, there has been an implicit assumption that true peer pressure, arguably the exclusive domain of the adolescent, is the only kind of influence that researchers should be concerned about.

However, we argue that it makes good sense to study these same influence processes in children for at least two reasons. First, it will be interesting to investigate patterns of developmental change in the process of peer influence. When does the desire to manipulate or change the behavior of peers emerge, and how does that desire play out in young dyads or groups? How do the techniques of influence change as children get older? Are the characteristics that make some adolescents effective influencers the same characteristics that make some children good at it, too, or does influence mean different things to different age groups? Similar questions may be asked from the perspective of the target of influence. What are the developmental precursors to having a particularly high or low level of conformity or susceptibility to influence?

It is also important to understand processes of peer influence in childhood because there is empirical evidence that children can indeed persuade each other to do things that might cause harm, and that they can be quite creative in their attempts to do so. For example, in one experimental study, 8- and 9-year-old boys and girls were successful in persuading a friend to travel a more high-risk path than the one the friend had initially chosen, regardless of the increased risk of injury. Those children in the role of influencer were found to use a variety of arguments to support their recommendation of a more dangerous path (Christensen & Morrongiello, 1997). This study highlights the need for further research on both the kinds of influence younger children exert on each other, as well as more underlying influence processes.

Our understanding of children's peer relationships will also be enhanced by examining how peers might influence one another to engage in positive behaviors. As discussed earlier, members of children's social networks tend to be similar in academic motivation (Kindermann, 1993). Group members are similar on academic motivation at the beginning of the year, suggesting that peers choose to affiliate with those similar to them. However, over the course of the school year, network members become even more similar to one another on academic motivation, suggesting that peers might be socializing one another in this domain. It would be fascinating and possibly helpful for intervention purposes to understand more about the social processes by which children influence one another to care more or less about doing well in school, as well as other positive behaviors.

In understanding peer social influence in middle childhood, it will be important to investigate how these processes differ in girls' and boys' peer groups. Two Cultures Theory suggests that boys' groups may encourage misbehavior and support risk taking more than girls' groups do (Maccoby, 1998). Ethnographic evidence suggests that in the middle childhood years, boys and girls may socialize one another differently in the domain of romantic relationships; girls talk about heterosexual relationships in terms of romance and intimacy, whereas boys regale one another with risqué statements about sexual activity (Thorne & Luria, 1986). Studies with older adolescents have not yet detected gender differences in the effects of peer social influence for specific negative behaviors, but few studies have examined carefully how the gender of the influencer and the person being influenced may interact (Hartup, 1999). Fewer studies still have examined how girls and boys may socialize one another during middle childhood, although Two Cultures Theory offers fascinating theoretical propositions (Maccoby, 1998). Given the intensity of children's feelings about belonging to their same-gender peer groups and the strong segregation between girls' and boys' groups in this age range, same gender groups of girls and boys likely exert powerful influences as they tackle increasing academic challenges, navigate the complexities of the friendships, and contemplate romantic relationships as they move toward adolescence.

ACKNOWLEDGMENT

This work was partially supported by NIMH grants R03 MH52110, R29 MH55992, and R01 MH63076.

REFERENCES

Aboud, F. E. (1989). Disagreement between friends. *International Journal of Behavioral Development, 12*, 495–508.

Asher, S. R., Parkhurst, J. T., Hymel, S., & Williams, G. A. (1990). Peer rejection and loneliness in childhood. In S. R. Asher & J. D. Coie (Eds.), *Peer rejection in childhood* (pp. 253–273). New York: Cambridge University Press.

Bagwell, C. L., Coie, J. D., Terry, R. A., & Lochman, J. E. (2000). Peer clique participation and social status in preadolescence. *Merrill-Palmer Quarterly, 46*, 280–305.

Bjorkqvist, K., Lagerspetz, K., & Kaukiainen, A. (1992). Do girls manipulate and do boys fight? Developmental trends in regard to direct and indirect aggression. *Aggressive Behavior, 18*, 117–127.

Brody, L. R. (1997). Beyond stereotypes: Gender and emotion. *Journal of Social Issues, 53*, 369–394.

Buhrmester, D. P. (1996). Need fulfillment, interpersonal competence, and the developmental contexts of early adolescent friendship. In W. M. Bukowski, A. F. Newcomb, & W. W. Hartup (Eds.), *The company they keep: Friendship in childhood and early adolescence* (pp. 159–185). New York: Cambridge University Press.

Burks, V. S., & Parke, R. D. (1996). Parent and child representations of social relationships: Linkages between families and peers. *Merrill-Palmer Quarterly, 42*, 358–378.

Cairns, R. B., & Cairns, B. D. (1994). *Lifelines and risks: Pathways of youth in our time.* New York: Cambridge University Press.

Cairns, R. B., Cairns, B. D., Neckerman, H. J., Ferguson, L. L., & Gariepy, J. (1989). Growth and aggression: 1. Childhood to early adolescence. *Developmental Psychology, 25* (2), 320–330.

Cairns, R. B., Cairns, B. D., Neckerman, H. J., Gest, S. D., & Gariepy, J. L. (1988). Social networks and aggressive behavior: Peer support or peer rejection? *Developmental Psychology, 24*, 815–823.

Christensen, S., & Morrongiello, B. A. (1997). The influence of peers on children's judgments about engaging in behaviors that threaten their safety. *Journal of Applied Developmental Psychology, 18*, 547–562.

Coie, J. D., Cillessen, A. H. N., Dodge, K. A., Hubbard, J. A., Schwartz, D., Lemerise, E. A., & Bateman, H. (1999). It takes two to fight: A test of relational factors and a method for assessing aggressive dyads. *Developmental Psychology, 35*, 1179–1188.

Coie, J. D., Dodge, K. A., & Coppotelli, H. A. (1982). Dimensions and types of social status. *Developmental Psychology, 18*, 557–569.

Coie, J. D., & Kupersmidt, J. B. (1983). A behavioral analysis of emerging status in boys' groups. *Child Development, 54*, 1400–1416.

Cole, P. M., Martin, S. E., & Dennis, T. A. (2004). Emotion regulation as a scientific construct: Methodological challenges and directions for child development research. *Child Development, 75*, 317-333.

Crick, N. R., & Grotpeter, J. K. (1995). Relational aggression, gender, and social-psychological adjustment. *Child Development, 66*, 710–722.

Crombie, G., & DesJardins, M. (1993, April). *Predictors of gender: The relative importance of children's play, games, and personality characteristics.* Paper presented at the Biennial Meeting of the Society for Research in Child Development, New Orleans, LA.

Deaux, K. (2000). Gender and emotion: Notes from a grateful tourist. In A. H. Fischer (Ed.), *Gender and emotion: Social psychological perspectives* (pp. 301–318). Cambridge: Cambridge University Press.

Denton, K., & Zarbatany, L. (1996). Age differences in support processes in conversations between friends. *Child Development, 67*, 1360–1373.

Dishion, T., McCord, J., & Poulin, F. (1999). When interventions harm: Peer groups and problem behavior. *American Psychologist, 54*, 755–764.

Eisenberg, N., & Fabes, R. A. (1999). Emotion, emotion-related regulation, and quality of socioemotional functioning. In L. Balter & C. S. Tamis-LeMonda (Eds.), *Child psychology: A handbook of contemporary issues* (pp. 318–335). Philadelphia: Psychology Press.

Erikson, E. H. (1968). *Identity, youth, and crisis.* New York: Norton.

Erikson, E. H. (1980). Elements of a psychoanalytic theory of psychosocial development. In S. I. Greenspan & G. H. Pollock (Eds.), *The course of life: Psychoanalytic contributions towards understanding personality development: Vol. 1, Infancy and early childhood* (pp. 11–61). Adelphi, MD: NIMH Mental Health Study Center.

Fagot, B. I. (1985). Beyond the reinforcement principle: Another step toward understanding sex role development. *Developmental Psychology, 21*, 1097–1104.

French, D. C. (1988). Heterogeneity of peer-rejected boys:

Aggression and non-aggressive subtypes. *Child Development, 59,* 976–985.

French, D. C. (1990). Heterogeneity of peer-rejected girls. *Child Development, 61,* 2028–2031.

Freud, S. (1905). Three essays on the theory of sexuality. In J. Strachey (Ed.), *The complete psychological works* (Vol. 7). New York: Norton.

Galen, B. R., & Underwood, M. K. (1997). A developmental investigation of social aggression among children. *Developmental Psychology, 33,* 589–600.

Gnepp, J., & Hess, D. L. (1986). Children's understanding of verbal and facial display rules. *Developmental Psychology, 22,* 103–108.

Gottman, J. M., & Mettetal, G. (1986). Speculations about social and affective development: Friendship and acquaintanceship through adolescence. In J. M. Gottman & J. G. Parker (Eds.), *Conversations with friends: Speculations on affective development* (pp. 192–237). New York: Cambridge University Press.

Harris, P. L. (1993). Understanding emotion. In M. Lewis & J. M. Haviland (Eds.), *Handbook of emotions* (pp. 237–246). New York: Guilford.

Hartup, W. W. (1970). Peer interaction and social organization. In P. H. Mussen (Ed.), *Carmichael's manual of child psychology*. New York: Wiley.

Hartup, W. W. (1979). The social worlds of childhood. *American Psychologist, 34,* 944–950.

Hartup, W. W. (1983). Peer relations. In E. M. Hetherington (Ed.), *Handbook of child psychology: Socialization, personality, and social development* (Vol. 4). New York: Wiley.

Hartup, W. W. (1989). Social relationships and their developmental significance. *American Psychologist, 44,* 120–126.

Hartup, W. W. (1999). Constraints on peer socialization: Let me count the ways. *Merrill-Palmer Quarterly, 45,* 172–183.

Hartup, W. W., & Abecassis, M. (2002). Friends and enemies. In P. K. Smith & C. H. Hart (Eds.), *Blackwell handbook of social development* (pp. 285–306). Oxford: Blackwell Publishers.

Hartup, W. W., French, D. C., Laursen, B. Johnston, M. K., & Ogawa, J. R. (1993). Conflict and friendship patterns in middle childhood: Behavior in a closed field situation. *Child Development, 64,* 445–454.

Hubbard, J. A., & Coie, J. D. (1994). Emotional correlates of social competence in children's peer relationships. *Merrill-Palmer Quarterly, 40,* 1–20.

Hubbard, J. A., Smithmyer, C. M., Ramsden, S. R., Parker, E. H., Flanagan, K. D., Dearing, K. F., Relyea, N., & Simons, R. F. (2002). Observational, physiological, and self-report measures of children's anger: Relations to reactive versus proactive aggression. *Child Development, 73,* 1101–1118.

Hymel, S., Wagner, E., & Butler, L. J. (1990). Reputational bias: View from the peer group. In S. R. Asher & J. D. Coie (Eds.), *Peer rejection in childhood* (pp. 156–186). New York: Cambridge University Press.

Jacklin, C. N., & Maccoby, E. E. (1978). Social behavior at 33 months in same sex and mixed-sex dyads. *Child Development, 49,* 557–569.

Kindermann, T. A. (1993). Natural peer groups as contexts for individual development: The case of children's motivation at school. *Developmental Psychology, 29,* 970–977.

Kohlberg, L., LaCrosse, J., & Ricks, D. (1972). The predictability of adult mental health from childhood behavior. In B. Wolman (Ed.), *Manual of child psychopathology* (pp. 1217–1284). New York: McGraw-Hill.

Kupersmidt, J. B. & Coie, J. D. (1990). Preadolescent peer status, aggression, and school adjustment as predictors of externalizing problems in adolescence. *Child Development, 61,* 1350–1362.

Kupersmidt, J. B., & Dodge, K. A. (Eds., 2004) *Children's peer relations: From developmental science to intervention.* Washington, DC: American Psychological Association.

Ladd, G. W., & Golter, B. S. (1988). Parents' management of preschooler's peer relations: Is it related to children's social competence? *Developmental Psychology, 24,* 109–117.

LaFontana, K.M., & Cillessen, A. H. N. (1998). The nature of children's stereotypes of popularity. *Social Development, 7,* 301–320.

LaFontana, K. M., & Cillessen, A. H. N. (2002). Children's perceptions of popular and unpopular peers: A multimethod assessment. *Developmental Psychology, 38,* 635–647.

Laursen, B. (1996). Closeness and conflict in adolescent peer relationships: Interdependence with friends and romantic partners. In W. M. Bukowski, A. F. Newcomb, & W. W. Hartup (Eds.), *The company they keep: Friendship in childhood and adolescence* (pp. 186–210). New York: Cambridge University Press.

Laursen, B., Hartup, W. W., & Koplas, A. L. (1996). Towards an understanding of peer conflict. *Merrill-Palmer Quarterly, 42*(1), 76–102.

Leaper, C. (1991). Influence and involvement in children's discourse: Age, gender, and partner effects. *Child Development, 62,* 797–811.

Lemerise, E. A., & Arsenio, W. F. (2000). An integrated model of emotion processes and cognition in social information processing. *Child Development, 71,* 107–118.

Lempers, J. D., & Clark-Lempers, D. S. (1992). Young, middle, and late adolescents' comparisons of the functional importance of five significant relationships. *Journal of Youth and Adolescence, 21*(1), 53–96.

Maccoby, E. E. (1990). Gender and relationships: A developmental account. *American Psychologist, 45* (4), 513–520.

Maccoby, E. E. (1994). Commentary: Gender segregation in childhood. In C. Leaper (Ed.) *Childhood gender segregation: Causes and consequences, New Directions in Child Development, 65,* 87–98.

Maccoby, E. E. (1998). *The two sexes: Growing up apart, coming together.* Cambridge: Harvard University Press.

Maccoby, E. E.. (2004). Aggression in the context of gender development. In M. Putallaz & K. L. Bierman (Eds.), *Aggression, Antisocial Behavior, and Violence among Girls: A Developmental Perspective* (pp. 3–22). NY: Guilford.

Maccoby, E. E., & Jacklin, C. N. (1987). Gender segregation in childhood. In H. Reese (Ed.), *Advances in child behavior and development.* New York: Academic Press.

Miller, P. M., Danaher, D. L., & Forbes, D. (1986). Sex-related strategies for coping of interpersonal conflict in children ages 5 to 7. *Development Psychology, 22,* 543–548.

Moely, B. E., Skarin K., & Weil, S. (1979). Sex differences in competition-cooperation behavior of children at two age levels. *Sex Roles, 5* (3), 329–342.

Moreno, J. L. (1934). *Who shall survive? A new approach to the problem of human interrelations.* Washington, DC: Nervous and Mental Disease Publishing.

Murphy, B., & Eisenberg, N. (1996). Provoked by a peer: Children's anger-related responses and their relation to social functioning. *Merrill-Palmer Quarterly, 42,* 103–124.

Newcomb, A. F., Bukowski, W. M., & Pattee, L. (1993). Children's peer relations: A meta-analytic review of popular, rejected, neglected, controversial, and average status. *Psychological Bulletin, 113,* 99–128.

Newman, P. R., & Newman, B. M. (1976). Early adolescence and its conflicts: Group identity vs. alienation. *Adolescence, 11*, 261–274.

Olweus, D. (1991). Bully/victim problems among schoolchildren: Basic facts and effects of a school-based intervention program. In D. J. Pepler & K. H. Rubin (Eds.), *The development and treatment of childhood aggression* (pp. 411–448). Hillsdale, NJ: Erlbaum.

Paquette, J. A., & Underwood, M. K. (1999). Young adolescents' experiences of peer victimization: Gender differences in accounts of social and physical aggression. *Merrill-Palmer Quarterly, 45*, 233–258.

Parke, R. D. (1978). The father's role in infancy: A re-evaluation. *Journal of Pediatric Psychology. 3*, 9–13.

Parke, R. D. (1994). Progress, paradigms, and unresolved problems: A commentary of recent advances in our understanding of children's emotions. *Merrill-Palmer Quarterly, 40*, 157–169.

Parker, J. G., & Asher, S. R. (1987). Peer relations and later personal adjustment: Are low-accepted children at greater risk? *Psychological Bulletin, 102*, 357–389.

Parker, J. G., & Asher, S. R. (1993). Friendship and friendship quality in middle childhood: Links between peer group acceptance and feelings of loneliness and social dissatisfaction. *Developmental Psychology, 29*(4), 611–621.

Parkhurst, J. T., & Hopmeyer, A. (1998). Sociometric popularity and peer-perceived popularity: Two distinct dimensions of peer status. *The Journal of Early Adolescence, 18*, 125–144.

Pettit, G. S., Dodge, K. A., Brown, M. M. (1988). Early family experience, social problem solving patterns, and children's social competence. *Child Development, 59*, 107–120.

Piaget, J. (1983). Piaget's theory. In P. H. Mussen (Ed.), *Handbook of child psychology: Vol. 1, history, theory and methods* (4th ed., pp. 1–25). New York: Wiley.

Rodkin, P. C., Farmer, T. W., Pearl, R., & Van Acker, R. (2000). Heterogeneity of popular boys: Antisocial and prosocial configurations. *Developmental Psychology, 36*, 14–24.

Rubin, K. H., Bukowski, W. & Parker, J. G. (1998). Peer interactions, relationships, and groups. In N. Eisenberg (Ed.), *Handbook of child psychology* (pp. 619–700). New York: Wiley.

Saarni, C. (1999). *The development of emotional competence.* New York: Guilford Press.

Saarni, C., & von Salisch, M. (1993). The socialization of emotional dissemblance. In M. Lewis & C. Saarni, (Eds.), *Lying and deception in everyday life* (pp. 106–125). New York: Guilford Press.

Serbin, L. A., Moller, L., Gulko, J., Powlishta, K. K., & Colbourne, K. A. (1994). The emergence of gender segregation in toddler playgroups. In C. Leaper (Ed.), *Childhood gender segregation: Causes and consequences, New Directions in Child Development, 65*, 7–18.

Serbin, L.A., Powlishta, K. K., & Gulko, J. (1993). The development of sex typing in middle childhood. *Monographs of the SRCD, 58*(2, Serial No. 232), 1–75.

Sullivan, H. S. (1953). *The interpersonal theory of psychiatry.* New York: W. W. Norton.

Terry, R., & Coie, J. D. (1991). A comparison of methods for defining sociometric status among children. *Developmental Psychology, 27*(5), 867–880.

Thorne, B., & Luria, Z. (1986). Sexuality and gender in children's daily worlds. *Social Problems, 33*, 176–190.

Underwood, M. K. (1992, April). Peer social status and the development of anger expression. In T. A. Kinderman (Chair), *Peer group networks as contexts for children's development.* Invited symposium conducted at the annual convention of the Western Psychological Association, Portland, Oregon.

Underwood, M. K. (1997). Peer social status and children's choices about the expression and control of positive and negative emotions. *Merrill-Palmer Quarterly, 43*(4), 610–634.

Underwood, M. K. (2003). *Social aggression among girls.* Guilford.

Underwood, M. K., Coie, J. D., & Herbsman, C. R. (1992). Display rules for anger and aggression in school-aged children. *Child Development, 63*, 366–380.

Underwood, M. K., Galen, B. R., & Paquette, J. A. (2001). Top ten challenges for understanding aggression and gender: Why can't we all just get along? *Social Development, 10*(2), 248–267.

Underwood, M. K., Hurley, J. C., Johanson, C. A., & Mosley, J. E. (1999). An Experimental, observational investigation of children's responses to peer provocation: Developmental and gender differences in middle childhood. *Child Development, 70*, 1428–1446.

Underwood, M.K., Schockner, A.S., & Hurley, J.C. (2001). Children's responses to provocation by same- and opposite-gender peers: An experimental, observational study with 8-, 10-, and 12-Year-Olds. *Developmental Psychology, 37*, 362–372.

Underwood, M. K., Scott, B. L., Galperin, M., Bjornstad, G. J., & Sexton, A. E. (2004). *An experimental, observational study of social aggression: Gender and developmental differences, Child Development, 75*, 1538–1555.

Urberg, K. (1992). Locus of peer influence: Social crowd and best friend. *Journal of Youth and Adolescence, 21*, 439–450.

Whitesell, N. R., & Harter, S. (1996). The interpersonal consequences of emotion: Anger with close friends and classmates. *Child Development, 67*, 1345–1359.

Zarbatany, L., Ghesquierre, K., & Mohr, K. (1992). A context perspective on early adolescents' friendship expectations. *Journal of Early Adolescence, 12*(1), 111–126.

Zarbatany, L., Hartmann, D. P., & Rankin, D. B. (1990). The psychological functions of preadolescent peer activities. *Child Development, 61*, 1067–1080.

Zarbatany, L., McDougall, P., & Hymel, S. (2000). Gender-differentiated experience in the peer culture: Links to intimacy in preadolescence. *Social Development, 9*, 62–79.

12

Appreciating the Meaning and Aesthetics of Spatial-Graphic Representations During Childhood

Lynn S. Liben

INTRODUCTION

All organisms live in a real, physical world. A core challenge for developmental psychologists is to explain how individuals come to know that world. Virtually any explanation—irrespective of whether it is rooted in a theory that emphasizes biological hard-wiring, associative learning, or self-directed constructive processes—recognizes the key role played by the individual's direct exploration of, and interaction with that real, physical world. As humans, however, we learn about our world not only by interacting with it directly, but also by using depictions of it, that is, external representations that convey information about some aspect of the physical world. Representations are as varied as verbal descriptions, photographs, maps, satellite images, paintings, television images, diagrams, graphs, blueprints, numerical equations, x-rays, and scale models (e.g., see Ittleson, 1996; Liben, 1999; Tversky, 2001).

It is readily apparent that one subset of these representations will be difficult for children to understand and will require social guidance to master. These are arbitrary or unmotivated representations, that is, those that do not have inherent similarities to their referents. Much of our educational curriculum is directed to teaching children how to understand and produce representations such as verbal language and mathematical notation whose referential meaning is assigned by convention.

At first glance, it may appear that another subset of these representations—those that have been called *spatial-graphic representations* (Liben, 1999)—will be easy to understand and will require little formal or informal instruction to master. These are two-dimensional representations in which at least some aspects of the way that graphic marks are arranged are motivated by (that is, correspond to, or are isomorphic with) the spatial features of the referents for which they stand. For example, a line drawing of a cat may be expected to be easy to interpret because the relative size, shape, and position of the head, ears, nose, and whiskers of the drawn cat are isomorphic with the size, shape, and position of the head, ears, nose, and whiskers of the real cat. Consistent with the expectation that spatial-graphic representations may be understood relatively easily is research showing that even infants categorize pictorial representations similarly to the way they categorize the objects they represent. For example,

DeLoache, Strauss, and Maynard (1979) reported that after 5-month-old infants were habituated to an actual object, they then responded to photographs similarly to the way they would if they had been presented with additional objects. That is, they remained habituated if the photograph showed the same object, but responded with renewed attention if the picture showed a novel object.

Despite the indications that even very young children can see through graphic representations to the referents that lie beneath them, there is ample evidence that young children do not understand spatial-graphic representations fully. In this chapter I review conceptual arguments and empirical data leading to the conclusion that mastery of spatial-graphic representations does not occur automatically and early, but instead follows a gradual and sometimes effortful process that extends well into (and even beyond) childhood.

The mastering of spatial-graphic representations is a multifaceted achievement. In the remainder of the introduction, I overview the representational, spatial, and aesthetic facets of mastery. In the second section, I highlight earlier developmental approaches to these three domains. In the third section I focus on our conceptual and empirical work on graphic representations. In keeping with the placement of the current chapter within Part III, Childhood, I draw most of my examples from work with children who have entered the school years. I do, however, include some material from both younger (preschool) and older (college) age groups as a way of addressing, respectively, the foundations on which the achievements of childhood rest and the more sophisticated levels of mastery to which at least some individuals may be presumed to be heading. In the closing section, I offer some conclusions based on work to date, and suggest some fruitful areas for additional research.

Facets of Understanding

The premise of the work discussed in this chapter is that understanding graphic representations involves a number of facets, summarized in Table 12.1. The first, *referential meaning,* is the most obvious: recognizing the denotative meaning of the representation. For example, when a viewer who is asked to interpret a painting of a cat answers "It's a cat," the viewer has demonstrated understanding of referential meaning. However, as Figure 12.1 reminds us, images like these are not, in fact, their referents. The painting of the cat is a *painting,* not a cat, just as the image in Figure 12.1 is a *photograph,* not a pipe. Being aware of a representation's own existence *as* a representation constitutes the second facet of understanding, *representational awareness.*

But even having interpreted the referential meaning of a representation and having recognized that the representation is a thing in itself, it remains challenging to appreciate these two roles simultaneously. Thus, a third facet of understanding, *representational duality,* is reconciling that something can have an existence in its own right and simultaneously carry meaning about something else (DeLoache, 1987; Potter, 1979). What is challenging is not only recognizing duality at the general level of the representation, but also at the level of individual parts of the representation (which have been called, respectively, "holistic" and "componential" levels, see Liben & Downs, 1991). For this third facet, the user must understand that some qualities of the representation are informative about the

TABLE 12.1
Facets of Understanding Spatial-Graphic Representations

Referential meaning	Identifying the referent
Representational awareness	Recognizing that there *is* a representation as distinct from the referent
Representational duality	Differentiating qualities that carry "stand for" meaning and qualities that adhere in the representation itself at both global and componential levels
Spatial meaning	Understanding representational vantage point; interpreting spatial qualities of and among referents; and integrating spatial relations among referent, representation, and user
Aesthetic awareness	Appreciating that there is an aesthetic quality of graphic representations
Aesthetic duality	Differentiating aesthetic qualities of the representation from aesthetic qualities of the referent

Figure 12.1   Photograph inspired by Magritte's painting, *Ceci ne'est pas une pipe*. Reproduced from Liben (2003a) with permission.

referent, and some are simply qualities of the representation itself. For example, the location of the ears on the photographic cat carries referential meaning about the location of the ears on the real cat, but neither the flatness nor size of the image implies anything about the flatness and size of the real animal. Instead, these latter qualities adhere in the representation.

A fourth facet involves understanding several kinds of *spatial meaning* contained in representations. Included is information about the vantage point from which the referent is depicted. As shown graphically in Figure 12.2, vantage point is defined along three spatial dimensions: *viewing distance* (the contrast between a close-up vs. a distant photograph of, for example, a pipe), *viewing angle* (the slant along the vertical axis, as in the contrast between viewing a pipe from directly overhead vs. viewing it from straight ahead), and *viewing azimuth* (the direction from which the referent is approached, as in the contrast between viewing a pipe from the side vs. from its end). Representations also provide information about spatial features of individual components of the referent (e.g., the curved shape of the pipe's bowl), spatial relations among components of the referent (e.g., the right

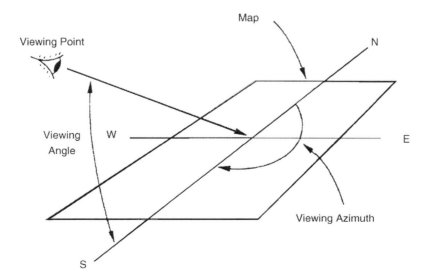

Figure 12.2   The three spatial qualities of representational vantage point. Modified from Downs (1981).

angular connection between the pipe's bowl and stem), and relations between one referent and another (e.g., the pipe is on the table).

The final facets of understanding listed in Table 12.1 lie in the aesthetic domain, focusing on the expressive nature of representations. *Aesthetic awareness* refers to understanding that the representation may be interpreted or experienced with respect to dimensions such as beauty or emotional impact; *aesthetic duality* refers to differentiating between expressive or aesthetic experiences that are afforded by the representation as distinct from those that would be afforded by the referent itself.

HISTORICAL BACKGROUND

The domains identified as relevant for understanding spatial-graphic representations—representation, space, and aesthetics—have important histories within developmental psychology. I next highlight past approaches and controversies within each.

Representation

Representations are the tools that enable the child to move from thinking and reasoning about the here and now, to thinking and reasoning about things that are not currently in view (e.g., a toy in the next room or a grandparent who visited last week), have never been in view (e.g., a new school), or could never be in view (e.g., a unicorn). Although there is little controversy that representation is central to cognition, there is considerable controversy about how early and in what form the ability to form and use representations emerges.

In a classic and broad theory of representational development, Piaget (1951) argued that infants' representational capacity develops only gradually. At first, infants interpret only *indices*. These are inherent parts of referents (e.g., smoke is an index of fire), and because they are not completely distinct from the referent, are not considered to be true representations. Piaget proposed that the true symbolic function develops gradually during the sensorimotor period (roughly the first two years of life). Infants first come to understand representations that are motivated by the referent (referred to as *symbols*, as in a picture of a cat), and then understand those connected to the referent by arbitrary assignment (referred to as *signs*, as in the word "cat"). Bruner (1964) proposed an expanded developmental progression, suggesting that children begin with action-based or *enactive* representations (as in representing a rattle with a shaking hand), then use visually-isomorphic images or *iconic* representations, and finally use arbitrary *symbols* such as words. Although their terminologies differ, Piaget and Bruner shared the view that the ability to understand representations is not inborn, and that there is an age-linked progression in the types and flexibility of representations available.

More recent work has suggested that the ability to create and access some kinds of representations is present extremely early. For example, even within a day or two of birth, infants have been found to imitate adults' facial actions, a finding taken to imply that infants encoded and stored and later retrieved some representation of the observed event (Meltzoff & Moore, 1977). Also taken as suggestive of babies' ability to form and use representations are demonstrations that information acquired from one sensory modality is extended to another. For example, 1-month-old infants given either a bumpy or smooth pacifier to suck (tactile modality) were found to prefer looking at the matching picture (visual modality) of that pacifier (Meltzoff & Borton, 1979). These and related recent empirical studies have resulted in some heated debates (e.g., see Haith, 1998; Mueller & Overton, 1998; Smith, 1999; Spelke, 1999) about whether there is true representation during infancy.

Once the focus is on toddlers or preschoolers, however, there is little question about the existence of representational thinking. By this age, the key questions concern whether representational systems undergo qualitative or merely quantitative development, what kinds of representational systems are available (e.g., numerical, linguistic, spatial), and whether young children are able to consider multiple (especially conflicting) representations simultaneously or in quick sequence (e.g., Zelazo, Mueller, Frye, & Marcovitch, 2003).

Another major research thrust has been aimed at identifying mechanisms that facilitate children's developing representational competence during and beyond the preschool years. For example, research has addressed the impact of parents' tendency to discuss objects, people, or events that are spatially or temporally distant (e.g., Sigel, 1978; Sigel & McGillicuddy-De Lisi, 1984), parents' guidance of their children's understanding of words and pictures (e.g., Gauvain, de la Ossa, & Hurtado, 2001; Snow & Ninio, 1986; Szechter & Liben, 2004), exposure to a bilingual environment (e.g., Bialystok & Martin, 2004), and experience with representational media such as videotape (e.g. Troseth, 2003). Researchers have also sought to catalogue children's emerging meta-cognitive understanding of specific representational systems and distinctions among them (e.g., Bialystok, 2000; Ferreiro & Teberosky, 1982).

Space

Space, like many other concepts that seem intuitively simple, is in actuality difficult to define. Philosophers have debated the question, *What is space?* since antiquity (see Jammer, 1954; Liben, 1981). Within psychology, space has been studied in a number of arenas. For example, questions about visual space (e.g., how people see distance, depth, or size of objects in their visual field) are studied within the field of visual perception (e.g., Gibson, 1979; Marr, 1982), those about motor space (e.g., how people interact with the immediately surrounding physical space as in walking through it or grasping at objects within it) are addressed within the field of kinesiology or motor performance (e.g., Rosenbaum, Meulenbroek, Vaughan, & Jansen, 2001), those of large-scale space (e.g., how people develop and then rely upon cognitive maps as they think about and travel through familiar neighborhoods or novel cities) are studied within the field of environmental psychology or behavioral geography (e.g., Downs & Stea, 1977; Lynch, 1960; Stokols & Altman, 1987), and questions about mental space (e.g., how people rotate mental images of objects or figures) are studied within cognitive psychology (e.g., Shepard & Cooper, 1986).

Within developmental psychology, the same kinds of questions have been addressed, but with a particular focus on describing and explaining at what point in life these skills emerge and mature. Developmental psychologists have also generally been more concerned than their nondevelopmental colleagues with the study of group and individual differences (e.g., Eliot, 1987; Liben, 1991, 2002; Linn & Petersen, 1985; Thomas & Turner, 1991) as a way to provide insights into how spatial development is linked to organismic variables (e.g., inherited spatial abilities, see Thomas, 1983) and experiential factors (e.g., participation in certain kinds of activities, see Signorella, Jamison, & Krupa, 1989).

The theoretical and empirical controversies surrounding spatial functioning are much like those concerning representational functioning discussed earlier. That is, research has involved cataloguing how early, and under what conditions, spatial processes and representations emerge. Again, it was Piaget (1954) who posited a gradual and extended period of spatial development. He suggested that it took the entire sensorimotor period for infants to develop such fundamental ideas as the understanding that they are separate entities from the space that envelopes them, that objects continue to exist in space even when unseen, and that the various perceptual spaces (e.g., visual space, tactile space, auditory space) can be integrated into a single, encompassing whole. Further, he argued that even those kinds of accomplishments fell under the relatively primitive domain of *spatial action* or *behavior*. It was not until children entered the preschool years that *spatial representation* was said to emerge.

With respect to spatial representation, Piaget and Inhelder (1956) posited that during the preschool years, children constructed topological concepts that involve "rubber sheet" spatial qualities, that is, those remain unchanged as a surface is stretched (e.g., open vs. closed figures; on vs. next to). Children were then said to construct projective and Euclidean (or metric) concepts. The former involve "point of view" qualities, that is, those that change with the viewer's perspective (e.g., right vs. left or in front vs. behind) and the latter involve the use of abstract spatial systems such as Cartesian coordinates, allowing conservation of distance and angle. As was true for representation, investigators who followed Piaget have reported far earlier emergence of spatial functions. For example, investigators have reported young infants succeeding in integrating cues across perceptual modalities (e.g.,

Starkey, Spelke, & Gelman, 1983), grasping accurately at objects in space (Jonsson & von Hofsten, 2003), and demonstrating sensitivity to locations with substantial metric precision (e.g., Newcombe & Huttenlocher, 2000).

The "early versus late" and "qualitative versus quantitative change" controversies that have been evident in the literature on spatial behaviors during infancy have likewise been evident in the literature on spatial concepts and representations during childhood. For example, in contrast to Piaget's description of the gradual and relatively late emergence of children's abilities to understand projective and metric concepts, others have reported very early metric and angular inferences in wayfinding (e.g., Landau, Gleitman, & Spelke, 1981) and uses of vertical and horizontal coordinate axes to locate points in space (Somerville & Bryant, 1985). Debates, often heated, concern what successes and failures do and do not mean (e.g., see Blaut, 1997a, 1997b; Downs & Liben, 1997; Liben, 1988, 2003a; Liben & Downs, 1989, 1997; Mandler, 1988; Newcombe & Huttenlocher, 2000; Morrongiello, Timney, Humphrey, Anderson, & Skory, 1995)

Aesthetics

Of the three domains, aesthetics has received the least attention, perhaps an index of a more general view that art is an expendable luxury in both academic research and public education. Yet, art appears to be a part of all human societies, even when physical survival is at risk (Winner, 1982). Its ubiquity, alone, makes it worthy of developmental inquiry. Further, aesthetic development may be linked to development in realms as varied as cognition, self-identity, self-esteem, and intergroup relations (see Liben & Szechter, 2002).

Most developmental work on aesthetics has centered on the visual arts. Parsons (1987), for example, proposed a five-stage model of children's developing understanding and appreciation of art that begins with idiosyncratic aesthetic preferences based on a specific feature (as in liking a painting because it is predominated by one's favorite color) and ends with judgments incorporating multiple factors such as style and artistic intent. Other developmental psychologists have been concerned primarily with children's developing artistic productions (e.g., Golomb, 2004; Milbraith, 1998).

Data from controlled empirical work are consistent with the notion that children begin by making aesthetic judgments by focusing on content, and only later develop an aesthetic that also includes style (e.g., Freeman, 1995; Gardner, 1970; Gardner & Gardner, 1970, 1973). Some investigators have suggested that full sensitivity to aesthetic properties such as composition (the way the components of an art work are organized) does not appear until adolescence (e.g., Winner, Rosenblatt, Windmueller, Davidson, & Gardner, 1986), although others have argued that even young children can display aesthetic sensitivity if given age-appropriate tasks and if an aesthetic stance is modeled by adults (e.g., Callaghan, 2000; Callaghan & MacFarlane, 1998; Hardiman & Zernich, 1985).

Taken together, the history of theory and research in all three topics—representation, space, and aesthetics—lead to the conclusion that it is probably more productive to avoid framing research questions in dichotomous terms (e.g., "Do children at age X have capacity Y?") and substitute more nuanced questions such as "Under what conditions and with what experiences is some representational, spatial, or aesthetic sensitivity evident?" We have tried to use the latter kinds of questions in guiding our program of research, described next.

RESEARCH ON CHILDREN'S DEVELOPING UNDERSTANDING OF SPATIAL-GRAPHIC REPRESENTATIONS

Overview

This section of the chapter is focused on our program of research. I begin by describing conceptual frameworks, and then sample from our empirical work on children's developing understanding of the representational, spatial, and aesthetic meaning of spatial-graphic representations.

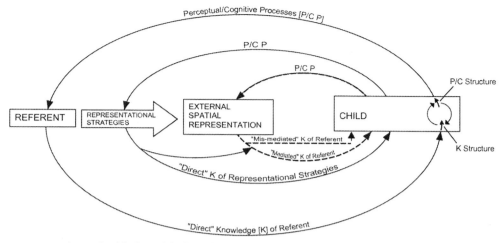

Figure 12.3   The Embedded Model of the developmental understanding of spatial-graphic representations. Adapted from Liben (1999) with permission.

Theoretical Foundations

Figure 12.3 depicts the "Embedded Model" that I have used to conceptualize children's developing understanding of spatial-graphic representations. Although the figure is graphically complex and requires an extended discussion to explicate it completely (see Liben, 1999), the core ideas are relatively straightforward and can be highlighted here briefly.

Most broadly, the model rejects a simple "transparency" view that assumes a viewer (here the child) automatically sees through the representation and understands the referent for which it stands. Instead, the model assumes that understanding a given representation relies on the viewer's use of constructive perceptual and cognitive processes directed at both the referent and the representation itself. The former allows the child to construct direct knowledge of the referent, and the latter to construct "mediated" knowledge. Further, the model posits that there is a third target to which these constructive processes are directed—representational strategies. Thus, to fully understand the meaning of a graphic representation, it is necessary to appreciate something about the media-specific techniques (e.g., photography or cartography) relevant to a particular representation. Absent this understanding, the child runs the risk of inappropriately inferring that some quality of a representation is meant to carry meaning about a quality of the referent, and thus leading to what I have called a "mis-mediated" understanding of the referent. As these processes continue, the child's understanding of which qualities reside in the referent and which qualities reside in the representation progresses. The milestones of understanding are summarized in Table 12.2, while Table 12.3 links these competencies to age.

Empirical Work

Referential Understanding

A core question concerning referential understanding concerns the emergence of understanding of the denotative meaning of representations. There is considerable research asking whether individuals show this understanding virtually from birth or if they instead must develop it gradually, and if the latter, what kinds of perceptual, neurological, physical, and social experiences contribute to its development. Most of the research exploring this foundational knowledge concerns the chronological period well before that covered by the current chapter. That is, errors suggesting general confusion between representations and referents are typically made by children younger than 3. For example, it is infants and toddlers who have difficulty appreciating that a location shown in a scale model stands for

TABLE 12.2
Progressive Competencies in Understanding External Spatial Representations

I.   **Referential Content**. The viewer begins to identify the referential meaning of the representation, with varying ease depending upon the physical similarity of representation and referent. Thus, the viewer "understands" the representation in the sense of identifying the denoted referent, but appears to confuse them (as in trying to pick up a depicted object).

II. **Global Differentiation.** The viewer identifies the denotative meaning of the representation, distinguishes the representation and referent, and responds to each differentially. The viewer does not, however, reflect upon the correspondence between the two. The "stand for" relation is implicit in identification, but not generally subject to intentional manipulation.

III. **Representational Insight.** The viewer distinguishes between representation and referent, and intentionally interprets or assigns "stand for" meaning to the representation. Representational insight occurs first for objects that are inherently representational (as a photograph) and only later for objects that do not normally function as representations, but rather are most salient as objects in their own right (as a scale model).

IV. **Attribute Differentiation.** The viewer comes to appreciate that some, but not all attributes of the representation are motivated by attributes of the referent, and that some, but not all attributes of the referent motivate graphic attributes of the representation. Until doing so, the viewer inappropriately expects that attributes of the representation necessarily mimic attributes of the referent (as in inferring that a red line means a red road) and that attributes of the referent will necessarily be mimicked by attributes of the representation (as in expecting that a large building will appear large in the representation).

V.   **Correspondence Mastery.** The viewer extends the prior understanding of attribute differentiation to develop understanding of the formal representational and geometric correspondences between representation and referent. The former allows the viewer to understand the referential content of symbols; the latter allows the viewer to understand the referential meaning of graphic space.

VI. **Meta-representation.** The viewer is able to reflect upon the mechanisms by which, and the purposes for which, graphic representations are created, including understanding that different correspondence rules and conventions are used in different media (as in maps vs. graphs), different traditions (as in Western vs. Asian art), and different renditions (as in a world map in a Mercator vs. a Peters projection). As a result, the viewer is able to understand representations not simply as convenient substitutions for referents, but rather as cognitive tools that enrich understanding of the referent, and to select among them appropriately for particular purposes.

Reproduced from Liben (1999) with permission.

the analogous location in the referent room (DeLoache, 1987); and who show signs of profound scale errors as in trying to sit down on a dollhouse-sized chair (DeLoache, Uttal, & Rosengren, 2004).

By the age of about 3 years, children are typically able to appreciate the referential intent of spatial-graphic representations as a whole, that is, to demonstrate facility in the first three competencies shown earlier in Table 12.2. It is at this age and beyond that we have concentrated our research. The specific studies I describe are those in which we show children spatial-graphic representations (either aerial photographs or maps) of large-scale environments (such as a city or a college campus), and ask them to identify the referential content.

In our initial work (Liben & Downs, 1991), we interviewed children age 3 to 6 years with a series of place representations such as a road map of Pennsylvania, a small scale aerial photograph of Chicago, and a medium scale aerial photograph of the local community. We began with general questions about the referent such as *What do you think this shows?* Even the youngest children answered correctly at the holistic level in that they almost uniformly provided some kind of place-related response, even if some were imprecise or inaccurate about the specifics (e.g., "A city ... because there's so much stuff in there–houses, roads, buildings." "It's a lots of buildings." "It's a big state." "That's the United States. Because the United States has a lot of people and a lot of cars and a lot of roads.").

Most of these young children were, however, confused when answering identification questions about specific components of the representations. Their errors implied that they were having difficulty differentiating between attributes of the representation and attributes of the referent (see Table 12.2), with spatial attributes proving to be especially troublesome. In discussing the challenges of spatial

TABLE 12.3
Developmental Progression in Understanding External Spatial Representations

Age Group	Competency					
	Referential Content	Global Differentiation	Representational Insight	Attribute Differentiation	Correspondence Mastery	Meta-Representation
Infants	(shaded)	o				
Toddlers	•	(shaded)	o			
Preschoolers	•	o	(shaded)	o		
Young Children	•	•	o	(shaded)	o	
Older Children	•	•	•	o	(shaded)	o
Adolescents +	•	•	•	•	o	(shaded)

Note. Shaded cells indicate focal competency under development. Cells marked with a closed circle indicate that the basic competence has been achieved, although further minor development may still be occurring. Cells marked with an open circle indicate that development of the competency is underway. Blank cells indicate that little development is yet under way. Definitions of competencies are given in Table 12.2

attributes, it is useful to return to the spatial features illustrated in Figure 12.2—viewing distance, viewing angle, and viewing azimuth.

Viewing distance affects the size of a depiction. For example, if one is representing (e.g., photographing) a building from a great distance, the representation of the building would be very small even though the building itself is very large. Viewing angle affects the shape of the representation. Thus, for example, a circular children's wading pool photographed or drawn from directly overhead (i.e., a vertical or nadir view) would be perfectly round, whereas one photographed or drawn from a slanted angle (an oblique view) would be elliptical. The task of identifying referential meaning of a component of a representation thus draws on understanding both scale and viewing angle.

Consistent with this analysis, we found that children often made errors of interpretation that could be attributed to confusion about scale. Children evidenced difficulty in separating out depicted (representational) size from actual (referent) size. One 4-year-old boy, for example, denied that a rectangular shape on an aerial photograph of campus could possibly be his father's office building because it was so small, and his father's building was "Huge! It's as big as this whole map!" Another denied that a line on a road map could show a road "because it's not fat enough for two cars to go on." Similarly, we found children made errors that could be attributed to confusion about viewing angle. Thus, for example, what was in actuality a triangular shaped parking area was misidentified by a preschooler as a "hill," an error that can readily be understood by assuming that the child was interpreting that part of the image as if it had been photographed from straight ahead (an elevation view) rather than from overhead. Similarly, we (Liben & Downs, 1991) and others (Spencer, Harrison, & Darvizeh, 1980) found preschoolers interpreting tennis courts as "doors." Again, this interpretation makes sense if one were to assume that this part of the image had been photographed from straight ahead (so that what were in reality the lines on the tennis court would appear to be panels of a door).

To study the role of viewing angle on children's ability to interpret aerial photographs more systematically, we (Liben, Dunphy-Lelli, & Szechter, in preparation) conducted a follow-up study in which preschoolers and adults were asked to identify a series of referents (e.g., baseball field, train tracks) that appeared on aerial photographs that differed in viewing angle (nadir vs. oblique views) and viewing distance (near vs. far). Consistent with the hypothesis that young children have particular problems in identifying referential meaning in spatial contexts that require interpretation of viewing angles that are unlike everyday eye-level views, children (although not adults) gave fewer correct identifications on nadir than on oblique photographs. Furthermore, the kinds of errors made by adults and children differed. Adults' errors were almost always within the domain of environmental referents and were at roughly the right scale, whereas children's errors often were not. For example, when a baseball diamond shown on a far nadir photograph was misidentified by adults, their errors were typically environmental referents such as "parking lot," "pond," or "park," whereas when it was misidentified by children, their errors included nonenvironmental referents such as "thermometer," "machine," "maze," and "dragon."

Given that the studies just described involved preschoolers, they address the lower limits of the age group relevant to the current chapter. A study that included both 8- to 10-year-old children and adults demonstrates that referential identification continues to be challenging well into childhood. In this study we asked respondents to identify seven components of three aerial images, all of which were nadir views, but varied in viewing distance. Although virtually all adults and the large majority of the children were successful in identifying referents correctly, or at least made conceptually sensible errors (e.g., identifying a parking lot as a "playground"), some children still offered some dramatic referential errors. For example, railroad tracks were identified as "an airplane in the air," "a big fly swatter," and an "oar to a boat," while a boat was identified as "a pencil," "a bird," "bird poop," and "outer space—where the world is" and, in a simple scale error, a building was identified as "a doll's house."

Taken together, these studies provide evidence that even children as young as 3 years can understand the referential meaning of spatial graphic representations at a general or holistic level, but that children considerably older are challenged in interpreting the identity of images that are depicted from unfamiliar viewpoints. It is not *only* spatial features of representations that continue to challenge children beyond toddlerhood. Young children may also find it difficult to separate out other kinds of referential versus representational qualities. Color appears to be particularly difficult for young children to ignore. Evidence for children's tendency to assume that the color of representations match the color of referents was first found in the interview study of preschoolers' interpretation of place representations mentioned earlier (Liben & Downs, 1991). Some charming examples of the conflation of representational and referential color were a number of preschool children who said that the red line on a road meant that the road itself was red, a child who insisted that a portion of a black-and-white aerial photograph of the local community could not possibly be a grassy area "because grass is green," and children who hypothesized that the yellow areas (cities) on a road map were "eggs" or "firecrackers."

A recent study (Myers & Liben, 2004) explored whether shared color of representation and referent continues to be a core assumption of children even as they are entering the school years. After completing a number of other mapping tasks that provided some experience in linking locations on a map to locations in a room, 5- and 6-year-old children watched two videotapes of two different adults adding dots to an oblique perspective map of a room. One adult displayed symbolic intent while adding green dots. She first picked up the paper and said, "I'm going to use this," and then, prior to placing each green dot, looked up as if watching someone else in the room, making comments such as, "Okay. Let's see. She put that one there, so [looking down at the paper] I should put my dot here." The other adult displayed a nonsymbolic (aesthetic) intent while adding red dots. This adult began by picking up the paper and said, "This isn't colorful! I'll make it prettier!" As she added dots, she mentioned her plan to hang it on the wall and selecting a red marker because red was her favorite color. Prior to placing each dot, she looked at only the paper itself, making comments such as, "I think I'll draw two red dots to make this part prettier."

After seeing the two tapes, children were then shown a photograph of each adult, and asked what each adult had been trying to do. Of the 40 children, only two could not demonstrate any understanding of either actor's intent; 25 were able to explain what both adults had been trying to do, and another 13 explained one or the other adult's intent. Children were then asked which drawing they would use to find hidden toy fire trucks. Although the adult with symbolic-intent never specified that it was fire trucks that were being hidden, she was explicit in commenting on placing the green dots to show hiding locations, whereas the adult with nonsymbolic intent was explicit in commenting on placing the red dots to make the paper look pretty. Of the 38 children who were correct in answering one or both of the manipulation-check questions about intent, 27 were *incorrect* in answering the question about which map they would use to help them find the toy fire trucks. That is, even though red dots had been placed on the paper simply to make it pretty, children thought that the map with red symbols would be more useful for finding toy fire trucks. Furthermore, among those children who selected the correct (green dot) map, only three of them explained their responses in a way that demonstrated representational understanding. The other eight were either unable to provide any rationale, or offered a rationale that still revealed a commitment to a color match between symbol and referent, as in a child who explained that the map he chose would be helpful because the fire trucks were green.

Although we have done no similar research with older participants, spontaneous comments and behaviors observed during our work (Liben & Downs, 1986) provide at least anecdotal evidence suggesting that the difficulty in distinguishing between qualities of representations and referents extends beyond kindergarten. For example, in a second grade classroom, children laughed aloud at the idea of using asterisks to stand for file cabinets on a map of their classroom because file cabinets do not look like stars; even many adults insist that water *must* be represented in blue (Liben, 2001; Liben & Downs, 1994).

Spatial Understanding

Vantage Point

As discussed earlier and as illustrated in Figure 12.2, any given representation has a particular vantage point that is determined by the combination of viewing distance, viewing angle, and viewing azimuth. Our empirical work has addressed children's developing appreciation of vantage point by examining their ability to distinguish among images that depict the same referent from different vantage points, and to produce representations that fit certain vantage-point specific qualities.

As one means of testing children's appreciation of the elements of vantage point shown in Figure 12.2, we (Liben & Szechter, 2001) prepared pairs of photographs with the same referent. Children were shown each pair of photographs and asked whether they were identical. Whenever children judged the photographs to be different, they were asked to say whether the photographs differed because something had changed in the scene itself, or because of something that had been done by the person who took the photograph. Irrespective of which attribution was given, the child was asked to explain what had happened, that is, what had changed, or what the photographer had done. Critical items were 15 pairs in which the photographer's vantage point had changed by altering viewing distance, viewing angle, or viewing azimuth (illustrated in Figure 12.4). To ensure that correct answers varied, there were also filler items in which either something in the scene had changed or in which the photographs were identical.

This spatial photo-pair task was given to children aged 3-, 5-, and 7-years, as well as to a comparison group of college students. For pairs that differed by viewing distance (so that a correct response would include explaining that the photographer had moved closer to, or further away from the depicted subject), only about 25% of the 3-year-old children were correct even on a single one of the five items; the rest were completely unable to explain anything about viewing distance. About 50% of the 5-year-old children were correct on four or all five items, with the rest distributed fairly evenly across the remaining lower scores; just over 75% of the 7-year-old children were correct on all or all but one items, and virtually all adults had errorless performance.

For pairs that differed by viewing angle or viewing azimuth, the pathway to mastery was more protracted. More specifically, for viewing-angle pairs, none of the 3-year-old children explained even a single item. Indeed, children of this age commonly failed to even notice that anything differed in the two photographs, focusing instead on the shared referential *content*. For example, when commenting on the viewing-angle pair (tulips) shown in Figure 12.4, one 3-year-old child said, "They're both the same." When the interviewer continued by saying, "Well, they're both of tulips, but is there anything different about the pictures?" the child answered in the negative, saying, "Nope. This one [pointing to one on the right] has the same stuff."

The 5-year-old children were more likely to notice a difference between the two images, but their explanations suggested they inferred that there had been a change in what had been in the scene rather than in the way that was photographed. Thus, for example, 5-year-olds accounted for the difference

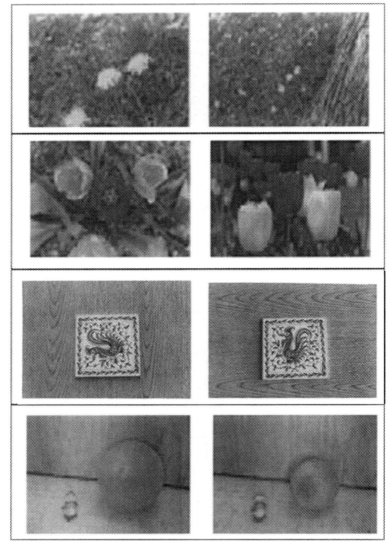

Figure 12.4 Sample pairs of photographs used in the photograph-pair task illustrating (top to bottom) changes in viewing distance, viewing angle, viewing azimuth, and referent. Reproduced from Liben (2003a) with permission.

between the tulip photographs by explaining that the photographer took "this one when [the tulips] were all curled up and those ones when they were all blooming," that the photographs were taken "in the spring [when] they were closed [and] then in the summer [when] they came out again," and that the photographer "took one sometime when they were closed and one sometime when they were open." About half of the 5-year-old children were able to provide correct explanations of at least one angle pair, sometimes extremely clearly as one child explained, "Um, that one you're looking that way [points straight ahead] and that one you're looking down, this way [bends over the picture]" or another who said, "Oh I like these... He [the photographer] went sort of on the side of them and then like up above them to get the middle [points hand down on top of the tulips and rises in chair]... because um, like this one is like straight across and this one's like you're looking down [flexes hand to point all fingers down onto the tulips]." By the age of 7, responses like these were common, and by adulthood, they were virtually universal.

The azimuth pairs showed an even more protracted period for mastery. Again, many 3-year-old children failed to note the difference between the two photographs, but even when they did, they commonly believed that there had been a change in the referent objects rather than a change in the photographer's position. To illustrate by reference to the rooster-tile azimuth example shown in Figure 12.4, many children (and even some adults) thought that what had changed was the orientation of the tile rather than the vantage point of the photographer. That it was, instead, the photographer's position that had changed is apparent from looking at the grain pattern of the wood surface on which the tile rests.

In a second task used to study the developing ability to understand vantage point, we gave digital cameras to 8- to 10–year-old children and adults, and asked them to reproduce model photographs. Specifically, respondents were asked to "try to take a picture so that yours will look as much like this photograph as you can make it" and then, after viewing the result on the display screen of the digital camera, to take a second photograph to try to improve the match. Figure 12.5 shows a sample of children's initial photographs for one model. Photographs were scored by assigning points to qualities of the photograph that reflected correct viewing distance, viewing angle, and viewing azimuth. An analysis of variance on scores totaled over four photographs revealed significant effects of age and trial, and a significant interaction showing that the improvement over trials was significant in children only.

We also studied understanding of vantage point by asking participants to create photographs that were consistent with some view-specific verbal description. For example, as participants approached an art museum at which two lion paw sculptures flanked the entrance they were asked to take a photograph with "just one paw in the picture." Adults were almost universally successful in implementing this request, usually by adjusting the direction the camera pointed (azimuth). Only 10% of the adult participants produced an image in which a second paw showed at the edge of the image, an error presumably accounted for by the fact that the area recorded on the image is slightly larger than that

Figure 12.5   Four sample responses to a request to reproduce a photographic model that was almost identical to the bottom right photograph. Reproduced from Liben (2003a) with permission.

(1) (2) (3)

(4) (5) (6)

Figure 12.6 Illustrative responses by children asked to create a photograph showing only one paw. Solutions involved (1) canonical azimuth (front view) but noncanonical distance (close up), (2) noncanonical azimuth (building entrance viewed from side), (3) noncanonical azimuth (back view), (4) noncanonical distance and azimuth (close and to the side), (5) noncanonical angle (overhead rather than eye-level), and (6) change in referent (child said he "waited for people walking by to block one of the paws from view.") Reproduced from Liben (2003a) with permission.

seen through the viewfinder. Errors were more common (32%) among children. Unlike adults, when children erred, the second paw typically appeared well within the frame of the image. The children who were successful used a variety of strategies involving distance, angle, and azimuth as illustrated in Figure 12.6.

Linking Location and Direction Information Across Spatial-Graphic Representations

Another way that we have studied the developing ability to understand the spatial meaning contained in graphic representations is to ask participants to transfer location or direction information gleaned from one spatial-graphic representation to another. Table 12.4 lists four representation-to-representation tasks discussed next. In each, participants were first given some kind of representation (such as an eye-level photograph, aerial photograph, or line drawing) of a space (such as a park, city, or local region) that was not currently in view. They were then asked to demonstrate their understanding of some information that could be gleaned from that representation (e.g., the location of a particular landmark in the represented park) by performing some task on another representation of that same referent space (e.g., placing a location dot on a plan map of the park). Success on tasks like these draws simultaneously and interactively on understanding the initial depiction (e.g., the eye-level photograph), on understanding of the representation on which responses must be made (e.g., the plan map), and on the skill (and care) needed to implement the required response (e.g., precision in placing the sticker on the plan map to show the landmark's location).

In the city aerial task (Liben & Downs, 1991), first and second graders were given individual copies of an aerial photograph of Chicago. After class discussion of the photograph and its general referent, children were asked to use it as a basis to draw (but not trace) a map of Chicago. Next, children were given a plan map, and were asked to identify what area of the photograph was depicted. An acetate sheet was then placed over each child's copy of the aerial photograph to outline the correct area and to

TABLE 12.4
Representation-To-Representation Tasks

Task name	Spatial information obtained from . . .	Response indicated on . . .	Query: Location?	Query: Orientation?
City aerial	Vertical aerial photo of large city	Plan map	Y	
School aerial	Oblique aerial photo of school neighborhood	Plan map		Y
Terrain perspective	Line drawings of local topography in oblique view	Contour map		Y
Photo-map	Eye-level photos of room, playground, & campus scenes	Plan map; oblique map	Y	Y

indicate eight locations. Children were asked to place stickers on the plan map to show the locations indicated on the aerial photograph.

With respect to location variables, and as hypothesized in the selection of the locations that were queried, items that allowed solution via topological concepts such as "on" or "next to" generally elicited better performance than items that required metric or quantitative reasoning. For example, the item at a clear and unique bend of the breakwater was answered correctly by 29% and 70% of the first and second graders, respectively, whereas an item located on one of many similar buildings whose identification required metric concepts (e.g., judging distances from some other distinct location) was answered correctly by only 0% and 19% of the same age groups.

With respect to user variables, one generalization that emerges from the data is clear improvement in performance with age. For example, the modal response (42%) in Grade 1 was failing to be correct on even a single item, a score that was almost unheard of (4%) by Grade 2. These data suggest that handling the simultaneous changes in graphic medium, scale, and different representational content of the two representations (i.e., the fact that the map represented only a portion of the area shown in the photograph) was completely overwhelming for many of the first but not the second graders. In addition, the maximum score was four correct in Grade 1 but seven correct in Grade 2, and an analysis of variance revealed significantly higher mean scores in the older children. The age difference is unlikely to be attributed to formal instruction given that neither aerial photographs nor mapping tasks like these were included in the children's elementary school curriculum. Instead, it is more likely to reflect general development in both representational and spatial skills during middle childhood. Equally or perhaps even more striking than the age-linked differences, is the wide range of performance within a given grade. For example, within Grade 2, performance ranged from erring on every single item out of eight, to erring on only one item.

The city aerial task could be expected to be challenging because the referent space (Chicago) was entirely unknown, the vertical perspective of both photograph and map which—although shared—was unfamiliar, and the viewing distance of the photograph was great. A different set of challenges was presented by the school aerial task given to first and second grade children (Liben & Downs, 1986). Introductory tasks familiarized children with directional arrow stickers, a map of the school neighborhood, and an aerial photograph of their school (see Figure 12.7). Children were then shown slides of eight aerial photographs of the school, and asked to place arrows on the map to show the direction from which the building had been photographed. This task could be expected to be somewhat easier than the city aerial task because the photographs depicted a familiar rather than an unfamiliar referent and used a smaller viewing distance with a somewhat more familiar viewing angle (oblique rather than nadir). However, the task could be expected to prove even more challenging because it required linking spatial information across representations with two different viewing angles (the oblique angle photograph and the vertical angle map) and queried children's understanding of viewing direction (azimuth) rather than simply location.

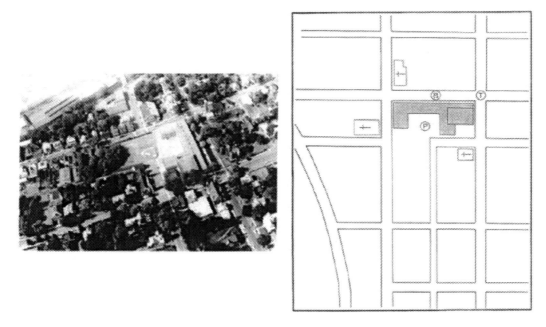

Figure 12.7 Aerial photograph and neighborhood map of school used in school aerial task.

Performance was scored by measuring the angular displacement from the correct arrow placement. Even using a lenient margin of error (± 45°), most children in both grades (93% and 87%, respectively) were correct on fewer than half the items, with no age-linked increase, and with no child performing perfectly or almost perfectly. These findings are consistent with the observation that projective (point-of-view) tasks continue to be challenging throughout childhood and even during adulthood.

The pattern of differential performance across items shows that although performance was low overall, it was not random. For example, there appeared to be some systematic tendency to mistake another centrally-located building for the school, or to mistake the rear of the school for its side. Unfortunately, we were unable to vary desired image variables (e.g., azimuth, distance) systematically because of constraints imposed by terrain, cloud cover, and possible flight paths at the time the aerial photographs were taken. Systematic control of viewing angle and azimuth was, however, possible in the terrain perspective task discussed next.

In this task, nine computer-generated line drawings of the local topography were created from different viewing azimuths and angles (see Liben & Downs, 1992). First and second grade children were asked to indicate the direction from which the topographical region had been drawn by placing an arrow sticker on a contour map, and, responses were scored for the degree of divergence from the correct angle. Although there was some slight age-linked advance in performance, again what was most striking were the similarly low scores in both grades (averaging, respectively, only 1.9 and 2.0 correct out of 9 possible). When the quality of the errors is taken into account, however, an age-linked difference is evident: in Grade 1, errors tended to be dispersed evenly over 360° whereas in Grade 2, errors tended to cluster near the correct response. Apparently older children are better able to understand the directional information, but still have difficulty in understanding or in demonstrating that understanding with precision. Interestingly, and consistent with earlier observations of the wide range of performance within any given age is the fact that even as roughly one-fifth of the children at each grade were correct on none of the items, a single child at each grade performed perfectly or nearly perfectly on all of them.

As on other tasks, different items elicited different performance systematically rather than randomly. In general, performance was better on the items for which the correct response faced toward one of the corners of the contour map than for items that faced toward one of the sides. Further research is needed to disentangle the extent to which the corner advantage is due to the match between the corners of both representations, and whether it would still be evident if only one or neither of the two representations had graphically-defined corners (implemented, for example, by using a circular rather than a square contour map).

The final task discussed in this section is the photo-map task (Liben, Kastens, & Stevenson, 2002). In this task, participants were shown eye-level photographs of everyday environments like parks, rooms, and campus vistas. With the photograph in view, participants were asked to place an arrow on a plan or oblique map to indicate where the photographer was standing, and the direction in which his camera was pointing when the picture was taken.

To date, the photo-map task has been given to several samples of fourth-grade children who have been participants in research designed to evaluate the efficacy of a map-use curriculum (see Liben et al., 2002), and to several samples of college students who have been participants in studies examining the role of individual differences and task variables on map use. To provide illustrative data, Figure 12.8 shows one photograph and composite maps of responses from one illustrative sample of each age.

Among the adults, a large cluster of responses (marked as cluster A in Figure 12.8 is correct within a generous margin of error. With two exceptions (responses E and F), even the erroneous arrow placements appear to reflect at least an understanding that the camera was aimed down a path between a building and a tower. Errors suggest inattention to or confusion about viewing direction, about which building appears in the photograph, or both. For example, responses B, C, and cluster G suggest a failure to appreciate that the camera must be positioned so that in the photograph, a building would be to the right rather than to the left of the tower. If one were inattentive to that right-left relation, it would be possible that building #2 or #3 could have been the building appearing in the photograph

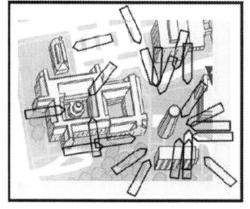

Figure I2.8 Composite of arrows placed by adults (left) and children (right) to show position and direction of camera for photograph shown above. Letters (for responses) and numbers (for key buildings) have been added to adult composite to facilitate discussion. Images reproduced from Liben et al. (2002) with permission.

(responses B and C), or that the camera was positioned near a different face of building #4 (response cluster G).

Among the children, not only are there very few correct responses, but performance is far more varied, and strategies are harder to discern. One clear contrast between the children's and adults' responses is that the children are not even uniformly able to identify the critical referential links between the photograph and map. For example, it appears that many of the children had difficulty identifying the representation of the free-standing, tower-like building on the map (labeled #6 on the adult composite). Several children placed their arrows to point at the tower-like part of the large building (#4). It should have been apparent from the photograph that it was the former (#6) rather than the latter (#4) given that the tower in the photograph goes down to ground level and is not embedded within a building. At least one child placed the arrow facing directly toward a rectilinear building with no tower-like structure in sight, and many showed right-left confusions like those discussed for adult respondents.

Taken together, these data suggest that as late as fourth grade, many children have difficulty interpreting the meaning of spatial-graphic representations, and that not only children, but also adults find it difficult to understand the links between representations of given referents when the task challenges point-of-view (or projective) concepts.

Insofar as the photograph is meant to be a proxy for the kind of visual experience one would have if one had actually been standing in the real environment, the photo-map task is transitional to the next category of tasks, that is, to tasks that assess respondents' ability to extract information from a real, currently experienced space, and communicate that information by performing some response on a spatial-graphic representation.

Linking Experienced Environments to Spatial-Graphic Representations

The research discussed in the prior section involves tasks in which there are representational challenges at both input and output. That is, to perform successfully on the described tasks, participants must be able to extract spatial meaning from one graphic representation and then demonstrate that understanding on another graphic representation. In contrast, the research discussed in the current section requires participants to use graphic representations for the output stage only; spatial information is gathered by looking at or moving around in the real, physical environment.

In a taxonomy of methods used to study spatial representation (Liben, 1997a), the former tasks would fall under the rubric of "Representational Correspondence Methods" because they require participants to relate two representations (e.g., a photograph and a plan map). The latter would fall under the rubric of "Production Methods" because they require participants to produce [or modify] a representation by using knowledge collected from a real, physical space. Before turning to illustrative "production" research, it is important to acknowledge that it is also possible to use tasks in which participants gather spatial information from a spatial-graphic representation and then demonstrate their understanding by an action in a real, physical space (called "Comprehension Methods"). To date there has been relatively little research of this kind, probably because of the greater practical difficulties it presents. For example, consider a task in which children are asked to record the location of a novel object placed in their classroom on a copy of a map (a production task) versus the reciprocal task in which children are asked to place the object at a location indicated on a map (a comprehension task). Only the first task permits many children to perform the task simultaneously and independently, and only the first task provides an automatic record of the child's response. Recording where the child places the real object in the real room creates what is in essence a comprehension task for the researcher, who may or may not have advanced enough spatial skills to record responses accurately him or herself. Ongoing research employs comprehension methods (e.g., Kastens & Liben, 2004) but until more data are available, it is not yet possible to know whether or not the two kinds of tasks—comprehension and production—are truly reciprocal. Table 12.5 lists three tasks discussed next to illustrate research in

TABLE 12.5
Environment-To-Representation Tasks

Task name	Stimulus (information obtained from . . .)	Response (indicated on . . .)	Query: Location?	Query: Orientation?
Object location	Surrounding familiar classroom; familiar objects	Plan map	Y	
Person location, direction	Surrounding familiar classroom; person standing and pointing	Plan map	Y	Y
Flag field task	Surrounding unfamiliar urban or rural campus; flags on campus	Plan map	Y	

which participants gather spatial information available in the surrounding environment and record it on a graphic representation.

The object location task (see Liben & Downs, 1986) was given to kindergarten, first- and second-grade children in their own classrooms. Children were first introduced to maps in general and then shown overhead transparencies of a map of their classroom. The first contained a scale map of the walls, door, and windows of the classroom, and the second added scale symbols for the classroom furniture. Group discussions involved collaborative identification of key features on the map (such as doors and windows) and of their link to the analogous features in the actual room (e.g., linking map lines to corresponding room walls). After general correspondences were established, a map was placed on each child's desk so that it was aligned with the room. Children were then asked to show on their map the location of six objects in their classroom. Because this task was designed to test children's ability to use a spatial-graphic representation to convey information about locations that were perceptually available (rather than, say, stored environmental knowledge about the room), children were first asked to point to a given object (e.g., the pencil sharpener), and only after all children were pointing correctly, to indicate its location on the map.

As in most earlier tasks, what is striking from the resulting data is less that there was an increment in performance with age (correct object locations were, by grade, 50%, 78%, and 87%), but rather the range of performance within each grade such that even some kindergarten children were correct on every item, and even some second-grade children were incorrect on every item.

Also as in earlier tasks, there was considerable variability in success across items. The most likely interpretation of the differences is that they reflect the degree to which similarly shaped, nearby landmarks are available for possible confusion. For example, in one classroom, children were very accurate (73% correct) in locating the blue box which was on the piano. The only similarly shaped and isolated piece of furniture was the teacher's desk which was at the opposite end of the room. In contrast, children in that class were very inaccurate (4% correct) in locating the red phone which was on a small shelf unit. In this case, there were several other nearby pieces of furniture of a similar size and shape that offered confusing alternatives.

The second illustrative task, the person location and direction task, was given to children in Kindergarten, Grade 1, Grade 2, and in a combined Grade 5/6 (Liben & Downs, 1993). This task was conceptually similar to the object location task, but extended it in several ways. First, rather than identifying locations of familiar objects already present in the classroom, target locations were defined by a person who moved to various places in the room. Because the person stood on the floor, this meant that locations were on undifferentiated areas of the map, thus involving metric definitions of location (e.g., "about a third of the way across the room") rather than only topological ones (e.g., "on the piano"). Second, children were asked to indicate the person's orientation as well as his location. Specifically, at each location, the person pointed straight ahead, and said, "Now I am the [color, e.g., blue] arrow. Put your [blue] arrow on the map to show where I am standing and which direction I am pointing." Finally, children were asked to complete the task twice, first when the map was aligned with the room, and second, after the map had been rotated by 180°. Under the latter condition, when a person was, say, to a child's right in the actual space, the correct location for the sticker on the map would be to the child's left. Whenever a map is out of alignment with the space (as often occurs in the real world, see Levine, Marchon, & Hanley, 1984), users must draw on projective spatial concepts to use the map successfully.

Performance was generally worse among younger children, but particularly so in the unaligned condition (Liben & Downs, 1993). This finding is consistent with the notion that reading or communicating point-of-view information (projective spatial concepts) is mastered later in childhood than is landmark or topological information. Again, data revealed a wide range of performance within grades. For example, even on the most difficult unaligned condition, a small percentage of the kindergarten children performed very well.

Patterns of responses to individual items are again useful in suggesting strategies, and in identifying what aspects of these tasks are difficult. Figure 12.9 shows the placement of arrows for one particular item in one of the first-grade classrooms. What is apparent is that under the aligned condition, most children place their stickers in the correct quadrant of the map, and almost all children orient the arrows in roughly the correct direction. They apparently have little difficulty differentiating what part of the map refers to the floor, and what part to furniture (only a single arrow is placed on a piece of furniture). In contrast, in the unaligned condition, few responses are in the correct quadrant and facing in the correct direction. There are some responses that appear to be the result of children placing their arrows on the map in relation to their own bodies, rather than in relation to the represented space. These arrows are in the opposite corner of the map (lower right, rather than upper left) and point in the opposite direction (facing the upper left rather than the lower right). Other children appear to realize that they need to take the unaligned position of the map into account as they answer and thus respond differently, but they do not understand how to adjust. Many responses suggest deep confusions: several arrows were placed on furniture (impossible, given that the person had not climbed on top of a desk) and some directions were correct neither in relation to the piece of paper, nor in relation to the child's own body (e.g., see arrows pointing to the upper right corner of the map).

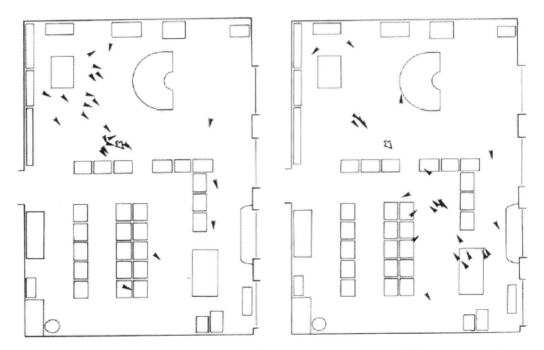

Figure 12.9 Composite of arrow placements (black arrows) by first-grade children asked to show the location and orientation of an adult (open arrow) when map was aligned (left) and unaligned (right) with the room. Reproduced from Liben and Downs (1993) with permission.

Response strategies are revealed not only by looking at arrow placements on individual items, but also by examining the distributions of responses across items. First, those items in which the pointing direction was parallel to one of the classroom walls tended to elicit better performance than those items that were at some oblique angle, perhaps because in the former case, the wall lines on the map provided guides for children's responses. Second, within the oblique items, the types of errors change dramatically by age. The oldest children's errors were virtually exclusively ones of precision. That is, when children in Grade 5/6 made a mistake, it was generally because they placed their arrow only a little bit off from the correct direction. In contrast, when the kindergarten children erred, their placements were generally distributed throughout 360° suggesting random responding. Children between these two ages (Grades 1 and 2) tended to err by placing their arrows directly opposite the correct orientation, suggesting that they were failing to compensate for the map rotation.

Because of practical constraints, most developmental map research (including our work) has employed maps of very small environments such as rooms or hallways rather than of large environments such as parks, campuses, or towns. The former are often not even considered to *be* maps by many children and adults (see Downs, Liben, & Daggs, 1988). Even more important, maps of such small spaces do not present many of the cognitive challenges presented by the kinds of maps that are typically used in daily life (e.g., for wayfinding or route planning) or in professional tasks (e.g., for recording distributions of regions affected by acid rain). For example, it is often difficult to orient maps of large environments because they may have less-differentiated landmarks (e.g., many similar paths, roads, buildings, vegetation, hills) than might be found in a small contained space such as a classroom, it is challenging to integrate information acquired sequentially (e.g., as in walking or driving through an environment) rather than simultaneously (as looking around a classroom while seated at a particular desk), and it is challenging to understand the relative scales of a very large, navigable environment and its scaled representation.

Many of these ecological challenges were incorporated into the flag location task designed as part of research (Liben et al., 2002) on the *Where Are We?* map-skills curriculum designed by Kastens (2000). First, eight colored flags were placed at various locations on campus field sites (either urban or rural settings). Fourth-grade children, unfamiliar with the sites, were then brought to the campus as part of a field trip, and as a group, were introduced to the map and the task in general. Each child was then launched on the task individually by an adult who gave the child a copy of the map, aligned the map with the space, and pointed out the child's current location and facing direction on the map. Children were then asked to explore the area, and when they found flags, to place colored stickers on their map to show the flags' locations.

The patterns of data showed that understanding the links between a real space and a graphic representation remains difficult during middle childhood. Scores ranged from zero correct to perfect performance, with the average in most samples at roughly 50% correct. As had been true for tasks described earlier, performance on individual items suggested differential challenges depending on relevant spatial concepts. For example, sticker placements for the black flag were closely clustered around the correct location whereas those for the red flag were scattered, not only near the correct location, but even in other sections of the map entirely. The former was on a statue that was the only statue symbolized on the map and thus topological concepts could be used to identify its location correctly ("on the statue"). In contrast, the latter was on a road which required projective concepts (to identify the correct end of the map) and Euclidean concepts (to identify the precise location along the extended linear symbol).

Conclusions

I have reviewed an assortment of tasks addressing children's developing ability to decode or communicate spatial information with spatial-graphic representations. It is important to point out explicitly that all the tasks discussed intentionally involve these representations. That is, they are not addressed to investigating what information participants may have about a space *independently* of these representations. For example, even without an external representation, individuals may be able to figure out where they are (e.g., in front of the library) and how to get from one place to another (e.g., from the library to the movie theatre) by using mental imagery, an intuitive sense of direction, a learned motor sequence, or other strategies. At the same time, when participants perform imperfectly on some task that uses spatial-graphic representations, their difficulty might be traced to incomplete or inaccurate "real-space" knowledge or skills, rather than to difficulty in meeting the representational challenges of the task. For example, participants who place stickers incorrectly on the map for the flag location task might err *not* because they have difficulty relating a location in the environment to a spot on the map, but rather because they have difficulty understanding where they are in the environment in the first place. Much additional research is needed to tease apart where the challenges lie for participants, and to understand the ways in which the use of spatial-graphic representations may aid individuals' knowledge of environments just as familiarity with environments may enhance individuals' facility in using spatial-graphic representations (Liben, 2000, 2002; Liben & Downs, 2001; Uttal, 2000).

Aesthetic Understanding

Overview

Most work on graphic representations within developmental psychology—including the work discussed in prior sections of this chapter—is embedded within the study of cognitive development. But once one appreciates that any given graphic representation is not a small, flat, singular replica of some portion of reality, the stage is set for considering a host of factors related to the creation of any particular representation (e.g., what was the creator's intent?) and to the impact of that particular representation (e.g., how does the graphic medium selected affect the emotional tone of the representation?). The former raises questions that are associated with research on theory of mind (e.g., Flavell, 1986), the latter raises questions that are associated with the study of aesthetic development. In the final section of this chapter, I focus on the latter. Thus, whereas in the prior sections I have discussed research that is addressed primarily to children's developing ability to see through graphic representations to the world that lies behind them, I now turn to empirical work that is concerned more directly with the representational surfaces themselves.

More specifically, the research described below concerns children's developing appreciation of the aesthetic nature of representational surfaces. Our work (e.g., Liben, 2003b; Liben & Szechter, 2002; Szechter & Liben, 2000b, 2003a; Szechter, 2003) has focused on one particular medium—photography. One reason for selecting this medium is practical: even very young children have the skills to produce photographic images and equipment is relatively inexpensive and portable. A second reason is conceptual, and is derived from the tendency for children and adults alike to think of photographs as if they were a means of capturing reality (e.g., see Beilin, 1991, 1999; Sontag, 1977). In actuality, any given photograph reflects many decisions: how it is framed, the kind of film, the lens, shutter speed, and aperture, lighting, printing process, and so on. Photographs thus provide a particularly strong test of participants' appreciation of the representational nature of graphics, of the extent to which the creator (rather than reality itself) controls the ultimate appearance of the representation, and of the range of substance and affect that may be communicated by a particular combination of choices. In an elegant statement that captures the intersection of the seeming opposing qualities of simplicity and complexity, Szarkowski (1973) wrote, "The simplicity of photography lies in the fact that it is very easy to make a picture. The staggering complexity of it lies in the fact that a thousand other pictures of the same subject would have been equally as easy" (p. 134).

Below I discuss three kinds of data bearing on aesthetics derived from asking participants to first, select and explain which photographs they liked most among a set they had themselves taken, second, to create a photograph with a requested expressive impact, and third, to reflect on photographic qualities in the course of comparing pairs or sorting photographs into categories.

Photographic Preferences

In a study of the bases for aesthetic judgments, 8-year-old children and college students were first taken on a walk through a college campus. As they walked, they were asked to take digital photographs, some of which were defined by the interviewer, and some of which left entirely to the participants' choice. After returning to the computer lab and downloading their images, participants were asked to select their three best- and three least-liked images, and to explain their selections.

Figure 12.10 provides a sample of best-liked selections and explanations given by children and adults. As illustrated there, children's explanations of their choices tended to focus on the referential content of the images, whereas adults' explanations were more likely to focus on what the surface of the image itself looked like (e.g., coloring, light patterns) or on some abstract idea or feeling the image itself conveyed (e.g., a sense of calm). To allow quantitative analyses, explanations were categorized as focused primarily on (a) the content of the photograph (i.e., on what was depicted), (b) the surface of the photograph (i.e., on how the image looked), (c) the technique used in creating it (e.g., a comment about camera position), or as (d) uncodable, either because the participant could not provide an explanation at all, or because the explanation could not be unambiguously assigned to one of the other categories (see Liben, 2003b). As would be expected given the examples provided in Figure 12.10, the quantitative data showed that when discussing most-like images, children gave greater attention to referents than did adults. Thus, the developmental progression reported for other visual arts (e.g., Freeman, 1995; Freeman & Parsons, 2001; Gardner, 1970; Parsons, 1987) in which an early focus on the referent gives way to a greater focus on the aesthetics of the image, appears to operate for photography as well.

(1)   (2)   (3)

(4)   (5)   (6)

Figure 12.10   Illustrative selections by children (top row) and adults (bottom row) of their "best liked" photographs. Children's explanations were: (1) "It was my favorite team's mascot." (2) "It shows a pretty sign and pretty flowers." (3) "I love beetles, and plus it is a yellow beetle and yellow is one of my favorite colors." Adults' explanations were (4) "Cause it just makes him look really cool. The close up of it. Just the effect of it." (5) "The way the sun beats down, it kind of distorts the image. You can see like spectrum colors." (6) "I like the colors . . . usually you look at pictures straight on [gestures straight ahead], but you're looking up." Original photographs were in color. Reproduced from Liben (2003a) with permission.

Creating an Expressive Photograph.

The second empirical example explores participants' ability to craft a photograph of a referent so that it conveys a particular emotional tone. Specifically, 8-year-old children and college students were asked to take a photograph of a lion statue so that it would "look kind of scary" (Liben & Szechter, 2001). Our expectation was that a scary effect could be achieved by using a close viewing distance. To provide an index of viewing distance, we printed each photograph to a fixed size, drew a circle around the head (extrapolating beyond the picture boundaries when necessary), and measured the head's diameter. On average, lion heads in children's photographs were significantly smaller than those in adults'. The top row of Figure 12.11 shows photographs that are of roughly the average sizes produced by children (left) and adults (right). Examination of the distributions as well as the mean sizes showed that both children and adults took close-up shots, but only children took photographs from a great distance and thus produced images with relatively small lions.

Viewing distance is not, however, the only possible means of affecting the expressive nature of the image, as illustrated by the two additional examples of photographs shown in the bottom row of Figure 12.11. Thus, we scored the photographs for other qualities as well. Data revealed that children and adults also differed in their manipulation of viewing azimuth, such that children were more likely to have the camera facing directly at the lion's face than elsewhere (65% vs. 35%), a pattern that was reversed among adults (33% vs. 67%) and of viewing angle, such that children were more likely to point the camera up than use a straight-ahead view (65% vs. 35%), a pattern reversed among adults (22% vs. 61%,; the remainder tilted the camera downward.) In addition, to evaluate whether these differences

Figure 12.11 Illustrations of "scary" lion photographs. Top row depicts average viewing distance of children's (left) and adults' (right) photographs; bottom shows a child's (left) and an adult's (right) photograph at roughly comparable viewing distances. Original photographs were in color. Reproduced from Liben (2003a) with permission.

in viewing distance, azimuth, and angle did, indeed, affect the expressive impact of the images, we obtained "scariness" ratings. College students were asked to use a seven-point scale ranging from "not scary at all" to "very scary" to rate the photographs (unmarked for photographer's age). Photographs taken by adults received significantly higher scariness ratings than those taken by children.

Although we had (in retrospect, regrettably) not asked participants to explain their strategies, in a few cases, they spontaneously offered revealing comments. One child, for example, commented that "If you want to make it look scary you can't take a picture of the face because the face isn't scary at all. The eyes are just circles and the mouth isn't growling. You have to take other angles to make it look scary." As is often the case with verbal statements, the words alone are ambiguous. The comment might be a sophisticated one, implying an appreciation of the expressive power of differing vantage points, or it might be an unsophisticated one, implying a belief that scariness rests entirely in the referent itself, and this lion's face is simply not frightening. Evidence that the latter interpretation is probably correct comes from the fact that after making this comment, the child proceeded to take a photograph of the lion's leg so that the claws—rather than the face—were the focus of the image. Another child's spontaneous comments also suggested her belief that it is something about the referent rather than the image of the referent that makes it scary. After taking one photograph as requested, this participant asked the interviewer to take a picture while she climbed up on the lion's back to "give him horns to make him scary." Only a single child verbalized a strategy that was aimed at affecting the image, saying he would make the picture blurry so "it looks like the lion's going to jump out at you." He was not, however, able to implement his strategy: He shook the camera immediately before and after, but not during, the exposure.

Responding to Photographs

A third empirical approach has been to explore age-linked and experience-linked sensitivity to the expressive qualities of photographs by using open-ended interview and observational techniques (Szechter, 2003; Szechter & Liben, 2003a, 2003b). In this work, 7- to 13-year-old children and their parents were asked to complete various photography-related tasks.

In one of the tasks, respondents were shown pairs of photographs that contained the same referential content, but that varied as a consequence of changing some aspect of the photographic process (e.g., shutter speed). Participants were asked to explain how the photographs differed. Consistent with findings discussed earlier showing children's focus on referential content of images, children were significantly more likely than adults to attribute differences to a change in the referent, even though the interviewer had begun by explicitly saying that both photographs "show the same thing." For example, in response to a pair of photographs of the same woman that differed in appearance as a result of adding a filter, 47% of the children but only 12% of the adults stated that the woman had changed her scarf. Furthermore, in describing the differences between the two images, children tended to offer more factual descriptions, as in "And the hat is darker in this one," whereas adults tended to offer comments about expressive effects, as in "The color of the cape and the background in this picture [pointing to one] are harmonious." Of course, these data alone may simply reflect adults' greater knowledge about photographic processes and greater verbal fluency, and thus it is useful to combine these findings with those from other components of the interviews.

In another of the tasks, respondents were shown five photographs. For each, they were asked three questions that had been identified by Barrett (1987) as useful for eliciting viewers' reflections on photographs: *What do you see? What does it mean? How do you know?* In their answers, children were significantly less likely than adults to comment on the photographer's role or technique, and they tended to offer concrete and literal descriptions of the photographs. For example, shown *Memphis*, a photograph by Eggleston that (in a literal description) shows a tricycle looming large in the foreground, with suburban ranch home in the background, a prototypical 8-year-old child's response to the questions was:

I see a little, like, bike. It has three wheels. Um there's houses behind it and a car. And, um, there are no clouds in the sky. Um, I think it means someone left their bicycle out and it got a lot [mumbles]. Because it looks flat there [points to bike]. That's all.

A sharp contrast is seen in one particularly articulate parent's response:

I see a tricycle on the sidewalk in front of a house... I guess in some ways I think about how normally kids are little, and houses and people and parents are big, and so it's like they're kind of turning that on its head and saying this is the kid's world and of course it's at a kid's eye level, it's not taken down this way [gestures down], but it's taken at kind of a level where the kid's at, so it's like this is what would be important to a kid. Um, I know because he took the trouble to get down, it's obviously, nobody's ya know, this tall [gesturing low to ground], so he's taken the trouble to lie on his stomach and compose it just so... maybe causing adults to see things from a child's perspective.

Converging data were provided from a sorting task, in which respondents were asked to complete multiple sorts of a dozen photographs that could conceivably be categorized by referent (e.g., animals, houses), photographic qualities (e.g., color vs. black and white; close-up vs. distant shots), emotional tone (e.g., happy vs. sad) and so on. Children were far less likely than adults to sort on the basis of photographic qualities, and instead, were more creative in finding endless referent-based groupings (e.g., "with or without walls, with or without houses, with or without windows, with or without doors, with or without people").

CONCLUSIONS AND FUTURE DIRECTIONS

In one sense, spatial-graphic representations are easy to interpret. Even infants are able to extract denotative meaning from motivated graphic representations relatively effortlessly. However, just as understanding or producing single words or even short sentences is not tantamount to mastering all that language offers, so, too, identifying the referential meaning of graphic representations is not tantamount to understanding the rich cognitive or expressive meanings that graphic images provide. I have proposed a more complete interpretation of what it means to understand graphic representations as summarized in Table 12.1. With this more differentiated conception of understanding, it is easy to appreciate the relevance of the range of perceptual, cognitive, and social processes encompassed by the Embedded Model shown in Figure 12.3. In concert, these diverse competencies and developmental processes set the stage for going beyond dichotomous questions and theories that have plagued theoretical debates in developmental psychology (Liben, 1997b; Overton, 2003). Rather than motivating research by yes-or-no questions such as *Is representation present from birth?* or *Do preschoolers have projective and Euclidean concepts?*, these more differentiated conceptualizations inspire questions about sequencing, about the conditions under which some competence is activated and applied successfully, and about the experiences that foster their emergence and application. Questions like these are of interest not only to theorists, but also to those whose goals are to optimize developmental outcomes.

The empirical work that I have reviewed in this chapter has addressed the development of a sample of competencies in the representational, spatial, and aesthetic domains. The research literature from which it draws is limited in a number of important ways, each of which presents opportunities for further research. First, unlike work on children's developing mastery of linguistic representations, the extant work on children's developing mastery of graphic representations typically samples rather sparsely and unsystematically over different chronological ages and populations. That is, most studies to date in this area have sampled participants of only two or three (often widely separated) ages drawn from largely homogenous populations (e.g., drawing adult samples from college psychology classes). Research is needed to provide descriptions of normative behaviors across the entire life course and across diverse populations.

Second, much of the extant literature focuses on measures of central tendency (e.g., presenting mean levels of performance by age, and testing the statistical significance of mean differences). It is not surprising that on any given task, older participants do better than younger participants. But what accounts for these differences? Do all individuals gradually become better and better, or do increasing proportions of individuals move out of an incompetent category and enter a competent one? What might these different profiles imply about developmental mechanisms? Scholars have developed methods that may be used to differentiate patterns of age-linked change (e.g., Thomas & Lohaus, 1993), and these methods that may be profitably applied in future work on graphic representation.

Third, and implicit in the previous point, is the observation that performance varies widely within any given age. For example, earlier in this chapter, I commented on tasks on which there were kindergarten children who performed very well and second-grade children who performed very badly. It is clear that age is not the *causal* factor in explaining levels of mastery. In our own work, we have attempted to identify factors other than age (e.g., intellectual skills; leisure activities) that correlate with better or worse performance (e.g., Liben, 2005; Liben & Downs, 1993). Although this approach is not unique to our work, it is also far less universal than it should be if we are to maximize the opportunity to formulate hypotheses about potential causal factors.

Fourth, as correlates of competencies are identified, it is important to evaluate whether they are merely related through some third factor (e.g., general intellectual ability; greater family resources) or whether they have causal power. One way to distinguish between these alternatives is through experimental research in which the hypothesized factor is manipulated. Illustrative of this approach in the graphic domain are studies in which children are taught to use pictorial symbols for communication (e.g., Callaghan, 1999), given photography lessons (Liben & Szechter, 2002), or exposed to home video (Troseth, 2003). Additional research of this kind is needed to provide experimental tests of whether the factors found to be associated with better understanding in correlational research actually have the power to facilitate better outcomes. In turn, research is needed to observe whether (and if so, how) these hypothesized mechanisms operate in the natural ecology. Illustrative are observing ways in which parents mediate graphic representations during picture-book reading (e.g., Szechter & Liben, 2004) or while examining museum exhibits (e.g., Fender & Crowley, 2003). To the degree that graphic representations are becoming increasingly pervasive in school, occupational, leisure, and public settings, it should become ever easier to find opportunities to observe relevant interactions beyond the walls of research laboratories.

In this chapter, I have argued that children's understanding of spatial graphic representations is multi-faceted, protracted, and complex. Programs of research can be no less multi-faceted, protracted, and complex if we are to understand the developmental processes that account for the evolution of children's understanding, and if we are to design educational experiences to facilitate it.

ACKNOWLEDGMENT

Work discussed in this chapter was supported, in part, by grants from the National Institute of Education (NIE-G-83-0025) and from the National Science Foundation (ESI 01-01758).

REFERENCES

Barrett, T. (1987). *Talking about student art.* Worchester, MA: Davis.

Beilin, H. (1991). Developmental aesthetics and the psychology of photography. In R. M. Downs, L. S. Liben, & D. S. Palermo (Eds.), *Visions of aesthetics, the environment, and development: The legacy of Joachim F. Wohlwill* (pp. 45–86). Hillsdale, NJ: Erlbaum.

Beilin, H. (1999). Understanding the photographic image. *Journal of Applied Developmental Psychology, 20,* 1–30.

Bialystok, E. (2000). Symbolic representation across domains in preschool children. *Journal of Experimental Child Psychology, 76,* 173–189.

Bialystok, E., & Martin, M. M. (2004). Attention and inhibition in bilingual children: Evidence from the dimensional change card sort task. *Developmental Science, 7,* 325–339

Blaut, J. M. (1997a). Children can. *Annals of the Association of American Geographers, 87,* 152—158.

Blaut, J. M. (1997b). Piagetian pessimism and the mapping abilities of young children: A rejoinder to Liben and Downs. *Annals of the Association of American Geographers, 87,* 168–177.

Bruner, J. S. (1964). The course of cognitive growth. *American Psychologist, 15,* 515–529.

Callaghan, T. C. (1999). Early understanding and production of graphic symbols. *Child Development, 70,* 1314–1324.

Callaghan, T. C. (2000). The role of context in preschoolers' judgments of emotion in art. *British Journal of Developmental Psychology, 18,* 465–474.

Callaghan, T. C., & MacFarlane, J. M. (1998). An attentional analysis of children's sensitivity to artistic style in paintings. *Developmental Science, 1,* 307–313.

DeLoache, J. S. (1987). Rapid change in the symbolic functioning of very young children. *Science, 238,* 1556–1557.

DeLoache, J. S., Strauss, M. S., & Maynard, J. (1979). Picture perception in infancy. *Infant Behavior and Development, 2*, 77-89.

DeLoache, J. S., Uttal, D. H., & Rosengren, K. S. (2004). Scale errors offer evidence for a perception-action dissociation early in life. *Science, 304*, 1027-1029.

Downs, R. M., & Liben, L. S. (1997). The final summation: The defense rests. *Annals of the Association of American Geographers, 87*, 178-180.

Downs, R. M., Liben, L. S., & Daggs, D. G. (1988). On education and geographers: The role of cognitive developmental theory in geographic education. *Annals of the Association of American Geographers, 78*, 680-700.

Downs, R. M., & Stea, D. (1977). *Maps in minds.* New York: Harper & Row.

Eliot, J. (1987). *Models of psychological space: Psychometric, developmental, and experimental approaches.* New York: Springer-Verlag.

Fender, J. G., & Crowley, K. (2003, April). *Adult explanations change children's encoding of everyday evidence.* Society for Research in Child Development, Tampa, FL.

Ferreiro, E., & Teberosky, A. (1982). *Literacy before schooling.* Portsmouth: NH: Heinemann.

Flavell, J. H. (1986). The development of children's knowledge about the appearance-reality distinction. *American Psychologist, 41*, 418-425.

Freeman, N. H. (1995). The emergence of a framework theory of pictorial reasoning. In C. Lange-Küttner & G. V. Thomas (Eds.), *Drawing and looking* (pp. 135-146). New York: Harvester Wheatsheaf.

Freeman, N. H., & Parsons, M. J. (2001). Children's intuitive understandings of pictures. In B. Torff & R. S. Sternberg (Eds.),*Understanding and teaching the intuitive mind: Student and teacher learning* (pp. 73-91). Mahwah, NJ: Erlbaum.

Gardner, H. (1970). Children's sensitivity to painting styles. *Child Development, 41*, 813-821.

Gardner, H., & Gardner, J. (1970). Developmental trends in sensitivity to painting style and subject matter. *Studies in Art Education, 12*, 11-16.

Gardner, H., & Gardner, J. (1973). Developmental trends in sensitivity to form and subject matter in paintings. *Studies in Art Education, 14*, 52-56.

Gauvain, M., de la Ossa, J. ., & Hurtado, M. T. (2001). Parental guidance as children learn to use cultural tools: The case of pictorial plans. *Cognitive Development, 16*, 551-575.

Gibson, J. J. (1979). *The ecological approach to visual perception.* Hillsdale, NJ: Erlbaum.

Golomb, C. (2004) *The child's creation of a pictorial world.* Mahwah, NJ: Erlbaum.

Haith, M. M. (1998). Who put the cog in infant cognition? Is rich interpretation too costly? *Infant Behavior and Development, 21*, 167-179.

Hardiman, G. W., & Zernich, T. (1985). Discrimination of style in painting: A developmental study. *Studies in Art Education, 26*, 157-162.

Ittleson, W. H. (1996). Visual perception of markings. *Psychonomic Bulletin and Review, 3*, 171-187.

Jammer, M. (1954). *Concepts of space.* Cambridge: Harvard University Press.

Jonsson, B. & von Hofsten, C. (2003). Infants' ability to track and reach for temporarily occluded objects. *Developmental Science, 6*, 86-99

Kastens, K. A. (2000). *Where are we?* Watertown, MA: Tom Snyder Productions.

Kastens, K. A., & Liben, L. S. (2004, May). *Where are we? Understanding and improving how children translate from a map to the represented space and vice versa.* Poster presented at the Instructional Materials Development PIs Meeting, National Science Foundation, Washington, D.C.

Landau, B., Gleitman, H., & Spelke, E. (1981). Spatial knowledge and geometric knowledge in a child blind from birth. *Science, 213*, 1275-1278.

Levine, M., Marchon, I., & Hanley, G. (1984). The placement and misplacement of You-Are-Here maps. *Environment and Behavior, 16*, 139-158.

Liben, L. S. (1981). Spatial representation and behavior: Multiple perspectives. In L. S. Liben, A. H. Patterson, & N. Newcombe (Eds.), *Spatial representation and behavior across the life span: Theory and application* (pp. 3-36). New York: Academic Press.

Liben, L. S. (1988). Conceptual issues in the development of spatial cognition. In J. Stiles-Davis, M. Kritchevsky, & U. Bellugi (Eds.), *Spatial cognition: Brain bases and development* (pp. 167-194). Hillsdale, NJ: Erlbaum.

Liben, L. S. (1991). The Piagetian water-level task: Looking beneath the surface. In R. Vasta (Ed.), *Annals of Child Development* (Vol. 8, pp. 81-143). London: Jessica Kingsley.

Liben, L. S. (1997a). Children's understanding of spatial representations of place: Mapping the methodological landscape. In N. Foreman & R. Gillett (Eds.), *A handbook of spatial research paradigms and methodologies.* (pp. 41-83). East Sussex, UK: Psychology Press.

Liben, L. S. (1997b). Standing on the shoulders of giants or collapsing on the backs of straw men? *The Developmental Psychologist,* Fall, 2-14.

Liben, L. S. (1999). Developing an understanding of external spatial representations. In I. E. Sigel (Ed.), *Development of mental representation: Theories and applications,* (pp. 297-321). Mahwah, NJ: Erlbaum.

Liben, L. S. (2000). Map use and the development of spatial cognition: Seeing the bigger picture. *Developmental Science, 3*, 270-274.

Liben, L. S. (2001). Thinking through maps. In M. Gattis (Ed.), *Spatial schemas and abstract thought* (pp. 44-77). Cambridge, MA: MIT Press.

Liben, L. S. (2002). Spatial development in children: Where are we now? In U. Goswami (Ed.), *Blackwell handbook of childhood cognitive development* (pp. 326-348). Oxford: Blackwell.

Liben, L. S. (2003a). Extending space: Exploring the expanding territory of spatial development. *Human Development, 46*, 61-68.

Liben, L. S. (2003b). Beyond point and shoot: Children's developing understanding of photographs as spatial and expressive representations. In R. V. Kail (Ed.), *Advances in child development and behavior: Vol. 31* (pp. 1-42). San Diego: Elsevier.

Liben, L. S. (2005). The role of action in understanding and using environmental place representations. In J. Rieser, J. Lockman, & C. Nelson (Eds.), *The Minnesota Symposium on Child Development* (pp. 323-361). Mahwah, NJ: Erlbaum.

Liben, L. S., & Downs, R. M. (1986). *Children's production and comprehension of maps: Increasing graphic literacy.* Final Report to National Institute of Education (#G-83-0025).

Liben, L. S., & Downs, R. D. (1989). Understanding maps as symbols: The development of map concepts in children. In H. W. Reese (Ed.), *Advances in child development and behavior: Vol. 22* (pp. 145-201). San Diego: Academic Press.

Liben, L. S., & Downs, R. M. (1991). The role of graphic representations in understanding the world. In R. M. Downs, L. S. Liben, & D. S. Palermo (Eds.), *Visions of aesthetics, the environment, and development: The legacy of Joachim Wohlwill* (pp. 139–180). Hillsdale, NJ: Erlbaum.

Liben, L. S., & Downs, R. M. (1992). Developing an understanding of graphic representations in children and adults: The case of GEO-graphics. *Cognitive Development, 7*, 331–349.

Liben, L. S., & Downs, R. M. (1993). Understanding person-space-map relations: Cartographic and developmental perspectives. *Developmental Psychology, 29*, 739–752.

Liben, L. S., & Downs, R. M. (1994). Fostering geographic literacy from early childhood: The contributions of interdisciplinary research. *Journal of Applied Developmental Psychology, 15*, 549–569.

Liben, L. S., & Downs, R. M. (1997). Can-ism and can'tianism: A straw child. *Annals of the Association of American Geographers, 87*, 159–167.

Liben, L. S., & Downs, R. M. (2001). Geography for young children: Maps as tools for learning environments. In S. L. Golbeck (Ed.), *Psychological perspectives on early childhood education* (pp. 220–252). Mahwah, NJ: Erlbaum.

Liben, L. S., Dunphy-Lelli, S., & Szechter, L. E. (in preparation). Children's and adults' interpretations of aerial photographs: The role of viewing distance and viewing angle. Unpublished manuscript, Pennsylvania State University.

Liben, L. S., Kastens, K. A., & Stevenson, L. M. (2002). Real-world knowledge through real-world maps: A developmental guide for navigating the educational terrain. *Developmental Review, 22*, 267–322.

Liben, L. S., & Szechter, L. E. (2001, October). *Understanding the spatial qualities of photographs*. In L. S. Liben (Chair), Cognitive development: A photographic view. Symposium conducted at the biennial meeting of the Cognitive Development Society, Virginia Beach, VA.

Liben, L. S., & Szechter, L. E. (2002). A social science of the arts: An emerging organizational initiative and an illustrative investigation of photography. *Qualitative Sociology, 25*, 385–408.

Linn, M. C., & Petersen, A. C. (1985). Emergence and characterization of sex differences in spatial ability: A meta-analysis. *Child Development, 56*, 1479–1498.

Lynch, K. (1960). *The image of the city*. Cambridge, MA: MIT Press.

Mandler, J. (1988). The development of spatial cognition: On topological and Euclidean representation. In J. Stiles-Davis, M. Kritchevsky, & U. Bellugi (Eds.), *Spatial cognition: Brain bases and development* (pp. 423–441). Hillsdale, NJ: Erlbaum.

Marr, D. (1982). *Vision*. New York: Freeman.

Meltzoff, A. N., & Borton, R. W. (1979). Intermodal matching by human neonates. *Nature, 282*, 403–404.

Meltzoff, A. N., & Moore, M. K. (1977). Imitation of facial and manual gestures by human neonates. *Science, 198*, 75–78.

Milbraith, C. (1998). *Patterns of artistic development in children*. Cambridge: Cambridge University Press.

Morrongiello, B. A., Timney, B. Humphrey, G. K., Anderson, S., & Skory, C (1995). Spatial knowledge in blind and sighted children. *Journal of Experimental Child Psychology, 59*, 211–233.

Mueller, U., & Overton, W. F. (1998). How to grow a baby: A re-evaluation of image-schema and Piagetian action approaches to representation. *Human Development, 41*, 71–111.

Myers, L. J., & Liben, L. S. (2004, May). *Children's understanding and use of symbolic intentions in graphic representations*. Poster presented at the American Psychological Society 16th Annual Convention, Chicago.

Newcombe, N., & Huttenlocher, J. (2000). *Making space*. Cambridge, MA: MIT Press.

Overton, W. F. (2003). Metatheoretical features of behavior genetics and development. *Human Development, 46*, 356–361.

Parsons, M. J. (1987). *How we understand art: A cognitive developmental account of aesthetic experience*. Cambridge: Cambridge University Press.

Piaget, J. (1951). *Play, dreams and imitation in childhood*. New York: Norton.

Piaget, J. (1954). *The construction of reality in the child*. New York: Ballantine Books.

Piaget, J., & Inhelder, B. (1956). *The child's conception of space*. New York: Norton.

Potter, M. C. (1979). Mundane Symbolism: The relations among objects, names, and ideas. In N. R. Smith & M. B. Franklin (Eds.), *Symbolic functioning in childhood* (pp. 41–65). Hillsdale, NJ: Erlbaum.

Rosenbaum, D. A., Meulenbroek, R. J., Vaughan, J., & Jansen, C. (2001) Posture-based motion planning: Applications to grasping. *Psychological Review, 108*, 709–734.

Shepard, R. N., & Cooper, L. A., (1986). *Mental images and their transformations*. Cambridge, MA: MIT Press

Sigel, I. E. (1978). The development of pictorial comprehension. In B. S. Randhawa & W. E. Coffman (Eds.), *Visual learning, thinking, and communication* (pp. 93–111). New York: Academic Press.

Sigel, I. E., & McGillicuddy-De Lisi, A. V. (1984). Parents as teachers of their children: A distancing behavior model. In A. D. Pellegrini & T. D. Yawkey (Eds.), *The development of oral and written language in social contexts* (pp. 71–92). Norwood, NJ: Ablex.

Signorella, M. L., Jamison, W., & Krupa, M. H. (1989). Predicting spatial performance from gender stereotyping in activity preferences and in self-concept. *Developmental Psychology, 25*, 89–95.

Smith, L. B. (1999). Do infants possess innate knowledge structures? The con side. *Developmental Science, 2*, 133–144.

Snow, C. E., & Ninio, A. (1986). The contracts of literacy: What children learn from learning to read books. In W. H. Teale & E. Sulzby (Eds.), *Emergent literacy: Writing and reading* (pp. 116–137). Norwood, NJ: Ablex.

Somerville, S. C., & Bryant, P. E. (1985) Young children's use of spatial coordinates. *Child Development, 56*, 604–613.

Sontag, S. (1977). *On photography*. New York: Anchor Books.

Spelke, E. S. (1999). Innateness, learning and the development of object representation. *Developmental Science, 2*, 145–148.

Spencer, C., Harrison, N., & Darvizeh, Z. (1980). The development of iconic mapping ability in young children. *International Journal of Early Childhood, 12*, 57–64.

Starkey, P., Spelke, E. S., & Gelman, R. (1983). Detection of intermodal numerical correspondences by human infants. *Science, 222*, 179–181.

Stokols, D., & Altman, I. (1987). *Handbook of environmental psychology*. New York: Wiley.

Szarkowski, J. (1973). *Looking at photographs: 100 pictures from the collection of the Museum of Modern Art*. New York: Museum of Modern Art.

Szechter, L. E. (2003). *Artistic expertise, parent-child interaction, and the development of aesthetic sensitivity*. Doctoral dissertation, Pennsylvania State University.

Szechter, L. E. & Liben, L. S. (2003a, May). *Parent-child interaction and the development of aesthetic awareness*. Poster presented at the American Psychological Society 15th Annual Convention, Atlanta.

Szechter, L. E., & Liben, L. S. (2003b, October) *Parent-child discussions of photography*. Poster presented at the Biennial Meeting of the Cognitive Development Society, Park City, UT.

Szechter, L. E., & Liben, L. S. (2004). Parental guidance in preschoolers' understanding of spatial-graphic representations. *Child Development, 75*, 869–885.

Thomas, H. (1983). Familial correlational analyses, sex differences, and the X-linked gene hypothesis. *Psychological Bulletin, 93*, 427–440.

Thomas, H., & Lohaus, A. (1993). Modeling growth and individual differences in spatial tasks. *Monographs of the Society for Research in Child Development, 58, No. 169*.

Thomas, H., & Turner, G. F. W. (1991). Individual differences and development in water-level task performance. *Journal of Experimental Child Psychology, 51*, 171–194.

Troseth, G. L. (2003). TV guide: Two-year-old children learn to use video as a source of information. *Developmental Psychology, 39*, 140–150.

Tversky, B. (2001). Spatial schemas in depictions. In M. Gattis (Ed.), *Spatial schemas and abstract thought* (pp. 79–112). Cambridge, MA : MIT Press.

Uttal, D. H. (2000). Seeing the big picture: Map use and the development of spatial cognition. *Developmental Science, 3*, 247–286.

Winner, E. (1982) *Invented worlds: The psychology of the arts*. Cambridge, MA: Harvard University Press.

Winner, E., Rosenblatt, E., Windmueller, G., Davidson, L., & Gardner, H. (1986). Children's perceptions of 'aesthetic' properties of the arts: Domain-specific or pan-artistic? *British Journal of Developmental Psychology, 4*, 149–160.

Zelazo, P. D., Mueller, U., Frye, D., & Marcovitch, S. (2003). The development of executive function. *Monographs of the Society for Research in Child Development, 68*(274).

13

The Role of Gender Stereotypes in Children's Preferences and Behavior

Cindy Faith Miller
Hanns Martin Trautner
Diane N. Ruble

INTRODUCTION

Gender serves as one of the most significant identifying labels throughout the life span. While originally a child's sex is based primarily on chromosomal and genital distinctions, this category will follow the child from the birthing room, operating as a life-long functional tag that will influence virtually every aspect of her or his experience. Our society uses sex categories to divide names, public restrooms, pronoun usage, school lines, toys, room decor, clothing and appearance options, hobbies, and occupations. Given societies' insistence on the functional use of sex categories (Bem, 1981), a child's physical, social, cognitive, and emotional milestones will all develop under a gendered umbrella. During some aspects of development, a child's gender tag will be at the forefront of experience while, other times, it will fade into the background providing minimal cues and effects to the situation. Regardless of the degree of salience, an individual's gender[1] has meaningful consequences that need to be considered when tackling issues related to child development.

An empirical and theoretical exploration of gender development can take many different forms. For example, researchers have recently highlighted the need to consider the multidimensionality of gender development (Eckes & Trautner, 2000; Hort, Leinbach, & Fagot, 1991; Huston, 1983; Liben & Bigler, 2002; Martin, 2000; Ruble & Martin, 1998; Signorella, 1999). This framework was first outlined in Huston's (1983) comprehensive review of the sex-typing literature and later modified in Ruble and Martin's (1998) updated chapter on gender development. This view recognizes the many distinct and possibly unrelated features of gender development (e.g., knowledge of gender stereotypes, gender attitudes, sex-role identity, sex-typed preferences) and allows researchers to locate their specific issue within a common frame of reference (Eckes & Trautner, 2000).

In the matrix outlined by Huston (1983) and Ruble and Martin (1998), this includes making a distinction between gender constructs and gender content areas. The content areas are divided according to biological/categorical sex, activities and interests, personal-social attributes, gender-based social relationships, styles and symbols, and gender-related values.[2] Within each of the six content areas, the four constructs that are considered include concepts or beliefs, identity or self-perception, preferences, and behavioral enactment. Thus, this matrix consists of twenty-four potential ways to locate specific research and theoretical issues related to gender development. This division is especially important because it allows researchers to consider developmental changes and possible relationships between dimensions for each of the unique facets of gender. For instance, research has proposed that knowledge of gender stereotypes increases with age while rigidity of gender attitudes decreases with age (see Signorella, Bigler, & Liben, 1993, and Ruble & Martin, 1998). Moreover, it has been suggested that there is little relationship between different preference areas such as same-sex peer preference and sex-typed toy preference (e.g., Campbell, Shirley, & Caygill, 2002; Shirley & Campbell, 2000). Nevertheless, increasing knowledge of the gender stereotypes associated with toys can influence preferences for those same toys (see Aubry, Ruble, & Silverman, 1999). It, therefore, seems clear that there are many facets to gender development and that a comprehensive and accurate picture would include an assessment of how each dimension is similar and different from the others, and how they influence each other.

In addition to recognizing the multidimensional nature of gender development, it is important to highlight that gender development occurs in a social and cultural context. While children might show particular sex-typed behaviors in front of their peers or with strangers, their behavioral enactment might change when they are surrounded by family or with people who are familiar to them. Incorporating these types of situational and social processes has been a challenge to developmental psychologists who have tended to focus on gender-related cognitions, preferences, and behaviors at the individual level (Eckes & Trautner, 2000; Maccoby, 2002a, 2002b). In contrast, examining social, contextual, and cultural factors related to gender has been of primary interest to social psychologists who, at the same time, have tended to ignore developmental changes and early experiences. This division between the developmental and social psychological approaches motivated Eckes and Trautner (2000) to edit a volume with the aim of integrating the two perspectives. In fact, in their introductory chapter, they broadened the Ruble and Martin (1998) matrix to include multiple levels of analysis. The proposed levels are the individual level, the interpersonal (or interactional) level, the group (or role) level, and the cultural (or societal) level. The addition of these levels produce a 96-cell matrix that will, hopefully, allow both social and developmental researchers to more deliberately pinpoint the questions that they are pursuing and the questions that still need answers.

After outlining the different dimensions and levels of gender development, we are better able to locate our specific research questions and goals of this chapter. Similar to the Aubry et al. (1999) chapter in the first edition of this volume, our aim is to explore children's knowledge of gender stereotypes for objects, activities, and attributes and the influence of this knowledge on children's behavior. While the chapter in the previous edition focused primarily on children's gender-related preferences, our review will expand the discussion to include the effect of stereotype knowledge on children's exploration and performance (i.e., behavioral enactment). This review mainly focuses on issues located at the individual level of analysis; however, other levels are considered when evidence is available and directly relevant to the topic.

Like the Aubry et al. (1999) chapter, our discussion begins with an outline of the different theoretical explanations of sex typing, paying attention to recent changes and debates that have stimulated the field. Given that our research is closely tied to cognitive approaches, we expand this section to review our particular view of gender development. The second section briefly describes the literature concerning knowledge and preference trends and the relationship between these two dimensions, and highlights research and issues that have been raised in this area since the first edition of this volume. Following this review, we present new longitudinal data on the relationship between children's gender stereotype knowledge and preferences and examine how this study provides additional support for cognitive views of gender development. In the last section, experimental studies that have assessed the effects of gender labels on children's exploration, preferences, and performance are explored and explanations for the observed findings are proposed.

THEORETICAL PERSPECTIVES OF GENDER DEVELOPMENT

What are the processes that account for gender differentiation? This question has stimulated theoretical debates that continue in the field today. The beginning of the controversy over the relative influences of social and cognitive factors can be traced back to Maccoby's (1966) book *The Development of Sex Differences*. In one chapter, Walter Mischel emphasized environmental influences by using principles of learning theory (e.g., rewards, punishments) and modeling to explain sex-typed behavior. In another chapter, Lawrence Kohlberg proposed a cognitive-developmental theory based on Piagetian principles, highlighting how developmental changes in cognitive structures account for gendered behaviors. While both theories have moved toward a middle ground with social learning theory incorporating cognitive factors (i.e., social cognitive theory) and cognitive theories recognizing environmental influences, there continues to be inconsistencies and confusions in the literature regarding which factors play a necessary and central role in early gender development (see Martin, Ruble, & Szkrybalo, 2002). In fact, this controversy was recently revived with Bussey and Bandura's (1999) updated presentation of their social cognitive theory of gender development. In addition to providing a comprehensive explanation of their theory, they critiqued cognitive theories of gender development on theoretical and empirical grounds. In response to this critique, Martin et al. (2002) defended assumptions proposed by cognitive theories with a review of supportive research and by addressing misconceptions in the field. Although these two publications are directly linked to Mischel and Kohlberg's 1966 accounts, the degree of overlap is much greater and the possibility of a comprehensive and integrative theory of gender development does not seem far away (Martin et al., 2002 Powlishta, Sen, Serbin, Poulin-Dubois, & Eichstedt, 2001). In the next section, we briefly review the basic tenets of each of these theories and discuss the assumptions that guide our own research. Given that biological theories of gender development have appeared to build momentum in recent years, we also provide a short account of this view.

Social-Cognitive Theory

Bussey and Bandura's (1999) most recent account proposes that children's development of sex-typed knowledge and competencies is promoted by modeling, enactive experience, and direct tuition. As in previous versions of their theory, observational learning continues to take center stage as the major conveyor of gender-typed information. Through cognitive functions such as attentional and representational processes, symbolic conceptions derived through modeling are able to be translated into behavioral courses of action. Whether children will actually perform the learned behaviors, however, will depend on the incentive motivators (i.e., direct, vicarious, or self-evaluative) associated with the outcomes. Through these social experiences, children also develop outcome expectancies and self-efficacy beliefs that become linked to sex-typed roles and conduct. These cognitions are then expected to regulate children's sex-typed behavior. For example, if a girl observes other girls in her classroom receive disapproval for engaging in rough and tumble play, she will expect that a similar outcome will occur if she attempts to perform the same behaviors. Thus, gender-linked sanctions serve an informational and motivational function that will influence subsequent courses of action. While these sanctions are originally socially prescribed, social cognitive theory asserts that they eventually become internalized to form personal standards that will allow children to regulate and exert direct influence over their own behaviors.

Based on the outline of Bussey and Bandura's (1999) recent description, it is clear that social learning theory has come a long way from just relying on simple stimulus-response principles to explain behavior. In fact, they promote a triadic reciprocal model of causation in which personal (e.g., cognitive, affective, biological factors), behavioral, and environmental factors interact to determine sex-linked conduct. Additionally, children are no longer seen as passive recipients of environmental influences, but are now viewed as active contributors to their gender development. Even though these theoretical additions have increased the overlap between social and cognitive perspectives, there continues to be confusions and differences regarding the necessary cognitive precursors of same-sex modeling, the evaluative and motivational consequences of gender identity, and the factors that are associated with children's active role in acquiring knowledge (see Martin et al., 2002).

Cognitive Theories of Gender Development

Cognitive-oriented theorists view children as active constructors of knowledge who seek, interpret, and act on information in an effort to match their behavior to their understanding of gender (Martin, 1993; Martin, 2000; Martin & Dinella, 2002; Martin et al., 2002, 2004; Martin & Ruble, 2004; Ruble, 1994). This idea was proposed by Kohlberg (1966) when he first outlined his cognitive-developmental theory of gender development. In his view, children's understanding of gender emerges as children undergo age-related changes in cognitive development. A key feature in his theory is *gender constancy*, which refers to the developing understanding that gender is a fixed characteristic that is not altered by situational changes in appearance, activities, or behavior. Once children have attained this level of understanding, they are expected to show increased motivation to seek out gender-linked information with the goal of mastering the gender norms of our culture. Thus, the acquisition of gender knowledge is, in part, initiated internally by the child and is a guiding determinant of sex-typed behaviors.

While Kohlberg's innovative theory stimulated enduring changes in the way researchers conceptualize gender development, lack of empirical support for some of his ideas has prompted theorists to reconsider and debate his original contentions. The main controversy has concerned the critical importance of children acquiring the last stage of gender constancy, called *gender consistency* (Slaby & Frey, 1975). For example, there have been confusions regarding whether Kohlberg even indicated that this level of knowledge was a necessary prerequisite for the emergence of sex-typed behaviors (Martin et al., 2002; Ruble & Martin, 1998). Although Kohlberg's (1966) theoretical description mostly refers to the primary importance of gender consistency, he also seems to suggest that basic gender category knowledge organizes gender development. Moreover, empirical findings support the notion that earlier levels of constancy understanding, such as the belief that gender categories are stable over time, may be more related to gendered behaviors than gender consistency (see Ruble & Martin, 1998 for a review). Not surprisingly, these inconsistencies in the literature have led researchers to develop more complex ideas regarding the consequences of different forms of gender category knowledge.

One such proposal views children's developing knowledge about gender as a social-cognitive transition that begins when children are just beginning to realize the significance of gender in their world (Ruble, 1994). As children progress through this transition, they are expected to show predictable changes in terms of how actively they seek out gendered information and the degree to which different types of information become salient and significant. In this model, gender consistency is characterized as a period of consolidation for conclusions about gender norms. Rather than serving as an initial organizer of gender development, gender consistency knowledge is intended to motivate children to be more focused on expanding their same-sex knowledge (Ruble, 1994; Stangor & Ruble, 1987). During this consolidation phase, children are also proposed to display an increase in rigidity in that they are less likely to process information and behave in a way that is inconsistent with their beliefs about gender (Frey & Ruble, 1992; Stangor & Ruble, 1989).

Kohlberg's ideas and the cognitive revolution in psychology also set the stage for another cognitive view of gender development referred to as gender schema theory (see Martin et al., 2002, for a current review of these theories). Similar to cognitive-developmental theory, gender schema theory emphasizes the primary function of children's cognitions and focuses on the ways children actively participate in their gender development (Bem, 1981; Martin & Halverson, 1981). In this view, there is an emphasis on the dynamic processes involved in the acquisition of gender-related knowledge and how this knowledge influences attention, perception, memory, and behavior. This process is stimulated by children's natural tendency to use categories that are salient and functional in the environment to organize and make sense of information (Bem, 1981; Martin & Halverson, 1981). Therefore, the development of sex-linked knowledge and associations is organized into gender schemas that continue to exert their influence on incoming information. In one version of gender schema theory, Bem (1981) proposes that children develop gender schemas by virtue of the pervasive gender messages in society and that sex-typing occurs when children's self-concept and self-esteem gets assimilated into gender schemas. Interestingly, Bem's theory also focuses on individual differences in the degree of being sex-typed. She asserts that "individual differences schemas" and "sexism schemas" can replace gender schemas when children are encouraged to process information according to the variability within groups and the historical roots and consequences of sex discrimination (Bem, 2000).

Martin and Halverson's (1981) gender-schema theory focuses on the ways that gender schemas organize, bias, and regulate thinking, attention, and behavior. The motivating force in this theory is the maintenance of cognitive consistency and the need for self-definition. According to this view, children attend to and remember more script-like information about same-sex activities than about opposite-sex activities. This suggests that children are more likely to approach, explore, ask questions, and learn detailed information about an activity when it is considered self-relevant. Thus, this model helps explain how gender stereotypes are maintained and how they may lead to differential preferences, abilities, and behaviors in girls and boys.

Biological Theories

In recent years, gender development researchers have called for an increased recognition of the integrative role of biological factors in the production of sex differences (e.g., Alexander, 2003; Kenrick & Luce, 2000; Maccoby, 2000, 2002b; Ruble & Martin, 1998; Zucker, 2001). Biological approaches to gender development have focused on issues ranging from the role of genes and hormones to the effects of evolution on sex differences in behavior. For example, research on the effects of hormones is generally based on the view that sex differentiated exposure to prenatal and/or postnatal hormones can cause behavioral and ability differences in males and females (see Collaer & Hines, 1995, and Berenbaum, 2002). One program of research that has shown promising results in this area has involved the investigation of girls with congenital adrenal hyperplasia (CAH). Individuals with CAH have a genetic condition that results in the overproduction of androgenic steroids during prenatal development. In addition to having either fully or partly masculinized external genitalia, girls with CAH have been shown to engage in more male-typical childhood play and have more masculine interests in adolescence and adulthood when compared to control samples (see Zucker, 2001 and Berenbaum, 2002). It is possible though that the masculinized behaviors of CAH girls may be partly due to socialization or cognitive responses to the ambiguous genitalia or overall condition (see Zucker, 2001, p. 108). Thus, future research that actively accounts for these factors is likely to produce interesting findings regarding the integrative and unique influences of biology.

Another biological perspective that has gained interest in recent years concerns evolutionary explanations of sex differences. Proponents of this view believe that sex-typed behavior is partly due to the differential demands and inherited adaptive strategies that have been linked to males and females during the ancestral past (see Kenrick & Luce, 2000). This perspective has been used to interpret sex differences in mate preferences (e.g., Buss & Schmitt, 1993 ; Trivers, 1972) and jealousy (e.g., Buss, Larsen, Westen, & Semmelroth, 1992) and, more recently, researchers have been using evolutionary principles to explain sex segregation (Maccoby, 2000, 2002b) and sex-typed toy preferences (Alexander, 2003) in childhood. For example, Alexander (2003) proposes that the categories of "masculine" and "feminine" toys have been partly influenced by evolved perceptual preferences (e.g., movement, color) that have had differential adaptive significance for males and females.

Conclusions

The descriptions provided concerning the theoretical explanations of sex differentiation allows us to place our own research and perspectives within this context. In general, our research questions and pursuits are heavily grounded in cognitive theories of gender development. We are guided by the view that children's cognitions are important determinants of their sex-typed behaviors. Mainly, this refers to the idea that the acquisition of gender knowledge (i.e., basic identity and stereotypic information) has evaluative, motivational, cognitive (e.g., information processing), and behavioral consequences. Along with this assumption is the idea that children are active information seekers who are intrinsically motivated to learn about and match their behavior to gender norms as an inherent part of gender identity development. We believe, however, that the environment provides the sources for information about gender norms through parental and teacher socialization, same-sex modeling, peer groups, the media, etc. Moreover, we are particularly interested in the developmental change patterns concerning children's gender cognitions and behaviors and believe that these changes are essential to a comprehensive understanding of gender development.

Although cognitive approaches emphasize the role of cognitions in gender differentiation, it is essential to highlight that theorists who adhere to this view do not assert that gender knowledge is the only determinant of sex-typed behaviors (see Aubry et al., 1999; Martin, 1993; Martin et al., 2002, 2004; Ruble & Martin, 1998). For example, it is clearly recognized that biological and social factors play a role in gender development. If a young girl is provided with dolls and is rewarded for engaging in doll play, she is likely to show a preference for dolls even if she has not yet labeled herself as a girl and acquired the knowledge that "dolls are for girls." In addition, it is recognized that girls and boys have biological differences that might predispose them to engage differently in the world. While this point has been made clear in other reviews (see Martin et al., 2002), researchers continue to use findings indicating that preferences appear before knowledge as evidence to critique cognitive accounts (Bandura & Bussey, 2004; Bussey & Bandura, 1999; Campbell et al., 2002; Shirley & Campbell, 2000). Given that cognitive theorists, including ourselves, believe that social and biological factors influence gender development, this is not a valid critique. In a similar vein, current cognitive approaches recognize that certain factors moderate the relationship between gender knowledge and sex-typed behaviors (see Martin et al., 2002). These factors might include toy attractiveness, salience of schemas, accessibility of specific knowledge, situational demands and contextual factors, personal skills, gender attitudes, and degree of gender identification. Cognitive theorists believe that these variables will influence whether children will match their behavior to their understanding of gender norms. It is also not valid then to use studies that do not find a direct relationship between knowledge and behavior as a means to conclude that gender cognitions do not influence gender-typed behavior. Taken together, some of the key questions for cognitive theorists include: What constitutes children's gender knowledge and sex-typed behaviors and how does knowledge and behavior change over time? When and how does children's gender knowledge influence their perceptions, attention, memory, judgements, and behaviors? What factors moderate the relationship between knowledge and behavior? In the next section, we tackle the first question by briefly examining the development of children's stereotype knowledge and sex-typed preferences. Following this review, we consider the relationship between these two forms of gender development.

STEREOTYPE KNOWLEDGE AND PREFERENCE TRENDS

In the first edition of this volume, Aubry et al. (1999) provided a detailed review of the literature concerning stereotype knowledge and preferences. Our aim in this section is to briefly summarize their presentation and to describe any new data that shed light on this issue.

Stereotype Knowledge

In terms of children's stereotype knowledge of concrete items and activities, it has been consistently found that this knowledge emerges during the preschool years and reaches ceiling levels by age 5 or 6 (see Ruble & Martin, 1998, for a review). For example, children as young as 3 are beginning to understand that items such as hairbrushes, dolls, domestic tools (e.g., iron, broom), and a needle and thread are associated with females while bats, balls, shovels, and cars are linked to males. Moreover, recent research has found that 4-year-olds show awareness of metaphorical gendered associations (Leinbach, Hort, & Fagot, 1997) and that 18-month-olds have formed metaphorical associations specific to the male role (Eichstedt, Serbin, Poulin-Dubois, & Sen, 2002). This type of knowledge refers to children's ability to perceive some abstract similarity among items that are associated with males or females. For example, hearts, the color pink, roundness, and softness are metaphorically associated with females while bears, the color blue, anger, and roughness are metaphorically associated with males. While there is some overlap between metaphorical and conventional knowledge, some theorists believe that abstracting metaphors requires going beyond direct associations and, therefore, may drive the acquisition of more conventional stereotypes (Eichstedt et al., 2002).

As children grow older, they continue to develop more detailed knowledge of concrete items and begin to learn about the stereotypes in other domains (Ruble & Martin, 1998). Specifically, research suggests that occupational stereotypes are learned around kindergarten and that attribute stereotypes emerges around age 5 and may continue to develop into adolescence (Aubry et al., 1999; Huston, 1983; Ruble & Martin 1998). Assessing knowledge of personality attributes has been complicated due to children's tendency to mainly attribute the positive items to their own sex and the negative items to the opposite sex regardless of the cultural stereotype (see Aubry et al., 1999). It has been found, however, that this same-sex bias is gradually replaced by more "accurate" associations during middle childhood (Aubry et al., 1999; Serbin, Powlishta, & Gulko, 1993).

In addition to expanding their stereotypic knowledge to include other domains, older children also seem to show increases in the ability to make more complex associations (Martin, Wood, & Little, 1990). This finding is based on the application of a component model of gender stereotype knowledge, which extends the assessment of gendered associations to include children's knowledge of "horizontal links" (see Martin, 1993). In addition to determining whether children can link certain attributes to a gender label (woman—dress), this type of assessment involves finding out if children can make a link for the attributes within (dress—high heels) or between (dress—nurturant) components. Research using these types of assessments have found that children are able to make horizontal associations for their own sex by age 6, but are unable to make opposite-sex horizontal links until about 8 years of age (Martin et al., 1990). It is important to note, however, that having more stereotyped knowledge and attaining the cognitive ability to make more complex gendered associations does not mean that children will continue to apply this information in a rigid fashion. In fact, just the opposite occurs; as children grow older, they become more flexible when assigning stereotypes. This idea is drawn from research that found that as children grow older, they are more likely to assign specific stereotypes to both sexes rather than stating that items are true for "only boys/men" or "only girls/women" (Trautner, 1992; Trautner, Ruble, Cyphers, Kirsten, Behrendt, & Hartmann, in press). It has been suggested that these developmental changes are partly due to children's advancing classification skills (Bigler, 1995; Trautner, 1992). Consistent with this belief, recent longitudinal research found that by 8 years old, children had similar levels of stereotype flexibility regardless of how rigid they were at earlier ages (Trautner, Ruble, Cyphers et al., in press). Moreover, children who showed earlier rigidity were even more flexible later on rather than less (Trautner, Ruble, Cyphers et al., in press). These results imply that young children's high levels of gender stereotype rigidity is part of a predictable developmental stage that occurs when they are first learning about and trying to make sense of gender.

The measures used to assess stereotype knowledge generally have children either verbally match pictures according to sex or have them sort into or point to male/female labeled boxes (e.g., Edelbrock & Sugawara, 1978; Leinbach, Hort, & Fagot, 1997). While these types of measures may seem age-appropriate for older children, it is possible that the tasks are too complicated to accurately detect the knowledge of children who are 3 or younger (Aubry et al., 1999). This indicates that children might develop stereotypic knowledge at much younger ages than is generally believed. In fact, recent studies using nonverbal looking-time tasks have found that infants age 2 years or younger have some knowledge of activities and objects that are associated with each gender (Eichstedt et al., 2002; Levy & Haaf, 1994; Serbin, Poulin-Dubois, Colburne, Sen, & Eichstedt, 2001; Serbin, Poulin-Dubois, & Eichstedt, 2002). For example, Serbin et al. (2001; Experiment 2) used an adaptation of the preferential looking paradigm to determine if 18- and 24-month-olds were able to correctly match gender-typed toys with the face of a boy or a girl. This first involved having children look at two identical pictures of either a masculine (i.e., vehicle) or feminine (i.e., doll) toy that was displayed on side-by-side computer screens. As the toy was shown, a gender ambiguous voice said, "See my doll (car)? That's my doll (car)!" After 5 seconds, a picture of a boy and a girl appeared on the screens accompanied by the statement, "Look at me!" The assumption in this procedure is that children who knew the gender stereotype associated with the toy would look at the matching face (e.g., girl after doll) longer than the mismatching face (e.g., boy after doll). The results indicated that there were no differences in the boys' looking time; however, the girls in both age groups looked significantly longer at the matched face when compared to the mismatched face.[3] This suggests that girls as young as 18 months are aware of the gender stereotypes associated with toys.

More recent studies using similar paradigms found that both boys and girls were aware of some of the gender stereotypes associated with adults (Eichstedt et al., 2002; Serbin et al., 2002). These studies, however, are based on the reverse assumption than the one that guided the Serbin et al. (2001) study. Instead of expecting children to look longer at the matched pictures, children who have knowledge of gender stereotypes are expected to look longer at the mismatched picture because it is seen as novel or surprising. For example, Serbin et al. (2002) showed 24-month-olds paired pictures of men and women engaging in identical activities that were either masculine (e.g., hammering, taking out the garbage), feminine (e.g., putting on make-up, feeding a baby) or neutral (e.g., reading, turning on a light). The results indicated that the children paid significantly more attention to the gender-inconsistent picture when the activities were feminine (e.g., man putting on make-up), but paid almost equal attention to the two pictures when the adults were performing a masculine activity. The stronger "mismatching" effect for feminine activities was consistent with the parents' report regarding the role division in the home. The report indicated that mothers were more likely to perform the feminine activities; however, the masculine activities were typically performed by either both parents or mostly mothers. In this case, the pictures of the women performing the masculine activities (e.g., woman taking out the garbage) was probably not seen as surprising or novel to the infants.

These results are somewhat inconsistent with another "surprise" study which found that 18- and 24-month olds were aware of the stereotypes associated with masculine stereotypes, but not feminine objects (Eichstedt et al., 2002). Like the earlier Serbin et al. (2001; Experiment 2) study, Eichstedt et al. (2002) used a sequential visual attention task, which involved presenting identical pictures of masculine (e.g., fire hat) or feminine (e.g., tiara) items accompanied by a gender-ambiguous voice saying, "This is the one I like. Can you look at me?" One male and one female adult face was shown after the objects and the only significant result found was that the children looked significantly longer at the female faces after the masculine items were presented. The authors suggest that the children displayed knowledge of masculine stereotypes, explaining the longer looking time at the female faces as evidence of "surprise." It is noteworthy though that this interpretation is the opposite of the assumption that was used to interpret the results in the Serbin et al. (2001) study. It is, therefore, unclear when "matched" or "mismatched" looking times should be used as evidence of gender stereotype knowledge. Until further research clarifies this confusion, the results from the infant paradigm studies should be interpreted with caution. Nonetheless, the results suggest that it is likely that children are developing at least some rudimentary knowledge of gender associations in the second year of life. Moreover, it is possible that girls may develop this knowledge quicker than boys (see also O'Brien et al., 2000) and that individual experiences may determine whether the initial learning of masculine and feminine stereotypes is acquired at different rates.

In addition to taking the target's sex into account when attempting to understand children's gender stereotype knowledge, it is also necessary to recognize that stereotypes are processed and activated within a situational context. This point was illustrated in a study of 6- and 7-year-old children in Scotland (Sani & Bennett, 2001). The researchers had children select cards to describe their own sex group (girls or boys) after they either performed the same procedure to describe opposite sex peers (girls or boys) or same-sex adults (women or men). Interestingly, the results revealed that the group of adjectives that were selected to describe the children's in-group depended on which out-group was used as a comparative reference. For example, when boys' comparative out-group was girls, their top two adjectives selected to describe boys were "strong" and "brave." In contrast, the most frequent adjectives selected when the reference group was men were "honest" and "happy." For girl participants, the top traits selected to describe their in-group were "friendly" and "happy" after they described boys and "kind" and "nice" after they described women. A similar study assessing 5- and 7-year old children also found that children's in-group descriptions depended on their frame of reference (Sani, Bennett, Mullally, & MacPherson, 2003). These studies provide some support for self-categorization theory, which asserts that the nature of stereotypes depends on the inter-group context. In this view, group stereotypes are considered to be highly flexible and variable rather than rigid and fixed. As discussed in the beginning of this chapter, these results highlight the need to consider levels of analysis beyond the individual when studying aspects of gender development.

Sex-Linked Preferences

The evidence is mixed concerning the development of children's sex-typed preferences for concrete toys and activities. Similar to the issue with assessing stereotype knowledge, the results seem to depend on the type of measure employed (see Aubry et al., 1999). For example, when asking children to make conscious choices based on verbal questions, children show sex-typed preferences as early as 3 years with well-established preferences by age 5 (Carter & Levy, 1988; Coker, 1984; Martin & Little, 1990; Perry, White, & Perry, 1984). On behavioral measures in which children's free play is observed to assess the amount of time they play with masculine and feminine toys, sex-typed preferences have been found in the second year (Weinraub, Clemens, Sockloff, Ethridge, Gracely, & Myers, 1984; Campbell et al., 2002). It is not clear, however, whether these types of behavioral measures are actually examining children's sex-typed preferences. For example, children may initially pick up and explore different toys because of familiarity or attractiveness and these factors may not be final determinants of actual, deliberate preferences. Even if behavioral measures do actually measure preferences, the influence of gender knowledge on children's deliberate choices is likely to be different than its role in an unstructured, novel play environment (Aubry et al., 1999).

After preschool and kindergarten, the developmental pattern of children's preferences for concrete items and activities is not straightforward. Earlier studies have found that boys continue to show an increased preference for masculine activities, whereas girls show a decline in preference for feminine activities and an increased interest in masculine pursuits (see Huston, 1983, for a review). Some more recent studies have continued to find this sex difference (Katz & Boswell, 1986; Katz & Walsh, 1991); however, others have either found that preferences remain stable after kindergarten (Serbin et al., 1993) or that they decline (Aubry et al., 1999; Welch-Ross & Schmidt, 1996). These inconsistent findings may be partly due to individual differences in the developmental course of children's sex-typed preferences (Ruble & Martin, 1998). For example, in a longitudinal study, Trautner (1992) observed two different patterns in children's sex-typed preferences. One pattern involved an increase in same-sex activity and toy preferences until age 7 at which point they either stabilized at a high level or decreased through age 10, whereas other children were already highly stereotyped by age 5 and remained at this level throughout the study. It is interesting though that while the first pattern was somewhat more typical for girls, more boys were observed showing the second pattern. Moreover, developmental patterns also seem to depend on whether children are asked about occupations, toys, or academic subjects (Etaugh & Liss, 1992), on the specific items used within domains such as chores versus attractive toys (see Aubry et al., 1999), and on whether children are asked about their preference for same-sex activities or their rejection of other-sex activities (Aubry et al., 1999; Bussey & Perry, 1982). In using items such as secretary, takes care of children, drives a truck, and boxing gloves to assess children's preferences, Aubry et al. (1999) found that preference trends tended to decline after kindergarten for both same-gender and opposite-gender items. Overall, this indicates that these specific items became less desirable with age. Does this mean that children also became less sex-typed with age? Not necessarily. The boys who liked boxing gloves and shovels in kindergarten might have a strong interest in football, video games, and race car drivers by third grade. This indicates that both boys and girls may continue to remain highly sex-typed with age, but that the way this is manifested may shift to include different same-gender interests, occupations, and traits. Furthermore, analyses need to consider children's same-sex and opposite-sex trends separately to reach a complete picture of children's sex-typed behaviors. While Aubry et al. (1999) found a declining interest in all items over time, children's decreased preference for other-gender items was more pronounced and reached much lower absolute levels by third grade. Taken together, measures assessing children's knowledge and preferences need to be clearly divided according to domain, provide separate same-sex and opposite-sex scores, and include a variety of different items to detect changing perceptions and interests with age.

In addition to examining children's preferences for gender stereotypical toys and activities, some research has examined whether children will tend to label themselves according to gender-typed personality attributes. Given that children do not show knowledge of stereotypes for personality attributes in preschool, it is not surprising that research has found that preschoolers will mainly attribute only positive characteristics to themselves regardless of the stereotypes (Cowan & Hoffman, 1986). However, it is unclear at what age children will begin to show a tendency to self-label according to gender-typed attributes. While some studies have found that children 8- or 9-years old will describe themselves according to gender-typed personality traits (see Aubry et al., 1999 and Ruble & Martin, 1998), a recent study that included both positive and negative attributes found that the same-sex bias observed in the assessment of children's knowledge may show a similar influence on children's willingness to label themselves with only stereotyped items (Aubry et al., 1999). For example, Aubry et al. (1999) found that even by third grade, children continued to endorse a high proportion of opposite-gender positive attributes and persisted in their reluctance to label themselves with same-gender negative attributes. It is possible that children may actually exhibit behavioral manifestations of gender-typed attributes, but their limited self-awareness and/or the demand characteristics of the testing situation influences their answers. Additionally, conducting assessments at the individual level may not adequately assess how children's behaviors are played out in different contexts. Maccoby (2002a) argues that children's gender-typical behavior is not consistent from one situation to another and that certain behaviors that occur at the group level are not apparent at the individual level. Maccoby's point illustrates the need to integrate the individual and group perspectives. Thus, researchers might advance the field of gender development by examining children's "gender signatures" in the same way that Walter Mischel and colleagues emphasize person-situation interactions and "personality signatures" (e.g., Mischel & Shoda, 1995; Shoda, Mischel, & Wright, 1994).

THE RELATIONSHIP BETWEEN KNOWLEDGE AND PREFERENCE

Researchers interested in gender development have gone beyond an assessment of developmental trends to examine the relationship between children's gender stereotypic knowledge and their preferences. One reason for interest in this research has been to test predictions made by cognitive theories of gender development. Cognitive theorists believe that having knowledge of gender stereotypes should influence whether children will match their behavior to gendered norms. As discussed in the section that reviewed theoretical perspectives, however, cognitive factors are not believed to be the only determinant. With that emphasized, we can now summarize the literature that has examined the relationship between knowledge and preferences with the goal of highlighting the status of this research and to point out methodological limitations and benefits that can be used as guides for future research. Given that this literature was reviewed in Aubry et al. (1999), we only present a brief summary here and provide a more detailed account of any recent studies.

Evidence for Independence

Several researchers have made the argument that gender knowledge and preferences are independent after observing that young children do not mention gender as a reason for their choices (Eisenberg,

Murray, & Hite, 1982), that gender preferences emerge before gender knowledge (Perry et al., 1984; Weinraub et al., 1984), and that there is no significant positive correlation between knowledge and preferences (Bussey & Bandura, 1992; Carter & Levy, 1988; Hort, Leinbach, & Fagot, 1991). As raised by Aubry et al. (1999), there were several methodological limitations in these studies that question the validity of their findings. For example, some of the research used different types of knowledge and preference tasks, with the knowledge task being far more challenging than the preference tasks (Bussey & Bandura, 1992; Weinraub et al., 1984). Moreover, one study used different items for the knowledge and preference tasks even when the tasks were more similar (Carter & Levy, 1988). Asking children about their knowledge of some activities (e.g., ironing, sweeping, boxing, digging) and assessing their preferences for other toys (e.g., kitchen set, doll, gun, truck) does not provide much information in terms of the relationship between these two dimensions.

Another difficulty with the literature assessing knowledge and preferences is that studies often use the Sex Role Learning Index (Edelbrock & Sugawara, 1978) to measure gender knowledge (Carter & Levy, 1988; Hort et al., 1991). Besides the fact that the items may be outdated, mostly all of the child feminine items include chores such as ironing, dishwashing, and sweeping. In this case, girls might show a reluctance to endorse these items even if they have the knowledge that they are stereotypically appropriate. Furthermore, a limitation of the Perry et al. (1984) study was that their results relied on using an analysis of variance method to explore developmental trends in knowledge and preference scores. This type of analysis does not detect whether individual children show knowledge-preference links, thereby raising the question of whether a correlational or regression analysis would have identified a significant relationship. A final concern is that longitudinal studies in this area are sparse. Thus, if there is a lag between the attainment of gender knowledge and the time it takes to influence children's preferences, an examination of only concurrent relationships might miss this important effect (Aubry et al., 1999).

Since the publication of the first edition of this volume, we are aware of one study that specifically addressed the role of gender knowledge in children's gendered preferences. In this study, Campbell et al. (2002) included measurements of gender-knowledge, peer preference, and toy preference in a sample of 2-year-olds. Interestingly, the gender knowledge measure was given by the child's mother and involved asking the child to point to either the boys' toy/game or the girls' toy/game after two opposite sex-typed toys/activities were pictorially presented. Using the same toys, children were observed in the same room with the mother and experimenter to see how long they played with each of the toys. Prior to this session, children were also observed in a group situation to see how long they played with other sex-typed toys, and same-sex and opposite-sex same-aged peers. Using an analysis of variance model in which children were categorized as knowing or not knowing stereotypes, the researchers did not find any significant effects when examining whether gender knowledge was associated with sex-typed behavior in either the group or individual observation sessions.[4] The authors, therefore, concluded that the impact of cognitive variables on children's sex-typed preferences might have been overemphasized. They stated that " . . . sex-congruent toy choice predates the ability to assign toys to male and female categories . . . " (p. 213) and assert that these data present a challenge to gender schema theory.

The conclusions drawn from this study do not seem justified for some of the same methodological reasons that were discussed regarding the earlier studies (e.g., differential processing demands of the tasks, using unattractive feminine toys, inappropriate analysis model). Moreover, the only significant sex difference found in terms of time spent with these toys was for doll play. Given that children were grouped solely on their overall success rate on the gender knowledge measure, it is unclear if the children who knew the gender labels of specific items (e.g., dolls) were the children who were more likely to approach or avoid these toys. It is noteworthy though that a correlational model may not have even detected a possible relationship. Overall, stereotypic knowledge was very low and, therefore, there was insufficient power to examine its possible effect on preferences. Thus, while it is reasonable to expect that the 2-year-olds in this study demonstrated sex-typed preferences before having stereotyped knowledge, the low levels of both stereotypic knowledge and sex differences in preferences make it difficult to draw firm conclusions. Moreover, even if the children did show preferences before knowledge, it would not constitute a challenge to the tenets of gender schema theory. It would be interesting, however, to follow the children in a longitudinal study to see if preferences shift once children do have knowledge.

In summary, prior conclusions that gender knowledge does not play a role in the development of sex-typed preferences seem premature. The data available to date are not convincing because of the myriad conceptual and methodological limitations of these studies. In fact, this claim is even more questionable when reviewing research that has found that gender knowledge relates to sex-typed preferences. These studies are summarized in the next section.

Evidence for a Relationship

Designing a study that directly addresses the relationship between gender knowledge and preferences is a challenging task. Nonetheless, a few studies that have avoided at least some of the limitations of the previously reviewed research have found that a relationship appears to exist (Aubry et al., 1999; Coker, 1984; Serbin et al., 1993). For example, using a Guttman scale analysis, Coker (1984) found that 3- to 6-year-olds had knowledge of the gender stereotypes associated with concrete objects before they showed preferences for those same items, and observed a significant positive correlation between knowledge and preferences for boys. Unfortunately, the author did not specify the specific items used in these tasks, which makes it impossible to speculate whether the nonsignificant correlation for girls was due to the inclusion of unattractive feminine items. However, Serbin et al. (1993) used a range of gender-typed items to assess 5- to 12-year-olds knowledge and preferences for activities, occupations, and traits and found that these two scores were significantly correlated for both girls and boys. Taken together, studies that have examined correlations, and used the same items and compatible tasks for the measures have found that a relationship exists between gender stereotype knowledge and preferences.

In addition to the limitations associated with the assessment tasks and analyses, it is also important to note that most of the studies examining the relationship between knowledge and preferences are confined to an assessment of concurrent relationships. This is especially problematic when considering that, in some situations, there may be a lag between the attainment of knowledge and the emergence of the associated preferences. For instance, this may occur when the gender-appropriate item is unattractive or when the new knowledge would require giving up a previously desired item (Aubry et al., 1999). Recognizing this issue, Aubry et al. (1999) conducted a 3-year longitudinal study to examine how knowledge of gender norms for concrete items and traits influences gender-related preferences in 4- to 8-year-old children. Using almost identical knowledge and preference tasks, they ran a series of regressions to examine both concurrent and lag predictions. For concrete objects, they found that knowledge of opposite-sex items in year 1 predicted a sizable decline for those same items the following year and that, for boys only, total gender knowledge in year 1 predicted greater preference for same-gender items relative to other gender-items in year 2. These results suggest that gender knowledge of objects may mostly influence behavior by predicting an avoidance of opposite-sex objects and that children's gender knowledge of concrete items tends to show a "lag" relationship with preferences.

To account for the same-sex bias phenomenon that has been found when assessing knowledge and self-descriptions in terms of attributes, Aubry et al. (1999) divided items into "no-conflict" items (i.e., positive same-sex and negative opposite-sex attributes) and "conflict items" (i.e., negative same-sex and positive opposite-sex attributes). In terms of the no-conflict items, the results suggested that boys who showed greater knowledge of same-gender positive attributes in year 3 were more likely to identify with those items the same year. The boys who were also aware of other-gender negative attributes in year 2 were less likely to identify with these items the following year. For conflict items, the findings indicated that knowledge of same-gender negative items in year 1 predicted identification with those items in year 2 for boys, and the girls who had knowledge of the same-gender negative items in year 3 were more likely to identify with those items the same year.

Overall, the results of this study illustrate that important gender knowledge effects can be missed when only examining concurrent relationships and when not considering the separate influences of same-sex and opposite-sex knowledge. For example, it may take time before the attainment of gender knowledge influences preferences. This was apparent when knowledge required that the children avoid opposite-sex objects and attributes or identify with negative attributes. This lag effect was less evident though for girls' endorsement of same-gender negative attributes. For some reason, girls may be less reluctant to self-identify with negative attributes. Nonetheless, girls' preferences, in general, seemed less affected by gender knowledge when compared to boys. This interesting finding is consistent with the literature and requires researchers to consider additional factors (e.g., status, gender identity) that may moderate the relationship between gender knowledge and preferences (Aubry et al., 1999).

The literature reviewed up to this point has examined children's existing knowledge of gender stereotypes and its relationship to children's sex-typed preferences. While some researchers have presented data to conclude that a relationship does not exist, the results from a few correlational studies have illustrated that this claim may be unwarranted. This inconsistency seems largely due to the theoretical and methodological limitations that exist in the research. Although studies have found significant relationships when addressing some of the methodological and theoretical critiques, conceptual challenges and confusions have continued to affect current research questions and design. Specifically, researchers have attempted to tackle the question of whether gender knowledge influences preferences from an all or none perspective. It should be clear by now that this approach to the issue is limited mainly because current theories of gender development do not predict a one-to-one correspondence between gender knowledge and behavior. Other factors such as attractiveness, situational demands, salience of schemas, knowledge accessibility, gender attitudes, and degree of gender identification are also likely to influence children's gendered behaviors. The inclusion of these factors in future studies would allow researchers to determine the variables that may moderate the influence of gender knowledge. For example, a girl who identifies highly with femininity, has rigid gender attitudes, and considers doll play to be an essential identifying feature of what it means to be a girl is likely to choose a doll over a truck. In contrast, the girl who identifies as a "tomboy," has egalitarian gender attitudes, and who does not consider doll play to be an essential feature of girls may be less likely to choose the doll over the truck. Thus, it is unrealistic to claim that gender knowledge always or never affects children's gender preferences. The next step in this line of research is to ask more sophisticated questions such as, when and how does gender knowledge influence children's preferences?

NEW LONGITUDINAL DATA

The question of when gender knowledge affects children's preferences was partly addressed in a recent longitudinal study of 5- to 10-year-old children. Trautner, Ruble, Kirsten, & Hartmann (2005) followed kindergarten children for 5 years and obtained yearly assessments of their gender knowledge of specific objects and activities and their verbal preferences for those same items. This study was part of a larger longitudinal research project on gender development in German children (see Trautner, 1992 and Trautner, Ruble, Cyphers et al., in press, for a detailed description of the sample and procedures). Like the Aubry et al. (1999) study, this research addressed many of the conceptual and methodological pitfalls in the literature by using identical knowledge and preference tasks and by employing correlational methods to assess concurrent and lag relationships. However, an additional advantage of this research is that it examined how rigidly children applied their gender knowledge to determine whether the relationship between knowledge and preferences depends, in part, on this factor.

The gender stereotyped items that were used for these analyses included 5 feminine (e.g., dolls, cooking and baking) and 8 masculine (e.g., trucks and car washing) concrete objects and activities.[5] For the gender knowledge measure, the child was presented with individual cards that had the items written on them. After the statement was read aloud, the child was asked to drop the card into one of five boxes representing *only males, more males than females, equal numbers of males and females, more females than males*, or *only females*. For the masculine items, a child was given a "correct" score if she or he placed the card in either the *only males* (score = 5) or *more males than females* box (score = 4). The reverse scoring system was used for the feminine items (e.g., only females = 5). A child's *total gender knowledge score* was calculated as the number of items correct out of the 13 items.

In addition to receiving a total score, children were rated according to how rigidly they applied their gender knowledge. The *rigidity score* was calculated as the number of items labeled as *only* characteristic of the appropriate gender. Using a median split, children were also classified according to their *age of peak rigidity* (i.e., early or late) and their *level of peak rigidity* (i.e., high or low). Age of peak rigidity was defined as the age at which a child gave her/his maximum number of correct "*only*" responses, and level of peak rigidity was calculated as the maximum number of correct "*only*" responses at any age[6] (see Trautner, Ruble, Cyphers et al., in press).

Children's preferences were assessed by presenting 24 black and white ink drawings of the objects and activities. They were arranged into four sets according to domain: toys, play activities, household chores, and occupational activities. Each set contained two feminine, two masculine, and two gender neutral items. The children were presented with the six items in each set and asked to choose the item that they liked best. The chosen card was then removed and the children were asked to choose their next favorite item. This procedure was continued until all six cards were rated from the best liked item to the least favorite item (i.e., 1 to 6).

In the present analyses, only the rankings for the 13 stereotyped concrete items were examined. Each child received a same-sex preference score and an opposite-sex avoidance score. The same-sex preference score was obtained by calculating a weighted sum of their 1st and 2nd choice rankings within each set. Children received a "2" if they picked a same-sex item for their first choice, and a "1" if they picked a same-sex item for their second choice. A "0" was given when children picked either a neutral or opposite-sex item for their top two choices. In contrast, the opposite-sex avoidance score was obtained by calculating a weighted sum of the 5th and 6th choice rankings. Namely, children received a "1" if their 5th choice was an opposite-sex item, and a "2" if their 6th choice was an opposite-sex item. A score of "0" was assigned when children picked either a same-sex or neutral item for their last two choices. To obtain an overall same-sex approach and opposite-sex avoidance score, a total of the weighted sums for each set were divided by the maximum possible score.[7]

The results are presented in two main sections. The first section describes the developmental trends that emerged from the individual knowledge and preference tasks. Following this analysis, we explore whether children's knowledge of gender stereotypes is related to their preferences for those same items. An examination of this relationship is conducted in three ways. Similar to Aubry et al. (1999), we present results from the cross-lagged-panel correlations between the stereotype knowledge and preference measures. We then describe the two analyses that focus on the association between rigidity of stereotyping and preferences. First, we examine whether developmental trends in children's preferences show a different pattern when the children are grouped according to their age of peak rigidity rather than age in years. Second, analyses of variance (ANOVAs) are used to examine whether individual differences in preferences are associated with variations in peak rigidity of stereotyping (i.e., early versus late, and high versus low).

Developmental Trends

The proportions of children showing gender stereotypic knowledge and rigid stereotyping are displayed in Figures 13.1 and 13.2. Consistent with the literature, children's stereotypic knowledge is already high at age 5, increases slightly when children reach 6 years, and then levels off until age 10. The increase in knowledge from age 5 to 6 is paired with an increase in rigidity. Once children reach their peak level of knowledge, however, their rigidity begins a steady decline. This illustrates that children become more flexible in their application of stereotypes once their knowledge is consolidated.

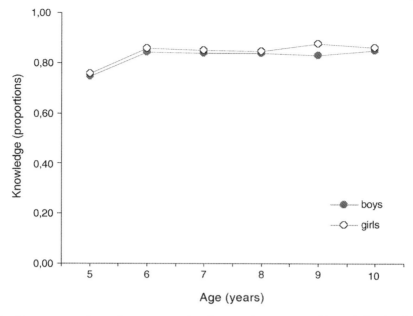

Figure 13.1   Mean proportions of responses showing gender sterotyped knowledge in girls and boys between 5 and 10.

As shown in Figure 13.3, boys' same-sex preferences remain slightly higher than girls' throughout the study. For boys, same-sex preferences remain generally constant from age 5 to 9 and only show a minimal increase at age 10. Girls' same-sex preference trends are also pretty flat even though they show some small fluctuations with age. In contrast to the generally flat trends in preference scores, children's opposite-sex avoidance scores exhibit more obvious changes with age (see Figure 13.4).

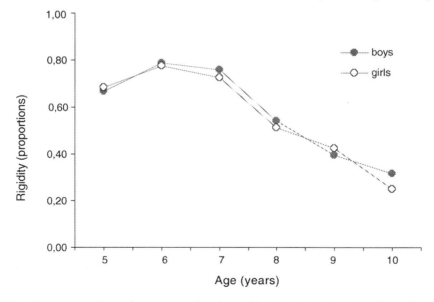

Figure 13.2   Mean proportions of responses showing rigid sterotyping in girls and boys between 5 and 10.

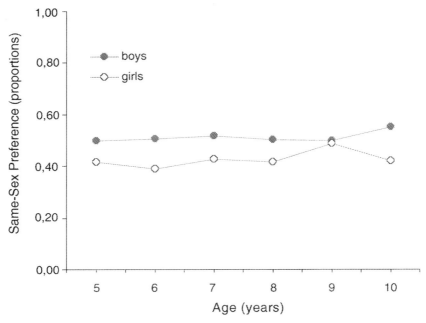

Figure 13.3 Developmental trends of girls' and boys' same-sex preference.

Boys demonstrate an increase in avoidance from age 5 to 9, whereas girls show an increase until age 7. Consistent with the results from Aubry et al. (1999), this suggests that developmental changes in sex-typing may be mostly reflected in children's avoidance of opposite-sex activities. It is possible, however, that the small number of items used in this study was not sufficient to detect the expansion of same-sex interests that might occur with age (e.g., make-up, sports).

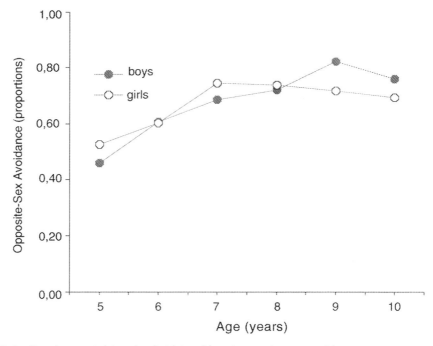

Figure 13.4 Developmental trends of girls' and boys' opposite-sex avoidance.

Cross-Lagged-Panel Correlations

The relationships between children's stereotyped knowledge and preference scores were examined using cross-lagged-panel correlations. This type of analysis allows us to assess whether there are concurrent relationships between these two dimensions, or whether children's knowledge predicts preferences after a time lag. In addition, the stability of knowledge and preferences over time can also be explored. Given that stereotype knowledge develops during ages 5 to 7, we focused on these lagged relations, though relations with later years were also examined.[8] In terms of the results for boys, same-sex preferences were reasonably stable across the first 3 years of the study ($r = .38^*$–$.58^{**}$), and preferences at age 5 were even correlated with preferences at age 10 ($r = .41^*$). For opposite-sex avoidance, stability was found only between years 2 and 3 ($r = .43^*$). In contrast, the nonsignificant auto-correlations for knowledge suggest that boys' understanding of stereotypes was not stable from 5 to 10. This observed instability is not surprising when considering that children's knowledge reaches ceiling levels between 5 and 7 and that there may have been differences in the timing of knowledge acquisition for boys at early ages. As expected, however, boys' knowledge of stereotypes at year 1 was associated with same-sex preferences at years 1 ($r = .57^{**}$), 2 ($r = .41^*$), and 3 ($r = .47^{**}$). That is, both concurrent and lagged effects were found for knowledge predicting same-sex preferences, but not the reverse. Moreover, a concurrent relation was found at age 5 between knowledge and opposite-sex avoidance ($r = .56^{**}$).

Unlike boys, girls' knowledge did not predict lagged preferences during the first 3 years. However, preferences and knowledge were reasonably stable, and concurrent relations were positive across this time period and significant for same-sex preferences at year 2 ($r = .38^*$). In contrast to predictions then, girls' level of stereotype knowledge did not relate subsequently to preferences. Indeed, the one significant lag correlation was in the opposite direction and difficult to interpret: girls' low opposite-sex avoidance at age 5 predicted higher knowledge at age 7. Thus, consistent with Aubry et al. (1999), the present findings indicate that increasing knowledge of stereotypes in young children does influence subsequent same-sex preferences, but only for boys. Unlike the Aubry et al. (1999) study though, there were no significant lag predictions for opposite-sex avoidance for either boys or girls. It is noteworthy that the present analyses used a total knowledge score instead of separating same-sex and opposite-sex knowledge, which may have contributed to this difference.

Peak Rigidity Age Groups

To detect whether same-sex and opposite sex preferences change as a function of stereotype rigidity, children's preference scores were charted before and after their age of peak rigidity. Figure 13.5 displays the same-sex preference trends for girls and boys. In contrast to the flat preference trends observed when children were grouped according to chronological age, there appear to be clear developmental changes in children's same-sex preferences in relation to the degree to which they rigidly apply their stereotype knowledge. Boys' same-sex preferences increase up until the point at which they reach their maximum level of rigidity and then their preferences tend to remain stable. This association between stereotype rigidity and preferences is less clear for girls. However, girls do show an increase in preferences for the 2 years before their age of peak rigidity. Overall, these patterns suggest that, at least for boys, same-sex preferences may develop at the same time as increasing rigidity of stereotyping.

Unlike their same-sex preferences, children's opposite-sex avoidance continues to increase past their age of peak rigidity (see Figure 13.6). While both girls and boys show an increase in avoidance during the 2 years before their age of peak rigidity, their avoidance scores continue to grow rather than level off. Mainly, boys' opposite-sex avoidance continues to increase 4 more years and girls' scores rise for an additional 2 years. Taken together, these findings suggest that changes in preferences occur in parallel with children's stereotype knowledge development. It is especially important to recognize that these apparent associations were missed when we relied on the examination of chronological age trends.

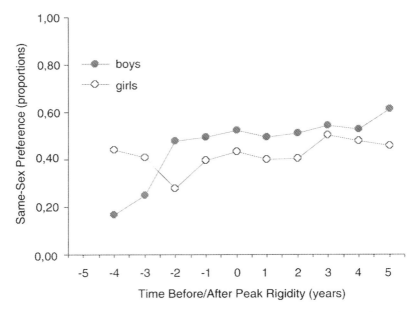

Figure 13.5 Girls' and boys' same-sex preference before and after their age of peak rigidity.

ANOVAs

A 2 (sex) × 2 (age of peak rigidity: early or late) × 2 (level of peak rigidity: high or low) × 6 (age) ANOVA was conducted separately on children's preference and avoidance choices. Sex of participant, age of peak rigidity, and level of peak rigidity were between subjects factors, and age of participant (i.e., time of measurement) was a within subjects factor. These analyses were explored to determine whether children's sex-typed choices were stronger in highly rigid and/or early rigid children. Based on the results from Trautner, Ruble, Cyphers et al. (in press) described earlier, we expected that early

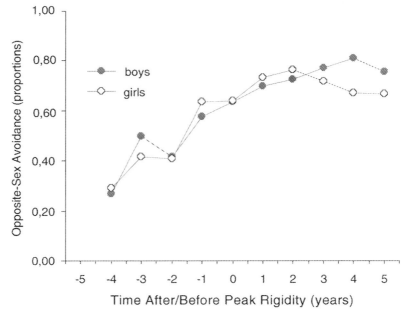

Figure 13.6 Girls' and boys' opposite-sex avoidance before and after their age of peak rididity.

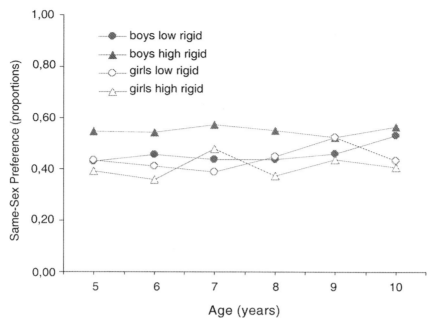

Figure 13.7   Same-sex preference of high rigid versus low rigid girls and boys between 5 and 10.

rigid children would start with a higher level of sex-typed preferences and would then show an earlier decrease in this behavior. In contrast, we did not expect differences between children who reached high versus low levels of rigidity at their peak.

For same-sex preferences, an interaction effect emerged between sex of participant and level of peak rigidity, $F(1, 60) = 5.05$, $p < .03$. As shown in Figure 13.7, high rigid boys surpassed low rigid boys in preferences during all years of the study, but especially in the first 3 years. Yet, there was little difference between high and low rigid girls during the first 3 years. During ages 8 to 10, though, high rigid girls tended to show less same-sex preferences when compared to low rigid girls. These data suggest once again that girls are less likely than boys to follow their ideas regarding gender norms.

The ANOVA conducted on opposite-sex avoidance revealed two- and three-way interaction effects. As expected, early rigid boys show a higher level of avoidance from the beginning when compared to late rigid boys (see Figure 13.8). In contrast to predictions, however, this difference continues across all ages, though it tends to become somewhat smaller up until both groups show a decrease in avoidance at age 10. Girls' avoidance trends show more support for our predictions. Compared to late rigid girls, early rigid girls display higher opposite-sex avoidance only until age 8. At this point, the avoidance of early rigid girls begins to decline and their avoidance is surpassed by the late rigid girls for the following 2 years. Taken together, it seems that boys may be more affected by their level of peak rigidity, whereas girls may be more influenced by the timing of their peak rigidity.

In summary, the analyses conducted in this study support the idea that stereotype knowledge and sex-typed preferences are related dimensions of gender development. In fact, this relationship is most likely to be detected as children are consolidating their knowledge of gender stereotypes (e.g., 5 to 7 years). As found in previous studies though (e.g., Aubry et al., 1999), boys seem generally more affected by their understanding of gender norms when compared to girls. Boys' knowledge of stereotypes was related concurrently to their choices at age 5 and 10, and predicted their same-sex preferences after a lag of 1 and 2 years. Girls, however, showed only weak concurrent relations and no lagged effects where knowledge predicted preferences.

Yet, a main goal of this study was to assess whether the relationship between knowledge and preferences depended on how rigidly children applied their understanding of gender norms. The results

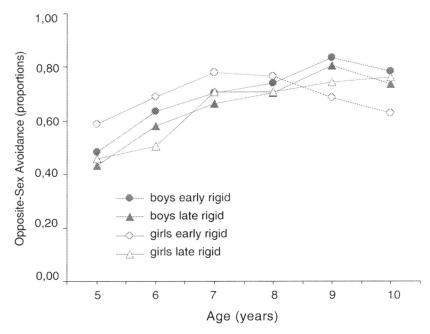

Figure 13.8 Opposite-sex avoidance of early versus late rigid girls and boys between 5 and 10.

from the two analyses that explored this factor suggest that children's rigidity development is related to their sex-typed choices. For example, children's preferences tended to vary as a function of the age that they reached their peak level of rigidity, though once again these relations were somewhat stronger for boys. Moreover, boys who displayed a higher level of peak rigidity and boys whose peak rigidity occurred earlier showed either stronger same-sex preferences or opposite-sex avoidance than boys who were less rigid. Interestingly, the link between rigidity and preferences for girls showed a clear developmental trend, such that opposite-sex avoidance depended on the age at which they most rigidly applied their gender knowledge. Thus, these analyses help advance our knowledge of gender development by suggesting that rigidity may moderate the relationship between gender stereotype understanding and sex-typed choices for concrete objects and activities. Future research that goes beyond the individual level of analysis will, hopefully, expand these findings by showing how children at different developmental stages are affected by situational and group factors.

EXPERIMENTAL EFFECTS OF GENDER KNOWLEDGE ON BEHAVIOR

So far, we have been concerned with correlational studies that have examined the relationship between knowledge and preferences. This research presents only part of the picture that represents our current understanding of the role of gender knowledge in children's behaviors. A series of experimental studies that have been mainly conducted in the 1970s and 1980s allows us to draw further conclusions regarding the predictions made by cognitive theories of gender development. Surprisingly, these studies have only recently been used as essential pieces of evidence in the debate regarding the cognitive underpinnings of gender development (see Martin et al., 2002; Martin & Dinella, 2002). Therefore, we chose to review this research here to provide a more complete analysis of the proposed influence of gender stereotypes on children's choices and behaviors. Moreover, revisiting this literature has also led us to draw some novel conclusions and questions that are relevant for a contemporary view of gender development.

The experimental design that has been used to study the influence of gender stereotypes has mostly involved manipulating the gender labels applied to novel toys and activities. This approach to the issue has offered some advantages over correlational and more naturalistic techniques. For example, the

TABLE 13.1
Gender Labeling Studies

Age	Outcome measure	Study	Neutral condition?[a]	Approach effect?	Avoidance effect?	Category label effect?	Ability label effect?
5 or under	Exploration	Masters et al. (1979)	No[b]	N/A	N/A	Yes	
		Bradbard & Endsley (1983)	Both	Yes	Yes	Yes	
		Bradbard et al. (1986)	Both	No[c]	No[c]	No	
	Preference	Thompson (1975)	No	N/A	N/A	Yes	
		Masters et al. (1979)	No[b]	N/A	N/A	Yes	
		Martin et al. (1995, study 3)	NL	Yes	No	Yes	
	Performance	Gold & Berger (1978)	Both	No[d]	Yes (boys only)[d]		Yes (boys only)
6 to 9	Exploration	Bradbard et al. (1986)	Both	Yes	Yes	Yes	
	Preference	Montemayor (1974)	NL	No	Yes	Yes	
		Etaugh & Ropp (1976)	No	N/A	N/A	No	
		White (1978)	Both	Yes (girls only)[e]	Yes	Yes	
		Herzog et al. (1982)	NL	No[c]	No[c]		No[f]
	Performance	Montemayor (1974)	NL	Yes (girls only)	No	Yes	
		Etaugh & Ropp (1976)	No	N/A	N/A	No	
		Herzog et al. (1982)	NL	No[c]	No[c]		No[f]
10 and older	Preference	Stein et al. (1971)	Both	Yes (boys only)[d]	Yes (boys only)[d]		Yes (boys only)
		Etaugh & Ropp (1976)	No	N/A	N/A	No	
	Performance	Etaugh & Ropp (1976)	No	N/A	N/A	No	
		Hargreaves et al. (1985)	No	N/A	N/A		Yes
		Davies (1986, 1989)	No	N/A	N/A		Yes
	Effort	Stein et al. (1971)	Both	Yes (boys only)[d]	Yes (boys only)[d]		Yes (only boys & high masc pref girls)

[a] All studies contained a same-sex label and an opposite-sex label condition. The studies that included a neutral condition either used a both boys and girls label (Both) or a No Label (NL) condition. [b] This study included a no labeling (NL) control condition; however it was not a neutral condition because the children observed either a same-sex or opposite-sex model engaging with the toys (i.e., modeling only condition). [c] This nonsignificant approach/avoidance finding is subsumed by an overall null gender labeling effect. [d] This nonsignificant approach/avoidance finding for girls is subsumed by an overall null gender labeling effect. [e] Girls showed significant approach behavior only when a female experimenter provided labels. This was not found when a male experimenter provided labels to girls. [f] Only 23% remembered or agreed with the label offered by the experimenter.

use of equally attractive novel toys and activities has allowed researchers to separate the influence of children's stereotypes of activities from children's prior history and experience with those activities (Martin et al., 2002; Martin & Dinella, 2002). This helps control for a couple of the potential factors (e.g., attractiveness, familiarity) that may have influenced the results in the other studies. Similarly, experimental studies allow researchers to make causal inferences regarding the influence of gender stereotypes on behaviors. Given that cognitive theories of gender development view cognitions as causal factors in children's gender-typed behaviors, experimental studies provide a more direct test of this prediction when compared to nonexperimental designs.

The following sections explore the research that has examined the effect of gender labels on children's exploratory behavior, preferences, and performance.[9] These studies are summarized in Table 13.1. While these studies generally show clear labeling effects, the results seem to depend on age, sex, type of dependent variable, whether approach or avoidance effects are examined, and by the type of label that is applied (i.e., category versus ability). Thus, the table is organized according to these factors. The following sections highlight the main conclusions regarding these variations and examine methodological issues that are relevant for future research. First, the general findings for each of the three dependent variables are presented and sex and age differences are described (see Martin & Dinella, 2002, for a detailed review of these studies). Following this review, we examine patterns in children's approach and avoidance behaviors, present two hypotheses that explain the inconsistencies in the literature in terms of the interaction between age and type of label, and illustrate alternative theoretical interpretations of the results.

The Effect of Gender Labels on Exploration, Preferences, and Performance

Exploration

The three studies that have examined the effects of gender stereotypes on children's exploration have found that children are more likely to approach same-sex labeled toys when compared to opposite-sex labeled toys (Bradbard & Endsley, 1983; Bradbard, Martin, Endsley, & Halverson, 1986; Masters, Ford, Arend, Grotevant, & Clark, 1979). For example, Bradbard et al. (1986) measured the amount of time 4 to 9-year-old children tactually explored novel objects after they were provided with same-sex, opposite-sex, and neutral labels. Although differential touching as a function of label was significant for the older children only, Bradford and Endsley (1983) found the same significant results for a sample of preschoolers when using almost the same procedure. Masters et al. (1979) found similar effects for preschoolers even when the labels were applied to more familiar toys (i.e., 2 balloons, 2 xylophones). Specifically, they found that children spent 75% of their time playing with same-sex labeled toys and 25% of their time playing with opposite-sex labeled toys. Overall, the results of these studies demonstrate that children's initial interest and contact with toys is affected by what they believe adults think is sex-appropriate.

Preferences

The research that has examined the effects of gender labels on verbal preferences has been less consistent than the exploration studies. This may be due to developmental changes in the ways children respond to gender labels. For example, all of the preference studies that assessed children under the age of 6 found significant gender labeling effects (Martin, Eisenbud, & Rose, 1995; Masters et al., 1979; Thompson, 1975). One of these studies is especially noteworthy because it is one of the only labeling studies that manipulated attractiveness for the toys and accounted for possible pressure to conform effects (Martin et al., 1995, study 3). Martin and colleagues showed children, between the ages of 4 to almost 6, novel toys that varied in attractiveness and that were labeled either for boys, for girls, or were given no label. One experimenter provided the labels and a second experimenter assessed the children's preferences and, at the end of the session, examined their memory for the gender labels. Not surprisingly, only children who remembered at least most of the labels (i.e., high recall children) showed the gender labeling effect. Moreover, the children who remembered the labels significantly liked attractive toys more than unattractive toys only when attractiveness comparisons were made within the same-sex and unlabeled toys.

The results from the studies that assessed the preferences of children 6 and older are less consistent in their findings when compared to the early childhood research. While half of the studies found a significant gender labeling effect (Liebert, McCall, & Hanratty, 1971;[10] Montemayor, 1974; White, 1978),[11] there were two studies that did not find any differences in preferences between conditions (Etaugh & Ropp, 1976; Herzog, Enright, Luria, & Rubin, 1982), and one study that found a preference effect for boys only (Stein, Pohly, & Mueller, 1971). It is interesting that the two studies that did not find any gender label influences were at least partly designed to replicate the frequently cited Montemayor (1974) study. In the Montemayor (1974) study, children 6 to 8 years old played a novel game ("Mr.

Munchie") that involved throwing as many plastic marbles as possible into a clown's body within a set time frame. Before playing the game, the children were either told that the game was "for boys, like basketball," "for girls, like jacks," or "for children your age" (i.e., neutral condition). Children in the same-sex and neutral conditions liked the game significantly more when compared to the children in the other-sex condition.

A review of the later Mr. Munchie studies offer some possibilities for why these findings were not replicated (Etaugh & Ropp, 1976; Herzog et al., 1982). First, even though Herzog et al. (1982) sought to replicate the original Mr. Munchie study, they may have altered the instructions in significant ways. Instead of telling children that the game was "for boys" or "for girls," they stated, "The people who made Munchie feel that girls (boys) can do much *better* than boys (girls) in the Munchie game." This finding, therefore, suggests that children 6 to 8 may be less likely to internalize gender stereotypes when they convey ability comparisons. In these situations, young children may ignore the external labels and rely on more comfortable modes of assessment such as toy attractiveness and self-oriented standards. Herzog's study lends some support for this idea in that they found that less than a quarter of the children accepted or agreed with the label provided by the experimenter (study 2).

The Etaugh and Ropp (1976) study differed from Herzog's in two ways that are relevant to this discussion. First, their sample consisted of third and fifth graders and, second, they employed labeling instructions that were almost identical to the original Munchie study. It is possible then that older children may be less likely to internalize general category labels ("for girls/boys") when they are confronted with a novel situation. Unfortunately, the manipulation check employed in this study was too limited to accurately test this hypothesis. Mainly, they did not include a "both girls and boys" option in their scale. Most of the children in Herzog et al. (1982) chose this option despite the labels, which raises the question of whether a significant number of Etaugh and Ropp's sample would have described Munchie as gender neutral if given the opportunity.

Performance

Do gender stereotypes influence children's actual performance on tasks? A review of this literature reveals that the effects seem to depend on age, type of label, and sex. In terms of age and type of label, the three Mr. Munchie studies (Etaugh & Ropp, 1976; Herzog et al., 1982; Montemayor, 1974) that were discussed with reference to the preference literature show the same issues regarding their findings on performance (i.e., number of successful tosses thrown into the toy). Namely, Montemayor (1974) found a significant gender labeling effect on children's performance, and the other two studies did not (Etaugh & Ropp, 1976; Herzog et al., 1982). Again, this is possibly due to developmental differences in the ways that children internalize and respond to alternative types of gender labels (i.e., older children may react more to ability labels while younger children may react more to category labels). Nonetheless, a study that assessed the problem-solving performance in children 3 to 5 showed that boys were affected by ability gender labels after the "...experimenter casually remarked that this was a task on which either boys or girls or both generally did well..." (Gold & Berger, 1978, p. 186). Given that this study had less than 10 boys in each condition and is the only ability labeling study that has been conducted with children younger than 6, caution needs to be used when drawing conclusions. This is especially important since the experimenters did not include a memory check in their design. This leaves open the possibility that the preschoolers did not even attend to or process the brief, casual label that was provided to the task.

In addition to considering the interaction of age and type of label, the gender labeling effects on performance also seem to depend on sex. Specifically, two performance studies found an effect for boys only (Gold & Berger, 1978; Stein et al., 1971). Interestingly, the Stein et al. (1971) study was different than each of the other performance studies described in that it examined indexes of motivation (i.e., time spent on each task) rather than actual performance. The analyses revealed that only boys spent significantly longer on the same-sex test when compared to the other tests (i.e., opposite-sex and neutral). An examination of sex-role preference scores though revealed that girls with high masculine preferences worked significantly longer on the masculine test than on the feminine test, whereas low-masculine preference girls worked an equal amount of time on each task. For boys, sex-role preference was not related to the time they spent on the tasks. These results suggest that gender identity factors may partially explain why some studies have found that boys are more affected by gender stereotype knowledge when compared to girls.

While the majority of gender labeling studies use direct stereotypes, a series of three studies found that the performance of both girls and boys is even affected by more subtle gender labels (Hargreaves et al., 1985; Davies, 1986, 1989). For example, Hargreaves et al. (1985) asked 10- and 11-year-olds to participate in a perceptual-motor steadiness task that involved passing a close-fitting metal ring around a 3 feet long bent wire without touching the wire. Children were either told "This is a test to see how good you would be at mechanics or at operating machinery" or "This is a test to see how good you would be at needlework—sewing and knitting." Both boys and girls made fewer errors on the task when it was labeled with a sex-appropriate stereotype than with a sex-inappropriate stereotype. Using an almost identical procedure, Davies (1986, 1989) confirmed these results in two studies that were conducted with 11-, 13-, and 16-year-old children. Overall, these studies illustrate that the performance of middle-elementary school children are influenced by subtle ability labels that imply gender stereotypes.

In summary, the experimental studies demonstrate that children's behavior is affected by their immediate knowledge of gender stereotypes. While there are clear effects for the exploration studies, the research has not shown completely consistent results when assessing preferences and performance. For example, consistent with the correlational studies, it seems that boys are more likely than girls to be influenced by gender labels. Further, developmental differences may affect whether boys and girls even attend to, accept, and process the different types of gender labels. Another issue is that other factors besides gender knowledge are likely to influence children's gender-typed behaviors. Stein et al. (1971) is one of the only experimental studies that assessed other factors and found that sex-role preference did, in fact, moderate the results. As raised when discussing the nonexperimental studies, this is an area that is lacking in the literature that addresses the relationship between gender stereotype knowledge and behavior. In terms of research design issues, these studies highlight the importance of examining children's memory and acceptance of gender labels. Moreover, attractiveness of specific toys appears to be an important influence on children's toy preferences. Thus, it is important in this research to use novel, equally interesting toys or to experimentally vary attractiveness in the design.

Approach versus Avoidance Effects

Many of the gender labeling studies included a neutral condition in their design, which involved either labeling the task as appropriate for both girls and boys or not applying any label to the task. The inclusion of this condition can help delineate whether the observed differences between same-sex and opposite-sex conditions is due to children approaching same-sex labeled tasks, avoiding opposite-sex labeled tasks, or both. This distinction can have important implications for the development of effective interventions that seek to counter the negative influence of gender stereotypes.

A list of the type of conditions that were used in each study is provided in Table 13.1. Within the relevant exploration comparisons that found overall gender labeling effects (Bradbard & Endsley, 1983; Bradbard et al., 1986, only 6- to 9-year-olds), it appears that children are likely to explore same-sex labeled toys as well as to avoid opposite-sex labeled toys. This finding seems to be the same for both girls and boys. The results from the preference studies, however, seem more variable. The one relevant study that assessed younger children found that preferences were only affected when the children felt the task was appropriate for them (Martin et al., 1995). In contrast, the two relevant studies for the middle age group (6 to 9 years old) are mixed and seem to be somewhat more dependent on gender. Both girls and boys illustrated avoidance behavior (Montemayor, 1974; White, 1978), but only girls showed approach behavior (White, 1978). The one relevant preference study for children 10 and older suggests that boys' preferences are affected by same-sex and opposite-sex labels, whereas girls show no effects (Stein et al., 1971). Similar to the preference studies, the results from the performance studies show gender differences in children's responses to the labels. While girls are less likely overall to show gender labeling effects, they seem to be more likely to show approach behavior when compared to avoidance behavior (Montemayor, 1974). On the other hand, boys seem to show avoidance behavior more consistently than approach behaviors (Gold & Berger, 1978).

An analysis of the approach/avoidance patterns offers two tentative conclusions. First, it seems that even though younger children show avoidance behavior when their exploration and performance is assessed, they might be less likely to tell an adult that they dislike opposite-sex toys (i.e., preferences). This difference suggests that preschool children's conscious statements might not always be reliable indicators of the extent to which they are affected by gender stereotypes. Second, this review implies that boys are more likely to show avoidance behaviors and that girls are more likely to show approach behaviors. It is important to recognize though that some gender labeling studies did find approach effects in boys and avoidance effects in girls. In addition, many studies found nonsignificant differences in the predicted direction that may have been significant with larger sample sizes (e.g., Montemayor et al., 1974; Gold & Berger, 1978). Therefore, more definite conclusions regarding these issues need to await future research.

Category Labels versus Ability Labels Effects

When describing the results of the experimental studies, we suggested that the different types of labels might interact with age to determine the gender labeling effects. In this section, we provide a more detailed analysis of the developmental trends and offer two developmental predictions regarding how susceptible children are to different types of labels. Table 13.1 divides the gender labeling experiments into two types of labeling studies: general category labeling (CL) studies and ability labeling (AL) studies. This information is marked by noticing whether the effects are reported in the CL or AL column. The CL studies employed labels that specified whether the task was "for boys" or "for girls." For example, Montemayor (1974) told children in the boy condition that Mr. Munchie was "a toy for boys like basketball." In contrast, the AL studies provided gender information regarding ability assessment. This was accomplished in two different ways. Four of the studies told children that the test was designed to see how good they would be at a particular task. Three of these studies (Hargreaves et al., 1985; Davies, 1986, 1989) used subtle labels (e.g., "This test is to see how good you would be at operating machinery.") and one study (Stein et al., 1971) made more explicit gender references ("This test helps to tell how good you might be at boy's subjects like shop and industrial arts."). The other two AL studies (Gold & Berger, 1978; Herzog et al., 1982) referred to how well girls or boys are expected to do on the task ("girls can do much better than boys in the Munchie game" or "boys generally do well on this task").

As shown in Table 13.1, almost all of the studies that used CL with the younger and middle-aged children found significant gender labeling effects. The two exceptions are the Bradbard et al. (1986) and the Etaugh and Ropp (1976) studies. Although Bradbard et al. (1986) did not find any significant results for the children under 5, the children aged 6 to 9 (i.e., mean age = 7.3 years) seemed to be affected by the gender labels. Using an almost identical design, however, Bradbard & Endsley (1983) did find significant exploration effects for 5-year-olds. It is possible then that children under the age of 5 find the objects that were used in these studies (e.g., hole puncher, shoe stretcher) generally less interesting when compared to children age 5 and older. For example, Bradbard et al. (1986) reported that the older children touched the objects significantly more than the younger group. Moreover, even though there were no significant differences in touching between the same-sex and opposite-sex objects for the younger children, their scores were in the predicted direction. This suggests that the children under 5 may have shown significant results if they spent more time attending to and tactually exploring the objects.

The Etaugh and Ropp (1976) study also did not find any category labeling effects for children 9 and younger. In fact, they did not find any effects for either the third or fifth graders in their study. This may be due to the fact that their sample was older than the samples in the other studies that used CL with children 6 to 9 years. The mean ages of the Etaugh and Ropp (1976) sample were 8.6 and 10.5 years. In contrast, the ages of the children in the other 3 studies were the following: mean age = 6.8 (Montemayor, 1974), 6–7 (White, 1978), and mean age = 7.3 (Bradbard et al., 1986).[12] Taken together, this information provides some support for the hypothesis that children older than 7 are less likely to respond to CL when compared to younger children.

A second reverse hypothesis can be gleaned from examining the AL studies. Specifically, we propose that older children are more likely to be influenced by AL when compared to younger children. For example, the two studies that used AL with children younger than 9 either did not find any effects (Herzog et al., 1982) or found effects for boys only (Gold & Berger, 1978). In contrast, 3 out of the 4 AL studies with older children (Davies, 1986, 1989; Hargreaves et al., 1985) found significant results for both girls and boys, and one study found effects for boys and the girls with high masculine preferences (Stein et al., 1971). Taken together, our two hypotheses suggest that there are developmental differences with respect to how vulnerable children are to different types of gender stereotypes. Next, we review some relevant research that lends some support for these ideas.

Why might older children be less susceptible to CL? The literature involving children's developing understanding of the mind might shed some light on this issue. For instance, there is a wide body of literature that suggests that children from preschool to adolescence progress from being cognitively egocentric to developing an understanding that different people can hold multiple perspectives (e.g., Flavell, 1992; Piaget, 1928; Selman, 1976, 1980). In fact, Selman's (1976) stages of social role-taking propose that children are unable to recognize that people can have different perspectives when given the same information until roughly 8 years of age. Furthermore, more recent research suggests that children under the age of 10 tend to believe that adults are the ultimate authority of information (Bar-Tal, Raviv, Raviv, & Brosch, 1991; Burton & Mitchell, 2003; Rosenberg, 1979). When asking children about the authority of their self-knowledge (e.g., "Who knows best what you want for your birthday?"), Burton & Mitchell (2003) found that children age 7 and younger were more likely to cite their parents, whereas 10-year-olds were more likely to cite themselves. These two areas of research imply that, unlike younger kids, older children understand that people can disagree about social information and are likely to trust their own beliefs about what they like and do not like rather than rely on an adult's authority. It seems possible then that older children will be less likely to passively accept an adult-imposed gender category label when compared to younger children. Instead, older children might use their own experience, toy attractiveness, or information from peers as guides for behavior.

Our next question is concerned with why older children might be more susceptible to AL when compared to younger children. First, the main differences between the CL and AL stereotypes are that AL is focused on *specific* gender information (e.g., ability) and actually provides the child with evidence that can be used for self-evaluation. Given that the literature indicates that there is a developmental progression in children's interest and capacity to use ability and social comparison information, we believe that older children will be more vulnerable to AL. For example, research suggests that children older than 7 years of age are more likely than younger children to utilize social comparison information to evaluate their own ability (e.g., Ruble, 1987; Ruble, Boggiano, Feldman, & Loebl, 1980; Ruble & Frey, 1991). While some research has also found that younger children can use social comparison information, it has been suggested that this is likely to depend on the complexity of the comparisons (see Butler, 1998). For children to be affected by AL (e.g., "girls can do much better than boys"), they need to attend to, process, retain, and use this abstract information in such a way that will affect their performance on a novel, future-oriented task. These processing requirements are likely to be quite complex for younger children, which may limit their motivation or ability to utilize this information.

Similar to their proposed interest and/or capacity to utilize social comparisons, it also appears that ability and performance concerns may be more salient and meaningful for older children (e.g., Ruble, 1994). For instance, Ruble (1994) suggests that as children begin to realize that their competence is stable and significant (between second and fourth grades), they are more likely to be focused on assessing their performance. Moreover, research has found that the perception of ability as a trait increases with age (Droege & Stipek, 1993) and is associated with greater interest in social comparison information among older children (Ruble & Flett, 1988). Consistent with this idea is evidence that suggests that young children tend to believe that effort and outcome are positively related to each other (Heyman, Gee, Giles, 2003; Nicholls, 1990). This implies that younger children tend to believe that if they try hard, they will do well on a task, which should presumably make ability information meaningless to them. Therefore, the existing literature provides some support for the ideas that children should show increasing vulnerability to AL and decreasing vulnerability to CL after approximately age 7. Whether these predictions will survive the tests of empirical research is, for now, an open question.

Mediating Mechanisms: Motivation versus Anxiety

The developmental predictions regarding how susceptible children are to CL and AL might be further explained by differences in the mechanisms that are triggered by these labels. Mainly, there are two main explanations that have been used to interpret the significant effects in the gender labeling studies. Initially, the results were explained in terms of motivational factors (e.g., Bradbard et al., 1986; Davies, 1986, 1989; Helper & Quinlivan, 1973; Montemayor, 1974). For example, cognitive theories suggest that children do not explore, choose, or perform well in opposite-sex tasks because they are *motivated* to define themselves according to the gender norms set forth by society. In this view, children make value judgements according to their self-categorization as either a boy or a girl and seek to behave in ways consistent with these values. Similarly, the proposed mechanism by social learning or social cognitive theory is also motivation. Children's *motivation* to avoid doing well or engaging in an opposite-sex task would then be explained by the outcome expectancies and self-efficacy beliefs that developed out of prior socialization experiences. However, Martin & Dinella (2002) recently suggested that the gender labeling effects could also be interpreted through the lens of stereotype threat theory. Stereotype threat theory asserts that, when individuals are in a situation in which they risk confirming a stereotype about their group (e.g., women taking a math test), they experience psychological distress (e.g., anxiety, distraction) that may hinder their performance (see Steele, 1997 and Steele, Spencer, & Aronson 2002 for a detailed review of this theory). Specifically, it is proposed that these threatening feelings are likely to arise when the individual's performance can be assessed according to a stereotype-relevant ability and when the individual considers the task to be pertinent to her or his self-definition. To illustrate, girls might perform better in an important task that favors the performance of girls ("girls do better") versus boys ("boys do better") because they do not experience the anxiety or distraction that is associated with the stereotype threat.

Instead of considering the explanations offered by stereotype threat and social/cognitive theories as competing mechanisms, it is possible to speculate the conditions that might promote either the motivation or anxiety effects. In light of the discussion regarding the focus and processing demand differences of CL and AL, it seems reasonable to link these two types of labels to the alternative explanations. Given that AL is focused on performance, it is possible that this type of label promotes stereotype threat conditions. In contrast, CL might be more likely to generate motivation effects in that it primarily conveys the message that either boys or girls should be interested in the specific task ("this task is for boys"). Thus, younger children might be more likely to display the motivation effects that are triggered by CL, whereas children older than 7 might be more vulnerable to the performance-impairing phenomenon that is induced by stereotype threat conditions. This hypothesis is consistent with the belief that stereotype threat processes require more complex developmental requirements than motivational mechanisms (see Martin & Dinella, 2002). Given that research has not yet examined the mediators responsible for the gender labeling effects, this analysis only provides tentative hypotheses regarding these issues. Therefore, these ideas offer exciting possibilities for future research.

CONCLUDING REMARKS

The purpose of this chapter was to provide a contemporary review of the literature that explores the effects of gender stereotypes on children's preferences and behavior. This began with a description of the major theoretical perspectives that guide the research in this area. While the theories continue to vary in terms of the degree to which they emphasize different factors, there has been an increasing emphasis on integration in recent years. In fact, our own research is heavily grounded in cognitive theories of gender development. Although we emphasize the important role of gender knowledge, we clearly recognize that biological and social factors are also important determinants in children's sex-typed behaviors. Given that we do not expect there to be a one-to-one relationship between gender knowledge and sex-typed behavior, we also believe that it is necessary to explore the factors that moderate this relationship. Like prior reviews (e.g., Aubry et al., 1999; Martin et al., 2002; Ruble & Martin, 1998), we highlighted these points throughout the chapter in an effort to clarify ongoing confusions regarding this issue.

In addition to presenting the research on children's preferences, we expanded the literature that was presented in Aubry et al. (1999) to include other content areas such as exploration and performance. This allowed us to provide a more complete analysis of the proposed influence of gender stereotypes on children's behavior. Even though the methodological and conceptual limitations involved in this research prevent us from drawing firm conclusions, the findings from these studies suggest that children are affected by their knowledge of gender stereotypes. Moreover, the new data presented in this chapter raised the possibility that stereotype rigidity may moderate the relationship between knowledge and preferences. Thus, children may be more likely to be affected by stereotypes when they are first learning and rigidly applying this knowledge. In addition, we raised the possibility that there are other developmental considerations such as the type of label that will determine when and how children will be influenced by gender stereotypes. For now, these predictions represent gaps in the literature that are waiting to be filled by future research.

NOTES

1. Some authors have previously distinguished the terms "sex" and "gender" in their writing based on whether they intended to convey biological based or socially based characteristics. We have not adopted this system in this chapter and, instead, use these terms interchangeably.

2. Gender-related values were added as a separate category in Ruble and Martin's (1998) modification of Huston's (1983) original matrix.

3. In Experiment 1, Serbin et al. (2001) used a reverse procedure that involved assessing how long the children looked at either the doll or the car after they were presented with identical faces of either a boy or girl. Although there were no significant gender stereotype effects, the authors suggest that the children's degree of interest in the toys may have interfered with the cognitive processing required for the stereotyped matches. This prompted the researchers to reverse the procedure in Experiment 2.

4. For the gender knowledge measure, children were placed in either the "labeler" or "nonlabeler" group based on the number of correct identifications made out of five trials. The labelers received a score of 4 or 5 and the nonlabelers received a score of 3 or less. The toy preference score was computed by subtracting time spent on sex-incongruent toys from time spent on sex-congruent toys.

5. There were originally 16 (8 masculine and 8 feminine) concrete items that were used in the stereotyped measures. However, 3 feminine items (i.e., make a drawing, writing on a typewriter, sitting at the cash desk of a store) were dropped because they were not clearly rated as feminine by the participants. In addition to these concrete items, the original stereotype measure included 22 gender stereotyped personality attributes of children and adults, which were not addressed in the present analyses.

6. The classification of children according to age and level of peak rigidity was based upon the 38 items of the original stereotype measure as described in Trautner, Ruble, Cyphers et al., in press. This resulted in the following grouping of children: Early Rigid = 55–73 months; Late Rigid = 74–113 months; Low Rigid = 16–31 "only" responses; High Rigid = 31–37 "only" responses.

7. For same-sex preference, the maximum score is 8 for girls and 12 for boys. For opposite-sex avoidance, the maximum score is 12 for girls and 8 for boys. The minimum score for each composite is 0. Given the proportional nature of the preference data, analyses were conducted after arcsine transformations.

8. Throughout this section, the level of significance of the correlation coefficients is indicated by the following notation: $^*p < .05$, $^{**}p < .01$.

9. The literature also includes studies that examine the effect of gender labels on attention and memory (see Martin & Dinella, 2002 for a review). Although this research tests key predictions proposed by gender schema theory, space limitations prevented us from including this literature.

10. It is important to note that instead of labeling novel toys, Liebert et al. (1971) mostly used familiar, masculine sex-typed toys for their gender labeling procedure (e.g., robot, dart gun, ball and bat, guitar). While they still found that both boys and girls significantly preferred toys that were labeled for their own sex, the children's prior preferences for specific toys seemed to complicate the analyses. Therefore, the results of this study are not included in the following analysis of the experimental literature.

11. Helper and Quinlivan (1973) is also among the gender labeling studies that found significant effects. When using an operant conditioning paradigm, they found that first and fourth grade girls' response frequency significantly increased after using "girls say that" as a "reinforcer." It is unclear whether this is a preference study though because the authors did not specify what questions they asked the girls.

12. Two of these studies did not divide the children into

groups based on their age (i.e., Montemayor, 1974; White, 1978). Out of these studies, only Montemayor (1974) provided the mean age of their sample.

ACKNOWLEDGMENTS

Preparation of this chapter were supported by a research grant from the National Institute of Mental Health (37215). The data presented in this chapter was based on a research cooperation between Hanns M. Trautner and Diane N. Ruble. The project was supported by a joint grant from the German American Academic Council of the Humboldt Foundation, Germany. The original longitudinal research had been supported by grants from the Volkswagen Foundation (36895) and The German Research Foundation (Tr 142/3) to Hanns M. Trautner.

We are grateful to Lisa Cyphers for assisting with the data analyses. We are also grateful to Kate Anderson for providing support in manuscript preparation.

REFERENCES

Alexander, G. M. (2003). An evolutionary perspective of sex-typed toy preferences: Pink, blue, and the brain. *Archives of Sexual Behavior, 32,* 7–14.

Aubry, S., Ruble, D. N., & Silverman, L. B. (1999). The role of gender knowledge in children's gender-typed preferences. In L. Balter & C. S. Tamis-LeMonda (Eds.), *Child psychology: A handbook of contemporary issues* (pp. 363–390). New York: Psychology Press.

Bandura, A., & Bussey, K. (2004). On broadening the cognitive, motivational, and sociostructural scope of theorizing about gender development and functioning: A reply to Martin, Ruble, and Szkrybalo. *Psychological Bulletin, 130,* 691–701.

Bar-Tal, D., Raviv, A., Raviv, A., & Brosh, M. E. (1991). Perception of epistemic authority and attribution for its choice as a function of knowledge area and age. *European Journal of Social Psychology, 21,* 477–492.

Bem, S. L. (1981). Gender schema theory: A cognitive account of sex typing. *Psychological Review, 88,* 354–364.

Bem, S. L. (2000). Gender schema theory and its implications for child development: Raising gender-aschematic children in a gender-schematic society. In K. A. Keough & J. Garcia (Eds.), *Social psychology of gender, race and ethnicity: Readings and projects* (pp. 112–121). New York: McGraw Hill.

Berenbaum, S. A. (2002). Prenatal androgens and sexual differentiation of behavior. In E. A. Eugster & O. H. Pescovitz (Eds.), *Developmental endocrinology: From research to clinical practice* (pp. 293–311). Totowa, NJ: Human Press.

Bigler, R. S. (1995). The role of classification skill in moderating the environmental influences on children's gender stereotyping: A study of the functional use of gender in the classroom. *Child Development, 66,* 1072–1087.

Bradbard, M. R., & Endsley, R. C. (1983). The effects of sex-typed labeling on preschool children's information-seeking and retention. *Sex Roles, 9,* 247–260.

Bradbard, M. R., Martin, C. L., Endsley, R. C., & Halverson, C. F. (1986). Influence of sex stereotypes on children's exploration and memory: A competence versus performance distinction. *Developmental Psychology, 22,* 481–486.

Burton, S., & Mitchell, P. (2003). Judging who knows best about yourself: Developmental change in citing the self across middle childhood. *Child Development, 74,* 426–443.

Buss, D. M., Larsen, R. J., Westen, D., & Semmelroth, J. (1992). Sex differences in jealousy: Evolution, physiology, and psychology. *Psychological Science, 3,* 251–255.

Buss, D. M., & Schmitt, D. P. (1993). Sexual strategies theory: An evolutionary perspective on human mating. *Psychological Review, 100,* 204–232.

Butler, R. (1998). Age trends in the use of social and temporal comparison for self-evaluations: Examination of a novel developmental hypothesis. *Child Development, 69,* 1054–1073.

Bussey, K., & Bandura, A. (1992). Self-regulatory mechanisms governing gender development. *Child Development, 63,* 1236–1250.

Bussey, K., & Bandura, A. (1999). Social cognitive theory of gender development and differentiation. *Psychological Review, 106,* 676–713.

Bussey, K., & Perry, D. G. (1982). Same-sex imitation: The avoidance of cross-sex models or the acceptance of same-sex models. *Sex Roles, 8,* 773–784.

Campbell, A., Shirley, L., & Caygill, L. (2002). Sex-typed preferences in three domains: Do two-year-olds need cognitive variables? *British Journal of Psychology, 93,* 203–217.

Carter, B. C., & Levy, G. D. (1988). Cognitive aspects of early sex-role development: The influence of gender schemas on preschoolers' memories and preferences for sex-typed toys and activities. *Child Development, 59,* 782–792.

Coker, D. R. (1984). The relationships among gender concepts and cognitive maturity in preschool children. *Sex Roles, 10,* 19–31.

Collaer, M. L., & Hines, M. (1995). Human behavioral sex differences: A role for gonadal hormones during early development? *Psychological Bulletin, 118,* 55–107.

Cowan, G., & Hoffman, C. C. (1986). Gender stereotyping in young children: Evidence to support a concept-learning approach. *Sex Roles, 14,* 211–224.

Davies, D. R. (1986). Children's performance as a function of sex-typed labels. *British Journal of Social Psychology, 25,* 173–175.

Davies, D. R. (1989-90). The effects of gender-typed labels on children's performance. *Current Psychology: Research, & Reviews, 8,* 267–272.

Droege, K. L., & Stipek, D. J. (1993). Children's use of dispositions to predict classmate's behavior. *Developmental Psychology, 29,* 646–654.

Eckes, T., & Trautner, H. M. (2000). Developmental social psychology of gender: An integrative framework. In T. Eckes & H. M. Trautner (Eds.), *The developmental social psychology of gender* (pp. 3–32). Mahwah, NJ: Erlbaum.

Edelbrock, C., & Sugawara, A. (1978). Acquisition of sex-typed preferences in preschool-aged children. *Developmental Psychology, 14,* 614–623.

Eichstedt, J. A., Serbin, L. A., Poulin-Dubois, D., & Sen, M. G. (2002). Of bears and men: Infants' knowledge of conventional and metaphorical gender stereotypes. *Infant Behavior & Development, 25,* 296–310.

Eisenberg, N., Murray, E., & Hite, T. (1982). Children's reasoning regarding sex-typed toy choices. *Child Development, 53,* 81–86.

Etaugh, C., & Liss, M. B. (1992). Home, school and playroom: Training grounds for adult gender roles. *Sex Roles, 26,* 129–147.

Etaugh, C., & Ropp, J. (1976). Children's self-evaluation of performance as a function of sex, age, feedback, and sex-typed label. *The Journal of Psychology, 94,* 115–122.

Flavell, J. H. (1992). Perspectives on perspective taking. In H. Belin & P. B. Pufall (Eds.), *Piaget's theory* (pp. 107–139). Hillsdale, NJ: Erlbaum.

Frey, K. S., & Ruble, D. N. (1992). Gender constancy and the "cost" of sex-typed behavior: A test of the conflict hypothesis. *Developmental Psychology, 28,* 714–721.

Gold, D., & Berger, C. (1978). Problem-solving performance of young boys and girls as a function of task appropriateness and sex identity. *Sex Roles, 4,* 183–193.

Hargreaves, D. J., Bates, H. M., & Foot, J. M. C. (1985). Sex-typed labeling affects task performance. *British Journal of Social Psychology, 24,* 153–155.

Helper, M. M., & Quinlivan, M. J. (1973). Age and reinforcement value of sex-role labels in girls. *Developmental Psychology, 8,* 142.

Herzog, E. W., Enright, M., Luria, Z., & Rubin, J. Z. (1982). Do gender labels yield sex differences in performance, or is label a fable? *Developmental Psychology, 18,* 424–430.

Heyman, G. D., Gee, C. L., & Giles, J. W. (2003). Preschool children's reasoning about ability. *Child Development, 74,* 516–534.

Hort, B. E., Leinbach, M. D., & Fagot, B. I. (1991). Is there coherence among the cognitive components of gender acquisition? *Sex Roles, 24,* 195–207.

Huston, A. C. (1983). Sex-typing. In P. H. Mussen (Ed.), *Handbook of child psychology* (4th ed., Vol. 4, pp. 387–467). New York: Wiley.

Katz, P.A., & Boswell, S. (1986). Flexibility and traditionality in children's gender roles. *Genetic, Social, and General Psychology Monographs, 112,* 103–147.

Katz, P. A., & Walsh, P. V. (1991). Modification of children's gender-stereotyped behavior. *Child Development, 62,* 338–351.

Kenrick, D. T., & Luce, C. L. (2000). An evolutionary life-history model of gender differences and similarities. In T. Eckes & H. M. Trautner (Eds.), *The developmental social psychology of gender* (pp. 35–63). Mahwah, NJ: Erlbaum.

Kohlberg, L. A. (1966). A cognitive-developmental analysis of children's sex-role concepts and attitudes. In E. E. Maccoby (Ed.), *The development of sex differences* (pp. 82-173). Stanford, CA: Stanford University Press.

Leinbach, M. D., Hort, B. E., & Fagot, B. I. (1997). Bears are for boys: Metaphorical associations in young children's gender stereotypes. *Cognitive Development, 12,* 107–130.

Levy, G. D., & Haaf, R. A. (1994). Detection of gender-related categories by 10-month-old infants. *Infant Behavior and Development, 17,* 457–459.

Liben, L. S., & Bigler, R. S. (2002). The developmental course of gender differentiation: Conceptualizing, measuring, and evaluating constructs and pathways. *Monographs of the Society for Research in Child Development, 67* (2, Serial No. 269).

Liebert, R. M., McCall, R. B., & Hanratty, M.A. (1971). Effects of sex-typed information on children's toy preferences. *The Journal of Genetic Psychology, 119,* 133–136.

Maccoby, E. E. (2000). Perspectives on gender development. *International Journal of Behavioral Development, 24,* 398–406.

Maccoby, E. E. (2002a). Gender and group process: A developmental perspective. *Current Directions, 11,* 54–58.

Maccoby, E. E. (2002b). The intersection of nature and socialization in childhood gender development. In C. von Hofsten & L. Backman (Eds.), *Psychology at the turn of the millennium* (Vol. 2, pp. 37–52). East Sussex, UK: Psychology Press.

Martin, C. L. (1993). New direction for investigating children's gender knowledge. *Developmental Review, 13,* 184–204.

Martin, C. L. (2000). Cognitive theories for gender development. In T. Eckes & H. M. Trautner (Eds.), *The developmental social psychology of gender* (pp. 91–121). Mahwah, NJ: Erlbaum.

Martin, C. L., & Dinella, L. M. (2002). Children's gender cognitions, the social environment, and sex differences in cognitive domains. In A. McGillicuddy-De Lisi & R. De Lisi (Eds.), *Biology, society, and behavior: The development of sex differences in cognition* (pp. 207–239). Westport, CT: Ablex.

Martin, C. L., Eisenbud, L., & Rose, H. (1995). Children's gender-based reasoning about toys. *Child Development, 66,* 1453–1471.

Martin, C. L., & Halverson, C. F., Jr. (1981). A schematic processing model of sex typing and stereotyping in children. *Child Development, 52,* 1119–1134.

Martin, C. L., & Little, J. K. (1990). The relation of gender understanding to children's sex-typed preferences and gender stereotypes. *Child Development, 61,* 1417–1439.

Martin, C. L., & Ruble, D. (2004). Children's search for gender cues: Cognitive perspectives on gender development. *Current Directions in Psychological Science, 13,* 67–70.

Martin, C. L., Ruble, D. N., & Szkrybalo, J. (2002). Cognitive theories of early gender development. *Psychological Bulletin, 128,* 903–933.

Martin, C. L., Ruble, D. N., & Szkrybalo, J. (2004). Recognizing the centrality of gender identity and stereotype knowledge in theorizing about gender development: Moving toward integration and inclusion. *Psychological Bulletin, 130,* 702–710.

Martin, C. L., Wood, C. H., & Little, J. K. (1990). The development of gender stereotype components. *Child Development, 61,* 1891–1904.

Masters, J. C., Ford, M. E., Arend, R., Grotevant, H. D., & Clark, L. V. (1979). Modeling and labeling as integrated determinants of children's sex-typed imitative behavior. *Child Development, 50,* 364–371.

Mischel, W. (1966). A social-learning view of sex differences in behavior. In E. E. Maccoby (Ed.), *The development of sex differences* (pp. 57–81). Stanford, CA: Stanford University Press.

Mischel, W., & Shoda, Y. (1995). A cognitive-affective system theory of personality: Reconceptualizing situations, dispositions, dynamics, and invariance in personality structure. *Psychological Review, 102,* 246–268.

Montemayor, R. (1974). Children's performance in a game and their attraction to it as a function of sex-typed labels. *Child Development, 45,* 152–156.

Nicholls, J. G. (1990). What is ability and why are we mindful of it? A developmental perspective. In R. J. Sternberg & J. Kolligian (Eds.), *Competence considered* (pp. 11–40). New Haven, CT: Yale.

O'Brien, M., Peyton, V., Mistry, R., Hruda, L., Jacobs, A., Caldera, Y., et al. (2000). Gender-role cognition in three-year-old boys and girls. *Sex Roles, 42,* 1007–1025.

Perry, D. G., White, A. J., & Perry, L. C. (1984). Does early sex typing result from children's attempts to match their behavior to sex role stereotypes? *Child Development, 55,* 2114–2121.

Piaget, J. (1928). *Judgment and reasoning in the child.* New York: Harcourt, Brace.

Powlishta, K. K, Sen, M. G., Serbin, L. A., Poulin-Dubois, D., & Eichstedt, J. A. (2001). From infancy through middle childhood: The role of cognitive and social factors in becoming gendered. In R. K. Unger (Ed.), *Handbook of the psychology of women and gender* (pp.116–132). New York: Wiley.

Rosenberg, M. (1979). *Conceiving the self.* New York: Basic Books.

Ruble, D. N. (1987). The acquisition of self-knowledge: A self-socialization perspective. In N. Eisenberg (Ed.), *Contemporary topics in developmental psychology* (pp. 243–270). New York: Wiley.

Ruble, D. N. (1994). A phase model of transitions: Cognitive and motivational consequences. In M .P. Zanna (Ed.), *Advances in experimental social psychology* (Vol. 26, pp. 163–214). San Diego, CA: Academic Press.

Ruble, D. N., Boggiano, A. K., Feldman, N. S., & Loebel, J. H. (1980). A developmental analysis of the role of social comparison in self-evaluation. *Developmental Psychology, 16,* 105–115.

Ruble, D. N., & Flett, G. L. (1988). Conflicting goals in self-evaluative information seeking: Developmental and ability level analysis. *Child Development, 59,* 97–106.

Ruble, D. N., & Frey, K. S. (1991). Changing patterns of comparative behavior as skills are acquired: A functional model of self-evaluation. In J. Suls, & T. A. Wills (Eds.), *Social comparison: Contemporary theory and research* (pp. 79–113). Hillsdale, NJ: Erlbaum.

Ruble, D. N, & Martin, C. L. (1998). Gender development. In W. Damon (Series Ed.) & N. Eisenberg (Vol. Ed.), *Handbook of child psychology: Vol. 3. Social, emotional, and personality development* (5th ed., pp. 933–1016). New York: Wiley.

Sani, F., & Bennett, M. (2001). Contextual variability in young children's gender ingroup stereotype. *Social Development, 10,* 221–229.

Sani, F., Bennett, M., Mullally, S., & McPherson, J. (2003). On the assumption of fixity in children's stereotypes: A reappraisal. *British Journal of Developmental Psychology, 21,* 113–124.

Selman, R. L. (1976). Social-cognitive understanding: A guide to educational and clinical practice. In T. Lickona (Ed.), *Moral development and behavior: Theory, research, and social issues* (pp. 299–316). New York: Holt, Rinehart and Winston.

Selman, R. L. (1980). *The growth of interpersonal understanding.* Orlando, FL: Academic Press.

Serbin, L. A., Poulin-Dubois, D., Colburne, K. A., Sen, M. A., & Eichstedt, J. A. (2001). Gender stereotyping in infancy: Visual preferences for and knowledge of gender-stereotyped toys in the second year. *International Journal of Behavioral Development, 25,* 7–15.

Serbin, L.A., Poulin-Dubois, D., & Eichstedt, J.A. (2002). Infants' response to gender-inconsistent events. *Infancy, 3,* 531–542.

Serbin, L. A., Powlishta, K. K., & Gulko, L. (1993). The development of sex typing in middle childhood. *Monographs of the Society for Research in Child Development, 58* (2, Serial No. 232).

Shirley, L. J., & Campbell, A. (2000). Same-sex preference in infancy: Visual preference for sex-congruent stimuli at three months. *Psychology, Evolution & Gender, 2.1,* 3–18.

Shoda, Y., Mischel, W., & Wright, J. C. (1994). Intraindividual stability in the organization and patterning of behavior: Incorporating psychological situations into the idiographic analysis of personality. *Journal of Personality and Social Psychology, 67,* 674–687.

Signorella, M. L. (1999). Multidimensionality of gender schemas: Implications for the development of gender-related characteristics. In W. Swann, J. Langlois, & L. Gilbert (Eds.), *Sexism and stereotypes in modern society* (pp. 107–126). Washington, DC: American Psychological Association.

Signorella, M. L., Bigler, R. S., & Liben, L. S. (1993). Developmental differences in children's gender schemata about others: A meta-analytic review. *Developmental Review, 13,* 147–183.

Slaby, R. G., & Frey, K. S. (1975). Development of gender constancy and selective attention to same-sex models. *Child Development, 52,* 849–856.

Stangor, C., & Ruble, D. N. (1987). Development of gender role knowledge and gender constancy. In L. S. Liben & M. L. Signorella (Eds.), *Children's gender schemata* (pp. 5–22). San Francisco: Jossey-Bass.

Stangor, C., & Ruble, D. N. (1989). Differential influences of gender schemata and gender constancy on children's information processing and behavior. *Social Cognition, 7,* 353–372.

Steele, C. M. (1997). A threat in the air: How stereotypes shape intellectual identity and performance. *American Psychologist, 52,* 613–629.

Steele, C. M., Spencer, S. J., & Aronson, J. (2002). Contending with group image: The psychology of stereotype and social identity threat. In M. P. Zanna (Ed.), *Advances in experimental social psychology* (Vol. 34, pp. 379–440). San Diego, CA: Academic Press.

Stein, A. H., Pohly, S. R., & Mueller, E. (1971). The influence of masculine, feminine, and neutral tasks on children's achievement behavior, expectancies of success, and attainment values. *Child Development, 42,* 195–207.

Thompson, S. K. (1975). Gender labels and early sex role development. *Child Development, 46,* 339–347.

Trautner, H. M. (1992). The development of sex-typing in children: A longitudinal analysis. *German Journal of Psychology, 16,* 183–199.

Trautner, H. M., Ruble, D. N., Cyphers, L., Kirsten, B., Behrendt, R., & Hartmann, P. (in press). Rigidity and flexibility of gender stereotypes in children: Developmental or differential? *Infant and Child Development.*

Trautner, H. M., Ruble, D. N., Kirsten, B., & Hartmann, P. (2005). Relationships between gender stereotypes and gender preferences in 5- to 10-year old children. Manuscript in preparation.

Trivers, R. L. (1972). Parental investment and sexual selection. In B. Campbell (Ed.), *Sexual selection and the descent of man 1871–1971* (pp. 136–179). Chicago: Aldine-Atherton.

Weinraub, M., Clemens, L. P., Sockloff, A., Ethridge, T., Gracely, E., & Myers, B. (1984). The development of sex role stereotypes in the third year: Relationships to gender labeling, gender identity, sex-typed toy preference, and family characteristics. *Child Development, 55,* 1493–1503.

Welch-Ross, M. K., & Schmidt, C. R. (1996). Gender-schema development and children's constructive story memory: Evidence for a developmental model. *Child Development, 67,* 820–835.

White, D. G. (1978). Effects of sex-typed labels and their source on the imitative performance of young children. *Child Development, 49,* 1266–1269.

Zucker, K. L. (2001). Biological influences on psychosexual differentiation. In R. K. Unger (Ed.), *Handbook of the psychology of women and gender* (pp. 101–115). New York: Wiley.

14

Motivational and Achievement Pathways Through Middle Childhood

Jacquelynne S. Eccles
Robert Roeser
Mina Vida
Jennifer Fredricks
Allan Wigfield

INTRODUCTION

Middle childhood is one of the least studied and yet one of the most exciting periods of life. Imagine a 5-year-old girl going to kindergarten for her first day of formal school. Now imagine this same girl at 12 years when she goes to secondary school. At 5 years, she is a cute child still anxious about separating from her parents as they leave her at the school. By 12, she will have grown into a young woman with secondary sex characteristics. In some populations, she will already have begun dating and she certainly will have begun menstruating in most American populations. In addition to starting school, she is likely to have experienced other institutional settings without her parents, settings in which she will be exposed to a variety of peers and adults as well as many opportunities learn new skills. Each of these new institutional settings (e.g., primary school, scouting, recreational programs, music lessons, etc.) will provide her with a series of new life experiences—experiences that will encourage the development of intellectual and interpersonal competencies, and introduce the child to new social roles in which status is conferred based upon competence and performance (e.g., Higgins & Parsons, 1983).

According to Erikson (1968), the accomplishment of a "sense of industry" during these years, as well as a sense of cooperation and mutuality in social interactions with peers and adults outside the home is critical to healthy development. If children fail to develop these requisite skills, and thereby meet the challenges of adaptation associated with entry into formal schooling and other skill-based activity settings, Erikson suggested that a "sense of inferiority" will develop that can exert long lasting consequences on children's intellectual, emotional, and interpersonal well-being.

Since the time of Erikson's (1959, 1968) seminal writings on children and youth, a great deal of research attention has focused on understanding how children's self-appraisals and behavioral competencies are related to the quality of their intellectual, social, and emotional functioning across the first two decades of life. Researchers have demonstrated that feelings of competence and personal esteem are critical for children's psychosocial well-being (see Eccles, 1993 Harter, 1998; Rosenberg, Schooler, & Schoenbach, 1989). For example, children who fail to develop positive self-perceptions of competence in the academic or social domains during the elementary school years report more internalizing and externalizing symptoms (e.g., depression and social isolation [Asher, Hymel, & Renshaw, 1984] and anger and aggression [Parkhurst & Asher, 1992]). Similarly, children's feelings of competence in various activity domains, especially academics, have been shown to protect children against both concurrent and later problem behaviors (e.g., Achenbach, Howell, Quay, & Conners, 1991; Lord, Eccles & McCarthy, 1994; Rae-Grant, Thomas, Offord, & Boyle, 1989). Finally, children who experience difficulties with learning early in school are at increased risk for behavioral, academic, and psychiatric difficulties and are particularly likely to both be retained in grade and then to drop out of school prior to the completion of high school (e.g., Alexander, Entwisle, & Horsey, 1997; Cairns, Cairns, & Neckerman, 1989; Hinshaw, 1992; Offord & Fleming, 1995; Roderick, 1994).

All of these findings suggest that academic success during middle childhood is critical to a successful developmental trajectory through this period and into adolescence precisely because academic success is critical to developing a healthy, positive view of one's competence and a positive motivational orientation to learning in school. Although we know that a distressingly large percentage of children in elementary and secondary schools experience academic difficulties, and are at-risk of academic failure and disengagement (e.g., 25%; Dryfoos, 1990, 1994), work documenting longitudinal changes in both ability self-concepts and academic motivation over this period is just beginning to emerge. There is even less work documenting the relation of early school adjustment and competence to the development of other personal difficulties in the late childhood and adolescent years. Finally, there are very few studies outside of the field of sport psychology assessing the role of experiences in other institutional settings, such as recreational sports and performing arts programs or scouting, in supporting the emergence of a sense of industry during the middle childhood years. The relative lack of cross-fertilization among the researchers interested in the different areas of a child's development has resulted in a fragmented understanding of developmental patterns of intellectual, emotional, social, and behavioral functioning. Although there is some cross-sectional evidence to suggest that academic problems are related to difficulties of adjustment in other domains of functioning (e.g., emotional, interpersonal, behavioral), few longitudinal studies have simultaneously examined the interweaving developmental lines of related experiences in skill acquisition settings and social-emotional adjustment from childhood to adolescence.

We have two goals in this chapter: First, we want to review the literature on longitudinal changes in skill-based self-concepts and motivational orientation. Second, we want to begin a discussion of the links between skill-based self-concepts, success in school and other skill-based settings, and emotional development. We do this primarily by linking different longitudinal patterns of school adjustment to individual differences in social/emotional development. By focusing on school adjustment, we test the notion that academic competence is an important part of the overall portrait of positive adjustment and more general interpersonal competency during both middle childhood and early adolescence (e.g., Eccles & Midgley, 1989; Erikson, 1968; Roeser et al., 1994).

Although we also bring in evidence from two other skill-based domains (sports and instrumental music), we emphasize the academic domain because all children are forced to attend school and thus all children must deal with developing a sense of industry or inferiority in this context. Some children also have the opportunity to participate in other skill-based contexts like youth sports programs or youth music programs. There has been very little work on the impact of such experiences on the emergence of a sense of industry in these other activity settings and there has been almost no work on how these experiences interact with school experiences to either support or undermine either children's more general sense of industry or children's more general socio-emotional development during the middle childhood years.

DEVELOPMENTAL PATTERNS ACROSS THE MIDDLE SCHOOL YEARS IN SKILL-BASED ABILITY SELF-CONCEPTS AND SUBJECTIVE TASK VALUES FOR ENGAGING IN VARIOUS SKILL-BASED ACTIVITIES

Over the years, psychologists have proposed many different components of achievement motivation. In an effort to systematize this vast literature, Eccles, Wigfield, & Schiefele (1998) suggested that one could group these various components under four basic questions: Can I succeed? Do I want to succeed? Why do I want to succeed? What do I have to do to succeed? We assumed that the answers to these questions would determine a child's engagement with academic and other skill-based tasks as well as their commitment to the educational and activity-related goals of their parents and teachers.

Children who develop positive and/or productive answers to these questions with regard to school are likely to engage their school work and to thrive in their school settings. Children who develop less positive answers to these questions with regard to school are likely to experience school failure and to withdraw their psychological attachments from the activities associated with school, thereby increasing the likelihood that they will turn to less productive and more risky activity settings for their psychological nurturance. Similar dynamics should apply in other skill-based areas as well. In this section, we review what is known about developmental changes over the middle childhood years in children's answers to these questions with a focus on school and academic achievement.

CAN I SUCCEED?

Several theorists have proposed constructs linked to this question. We focus here on those related to ability self-perceptions and expectations of success.

Eccles et al. Expectancy-Value Theory

Eccles and her colleagues have elaborated and tested an expectancy-value model of achievement-related choices and engagement, (Eccles, 1987; Eccles [Parsons] et al., 1983; Eccles, Adler, & Meece, 1984; Eccles & Wigfield, 1995; Meece, Wigfield, & Eccles, 1990; Wigfield & Eccles, 1992). The most recent version of this model is depicted in Figure 14.1. Expectancies and values are assumed to di-

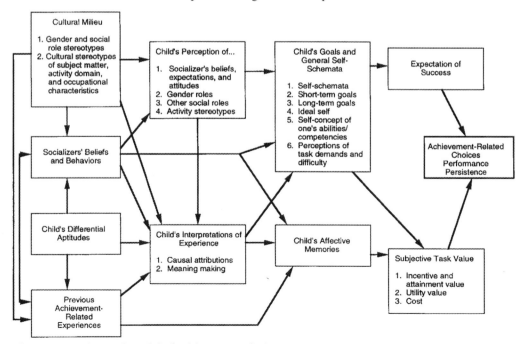

Figure 14.1 General model of achievement choices.

rectly influence performance, persistence, and task choice. Expectancies and values are assumed to be influenced by task-specific beliefs such as perceptions of competence, perceptions of the difficulty of different task, and individuals' goals and self-schema. These social cognitive variables, in turn, are influenced by individuals' perceptions of other peoples' attitudes and expectations for them, by their own interpretations of their previous achievement outcomes, and by their affective memories of, or affective expectations about, similar tasks. Individuals' task-perceptions and interpretations of their past outcomes are assumed to be influenced by socializer's behavior and beliefs, by their own histories of success and failure, and by cultural milieu and unique historical events.

Eccles [Parsons] et al. (1983) defined expectancies for success as children's beliefs about how well they will do on either immediate or future tasks. In contrast, they (1983) defined beliefs about ability as children's more general evaluations of their competence in different areas. Interestingly even though these two constructs are theoretically distinguishable form each other, Eccles and her colleagues have found empirically that children and adolescents do not distinguish between these two different levels of beliefs. Apparently, even though these constructs are theoretically distinguishable from each other, in real-world achievement situations they are highly related and empirically indistinguishable.

Self-Efficacy Theory

Bandura has also proposed a social cognitive model of motivated behavior that emphasizes the role of perceptions of efficacy and human agency in determining individuals' achievement strivings. Bandura (1977) defined self-efficacy as individuals' confidence in their ability to organize and execute a given course of action to solve a problem or accomplish a task. In his more recent writings (Bandura, 1994), Bandura characterizes self-efficacy as a multidimensional construct that can vary in strength, generality, and level (or difficulty). That is, some people have a strong sense of self-efficacy and others do not; some individuals' efficacy beliefs encompass many situations whereas others have narrow efficacy beliefs; and some individuals believe they are efficacious even on the most difficult tasks, whereas others do not.

As in expectancy-value theory, Bandura's self-efficacy theory focuses on expectancies for success. Although Bandura distinguished between two kinds of expectancy beliefs (outcome expectations [i.e., beliefs regarding which behaviors would lead to specific outcomes] vs. efficacy expectations [beliefs about whether one can effectively perform the behaviors necessary to produce the outcome]), Bandura proposed that efficacy expectations were the major determinant of goal setting, activity choice, willingness to expend effort, and persistence (see Bandura, 1994). By and large, the evidence supports these predictions. For example, high personal academic expectations predict subsequent performance, course enrollment, and occupational choice for all ethnic groups studied (see Eccles, Vida, & Barber, 2004; Eccles & Vida, 2003; Pintrich & Schunk, 2002; Schunk, 1991; Zimmerman, et al., 1992). Similarly, high personal sport expectations predict subsequent engagement in competitive sport activities (Barber, Eccles & Stone, 2001; Eccles & Barber, 1999).

Bandura (1994) proposed that individuals' perceived self-efficacy is determined by four main things: Previous performance (people who succeed will develop a stronger sense of personal efficacy than those who do not), vicarious learning (watching a model succeed on a task will improve one's own self-efficacy regarding the task), verbal encouragement by others, and the level of one's physiological reaction to a task or situation. Bandura (1994) also proposed hypotheses regarding the development of self-efficacy. First, he proposed that experiences controlling proximal stimuli provide the earliest sense of personal agency. Through these experiences, infants learn that they can influence and control their environments. If adults do not provide infants with these experiences, they are not likely to develop a strong sense of personal agency. Second, because self-efficacy requires the understanding that the self produced an action and an outcome, Bandura (1994) hypothesized that a more mature sense of self-efficacy should not emerge until children have at least a rudimentary self-concept and can recognize that they are distinct individuals. This recognition happens sometime during the second year of life (see Harter, 1998).

Through the preschool period, children are exposed to extensive performance information that should be crucial to their emerging sense of self-efficacy. However, just how useful such information proves to be is likely to depend on children's ability to integrate it across time, contexts, and domains. Because these cognitive capacities emerge gradually over the preschool and early elementary school years, young children's efficacy judgments should depend more on immediate and apparent outcomes than on a systematic analysis of their performance history in similar situations (see also Parsons & Ruble, 1972, 1977; Stipek & MacIver, 1989). Thus, similar to Erikson, Bandura's theoretical analysis points to the importance of the middle childhood years for the consolidation of children's sense of personal efficacy.

The Development of Competence-Related and Efficacy Beliefs

Most of the work on the development of children's achievement-related beliefs has looked at the development of children's ability and expectancy-related beliefs (e.g., see Eccles, et al., 1998; Stipek & Mac Iver, 1989). Researchers have studied three kinds of age-related changes in these beliefs: change in the factor structure of these beliefs, change in children's understanding of these concepts, and change in their mean levels. Due to limited space we focus on the second and third. We also discuss various ways of assessing and describing longitudinal patterns of change at the level of the individual.

Changes in Children's Understanding of Competence-Related Beliefs

It is important to understand how children conceptualize the different constructs in order to interpret comparisons of different-aged children's beliefs meaningfully. Several researchers have investigated these concepts, focusing primarily on children's understanding of ability and intelligence. For example, Nicholls and his colleagues asked children questions about ability, intelligence, effort, and task difficulty, and how different levels of performance can occur when children exert similar effort (e.g., Nicholls, 1990; Nicholls et al., 1990). They found four relatively distinct levels of reasoning: At level one (ages 5 to 6), effort, ability, and performance are not clearly differentiated in terms of cause and effect. At level two (ages 7 to 9), effort is seen as the primary cause of performance outcomes. At level three (ages 9 to 12), children begin to differentiate ability and effort as causes of outcomes, but they do not always apply this distinction. Finally, at level four, adolescents clearly differentiate ability and effort, and understand the notion of ability as capacity and believe that ability can limit the effects of additional effort on performance, that ability and effort are often related to each other in a compensatory manner, and, consequently, that a success which required a great deal of effort likely reflects limited ability.

Nicholls' analysis suggests that children early in the middle childhood period of life are likely to believe that they can get better by working harder and that failures result primarily from a lack of effort. If they live in a culture that stresses the moral importance of working hard (vs. being lazy), failures during this period may make children feel guilty rather than incompetent. Both Burhans and Dweck (1995) and Harter (1998) found that preschool children do report thinking they are bad people if they fail at tasks their parents and teachers highly value. Similarly, Heyman, Dweck, and Cain (1993) and Stipek, Recchia, and McClintic (1992) found that some children as young as 2 react both behaviorally and emotionally to failure experiences. On the positive side, such attributions leave open the belief that one can get better.

Dweck and her colleagues (see Dweck, 1999) focused on children's notions about the controllability and modifiability of their own abilities in various domains. They believe that children hold one of two views of intelligence or ability: An entity view that intelligence and other skill-based abilities are stable traits, or an incremental view that skill-based abilities are changeable and can be increased through effort. Like Nicholls (1990), Dweck stressed how children's conceptions of ability and intelligence have important motivational consequences. Believing that ability is an entity increases the debilitating effects of failure. Children holding this view likely believe that they have little chance of ever doing well, because their ability cannot be improved after failure. In contrast, believing that effort can improve performance should protect children from a learned helpless response to failure precisely because these children should continue to try even if they are not doing well on a given task. Although Nicholls' work suggests that younger children may be less likely to believe ability is stable or fixed, Burhans and Dweck (1995) concluded that some preschool-aged children already have doubts about their ability to do certain tasks, even if they are trying hard.

Both the Nicholls and Dweck perspectives point to the importance of developmental changes for understanding the emergence of a sense of industry versus inferiority during the middle childhood years. If children begin to think of ability as more entity-like during these years then the consequences of learning difficulties for developing a sense of industry increase. Evidence from a few studies (see Dweck, 1999) suggests that this is exactly what happens to children growing up in the United States. Furthermore, evidence is beginning to emerge suggesting that the developmental increase in entity beliefs is due in part to an increased emphasis by the adults (both teachers and coaches) on social comparative evaluative feedback and stress on doing better than others rather than improving one's own competence over time (see Dweck, 1999; Eccles, Midgley & Adler, 1984; Midgley, 2002)

Change in the Mean Level of Children's Competence-Related Beliefs

Several researchers have found that children's competence-related beliefs for different tasks decline across the elementary school years and into the middle school years (see Eccles et al., 1998; Eccles & Midgley, 1989; Fredricks & Eccles, 2002; Jacobs et al., 2002; Stipek & Mac Iver, 1989). To illustrate, in Nicholls (1979) most first graders ranked themselves near the top of the class in reading ability, and there was essentially no correlation between their ability ratings and their performance level. In contrast, the 12- year-olds' ratings were more dispersed, and their correlation with school grades was .70 or higher. Similar results have emerged in cross-sectional and longitudinal studies of children's competence beliefs in a variety of academic and nonacademic domains by Eccles and her colleagues (e.g., Eccles et al. 1993; Fredricks & Eccles, 2002; Jacobs et al., 2002; Wigfield et al. 1997) and Marsh (1989). These declines often continue into and through secondary school (e.g., Jacobs et al., 2002).

Some of the findings from our work on the Childhood and Beyond Study (CAB) are summarized in Figures 14.2 and 14.3, which illustrate the longitudinal changes in children's ability self-concepts for math and sports from Grade 1 through Grade 12. A set of predominantly white middle class children ($N = 615$), initially in first, second, and third grades, were given a survey in their classrooms each year for 3 consecutive years during elementary school (yielding data from Grade 1–6) and then again each year for 4 consecutive years 4 years later (yielding data from Grade 7–12). This survey contained items assessing their competence beliefs for math, reading, sports, and instrumental music (see Eccles et al., 1993). The items were read aloud to the children in the first three waves and given as a self-administered survey in the secondary school years. Scales were created from several items responded to on a 7-point scale anchored with verbal labels at the extreme endpoints and the midpoint (see Eccles et al., 1993; Fredricks & Eccles, 2002; Jacobs et al., 2002; and Wigfield et al., 1997 for full details).

Using Hierarchial Linear Modelling (HLM) techniques, these data can be used to create a picture of the developmental changes over the entire Grade 1–12 school period. The results of our HLM analyses for math and sports are shown in Figures 14.2 and 14.3 (see Fredricks & Eccles, 2002). For each of these domains, as well as for reading/English and instrumental music, there is a steady decline in the children's ability self-concepts as they move through the elementary and secondary school years. These declines are quite marked during middle childhood and early adolescence and they occur in children with all initial ability levels. Interestingly, the declines are least extreme for children whose parents rate their children's ability in each domain quite high, even after the children's actual ability levels are controlled. Thus, having a parent who thinks you are very competent protects you from the impact of negative performance experiences and teacher bias on your own confidence in your abilities.

Similar results have been found in the Michigan Study in Adolescent Life Transitions (MSALT, a mixed social class and ethnic sample from southeastern Michigan), (see Eccles et al., 1989 and Wigfield

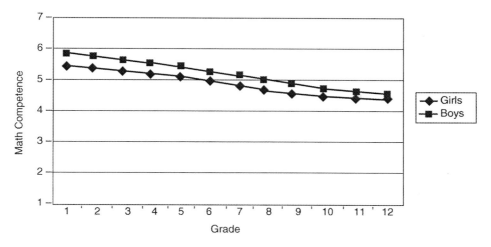

Figure 14.2   Developmental changes in girls' and boys' math ability self concepts.

et al., 1991 for details of study). These students were studied at four time points over the junior high school transition (two times in the sixth grade and two times in the seventh grade). Students' confidence in their math and English abilities and self-esteem were assessed at each time point. Confidence in both academic domains showed a marked decline over this school transition and continued to decline during the first year of junior high school. Self-esteem also showed a marked drop over the school transition followed by a partial rebound during the seventh grade school year (Wigfield et al., 1991). Most importantly for this chapter, confidence in one's abilities in math, sports, and reading predicted reduced declines in the self-esteem across this school transition (Lord, Eccles & McCarthy, 1994).

Expectancies for success also decrease during the elementary school years. In most laboratory-type studies, 4- and 5-year-old children's expect to do quite well on specific task, even after repeatedly failure (e.g., Parsons & Ruble, 1977; Stipek, 1984). Across the elementary school years, the mean levels of children's expectancies for success both decline and become more sensitive to both success and failure experiences. Consequently, both competence beliefs and expectancies more accurate or realistic in terms of their relation to actual performance history (see Eccles, Midgley, & Adler, 1984, Parsons & Ruble, 1972, 1977; Stipek, 1984).

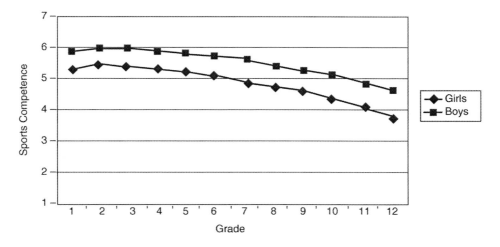

Figure 14.3   Developmental changes in girls' and boys' sports ability self concepts.

In summary, there is a drop in children's ability self-concepts and expectations for success over the elementary school years. In part this drop reflects the initially high expectations of kindergarten and first-grade children. Stipek (1984) argued that young children's optimistic expectancies may reflect hoped for outcome rather than real expectations; in contrast, Parsons & Ruble (1977) suggested that, since young children's skills do, in fact improve rapidly, high expectancies for future success may be based on experience. As the rate of improvement slows, children may learn that current failures are more predictive of subsequent performance. Other changes also likely contribute to this decline—changes such as increased exposure to failure feedback, increased ability to integrate success and failure information across time to form expectations more closely linked with experience, increased ability to use social comparison information, and increased exposure to teachers' expectations (see Harter, 1998; Stipek & Mac Iver, 1989).

Some of these changes are directly linked to the transition into elementary school. Entrance into elementary school and then the transition from kindergarten to first grade introduces several systematic changes in children's social worlds. First, classes are age stratified, making within-age ability social comparison much easier. Second, formal evaluations of competence by "experts" begin. Third, formal ability grouping begins usually with reading group assignment. Fourth, peers have the opportunity to play a much more constant and salient role in children' lives. Each of these changes should impact children's motivational development. Such changes could contribute to the increase in children's response to failure feedback as they move from preschool and kindergarten into the first grade (Parsons & Ruble, 1972, 1977; Stipek, 1984). Parents' expectations for, and perceptions of, their children's academic competence are also influenced by report card marks and standardized test scores given out during the early elementary school years, particularly for mathematics (Alexander & Entwisle, 1988; Arbreton & Eccles, 1994). More systematic studies of the effects of transition into elementary school, and transitions from kindergarten to first grade, on motivation are needed.

There are significant long-term consequences of children's experiences in the first grade, particularly experiences associated with ability grouping and within-class differential teacher treatment. For example, teachers use a variety of information to assign first graders to reading groups including temperamental characteristics like interest and persistence, race, gender, and social class (e.g., Alexander, Dauber & Entwisle, 1993). Alexander et al. (1993) demonstrated that differences in first grade reading group placement and teacher-student interactions have a significant effect (net of beginning differences in competence) on motivation and achievement several years later. Furthermore, these effects are mediated by both differential instruction and the exaggerating impact of ability group placement on parents' and teachers' views of the children's abilities, talents, and motivation (Pallas et al., 1994).

Further changes in ability self-concepts occur as children move from elementary school into middle or junior high school (see Eccles et al., 1993). These changes appear to reflect the impact of the types of changes in the classroom and school environments that often accompany this school transition, such as increased competitive and performance rather than task-mastery motivational strategies, increased ability tracking, and increased whole class instruction (see Maehr & Midgley, 1996; Midgley, 2002). Early adolescents who do not experience these types of changes in the classroom environments as they make this school transition do not show as marked declines in the ability self-concepts and expectations for educational success.

Individual Differences in Developmental Trajectories

All of the data reported above focused on mean level changes at the population level. Changes at this level likely reflect either shared maturational influences or shared changes in school characteristics (see Eccles, Midgley, & Adler, 1984; Eccles et al., 1998). These findings, however, mask individual differences in these developmental trajectories. Work in the arenas of underachievement, test anxiety, and learned helpless (reviewed later) provides clear evidence of strong individual differences in these trajectories: Some children evidence a negative self-concept pattern as soon as they enter the first grade and remain low throughout their schooling years; others start high and show the type of gradual decline evident in the mean level graphs; still others start low and rebound.

We have been exploring these individual differences in our Childhood and Beyond (CAB) study. This study was designed to look at two issues: (1) individual differences in the trajectories of children's academic ability self-concept, and (2) the relation of these different trajectories to other indicators of social development and mental health. We describe the results relevant to the first goal here; the results relevant to the second goal are presented later.

To assess trajectories of academic risk and resilience, we grouped children based upon their level of academic functioning at the two points in time: during early elementary school and later in middle school. We then examined a constellation of related indices of academic functioning as a means of corroborating our characterizations of children and youth as "academically at-risk" or "not-at-risk" during these times (for full details see Eccles, Roeser, Wigfield & Freedman-Doan, 1999). Because the criteria by which children judge their academic competence are known to change with development and increasing cognitive sophistication and because so many young children express such optimistic expectations and ability self-concepts (Eccles, Wigfield, & Schiefele, 1998), we relied on teacher reports of children's academic competence during the early grades to assess academic risk status. We did this by asking teachers to rate each child's academic abilities (in reading and math) and chances of future academic success relative to her same-aged peers.

When the youth were in Grade 7 and 8, we relied upon their own self-reports of academic competence to assess their academic risk status. Similar to the questions asked of teachers during the early elementary school years, several of the items in the self-report academic competence scale assessed how these early adolescents felt they compared to their same-aged peers in terms of their abilities in reading and math. By the early adolescent years, the use of social comparison information to determine one's abilities in a given domain is, for better or worse, a functional part of youth's self-assessments (e.g., Harter, 1998).

To identify children at risk at Time 1, we created a composite measure of teacher's perceptions of children's academic competence in reading and math, as well as their expectancies for children's future academic success. The children were identified as at academic risk at Time 1 if they were rated in the lowest 33% of the distribution of their teachers' ratings. Our original sample consisted of 397 first and second graders during the 1988 school year. Of these children, 137 (35%) were categorized as having poor school adjustment, and were thus designated as "academically at-risk." The remaining 260 children we categorized as academically "not-at-risk." Boys and girls were equally represented in each category.

We then assessed the relation of category membership to other indicators of developmental functioning. The Time 1 at-risk children scored significantly worse than the other children on the following measures: Teachers' ratings of the children's social competence, academic effort and persistence, adjustment to school, general anxiousness, and aggressive/impulsiveness; mothers' ratings of their children's academic competence; and the children's ratings of the value they attached to doing well in school and their own general sense of self-worth (see Eccles, Roeser, Wigfield & Freedman-Doan, 1999 for details). Interestingly, the two groups did not differ in the children's ratings of their own academic competence at either Time 1 or the next two annual waves of data collection. Clearly, being at academic risk early in elementary school is linked to wide range of other indicators of developmental functioning.

To identify the children at risk in Grade 7 or 8, we used adolescent self-report measures of their academic competence in reading and math. Criteria similar to those used during the early elementary school years were used to characterize adolescents as academically "at-risk" or "not-at-risk." Youth who were in the lowest 33% of the overall sample distribution on a measure of their self-reported academic competence were again designated as "academically at-risk." Youth in the upper 66% percent of the distribution were categorized as "not-at-risk." Of the sample of 363 seventh and eighth graders who were available for follow-up during the 1994 school year, 109 (30%) were categorized as being "academically at-risk," and 254 as "not-at-risk." Again boys and girls were equally represented in both categories but by junior high school there was a trend ($p < .10$) for boys to be slightly over-represented in the "at-risk" group.

Again we compared the two groups on a range of other self-report indicators of developmental well-being. The academic at risk early adolescents reported less academic valuing, lower grade point averages, lower self-worth, life satisfaction, and ego-resilience, higher probability of dropping out of school, and higher frequency of depression and anger than their not-at-risk academic peers (see Eccles, Roeser et al., 1999). We did not have either teacher or parent ratings at this wave of data collection. Thus, just as was true in early elementary school, being at academic risk in terms of one's academic ability self-concepts is linked with also being at risk on a wide range of other indicators of developmental well-being.

Next, we used these risk scores to identify different patterns of changes in risk status across the years that span middle childhood to early adolescence. To do this, we grouped children into four "academic risk trajectory" groups. These included children who were or were not at risk at both times, children who evidenced academic risk early on but not later, and children who did not evidence academic risk early on but did so later. Sixty-two percent remained in the same risk category across time. Nonetheless, the Chi-squared statistic for this two by two table was significant ($\chi^2 [1,289] = 17.85, p = .001$), indicating significant instability in this matrix as well. Twenty-eight percent moved from at-risk to the not-at-risk category and ten percent moved from the not-at-risk category to the at-risk category.

How did the changers differ from one another and from the associated stable groups? As noted above, they did not differ in their academic ability self-concepts at Time 1. There were three very important differences in these groups at Time 1. First, the increasers started with lower self-reported academic value than the stable not-at-risk group. By the second wave of data collection this difference had disappeared and by Grade 7–8, both the stable not-at-risk and the increaser groups attached higher value to academic success than the stable at-risk and the decliner group. Somewhere between the end of Grade 3–4 and Grade 7–8, the children in the Grade 7–8 at-risk group (both the decliners and the stable at-risk groups) experienced a major decline in the value they attached to doing well in school.

Second, the four groups showed different trajectories of self-worth. This is illustrated in Figure 14.4. As you can see, the decliners had the lowest levels of self-worth at the second wave of measurement; the stable not-at-risk children had the highest self-worth at this same point in time. By Time 4, the stable not-at-risk and the increasers reported similarly high self-worth, higher than both the stable at-risk and the decliner groups.

Finally, as shown in Figure 14.4, the actual school performance grades showed a pattern consistent with the motivational and mental health differences between the four groups. Although the increasers started with lower academic performance than the decliners and the stable not-at-risk group, by Time 3, their academic performance had caught up with the decliners. In addition, by Time 4, the increasers' academic performance had surpassed all groups except the stable not-at-risk group. Clearly, the increaser group had overcome both the motivational and performance problems they evidenced early in elementary school by Time 4. Their first grade teachers had been wrong about their potential. We do not yet know what is responsible for this turn around. We plan to explore the possibilities in the future.

Apparently, although children's confidence in their academic abilities declines over time on the average, a substantial number of children identified as at risk by their teachers due to their academic limitations appear to enter adolescence with reasonably high ability self-concepts and good academic records. We discuss exactly who these children are later, but before leaving this discussion it is important to point out that one needs to be careful about assuming that the mean level declines in academic self-concepts represent the tip of dangerous iceberg. Instead, some of this decline likely reflects the overly optimistic scores of young children. Furthermore, even though first-grade teacher ratings have emerged in several studies as significant predictors of adolescent school achievement, these data clearly indicate that a nontrivial number of the children rated by their first-grade teachers as at academic risk look fine by the time they are in middle school.

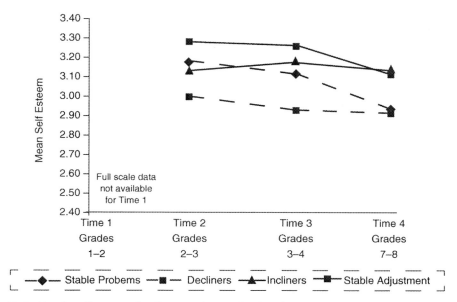

Figure 14.4   Youth self-report of self esteem by academic risk trajectory.

Control Theories

Control theorists have also proposed motivational components related to the question "Can I succeed" that are related to other aspects of social development, such as, individual's feelings of efficacy and industry, and general mental health. More specifically, these theorists propose that individuals with a strong sense of internal locus of control will be more likely to engage in, and succeed at, academic tasks and will feel better about themselves more generally. Empirical work has confirmed these predictions (see Weisz, 1984).

Connell and Wellborn (1991) integrated control beliefs into a broader theoretical framework in which they proposed three basic psychological needs for competence, autonomy, and relatedness (see also Ryan, 1992). They linked control beliefs to competence needs: Children who believe they can control their achievement outcomes should feel more competent. They hypothesized that the extent to which these three needs are fulfilled is influenced by following characteristics of the contexts: the amount of structure, the degree of autonomy provided, and the level of involvement in the children's activities. Finally, they proposed that the ways in which these needs are fulfilled determine engagement in different activities. When the needs are fulfilled, children will be fully engaged. When one or more of the needs is not fulfilled, children will become disaffected (see Connell, Spencer, & Aber, 1994; Skinner & Belmont, 1993, for supportive evidence). In this way Connell and Wellborn have also linked control beliefs to more general psychological functioning.

Developmental Changes in Control Beliefs

In her discussion of the ontogeny of control beliefs, Skinner (1995) stressed the importance of perceived contingency between individuals' actions and their successes. She also stressed the importance of success itself for developing positive control beliefs. Finally, she discussed how children's understanding of causality and explanations for outcomes likely changes over age with these beliefs becoming more differentiated as children get older. What is similar across all ages is the importance of fulfilling the need for competence.

In their review of studies of children primarily 8–9 years and older, Skinner and Connell (1986) concluded that there is an increase in perceptions of internal control as children get older. In contrast, based on series of studies of children's understanding of skill vs. chance events, Weisz (1984) concluded that the developmental sequence is more complex. The kindergarten children in these studies believed outcomes of chance tasks were due to effort, whereas the oldest groups (eighth graders and college students) believed that such outcomes were due to chance; fourth graders were confused about the distinction. Thus, in this work, the youngest children had strong internal control beliefs- so strong in fact that they believed in internal control over outcomes even when none was possible, suggesting that with age children came to understand better which kinds of events they can control, and which they can't. Perhaps this exaggerated confidence in one's ability to control even chance events helps to explain the high levels of ability self-concepts held by children during their preschool and early elementary school years.

In summary, children's competence beliefs and expectancies for success become more negative as they get older, at least through the early adolescence time period. The negative changes in children's achievement beliefs have been explained in two ways: (1) Because children become much better at understanding, interpreting, and integrating the evaluative feedback they receive, and engage in more social comparison with their peers, many children should become more accurate or realistic in their self-assessments, leading some to become relatively more negative (see Eccles et al., 1998; Nicholls, 1984; Parsons & Ruble, 1977; Stipek & Mac Iver, 1989). (2) Because school environments change in ways that makes evaluation more salient and competition between students more likely, some children's self-assessments will decline as they get older (e.g., see Eccles, Midgley, & Adler, 1984; Eccles & Midgley, 1989; Midgley, 2002; Stipek & Daniels, 1988). For example, there has been some speculation that the declines in ability self-concepts between Grade 2 and 4 and again over the transitions into and through secondary school reflect changes in the teachers' grading practices and stress on competition among students at about the third grade. However, evidence regarding these types of changes is just beginning to accumulate (see Eccles et al., 1998; Midgley, 2002).

We also discussed individual differences in these patterns of change. Some children show these declines; others do not. Some start quite low and remain low; others start high and remain quite high throughout their elementary school years. Very little work has been done on identifying the characteristics of children and their social environments that distinguish these groups from each other. More work is badly needed.

THEORIES CONCERNED WITH THE QUESTION "DO I WANT TO DO THIS TASK?"

Although theories dealing with competence, expectancy, and control beliefs provide powerful explanations of individuals' performance on different kinds of achievement tasks, these theories do not systematically address another important motivational question: does the individual want to do the task? Even if people are certain they can do a task, they may not want to engage in it. The theories presented in this section focus on this aspect of motivation.

Eccles, Wigfield, and Colleagues' Work on Subjective Task Values

Eccles and her colleagues have elaborated the concept of subjective task value. Building on earlier work on achievement values (e.g., Battle, 1966), intrinsic and extrinsic motivation (e.g., Deci, 1975; Gottfried, 1990), and on Rokeach's (1979) view that values are shared beliefs about desired end-states, Eccles (Parsons) et al. (1983) outlined four motivational components of task value: attainment value, intrinsic value, utility value, and cost. Like Battle (1966), they defined attainment value as the personal importance of doing well on the task. Drawing on self-schema and identity theories (e.g., Markus & Nurius, 1984), as well as the work by Feather (1982, 1992) and Rokeach, they also linked attainment value to the relevance of engaging in a task for confirming or disconfirming salient aspects of one's self-schema (see Eccles, 1987).

Like Harter (1985, 1998), Deci and his colleagues (e.g., Deci & Ryan, 1985), Csikszentmihalyi (1988), Gottfried (1990), and Renninger (1990), they defined intrinsic value in terms of the enjoyment the individual gets from performing the activity, or the subjective interest the individual has in the subject.

They defined utility value in terms of how well a task relates to current and future goals, such as career goals. A task can have positive value to a person because it facilitates important future goals, even if he or she is not interested in task for its own sake. For instance, students often take classes that they do not particularly enjoy but that they need in order to pursue other interests, to please their parents, or to be with their friends. In one sense then, this component captures the more "extrinsic" reasons for engaging in a task (see Deci & Ryan, 1985; Gottfried, 1985; Harter, 1985), but it also relates directly to the internalized short- and long-term goals an individual may have.

Finally, Eccles and her colleagues identified "cost" as a critical component of value (Eccles et al., 1983; Eccles, 1987). Cost is conceptualized in terms of the negative aspects of engaging in the task, such as performance anxiety, fear of both failure and success, the amount of effort that needed to succeed and the lost opportunities that result from making one choice rather than another.

Eccles and her colleagues have conducted extensive empirical tests of different aspects of this model. For example, they have shown that ability self-concepts and performance expectancies predict performances in mathematics and English, whereas task values predict course plans and enrollment decisions in mathematics, physics, and English and involvement in sport activities even after controlling for prior performance levels (Eccles, 1984; Eccles et al., 1983; Eccles & Barber 1999; Eccles Adler, & Meece, 1984; Eccles & Harold, 1991; Meece et al., 1990; Updegraff et al., 1996). They have also shown that both expectancies and values predict career choices (see Eccles, Barber, & Jozefowicz, 1999; Eccles, Vida, & Barber, 2004). Recent studies show that both ability self-concepts and subjective task value predict activity/course/career choices (Eccles & Vida, 2003; Updegraff et al., 1996).

Development of Subjective Task Values

There has been much less work on the development of subjective task values during the middle childhood years. Eccles, Wigfield, and their colleagues have examined change in the structure of children's task values, as well as mean level change in children's valuing of different activities. Even young children distinguish between their competence beliefs and their task values. In Eccles et al. (1993), Eccles & Wigfield (1995) and Wigfield et al. (1995), children's competence-expectancy beliefs and subjective values within the domains of math, reading, and sports formed distinct factors at all grade levels from first through twelfth. Thus, even during the very early elementary grades children appear to have distinct beliefs about what they are good at and what they value.

As with competence-related beliefs, studies generally show age-related declines in children's valuing of certain academic and nonacademic achievement tasks (e.g., Eccles et al., 1983, 1993; Eccles & Midgley, 1989; Fredricks & Eccles, 2002; Gottfried, Fleming & Gottfried, 2001; Jacobs et al., 2002; Wigfield & Eccles, 1992). For instance, in longitudinal analysis of elementary school children, beliefs about the usefulness and importance of math, reading, instrumental music, and sports activities decreased over time (Wigfield et al., 1997). In contrast, the children's interest decreased only for reading and instrumental music, not for either math or sports. The data for interest in, and perceived importance of, math and sports is illustrated in Figures 14.5 and 14.6. A similar pattern exists for reading and instrumental music.

Using data from other samples, the decline in valuing of math continues through high school (Eccles, 1984). Eccles et al. (1989) and Wigfield et al., (1991) also found that children's ratings of both the importance of math and English and their liking of these school subjects decreased across the transition to junior high school. In math, students' importance ratings continued to decline across seventh grade, whereas their importance ratings of English increased somewhat during seventh grade.

Researchers have not yet addressed changes in children's understandings of the components of task value identified by Eccles et al. (1983), although there likely are age-related differences in these understandings. An 8-year-old is likely to have a different sense of what it means for a task to be "useful" than an 11-year-old does. Further, it also is likely that there are differences across age in which

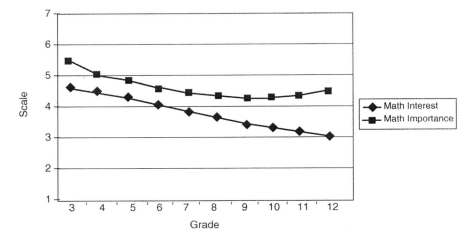

Figure 14.5   Developmental changes in girls' and boys' ratings of math interest and importance.

of the components of achievement values are most dominant. Wigfield and Eccles (1992) suggested that interest may be especially salient during the early elementary school grades. If so, then young children's choices of different activities may be most directly related to their interests. And if young children's interests shift as rapidly as their attention spans, it is likely that they will try many different activities for a short time each before developing a more stable opinion regarding which activities they enjoy the most. As children get older the perceived utility and personal importance of different tasks likely become more salient, particularly as they develop more stable self-schema and long range goals and plans. These developmental patterns have yet to be assessed empirically.

A related developmental question is how children's developing competence beliefs relate to their developing subjective task values? According to both the Eccles et al. model and Bandura's self-efficacy theory, ability self-concepts should influence the development of task values. In support of this prediction, Mac Iver, Stipek, and Daniels (1991) found that changes in junior high school students' competence beliefs over a semester predicted changes in children's interest much more strongly than vice versa. Does the same causal ordering occur in younger children? Recall that Bandura (1994) argued that interests emerge out of one's sense of self-efficacy and that children should be more interested in challenging than in easy tasks. Taking a more developmental perspective, Wigfield (1994)

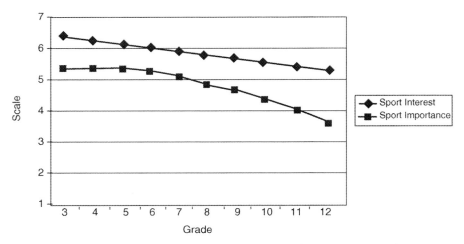

Figure 16.6   Developmental changes in girls' and boys' ratings of sport interest and importance.

proposed that initially young children's competence and task value beliefs are likely to be relatively independent of each other. This independence would mean that children might pursue some activities in which they are interested regardless of how good or bad they think they are at the activity. Over time, particularly in the achievement domain, children may begin to attach more value to activities on which they do well for several reasons: First, through process associated with classical conditioning, the positive affect one experiences when one does well should become attached to the activities yielding success (see Eccles, 1984). Second, lowering the value one attaches to activities that one is having difficulty with is likely to be an effective way to maintain a positive global sense of efficacy and self-esteem. Thus, at some point the two kinds of beliefs should become more positively related to one another. In partial support of this view, Wigfield et al. (1997) found that relations between children's competence beliefs and subjective values in different domains indeed are stronger among older than younger elementary school-aged children. A recent conference paper confirms this finding using our CAB (Childhood and Beyond) data (Denison, Zarrett & Eccles, 2004). The causal direction of this relation, however, has not yet been tested empirically.

Two recent studies in our laboratories have begun to unravel the causal direction story. Unfortunately, the story is not going to be simple. In the first such study, Jacobs et al. (2002) used the CAB data to link the developmental declines in academic self-concepts with these developmental declines in subjective task value over an extended longitudinal period (first to 12th grade). Using HLM with a time varying covariate, they found that the declines in subjective task value for both mathematics, and English were substantially reduced if one controlled for the declines in the same subject area academic ability self-concepts. These findings suggest that the age-related declines in academic ability self-concepts contribute to the age-related declines in the value the children attach to both mathematics and English.

Using our Michigan Study of Adolescent Life Transitions, Yoon (1996) investigated the links between performance, ability self-concepts and subjective task values for mathematics over the junior high school transition. He used structural equation modeling to compare all of the possible cross-lagged relations. In contrast to the Jacobs et al. findings (2002) and the Mac Iver et al. (1991) findings, his analyses suggest that subjective task values predict changes in ability self-concepts to a greater extent that vice versa, especially for early adolescent girls. In addition, changes in performance over the junior high school transition predicted changes in both math ability self-concepts and the value attached to doing well in math for both girls and boys.

In summary, our own studies find evidence that the causal relations among performance, ability self-concepts and subjective task values are likely to be reciprocal; they influence each other over time in a bi-directional manner. It seems quite likely that these reciprocal influences serve important psychological functions. For example, if one is doing quite well at particular activities, then one should develop a high estimate of one's ability at that activity as well as coming to place high value on success at this activity through processes associated with accurate information processing and classical conditioning. In contrast, if one is doing poorly at a particular activity, then it makes sense that one would develop a less positive view of one's abilities at that activity. It also makes sense that one would then lower the value attached to that activity in order to maintain a high sense of self-esteem. Reducing the value one attaches to a particular activity domain is a very adaptive way of responding to failure provided that one can then withdraw from that activity domain without great cost. If, however, a child is forced to continue to engage in those activity domains that he or she is having great difficulty mastering and the context focuses the child's attention on his or her relative performance rather than on his or her improvement over time, it is likely the child will be unable to reduce the value attached to that domain and, as a consequence, that his or her self-esteem and sense of self-worth will be at risk.

It is also likely that children will invest more time in activities that they enjoy. As a result, they should develop both greater competence in these activities and a more positive view of their abilities in these activities. Thus, it is no surprise that the influences among these constructs are bi-directional. The exact nature of these bi-directional relations is likely to vary depending on the child's cognitive maturity, the support provided at home, in school, and among his or peers for various causal interpretations of one's achievement experiences, and the amount of autonomy the child is provided for picking and choosing exactly how he or she wants to invest his or her time and energy.

Interest Theories

Closely related to the intrinsic interest component of subjective task value is the work on "interest" (Alexander, Kulikovich, & Jetton, 1994; Hidi, 1990; Renninger, Hidi & Krapp, 1992; Schiefele, 1991). Researchers in this tradition differentiate between individual and situational interest. Individual interest is a relatively stable evaluative orientation toward certain domains; situational interest is an emotional state aroused by specific features of an activity or a task. Two aspects or components of individual interest are distinguishable (Schiefele, 1991): feeling-related and value-related valences. Feeling-related valences refer to the feelings that are associated with an object or an activity itself—feelings like involvement, stimulation, or flow. Value-related valences refer to the attribution of personal significance or importance to an object. In addition, both feeling-related and value-related valences are directly related to the object rather than to the relation of this object to other objects or events. For example, if students associate mathematics with high personal significance because mathematics can help them get prestigious jobs, then we would not speak of interest.

Much of the research on individual interest has focused on its relation to the quality of learning (see reviews by Alexander et al., 1994; Renninger, Hidi & Krapp, 1992, and Schiefele, 1991). In general, there are significant but moderate relations between interest and text learning. More importantly, interest is more strongly related to indicators of deep-level learning (e.g., recall of main ideas, coherence of recall, responding to deeper comprehension questions, representation of meaning) than to surface-level learning (e.g., responding to simple questions, verbatim representation of text, Schiefele, 1996).

Most of the research on situational interest has focused on the characteristics of academic tasks that create interest. (e.g., see Hidi 1990; Teigen, 1987). Among others, the following text features arouse situational interest: personal relevance, novelty, activity level, and comprehensibility (Hidi 1990). Empirical evidence has provided strong support for the relation between situational interest and text comprehension and recall (see Schiefele, 1991).

Developmental Changes in Interest

Travers (1978) analyzed the earliest phase of interest development. He assumed that only "universal" interests would be evident in very young children, for example, the infant's search for structure or control. Later, depending on the general cognitive development of the child, these universal interests should become more differentiated and individualized. According to Roe and Siegelmann (1964), the earliest differentiation occurs between interest in the world of physical objects versus interest in the world of people. Todt (1990) argued that this early differentiation eventually leads to individual differences in interests in the social vs. the natural sciences.

The next phase of interest development—between 3 and 8 years of age—is characterized by the formation of gender-specific interests. According to Kohlberg (1966), the acquisition of gender identity leads to gender-specific behaviors, attitudes, and interests. Children strive to behave consistently with themselves and, thus, evaluate "male" and "female" activities or objects differently. Activities or objects that are consistent with the children's gender identity will be more positively evaluated than other activities or objects. As a consequence, boys and girls develop gender role stereotypes interests (see Eccles, 1987; Eccles & Bryan, 1994).

Like the work of Eccles and colleagues discussed earlier, several European researchers have found that interest in different school subject areas declines continuously during the school years. This is especially true for the natural sciences (e.g., Baumert, 1995; Hedelin & Sjîberg, 1989; Lehrke, Hoffmann, & Gardner, 1985). For example, Hedelin and Sjîberg (1989) investigated students in Grade 1–9 of the Swedish comprehensive school. Similar to the findings of Eccles, Wigfield, and their colleagues in studies of American children (e.g., Eccles et al., 1993; Wigfield et al., 1991), the students' ratings of their interest in mathematics and Swedish reading and writing showed declines over time, especially in mathematics. These researchers have identified a number of instructional variables that contribute positively or negatively to interest in school mathematics and science. Among these factors are: clarity of presentation, monitoring of what happens in the classroom, supportive behavior, cognitively stimulating experiences, self-concept of the teacher (educator vs. scientist), and achievement pressure (e.g., Baumert, 1995; Eder, 1992; Lehrke, 1992).

Intrinsic Motivation Theories

The theories described in this section deal with the distinction when intrinsic motivation and extrinsic motivation. When individuals are intrinsically motivated they do activities either because they enjoy doing them or because they want to do them. When extrinsically motivated, individuals do activities for instrumental or other reasons, such as receiving a reward.

Self-Determination Theory

Two basic assumptions about behavior underlie Deci and Ryan's self-determination theory: (1) the assumption that humans are motivated to maintain an optimal level of stimulation, and (2) the assumption that basic needs for competence and self-determination underlie intrinsically motivated behavior. They argued that intrinsic motivation is maintained only when actors feels competent and self-determined. Evidence that intrinsic motivation is reduced by the use of external control and negative competence feedback supports this hypothesis (see Deci and Ryan, 1985; Gottfried & Gottfried, 2004).

Deci and Ryan (1985) also argued, however, that the basic needs for competence and self-determination play a role in more extrinsically motivated behavior. Consider, for example, a student who consciously and without any external pressure selects a specific major because it will help him earn a lot of money. This student is guided by his basic needs for competence and self-determination but his choice of major is based on reasons totally extrinsic to the major itself. Finally, Deci and Ryan (1985) postulated that a basic need for interpersonal relatedness explains why people turn external goals into internal goals through internalization.

Individual Difference Theories of Intrinsic Motivation

Until recently, intrinsic motivation researchers like Deci and Ryan and Csikszentmihalyi have dealt with conditions, components, and consequences of intrinsic motivation without making a distinction between intrinsic motivation as a state versus intrinsic motivation as a trait-like characteristic. However, interest in trait-like individual differences in intrinsic motivation is growing particularly among educational and sport psychologists (see Amabile et al., 1994; Gottfried, 1990; Harter, 1998; Nicholls, 1989; Schiefele, 1991). These researchers define this enduring intrinsic motivational orientation in terms of three components: (1) preference for hard or challenging tasks, (2) learning that is driven by curiosity or interest, and (3) striving for competence and mastery. The second component is most central to the idea of intrinsic motivation. Both preference for hard tasks and striving for competence can be linked to either extrinsic or more general need-achievement motivation. Nonetheless, empirical findings suggest that the three components are highly correlated. In addition, evidence suggests that high levels of trait-like intrinsic motivation facilitate self-esteem (Ryan, Connell & Deci, 1985), mastery-oriented coping with failure (Dweck, 1999), high academic achievement (Benware & Deci, 1984; Schiefele & Schreyer, 1994), and use of appropriate learning strategies (Schiefele & Schreyer, 1994).

Developmental Changes in Intrinsic Motivation

Researchers in both Europe and the United States have found that mean levels of intrinsic motivation decline over the elementary school years (Gottfried et al., 2001; Harter, 1998; Helmke, 1993). The continuity or stability of intrinsic motivation, however, increases over the elementary and secondary school years. Mean levels of intrinsic motivation for particular school subjects also decline as children make the transition from elementary to middle school (see Eccles et al., 1993). As noted earlier, these declines seem directly linked to changes in the school environments that often coincide with these school transitions (Eccles et al., 1993; Midgley, 2002). Such changes in motivation likely contribute to the declines in school engagement often found during the early adolescent years.

Why Am I Doing This?

Achievement goal theory is the newest motivational approach to understanding children's engagement in various skill-based activities like school and sports (see Midgley, 2002). This theory focuses on why children think they are engaging in particular achievement-related activities and what they hope to accomplish through their engagement. Although the work related to this theory has progressed independently of the work discussed earlier on the valuing of an activity and on intrinsic versus extrinsic motivation, the concepts have strong theoretical links to these other theoretical perspectives. We include it in this chapter because individual differences in goals are likely to affect task engagement, as well as the relations of performance outcomes and engagement in mental health and ability self-concepts.

Nicholls and his colleagues (e.g., Nicholls, 1979; Nicholls et al., 1990) defined two major kinds of motivationally relevant goal patterns or orientations: ego-involved goals and task-involved goals. Individuals with ego-involved goals seek to maximize favorable evaluations of their competence and minimize negative evaluations of competence. Questions like "Will I look smart?" and "Can I outperform others?" reflect ego-involved goals. In contrast, with task-involved goals, individuals focus on mastering tasks and increasing one's competence. Questions such as "How can I do this task?" and "What will I learn?" reflect task-involved goals.

Dweck and her colleagues provide a complementary analysis distinguishing between performance goals (like ego-involved goals), and learning goals (like task-involved goals) (see Dweck, 1999; Dweck & Leggett, 1988). Similarly, Ames (1992) and Midgley (2002) distinguish between the association of performance (like ego-involved) goals and mastery goals (like task-focused goals) with both performance and task choice. With ego-involved (or performance) goals, children try to outperform others, and are more likely to do tasks they know they can do. Task-involved (or mastery-oriented) children choose challenging tasks and are more concerned with their own progress than with outperforming others.

Other researchers (e.g., Ford, 1992; Wentzel, 1991) have adopted a more complex perspective on goals and motivation, arguing that there are many different kinds of goals individuals can have in achievement settings. For example, Ford (e.g., Ford, 1992; Ford & Nichols, 1987) defined goals as desired end states people try to attain through the cognitive, affective and biochemical regulation of their behavior. Similar to Rokeach's (1979) human values and Eccles' attainment value (Eccles, 1983), Fords' set of goals included affective goals (e.g., happiness, physical well-being), cognitive goals (e.g., exploration, intellectual creativity), and subjective organization goals (e.g., unity, transcendence). Like Deci and Ryan's self-determination theory, his list of important goals also included self-assertive goals such as self-determination and individuality, integrative social relationship goals such as belongingness and social responsibility, and task goals such as mastery, material gain, and safety. Finally, Ford's goals included specific goals related to impacting on, or controlling/mastering, various aspects of the contexts one inhabits such as building a fort or winning a specific game or completing an important school assignment.

Development of Children's Goals

To date there has been surprisingly little empirical work on how children's goals develop. Nicholls (e.g., 1990) documented that both task goals and ego goals are already developed by second grade

(Nicholls et al., 1990). However, Nicholls (1989) also suggested that the ego-goal orientation becomes more prominent for many children as they get older, in part, because of developmental changes in their conceptions of ability and, in part, due to systematic changes in school context. Dweck and her colleagues (see Dweck, 1999) also predicted that performance goals should get more prominent as children go through school because they develop a more entity view of intelligence as they get older and that children holding an entity view of intelligence are more likely to adopt performance goals. Evidence supports these predictions (see Dweck, 1999; Midgley, 2002). In terms of mental health and engagement, this developmental shift is likely to lead more to increased disengagement and lower self-esteem for those children who have difficulty with school-based learning tasks.

It is also likely that the relation of goals to performance changes with age due to the changing meaning of ability and effort. Butler's work is directly related to this hypothesis. In a series of studies looking at how competitive and noncompetitive conditions, and task and ego-focused conditions, influence pre- and elementary school aged children's interests, motivation self-evaluations, she identified several developmental changes: First, competition decreased children's subsequent interest in a task only among children who judged their ability based on how their performance compared to the performances of other children (Butler, 1989a, 1990). Competition also increased older, but not younger, children's tendency to engage in social comparison (Butler, 1989a, 1989b). Second, although children of all ages engaged in social comparison, younger children seemed to be using the social comparison information primarily to determine how well they were mastering the task; in contrast the older children seemed to be using the social comparison information primarily as a way of judging their own ability (Butler, 1989b). As a result, the younger children were able to use the social comparison information to improve their performance. In contrast, engaging in social comparison had more mixed consequences for the older students. If they were doing better than the other children, they felt good about themselves and their competence; if they were doing worse than other children, they felt bad about themselves and were not able to effectively use the social comparison information to improve their own performance. Instead, they tended to withdraw from the activity and to evidence learned helpless behaviors. Third, whereas, 5-, 7-, and 10-year-old-children's self-evaluations were quite accurate under mastery conditions, under competitive conditions 5- and 7-year-olds inflated their performance self-evaluations more than 10-year-olds (Butler, 1990). Apparently the influence of situationally-induced performance goals on children's self-evaluations depends on the children's age and cognitive sophistication.

Finally, Butler and Ruzany (1993) found evidence that different patterns of socialization influence children's ability assessments and reasons for social comparison. In a study comparing kibbutz-reared with city-reared Israeli children, the kibbutz children adopted a normative ability concept earlier than urban children. However, only the urban children's reasons for engaging in social comparison were influenced by their concept of ability: once they adopted a normative view they used social comparison to compare their abilities to those of other children. In contrast, the kibbutz children used social comparison primarily for mastery reasons, regardless of their conception of ability.

Summary

In this section, we have reviewed the evidence for changes in children's goals for doing school work. Because interest in this area of motivation is fairly recent, much less empirical and theoretical work has been done on developmental changes; most of the work has focused instead on individual differences in goal orientation. The little available developmental work reveals a pattern of change not unlike the patterns discussed earlier for expectancy-related beliefs and values. At the population level, there appears to be an increase in ego-focused goals and competitive motivation. Given what we know about individual differences in goal orientation, such a shift is likely to lead at least some children (particularly those doing poorly in school) to disengage from school as they get older. We talk more about this in the sections on motivational problems and self-worth theory.

In the next section, we focus on work directly linking motivational constructs to healthy functioning. Much of this work has grown out of concern over particular motivational problems like test anxiety and learned helpless. We discuss this work first. More recently, researchers have been studying the link between motivational constructs and mental health directly. We discuss this work second.

THE DEVELOPMENT OF MOTIVATIONAL PROBLEMS

An increasing number of children begin to experience motivational problems during the elementary school years (Eccles et al., 1998). These problems include lack of confidence in one's abilities, anxiety, and the belief that one can not control one's achievement outcomes. In this section, we focus on performance anxiety and learned helplessness.

Test Anxiety

In one of the first longitudinal studies of performance anxiety, Hill and Sarason (1966) found that anxiety both increases across the elementary and junior high school years and becomes more negatively related to subsequent grades and test scores. They also found that highly anxious children's achievement test scores were up to 2 years behind the scores of their low anxious peers and that girls' anxiety scores were higher than boys'. Subsequent research has provided estimates of just how many children in the United States suffer from extreme forms of test anxiety: For example, Hill and Wigfield (1984) estimated that as many as 10 million U.S. children and adolescents experience significant evaluation anxiety.

What explains individual differences in test anxiety? Researchers point to both biological and social factors. For example, some research suggests that having parents who have overly high expectations and put too much pressure on their children contributes to high levels of test anxiety; (see Hill & Wigfield, 1984; Wigfield & Eccles, 1989). The fact that the prevalence of high test anxiety increases across the school years suggests that both cognitive maturational and school characteristics such as the increased frequency of social comparative and high stakes evaluation coupled with increasing are important influences (see Eccles et al., 1998, Midgley, 2002). Evidence from sport psychology suggests similar situational characteristics in the link between coaches' behaviors and levels of performance anxiety among young athletes (see Duda & Ntoumanis , 2005; Scanlon, Babkes, & Scanlan , 2005).

The nature of anxiety may also change with age. Typically, researchers in this area distinguish between two components of anxiety: a worry component and an emotional physical component. Wigfield and Eccles (1989) proposed that anxiety initially may be characterized more by emotionality, but as children develop cognitively, the worry aspect of anxiety should become increasingly salient. This proposal also remains to be tested, but we do know that worry is a major component of the thought processes of highly anxious fifth and sixth graders (Freedman-Doan, 1994). This hypothesis also points to the importance of middle childhood for the development of performance anxiety because these cognitive changes occur most rapidly during the 6- to 9-year-old period of life (Harter, 1998).

In addition, we know that academic performance anxiety predicts decreases in self-worth over the junior high school transition (Lord, Eccles, & McCarthy, 1994) which in turn predicts increases in depression, truancy, dropping out of school and alcohol use over the secondary school years (Eccles et al., 1998). Academic performance anxieties in late middle childhood also predict lowered educational and occupational aspirations much later in life (Vida & Eccles, 1999). For example, using Structural Equation Modelling (SEM) with data from our MSALT study, Vida and Eccles investigated the relation of sixth- and seventh-grade academic performance anxieties to occupational values, a sense of personal efficacy for jobs in business and science, and ability self- concepts for skills in leadership, independence and intellectual activities at age 20. The results from this analysis are illustrated in Figure 14.7. After controlling for actual GPA in junior high school, intellectual anxieties in early adolescence predicted valuing a job that is easy and not demanding at age 20. The intellectual anxieties also predicted lower ability self-concepts and reduced efficacy for jobs in business and science. Because we controlled for

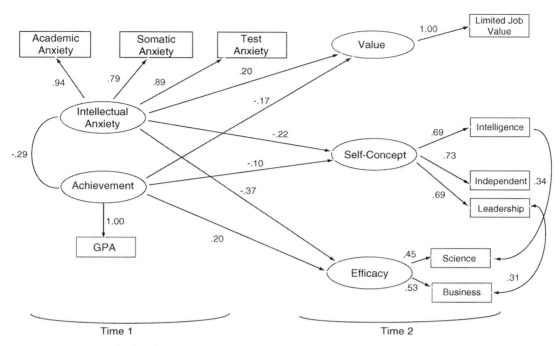

Figure 14.7 Standardized structural paths from early anxieties to later occupational ability self concepts and values

actual school performance, we can conclude that early intellectual anxieties undermine otherwise academically competent students' confidence in their abilities to succeed at demanding adult careers as well as the value they attach to such careers. In other analyses, we have also shown that early intellectual performance anxieties are related to higher levels of mental health problems among 18- to 24- year-olds (Vida & Eccles. 1999).

Anxiety Intervention Programs

Many programs to reduce anxiety have been developed (see Wigfield & Eccles, 1989). Earlier intervention programs emphasized the emotional aspects of anxiety and focused on various relaxation and desensitization techniques. Although these programs did succeed in reducing anxiety, they did not always lead to improved performance. Anxiety intervention programs linked to the worry aspect of anxiety focus on changing the negative, self-deprecating thoughts of anxious individuals and replacing them with more positive, task-focused thoughts. These programs have been more successful both in lowering anxiety and improving performance. An important issue that has not been adequately addressed is how programs should be tailored for different-aged children. This consideration is particularly important for elementary school-aged children (see Wigfield & Eccles, 1989). Further, because children's anxiety depends so much on the kinds of evaluations they experience in school, changes in school testing and other evaluation practices could help reduce anxiety.

Learned Helplessness

As defined by Dweck and Goetz (1978), "learned helplessness ... exists when an individual perceives the termination of failure to be independent of his responses" (p. 157). Learned helplessness has been related to individuals' attributions for success and failure: Helpless individuals are more likely to attribute their failures to uncontrollable factors, such as lack of ability, and their successes to unstable factors (see Dweck & Goetz, 1978). Dweck and her colleagues have documented several interesting differences between helpless and more mastery oriented children's responses to failure: When confronted by difficulty (or failure), mastery oriented children persist, stay focused on the task, and sometimes even use more sophisticated strategies. In contrast, helpless children's performance deteriorates, they ruminate about their difficulties, and often begin to attribute their failures to lack of ability. Further, helpless children adopt the "entity" view that their intelligence is fixed, whereas mastery oriented children adopt the incremental view of intelligence. Everything we have discussed thus far suggests that the prevalence of learned helplessness should increase during the middle childhood years (see Dweck, 1999, Fincham & Cain, 1986, and Weisz, 1984 for similar arguments). The little available empirical research supports this prediction (e.g., Parsons & Ruble, 1972; Pintrich & Schunk, 2002; Rholes et al., 1980; Stipek et al., 1992). However, Burhans and Dweck (1995) found that even some quite young (5- and 6-year-old) children respond negatively to failure feedback, judging themselves to be bad people (see also Stipek et al., 1992). These rather troubling findings show that negative responses to failure can develop quite early on.

As noted earlier, Burhans and Dweck proposed that very young children's helplessness is based more on their judgments that their worth as persons is contingent on their performance than on having the kind of entity views of intelligence that emerge during the middle childhood and early adolescent years. So what produces learned helplessness in children, even at these early ages, and do the causes change as the children mature? It seems likely that the very early sources of performance anxiety lie either in the affective reactions of parents to their young children's mastery attempts and performance failures or in genetically-based individual differences in various temperamental traits related to timidity and anxiety. The subsequent increases in the prevalence of test anxiety are probably linked to changes in the children's cognitive understanding of the nature of ability, changes in the nature of performance feedback and other social messages about the meaning of failure, and the interaction of genetic dispositions with these environmental changes. For example, Dweck and Goetz (1978) proposed that individual differences in learned helplessness during middle childhood depend on whether children receive feedback from the teachers and parents that imply that their failures reflect the lack of entity-type abilities. In support of this suggestion, Hokoda and Fincham (1995) found that mothers of helpless third-grade children (in comparison to mothers of mastery-oriented children) gave fewer positive affective comments to their children, were more likely to respond to their children's lack of confidence in their ability by telling them to quit, were less responsive to their children's bids for help, and did not focus them on mastery goals.

Alleviating Learned Helplessness

There are numerous studies designed to alleviate learned helplessness by changing attributions for success and failure so that learned helpless children learn to attribute failure to lack of effort rather than lack of entity-type abilities (see review by Forsterling, 1985). Various training techniques (including operand conditioning and providing specific attributional feedback) have been used successfully in changing children's failure attributions from lack of ability to lack of effort, improving their task persistence, and performance (e.g., Dweck, 1975). Two problems with these approaches have been noted. First, what if the child is already trying very hard? Then the attribution retraining may be counter productive. Second, telling children to "try harder" without providing specific strategies that are designed to improve their performance is likely to back fire- children may put in massive amounts of effort and still not succeed if they don't know how to apply that effort. Therefore, some researchers (e.g., Borkowski et al., 1990) now advocate using strategy retraining in combination with attribution retraining so that the lower achieving and/or learned helpless children are provided with specific ways to remedy their achievement problems. Borkowski and his colleagues, for example, have shown that a combined program of strategy instruction and attribution retraining is more effective than strategy instruction alone in increasing reading motivation and performance in underachieving students (e.g., Borkowski & Muthukrisna, 1995; Paris & Byrnes, 1989; Pressley & El-Dinary, 1993).

<u>Self-Efficacy Training</u>

Self-efficacy training has also been used to alleviate learned helplessness. For example, Schunk and his colleagues have done several studies designed to improve elementary school-aged children's (often low-achieving children) math, reading and writing performance through (see Schunk, 1994; Pintrich & Schunk, 2002). The training often includes skill training, enhancement of self-efficacy, attribution retraining, and training children how to set goals. Modeling often is an important aspect of this type of training. A number of findings have emerged from this work. First, the training increases both children's performance and their sense of self-efficacy. Second, attributing children's success to ability has a stronger impact on their self-efficacy than does either effort feedback, or ability and effort feedback (e.g., Schunk, 1983). Third, training children to set proximal, specific, and somewhat challenging goals enhances their self-efficacy and performance. Finally, like the work of Borkowski and his colleagues, Schunk and his colleagues have found that combining strategy training, goal emphases, and feedback to show children how their learning of strategies relate to their performance has some of the strongest effects on subsequent self-efficacy and skill development.

Summary

In summary, work on anxiety and helplessness shows that some children suffer from motivational problems that can undermine their performance in achievement situations. Although most of the work in developmental and educational psychology has focused on these two problems, there likely are other important motivational problems as well. In particular, some children may set maladaptive achievement goals, others may have difficulty regulating their achievement behaviors, and still others come to de-value achievement. More comprehensive work on these kinds of motivational problems and how they affect children's achievement is needed.

Researchers interested in the remediation of these motivational difficulties have turned increasingly to programs targeting both cognitive and motivational components. These studies illustrate both the need to attend to both motivational and cognitive factors, and the fact that different kinds of strategy instruction are more or less effective in enhancing performance, depending on how they influence motivation. This work now needs to be extended to children of different ages to determine whether the strategy instruction and motivation enhancement techniques need to be modified for younger and older children. Further, work is needed to develop programs that integrate various approaches, particularly those approaches associated with self-efficacy, goal setting, and self-regulation. More broadly, however, as valuable as these individual-focused programs are, they are likely to have little lasting benefit if home and school environments do not facilitate and support the changes. Therefore, some researchers have turned to changing school and classroom environments to facilitate motivation, rather than changing individual children (see Maehr & Midgley, 1996; Midgley, 2002).

Other theorists have focused more generally on the link between school experiences and emotional experiences. These theorists have been concerned with two issues: (1) the possible link between experiences in school and more general mental health, and (2) the emergence of what appear to be less adaptive motivational strategies as a means to protect one's mental health. Some of this work was summarized in the introduction to this chapter. In the next section, we focus on the work by Covington (1992) and on the work by Roeser (Roeser, 1998; Roeser & Eccles, 1998; Roeser, Eccles & Freedman-Doan, 1999; Roeser, Lord, & Eccles, 1994; Roeser, Midgley & Urdan, 1996) and Eccles (Eccles et al., 1998).

SELF-WORTH THEORY

Covington is concerned with children's need to maintain positive self-esteem particularly when they are faced with repeated failure experiences in school and other skill-based activity settings. Covington (1992) defined the motive for self-worth as the tendency to establish and maintain a positive self-image, or sense of self-worth. Because children spend so much time in classrooms and are evaluated so frequently there, Covington argued that they must protect their sense of academic competence in order to maintain their sense of self-worth. One way to accomplish this goal is by using those causal attribution patterns that enhance one's sense of academic competence and control: attributing success to ability and effort and failure to insufficient effort (Covington & Omelich, 1979; Eccles et al., 1982). Attributing failure to lack of ability is a particularly problematic attribution that students usually try to avoid. However, school evaluation, competition, and social comparison make it difficult for many children to maintain the belief that they are competent academically. Covington (1992) discussed the strategies many children develop to avoid appearing to lack ability. These include procrastination, making excuses, avoiding challenging tasks, and most importantly, not trying. Although trying is critical for success, if children try and fail, it is difficult to escape the conclusion that they lack ability. Therefore, if failure seems likely, some children will not try, precisely because trying and failing threatens their ability self-concepts. Further, Covington discussed how even some high achieving students can be failure avoidant. Rather than responding to a challenging task with greater effort, these students may try to avoid the task in order to maintain both their own sense of competence, and others' conclusions regarding their competence. Covington (1992) suggested that reducing the frequency and salience of competitive, social comparative, and evaluative practices, and focusing instead on effort, mastery, and improvement, would allow more children to maintain their self-worth without having to resort to the failure-avoiding strategies just described. These suggestions have been incorporated successfully into many other motivation theorists' recommendations for changing schools to enhance motivation (e.g., Ames, 1992; Maehr & Midgley, 1996; Midgley, 2002).

ACADEMIC SELF-PERCEPTIONS AND MENTAL HEALTH

We have also begun to assess the link between academic self-perceptions and mental health with our CAB (Childhood and Beyond) data. Earlier we summarized the patterns of change across middle childhood in children's academic risk status. We reported that a substantial number of children identified as at-risk in the first grade are doing fine in terms of both their academic self-concepts and their academic performance by the time they reach middle school/junior high school. Now we discuss in more detail both who those children might be and the link between academic outcomes and mental health. First, we looked at was the co-occurrence of academic and mental health risks. As summarized earlier, children identified as at academic risk in both early elementary school and early adolescence also have more mental health problems than their not-at-risk peers.

But more importantly, we found that variations in mental health related to the trajectories of change in risk status. These results were summarized in Figure 14.3. The incliners had significantly higher self-worth than the decliners at Time 2 even though they were performing more poorly in terms of their grades (see Figure 14.4) at that time. Furthermore, when they were adolescents (at Time 4), they still had significantly higher self-worth; in addition, they were more satisfied with their lives and reported higher levels of ego resilience and less anger than the decliner group.

We looked at the issue of co-occurrence in one other way (Roeser & Eccles, 1998). Using only the middle cohort of children in the CAB study (those in Grade 2 at the start of the study), we clustered the children based on indicators of academic motivation (ability self-concept and academic valuing) and mental health (a composite of scores on depressive affect, self-esteem, and anger scales) when they were in Grade 8. Four distinct clusters of approximately equal size emerged: a well functioning group (high on all three indicators), a poor motivation group (low on the motivation indicators but high on mental health), a poor mental health group (low on mental health but high on the motivation indicators), and a multiple risk group (low on all three indicators). These results indicate that these two sets of indicators of social adjustment sometimes co-occur in the same individual and sometimes do not. We then looked at the data for these four groups when they were in Grades 2 and 3 and compared their academic competence beliefs and grade point average.

Several interesting patterns emerged. As one might expect, the well functioning group scored the highest on both indicators. In contrast, there were no differences in academic self-competence among the other three groups at Grade 2. In contrast, by Grade 3 the multiple risk group had the lowest academic ability self-concepts and remained the lowest from that point on. The multiple risk group also had a lower grade point average than the other three groups in Grades 1–3 and 8 and they were the only group to show a decline in academic marks from the fourth to the eighth grade; the other groups showed an increase in marks over this period.

Clearly, these four groups of children had different trajectories of change in both their academic motivation and their mental health over the middle childhood years. We present these findings because they demonstrate the importance of taking a person-centered orientation to studying developmental trajectories. These patterns of individual differences would have gone unnoticed if we had relied only on population-centered and variable-centered analyses. Our next steps will be to identify the psychological, family, school, and peer-group characteristics that distinguish these four groups of children. We will focus on the child's own ability to regulate his or her behavior to the demands of the situation, on the quality of family support for effective problem solving during the preschool years; and on the nature of classroom environments these children must cope with as they pass through elementary school.

SUMMARY

We had two goals in this chapter: (1) to describe the developmental pathways associated with academic motivation and school engagement during middle childhood, and (2) to explore the link between academic adjustment and mental health during this same developmental period.

With regard to our second goal, the picture varies somewhat depending on whether one takes a population- and/or variable-centered approach or an individual difference or person-centered approach. At the population level, there is clearly a link between psychological functioning in the domain of school and general mental health. At the individual differences level, there is a strong relation between these two domains of functioning in some children and no relation (or only a very weak relation) in other children. Additional work is badly needed before we can understand these individual variations.

The findings regarding our first goal also yield somewhat different conclusions depending on whether one adopts a variable- versus a person-centered approach. Evidence for change at the population level points fairly consistently to declines in children's academic motivation and school attachment/engagement during the elementary school years. On average, children begin elementary school quite confident of their own abilities and quite enthusiastic about school; and, on average, both of these sets of beliefs decline over the elementary school years, particularly between Grades 2 and 4. Both psychological and situational causes for these patterns were discussed.

A different picture emerges when one conducts person-centered analyses. There are clear and consistent patterns of individual differences in these trajectories. Although it is the case that the vast majority of children do start elementary school with very high estimates of their own abilities, not all of these children evidence declines over the elementary school years, and the rate of decline varies in systematic ways across children with different psychological resources (assessed primarily in terms of self-esteem in the studies reported in this chapter).

The CAB results we discussed in detail identified two pathways to diminished academic and social-emotional functioning in early adolescence—the straight path of chronic academic difficulties, and the less common path of declining academic performance and feelings of competence over time. Although these pathways suggest the possibility of different underlying mechanisms, one common characteristic of both of these groups of children is clear: Somewhere between the upper elementary years and the transition to middle school, these youth experience a serious decline in their academic motivation. It could be that children who are vulnerable in terms of academic motivation and achievement, either due to long term problems or some other factor during childhood, are most susceptible to the stresses involved with bio-psycho-social transitions during early adolescence (e.g., Eccles & Midgley, 1989, Simmons & Blyth, 1987). Although speculative, these data certainly suggest a disruption between the late elementary and middle school years in the two groups of children who ended up academically at-risk during early adolescence. In support of this suggestion, in our Michigan Study of Adolescent Life Transitions we found that children with high performance anxiety, low confidence in their academic, social and/or athletic abilities and troubled relationships with their parents were most susceptible psychologically to the negative effects of the junior high school transition (Lord, Eccles, & McCarthy, 1994).

The "decliner" group certainly seemed to be a group of children who were capable, but seemed to have difficulties that went largely unnoticed in their elementary school years when they still appeared to be engaged in school. It could be that these children manifested their distress in an internalizing way that was not picked up on by their early teachers (e.g., Loeber et al., 1990; Lord et al., 1994), or that the problems they experienced later during adolescence resulted from events occurring during the later elementary school years or the transition into secondary school. Whatever the case, it is clear that these children, despite their ability to do well in school, end up very disengaged from academics by the seventh or eighth grade—so much so that they were already entertaining the notion that they might drop out of school before finishing.

The findings from these analyses also documented two pathways toward positive academic and social-emotional adjustment during early adolescence. The majority of children in the CAB study evidenced positive academic and social emotional adjustment over time. This is as one might expect. However, we also identified a group of "academically resilient" children who, despite early difficulties, went on to achieve at a fairly high level during early adolescence. Despite their lower academic marks, less favorable teacher beliefs concerning their abilities, and slightly lower intelligence scores early in elementary school, these children showed a positive profile of academic competence, value, and self-esteem beliefs all the way from childhood to early adolescence. These findings suggest that the optimism these children felt when they entered school protected them from the negative effects of lower academic performance and lower teacher expectations. We plan to investigate exactly which social and personal resources and contextual experiences distinguished these resilient youth from their less resilient peers.

The results presented in this chapter also raise several interesting issues regarding how children compensate for difficulties they experience in the academic domain. This question is important given the fact that the academic realm is a central sphere of experience and "work" for the child and adolescent, and competence and achievement is thus centrally relevant to a child's self-esteem (e.g., Eccles [Parsons] et al., 1983; Erikson, 1959; Harter, 1985). What happens when youth do not feel that they are academically competent? One the one hand, the findings presented earlier, as well as other work by Roeser and his colleagues (e.g., Roeser & Eccles, 1998; Roeser et al., 1995), suggest some of them will experience diminished self-esteem and general well-being. On the other hand, our findings also provide evidence of at least one mechanism of compensation: Youth who ended up feeling less academically competent and received lower performance marks also devalued academics the most. Beginning with William James, several self theorists have suggested that one way to maintain self-esteem in the face of relative incompetence in an achievement domain is to devalue that domain (Covington, 1992; Eccles [Parsons] et al., 1983; Harter, 1985; Wigfield & Eccles, 1992). This may be one explanation of what occurred with the children in the "stable difficulties" and "decliner" groups. That is, youth who experience more and more difficulties in school may adjust their perceptions of the importance, usefulness, and interest value of their academic subjects by the time they reach seventh or eighth grade. This is particularly distressing given that "not liking school" is one of the major reason youth give for why they drop out of school.

Another possible mechanism of compensation children might use is to increase their valuing of, and engagement, in achievement-related activities in other relevant life domains, domains in which they feel more competent and socially supported. Although there are several "culturally mandated" dimensions of self that are likely central to esteem, including academics (e.g., Stein, Roeser, & Markus,

Markus & Roeser, 1998), some children may be able to compensate for difficulties in one area by achievement in another. For instance, in the Eccles et al. expectancy-value formulation of achievement motivation, Eccles [Parsons] et al. (1983) suggested that competence and valuing of any number of achievement domains, including the performing and fine arts, sports, and the social sphere, can serve as relevant sources of esteem. Furthermore, in this model, self-perceptions of relative incompetence in one area are assumed to relate to children's feelings of competence and value in other domains: those children with very low academic competence beliefs may develop other strengths and competencies to compensate for their relative lack of success at school. If successful, this strategy can provide the children with another ecological niche in which to develop a sense of efficacy. Unfortunately, given that children must attend school until they are 16, this strategy is also likely to lead them to feel quite disaffected from the setting in which they must spend most of their time.

REFERENCES

Achenbach, T. M., Howell, C. T., Quay, H. C., & Conners, C. K. (1991). National survey of problems and competencies among four to sixteen year olds. *Monographs for the Society of Research in Child Development, 56*(3).

Alexander, K. L., & Entwise, D. (1988). Achievement in the first two years of school: Patterns and processes. *Monographs of the Society for Research in Child Development, 53*(2, Serial No. 218).

Alexander, K. L., Dauber, S. L., & Entwisle, D. R. (1993). First-grade classroom behavior: Its short- and long-term consequences for school performance. *Child Development, 64,* 801–803.

Alexander, P. A., Entwisle, D. R., & Horsey, C. S. (1997). From first grade forward: Early foundations of high school dropout. *Sociology of Education, 70,* 87–10

Alexander, P. A., Kulikowich, J. M., & Jetton, T. L. (1994). The role of subject-matter knowledge and interest in the processing of linear and nonlinear texts. *Review of Educational Research, 64,* 201–252.

Amabile, T. M., Hill, K. G., Hennessey, B. A., & Tighe, E. M. (1994). The Work Preference Inventory: Assessing intrinsic and extrinsic motivational orientations. *Journal of Personality and Social Psychology, 66,* 950–967.

Ames, C. (1992). Classrooms: Goals, structures, and student motivation. *Journal of Educational Psychology, 84,* 261–271.

Ames, C., & Ames, R. (Eds.). (1989). *Research on motivation in education (Vol. 3: Goals and cognitions).* San Diego: Academic Press.

Arbreton, A. J., & Eccles, J. S. (1994). *Mother's Perceptions of Their Children During the Transition from Kindergarten to Formal Schooling: The Effect of Teacher Evaluations on Parents' Expectations for Their Early Elementary School Children.* American Educational Research Association Conference, New Orleans, LA.

Asher, S. R., Hymel, S., & Renshaw, P. D. (1984). Loneliness in Children. *Child Development, 55,* 1456–1464.

Bandura, A. (1977). Self-efficacy: Toward a unifying theory of behavioral change. *Psychological Review, 84,* 191–215.

Bandura, A. (1986). *Social foundations of thought and action: A social cognitive theory.* Englewood Cliffs, NJ: Prentice-Hall.

Bandura, A. (1994). *Self-efficacy: The exercise of control.* New York: W. H. Freeman.

Barber, B. L., Eccles, J. S., & Stone, M. R. (2001). Whatever happened to the Jock, the Brain, and the Princess?: Young adult pathways linked to adolescent activity involvement and social identity. *Journal of Adolescent Research, 16,* 429–455.

Battle, E. (1966). Motivational determinants of academic competence. *Journal of Personality and Social Psychology, 4,* 534–642.

Baumert, J. (1995, April). *Gender, science interest, teaching strategies and socially shared beliefs about gender roles in 7th graders—a multi-level analysis.* Paper presented at the annual meeting of the American Educational Research Association, San Francisco.

Benware, C. A. & Deci, E. L. (1984). Quality of learning with an active versus passive motivational set. *American Educational Research Journal, 21,* 755–765.

Borkowski, J. G., & Muthukrisna, N. (1995). Learning environments and skill generalization: How contexts facilitate regulatory processes and efficacy beliefs. In F. Weinert & W. Schneider (Eds.), *Recent perspectives on memory development.* (pp. 283–300). Hillsdale, NJ: Erlbaum.

Borkowski, J. G., Carr, M., Relliger, E., & Pressley, M. (1990). Self-regulated cognition: Interdependence of metacognition, attributions, and self-esteem. In B. Jones & L. Idol (Eds.), *Dimensions of thinking and cognitive instruction* (Vol. 1) (pp. 52-92). Hillsdale, NJ: Erlbaum.

Burhans, K. K., & Dweck, C. S. (1995). Helplessness in early childhood: The role of contingent worth. *Child Development, 66,* 1719–1738.

Butler, R. (1989a). Interest in the task and interest in peers' work: A developmental study. *Child Development, 60,* 562–570.

Butler, R. (1989b). Mastery versus ability appraisal: A developmental study of children's observations of peers' work. *Child Development, 60,* 1350–1361.

Butler, R. (1990). The effects of mastery and competitive conditions on self-assessment at different ages. *Child Development, 61,* 201–210.

Butler, R. (1993). Effects of task- and ego-achievement goals on information seeking during task engagement. *Journal of Personality and Social Psychology, 65,* 18–31.

Butler, R., & Ruzany, N. (1993). Age and socialization effects on the development of social comparison motives and normative ability assessments in kibbutz and urban children. *Child Development, 64,* 532–543.

Cairns, R. B., Cairns, B. D., & Neckerman, H. J. (1989). Early School Dropout: Configurations and Determinants. *Child Development, 60,* 1437–1452.

Connell, J. P., & Wellborn, J. G. (1991). Competence, autonomy, and relatedness: A motivational analysis of self-system processes. In R. Gunnar & L. A. Sroufe (Eds.), *Minnesota symposia on child psychology* (Vol. 23, pp. 43–77). Hillsdale, NJ: Erlbaum.

Connell, J. P., Spencer, M. B., & Aber, J. L. (1994). Educational risk and resilience in African American Youth: Context, self, and action outcomes in school. *Child Development, 65*, 493–506.

Covington, M. (1992). *Making the grade: A self-worth perspective on motivation and school Reform.* New York: Cambridge University Press.

Covington, M. V., & Omelich, C. L. (1979). Effort: The double-edged sword in school achievement. *Journal of Educational Psychology, 71*, 169–182.

Csikszentmihalyi, M. (1988). The flow experience and its significance for human psychology. In M. Csikszentmihalyi & I. S. Csikszentmihalyi (Eds.), *Optimal experience* (pp. 15–35). Cambridge: Cambridge University Press.

Deci, E. L. (1975). *Intrinsic motivation.* New York: Plenum Press.

Deci, E.L., & Ryan, R. M. (1985). *Intrinsic motivation and self-determination in human behavior.* New York: Plenum Press.

Denison, J. A, Zarrett, N. R., & Eccles, J. S. (under review) I like to do it, I am able and I know it: Longitudinal coupling between domain specific ability/achievement, self concepts and interests. Manuscript under review.

Dryfoos, J. G. (1990). *Adolescents at risk: Prevalence and prevention.* New York: Oxford University Press.

Dryfoos, J. G. (1994). *Full service schools: A revolution in health and social services for children, youth, and families.* San Francisco: Jossey-Bass Publishers.

Duda, J. L. & Ntoumanis, N. (2005). After-school sport for children: Implications of a task-involving motivational climate. In J. L. Mahoney, R. W. Larson, & J. S. Eccles (Eds.), *Organized activities as contexts of development: Extracurricular activities, after-school and community programs.* (pp. 311-330). Mahwah, NJ: Erlbaum.

Dweck, C. S. (1975). The role of expectations and attributions in the alleviation of learned helplessness. *Journal of Personality and Social Psychology, 31*, 674–685.

Dweck, C. S. (1999). *Self-theories: Their role in motivation, personality, and development.* Philadelphia: Psychology Press,

Dweck, C. S., & Goetz, T. E. (1978). Attributions and learned helplessness. In J. H. Harvey, W. Ickes, & R. F. Kidd (Eds.), *New directions in attribution research* (Vol. 2). Hillsdale, NJ: Erlbaum.

Dweck, C. S., Davidson, W., Nelson, S., & Enna, B. (1978). Sex differences in learned helplessness: II. The contingencies of evaluative feedback in the classroom, and III. An experimental analysis. *Developmental Psychology, 14*, 268–276.

Dweck, C. S., & Leggett, E. (1988). A social-cognitive approach to motivation and personality. *Psychological Review, 95*, 256–273.

Eccles, J. S. (1987). Gender roles and women's achievement-related decisions. *Psychology of Women Quarterly, 11*, 135–172.

Eccles, J. S. (1993). School and family effects on the ontogeny of children's interests, self-perceptions, and activity choice. In J. Jacobs (Ed.), *Nebraska Symposium on Motivation, 1992: Developmental perspectives on motivation* (pp. 145–208). Lincoln: University of Nebraska Press.

Eccles, J. S., Adler, T. F., & Meece, J. L. (1984). Sex differences in achievement: A test of alternate theories. *Journal of Personality and Social Psychology, 46*, 26–43.

Eccles, J. S., & Barber, B. L. (1999). Student council, volunteering, basketball, or marching band: What kind of extracurricular involvement matters? *Journal of Adolescent Research, 14*, 10–43.

Eccles, J. S., Barber, B., & Jozefowicz, D. (1999). Linking gender to education, occupation, and recreational choices:

Applying the Eccles et al. model of achievement-related choices. In W. B. Swann, J. H. Langlois, & L. A. Gilbert (Ed.), *Sexism and stereotypes in modern society: The gender science of Janet Taylor Spence* (pp. 153–192). Washington, DC: APA Press.

Eccles, J., & Bryan, J., (1994). Adolescence: Critical crossroad in the path of gender-role development. In M. R. Stevenson (Ed.), *Gender roles through the life span* (pp. 110-147). Muncie, IN: Ball State University Press

Eccles, J. S., & Midgley, C. (1989). Stage-environment fit: Developmentally appropriate classrooms for young adolescents. In C. Ames & R. Ames (Eds.), *Research on motivation in education: Vol. 3, goals and cognitions* (pp. 13–44). New York: Academic Press.

Eccles, J. S., Midgley, C., & Adler, T. (1984). Grade related changes in the school environment: Effects on achievement motivation. In J. Nicholls (Ed.), *Advances in motivation and achievement* (Vol. 3, pp. 283–331). Greenwich: JAI Press.

Eccles, J. S., Midgley, C., Wigfield, A., Buchanan, C. M., Reuman, D., Flanagan, C., & MacIver, D. (1993). Development during adolescence: The impact of stage-environment fit on adolescents' experiences in schools and families. *American Psychologist, 48*, 90–101.

Eccles, J. S., Roeser, R. Wigfield, A., & Freedman-Doan, C. (1999). Academic and motivational pathways through middle childhood. In L. Balter & C. S. Tamis-Lemonda (Eds.), *Child psychology: A handbook of contemporary issues* (pp. 287–317). London: Taylor & Francis.

Eccles, J. S., Vida, M. N., & Barber, B. (2004). The relation of early adolescents' college plans and both academic ability and task-value beliefs to subsequent college enrollment. *Journal of Early Adolescence, 24*, 63–77.

Eccles, J. S., & Wigfield, A. (1995). In the mind of the actor: The structure of adolescents' achievement task values and expectancy-related beliefs. *Personality and Social Psychology Bulletin, 21*, 215–225.

Eccles, J. S., Wigfield, A., Flanagan, C., Miller, C., Reuman, D., & Yee, D. (1989). Self-concepts, domain values, and self-esteem: Relations and changes at early adolescence. *Journal of Personality, 57*, 283–310

Eccles, J. S., Wigfield, A., Harold, R., & Blumenfeld, P. (1993). Age and gender differences in children's self- and task perceptions during elementary school. *Child Development, 64*, 830–847.

Eccles, J. S., Wigfield, A., & Schiefele, U. (1998). Motivation. In N. Eisenberg (Ed.), *Handbook of child psychology* (pp. 1017–1095). New York: Wiley.

Eccles-Parsons, J., Adler, T. F., Futterman, R., Goff, S.B., Kaczala, C. M., Meece, J. L., & Midgley, C. (1983). Expectancies, values, and academic behaviors. In J. T. Spence (Ed.), *Achievement and achievement motivation* (pp. 75–146). San Francisco: W. H. Freeman.

Eccles-Parsons, J., Meece, J. L., Adler, T. F., & Kaczala, C. M. (1982). Sex differences in attributions and learned helplessness. *Sex Roles, 8*, 421–432.

Eder, F. (1992). Schulklima und Entwicklung allgemeiner Interessen. In A. Krapp & M. Prenzel (Eds.), *Interesse, lernen, leistung* (pp. 165-194). Munster: Aschendorff.

Erikson, E. H. (1959). Identity and the life cycle. *Psychological Issues, 1*, 18–164.

Erikson, E. H. (1968). *Identity, youth and crisis.* New York: Norton.

Feather, N. T. (1982). *Expectations and actions: Expectancy-value models in psychology.* Hillsdale, NJ: Erlbaum

Feather, N. T. (1992). Values, valences, expectations, and actions. *Journal of Social Issues, 48*, 109–124.

Fincham, F. D., & Cain, K. M. (1986). Learned helplessness

in humans: A developmental analysis. *Developmental Review, 6*, 301–333.

Ford, M. E. (1992). *Human motivation: Goals, emotions, and personal agency beliefs.* Newbury Park, CA: Sage.

Ford, M. E., & Nichols, C. W. (1987). A taxonomy of human goals and some possible application. In M. E. Ford & D. H. Ford (Eds.), *Humans as self-constructing living systems: Putting the framework to work* (pp. 289–311). Hillsdale NJ: Erlbaum.

Fosterling, F. (1985). Attributional retraining: A review. *Psychological Bulletin, 98*, 495–512.

Fredricks, J. A., & Eccles, J. S. (2002). Children's competence and value beliefs from childhood through adolescence. *Developmental Psychology, 38*(4), 519–533.

Freedman-Doan, C. R. (1994). Factors influencing the development of general, academic, and social anxiety in normal preadolescent children. Unpublished doctoral dissertation, Detroit, MI: Wayne State University.

Gottfried, A. E. (1990). Academic intrinsic motivation in young elementary school children. *Journal of Educational Psychology, 82*, 525–538.

Gottfried, A. E., Fleming, J. S., & Gottfried, A. W. (2001). Continuity of academic-intrinsic motivation from childhood through late adolescence: A longitudinal study. *Journal of Educational Psychology, 93*, 3–13.

Gottfried, A. E. (1985). Academic intrinsic motivation in elementary and junior high school students. *Journal of Educational Psychology, 77*, 631–645.

Harter, S. (1985). Competence as a dimension of self-evaluation: Toward a comprehensive model of self-worth. In R. L. Leahy (Ed.), *The development of the self.* New York: Academic Press.

Harter, S. (1998). The development of self-representations. In W. Damon & N. Eisenberg (Eds.), *Handbook of child psychology, fifth edition, vol. 3: Social, emotional, and personality development* (pp. 553–618). New York: Wiley.

Hedelin, L., & Sjiberg, L. (1989). The development of interests in the Swedish comprehensive school. *European Journal of Psychology of Education, 4*, 17–35.

Helmke, A. (1993). Die entwicklung der lernfreude vom kindergarten bis zur 5. klassenstufe. *Zeitschrift fÄr PÑdagogische Psychologie, 7*, 77–86.

Heyman, G. D., Dweck, C. S., & Cain, K. M. (1993). Young children's vulnerability to self-blame and helplessness: Relationships to beliefs about goodness. *Child Development, 63*, 401–415.

Hidi, S. (1990). Interest and its contribution as a mental resource for learning. *Review of Educational Research, 60*, 549–571.

Higgins, E. T., & Parsons, J. E. (1983). Social cognition and the social life of the child: Stages as subcultures. In E. T. Higgins, D. N. Ruble, & W. W. Hartup (Eds.), *Social cognition and social development* (pp. 15–62). Cambridge: Cambridge University Press.

Hill, K., & Sarason, S. B. (1966). The relation of test anxiety and defensiveness to test and school performance over the elementary school years: A further longitudinal study. *Monographs for the Society for Research in Child Development, 31* (2, Serial No. 104).

Hill, K. T., & Wigfield, A. (1984). Test anxiety: A major educational problem and what to do about it. *Elementary School Journal, 85*, 105–126.

Hinshaw, S. P. (1992). Externalizing behavior problems and academic underachievement in childhood and adolescence: Causal relationships and underlying mechanisms. *Psychological Bulletin, 111*, 127–155.

Hokoda, A., & Fincham, F. D. (1995). Origins of children's helpless and mastery achievement patterns in the family. *Journal of Educational Psychology, 87*, 375–385.

Jacobs, J. E., Hyatt, S., Osgood, W. D., Eccles, J. S., & Wigfield, A. (2002). Changes in children's self-competence and values: Gender and domain differences across grades one through twelve. *Child Development, 73*(2), 509–527.

Lehrke, M. (1992). Einige lehrervariablen und ihre beziehungen zum interesse der schuler. In A. Krapp & M. Prenzel (Eds.), Interesse, lernen, leistung (pp. 123–136). Munster: Aschendorff.

Lehrke, M., Hoffmann, L. & Gardner, P. L. (Eds.). (1985). *Interests in science and technology education.* Kiel: Institut fur die Padagogik der Naturwissenschaften.

Loeber, R., Green, S. M., & Lahey, B. B. (1990) Mental health professionals' perception of the utility of children, mothers, and teachers as informants on childhood psychopathology. *Journal of Clinical Child Psychology, 19*, 136–143.

Lord, S. E., Eccles, J. S., & McCarthy, K. (1994). Surviving the junior high school transition: Family processes and self-perceptions as protective and risk factors. *Journal of Early Adolescence, 14*, 162–199.

Mac Iver, D. J., Stipek, D. J., & Daniels, D. H. (1991). Explaining within-semester changes in student effort in junior high school and senior high school courses. *Journal of Educational Psychology, 83*, 201–211.

Maehr, M. L. & Midgley, C. (1996). *Transforming school cultures.* Boulder, CO: Westview Press. 1996

Markus, H. J., & Nurius, P. S. (1984). *Self-understanding and self-regulation in middle childhood. The status of basic research on school-aged children.* Washington DC: National Academy of Sciences.

Marsh, H.W. (1989). Age and sex effects in multiple dimensions of self-concept: Preadolescence to early adulthood. *Journal of Educational Psychology, 81*, 417–430.

Meece, J. L., Wigfield, A., & Eccles, J. S. (1990). Predictors of math anxiety and its consequences for young adolescents' course enrollment intentions and performances in mathematics. *Journal of Educational Psychology, 82*, 60–70.

Midgley, C. M. (2002). *Goals, goal structures, and patterns of adaptive learning.* Mahwah, NJ: Erlbaum.

Nicholls, J. . (1979). Development of perception of own attainment and causal attributions for success and failure in reading. *Journal of Educational Psychology, 71*, 94–99.

Nicholls, J. G. (1989). *The competitive ethos and democratic education.* Cambridge: Havard University Press.

Nicholls, J. G., Cobb, P., Yackel, E., Wood, T., & Wheatley, G. (1990). Students' theories of mathematics and their mathematical knowledge: Multiple dimensions of assessment. In G. Kulm (Ed.), *Assessing higher order thinking in mathematics* (pp. 137–154). Washington, DC: American Association for the Advancement of Science.

Nicholls, J. G. (1984). Achievement motivation: Conceptions of ability, subjective experience, task choice, and performance. *Psychological Review, 91*, 328–346.

Nicholls, J. G. (1990). What is ability and why are we mindful of it? A developmental perspective. In R. Sternberg & J. Kolligan (Eds.), *Competence considered.* New Haven, CT: Yale University Press.

Offord, D. R., & Fleming, J. E. (1995). Child and adolescent psychiatry and public health. In M. Lewis (Ed.), *Child and adolescent psychiatry: A comprehensive textbook,* (2nd ed.). Baltimore : Williams & Wilkins.

Ollendick, T. H., Greene, R. W., Weist, M. D., & Oswald, D. P. (1990). The predictive validity of teacher nominations: A five year follow-up of at-risk youth. *Journal of Abnormal Child Psychology, 18*, 699–713.

Pallas, A. M., Entwisle, D. R., Alexander, K. L., & Stluka, M. F. (1994). Ability group effects: Instructional, social, or institutional? *Sociology of Education, 67,* 27–46.

Paris, S. G., & Byrnes, J. P (1989). The constructivst approach to self-regulation and learning in the classroom. In B. J. Zimmerman & D. H. Schunk (Eds.), *Self-regulated learning and academic achievement: Theory, research, and practice.* New York: Springer-Verlag.

Parkhurst, J. T., & Asher, S. R. (1992). Peer rejection in middle school: Subgroup differences in behavior, loneliness, and interpersonal concerns. *Developmental Psychology, 28,* 231–241.

Parsons, J., & Ruble, D. (1972). Attributional processes related to the development of achievement-related affect and expectancy. *APA Proceedings,* 80th Annual Convention, 105-106.

Parsons, J. E., & Ruble, D. N. (1977). The development of achievement-related expectancies. *Child Development, 48,* 1075–1079.

Pintrich, P. R. (2000). Issues in self-regulation theory and research. *Journal of Mind & Behavior, 21,* 213–219.

Pintrich, P. R. (2000). Multiple goals, multiple pathways: The role of goal orientation in learning and achievement. *Journal of Educational Psychology, 92,* 544–555.

Pintrich, P. R. & Schrauben, B. (1992). Students' motivational beliefs and their cognitive engagement in classroom academic tasks. In D. H. Schunk & J. L. Meece)Eds.), *Student perceptions in the classroom* (pp. 149-183). .: Hillsdale, NJ Erlbaum. .

Pintrich, P. R. & Schunk, D. H., (2002). *Motivation in education: Theory, research, and applications.* Upper Saddle River, NJ: Merrill.

Pressley, M., & El-Dinary, P. B. (Eds.). (1993). Strategies instruction (Special issue). *Elementary School Journal, 94*(2), entire issue

Rae-Grant, N., Thomas, H., Offord, D. R., & Boyle, M. H. (1989). Risk, protective factors, and the prevalence of behavioral and emotional disorders in children and adolescents. *Journal of American Academy of Child and Adolescent Psychiatry, 28,* 262–268.

Renninger, K. A. (1990). Children's play interests, representation, and activity. In R. Fivush & J. Hudson (Eds.), *Knowing and remembering in young children* (pp. 127–165). Cambridge: Cambridge University Press.

Renninger, K. A., Hidi, S. & Krapp, A. (Eds.). (1992). *The role of interest in learning and development.* Hillsdale, NJ: Erlbaum.

Rholes, W. S., Blackwell, J., Jordan, C., & Walters, C. (1980). A developmental study of learned helplessness. *Developmental Psychology, 16,* 616–624.

Roderick, M. (1994). Grade retention and school dropout: Investigating the association. *American Educational Research Journal, 31,* 729–759.

Roe, A., & Siegelman, M. (1964). *The origin of interests.* Washington: American Personnel and Guidance Association.

Roeser, R. W., Lord, S. E., & Eccles, J. S. (1994, February). *A portrait of academic alienation in early adolescence: Motivation, mental health and family indices.* Paper presented at the Society for Research on Adolescence, San Diego.

Roeser, R. W., Midgley, C., Urdan, T. (1996). Perceptions of the school psychological environment and early adolescents' psychological and behavioral functioning in school: The mediating role of goals and belonging. *Journal of Educational Psychology, 88,* 113-131.

Rokeach, M. (1979). From individual to institutional values with special reference to the values of science. In M. Rokeach (Ed.), *Understanding human values* (pp. 47–70). New York: Free Press.

Rosenberg, M., Schooler, C., & Schoenbach, C. (1989). Self-esteem and adolescent problems: Modeling reciprocal effects. *American Sociological Review, 54,* 1004–1018.

Ryan, R. M., Connell, J. P. & Deci, E. L. (1985). A motivational analysis of self-determination and self-regulation in education. In C. Ames & R. Ames (Eds.), *Research on motivation in education. Vol. 2: The classroom milieu* (pp. 13–51). London: Academic Press.

Ryan, R. M. (1992). Agency and organization: Intrinsic motivation, autonomy, and the self in psychological development. In J. Jacobs (Ed.), *Nebraska Symposium on Motivation* (Vol., 40, pp. 1–56). Lincoln: University of Nebraska Press.

Scanlon, T. K., Babkes, M. L., & Scanlan, L. A. (2005). Participation in sport: A developmental glimpse at emotion. In J. L. Mahoney, R. W. Larson, & J. S. Eccles (Eds.), *Organized activities as contexts of development: Extracurricular activities, after-school and community programs.* (pp. 275-310). Mahwah, NJ: Erlbaum.

Schiefele, U. (1996). Topic interest, text representation, and quality of experience. *Contemporary Educational Psychology, 21,* 3–18.

Schiefele, U. (1991). Interest, learning, and motivation. *Educational Psychologist, 26,* 299–323.

Schunk, D. H. (1983). Ability versus effort attributional feedback: Differential effects on self-efficacy and achievement. *Journal of Educational Psychology, 75,* 848–856.

Schunk, D. H. (1990). Goal setting and self-efficacy during self-regulated learning. *Educational Psychologist, 25,* 71–86.

Schunk, D. H. (1991) Self-efficacy and academic motivation. *Educational Psychologist, 26,* 207–231.

Schunk, D. H. (1994). Self-regulation of self-efficacy and attributions in academic settings. In D. H. Schunk & B. J. Zimmerman (Eds.), *Self-regulation of learning and performance.* Hillsdale, NJ: Erlbaum.

Simmons, R. G., & Blyth, D. A. (1987). *Moving into adolescence: The impact of pubertal change and school context.* Hawthorn, NY: Aldine de Gruyler.

Skinner, E. A. (1995). *Perceived control, motivation, and coping.* Thousand Oaks, CA: Sage Publications.

Skinner, E. A., & Belmont, M. J. (1993). Motivation in the classroom: Reciprocal effects of teacher behavior and student engagement across the school year. *Journal of Educational Psychology, 85,* 571–581.

Skinner, E. A., & Connell, J .P. (1986). Control understanding: Suggestions for a developmental framework. In M. M. Baltes & P. B. Baltes (Eds.), *The psychology of control and aging.* Hillsdale, NJ: Erlbaum.

Stein, K. F., Roeser, R. W., & Markus, H. R., (1998). Self-schemas and possible selves as predictors and outcomes of risky behaviors in adolescents. *Nursing Research, 47,* 96-106.

Stevenson, H. W., Parker, T., Wilkinson, A., Hegion, A., & Fish, E. (1976). Predictive value of teacher's ratings of young children. *Journal of Educational Psychology, 68,* 507–517.

Stipek, D. (1984). Young children's performance expectations: Logical analysis or wishful thinking? In J. Nicholls (Ed.), *Advances in achievement motivation (Vol. 3): The development of achievement motivation* (pp. 33–56). Greenwich, CT: JAI.

Stipek, D. J., & Daniels, D. H. (1988). Declining perceptions of competence: A consequence of changes in the child or in the educational environment? *Journal of Educational Psychology, 80,* 352–356.

Stipek, D. J., & Mac Iver, D. (1989). Developmental change in children's assessment of intellectual competence. *Child Development, 60*, 521–538.

Stipek, D. J., Recchia, S., & McClintic, S. M. (1992). Self-evaluation in young children. *Monographs of the Society for Research in Child Development, 57* (2, Serial No. 226)

Teigen, K. H. (1987). Intrinsic interest and the novelty-familiarity interaction. *Scandinavian Journal of Psychology, 28*, 199–210.

Todt, E. (1990). Entwicklung des interesses. In H. Hetzer (Ed.), *Angewandte entwicklungspsychologie des kindes— und jugendalters*. Wiesbaden: Quelle & Meyer.

Travers, R. M. W. (1978). *Children's interests* (unpublished manuscript). Kalamazoo, Michigan: Michigan University, College of Education.

Updegraff, K. A., Eccles, J. S., Barber, B. L., & O'Brien, K. M. (1996). Course enrollment as self-regulatory behavior: Who takes optional high school math courses. *Learning and Individual Differences, 8*, 239–259.

Vida, M. N. & Eccles, J. S. (April, 1999). *The relation of early adolescent anxieties to young adults' occupational self concepts.* Paper presented at the biennial meeting of the Society for Research on Child Development, Albuquerque, New Mexico.

Weisz, J. P. (1984). Contingency judgments and achievement behavior: Deciding what is controllable and when to try. In J. G. Nicholls (Ed.), *The development of achievement motivation* (pp. 107–136). Greenwich, CT: JAI Press.

Wentzel, K. R. (1991). Social competence at school: Relation between social responsibility and academic achievement. *Review of Educational Research, 61*, 1–24.

Wigfield, A. (1994). Expectancy-value theory of achievement motivation: A developmental perspective. *Educational Psychology Review, 6*, 49–78.

Wigfield, A., & Eccles, J. S. (1989). Test anxiety in elementary and secondary school students. *Educational Psychologist, 24*, 159–183.

Wigfield, A., & Eccles, J. S. (1992). The development of achievement task values: A theoretical analysis. *Developmental Review, 12*, 1–41.

Wigfield, A., Eccles, J. S., Mac Iver, D., Reuman, D. A. & Midgley, C. (1991). Transitions during early adolescence: Changes in children's domain-specific self-perceptions and general self-esteem across the transition to junior high school. *Developmental Psychology, 27*, 552–565.

Wigfield, A., Eccles, J. S., Yoon, K. S., Harold, R. D., Arbreton, A. J., Freedman-Doan, C. R., & Blumenfeld, P. C. (1997). Changes in children's competence beliefs and subjective task values across the elementary school years: A three year study. *Journal of Educational Psychology, 89*, 451–469.

Yoon, K. S. (1996). *Testing reciprocal causal relations among expectancy, value, and academic achievement of early adolescents: A longitudinal study.* Dissertation at the University of Michigan.

Zimmerman, B. J., Bandura, A., & Martinez-Pons, M. (1992). Self-motivation for academic attainment: The role of self-efficacy beliefs and personal goal setting. *American Educational Research Journal, 29*, 663–676.

15

Emotion Regulation and Children's Socioemotional Competence

Nancy Eisenberg
Richard A. Fabes

INTRODUCTION

In recent years, interest in the role of emotion in development has grown enormously. For a long time, emotion was considered inconsequential or a nuisance variable (Campos, 1984). However, in the last two decades, it has become a central variable in research on social development and developmental psychopathology. For example, emotion and its regulation are foci of investigation in work on attachment, social competence, moral development, problems with adjustment, socialization in the home, and many other topics (see Eisenberg & Morris, 2002; Eisenberg, Smith, Sadovsky, & Spinrad, 2004; Saarni, Mumme, & Campos, 1998).

Like many other psychologists, our focus on emotion and its regulation emerged in the last two decades. It initially grew out of an interest in prosocial motivation (i.e., empathy); this interest expanded to include the role of emotion and its regulation in social competence and problem behavior more generally. Because our thinking about emotion grew out of work on empathy and empathy-related responding (i.e., sympathy and personal distress) and its role in prosocial behavior, we first briefly summarize this work. Next, recent research on the relations of individual differences in emotionality and regulation to empathy-related responding is reviewed, followed by examples of research on the role of emotion and emotion-related regulation in children's problem behavior and competent social functioning.

EMPATHY-RELATED RESPONDING AND PROSOCIAL BEHAVIOR

Numerous philosophers and psychologists have suggested that empathy-related processes motivate prosocial behavior (Blum, 1980; Hoffman, 2000; Hume, 1777/1966; Staub, 1979)—that when people experience others' negative emotions, they are likely to engage in prosocial behavior. However, in 1982 Underwood and Moore published a review in which they found, contrary to most theories, *no* empirical relation between empathy and prosocial behavior. Upon careful consideration of this literature, it became clear that most of the work before 1982 had been conducted with children using self-report measures and hypothetical vignettes that were problematic and that there were conceptual problems with most of the existing research (Eisenberg & Lennon, 1983; Eisenberg & Miller, 1987).

The conceptual problems were of several sorts. One problem was that most investigators had not differentiated among the different types of empathy-related responding that would be expected to involve different affective motivations. Batson (1991) first differentiated between empathy and personal distress in the late 1970s. One can further differentiate among empathy, sympathy, and personal distress. Although definitions differ, we define *empathy* as an affective response that stems from the apprehension or comprehension of another's emotional state or condition, and which is similar to what the other person is feeling or would be expected to feel. For example, if a child views a sad person and consequently feels sad him or herself, that child is experiencing empathy.

In most situations, empathy with another's negative emotion is likely to evolve into one or another related emotional reactions (or into both): sympathy and personal distress. *Sympathy* is an emotional response stemming from the apprehension or comprehension of another's emotional state or condition that is not the same as what the other person is feeling (or is expected to feel in that situation) but consists of feelings of sorrow or concern for the other. Thus, if a girl sees a sad peer and feels concern for the peer, she is experiencing sympathy. Such a sympathetic reaction often is based upon empathic sadness, although sympathy also may be generated by cognitive perspective taking or accessing encoded cognitive information relevant to another's situation or need (Eisenberg, Shea, Carlo, & Knight, 1991; Karniol, 1982). However, empathy also can lead to *personal distress*—a self-focused, aversive affective reaction to the apprehension of another's emotion (e.g., discomfort, anxiety).

The distinction between sympathy and personal distress is critical because these two empathy-related reactions are expected to result in different motivations and, consequently, different behavior. Batson (1991) hypothesized that a sympathetic reaction is associated with the desire to reduce the other person's distress or need and therefore is likely to lead to altruistic behavior. In contrast, personal distress, because it is an aversive experience, is considered to be associated with the motivation to reduce one's own distress. Consequently, personal distress is believed to result in the desire to avoid contact with the needy or distressed other if possible. People experiencing personal distress are expected to assist others in the distressing situation only when helping is the easiest way to reduce the helper's own distress.

In studies with adults, Batson (1991; Batson et al., 1988) found some empirical evidence to support the aforementioned relations between prosocial behavior and sympathy or personal distress. However, the experimental methods and self-report measures he used generally were inappropriate for use with children. Thus, we conducted a series of studies designed to develop alternative methods of assessing empathy-related responding and to examine the relations of sympathy and personal distress to children's prosocial behavior.

Briefly, in this work we used self-report, facial, and physiological markers of sympathy and personal distress. The experience of personal distress was expected to be associated with higher levels of physiological distress than sympathy, self-reports of distress, and facial distress, whereas sympathy was expected to be linked to facial concern, reports of sadness or sympathy for others, and heart rate deceleration (an index of outwardly oriented attention; Cacioppo & Sandman, 1978; Lacey, Kagan, Lacey, & Moss, 1963). In the first set of studies, we found that, in general, when children or adults were in situations likely to induce a reaction akin to personal distress, they exhibited higher heart rate and skin conductance than in analogous situations likely to induce sympathy. Moreover, children and adults tended to exhibit facial concerned attention rather than facial distress in sympathy-inducing contexts, and older children's and adults' self-reports also were somewhat consistent with the emotional context (although findings for report of distress were mixed; Eisenberg & Fabes, 1990; Eisenberg, Fabes, et al., 1988; Eisenberg, Fabes, Schaller, Miller, et al., 1991; Eisenberg, Schaller, et al., 1988). These findings provided some evidence that we could differentiate sympathy and personal distress with a variety of measures.

Using the aforementioned measures of sympathy and personal distress, we examined children's and adults' sympathetic or personal distress reactions to empathy-inducing films about others in distress or need. Specifically, we examined the relations between physiological, facial, and self-reported reactions to these films and actual helping or sharing with the needy/distressed individuals in the film (or others like them) when it was easy to avoid contact with the needy other (e.g., sharing of a prize or engaging in a boring task that would benefit the needy others rather than playing with toys). Consistent with theory, markers of sympathy generally were positively related to prosocial behavior whereas markers of personal distress were negatively related to prosocial behavior, the latter particularly for children. Thus, sympathy and personal distress seemed to reflect different motivational states (Eisenberg et al., 1989, 1990; see Eisenberg & Fabes, 1990, 1991, 1998, for reviews).

The differing relations of personal distress and sympathy to prosocial behavior are consistent with the conclusion that the subjective experiences of sympathy and personal distress are quite different. Prior to the time that sympathy and personal distress were consistently differentiated in the research, Hoffman (1982) suggested that overarousal due to empathy results in a self-focus. Consistent with this view, we (Eisenberg, Fabes, Murphy, et al., 1994) hypothesized that empathic overarousal in situations involving negative emotion results in an aversive emotional state, which leads to a self-focus—that is, personal distress. Children and adults who cannot maintain their emotional reactions to others' emotions within a tolerable range (and become overaroused) would be expected to focus on their own emotional needs, a response that is likely to undermine positive social interactions in situations involving negative emotion (including one's own or that of other people). Evidence consistent with the notion that empathic overarousal results in self-focused personal distress includes the following: (a) negative emotional arousal is associated with a focus on the self (Wood, Saltzberg, & Goldsamt, 1990); (b) people exhibit higher skin conductance, and sometimes report more distress, in situations likely to elicit personal distress (in contrast to sympathy; Eisenberg, Fabes, Schaller, Miller, et al., 1991; Eisenberg, Fabes, Schaller, Carlo, & Miller, 1991); and (c) personal distress sometimes has been associated with lower heart rate variability (the degree to which heart rate goes up and down as reflected in its variance), which can be viewed as a rough index of low physiological regulation (see Fabes, Eisenberg, & Eisenbud, 1993).

Conversely, children and adults who can maintain their vicarious emotional arousal at a moderate level, which is arousing but not aversive, would be expected to experience sympathy. Consistent with this view is the type of evidence just discussed: (a) skin conductance and heart rate are lower when people are viewing sympathy-inducing, in comparison to distressing, films (Eisenberg, Fabes, Schaller, Miller, et al., 1991; Eisenberg, Fabes, Schaller, Miller, & Carlo, 1991; Eisenberg, Schaller, et al., 1988); and (b) higher situational sympathy (as indexed by facial concern) has been correlated with high heart rate variability (which is correlated with a measure of physiological regulation, vagal tone; see Fabes, Eisenberg, & Eisenbud, 1993; also see Eisenberg, Fabes, Murphy, et al., 1996).

Conceptualizing personal distress and sympathy in this manner led to the next logical question: What factors account for individual differences in the tendencies to experience personal distress and sympathy and, on a broader level, in a host of behaviors that are at least in part driven by emotional reactivity? One possible set of contributing factors is environmental, including socialization; another is biological (e.g., heredity, biological outcomes due to prenatal factors). Thus, in some research, investigators have focused on the familial (environmental) or genetic (biological) contributors to emotionality and emotion-related regulation (see Eisenberg, Cumberland, & Spinrad, 1998; Goldsmith, Buss, & Lemery, 1997; Parke & Buriel, 1998; Zahn-Waxler, Schiro, Robinson, Emde, & Schmitz, 2001). Another approach is to consider person variables—which likely reflect both environmental and biological factors—that influence whether individuals become emotionally overaroused in social contexts involving emotion.

DETERMINANTS OF EMOTIONAL RESPONSIVITY

We have focused on two categories of person variables that we believe affect whether children and adults become emotionally overaroused in social contexts: (1) individuals' dispositional levels of emotional responsivity, particularly the intensity and/or quantity of responding, and (2) individuals' ability to regulate (modulate) their emotional reactions and emotion-related behavioral and cope constructively with the evocative situation.

Emotionality

Children's emotional responsivity is reflected in the intensity and frequency with which they experience negative emotions. By emotional intensity, we mean stable individual differences in the typical intensity with which individuals experience their emotions (i.e., affective intensity, as defined by Larsen & Diener, 1987). Both the intensity of emotional experiences and the ease with which individuals respond intensely (which likely is highly related to quantity of responding) are expected to contribute to the degree to which individuals become emotionally aroused in a given situation. Similar to others, we view emotional intensity as having a temperamental or biological/constitutional basis, and as a characteristic that is considerably consistent over time (Larsen & Diener, 1987; Rothbart & Bates, 1998; also see Plomin & Stocker, 1989).

In initial early work on this topic, dispositional emotional intensity was associated with the degree of positive or negative emotion experienced in specific contexts (Larsen & Diener, 1987), as well as with adults' physiological arousal to empathy-inducing stimuli (Eisenberg, Fabes, Schaller, Miller, et al., 1991). Thus, individual differences in emotional intensity seemed to be a likely predictor of the tendency to become emotionally overaroused in emotional contexts.

Emotion-Related Regulation

Conceptualization

Despite abundant interest in recent years in emotion-related regulation, there is little consensus on its conceptualization or definition. Campos and colleagues suggested that emotion regulation can take place at three general loci: at the level of sensory receptors (input regulation), at central levels where information is processed and manipulated (central regulation), and at the level of response selection (labeled output regulation; Campos et al., 1994). Thompson (1994) defined emotion regulation as the "extrinsic and intrinsic processes responsible for monitoring, evaluating, and modifying emotional reactions, especially their intensive and temporal features, to achieve one's goals" (pp. 27–28). He discussed various domains for emotion regulation, including neurophysiological responses, attentional processes, construals of emotionally arousing events, encoding of internal emotion cues, access to coping resources, regulating the demands of familiar settings, and selecting adaptive response alternatives. Taking a slightly different approach, Cicchetti, Ganiban, and Barnett (1991) defined emotional regulation as "the intra- and extraorganismic factors by which emotional arousal is redirected, controlled, modulated, and modified to enable an individual to function adaptively in emotionally arousing situations" (p. 15; also see Kopp & Neufeld, 2003).

In our view, emotion regulation can occur prior to, during, and after the occurrence of emotion (or its possible occurrence; see below). Thus, building on the work of others (e.g., Campos et al., 1994; Cole, Michel, Teti, 1994; Thompson, 1994), we define emotion-related regulation as the process of initiating, avoiding, inhibiting, maintaining, or modulating the occurrence, form, intensity, or duration of internal feeling states, emotion-related physiological, attentional processes, motivational states, and/or the behavioral concomitants of emotion in the service of accomplishing affect-related biological or social adaptation or achieving individual goals (Eisenberg & Spinrad, 2003).

Thus, emotion-related regulation involves the modulation or modification of internal emotion-relevant states and processes (e.g., attentional, physiological, and motivational states), emotion-related behavior (including the expression of emotion), and/or situations that have evoked, or are likely to evoke, emotion. Emotion regulation is not always successful and sometimes may even worsen problems in some contexts (Thompson & Calkins, 1996). Moreover, what is considered appropriate regulation depends, in part, on the particular context, the age, and other characteristics of the individual (e.g., gender). Thus, effective emotion-related regulation is viewed as flexible and relevant to one's goals (Cole et al., 1994; Eisenberg & Fabes, 1992), and individuals skilled in regulation adjust their behavior in accordance with the context.

Prior Research and Theory on Emotion-Related Regulation

The construct of emotion regulation has been considered in several bodies of work. For example, it has been discussed in depth by temperament theorists who define regulation in terms of modulating internal reactivity (Rothbart & Bates, 1998). In the temperament literature, emotion regulation frequently is operationalized as involving attentional processes such as the abilities to shift and focus attention as needed (Derryberry & Rothbart, 1988; Windle & Lerner, 1986). Similarly, in the literature on stress and coping, investigators discuss attentional processes such as cognitive distraction and positive cognitive restructuring of a situation (e.g., thinking of a negative situation in a positive light) that, if successfully applied, modify the individual's internal psychological, emotional, and/or physiological reactions. Indeed, in their early work, Lazarus and Folkman (1984) viewed emotion-focused coping—efforts to reduce emotional distress in contexts appraised as taxing or exceeding the resources of the individual—as a major category of coping reactions.

People who can regulate their emotional reactivity in social or nonsocial contexts through allocating attention appear to respond relatively positively to stressful events. For example, the abilities to shift and re-focus attention have been associated with lower levels of distress, frustration, and other negative emotions (Bridges & Grolnick, 1995; Calkins & Dedmon, 2000; Eisenberg, Fabes, Guthrie, & Reiser, 2000; Kochanska, Coy, Tjebkes, & Husarek, 1998; Rothbart, Ziaie, & O'Boyle, 1992; Sethi, Mischel, Aber, Shoda, & Rodriguez, 2000; Wilson, 2003; also see MacLeod, Rutherford, Campbell, Ebsworthy, & Holker, 2002). Shifting attention from a distressing stimulus likely decreases arousal (see Derryberry & Reed, 2002). Focusing attention on positive aspects of the situation or on means by which to cope also can decrease negative emotion and increase positive emotion, whereas focusing attention on nonthreatening ideas or objects can distract a person from a distressing event or cognition.

Other frequently studied aspects of regulation are the abilities to inhibit or activate behavior as needed to adapt and achieve goals, especially if one does not feel like doing so. These abilities, labeled as inhibitory and activational control by Rothbart and Derryberry (e.g., Derryberry & Rothbart, 1988; Rothbart et al., 2001), have frequently been studied by temperament researchers. Furthermore, other theorists and researchers in clinical, developmental, and personality psychology have discussed constructs such as inhibition, self-regulation, constraint, impulsivity, or ego control, all of which involve the ability (or inability) to modulate the behavioral expression of impulses and feelings (Block & Block, 1980; Kochanska et al., 2001; Kopp, 1982; Mezzacappa, Kindlon, Sauls, & Earls, 1998; Olson, Schilling, & Bates, 1999; Oosterlaan, Logan, & Sergeant, 1998; Tellegen, 1985).

In our view, some of these processes are not voluntarily modulated by individuals and voluntary efforts should be labeled as self-regulation whereas less voluntary should not. (Researchers differ in their willingness to include the modulation of affect or behavior due to another person's efforts or behavior [often the parent's] in the definition of "regulation," but there might be agreement that such regulation is not self-regulation; see Cole et al., 2004; Eisenberg & Spinrad, 2004). For example, if a child is inhibited because of involuntary freezing in response to novelty or fear-inducing stimuli, this is not regulation (see Eisenberg & Morris, 2002, for more discussion of this issue). More effortful aspects of regulation such as voluntarily modulating attention or inhibiting or activating behavior have been labeled as effortful control (Rothbart et al., 2001). In contrast, we have labeled approach or inhibition of behavior that is hard to voluntarily control—as exhibited by impulsive individuals who are "pulled" to action with little voluntary control or behaviorally inhibited children who are seem unable to control their constrained, rigid, and inflexible behavior—as reactive or less voluntary control (also see Derryberry & Rothbart, 1997). Similarly, some attentional processes are more voluntarily managed than others, whereas others, such as anxious people's tendency to attend to threatening stimuli, can be viewed as involving reactive control (see Derryberry & Reed, 2002; MacLeod et al., 2001; Nigg, 2001).

The control of situations, which we consider an aspect of emotion-related regulation, often has been studied by coping theorists who are interested in instrumental or problem-focused coping (i.e., actions taken to solve the problem) in stressful contexts (e.g., Lazarus & Folkman, 1984; Sandler et al., 1994, 2000). In addition, regulation of situations can occur prior to an emotion being elicited. Aspinwall and Taylor's (1997) defined such regulation as proactive coping or "efforts undertaken in advance of a potentially stressful event to prevent it or to modify its form before it occurs" (p. 417). Similarly, Gross (1999) discussed antecedent emotion regulation, which involves not only proactive coping, but also using attentional and cognitive processes to choose the situations that are focused upon and how they are interpreted. For instance, shy people might reduce their anxiety when planning a party by keeping the number of participants low or they might conceptualize a party with co-workers as a casual gathering of friends rather than a work-related event during which he or she is likely to be evaluated. Thus, emotion self-regulation can occur by preventing the occurrence of an emotion, as well as by managing circumstances in a way that fosters a different (often, but not always, more positive) emotional experience. Unfortunately, such proactive regulation seldom has been studied in children.

MODES OF REGULATION/CONTROL

In our view, emotionality and emotion-relevant regulation, albeit related conceptually and empirically, are also somewhat distinct. We have proposed that they can be associated in a variety of different ways and in combination predict more variance in diverse outcomes than does either alone. Moreover, we have argued that different aspects of regulation and reactive control sometimes provide unique prediction of adjustment and quality of social functioning.

Eisenberg and Morris (2002) differentiated among three styles of regulation or control—highly inhibited, undercontrolled, and optimally regulated—and developed a heuristic model regarding how these types of regulation or reactive control predict social behavior and adjustment. *Highly inhibited* individuals are viewed as high in involuntary inhibition of behavior (often labeled behavioral inhibition in the temperament literature, e.g., inhibition in novel and stressful contexts, rigidity of behavior; Derryberry & Rothbart, 1997; Kagan & Fox, in press), low to average in voluntary inhibitory control, low in activation control, and low to moderate in attentional regulation (e.g., the abilities to voluntarily shift and focus attention). *Undercontrolled* individuals are hypothesized to be low in effortful and involuntary (reactive) modes of control, including attentional, inhibitory, and activational control, and high in reactive approach (or impulsive) tendencies. Undercontrolled individuals are expected to be prone to externalizing problem behaviors and to be low in social competence, especially if they are prone to experience negative emotions.

In contrast to highly inhibited or undercontrolled individuals, *optimally regulated* people are hypothesized to be relatively high in various modes of effortful regulation, including attentional, inhibitory, and activational control. However, because effortful modes of control can be activated voluntarily as needed, these individuals are expected to be flexible and appropriate in their use of regulatory behavior. They are also expected to be high in planful instrumental coping, proactive coping, and antecedent emotion regulation. Because they are viewed as moderate in the use of involuntary control and approach, these people are not expected to be overly impulsive or overly inhibited. Thus, optimally regulated individuals are hypothesized to be well adjusted, socially competent (including well-liked by peers), and resilient in stressful and negative situations.

We further hypothesized that individual differences in individuals' proneness to experience negative emotions may moderate or alter the relations of regulation (and perhaps reactive control) to children's socially competence behavior and adjustment. For example, undercontrolled people who are also high in emotional intensity, especially intensity of negative emotions such as anger, were expected to be particularly out of control and prone to reactive (emotionally driven) aggression and other behaviors that are based on unregulated emotion. Internalizing problem behaviors (e.g., fearfulness, social avoidance and shyness, and behavioral inhibition to novelty and new people), as well as low social competence, were expected to be predicted by the combination of high negative emotionality (especially intensity and frequency of emotions such as sadness, anxiety, or fear) with low regulation (especially of internal emotion-related processes such as attention), low instrumental coping (due to their high reactive inhibition of behavior, which would reduce instrumental coping), and high levels of behavioral inhibition (e.g., high levels of reactive withdrawn behavior).

In summary, we have argued that individual differences in emotionality and regulation jointly contribute to the prediction of numerous aspects of social functioning, including socially appropriate and problem behavior, popularity with peers, shyness, sympathy and prosocial behavior. In some cases the contributions of emotionality and regulation are expected to be additive; in other cases, we predict interactive or moderating effects with the predisposition to experience negative emotionality.

EMPIRICAL FINDINGS

Empathy-Related Responding

Predictions

Because work on empathy was the genesis of our thinking about emotionality and regulation, much of our initial work on emotionality/regulation concerned empathy-related responding. According to our model (Eisenberg & Fabes, 1992), and based on the notion that sympathy involves optimal regulation, we made the following predictions: (1) In general, regulation was expected to be positively and linearly related to sympathy. (2) Conversely, low levels of regulation, especially low levels of regulation of internal emotion-related processes (e.g., by mechanisms such as attentional control), were expected to be associated with personal distress; this is because personal distress is believed to reflect high levels of unmodulated negative emotion. (3) Emotional intensity, in general (i.e., for both positive and negative emotions) or for emotions such as sadness, was predicted to be moderately positively associated with sympathy (in that somewhat higher sympathy was expected for higher intensity people), particularly for individuals who could voluntarily modulate their emotional arousal as needed to maintain a moderate level of arousal. (4) People high in intensity and frequency of negative emotion were expected to be high in personal distress, *particularly* if they were low in the ability to regulate negative emotion. In addition, the relations were expected to vary depending on the negative emotion. For example, anger was expected to be negatively related to sympathy whereas sadness (especially intensity rather than frequency) was predicted to be positively related to sympathy.

In addition, sympathy was expected to be associated with a disposition toward experiencing positive emotions because sympathy and positive emotion may be an outcome or correlate of an optimal level of emotional regulation (Eisenberg & Fabes, 1992). Moreover, individuals who tend to experience positive emotion may be more benign toward others due to mood effects or a relation between an ongoing sense of well being and a positive view of other people (Cialdini, Kenrick, & Baumann, 1982; Staub, 1984). In contrast, personal distress—which by definition involves feelings of distress, anxiety, or discomfort—was expected to be correlated with high frequency (as well as intensity) of negative affectivity and low levels of positive emotion.

The Data

In reviewing relevant data, we begin with brief summaries of initial studies with adult samples and then discuss research with children. We studied various ages to see if findings were consistent across ages and because we could use different methods with different age groups (e.g., adults can provide self-reports of their emotion and regulation more easily than children, whereas it is easier to obtain reports from real-life observers such as parents and teachers when studying children).

Dispositional Empathy-Related Responding

In general, we have obtained empirical support for the hypothesis that individual differences in emotionality and regulation predict differences among individuals in dispositional sympathy and personal distress. In an initial study with college students (Eisenberg, Fabes, Murphy, et al., 1994), we found that self-reported dispositional personal distress (assessed with Davis', 1994, questionnaire) was related to low levels of both self-reported regulation (behavioral and attentional) and friends' reports of students' coping. Although self-reported sympathy was unrelated to regulation in zero-order correlations, it was significantly positively related to regulation once the effects of negative emotional intensity were controlled (see Okun, Shepard, & Eisenberg, 2000, for similar findings with older people). Consistent with the notion that empathic people are high in emotional intensity, both personal distress and sympathy were positively related with intensity of negative emotion (including a variety of emotions) and dispositional proneness to experience sadness. However, friends' reports of negative emotionality (both intensity and frequency) related positively with students' personal distress, but not with sympathy. The aforementioned effects generally held even when scores on social desirability were controlled.

In regression analyses from the same study (Eisenberg, Fabes, Murphy, et al., 1994), regulation and emotionality contributed unique variance to the prediction of dispositional sympathy and personal distress. In general, the predicted moderational effects were not obtained in this study. Finally, frequency of positive emotion was negatively related to dispositional personal distress whereas intensity of positive emotion was positively correlated with sympathy.

In a similar study with elderly adults (Eisenberg & Okun, 1996), the pattern of findings was even more consistent with expectations. Self-reported regulation, especially emotion regulation, was positively related to sympathy and negatively related to personal distress. Negative emotional intensity was positively related to both personal distress and sympathy, although the relation was somewhat stronger for the former. Moreover, for women only (most of the elderly study participants were women), there was an interaction between negative emotional intensity and regulation (a composite of emotional and behavioral regulation) when predicting personal distress. Personal distress decreased with increasing levels of regulation for women at all levels of negative emotional intensity, but particularly for women who were low or average in negative emotional intensity. Thus, the relation between regulation and sympathy was stronger for women who were not prone to intense negative emotions. Apparently elderly women who were high in negative emotional intensity, were somewhat more likely than other women to be overwhelmed by vicariously induced negative emotion, even if they were high in regulation. However, even these women showed a significant drop in personal distress as a function of increasing regulation; the drop was simply less dramatic than for women moderate or low in negative emotional intensity.

The empirical findings regarding the relation of children's empathy-related responding to their regulation were similar to the findings with adults, whereas findings in regard to emotionality differed. In a study of 6- to 8-year-old school children, we obtained teachers' and children's reports of sympathy (on questionnaire measures) and parents' and teachers' reports of children's emotionality and regulation (Eisenberg, Fabes, Murphy, et al., 1996). Specifically, adults reported on children's emotional intensity with regard to negative, positive, and unspecified (general) emotions, frequency of children's negative and positive emotions, children's abilities to shift and focus attention, and children's abilities to inhibit and regulate their overt behavior. In general, adults' reports of children's regulation were positively related to children's dispositional sympathy. Further, vagal tone, a marker of physiological regulation (Porges, Doussard-Roosevelt, & Maiti, 1994), was positively related to self-reported sympathy for boys (although the relation was negative for girls). Further, there was evidence that for boys, physiological arousal (heart rate, skin conductance) when exposed to a relatively distressing film clip was related to low dispositional sympathy. Thus, boys prone to physiological overarousal appeared to be low on dispositional sympathy. In 2- and 4-year follow-ups of this sample, similar relations between adult-reported regulation and children's dispositional sympathy were found, both within a given assessment time and often across 2 or 4 years (Eisenberg et al., 1998; Murphy, Shepard, Eisenberg, Fabes, & Guthrie, 1999).

Moreover, in a study conducted with Indonesian third graders, the pattern of findings was similar to that found in the United States. Specifically, we found a positive relationship between children's adult-reported sympathy and their regulation (Eisenberg, Liew, & Pidada, 2001). This finding in Indonesia was replicated 3 years later, albeit at this age, primarily for boys (Eisenberg, Liew, & Pidada, 2003). Thus, the initial data are consistent with the view that role of regulation in children's sympathy may be similar in fairly different cultures.

Moreover, in general, children's negative emotionality in our longitudinal study was negatively related to their sympathy; this finding was primarily for boys at the first assessment, but not in the latter ones. A similar relation between sympathy and dispositional negative emotionality was obtained in Indonesia (Eisenberg, Liew, & Pidada, 2001). Recall that in the research with adults, intensity and/or frequency of negative emotion was positively related to both sympathy and personal distress. It is likely the reversed pattern of findings for children is due to the types of children's negative emotions that are salient to adults. In general, researchers have found that boys exhibit more anger than do girls (Birnbaum & Croll, 1984; Fabes, Eisenberg, Nyman, & Michealieu, 1991; see Eisenberg, Martin, & Fabes, 1996). Probably adults' (particularly teachers') reports of children's negative emotionality reflect predominantly externalizing emotions such as anger and frustration, as well as overt distress (see Eisenberg et al., 1993; Eisenberg, Fabes, Nyman, et al., 1994); these sorts of negative emotions are likely to be particularly visible and salient to adults, and especially noticeable in boys. Parents may be likely to report internalizing negative emotions, as well as externalizing negative emotions, when reporting on children's negative emotionality; however, a dispositional tendency to experience or express internalizing negative emotions, like externalizing emotions, is expected to be related to personal distress (Eisenberg & Fabes, 1992). In addition, teachers', but not parents', reports of children's positive emotionality were positively related to teachers' reports of girls' sympathy and boys' self-reported sympathy.

At the first assessment, there also was an interaction between general emotional intensity and regulation when predicting teacher-reported child sympathy (Eisenberg, Fabes, Murphy, et al., 1996). General emotional intensity is the general tendency to feel emotions strongly, without reference specifically to valence of the emotion (positive or negative). Children low in regulation were low in sympathy regardless of their general emotional intensity; such children were likely to be overwhelmed by their vicarious emotion when it was experienced. In contrast, for children who were moderate or relatively high in their regulation, sympathy increased with the level of general emotional intensity. Thus, children who were likely to be emotionally intense were sympathetic if they were at least moderately well regulated. Such children would be expected to experience vicariously others' emotions yet not become overaroused and overwhelmed by this emotion. A similar interaction was noted two years later, but only for boys (Eisenberg et al., 1998). (Note that the sample was small and power was limited.)

In brief, across studies, we generally (albeit not always) have found that regulation is correlated with high dispositional sympathy and low dispositional personal distress. Despite the use of differing methods for different age groups, regulation predicted dispositional sympathy for both adults and children. In contrast, the relation of emotionality with empathy-related responding appears to vary depending for children and adults. This is likely due, at least in part, to the fact that different measures of negative emotionality were used with children and adults. In general, adults reported on their own negative emotionality (although we did have friends' reports of adults' negative emotionality in one study), whereas other people (teachers or parents) reported on children's negative emotionality. In general, emotionally intense adults who report they are prone to negative emotion tend to score high on both dispositional sympathy and personal distress, particularly the latter. In contrast, friends' reports of adults' negative emotional intensity and frequency of negative emotion were related to college students' personal distress, but not sympathy. In addition, adults' reports of children's negative emotional intensity and frequency of negative emotion tended to be related to low dispositional sympathy in children, probably because children who exhibit high levels of negative emotionality are prone to overarousal and emotions such as anger that are unlikely to be linked to sympathy. In contrast, normal adults who report high levels of negative emotions may be those who are willing to think about and acknowledge their negative emotions; such people may be especially susceptible to vicariously induced emotion.

In addition, there is initial evidence that the joint contributions of general emotionality and regulation sometimes are useful for predicting individual differences in children's empathy-related behavior. Children who were prone to relatively intense emotions (both positive and negative) and who were well regulated were especially high in teacher-reported sympathy. Finally, it is important to note that although adults' reports of negative emotionality frequently were negatively related to children's dispositional sympathy, the tendency to be emotionally intense in general was positively related to teacher-reported dispositional sympathy for children who are moderately and highly regulated.

Situational Empathy-Related Responding

Prior to leaving the topic of empathy-related responding, it is worth noting that relations between situational measures of empathy-related responding and measures of dispositional regulation and emotionality are considerably weaker than findings for dispositional empathy-related responding. For example, Eisenberg, Fabes, Murphy, et al. (1994) found that adults' self-reported sympathy, sadness, and distress in response to empathy-inducing films were not only positively related to measures of intensity of emotion, but also negatively related to a self-reported measure of emotion regulation. Facial reactions to the films, including sadness, concerned attention, and distress, were all related to some of the measures of emotionality, but they were unrelated to measures of regulation. Men's heart rate acceleration during an evocative portion of the film (a marker of personal distress) was positively correlated with frequency and intensity of dispositional negative emotion, and negatively related to emotion regulation. Thus, the relations of measures of situational empathy-related responding varied with the specific measure and sex of the individual.

Most of our research on situational empathy-related responding has been conducted with children. In a study of children aged 4 to 6 years, more consistent relations between situational sympathy and dispositional regulation were found, at least for the measure of facial concerned attention in response to a film about peer conflict (a child being bullied; Eisenberg & Fabes, 1995). Children's facial reactions to the conflict film were videotaped and their self-reported reactions were assessed after the film. For children who viewed the conflict film first (effects were diluted for the group who viewed another film first), those high in facial concerned attention were rated by teachers as high on attentional control and low on negative dispositional emotional intensity and nonconstructive (acting out versus avoidant) coping. Facial distress and sadness reactions, as well as self-reported reactions, were infrequently related to measures of dispositional regulation and emotionality.

Moreover, in a study of nearly 200 children in kindergarten to third grade (Guthrie et al., 1997), children who evidenced sympathy (e.g., facial sadness, mean heart rate decline, and self-reported sympathy) in response to an empathy-inducing film generally were rated higher in regulation and resiliency, although findings sometimes were obtained for only one sex and often were weak. For example, facial sadness in response to the sympathy segment of the film was positively related to teachers' ratings of attention shifting and resiliency (the latter particularly for girls), as well as teachers' and parents' ratings of general emotional intensity. Children who evidenced personal distress (e.g., facial distress) were rated relatively high in emotionality. Girls' (but not boys') reports of sympathy were positively related to teachers' ratings of attentional control. Moreover, self-reports of situational sympathy for both boys and girls were negatively related to parents' ratings of negative emotionality, whereas self-reports of sadness were positively related to parents' ratings of general emotional intensity and fathers' ratings of negative emotionality (this was particularly true for boys).

Thus, although situational measures of empathy-related responding tend to be related to emotionality and sometimes regulation, the findings are complex and relatively weak. Given that emotional responding in any particular context may or may not be a very reliable index of general empathy-related dispositions, it is not really surprising that the relations between situational measures of empathy-related responding and dispositional emotionality and regulation are weak. If numerous situational empathy-related reactions were aggregated across different events and settings, the relation of these aggregated responses to enduring personality characteristics such as emotionality and regulation probably would be stronger (Rushton, Brainerd, & Pressley, 1983).

Social Competence and Problem Behavior

Because many of the same predictions regarding the relation of individual differences in emotionality and regulation to empathy-related responding logically would be expected to apply to the broader domain of social competence and problem behavior, we have also have examined the role of individual differences in emotionality and regulation in children's social competence and problem behavior.

Predictions

As for the study of sympathy and personal distress, we have been interested in the additive and multiplicative contributions of emotionality and regulation. In general, we predicted that high emotionality, particularly frequency and intensity of negative emotion, combined with low regulation, would be associated with externalizing types of behavior problems and low social competence. In contrast, low regulation of emotion (e.g., through low attentional control) combined with high behavioral inhibition/low impulsivity and high emotionality (especially negative emotionality) was expected to predict internalizing types of problems such as high levels of shyness and withdrawn behavior. For both externalizing and internalizing behavior, prediction is expected to be greater when measures of both emotionality and regulation are obtained. Further, we hypothesized that moderational effects would be found for emotionally driven internalizing or externalizing problem behaviors (e.g., that regulation would be a better predictor of externalizing problem behaviors for children prone to experience intense negative emotions).

When we started doing research on these issues, researchers had linked negative emotionality to quality of social functioning (e.g., Barron & Earls, 1984; Teglasi & MacMahon, 1990), but intensity of emotion seldom was examined and often data on both emotionality and social functioning were provided by the same reporter. Although some investigators also had examined the relation between regulation and social functioning, such research was limited in quantity, often a single reporter provided all data (particularly in the studies of temperament or coping, e.g., Kyrios & Prior, 1990; Teglasi & MacMahon, 1990), the findings on regulation pertained primarily to behavioral rather than emotion regulation (e.g., Block & Block, 1980; Kochanska, Murray, Koenig, & Vandegeest, 1996; Pulkkinen, 1982), and the existing data on emotion regulation were collected primarily with infants (e.g., Bridges & Grolnick, 1995; Rothbart et al., 1992). Nonetheless, in the last decade, numerous investigators have examined the relations of regulation and emotionality to adjustment and social competence and many have found that negative emotionality and low regulation are related to low levels of social competence or moral development and to high levels of problem behaviors (e.g., Belsky, Friedman, & Hsieh, 2001; Calkins, Gill, Johnson, & Smith, 1999; Caspi, Henry, McGee, Moffitt, & Silva, 1995; Gilliom, Shaw, Beck, Schonberg, & Lukon, 2002; Kochanska & Knaack, 2003; Kochanska, Murray, & Coy, 1997; Olson, Schilling, & Bates, 1999; Rothbart, Ahadi, & Hershey, 1994; for reviews, see Eisenberg, Fabes, Guthrie, & Reiser, 2000; Eisenberg, Smith, et al., 2004; Rothbart & Bates, 1998, in press)

The Data

We now review some representative examples of the findings to illustrate the overall pattern of results in our work. In general, our findings tend to be consistent with those of others, although we have examined some issues in more detail or in different ways than other researchers.

Social Competence and Externalizing Problem Behaviors

In an initial study with 4- to 6-year-olds (Eisenberg et al., 1993), children's socially appropriate behavior was rated by undergraduates who observed the children's naturally occurring interactions with peers and teachers at school for extended periods of time. For example, the observers rated if the children had good social skills, tended to get into trouble because of their actions, and acted appropriately. Moreover, peer evaluations of sociometric status (popularity) were obtained by asking children to sort pictures of their classmates into piles that indicated how much they liked to play with each peer. Teachers and mothers also rated children on their negative emotional intensity, frequency of negative emotion, attentional regulation (the abilities to shift and focus attention), constructive coping (instrumental coping or trying to take care of the problem by fixing the problem and seeking support), and nonconstructive coping (aggression and venting emotion versus avoidance) coping. Boys who were viewed as socially appropriate and who were popular with peers, were high in teacher-rated attentional regulation, were reported by teachers as exhibiting high levels of constructive coping and low levels of nonconstructive coping, and were low in both intensity and frequency of negative emotion (as rated by teachers). Fewer relations were obtained for girls, although socially appropriate girls were low in nonconstructive coping and in negative emotionality intensity. Many of the correlations ranged from about .40 to .65 (and emotionality and attentional regulation combined accounted for about 50% of the variance in boys' and girls' socially appropriate behavior), even though information on social functioning and regulation or emotionality was obtained from different sources (thereby minimizing common method variance). In addition, children who were both low in attentional regulation and high in negative emotional intensity were particularly likely to be low in socially appropriate behavior and popularity. The findings based on mothers' reports of children's emotionality and regulation were less impressive, although there were some interesting associations. For example, boys viewed by their mothers as being high in negative emotional intensity were rated as low in peer status and observed social competence.

Further, individual differences in regulation and emotionality predicted real-life behavior when children were angered in their social interactions at school (Eisenberg, Fabes, Nyman, et al., 1994). Real-life, naturally occurring events involving anger and frustration were observed over the school year. Children who were relatively likely to use nonabusive verbalizations to deal with anger—a constructive strategy—were high in teacher-rated constructive coping and attentional control (both of these finings were only for boys) and low in nonconstructive coping and negative emotional intensity (for boys and girls). In addition, such children were viewed by mothers as high in instrumental coping and coping by seeking support, and low in aggressive coping and negative emotional intensity (Eisenberg, Fabes, Nyman, et al., 1994). There were fewer findings for other modes of coping with anger, although, for example, teachers' reports of children's negative emotional intensity were related to girls' venting of emotion, children's use of physical retaliation, and low levels of children's avoidant behavior when angered.

Data for these children were also obtained 2, 4, and 6 years later, when children were aged 6- to 8-, 8- to 10-, and 10- to 12-years old. At the 2-year follow-up, teachers' reports of children's socially appropriate/nonaggressive behavior and prosocial/sociable behavior were linked to contemporaneous teacher ratings of high regulation (behavioral and attentional control combined), either high constructive coping or low nonconstructive coping, and low negative emotionality. Thus, when the children were aged 6 to 8, teachers' ratings of children's social functioning were related to their ratings of emotionality and regulation. Of more interest, teachers' reports of children's social functioning at age 6 to 8 correlated with reports of attentional regulation, constructive coping, low nonconstructive coping (for socially appropriate/nonaggressive behavior only), and low emotional intensity provided by different teachers 2 years earlier (at age 4 to 6). Parental reports of regulation and emotionality were infrequently related to teachers' reports of social functioning; however, such reports obtained when the children were aged 6 to 8 were correlated with reports of externalizing problem behaviors in the home concurrently (at age 6 to 8). Moreover, parental reports of attentional regulation and negative emotionality taken at age 4 to 6 correlated, to some degree, with parents' reports of problem behavior at age 6 to 8, albeit primarily for boys.

At the 4-year follow-up, when the children were aged 8 to 10, a composite index of socially competent behavior was computed (see Eisenberg, Fabes, Shepard, et al., 1997). Included in this measure were teachers' reports of children's socially appropriate behavior (in the manner described previously), popularity, prosocial behavior, and aggressive and disruptive behavior. Also included were ratings of how friendly versus hostile children were when they acted out with puppets what they would do in five hypothetical situations involving the potential for conflict with peers (e.g., when the child is excluded from activities or called a "baby"). This aggregate measure of social functioning generally was related to both teachers' and parents' report of high regulation and low negative emotionality, particularly the latter, contemporaneously (at age 8 to 10) as well as when assessed 2 and 4 years earlier. Parents' and teachers' reports of children's nonconstructive coping also tended to predict quality of social functioning. Parents' reports of low regulation, high negative emotionality, and high destructive coping at age 8 to 10 as well as 2 or 4 years earlier tended to predict parents' reports of problem behavior, although findings for father-reported problem behavior held primarily for boys whereas maternal reports of emotionality/regulation also predicted girls' problem behavior (Eisenberg, Fabes, Shepard, et al., 1997).

When the children in this study were 10- to 12-years old, teachers' reports of children's social competence and adjustment continued to be related with teachers' and parents' reports of children's regulation concurrently as well as 2, 4, and 6 years earlier, as well as with teachers' reports of children's low negative emotionality years earlier (and parents' reports of low negative emotionality for boys). Moreover, parents' reports of children's problem behaviors were related to their reports of children's low regulation and high negative emotionality, but only for up to 4 years earlier (i.e., ratings by parents when the children were in preschool were not related to problem behaviors at age 10 to 12; Murphy et al., 2004). Thus, in general, high regulation and low intensity and frequency of negative emotionality predicted socially competent behavior and low levels of problem behavior contemporaneously and across time, albeit primarily in the home context for parental reports of problem behavior. A number of the aforementioned relations held even at age 10 to 12 when the level of children's problem behaviors at younger ages were controlled in the analysis. The fact that parents' reports of problems with adjustment did not relate to teachers' reports of regulation and emotionality at school is probably due to at least two factors: (1) children undoubtedly display somewhat different patterns of problems at school and at home (due to the difference in the people around them, the tasks, and what is expected or allowed in different contexts), and (2) teachers probably are less aware than parents of children's feelings of relatively subtle negative emotions such as anxiety and sadness. Consequently, it is useful to assess children's adjustment and their dispositional regulation and emotionality in multiple settings using a variety of reporters.

As expected, we frequently found that the effects of emotionality and regulation were additive as well as overlapping when predicting social functioning within a given setting (i.e., home or school), even over time (see Eisenberg, Fabes, Shepard, et al., 1997). Of particular interest, at age 8 to 10, there was an interaction of teacher-reported general emotional intensity and regulation when predicting social competence; social competence increased with regulation at all levels of emotional intensity, but the association was strongest for children high in general emotional intensity. A similar interaction was identified at age 6 to 8 years; moreover, similar interactions were obtained when negative emotionality rather than general emotional intensity was used as a predictor. Thus, regulation generally was a predictor of social competence, but especially for children prone to intense emotion. In contrast, negative emotionality did not moderate the relation between regulation and parents' reports of problem behavior.

The sample in the aforementioned study was relatively small (64 to 93 children were in the study, with fewer children at the last assessment), so it was difficult to obtain significant interaction effects when predicting problem behavior (due to lack of power), although some were obtained for the aggregate measure of social competence. However, we also examined the relation of dispositional regulation and emotionality to teacher- and parent-reported problem behavior and social competence in two other large samples. In a study of nearly 200 school children (Eisenberg, Fabes, Guthrie, et al., 1996), parents reported on a number of children's externalizing problem behaviors such as starting fights, being disobedient, breaking rules, lying, and being sneaky. The primary parent (usually mothers) and teachers also provided information on children's attentional regulation, ego control (primarily behavioral control; see Block & Block, 1980), and ego resiliency (resourceful adaptation to changing circumstances and contingencies, flexible use of the available repertoire of coping strategies, the ability to rebound from stress; see Block & Block, 1980). In addition, children played a game in which their persistence and resistance to cheating were assessed; this measure was viewed as an index of behavioral regulation. Gaze aversion during a distressing film segment also was assessed as an index of attentional control (i.e., the ability to shift attention briefly when needed to lower arousal). Further, baseline facial and heart rate responding were obtained while children viewed the film. Low baseline heart rate has been associated with externalizing problem behaviors in prior work, for example, in the criminology literature (Fowles, 1993; Lahey, Hart, Pliszka, Applegate, & Williams, 1990).

In general, there were consistent relations between reported problem behavior and low regulation, as measured by both adults' reports and by the behavioral (persistence/cheating) task. Moreover, reported problem behavior often was associated with low resiliency. Generally findings were obtained when one reporter (the primary care giving parent or teacher) provided information on emotionality and regulation and another reporter (mother, father, or teacher) provided information on externalizing problem behavior. Additionally, children who tended to use gaze aversion while watching a distressing film segment were relatively low in problem behaviors.

Children with problem behaviors also were viewed as high in negative emotionality (frequency and intensity) and, to some degree, as high in general and positive emotional intensity by parents and teachers (although generally not for correlations with mothers' reports of daughters' problem behavior). Teachers' reports of children's problem behaviors generally were substantially predicted by parents' reports of children's emotionality and vice versa.

Of most interest was the finding that the relation between problem behaviors and regulation sometimes was moderated by children's negative emotionality. For example, teachers' reports of regulation were related to teachers' reports of low problem behavior at all levels of negative emotion; however, the relation was strongest for children high in negative emotionality. Thus, regulation was most important for predicting problem behavior of children prone to negative emotion. A moderating effect also was found when teachers' reports of regulation and emotionality were used to predict parents' reports of problem behavior (averaged across parents). In this case, the relation between regulation and parents' reports of problem behavior was significant for children moderate and high in negative emotionality, but not for children low in negative emotion (who tended to be low in problem behavior). Moderation effects were obtained less frequently when parents' (usually mothers') reports of emotionality and regulation were used in the analyses; however, an interaction effect was obtained for the prediction of fathers' reports of boys' problem behavior. Maternal report of regulation was unrelated to fathers' reports of problem behavior for boys low and moderate in negative emotionality (who were relatively low in problem behavior), but for boys high in negative emotionality, problem behavior decreased with increasing regulation. Thus, in general, regulation appeared to be a particularly important predictor of children's problem behavior for children prone to frequent and intense negative emotions.

Finally, children's heart rate and facial distress during a baseline period (while seeing a calm film) were at least marginally, negatively related to problem behavior; findings held for mother- and father-rated problem behavior for heart rate and for problem behavior as rated by all three reporters for facial distress. This finding is consistent with prior work in which children and adults with low baseline physiological arousal are prone to problem behavior. People with low baseline arousal may seek out stimulation and exciting sensations.

An analysis of the relations of regulation, resiliency (i.e., resourceful adaptation to changing circumstances and contingencies, flexible use of the available repertoire of coping strategies, the ability to rebound from stress), and emotionality to positive social functioning in this sample illustrates the importance of attending to both moderation and mediation in thinking about the prediction of social behavior. In some of the aforementioned studies, we examined moderation effects, but not mediation. Thus, in this sample (Eisenberg, Guthrie, et al., 1997), we examined the possibility that kindergarten to third grade children's socially competent behavior was predicted by the interaction of individual differences in emotionality and regulation, and that the interactive effects of emotionality and regulation on social functioning were mediated by individual differences in resiliency. That is, we expected regulation to predict higher resiliency, which in turn would predict higher social competence, and that the relation between regulation and resiliency would be higher for children prone to negative emotion. Both attentional regulation (teacher- and parent-reported attention shifting and focusing) and behavioral control (including parent and teacher reports of inhibitory control and ego control, as well as the puzzle box persistence task) were assessed. For the puzzle box persistence task, children worked to complete a wooden puzzle for a prize. The puzzle was in a large wooden box and children put their arms into the box through sleeves. Children were not supposed to look into the box at the puzzle, but it was easy to cheat and peak by lifting the sleeves and looking under the cloth blocking the view of the puzzle. The children were left alone to work on the puzzle; the time they persisted on this task while not cheating (and not going off-task) was recorded by observers by means of a hidden camera (the box of the box facing the camera was plexiglass).

Regulation was expected to predict resiliency, which in turn was expected to predict social functioning—in this case, popularity with peers and socially appropriate/prosocial behavior. However, we expected these relations to be stronger for children high in negative emotionality because regulation is more important for those children. The data were analyzed using EQS (a structural modeling program). The effects of attentional (i.e., emotional) control on social status and socially appropriate behavior were mediated by resiliency; in addition, the path from attentional control to resiliency, albeit significant for children both high and low in negative emotionality, was higher for children prone to negative emotion. Thus, children who could regulate their attention appeared to be resilient to stress and, perhaps as a consequence, were better liked by peers and viewed as being more socially appropriate or prosocial by teachers and peers. However, level of attentional control was particularly important for predicting socially appropriate behavior for children prone to negative emotion.

The relation between behavioral regulation and socially appropriate behavior was not mediated by resiliency. Rather, individual differences in behavioral control were directly related to socially appropriate behavior (but not social status). Moreover, this direct effect held only for children high in dispositional negative emotionality. As expected, behavioral control was particularly important for children likely to experience negative emotions because they have more frequent and intense emotions to manage.

At the 2-year follow-up of this sample, the model described above in regard to the prediction of popularity and socially appropriate behavior was replicated; the primary difference was that the positive, significant relation of attentional regulation to resiliency did not differ for children who were low versus high in negative emotionality (Eisenberg, Fabes, et al., 2000). We also found that resiliency did not mediate the relations of attentional regulation and behavioral control to children's externalizing problems. Rather, in a structural equation model, we found similar relations at the first and second assessment: high attentional regulation and behavioral control both provided some unique (nonoverlapping) prediction of low levels of problem behaviors in the children. In addition, there was evidence that the negative relations of attentional regulation and behavioral control (especially the former) to children's problem behavior was greater for children who were prone to experience intense and frequent negative emotion (Eisenberg, Guthrie, et al., 2000).

Relations of Effortful Control (Regulation), Reactive Control, and Specific Negative Emotions (Anger and Sadness) to Children's Adjustment

In the models that we have discussed thus far, we used attentional regulation versus behavioral control as the two aspects of control predicting children's adjustment and social competence. In our more recent studies, we have started to differentiate between effortful (or voluntary) aspects of control and less voluntary, reactive aspects of control. In addition, because it is likely that anger and sadness are differentially related to adjustment and social behavior, in our most recent study we have obtained measures of both of these aspects of negative emotionality. We now illustrate the usefulness of these decisions by reporting findings from two samples on the relations of effortful and reactive control to children's adjustment (i.e., problem behaviors).

With the longitudinal sample that we have just discussed, for example, we completed another 2-year follow-up (4 years after the initial assessment) and computed structural equation models to examine the relations of effortful and reactive control to externalizing problem behaviors, from the first assessment (Time 1 or T1) to the third assessment (T3) (Valiente et al., 2003). At T3, parents (usually mothers) and teachers reported on children's effortful attention shifting, attention focusing, and inhibitory control, reactive over- versus under-control (selected items from Block & Block's, 1980, ego control scale), negative emotionality, and externalizing behavior. In addition, children's persistence on a difficult puzzle task (the puzzle box persistence task) rather than cheating or quitting (they were working to win a prize)—an index of effortful control—was assessed at all three assessments. In T1, T2, and T3 concurrent models (i.e., models containing variables only from one given assessment), we successfully grouped the measures of regulation/control into effortful control (attentional control, inhibitory control, persistence) and reactive overcontrol versus undercontrol (ego control). Although at T3 all measures of effortful or reactive over- versus. undercontrol were significantly correlated with low externalizing, in models including both the T1 to T3 model or only the T3 data, T3 effortful control, but not ego over- versus undercontrol, had a unique negative relation to externalizing (i.e., the relation was significant when simultaneously controlling for the effects of other predictors; see Figure 15.1 for the longitudinal model). In contrast, at T1, both effortful control and reactive control had significant unique relations to externalizing problems. In the longitudinal model, autoregressive paths from a given variable at T1 (e.g., externalizing problems) to the same variable at T3 were included, so the model took into account the consistency of the various variables across time (that is, the effects of a predictor on a dependent variables were unique from the effects of consistency of the dependent variable over time). Thus, the findings supported the idea that with age, effortful control increasingly modulates the overt effects of ego control when predicting externalizing. We also obtained evidence that the negative relation of effortful control to externalizing behavior was significant for all children

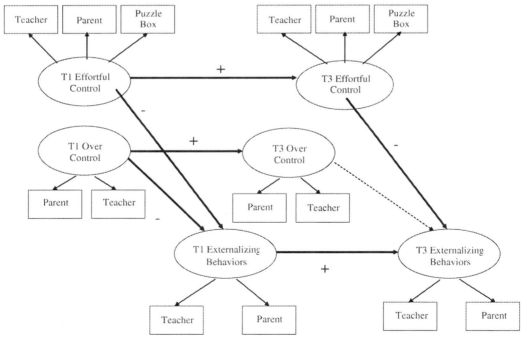

Figure 15.1 A structural equation model of the relations of effortful control (regulation) and reactive overcontrol to externalizing problem behaviors at two points in time, four years apart. Bold paths are significant; dotted lines are nonsignificant. Adapted from Valiente et al. (2003).

but stronger for those prone to negative emotion (this same interaction was marginally significant for ego control with negative emotionality; Valiente et al., 2003).

In all of the research we have already discussed on children's emotion-related regulation, our samples were unselected samples of typical school children. Yet behavioral inhibition and high social withdrawal are relatively rare in nonclinical samples (Coll et al., 1984; Strauss, 1988) and problems with effortful control and impulsivity may be more limited. Thus, we began to examine our hypotheses in a sample that is more diverse in terms of problem behavior. Therefore, we selected a sample of school children using primary caregivers' reports of children's problem behaviors. Children age 4.5 through 7 years were recruited from local preschools and elementary schools, a newspaper ad, and flyers at after school programs. Out of a pool of 315 children, we selected all children with relatively high scores on externalizing and/or internalizing problem behaviors and matched these children with control children of the same sex and race, similar social class, and about the same age (when possible). Control children were those scores below the level that indicates at-risk or clinical levels of problem behaviors (i.e., internalizing or externalizing problems). The final sample included 214 children, about three-fourths of whom were non-Hispanic European American.

Children came to the laboratory where they engaged in a variety of tasks; moreover, we obtained information from parents and teachers on numerous aspects of children's functioning. In the first major analyses from these data, we examined the relations of specific types of regulation (that is, effortful control) and reactive undercontrol (i.e., impulsivity) to children's categorization as an internalizer (e.g., prone to social withdrawal, anxiety, and depression), externalizer (e.g., aggressive, delinquent behavior), or nondisordered control child (using scores on Achenbach's, 1991, Child Behavior Checklist). We used teachers' and one parent's reports of children's effortful attention shifting, attention focusing, and inhibitory control, as well as impulsivity. We also administered several observed measures of children's effortful regulation. These tasks assessed children's abilities to persist rather than cheating on a puzzle when working for a prize (our puzzle box persistence task), sit still when asked to do so before being left alone with physiological equipment on them (e.g., they had heart rate and skin conductance electrodes on their chests and hands), and exhibit positive versus negative facial or verbal reactions to a disappointing prize. The latter task involved the children getting an unattractive prize at the end of the laboratory session when they expected to get a very attractive prize. Children's facial, gestural, vocal, and verbal reactions when receiving the gift from the experimenter were videotaped and coded to see if children hid their disappointment. In addition, mothers, fathers, and teachers reported on children's internalizing and externalizing problems, and, based on these reports, we divided children into groups of control (nondisordered) children, externalizing children (children high on externalizing but not internalizing problems), internalizing children (those high on internalizing problems but not externalizing problems), and co-morbid children (those high on both internalizing and externalizing problems).

Consistent with the previously discussed theory and hypotheses, children high on externalizing (externalizing only and co-morbid children combined), in comparison to nondisordered children, were low in adult-reported effortful control (attention shifting, focusing, and inhibitory control), high in adult-reported impulsivity, and low on some behavioral measures of regulation. For example, they had more difficulty than control (nondisordered) children in sitting still when asked to do so and in persisting rather than cheating or going off-task on the puzzle box persistence task. Thus, children with externalizing symptoms were low in both effortful and reactive control. They also were reported by adults to be prone to anger and, to a lesser degree, sadness. Internalizers, in comparison to controls, were low in attentional regulation (i.e., attention shifting and focusing) and impulsivity, did not differ much on observed regulation (on the behavioral tasks) or reported inhibitory control, and were higher in reported sadness. Compared to externalizers, internalizers were higher in attentional control and inhibitory control, more regulated on some behavioral measures, lower on impulsivity, and less angry. For example, internalizers showed less negative emotion than externalizers in response to a disappointing gift and internalizing boys exhibited more persistence on the puzzle box persistence task than externalizing did boys (Eisenberg, Cumberland, et al., 2001).

Thus, internalizers, but not externalizers, were relatively low on involuntarily reactive undercontrol (as tapped with impulsivity), whereas externalizers were quite high on reactive undercontrol. Of interest, both externalizers and internalizers were low in attentional modes of effortful control—the types of regulation that would be expected to help modulate the experience of negative emotions such as anxiety, fear, or anger. Because externalizers were also low in the ability to willfully inhibit behavior, they would be expected to have more problems than internalizers with displays of inappropriate behavior.

We followed up the aforementioned sample of children 2 years later (Eisenberg, Spinrad, et al., 2004) and used these data to examine longitudinal relations between measures of control/regulation, emotionality, and adjustment. In these analyses, children were not divided into adjustment groups; rather, continuous scores on internalizing and externalizing problems were used. In initial structural equation measurement models using multiple indicators of all constructs (e.g., teachers' and parents' reports), we found that using the two latent constructs of effortful control (attention shifting, attention focusing, and inhibitory control, as well as persistence on the puzzle box persistence task) and reactive control (impulsivity) fit the data better than when we created separate constructs for attentional control (attention shifting and focusing) and behavioral control (impulsivity, inhibitory control, and persistence on the puzzle box persistence task).

Based on these analyses, we then used structural equation modeling to predict both externalizing and internalizing problems (correlating the two latent constructs) from effortful control and impulsivity, with relations to internalizing being mediated by resiliency. Effortful control was assessed with adults' reports of inhibitory control and attentional regulation; at T1, a behavioral measure of regulation (persistence on our puzzle box task) also contributed to the latent construct (it did not load significantly at T2). Impulsivity was the sole index of reactive (over)control. Impulsivity, resiliency, externalizing, and internalizing were indicated by reports from teachers and primary caregiving parents, and fathers as well as mothers provided data on adjustment. In these analyses, experts' ratings were used to drop items on the regulation, emotion, and adjustment scales that were confounded with one another (e.g., adjustment items rated by experts as assessing temperamental emotion were dropped from externalizing or internalizing scales).

In the models, we predicted adjustment (i.e., externalizing and internalizing behavior problems) from both effortful control and impulsivity so we could assess their unique prediction of both types of problem behaviors. In addition, autoregressive paths from a given variable at T1 (e.g., externalizing problems) to the same variable at T2 were included to take into account the consistency of the various variables across time. We also tested whether the relations to internalizing were mediated by resiliency; children with internalizing problems, who were prone to reactive overcontrol, were hypothesized to be rigid and overly inhibited in their behavior, in part due to low resiliency. To test bidirectional effects (from adjustment to regulation/control as well as vice versa), cross-lagged paths were included (i.e., paths from T1 problem behaviors to T2 effortful control, impulsivit, and resiliency, and from T1 effortful control, impulsivity, and resiliency to T2 resiliency and problem behaviors).

As shown in Figure 15.2, impulsivity and effortful control were both significant, positive predictors of resiliency. Resiliency mediated the relations of effortful control and impulsivity to internalizing at both ages. In contrast, externalizing was predicted directly by low effortful control and high impulsivity, although at T1, in the longitudinal (but not the T1 only model), there also was mediation through resiliency from EC and impulsivity to externalizing problems. These relations held at T2 even when controlling for levels of the various constructs at T1 with one exception: the path from impulsivity to externalizing problems became nonsignificant. Thus, with the exception of that one path, relations at T2 were not due merely to the consistency of relations and variables at T1 over time. One possible explanation of the fact that impulsivity was a weaker predictor of externalizing problems in the T2 model (concurrent and longitudinal) is that effortful control is more important than impulsivity in predicting older children's externalizing problems because children with higher effortful control can better minimize outer manifestations of impulsivity. This finding is consistent with the nonsignificant prediction of adjustment from reactive control (i.e., ego control) at T3 in the previously discussed model from our other sample.

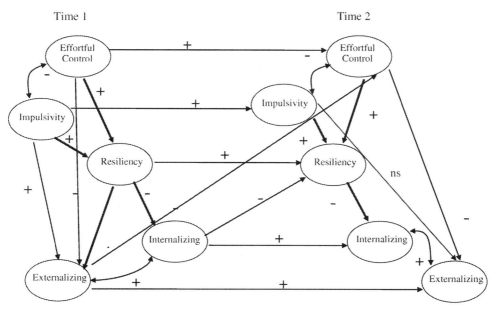

Figure 15.2 A structural equation model of the relations of effortful control and impulsivity to resiliency, externalizing problems, and internalizing problems at two points in time, two years apart. Bold paths are significant; dotted lines are nonsignificant. Adapted from Eisneberg, Spinrad, et al. (2004).

In addition, in the longitudinal model there were negative paths from T1 externalizing to T2 effortful control and from T1 internalizing to T2 resiliency. Thus, adjustment appeared to predict effortful and reactive control and resiliency, as well as vice versa. Moreover, when we computed an additional model with only cross-lagged paths (and correlations among the T1 latent constructs and those at T2 that required correlating), the same cross-lagged paths were found, as well as paths from T1 effortful control to high T2 resiliency and lower levels of T2 externalizing (see Figure 15.3). Thus, there was evidence of bi-directionality of relations among these variables.

There also was evidence that anger, but not sadness, moderated some of the relations in the model. Based on composite measures of adjustment, EC, and impulsivity, teacher-reported anger moderated the direct path of effortful control (or impulsivity) to externalizing at both T1 and T2 (relations of effortful control or impulsivity to externalizing were significant for all groups, but more so for children prone to anger).

Note in the models that resiliency was positively related to effortful control and impulsivity. One would expect children high in effortful control to be resilient because they can adjust their level of control as needed to adapt successfully. However, it might initially seem odd that impulsivity was also *positively* related to personality resiliency. Block and Kremen (1996) asserted that "the human goal is to be as undercontrolled as possible and as overcontrolled as necessary. When one is more undercontrolled than is adaptively effective or more overcontrolled than is adaptively required, one is not resilient" (p. 351). If they are correct, children not only high in effortful control but also moderate to moderately high in reactive undercontrol, who are relatively spontaneous and impulsive, would be expected to be more likely than overcontrolled children to deal well with stress. In fact, we have found positive linear relations between reactive undercontrol (low ego control or high impulsivity) and resiliency in 3 samples of younger children, as well as quadratic relations in 2 samples (Cumberland et al., 2004; Eisenberg, Spinrad, et al., 2004; Eisenberg, Valiente, et al., 2003). Young children who are moderate or sometimes high on impulsivity tend to be more resilient than those who are high in reactive overcontrol (or low in impulsivity). By mid- to late-elementary school, only the quadratic relation remains and it appears that this relation dissipates further with age.

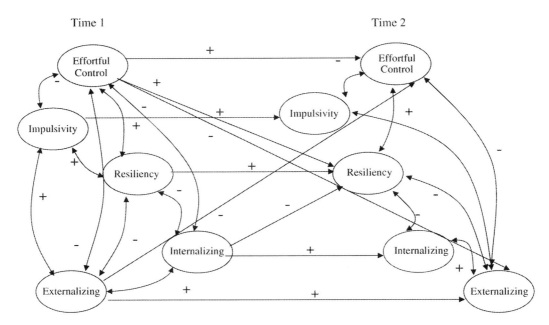

Figure 15.3 A structural equation model of the bi-directional relations of effortful control, impulsivity, and resiliency with adjustment across two years of time. Nonsignificant paths across time are not shown. Curved lines indicate that the constructs were correlated within time.

SUMMARY

In our work we have documented the importance of individual differences in emotionality and regulation in both positive and negative aspects of social functioning. We found that one can make more sense of the empirical data by considering moderational and mediational relations, as well as additive effects. For example, socially competence and problems behaviors often are predicted by both high regulation and low negative emotionality, although regulation is a better predictor of outcomes for children prone to negative emotion. We also have found that we can learn more by considering various types of regulation and emotional reactions and by using multiple reporters and a multi-method approach to data collection. Sometimes our facial or physiological data added information that was different than that provided by self- or other-report data; for example, relations between children's prosocial behavior and empathy-related responding have been much more consistent for these nonverbal measures than for self-report measures. Children may have difficulty assessing and reporting their internal states, and their reports may be contaminated by concerns about providing socially desirable responses. In general, each type of measure has different strengths and weaknesses, and provides somewhat different kinds of information. Nonetheless, facial or physiological measures may be especially useful for younger children because their self-reports often are not very predictive of outcomes. Overall, our data support the current emphasis on process (mediation) and moderating relations in the study of socioemotional development.

In regard to future directions, relatively little is known about the role of positive emotionality in the development and prediction of children's social competence and problem behaviors. It is likely that children prone to positive emotionality are relatively resilient and socially competent. In addition, it would be useful to further differentiate among various negative emotions when predicting outcomes for children (e.g., examine anxiety as well as anger and sadness). Anger/frustration and emotions such as sadness appear to be related somewhat differently to internalizing and externalizing problem

TABLE 15.1
Summary of Major Constructs Predicting Quality of Socioemotional Functioning

Emotionality

1. Emotional intensity—stable individual differences in the typical intensity with which individuals experience their emotions (one can also look at emotional intensity in specific contexts)
   a. intensity of negative emotions
   b. intensity of positive emotions
   c. intensity of general emotionality—the general tendency to feel emotions strongly, without reference specifically to valence of the emotion (positive or negative)
2. Emotional frequency—individual differences in the frequency of experiencing emotions
   a. frequency of negative emotions
   b. frequency of positive emotions

Emotion-related Regulation (sometimes labeled *emotion regulation* for brevity)

1. The process of initiating, avoiding, inhibiting, maintaining, or modulating the occurrence, form, intensity, or duration of internal feeling states, emotion-related physiological, attentional processes, motivational states, and/or the behavioral concomitants of emotion in the service of accomplishing affect-related biological or social adaptation or achieving individual goals.

   This, emotion-related regulation includes the following:
   a. regulation of internal feeling states, attention (*attentional control*), cognitions, motivation, and physiological reactions that are related to (or part of) emotion
   b. *behavioral regulation*: regulation of observable facial and gestural responses and other behaviors that stem from, or are associated with, internal emotion-related psychological or physiological states and goals, often through either inhibitory control (i.e., the capacity to suppress approach tendencies as needed) or activation control (the capacity to perform an action when there is a strong tendency to avoid it).
   c. attempts to alter or manage the emotion-inducing context causing the emotion (often called instrumental or problem-focused coping).

Effortful Control

Effortful control is defined as "the ability to inhibit a dominant response to perform a subdominant response" (Rothbart & Bates, 1998, p. 137) or the "efficiency of executive attention, including the ability to inhibit a dominant response and/or to activate a subdominant response, to plan, and to detect errors" (Rothbart & Bates, in press). Effortful control pertains to the ability to willfully or voluntarily inhibit, activate, or change (modulate) attention and behavior.

Reactive Control

Reactive control: relatively involuntary motivational approach and avoidance systems of response reactivity that, at extreme levels, result in impulsive undercontrol and rigid overcontrol. Measures typically tap (but are not confined to):
   (a) *impulsivity or reactive undercontrol*: pertains to speed of response initiation
   (b) *reactive overcontrol* (rigid, constrained behavior; low ego control) and *behavioral inhibition* (slow or inhibited approach in situations involving novelty or uncertainty).

behaviors. Moreover, some aspects of regulation may be more effective than others in moderating the relations between various emotions and specific outcomes. For example, effortful inhibitory control may be more crucial for managing anger/frustration than sadness whereas attention shifting may more particularly linked to moderating the relation of anxiety or sadness to social behavior and internalizing problems. Thus, in the future, more differentiation among various emotions and types of regulation is desirable in research on the role of these aspects of functioning in the quality of social functioning.

Finally, although not a topic of this chapter, we know that children's regulation does vary with socialization experiences (see Eisenberg et al., 1998; Eisenberg, Valiente, et al., 2001). We also know that preventative interventions can improve children's emotional competence and reduce their aggression and other problem behaviors (Kam, Greenberg, & Walls, 2003; Greenberg, Kusche, Cook, & Quamma, 1995). Thus, it is very likely that parents, teachers, and other socializers affect the degree to which children are well-regulated. Given the importance of self-regulation for children's social competence and adjustment, behavioral scientists should continue to study ways to foster it in childhood.

ACKNOWLEDGMENTS

Work on this chapter was supported by grants from the National Institutes of Mental Health (2 R01 MH60838) to the authors and a grant from the National Institutes of Drug Abuse to Nancy Eisenberg.

REFERENCES

Achenbach, T. M. (1991a). *Manual for the child cehavior checklist/4-18 and 1991 profile*. Burlington, VT: University of Vermont Department of Psychiatry.

Aspinwall, L. G., & Taylor, S. E. (1997). A stitch in time: Self-regulation and proactive coping. *Psychological Bulletin, 121*, 417–436.

Barron, A. P., & Earls, F. (1984). The relation of temperament and social factors to behavior problems in three-year-old children. *Journal of Child Psychology and Psychiatry, 25*, 23–33.

Batson, C. D. (1991). *The altruism question: Toward a social-psychological answer*. Hillsdale, NJ: Erlbaum.

Batson, C. D., Dyck, J. L., Brandt, J. R., Batson, J. G., Powell, A. L. McMaster, M. R., & Griffitt, C. (1988). Five studies testing two new egotistic alternatives to the empathy-altruism hypothesis. *Journal of Personality and Social Psychology, 55*, 52–77.

Belsky, J., Friedman, S. L., & Hsieh, K. H. (2001). Testing a core emotion-regulation prediction: Does early attentional persistence moderate the effect of infant negative emotionality on later development? *Child Development, 72*, 123–133.

Birnbaum, D. W., & Croll, W. L. (1984). The etiology of children's stereotypes about sex differences in emotionality. *Sex Roles, 10*, 677–691.

Block, J. H., & Block, J. (1980). The role of ego-control and ego-resiliency in the organization of behavior. In W. Andrew Collins (Ed.), *Development of cognition, affect, and social relations. The Minnesota symposia on child psychology*. (Vol. 13, pp. 39–101). Hillsdale, NJ: Erlbaum.

Block, J., & Kremen, A. M. (1996). IQ and ego-resiliency: Conceptual and empirical connections and separateness. *Journal of Personality and Social Psychology, 70*, 349–360.

Blum, L. A. (1980). *Friendship, altruism and morality*. London: Routledge and Kegan Paul.

Bridges, L. J., & Grolnick, W. S. (1995). The development of emotional self-regulation in infancy and early childhood. In N. Eisenberg (Ed.), *Review of personality and psychology*. Newbury Park: Sage.

Cacioppo, J. T., & Sandman, C. A. (1978). Physiological differentiation of sensory and cognitive tasks as a function of warning processing demands and reported unpleasantness. *Biological Psychology, 6*, 181–192.

Calkins, S. D., & Dedmon, S. E. (2000). Physiological and behavioral regulation in two-year-old children with aggressive/destructive behavior problems. *Journal of Abnormal Child Psychology, 28*, 103–118.

Calkins, S. D., Gill, K. L., Johnson, M. C., & Smith, C. L. (1999). Emotional reactivity and emotional regulation strategies as predictors of social behavior with peers during toddlerhood. *Social Development, 8*, 310–334.

Campos, J. (1984). A new perspective on emotions. *Child Abuse and Neglect, 8*, 147–156.

Campos, J. J., Mumme, D. L., Kermoian, R., & Campos, R. G. (1994). A functionalist perspective on the nature of emotion. In N. A. Fox (Ed.), The developmental of emotion regulation: Biological and behavioral considerations. *Monographs of the Society for Research in Child Development, 59*(Serial No. 240), 284–303.

Caspi, A., Henry, B., McGee, R.O., Moffitt, T.E., & Silva, P.A. (1995). Temperamental origins of child and adolescent behavior problems: From age 3 to age 15. *Child Development, 66*, 55–68.

Cialdini, R. B., Kenrick, D. T., & Baumann, D. J. (1982). Effects of mood on prosocial behavior in children and adults. In N. Eisenberg (Ed.), *The development of prosocial behavior* (pp. 339–359). New York: Academic Press.

Cicchetti, D., Ganiban, J., & Barnett, D. (1991). Contributions from the study of high risk populations to understanding the development of emotion regulation. In K. Dodge & J. Garber (Eds.), *The development of emotion regulation* (pp. 15–48). New York: Cambridge University Press.

Cole, P. M., Martin, S. E., & Dennis, T. A. (2004). Emotion regulation as a scientific construct: Methodological challenges and directions for child development research. *Child Development*.

Cole, P. M., Michel, M. K., Teti, L. O. (1994). The development of emotion regulation and dysregulation: A clinical perspective. *Monographs of the Society for Research in Child Development, 59*(Serial No. 240), 73–100.

Coll, C. G., Kagan, J., & Reznick, J. S. (1984). Behavioral inhibition in young children. *Child Development, 55*, 1005–1019.

Cumberland, A., Eisenberg, N., & Reiser, M. (2004). Relations of young children's agreeableness and resiliency to effortful control and impulsivity. *Social Development, 13*, 191–212.

Davis, M. H. (1994). *Empathy: A social psychological approach*. Madison, WI: Brown & Benchmark.

Derryberry, D., & Reed, M. A. (2002). Anxiety-related attentional biases and their regulation by attentional control. *Journal of Abnormal Psychology, 111*, 225–236.

Derryberry, D., & Rothbart, M. K. (1988). Arousal, affect, and attention as components of temperament. *Journal of Personality and Social Psychology, 55*, 958–966.

Eisenberg, N., Cumberland, A., & Spinrad, T. L. (1998). Parental socialization of emotion. *Psychological Inquiry, 9*, 241–273.

Eisenberg, N., Cumberland, A., Spinrad, T. L., Fabes, R. A., Shepard, S. A., Reiser, M., Murphy, B. C., Losoya, S. H., & Guthrie, I. K. (2001). The relations of regulation and emotionality to children's externalizing and internalizing problem behavior. *Child Development, 72*, 1112–1134.

Eisenberg, N., & Fabes, R. A. (1990). Empathy: Conceptualization, assessment, and relation to prosocial behavior. *Motivation and Emotion, 14*, 131–149.

Eisenberg, N., & Fabes, R. A. (1991). Prosocial behavior and empathy: A multimethod, developmental perspective. In P. Clark (Ed.), *Review of personality and social psychology* (Vol. 12, pp. 34–61). Newbury Park: Sage.

Eisenberg, N., & Fabes, R. A. (1992). Emotion, regulation, and the development of social competence. In M. S. Clark (Ed.), *Review of personality and social psychology*. Vol. 14. *Emotion and social behavior* (pp. 119–150). Newbury Park, CA: Sage.

Eisenberg, N., & Fabes, R. A. (1995). The relation of young children's vicarious emotional responding to social competence, regulation, and emotionality. *Cognition and Emotion, 9*, 203–229.

Eisenberg, N., & Fabes, R. A. (1998). Prosocial development. In W. Damon (Series Ed.), N. Eisenberg (Vol. Ed.), *Handbook of child psychology: Vol. 3. Social, emotional, and personality development* (5th ed., pp. 701–778). New York: Wiley.

Eisenberg, N., Fabes, R. A., Bernzweig, J., Karbon, M., Poulin, R., & Hanish, L. (1993). The relations of emotionality and regulation to preschoolers' social skills and sociometric status. *Child Development, 64,* 1418–1438.

Eisenberg, N., Fabes, R. A., Bustamante, D., Mathy, R. M., Miller, P., Lindholm, E. (1988). Differentiation of vicariously-induced emotional reactions in children. *Developmental Psychology, 24,* 237–246.

Eisenberg, N., Fabes, R. A., Carlo, G., Troyer, D., Speer, A. L., Karbon, M., & Switzer, G. (1992). The relations of maternal practices and characteristics to children's vicarious emotional responsiveness. *Child Development, 63,* 583–602.

Eisenberg, N., Fabes, R. A., Guthrie, I. K., Murphy, B. C., Maszk, P., Holmgren, R., & Suh, K. (1996). The relations of regulation and emotionality to problem behavior in elementary school children. *Development and Psychopathology, 8,* 141–162.

Eisenberg, N., Fabes, R. A., Guthrie, I. K., & Reiser, M. (2000). Dispositional emotionality and regulation: Their role in predicting quality of social functioning. *Journal of Personality and Social Psychology, 78,* 136–157.

Eisenberg, N., Fabes, R. A., & Losoya, S. (1997). Emotional responding: Regulation, social correlates, and socialization. In P. Salovey & D. J. Sluyter (Eds.), *Emotional development and emotional intelligence: Educational implications* (pp. 129–163). New York: Basic Books.

Eisenberg, N., Fabes, R. A., Miller, P. A., Fultz, J., Mathy, R. M., Shell, R., & Reno, R. R. (1989). The relations of sympathy and personal distress to prosocial behavior: A multimethod study. *Journal of Personality and Social Psychology, 57,* 55–66.

Eisenberg, N., Fabes, R. A., Miller, P. A., Shell, C., Shea, R., May-Plumlee, T. (1990). Preschoolers' vicarious emotional responding and their situational and dispositional prosocial behavior. *Merrill-Palmer Quarterly, 36,* 507–529.

Eisenberg, N., Fabes, R. A., Murphy, B., Karbon, M., Maszk, P., Smith, M., O'Boyle, C., & Suh, K. (1994). The relations of emotionality and regulation to dispositional and situational empathy-related responding. *Journal of Personality and Social Psychology, 66,* 776–797.

Eisenberg, N., Fabes, R. A., Murphy, B., Karbon, M., Smith, M., & Maszk, P. (1996). The relations of children's dispositional empathy-related responding to their emotionality, regulation, and social functioning. *Developmental Psychology, 32,* 195–209.

Eisenberg, N., Fabes, R. A., Murphy, M., Maszk, P., Smith, M., & Karbon, M. (1995). The role of emotionality and regulation in children's social functioning: A longitudinal study. *Child Development, 66,* 1239–1261.

Eisenberg, N., Fabes, R. A., Nyman, M., Bernzweig, J., & Pinuelas, A. (1994). The relations of emotionality and regulation to children's anger-related reactions. *Child Development, 65,* 109–128.

Eisenberg, N., Fabes, R. A., Schaller, M., Carlo, G., & Miller, P. A. (1991). The relations of parental characteristics and practices to children's vicarious emotional responding. *Child Development, 62,* 1393–1408.

Eisenberg, N., Fabes, R. A., Schaller, M., Miller, P. A., Carlo, G., Poulin, R., Shea, C., & Shell, R. (1991). Personality and socialization correlates of vicarious emotional responding. *Journal of Personality and Social Psychology, 61,* 459–471.

Eisenberg, N., Fabes, R. A., Shepard, S. A., Murphy, B. C., Guthrie, I. K., Jones, S., Friedman, J., Poulin, R., & Maszk, P. (1997). Contemporaneous and longitudinal prediction of children's social functioning from regulation and emotionality. *Child Development, 68,* 642–664.

Eisenberg, N., Fabes, R. A., Shepard, S. A., Murphy, B. C.,

Jones, S., & Guthrie, I. K. (1998). Contemporaneous and longitudinal prediction of children's sympathy from dispositional regulation and emotionality. *Developmental Psychology, 34,* 910–924.

Eisenberg, N., Guthrie, I. K., Fabes, R. A., Reiser, M., Murphy, B. C., Holmgren, R., Maszk, P., & Losoya, S. (1997). The relations of regulation and emotionality to resiliency and competent social functioning in elementary school children. *Child Development, 68,* 295–311.

Eisenberg, N., Guthrie, I. K., Fabes, R. A., Shepard, S., Losoya, S., Murphy, B., Jones, S., Poulin, R., & Reiser, M. (2000). Prediction of elementary school children's externalizing problem behaviors from attentional and behavioral regulation and negative emotionality. *Child Development, 71,* 1367–1382.

Eisenberg, N., & Lennon, R. (1983). Gender differences in empathy and related capacities. *Psychological Bulletin, 94,* 100–131.

Eisenberg, N., Liew, J., & Pidada, S. (2001). The relations of parental emotional expressivity with the quality of Indonesian children's social functioning. *Emotion, 1,* 107–115.

Eisenberg, N., Martin, C. L., & Fabes, R. A. (1996). Gender development and gender differences. In D. C. Berliner & R. C. Calfee (Eds.), *The handbook of educational psychology* (pp. 358–396). New York: Macmillan Publishing.

Eisenberg, N., & Miller, P. (1987). The relation of empathy to prosocial and related behaviors. *Psychological Bulletin, 101,* 91–119.

Eisenberg, N., & Morris, A. S. (2002). Children's emotion-related regulation. In R. Kail (Ed.), *Advances in child development and behavior* (Vol. 30, pp. 190–229). Academic Press: Amsterdam.

Eisenberg, N., & Okun, M. (1996). The relations of dispositional regulation and emotionality to elders' empathy-related responding and affect while volunteering. *Journal of Personality, 64,* 157–183.

Eisenberg, N., Shea, C. L., Carlo, G. & Knight, G. (1991). Empathy-related responding and cognition: A "chicken and the egg" dilemma. In W. Kurtines & J. Gewirtz (Eds.), *Handbook of moral behavior and development: Vol. 2, research* (pp. 63–88). Hillsdale, NJ: Erlbaum.

Eisenberg, N., Schaller, M., Fabes, R. A., Bustamante, D., Mathy, R., Shell, R., & Rhodes, K. (1988). The differentiation of personal distress and sympathy in children and adults. *Developmental Psychology, 24,* 766–775.

Eisenberg, N., Smith, C. L., Sadovsky, A., & Spinrad, T. L. (in press). Effortful control: Relations with emotion regulation, adjustment, and socialization in childhood. In R. F. Baumeister & K. D. Vohs (Eds.), *Handbook of self-regulation research.* New York: Guilford Press.

Eisenberg, N., & Spinrad, T. L. (2003). *Emotion-related regulation: Sharpening the definition.* Paper submitted for editorial review.

Eisenberg, N., Spinrad, T. L., Fabes, R. A., Reiser, M., Cumberland, A., Shepard, S. A., Valiente, C., Losoya, S. H., Guthrie, I. K., &, Thompson, M. (2004). The relations of effortful control and impulsivity to children's resiliency and adjustment. *Child Development, 75,* 25–46.

Eisenberg, N., Valiente, C., Fabes, R. A., Smith, C. L., Reiser, M., Shepard, S. A., Losoya, S. H., Guthrie, I. K., Murphy, B. C., & Cumberland, A. (2003). The relations of effortful control and ego control to children's resiliency and social functioning. *Developmental Psychology, 39,* 761–776.

Eisenberg, N., Valiente, C., Morris, A. S., Fabes, R. A., Cumberland, A., Reiser, M., Gershoff, E. T., Shepard, S. A., & Losoya, S. (2003). Longitudinal relations among parental emotional expressivity, children's regulation, and quality of socioemotional functioning. *Developmental Psychology*, 39, 2–19.

Fabes, R. A., Eisenberg, N., & Eisenbud, L. (1993). Behavioral and physiological correlates of children's reactions to others' distress. *Developmental Psychology*, 29, 655–663.

Fabes, R. A., Eisenberg, N., Nyman, M., & Michealieu, Q. (1991). Young children's appraisals of others' spontaneous emotional reactions. *Developmental Psychology*, 27, 858–866.

Fowles, D. C. (1993). Electrodermal activity and antisocial behavior: Empirical findings and theoretical issues. In J. C. Roy, W. Boucsein, D. Fowles, & J. Gruzelier (Eds.), *Progress in electrodermal research* (pp. 1–14). London: Plenum Press.

Fox, N. A. (1989). Psychophysiological correlates of emotional reactivity during the first year of life. *Developmental Psychology*, 25, 364–372.

Gilliom, M., Shaw, D. S., Beck, J. E., Schonberg, M. A., & Lukon, J. L. (2002). Anger regulation in disadvantaged preschool boys: Strategies, antecedents, and the development of self-control. *Developmental Psychology*, 38, 222–235.

Goldsmith, H. H., Buss, K. A., & Lemery, K. S. (1997). Toddler and childhood temperament: Expanded content, stronger genetic evidence, new evidence for the importance of environment. *Developmental Psychology*, 33, 891–905.

Greenberg, M. T., Kusche, C. A., Cook, E. T., Quamma, J. P. (1995). Promoting emotional competence in school-aged children: The effects of the PATHS curriculum. *Development and Psychopathology*, 7, 117–136.

Gross, J. J. (1999). Emotion and emotion regulation. In L. A. Pervin & O. P. John (Eds.), *Handbook of personality: Theory and research* (2nd ed., pp. 525–552). New York: Guilford Press.

Guthrie, I. K., Eisenberg, N., Fabes, R. A., Murphy, B. C., Holmgren, R., Mazsk, P., & Suh, K. (1997). The relations of regulation and emotionality to children's situational empathy-related responding. *Motivation and Emotion*, 21, 87–108.

Hoffman, M. L. (1982). Development of prosocial motivation: Empathy and guilt. In N. Eisenberg (Ed.), *The development of prosocial behavior* (pp. 281–313). New York: Academic Press.

Hoffman, M. L. (2000). *Empathy and moral development: Implications for caring and justice*. Cambridge: Cambridge University Press.

Hume, D. (1966). *Enquiries concerning the human understanding and concerning the principles of morals* (2nd ed). Oxford: Clarendon Press. (Originally published, 1777).

Kagan, J. (1989). The concept of behavioral inhibition to the unfamiliar. In J. S. Reznick (Ed.), *Perspectives on behavioral inhibition* (pp. 1–23). Chicago: Chicago University Press.

Kagan, J., & Fox, N. (in press). Biology, culture, and temperamental biases. In W. Damon & R. M. Lerner (Eds.) and N. Eisenberg (Vol. Ed.), *Handbook of child psychology*. New York: Wiley.

Kam, C-M., Greenberg, M. T., & Walls, C. T. (2003). Examining the role of implementatrion quality in school0based prevention using the PATHS curriculum. *Prevention Science*, 4, 55–63.

Karniol, R. (1982). Settings, scripts, and self-schemata: A cognitive analysis of the development of prosocial behavior. In N. Eisenberg (Ed.), *The development of prosocial behavior* (pp. 251–278). New York: Academic Press.

Kliewer, W., (1991). Coping in middle childhood: Relations to competence, type A behavior, monitoring, blunting, and locus of control. *Developmental Psychology*, 27, 689–697.

Kochanska, G., & Knaack, A. (2003). Effortful control as a personality characteristic of young children: Antecedents, correlates, and consequences. *Journal of Personality*, 71, 1087–1112.

Kochanska, G., Coy, K. C., & Murray, K. T. (2001). The development of self-regulation in the first four years of life. *Child Development*, 72, 1091–1111.

Kochanska, G., Coy, K. C., Tjebkes, T. L., & Husarek, S. J. (1998). Individual differences in emotionality in infancy. *Child Development*, 64, 375–390.

Kochanska, G., Murray, K., & Coy, K. (1997). Inhibitory control as a contributor to conscience in childhood: From toddler to early school age. *Child Development*, 68, 263–277.

Kochanska, G., Murray, K., Jacques, T. Y., Koenig, A. L., & Vandegeest, K. A. (1996). Inhibitory control in young children and its role in emerging internalization. *Child Development*, 67. 490–507.

Kopp, C. B. (1982). Antecedents of self-regulation: A developmental perspective. *Development Psychology*, 18, 199–214.

Kopp, C. B., & Neufeld, S. J. (2003). Emotional development during infancy. In R. Davidson, K. R. Scherer, & H. H. Goldsmith (Eds.), *Handbook of affective sciences* (pp. 347–374). Oxford: Oxford University Press.

Kyrios, M., & Prior, M. (1990). Temperament, stress and family factors in behavioural adjustment of 3-5-year-old children. *International Journal of Behavioral Development*, 13, 67–93.

Lacey, J. I., Kagan, J., Lacey, B. C., & Moss, H. A. (1963). The visceral level: Situational determinants and behavioral correlates of autonomic response patterns. In P. H. Knapp (Ed.), *Expression of the emotions in man* (pp. 161–196). New York: International Universities Press.

Lahey, B. B., Hart, E. L, Pliszka, S., Applegate, B., & McBurnett, K. (1993). Neurophysiological correlates of conduct disorder: A rationale and review of the research. *Journal of Clinical Child Psychology*, 22, 141–153.

Larsen, R. J., & Diener, E. (1987). Affect intensity as an individual difference characteristic: A review. *Journal of Research in Personality*, 21, 1–39.

Lazarus, R. S., & Folkman, S. (1984). *Stress, appraisal, and coping*. New York: Springer.

Lemery, K. S., Essex, M. J., & Snider, N. A. (2002). Revealing the relation between temperament and behavior problem symptoms by eliminating measurement confounding: Expert ratings and factor analyses. *Child Development*, 73, 867–882.

MacLeod, C., Rutherford, E., Campbell, L., Ebsworthy, G., & Holker, L. (2002). Selective attention and emotional vulnerability: Assessing the causal basis of their association through the experimental manipulation of attentional bias. *Journal of Abnormal Psychology*, 111, 107–123.

Mezzacappa, E., Kindlon, D., Saul, J. P., & Earls, F. (1998). Executive and motivational control of performance task behavior, and autonomic heart-rate regulation in children: Physiological validation of two-factor solution inhibitory control. *Journal of Child Psychology and Psychiatry*, 39, 525–531.

Murphy, B. C., Shepard, S. A., Eisenberg, N., Fabes, R. A., & Guthrie, I. K. (1999). Contemporaneous and longitudinal relations of young adolescents' dispositional sympathy to their emotionality, regulation, and social functioning. *Journal of Early Adolescence*, 19, 66–97.

Murphy, B. C., Shepard, S. A., Eisenberg, N., & Fabes, R. L. A. (2004). Concurrent and across time prediction of young adolescents' social functioning: The role of emotionality and regulation. *Social Development*, 13, 56–86.

Nigg, J. T. (2000). On inhibition/disinhibition in developmental psychopathology: Views from cognitive and personality psychology and a working inhibition taxonomy. *Psychological Bulletin, 126,* 230–246.

Okun, M. A., Shepard, S. A., & Eisenberg, N. (2000). The relations of emotionality and regulation to dispositional empathy-related responding among volunteers-in-training. *Personality and Individual Differences, 28,* 367–382.

Olson, S. L., Schilling, E. M., & Bates, J. E. (1999). Measurement of impulsivity: Construct coherence, longitudinal stability, and relationship with externalizing problems in middle childhood and adolescence. *Journal of Abnormal Child Psychology, 27,* 151–165.

Oosterlaan, J., Logan, G. D., & Sergeant, J. A. (1998). Response inhibition in AD/HD, CD, comorbid AD/HD + CD, anxious, and control children: A meta-analysis of studies with the stop task. *Journal of Child Psychology & Psychiatry & Allied Disciplines, 39,* 411–425.

Parke, R. D., & Buriel, R. (1998). Socialization in the family: Ethnic and ecological perspectives. In W. Damon (Series Ed.) and N. Eisenberg (Vol. Ed.), *Handbook of child psychology. Vol. 3, social, emotionality, and personality development* (5th ed., pp. 463–552. New York: Wiley

Plomin, R., & Stocker, C. (1989). Behavioral genetics and emotionality. In J. S. Reznick (Ed.), *Perspectives on behavioral inhibition* (pp. 219–240). Chicago: Chicago University Press.

Porges, S. W., Doussard-Roosevelt, J. A., & Maiti, A. K. (1994). Vagal tone and the physiological regulation of emotion. *Monographs of the society for Research in Child Development, 59* (Serial No. 240), 167–186.

Pulkkinen, L. (1982). Self-control and continuity from childhood to late adolescence. In P. B. Baltes & O. Brim, Jr. (Eds.), *Life-span development and behavior* (Vol. 4, pp. 63–105). New York: Academic Press.

Rothbart, M. K., Ahadi, S. A., & Hershey, K. L. (1994). Temperament and social behavior in childhood. *Merrill-Palmer Quarterly, 40,* 21–39.

Rothbart, M. K., Ahadi, S. A., Hershey, K. L., & Fisher, P. (2001). Investigations of temperament at three to seven years: The children's behavior questionnaire. *Child Development, 72,* 1394–1408.

Rothbart, M. K., & Bates, J. E. (1998). Temperament. In W. Damon (Series Ed.), N. Eisenberg (Vol. Ed.), *Handbook of child psychology: Vol. 3, social, emotional, personality development* (pp. 105–176). New York: Wiley.

Rothbart, M. K., & Bates, J. E. (in press). Temperament. In W. Damon & R. M. Lerner (Series Eds.) and N. Eisenberg (Vol. Ed.), *Handbook of Child Psychology. Vol. 3. Social, emotional, personality development* (6th ed.). New York: Wiley.

Rothbart, M. K., Ziaie, H., & O'Boyle, C. G. (1992). Self-regulation and emotion in infancy. *New Directions in Child Development, 55,* 7–23.

Rushton, J. P., Brainerd, C. J., & Pressley, M. (1983). Behavioral development and construct validity: The principle of aggregation. *Psychological Bulletin, 94,* 18–38.

Saarni, C., Mumme, D. L., & Campos, J. J. (1998). Emotional development: Action, communication, and understanding. In W. Damon (Series Ed.), N. Eisenberg (Vol. Ed.), *Social, emotional and personality development: Vol. 3, handbook of child psychology* (pp. 237–309). New York: Wiley.

Sandler, I. N., Tein, J., & West, S. G. (1994). Coping, stress and the psychological symptoms of children of divorce: A cross-sectional and longitudinal study. *Child Development, 65,* 1744–1763.

Sethi, A., Mischel, W., Aber, J. L., Shoda, Y., & Rodriguez, M. L. (2000). The role of strategic attention deployment in development of self-regulation: Predicting preschoolers' delay of gratification from mother-toddler interactions. *Developmental Psychology, 36,* 767–777.

Staub, E. (1979). *Positive social behavior and morality: Vol. 2, socialization and development.* New York: Academic Press.

Staub, E. (1984). Steps toward a comprehensive theory of moral conduct: Goal orientation, social behavior, kindness and cruelty. In J. Gewirtz & W. Kurtines (Eds.), *Morality, moral development, and moral behavior: Basic issues in theory and research* (pp. 241–260). New York: Wiley.

Stocker, C., & Dunn, J. (1990). Sibling relationships in childhood: Links with friendships and peer relationships. *British Journal of Developmental Psychology, 8,* 227–244.

Strauss, C. C. (1988). Social deficits of children with internalizing disorders. In B. B. Lahey & A. E. Kazdin (Eds.), *Advances in clinical child psychology. Vol. 11* (pp. 159–191). New York: Plenum Press.

Teglasi, H., & MacMahon, B. H. (1990). Temperament and common problem behaviors of children. *Journal of Applied Developmental Psychology, 11,* 331–349.

Tellegen, A. (1985). Structures of mood and personality and their relevance to assessing anxiety, with an emphasis on self-report. In A. H. Tuma & J. D. Maser (Eds.), *Anxiety and anxiety disorders* (pp. 681–706). Hillsdale, NJ: Erlbaum.

Thomas, A., Chess, S., & Birch, H. G. (1968). *Temperament and behavior disorders in children.* New York: New York University Press.

Thompson, R. A. (1994). Emotional regulation: A theme in search of definition. *Monographs of the Society for Research in Child Development, 59* (Serial No. 240), 25–52.

Thompson, R. A., & Calkins, S. D. (1996). The double -edged sword: Emotional regulation for children at risk. *Development and Psychopathology, 8,* 163–182.

Underwood, B., & Moore, B. (1982). Perspective-taking and altruism. *Psychological Bulletin, 91,* 143–173.

Valiente, C., Eisenberg, N., Smith, C. L., Reiser, M., Fabes, R. A., Losoya, S., Guthrie, I. K., & Murphy, B.C. (2003). The Relations of effortful control and reactive control to children's externalizing problems: A longitudinal assessment. *Journal of Personality, 71,* 1179–1205.

Wilson, B. (2003). The role of attentional processes in children's prosocial behavior with peers: Attention shifting and emotion. *Development and Psychopathology, 15,* 313–329.

Windle, M., & Lerner, R. M. (1986). Reassessing the dimensions of temperamental individuality across the life span: The revised dimensions of temperament survey (DOTS-R). *Journal of Adolescent Research, 1,* 213–230.

Wood, J. V., Saltzberg, J. A., & Goldsamt, L. A. (1990). Does affect induce self-focused attention? *Journal of Personality and Social Psychology, 58,* 899–908.

Zahn-Waxler, C., Schiro, K., Robinson, J. L., Emde, R. N., & Schmitz, S. (2001). Empathy and prosocial patterns in young MZ and DZ twins: Development and genetic and environmental influences. In R. N. Emde & J. K. Hewitt (Eds.), *Infancy to early childhood: Genetic and environmental influences on developmental change* (pp. 141–162). Oxford: Oxford University Press.

Part IV

Adolescence

16

Transition Into Adolescence
The Role of Pubertal Processes

Laura M. DeRose
Jeanne Brooks-Gunn

INTRODUCTION

The onset of adolescence is considered a crucial developmental transition marked by a confluence of changes (Brooks-Gunn, 1984; Graber & Brooks-Gunn, 1996; Hamburg, 1974). In addition to the drastic physical changes that occur, the adolescent decade is defined by the restructuring of social roles, expectations, and relationships within the family, peer group and school environment (Feldman & Elliott, 1990; Graber & Brooks-Gunn, 1996). The pubertal transition is considered an impetus for some of the behavioral and social changes that occur during adolescence (Brooks-Gunn & Petersen, 1983; Graber & Brooks-Gunn, 2002). As individuals develop adult-like features during puberty, family, friends, and teachers may react to them differently and expectations of them may change. New behaviors related to sexual feelings and interest are emerging for the adolescent (Graber & Brooks-Gunn, 2002). Additionally, the internal changes of puberty, such as hormonal changes, have also been associated with variations in affect and behavior (Brooks-Gunn, Graber, & Paikoff, 1994; Buchanan, Eccles, & Becker, 1992; Susman, Dorn, & Chrousos, 1991). In other words, behavioral changes during adolescence may be influenced directly by physiological and physical changes, may be more generally related to the effects of age and grade in school, or may be linked to pubertal growth through social or contextual factors (Brooks-Gunn & Reiter, 1990). As such, interactive models have been developed in the field of puberty research to address the psychosocial implications of pubertal processes.

The timing of the transitions is salient for at least three reasons, the first having to do with level of development at the time of the transition, the second with the vulnerabilities of the psychological state at the time of change, and the third with social context (Rutter, 1989). These reasons have been illustrated using examples related to timing of puberty (Graber, Petersen, & Brooks-Gunn, 1996). First, any biological effects of the pubertal experience will differ depending on the level of development of the biological system at the time. For example, it has been suggested that puberty curtails lateralization of function between the two hemispheres of the brain, resulting in different cognitive abilities depending on timing of the pubertal transition (Waber, 1977). For the most part, research on pubertal timing effects on biological systems has been sparse. Second, any influences on the psychological state of the individual depend on the sensitivities and vulnerabilities of the psychological state at the time of change. For example, experiencing the pubertal transition earlier than others may not only result in being less prepared cognitively and emotionally, but also socially. This may make it more difficult for early maturers to successfully navigate the pubertal transition. Third, timing of puberty may interact with social context. Experiencing the pubertal transition either earlier or later than one's peers may have negative effects on the individual as he or she is perceived as deviating from normative development (Brooks-Gunn & Petersen, 1983; Neugarten, 1979). For example, earlier-maturing girls gain weight at a time when most girls still have childlike physical appearance, which may be one reason why early-maturing girls have reported poorer self-esteem especially related to their body image (Brooks-Gunn & Warren, 1985; Tobin-Richards, Boxer, Petersen, & Albrecht, 1990).

Before the 1980s, only two major studies were conducted on the effects of pubertal development—the California and the Fels Longitudinal Growth Studies. The 1970s were marked by two seminal works that described the lack of systematic study of pubertal development during adolescence (Hamburg, 1974; Lipsitz, 1977). Researchers were also reconsidering whether "storm and stress" was an appropriate characterization of the experience and behavior of young adolescents and whether alterations in self-image and emotionality during early adolescent transitions were influenced by context as well as pubertal changes (Nesselroade & Baltes, 1974; Offer, 1987). Pubertal processes became a subject of study in the 1980s, beginning in 1981 with a conference on girls at puberty (Brooks-Gunn & Petersen, 1983). The 1990s were marked by an increase in studies that address the psychosocial implications of pubertal changes (Alsaker, 1995, 1996; Brooks-Gunn, Graber et al., 1994; Brooks-Gunn, Petersen, & Compas, 1995; Brooks-Gunn & Reiter, 1990; Buchanan et al., 1992; Connolly, Paikoff, & Buchanan, 1996; Graber et al., 1996; R. L. Paikoff & Brooks-Gunn, 1991; Susman & Petersen, 1992; Susman & Ponirakis, 1997).

The current chapter will begin with a description of the biological aspects of pubertal development, with attention to the gender differences in development. Next, methods of measuring puberty, the age of pubertal onset, and the psychological correlates of pubertal development are addressed. In the third section, models linking pubertal development with psychosocial adjustment and the research supporting them are presented, along with proposed mechanisms underlying the models. Finally, we provide some suggestions for the next wave of research.

BIOLOGICAL ASPECTS OF PUBERTAL DEVELOPMENT

Pubertal development is a series of interrelated processes resulting in maturation and adult reproductive functioning. The physiological changes of puberty primarily involve the hypothalamic-pituitary-adrenal (HPA) axis and hypothalamic-pituitary-gonadal (HPG) axis. Pubertal development begins in middle childhood and takes five to six years for most adolescents to complete (Brooks-Gunn & Reiter, 1990; Petersen, 1987). A wide range of individual differences exists in the timing of onset and rate of puberty. The following sections describe the physiological, physical, and central nervous system changes of pubertal development, with attention to gender differences in development. An explanation of how the different aspects of pubertal development are measured is also provided.

Physiological Changes of Puberty

Puberty is part of a continuum of events initiated at conception, mostly involving the hypothalamic-pituitary-gonadal (HPG) axis. The hypothalamic gonadotropin releasing hormone (GnRH) pulse generator, or "gonadostat" is active prenatally and during early infancy, suppressed during childhood, then reactivated at the onset of puberty (Fechner, 2003).[1] In order for puberty to begin, the brain's sensitivity to the negative feedback of gonadal sex steroids (testosterone in males and estrogen in females) decreases, which then releases the HPA axis from inhibition. Puberty begins with the release of GnRH pulses, which activates pulsatile bursts of gonadotropins, luteinizing hormone (LH), and follicle stimulating hormone (FSH), from the pituitary gland. The LH and FSH pulses secreted in response to the GnRH occur first at night and then during the day. Increases in LH and FSH are some of the earliest measurable hormonal indications of pubertal development, and they have been found to rise progressively during puberty (Reiter & Grumbach, 1982). Episodic nocturnal bursts of low-levels of LH are indicative of early pubertal stages (Grumbach & Styne, 1998). The gonads respond to LH and FSH by enlarging, maturing, and secreting increased amounts of gonadal sex steroids, androgens and estrogens.

Gender Differences in Physiological Changes

Multiple gender differences in the mean levels and functions of hormone secretions are evident during the period of pubertal development. In females, the function of LH and FSH is to initiate follicular development in the ovaries, which stimulates them to produce estrogen. Estrogen sensitive tissues, such as the breasts and uterus, then respond to the increase (Fechner, 2003). In males, increased LH stimulates the testes to secrete testosterone, resulting in an increase in testicular size, and FSH stimulates spermatogenesis. LH levels increase in both girls and boys at puberty, while FSH is higher in girls than boys during the prepubertal and pubertal years. Increased FSH levels simulate the ovaries to produce estrogen. Whereas LH and FSH levels in both sexes are regulated by the negative feedback of the gonadal steroids and by the hormone inhibin, girls have a second control mechanism associated with their menstrual cycles which is under positive feedback and is cyclic. When estradiol level is high enough, it triggers an LH, and to a lesser extent, an FSH surge, each which lasts less than 2 days and stimulates ovulation. A corpus luteum forms from the ruptured follicle and begins to secrete progesterone. In the absence of pregnancy, the corpus luteum regresses and the progesterone and estrogen levels drop, triggering withdrawal bleeding and menstruation (Fechner, 2002).

Estrogen and testosterone levels also differ between the two sexes at puberty. Estradiol levels at puberty increase in females then remain elevated during periods of each menstrual cycle. In males, estradiol levels increase until their growth spurt (at midpuberty) then decrease again. On the other hand, while males experience substantial increases in testosterone and androstenedione (a weaker androgen than testosterone) at puberty, there is only a slight rise in females. The sexes also differ in their levels of dehydroepiandrosterone (DHEA) and DHEAS (sulfated form of DHEA), hormones which mark the beginning of adrenarche, the period of initial increases in adrenal androgen hormones, at 6 to 7 years of age in both sexes. Levels of DHEA and DHEAS are similar between the sexes until late puberty, when males begin to have higher levels than females. This difference persists into adulthood (Fechner, 2002).

Physical Changes of Puberty

In females, secondary sexual characteristic development is a result of estrogens from the ovaries. Breast budding is generally the first sexual characteristic to appear, and is most commonly classified by Marshall and Tanner's (1969) 5 stages of development, as illustrated in Table 16.1. Breast development begins in the United States between ages 8 and 13, with a mean age of 9.96 for White girls and a mean age of 8.87 for African American girls (Herman-Giddens et al., 1997). The process of developing mature breasts from breast budding takes approximately 4.5 years, regardless of whether or not girls enter puberty earlier or later than average (Brooks-Gunn & Reiter, 1990). Pubic hair development typically begins shortly after breast budding; however approximately 20 percent of girls experience pubic hair development prior to breast budding.

Pubic hair development begins in the United States between the ages of 8 and 13 years, with a mean age 10.5 years in White girls and 8.8 years for African American girls (Herman-Giddens et al., 1997). Table 16.1 illustrates the 5 stages of pubertal hair development in girls. Menarche is a late sign of pubertal development in girls and occurs following the peak in height velocity and during the rapid increase in weight and body fat (Tanner, 1978). The mean age of menarche in North America is 12.88 years for White girls and 12.16 years for African American girls (Herman-Giddens et al., 1997).

In males, secondary sexual characteristic development is a result of testosterone from the testes. The onset of testicular growth is the initial sign of pubertal development, which occurs on average

Table 16.1
The Five Pubertal Stages for Breast and Pubic Hair Growth in Girls

Stage	Pubic Hair Development	Breast Development
1.	No pubic hair	No breast development
2.	There is a small amount of long pubic hair chiefly along vaginal lips.	The first sign of breast development has appeared. This stage is sometimes referred to as the breast budding stage. Some palpable breast tissue under the nipple, the flat area of the nipple (areola) may be somewhat enlarged.
3.	Hair is darker, coarser, and curlier and spreads sparsely over skin around vaginal lips.	The breast is more distinct although there is no separation between contours of the two breasts.
4.	Hair is adult in type, but area covered is smaller than in most adults. There is no pubic hair on the inside of the thighs.	The breast is further enlarged and there is greater contour distinction. The nipple including the areola forms a secondary mound on the breast.
5.	Hair is adult in type, distributed as an inverse triangle. There may be hair on the inside of the thighs.	Mature stage size may vary in the mature stage. The breast is fully developed. The contours are distinct and the areola has receded into the general contour of the breast.

Source: Table adapted and reproduced from W.A. Marshall and J.M. Tanner, Variations in the pattern of pubertal changes in girls, *Archives of Disease in Childhood*, 44 [1969], pp. 291-303. Copyright 1969 by BMJ Publishing Group.

between ages 11 and 11.5, but can begin as early as age 9.5 (Brooks-Gunn & Reiter, 1990). Similar to girls, the most common classification of testicular and pubic hair development in males is Tanner's 5 stages of development (Marshall & Tanner, 1969), as illustrated in Table 16.2. Pubic hair growth begins on average at about age 12, however, 41% of boys are in Tanner Stage 4 of testicular growth when initial pubic hair growth begins. The average length of time between initial genital growth and

TABLE 16.2
The Five Pubertal Stages for Penile and Pubic Hair Growth in Boys

Stage	Pubic Hair Development	Penile Development
1.	There is no pubic hair, although there may be a fine velus over the pubes similar to that over other parts of the abdomen.	The infantile state that persists from birth until puberty begins. During this time the genitalia increase slightly in overall size but there is little change in general appearance.
2.	Sparse growth of lightly pigmented hair, which is usually straight or only slightly curled. This usually begins at either side of the base of the penis.	The scrotum has begun to enlarge, and there is some reddening and change in texture of the scrotal skin.
3.	The hair spreads over the pubic symphysis and is considerably darker and coarser and usually more curled.	The penis has increased in length and there is smaller increase in breadth. There has been further growth of the scrotum.
4.	The hair is adult in character but covers an area considerably smaller than in most adults. There is no spread to the medial surface of the thighs.	The length and breadth of the penis have increased further and the glans has developed. The scrotum is further enlarged and the scrotal skin has become darker.
5.	The hair is distributed in an inverse triangle as in the female. It has spread to the medial surface of the thighs but not up the linea alba or elsewhere above the base of the triangle.	The genitalia are adult in size and shape. The appearance of the genitalia may satisfy criteria for one of these stages for a considerable time before the penis and scrotum are sufficiently developed to be classified as belonging to the next stage.

Source: Table adapted and reproduced from N.M. Morris and J.R. Udry, Validation of a self-administered instrument to assess stage of adolescent development, *Journal of Youth and Adolescence*, 9 [1980], pp. 275-276. Reprinted with kind permission of Springer Science and Business Media.

the development of mature genitalia in boys is 3 years (Brooks-Gunn & Reiter, 1990). Spermarche, or first ejaculation, usually occurs between 13 and 14 years of age. More noticeable physical changes in boys include voice changing and the development of facial hair, which occur predominantly in early adolescence (Brooks-Gunn & Reiter, 1990).

Compared to girls, not as many studies have been conducted with boys that compare timing of pubertal onset across ethnic groups. Based on data from the Third National Health and Nutrition Examination Survey (NHANES III), conducted between 1988 and 1994, African American boys had earlier median and mean ages for Tanner stages than the White and Mexican American boys (Sun et al., 2002). These findings parallel the findings that African American girls begin puberty earlier than White girls (Herman-Giddens et al., 1997).

Gender Differences in Physical Change

The developmental course of physical changes during puberty for girls and boys is demonstrated in Figures 16.1 and 16.2, respectively. Boys typically begin pubertal development about a year later than girls. Gender differences are also evident in regards to the alterations in linear growth, body composition, and the regional distribution of body fat during puberty. The pubertal growth spurt begins about 2 years earlier for females compared to males, and it also occurs at an earlier stage in puberty in girls than it does it boys (Fechner, 2003). Girls average a peak height velocity of 9 cm/yr at Tanner stage 2, and a total height gain of 25 cm during pubertal growth (Marshall & Tanner, 1969). Boys attain a mean peak height velocity of 10.3 cm/yr during Tanner stage 4 and gain 28 cm in height total (Marshall & Tanner, 1970). Increases and/or redistribution of body fat also occur in girls and boys during puberty. Prepubertally, lean body mass, bone mass, and body fat are about equal in boys and girls. However, postpubertal boys have 1.5 times the lean body mass and bone mass of postpubertal girls, and postpubertal girls have twice as much body fat as postpubertal boys (Grumbach & Styne, 1998).

Central Nervous System and Tissue Sensitivity to Sex Steroids

Levels of circulating steroid hormones explain on average less than half the variance in morphological pubertal development and growth in girls and boys (Nottelmann et al., 1987). One reason for this is that most hormone measurements are collected at only one point in time. Some of the variance could also be accounted for by structural differences in the CNS or in peripheral target tissues such as the

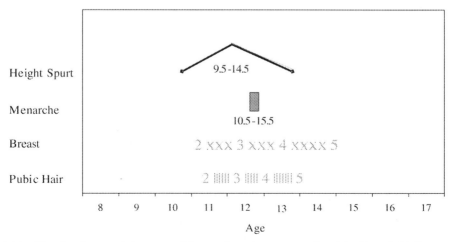

Figure 16.1 The developmental course of four pubertal processes for girls. From J. M. Tanner (1962), *Growth at Adolescence*, p. 36. Oxford: Blackwell Scientific. Copyright 1962 by Blackwell Scientific, reprinted with permission.

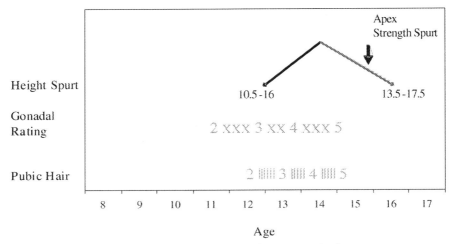

Figure 16.2 The developmental course of four pubertal processes for boys. From J. M. Tanner (1962), *Growth at Adolescence*, p. 30. Oxford: Blackwell Scientific. Copyright 1962 by Blackwell Scientific, reprinted with permission.

breast. For example, breast development is partly controlled by the number and type of breast tissue receptors and other intracellular conditions (Layman, 1995). End-organ sensitivity in the CNS, that is, how reactive neural tissues are to hormones and neurotransmitters, may also play a role, although more research is needed in this area (Sanborn & Hayward, 2003).

Steroid hormones may affect sexual differentiation of the brain via influencing cell proliferation, cell migration, ontogenetic cell death, synaptogenesis, and neuroregulation (Casper, 1998; MacLusky & Naftolin, 1981; Phoenix, Goy, Gerall, & Young, 1959). As most sexual dimorphisms in brain morphology are established prenatally, changes human brain anatomy have not been well studied during the pubertal development period (Giedd, Castellanos, Rajapakse, Vaituzis, & Rapoport, 1997). In one cross-sectional study that examined brain dimorphisms in children between 4 and 18 years of age, amygdala and hippocampal volume increased for both sexes but with the amygdala increasing significantly more in males than females and hippocampal volume increasing more in females (Giedd et al., 1997). Research with rats that involves highly specific probes for estrogen action in the CNS has uncovered new classes of estrogen receptors in the rat brains (Laflamme, Nappi, Drolet, Labrie, & Rivest, 1998; Mitchner, Garlick, & Ben-Jonathon, 1998; Osterlund, Kuiper, Custafsson, & Hurd, 1998). The nature of these estrogen receptors in humans, and how they may relate to pubertal variation between individuals, is not known.

MEASURING PUBERTY

Self- and Parent-Report Measures

The majority of studies that assess secondary sexual characteristic development include self- or parent-report ratings of Tanner's 5 stages of development (Marshall & Tanner, 1969). Although the most accurate Tanner ratings are those assessed by health professionals via visual inspection and sometimes palpation of the breast, self- or parent-report ratings are much more feasible to obtain. Studies report correlations between parent and examiner ratings of Tanner stages ranging from 0.75 to 0.87 (Brooks-Gunn, Warren, Rosso, & Gargiulo, 1987; Dorn, Susman, Nottelmann, Inoff-Germain, & Chrousos, 1990). Studies have also examined the validation of self-reported maturation based on Tanner drawings. Pearson correlation coefficients, when excluding testicular size, have been reported as .6 or above for the self- and physician-reports (Morris & Udry, 1980). Dorn and colleagues (1990) reported correlations between self- and physician-reports ranging between 0.77 and 0.91, which were slightly more accurate than the parent ratings in the same study. The Pubertal Development Scale (PDS) is another commonly used measure that includes questions about growth spurt, body hair (not specifically pubic hair) and skin change in boys and girls, facial hair growth and voice change in boys, and breast development and menarche in girls, rated on 4-point scales ("no development" to "development already completed"; Petersen, Crockett, Richards, & Boxer, 1988). Correlations between physician Tanner ratings and self-reports of the PDS were between .61 and .67 (Brooks-Gunn et al., 1987).

When physician ratings are feasible, concerns have been raised regarding the validity of assessing breast development via visual inspection without palpation. The reason is that by visual inspection only, it is sometimes difficult to distinguish fat tissue from real breast tissue, especially in overweight girls. In the Herman-Giddens and colleagues (1997) study of pubertal development in girls in pediatric settings, the data only included ratings of breast development by visual inspection. However, 39% of physicians assessed breast stage by palpation, as well as visual inspection. Only 4% of the girls with breast development by inspection had no breast tissue by palpation, and only 1.7% of girls who had no breast development by inspection had breast tissue by palpation (Kaplowitz, Slora, Wasserman, Pedlow, & Herman-Giddens, 2001). In addition, findings showed that the occasional misclassification of breast tissue was just as likely to occur in thin girls as in overweight girls. This follow-up evaluation of the pediatric setting study supports Tanner staging via inspection of breast development as a valid method of assessment, regardless of whether the girls are overweight.

In regards to measuring height, self-report data are fairly accurate, even for young adolescents. Correlations between self- and actual reports of weight and height range between .75 and .98 (Brooks-Gunn et al., 1987; Goodman, Hinden, & Khandelwal, 2000). It is unusual for researchers to ask parents to measure their children at home, so to our knowledge, parental-reports of height have not been validated.

Hormone Measures

Pubertal development can also be assessed via measuring hormonal biomarkers. As explained in the previous section, a major hormone involved in the regulation of puberty is GnRH. However, it is difficult to measure GnRH because it has a short half-life and is transported directly to the pituitary (Rockett, Lynch, & Buck, 2004). Therefore, pubertal development is most often measured through hormones regulated directly or indirectly by GnRH, including the gonadotropins (LH, FSH) and sex steroid hormones (testosterone and estrogen). Methods for measuring these hormones include blood draws, salivary collection, blood spots, and urinary collection.

Compared to blood draws, advantages of salivary and urinary assessments are that they are noninvasive, painless, and highly acceptable to most research participants. Drawbacks are that salivary and urinary studies provide limited estimates of total output by peripheral glands and preclude evaluation of central neuroendocrine regulation. Also, there are technical demands on salivary and urinary assays for steroids of low concentrations (e.g., estradiol), which may prevent their use in some developmental studies. Advantages of blood spots are that they are minimally invasive and require very little blood, they allow for multiple collections so that mean hormone concentrations can be measured, few factors compromise validity of blood spot samples for analysis, and assays for blood are more sensitive than the assays for urine or saliva (Worthman & Stallings, 1997).

Important Issues to Consider When Measuring Puberty

The appropriate measure(s) of puberty to use in a study must be "purpose-dependent" (Hayward, 2003). Indicators of puberty are correlated, but not equivalent, as each indicator captures a different aspect of the pubertal process (Brooks-Gunn & Warren, 1985; Graber et al., 1996). Each indicator involves limitation in how it is measured. For example, validity of Tanner self-ratings may vary by degree of body image disturbance (Hick & Katzman, 1999; Litt, 1999); and cross-sectional measurements of hormonal levels are difficult to interpret (Hayward, 2003). The ideal way to measure the pubertal process would be multiple indicators of puberty collected longitudinally.

It is also important to note that at different stages of puberty, the correlations between the various manifestations of puberty change dramatically (Angold, Worthman, & Costello, 2003). For example, as girls begin to cycle, age and Tanner stage may not be as correlated with FSH, LH, and estrogen, because their levels become primarily controlled by the menstrual cycle. Even though circulating hormone levels are the best available correlate of hormonal action in the CNS, self-report of breast development is a better measure of breast development than is circulating estrogen level (Angold et al., 2003). Therefore, researchers must consider the meaning of the pubertal indicator and the developmental range when designing studies involving puberty.

THE DECREASING AGE OF PUBERTAL ONSET

The data presented in the previous section on average age of breast and pubic hair development in girls and boys in the United States stem from study conducted by 225 clinicians in pediatric practices belonging to Pediatric Research in Office Settings (PROS), a practice-based research network that is part of the American Academy of Pediatrics (Herman-Giddens et al., 1997). Previous to this study, the study most often quoted as defining normative ages for puberty was the Marshall and Tanner (1969) longitudinal study of 192 White girls living in a children's home, assessed every 3 months from age 8 through age 18. Studies of pubertal onset comparable in scope to the British (Marshall and Tanner) study had not been conducted in the United States. The PROS study was cross-sectional, consisting of 17,000 girls between the ages of 3 and 12 whose breast and pubic hair development was assessed via practitioner ratings (Herman-Giddens et al., 1997). Findings from this study indicate that the mean age of pubertal onset for girls has decreased by as much as a year, compared to the Marshall and Tanner data. Furthermore, the study found that African American girls are beginning breast and pubic hair development about 6 months to a year earlier than White girls, although the reasons for the earlier age of secondary sexual characteristic onset for African American girls are not clear.

The National Health and Nutrition Examination Survey (third cycle) found similar results (Wu, Mendola, & Buck, 2002). Physician-ratings of Tanner stages of breast and pubic hair development were available for 1,623 girls between ages 8 and 16 years. Mean age of onset of pubic hair and breast development was 9.5 and 9.5 years for African American girls, 10.3 and 9.8 years for Mexican American girls, and 10.5 and 10.3 years for White girls. These ethnic differences remained even after adjustment for current body mass index and several social and economic variables (Wu et al., 2002).

Changes in the age of menarche in the United States across the past few decades are not as clear. In a large study of puberty in girls conducted between 1966 and 1970, the U.S. National Health Examination Survey, assessed age of menarche in girls between the ages of 12 and 17 (Harlan, Harlan, & Grillo, 1980). Data from this study indicated that age of menarche was 12.8 years for White girls and 12.5 years for African American girls. The age of menarche for White girls in the PROS study, 12.88 years, was similar to the 1980 report, whereas the age for African American girls in the PROS study, 12.16 years, was slightly lower (Herman-Giddens et al., 1997). A study based in Chicago neighborhoods in the mid- to late 1990s, which included African American, White, and Latina girls from low-, middle-, and high-socioeconomic status reported younger ages of menarche than the previously mentioned studies (Obeidallah, Brennan, Brooks-Gunn, Kindlon, & Earls, 2000). Results showed that Latina girls reached menarche at a younger age (11.58 years) than African American girls (11.93 years), after controlling for socioeconomic factors. Adjusting for socioeconomic status, no significant differences were found between White girls (12.04 years) and Latinas or between White girls and African American girls. It should be noted that not all girls in this study had begun to menstruate, so the means are lower than they ultimately will be, although the ethnic differences should hold.

Although findings for boys indicate that there may be variations in puberty onset by race (Sun et al., 2002), no clear data indicate that boys are entering puberty earlier now than they were twenty or thirty years ago. Implications for potential effects of earlier pubertal timing on depression in girls will be reviewed later in the chapter.

Potential Explanations for the Decreasing Age of Pubertal Onset

Several hypotheses that have been proposed that focus on environmental factors as an explanation for the earlier age of pubertal onset in girls. One such hypothesis is that exposure to environmental toxins may mimic estrogens in the body and thus stimulate pubertal development. Two epidemics of early puberty, one in Italy and the other in Puerto Rico, are suspected to have been caused by exposure to estrogens in food, specifically meat and poultry (Fara et al., 1979; Saenz de Rodriguez, Bongiovanni, & Conde de Borrego, 1985). However, no localized outbreaks of early breast development have been reported in the continental United States (Kaplowitz, 2004) and no published data provide evidence that an increased overall exposure to environmental estrogens leads to earlier puberty (Paretsch & Sippell, 2001). Another hypothesis is that manufactured compounds being released into the environment may interfere with the human endocrine system. Studies in this area are difficult because pubertal onset may occur many years after exposure to the chemical in question (Kaplowitz, 2004). Although a few studies have managed to collect data on exposure to environmental contaminants at the time of birth and relate it to growth and development (Colon, Caro, Bourdony, & Rosario, 2000; Gladen, Ragan, & Rogan, 2000; Krstevska-Komstantinova et al., 2001; Michels Blanck et al., 2000), the results do not provide enough compelling evidence that the overall trend for earlier puberty is linked with environmental contaminants. Hormone-containing hair products have been targeted as reason for earlier pubertal onset (Zimmerman, Francis, & Poth, 1995), but this hypothesis requires further examination.

Other hypotheses regarding the earlier onset of puberty focus on more intrinsic factors. For example, perinatal factors, such as birth weight, have been found to play a role in subsequent pubertal development. In one study, girls who were smaller at birth but had a rapid "catch-up" period of growth between birth and age 6 were earlier maturers (Persson et al., 1999). Mechanisms for this association are not clear, but it is likely that the prenatal environment may influence subsequent timing of onset of development, given that sex hormones are active prenatally in organizing the brain for subsequent pubertal development and reproductive functioning (Fechner, 2002). A more widely discussed hypothesis is that higher body fat is associated with earlier maturation. In general, overweight girls tend to mature earlier than girls of normal weight, and thin girls tend to mature later. Numerous studies have indicated that in the past thirty years, there is an increasing prevalence of obesity in both sexes, at all ages, and in all racial and ethnic groups. Since obesity is widespread and prevalent throughout all parts of the United States, it makes sense to examine obesity as a link to earlier pubertal onset. Kaplowitz and colleagues (2001) examined the role of body mass index (BMI) in earlier pubertal onset using data from the PROS study. BMI standard deviation scores (z scores) were computed in order to compare each girl's BMI with what was normal for her age. A key finding of the study was that 6- to 9-year-old girls with early breast development had significantly higher BMI scores than the girls of the same age and race who were prepubertal. When the difference in BMI z scores between African American and White girls was controlled, African American girls still had an earlier onset of puberty than did White girls. Furthermore, African American and White girls who had pubic hair but no breast development were also more overweight than prepubertal girls, even though hormonal regulation of pubic hair and breast development is quite different (Kaplowitz et al., 2001). The hormone leptin has been proposed as a mechanism linking body mass index with puberty (Clayton & Trueman, 2000). Leptin, a protein produced by fat cells, is involved in regulation of appetite and body composition. Evidence has accrued over the past 10 years that leptin also plays a role in the regulation of puberty (Barash et al., 1996). Leptin levels rise progressively during puberty in normal girls, beginning at age 7 to 8; their rise occurs before increases in LH and estradiol, which means that leptin could be a trigger for the production of puberty hormones (Ahmed et al., 1999; Blum et al., 1997; Garcia-Mayor, Andrade, Rios, Lage, Dieguez, & Casanueva, 1997).

A final hypothesis to be discussed is that psychosocial or environmental stress is associated with earlier puberty. In particular, stressful family situations have been linked to earlier onset of puberty

(Graber, Brooks-Gunn, & Warren, 1995; Moffitt, Caspi, Belsky, & Silva, 1992; Surbey, 1990). Lower warmth in parent–child relationships has been associated with earlier age at menarche after controlling for the effect of maternal age at menarche and level of breast development (Graber et al., 1995). Father's absence in the childhood years has been predictive of earlier maturation (Ellis & Garber, 2000; Surbey, 1990). In girls not living with their biological parents, the presence of a stepfather rather than the absence of a father was more strongly associated with earlier pubertal maturation (Ellis & Garber, 2000). A Polish study found that age of menarche in girls who experienced stressful family dysfunction was 0.4 years earlier than age of menarche in girls from families free of major trauma. Mechanisms for the relationship between family stress and early puberty are not clear. Estrogens may play a role, as there is an increasing body of evidence showing effects of stress on estrogen systems in adults (McEwen, 1994).

Potential Reasons for Ethnic Differences in Age of Pubertal Onset

A finding across three large-scale studies conducted in the 1980s and 1990s, the PROS study (Herman-Giddens et al., 1997), NHANES III (Wu et al., 2002), and the National Heart, Lung, and Blood Institute Growth and Health Study (Morrison et al., 1994), is that African American girls begin breast and pubic hair development about a year earlier than White girls and begin menses about half a year earlier. The reasons for the earlier age of secondary sexual characteristic onset for African American girls are not clear. Possible factors to consider include differences in diet and weight, environmental hazards or environmental estrogens, or differences in contextual stress and cultural attitudes between ethnic groups (Graber, 2003). Physiological differences that have been hypothesized to play a role in timing of pubertal onset include lower insulin sensitivity (Arslanian, Suprasongsin, & Janosky, 1997) and higher serum leptin levels (Wong et al., 1998) in African American children compared to White children. None of these hypotheses have been investigated extensively.

PSYCHOLOGICAL MEANING OF PUBERTAL CHANGE

Meaning of Pubertal Changes to Girls

The majority of studies on the psychological meaning of pubertal change were conducted in the 1970s and 1980s; more current research has not examined this issue. The meaning of menarche to girls has been examined the most extensively, as menarche is a salient and singular event (Brooks-Gunn & Petersen, 1983; Brooks-Gunn & Ruble, 1982; Greif & Ulman, 1982; Koff, Rierdan, & Sheingold, 1982). In studies conducted by Brooks-Gunn and Ruble (1982), girls were interviewed within two or three months of getting their periods for the first time. Twenty percent of girls reported only positive reactions, 20% reported only negative reactions, 20% reported ambivalent feelings, such as "felt same" or "felt funny," and the last 40% reported both positive and negative reactions. Girls who are early or unprepared for menarche reported more negative experiences than on-time ore prepared girls. Also, girls are at first reluctant to discuss menarche, except with their mothers. Girls only begin to share their experiences with their friends about 6 months after reaching menarche (Brooks-Gunn, 1987; Brooks-Gunn, Warren, Samelson, & Fox, 1986; Ruble & Brooks-Gunn, 1982).

Brooks-Gunn and colleagues have also examined the significance of breast and pubic hair development to adolescent girls in the fifth and sixth grades (Brooks-Gunn, 1984; Brooks-Gunn & Warren, 1988). The majority of girls (82%) reported that breast growth was more significant to them than pubic hair growth because "other people can tell." Girls also reported that mothers talked to them more about their breast than their pubic hair development. Onset of breast growth was associated with positive peer relationships, greater salience of sex roles linked with reproduction, and a positive body image, while the onset of pubic hair growth was not (Brooks-Gunn & Warren, 1988). However, girls were likely to experience teasing by family members and boys about their breast development (Brooks-Gunn, Newman, Holderness, & Warren, 1994; Brooks-Gunn & Warren, 1988).

Girls tend to experience the normal height and weight changes of puberty negatively, particularly increases in weight and/or fat. More advanced pubertal development has been associated with less satisfaction with weight and to perceptions of being overweight for girls but not for boys (Tobin-Richards et al., 1990; Tyrka, Graber, & Brooks-Gunn, 2000). Weight-related negative body image, weight dissatisfaction, and weight concerns were associated with increased depressive symptoms in a sample of early adolescent girls, even when controlling for objective weight status (Rierdan & Koff, 1997). It is likely that girls more often experience increased body size negatively due to the media images in Western cultures that value the thin physique of a prepubertal body over the mature body for girls (Attie & Brooks-Gunn, 1989; Parker et al., 1995).

Meaning of Pubertal Changes to Boys

Very little is known about the meaning of pubertal changes for boys. In a small qualitative study, middle adolescent boys were interviewed about their reactions to their first ejaculation (spermarche), their preparedness for the event and sources of information, and the extent to which they discussed this with friends (Gaddis & Brooks-Gunn, 1985). Responses from boys were more positive than negative, although two-thirds of the boys reported being a little frightened, which is comparable to girls' reactions to menarche. The boys were very reluctant to discuss their experience of first ejaculation with parents or peers. This secrecy may stem in part from spermarche's link with masturbation. Although studies have not focused on boys' responses to increases in height and weight during puberty, these are most likely positive changes for boys. However, it has been suggested that media images of men are becoming as unrealistic and unattainable as media images of women (Leit, Gray, & Pope, 2002). The "pumped up" physique is becoming prevalent in the media, men with large shoulders and muscular abdomens. Although the effects of this portrayal of men in the media have not been studied, it could potentially be linked with body dissatisfaction, obsessive weight lifting, or steroid use in adolescent boys.

MODELS LINKING PUBERTAL PROCESSES AND PSYCHOSOCIAL ADJUSTMENT

The research that links puberty with psychosocial adjustment involves two main categories of models—pubertal status and timing of puberty (Brooks-Gunn, Graber et al., 1994; Buchanan et al., 1992; Graber, Brooks-Gunn, & Archibald, 2005; Graber, Brooks-Gunn, & Warren, in press). Pubertal status models refer to adolescents' degree of physical maturation and their hormone levels. Models that examine hormone levels are considered direct effect models, and those that measure physical change secondary to hormone changes are considered indirect effect models. The theory behind status models is that girls may experience negative reactions or receive negative feedback from others about their development when they reach certain stages, or they may feel that certain behaviors are expected with increasing physical development. Pubertal timing models suggest that being either an early maturer or out-of-synch (earlier or later) with one's peers is what affects depressive outcomes. Other types of models suggest that it is not pubertal development per se, but factors that interact with the challenges of pubertal development that lead to more adjustment problems (Nolen-Hoeksema & Girgus, 1994). For example, risk factors for depression may be more common in girls than in boys before adolescence, but depression results when these factors interact with the challenges specific to early adolescence, such as pubertal development.

In general, any model describing the relationship between pubertal and social events in adjustment outcomes should be mediated rather than direct, bidirectional rather than unidirectional, and interactive rather than additive (Brooks-Gunn, Graber et al., 1994), as Figure 16.3 illustrates. A framework with three potential mediational processes between the hormonal changes of puberty and short-term effects on affective states is illustrated. The first mediational pathway shows the effect that timing of secondary sexual characteristic development links hormonal changes and affective states. The second mediational pathway highlights the effect of social experiences, including perceptions of puberty,

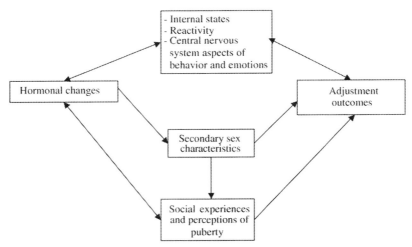

Figure 16.3 Theoretical framework model linking puberty with adjustment outcomes in girls. Adapted from Brooks-Gunn, J., Graber, J. A., & Paikoff, R. L., "Studying links between hormones and negative affect: Models and measures," *Journal of Research on Adolescence*, 4, 469–486. Copyright 1994, reprinted with permission from Blackwell Publishing.

on affective states; this effect stems partly from hormonal changes and is also a response to changes in physical development during puberty. The third mediational link refers to internal states, such as central nervous system changes that stem from the hormonal changes, and individual differences in arousal and physiological reactivity. Figure 16.3 illustrates that some of the pathways are bidirectional, which means that girls' social experiences and behaviors may have effects on the hormonal systems, which may affect the timing of pubertal development. The following sections review the empirical evidence associated with the different aspects of this theoretical framework. More studies on links between puberty and adjustment have been conducted with girls than with boys. Also, studies have more often examined internalizing behaviors than externalizing behaviors.

Hormone Effects

Findings from studies that focus on pubertal hormones and adjustment reveal that effects vary across study, by gender, by hormone, and by outcome. In research focused on hormone-behavior links in girls only, findings indicate that increases in estradiol, specifically during the most rapid period of increase during puberty, have been associated with negative affect (Brooks-Gunn & Warren, 1989; Warren & Brooks-Gunn, 1989). Estradiol levels increase dramatically during puberty, and they correlate strongly with many of the other hormone levels. In the first set of analyses, ordinary least-squares regressions (OLS) were performed in order to compare findings with those of other researchers. Age and five hormones, FSH, LH, estradiol, testosterone, and DHEAS, were entered as possible predictors. None of the individual variables had significant beta weights in the linear analysis.

The second set of analyses tested both linear and nonlinear effects (the square of each hormone was entered in order to test for nonlinear associations). Findings indicated a nonlinear effect of estradiol for depressive affect and a negative linear effect of DHEAS for aggressive affect. Based on the significant nonlinear estradiol finding, girls were categorized into 4 hormonal stages based on the range of their estradiol levels; each range affects reproductive organs and functioning of the reproductive system differently. Stage I girls were considered prepubertal, stage II girls were experiencing beginning pubertal development, stage III girls were considered to be in mid- or late- puberty, and stage IV girls were experiencing cyclic menstrual function. Estradiol levels were 0–25, 26–50, 51–74, and greater than 75 pg/mL, respectively, for each stage.

As seen in Figure 16.4, results indicated a significant quadratic effect for girls' depressive affect while controlling for age, with highest levels of depressive affect in the groups (stages II and III) that demonstrated initial increases in estradiol (Brooks-Gunn & Warren, 1989; Warren & Brooks-Gunn, 1989). In follow-up analysis, this hormone-affect association was found to persist over the course of one year (Paikoff, Brooks-Gunn, & Warren, 1991). The curvilinear nature of the hormone-affect association fits the premise that activational effects may be greatest when the endocrine system is being turned on. However, the magnitude of the hormone effect was small, accounting for only 4% of the variance in negative affect. Other studies have also indicated that when hormone-affect associations are found, they generally account for a small portion of variance in behavior (e.g., Buchanan et al., 1992). Social factors, as measured in this study by positive and negative life events, accounted for more variance than hormonal pubertal factors alone (8%–18%), as did the interaction between negative life events and pubertal factors (9%–15%). Thus, hormone effects on affect may be overshadowed by environmental events.

Angold and colleagues have conducted a number of studies on links between pubertal factors and depression. The first study assessed age, pubertal timing, and Tanner stage on the probability of depression in both boys and girls over four waves of data collection from the Great Smoky Mountains Study (Angold, Costello, & Worthman, 1998). Depression included three diagnoses: *DSM-IV* major depressive episode, dysthymia, and minor depressive disorder. Findings revealed that only after the transition to mid-puberty (Tanner Stage III and above) were girls more likely than boys to be depressed. Timing of the pubertal transition did not affect depression, whether measured by onset of menarche or Tanner stage development. These findings imply that some aspect of puberty itself was related to depression, rather than the age at which the pubertal level was achieved. Further analyses considered HPG axis hormonal effects on depression in girls, in order to disentangle the effects of the morphological changes of puberty and the hormonal changes underlying them (Angold, Costello, Erkanli, & Worthman, 1999). Results indicated that the effects of testosterone and estrogen in the model eliminated the apparent effect of Tanner stage. The Odds Ratio associated with Tanner stage was reduced from 2.9 to 1.0 by the addition of these hormones, meaning that before the hormones were added to the model, the likelihood of depression for girls at Tanner stage III and above was nearly three times as great as the likelihood of depression for girls below Tanner stage III. An Odds Ratio of "1" indicates that there is no difference in the likelihood of depression based on Tanner stage grouping). In order to examine the possibility that hormone thresholds may be present, the researchers divided the ranges of testosterone and estrogen into quintiles and plotted rates of depression for each quintile. The effect of testosterone was particularly marked and was manifested only above a certain threshold, above the 60th percentile of testosterone levels in this sample (corresponding to a

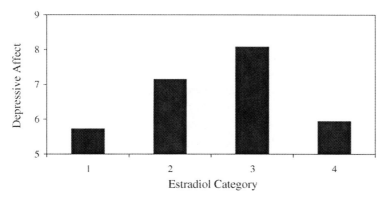

Figure 16.4 Significant quadratic effect of estradiol categories on depressive affect in girls. Adapted from Warren, M. P., & Brooks-Gunn, J., "Mood and behavior at adolescence: Evidence for hormonal factors," *The Journal of Clinical Endocrinology and Metabolism*, 69, 77–83. Copyright 1989, The Endocrine Society.

level of 24.7 ng/dl). The relationship between testosterone and depression was nonlinear in that there is a sharp jump between the third and fourth quintiles, whereas the effects of estrogen on depression appeared to be reasonably linear. In this study, levels of FSH and LH had no effect on depression rates over and above those accounted for by testosterone and estrogen. The findings of this study parallel previous findings that negative affect is associated with higher levels of androgens and estrogens in adolescent girls and imply that hormones rather than physical status are the 'active ingredient' in the effects of puberty on depression in girls (Angold et al., 1999).

More recently, Angold and colleagues hypothesized that the apparent effects of both testosterone and estrogen could represent an intracellular estrogenic effect (Angold et al., 2003), since when behavioral effects of testosterone in animals have been investigated at the level of the brain receptors involved, most have proven to occur via estrogen receptors following intracellular aromatization, or conversion, of testosterone to estrogen (Hutchison, Schumacher, Steimer, & Gahr, 1990; Rasmussen, Torres-Aleman, MacLusky, Naftolin, & Robbins, 1990). Using the same sample of girls from previously described studies, the researchers combined levels of testosterone and estrogen, instead of entering testosterone and estrogen separately in analyses. The rationale for this decision was that both may act on the same receptors in their effects on depression. The sum of the measured molarities of testosterone and estrogen was called sex steroid level (SSL). The distribution of SSL was divided into deciles, and the prevalence of depression was plotted in the deciles. The plot showed pronounced threshold effects of SSL groups based on 3 cutpoints; the difference between each group was significant, with the highest rate of depressive symptoms for the SSL group in the 80th percentile and above. Additional analyses showed that the effects of pubertal hormone status were not explained by either changes in levels of life events or by the interaction of life events and SSL status. The threshold effect of the SSL hormones is similar to the findings of Brooks-Gunn and Warren (1989), in which a significant quadratic effect was found for girls' depressive symptoms, with highest levels of depressive symptoms in the groups that demonstrated initial increases in hormones. Both studies underscore the need to consider linear and nonlinear models when examining effects of hormones on behaviors.

Pubertal Status Effects

Examining links between pubertal status and adjustment involves comparisons of outcomes among adolescents at different levels or stages of key external signs of pubertal development (e.g., breast growth, pubic hair, testicular changes). Pubertal staging is usually indexed by some measure of Tanner stages that range from no signs of development to completed development. Pubertal status is considered important because it signifies that the adolescent is more adult-like in appearance, which may result in different responses from family and peers in the adolescents' social world, as well as changes in how adolescents view themselves.

Since hormonal changes are the cause of the changes in physical growth and development, it is often difficult to disentangle hormonal and status effects on adjustment. For example, as described in the previous section, a study by Angold and colleagues (1998) found that only after reaching Tanner stage III were girls more likely than boys to experience higher rates of depressive disorder. However, subsequent analyses showed that effects of elevated estradiol and testosterone levels eliminated effects due to secondary sexual characteristics (Angold et al., 1999). This study suggests that when pubertal status effects on adjustment are found, they are likely be driven by hormonal changes.

Pubertal Timing Effects

A large body of literature involves studies examining links between pubertal timing and adjustment in adolescents, mainly because there is substantial variation among individuals regarding when puberty begins and how it progresses (Tanner, 1970). Girls typically exhibit the external manifestations of puberty about 1 or 2 years earlier than boys. Early-maturing girls can therefore develop 3 to 6 years ahead of boys as well as developing earlier than on-time or late-maturing girls. Variations in pubertal timing are most likely a combination of genetic differences and environmental factors such as nutrition, exercise, and health conditions.

Classifications of maturational timing may differ by study, even when the same pubertal status measure is used, such as the Tanner. Many studies group adolescents using population norms (Duke-Duncan, Ritter, Dornbusch, Gross, & Carlsmith, 1985) or classify adolescents according to sample distribution into early, on-time, and late developers. Researchers have typically considered the earliest 20% within the distribution for that sample as the "early" developers and the latest 20% as the "late" developers (Brooks-Gunn & Warren, 1985; Graber et al., 1996). Another method is to use sample values to indicate the deviation from the mean, such as defining more than one standard deviation above or below the group mean as the threshold for early or late pubertal maturation (Alsaker, 1992). Some researchers have used ratings of perceived pubertal timing, in which adolescents rate their timing as earlier, the same, or later than their peers (Dubas, Graber, & Petersen, 1991; Graber, Lewinsohn, Seeley, & Brooks-Gunn, 1997; Graber, Seeley, Brooks-Gunn, & Lewinsohn, 2003; Obeidallah, Brennan, Brooks-Gunn, & Earls, 2004). These varied methods result in cross-study variation in the maturational and chronological ages of adolescents classified in the same timing group. In the cases where the same classification system is used, different samples, having different distributions, may exhibit various percentages of off-time and on-time girls (even if same definition of timing is used). It is also important to consider that when assessing pubertal timing, studies often do not include a complete design, in that at any one grade level or age, a complete range of pubertal growth will not be seen, resulting in restricted ranges (Brooks-Gunn, Petersen, & Eichorn, 1985).

A few hypotheses have emerged to explain links between pubertal timing and psychological development. The "off-time" hypothesis is the most general one; it predicts that both earlier and later development in girls and boys compared to one's same-age, same-gender peers is a risk factor for problem behaviors (Caspi & Moffitt, 1991). A more specific hypothesis is the gendered "deviation" pattern of pubertal timing effects, where early maturation is a risk factor for females but late maturation is a risk factor for males. This hypothesis is based on the developmental pattern that girls, on average, mature earlier than boys. Girls who mature earlier than their peers or boys who mature later than their peers are considered to be in the "deviant" categories (Brooks-Gunn et al., 1985; Petersen & Taylor, 1980).

The "early maturation" hypothesis is also referred to as the "stage-termination" hypothesis (Petersen & Taylor, 1980). This hypothesis posits that early maturation is a risk factor for adjustment problems among both females and males across a range of outcomes (Brooks-Gunn et al., 1985; Caspi & Moffitt, 1991; Ge, Conger, & Elder, 1996; Tschann et al., 1994). Early maturation may be disadvantageous because early maturers experience social pressure to adopt more adult norms and engage in adult behaviors, even though they may not be socially, emotionally, or cognitively prepared (Brooks-Gunn et al., 1985; Caspi & Moffitt, 1991) for the new experiences. This hypothesis involves the notion of stage termination (Petersen & Taylor, 1980), which means that early maturation disrupts the normal course of development such that early maturers have less time and are less experienced to handle adult behaviors.

Effects of Pubertal Timing on Internalizing Symptoms

Early maturation has been repeatedly associated with more internalizing symptoms and psychological distress in girls, compared to on-time or later maturing peers (Brooks-Gunn et al., 1985; Ge et al., 1996; Graber et al., 1997; Graber et al., 2003; Hayward et al., 1997; Stattin & Magnusson, 1990). During early adolescence, girls begin to manifest higher levels of diagnosed depression and depressive symptoms than boys. By adulthood, rates of depression are approximately 2 to 3 times higher among women than men (Culbertson, 1997; Petersen et al., 1993). In a longitudinal study investigating links between pubertal transition and depressive symptoms in rural White youth living in Iowa, girls began to experience more depression than boys in the eighth grade and this difference persisted through mid- and late adolescence (Ge, Conger, & Elder, 2001a). Girls who experienced menarche at a younger age subsequently experienced a higher level of depressive symptoms than their on-time and late-maturing peers, at each annual assessment during the 6-year study. Additionally, the interaction between early menarche and recent life events predicted subsequent depressive symptoms for girls. Interestingly, the significant main effect of gender on depressive symptoms disappeared when pubertal transition, recent life events, and their interaction were included in models, suggesting that pubertal factors may explain a significant part of the observed gender differences in depressive symptoms during adolescence.

In one of the only studies that has examined long-term consequences of pubertal timing on psychopathology in young adults, young women who had been early maturers (based on self-reports of perceived timing relative to one's peers) continued to have higher lifetime prevalence rates of major depression, anxiety, disruptive behavior disorders, and hence any Axis I psychiatric disorder, as well as higher lifetime rates of attempted suicide in comparison to other women. The on-time and late maturers did not "catch up" in rates of disorder (at least by age 24), and differences in lifetime prevalence rates were maintained into adulthood (Graber et al., 2003).

On the other hand, in boys, findings on links between pubertal timing and internalizing symptoms are more inconsistent. Many of the earlier studies on pubertal timing in boys found that early-maturing boys were better off than their later-maturing counterparts, on measures of social, psychological, and behavioral outcomes (Jones, 1957, 1965; Mussen & Jones, 1957). Studies since the 1950s and 1960s have found more mixed effects. In the NIMH study of puberty and psychopathology, a higher rate of negative emotional tone has been found in late maturing boys in mid and late adolescence as compared to their agemates (Nottelmann et al., 1987). However, studies have also found that early-maturing boys experience more internalizing symptoms (Petersen & Crockett, 1985; Susman et al., 1991; Susman et al., 1985) or that both early- and late maturing boys show more depressive tendencies (Alsaker, 1992). Graber and colleagues (1997) found that late maturing boys experienced more internalizing symptoms than their on-time peers, and that both early- and late maturing boys showed significantly higher rates of depression than on-time maturing boys. In a longitudinal study with White boys living in a rural area, early-maturing boys, compared to their on-time and late-maturing peers, exhibited more internalized distress (Ge, Conger, & Elder, 2001b). Results from a large-scale study of African American boys also indicated that early-maturers reported higher levels of internalizing symptoms (Ge, Brody, Conger, & Simons, in press). In sum, more recent studies of pubertal timing in boys show a trend for early- and late-maturing boys to experience more internalizing symptoms than their on-time peers.

According to the early maturation, or stage-termination, hypothesis, if African American girls are indeed developing earlier than their White counterparts (they are the earliest to mature across ethnic groups), and thus should experience the most stress. So far a few studies have tested links between pubertal timing and adjustment across ethnic groups. While one study found associations between early menarche and depressive symptoms in White girls but not African American or Hispanic girls (Hayward, Gotlib, Schraedley, & Litt, 1999), another study including only African American children ($N = 639$), results showed that early maturing African American girls had higher rates of depressive symptoms (Ge et al., 2003). A study that examined pubertal timing effects across Latina, African American, and White children from economically diverse Chicago neighborhoods found that girls in each ethnic group who matured "off-time," that is, earlier or later than their same-age, same-gender peers, experienced more clinical levels of depression/anxiety, with strongest effects found in White girls (Foster & Brooks-Gunn, manuscript under review). It is important for researchers to further address associations between pubertal change and adjustment in non-White girls and boys, as this group has been understudied. It is possible that girls of different ethnic groups may differ from White children in theoretically important ways, such as in their preparation for puberty or in the responses from others within their ethnic group to their pubertal changes and attitudes about it.

Links Between Pubertal Timing and Externalizing Behaviors

Early maturation in girls has also been identified as a risk factor for externalizing behaviors. Studies show that early maturing girls tend to engage in risky behaviors, such as delinquency, earlier in adolescence and more frequently than their same-age peers (Caspi & Moffitt, 1991; Flannery, Rowe, & Gulley, 1993; Magnusson, Stattin, & Allen, 1985). Early maturing girls display more adverse outcomes if they had a history of behavior problems prior to puberty (Caspi & Moffitt, 1991) and have higher lifetime histories of disruptive behavior disorder in the high school years (Graber et al., 1997). Additionally, early-maturing girls show earlier onset and higher levels of substance abuse behaviors, such as cigarette smoking and alcohol drinking, compared to their on-time and late maturing age-mates (Aro & Taipale, 1987; Dick, Rose, Viken, & Kaprio, 2000; Magnusson et al., 1985). In the National Longitudinal Study of Adolescent Health, early-maturing girls in the seventh grade were three times more likely to be in the most advanced stage of substance use (involving alcohol use, drunkenness, cigarette use, and marijuana use) than the girls in the on-time/late group and in general, early developers were more likely to advance in substance use, regardless of their level at Grade 7 (Lanza & Collins, 2002). Early maturers show a higher current and lifetime prevalence for substance use (Graber et al., 1997), although other longitudinal data suggests that the association between early maturation and substance use holds only for girls whose advanced developmental status, relative to same-age peers, remained stable between the ages of 12 and 14 (Dick, Rose, Pulkkinen, & Kaprio, 2001).

For boys, the research on externalizing behaviors has mostly indicated effects for early maturers, or for both early- and late-maturing boys compared to their on-time peers. For example, both early- and late maturing boys have been found to have higher rates of delinquency than their on-time maturing peers (Williams & Dunlop, 1999). Early-maturing boys have been found to be at higher risk for early onset of sexual activity and tobacco and alcohol use (Graber et al., 1997; Kaltiala-Heino, Rimpela, Rissanen, & Rantanen, 2001; Wichstrom, 2001). On the other hand, in their examination of long-term consequences of pubertal timing, Graber and colleagues (2003) found that it was the late maturers, in comparison to other men, who had elevated onset of disruptive behavior and substance use disorders during the transition to adulthood.

In sum, early maturation is a consistent predictor to the onset of internalizing symptoms and externalizing behaviors in girls. Effects of both early and late maturation have been found for boys. Pubertal timing effects may be most pronounced during early adolescence and decrease during late adolescence (Weichold, Silbereisen, & Schmitt-Rodermund, 2003), although the literature on this point is rather limited. When inconsistencies in findings occur, possible reasons may be the different methods of measuring pubertal timing and the different ways of assessing outcome variables. It should be noted that the majority of research on pubertal timing has focused on its short-term consequences and more research on the long-term consequences is needed. Also, researchers should consider the duration of timing status, that is, how long adolescents remain consistently early or late, as one study has suggested that effects of timing were found only when interindividual differences in timing remained stable over adolescence (Dick et al., 2000).

Examining Effects of Earliest Pubertal Changes on Mood in Preadolescent Girls

Our group has conducted an exploratory investigation in order to examine pubertal and hormonal effects on mood during the time when pubertal hormones are expected to be increasing prior to and along with early changes in secondary sexual characteristics (Archibald, Graber, & Brooks-Gunn, 2004). Participants were 76 preadolescent girls of varied ethnic backgrounds: White ($n = 36$), African American ($n = 25$), and Latina ($n = 15$). Girls were recruited in 1995 from public and parochial schools from integrated, working- and middle-class communities in outlying areas of New York City. Mean age of girls at the first (Time 1) and second time (Time 2) of assessment was 8.34 years ($SD = .48$) and

9.25 years (*SD* = .44), respectively. The majority of girls (69%) were living in two-parent households (55% with biological parents). About a quarter (24%) of the girls' families were living below the federal poverty level (based on income-to-needs ratio); 42% of the girls' families were living at the 1995 U.S. median/modal annual income of $34,500.

Girls completed Daily Mood Diaries (Buchanan, 1991) on two consecutive evenings at Time 1 and at Time 2. Girls rated on a 5-point Likert scale the degree to which they experienced a range of feelings (excited, sad, impatient, happy, tired, friendly, ashamed, nervous, proud) on the particular day that they completed the diary. Principal components factor analyses were conducted to determine how many underlying constructs or dimensions accounted for the majority of variance in the Daily Mood Diary. A "positive mood" dimension emerged, which consisted of happy, excited, and proud moods. Girls' scores on these three moods were averaged across the two days at each time point to yield positive mood scores. The negative moods on the Daily Mood Diary failed to significantly load together on one or more factors, and thus, failed to result in a reliable mood composite. It appeared that anger and sadness were the more distinct emotions or feelings and they were therefore used as separate dependent variables. Girls' scores on each of these negative moods were separately averaged across each of the 2 days at each time point to yield composite mood scores at Time 1 and Time 2. Mood composite scores served as indices of mood intensity. Consistent with the technique used by Buchanan (1991), variability of each mood was defined as the variance of each girl's daily mood composite over the 2 days at each time point.

To assess pubertal status, mothers completed Tanner ratings (Marshall & Tanner, 1969) of their daughters' breast and pubic hair development. A combined pubertal status variable was created by taking the mean of each girl's breast development and pubic hair development stage at each time of assessment. Additionally, change scores were computed to determine degree of change in pubertal status from Time 1 to Time 2. To assess pubertal hormone levels, girls separately collected morning and afternoon urine samples on two consecutive days. Samples were assayed for levels of gonadotropins, luteinizing hormone (LH) and follicle stimulating hormone (FSH) by a physician-trained lab technician. For the analyses, a ratio of morning hormone levels was used because of their relative uniformity and high concentration (Saketos, Sharma, Adel, Raghuwanshi, & Santoro, 1994) and because single daytime measurements do not reliably indicate stage of puberty (Grumbach & Styne, 1998). Since LH shows periodic bursts while FSH increases more steadily in the earliest stages of puberty, a LH/FSH ratio should tap "bursting/pulsing." Change scores were also computed to determine the degree of change in ratio of morning hormone levels from Time 1 to Time 2. Pubertal timing was categorized as "early-maturing girls" (Tanner stage 2 or greater at Time 1; *n* = 31) versus "physically prepubertal girls" (*n* = 45).

The first research question addressed whether the three aspects of puberty (status, hormone levels, and early timing) were linked to girls' moods at Time 1. Separate ordered regression models were tested to examine direct associations between girls' moods and each pubertal predictor, controlling for age. No significant concurrent associations were found between girls' moods and hormones, secondary sexual characteristics or pubertal timing at Time 1. The lack of association between concurrent pubertal status and mood is not surprising given the few and relatively small links found in previous studies (Buchanan, 1991; Richards & Larson, 1993). Perhaps hormone levels and secondary sexual characteristic development are predictive of moods at a later time point.

The second question assessed whether longitudinal changes in the three aspects of puberty were linked to dimensions of girls' moods at Time 2. Separate ordered regression models were tested to examine the direct effects of girls' moods at Time 2 of changes in secondary sexual characteristics and hormone levels, controlling for age. Increases in LH/FSH over the two time points were predictive of greater anger intensity at Time 2. This relationship remained significant after accounting for increases in secondary sexual characteristic development in follow-up analyses. This finding suggests that girls experience the earliest hormonal changes of puberty negatively, as evidenced by higher anger intensity

Because no significant effects were found when testing linear associations between secondary sexual characteristic change and mood indices, an alternative approach to these analyses was undertaken to determine if patterns of change in secondary sexual characteristics were more salient than difference scores. Five groups of Tanner pubertal status change were identified over time:

1. Prepubertal: combined Tanner stage of 1 at each time point
2. Beginning puberty: moving from *prepubertal* at Time 1 to low-mid stages of puberty at Time 2
3. Stable in lower stages of puberty: combined Tanner score of 1.5 at each time point
4. Lower stages of puberty and increasing: Tanner score of 1.5 at Time 1 and increasing to mid-puberty by Time 2
5. Mid-pubertal and increasing: combined Tanner stage 2 or 3 at Time 1 and increasing to 4 or 5 at Time 2 Separate Tanner Change Group × Time Point (5 × 2) repeated measures analysis of variance models were tested using mood intensity and variability scores as the outcome variables. A significant Tanner Change Group × Time Point interaction was found for positive mood intensity, in that girls who were in the *stable low puberty* group were experiencing the most positive mood at each time point and remained highly positive in their mood over time. Girls who were *beginning puberty* showed the greatest decreases in positive mood over time, and had the lowest positive mood scores at Time 2. A trend-level Tanner Change Group × Time Point interaction was found for sad intensity, in that girls who were *beginning* puberty showed the greatest increases in sad mood over time, and were experiencing the most sadness at Time 2 of all the girls. Girls who were *mid-pubertal at Time 1 and increasing at Time 2* were experiencing more sad intensity at Time 1, but had decreased by Time 2. Girls in the other groups remained fairly stable over time. This finding is illustrated in Figure 16.5.

Regression results showed that girls' early pubertal timing predicted their increased positive mood at Time 2. Separate Pubertal Timing × Time Point repeated measures analysis of variance models were also tested to assess if early pubertal timing accentuated the experience of more intense or variable

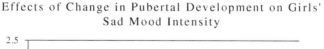

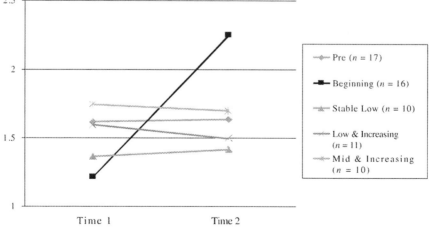

Figure 16.5   Tanner Change Group × Time Point Interaction for sad mood intensity. Girls who were beginning puberty showed the greatest increases in sad mood over time, and were experiencing the most sadness at Time 2 of all the girls. Girls who were mid-pubertal at Time 1 and increasing at Time 2 were experiencing more sad intensity at Time 1, but had decreased by Time 2. Girls in the other groups remained fairly stable over time. From Archibald, Graber, and Brooks-Gunn (2005).

moods over time. Contrary to prior literature, results indicated that early maturing girls had higher positive mood scores at Time 1 and increased in positive moods over the two time points, with other girls showing decreases in positive moods over the two time points. Girls' anger intensity and variability increased over time regardless of pubertal timing group. Given that most of the existing literature on pubertal timing examined effects for girls in the later or post-pubertal years, the present early timing effects on positive mood in younger girls may not be inconsistent. Possibly, the negative effects of early maturation may not be evident until around the age the girls begin middle school, which would suggest contextual effects of puberty. Stattin and Magnusson (1990) found that most negative effects occur when girls are nearly fully developed, viewed by others as older than they are, and unable to meet the social pressures this may impose.

In sum, findings of this study suggest that beginning secondary sexual characteristic development may be experienced most negatively by girls over the short-term, and that stability or lack of change in development (at least in the earliest stages of puberty) may be experienced most positively. The implication of these findings is that a faster *rate* of pubertal change, specifically during early puberty, may be most salient to mood. Even though the groups of girls for these analyses were particularly small, these should be viewed as preliminary findings that illuminate the need for researchers to consider not only stage of pubertal development, but also the rate and possibly sensitive periods of pubertal development.

PROPOSED MECHANISMS FOR EXPLAINING PUBERTAL EFFECTS ON ADJUSTMENT

Although tests of specific pathways that might be predicted from each of the preceding hypotheses have not been conducted, several pathways have been proposed. One such pathway is the individual diathesis-stress model. This model is based on the idea that it is not puberty per se that is associated with more negative developmental outcomes, but that puberty accentuates the effects of psychosocial factors that exist prior to the onset of puberty. The transitional stress model posits that pubertal development is a biological transition that may be linked with increases in emotional arousal or distress. Finally, contextual models will be described, which focus on the role of the social factors and contexts that coincide with the period of pubertal development.

Individual Diathesis-Stress Model

The individual diathesis-stress model posits that psychosocial vulnerability factors that exist prior to adolescence accentuate the probability of increases in emotional distress in interaction with pubertal development (Caspi & Moffitt, 1991; Dorn & Chrousos, 1997; Nolen-Hoeksema & Girgus, 1994; Susman, Dorn, & Schiefelbein, 2003). For example, this model was supported by a longitudinal study of the behavioral responses of adolescent girls to the onset of menarche (Caspi & Moffitt, 1991). Beginning at age 3, girls were assessed with a battery of psychological, medical, and sociological measures every 2 years, through age 15. Systematic interactions between premenarcheal personality and age of onset of menarche were examined. Results indicated that the early onset of menarche magnified and accentuated behavioral problems among girls who were predisposed to behavior problems earlier in childhood. The group that experienced the most adjustment difficulties throughout adolescence was the early maturing girls with a history of behavioral problems earlier in childhood. In order to further test this model, longitudinal studies are needed in which levels of adjustment, the risk factors for poor adjustment, and the pubertal challenges with which these risk factors might interact are tracked as children transition from childhood into adolescence (Nolen-Hoeksema & Girgus, 1994). Studies on puberty have rarely explored the full range of adolescence, including the transition from childhood and the transition into adulthood. As such, many studies miss the onset of puberty for a portion of their samples, which makes it challenging to validate this model.

Transitional Stress Model

The basis of the transitional stress model is that reproductive transitions are periods of development that involve reorganization of biological and behavioral systems (Susman, 1997, 1998). This reorganization may increase emotional arousal and the onset of psychiatric disorders (Dorn & Chrousos, 1997). For example, in the case of depression, aroused physiological states may trigger increased moodiness, sudden mood changes, feelings of self-consciousness, or elevated intensity of moods, all of which, if interpreted negatively, could lead to adjustment problems. The following study by our research group uses the transitional stress model as its underlying theoretical framework.

Examining Pathways Between Pubertal Effects and Adjustment in Girls

Proposed pathways between pubertal effects and adjustment were examined in a study of 100 adolescent girls between the ages of 10 to 14 (Graber, Brooks-Gunn, & Warren, in press). Girls were from well-educated, middle to upper-middle class families in a major northeastern urban area. Measures of pubertal status included Tanner ratings for breast and pubic hair development. Pubertal timing comparisons were made for early maturing versus other girls; girls were classified as early using norms for Tanner Stages by age from the National Health Examination Survey (Duke, Jennings, Dornbusch, & Siegel-Gorelick, 1982). Blood samples were obtained from each girl in the mid-afternoon at the time of the laboratory visit. Samples were assayed for estradiol, testosterone, LH (luteinizing hormone), FSH (follicle stimulating hormone), and DHEAS (dehydroepiandosterone sulfate). Since prior studies with this sample have found effects for estradiol and DHEAS on depression and aggression, respectively, (Brooks-Gunn & Warren, 1989; Warren & Brooks-Gunn, 1989), this study only examined these hormones in order to follow up on underlying pathways for prior effects. Estradiol categories were created (0/1 code) to designate girls experiencing rapid change in estradiol levels versus those at stable levels (see Warren & Brooks-Gunn, 1989). DHEAS was examined as a continuous variable. Outcome measures include the depressive affect and aggression subscales of the Youth Self-Report (Achenbach, 1991). Three potential mediators of timing effects were examined - emotional arousal, attention difficulties, and negative life events. A measure of emotional arousal was created from 6 items on the YSR, predominantly from the Anxious-Obsessive subscale, based on a conceptual framework for emotional arousal. Similarly, an attention scale was created from 5 YSR items. Girls also completed a measure of life events covering the domains of family, school, and peer events, and sum score of negative life events across contexts was computed.

A series of regression models were run to examine the potential mediated pathways from either hormonal levels or pubertal timing to depressive affect or aggression, controlling for age. Despite the hypothesis that estradiol would lead to emotional arousal which would lead to depression, there was no support for this pathway in the analyses. However, as seen in Figure 16.6, the effect of pubertal timing on depressive affect was mediated by emotional arousal. The fact that emotional arousal did not explain the estradiol effect on depressive affect as expected warranted further exploration. Because links between adrenal response (e.g., cortisol response) and psychosocial stress have been extensively noted, DHEAS levels (another indicator of adrenal response) were examined in association with early maturation. The interaction between hormonal arousal (the upper third of the distribution of DHEAS considered high hormonal arousal) and timing (early versus other) was predictive of depressive affect and had a trend toward predicting the emotional arousal construct. Figure 16.7 illustrates that girls who were early maturers and who had high hormonal arousal as tapped by higher levels of DHEAS had the highest reports of depressive affect; a similar pattern is seen for emotional arousal. That is, this subgroup of early-maturing girls about age 12 with increased levels of DHEAS showed elevated emotional arousal and depressive affect.

The findings for aggression in this study are more difficult to explain. Pubertal timing was not associated with aggression in these analyses despite previous findings of an early maturation effect for conduct disorder in girls (e.g., Graber et al., 1997). Two reasons are suggested that may explain the lack of association. First, other studies examined delinquency or conduct disorder as outcomes, while this study analyzed mostly verbal aggression. Second, it has been found that early-maturing girls in mixed-gender schools had higher levels of behavior problems than other girls; however, early-maturing girls in single-sex schools did not have elevated behavior problems (Caspi, Lynam, Moffitt, & Silva, 1993). Since the sample of girls in the present study was drawn predominantly from private girls' schools, perhaps the absence of an effect of timing on aggression is consistent with the interaction of timing and school context found by Caspi and colleagues (1993).

Although aggression was not associated with early timing, it was associated with hormonal measures and some mediated pathways were identified. Mediated associations with aggression via negative life events were found for both estradiol category and DHEAS, as seen in Figure 16.8. Rapidly changing estradiol levels were associated with reporting more negative life events which predicated increased aggression. A similar mediation occurred for DHEAS, except that DHEAS was negatively associated with negative life events and aggression. The negative association between DHEAS and aggression has been found by others (e.g., Susman et al., 1987). Also, persistent low levels of cortisol, another adrenal hormone, have been linked with higher rates of aggression in boys (McBurnett, Lahey, Rathouz, & Loeber, 2000).

In sum, a goal of this study was to move beyond the demonstration of main effects and to better understand potential pathways that underlie effects. Results indicate that unique associations between different hormonal axes (HPG and HPA) and affect (depressive and aggressive) may be occurring. One limitation to the study is that it has a cross-sectional design, therefore, bi-directional associations were not tested. The sample included White, middle- and upper-middle-class families, so it is unclear whether effects can be generalized to more diverse samples. Two of the mediating constructs, emotional arousal and attention difficulties, were measured using scales created for this study (comprised of YSR items) based on conceptual frameworks. The validity of these scales has not been established. A future direction for the examination of pathways linking pubertal effects and adjustment would be to develop more comprehensive assessment of various aspects of arousal.

Contextual Models

Another proposed pathway linking pubertal changes with adjustment takes social factors such as familial support and peer relations into account. The biological and social changes of puberty may vary systematically with the family, peer, school, or neighborhood contexts in which they occur (Petersen & Taylor, 1980). Different contexts may amplify or attenuate the effects of pubertal factors on adjustment. Factors that have been shown to amplify negative effects of pubertal timing include association with deviant peers, adverse parenting, living in dangerous neighborhoods, or negative life events in general (Brooks-Gunn & Warren, 1989; Ge, Conger, Lorenz, & Simons, 1994). Conversely, positive factors such as parental support and warmth have been found to buffer the potential stressful effects of the pubertal transition (Ge et al., 1994; Petersen, Sargiani, & Kennedy, 1991).

A study by Brooks-Gunn and Warren (1985) illustrates how effects of puberty are mediated by social context. The study examined effects of menarcheal timing in a sample of ballet dancer and nondancer girls aged 14 to 18. Girls who were 1.2 years earlier or later than the mean menarcheal age of 12.6 to 12.8 years for American White adolescents (Damon, Damon, Reed, & Valadian, 1969) were classified as early or late maturers. In the nondance school sample, 11% of the girls were early, 59% were on time, and 57% were late. In contrast, 6% of the dance students were early, 38% on time, and 57% late. Another difference between groups was that dancers weighed less and were leaner than nondancers, and dancers expressed more concern about their weight. Since so few dancers were early, only on-time and late maturers were compared across social context. On-time dancers had higher psychopathology, perfection, and bulimia scores and lower body image scores than the late maturing dancers; while these effects were not found for the nondancers. The different self-standards of dancers, particularly in regards to maintaining a low body weight, seem to account for the sample differences. Additional analyses with the same sample showed that effects of physical maturation on dating differed between dancers and nondancers (Gargiulo, Attie, Brooks-Gunn, & Warren, 1987). Postmenarcheal dancer girls had higher dating scores than premenarcheal dancer girls, while menarcheal status was not associated with dating behavior in the nondance sample. Although speculative, it is possible that menarche may mean something different to the dancer, or that the postmenarcheal dancer may identify less with the ideals of the dance world and thus begin to date. The results of these studies illustrate a goodness of fit between the requirements of a social context and a person's physical and behavioral characteristics.

FUTURE DIRECTIONS/CONCLUSIONS

Puberty is considered the most salient developmental milestone during adolescence, involving pervasive physical and psychological changes. An accumulating body of research in the past few decades has documented how certain aspects of the pubertal transition have effects on adolescents' psychosocial adjustment. In general, these studies have more often focused on girls than boys. The three main dimensions of puberty studied have been hormone changes, secondary sexual characteristic development and menarche, and timing of the pubertal transition compared to one's peers. Although the majority of children adapt well to pubertal changes and do not experience mental health problems during or after the transition (e.g., Offer, 1987), the research indicates that pubertal changes, as well as interactions between pubertal changes and social factors, contribute to adjustment difficulties. One of the most consistent findings has been that early-maturing girls tend to experience more adjustment difficulties than their on-time and late-maturing peers. For boys, findings are more mixed, although early- and late-maturers, compared to their on-time peers, seem to be most at risk. Inconsistencies in the literature most likely stem from different ways of measuring and classifying pubertal development,

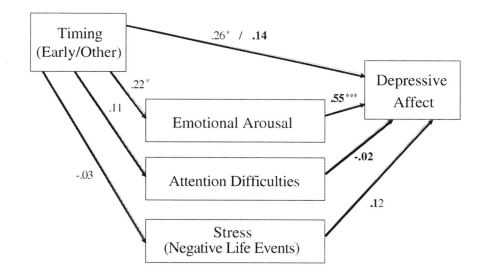

$R^2 = .37$; $F(5, 90) = 9.89$, $p < .0001$; Mediated Pathway via Arousal

Figure 16.6 Path model showing significant mediated pathway between pubertal timing and depressive affect, via emotional arousal. On the left side of the model, the β values were calculated separately for each pathway for each potential mediator. The β coefficients on the right side of the model (shown in bold type) were calculated with all variables (predictors and mediators) entered simultaneously into the model; there are two β coefficients for pubertal timing to depressive affect. From Graber, Brooks-Gunn, & Warren (in press).

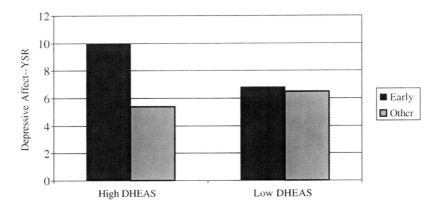

Figure 16.7 The interaction of high DHEAS levels (as an Index of High Adrenal Activity) and early maturation on girls' depressive affect. From J. A. Graber, J. Brooks-Gunn, J., & A. B. Archibald, "Links between puberty and internalizing and externalizing behavior in girls: Moving from demonstrating effects to identifying pathways, in D. M. Stoff & E. J. Susman (Eds.), *Developmental psychobiology of aggression.* Copyright 2005, Cambridge University Press.

different ages at time of outcome assessment, and different conceptual frameworks (i.e., deviance of stage termination hypotheses).

Although the past few decades have been marked by many pioneering studies on the effects of the pubertal transition on adjustment, there are a few key areas to focus on for future research studies. First, as outlined in this chapter, puberty is associated with a multitude of significant biological, psychological, and social changes. Studies that assess interactions between changes in these multiple

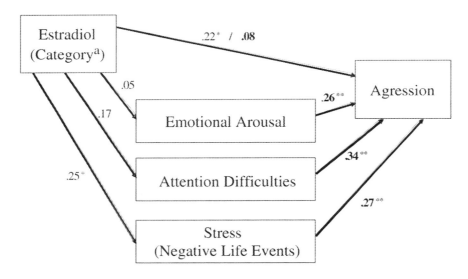

$R^2 = .41$; $F(5, 90) = 11.60$, $p < .0001$; Mediated Pathway via Life Events

Figure 16.8 Path model for estradiol category to aggression, via negative life events. On the left side of the model, the β values were calculated separately from estradiol category to aggression and to each potential mediator. The β coefficients on the right side of the model (shown in bold type) were calculated with all variables (predictors and mediators) entered simultaneously into the model; there are two β coefficients for estradiol category to aggression. From Graber, Brooks-Gunn, & Warren (in press).

domains represent an area of promising future research. Second, the majority of studies on the psychosocial implications of pubertal development have included White samples of children. Especially considering the noted differences between age of pubertal onset and age of menarche for White and African American girls, pubertal research is needed with more ethnically and socioeconomically diverse samples. Third, studies on pubertal development have tended to begin when adolescents are already experiencing the changes of mid- to late puberty. Examining the earliest changes of puberty, such as the initial increases of luteinizing hormone, would give a more complete picture of how adolescents adjust to the entry into puberty. Additionally, some studies have indicated that rate of pubertal development and duration of pubertal timing status may have effects on adjustment outcomes (e.g., Archibald et al., 2004; Dick et al., 2000). Future studies need to further explore the effects of rate and duration of pubertal development on adjustment. Fourth, there is a need for longitudinal studies that follow children throughout the span of pubertal development and beyond, in order to better understand the longer-term effects of the pubertal transition on adjustment. Most studies from the past few decades have been cross-sectional or short-term, so it is not clear whether the effects of puberty persist over time. Finally, there has been a disconnect on the literature on factors affecting pubertal onset and pubertal factors associated with adjustment outcomes (see Graber, 2003). A future direction for research would be to jointly explore the precursors of puberty and the outcomes of puberty, in order to determine whether processes associated with onset of puberty also play a role in whether puberty influences subsequent adjustment outcomes.

ACKNOWLEDGMENTS

Preparation of this chapter was supported in part by the National Institute of Mental Health, the National Institute of Child Health and Human Development, the National Institute of Child Health and Human Development Research Network on Child and Family Well-Being, the Marx Family Foundation, and the William T. Grant Foundation.

NOTE

1. During early infancy, it may be the case that the gonadostat is not completely mature, meaning it is insensitive to the presence of gonadal sex steroids (Fechner, 2003). Maturation of the gonadostat could be described as increased sensitivity to the negative feedback of gonadal sex steroids, which inhibits the GnRH pulse activator during childhood. The mechanism by which the GnRH pulse activator t is "dis-inhibited" in order for puberty to commence is not clear.

REFERENCES

Achenbach, T. M. (1991). *Manual for the Youth Self-Report and 1991 Profile*. Burlington: University of Vermont, Department of Psychiatry.

Ahmed, M. L., Ong, K. K. L., Morrell, D. J., Cox, L., Drayer, N., Perry, L., et al. (1999). Longitudinal study of leptin concentrations during puberty: Sex differences and relationship to changes in body composition. *Journal of Clinical Endocrinology and Metabolism, 84*, 899–905.

Alsaker, F. D. (1992). Pubertal timing, overweight, and psychological adjustment. *Journal of Early Adolescence, 12*, 396–419.

Alsaker, F. D. (1995). Tiiming of puberty and reactions to pubertal changes. In M. Rutter (Ed.), *Psychosocial disturbances in young people: challenges for prevention* (pp. 37–82). Cambridge: Cambridge University Press.

Alsaker, F. D. (1996). Annotation: the impact of puberty. *Journal of Child Psychology and Psychiatry, 37*, 249–258.

Angold, A., Costello, E. J., Erkanli, A., & Worthman, C. W. (1999). Pubertal changes in hormone levels and depression in girls. *Psychological Medicine, 29*, 1043–1053.

Angold, A., Costello, E. J., & Worthman, C. W. (1998). Puberty and depression: the roles of age, pubertal status and pubertal timing. *Psychological Medicine, 28*, 51–61.

Angold, A., Worthman, C. M., & Costello, E. J. (2003). Puberty and depression. In C. Hayward (Ed.), *Gender differences at puberty* (pp. 137–164). New York: Cambridge University Press.

Archibald, A. B., Graber, J., & Brooks-Gunn, J. (2005). Effects of the earliest pubertal and hormonal changes on pre-adolescent girls' moods: A short-term longitudinal study. Manuscript submitted for publication.

Aro, H., & Taipale, V. (1987). The impact of timing of puberty on psychosomatic symptoms among fourteen- to sixteen-year-old Finnish girls. *Child Development, 58*, 261–268.

Arslanian, S., Suprasongsin, C., & Janosky, J. (1997). Insulin secretion and sensitivity in black vs. white prepubertal healthy children. *Journal of Clinical Endocrinology and Metabolism, 82*, 1923–1927.

Attie, I., & Brooks-Gunn, J. (1989). Development of eating problems in adolescent girls: A longitudinal study. *Developmental Psychology, 25*, 70–79.

Barash, I. A., Cheung, C. C., Weigle, D. S., Ren, H., Kabigting, E. B., Kuijper, J. L., et al. (1996). Leptin is a metabolic signal to the reproductive system. *Endocrinology, 137*, 2144–3147.

Blum, W. F., Englaro, P., Hanitsch, S., Juul, A., Hertel, N. T., Muller, J., et al. (1997). Plasma leptin levels in healthy children and adolescents: Dependence on body mass index, body fat mass, gender, pubertal stage, and testosterone. *Journal of Clinical Endocrinology and Metabolism, 82*, 2904–2910.

Brooks-Gunn, J. (1984). The psychological significance of different pubertal events to young girls. *Journal of Early Adolescence, 4*, 315–327.

Brooks-Gunn, J. (1987). Pubertal processes and girls' psychological adaptation. In R. Lerner & T. T. Foch (Eds.), *Biological-psychosocial interactions in early adolescence:*

A *life-span perspective* (pp. 123–153). Hillsdale, NJ: Erlbaum.

Brooks-Gunn, J., Graber, J., & Paikoff, R. L. (1994). Studying links between hormones and negative affect: Models and measures. *Journal of Research on Adolescence, 4,* 469–486.

Brooks-Gunn, J., Newman, D. L., Holderness, C., & Warren, M. P. (1994). The experience of breast development and girls' stories about the purchase of a bra. *Journal of Youth and Adolescence, 23,* 539–565.

Brooks-Gunn, J., & Petersen, A. C. (1983). *Girls at puberty: Biological and psychosocial perspectives.* New York: Academic.

Brooks-Gunn, J., Petersen, A. C., & Compas, B. (1995). Physiological processes and the development of childhood and adolescent depression. In I. M. Goodyer (Ed.), *The depressed child and adolescent: Developmental and clinical perspectives* (pp. 81–109). New York: Cambridge University Press.

Brooks-Gunn, J., Petersen, A. C., & Eichorn, D. (1985). The study of maturational timing effects in adolescence. *Journal of Youth and Adolescence, 14,* 149–161.

Brooks-Gunn, J., & Reiter, E. O. (1990). The role of pubertal processes. In S. S. Feldman & G. R. Elliott (Eds.), *At the threshold: The developing adolescent* (pp. 16–53). Cambridge: Harvard University Press.

Brooks-Gunn, J., & Ruble, D. N. (1982). The development of menstrual–related beliefs and behaviors during early adolescence. *Child Development, 53,* 1567–1577.

Brooks-Gunn, J., & Warren, M. P. (1985). Measuring physical status and timing in early adolescence: a developmental perspective. *Journal of Youth and Adolescence, 14,* 163–189.

Brooks-Gunn, J., & Warren, M. P. (1988). The psychological significance of secondary sexual characteristics in nine- to eleven-year-old girls. *Child Development, 59,* 1061–1069.

Brooks-Gunn, J., & Warren, M. P. (1989). Biological and social contributions to negative affect in young adolescent girls. *Child Development, 60,* 40–55.

Brooks-Gunn, J., Warren, M. P., Rosso, J., & Gargiulo, J. (1987). Validity of self-report measures of girls' pubertal status. *Child Development, 58,* 829–841.

Brooks-Gunn, J., Warren, M. P., Samelson, M., & Fox, R. (1986). Physical similarity of and disclosure of menarcheal status to friends: Effects of age and pubertal status. *Journal of Early Adolescence, 6,* 3–14.

Buchanan, C. M. (1991). Pubertal status in early-adolescent girls: Relations to moods, energy, and restlessness. *Journal of Early Adolescence, 11,* 185–200.

Buchanan, C. M., Eccles, J. S., & Becker, J. B. (1992). Are adolescents the victims of raging hormones: Evidence for activational effects of hormones on moods and behavior at adolescence. *Psychological Bulletin, 111,* 62–107.

Casper, R. (1998). Growing up female. In R. Casper (Ed.), *Women's health: hormones, emotions, and behavior* (Vol. XVIII, pp. 1–14). Cambridge: Cambridge University Press.

Caspi, A., Lynam, D., Moffitt, T. E., & Silva, P. A. (1993). Unraveling girls' delinquency: Biological, dispositional, and contextual contributions to adolescent misbehavior. *Developmental Psychology, 29,* 19–30.

Caspi, A., & Moffitt, T. E. (1991). Individual differences are accentuated during periods of social change: The sample case of girls at puberty. *Journal of Personality and Social Psychology, 61,* 157–168.

Clayton, P. E., & Trueman, J. A. (2000). Leptin and puberty. *Archives of Disease in Childhood, 83,* 1–4.

Colon, I., Caro, D., Bourdony, C. J., & Rosario, O. (2000). Identification of phthalate esters in the serum of young Puerto Rican girls with premature breast development. *Environmental Health Perspectives, 108,* 895–900.

Connolly, S. D., Paikoff, R. L., & Buchanan, C. M. (1996). Puberty: the interplay of biological and psychosocial processes in adolescence. In G. R. Adams, R. Montemayor & T. P. Gullotta (Eds.), *Psychosocial development during adolescence* (pp. 173–188). Thousand Oaks, CA: Sage.

Culbertson, F. M. (1997). Depression and gender: An international review. *American Psychologist, 52,* 25–31.

Damon, A., Damon, S. T., Reed, R. B., & Valadian, I. (1969). Age at menarche of mothers and daughters, with a note on accuracy of recall. *Human Biology, 41,* 161–175.

Dick, D. M., Rose, R. J., Pulkkinen, L., & Kaprio, J. (2001). Measuring puberty and understanding its impact: A longitudinal study of adolescent twins. *Journal of Youth and Adolescence, 30,* 385–399.

Dick, D. M., Rose, R. J., Viken, R. J., & Kaprio, J. (2000). Pubertal timing and substance use: associations between and within families across late adolescence. *Developmental Psychology, 36,* 180–189.

Dorn, L. D., & Chrousos, G. P. (1997). The neurobiology of stress: Understanding regulation of affect during female biological transitions. *Seminars in Reproductive Endocrinology, 15,* 19–35.

Dorn, L. D., Susman, E. J., Nottelmann, E. D., Inoff-Germain, G., & Chrousos, G. P. (1990). Perceptions of puberty: Adolescent, parent, and health care personnel. *Developmental Psychology, 26,* 322–329.

Dubas, J. S., Graber, J. A., & Petersen, A. C. (1991). The effects of pubertal development on achievement during adolescence. *American Journal of Education, 99,* 444–460.

Duke, P. M., Jennings, D. J., Dornbusch, S. M., & Siegel-Gorelick, B. (1982). Educational correlates of early and late sexual maturation in adolescence. *Journal of Pediatrics, 100,* 633–637.

Duke-Duncan, P. M., Ritter, P., Dornbusch, S. M., Gross, R. T., & Carlsmith, J. M. (1985). The effects of pubertal timing on body image, school behavior, and deviance. *Journal of Early Adolescence, 14,* 227–235.

Ellis, B. J., & Garber, J. (2000). Psychosocial antecedents of variation in girls' pubertal timing: maternal depression, stepfather presence, and marital and family stress. *Child Development, 71,* 485–501.

Fara, G. M., Del Corvo, S., Bernuzzi, S., Bigatello, A., Di Pietro, C., Scaglioni, S., et al. (1979). Epidemic of breast enlargement in an Italian school. *Lancet, II,* 295–297.

Fechner, P. Y. (2002). Gender differences in puberty. *Journal of Adolescent Health, 30,* 44–48.

Fechner, P. Y. (2003). The biology of puberty: new developments in sex differences. In C. Hayward (Ed.), *Gender differences at puberty* (pp. 17–28). New York: Cambridge University Press.

Feldman, S., & Elliott, G. (1990). *At the threshold: The developing adolescent.* Cambridge: Harvard University Press.

Flannery, D. J., Rowe, D. C., & Gulley, B. L. (1993). Impact of pubertal status, timing, and age on adolescent sexual experience and delinquency. *Journal of Adolescent Research, 8,* 21–40.

Foster, H., & Brooks-Gunn, J. Pubertal timing effects by gender and ethnicity in the transition to adolescence. Manuscript under review.

Gaddis, A., & Brooks-Gunn, J. (1985). The male experience of pubertal change. *Journal of Youth and Adolescence, 14,* 61–69.

Garcia-Mayor, R. V., Andrade, A., Rios, M., Lage, M., Dieguez, C., & Casanueva, F.F. (1997). Serum leptin levels in normal children: Relationship to age, gender, body mass index, pituitary-gonadal hormones, and pubertal stage. *Journal of Clinical Endocrinology and Metabolism, 82,* 2849–2855.

Gargiulo, J., Attie, I., Brooks-Gunn, J., & Warren, M. P. (1987). Girls' dating behavior as a function of social context and maturation. *Developmental Psychology, 23,* 730–737.

Ge, X., Brody, G. H., Conger, R. D., & Simons, R. L. (in press). Pubertal transition and African American children's internalizing and externalizing symptoms. *Journal of Youth and Adolescence.*

Ge, X., Conger, R. D., & Elder, G. H., Jr. (1996). Coming of age too early: Pubertal influences on girls' vulnerability to psychological distress. *Child Development, 67,* 3386–3400.

Ge, X., Conger, R. D., & Elder, G. H., Jr. (2001a). Pubertal transition, stressful life events, and the emergence of gender differences in adolescent depressive symptoms. *Developmental Psychology, 37,* 404–417.

Ge, X., Conger, R. D., & Elder, G. H., Jr. (2001b). The relationship between puberty and psychological distress in adolescent boys. *Journal of Research on Adolescence, 11,* 49–70.

Ge, X., Conger, R. D., Lorenz, F. O., & Simons, R. L. (1994). Parents' stressful life events and adolescent depressed mood. *Journal of Health and Social Behavior, 35,* 28–44.

Ge, X., Kim, I. J., Brody, G. H., Conger, R. D., Simons, R. L., Gibbons, F. X., et al. (2003). It's about timing and change: pubertal transition effects on symptoms of major depression among African American youths. *Developmental Psychology, 39,* 430–439.

Giedd, J. N., Castellanos, F. X., Rajapakse, J. C., Vaituzis, A. C., & Rapoport, J. L. (1997). Sexual dimorphism of the developing human brain. *Progress in Neuro-Psychopharmacology and Biological Psychiatry, 21,* 1185–1201.

Gladen, B. C., Ragan, N. B., & Rogan, W. J. (2000). Pubertal growth and development and prenatal and lactational exposure to polychlorinated biphenyls and dichlorodiphenyl dichloroethene. *Journal of Pediatrics, 136,* 190–196.

Goodman, E., Hinden, B. R., & Khandelwal, S. (2000). Accuracy of teen and parental reports of obesity and body mass index. *Pediatrics, 106,* 52–58.

Graber, J. A. (2003). Puberty in context. In C. Hayward (Ed.), *Gender differences at puberty* (pp. 307–325). New York: Cambridge University Press.

Graber, J. A., & Brooks-Gunn, J. (1996). Transitions and turning points: Navigating the passage from childhood through adolescence. *Developmental Psychology, 32,* 768–776.

Graber, J. A., & Brooks-Gunn, J. (2002). Adolescent girls' sexual development. In G. M. Wingood & R. J. DiClemente (Eds.), *Handbook of women's sexual and reproductive health* (pp. 21–42). New York: Kluwer Academic/Plenum.

Graber, J. A., Brooks-Gunn, J., & Archibald, A. B. (2005). Links between girls' puberty and externalizing and internalizing behaviors: Moving from demonstrating effects to identifying pathways. In D.M. Stoff & E. J. Susman (Eds.), *Developmental psychobiology of aggression* (pp. 87–116). New York: Cambridge University Press.

Graber, J. A., Brooks-Gunn, J., & Warren, M. P. (1995). The antecedents of menarcheal age: Heredity, family environment, and stressful life events. *Child Development, 66,* 346–359.

Graber, J. A., Brooks-Gunn, J., & Warren, M. P. (in press). Pubertal effects on adjustment in girls: Moving from demonstrating effects to identifying pathways. *Journal of Youth and Adolescence.*

Graber, J. A., Lewinsohn, P. M., Seeley, J. R., & Brooks-Gunn, J. (1997). Is psychopathology associated with the timing of pubertal development? *Journal of the American Academy of Adolescent Psychiatry, 36,* 1768–1776.

Graber, J. A., Petersen, A. C., & Brooks-Gunn, J. (1996). Pubertal processes: methods, measures, and models. In J. A. Graber, J. Brooks-Gunn & A. C. Petersen (Eds.), *Transitions through adolescence: Interpersonal domains and context* (pp. 23–53). Mahwah, NJ: Erlbaum.

Graber, J. A., Seeley, J. R., Brooks-Gunn, J., & Lewinsohn, P. M. (2003). Is pubertal timing associated with psychopathology in young adulthood? Manuscript submitted for publication.

Greif, E. B., & Ulman, K. J. (1982). The psychological impact of menarche on early-adolescent females: A review of the literature. *Child Development, 53,* 1413–1430.

Grumbach, M. M., & Styne, D. M. (1998). Puberty: Ontogeny, neuroendocrinology, physiology, and disorders. In J. D. Wilson, D. W. Foster & H. M. Kronenberg (Eds.), *Williams textbook of endocrinology* (pp. 1509–1625). Philadelphia: W.B. Saunders.

Hamburg, B. A. (1974). Coping in early adolescence. In S. Arieti (Ed.), *American handbook of psychiatry* (2nd ed., pp. 212–236). New York: Basic Books.

Harlan, W. R., Harlan, E. A., & Grillo, C. P. (1980). Secondary sex characteristics of girls 12–17 years of age: The U.S. Health Examination Survey. *Journal of Pediatrics, 96,* 1074–1078.

Hayward, C. (2003). Methodological concerns in puberty-related research. In C. Hayward (Ed.), *Gender differences at puberty* (pp. 1–16). New York: Cambridge University Press.

Hayward, C., Gotlib, I., Schraedley, P. K., & Litt, I. F. (1999). Ethnic differences in the association between pubertal status and symptoms of depression in adolescent girls. *Journal of Adolescent Health, 25,* 143–149.

Hayward, C., Killen, J. D., Wilson, D. M., Hammer, L. D., Litt, I. F., Kraemer, H. C., et al. (1997). Psychiatric risk associated with early puberty in adolescent girls. *Journal of the American Academy of Child and Adolescent Psychiatry, 36,* 255–262.

Herman-Giddens, M. E., Slora, E. J., Wasserman, R. C., Bourdony, C. J., Bhapkar, M. V., Koch, G. G., et al. (1997). Secondary sexual characteristics and menses in young girls seen in office practice: a study from the pediatric research in office settings network. *Pediatrics, 99,* 505–512.

Hick, K. M., & Katzman, D. K. (1999). Self-assessment of sexual maturation in adolescent females with anorexia nervosa. *Journal of Adolescent Health, 24,* 206–211.

Hutchison, J. B., Schumacher, M., Steimer, T., & Gahr, M. (1990). Are separable aromatase systems involved in hormonal regulation of the male brain? *Journal of Neurobiology, 21,* 743–759.

Jones, M. C. (1957). The later careers of boys who were early- or late-maturing. *Child Development, 28,* 113–128.

Jones, M. C. (1965). Psychological correlates of somatic development. *Child Development, 36,* 899–911.

Kaltiala-Heino, R. A., Rimpela, M., Rissanen, A., & Rantanen, P. (2001). Early puberty and early sexual activity are associated with bulimic-type eating pathology in middle adolescence. *Journal of Adolescent Health, 28,* 346–352.

Kaplowitz, P. B. (2004). *Early puberty in girls.* New York: The Random House Publishing Group.

Kaplowitz, P. B., Slora, E. J., Wasserman, R. C., Pedlow, S. E., & Herman-Giddens, M. E. (2001). Earlier onset of puberty in girls: Relation to increased body mass index and race. *Pediatrics, 108,* 347–353.

Koff, E., Rierdan, J., & Sheingold, K. (1982). Memories of menarche: Age, preparation, and prior knowledge as determinants of initial menstrual experience. *Journal of Youth and Adolescence, 11*, 1–9.

Krstevska-Komstantinova, M., Charlier, C., Craen, M., Du Caju, M., Heinrichs, C., de Beaufort, C., et al. (2001). Sexual precocity after immigration from developing countries to Belgium: Evidence of previous exposure to organochlorine pesticides. *Human Reproduction Update, 16*, 1020–1026.

Laflamme, N., Nappi, R. E., Drolet, G., Labrie, C., & Rivest, S. (1998). Expression and neuropeptidergic characterization of estrogen receptors (ER alpha and ER beta) throughout the rat brain: anatomical evidence of distinct roles of each subtype. *Journal of Neurobiology, 36*, 357–378.

Lanza, S. T., & Collins, L. M. (2002). Pubertal timing and the onset of substance use in females during early adolescence. *Prevention Science, 3*(1), 69–82.

Layman, L. C. (1995). Molecular biology in reproductive endocrinology. *Current Opinion in Obstetrics and Gynecology, 7*, 328–339.

Leit, R. A., Gray, J. J., & Pope, H. G. (2002). The media's representation of the ideal male body: A cause for muscle dysmorphia? *International Journal of Eating Disorders, 31*, 334–338.

Lipsitz, J. (1977). *Growing up forgotten: A review of research and programs concerning young adolescents.* Lexington, MA: D.C. Heath.

Litt, I. F. (1999). Self-assessment of puberty: problems and potential (editorial). *Journal of Adolescent Health, 24*, 157.

MacLusky, N., & Naftolin, F. (1981). Sexual differentiation of the central nervous system. *Science, 211*, 1294–1302.

Magnusson, D., Stattin, H., & Allen, V. (1985). Biological maturation and social development: A longitudinal study of some adjustment processes from mid-adolescence to adulthood. *Journal of Youth and Adolescence, 14*, 267–283.

Marshall, W. A., & Tanner, J. M. (1969). Variations in the pattern of pubertal changes in girls. *Archives of Disease in Childhood, 44*, 291–303.

Marshall, W. A., & Tanner, J. M. (1970). Variations in the pattern of pubertal changes in boys. *Archives of Disease in Childhood, 45*, 13–23.

McBurnett, K., Lahey, B. B., Rathouz, P. J., & Loeber, R. (2000). Low salivary cortisol and persistent aggression in boys referred for disruptive behavior. *Archives of General Psychiatry, 57*, 38–43.

McEwen, B. S. (1994). How do sex and stress hormones affect nerve cells? *Annals of the New York Academy of Sciences, 743*, 1–18.

Michels Blanck, H., Marcus, M., Tolbert, P. E., Rubin, C., Henderson, A. K., Hertzberg, V. S., et al. (2000). Age at menarche and Tanner stage in girls exposed in utero and postnatally to polybrominated biphenyl. *Epidemiology, 11*, 641–647.

Mitchner, N. A., Garlick, C., & Ben-Jonathon, N. (1998). Cellular distribution and gene regulation of estrogen receptors alpha and beta in the rat pituitary gland. *Endocrinology, 139*, 3976–3983.

Moffitt, T. E., Caspi, A., Belsky, J., & Silva, P. A. (1992). Childhood experience and the onset of menarche: A test of a sociobiological model. *Child Development, 63*, 47–58.

Morris, N. M., & Udry, J. R. (1980). Validation of a self-administered instrument to assess stage of adolescent development. *Journal of Youth and Adolescence, 9*, 271–280.

Morrison, J. A., Barton, B. A., Biro, F., Sprecher, D. L., Falkner, F., & Obarzanek, E. (1994). Sexual maturation and obesity in 9- and 10-year old black and white girls: The National Heart, Lung, and Blood Institute Growth and Health Study. *Journal of Pediatrics, 124*, 889–895.

Mussen, P. H., & Jones, M. C. (1957). Self-conceptions, motivations, and interpersonal attitudes of late- and early-maturing boys. *Child Development, 28*, 243–256.

Nesselroade, J. R., & Baltes, P. B. (1974). Adolescent personality development and historical change: 1970-1972. *Monographs of the Society for Research in Child Development, 39*, ser. no. 154.

Neugarten, B. L. (1979). Time, age and life cycle. *American Journal of Psychiatry, 136*, 887–894.

Nolen-Hoeksema, S., & Girgus, J. S. (1994). The emergence of gender differences in depression during adolescence. *Psychological Bulletin, 115*, 424–443.

Nottelmann, E. D., Susman, E. J., Inoff-Germain, G., Cutler, G. B., Loriaux, D. L., & Chrousos, G. P. (1987). Developmental processes in American early adolescence: Relations between adolescent adjustment problems and chronologic age, pubertal stage and puberty-related serum hormone levels. *Journal of Pediatrics, 110*, 473–480.

Obeidallah, D. A., Brennan, R. T., Brooks-Gunn, J., & Earls, F. (2004). Links between puberty timing, neighborhood contexts, and girls' violent behavior. *Journal of the American Academy of Child and Adolescent Psychiatry, 43*, 1460–1468.

Obeidallah, D. A., Brennan, R. T., Brooks-Gunn, J., Kindlon, D., & Earls, F. (2000). Socioeconomic status, race, and girls' pubertal maturation: Results from the Project on Human Development in Chicago Neighborhoods. *Journal of Research on Adolescence, 10*, 443–488.

Offer, D. (1987). In defense of adolescents. *Journal of the American Medical Association, 257*, 3407–3408.

Osterlund, M., Kuiper, G. G., Custafsson, J. A., & Hurd, Y. L. (1998). Differential distribution and regulation of estrogen receptor-alpha and -beta mRNA within the female rat brain. *Brain Research: Molecular Brain Research, 54*, 175–180.

Paikoff, R., Brooks-Gunn, J., & Warren, M. P. (1991). Predictive effects of hormonal change on affective expression in adolescent females over the course of one year. *Journal of Youth and Adolescence, 20*, 191–214.

Paikoff, R. L., & Brooks-Gunn, J. (1991). Do parent-child relationships change during puberty? *Psychological Bulletin, 110*, 47–66.

Paretsch, C.-J., & Sippell, W. G. (2001). Pathogenesis and epidemiology of precocious puberty: Effects of exogenous oestrogens. *Human Reproduction Update, 7*, 292–302.

Parker, S., Nichter, M., Nichter, M., Vuckovic, N., Sims, C., & Ritenbaugh, C. (1995). Body image and weight concerns among African American and white adolescent females: Differences that make a difference. *Human Organization, 54*, 103–114.

Persson, I., Ahlsson, F., Ewald, U., Tuvemo, T., Qingyuan, M., von Rosen, D., et al. (1999). Influence of perinatal factors on the onset of puberty in boys and girls: Implications for interpretation of link with risk of long term diseases. *American Journal of Epidemiology, 150*, 747–755.

Petersen, A. C. (1987). The nature of biological-psychosocial interactions: The sample case of early adolescence. In R. M. Lerner & T. T. Foch (Eds.), *Biological-psychosocial interactions in early adolescence: A life-span perspective* (pp. 35–61). Hillsdale, NJ: Erlbaum.

Petersen, A. C., Compas, B., Brooks-Gunn, J., Stemmler, M., Ey, S., & Grant, K. (1993). Depression in adolescence. *American Psychologist, 48*, 155–168.

Petersen, A. C., Crockett, L., Richards, M., & Boxer, A. (1988).

A self-report measure of pubertal status: Reliability, validity, and initial norms. *Journal of Youth and Adolescence, 17*, 117–133.

Petersen, A. C., & Crockett, L. J. (1985). Pubertal timing and grade effects on adjustment. *Journal of Youth and Adolescence, 14*, 191–206.

Petersen, A. C., Sargiani, P. A., & Kennedy, R. E. (1991). Adolescent depression: Why more girls? *Journal of Youth and Adolescence, 20*, 247–271.

Petersen, A. C., & Taylor, B. (1980). The biological approach to adolescence: Biological change and psychological adaptation. In J. Adelson (Ed.), *Handbook of adolescent psychology* (pp. 117–155). New York: Wiley.

Phoenix, C. H., Goy, R. W., Gerall, A. A., & Young, W. C. (1959). Organizing action of prenatally administered testosterone propionate on the tissues mediating mating behavior in the female guinea pig. *Endocrinology, 65*, 369–382.

Rasmussen, J. E., Torres-Aleman, I., MacLusky, N. J., Naftolin, F., & Robbins, R. J. (1990). The effects of estradiol on the growth patterns of estrogen receptor-positive hypothalamic cell lines. *Endocrinology, 126*, 235–240.

Reiter, E. O., & Grumbach, M. M. (1982). Neuroendocrine control mechanisms and the onset of puberty. *Annual Review of Physiology, 44*, 595–613.

Richards, M., & Larson, L. (1993). Pubertal development and the daily subjective states of young adolescents. *Journal of Research on Adolescence, 3*, 145–169.

Rierdan, J., & Koff, E. (1997). Weight, weight-related aspects of body image, and depression in early adolescent girls. *Adolescence, 32*, 615–624.

Rockett, J. C., Lynch, C. D., & Buck, G. M. (2004). Biomarkers for assessing reproductive development and health: Part I-Pubertal Development. *Environmental Health Perspectives, 112*, 105–112.

Ruble, D. N., & Brooks-Gunn, J. (1982). The experience of menarche. *Child Development, 53*, 1557–1566.

Rutter, M. (1989). Pathways from childhood to adult life. *Journal of Child Psychology and Psychiatry and Applied Disciplines, 30*, 23–51.

Saenz de Rodriguez, C. A., Bongiovanni, A. M., & Conde de Borrego, L. (1985). An epidemic of precocious pubertal development in Puerto Rican children. *Journal of Pediatrics, 107*, 393–396.

Saketos, M., Sharma, N., Adel, T., Raghuwanshi, M., & Santoro, N. (1994). Time-resolved immunofluorometric assay and specimen storage conditions for measuring urinary gonadotropins. *Clinical Chemistry, 40*, 749–753.

Sanborn, K., & Hayward, C. (2003). Hormonal changes at puberty and the emergence of gender differences in internalizing disorders. In C. Hayward (Ed.), *Gender differences at puberty* (pp. 29–58). New York: Cambridge University Press.

Stattin, H., & Magnusson, D. (1990). *Pubertal maturation in female development.* Hillsdale, NJ: Erlbaum.

Sun, S. S., Schubert, C. M., Cameron, W. C., Roche, A. F., Kulin, H. E., Lee, P. A., et al. (2002). National estimates of the timing of sexual maturation and racial differences among US children. *Pediatrics, 110*, 911–919.

Surbey, M. K. (1990). Family composition, stress, and the timing of human menarche. In T. E. Ziegler & F. B. Bercovitch (Eds.), *Socioendocrinology of primate reproduction* (pp. 11–32). New York: John Wiley.

Susman, E. J. (1997). Modeling developmental complexity in adolescence: Hormones and behavior in context. *Journal Of Research on Adolescence, 7*, 283–306.

Susman, E. J. (1998). Biobehavioural development: An inte-grative perspective. *International Journal of Behavioral Development, 22*, 671–679.

Susman, E. J., Dorn, L. D., & Chrousos, G. P. (1991). Negative affect and hormone levels in young adolescents: Concurrent and predictive perspectives. *Journal of Youth and Adolescence, 20*, 167–189.

Susman, E. J., Dorn, L. D., & Schiefelbein, V. (2003). Puberty, sexuality, and health. In M. Lerner, M. A. Easterbrooks & J. Mistry (Eds.), *The Comprehensive Handbook of Psychology* (Vol. 6, pp. 295–324). New York: Wiley.

Susman, E. J., Inoff-Germain, G., Nottelmann, E. D., Loriaux, D. L., Cutler, G. B., & Chrousos, G. P. (1987). Hormones, emotional dispositions, and aggressive attributes in young adolescents. *Child Development, 58*, 1114–1134.

Susman, E. J., Nottelmann, E. D., Inoff-Germain, G., Dorn, L. D., Cutler, G. B., Loriaux, D. L., et al. (1985). The relation of relative hormonal levels and physical development and social-emotional behavior in young adolescents. *Journal of Youth and Adolescence, 14*, 245–264.

Susman, E. J., & Petersen, A. C. (1992). Hormones and behavior in adolescence. In E. R. McAnarney, R. E. Kreipe, D. P. Orr & G. D. Comerci (Eds.), *Textbook of adolescent medicine* (pp. 125–133). New York: W.B. Saunders.

Susman, E. J., & Ponirakis, A. (1997). Hormones-context interactions and antisocial behavior in youth. In A. Raine & e. a. n. o. editors) (Eds.), *Biological Bases of Violence* (pp. 251–269). New York: Plenum Press.

Tanner, J. M. (1970). Physical growth. In P. H. Mussen (Ed.), *Carmichael's manual of child psychology* (pp. 77–155). New York: Wiley.

Tanner, J. M. (1978). *Fetus into man: Physical growth from conception to maturity.* Cambridge: Harvard University Press.

Tobin-Richards, M. H., Boxer, A. W., Petersen, A. C., & Albrecht, R. (1990). Relation of weight to body image in pubertal girls and boys from two communities. *Developmental Psychology, 26*, 313–321.

Tschann, J. M., Adler, N. E., Irwin, C. E., Millstein, S. G., Turner, R. A., & Kegeles, S. M. (1994). Initiation of substance use in early adolescence: The roles of pubertal timing and emotional distress. *Health Psychology, 13*, 326–333.

Tyrka, A. R., Graber, J. A., & Brooks-Gunn, J. (2000). The development of disordered eating: Correlates and predictors of eating problems in the context of adolescence. In A. J. Sameroff, M. Lewis & S. M. Miller (Eds.), *Handbook of developmental psychopathology* (2nd ed., pp. 607–627). New York: Plenum.

Waber, D. P. (1977). Sex differences in mental abilities, hemispheric lateralization, and rate of physical growth at adolescence. *Developmental Psychology, 13*, 29–38.

Warren, M. P., & Brooks-Gunn, J. (1989). Mood and behavior at adolescence: Evidence for hormonal factors. *Journal of Clinical Endocrinology and Metabolism, 69*(1), 77–83.

Weichold, K., Silbereisen, R. K., & Schmitt-Rodermund, E. (2003). Short-term and long-term consequences of early versus late physical maturation in adolescents. In C. Hayward (Ed.), *Gender differences at puberty* (pp. 241–276). New York: Cambridge University Press.

Wichstrom, L. (2001). The impact of pubertal timing on adolescents' alcohol use. *Journal of Research on Adolescence, 11*, 131–150.

Williams, J. M., & Dunlop, L. C. (1999). Pubertal timing and self-reported delinquency among male adolescents. *Journal of Adolescence, 22*, 157–171.

Wong, W. W., Nicolson, M., Stuff, J. E., Butte, N. F., Ellis,

K. J., Hergenroeder, A. C., et al. (1998). Serum leptin concentrations in Caucasian and African–American girls. *Journal of Clinical Endocrinology and Metabolism, 83*, 3574–3577.

Worthman, C. M., & Stallings, J. F. (1997). Hormone measures in finger–prick blood spot samples: New field methods for reproductive endocrinology. *American Journal of Physical Anthropology, 104*, 1–21.

Wu, T., Mendola, P., & Buck, G. M. (2002). Ethnic differences in the presence of secondary sex characteristics and menarche among US girls: The third National Health and Nutrition Examination Survey, 1988–1994. *Pediatrics, 110*, 752–757.

Zimmerman, P. A., Francis, G. L., & Poth, M. (1995). Hormone–containing cosmetics may cause signs of early sexual development. *Military Medicine, 160*, 628–630.

17

Friendships Among Black, Latino, and Asian American Adolescents in an Urban Context

Niobe Way
Bronwyn E Becker
Melissa L. Greene

INTRODUCTION

Theory and research have repeatedly underscored the importance of friendships in satisfying adolescents' desire for intimacy; enhancing their interpersonal skills, sensitivity, and understanding; and contributing to their cognitive and social development and psychological adjustment (Crockett, Losoff, & Petersen, 1984; Csikszentmihalyi & Larson, 1984; Hartup, 1996; Savin-Williams & Berndt, 1990). During adolescence, the significance of friendships becomes even more paramount as adolescents begin to spend increased time with their friends (Crockett et al., 1984). However, despite the fact that friendships appear critical for all adolescents (Hinde, 1987; Patterson, Dishion, & Yoerger, 2000; Sherer, 1991), few studies have examined these processes among ethnic minority adolescents. Indeed, the vast majority of research on friendships has been conducted with White, middle-class adolescents, raising questions about the generalizability of findings to ethnic minority and/or poor and working class adolescents.

Such oversight is not trivial, considering that by the year 2050, it is estimated that "ethnic minorities" as a group will no longer be numerical minorities in the United States and that even at present, 32% of the population in the United States is Black, Latino, or Asian American. Furthermore, although Latinos represent the largest and fastest growing ethnic minority group in the United States and are expected to make up nearly a quarter of the population by 2050 (U.S. Census Bureau, 2004), the small body of research that has explored friendships among ethnic minority adolescents has focused almost exclusively on Black adolescents. Accordingly, given the rapidly changing ethnic and racial composition of the adolescent population in the U.S. and the increasing significance of friendships during childhood and adolescence (Gavin & Furman, 1989; O'Brian & Bierman, 1988), understanding the experiences of friendships among Black, Latino, and Asian American adolescents becomes critical.

To date, a few researchers have examined friendships among ethnic minority youth (e.g., Cauce, 1986; Cote, 1996; Dubois & Hirsch, 1990; Hamm, 2000). These studies have tended to be comparative in nature striving to detect ethnic/racial differences in the *characteristics* or *quality* of friendships between Black adolescents and their White counterparts (Hagan & Conley, 1994). Research on friendship characteristics has typically examined the extent to which African American and European American youth have cross-ethnic/racial friends and has shown that, particularly during adolescence, both ethnic minority and majority youth often seek friends from their own ethnic/racial group (Shrum, Cheek, & Hunter, 1987; Zisman & Wilson, 1994). Other studies have revealed differences in the characteristics of African American and European American adolescents' friendships, with findings showing African American youth more likely to report having best friends from their neighborhoods and European American adolescents more likely to indicate having school-based best friends (Clark & Ayers, 1991; DuBois & Hirsch, 1990).

Research on the quality of friendships among ethnic minority youth has focused primarily on gender and ethnic differences in friendship support and intimacy across and within ethnic minority and majority groups. These studies have typically found gender differences in levels of support in friendships among European American adolescents but not among African American youth (DuBois & Hirsch, 1990). Moreover, ethnic differences in levels of friendship intimacy have also been suggested with African American boys reporting higher levels of intimacy with their male friends than European American boys (Jones, Costin, & Ricard, 1994). Taken as a whole, extant literature showing both commonalities and differences in the friendships of European American and African American youth underscores the need for further exploration of friendships among ethnically diverse groups of adolescents, and draws attention to the problem of making generalizations about friendships solely from the experiences of European American adolescents.

In our own research over the past decade, we have conducted mixed methods longitudinal studies on the development of friendships among Black, Latino, and Asian American high school students from low-income families living in urbant contexts. These studies, like those mentioned in the previous paragraph, have examined gender and ethnic differences in the characteristics and quality of friendships. However, the crux of our research has taken a more ecological approach to the study of friendships than is typical of the literature, examining the ways in which contexts such as families, schools, and neighborhoods shape the quality of friendships among ethnic minority adolescents.

The primary goal of this chapter is to describe key themes in our research and how these themes relate to other studies on adolescent friendships. The chapter begins with a review of the ecological framework in which our work is embedded. Following this discussion, we detail the methods we employed to investigate the development of friendships among ethnic minority youth. Next, we describe our findings regarding contextual-level predictors (i.e., family, school, and neighborhood) of friendships among adolescents. We then discuss our research on the characteristics and quality of friendships among ethnic minority adolescents. Although our focus is on ethnic minority youth, whenever relevant, we also briefly review what is known regarding contextual-level predictors, characteristics, and quality of friendships among ethnic majority youth in an attempt to highlight potential similarities and differences among ethnic minority and majority adolescents. We conclude the chapter with recommendations for further exploration of the friendship experiences of adolescents from a diverse range of racial/ethnic, socioeconomic, and geographic backgrounds.

AN ECOLOGICAL MODEL OF HUMAN DEVELOPMENT

Our work on friendship is grounded in an ecological understanding of human development (Bronfenbrenner, 1979, 1989). An ecological framework draws attention to the adolescent's immediate developmental milieu, interrelations among major settings, and specific social structures that exert indirect influence on proximal environments in which the adolescent lives. Considering that the child exists within multiple intersecting and overlapping contexts that determine what is adaptive or normative, the various levels (child, relationships, and settings) of the ecological system should not be considered in isolation from one another.

Over the past decade, there has been a surge of research directed at understanding the ways in which multiple settings or contexts influence child development (Brooks-Gunn, Duncan, Klebanov, & Sealand, 1993; Burton, Allison, & Obeidallah, 1995; Seidman, 1991). This research has indicated that contexts such as families, peers, schools, and neighborhoods exert an important influence on adolescent development, with each context influencing the ways in which adolescents experience other contexts. For example, how an adolescent experiences high school is influenced not only by the type of school attended previously, but also by the attitude his/her family has toward school, the perceived safety of the neighborhood, and the quality of peer relations in school (Epstein & Karweit, 1983). Exploring the ways in which each of these contexts shape the experience of other contexts allows for a greater understanding of the processes that shape adolescent development (Phelan, Yu, & Davidson, 1994). Yet little attention has been paid to how contexts, settings, or sets of relationships influence each other. This gap is evident throughout the research on adolescent development but is particularly true for research on friendships. Although an ecological framework has become almost de rigueur in some areas of psychological research, such model has rarely been employed in research on adolescent friendship (exceptions include Crosnoe, Cavanagh, & Elder, 2003).

Our work is also grounded in the belief that subjective experience is a large part of what truly matters in studies of human development (Bronfenbrenner, 1979; Lewin, 1951). How a child or adolescent perceives his or her world is a fundamental component of his or her development. Disregarding adolescents' own experiences of their environments leads to an inadequate understanding of adolescents or of the environments in which they exist. For example, our research has suggested that although schools on the outside may appear hostile or supportive, they are not necessarily perceived as such by the adolescents themselves. This discrepancy has direct implications for understanding the effects of those environments on adolescent development. Thus, in our research on friendships, we focus in particular on how adolescents themselves perceive their friendships and other contextual-level variables such as family relationships, school climate, and neighborhood cohesion.

OUR RESEARCH

Goals and Method

We have conducted two longitudinal, mixed methods research projects over the past decade focusing on the following three sets of questions: (1) What are the characteristics and quality of friendships among ethnic minority, low-income, urban adolescents and how do the characteristics and quality of their friendships vary by gender, ethnicity, and age?; (2) What are the ways in which adolescents' perceptions of family relationships, school and neighborhood climate (i.e., contextual-level predictors) shape adolescents' perceptions of the quality of their friendships?; and (3) Are these patterns moderated by ethnicity or gender? In our research we distinguish between *closest* friends and friends *in general* as adolescents themselves are known to make sharp distinctions between these types of friendships (Newcomb & Bagwell, 1996; Shulman, 1993; Way, 1998) and the associated correlates vary depending on the type of relationship to which the adolescent is referring (Harter, 1990; Reyes, Goyette, & Bishop, 1996; Robinson, 1995; Way & Pahl, 2001). Closest friends refer to those whom the adolescent feels closest (i.e., best friends), while friends in general refer to a large array of friends, some of whom may not be close.

Data collection involved administering standardized measures and semi-structured interviews with urban, ethnic minority, low-income adolescents each year, over a 4- or 5-year period (depending on the study), beginning in the first year of high school. Intensive participant observation over a 4- or 5-year period was also conducted. Each study was conducted in a public high school located in a low-income neighborhood in New York City and was successful in recruiting 86–95% of the freshman population during the first year. Our recruitment effort resulted in sample sizes that ranged from 213 (study 1) to 225 (study 2) for the quantitative component. The qualitative component of each study involved interviewing a total of 242 adolescents (132 in study 1 and 110 in study 2) during their freshman year; adolescents were re-interviewed each year of high school. The interview sample was selected based on our goal of having a representative sample of girls, boys, Blacks, Latinos, and Asian Americans that reflected the student body in each of the schools. For both the quantitative and qualitative component, we had at least a 60% retention rate over a 4- or 5-year period depending on the study, which is typical of longitudinal studies of low-income, urban adolescents (see Seidman, 1991). It is important to note, however, that we had a 90–96% retention rate in both schools among those participants who remained in the school during the study. Those adolescents who were retained for our studies did not differ on any of our demographic variables from those who were not retained.

Participants

The mean age of the respondents at Time 1 was 14.33 (Study 1) and 14. 21 (Study 2). The vast majority (over 90%) of participants in both studies identified themselves as Black (almost exclusively African American), Latino (primarily Puerto Rican and Dominican) or Asian American (almost exclusively Chinese American). These ethnic groups are reflective of the dominant ethnic groups in the schools in which we collected the data. The majority of the students (80–90%) in each of the two schools were eligible for federal assistance through the free or reduced-price lunch program.

Procedure

Students were recruited from "mainstream" English classes (not from bilingual English classes) in order to assure English fluency for the qualitative component of the interview. Approximately 90% of the students in both schools were registered in mainstream English classes. For all waves of data collection, adolescents were required to return signed parental consent forms that were in English, Spanish, or Chinese. The questionnaires and one-to-one, semi-structured interviews in both studies were administered during English classes, free periods, lunch periods, or after school. Questionnaires took approximately 90 minutes to complete (two class periods) and the interviews were approximately 90 minutes to 120 minutes depending on the year of the assessment (the longer interviews took place during the latter years of the studies). Ethnically diverse research assistants who had been extensively trained in interviewing techniques administered both questionnaires and interviews. Participants were paid $5.00 to complete the questionnaires and $10.00 to complete the interviews in Year 1; each participant received an additional $5.00 for participating in each new wave of data collection (Times 2, 3, and 4).

Measures

All measures employed in our research have been used with ethnically and socioeconomically diverse urban populations and have been found to have good to excellent internal reliability and external validity (Buhrmester, 1990; Way & Chen, 2000; Way, Cowal, Gingold, Pahl, & Bissessar, 2001; Wheelock & Erickson, 1996).

For the assessment of the quality of *closest* same-sex friendship and the quality of relationships with mother and father, we used a 20-item version of Furman and Buhrmester's (1985) Network of Relationships Inventory. This measure investigates multiple dimensions of relationship quality (i.e., intimacy, affection, reliable alliance, satisfaction, companionship, conflict and antagonism) using a 5-point Likert Scale. The "positive" dimensions (i.e., intimacy, affection, reliable alliance, satisfaction, and companionship) were highly correlated with each other and thus, for the purposes of our study, were summed into one score that represented overall support. Our decision to combine these five dimensions into one score is based on previous research that indicates that the positive dimensions on the NRI comprise one factor (Gavin & Furman, 1996). To investigate the quality—overall level of perceived support—of *general* friendships and family relationships, we relied on The Perceived Social Support Scale for Family and Friends (PSS-FA Procidano & Heller, 1983). The Network of Relationships Inventory is focused on particular dyadic relationships (i.e., closest friend, mother, or father) while the Perceived Social Support Scale is focused on relationships more generally (i.e., friends in general and family members).

Adolescents' perceptions of the climate of their school was assessed using a shortened version of the School Climate Scale (Haynes, Emmons, & Comer, 1993). This measure examines three dimensions (teacher/student relationships, student/student relationships, and order/safety) of school climate on a 5-point Likert scale. To investigate adolescents' perceptions of their neighborhood, we used on the Neighborhood Cohesion Scale (Adolescent Pathways Project, 1992), which assesses perceptions of neighborhood safety, cohesion, and satisfaction using a 4-point Likert scale.

Interview Protocol

In order to explore adolescents' experiences of friendships, family relationships, schools, and neighborhoods, one-to-one, semi-structured interviews were conducted each year with adolescents over a 4- to 5-year period. The interview protocol included questions regarding general descriptions (e.g., tell me about your relationships with your best friend?) as well as more specific probes (e.g., in what ways do you trust your best friend?). Each interview, during Times 2, 3, and 4, began with the following question: "What has changed for you over the past year?" This question allowed us to better understand adolescent responses during the remainder of the interview. Although each interview included a standard set of questions, follow-up probes and questions allowed us to capture the adolescents' own ways of describing their friendships.

Data Analysis

Data analysis of our quantitative data involved methods ranging from Hierarchical Regression Analysis to Growth Curve modeling (see Rogosa & Willett, 1985; Willett, Singer, & Martin, 1998). For our qualitative data, we used analytic techniques such as Narrative summaries (Miller, 1991), conceptually clustered matrices (Miles & Huberman, 1995), and the Listening Guide (Brown, Tappan, Gilligan, Miller, & Argyris, 1989).

CONTEXTUAL LEVEL INFLUENCES ON ADOLESCENT FRIENDSHIPS: FAMILIES, SCHOOLS, AND NEIGHBORHOODS

The Family Context

Family/Parental Support

Research on the links between the quality of relationships with family members and with peers has been based primarily on attachment and/or social support theories (Updegraff et al., 2001) and has typically found the quality of family relationships to be positively associated with the quality of friendships (Greenberg, Siegel, & Leitch, 1983; Kerns, 1994; Kerns & Stevens, 1996; Procidano & Smith, 1997; Youngblade, Park, & Belsky, 1993). According to attachment theorists, children internalize their parents' responsiveness toward them in the form of internal working models of the self (Ainsworth & Bowlby, 1991). These internal working models in turn influence non-familial relationships, as children provided with security, warmth, and trust are more likely than others to seek out and experience similar qualities in their relationships with their peers (Armsden & Greenberg, 1987; Greenberg et al., 1983; Kerns & Stevens, 1996; Sroufe & Waters, 1977). Attachment theorists also emphasize the enduring and stable nature of attachment styles, showing significant associations between current parent attachment and peer relationships (Armsden & Greenberg, 1987; Cauce, Mason, Gonzales, Hiraga, & Liu, 1996).

In a similar vein, social support theorists also maintain that a positive association exists between adolescents' perceived support from families and from friends (Procidano, 1992; Procidano & Smith, 1997). In the social support literature, perceived family support is generally understood as the extent to which adolescents feel they can depend on family for advice, guidance, and emotional support.

When a child's need for support is met at home, that child will likely experience others outside of the home as supportive as well (Bartholomew, Cobb, & Poole, 1997; Sarason, Pierce, & Sarason, 1990).

Although the vast majority of attachment and social support-based research has been focused on European American adolescents, a few studies have examined the links between parent-child closeness and adolescent friendships among ethnic minority youth as well (see Cote, 1996; Updegraff et al., 2001). This research has suggested that the association between parent and peer relationships varies as a function of culture, race/ethnicity, and/or gender. For example, using a sample of early adolescents from Latino and European American families, Updegraff and her colleagues (2002) examined adolescents' experiences with their mothers, fathers, and best friends and found both mother and father acceptance to be significantly linked to friendship intimacy among European American adolescents. For Latino adolescents, however, only mother acceptance was related to friendship intimacy.

In our own research on family and friendship support among ethnic minority youth, we have found patterns that are both consistent and inconsistent with previous findings (Way, 1998; Way & Chen, 2000; Way, Greene, & Pahl, 2004; Way & Pahl, 2001). Similar to Updegraff and her colleagues (2002), our longitudinal analyses showed that over a one-year period, father support was unrelated to friendship support among Latino, Black, and Asian American adolescents. However, perceived support from mothers at Time 1 was significantly associated with change over time in the quality of both general and closest friendship support (Way & Pahl, 2001). These findings extend the significance of mother support to other ethnic minority groups (e.g., African American and Asian American). Strikingly, though, adolescents who reported the least amount of support from their mothers at Time 1 showed the sharpest increases over time in reported levels of support from friends. Although one might interpret such findings as a "ceiling effect" (i.e., those adolescents who reported initial high scores had less room to grow over time than those who initially reported low scores), the analysis indicated that there was no concurrent association between mother and friendship support. In other words, adolescents who reported the lowest mother support were not necessarily the same adolescents who reported the lowest levels of friendship support. Although the *increase over time* in friendship support was significantly sharper among adolescents reporting the lowest levels of mother support, the mean level of friendship support was not the lowest among these groups. In fact, the mean level of friendship support at Time 2 for those who reported the lowest mother support at Time 1 was significantly *higher* than the mean levels of friendship support at Time 2 for those who reported the highest mother support at Time 1 (see Figure 17.1). These patterns suggest a compensatory rather than a "ceiling" effect.

Growth curve analyses examining the dynamic associations between perceptions of family support[1] and general and closest friendship quality over a 5-year period showed that improvements over time in reports of family support were significantly associated with improvements over time in levels of general and closest friendship support (Way & Greene, in press). In addition, similar to what we found in our analysis of two waves of data (Way & Pahl, 2001), adolescents who reported lower mean levels of family support (averaged over time) experienced sharper improvements in general friendship quality over a 5-year period than those adolescents with higher mean levels of family support. These associations were robust across grade and ethnicity.

Thus, our longitudinal analyses provide evidence for both attachment-like and compensatory-like patterns between family and friendships. Attachment-like associations were indicated in the growth curve findings showing that an increase over time in perceptions of family support were significantly associated with an increase over time in perceptions of friendship support. Compensatory patterns were apparent in the findings suggesting that those adolescents who reported lower mother or family support revealed sharper increases over time in perceptions of friendship support than those who reported higher mother or family support (Way & Greene, in press; Way & Pahl, 2001). Although these findings seem contradictory, they are consistent with much of what we know about the development of relationships. Overall, improvements in one type of relationship (i.e., family members) may be associated with improvements in another type of relationship (i.e., friends). However, the sharpest

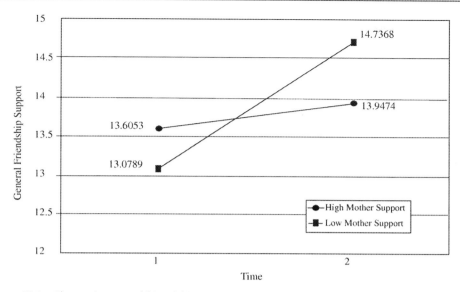

Figure 17.1   Change in general friendship support over time as a function of mother support at Time 1.

improvements may be seen in those relationships (i.e., friends) that compensate for the lack of support in other relationships (see also Cicchetti, Lynch, Shonk, & Manly, 1992).

To further explore the prevalence of these attachment-like and compensatory-like relationships, we conducted a cluster analysis of perceived mother, father, and friendship support. Our findings indicated that adolescents are as likely to report compensatory-like patterns (e.g., high friendship support and low mother *and* father support) as attachment-like patterns (e.g., high mother, father, and friend support; Williams, 2004[2]). Given the dearth of longitudinal research on the association between family relationships and friendships among adolescents in general, it is impossible to know the extent to which our findings regarding the presence of both attachment- and compensatory-like patterns among ethnic minority youth are particular to the population under investigation. The existing research on family and friend relationships emphasizes attachment models of relationships, rarely considering compensatory effects or attempting to integrate the two models of relationships. Our research underscores the importance of considering both theoretical models.

Parental Monitoring, Attitudes, and Rules

In addition to studies examining the association between the quality of family support and peer relationships, a growing body of research based on social learning theories has examined the links between parental attitudes and adolescent friendships. According to social learning theorists, children acquire the requisite skills for friendships through modeling and observational learning (Mischel, 1966). Such research has primarily focused on issues of parental monitoring, examining how parental monitoring at home influences the quality and characteristics of peer relationships (Brown, Mounts, Lamborn, & Steinberg, 1993; Fuligni & Eccles, 1993; Snyder & Hoffman, 1990). Findings from these studies have suggested that there is a clear association between the extent of parental monitoring and a range of adolescent outcomes including involvement with deviant peers (Ary, Duncan, Duncan, & Hops, 1999; Snyder, Dishion, & Patterson, 1986) and, positive peer contact (Brown et al., 1993; Mounts, 2001). The degree of parental monitoring has also been related to friendship development, with the two extremes of monitoring—excessively high and excessively low—being shown to interfere with children's abilities to establish friendships (Patterson & Stouthamer-Loeber, 1984). Our survey-based research with ethnic minority youth has found parental monitoring to be significantly related to the perceived quality of closest and general friendships among youth. Adolescents who reported their parents as knowing their whereabouts, what they are doing after school, how they spend their money, and where they are during the day and evening hours, reported having more supportive closest friendships and general friendships (Rosenbaum, 2000[3]).

Parental guidance, or the degree to which parents directly assist adolescents with making friends, has also been examined. Vernberg and colleagues (1993), for example, documented various strategies used by parents to help their seventh- and eighth-grade children develop friendships after moving to a new school district, such as meeting with other parents, facilitating proximity to peers, talking with their adolescent children about peer relationships, and encouraging their children to participate in activities with other adolescents. More recently, in a study of Latino and European American adolescents and their parents, Updegraff and colleagues (2001) reported that parents—mothers in particular—often got to know and spent time with their children' friends as a way to influence these relationships. Mounts (2004; 2001; 2002) has also described various strategies parents use to influence their adolescents' friendships, such as guiding (i.e., talking about the consequence of being friends with particular people), neutrality (i.e., not interfering with their children's peer relationships), prohibiting (i.e., forbidding adolescents' associations with particular peers) and supporting (i.e., providing an environment at home where adolescents can have their friends over).

Our studies of ethnic minority adolescents have indicated that parental rules and attitudes regarding their adolescents' friends are also critically related to friendship quality. In a concurrent analysis, adolescents' perceptions of parental rules and attitudes was significantly associated with the quality of closest friendships over and above the effect of mother and family support. Those adolescents who perceived themselves as having parents with a more encouraging attitudes (e.g., "my parents think it is important to have friends") and rules (e.g., "my parents allow me to spend time with my friends during the weekends or after school") toward friendships reported having more supportive close friendships. Indeed, parenting rules and attitudes about friendships emerged as the only significant family-level predictor of closest same-sex friendship quality when included in a hierarchical regression model with adolescents' perceptions of family support and parental monitoring as independent predictors (Rosenbaum, 2000[3]). In a prospective analysis, only parental attitudes about friendships predicted change over time in perceived close friendship quality. Adolescents who perceived their parents to have increasingly more positive attitudes about friendships over time also reported having increasingly more supportive close friendships (Way & Greene, 2005). Our concurrent and prospective analysis suggest that in addition to family support, parental monitoring, guidance, attitudes and rules pertaining to friendships are critical correlates of the ways in which adolescents perceive the quality of their close friendships.

Our qualitative data suggest ethnic differences in parents' attitudes about friendships. Our interview data indicated that the adolescents, particularly the Black and Asian American adolescents, perceive their parents to be extremely wary of non-familial friendships (Gingold, 2003[3]; Way, 1998; Way & Pahl, 1999; Way & Greene, 2005). For example, Michael, an Asian American adolescent, says: "My mom doesn't think friends are important because they may betray you or something they can have a bad influence on you." Like Michael, adolescents indicated that their parents, grandparents, cousins, aunts, and uncles warned them repeatedly of the tendency for non-familial friends to be deceptive and deviant. Previous research has suggested that many families from low-income and/or ethnic minority backgrounds maintain belief systems—due to a history of discrimination and oppression—that those who are not part of one's immediate or extended family should not be trusted (Salguero & McCusker, 1996; Stack, 1974; Way, 1998). Thus, while parental attitudes about friendships may influence the quality of friendships of adolescents from a wide range of backgrounds, the particular attitudes that parents have about friendships may be group specific.

Notably, qualitative findings from our research also demonstrate that the influence of parental concerns and warnings about friendships appear to vary depending on adolescents' perceived parental closeness. Adolescents who reported being close to their parents were more likely to report being extremely careful regarding the selection and maintenance of their own friendships. Those adolescents who reported being less close to their parents were more likely to disregard parental warnings and be less cautious of friendships in general (Gingold, 2003[3]). Like our survey data, which showed significant associations between the quality of parent and friend relationships, these qualitative findings suggest a compensatory pattern for those adolescents who report low levels of parental closeness. However, the compensatory mechanism appears to entail rejecting parents' warnings by seeking out friendships rather than having friends to compensate for the lack of support within their families.

Summary of the Family Context

Previous attachment and social support-based research with predominantly White, middle-class adolescents, coupled with our own research with urban, low SES, ethnic minority youth indicate attachment-like associations between the quality of mother and/or family relationships and adolescent friendships. However, our research also suggests patterns of compensatory associations between mother and friendship support that are as likely to exist among the adolescents in our studies as attachment-like associations. Longitudinal and mixed method research with European American adolescents and middle to upper SES ethnic minority youth is thus warranted to elucidate whether this combination of compensatory and attachment-based patterns is evident in other populations of youth.

Corroborating the existing research on ethnic minority youth (see Updegraff et al., 2001), our research shows that ethnic minority adolescents' perceptions of father support is not linked with perceptions of friendship quality. The lack of findings with respect to the influence of father support may be due to lower levels of father involvement, which decrease the opportunities for fathers to influence their children. However, fathers' residential status did not make a difference in the association between adolescents' perceptions of father and friendship support (Way & Chen, 2000). Substantiating these findings, Mott (1994) showed little evidence for detrimental effects of father absence on peer relationships among African American youth (although there were negative effects for White adolescents). Of note, many of the adolescents in our studies perceived their fathers as "too busy" working two or three jobs to be available for support and guidance. Thus, rather than the residential status of fathers, father's work schedules may be a primary reason for the lack of association between perceived father support and friendship quality. Furthermore, there are other ways in which fathers may influence the quality of their children's friendships (e.g., by regulating access to peers and peer-related activities, modeling or teaching appropriate peer behavior; see Parke et al., 2002).

Previous social learning based studies and our own research show parental monitoring and guidance to be linked with better perceptions of friendship quality. Extending this research, our concurrent and longitudinal findings indicate that adolescents' perceptions of their parents' rules and/or attitudes about friendships are also important components of how parents influence their children's friendships. The association, however, between parents' attitudes and the quality of adolescent friendships appears mediated by adolescents' perceptions of parental closeness. Those adolescents who reported feeling closer to their parents were more likely to heed the warnings of their parents about friendships than those who felt less close to their parents. Additional qualitative research is needed to further understand how adolescents, despite warnings by family members of the hazards of peer relationships, continue to find and maintain close friendships with non-familial peers.

Although our findings do suggest ethnic group differences in the attitudes that parents have about friendships (see Way and Greene, 2005)—with Asian American and African American adolescents reporting more negative parental attitudes about friendships than their Latino peers—our findings show no gender or ethnic differences in the associations between the quality of family relationships or parental attitudes, rules, or level of monitoring and adolescents' perceptions of the quality of their friendships. A lack of ethnic differences is not consistent with research that has shown ethnic differences in the association between parent and friendship support (see Updegraff et al., 2002). Yet such research has typically compared European Americans with ethnic minority groups. Thus, it is possible that our research failed to detect ethnic differences in associations between family-level factors and perceptions of friendship quality due to the fact that our studies have not included European American, middle class adolescents. Ethnic differences in the association between parent and peer relationships may be more likely if one compares groups who do not share similar fundamental beliefs about family relationships (e.g., European-American vs. Latino) than groups who share such beliefs (Cooper, 1999).

The School Context

In addition to familial influences, researchers have emphasized the significance of adolescents' perceptions of the school environment in studies of contextual-level influences on adolescent development (Epstein & Karweit, 1983; Kuperminc, Leadbeater, Emmons, & Blatt, 1997; Minuchin & Shapiro, 1983; Roeser & Eccles, 1998). Perceptions of the school climate, or the quality of interactions and feelings of trust, respect, and support that exist within the school community, have been found to influence (both concurrently and prospectively) students' self-esteem, psychological adjustment, level of anxiety, problem behavior, academic self-concept (Grobel & Scharzer, 1982; Kuperminc et al., 1997; Roeser & Eccles, 1998), and school behavior (Hoge, Smit, & Hanson, 1990; Sommer, 1985).

Theorists also argue that students who perceive the school environment as respectful, supportive, equitable, safe, and dependable, will find it easier, and will be more willing to make and maintain supportive friendships with their peers than those who perceive the school as hostile (Epstein & Karweit, 1983; Minuchin & Shapiro, 1983). Epstein and Karweit (1983) note: "Negative features in a school environment—ridicule, discrimination, low expectations, stereotypes, repressions, punishment, isolation—may increase the disassociative quality of the setting and affect the thought processes and social behavior of the students" (p. 60). Although the "objective reality" of the school (e.g., number of students in school, ethnic diversity) is likely associated with the characteristics and quality of friendships, adolescents' perceptions of the relational (e.g., teacher/student and student/student relationships) and organizational (e.g., sense of safety in the school) climate may also have a powerful influence (Andersen, 1982; Roeser & Eccles, 1998).

Whereas much research has investigated the ways in which perceptions of school climate influence adolescents' psychological and academic development (Hoge et al., 1990; Kuperminc et al., 1997; Roeser, Eccles, & Strobel, 1998; Way & Robinson, 2003), substantially less attention has been directed at exploring the ways in which adolescents' perceptions of school climate shape their social development (Eccles & Roeser, 2003). To our knowledge, save for one study (see Crosnoe et al., 2003), our work is the only research to date that has specifically examined the influence of adolescents' perceptions of the climate of their school on their perceptions of their friendships. This absence in the research literature is particularly striking given that most adolescents spend much of their time in school, thus making and/or maintaining many of their friendships within the school context.

Findings from our quantitative and qualitative research have shown students' perception of school climate (i.e., teacher/student relations, student/student relations, and order, discipline, and safety in the school) to be significantly associated with changes over time in perceptions of general and closest friendships; the effects of adolescents' perceptions of school climate on friendship quality is significant over and above the influence of family relationships and psychological adjustment (Way & Pahl, 2001). Moreover, growth curve analyses of our 5-year survey data demonstrated that changes in two dimensions of school climate in particular (i.e., teacher/student relations and student/student relations) are significantly associated with changes over time in adolescent perceptions of friendship quality. When students reported improvements in their relationships with their teachers and high levels of support from other students, they also reported improvements in the quality of friendships in general (Way & Greene, in press). When examined together with perceptions of family relationships, teacher/student and student/student relationships remain significant predictors of change over time in adolescents' perceptions of the quality of friendships in general. We did not find any gender or ethnic differences in our analyses of the effects of school climate on perceived friendship quality.

Moreover, our findings showed that adolescents' perceptions of the school climate had a greater influence on their perceptions of friendships in general than on their closest friendships. We initially hypothesized that such patterns were the result of fact that many of the adolescents in our studies reported having general friendships that were school-based and closest friendships that were neighborhood-based; thus making the influence of the school more pronounced in school-based, general friendships than in non-school-based, close friendships. However, post-hoc analyses showed school-based friendships were no more influenced by perceptions of school climate than were non-school-based friendships. Thus, it may be that closest friendships—by virtue of being close—are simply less vulnerable to the fluctuations of students' perceptions of school climate (see Way & Pahl, 2001).

Significantly, our ethnographic work with adolescents in schools has suggested that the racial/ethnic dynamics of the school are strongly associated with the quality and characteristics of friendships (Rosenbloom & Way, 2004). In the urban, exclusively ethnic minority high schools in which we have conducted our two research studies, Black and Latino students are typically in either mainstream or special education classes while Asian American students are generally overrepresented in honors classrooms. According to many of the teachers we have spoken with, these divisions are often made irrespective of the actual abilities of students, with Asian American students with very low literacy skills being placed in honors classes so that he/she can "be with their peers"(Baolin-Qin, Way, & Pandey, under review). Such actions not only openly and actively reinforce the model minority myth of Asian American students, they also reinforce the stereotype that Black and Latino students are not smart enough for honors classes (Tatum, 1998). Black and Latino students were often seen by the participant observers in our studies harassing Asian American students. Our observations suggest that this harassment was provoked, at least in part, by the frustration and anger among Black and Latino students about the preference by their teachers for the Asian American students (see Rosenbloom & Way, 2004). The ethnic/racial class divisions created a hostile school climate in which friendships across racial/ethnic lines were discouraged and segregation was a normal part of everyday school life, especially among the Asian American students who often reported being fearful of the Black and Latino students (Rosenbloom & Way, 2004).

Remarkably, such a negative and hostile relational climate in the schools also appeared to make it difficult for students to form supportive friendships even within their own ethnic/racial group (Way et al., 2004). Our interview data indicated, for example, that those students who reported school as being a particularly hostile place (usually based on incidents of racism and discrimination) often indicated having the most contentious friendships—irrespective of the ethnicity/race of their friendships. Students, on the other hand, who recounted more positive school experiences (e.g., good teachers) tended to describe more stable, secure, and supportive friendships (Rosenbloom, 2004[3]). Although the direction of effect for this pattern is unclear, feeling unsupported in school was clearly associated with feeling unsupported by friends (Way et al., 2005).

Summary of the School Context

It is typically assumed that family relationships—both the quality of these relationships and the level of parental guidance and monitoring—are the most important factors shaping adolescents' experiences of their friendships. However, such beliefs ignore the significant role of the school context (Rosenbloom & Way, 2004; Way et al., 2004; Way & Pahl, 2001). Both perceptions of teacher/student and student/student relationships in school appear to be significantly associated with the trajectories of perceived friendship quality over time even after considering the effect of family relationships. Moreoever, although no moderating effects of ethnicity/race in the association between perceptions of school climate and friendship quality were detected in our quantitative data, our qualitative interviews suggested that ethnicity/race plays a major role in the relational climate of the school (Rosenbloom & Way, 2004; Way et al., 2004). Thus, our quantitative and qualitative findings underscore the need for research examining the role of school climate (including the racial/ ethnic climate) in the quality and development of adolescent friendships.

The Neighborhood Context

Recent studies have indicated that friendship experiences vary depending on the quality and characteristics of the neighborhood (Berg & Medrich, 1980; DuBois & Hirsch, 1990; Epstein, 1989); Homel & Burns, 1989). Children, for example, living in neighborhoods with easily accessible "play spaces" have more contact with friends outside of school and more friends in general than those who live in neighborhoods without such places (Berg & Medrich, 1980; Homel & Burns, 1989). Similarly, youth residing in dangerous neighborhoods with a high prevalence of violence tend to have fewer neighborhood friends and less contact with their friends outside of school than their peers who live in less violent neighborhoods (Rosenbaum, 2000[3] ;Way, 1998).

Neighborhood climate has also been shown to influence friendship satisfaction. For example, in their study of urban low-income early adolescents, Homel and Burns (1989) found neighborhood social problems (e.g., crime, delinquency) to predict lower levels of perceived satisfaction with friends and a lower probability of liking one's classmates. Other studies have found family's residence to be strongly linked to the quality of social opportunities (Berg & Medrich, 1980; DuBois & Hirsch, 1990; Hirsch & DuBois, 1990).

Our research also indicates that adolescents' perceptions of their neighborhood shape the quality and characteristics of their friendships. In our qualitative studies, Black and Latino boys often report choosing not to spend time with neighborhood friends because doing so meant being stopped and harassed by policemen or by groups of boys "looking for trouble" (Way, 1998). As a consequence, some of the boys chose instead to spend time alone or with family members. For example, one male Puerto Rican sophomore stated in his interview that he did not have friends from the neighborhood because he did not like "hangin' with people getting killed" (Way, 1998, p. 119) instead preferring to stay at home during non-school hours. Similarly, when a Black 11th-grade male was asked why he thought he had not found a close friend he could trust, he replied that "backstabbing" which was typical in his neighborhood led people to further "diss" one another in order to "feel important" (Way, 1998, p. 118). After learning that his closest friend was talking about him "all throughout my neighborhood," this young man decided not to "really bother with it, you know, trying to make best friends" (Way, 1998, p. 116).

Experiences of betrayal in and around their neighborhoods significantly affected adolescents' willingness to spend time with their neighborhood friends. Those adolescents, particularly boys, who spoke of not wanting to spend time with their friends outside of school also spoke of not having close or best friends because they could not trust anyone. In fact, quantitative findings revealed that for Black, Latino, and Asian American youth, perceptions of neighborhood cohesion (defined as levels of trust, familiarity, and reliability among neighbors and level of safety in the neighborhood) were significantly associated with reported levels of general friendship support (Rosenbaum, 2000[3]). Similar, however, to the pattern of findings for school climate, the effects of neighborhood cohesion was not detected for closest friendships. It may be that closest friendships are not as influenced by the nuances of one's neighborhood (or school) because by their very nature (e.g., characterized by consistent support) they are more resistant to the effects of hostile contexts.

Summary of the Neighborhood Context

Quantitative and qualitative research on the links between neighborhoods and adolescent friendships has consistently found neighborhoods to influence the ways in which adolescents obtain, engage, and maintaining friendships with peers (Brooks-Gunn et al., 1993; Jencks & Mayer, 1990; Seidman, 1991). In our own research, however, when adolescent perceptions of the neighborhood climate were considered in combination with the effects of family and school contexts, the relative influence of neighborhood climate on adolescent friendship quality was lost. Such findings underscore the limitations of evaluating contextual influences in isolation. It is also possible, as our qualitative data suggest, that although the neighborhood climate may indeed influence the extent to which adolescents choose to spend time with friends outside of school, it may have less of an affect on adolescents' perceptions of friendship *quality* of their friendships.

Ethnic and Gender Differences

Strikingly, our quantitative analyses have suggested few gender or ethnic differences in the association between various contextual-level variables and adolescent friendships. However, our qualitative data has indicated that gender and ethnicity shape the ways in which adolescents experience contexts such as schools, neighborhoods, and friendships. For example, our interviews suggest that Black and Latino students' frustration with the preferential treatment by teachers shown toward Asian American students in school creates a hostile peer climate for Asian American students. Furthermore, boys, particularly Black and Latino (the boys who are most likely to be the victims of violence in urban areas), express frustration with the violence and "backstabbing" in their neighborhoods and respond by "keeping to themselves" rather than spending time with their friends outside of school. Finally, the wariness of adolescents' parents toward non-familial friends may be influenced by being a part of an oppressed minority group. Although this theme may also be evident among European American, middle-class families as well, the level of distrust of non-family members within Black, Latino, and Asian American, low SES families is likely to be more severe given their history of ethnic/racial and SES discrimination.

THE CHARACTERISTICS AND QUALITY OF ADOLESCENT FRIENDSHIPS

While few researchers have examined the contextual-level predictors of friendship quality among ethnic minority adolescents, there has been an increasing number of studies examining the characteristics (e.g., number of cross-ethnic/racial friendships) and quality (e.g., level of support or intimacy) of friendships among ethnically diverse youth. This body of research has, for the most part, suggested that the characteristics and quality of friendships are influenced by race, ethnicity, gender and/or social class (Cauce, 1986, 1987; DuBois & Hirsch, 1990; Hamm, 1994; Way, 1996, 1998).

The Characteristics of Adolescent Friendships

Research focused on the extent to which ethnic minority and majority youth have cross ethnic/racial friendships has, for the most part, suggested that adolescents, including those who attend ethnically diverse schools, are less likely to befriend peers from other ethnic/racial groups than they are peers from their own ethnic/racial group (Brown, 1990; Hamm, 1998; Tatum, 1997). Inconsistencies, however, are evident in the research literature regarding the prevalence of cross-ethnic/racial friendships. Some studies show African American and/or European American youth as unlikely to have any cross ethnic friendships (Shrum et al., 1987; Way & Chen, 2000), while others depict adolescents who attend ethnically diverse schools as more commonly experiencing cross-race friendships (Hamm, 1998).

In addition, some findings show that the likelihood of cross ethnic/racial friendships differs depending on the race/ethnicity of the adolescent (Clark & Ayers, 1991; DuBois & Hirsch, 1990; Hamm, 1998). However, like the pattern of prevalence of cross ethnic/racial friendships, findings have been contradictory. Hamm (1998) showed, for example, 75% of the Asian American and Latino adolescents in her study as reportedly having at least one cross-ethnic/race friend, whereas this was true for only 50% of the African American and European American adolescents. Other scholars have shown, in contrast, that African American adolescents are almost twice as likely as their White peers to report having cross-ethnic/race friends (Clark & Ayers, 1991; DuBois & Hirsch, 1990).

In our own research, we find that the vast majority (>73%) of Black, Latino, and Asian American students report having same-race/ethnic friendship networks (Way & Chen, 2000). However, in contrast to Hamm's (1998) findings, Asian American students are most likely *not* to report having cross racial/ethnic friendships (85% of Asian American students in comparison to 73% and 64% of Latino and African American students, respectively). The discrepancy in findings regarding prevalence of cross-ethnic/race friendships as well as the ethnic/racial group least or most likely to report having such friendships draws attention to the importance of examining the context in which friendships are embedded. Cross-ethnic/race friends may be more likely in school contexts in which there are academic and extracurricular activities that implicitly or explicitly encourage such friendships (Phelan, Davidson, & Cao, 1991). Furthermore, the ethnic/racial diversity of the school as well as the dominance of particular ethnic/race groups within the school is likely to influence the prevalence of cross-ethnic/race friendships (Joyner & Kao, 2000). The discrepancy in findings may also be due to the type of friendship being examined. Closest friendships may be less likely to cross the racial/ethnic divide than friendships in general. Our quantitative findings suggest that closest friendships are more segregated by race/ethnicity than are friendships in general.

The prevalence of cross-ethnic/race friendships within particular ethnic/racial groups is also likely influenced by the social status and language use of the ethnic/racial group within the school (Suárez-Orozco & Suárez-Orozco, 2001). In our research, Asian American students, although representing the second largest pan ethnic group in the school, were very low on the social hierarchy and were harassed by their Black and Latino peers (see Way, Kim, & Santos, 2005). Consequently, the Asian American students reported fearing Black and Latino students and felt the need to keep to themselves (Rosenbloom & Way, 2004; Way et al., 2005). In addition, Asian American students were most likely among the adolescents in our research to speak a non-English language at home. Thus, speaking another language with their friends may enhance the segregation of their friendships.

Although most studies have not explored gender differences in the likelihood of cross-ethnic/racial friendships, findings from our research show girls to be slightly more likely to report having same-ethnic/race friendships than boys, with approximately 78% of the girls and 67% of the boys reporting same-race/ethnic friendship networks (Way & Chen, 2000). Qualitative interview data from our research reveal boys to be more flexible regarding friendship selection than girls. Such patterns may be the product of boys more active engagement in sports which puts them in contact with adolescents from different ethnic/racial groups. However, despite these gender and ethnic/racial differences in the likelihood of having cross-ethnic/race friendships, substantially more than half of the girls and boys from all ethnic/racial groups in our research have been more likely to report same-ethnic/race friendships than cross-ethnic/race friendships.

The research on the characteristics of ethnic minority adolescent friendships has also shown context-specific differences in the source of friendships. DuBois and Hirsch (1990), for example, found Black adolescents to be more likely than their White peers to report having a large network of neighborhood friends while White adolescents reported having more school-based friendships. Supporting this finding, Clark and Ayers (1991) showed African American adolescents as having more contact with their best friends outside of school, whereas White adolescents' best friendships were more likely to take place within the school context.

In our own research, we find that although most adolescents report having school-based friendships, less than half, particularly in the first 2 years of high school, indicate having *best* friends who attend the same school. In the ninth grade, for example, only 25% of the Black students, 40% of the Latino students, and 38% of the Asian American students reported having best friends who attended the same school (Way & Chen, 2000). Such findings are consistent with previous research that suggest that the friendships of ethnic minority youth are not necessarily school-based and underscore the importance of examining the diversity of friendship characteristics among youth and of distinguishing between types of friendships (e.g., school vs. neighborhood, closest vs. general friendships).

Summary of the Characteristics of Friendships

The research on characteristics of friends among ethnic minority youth reveals variation in the extent to which adolescents seek out cross-ethnic/race friendships which is likely due to the context in which these friendships are embedded. The same factors that influence the quality of friendships (family relationships, school climate, and neighborhood climate) may also predict the extent to which, for example, adolescents seek out cross-ethnic/race friendships. The characteristics of friendships also appear to vary by ethnicity/race with European American youth reporting fewer neighborhood-based friendships than Black youth. These patterns are likely influenced by a multitude of factors including the mobility patterns of the people who live in the neighborhoods, the ethnic/racial composition of the adolescents in the neighborhood of the school, and the extent to which adolescents from the neighborhood attend the neighborhood school. These findings regarding the characteristics of friendships underscore, once again, the importance of understanding the contexts in which friendships are embedded and the ways in which friendships respond to and shape these contexts.

The Quality of Friendships: Quantitative Data

Gender and Ethnic Differences

Research on the quality of adolescent friendships has typically been grounded in Weiss's (1974) contention that children and adolescents seek social provisions in their close friendships (Furman, 1996). Such provisions include intimacy (e.g., sharing secrets together), affection (e.g., showing affection toward one another), companionship (e.g., having fun together), and satisfaction (Shulman, 1993). A large body of research over the past decade has focused on understanding the prevalence and correlates of these dimensions of friendship quality (see Buhrmester, 1990; Bukowski, Newcomb, & Hartup, 1996; Collins & Laursen, 1992; Furman & Buhrmester, 1985), and the extent to which they vary by gender and, more recently, by ethnicity/race.

Studies have found that the quality of friendships do vary by gender and ethnicity/race. Jones, et al. (1994), for example, explored friendship quality among Mexican American, African American, and European American sixth and ninth graders and found that African American males were more likely to reveal their personal thoughts and feelings with their male friends than were Mexican American and European American boys. Furthermore, significant gender differences in levels of self-disclosure in their same-sex friendships were only apparent among European American adolescents; European American girls were more likely to reveal their personal thoughts and feelings to their friends than were European American boys. Similarly, in their study of Black and White, socio-economically diverse, middle school children, Dubois and Hirsch (1990) showed White girls as reporting significantly more supportive friendships than White boys. No gender differences were detected among Black youth. Black boys were also more likely to report having intimate conversations with their best friends than were White boys; no differences were found between Black and White girls.

Our quantitative analyses have consistently shown that Black and Latino adolescents reporting higher levels of friendship support than their Asian American peers (Way & Chen, 2000; Way & Greene, in press). Our qualitative data support these findings with Asian American adolescents commonly reporting being unhappy with their friendships and yearning for friendships that are more supportive. Moreover, gender differences have also been suggested in our quantitative data with Latinas reporting, during the first years of our studies, more supportive friendships than Latino boys (Way & Chen, 2000). The lack of gender differences in perceived friendship quality among Black youth is consistent with previous research (Dubois & Hirsch, 1990). It is not clear from our quantitative or qualitative data, however, why such gender differences are evident during the early years of high school among Latino youth but not among Black or Asian American adolescents. By the latter years of the studies, no gender differences are indicated in levels of friendship support within or across any ethnic/racial group.

Age-Related Changes: Quantitative Data

The focus of the vast majority of theoretical and empirical work on change over time in the perceived quality of friendships has focused on the changes that occur from childhood to early or middle adolescence (Berndt, 2004). According to theory and research, as children become less dependent on their parents, cognitively more advanced, and develop a greater need for collaborative relationships (Ainsworth, 1989; Blos, 1967; Sullivan, 1954; Youniss & Smollar, 1985), they increasingly turn to their friends for emotional support and experience more intimacy in their friendships (Berndt, 2004). Theories of social support (Cauce, 1994; 1996), attachment (Ainsworth, 1989; Bowlby, 1969/1982), identity development (Erikson, 1968), and interpersonal development (Selman, 1980; Sullivan, 1954; Youniss & Smollar, 1985) also suggest, however, that an increase in emotional support and intimacy in friendships are evident *during* adolescence, as well as youth become better able to find mutually supportive and validating friendships and as they explore and achieve their own identities. In addition, an increase in romantic interests and involvement during adolescence may also precipitate an increase in perceived intimacy and support in friendships as friendships provide a forum in which adolescents can discuss these newly developed interests (Azmitia et al., 1998; Furman & Buhrmester, 1992). Despite these theoretical assumptions, few researchers have examined the trajectories of perceptions of friendship quality during adolescence.

The few exceptions to this pattern include cross-sectional research on White, middle-class youth. Such research has found that perceptions of friendship support do, in fact, increase during adolescence (Furman & Buhrmester, 1992; Hunter & Youniss, 1982; Sharabany et al, 1981). Findings have also indicated that gender differences in friendship quality become less apparent as girls *and* boys mature and begin to rely more on friends to help solve their problems (Azmitia, Kamprath, & Linnet, 1998; Berndt, 1989; Furman & Burhmester, 1992; Rice & Mulkeen, 1995; Sharabany, Gershoni, & Hofman, 1981; Youniss & Smollar, 1985). These studies, however, do not typically examine the changes that occur from middle to late adolescence, a time in which the increase in perceived levels of support may be most dramatic (Allan & Land, 1999; Buhrmester, 1992; Hartup, 1993). Furthermore, cross-sectional studies do not offer insight into the patterns of individual trajectories of change over time.

Using growth curve analysis to examine the trajectories of change in perceptions of the quality of general and closest same-sex friendships from early to late adolescence, our longitudinal studies have shown patterns of increase over time among Black, Latino, and Asian American youth (Way & Greene, in press). On average, the perceived level of support for friendships in general as well as closest friendships increases over time from ages 13 to 18. These findings support theory and research indicating that as young people become increasingly self- aware, cognitively skilled, and confident in their identities (McCarthy & Hoge, 1982), they become better able to have mutually supportive and satisfying friendships. We have also found that the rate of improvements over time in friendship quality is similar for Asian American, Latino, and Black adolescents. Boys, however, show steeper improvements over time than girls in the quality of closest same-sex friendships even though the mean level of friendship quality at age 16 showed no gender difference (Way & Greene, in press) (see Figure 17.2). This latter finding is consistent with previous longitudinal research with predominantly White adolescents suggesting that intimacy in best friendship increases at a sharper rate for boys than for girls from 8th through 12th grade (Rice & Mulkeen, 1995).

Summary of Quality of Friendships: Quantitative Data

Although gender differences are often detected in samples of European American and Latino adolescents, such gender differences are rarely indicated among African American (DuBois & Hirsch, 1990; Rosenbloom, 2004[2]; Way & Chen, 2000) or Asian American youth (Way & Chen, 2000). One possible explanation for the lack of gender differences among African American youth may be that African American boys experience more supportive friendships than both European American or Latino boys and thus mean level differences in friendship support among African American boys and girls are not significant. This interpretation is corroborated by recent survey-based research showing that although African American and White girls report similar levels of friendship quality, African American boys report having more intimate close friendship than White and/or Latino adolescent boys (DuBois & Hirsch, 1990; Jones et al., 1994).

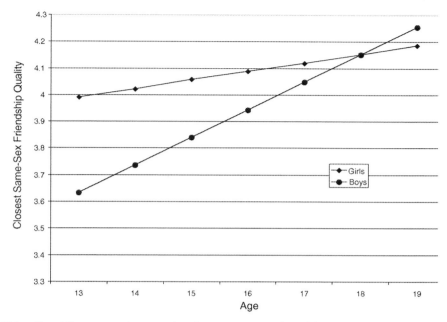

Figure 17.2   Fitted linear growth curves for closest same-sex friendship quality a function of gender.

With regard to gender differences, our research indicates that boys tend to experience sharper improvements over time than girls in the perceived quality of closest friendships. Although boys begin high school reporting lower levels of support in their closest friendships than girls, by their latter years of high school, boys and girls report comparable mean levels of support from their closest friends (see Figure 17.2). Previous research has also shown gender differences in perceptions of friendship support to be more pronounced among young adolescents than older adolescents (Azmitia et al., 1998). Boys may start high school being particularly wary of intimate or close friendships with other boys due to heightened fears of being perceived as gay (see McAnGhaill, 1996; Raymond, 1994). Scholars have noted the extent to which early adolescents, in particular, are consumed with concerns about sexuality and the way others perceive them (Chu, 2004; Tolman, 2002). This period of development may be particularly difficult for boys because the homophobic culture in which they develop implicitly and explicitly discourages intimate, male friendships (Chu, 2004; Raymond, 1994). Yet as boys become more secure in their own identities and involved in romantic relationships, they may become more willing and interested in engaging in intimate, male friendships (Azmitia et al., 1996). Gender differences in rates of improvements in perceived friendship quality may also be due to the differing socialization practices of boys and girls. The socialization of girls often emphasizes relational skills and interpersonal understanding (see Gilligan, 1982), while the socialization of boys often emphasizes autonomy and individuation (Kimmel, 2004). Thus, girls may acquire the necessary interpersonal and cognitive skills needed for close and supportive friendship at an earlier age than boys. Additional research is needed to understand the reasons for such gender differences in trajectories of friendship quality.

The Quality of Friendships: Qualitative Data

Although research has examined *the extent to which* adolescents feel intimate or supported in their friendships, very little research has focused on how adolescents make meaning of or experience their friendships in the first place. There has been an implicit and explicit assumption in the friendship research that we already know *how* adolescents experience their friendships and thus should focus instead on the frequencies or intensity of these experiences. Yet descriptive research on how adolescents experience friendships is not only dated (Sullivan, 1954; Selman, 1980; Youniss & Smollar, 1985), it is also based primarily on White middle class adolescents. Furthermore, research has rarely explored how friendship experiences and meanings vary by age, gender, or race/ethnicity (exceptions include Azmitia et al., 1998). Our longitudinal studies of ethnic minority, low-income adolescents are one of the only sets of studies that has explored the ways in which adolescents experience their friendships from early to late adolescence and how these experiences *during* adolescence vary by age, gender, and race/ethnicity.

In-depth interviews over a 4- to 5-year period revealed themes of *closeness, desire, and distrust*, and subthemes within each of these themes, in the friendships of urban, low SES, ethnic minority youth (Way et al., 2004; Way & Pahl, 2001). For example, closeness is experienced not only as a result of intimate disclosures but also as a result of borrowing and loaning money. Furthermore, these three themes are interwoven such that, for example, the theme of distrust (i.e., not trusting anyone) formed a type of "context" for the experience of closeness. Over the next few pages, we describe these three overarching patterns, the subthemes within each pattern, and the ways in which these patterns vary by gender, ethnicity, and age.

I. Closeness

In our interviews, adolescents spoke at length about the ways in which they felt close to their best friends. Interestingly, when asked why they felt close to their best friends (or how their best friend was different from their other friends), commonly expressed sentiments included claims that they could trust their best friends with their *secrets* and their *money*. In addition, adolescents voiced feelings that they could trust closest friends to *protect them from harm* and that they would "be there" when needed. Although trust was consistently the foundation of closeness in friendships, the ways in which the adolescents in our studies trusted their friends varied across gender and occasionally ethnicity. Finally, adolescents conveyed feelings of closeness to their best friends due to the fact that their *family knew their friends and their friends' families* (and vice versa). Thus, while the literature typically characterizes adolescent friendship closeness by the extent to which each partner in the friendship shares intimate details of their lives (Savin-Williams & Berndt, 1990), the adolescents in our studies revealed that the experience of closeness (and trust) stems from a much broader array of experiences.

Sharing Secrets

As predicted from the theoretical and research literature, the vast majority of adolescents spoke with great passion and conviction about their best friend(s) with whom they trusted to share "everything." When Amanda was asked what she liked about her best friend, she replied, "She keeps everything a secret, whatever I tell her." Maria responded similarly saying, "Like the back of their hands....I can talk to her about anything, like if I call her, I'm hysterically crying or something just happened or whatever,...and maybe she'll be doing something, she'll stop doing that to come and talk to me and to help me." Brian stated about his best friends, "I tell them anything about me and I know they won't tell anybody else unless I tell them to."

A key part of this sharing process appeared to be mutuality. When asked to define a best friend, Justin responded, "He could just tell me anything and I could tell him anything. Like I always know everything about him.... We always chill, like we don't hide secrets from each other." In responding to a question probing what he liked about his friend, Justin replied, "If I have a problem, I can go tell him. If he has a problem, he can go tell me." Similarly, Steven stated about his best friends, "We share secrets that we don't talk about it in the open." When asked to explain why he felt close to his friends, he stated, "If I'm having problems at home, they'll like counsel me, I just trust them with anything, like deep secrets, anything." When Jerome, a 16-year-old West Indian boy was asked to describe his best friend, he said,

He's like a brother, I could tell him anything, anything. If I ask him to keep it a secret, he will keep it a secret. If he tells me something, he tells me not to tell nobody. I keep it a secret. If I need him, I know he's going to be there...When I talk about problems...he'll tell me or give me ideas or things to do.

Expressing "deep depth secrets" and "private stuff" was a central part of the friendships of the boys and girls in our studies.

Sharing Money

In addition to the sharing of secrets, sharing money was another way in which adolescents, especially boys, expressed closeness with each other in their friendships. Like a mantra, most of the boys and some of the girls stated, in response to a question of how/why they felt close to their friends, that sharing secrets and money made them feel close to their best friends. To illustrate, when Randall was asked how he felt close to his friends, he replied because he can "trust them completely." When asked to explain how he trusted his friends, he responded, "I trust them to hold my money, and I trust them to, if I lend them money they'll pay me back." In answering the same set of questions, Nathan replied, "I could leave any amount of money with him. He gave me money, I give him money. If I need something, he gives it to me, I give it to him [if he needs something]...." In a few instances, sharing of money was also reported by girls, as was the case with Nicole. When asked to describe her best friend, Nicole stated that she is a friend she can "really trust." When asked about a recent time that she trusted her best friend, Nicole replied, "We went shopping and I put money in her pocket, but I forgot about how much I had given her. And then she gave me the right amount back...." In addition to knowing that friends would pay them back, the adolescents also emphasized their willingness to loan their friends money. Sharing, borrowing, and loaning money were distinct components of feelings of closeness in friendships.

Protection From Harm

Among the Black and Latino boys, closeness was also experienced in the knowledge that one's friend would protect them from harm. Although some of the girls and the Asian American boys also voiced this theme, it was especially apparent among Black and Latino boys who repeatedly emphasized the importance of knowing that their closest friends would protect them in fights and that they would, in turn, reciprocate the protection. For example, when Raphael was asked by an interviewer, "What kinds of things could you trust with your [closest] friends?" he replied, "Let's just say I had a big fight, I got beat up, I had like five guys against me, they'll come and they'll help me out." Similarly, Akil responded to the same question, "You get into a fight with somebody else; [my best friend] will tell me to calm down, child...like when someone jumps me, he will help me." Armondo also discussed how the bonds between he and his friends were enhanced by the protection of each other in fights. He described a time when he and his three male friends were confronted by another group of boys who wanted to fight, explaining to the interviewer how it was up to him to protect his friends, "And I'm behind my friend....if something happened to him where it was like he couldn't react fast enough and I was behind him, it would have been up to me to...protect him and help him out." Armondo further explained that had he not protected his friend, consequent exclusion by his friends would have ensued, "If something had happened and I didn't do anything, I'm just standing like a big dummy, you know, I mean, none of them would ever want to hang out with me again, and it would be the same with any of them. So, it's a trust thing." As a result of this incident, Armondo stated that he and his friends felt closer to each other knowing each would protect the other if necessary.

Like the theme of shared secrets and shared money, the theme of protection was often evident in the adolescents' responses regarding how they trusted their friends rather than how they felt close to their friends. However, the interviewer's questions regarding the experience of trust was almost always in response to adolescents claiming that they felt close to their friends because they could trust them.

These stories of protection from harm were striking in the boys' willingness to express feelings of vulnerability. Although boys voiced beliefs that they and their best friends protected each other, they did not emphasize, as one might expect based on images of "hypermasculinity" (Stevenson, 2004), the protection of their friends. Rather, the boys' emphasis was more on how their friends would protect them if needed. African American and Latino boys, in particular, openly referred to and seemed proud of such interdependency with their closet male friends.

The Family-Friend Connection

Among the Black and Latino adolescents, in general, closeness also appeared to be experienced as a result of their families knowing each other. Anthony's aunt (who is his primary caretaker) used to baby sit Pedro who is his best friend. His other best friend's mom is the best friend of his aunt. These connections, he said, were one of the primary reasons why he trusted his friends to keep his secrets. The mother of Minda's best friend is the best friend of her mother. Minda claimed that the fact that she and her mother have best friends from the same family made her feel closer not only to her mother but also to her best friend. Michael made similar claims about his best friend, saying, "Since we were real small I have known his whole family, he knows everybody in my house, we just walk over to his crib, open his fridge without asking or something, that's how long we've know each other." Similarly, Armando responded when asked what makes him close to his best friend, "Um basically 'cause he knows my family. If you know somebody's parents, then you know how far the trust can be stretched." Bringing their friends into the fold of their families and becoming part of their friends' family allowed the adolescents to trust and feel close to their friends.

Change Over Time in Experiences of Closeness

Sharing secrets, sharing money, protection from harm, and having family/friend connections comprised the primary ways in which adolescents trusted and consequently felt close to their friends. For the most part, these themes of closeness did not vary over time. The content of these themes, however, shifted over time. For example, although the secrets that were shared during the first year of the study included revealing a crush on a girl or boy or a score on a test from class, by the fourth year "shared secrets" focused more on struggles in romantic relationships or family conflicts. Similarly, although protection from harm involved protection in physical fights during the first few years of the study, by the latter years it entailed protecting each other from emotional (e.g., being betrayed) as well as physical harm. The only exception to this pattern of stability in the themes of closeness was the experience of shared money which seemed less evident in the interviews during the latter years of the study than in the earlier years. This shift may be due to the fact that the adolescents by this time were working and thus borrowing money was, perhaps, less necessary.

II. Desire

With a clarity that is striking in light of the dominant beliefs about boys' friendships, the boys who reported not having closest same-sex friendships (10–30% depending on the year) consistently expressed a strong yearning for such friendships. For example, Albert told the interviewer, "I would like a friend that if I got anything to say to him or like any problems or anything I'll tell him and he'll tell me his problems." In contrast to what the research literature suggests (Belle, 1989; Buhrmester & Furman, 1987), Albert's wish for a close friend was not based on a desire for friends with whom to "do things," but instead, to discuss personal problems. After describing the betrayals of friends who will "talk behind your back" Victor similarly stated, "Basically I hate it, I hate it, cause you now I wouldn't mind talking to somebody my age that I can relate to 'em on a different basis." Boys, like Albert and Victor, expressed yearning for friends who "would really be there" and with whom they could share their "true feelings."

Significantly, these stories of desire for friendships that involve high levels of self-disclosure were not stories revealed exclusively by acutely sensitive boys who were socially isolated in the school context. They were stories heard from popular boys who were members of athletic teams as well as those involved in theater arts. These stories were heard from straight "A" students and students who were struggling academically. The language of yearning for intimacy with other males was used by laid back, macho, "hip hop" boys wearing low riding pants, a Walkman around their necks, baseball caps drawn low over their brows, and untied sneakers. Boys, who have been portrayed in popular culture as more interested in shooting each other than in sharing their thoughts and feelings, spoke to us about wanting male friendships with whom they could "share their secrets," "tell everything," and "get inside."

III. Distrust

In striking contrast to the themes of intimacy and desire, one of the most pervasive themes we heard among all of the adolescents in our studies was a distrust of peers. Adolescents often spoke of a world in which peers will "try to take over you and take you for everything you've got and step on you." For example, in response to a question about his male peers in general, Anthony responded, "I don't trust [them], I trust me, myself, and I. That's the way I am. I trust nobody." Although he reported having a best friend during all 4 years of the study, a friend in whom he voiced being able to confide in and to whom he felt close to, his overall perception of his peers in general involved much mistrust. Richard too, spoke about distrusting his male peers, saying, "Can't trust anybody nowadays. They are trying to scam you, or scheme, or talk about you." Richard admitted that although he had never directly experienced these types of betrayals from his male peers, he "know[s] what most of [them] are like."

Interestingly, during the early high school years, themes of distrust of peers seemed almost cliché, something that the adolescents perpetuated among themselves but did not really believe. However, by the junior and senior years in high school, most of the adolescents discussed actual experiences of betrayal and thus of feeling like they could no longer trust their friends. For example, although Joseph, a Dominican student, reported having a best friend when he was in the ninth and tenth grades, by his junior year of high school the situation had changed.

> Interviewer: Do you have a close or best friend?
>
> Joseph: No, I don't trust nobody.
>
> Interviewer: You don't trust nobody? How come?
>
> Joseph: Can't trust nobody these days.
>
> Interviewer: Have you had bad experiences with people?
>
> Joseph: Yeah, especially this year

Like Joseph, many of the boys and girls indicated, particularly during late adolescence, struggling to trust their friends and maintain close friendships.

Notably, when girls spoke about distrusting their peers, they often referred only to other girls generally believing that boys, in contrast, could be trusted. For example, when asked to compare her male friends with her female friends, Monique replied, "Well in a way I think I'm closer to guy friends than girls 'cause girls stab you in your back and you can't really talk to them that much because they spread rumors around about you." Anna similarly stated, "I prefer hanging out with guys because I think they won't talk about you...I only tell my best [female] friend like secrets and stuff but with boys it's like a friendship. Like we all go in groups to the movies and we hang out." Elizabeth also responded, "To me I feel more comfortable with the guys than the girls because the girls are like always talking about other girls. This girl did this, this girl did that.... The girls might talk about one certain girl that they can't stand or something and I might know her."

The striking aspect of girls' stories of trusting boys was that in the same breath that girls spoke about trusting boys more than girls, their closest friends were almost always girls. Similar to the theme of distrust of peers in the early years of the studies, distrusting other girls had a cliché quality to it ("girls are catty") since the girls' beliefs about not trusting other girls did not appear to influence who they chose as best friends.

Contradiction was also evident in adolescents' stories of close friendships. Distrusting one's peers, even distrusting "everybody," was discussed at the same time that adolescents discussed the ways they felt close to, passionate about, and loyal toward their best same-sex friends. The juxtaposition of vigorous statements of "trusting no one" alongside statements of love and affection for one's best friend suggested a type of "relational resilience" in which adolescents maintained close relationships with their peers despite a context characterized by distrust. This resilience is evident each year of the interviews but seems especially prevalent in latter years. As the feelings of distrust of peers intensified over time, the feelings of closeness also seemed to intensify. This pattern of improvement in perceptions of one's closest friend over time is confirmed in our quantitative data (Way & Greene, in press). The context of distrust of one's peers may make adolescents more selective regarding who they consider a best friend; thus also possibly enhancing adolescents' sense of closeness with those friends who can be trusted.

Summary of Quality of Friendships: Qualitative Data

Similar to what the research literature has suggested (Savin-Williams & Berndt, 1990), shared secrets were a critical part of the experience of closeness for the adolescents in our studies. Contrary to the existing literature on friendships, however, shared secrets or the desire to share secrets was just as important for boys as for girls. Perhaps among adolescents who come from more interdependent cultures (e.g., poor and working class, African American, Latino, and Asian American families), sharing the intimate details of one's life with close friends is more normative than among adolescents who come from more autonomy-focused cultures (e.g., European American, middle-class families). It is also possible that our findings are more a product of methodology than of sample demographics. The ways in which we conduct qualitative research entails creating a safe space for young people to share their thoughts and feelings and encouraging them to speak about what they find most meaningful (see Way, 1998). Such research may be better equipped to "unpack" the meaning of closeness than more close-ended surveys typically used in quantitative research. Indeed, Chu (2004) also found in her qualitative research with primarily White, middle-class adolescent boys that sharing secrets was an important part of friendships for these boys as well.

Moreover, results from our qualitative findings suggest that in addition to the sharing of secrets, closeness was based on sharing money, physical and emotional protection, and having family/friend connections. Again, it is unclear whether these elements of closeness are unique to the ethnic minority low SES, urban adolescents in our studies, or whether similar variations in the meaning of closeness would be evident for youth of different backgrounds. It is likely, however, that the sharing of money is more relevant for those who have less money than for those for whom money is not a concern. Similarly, protection from harm may be particularly critical for those raised in environments where they do not feel safe. Finally the value of family/friend connections might be especially important for those adolescents coming from cultures in which family relationships are strongly emphasized. "Fictive kin" has been explored for decades in the research on African American family relationships (Stack, 1974) and our research suggests that these fictive kin networks are also important for understanding adolescent friendships. Themes connecting friends and family, however, were not evident among Asian American adolescents which may be due to parents' values and beliefs (Way & Chen, 2000). Asian American adolescents in our studies often spoke of their parents being distrustful of their peers, particularly peers who were not Asian, and not allowing their children's friends to come to their homes (Way & Pahl, 2001; Way & Greene, 2005). This prohibition may influence the extent to which non-familial friends and family members blend together.

Distrust of peers was also a significant theme in our data. Reasons for the high levels of distrust might lie with the racism and harassment experienced by the adolescents on a daily basis (see Rosenbloom & Way, 2004). This lack of trust likely affects adolescents' ability to trust each other (Epstein & Karweit, 1983). Increases in distrust over time, particularly distrust of same-sex peers, may also be due to the increased likelihood of having actually experienced a betrayal by a friend and by the "compulsory heterosexuality" (see Tolman, 2002) that weighs down on girls and boys particularly during middle and late adolescence, often leading them to betray their same-sex friends. Adolescents, particularly the boys, found it increasingly difficult to find and maintain same-sex friendships as they grew older which is likely due, at least in part, to gender expectations regarding what it means to be "a man" or "woman" and the embedded homophobia in mainstream messages regarding masculinity and femininity (Chu, 2004; McAnGhaill, 1996; Raymond, 1994). Nevertheless, these feelings of distrust, for the most part, did not preclude close, trusting friendships from flourishing. Indeed, although the context of friendships was one of mistrust, the friendships themselves appeared quite trustworthy and close. Understanding what allows for or supports adolescents' "relational resilience" is an important area for future investigation.

IMPLICATIONS FOR FUTURE RESEARCH

Having described our efforts to understand ethnic minority low SES, urban adolescents' experiences of friendships, we dedicate the remaining portion of this chapter to describing prevailing gaps in the literature, with the hope of inspiring further inquiry into the peer experiences of adolescents from ethnically, socioeconomically, and geographically diverse backgrounds. We believe that such research is critical, for despite changing demographics—resulting in a proliferation of ethnic minority adolescents in the United States (U.S. Census Bureau, 2004)—there remains a dearth of research on ethnic minority adolescents' experiences in the world (Fitzgerald, Lester, & Zuckerman, 1995; Garcia Coll, Akerman, & Cicchetti, 2000; Garcia Coll et al., 1996; Graham, 1992, 1994; Way & Chen, 2000).

Indeed, in order to respond to the needs of such an increasingly diverse adolescent population, several important research agendas should be explored. Future research should examine the multiple intersecting and overlapping contexts that shape the ways in which adolescents experience their friendships and how friendships change and shape the contexts in which they are embedded. Furthermore, multimethod, longitudinal research exploring how the predictors of friendships or the processes affecting adolescent peer experiences change over time is needed. As our own research suggests, exclusive reliance on survey, questionnaire, or observational methods may seriously constrain our understanding of adolescents' friendships.

Contextual-Correlates of Friendships

As noted throughout this chapter, relatively little attention has been paid to the ways in which adolescent friendships are embedded within multiple social networks. In fact, the majority of friendship research has focused on the correlates (e.g., psychological adjustment) and consequences of friendships (e.g., delinquency, drug use, academic outcomes), without concomitant attention to understanding the contextual variables that shape the friendship experiences and the ways in which friendships, in turn, alter these contexts. Such neglect is especially surprising given the proliferation of research exploring how multiple settings or contexts influence child development (Brooks-Gunn et al., 1993; Burton et al., 1995; Seidman, 1991). Despite the fact that adolescents' experiences with peers take place in multiple contexts—including families, schools, neighborhoods, and communities—few studies have used an ecological framework to explore how these contexts influence the nature, type, quality, or experiences of adolescent friendships (DuBois & Hirsch, 1990; Epstein, 1989; Phelan et al., 1994). Accordingly, future research should consider how contextual-features interact with children's friendship experiences. In all probability, the experience of friendships may be quite different for adolescents living in, for example, single- versus two-parent homes, first versus second generation families, dangerous versus safe neighborhoods, economically disadvantaged versus well-funded schools (Elias & Dilworth, 2003); the list is endless.

Adolescents' Experience of Friendships

Relatedly, a second limitation to the friendship literature is a failure to consider adolescents' actual friendship experiences. This is surprising given the fact that the degree to which adolescents attach importance to various traits and behaviors will likely vary by the extent that they (1) are exposed to various norms and values in the larger society and (2) associate with peers who come from differing racial/ethnic backgrounds (Aboud, 1987). Thus, although many researchers have argued that people tend to make distinct causal attributions for similar behaviors (Triandis, 1976; Triandis, Vassiliou, Vassiliou, Tanaka, & Shanmungan, 1972), the ever-increasing diversity of schools and other significant socializing contexts encountered by adolescents (e.g., neighborhood/community) will likely impact adolescent experiences of friendships. This is especially true given that over the course of adolescence, friends increase significantly in importance (Blyth, Hill, & Thiel, 1982; Brown, Eicher, & Petrie, 1986), with most free time spent in the company of peers (Csikszentmihalyi & Larson, 1984), from both in-and out-of-school contexts (Blyth et al., 1982; Montemayor & Van Komen, 1980). Understanding the extent to which variations in cultural (e.g., ethnicity, race, immigration history, SES, gender etc.) beliefs and values interact with other socializing agents to shape the friendship experiences of ethnically and socioeconomically diverse groups of adolescents is clearly warranted.

Age-related Changes in Friendship Experiences

Additional longitudinal studies investigating how friendships change over time during adolescence and from adolescence to young adulthood are also warranted. Indeed, with regard to friendships, researchers have noted repeatedly (e.g., Newcomb & Bagwell, 1996) that longitudinal research is extremely limited, with much of it conducted over brief periods of time, with middle-class, White adolescents (e.g., Buhrmester & Furman, 1987) or with young children (e.g., Ladd, 1990). Notwithstanding, the extant research has suggested that over time, friendships become more intimate and self-disclosing, with gender differences in friendship quality becoming more pronounced during the transition from childhood to early adolescence (Berndt, 1989; Crockett et al., 1984; Furman & Burhmester, 1992; Hirsch & Rapkin, 1987; Youniss & Smollar, 1985) but less pronounced from early to late adolescence (Azmitia et al.,1998). Our research suggests a similar pattern but also indicates that gender differences may be context-specific.

As adolescents mature, more sophisticated thought processes enable them to make comparisons between themselves and others (Barenboim, 1981). Such comparisons not only enhance adolescents' understanding of their own beliefs, behaviors, and characteristics, but also promote friendship formation based on similarly shared beliefs and expectations, or on the flip side, discouraging relationships with dissimilar peers (Youniss & Smollar, 1985). Paralleling the maturation of adolescent thought processes, adolescent exposure to diverse groups of peers increases, with middle and high schools providing some adolescents their first contact with youth from diverse ethnic backgrounds (Epstein & Karweit, 1983; Hamm, 1998). Consequently, with regard to cross-ethnic/race friendships, this exposure may contribute to increased experiences of discrimination and a tendency to judge others in terms of existing stereotypes (Hamm, 1998). Future research, taking into account intrapersonal, interpersonal, and contextual antecedents and consequences of friendship quality, characteristics, and formation *over time*, is warranted (Hamm, 2000). Examining the dynamic process of friendship development over time and in context will enhance our understanding of friendships in particular and also of adolescent development more broadly.

Qualitative Understanding of Adolescent Friendships

As described in this chapter, implications from our own qualitative research (Way, 1998; Way & Pahl, 1999) suggest that longitudinal studies would also benefit from the inclusion of a qualitative component aimed at understanding the experiences of friendships themselves. Indeed, our qualitative findings indicate that what some presume to be the typical friendship patterns of adolescent boys (based primarily on survey research) inadequately represents the types of friendships that, at the very least, urban, ethnically diverse adolescent boys from low-income families actually experience or desire. We believe that such qualitative findings have significant implications for future studies of adolescents' friendships, and development more broadly. By relying exclusively on survey research for descriptions of adolescent processes, resulting theoretical predictions and explanations of such processes may be based on insufficient grounding. Taking into account participants' voices and personal experiences, qualitative, interview based research with ethnically diverse groups of youth should strengthen current understanding of adolescent development and, consequently, human development.

Concluding Remarks

There continues to be only a small body of developmental research on the friendships of racial and ethnic minorities (Fitzgerald et al., 1995; Garcia Coll et al., 2000, 1996; Graham, 1992, 1994). This is especially troubling given the centrality of peer relationships during adolescence. Moreover, few studies have examined the ways in which contexts or settings shape adolescent friendships (and vice versa) or the ways in which friendships are experienced within diverse contexts. Thus, longitudinal research that considers competing and corresponding socializing messages originating in and reinforced by the family, peer, school, and neighborhood contexts is critical (Phelan, Davidson, & Cao, 1991). Bronfenbrenner's (1977; 1979) ecological model of human behavior provides a framework that is particularly suitable for understanding the ways in which contexts influence friendships or how youth experience varying contexts and/or relationships. In order to adequately understand the development of friendships among adolescents, future research must move beyond uni-dimensional, uni-methodological, and uni-population approaches to explore the contextual correlates, characteristics, and quality of friendships among adolescents from ethnically, socio-economically, and geographically diverse backgrounds using multimethod approaches.

NOTES

1. Family support was highly correlated with mother support and less correlated with father support thus indicating that family support was in large part an assessment of mother support.
2. This citation is from a Masters Thesis completed at New York University based on the data from Dr. Niobe Way's studies of friendship development among ethnic minority, low-income, urban adolescents.
3. This citation is from a Doctoral Dissertation based on the data from Dr. Niobe Way's studies of friendship development among ethnic minority, low-income, urban adolescents

REFERENCES

Aboud, F. E. (1987). The development of ethnic self-identification and attitudes. In J. S. Phinney & M. J. Rotherman (Eds.), *Children's ethnic socialization: Pluralism and development* (pp. 32–55). Newbury Park, CA: Sage.

Adolescent Pathways Project. (1992). Pennsylvania State University.

Ainsworth, M. D., & Bowlby, J. (1991). An ethological approach to personality development. *American Psychologist, 46,* 333–341.

Andersen, C. S. (1982). The search for school climate: A Review of the research. *Review of Educational Research, Review of Educational Research, 368*–420.

Armsden, G. C., & Greenberg, M. T. (1987). The Inventory of Parent and Peer Attachment: Individual differences and their relationship to psychological well-being in adolescence. *Journal of Youth & Adolescence, 16,* 427–454.

Ary, D. V., Duncan, T. E., Duncan, S. C., & Hops, H. (1999). Adolescent problem behavior: The influence of parents and peers. *Behaviour Research & Therapy, 37,* 217–230.

Azmitia, M., Kamprath, N., & Linnet, J. (1998). Intimacy and conflict: The dynamics of boys' and girls' friendships during middle childhood and early adolescence. In L. Meyer, H. Park, M. Grnot-Scheyer, I. Schwartz & B. Harry (Eds.), *Making friends: The influences of culture and development* (pp. 171–189). Baltimore: Brookes Publishingy.

Barenboim, C. (1981). The development of person perception in childhood and adolescence: From behavioral comparisons to psychological constructs to psychological comparisons. *Child Development, 52,* 129–144.

Bartholomew, K., Cobb, R. J., & Poole, J. A. (1997). Adult attachment patterns and social support processes. In G. R. Pierce, B. Lakey, I. Sarason & B. R. Sarason (Eds.), *The sourcebook of social support and personality* (pp. 359–378). New York: Plenum Press.

Belle, D. (Ed.). (1989). *Children's social networks and social supports.* Oxford, UK: Wiley.

Berg, M., & Medrich, E. A. (1980). Children in four neighborhoods: The physical environment and its effect on play and play patterns. *Environment and Behavior, 12,* 320–348.

Berndt, T. (1989). The nature and significance of children's friendships. In R. Vasta (Ed.), *Annals of Child Development* (Vol. 5, pp. 155–186). Greenwich, CT: JAI Press.

Blyth, D. A., Hill, J. P., & Thiel, K. S. (1982). Early adolescents' significant others: Grade and gender differences in perceived relationships with familial and non-familial adults and young people. *Journal of Youth & Adolescence, 11,* 425–450.

Bronfenbrenner, U. (1977). Toward an experimental ecology of human development. *American Psychologist, 32,* 513–530.

Bronfenbrenner, U. (1979). *The ecology of human development: Experiments by nature and design.* Cambridge: Harvard University Press.

Bronfenbrenner, U. (1989). Ecological systems theory. *Annals of Child Development, 6,* 187–249.

Brooks-Gunn, J., Duncan, G. J., Klebanov, P., & Sealand, N. (1993). Do neighborhoods influence child and adolescent development? *American Journal of Sociology, 99,* 353–395.

Brown, B., Eicher, S. A., & Petrie, S. (1986). The importance of peer group ("crowd") affiliation in adolescence. *Journal of Adolescence, 9,* 73–96.

Brown, B., Mounts, N., Lamborn, S., & Steinberg, L. (1993). Parenting practices and peer group affiliation in adolescence. *Child Development, 69,* 771–791.

Brown, B. B. (1990). Peer groups and peer cultures. In S. S. Feldman & G. R. Elliot (Eds.), *At the threshold: The developing adolescent* (pp. 171–195). Cambridge: Harvard University Press.

Brown, L., Tappan, M., Gilligan, C., Miller, B., & Argyris, D. (1989). Reading for self and moral voice: A method for interpreting narratives of real-life moral conflict and choice. In M. Packer & R. Addison (Eds.), *Entering the circle: Hermeneutic investigation in psychology* (pp. 141–164). Albany: SUNY Press.

Buhrmester, D. (1990). Intimacy of friendship, interpersonal competence, and adjustment during preadolescence and adolescence. *Child Development, 61,* 1101–1111.

Buhrmester, D., & Furman, W. (1987). The development of companionship and intimacy. *Child Development, 58,* 1101–1113.

Bukowski, W. M., Newcomb, A. F., & Hartup, W. W. (1996). *The company they keep: Friendship in childhood and adolescence.* New York: Cambridge University Press.

Burton, L. M., Allison, K. W., & Obeidallah, D. (1995). Social context and adolescence: Perspectives on development among inner-city African-American teens. In L. J. Crockett & A. C. Crouter (Eds.), *Pathways through adolescence: Individual development in relation to social contexts* (pp. 119–138). Mahwah, NJ: Erlbaum.

Cairns, R. B., Xie, H., & Leung, M. (1998). The popularity of friendship and the neglect of social networks: Toward a new balance. In W. M. Bukowski & A. H. Cillessen (Eds.), *Sociometry then and now: Building on six decades of measuring children's experiences with the peer group: No 80. New directions for child development* (pp. 5–24). San Francisco: Jossey-Bass.

Cauce, A. M. (1986). Social networks and social competence: Exploring the effects of early adolescent friendships. *American Journal of Community Psychology, 14,* 607–628.

Cauce, A. M. (1987). School and peer competence in early adolescence: A test of domain-specific self-perceived competence. *Developmental Psychology, 23,* 287–291.

Cauce, A. M., Mason, C. A., Gonzales, N., Hiraga, Y., & Liu, G. (1996). Social support during adolescence: Methodological and theoretical considerations. In K. Hurrelmann & S. F. Hamilton (Eds.), *Social problems and social contexts in adolescence* (pp. 131–153). Hawthorne, NY: Aldine.

Chu, J. (2004). A relational perspective on adolescent boys' identity development. In N. Way & J. Chu. (Eds.), *Adolescent boys: Exploring diverse cultures beyond boyhood* (pp. 78–104). New York: New York University Press.

Cicchetti, D., Lynch, M., Shonk, S., & Manly, J. T. (1992). An organizational perspective on peer relations in maltreated children. In R. D. Parke & G. W. Ladd (Eds.), *Family-peer relationship: Modes of linkage* (pp. 345–383). Hillsdale, NJ: Erlbaum.

Clark, M. L., & Ayers, M. (1991). Friendship similarity during early adolescence: Gender and racial patterns. *Journal of Psychology, 126,* 393–405.

Collins, A. W., & Laursen, B. (1992). Conflicts and relationships in adolescence. In C. Shantz & W. W. Hartup (Eds.), *Conflict in Child and Adolescent development* (pp. 216–241). New York: Cambridge University Press.

Cooper, C. (1999). Multiple selves, multiple worlds: Cultural perspectives on individuality and connectedness in adolescent development. In A. Masten (Ed.), *Cultural processes in child development. The Minnesota symposia on child psychology. Vol. 29.* (pp. 25–57)

Cote, J. E. (1996). Sociological perspectives on identity formation: The culture-identity link and identity capital. *Journal of Adolescence, 19,* 417–432.

Crockett, L. J., Losoff, M., & Petersen, L. (1984). Perceptions of the peer group and friendship in early adolescence. *Journal of Early Adolescence, 4,* 155–181.

Crosnoe, R., Cavanagh, S., & Elder, G. H. (2003). Adolescent friendships as academic resources: The intersection of social relationships, social structure, and institutional context. *Sociological Perspectives, 46,* 331–352.

Csikszentmihalyi, M., & Larson, R. (1984). *Being adolescent: Conflict and growth in the teenage years.* New York: Basic Books.

DuBois, D. L., & Hirsch, B. J. (1990). School and neighborhood friendship patterns of blacks and whites in early adolescence. *Child Development, 61,* 524–536.

Eder, D. (1985). The cycle of popularity: Interpersonal relations among female adolescents. *Sociology of Education, 58,* 154–165.

Eder, D., Evans, C. C., & Parker, S. (1995). *School talk: Gender and adolescent culture.* New Brunswick, NJ: Rutgers University Press.

Elias, M. J., & Dilworth, J. E. (2003). Ecological/developmental theory, context-based best practice, and school-based action research: cornerstones of school psychology training and policy. *Journal of School Psychology, 41,* 293–297.

Epstein, J. L. (1989). The selection of friends: Changes across the grades in different school environments. In T. J. Berndt & G. W. Ladd (Eds.), *Peer relationships in child development* (pp. 158–187). New York: Wiley.

Epstein, J. L., & Karweit, N. (1983). *Friends in school: Patterns of selection and influence in secondary schools.* New York: Academic Press.

Farmer, E. M., & Rodkin, P. C. (1996). Antisocial and prosocial correlates of classroom positions: The social network centrality perspective. *Social Development, 5,* 174–188.

Fitzgerald, H. E., Lester, B. M., & Zuckerman, B. S. (1995). *Children of poverty: Research, health, and policy issues.*

Fuligni, A. J., & Eccles, J. S. (1993). Perceived parent-child relationships and early adolescents' orientation toward peers. *Developmental Psychology, 29,* 622–632.

Furman, W. (1996). The measurement of friendship perceptions: Conceptual and methodological issues. In W. M. Bukowski & F. Newcomb (Eds.), *The company they keep: Friendships in Childhood and Adolescence* (pp. 41–65). New York: Cambridge University Press.

Furman, W., & Buhrmester, D. (1985). Children's perceptions of the personal relationships in their social networks. *Developmental Psychology, 21,* 1016–1024.

Furman, W., & Buhrmester, D. (1992). Age and sex differences in perceptions of networks of personal relationships. *Child Development, 65,* 103–115.

Garcia Coll, C., Akerman, A., & Cicchetti, D. (2000). Cultural differences on developmental processes and outcomes: Implications for the study of development and psychopathology. *Development & Psychopathology, 12,* 333–356.

Garcia Coll, C., Lamberty, G., Jenkins, R., McAdoo, H. P., Crnic, K., Wasik, B. H., et al. (1996). An integrative model for the study of developmental competencies in minority children. *Child Development, 67,* 1891–1914.

Gavin, L. A., & Furman, W. (1989). Age difference in adolescents' perceptions of their peer groups. *Developmental Psychology, 25,* 827–834.

Gest, S. D., Graham-Bermann, S. A., & Hartup, W. (2001). Peer experience: Common and unique features of number of friendships, social network centrality, and sociometric status. *Social Development, 10,* 23–40.

Gifford-Smith, M. E., & Brownell, C. A. (2003). Childhood peer relationships: social acceptance, friendships, and peer networks. *Journal of School Psychology, 41,* 235–284.

Gingold, R. (2003). *The influence of parenting beliefs and messages about friendships on adolescent friendships.* Unpublished dissertation completed at Yeshiva University.

Graham, S. (1992). "Most of the subjects were White and middle class": Trends in published research on African Americans in selected APA journals. *American Psychologist, 47,* 629–639.

Graham, S. (1994). Motivation in African Americans. *Review of Educational Research, 64,* 55–117.

Greenberg, M. T., Siegel, J. M., & Leitch, C. J. (1983). The nature and importance of attachment relationships to parents and peers during adolescence. *Journal of Youth & Adolescence, 12,* 373–385.

Grobel, J., & Scharzer, R. (1982). Social comparison, expectations, and emotional reactions in the classroom. *School Psychology International, 3,* 49–56.

Hagan, J. W., & Conley, A. C. (1994). Ethnicity and race of children studied in Child Development, 1980–1993. *Society for Research in Child Development Newsletter,* 6–7.

Hamm, J. V. (1994). *Similarity in the face of diversity? African American, Asian American, European-American, and Hispanic-American adolescents' best friendships in ethnically diverse high school.* Paper presented at the biennial meeting of the Society for Research on Adolescence, San Diego, CA.

Hamm, J. V. (1998). Negotiating the maze: Adolescents' cross-ethnic peer relations in ethnically diverse schools. In L. H. Meyer, H. S. Park, M. Grenot-Scheyer, I. S. Schwartz, & B. Harry (Eds.), *Making friends: The influences of culture and development* (pp. 243–261). Baltimore: Paul H. Brookes Publishing.

Hamm, J. V. (2000). Do birds of a feather flock together? The variable bases for African American, Asian American, and European American adolescents' selection of similar friends. *Developmental Psychology, 36,* 209–219.

Harter, S. (1990). Causes, correlates, and the functional role of global self-worth: A life-span perspective. In R. J. Sternberg & J. Kolligan (Eds.), *Competence considered* (pp. 67–97). New Haven, CT: Yale University Press.

Hartup, W. W. (1996). The company they keep: Friendships and their developmental significance. *Child Development, 67,* 1–13.

Hawley, P. H. (2002). Social dominance and prosocial and coercive strategies of resource control in preschoolers. *International Journal of Behavioral Development, 26,* 167–176.

Haynes, N., Emmons, C., & Comer, J. P. (1993). *Elementary and middle-school climate survey. Unpublished Manuscript:* Yale University Child Study Center.

Hinde, R. A. (1987). *Individuals, relationships, and culture.* Cambridge: Cambridge University Press.

Hirsch, B., & Rapkin, B. (1987). The transition to junior high school: A longitudinal study of self-esteem, psychological symptomatology, school life, and social support. *Child Development, 58,* 1235–1243.

Hirsch, B. J., & DuBois, D. L. (1990). The school-nonschool ecology of early adolescent friendships. In D. Belle (Ed.), *Children's social networks and social supports* (pp. 260–274). New York: Wiley.

Hoge, D. R., Smit, E. K., & Hanson, S. L. (1990). School experiences predicting changes in self-esteem of sixth- and seventh-grade students. *Journal of Educational Psychology, 82,* 117–127.

Homel, R., & Burns, A. (1989). Environmental quality and the wellbeing of children. *Social Indicators Research, 21,* 133–158.

Jencks, C., & Mayer, S. E. (1990). The social consequences of growing up in a poor neighborhood. In L. E. Lynn & M. McGeary (Eds.), *Inner city poverty in the United States* (pp. 111–186). Washington, DC: National Academy Press.

Jones, D. C., Costin, S. E., & Ricard, R. J. (1994, February). *Ethnic and sex differences in best friendship characteristics among African American, Mexican American, and European American adolescents.* Paper presented at the Society for Research on Adolescence, San Diego, CA.

Joyner, K., & Kao, G. (2000). School racial composition and adolescent racial homophily. *Social Science Quarterly, 81,* 810–825.

Kerns, K. A. (1994). A longitudinal examination of links between mother-child attachments and children's friendships in early childhood. *Journal of Social and Personal Relationships, 11,* 379–381.

Kerns, K. A., & Stevens, A. C. (1996). Parent-child attachment in late adolescence: Links to social relations and personality. *Journal of Youth & Adolescence, 25,* 323–342.

Kuperminc, G., Leadbeater, B. J., Emmons, C., & Blatt, S. J. (1997). Perceived school climate and problem behaviors in middle-school students: The protective function of a positive educational environment. *Journal of Applied Developmental Science, 1,* 76–88.

Ladd, G. W. (1990). Having friends, Keeping friends, making friends, and being liked by peers in the classroom: Predictors of children's early school adjustment? *Child Development, 61,* 1081–1100.

Lewin, K. (1951). *Field theory in social science. Selected theoretical papers.* Oxford, UK: Harpers.

Luthar, S. S., & McMahon, T. (1996). Peer reputation among inner city adolescents: Structure and correlates. *Journal of Research on Adolescence, 6,* 581–603.

McCarthy, J. D., & Hoge, D. R. (1982). Analysis of age effects in longitudinal studies of adolescent self-esteem. *Developmental Psychology, 18,* 372–379.

McLoyd, V. C. (1998). Changing demographics in this American population: Implications for research on minority children and adolescents. In V. C. McLoyd & L. Steinberg (Eds.), *Studying minority adolescents: Conceptual, methodological, and theoretical issues* (pp. 3–28). Mahwah, NJ: Erlbaum.

Miles, M. B., & Huberman, A. M. (1995). *Qualitative data analysis: An expanded sourcebook of new methods* (2nd ed.). Thousand Oaks, CA: Sage.

Minuchin, P. P., & Shapiro, E. K. (1983). The school as a context for social development. In P. H. Mussen (Ed.),

Handbook of child psychology: Vol. 4. Socialization, personality, and social development (pp. 197–275). New York: John Wiley.

Mischel, W. A. (1966). A social learning view of sex differences in behavior. In E. E. Maccoby (Ed.), *The development of sex differences* (pp. 56–81). Stanford, CA: Stanford.

Montemayor, R., & Van Komen, R. (1980). Age segregation of adolescents in and out of school. *Journal of Youth and Adolescence, 9*, 371–381.

Mott, F. L. (1994). Sons, daughters, and fathers' absence: Differentials in father-leaving probabilities and in home environments. *Journal of Family Issues, 15*, 97–128.

Mounts, N. (2004). Adolescents' perceptions of parental management of peer relationships in an ethnically diverse sample. *Journal of Adolescent Research, 19*, 428–445.

Mounts, N. S. (2001). Young adolescents' perceptions of parental management of peer relationships. *Journal of Early Adolescence, 21*, 92–122.

Mounts, N. S. (2002). Parental management of adolescent peer relationships in context: The role of parenting style. *Journal of Family Psychology, 16*, 58–69.

Newcomb, A., & Bagwell, C. L. (1996). The developmental significance of children's friendship relations. In W. Bukowski, A. Newcomb, & W. Hartup (Eds.), *The company they keep: Friendship in childhood and adolescence* (pp. 289–321). New York: Cambridge University Press.

O'Brian, S. F., & Bierman, K. L. (1988). Conceptions and perceived influence of peer groups: Interviews with preadolescents and adolescents. *Child Development, 59*, 1360–1365.

Parke, R. D., McDowell, D. J., Kim, M., Killian, C., Dennis, J., Flyr, M. L., et al. (2002). Fathers' contributions to children's peer relationships. In C. S. Tamis-LeMonda & N. Cabrera (Eds.), *Handbook of father involvement: Multidisciplinary perspectives* (pp. 141–168). Mahwah, NJ: Erlbaum.

Patterson, G. R., Dishion, T. J., & Yoerger, K. L. (2000). Adolescent growth in new forms of problem behavior: Macro- and micro-peer dynamics. *Prevention Science, 1*, 3–13.

Patterson, G. R., & Stouthamer-Loeber, M. (1984). The correlation of family management practices and delinquency. *Child Development, 55*, 1299–1307.

Phelan, P., Davidson, A. L., & Cao, H. T. (1991). Students' multiple worlds: Negotiating the boundaries of family, peer, and school cultures. *Anthropology and Education Quarterly, 22*, 224–250.

Phelan, P., Yu, H. C., & Davidson, A. L. (1994). Navigating the psychosocial pressure of adolescence: The voices and experiences of high school youth. *American Educational Research Journal, 31*, 415–447.

Procidano, M. (1992). The nature of perceived social support: Findings of meta-analytic studies. In C. D. Spielberger & J. N. Butler (Eds.), *Advances in personality assessment* (Vol. 9, pp. 1–26). Hillsdale, NJ: Erlbaum.

Procidano, M., & Heller, K. (1983). Measure of perceived social support from friends and family. *American Journal of Psychology, 11*(1–24).

Procidano, M., & Smith, W. W. (1997). Assessing perceived social support: The importance of context. In G. R. Pierce, B. Lakey, I. Saraivson & B. R. Sarason (Eds.), *The sourcebook of social support and personality* (pp. 93–106). New York: Plenum Press.

Raymond, D. (1994). Homophobia, identity, and the meanings of desire: Reflections on the culture construction of gay and lesbian adolescent sexuality. In J. Irvine (Ed.). *Sexual cultures and the construction of adolescent identities* (pp. 115–150). Philadelphia: Temple University Press.

Reyes, G. M., Goyette, M. K., & Bishop, J. A. (1996, March). *Friendship, peer acceptance, and social behaviors: Contributors to self-esteem.* Paper presented at the Society for Research on Adolescence, Boston, MA.

Rice, K., & Mulkeen, P. (1995). Relationships with parents and peers: A longitudinal study of adolescent intimacy. *Journal of Adolescent Research.* Vol. 10, 338–357.

Robinson, N. S. (1995). Evaluating the nature of received support and its relation to perceived self-worth in adolescents. *Journal of Research on Adolescence, 5*, 253–280.

Rodkin, P. C., Farmer, T. W., Pearl, R., & Van Acker, R. (2000). Heterogeneity of popular boys: Antisocial and prosocial configurations. *Developmental Psychology, 36*, 14–24.

Roeser, R. W., & Eccles, J. S. (1998). Adolescents' perceptions of middle school: Relation to longitudinal changes in academic and psychological adjustment. *Journal of Research on Adolescence, 8*, 123–158.

Roeser, R. W., Eccles, J. S., & Strobel, K. R. (1998). Linking the study of schooling and mental health: Selected issues and empirical illustrations at the level of the individual. *Educational Psychologist, 33*, 153–176.

Rogosa, D. R., & Willett, J. B. (1985). Understanding correlates of change by modeling individual differences in growth. *Psychometrika, 50*, 203–228.

Rosenbaum, G. (2000). *An investigation of the ecological factors associated with friendship quality in urban, low-income, racial and ethnic minority adolescents.* Unpublished Doctoral Dissertation completed at New York University.

Rosenbloom, S., & Way, N. (2004). Experiences of discrimination among African American, Asian American, and Latino adolescents in an urban high school. *Journal of Youth and Society.*

Rosenbloom, S. R. (2004). *The influence of the school context on urban adolescent friendships.* Unpublished Dissertation completed at New York University.

Salguero, C., & McCusker, W. (1996). Symptom expression in inner-city Latinas: Psychopathology or help-seeking? In B. J. Leadbeater & N. Way (Eds.), *Urban girls: Resisting stereotypes, creating identities.* New York: New York University Press.

Sarason, B. R., Pierce, G. R., & Sarason, I. G. (1990). Social support: The sense of acceptance and the role of relationships. In B. R. Sarason, I. G. Sarason & G. R. Pierce (Eds.), *Social support: An interactional view.* New York: John Wiley.

Savin-Williams, R. C., & Berndt, T. (1990). Friendship and peer relations. In S. S. Feldman & D. S. Elliot (Eds.), *At the threshold: The developing adolescent* (pp. 277–307). Cambridge, MA: Harvard University Press.

Seidman, E. (1991). Growing up the hard way: Pathways of urban adolescents. *American Journal of Community Psychology, 19*, 169–205.

Sharabany, R., Gershoni, R., & Hofman, J. (1981). Girlfriend, boyfriend: Age and sex differences in intimate friendship. *Developmental Psychology, 17*, 800–808.

Sherer, M. (1991). Peer group norms among Jewish and Arab juveniles in Israel. *Criminal Justice and Behavior, 18*, 267–286.

Shrum, W., Cheek, N. H., & Hunter, S. M. (1987). Friendship in school: General and racial homophily. *Sociology of Education, 61*, 227–239.

Shulman, S. (1993). Close friendships in early and mid adolescence: Typology and friendship reasoning. In B. Laursen (Ed.), *Close friendships in adolescence* (pp. 55–71). San Francisco: Jossey-Bass.

Snyder, J., Dishion, T. J., & Patterson, G. R. (1986). Determinants and consequences of associating with deviant peers during preadolescence and adolescence. *Journal of Early Adolescence, 6*, 29–43.

Snyder, T. D., & Hoffman, C. M. (1990). *Digest of educational statistics, 1990*. Washington, DC: National Center for Educational Statistics, U.S. Department of Education.

Sommer, B. (1985). What's different about truants? A comparison study of eighth graders. *Journal of Youth & Adolescence, 14*, 411–422.

Sroufe, L. A., & Waters, C. (1977). Attachment as an organizational construct. *Child Development, 48*, 1184–1199.

Stack, C. (1974). *All our kin: Strategies for survival in a black community*. New York: HarperCollins.

Stevenson, H. C. (2004). Boys in men's clothing: Racial socialization and neighborhood safety as buffers to hypervulnerability in African American adolescent males. In N. Way & J. Chu (Eds.), *Adolescent boys: Exploring diverse cultures of boyhood* (pp. 59–77). New York: New York University Press.

Suárez-Orozco, C. (2004). Formulating identity in a globalized world. In M. Suárez-Orozco & D. B. Qin-Hillard (Eds.), *Globalization: Culture and education in the new millennium* (pp. 173–202). Berkeley: University of California Press.

Suárez-Orozco, C., & Suárez-Orozco, M. M. (2001). *Children of immigration*. Cambridge, MA: Harvard University Press.

Tatum, B. D. (1997). *Why are all the black kids sitting together in the cafeteria?* New York: Basic.

Triandis, H. (1976). *Variations in black and white perceptions of the social environment*. Urbana: University of Illinois Press.

Triandis, H. C., Vassiliou, V., Vassiliou, G., Tanaka, Y., & Shanmungan, A. (1972). *The analysis of subjective culture*. New York: Wiley.

U.S. Census Bureau. (1999). *CenStats Databases*, http://tier2. census.gov/dbappweb.htm

U.S. Census Bureau. (2004). *CenStats Databases*, http://tier2. census.gov/dbappweb.htm

Updegraff, K. A., Madden-Derdich, D. A., Estrada, A. U., Sales, L. J., & Leonard, S. A. (2002). Young adolescents' experiences with parents and friends: Exploring the connections. *Family Relations: Journal of Applied Family & Child Studies, 51*, 72–80.

Updegraff, K. A., McHale, S. M., Crouter, A. C., & Kupanoff, K. (2001). Parents' involvement in adolescents' peer relationships: A comparison of mothers' and fathers' roles. *Journal of Marriage & the Family, 63*, 655–668.

Vernberg, E. M., Beery, S. H., Ewell, K. K., & Absender, D. A. (1993). Parents' use of friendship facilitation strategies and the formation of friendships in early adolescence: A prospective study. *Journal of Family Psychology, 7*, 356–369.

Way, N. (1996). Between experiences of betrayal and desire: Close friendships among urban adolescents. In B. J. Leadbeater & N. Way (Eds.), *Urban girls: Resisting stereotypes, creating identities* (pp. 173–93). New York: New York University Press.

Way, N. (1998). *Everyday courage: The lives and stories of urban teenagers*. New York: New York University Press.

Way, N. (2004). Intimacy, desire, and distrust in the friendships of adolescent boys. In N. Way & J. Y. Chu (Eds.), *Adolescent boys: Exploring diverse cultures of boyhood* (pp. 167-196). New York: New York University Press.

Way, N., & Chen, L. (2000). Close and general friendships among African American, Latino, and Asian American adolescents from low-income families. *Journal of Adolescent Research, 15*, 274-301.

Way, N., Cowal, K., Gingold, R., Pahl, K., & Bissessar, N. (2001). Friendship patterns among African American, Asian American, and Latino adolescents from low-income families. *Journal of Social and Personal Relationships, 18*, 29-53.

Way, N., & Greene, M. L. (under review). Changes in friendship quality from early to late adolescence among ethnic minority youth: Using Growth Curve Analysis to examine the patterns and predictors. *Journal of Research on Adolescence*.

Way, N., Greene, M. L., & Pahl, K. (2004, March). *School as a context for the development of social identities*. Paper presented at the Baltimore, MD, Society for Research on Adolescence.

Way, N., & Greene, M.L. (2005, April). Adolescents' Perceptions of their Parents Rules and Attitudes about Friendships: Ethnic differences and similarities. Paper presented at the Atlanta GE, Society for Research on Child Development.

Way, N., & Pahl, K. (1999). Friendship patterns among urban adolescent boys: A qualitative account. In M. Kopala & L. Suzuki (Eds.), *Using qualitative methods in psychology* (pp. 145-161). Thousand Oaks, CA: Sage Publications.

Way, N., & Pahl, K. (2001). Individual and contextual-level predictors of perceived friendship quality among ethnic minority, low-income adolescents. *Journal of Research on Adolescence, 11*, 325-349.

Way, N., & Robinson, M. (2003). The influence of family and friends on the psychological adjustment of ethnic minority, low-income adolescents. *Journal of Adolescent Research, 18*, 324-347.

Weiss, R. S. (1974). The provisions of social relationships. In Z. Rubin (Ed.), *Doing unto others* (pp. 17-26). Englewood Cliffs, NJ: Prentice Hall.

Wheelock, M. A., & Erickson, C. (1996). *Self-esteem: Examining gender, ethnic, socioeconomic status, and developmental differences*. Paper presented at the Association for Women in Psychology, Indianapolis, IN.

Willett, J. B., Singer, J. D., & Martin, N. C. (1998). The design and analysis of longitudinal studies of development and psychopathology in context: Statistical models and methodological recommendations. *Development and Psychopathology, 10*, 395-426.

Youngblade, L. M., Park, K. A., & Belsky, J. (1993). Measurement of young children's close friendship: A comparison of two independent assessment systems and their associations with attachment security. *International Journal of Behavioral Development, 16*, 563-587.

Youniss, J., & Smollar, J. (1985). *Adolescent relations with mothers, fathers, and friends*. Chicago: University of Chicago Press.

Zisman, P. M., & Wilson, V. (1994). Table Hopping in the Cafeteria: An Exploration of 'Racial' Integration in Early Adolescent Social Groups. *Multicultural Education Annual Editions*, 104-115.

18

Toward a New Vision and Vocabulary About Adolescence
Theoretical, Empirical, and Applied Bases of a "Positive Youth Development" Perspective[1]

Richard M. Lerner
Jacqueline V. Lerner
Colleagues in the Institute
for Applied Research
in Youth Development[2]

INTRODUCTION

How do we know if adolescents are doing well in life? What vocabulary do researchers, parents, teachers, policy makers, and often young people themselves, use to describe a young person who is showing successful development?

All too often in the United States and internationally, we discuss positive development in regard to the absence of negative or undesirable behaviors. Typically, such descriptions are predicated on the assumption that children are "broken" or in danger of becoming broken (Benson, 2003), and thus that young people are "problems to be managed" (Roth, Brooks-Gunn, Murray, & Foster, 1998). As such, when we describe a successful young person we speak about a youth whose problems have been managed or are, at best, absent. We might say, then, that a youth who is manifesting behavior indicative of positive development is someone who is *not* taking drugs or using alcohol, is *not* engaging in unsafe sex, and is *not* participating in crime or violence.

Benson (2003) believes that the focus on problems in Americans' discussions of youth, and the use in the United States of a vocabulary that stresses the risks and dangers of young people, occurs because we have "a culture dominated by deficit and risk thinking, by pathology and its symptoms" (p. 25) and he points out that "Intertwined with this social phenomenon is the contemporary dominance of what is often called the deficit-reduction paradigm. In this paradigm, research and practice are steered to naming, counting, and reducing the incidence of environmental risks (e.g., family violence, poverty, family disintegration) and health-compromising behaviors (e.g., substance use, adolescent pregnancy, interpersonal violence, school dropout)" (p. 24). The deficit model of youth that shapes our vocabulary about the behaviors prototypic of young people results, then, in an orientation in America to discuss positive youth development as the absence of negative behaviors (Pittman & Fleming, 1991)

For instance, Catalano, Berglund, Ryan, Lonczak, and Hawkins (1999, p. vi) noted that "Currently, problem behaviors are tracked more often than positive ones and, while an increasing number of positive youth development interventions are choosing to measure both, this is still far from being the standard in the field." They go on to note that "A major obstacle to tracking indicators of positive youth development constructs is the absence of widely accepted measures for this purpose . . . [M]any aspects of positive youth development go unassessed due to the underdeveloped state of the assessment tools" (Catalano et al., 1999, pp. vi–vii). The absence of an accepted vocabulary for the discussion of positive youth development is a key obstacle to evaluating the effectiveness of programs or policies aimed at promoting such change.

In short, characterizations of young people as problems to be managed or as primarily people in need of fixing reflect a deficit-based belief that there is some shortcoming of character or personality that leads youth to become involved in risky or negative behaviors. Given the presence of such a deficit, the appropriate and humane actions to take in regard to young people are to prevent the actualization of the otherwise inevitable problems they will encounter. Indeed, policy makers and practitioners are pleased when their actions are associated with the reduction of problem behaviors, such as teenage pregnancy and parenting, substance use and abuse, school failure and dropout, and delinquency and violence.

Everyone should, of course, be pleased when such behaviors diminish. However, it is very dispiriting for a young person to learn that he or she is regarded by adults as someone who is likely to be a problem for others as well as for himself or herself. It is very discouraging for a young person to try to make a positive life when he or she is confronted by the suspicion of substance use and abuse, unsafe sexual practices, and a lack of commitment to supporting the laws and mores of society. What sort of message is sent to youth when they are spoken of as inevitably destined for trouble unless parents or practitioners take preventive steps? How do such messages affect the self-esteem of young people, and what is the impact of such messages on their spirit and motivation?

There are, of course, some words for describing positive behaviors about youth, for example, pertaining to academic achievement, getting along with others, and activities relating to current or potentially successful entrepreneurship. Nevertheless, the vocabulary for depicting youth as "resources to be developed" (Roth, et al., 1998) is not as rich or nuanced as the one available for depicting the problematic propensities of young people (King, et al., 2004, 2005). Moreover, there have been relatively few positive indicators to which people may point in order to reflect the desirable, healthy, and valued behaviors among its children and adolescents (Lerner, 2004). This situation is changing, however.

A STRENGTH-BASED VIEW OF YOUTH DEVELOPMENT

In these early years of the twenty-first century, a new vision and vocabulary for discussing young people has begun to emerge (King et al., 2004). Propelled by the increasingly more collaborative contributions of scholars (e.g., Benson, 2003; Damon & Gregory, 2003; Lerner, Dowling, & Anderson, 2003; Roth, Brooks-Gunn, Murray, & Foster, 1998), practitioners (e.g., Pittman, Irby, & Ferber, 2001; Wheeler, 2000, 2003), and policy makers (e.g., Cummings, 2003; Gore, 2003; Gore & Gore, 2002), youth are viewed as resources to be developed. The new vocabulary emphasizes the strengths present within all young people and involves concepts such as developmental assets (Benson, 2003), positive youth development (Benson, 1990; Little, 1993), moral development and noble purpose (Damon, 1990; Damon, Menon, & Bronk, 2003), civic engagement (e.g., Flanagan & Faison, 2001; Flanagan & Sherrod, 1998; Youniss, McClellan, & Yates, 1999), well-being (Bornstein, 2003), and thriving (Dowling, et al., 2003, 2004; King, et al., in press; Lerner, 2004; Scales, Benson, Leffert, & Blyth, 2000; Theokas et al., 2005). All concepts are predicated on the idea that *every* young person has the potential for successful, healthy development and the belief that *all* youth possess the capacity for positive development.

This vision for and vocabulary about youth has evolved over the course of a scientifically arduous path (Lerner, 2004; Lerner et al., 2002). Complicating any new conceptualization of the character of youth as resources for the positive development of self, families, and communities was an antithetical theoretical approach to the nature and development of young people, one characterized by a deficit view that conceptualized youth behaviors as deviations from normative development (see Hall, 1904). Understanding such deviations was not seen as being of direct relevance to scholarship aimed at discovering the principles of basic developmental processes. Accordingly, the characteristics of youth were regarded as issues of "only" applied concern—and thus of secondary scientific interest. Not only did this model separate basic science from application but, as well, it disembedded the adolescent from the study of normal or healthy development. In short, the deficit view of youth as problems to be managed split the study of young people from the study of health and positive development (Lerner et al., 2002; Overton, 1998).

Other types of "splits" were associated with this deficit model of youth development. The conception of developmental process typically associated with this model often involved causal splits between individual and context, between organism and environment, or—most generally—between nature and nurture (Gottlieb, 1997; Lerner, 2002; Overton, 1998). In short, scholars studying human development, in general, and youth development, in particular, used a theoretical model that was not useful in understanding the integrated, or relational, character of development (Overton, 1998); the synthesis between basic and applied science; or how young people developed in normative, healthy, or positive ways. However, the integration of person and context, of basic and applied scholarship, and of young people with the potential for positive development were legitimated by the relational models of development that emerged as cutting-edge scholarship by the end of the twentieth century (Damon, 1998).

DEVELOPMENTAL SYSTEMS AND INDIVIDUALS ← → CONTEXT RELATIONS

The forefront of contemporary developmental theory and research is associated with ideas stressing that systemic (bidirectional, fused) *relations* between individuals and contexts provide the bases of human behavior and developmental change (e.g., Damon, 1998; Ford & Lerner, 1992; Gottlieb, 1997; Overton, 1998). Within the context of such developmental systems theories, changes across the life span are seen as propelled by the dynamic relations between individuals and the multiple levels of the ecology of human development (e.g., families, peer groups, schools, communities, and culture), all changing interdependently across time (history) (Lerner, 2002). History—temporality—infuses the system of relations between individuals and contexts with the potential for change (Baltes, Lindenberger, & Staudinger, 1998; Elder, 1998).

Developmental systems theory eschews the reduction of individual and social behavior to fixed genetic influences and, in fact, contends that such a hereditarian conception is counterfactual (Gottlieb, 1997, 1998; Lerner, 2002). Instead, developmental systems theory stresses that mutually influential (i.e., bidirectional or fused) relations exist among variables from all the levels of organization comprising the individual (e.g., the genetic and physiological) and the contextual tiers that we have noted comprise the ecology of human development (Bronfenbrenner, 1979, 2001, 2005). The fusion of these levels creates a fully coactional system (Gottlieb, 1997, 1998, 2004) that, because of the temporality of change derived from the embeddedness of the system in history, makes human development both lawfully probabilistic (i.e., probabilistic epigenetic; Gottlieb, 1997, 1998) and *relatively plastic*. This concept means that, because of the reciprocity between the individual and the context (which may be represented as individual ← → context), there is always at least some potential for systematic change in behavior.

The relative plasticity of development means that one may expect that there may be means found to improve human life. Such plasticity legitimizes an optimistic view of the potential for promoting positive changes in humans. As such, plasticity is a strength present within all people. Plasticity directs both science and applications of science—for example, involving public policies and the programs of community-based organizations (CBOs)—to find ways to create optimal matches between individuals and their social worlds in order to capitalize on the potential for positive change in people and thereby promote positive development.

The optimistic view of the potential of the developmental systems model to promote positive human development is linked also to the concept of "developmental regulation," that is, to the idea that individual ← → context relations constitute the basic process of change within developmental systems models. Developmental regulations may act to promote variation over time in how an individual interacts in his or her world and/or to promote consistencies in positive behaviors, e.g., continued resistance to engaging in health compromising behaviors. Cairns and Hood (1983) explain that such behavioral continuity may necessitate new means (strategies) at different points in life; thus, plasticity is involved in the production of both change and constancy in human development.

In essence, then, the systemic variability of developmental regulations, produced by the temporality of the developmental system, enables potential plasticity to be instantiated. Our interactions with our contexts can involve new means to positive outcomes and/or finding means to maintain health in the face of new risks (Baltes et al., 1998; Cairns & Hood, 1983). Thus, the concept of developmental regulation underscores an optimistic view of human potential. The concepts of relative plasticity and developmental regulation frame a conceptualization of a life-span developmental process for positive development, a process that may be labeled as "thriving."

A young person may be said to be *thriving* if he or she is involved across time in healthy, positive individual ← → context relations and on the path to what Csikszentmihalyi and Rathunde (1998) describe as "idealized personhood" (an adult status marked by making culturally valued contributions to self, others, and institutions). While the structure of individual ← → context relations (of developmental regulations) remains invariant (e.g., involving bidirectionality and relative plasticity), the components of the individual-psychological and social relational features of individual ← → context relations may show inter-individual and inter-cultural differences as they change over time to comprise the thriving process. Nevertheless, despite individual and contextual variation, Lerner (2004) believes that the probability of thriving can be maximized in the context of developmental regulations that assure individual liberty and that reflect the democratic institutions of civil society. Such relations promote the individual development of the person and support institutions that are designed to protect and further such promotion.

Because of temporality and contextual variation, the instantiation of the relation between individual liberty and civil society may be different across cultures, in different nations, or across historical epochs. For example, attributes such as competence, confidence, character, social connection, and caring or compassion, which are characteristics that have been labeled as the "Five Cs" of positive youth development (e.g., Eccles & Gootman, 2002; Roth et al., 1998; Lerner, 2004; Lerner, Fisher, & Weinberg, 2000), are often regarded as healthy outcomes of functionally appropriate (adaptive) developmental regulations in the contemporary United States (Lerner, 2004).

The Five Cs of Positive Youth Development

In our theoretical discussions of the Five Cs (Lerner, 2004; Lerner et al., 2005, we have suggested that they may be latent constructs that capture the essence of to-be-developed indicators of the numerous mental, behavioral, and social relational elements that could comprise positive youth development (PYD). Initially proposed by Little (1993), these theoretical latent constructs were first discussed as Four Cs, i.e., competence, confidence, (positive social) connection, and character. Eccles and Gootman (2002), Roth and Brooks-Gunn (2003a, 2003b), and Lerner (2004) reviewed evidence from research and practice that converges in stressing the use of these Cs and potentially of a fifth C, caring (or compassion), in understanding the goals and outcomes of community-based programs aimed at enhancing youth development.

Derived from this literature, the current working definitions of these Cs are presented in Table 18.1. As explained below, these definitions frame the measurement model and the structural equation modeling procedures undertaken in the research on PYD we will discuss in this chapter.

Little (personal communication, March 2000) and Lerner (2004; Lerner et al., 2003a) have suggested that when these Five Cs are present in a young person there emerges a Sixth C, contribution.

TABLE 18.1
"Working Definitions" of the 5Cs of Positive Youth Development

C	Definition
Competence	Positive view of one's actions in domain specific areas including social, academic, cognitive, and vocational. Social competence pertains to interpersonal skills (e.g., conflict resolution). Cognitive competence pertains to cognitive abilities (e.g., decision making). School grades, attendance, and test scores are part of academic competence. Vocational competence involves work habits and career choice explorations.
Confidence	An internal sense of overall positive self-worth and self-efficacy; one's global self-regard, as opposed to domain specific beliefs.
Connection	Positive bonds with people and institutions that are reflected in bidirectional exchanges between the individual and peers, family, school, and community in which both parties contribute to the relationship.
Character	Respect for societal and cultural rules, possession of standards for correct behaviors, a sense of right and wrong (morality), and integrity.
Caring and Compassion	A sense of sympathy and empathy for others.

Note. Derived from Lerner (2004) and Roth & Brooks Gunn (2003a).

That is, a young person enacts behaviors indicative of the Five Cs by contributing positively to self, family, community, and—ultimately—civil society (Lerner, 2004). Such contributions are envisioned to have both a behavioral (action) component and an ideological component (that is, the young person possesses an identity that specifies that such contributions are predicated on moral and civic duty; Lerner et al., 2003a). In other words, when youth believe they should contribute to self and context and when they act on these beliefs, they will both reflect and promote further advances in both their own positive development and, as well, the "health" of their social world. Theoretically, there will be adaptive individual ← → context developmental regulations.

The developmental course of the ideological and behavioral components of contributions to self and society remains to be determined. For example, given the orthogenetic principle (Werner, 1957), it may be that these components are differentiated (e.g., weakly correlated) in early developmental periods (e.g., at the beginning of adolescence) and become integrated later in ontogeny. However, as we discuss below, there is reason to believe that both positive development and youth contributions to self and to their ecology are likely to take place in the context of community-based, youth development programs.

THE POTENTIAL OF YOUTH DEVELOPMENT PROGRAMS TO PROMOTE POSITIVE YOUTH DEVELOPMENT

Numerous scholars, practitioners, advocates for youth, and policy makers have studied and discussed effective youth programs (e.g., Benson, 1997; Blum, 2003; Carnegie Corporation of New York, 1995; Damon, 1997; Dryfoos, 1990, 1998; Lerner, 2004; Lerner & Galambos, 1998; Little, 1993; Pittman, 1996; Roth & Brooks-Gunn, 2003a, 2003b; Roth et al., 1998; Schorr, 1988, 1997; Villarruel et al., 2003; Wheeler, 2003). Although all contributors to this discussion may have their own ways of phrasing their conclusions, it is possible to provide an overview of the ideal features—the *best practices*—that should be integrated into effective positive youth development programs. It is clear that these features of best practice involve coordinated attention to the youth's characteristics of individuality and to the specifics of his or her social context.

Moreover it is also clear that community-based programs that seek only to prevent problems are not, in the main, successful in promoting the development of the clusters of behaviors associated with the Five Cs of PYD (Roth & Brooks-Gunn, 2003a). Adoption of only a prevention orientation fails in promoting positive youth development because such an effort does not provide the program features—or more broadly the individual and contextual resources or, what Benson and his colleagues from Search Institute (Benson, 2003, Benson et al., 1998) term the "developmental assets"—fostering the thriving youth ← → civil society relation. What does assure, or at least increase the likelihood, of the provision of these developmental assets, of the engagement of youth with their communities, and of PYD?

Catalano et al. (1999) define positive youth development and the programs linked to its occurrence as involving attempts to promote characteristics associated with several of the Five Cs or with some of the ecological developmental assets specified by Search Institute (Benson, 1997, 2003). Roth and Brooks-Gunn (2003a) also use the Five Cs as a frame for evaluating the effectiveness of programs aimed at promoting positive youth development.

For instance, programs promote positive youth development when they instill in youth attributes of competence such as self-efficacy, resilience, or social, cognitive, behavioral, and moral competence; attributes of confidence such as self-determination and a clear and positive identity; and attributes of social connection such as bonding; attributes of character such as spirituality and a belief in the future (Catalano et al., 1999). In addition, programs promote positive youth development when they enhance ecological assets related to empowerment such as recognition for a young person's positive behaviors, provide opportunities for prosocial involvement, and support prosocial norms or standards for healthy behavior (Catalano et al., 1999). In this regard, Roth and Brooks-Gunn (2003a) compare programs that seek to promote the Five Cs—programs that are aimed at youth *development*—with programs that just have a youth focus but are not developmental in orientation and, in particular, are not aimed at the promotion of positive development. Roth and Brooks-Gunn (2003a, p. 217) note that the former, youth development programs are "more successful in improving participants' competence, confidence, and connections."

The "Big Three" Components of Effective Youth Development Programs

What are the specific actions taken by youth development programs that make them effective in promoting the Five Cs? Catalano et al. (1999) find that the preponderant majority (about 75%) of effective positive youth development programs focus on what Lerner (2004) termed the "Big Three" design features of effective positive youth development (YD) programs. YD programs involving the Big Three provide:

1. Opportunities for youth participation in and leadership of activities; that
2. Emphasize the development of life skills; within the context of
3. A sustained and caring adult-youth relationship.

For instance, Catalano et al. (1999, p. vi) note that effective positive youth development programs "targeted healthy bonds between youth and adults, increased opportunities for youth participation in positive social activities,... [involved] recognition and reinforcement for that participation," and often used skills training as a youth competency strategy. These characteristics of effective positive youth development programs are similar to those identified by Roth and Brooks-Gunn (2003b), who noted that such programs transcend an exclusive focus on the prevention of health compromising behaviors to include attempts to inculcate behaviors that stress youth competencies and abilities through "increasing participants' exposure to supportive and empowering environments where activities create multiple opportunities for a range of skill-building and horizon-broadening experiences" (p. 94). In addition, Roth and Brooks-Gunn (2003b) indicate that the activities found in these programs offer both "formal and informal opportunities for youth to nurture their interests and talents, practice new skills, and gain a sense of personal and group recognition. Regardless of the specific activity, the emphasis lies in providing real challenges and active participation" (p. 204).

In this regard, Roth and Brooks-Gunn (2003a) note that when these activities are coupled with the creation of an atmosphere of hope for a positive future among youth, when the program "conveys the adults' beliefs in youth as resources to be developed rather than as problems to be managed" (p. 204), then the goals of promoting positive youth development are likely to be reached. In other words, when activities that integrate skill building opportunities and active participation occur in the presence of positive and supportive adult ← → youth relations, positive development will occur.

Blum (2003) agrees. He notes that effective youth programs offer to youth activities through which to form relationships with caring adults, relations that elicit hope in young people. When these programs provide as well the opportunity for youth to participate in community development activities, positive youth development occurs (Blum, 2003).

The role of positive adult ← → youth relationships has been underscored as well by Rhodes (2002; Rhodes & Roffman, 2003). Focusing on volunteer mentoring relationships, for instance, Rhodes and Roffman (2003) note that these nonparental "relationships can positively influence a range of outcomes, including improvements in peer and parental relationships, academic achievement, and self-concept; lower recidivism rates among juvenile delinquents; and reductions in substance abuse" (p. 227).

However, Rhodes and Roffman (2003) also note that there is a developmental course to these effects of volunteer mentoring on youth. When young people are in relationships that last a year or longer, they are most likely to experience improvements in academic, psychological, social, and behavioral characteristics. On the other hand, when youth are in relationships that last for only between 6 and 12 months, fewer positive outcomes of mentoring are evident. When young people are in mentoring relationships that end relatively quickly, it appears that mentoring may actually be detrimental. Decrements in positive functioning have been reported in such circumstances (Rhodes, 2002; Rhodes & Roffman, 2003).

Of course, parents may also serve as the adults in positive adult ← → youth relations. Bornstein (2003) notes that the positive influences of parents on their children's healthy development may be enhanced when parents have several "tools" to facilitate their effective parenting behaviors. These tools include possessing accurate knowledge about child and adolescent development, having good skills at observing their children, possessing strategies for discipline and for problem prevention, having the ability to provide to their children effective supports for their emotional, social, cognitive, and language development. An additional resource for positive parenting is for adults to have their own sources of social support (Bornstein, 2003).

In addition to the Big Three components of programs that effectively support PYD, there are, of course, other program characteristics that are effective in promoting such development. Among these are the presence of clear program goals; attention to the diversity of youth and of their families, communities, and cultures; assurance that the program represents a safe space for youth and that it is accessible to them; integration of the developmental assets within the community into the program; a collaborative approach with other youth-serving organizations and programs; contributing to the provision of a "seamless" social support across the community; engagement in program evaluation; and advocacy for youth (Dryfoos, 1990, 1998; Eccles & Gootman, 2002; Lerner, 1995; Little, 1993; Roth & Brooks-Gunn, 2003a, 2003b; Schorr, 1988, 1997). However, youth participation, adult mentorship, and skill building are the bedrocks upon which effective programs must be built. Indeed, Scales et al. (2000), in an assessment of thriving among 6,000 youth participating in the 1999–2000 Search Institute Profiles of Student Life—Attitudes and Behaviors Survey (PSL-AB) of developmental assets, found that spending time in youth programs was the key developmental asset promoting thriving.

The Empirical Composition of the Five Cs and Their Association With YD Programs

Certainly, given the idea that participation in YD programs is associated with PYD, a direct demonstration of the relation between participation in youth development programs and positive youth development would be quite significant for planning and implementing efforts to promote healthy adolescent development. However, as made clear in the Eccles and Gootman (2002) National Academy of Sciences report, as well as by other reviews of the literature of youth development (e.g., Blum, 2003; Lerner, 2004; Roth & Brooks-Gunn, 2003a, 2003b), there are relatively few data—and certainly none derived from large-scale longitudinal studies—pertinent to the empirical composition of any of the Five Cs of positive youth development or contribution, to the role of individual and ecological developmental assets in moderating their development, and to the distinctive role of the programs of community-based youth development organizations in serving as a key developmental asset within the ecology of human development. Similarly, there are no longitudinal data indicating that PYD varies positively with youth contributions and negatively with risk behaviors (e.g., substance use and abuse) or with internalizing problems (e.g., depression, anxiety).

As we explain in this chapter, the 4-H Study of Positive Youth Development constitutes a large, longitudinal study. A project funded by the National 4-H Council, and conducted within the Institute for Applied Research in Youth Development in the Eliot-Pearson Department of Child Development of Tufts University, the 4-H Study is designed to ascertain whether empirical evidence can be found for the Five Cs of PYD. The study also seeks to describe the individual and ecological asset bases of the Cs, including, in particular, community-based YD programs, such as those of 4-H and others (e.g., Boys and Girls Clubs and the YMCA). The potential contributions of youth development programs are contrasted with (a) programs for youth that are not directed to promoting their positive development, e.g., programs that focus on the reduction of a risk behavior (see Roth, et al., 1998); (b) individual activities, such as music or art lessons; and (c) no participation in programs or activities.

In essence, then, the goal of the 4-H Study is to understand the latent and manifest variables that constitute PYD, and the components of the developmental system that combine to enhance the likelihood of positive development and decrease the likelihood of problematic development, that is, that create conditions for healthy functioning at any one point in time (i.e., what we term "well-being;" Lerner, Bornstein, & Smith, 2003b; Lerner et al., 2003a) and that support the development of exemplary PYD across the adolescent years. The 4-H Study is interested in understanding what propels the young person along a healthy developmental trajectory (i.e., what fosters the process of thriving; Lerner, 2004; Lerner et al., 2003a), and thus what leads youth toward an "idealized" adulthood, one marked by effective contributions to self, family, community, and civil society (Csikszentmihalyi & Rathunde, 1998; Hein, 2003; Lerner et al., 2003a).

Figure 18.1 presents the theoretical model of the thriving process that we have used to frame the research conducted within the 4-H Study (Lerner, 2004; Lerner et al., 2003a). Derived from the developmental systems conception that mutually beneficial developmental regulations, that is, adaptive individual ← → context relations, propel a person along a healthy developmental trajectory across life (and that at any one point in time enable a person to be in a state of well-being), the model specifies that when there is an alignment between individual strengths and ecological assets that promote healthy development, the Five Cs will evolve over the course of an individual's development. This development of the Five Cs will result in the above-noted, idealized adulthood, and thus in the sixth C of contribution, that is, in multifaceted contributions of individuals to their selves and their contexts that maintain and perpetuate adaptive individual ← → context relations.

In short, Figure 18.1 illustrates the idea that adaptive developmental regulation results in the emergence among young people of an orientation to transcend exclusive self-interest and place value on, and commitments to, actions supportive of their social system. This regulatory system enables the individual and individual initiative to prosper. As such, it is this relation—between an individual engaged in support of a democratic system that, in turn, supports the individual—that is the essence of the mutual, individual ← → context benefits defining healthy developmental regulation.

In sum, this vision of the development and import for self and society of exemplary positive development, or thriving, among youth, frames the 4-H Study. Predicated on the optimistic view of young people, and on the belief that all youth have strengths, and that in all contexts developmental assets may be found to combine with youth strengths in order to actualize positive developmental potentials, the 4-H Study is designed to generate heretofore unavailable longitudinal data elucidating how community-based YD programs contribute to the positive, healthy course of development among American youth. As we explain, such information is vital and timely.

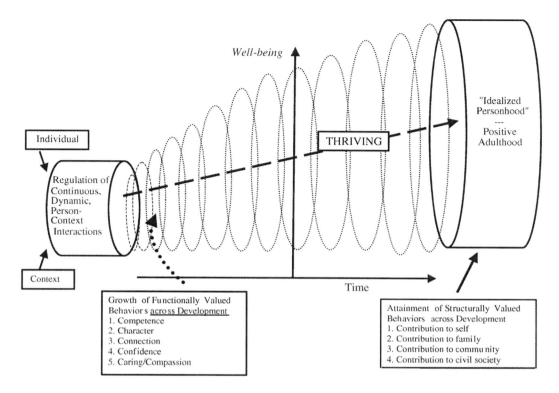

Figure 18.1   A developmental contextual view of PYD.

THE 4-H STUDY OF POSITIVE YOUTH DEVELOPMENT

American youth, and the nation that seeks to nurture and support them, face a set of problems of historically unprecedented scope and severity that, together, limit the opportunities for active and constructive participation by young people in community life and civil society. Estimates are that 50% of American youth engage in two or more of the four major categories of risk behaviors (substance use and abuse, crime and violence, unsafe sex and teenage pregnancy and parenting, and school failure) and that 10% engage in all four sets (Dryfoos, 1990, 1998; Perkins & Borden, 2003). Moreover, since the 1980s there continues to be a strikingly alarming rate of youth poverty—involving a fifth of the children and adolescents in the United States. Rates of all of the above-noted problem behaviors are higher among poor youth (McLoyd, 1998).

It is clear, then, that American communities need to have greater access to existing effective youth-serving programs. Furthermore, given the unprecedented scope of the contemporary challenges to the healthy development of American children and adolescents, new efforts must be devised, studied and, if effective, sustained (e.g., through new social policies; Lerner, 2004). If the developmentally nurturing resources, or developmental assets, possessed by communities are integrated on behalf of youth, as identified in developmental systems theories, this potential may be realized; that is, positive development may be promoted.

The longitudinal, 4-H Study of Positive Youth Development began with youth in the fifth grade and assesses—through use of a measurement model that operationalizes the Five Cs of positive youth development (PYD) and, as well, the Sixth C of contribution—characteristics of young people theoretically believed to be key facets of PYD. The research evaluates also the impact on PYD of key ecological assets—families, communities and, in particular, community-based programs for youth—especially 4-H youth development programs.

Although the 4-H Study is designed to follow fifth graders through their adolescence and has completed its second wave of testing, at this writing the research has completed analyses only of the first wave of data collection (i.e., the 2002–2003 Wave). As such, in this chapter we summarize the cross-sectional information presently available. These data will not enable us to specify the developmental course of the Five Cs, since only change-sensitive data (e.g., data derived from longitudinal research) can do this. Accordingly, in the present chapter we evaluate the unitemporal status of the Five Cs (and thus, in regard to the model presented in Figure 18.1, appraise well-being). These analyses provide a baseline for subsequent reports of developmental change in both PYD and for the association between youth participation in community-based, youth development programs and the presence of the Cs of PYD.

We discuss findings that addresses three questions about the unitemporal patterns of covariation present within the Wave 1 4-H Study data set: (1) Is there empirical evidence for the conception that PYD may be instantiated by the Five Cs of competence, confidence, connection, character, and connection?; (2) Is there empirical evidence for the theoretically-specified relation between PYD and (a) self and context contributions and (b) lower risk behaviors?; and (3) Is there evidence that YD programs—as potentially key instances of the developmental assets present in the ecology of adolescent development—are associated with PYD, contribution, and lower risk behaviors?

Methods of the 4-H Study

In the first wave of the 4-H Study, we secured cooperation from sites in 40 cities or towns located in 13 states that, together, provided regional, rural-urban, racial/ethnic, and religious variation. In turn, in order to identify the association between community-based YD programs and PYD, we sought also to develop a sample that would reflect variation of youth participation in such organizations and in other types of school- and community-based youth activities (i.e., in programs that did not have a youth development mission or in individually focused youth activities). We sampled also youth who were not involved in any individual or group activity.

Participants

Given our interest in ascertaining if PYD varies positively with the development of contribution and negatively with the appearance of risk behaviors and internalizing problems, and if youth development programs promote PYD and prevent or delay the emergence of problem behaviors and/or slow their growth, the study was launched with fifth graders in order to obtain baseline levels of behaviors from which to measure change over time. The literature shows that one may expect low levels of risk among youth of this grade level (e.g., Dryfoos, 1990; Perkins & Borden, 2003).

Accordingly, Wave 1 youth participants were a diverse group of 1,700 fifth grade adolescents (47.2% males; mean age = 11.1 years, SD = .53 years; 52.8% females, mean age = 10.9 years, SD = .46 years) and 1,117 of their parents (82.5% mothers, mean age = 38.4 years, SD = 6.8 years; 13.9% fathers, mean age = 41.6 years, SD = 6.2 years; only one parent per student was sampled). Other adults who completed the survey were grandparents 1.3%, other adults .4%, stepmothers .4%, stepfathers .2%, and foster parents .2%. The remaining 1.2% of adults did not specify their relation to the child. The overall rate of parent (or other adult) participation was 65.7%. The sample was predominantly Catholic (50.0%) or Protestant (18.7%); educated (more than 67% of the sample had at least some college education); from families with two, married parents (73.5%); European American (57.9%), and at least middle income (e.g., 58.8% of the youth lived in families that reported incomes of at least $45,000 a year). Complete details about the demographic characteristics of the participants and their families are presented in Lerner et al., 2005.

Study Sites

Wave 1 data were collected in 57 schools and in four after school programs. The schools varied in type (public/private), size, grades and students served, and along various socioeconomic characteristics (e.g., percent students eligible for free or reduced lunch). Moreover, the schools were distributed fairly evenly across four regions of the country: Northeast, North Central, South, and West. The four after school programs were located in diverse urban communities, and served primarily minority and low-income children and families.

Measures

The measurement model used to initiate this study was designed to provide indices of the six Cs of PYD, of risks and problem behaviors, of the purported individual and ecological assets theoretically linked to the development of the Cs, and of the diminution of problem behaviors among youth. To index constructs related to developmental assets we relied on the Search Institute PSL-AB survey (Benson, 1997, 2003; Benson et al., 1998). Given the person ← → context systems model framing our approach to the study of adolescence, we also attempted to assess the regulation of mutually influential relations between youth and their contexts. This assessment included both indices of current regulatory functioning and goal oriented behaviors. The key measure used here was the Selection, Optimization, and Compensation (SOC) questionnaire (Freund & Baltes, 2002; Freund, Li, & Baltes, 1999)

In addition to standard demographic questions about youth and their families (sex, date of birth, race/ethnicity, household composition, number of years in current neighborhood, and time spent without an adult present), items were also included to assess youth participation in activities and involvement with community-based organizations. Finally, given that pubertal variation and ego development have been linked repeatedly within the adolescent literature to a range of positive and problem behaviors in adolescence (Nurmi, 2004; Susman & Rogol, 2004), we assessed these constructs for exploratory purposes.

Our measures were embedded in one of two questionnaires. A Student Questionnaire (SQ) was composed of measures pertinent to the Cs of PYD, problem behaviors, pubertal level of development, individual and ecological assets, developmental regulation, activities, and demographics. One parent/guardian per youth participant was asked to complete the Parent Questionnaire (PQ) for each child participating in the study. The PQ was composed of two types of items: (1) Items about the parent/guardian and (2) items about the child. Items about the parent/guardian included relationship to the child; age; sex; current marital status; race/ethnicity; religion; health status; education level; mother's education level (if the person completing the survey was not the mother); number of years spent in their current neighborhood; SES; number of children in the household; number of people in the household; primary language spoken in the household; and importance of religion in the participant's family life.

Items about the child included: birth date; birth order; height; weight; race/ethnicity; religion; hours of sleep per night; and clubs, groups, and activities in which the child participated in, both now and in the past. The list of options for these activities included: 4-H Clubs, Boys Clubs/Girls Clubs, YMCA/YWCA, Girl Scouts/Boy Scouts, Big Brother/Big Sister, religious youth groups, school band, martial arts, acting/drama, dance, music, arts/crafts, academic clubs, school government, religious education, sports, after-school child care programs, volunteer work, paid work, mentoring/peer advising, tutoring, and others. Many of these items were included in the PQ in order to cross-validate the information provided by the child.

Tables 18.2 and 18.3 present the measures included in the SQ and the PQ, respectively. Across the questionnaires, measures were combined to provide indices of the latent constructs on interest in the 4-H Study (e.g., the Five Cs, PYD). As explained below, this combination was an iterative process, as we sought to use our data set to identify a measurement model of the latent constructs that maximized

TABLE 18.2
Measures and Constructs Used in the Student Questionnaire of the 4-H Study

Constructs	Measure
Demographic information about youth and their families	Questions about sex, date of birth, race/ethnicity, household composition, number of years in current neighborhood, time spent without an adult present.
Developmental assets and thriving indicators	99 items from the Search Institutes' Profiles of Student Life—Attitudes and Behaviors Survey (PSL-AB) (Benson, Leffert, Scales, Blyth, 1998). Assesses internal and external developmental assets as well as thriving behaviors. Scale development for these 99 items is reported in Theokas et al. (2005).
Parental warmth	Paternal and maternal subscales of parental warmth from Child's Report of Parenting Behaviors Inventory (Schludermann & Schludermann, 1970).
Parental monitoring	Parental monitoring scale (Small & Kerns, 1993)
Target based expectations	Three subscales (Prosocial, Difficult, and Alienated) from the Target-Based Expectations Scale (Buchanan and Hughes, 2004). Assesses adolescents' beliefs about what behavior and traits will characterize them during adolescence.
Self-perceived competencies and global self-worth	Self-Perception Profile for Children (Harter, 1983) with six subscales was used to assess self-perceived academic, social, and physical competencies, as well as physical appearance, conduct/behavior adequacy, and self-worth.
Peer support	Peer Support Scale (Armsden & Greenberger, 1987)
Sympathy	Eisenberg Sympathy Scale (Eisenberg et al., 1996) was used to assess the degree to which participants feel sorry for the distress of others.
Social responsibility	Social Responsibility Scale (Greenberger & Bond, 1984) assesses adolescents' contribution to community and society.
Ideology concerning community contribution	Set of three open-ended questions developed for this study assessing whether or not youth think that positive development includes giving back to the world around them.
Barriers to participation in community activities	Six items associated with "Reasons for not participating in community activities" items set were used to assess the frequency of factors that may not allow or may impede children from participating in different activities. This items set was derived from the Teen Assessment (TAP) Survey Question Bank (Small, & Rodgers, 1995).
Healthy life style behaviors	Five items associated with the "Healthy life style behavior" items set from TAP (Small, & Rodgers, 1995) were used to assess health-related behaviors such as exercising and sleeping.
Depression	Center for Epidemiological Studies Depression Scale (CES-D; Radloff, 1977)
Risk behaviors and delinquency	Set of questions developed for this study to assess the frequency of substance use and frequency of delinquent behaviors. Questions were modified from items included in PSL-AB (Leffert, et al., 1998) and the Monitoring the Future Questionnaire (2000).
Regulation and goal-oriented behaviors	Selection, Optimization, and Compensation (SOC) Questionnaire (Freund & Baltes, 2002) was used to measure behaviors in selection of goals, acquisition and investment of goal-relevant means to achieve one's goals, and the use of alternative means to maintain a given level of functioning when specific goal-relevant means are not available anymore.
School and career aspirations/expectations	Four open-ended questions assessed the highest level of education adolescents' dream of completing, the highest level of education they believe they would actually complete, the job they would like to have as an adult, if they really thought they would attain the job, and if not what job they thought they would actually have.
Thinking about the future	Set of questions created for this study that assessed students' perception of the chances that some things (e.g. graduating from college, being healthy, being safe, etc.) are going to happen to them in future.
Pubertal development	Puberty Development Scale (Petersen, Crockett, & Boxer, 1988)
Psychosocial development	Three subscales of Erikson Psychosocial Stage Inventory (Rosenthal, Gurney, & Moore, 1981) were used to assess the resolution of the conflict associated with Erikson's developmental stages of early adolescence: Industry, Identity, and Intimacy.
Participation in activities	Set of 21 questions created for the purpose of this study which assessed students' involvement in different clubs and groups.

TABLE 18.3
Measures Included in the Parent Questionnaire of the 4-H Study

Items about the parent/guardian	Questions included relationship to the child, age, sex, current marital status, race/ethnicity, religion, health status, education level, mother's education level (if the person completing the survey was not the mother), number of years spent in current neighborhood, SES, number of children in the household, number of people in the household, primary language spoken in the household, and importance of religion in the participant's family life.
Items about the child	Questions included birth date, birth order, height, weight, race/ethnicity, religion, hours of sleep per night, and clubs groups, and activities in which the child participated, both now and in the past.

goodness-of-fit with our theory. Table 18.4 presents the measurement model employed finally to index each of the Cs. The several steps followed to arrive at the measurement model for the Five Cs and PYD are discussed below.

Results

This analyses of the 4-H Study Wave 1 data were conducted to bring information to bear on the developmental systems view of the thriving process shown in Figure 18.1. In our initial analyses we focused on testing the empirical validity of the conception of positive development as instantiated

TABLE 18.4
Measurement Model of the Five Cs and PYD

		Standardized ML Estimate	Residual Error
Confidence			
1	Positive identity	.91	.18
2	Self-worth	.64	.50
Competence			
3	Academic competence	.51	.74
4	Grades	.56	.69
5	School engagement	.72	.48
6	Social competence	.46	.79
Character			
7	Personal values	.76	.42
8	Social conscience	.79	.37
9	Values diversity	.70	.51
10	Interpersonal values and skills	.67	.54
Caring			
11	Sympathy: Disadvantaged	.72	.48
12	Sympathy: Loneliness	.81	.30
13	Sympathy: Unfortunate	.74	.46
14	Sympathy: Pain	.80	.37
15	Sympathy: Rejection	.76	.43
Connection			
16	Family	.60	.64
17	School	.71	.40
18	Community	.44	.81
19	Peers	.43	.81
PYD			
1	Confidence	.77	.41
2	Competence	.82	.33
3	Character	.82	.32
4	Caring	.49	.76
5	Connection	.91	.18

by the Five Cs, and proposed a measure of contribution for fifth graders that could be analyzed in relation to PYD. Future reports from the 4-H Study, which will capitalize on the longitudinal design of this research, will extend model testing to include the relationship between assets, contribution, and the growth of the Five Cs.

Descriptive analyses were conducted first to determine whether there was systematic variation in the measures described above with selected youth and parent background variables: sex, race/ethnicity, and social class. Accordingly, correlations were computed among the youth and parent background variables, such as youth sex, youth race/ethnicity (recoded as European American/nonEuropean American), household income, mother's education, and number of children in the household. Youth sex was not correlated with the other variables. Household income and mothers' education were significantly and positively correlated and both were negatively correlated with the number of children in the household. Being European American was positively correlated with household income and mothers' education and negatively correlated with number of children in the home.

Hierarchical multiple regression analyses were computed for each scale score as the dependent variable and sex, race/ethnicity, household income, mother's education, and number of children in the home as a set of independent variables. In addition, two-way interactions between race/ethnicity and sex, and race/ethnicity and household income were tested as a second set of independent variables. Race/ethnicity was assessed through the use of three dummy variables (European American, African American, Latino/a vs. the reference category of all other designations). These analyses are based on participants whose parents answered the PQ, with a maximum sample size of 1,117.

Because there were 48 measures included in these analyses, the significance level was adjusted to control for Type I error. Starting with a p-value of .05, we adjusted our p-value to be .001, using the standard correction of p-value/N of analyses (.05/48). Using this corrected p-value, none of the 2-way interactions were significant. Number of children as a variable also was dropped from the analyses because it never added a significant proportion of variance after other variables were included.

Youth sex and household income were significantly related to the measures in expected ways: Girls have higher scores for, and household income is positively related to, most of the measures. Once household income is controlled for there remained a few significant relationships with race/ethnicity. The race/ethnicity effects that were present show that Latino/a fifth graders reported greater parent involvement, value interpersonal relationships and skills, valued diversity in their relationships, and thought about the future more than fifth graders from other groups. Compared to other youth, African American fifth graders reported lower support from peers, and engaged in more delinquent behaviors but reported greater risk avoidance. European American fifth graders reported higher perceived social and physical competence, and greater self-worth than youth in the other race/ethnicity groups. Future work will explore the complex relationships among these variables within our model of positive youth development.

PYD AND THE FIVE CS

As we have noted, specification of the measurement model of the Five Cs proceeded through multiple steps. First, an extensive literature review was conducted to identify a set of measures that would serve as indicators for each of the Five Cs. Second, these measures were assessed in a pilot study involving 339 youth from five cities and towns in Massachusetts. Scales were assessed in relation to their ability to capture the essential definitions of the Five Cs developed for use in this study (see Table 18.1). Following the evaluation of the pilot results, the survey was revised to better represent the constructs. Third, and concurrent with Wave 1 data collection, the factor structure of internal and external developmental assets, as measured by the Search Institutes' PSL-AB measure (Benson et al., 1998), was reevaluated and restructured to reflect both empirical and substantive considerations (see Theokas et al., 2005). These modifications lead to revisions of the initial measurement model.

To accomplish these revisions, several of the authors independently categorized all scales included in the SQ as either an index of one of the Five Cs, an index of the sixth C of contribution, an index of internal assets, an index of external assets, an index of regulation, or as not relevant to any of the constructs (e.g., pubertal maturation, race, and sex were constructs placed by all authors/raters into this last category). When at least 80% of all raters categorized a measure as reflecting one of the constructs, this measure was considered as an operationalization of it.

Confirmatory factor analysis (CFA) was conducted to assess the degree to which the Five Cs/PYD model fit the data. Model-fitting analyses were conducted to assess the adequacy of the a priori model; subsequent analyses were used to assess model improvement following theoretically-sound modifications. LISREL 8.54 (Jöreskog & Sörbom, 1996a), using Maximum Likelihood (ML) estimation on raw data within a PRELIS 2.0 (Jöreskog & Sörbom, 1996b) file, was used for all CFA analyses.

The initial model contained 19 manifest indicators, five first-order latent factors, one for each of the Five Cs, and one second-order latent factor, representing the PYD construct. All hypothesized pathways were significant but the model had a relatively poor fit ($\chi^2 = 1933$, $df = 147$; RMSEA = 0.085; GFI = 0.89; CFI = 0.94; NNFI = 0.94). The Five Cs/PYD model was therefore retained and subjected to model-improving modifications.

Inspection of the modification indices suggested several changes to improve model fit. Considering that we found high intercorrelations among the indicators, modifications to allow correlated residual errors among the indicators were implemented. Specifically, residuals from three indicators, social competence, academic competence, and self-worth, were allowed to correlate on the assumption that scores on these scales, having all come from the Harter SPPC scale (Harter, 1998), shared method variance not accounted for by the model. The freeing of these residuals resulted in a significantly better model ($\chi^2 = 1455$, $df = 144$; $p < .01$; RMSEA = 0.073; GFI = 0.92; CFI = 0.96; NNFI = 0.95).

Next, residual errors were allowed to correlate between indicators within factors. Consistent with the definitions presented by Roth and Brooks-Gunn (2003a), within competence, residuals between grades and academic competence and between school engagement and social competence were allowed to correlate. Within character, residuals between personal values and social conscience and between values diversity and interpersonal values were allowed to correlate. Within caring, residuals between sympathy for disadvantaged and sympathy for unfortunate and between sympathy for rejected and sympathy for loneliness were allowed to correlate. Finally, within connection, residuals between connection to family and connection to community and between connection to school and connection to community were allowed to correlate. All together, these modifications significantly improved model fit ($\chi^2 = 662$, $df = 136$; $p < .01$; RMSEA = 0.048; GFI = 0.96; CFI = 0.98; NNFI = 0.98).

The modification indices suggested that for the revised model indicated that model fit could be further improved by correlating two more pairs of residuals: positive identity with academic competence and positive identity with social competence. Such relations may reflect the theoretically and empirically established relations between adolescent achievements in academic and social areas and their positive self-regard (e.g., Brown, 2004; Eccles, 2004; Harter, 1998). Following these modifications, model fit was again improved ($\chi^2 = 552$, $df = 134$; $p < .01$; RMSEA = 0.043; GFI = 0.97; CFI = 0.99; NNFI = 0.98). These modifications, however, were not sufficient to specify a model that optimally fit the data.

Inspection of the revised modification indices suggests that additional structure in the relationships among the first order factors has not been exhausted by either the correlated residuals among the respective indictors or their respective loading on the second-order factor of PYD. Specifically, two pairs of first-order factors, confidence/competence and character/caring, continued to share variance not accounted for by the model. Rather than specifying additional structure to the model, we retained the more parsimonious model described below, and allocated additional refinement of and evaluation of sample specific effects on the model to future waves of the 4-H study—waves that would allow us to take advantage of longitudinal data and retest control samples for purposes of cross-validating the model (cf. Browne & Cudeck, 1993; Cudeck & Browne, 1983).

The retained model is depicted in Figure 18.2. While the model Chi-Square was significant at 4-times the model degrees of freedom ($\chi^2 = 552$, df = 134, $p < .01$), it is sensitive to sample size. With large sample sizes, the χ^2 statistic becomes unreasonably powerful at detecting discrepancies between the model and the data and under realistic conditions perfect model fit is not to be expected (Bollen, 1989, pp. 266–269). Following prior recommendations (e.g., Raykov, Tomer, & Nesselroade, 1991; McDonald & Ho, 2002; Tomer & Pugesek, 2003), we evaluated a variety of fit indices. For this model, the Goodness-of-Fit index (GFI, Jöreskog & Sörbom, 1996a), a measure of absolute fit, was 0.97, well above the 0.90 minimum criterion of close fit suggested by Hoyle and Panter (1995). The Comparative Fit Index (CFI, Bentler, 1990) was 0.99, suggesting that the specified model is 99% better than an independence model where all observed variables are assumed to be uncorrelated. Likewise, the Non-Normed Fit Index (NNFI, Bentler & Bonett, 1980), which takes into account model complexity and performs well with large sample sizes was 0.98, again indicating close fit. Finally, the Root Mean Square Error of Approximation (RMSEA, Steiger & Lind, 1980), which is a measure of fit per degree of freedom and is sensitive to model misspecification (Hu & Bentler, 1995), was 0.043 with a 90% confidence interval of 0.039 to 0.047. A value of .05 or less indicates a close fit (Browne & Cudeck, 1993).

Standardized factor loadings for the 19 manifest variables ranged from .43 to .91, indicating that the Five Cs factors accounted for 18–83% of the indicators' variance. In turn, the second-order factor of PYD accounted for an average of 60% of the variance in the latent factors for the Five Cs. This explained variance (or common variance) ranged from 24% for Caring to 83% for Connection.

Latent factor scores for the Five Cs and PYD were calculated in LISREL 8.54 for use in remaining analyses (Jöreskog, Sörbom, du Toit, & du Toit, 2001). These scores should be treated with caution since they are indeterminate, with individual-level rank ordering on a specified factor varying widely depending upon how the scores are calculated (Bollen, 1989). It should be noted, however, that correlations between the LISREL-computed factor scores and mean scores calculated from the standardized indicator variables (so called "coarse factor scores," e.g., Grice, 2001) were all high (> 0.93).

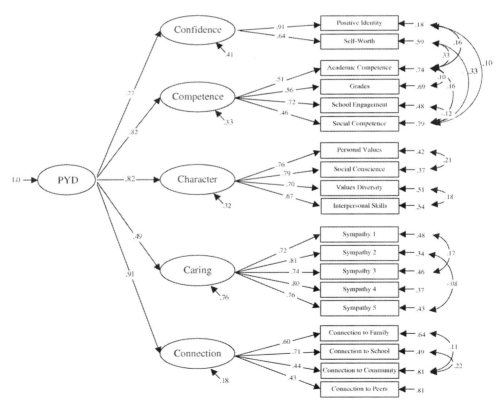

Figure 18.2 Retained factor model with standardized maximum likelihood estimates. *Note:* All estimates are significant at the 0.005 level.

In addition, hierarchical multiple regression analyses were computed using factor score as the dependent variable and sex, race/ethnicity, household income as predictor variables to provide comparable background information as for the indicator scale scores. Girls have higher scores than boys on caring, character, competence, connection, and PYD. European American and Latino/a youth have higher confidence scores than other youth. Youth from families with higher incomes have higher scores on all but the caring constructs. These scores, therefore, appear to be reliable and to have some predictive validity.

Youth Contribution

Using the indicators of contribution present in the Wave 1 data, two measures were constructed which are distinct and which match the definition of contribution we have used in our work (Lerner, 2004; Lerner et al., 2003a), i.e., that within adaptive individual ← → context developmental regulations there is both an ideological and a behavioral component to youth contributions. The first measure reflects ideology of contribution and was obtained by coding responses to two open-ended questions. These questions asked youth to describe themselves as they would like to be and as they actually are, in terms of what they are like and what sorts of things they do. Responses that reflect a desire for or commitment to giving back to the world around them were coded as absent (0), present (1), or important (2). The second measure pertains to the behavioral component of contribution, and describes the amount of participation in activities that reflect active engagement with the world around oneself such as being a leader in a group, helping friends and neighbors, participating in school government, sports, religious youth groups, mentoring, and volunteering in the community.

The items used to measure contribution were considered a variable set and a sum score was computed for all youth with the ideology and participation scores equally weighted. Higher scores represent a composite indicating more involvement in contribution activities and/or an ideology of giving back to the world around oneself. This sum score was analyzed as an outcome regressed on youth sex, race/ethnicity, and household income and then compared with factor scores on each of the five Cs and PYD. Because fewer parents answered the questionnaire, the sample size drops significantly when household income is included in the analyses so the results are displayed with and without household income. When included in the analyses, household income is significantly and negatively related to contribution in fifth graders. However, the results are nearly identical for the other variables whether or not income is controlled for.

Females have significantly higher contribution scores than males and there are no significant differences for the race/ethnicity variables. PYD is significantly related to contribution when the background variables are controlled for. When the Five Cs are entered as a group instead of PYD, the joint contribution is significant (e.g., the change in R^2 (5, 1047) = .037, $p < .001$ without controlling for income). The pattern for the individual Cs varies somewhat when income is not included: confidence and character are significantly related to contribution when income is not controlled for; and competence alone is significant when income is controlled for. This difference is likely due to sample size variation with the inclusion of parent variables.

These results provide empirical support for the theoretically-specified relationship between PYD and the Five Cs and contribution. Of course, these results represent a one-time pattern of covariation among the constructs. The longitudinal data from the subsequent waves of data collection to occur within the 4-H Study will permit assessment as to whether PYD and/or particular Cs at an earlier point in time predict the growth of contribution beyond any within-time relationships among the constructs. In addition, such data will enable analysis of the reverse direction of influence seen as possible within the developmental systems theoretical perspective, that is, contribution at an earlier time may promote positive growth (Lerner, 2004). In fact, if youth are engaged in community-based, youth development programs that foster civic engagement, the development of positive behaviors and the diminution of risk behaviors would, in fact, be expected. The final set of analyses conducted to date with the Wave 1 data were aimed at appraising the association of participation in such YD programs with PYD, risk reduction, and contribution, and will elucidate this possibility.

Youth Development Program Participation, the Five Cs, Risk Reduction, and Contribution

Given that youth development programs have been identified in theory (Lerner, 2004) and research (Roth & Brooks-Gunn, 2003a, 2003b; Scales et al., 2000) as key assets in promoting positive development among youth, we address the question of whether the level of participation in YD programs is associated with either PYD or contribution. Our view is that youth development programs promote youth contribution by having the Big Three features of effective programs that we have previously discussed, i.e., by assuring that the young person has a sustained relationship with at least one committed adult who provides skill building opportunities to the youth and who acts to enhance the young person's healthy and active engagement with the context (Lerner, 2004).

To reflect this orientation toward youth development programs, a measure of participation in youth development programs was designed to describe a youth's maximum depth of involvement with any of four kinds of programs: 4-H, Boy and Girl Scouts, YMCA or YWCA programs, and Boys' and Girls' Clubs. These programs were selected from among the many activities we asked youth to report on because their mission statements specifically emphasize a positive youth development perspective. Since we were interested in a sustained level of involvement, current and past participation was included and indexed by amount of participation per month in the activity with the greatest level of participation. For example, if a youth was active a couple of times a week in 4-H and went to the Boys' and Girls' Club twice a month, the activity level in 4-H of eight times per month was their participation score. Thus, this measure was developed to assess depth of participation rather than the number of programs in which youth participated.

Three regression analyses were conducted to address the question of the relationships among PYD, participation in youth development programs, and contribution. This analysis was done in an exploratory fashion as a first step toward assessing, while controlling for youth sex and race/ethnicity, whether participation contributes to the relationship between PYD and contribution for the fifth graders in this study.

In this sample, at Wave 1, both PYD and program participation are significantly related to contribution. The relationship between PYD and program participation is not significant. This pattern of results suggests that for this age group, PYD and program participation are each independently related to contribution rather than PYD being moderated by program participation. In addition, analysis of risk behaviors for Wave 1 indicated that, overall, adolescents reported relatively low incidences of substance use and delinquency. In addition, across the sample, the level of depression reported by adolescents was not indicative of risk. Based on the extant literature (e.g., Perkins & Borden, 2003), we expect that in future waves within this study the incidence and variability of these risk indicators will increase. Such changes will afford a more in-depth analysis of the relationship between the role of youth development programs in promoting the Five Cs and in diminishing problem behaviors. Thus, analyses of future waves of data will allow us to refine this finding and determine if there is a causal link between PYD and program participation and the nature and direction of the link.

CONCLUSIONS: INTEGRATING THEORY, RESEARCH, AND APPLICATION

Data from the first wave of the 4-H Study of Positive Youth Development provide cross-sectional information that constitutes a baseline (foundation) for subsequent, longitudinal reports of the nature of developmental change in PYD, in the ideological and behavioral components of youth contributions, and in the relationships among participation in YD programs, the Cs of PYD, and youth contributions. Building on this foundation, future analyses will further refine the model of the Five Cs presented in this chapter. As an example, the correlations that exist among the Five Cs will be explored, and their significance to the conceptual model of PYD will be addressed. Furthermore, data from future waves of the study will allow for a more comprehensive appraisal of the model presented in Figure 18.1, and for the assessment of constructs not addressed in this chapter, such as regulation and the role of select individual and contextual assets.

While we provided preliminary, descriptive information about the behavior of all the measures included in the measurement model employed for Wave 1 of the study, the main analyses in the present report focused on only those measures that enabled us to address three issues, i.e., the nature of the empirical evidence for: (1) the conception that PYD may be instantiated by the Five Cs of competence, confidence, connection, character, and caring, and assessed in the present report through the unitemporal patterns of covariation available in the Wave 1 data set; (2) for the theoretically-specified relation between PYD and contribution; and (3) for the purported relations among participation in youth development programs, PYD, and contribution.

The results of the preliminary data analyses suggested that all the previously used measures and the scale scores derived from them behaved as expected, based on prior results reported in the adolescent development literature (e.g., Harter, 1998). Levels of reliability and validity reported in past research were replicated within the Wave 1 data analyses. In addition, the measures that were devised for use in the present research (e.g., the assessment of youth ideology of contribution) were found to possess moderate to high response or coding reliability; the theoretically expected patterns of association between these measures and other assessments within our measurement model (e.g., with the Cs of PYD) suggest the validity of these measures as well.

In regard to differential behavior of the scores in our data set across subgroups of the youth participants, we found that—given the number of preliminary comparisons made and the power of these analyses—relatively few instances of systematic variation existed in relation to major demographic categories within the sample, e.g., gender, race/ethnicity, household income, and mother's education. Nevertheless, girls more so than boys, and youth with higher family incomes, did tend to show higher scores on the Five Cs and contribution. However, given that these differences reflect unitemporal patterns of covariation, and therefore that their developmental significance cannot be ascertained through cross-sectional analyses, we believe that it is prudent to delay interpretation of the possible significance of such variation pending the replication of these differences in our longitudinal data.

Moreover, even when these few differences arose, they reflected contrasts between groups evidencing overall positive, healthy behaviors. That is, other general findings from the descriptive analyses indicated that the participants in this study were reporting their behavior to be positive and/or healthy. Of course, the location of these central tendencies in our data may reflect the often-reported positive bias in dependent variables associated with people agreeing to participate in a longitudinal study (e.g., Baltes, Reese, & Nesselroade, 1977; Schaie & Strother, 1968) and/or the fact that America's contemporary cohorts of young people exist in a far more positive state than prior deficit-based accounts of today's youth would predict (cf. Benson, 2003).

The viability of these two, nonmutually exclusive interpretations may be better ascertained as the 4-H Study continues its waves of data collection and participants enter the higher risk years of middle and late adolescence (Dryfoos, 1990; Perkins & Borden, 2003) and, in addition, are compared to retest control participants. In any event, we regarded the evidence we found for the psychometric quality of the present set of measures and the magnitude of the comparable behavior of the measures across demographic categories within the sample supportive of the use of these assessment tools in the analyses we conducted to address the three key issues discussed in this chapter.

Turning to the first issue—whether the unitemporal instantiation of PYD that was tested may be represented by the Five Cs—this chapter presents evidence of the empirical reality of these Five "Cs" and of their convergence on a second-order latent variable of PYD. The structural model initially tested in an attempt to verify the presence of these Cs and of PYD was derived from our interpretation of the extant theoretical and meta-evaluation evidence pertinent to the conceptualization of PYD (e.g., Benson, 2003; Damon, 1997; Lerner, 2004; Eccles & Gootman, 2002; Roth & Brooks-Gunn, 2003a, 2003b; Scales et al., 2000). While the results of the SEM analyses testing this model proved to be adequate, model fit was substantially improved in the model that derived from, first, a content analysis procedure regarding the specific substantive character of the items involved in the several measures used to assess the Cs and, second, from the subsequent modifications made to the model. Although an ideal model assumes low correlation between the manifest variables, we did not expect this to be the case, as these measures are expected to overlap somewhat conceptually (e.g., self-worth and positive identity should be related). As expected, we found that allowing the residuals of scales within the same latent variable to correlate resulted in a better fit of the model to the data.

Of course, even the revised model can be improved. The apparent shared variance between the first order factors of confidence/competence and character/caring that are not accounted for by the model suggest the presence of an additional structure. There are three potential ways in which these results can be interpreted. First, some of the Cs may represent the same latent construct, resulting in fewer than five Cs. Second, there may be an additional level of latent constructs present in our model, for instance, between the first order factors and the second order factor. Third, these findings may have resulted from the fact that all latent constructs are measured by self-report. For example, our working definition of competence clearly articulates that a purer measure of competence would result if the actions of youth were directly measured. These different possible interpretations of our Wave 1 findings will require cross-validation in subsequent waves of the 4-H Study, as well as in independent research that both uses the present measurement model and other potential indices of the Five Cs.

Furthermore, some of the latent constructs of the revised model are underspecified. As an example, the construct of caring seems not to be conceptually complete, as may be reflected in the lower correlations between caring and the other Cs, as compared to the correlations among the other Cs. Steps to improve the model have already been taken in subsequent waves of the 4-H Study. For example, in Wave 2 we added items to improve the measure of caring. This refinement process will continue through future waves of the study. Nevertheless, the current data provide strong, albeit preliminary and cross-sectional, evidence about the empirical reality of the constructs associated with the new vision and vocabulary about healthy youth development (e.g., Benson, 2003; Damon, Menon, & Bronk, 2003; Lerner, 2004; Roth & Brooks-Gunn, 2003a, 2003b).

There are also provocative preliminary findings from the first wave of the 4-H Study that are pertinent to the Sixth C, contribution, and thus to the second key issue of interest we addressed, i.e., the nature of the theoretically-specified relation between PYD and contribution. Both PYD and the Cs were related to the construct of contribution, which was indexed by combining scores for each of the two components of this construct (i.e., of ideology and of action) we believe comprise youth contributions. However, the strength of the relations we identified may be attenuated by the fact that the means by which fifth grade youth in America can contribute to their communities is relatively constricted by prototypic ecological circumstances (e.g., 10-year-old youth cannot drive themselves to community service sites and, in some cases, there is not public transportation that is convenient or even available). Nevertheless, the positive relations found among PYD and contribution are consistent with theoretical expectations (Damon, 1997; Damon et al., 2003; Lerner, 2004).

Moreover, these theoretical ideas, that suggest that there exists a bidirectional relation between youth civic engagement and thriving (Lerner, 2004; Sherrod, Flanagan, & Youniss, 2002), require time-ordered, lagged data for adequate testing. Accordingly, a key question to be addressed when at least three waves of data are available within the 4-H Study is the nature of the antecedent-consequent relations between contribution and PYD (thriving), that is, in the civically engaged youth ← → thriving relationship, does one direction of effect lead the other in its influence on the course of development?

Of course, the opportunity for youth to contribute to their communities often occurs within the context of their participation in community-based, youth development programs. As such, the third key question addressed in this chapter was about the association between participation in youth development programs, PYD, and contribution. As with the engaged youth ← → thriving relationship, data fully adequate to address this question must be, at the least, longitudinal in character. Nevertheless, the Wave 1 findings we have summarized above offer some provocative ideas that will be tested as the 4-H Study moves into its longitudinal phases.

The present research indexed depth of participation in youth development programs and found that these scores for participation constituted a source of variation in youth contributions that was independent of scores for PYD. Given the theoretical belief in the bidirectional associations among PYD, youth development program participation, and contributions by youth to self and context (Lerner,

2004; Lerner et al., 2003a; Scales et al., 2000), the independent contributions of program participation and PYD to contributions is puzzling. However, it may be that future, developmental analyses across the adolescent years will elucidate the relation among these three domains of youth functioning. Developmentally, and again recalling the orthogenetic principle (Werner, 1957), it may not be until a more developmentally mature portion of adolescence emerges that an integration among PYD, youth development program participation, and self ← → context contribution is evidenced. Once again, this possibility can only be appraised through analyses of the 4-H Study data set that include information from additional waves of observation.

Such analyses may be usefully extended by ascertaining the personological and ecological characteristics of youth participating in specific clusters of particular YD programs, and/or by considering both hours per week of participation as well as the number of programs per se in which a youth participates. The results of such analyses will then be able to inform subsequent longitudinal analyses (e.g., wherein number of programs or frequency of participation at Time 1 can be used as a covariate in analyses of the relations at Time 2 among program participation, PYD, and risk).

Furthermore, the questions that remain to be addressed in regard to the third issue addressed in this study, i.e., the issue of the association between YD program participation and the positive development of youth, are just a sample of the questions that we need to investigate in further analyses of Wave 1 and subsequent data in the 4-H Study. For instance, further analyses will address key facets of the theoretical model of PYD we discussed in this chapter and, specifically, the role of individual ← → context developmental regulations involving the internal and ecological developmental assets of youth in promoting PYD. Although the 4-H data set includes a measure of developmental regulation, i.e., the SOC measure (Freund & Baltes, 2002; Freund, Li, & Baltes, 1999), the analyses we have conducted to date (Lerner et al., 2005) have not focused on the developmental regulation component of our theoretical model, despite its fundamental significance within the conceptualization we present of PYD. This decision was based primarily on the fact that developmental regulation can only be understood with change-sensitive data. Moreover, although cross-sectional data sets can be used to test hypotheses that conform to certain causal hypotheses, to test hypotheses reflecting dynamic, causal models longitudinal data are optimal. As such, these analyses remain priorities for future reports of the 4-H Study data set.

In addition, given the relative power and richness of the data set, we will be able to focus future work on patterns of individual differences in the youth development trajectories we will be able to assess across the waves of this longitudinal study. For instance, we will be able to also ascertain how different groups of youth (e.g., males and females, adolescents from different regions, youth involved in different constellations of activities, or adolescents having different family experiences) may differ in regard to the structure and levels of the Five Cs, PYD, and contribution.

As noted earlier, these analyses will be enhanced by improvement of the measurement model we use to index key constructs in our structural model of the adolescent ← → context relation, e.g., developmental assets and, particularly, external developmental assets which can be indexed objectively through measures of the actual ecology of human development (Theokas & Lerner, in press); they can also be conceptualized as distinct from the Cs of PYD with which (as evidenced by the nature of our revised measurement model) the perceived internal assets indexed by the PSL-AB covary substantially. Indeed, the opportunity in future waves to index constructs through both self-report and independent and objective means will enhance the level of triangulation within the data set and, as well, will diminish the possibility that method variance may constrain our ability to generate valid and generalizable data. The changes in the measurement model for the Five Cs that was introduced by the formulation of our revised measurement model, and the use of an enhanced measurement model for such constructs as ecological developmental assets or contribution (which can be indexed through school- and community-based records), will enable us to better appraise the developmental systems notion that adaptive developmental regulation—mutually beneficial individual ← → context relations—are linked to PYD.

A key asset to be provided by the analysis of further waves of data from the 4-H Study is that causality can be modeled, which of course cannot be done by cross-sectional, unitemporal data. Accordingly, reports of the results of analyses of the dynamic influences on PYD of the system of relations within which a young person is developing will be a key contribution of the work deriving from the future waves of this longitudinal study.

In sum, the analyses from the first wave of the 4-H Study provide empirical support for the conceptualization of positive youth development as competence, confidence, connections, character, and caring, for the conception of youth contribution presented in this article, and for the role that youth development programs play in PYD. These findings, together with future publications of the 4-H Study that will be focused on a comprehensive model of PYD, provide important information to scholars, practitioners, and policy makers who have called for a model of the strengths that young people possess. This important work can facilitate efforts to promote and support thriving among young people and their families through applications to community-based youth developmental programs and to broaden and sustain such applications to youth development social policies.

Such policies should be developed to enhance in communities the capacities of families to provide individual and ecological developmental assets (Benson, 2003; Damon, 1997; Damon, et al., 2003; Lerner et al., 2002; Lerner et al., 2000). Within such a policy context, asset rich communities would enact activities (e.g., programs) that would provide young people with the resources needed to build and to pursue healthy lives that make productive contributions to self, family, and community. Such resources include a healthy start, a safe environment, education for marketable skills, the opportunity to "give back" to (to serve) the community, and freedom from prejudice and discrimination (Lerner et al., 2000).

Thriving will more likely emerge when youth develop in such a policy and community action/program context (Benson, 2003; Lerner et al., 2000; Pittman et al., 2001; Roth et al., 1998). In contemporary American society a competent, confident, connected, caring youth, who also possesses character, will have the moral orientation, the civic allegiance, and the behavioral skills to promote in his or herself (and when a parent, in his or her children), behaviors that "level the playing field" for all individuals. Committed—behaviorally, morally, and spiritually—to a better world beyond themselves, such youth will act to sustain for future generations a society marked by social justice, equity, and democracy and a world wherein all young people may thrive.

NOTES

1. The writing of this chapter was supported in part by grants from the National 4-H Council and by the William T. Grant Foundation. Jacqueline V. Lerner and Elise Christiansen are affiliated with Boston College. Alexander von Eye is affiliated with Michigan State University. All other authors are affiliated with Tufts University. Portions of the theory of positive youth development presented in this chapter have been derived from Lerner (2004). The data presented in this chapter were reported originally in Lerner et al. (in press).

2. The colleagues at the Institute coauthoring this chapter include Jason Almerigi, Christina Theokas, Erin Phelps, Sophie Naudeau, Steinunn Gestsdottir, Lang Ma, Helena Jelicic, Amy Alberts, Lisa Smith, Isla Simpson, Elise Christiansen, Daniel Warren, and Alexander von Eye.

REFERENCES

Armsden, G., & Greenberger, M. (1987). The inventory of parent and peer attachment: Individual differences and their relationship to psychological well-being in adolescence. *Journal of Youth and Adolescence, 16*(3), 427–452.

Baltes, P.B., Lindenberger, U., & Saudinger, U. M. (1998). Life-span theory in developmental psychology. In W. Damon (Series Ed.) & R. M. Lerner (Vol. Ed.), *Handbook of child psychology: Vol.1 Theoretical models of human development* (5th ed., pp. 1029–1144). New York: Wiley.

Baltes, P. B., Reese, H. W., & Nesselroade, J. R. (1977). *Life-span developmental psychology: Introduction to research methods.* Monterey, CA: Brooks Cole.

Benson, P. L. (1990). *The troubled journey: A portrait of 6th–12th grade youth.* Minneapolis, MN: Search Institute.

Benson, P. L. (1997). *All kids are our kids: What communities must do to raise caring and responsible children and adolescents.* San Francisco: Jossey-Bass.

Benson, P. L. (2003). Developmental assets and asset-building community: Conceptual and empirical foundations. In R. M. Lerner & P. L. Benson (Eds.), *Developmental assets and asset-building communities: Implications for research, policy, and practice* (pp. 19–43). Norwell, MA: Kluwer Academic.

Benson, P. L., Leffert, N., Scales, P. C., & Blyth, D. A. (1998). Beyond the "village" rhetoric: Creating healthy communities for children and adolescents. *Applied Developmental Science, 2*(3), 138–159.

Bentler, P. M. (1990). Comparative indexes in structural models. *Psychological Bulletin, 107,* 238–246.

Bentler, P. M., & Bonett, D. G. (1980). Significance tests and goodness-of-fit in the analysis of covariance structures. *Psychological Bulletin, 88,* 588–606.

Blum, R. W. (2003). Positive youth development: A strategy for improving health. In. F. Jacobs, D. Wertlieb, & R. M. Lerner (Eds.), *Enhancing the life chances of youth and families: Contributions of programs, policies, and service systems. Handbook of applied developmental science: Promoting positive child, adolescent, and family development through research, policies, and programs* (Vol. 2, pp. 237–252). Thousand Oaks: CA: Sage.

Bollen, K. A. (1989). *Structural equations with latent variables.* New York: Wiley.

Bornstein, M. H. (2003). Positive parenting and positive development in children. In. R. M. Lerner, F. Jacobs, & D. Wertlieb (Eds.), *Applying developmental science for youth and families: Historical and theoretical foundations. Handbook of applied developmental science: Promoting positive child, adolescent, and family development through research, policies, and programs* (Vol. 1, pp. 187–209). Thousand Oaks, CA: Sage.

Bronfenbrenner, U. (1979) *The ecology of human development: Experiments by nature and design.* Cambridge: Harvard University Press.

Bronfenbrenner, U. (2001). Human development, bioecological theory of. In N. J. Smelser & P. B. Baltes (Eds.), *International encyclopedia of the social and behavioral sciences* (pp. 6963–6970). Oxford: Elsevier.

Bronfenbrenner, U. (2005). *Making human beings human: Bioecological perspectives on human development.* Thousand Oaks, CA: Sage.

Brown, B. B. (2004). Adolescents' relationships with peers. In. R. M. Lerner & L. Steinberg (Eds.), *Handbook of adolescent psychology* (2nd ed., pp. 363–394). Hoboken, NJ: Wiley.

Browne, M. W., & Cudeck, R. (1993). Alternative ways of assessing model fit. In K. A. Bollen & J. S. Long (Eds.), *Testing structural equation models.* Newbury Park, CA: Sage.

Buchanan, C. M., & Hughes, J. L. (2004). Can expecting storm and stress in adolescence create "storm and stress"? : Expectations for adolescence as related to early-adolescent behaviors and relationships. Manuscript in preparation. Wake Forest University: Winston-Salem, North Carolina.

Cairns, R. B., & Hood, K. E. (1983). Continuity in social development: A comparative perspective on individual difference prediction. In P. B. Baltes & O. G. Brim, Jr. (Eds.), *Life-span development and behavior* (Vol. 5, pp. 301–358). New York: Academic Press.

Carnegie Corporation of New York. (1995). *Great transitions: Preparing adolescents for a new century.* New York: Author.

Catalano, R. F., Berglund, M. L., Ryan, J. A. M., Lonczak, H. S., & Hawkins, J. D. (1999). *Positive youth development in the United States: Research findings on evaluations of youth development programs.* Washington, DC: U.S. Department of Health and Human Services.

Csikszentmihalyi, M., & Rathunde, K. (1998). The development of the person: An experiential perspective on the ontogenesis of psychological complexity. In W. Damon (Series Ed.) & R. M. Lerner (Volume Ed.), *Handbook of child psychology: Vol. 1 Theoretical models of human development* (5th ed., pp. 635–684). New York: Wiley.

Cudeck, R., & Browne, M. W. (1983). Cross-validation of covariance structures. *Multivariate Behavioral Research, 18*, 507–534.

Cummings, E. (2003). Foreword. In D. Wertlieb, F. Jacobs, & R. M. Lerner (Eds.), *Promoting positive youth and family development: Community systems, citizenship, and civil society. Handbook of applied developmental science: Promoting positive child, adolescent, and family development through research, policies, and programs* (Vol. 3, pp. ix–xi). Thousand Oaks, CA: Sage.

Damon, W. (1990). *The moral child.* New York: Free Press.

Damon, W. (1997). *The youth charter: How communities can work together to raise standards for all our children.* New York: The Free Press.

Damon, W. (Ed.). (1998). *Handbook of child psychology* (5th ed.). New York: Wiley.

Damon, W., & Gregory, A. (2003). Bringing in a new era in the field of youth development. In R. M. Lerner & P. L. Benson (Eds.), *Developmental assets and asset-building communities: Implications for research, policy, and practice* (pp. 47–64). Norwell, MA: Kluwer Academic.

Damon, W., Menon, J., & Bronk, K. C. (2003). The development of purpose during adolescence. *Applied Developmental Science, 7*, 119–128.

Dowling, E., Gestsdottir, S., Anderson, P., von Eye, A., Almerigi, J., & Lerner, R. M. (2004). Structural relations among spirituality, religiosity, and thriving in adolescence. *Applied Developmental Science, 8*, 7–16.

Dowling, E., Gestsdottir, S., Anderson, P., von Eye, A., & Lerner, R. M. (2003). Spirituality, religiosity, and thriving among adolescents: Identification and confirmation of factor structures. *Applied Developmental Science, 7*, 253–260

Dryfoos, J. (1990) *Adolescents at risk: Prevalence and prevention.* New York: Oxford University Press.

Dryfoos, J. G. (1998). *Safe passage: Making it through adolescence in a risky society.* New York: Oxford University Press.

Eccles, J. S. (2004). Schools, academic motivation, and stage-environment fit. In R. M. Lerner & L. Steinberg (Eds.), *Handbook of adolescent psychology: Volume 2* (pp. 125–153). Hoboken, NJ: Wiley.

Eccles, J., & Gootman, J. (Eds.). (2002). *Community programs to promote youth development.* Washington DC: National Academy Press.

Eisenberg, N., Fabes, R. A., Murphy, B. C., Karbon, M., Smith, M., & Maszk, P. (1996). The relations of children's dispositional empathy-related responding to their emotionality, regulation, and social functioning. *Developmental Psychology, 32*, 195–209.

Elder, G. H., Jr. (1998). The life course and human development. In W. Damon (Series Ed.) & R. M. Lerner (Vol. Ed.), *Handbook of child psychology: Vol. 1 Theoretical models of human development* (5th ed., pp. 939–991). New York: Wiley.

Flanagan, C., & Faison, N. (2001). Youth civic engagement: Implications of research for social policy and programs. *Social Policy Report, 15*, 3–16.

Flanagan, C., & Sherrod, L. (Eds.). (1998). Political development: Youth growing up in a global community. *Journal of Social Issues, 54*(3), 457–475

Ford, D. L., & Lerner, R. M. (1992). *Developmental systems theory: An integrative approach.* Newbury Park, CA: Sage.

Freund, A. M., & Baltes, P. B. (2002). Life-management strategies of Selection, Optimization and Compensation: Measurement by self-report and construct validity. *Journal of Personality and Social Psychology, 82*(4), 642–662.

Freund, A. M., Li, Z. H., & Baltes, P. B. (1999). The role of selection, optimization, and compensation in successful aging. In J. Brandtstädter & R. M. Lerner (Eds.), *Action and development: Origins and functions of intentional self-development* (pp. 401–434). Thousand Oaks, CA: Sage.

Gore, A. (2003). Foreword: In R. M. Lerner & P. L. Benson (Eds.), *Developmental assets and asset-building* communities: Implications for research, policy, and practice (pp. xi–xii). Norwell, MA: Kluwer Academic.

Gore, A., & Gore, T. (2002). Joined at the heart: The transformation of the American family. New York: Henry Holt and Company.

Gottlieb, G. (1997). Synthesizing nature-nurture: Prenatal roots of instinctive behavior. Mahwah, NJ: Erlbaum.

Gottlieb, G. (1998). Normally occurring environmental and behavioral influences on gene activity: From central dogma to probabilistic epigenesis. Psychological Review, 105, 792–802.

Gottlieb, G. (2004). Normally occurring environmental and behavioral influences on gene activity. In C. Garcia Coll, E. Bearer, & R. M. Lerner (Eds.), Nature and nurture: The complex interplay of genetic and environmental influences on human behavior and development (pp.85–106). Mahwah, NJ: Erlbaum.

Greenberger, E., & Bond, L. (1984). Psychosocial maturity inventory. Department of Social Ecology, University of California, Irvine.

Grice, J. W. (2001). Computing and evaluating factor scores. Psychological Methods, 6(4), 430–450.

Hall, G. (1904). Adolescence. New York: Appleton.

Harter, S. (1983). Supplementary description of the Self-Perception Profile for Children: Revision of the Perceived Competence Scale for Children. Unpublished Manuscript. Denver, CO: University of Denver.

Harter, S. (1998). The development of self-representations. In W. Damon (Series Ed.) & N. Eisenberg (Vol. Ed.), Handbook of child psychology, Vol. 3, Social, emotional, and personality development (5th ed., pp. 553–617). New York: Wiley.

Hein, K. (2003) Enhancing the assets for positive youth development: The vision values, and action agenda of the W.T. Grant Foundation. In R. M. Lerner & P. L. Benson (Eds.). Developmental assets and asset-building communities: Implications for research, policy, and practice (pp. 97–117). Norwell, MA: Kluwer Academic.

Hoyle, R. H., & Panter, A. T. (1995). Writing about structural equation models. In R. Hoyle (Ed.), Structural equation modeling: Concepts, issues and applications (pp. 158–176). Thousand Oaks, CA: Sage.

Hu, L., & Bentler, P. M. (1995). Evaluating model fit. In R. H. Hoyle (Ed.), Structural equation modeling: Concepts, issues and applications (pp. 76–79). Thousand Oaks, CA: Sage.

Jöreskog, K. G., & Sörbom, D. (1996a). LISREL 8: User's reference guide. Chicago: Scientific Software International.

Jöreskog, K. G., & Sörbom, D. (1996b). PRELIS 2: User's reference guide. Chicago: Scientific Software International.

Jöreskog, K. G., Sörbom, D., du Toit, S., & du Toit, M. (2001). LISREL 8: New statistical features. Chicago: Scientific Software International.

King, P. E., Shultz, W., Mueller, R. A., Dowling, E. M., Osborn, P., Dickerson, E., & Lerner, R. M. (2004). Positive youth development (PYD): Is there a nomological network of concepts used in the developmental literature? Unpublished manuscript.

King, P. E., Dowling, E. M., Mueller, R. A., White, K., Schultz, W., Osborn, P., Dickerson, E., Bobek, D. L., Lerner, R. M., Benson, P. L., & Scales, P. C. (2005). Thriving in adolescence: The voices of youth-serving practitioners, parents, and early and late adolescents. Journal of Early Adolescence, 25(1), 94–112..

Leffert, N., Benson, P. L., Scales, P. C., Sharma, A. R., Drake, D. R., & Blyth, D. A. (1998). Developmental assets: Measurement and prediction of risk behaviors among adolescents. Applied Developmental Science, 2, 209–230.

Lerner, R. M. (1995). America's youth in crisis: Challenges and options for programs and policies. Thousand Oaks, CA: Sage.

Lerner, R. M. (2002). Concepts and theories of human development (3rd ed.). Mahwah, NJ: Erlbaum.

Lerner, R. M. (2004). Liberty: Thriving and civic engagement among American youth. Thousand Oaks, CA: Sage.

Lerner, R. M., Bornstein, M. H., & Smith C. (2003b). Child well-being: From elements to integrations. In M. H. Bornstein, L. Davidson, C. M. Keyes, K. Moore, & The Center for Child Well-Being. Well-being: Positive development across the life course (pp. 501–523). Mahwah, NJ: Erlbaum.

Lerner, R. M., Brentano, C., Dowling, E. M., & Anderson, P. M. (2002). Positive youth development: Thriving as a basis of personhood and civil society. In R. M. Lerner, C. S. Taylor, & A. von Eye (Eds.), G. Noam (Series Ed.), Pathways to positive development among diverse youth. In New directions for youth development: Theory, practice and research (Vol. 95, pp. 11–34). San Francisco: Jossey-Bass.

Lerner, R. M., Dowling, E. M., & Anderson, P. M. (2003a). Positive youth development: Thriving as a basis of personhood and civil society. In Furrow, J. & Wagener, L. (Eds.), [Special Issue], Applied Developmental Science, 7(3), 172–180.

Lerner, R. M., Fisher, C. B., & Weinberg, R. A. (2000). Toward a science for and of the people: Promoting civil society through the application of developmental science. Child Development, 71, 11–20.

Lerner, R. M., & Galambos, N. L. (1998). Adolescent development: Challenges and opportunities for research, programs, and policies. In J. T. Spence (Ed.), Annual Review of Psychology (Vol. 49, pp. 413–446). Palo Alto, CA: Annual Reviews.

Lerner, R. M., Lerner, J. V., Almerigi, J., Theokas, C., Naudeau, S., Gestsdottir, S., Jelicic, H., Alberts, A. E., Ma, L., Smith, L. M., Bobek, D. L. Simpson, I., Christiansen, E. D., & von Eye, A. (2005). Positive youth development, participation in community youth development programs, and community contributions of fifth grade adolescents: Findings from the first wave of the 4-H Study of Positive Youth Development. Journal of Early Adolescence, 25(1), 17–71.

Little, R. R. (1993). What's working for today's youth: The issues, the programs, and the learnings. Paper presented at the Institute for Children, Youth, and Families Fellows' Colloquium, Michigan State University.

McDonald, R. P., & Ho, M-H. R. (2002). Principles and practice in reporting structural equation analyses. Psychological Methods, 7, 64–82.

McLoyd, V. C. (1998). Children in poverty: Development, public policy, and practice. In W. Damon (Ed.), I. E. Sigel & K. A. Renninger (Vol. Eds.), Handbook of psychology: Child psychology in practice (Vol. 4, pp. 135–208). New York: Wiley.

Monitoring the Future (2000). National survey on drug use, 1975–2000. Bethesda, MD: National Institute on Drug Abuse.

Nurmi, J-E (2004). Socialization and self-development: Channeling, selection, adjustment, and reflection. In R. M. Lerner & L. Steinberg (Eds.), Handbook of adolescent psychology (2nd ed., pp. 85–124). New York: Wiley.

Overton, W. F. (1998). Developmental psychology: Philosophy, concepts, and methodology. In R. M. Lerner (Ed.), Theoretical models of human development. Vol. 1. The handbook of child psychology (5th ed., pp. 107–189). New York: Wiley.

Perkins, D. F., & Borden, L. M. (2003). Positive behaviors, problem behaviors, and resiliency in adolescence. In R. M. Lerner, M. A. Easterbrooks, & J. Mistry (Eds.), *Handbook of psychology: Vol. 6. Developmental psychology* (pp. 373–394). New York: Wiley.

Petersen, A. C., Crockett, L., Richards, M., & Boxer, A. (1988). A self-report measure pf pubertal status: Reliability, validity, and initial norms. *Journal of Youth and Adolescence, 17,* 117–133.

Pittman, K. (1996). Community, youth, development: Three goals in search of connection. *New Designs for Youth Development,* Winter, 4–8.

Pittman, K. J., & Fleming, W. E. (1991, September). *A new vision: Promoting youth development.* Written transcript of live testimony by Karen J. Pittman given before the House Select Committee on Children, Youth and Families. Washington DC: Center for Youth Development and Policy Research.

Pittman, K., Irby, M., & Ferber, T. (2001). Unfinished business: Further reflections on a decade of promoting youth development. In P. L. Benson & K. J. Pittman (Eds.), *Trends in youth development: Visions, realities and challenges* (pp. 4–50). Norwell, MA: Kluwer Academic.

Radloff, L. S. (1977). The CES-D scale: A self-report depression scale for research in the general population. *Applied Psychological Measurement, 1,* 385–401.

Raykov, T., Tomer, A., & Nesselroade, J. R. (1991). Reporting structural equation modeling results in *Psychology and Aging*: Some proposed guidelines. *Psychology and Aging, 6,* 499–503.

Rhodes, J. E. (2002). *Stand by me: The risks and rewards of mentoring today's youth.* Cambridge: Harvard University Press.

Rhodes, J. E., & Roffman, J. G. (2003). Relationship-based interventions: The impact of mentoring and apprenticeship on youth development. In F. Jacobs, D. Wertlieb, & R. M. Lerner (Eds.), *Enhancing the life chances of youth and families: Public service systems and public policy perspectives. Handbook of applied developmental science: Promoting positive child, adolescent, and family development through research, policies, and programs* (Vol. 2, pp. 225–236). Thousand Oaks, CA: Sage.

Rosenthal, D. A., Gurney, R. M., & Moore, S. M. (1981). From trust to intimacy: A new inventory for examining Erikson's stages of psychosocial development. *Journal of Youth & Adolescence, 10,* 525-537.

Roth, J. L., & Brooks-Gunn, J. (2003a). What is a youth development program? Identification and defining principles. In F. Jacobs, D. Wertlieb, & R. M. Lerner (Eds.), *Enhancing the life chances of youth and families: Public service systems and public policy perspectives. Handbook of applied developmental science: Promoting positive child, adolescent, and family development through research, policies, and programs* (Vol. 2, pp. 197–223). Thousand Oaks, CA: Sage.

Roth, J. L., & Brooks-Gunn, J. (2003b). What exactly is a youth development program? Answers from research and practice. *Applied Developmental Science, 7,* 94–111.

Roth, J., Brooks-Gunn, J., Murray, L., & Foster, W. (1998). Promoting healthy adolescents: Synthesis of youth development program evaluations. *Journal of Research on Adolescence, 8,* 423–459.

Scales, P., Benson, P., Leffert, N., & Blyth, D. A. (2000). The contribution of developmental assets to the prediction of thriving among adolescents. *Applied Developmental Science, 4,* 27–46.

Schaie, K. W., & Strother, C. R. (1968). A cross-sequential study of age changes in cognitive behavior. *Psychological*

Bulletin, 70, 671–680.

Schludermann, E., & Schluderman, S. (1970). Replicability of factors in children's reports of parent behavior (CRPBI). *Journal of Psychology,* 76, 239–249.

Schorr, L. B. (1988). *Within our reach: Breaking the cycle of disadvantage.* New York: Doubleday.

Schorr, L. B. (1997). *Common purpose: Strengthening families and neighborhoods to rebuild America.* New York: Doubleday.

Sherrod, L., Flanagan, C., & Youniss, J. (Guest Eds.). (2002). Growing into citizenship: Multiple pathways and diverse influence. Special Issue of *Applied Developmental Science, 6(4),* 264–272.

Small, S. A., & Kerns, D. (1993). Unwanted sexual activity among peers during early and middle adolescence: Incidence and risk factors. *Journal of Marriage and the Family, 55,* 941–952.

Small, S. A., & Rodgers, K. B. (1995). *Teen Assessment Project (TAP) Survey Question Bank.* Madison: University of Wisconsin-Madison.

Steiger, J. H., & Lind, J. M. (1980, June). Statistically based tests for the number of common factors. Paper presented at the annual meeting of the Psychometric Society, Iowa City, IA.

Susman, E. J. & Rogol, A. (2004). Puberty and psychological development. In R. M. Lerner & L. Steinberg (Eds.). *Handbook of adolescent psychology* (2nd ed., pp. 15–44). Hoboken, NJ: Wiley.

Theokas, C., Almerigi, J., Lerner, R. M., Dowling, E., Benson, P., Scales, P. C., von Eye, A. (2005). Conceptualizing and modeling individual and ecological asset components of thriving in early adolescence. *Journal of Early Adolescence, 25(1),* 113-143.

Theokas, C., & Lerner, R. M. (2005). Promoting positive development across variations in socioeconomic status and poverty: Framing the Corwyn and Bradley structural equation modeling approach with a developmental systems perspective. In A. Acock, K. Allen, V. L. Bengtson, D. Klein and P. Dilworth-Anderson (Eds.) *Sourcebook of family theory and research.* Thousand Oaks, CA: Sage.

Tomer, A., & Pugesek, B. H. (2003). Guidelines for the implementation and publication of structural equation models. In B. H. Pugesek, A. Tomer, & A. von Eye (Eds.). *Structural equation modeling* (pp. 125–140). Cambridge: Cambridge University Press.

Villarruel, F. A., Perkins, D. F., Borden, L. M., & Keith, J. G. (Eds.). (2003). *Community youth development: Programs, policies, and practices.* Thousand Oak, CA: Sage.

Werner, H. (1957). The concept of development from a comparative and organismic point of view. In D. B. Harris (Ed.), *The concept of development* (pp. 125–148). Minneapolis, MN: University of Minnesota Press.

Wheeler, W. (2000). Emerging organizational theory and the youth development organization. *Applied Developmental Science, 4, Supplement 1,* 47–54.

Wheeler, W. (2003). Youth leadership for development: Civic activism as a component of youth development programming and a strategy for strengthening civil society. In R. M. Lerner, F. Jacobs, & D. Wertlieb (Eds.), *Enhancing the life chances of youth and families: Public service systems and public policy perspectives. Handbook of applied developmental science: Promoting positive child, adolescent, and family development through research, policies, and programs* (Vol 2., pp. 491–505). Thousand Oaks, CA: Sage.

Youniss, J., McLellan, J. A., & Yates, M. (1999). Religion, community service, and identity in American youth. *Journal of Adolescence, 22,* 243–253.

19

What Does It Mean
to Be an Adult?
Young People's Conceptions of Adulthood

Jeffrey Jensen Arnett

INTRODUCTION

When does a person become an adult in American society? How does the conception of the transition to adulthood held by today's young Americans compare to the conceptions held by people in traditional cultures and in previous centuries of American and Western society? Anthropologists have found that in most cultures, and particularly in the more traditional, non-Western cultures of the world, marriage is often designated explicitly as the event that marks the transition from boy to man and from girl to woman (Gilmore, 1990; Schlegel & Barry, 1991). Historically, too, in the United States and other Western countries, marriage has loomed large as the definitive transition to adulthood, at least until recently (Ben-Amos, 1994; Modell, 1989). But are there transitions other than marriage that have been viewed as an important part of the transition to adulthood, cross-culturally and historically? And how do these perspectives from other places and times compare to the perspectives of young people in the United States today?

In the course of this chapter I will address these questions by presenting conceptions of the transition to adulthood held by people in other places and times, based on the anthropological, sociological, and historical literatures. These perspectives will then be contrasted with research on conceptions of the transition to adulthood among today's young Americans in their teens and twenties. This analysis will show that there is substantial evidence that the transition to adulthood is widely regarded as a process extending over several years, including adolescence and sometimes an additional period beyond adolescence. However, in most places and times this gradual transition has been viewed as culminating in marriage, the quintessential transition event marking the attainment of adult status.

In contrast, the conception of the transition to adulthood held by the current generation of young people in American society rejects marriage and other role transitions as essential markers of adulthood, in favor of criteria that are distinctly *individualistic*. The criteria most important to young Americans as markers of adulthood are those that represent becoming independent from others (especially from parents) and attaining self-sufficiency. The three individualistic criteria that emerge repeatedly in studies of young Americans' conceptions of the transition to adulthood are *accepting responsibility for one's self, making independent decisions,* and *financial independence.*

In addition to being individualistic, I regard the capacities for accepting responsibility for one's self and for making independent decisions as *qualities of character*. By this I mean that they are qualities that are part of the individual's psychological and moral identity, so that they manifest themselves in a wide variety of situations. The term character has a moral connotation and these qualities are regarded in a distinctly moral light, as the *right* way for an adult to be and to behave.

We will see that other character qualities have been valued as part of the transition to adulthood in other places and times, for example qualities such as reliability, diligence, and (especially) impulse control. However, in other places and times marriage has held the status of the transition event that marked a definite, ritualized, unambiguous entry into adulthood, whatever character qualities a young person may have been required to develop in order to be considered ready for marriage. In contrast, for young Americans the transition to adulthood is considerably more indefinite and ambiguous because it is based principally on intangible qualities of character, and marriage is no longer regarded as the culminating event that marks the incontestable attainment of adulthood. As we will see, there is considerable consistency in this view of what it means to be an adult across ethnic groups in American society, although there are some variations. Similarly, evidence from other industrialized countries indicates that there is considerable cross-national consistency as well, again with some variations.

HISTORICAL BACKGROUND

Other Places: Marriage and Gender Issues

According to anthropologists, marriage has long been almost universally regarded as the definitive transition to adulthood in traditional cultures worldwide (Schlegel & Barry, 1991). For many young people, this means making the transition to adulthood in the late teens or very early twenties. In Schlegel & Barry's (1991) analysis of adolescent development in 186 traditional/preindustrial cultures the typical marriage age was 18 for women and 20 for men.[1] In such cultures, the timing of marriage (and therefore of the transition to adulthood it confers) is often chosen not by young people themselves but by their families, according to family interests and cultural expectations of the appropriate age of marriage. As Schlegel & Barry (1991) observe, "the length of adolescence... is determined in most societies by the age of marriage, which in turn is the consequence of decisions made by persons controlling the marriages of very young people, who are rarely in an economic or political position to make such determinations themselves" (p. 106).

One possible consequence of this traditional pattern is that young people may have found themselves designated as adults by their cultures, through marriage, before they would have considered themselves to have reached adulthood according to their individual perceptions of their developmental maturity. It is also possible that young people in traditional cultures "feel adult" earlier than young people in the United States and other industrialized societies, as a result of being given considerable work and family responsibilities from an early age (e.g., Whiting & Edwards, 1988). A third possibility is that young people in traditional cultures accept marriage as the ultimate marker of adulthood because they have been socialized to hold cultural beliefs that the guidelines for many aspects of life are set by the group rather than by the individual (Arnett, 1995; Triandis, 1995).

It is difficult to know which of these possible interpretations to favor because few anthropological studies have asked young people directly about their conceptions of adulthood. However, there are some suggestive sources of evidence. One important source is Susan and Douglas Davis' ethnography on adolescents in rural Morocco (Davis & Davis, 1989). They asked young people (aged 9–20) "How do you know you're grown up?" as part of their basic interview. They found that the two most prominent types of responses were (1) those that emphasized physical development or chronological age, and (2) those that emphasized character qualities the authors categorized as "behavioral, moral, or mental changes" (p. 52). Few of the young people mentioned marriage as a criterion, even though Davis & Davis state that in Moroccan culture generally, "after marriage, one is considered an adult" (p. 59). It should be noted that the question concerned being "grown up" rather than adulthood per se, and that their responses may reflect the increasing Westernization of Moroccan society. Nevertheless, the results suggest that further investigation of young people's conceptions of adulthood in various cultures may prove enlightening, and that their conceptions may not match the conception of adulthood held by adults.

Davis & Davis (1989) also reported evidence that Moroccan adults view the development of qualities of character as important in their conception of adolescence and the transition to adulthood. The key character quality in this conception is *'aql*, an Arabic word with connotations of rationality and impulse control. To possess it means to be capable of making reasoned, informed judgments, and to have control over one's needs and passions. Moroccans see this as a quality expected of adults and often lacking in adolescents. Although both males and females are expected to develop *'aql* in the course of adolescence, males are viewed as taking a decade longer to develop it fully, perhaps because females take on greater responsibilities at an earlier age, as they do in most traditional cultures (Schlegel & Barry, 1991).

Kirkpatrick's (1987) ethnography of the people of the Marquesas Islands of Polynesia provides similar evidence of a conceptualization of the transition to adulthood that includes character qualities. In the Marquesas Islands, by age 14 girls and boys are working alongside adults and are considered to be capable of adult work. However, they are not yet considered to be adults, and not only because they have not yet married. They are also seen (by adults) as lacking the qualities of character necessary for adult status. The term *taure'are'a* is used to describe the lack of these qualities in adolescents. Translated by Kirkpatrick as "errant youth," it is a term that includes unreliability, laziness, and lack of impulse control. To become an adult, then, means growing out of *taure'are'a* by gradually developing the character qualities necessary for the fulfillment of adult role responsibilities.

Another source of evidence comes from Condon's (1987) ethnography on Inuit adolescents in the Canadian Arctic. Condon explored conceptions of the transition to adulthood by asking young people in their teens to assign life stage categories to various people in the community and explain the reason for their designations. Their responses reflected a variety of criteria for the transition to adulthood, including marriage, parenthood, chronological age, and employment. Most important was establishing a permanent pair-bond by moving into a separate household with a prospective spouse—a marriage-like relationship, but not necessarily involving a formal ceremony or legal tie. Chronological age also mattered; young people living with a prospective spouse but remaining in the parental household of one partner or the other were considered adults if they were beyond their teen years.

In addition, certain character qualities were viewed as distinguishing adolescents from adults. Adolescents spend a great deal of their time "running around," which means visiting each other at all hours of the day and night and (for the boys) playing team sports such as hockey, baseball, and football. Becoming an adult means developing character qualities of self-restraint, reliability, and seriousness of purpose. This is expected to be reflected in spending less time running around, and more time at home with one's spouse/partner and visiting other households accompanied by one's spouse/partner.

Evidence of the relationship between the development of character qualities and preparation for adult roles has been compiled by Gilmore (1990), who analyzed information from a variety of ethnographies in an effort to explore cross-cultural similarities and differences in conceptions of manhood and the passage from boyhood to manhood status. Gilmore concurred that marriage commonly marks the ultimate passage to manhood in traditional cultures around the world. However, he focused on the years of preparation for manhood, especially on the skills that are developed by boys during adolescence as preparation for taking on adult roles.

According to Gilmore's analysis, there are three capacities that boys in traditional cultures must develop in the course of adolescence in order to be considered fit to enter manhood: *provide*, *protect*, and *procreate*. They must learn to *provide* economically for themselves and for their wives and children. They learn this by acquiring the knowledge and skills that are necessary for economic performance in their culture—hunting, fishing, and farming are typical examples. They must learn to contribute to the *protection* of their family, kinship group, tribe, and other groups to which they belong, from attacks by human enemies and/or animal predators. They learn this by acquiring the skills of warfare. Also, they must learn to *procreate*, that is, they must gain some degree of sexual experience before marriage, so that in marriage they will be able to perform well enough sexually to produce children. Although Gilmore claims no similar set of requirements exist for girls in preparation for womanhood, Schlegel and Barry (1991) and other anthropologists (e.g., Chinas, 1991; Davis & Davis, 1989) have noted that girls in traditional cultures are typically expected to be capable of *caring for children* and *running a household* before they are considered to be ready for marriage and the adult status it confers.

In addition to the development of specific skills, the cultures described by Gilmore (1990) also require the development of qualities of character in tandem with those skills, in order for adult status to be obtained. Learning to provide requires the development of diligence and reliability. Learning to protect means cultivating courage and fortitude in battle. Learning to procreate requires boldness and confidence in heterosexual relations and sexual performance. For girls, too, learning to care for children and run a household means developing character qualities such as diligence and reliability.

In sum, anthropological studies indicate that many traditional cultures view marriage as the ultimate marker of the transition to adulthood. However, marriage is typically viewed not as the sole and isolated marker of adult status but as the culmination of a transition to adulthood lasting several years. The focus of this period is on the development of character qualities along with the development of gender-specific skills.

Other Times: Marriage and More

Historians have noted that the conception of adolescence as a time of prolonged institutional education and exclusion from the adult workplace through the late teens arose in the West only in the late nineteenth century (Kett, 1977). However, in a more general sense, as a period of acquiring the skills and character qualities required for attaining adult status, adolescence and an extended transition to adulthood have a long history in the West, reaching back at least 500 years (Hanawalt, 1986).

Particularly striking is the scholarship on early modern English society (during the years 1500–1700) summarized by Ben-Amos (1994). This work indicates that people in early modern English society viewed the transition to adulthood as an extended and gradual transition, in which legal, social, and economic rights and obligations were granted gradually as young people developed the appropriate character qualities in the course of many years after puberty. The transition to adulthood became complete for most people when they married in their late twenties.

The median age of marriage in early modern English society was high, about 26 for women and 28 for men. A key reason for the lateness of marriage was that most young people took part in what historians term "life-cycle service," a period in their late teens and early-to-mid-twenties in which young people would engage in domestic service, farm service, or apprenticeship in various trades and crafts. This involved moving out of their family household and into the household of the "master" to whom they were in service, for a period lasting (typically) 7 years. Young women were somewhat less likely than young men to engage in life-cycle service, but even among women a majority left home before marriage, most often for employment in domestic service.

Adults in early modern English society held a view of adolescence (which they termed "youth") and the transition to adulthood that emphasized character qualities. They viewed youth as a distinct stage of life, characterized by character qualities such as lack of impulse control (especially with regard to sexual behavior), emotional extremes (especially anger), and reckless and riotous behavior (the Prodigal Son theme was popular in plays and songs). They also viewed this period as a time of developing favorable character qualities such as open-mindedness and rationality. Rights and obligations were gradually conferred on young people in the course of their teens and twenties according to societal perceptions of their character development. Marriage was the culmination of these developments, "the single most important event in the entry of most young people into adult life" (Ben-Amos, 1994, p. 208), but as in the traditional cultures discussed in the previous section, marriage was seen as "the culmination of a series of transformations rather than a sudden transition into adult life" (Ben-Amos, 1994, p. 208).

The transition to adulthood in early American society was similar in some ways to that of early modern English society. Rotundo (1993) takes up the historical trail where Ben-Amos (1994) left off, focusing on males and tracing the development of conceptions of manhood in the American middle class from the seventeenth century to the present. In Rotundo's account, the seventeenth and eighteenth centuries in colonial New England were characterized by communities that were small, tightly-knit, and strongly based in religion. In this phase of what Rotundo terms "communal manhood," the focus of the transition to adulthood was on assuming adult role responsibilities in work and marriage. The role of "head of the household" was seen as especially important, with the man as provider and protector of wife and children (a striking correspondence to Gilmore's (1990) description of the requirements of manhood in traditional cultures). Women prepared for complementary adult role responsibilities as wife and mother (again, highly similar to traditional cultures). Life-cycle service was sometimes part of preparation for adult roles, as it was in early modern England, but in colonial New England such service was less common and usually took place in the home of a relative or family friend.

In the nineteenth century, as the American population grew and industrialization proceeded, communities became more fluid and young people became more likely to leave home in their late teens for a setting (often urban) where they neither knew nor were known by others. This was an era in which individualism grew in strength, as the bonds of community diminished. The movement into adulthood became "variable in definition and loose in the definition of its boundaries" (Rotundo, 1993, p. 56), and there was an explicit emphasis on the importance of developing the character qualities necessary for adulthood. "Decision of character" became a popular term to describe the passage of a young person from high-spirited but undisciplined youth to an adult status characterized by self-control and a strong will for carrying out independent decisions (see Kett, 1977). Nevertheless, the focus of the transition to adulthood remained role-related: work and marriage for young men, marriage and motherhood for young women. Marriage (which took place in the mid-twenties for most young people during the ninteenth century) was the mark of full adulthood, the event that "completed the social identity" (Rotundo, 1993, p. 115) of the adult. Thus even as individualism rose in strength in American society from the seventeenth through the ninnettenth centuries, and qualities of character gained an explicit prominence as criteria for adulthood, marriage remained central to the transition to adulthood.

In the first half of the twentieth century, marriage continued to hold its status as the definitive transition to adulthood. In fact, its status as a transition event may even have risen, as the median age of marriage declined steadily and marriages become more elaborate as social and communal events (Modell, 1989). However, this pattern changed markedly beginning about 1960. The median age of marriage began to rise steeply, and by 2000 had reached its highest level ever in American society (age 25 for women and age 27 for men).

This rise, along with a corresponding rise in the strength of American individualism (Alwin, 1988; Bellah et al., 1985), led ultimately to the demise of marriage as a significant marker of the transition to adulthood in favor of the individualistic character qualities described in the following section. Modell (1989), in his comprehensive analysis of changes in the timing of marriage and other transition events in the course of the twentieth century, concluded that during recent decades "young individuals have gained more control over the resources that allow them to choose the timing of their own life course events and have come increasingly to value the expression of personal choice in this as in other aspects of their own lives…Conformity to (adult) expectations…has come to matter less. One's own identity has come to matter correspondingly more" (pp. 330–331).

THEORETICAL AND EMPIRICAL CONSIDERATIONS

Although the transition to adulthood has been a topic of research for decades in the social sciences, particularly in sociology, this research has focused on demographic patterns and has rarely included studies of how young people themselves view the transition. However, in recent years numerous studies have investigated young Americans' perspectives on the transition to adulthood (Arnett, 1994, 1997, 1998, 2000, 2001, 2004; Crockett, 2000; Greene, Wheatley, & Aldava, 1992; Scheer, Unger, &

Brown, 1994). The findings of these studies, conducted on samples of various ages using a variety of methods, converge so strongly as to suggest the existence of a pervasive, coherent conception of the transition to adulthood among young people in American society. The three criteria found to be most important as criteria for the transition to adulthood are: *accepting responsibility for one's self, making independent decisions*, and *financial independence*.

Specifically, Scheer et al. (1994) surveyed adolescents aged 13–19 about the criteria they viewed as marking the transition to adulthood. Participants were asked to mark one of eight options as the *most important* factor for them in becoming adults, with the options based on a previous interview study (Scheer & Palkovitz, 1995). The top three responses were "taking responsibility for my actions," "making my own decisions," and "financial independence/having a job." Legal age thresholds and role transitions such as marriage, parenthood, and finishing education ranked low.

Greene et al. (1992) asked high school (12th grade) and college students to respond in writing to the question, "In your perception, what characteristics and/or experiences make a person an adult?" They found the top three criteria to be the same for both high school and college students: responsible behavior, autonomous decision making, and financial independence. Chronological age, physical changes, legal thresholds, and role transitions were rarely mentioned.

Also, Arnett (1994) used a 40-item questionnaire to examine college students' (aged 18–23) conceptions of the transition to adulthood. They were asked to "Indicate whether you think each of the following must be achieved before a person can be considered an adult," by marking yes or no. The three criteria endorsed by the highest percentage of students were "accept responsibility for the consequences of your actions" (92%), "decide on beliefs and values independently of parents or other influences," (80%), and "establish a relationship with parents as an equal adult" (72%), with "support self financially" (66%) close behind. As in the Greene et al. (1992) and Scheer et al. (1994) studies, criteria such as chronological age and role transitions ranked very low. Similar results were found in a community sample of 12- to 55-year-olds, with few differences between age groups (Arnett, 2001).

These studies indicate that the conception of the transition to adulthood held by contemporary Americans in their teens and early twenties is notably *individualistic* and emphasizes *qualities of character*. The top three criteria—accepting responsibility for one's self, making independent decisions, and financial independence—have a common theme of individualism, in that they emphasize the capacity of the individual to stand alone as a self-sufficient person, without relying upon anyone else. Furthermore, accepting responsibility for one's self and making independent decisions are character qualities rather than specific events.

But how do young people explain the importance of these criteria, and how do they apply them to their own progress through the transition to adulthood? To answer this question, I will describe one of my studies of conceptions of adulthood among contemporary young Americans in more detail (Arnett, 1998).

A Study of Conceptions of the Transition to Adulthood

The participants in the study were 140 persons aged 21–28 (50% were aged 21–24, 50% were aged 25–28), part of the age period scholars now refer to as "emerging adulthood" (Arnett, 2000; 2004). Participants were contacted from mid-Missouri high school enrollment lists from 3–10 years earlier, and 72% agreed to participate in the study. For married persons contacted, spouses were also invited to participate. Participants were predominantly White (94%), and about evenly divided between males and females (47% female, 53% male). Forty percent of the participants were married and 27% had had at least one child. There was a wide range of educational attainment and socio-economic status (SES) background. Level of education varied from high school or less (16%) to some college (52%) to college degree (19%) to some graduate school or graduate school degree (13%). Father's education varied from high school or less (32%) to some college (15%) to college degree (24%) to some graduate school or graduate school degree (30%).

Participants filled out a questionnaire containing 38 possible criteria for adulthood (see Table 19.1). The items were drawn from a wide range of empirical and theoretical perspectives in psychology,

TABLE 19.1
Criteria for Adulthood Questionnaire Responses

	Necessary for adulthood? Percent indicating "yes"
Individualism	
Accept responsibility for the consequences of your actions	94
Decide on personal beliefs & values independently of parents or other influences	78
Financially independent from parents	73
Establish relationship with parents as an equal adult	69
No longer living in parents' household	60
Family capacities	
Capable of running a household (man)	72
Capable of running a household (woman)	67
Capable of keeping family physically safe (man)	52
Capable of supporting a family financially (man)	50
Capable of caring for children (woman)	50
Capable of caring for children (man)	50
Capable of keeping family physically safe (woman)	47
Capable of supporting a family financially (woman)	42
Norm compliance	
Avoid committing crimes like shoplifting and vandalism	66
Use contraception if sexually active and not trying to conceive a child	65
Avoid drunk driving	55
Avoid using illegal drugs	41
Drive safely and close to the speed limit	32
Avoid becoming drunk	30
Have no more than one sexual partner	29
Avoid using profanity/vulgar language	18
Biological transitions	
Capable of fathering children (man)	30
Capable of bearing children (woman)	29
Grow to full height	13
Have had sexual intercourse	9
Legal/chronological	
Reached age 18	39
Reached age 21	31
Obtained driver's license	24
Role transitions	
Settle into a long-term career	21
Married	17
Employed full-time	17
Have at least one child	14
Finished with education	10
Other	
Learn always to have good control of your emotions	50
Make lifelong commitments to others	36
Not deeply tied to parents emotionally	19
Purchased a house	17
Committed to a long-term love relationship	16

Note. For each item, participants were asked to "Indicate whether you think each of the following must be achieved before a person can be considered an adult," and they responded by indicating yes or no.

sociology, and anthropology, as well as from pilot studies. More detailed explanation of the basis for including particular items will be included in the context of the results.

Participants also took part in a structured interview. Two two-part questions from that interview concerned their conceptions of adulthood. One question applied to themselves: "Do you feel like you have reached adulthood? In what ways do you feel you have or have not?" This question was asked in order to explore the criteria they applied to their own transition to adulthood, for comparison with their general conception of the transition to adulthood as indicated on the questionnaire. The second question was specific to gender: "What would you say makes a person a woman, as opposed to a girl? What would you say makes a person a man, as opposed to a boy?" This question was asked because (as previously described) historical and anthropological evidence indicates that the requirements for adult status have often been gender-specific in other times and places, and in light of this it seemed appropriate to explore the possibility of gender-linked criteria. Female participants were asked the woman/girl part of the question first, and then the man/boy part; for male participants, the order was reversed.

Responses to the interview questions were coded by the author using a categorical system based on the questionnaire (see Table 19.2). A second person also coded 10% of the interviews (randomly selected), and the rate of agreement between the coders was 89%. Both the questionnaire and the interview results confirmed the findings of other studies indicating that the conception of the transition to adulthood held by young people in the American majority culture especially emphasizes three specific criteria: accepting responsibility for one's self, making independent decisions, and financial independence. These findings were unrelated to socioeconomic status; neither participants' education nor their fathers' education were notably related to their responses on the questionnaire.[2]

TABLE 19.2
Criteria for Adulthood: Coded Responses From Interview Questions

Criterion	Personal Conception		Man/Boy–Woman/Girl	
	Rank	Percent	Rank	Percent
Accept responsibility for one's self	1	43	1	60
Financial independence	2	40	4	15
Independent decision making	3	25	2	24
General independence/self-sufficiency	4	25	5	12
Independent household	5	22	13–14	2
Become a parent	6	19	9–10	5
Spontaneous, fun-loving, adventurous, nonconforming (as *not* adult)	7	17	15	1
Employed full-time	8	15	11	4
Avoiding reckless behavior	9	12	9–10	5
Emotional maturity	10	12	8	7
Marriage	11	8	13–14	2
Finish education	12–13	5	16–19	0
Cognitive maturity	12–13	5	6	10
Consideration for others	14	4	3	16
Purchase house	15	3	16–19	0
Military service	16–19	1	16–19	0
Committed to long-term relationship	16–19	1	16–19	0
Any physical/biological	16–19	1	7	8
Any legal/chronological	16–19	1	12	3

Note. The percentages indicate the percentage of participants who mentioned each criterion in response to the interview question indicated. The numbers under Rank indicate the rank-order of prevalence for each criterion for each interview question (with tied rankings indicated by dashes, e.g., 12–13). For "Personal Conception," the whole question was "Do you feel like you have reached adulthood? In what ways do you feel you have or have not?" For the "Man–Boy/Woman–Girl" question, the whole question was "What would you say makes a person a woman, as opposed to a girl? What would you say makes a person a man, as opposed to a boy?" For this question, males were asked the man–boy part first and females were asked the woman–girl part first. Because the majority (72%) of the participants indicated that the criteria were the same for males and females, only the first part of this question was coded (man–boy for males, woman–girl for females).

For all criteria, more participants endorsed specific criteria on the questionnaire than mentioned those same criteria in the interview. This is a predictable consequence of the two different methodologies—people are likely to check off more criteria on a questionnaire than they are to mention spontaneously in an interview. Nevertheless, the convergence of findings using the two methodologies testifies to the robustness of the results. With both methods, accepting responsibility for one's self, independent decision making (deciding specifically on beliefs and values, on the questionnaire), and financial independence ranked highest.

The questionnaire findings and coded interview responses confirmed the results of previous studies with respect to the criteria viewed as the most important markers of the transition to adulthood. Now we turn to examples from the interviews, to explore how emerging adults explain the importance of these criteria and how they apply them to their own lives.

The Preeminence of Accepting Responsibility for One's Self

Accepting responsibility for one's self was far and away the top criterion for adulthood, in both the questionnaire and the interview. The endorsement of the questionnaire item "accept responsibility for the consequences of your actions" as necessary for adulthood was nearly unanimous—94% (see Table 19.1). With respect to the interview questions, the proportion mentioning responsibility for one's self was higher than for any other criterion, in response to both questions (see Table 19.2).

Thus the idea of "responsibility" looms large in the conception of adulthood held by American emerging adults, and, for the most part, it is an individualistic kind of responsibility they endorse, responsibility *for one's self* rather than responsibility *to or for others*. The item in the questionnaire stated specifically, "accept responsibility for the consequences of your actions," and this view was expounded repeatedly in the interviews. Indeed, the questionnaire item was developed on the basis of pilot interviews in which responsibility was often placed in this context.[3] Notice the contrast between this individualistic kind of responsibility and traditional cultures' criteria of provide, protect, and procreate, all of which involve responsibilities toward others (Gilmore, 1991). Marriage, too, carries definite responsibilities toward others—specifically, a marriage partner and his/her kin—particularly in traditional cultures.

Examples of emerging adults' responses from the interviews illustrate the individualistic nature of their conception of responsibility. One 24-year-old man stated that becoming an adult means "just being accountable for your actions and being responsible. I describe it as taking care of your own actions, and not looking to other people to help you along." A 28-year-old woman was similarly concise and individualistic, explaining that she felt she had reached adulthood "because I finally realized that I'm responsible for everything that I do and say and believe, and no one else is. Just me. That's all. So, I'm an adult."

Thus, responsibility is seen as the key to adult status because it has such strong connotations of self-sufficiency and self-reliance. The prominence of this criterion reflects the individualistic cultural beliefs of American society. In this society, accepting responsibility for one's self is the character quality that is essential to the attainment of adult status.

Independent Decision Making

The second most-endorsed item on the questionnaire was "decide on personal beliefs and values independently of parents or other influences" (endorsed by 78%), and independent decision making was also among the top three criteria for adulthood in response to both interview questions. The questionnaire item was based on psychological studies of the transition to adulthood, particularly a well-known study by Perry (1970). Perry studied Harvard undergraduates through the course of their college careers, and concluded that the typical path of cognitive development during the transition to adulthood begins with adherence to absolute truths at the beginning of the college experience, followed by a swing to relativism midway through college, and finally landing on a set of individualized and self-chosen beliefs and values by the end of college, as the cognitive transition to adulthood is completed. The item was also based partly on Erikson's (1963) idea that part of identity formation in adolescence means developing and clarifying a set of beliefs and values. One might expect that if making decisions about one's beliefs and values is part of identity formation in adolescence, reaching fruition in this process would prompt a subjective sense of having reached adulthood.

The validity of Perry's (1970) and Erikson's (1963) views for today's emerging adults seems to be supported by the widespread endorsement of the item "decide on personal beliefs and values…" on the questionnaire. The importance of deciding on one's beliefs was also stated frequently in response to the interview questions. For example, a 25-year-old woman described how she had grown up in a highly religious household, and said that becoming an adult for her meant that "I learned to believe what I believe and not let my parents or anyone else tell me what to believe. And I think once you establish your own beliefs and control your own life, then you're an adult."

In the interviews, however, the importance of decision making as a criterion for adulthood was not restricted to the formation of beliefs and values, but applied to a variety of aspects of life. An adult is not only someone who has decided on a set of guiding beliefs and values, but also someone who has the maturity of character to make sensible, *independent* decisions about any issues that come up in the course of daily life. To this 22-year-old woman, it was self-evident: "I mean, that's what being an adult *is*, thinking for yourself and making the right decisions and taking care of yourself." A 24-year-old man described the crossing of the threshold from boyhood to manhood in these individualistic decision-making terms: "All of a sudden, you've just got to decide, 'Okay, I'm a man. I'm going to do this how I want to. It's going to be my life, and this is how I'm going to run it.'" Responses such as this echo the idea of "decision of character" that was such an important criterion for the transition to adulthood in American society during the nineteenth century (Kett, 1977), in that it combines a sense of making independent decisions with a self-consciously strong-willed intention to carry them out.

Making independent decisions means becoming less dependent on parents, in particular, for guidance. Describing her passage to adulthood, a 28-year-old woman said, "I had always been very, very dependent on my parents in making decisions. I wanted to make sure I had their stamp of approval. Now, I certainly don't worry as much about that. I feel confident in being able to make decisions." Although "establish an equal relationship with parents" was rarely stated explicitly in the interviews, it was one of the most widely endorsed questionnaire items (69%), and it was implicit in interview responses such as these.

Evident in all of these responses is that the capacity for making decisions, like accepting responsibility, has strongly individualistic connotations. Becoming an adult means not just that you have developed the cognitive maturity to weigh a variety of considerations before deciding among a range of choices, but that you make these decisions *independently*, *self-sufficiently*, without relying on anyone else—especially your parents—to advise you (Moore, 1987). Also like accepting responsibility, the capacity for making decisions is reflected in behavior but is essentially a quality of character, part of the individual's psychological and moral identity.

Financial Independence

The third of the top three criteria, financial independence, also has connotations of individualism. However, financial independence is more tangible, more definite and measurable than accepting responsibility for one's self or the capacity for making independent decisions. It is a yardstick by which young people can measure quite definitely their progress toward adulthood. A 25-year-old woman viewed herself as mostly but not entirely finished with the transition to adulthood, because "I'm paying for everything. I'm paying for school, I'm paying for my car, I'm paying for my credit card bills that were my fault a long time ago… The only thing is, I'm not paying for rent, and I think that's a part of adulthood." A 28-year-old man recalled the significance of a single event that denoted his financial independence, and at the same time his movement into adulthood: "I would say the first time it ever hit me in the face was the first time I ever had to sign on the dotted line for a car loan. To me, being an adult was signing on the dotted line and knowing I had a big payment every month."

Like decision-making competence, financial independence often means, specifically, independence from parents (Moore, 1987). A 23-year-old man observed that becoming an adult means "not going to Mom and Dad and saying, 'Can I have $300 to go to Florida with the guys for Spring Break?'" A 24-year-old woman said that she does not feel like an adult "when I have my mom pay half the rent . . . when she helps me out with that, it makes me feel like a kid again."

Although independent decision making and financial independence rank high as criteria for the transition to adulthood, and both have connotations of independence from parents, it is interesting to note that several studies of relationships with parents among adolescents and emerging adults emphasize that these forms of independence do not signify emotional separation from parents. This literature stresses that autonomy (independence of thought and behavior) and relatedness (emotional closeness and support) are complementary rather than opposing dynamics in parent-child relationships during adolescence and emerging adulthood in the American middle class (Arnett, 2004; Allen, Hauser, Bell, & O'Connor, 1994; Ryan & Lynch, 1989; O'Connor, Allen, Bell, & Hauser, 1996). In fact, it is a consistent finding in these studies that young people who are more self-reliant also report *closer* relationships to their parents. In the present study, this is reflected in the finding that "not deeply tied to parents emotionally" ranks very low as a criterion for adulthood even though a variety of criteria indicating autonomy from parents rank high (Table 19.1).

At the same time, the difference between traditional cultures and Western cultures in relationships with parents during adolescence and adulthood should not be underestimated. Numerous studies show that expectations of continued interdependence with parents through adolescence and into adulthood is the norm for traditional cultures (for example in China [Yang, 1988] and Japan [Shand, 1985]). Although relationships between parents and adolescents in American society tend to seek a balance of autonomy and relatedness, the degree of autonomy allowed and expected for American adolescents is considerably greater than in traditional cultures (Shand, 1985). What is considered emotionally close by American adolescents and their parents may seem relatively distant to parents and adolescents in traditional cultures (Kagitcibasi, 1996).

In sum, individualism is the predominant feature of young people's conceptions of the transition to adulthood in American society. The three top criteria for becoming an adult—accepting responsibility for one's self, independent decision making, and financial independence—all signify the developing capacity of the individual to be independent, self-reliant, and self-sufficient.

Furthermore, the top two criteria, accepting responsibility and making independent decisions, are qualities of character. Qualities of character are also important to the transition to adulthood cross-culturally and historically, as we have seen. However, in other places and times the attainment of the appropriate character qualities has been capped by marriage as a definite, explicit marker of reaching adulthood. For today's young Americans, in contrast, marriage ranks low as a criterion for adulthood, and consequently it is qualities of character that play the largest part in marking their transition to adulthood.

Modifications of the Individualistic Theme

Although the conception of the transition to adulthood held by adolescents and emerging adults is characterized by individualism, it is not necessarily an unbridled or selfish individualism. On the contrary, for many young people becoming an adult necessarily means that individualism is tempered by the development of character qualities that emphasize social and communal considerations. Egocentrism and selfishness are character qualities they see as part of adolescence, and becoming an adult means overcoming these tendencies and learning to take other people's interests and needs into account. Modifications of the individualistic theme fell into three general areas: consideration for others, avoiding reckless behavior, and becoming a parent.

Consideration for others was not included as a specific item on the questionnaire, but it came up often as a theme in the interviews. In response to the woman-girl man-boy question, it was the third most common theme. Being a man involves, to one 24-year-old man, "putting others in front of yourself. When you make a decision with others in mind before yourself, that probably makes you a man." A 28-year-old woman said that for her, becoming an adult means learning "not to be selfish, to take other people into account—their feelings, needs, and wishes."

In addition to cultivating a general sense of consideration for others, making the transition to adulthood also means avoiding behavior that might be harmful to others. On the questionnaire, three types of risk behavior concerning crime, sexual behavior, and automobile driving were viewed by a majority of participants as important to avoid as part of becoming an adult. The specific items were: "avoid committing petty crimes like shoplifting & vandalism" (endorsed by 66%), "use contraception if sexually active and not trying to conceive a child" (65%), and "avoid drunk driving" (55%). All three involve behavior that may affect others. In the interviews as well, avoiding various types of risk behavior was occasionally stated as an important criterion for adulthood, although it was not among the top criteria (see Table 19.2). For example, a 22-year-old woman who had recently been stopped by the police and charged with driving while intoxicated said the experience had "made me think about things… like drinking and driving, that you need to be responsible and not just think about where you want to go but how it's going to affect someone else."

The third kind of response that indicated a communal counterpoint to their individualistic conception of adulthood was becoming a parent. This was rated quite low on the questionnaire as a necessary marker of adulthood, endorsed by only 14% (see Table 19.1). However, in the interviews it ranked sixth highest in participants' responses concerning criteria they considered important in their own transition to adulthood (see Table 19.2). More importantly, one-fourth of the participants had had at least one child, and for them having a child was mentioned *more often than any other criterion* (61%) as a marker of their own transition to adulthood. (In contrast, those who were married were no more likely than those who were unmarried to name marriage as a key transition, either for themselves or more generally). This is consistent with other studies indicating that becoming a parent adds considerably to the sense of being adult for many people (Feldman, Biringen, & Nash, 1981; Galinsky, 1981). Many of the parents in the present study saw children as having the effect of puncturing one's egocentrism and directing one's concerns to others, in an inescapable and even involuntary way. "Children can definitely make you feel like an adult," said a 25-year-old woman with two children, "because you have responsibilities, and it's not so much myself anymore, because you have to raise someone else."

Unlike character qualities, which tend to develop gradually, having a child is an event that some describe as a sudden thrust into adulthood, as numerous weighty responsibilities descend simultaneously. "I have two daughters, and if you want to grow up fast, that's a sink or swim" said a 26-year-old man. "I went from happy-go-lucky to 'You've got a baby to take care of. You've got to put a roof over its head. You've got to do this and this and this.'" A 22-year-old woman responded to the question of whether she had reached adulthood by saying "With kids, definitely! Adulthood overnight, you know! [What is it about having kids?] The attention that you have to put on them. The focus is on them and not on you… You think of that other person before you think of yourself."

These comments suggest that young Americans may incorporate "provide" and "protect" into their conception of adulthood more centrally after they procreate (Gilmore, 1990). It is also worth noting here the prominence of parenthood as a criterion for adulthood in some traditional cultures (e.g. Herdt, 1987; Nsamenang, 1992; see Schlegel & Barry, 1991, p. 11). Perhaps parenthood would loom larger in American's conceptions of the transition to adulthood if it took place as early—the mid-to-late teens—as it does in most traditional cultures (Schlegel & Barry, 1991).

In sum, although the view of the transition to adulthood held by young people in their twenties is distinctly individualistic, it is not necessarily a selfish individualism. On the contrary, their individualism is often tempered in a number of ways that reflect sensitivity to and concern for the rights and needs of others. They are not egoists, but social individuals (Jensen, 1998).

The Absence of Gender-Specific Criteria

In contrast to the strict demarcation of gender expectations in the preparation for the transition to adulthood in traditional cultures—with provide/protect/procreate as requirements for males, and care for children/run a household as requirements for females—it is striking how little the views of the emerging adults described here were linked to gender. The questionnaire items specific to gender, and the interview question on woman/girl and man/boy distinctions, were intended to explore this issue, and were based directly on the work of anthropologists, as summarized by Gilmore (1990) and Schlegel & Barry (1991). The results indicate that for young Americans gender has little relevance to the transition to adulthood. Learning to provide for and protect a family, care for children, and run a household were all viewed as quite important criteria in the transition to adulthood (Table 19.1), but for males and females equally, not as gender-linked criteria.

Also, for all 38 items on the questionnaire, males and females were highly similar in their responses.[4] Furthermore, even though one of the interview questions asked specifically about distinctions between males and females in the transition to adulthood (woman–girl, man–boy), most participants stated that there was no important distinction between the genders in this respect. Their responses to this part of the question were also coded, and the results indicated that 72% held the view that adult status is defined no differently for males and females, 21% believed there were gender differences in the most important criteria for adulthood, and the remaining 6% were unsure. This is a stark contrast to the gender-distinct pattern in traditional cultures and historically in the West, and perhaps reflects the fact that today's emerging adults have grown up in a time and a culture in which gender role distinctions are relatively nebulous, in comparison to many other places and times.

What Does *Not* Matter: Marriage, Age, Finishing School, Getting a Job

Just as interesting as what matters to emerging adults in defining adulthood is what does *not* matter to them. We have already seen that marriage now matters little as a marker of adulthood, despite its traditional importance as the ultimate marker. Through most of American history, until late in the twentieth century, getting married meant reaching full adulthood.

Marriage no longer has this meaning in American society. It is meaningful in other important ways, of course, but its status as a marker of adult status has passed. In the many studies I and others have conducted on what people of various ages believe defines the transition to adulthood, marriage consistently ranks near rock-bottom (Arnett 1994, 1997,; 1998, 2001, 2003; Mayseless & Scharf, 2003; Nelson & Badger, 2004). In interviews, when people are given a chance to state their views about what is important to them personally as markers of their progress toward adulthood, marriage is almost never mentioned—even by people who are married.

What explains the demise of marriage as a marker of adulthood? Perhaps most important is that marriage is a much less dramatic transition than it used to be even 40 or 50 years ago. By the time they marry, the majority of today's emerging adults have already known each other for several years, had a regular sexual relationship, and lived in the same household. Being married may feel different to them psychologically than cohabiting did, but in fact not much changes in their daily lives. For example, one 24-year-old woman married 4 months ago, but says it had nothing to do with making her feel more like an adult: "We had been together for four years and I just felt like it was a continuation of our relationship. I mean, we lived together anyway, so I don't think it's changed much." Compare this to the situation historically—when getting married usually involved leaving your parents' household for the first time, having a sexual relationship for the first time, and living for the first time with someone outside your immediate family—and it is easy to see why marriage would have had greater significance as a transition to adulthood in the past than it does now.

As Table 19.1 shows, emerging adults have the same lack of regard for other traditional markers of adulthood, such as turning age 18, finishing school, and holding a full-time job.

Turning age 18 marks the attainment of a wide range of legal rights and responsibilities in American society. At age 18, a person becomes able to vote and to sign legally-binding contracts. Becoming 18 has also meant becoming subject to the military draft during major wars, and even now young men are obligated to register with the Selective Service Program when they turn 18. Eighteen year-olds are also tried as adults when accused of criminal activity (although some states try younger teens as adults as well).

All of this makes it seem that turning 18 must be a momentous occasion in the lives of young people, but emerging adults do not see it as having anything to do with reaching adulthood. In the interviews they never mentioned turning 18 as a milestone of adulthood, and on the questionnaires few of them indicated turning 18 (or 21) as important. They are focused on their personal passage to adulthood, as defined by their progression toward self-sufficiency, and the idea that simply reaching a certain age makes them adults would strike them as nonsense. The entrance into emerging adulthood usually takes place at age 18 because that is the age which people typically graduate from high school and leave home (Goldscheider & Goldscheider, 1994), but for most people full adulthood is a long way off at that point.

Finishing school is another transition that has been traditionally regarded as an important marker of adult status (Hogan & Astone, 1986), but for today's emerging adults it does not have this significance. Graduating from high school means little, because a high school degree alone has little value in the workplace, and the great majority of high school graduates expect to go on to college. Even graduating from college holds little significance today as a marker of adulthood. Perhaps this is because so many college graduates expect to obtain further education at some point, and they do not see their movement toward adulthood as delayed for this reason.

Sometimes in interviews emerging adults mention college graduation as an important step toward adulthood, not because the graduation itself has this significance but because graduating means new responsibilities and a major step toward self-sufficiency. For example, a 22-year-old recent college graduate said that he started to feel like an adult "probably when I graduated, because all of a sudden I felt like I had responsibility and I had to pay bills." A 27-year-old man who graduated 3 years earlier recalled a similar experience, "When I graduated from college and I was responsible for myself, I think that's when I reached it. Once you graduate from college and you get out on your own, that's when you realize that there's nobody else to fall back on but yourself."

Obtaining a full-time job also lacks significance as a marker of adulthood for today's emerging adults. Perhaps this is because so many young people today begin working twenty or more hours a week while still in high school, and college students usually work as well, so that moving into a full-time job is a gradual process rather than an abrupt and momentous transition. In 1940 less than 5% of high school students were employed, but this figure ballooned in the 1970s and 1980s, and by now over 80% of high school seniors have held at least one part-time job (Barling & Kelloway, 1999) With working part-time so prevalent beginning in adolescence, the transition to full-time work no longer marks a major change in the lives of emerging adults. Some sociologists continue to argue for the importance of role transitions in young people's conceptions of adulthood. In 2003 a national study conducted by the National Opinion Research Center (NORC) claimed that "finish education" was perceived as the top criterion for adulthood (Associated Press, 2003). However, the study did not allow people to state their own view of what was most important for adulthood, but gave them a narrow range of choices that included only role transitions (e.g., in addition to finish education, there was marriage, parenthood, and obtaining a full-time job). In contrast to the NORC findings, numerous studies have been conducted on this topic, in many parts of the United States, using a variety of different methods (interviews as well as questionnaires), and finish education has never been any where near the top criteria (Arnett 1994; 1997; 1998; 2001; 2003; Mayseless & Scharf, 2003; Nelson, 2003), so there is good reason to question whether the NORC findings are valid. They are an artifact of the restrictive method of offering respondents only a narrow range of possible choices.

Ethnic Similarities and Differences

The study described thus far was conducted on a nearly all-White sample. However, a recent study of mine included 574 emerging adults (ages 18–29) from a variety of ethnic groups in American society, who were approached in public places in San Francisco, thus making it possible to obtain a diverse community sample. A subsample also took part in a structured interview. A strong degree of

TABLE 19.3
Selected Criteria for Adulthood, American Ethnic Groups

| | Necessary for Adulthood? Percent Yes | | | |
	African American	Latino	Asian American	White
Accept responsibility for the consequences of your actions	89	85	93	91
Decide on personal beliefs and values independently of parents or other influences	80	72	82	82
Financially independent from parents	72	79	75	71
No longer living in parents' household	55	56	49	52
Become less self-oriented, develop greater consideration for others	75	75	80	73
Avoid drunk driving	62	64	72	60
Use contraception if sexually active and not trying to conceive a child	63	65	65	56
Make life-long commitments to others	42	46	52	37
Become employed full-time	43	50	35	19
Married	14	32	13	5
Reached age 18	41	52	35	34
Reached age 21	43	47	40	30
Finish education	23	24	32	14
Have at least one child	16	32	10	5

Note. The questionnaire asked participants to "Indicate whether you think each of the following must be achieved before a person can be considered an adult." N = 109 Whites, 122 African Americans, 96 Latinos, and 247 Asian Americans.

consistency was found among across ethnic groups in their conceptions of adulthood (Arnett, 2003). Whites, African Americans, Latinos, and Asian Americans all agreed that self-sufficiency is at the heart of what it means to be an adult, specifically accepting responsibility for yourself, making independent decisions, and becoming financially independent. As Table 19.3 illustrates, in all four groups in this study these were the most widely favored criteria, on the questionnaire of markers of adulthood.

However, two ethnic differences are worth noting. One is that emerging adults who are Asian American tend to place more emphasis on obligations to others as part of becoming an adult than do Whites. On the questionnaire of possible markers of adulthood Asian American more often favored criteria such as "Make life-long commitments to others." In the interviews they more often mentioned obligations to others, especially to parents. An important part of many Asian cultural traditions is the idea of *filial piety*, meaning that children owe their parents duty, love, even reverence, not just during childhood but all their lives. Even growing up in the United States, many Asian American emerging adults have maintained some sense of filial piety. There is especially a feeling that they should take care of their parents when their parents reach old age. Consequently, becoming an adult may mean becoming capable of caring for one's parents. For example, a 22-year-old Chinese American woman said, "I think that as an adult I should be able to take care of my parents, which I'm not able to. They're taking care of me right now, so in that way, I'm not an adult yet." Thus the criterion "Make life-long commitments" appears to apply to this obligation to parents for Asian American emerging adults, as they were no more likely than those in other ethnic groups to endorse marriage or having a child as markers of adulthood and did not mention these as important markers of adulthood in the interviews.

The other notable ethnic difference was that African American emerging adults were more likely than emerging adults in any other group to state that they believed they had reached adulthood. In response to the question, "Do you think that you have reached adulthood?" a majority of African Americans (59%) and nearly half of Latinos (48%) responded "yes." A smaller proportion of Whites (36%) and Asian Americans (38%) responded "yes." A majority of Whites (60%) and Asian Americans (54%) responded "in some respects yes, in some respects no." Less than half of African Americans (34%) and Latinos (44%) gave this response. Relatively few persons in each group answered "no": 7% African Americans, 8% Latinos, 9% Asian Americans, and 4% Whites.

Why do African Americans, by their own evaluation, seem to reach adulthood earlier than Whites? Two themes in the interviews seemed to explain the difference. One is that African Americans are often called upon at a young age to take on household responsibilities. Because nearly 70% of African American children grow up in a home with a single mother, their mothers often need them to provide a great deal of help in order for the household to function. A 25-year-old man recalled, "Even as a child I had a lot of responsibilities that were adult responsibilities. I was the father figure for my brothers and sisters. I cooked the meals, I cleaned the house, I sent my brothers and sisters to school when I was 8-and 9-years-old." This 23-year-old man had a similar story, "I had to do a lot of the manly things of the house being that my father wasn't there. It was just me and my mother, and I felt like I was the man of the house. I did odd jobs, cut the grass, whatever it took to make the ends meet. Took care of my sisters and help raise them while she worked."

The other reason why African Americans often reach adulthood relatively early is that African American women are more likely than White women to have a child and become a single mother at a young age. We have already seen how having a child can propel young people suddenly into adulthood even when they are in their early twenties and already married. How much more abrupt must it be for a young woman who has a child in her teens, without a husband or partner to share the responsibilities? One 28-year-old woman, who had her first child at age 16, said that is when she became an adult: "When I had the kids, I felt like I was real responsible and I had to take care of somebody else." A 23-year-old woman said that she became an adult at "18, because of having a child and moving out on my own, and beginning to take care of my own responsibilities, and work and make my own money." For this 25-year-old woman, having her daughter when she was 19 led her to an abrupt realization of the urgency of becoming an adult: "When I had my daughter it really dawned on me, you know, 'You have to grow up *now* in order to take care of her.'"

Cross-National Similarities and Differences

The idea of studying how young people think about what it means to become an adult is fairly new, and as previously noted, until recently studies on this topic have been limited mostly to White Americans representing the American majority culture. However, several papers have come out recently that provide insights into how people in a variety of different cultures think about what it means to be an adult and consider their responses in the context of the distinctive characteristics of their culture. In addition to the new data described on American ethnic groups, these studies have examined conceptions of adulthood among Israelis (Mayseless & Scharf, 2003), Argentines (Facio & Micocci, 2003), and American Mormons (Nelson, 2003). Both cultural similarities and cultural differences have been found.

The cultural distinctiveness of conceptions of adulthood is one of the notable themes of studies conducted in different cultures. Two-thirds of the young Israelis in the Mayseless & Scharf (2003) study viewed completing their required term of military service as an important part of becoming an adult. For young Argentines (Facio & Micocci, 2003), the economic upheavals that have taken place in recent years in their country make the prospect of entering the adult world more daunting than it might be in places with greater economic stability. Facio and Micocci (2003) suggest that these upheavals explain in part the tendency of Argentinian emerging adults to emphasize family capacities (e.g., being able to support a spouse and children financially) as criteria for adulthood, because they value family as a source of stability in a way that the working world is not. Among the Mormons described by Nelson (2003), the roles and rites of passage unique to their religion—such as attending the Temple or completing mission service—have considerable meaning to them as markers of adult status.

As for similarities, one common theme across several studies has been that criteria for adulthood reflecting collectivistic values were found to be more important than in previous studies of White Americans. In the Facio and Micocci (2003) study of Argentine emerging adults, criteria reflecting communal, collectivistic values (such as care and consideration for others) were nearly equal in prominence to the individualistic criteria. In the Mayseless and Scharf (2003) study, Israelis endorsed communal value items (e.g., avoid drunk driving) much more widely than did Americans. Together, these findings highlight the unusually high individualism of American Whites and the tendency even in other cultures that are Western and industrialized to balance individualism with a stronger measure of collectivism.

Nevertheless, a great deal of similarity has been found across cultures in conceptions of adulthood in regard to the cultures studied thus far. In Israel, in Argentina, in every American ethnic group, and among Mormons, the most widely-supported criteria for adulthood were those that reflected values of independence and individualism, just as in previous studies of American middle-class Whites (Arnett, 1994, 1997, 1998, 2001, 2003). Accepting responsibility for one's self, deciding on one's own beliefs and values, and becoming financially independent tend to be at the top in every study.

FUTURE DIRECTIONS

The widespread endorsement of individualistic criteria across the different studies is striking. However, this does not mean that we can in any sense draw conclusions about a universal, worldwide conception of what it means to be an adult. The different studies conducted thus far represent diverse cultures in several regions of the world. However, all the samples have consisted mainly of young people from the urban middle-class sector of their societies. Future research will have to explore other possible differences both within and between countries.

Rural-urban differences are one such possible difference. These differences may not be large in industrialized countries. For example, a mostly-rural sample of emerging adults in Missouri (Arnett, 1998) held conceptions of the transition to adulthood almost identical to the emerging adults in San Francisco (Arnett, 2003). However, rural-urban differences may be larger in economically developing countries, because young people living in the two areas are likely to be much more different culturally (e.g., education, economic basis, exposure to media) than is the case in economically developed countries.

In short, country does not equal culture, and there may be cultural differences within countries that are as great or greater than differences between similar groups across countries. The studies by Nelson (2003) and by Arnett (2003) are illustrative. The Mormon emerging adults described by Nelson are part of American society and embrace many individualistic criteria for adulthood, yet certain aspects of their conception of the transition to adulthood are starkly different than for emerging adults in the majority culture. Specifically, their religious beliefs are the basis for some of the criteria for adulthood that are important to many of them, such as participating in religious rites of passage and being admitted into the gender-specific adult organizations that are part of their religious institution. Similarly, the emerging adults in the ethnic minority groups described by Arnett (2003) support a variety of individualistic criteria for adulthood, just as White American emerging adults do, but they are more likely than Whites to favor certain criteria for adulthood that reflect the more collectivistic values of their cultures.

And what of the rest of the world, the vast regions and diverse areas not discussed in this chapter? Africa, Asia, Central America, Eastern Europe? Clearly there is much that remains to be discovered about how young people around the world think about what it means to be an adult. Of particular interest are the conceptions of adulthood that exist among young people in traditional, tribal cultures that are as yet little touched by globalization or industrialization. Here is where the sharpest contrast may be found to the individualistic conception of adulthood favored by many young people in industrialized societies. Many of these cultures are more collectivistic in their values than industrialized countries are, and their criteria for adulthood may be expected to vary accordingly, perhaps with greater emphasis on marriage, parenthood, and culture-specific roles that entail obligations to others. We can only speculate at this point, but this is certainly an important and compelling topic for future research.

Research on conceptions of the transition to adulthood is a central part of the growing field of emerging adulthood, which focuses on the developmental characteristics of young people from their late teens through their twenties. So far, research in this area has turned up many fascinating and surprising findings, as this chapter illustrates. As the study of emerging adulthood grows and spreads further around the world, more such findings will surely be discovered. Explorations of emerging adults' views of the transition to adulthood are important to a fuller understanding of what it means to be an adult, as well as to an understanding of the different balances between individualism and collectivism that cultural groups may devise in contemporary societies.

NOTES

1. It is, of course, recognized that there is also considerable diversity among traditional cultures. However, Schlegel & Barry (1991) make an effective case that patterns common to many of them can also be discerned, and that is the view taken in this chapter as well.
2. Father's education was examined in relation to all 40 of the criteria for the transition to adulthood, using correlations. There was only one significant correlation ($p < .001$): Those with relatively lower father's education were relatively more likely to indicate that a man should be capable of supporting a family financially in order to be considered an adult. Participant's own level of education was also examined in relation to the 40 criteria for the transition to adulthood, using correlations. There were two significant correlations (both $p < .01$): Participants with relatively less education were more likely to indicate that a man should be capable of supporting a family financially and also that a woman should be capable of supporting a family financially, in order to be considered an adult.
3. It should be noted that "accepting responsibility for one's self" was coded only if the focus of the response was on responsibility for one's self as a general characteristic. Specific references to, for example, financial responsibilities or taking responsibility for children, or to any aspect of responsibility that concerned responsibility to or for others rather than for one's self, were coded according to the specific context mentioned rather than for "responsibility."
4. Gender differences on the questionnaire were examined for each of the 38 items, using the SPSSPC cross tabulations procedure. There were only two significant differences out of the 38 items, both at $p < .05$, which is no more than would be expected by chance in the course of 38 analyses.

REFERENCES

Allen, J. P., Hauser, S. T., Bell, K. L., & O'Connor, T. G. (1994). Longitudinal assessment of autonomy and relatedness in adolescent-family interactions as predictors of adolescent ego development and self-esteem. *Child Development, 65*, 179–194.

Alwin, D. F. (1988). From obedience to autonomy: Changes in traits desired in children, 1924–1978. *Public Opinion Quarterly, 52*, 33–52.

Arnett, J. J. (1994). Are college students adults? Their conceptions of the transition to adulthood. *Journal of Adult Development, 1*, 154–168.

Arnett, J. J. (1995). Broad and narrow socialization: The family in the context of a cultural theory. *Journal of Marriage and the Family, 57*, 617–628.

Arnett, J. J. (1997). Young people's conceptions of the transition to adulthood. *Youth & Society, 29*, 1–23.

Arnett, J. J. (1998). Learning to stand alone: The contemporary American transition to adulthood in cultural and historical context. *Human Development, 41*, 295–315.

Arnett, J. J. (2000). Emerging adulthood: A theory of development from the late teens through the twenties. *American Psychologist, 55*, 469–480.

Arnett, J. J. (2001) Conceptions of the transition to adulthood: Perspectives from adolescence to midlife. *Journal of Adult Development, 8*, 133–143.

Arnett, J. J. (2003). Conceptions of the transition to adulthood among emerging adults in American ethnic groups. *New Directions in Child and Adolescent Development, 100*, 63–75.

Arnett, J. J. (2004). *Emerging adulthood: The winding road from the late teens through the twenties*. New York: Oxford University Press.

Arnett, J. J., & Taber, S. (1994). Adolescence terminable and interminable: When does adolescence end? *Journal of Youth and Adolescence, 23*, 1–21.

Barling, J., & Kelloway, E. K. (1999). *Young workers: Varieties of experience*. Washington, DC: American Psychological Association.

Bellah, R. N., Madsen, R., Sullivan, W. M., Swidler, A., & Tipton, S.M. (1985). *Habits of the heart: Individualism and commitment in American life*. New York: Harper & Row.

Ben-Amos, I. K. (1994). *Adolescence and youth in early modern England*. New Haven, CT: Yale University Press.

Chinas, L. (1991). *The Isthmus Zapotecs: A matrifocal culture of Mexico*. New York: Harcourt Brace Jovanovich College Publishers.

Condon, R. G. (1987). *Inuit youth: Growth and change in the Canadian Arctic*. New Brunswick, NJ: Rutgers University Press.

Crockett, L. *What makes an adult? Straight from the horses' mouths*. Paper presented at the biennial meeting of the Society for Research on Adolescence, Chicago, Illinois, March 2000.

Davis, S. S., & Davis, D. A. (1989). *Adolescence in a Moroccan town*. New Brunswick, NJ: Rutgers University Press.

Erikson, E. (1963). *Childhood and Society* (2nd ed.). New York: W.W. Norton.

Facio, A., & Micocci, E. (2003). Emerging adulthood in Argentina. *New Directions in Child and Adolescent Development, 100*, 21–31.

Feldman, S. S., Biringen, Z. C., & Nash, S. C. (1981). Fluctuations of sex-related self-attributions as a function of stage of family life. *Developmental Psychology, 17*, 24–35.

Galinsky, E. (1981). *Between generations: The six stages of parenthood*. New York: Berkeley.

Gilmore, D. (1990). *Manhood in the making: Cultural concepts of masculinity*. New Haven, CT: Yale University Press.

Goldscheider, F., & Goldscheider, C. (1994). Leaving and returning home in 20th century America. *Population Bulletin, 48*(4). Washington, DC: Population Reference Bureau.

Greene, A. L., Wheatley, S. M., & Aldava, J. F., IV. (1992). Stages on life's way: Adolescents' implicit theories of the life course. *Journal of Adolescent Research, 7*, 364–381.

Hanawalt, B. A. (1986). *The ties that bound: Peasant families in medieval England*. New York: Oxford University Press.

Herdt, G. (1987). *The Sambia: Ritual and gender in New Guinea*. New York: Holt, Rinehart, & Winston.

Hogan, D. P., & Astone, N. M. (1986). The transition to adulthood. *Annual Review of Sociology, 12*, 109–130.

Jensen, L. A. (1998). Different habits, different hearts: The divergent moral languages of the culture war. *The American Sociologist, 29*, 83–101.

Kagitcibasi, C. (1996). *Family and human development across cultures: A view from the other side*. Mahway, NJ: Erlbaum.

Kett, J. F. (1977). *Rites of passage: Adolescence in America, 1790 to the present*. New York: Basic Books.

Kirkpatrick, J. (1987). *Taure'are'a*: A liminal category and passage to Marquesan adulthood. *Ethos, 15*, 382–405.

Mayseless, O., & Scharf, M. (2003). What does it mean to be an adult? The Israeli experience. *New Directions in Child and Adolescent Development, 100*, 5–20.

Modell, J. (1989). *Into one's own: From youth to adulthood in the United States, 1920–1975*. Berkeley: University of California Press.

Moore, D. (1987). Parent-adolescent separation: The construction of adulthood by late adolescents. *Developmental Psychology, 23*, 298–307.

Nelson, L. J., Badger, S., & Wu, B. (2004). The influence of culture in emerging adulthood: Perspectives of Chinese college students. *International Journal of Behavioral Development, 28*, 26–36.

Nsamenang, A. B. (1992). *Human development in cultural context: A Third World perspective*. Newbury Park, CA: Sage.

O'Connor, T. G., Allen, J. P., Bell, K. L., & Hauser, S. T. (1996). Adolescent-parent relationships and leaving home in young adulthood. *New Directions in Child Development, 71*, 39–52.

Perry, W. G. (1970). *Forms of intellectual and ethical development in the college years*. New York: Holt, Rinehart & Winston.

Rotundo, E. A. (1993). *American manhood: Transformations in masculinity from the revolution to the modern era*. New York: Basic Books.

Ryan, R. M., & Lynch, J. H. (1989). Emotional autonomy versus detachment: Revisiting the vicissitudes of adolescence and young adulthood. *Child Development, 60*, 340–356.

Scheer, S. D., & Palkovitz, R. (1995). Adolescents-to-adults: Social status and cognitive factors. *Sociological Studies of Children, 6*, 125–140.

Scheer, S. D., Unger, D. G., & Brown, M. (1994, February). Adolescents becoming adults: Attributes for adulthood. Poster presented at the biennial meeting of the Society for Research on Adolescence, San Diego, CA.

Schlegel, A., & Barry, H., III (1991). *Adolescence: An anthropological inquiry*. New York: Free Press.

Shand, N. (1985). Culture's influence on Japanese and American maternal role perception and confidence. *Psychiatry, 48*, 52–67.

Spitze, G. D. (1978). Role experiences of young women: A longitudinal test of the role hiatus hypothesis. *Journal of Marriage and the Family, 40*, 471–480.

Triandis, H. C. (1995). *Individualism and collectivism*. Boulder, CO: Westview Press.

Whiting, B. B., & Edwards, C. P. (1988). *Children of different worlds: The formation of social behavior*. Cambridge: Harvard University Press.

Yang, K-S. (1988). Will societal modernization eventually eliminate cross-cultural psychological differences? In M. H. Bond (ed.), *The cross-cultural challenge to social psychology* (pp. 67–85). London: Sage.

Part V

Ecological Influences

20

The Family Environment

Robert H. Bradley
Robert F. Corwyn

INTRODUCTION

> When Gamini finished surgery in the middle of the night, he walked back through the compound into the east buildings, where the sick children were. The mothers were always there. Sitting on stools, they rested their upper torso and head on their child's bed and slept holding the small hands. . . . He watched the children, who were unaware of their parents' arms. Fifty yards away in Emergency he had heard grown men scream for their mothers as they were dying. . . . He turned away from every person who stood up for war. . . . He believed only in the mothers sleeping against their children, the great sexuality in them, the sexuality of care, so the children would be confident and safe during the night. (Ondaatje, 2000, p. 119)

This piquant passage is from *Anil's Ghost* by Michael Ondaatje. The story is set in war-ravaged Sri Lanka, a near armageddon of ethnic cleansing, brutal subjugation, and political intrigue. The passage conveys two basic beliefs about parenting. First, there is something elemental about parental caregiving, with near universal agreement as to its significance in children's lives. Second, the context in which parenting occurs shapes both its goals and its tactics. As a result, what children experience as part of their home life is enormously varied despite the fact that all children share many common needs for parental care.

Our research has been concerned with what parents do to help their children thrive, why and how they do it, what factors help determine what they do, and how it matters in children's lives. It is a journey of some 30 years. In some respects it has been a journey much like the journey a dog takes when tied to a tree. We have gone for a while in one direction, then for a while in a second, but ultimately we have circled back to one central issue: what children themselves experience as part of their care at home and how that pertains to their well-being. We have done so believing that these experiences exert significant influence on the character and quality of children's lives. In this chapter we describe a series of interconnected studies about children's experiences at home, how those experiences reflect the context of family life and the persons who act as parents, and how those experiences are reflected in children's behavior and development.

The chapter is organized around four questions concerning parenting: (1) What are the central tasks of parenting? (2) What difference does parenting make in the lives of children? (3) How does context affect parenting? (4) Why do parents invest in their children? Throughout we discuss issues pertaining to the measurement of *parenting* (a.k.a., the home environment) because it is through the process of measurement that answers about parenting are both realized and constrained.

493

WHAT ARE THE CENTRAL TASKS OF PARENTING?

It is at once both easy and difficult to describe the central tasks of parenting. Said simply, the central tasks of parenting are those actions parents must take to assure survival and promote optimal development in their offspring. But this banal response masks the true intricacies of providing care for children. There is now a 5-volume reference work on the issues and concerns of parenting that makes the complexities of child rearing abundantly clear (Bornstein, 2002). The fact is, what adults do in their role as parents has changed over the centuries, a function of technological, social, and economic adjustments. That said, the goal of parenting has remained essentially the same, to enable children to become competent, caring adults who are able to function well within society (Maccoby, 1992). For any place and any era, attaining the goal is no mean feat. This seemingly innocuous generic prescription requires a plethora of specific parenting actions carried out over a lengthy period of time fitted to a particular child's needs and executed within the boundaries of the resources and constraints present.

About a decade ago, we constructed a system for organizing the tasks of parenting (Bradley & Caldwell, 1995). It derives from systems theory, and is organized around the concept that the environment (parenting) helps to regulate the course of development (Sameroff, 1983). Central to our framework is the notion that *optimal parenting* (a facilitative home environment) is best conceived of as a set of regulatory acts and conditions aimed at successful adaptation and at successful exploitation of opportunity structures for children (Saegert & Winkel, 1990). Such a conception seems in keeping with ecological developmental theories that portray human beings as phylogenetically advanced, self-constructing organisms and the environment as a regulator (actually, coregulator) of complex developmental processes (Ford & Lerner, 1992). This framework is also consonant with the idea that children are conscious agents who are active in adapting to their environments (Lewis, 1997). Finally, it is consistent with recent notions about the value of building positive personal assets (Scales & Leffert, 1999). Starting from this basic notion, we identified six basic regulatory tasks (or functions) performed by parents: (a) sustenance/safety, (b) stimulation, (c) support, (d) structure, (e) surveillance, and (f) social integration.

The first three regulatory functions derive from what is known about human needs and arousal systems. Specifically, Maslow (1954) contended that human beings need environments that promote survival, provide information (including enlistment of attention), and affirm worth. For complex living systems such as human beings, the task of maintaining internal unity is quite complicated due to the large number of component subsystems involved and the elaborateness of their organization (Ford & Lerner, 1992). To deal with the child's individuality and complexity, parents must perform other functions to assure that the direct inputs designed to sustain, stimulate, and emotionally support the child are maximally fitted to the child's current needs, proclivities, and competencies; hence, structure, surveillance, and social integration.

Sustenance/Safety

From time immemorial, promoting the physical well-being of children has been considered the *sine qua non* of parental responsibility. Those acts and conditions designed to promote biological integrity we have organized under the joint class, sustenance/safety. Parents must provide adequate nutrients, shelter, and health care to ensure both survival and the level of biological integrity needed for physical and psychological development (Pollitt, 1988). As well, children face numerous potential threats of direct harm: from violence and natural disasters to dangerous objects and physical conditions (La Greca, Silverman, Vernberg, & Roberts, 2002; Peterson & Gable, 1998). In our analysis of data from the National Longitudinal Survey of Youth, we found that between one fourth and one third of children in the United States live in homes with potentially dangerous structural or health hazards (Bradley, Corwyn, McAdoo, & Garcia Coll, 2001). Parents must afford protection from such conditions. Likewise, they must protect children from pathogenic conditions such as pollutants, passive cigarette smoke, and exposure to heavy metals (Evans et al., 1991; J. L. Jacobson, Jacobson, Padgett, Brummitt, & Billings, 1992; Tong & McMichael, 1992).

Stimulation

To ensure competence and continued effort toward life-enhancing goals, the environment must provide sensory data that engage attention and provide information (i.e., stimulation). According to Kagan (1984), the main catalyst for environmentally-mediated change is stimulation. Indeed, there is an abundance of both psychological theory and empirical data to buttress the significance of stimulation for cognitive, psychomotor, and social development (Horowitz, 1987; Shonkoff & Phillips, 2002). Illustrative evidence of the value of stimulation comes from studies of parent talk. The research of Hart & Risley (1995) and Hoff (2003) provide compelling documentation of the value of providing children more labels for objects, responding contingently to children's speech, making efforts to elicit conversation from children, sustaining conversations with children, and just talking to them more often.

Support

Optimal social-emotional development depends on having an environment that responds to human social and emotional needs (Bretherton & Waters, 1985). Such acts and conditions we call support. Some acts of support are given in anticipation of unexpressed needs, others following expressed needs. Emotions function to prepare human beings to take action in their own best interest (Grinker et al., 1956). Parents must assist in enlisting and modulating the motivational properties of emotions to help ensure optimal fit with environmental demands (Eisenberg, Cumberland, & Spinard, 1998).

There also is evidence that children benefit from positive affirmation of worth (Ausubel, 1968; Roberts, 1986). That is, to be supportive, parents must be reinforcing (in a proactive sense) as well as responsive (in a reactive sense). How worth is affirmed varies substantially from culture to culture. In some societies worth is closely tied to individual accomplishments or status; in others, it is more strongly tied to collective commitments and involvement. Finally, a supportive environment is one that provides guidance or direction for adequate functioning in other environments (Pettit, Dodge, & Brown, 1988). At its base, support is motivational preparation for encountering other environments.

Structure

Although children need sustenance, stimulation, and support for optimal growth and development, there also is evidence that the relation between these inputs and either growth or development is not constant. Receiving equal amounts of these inputs does *not* seem to result in equal amounts of "good" growth and development. The arrangement of inputs may be as crucial to development as the amount. In sum, optimal parenting consists not only in ensuring that sufficient amounts of stimulation, sustenance, and support reach a child, but also in configuring or structuring a child's encounters with those direct inputs so that "fit" is achieved (Wachs, 2000). According to the Committee on Developments in the Science of Learning, "Parents and others who care for children arrange their activities and facilitate learning by regulating the difficulty of the tasks" (Bransford, Brown, & Cocking, 2000, p. 103). What fits one child's needs may not be suitable at all for another child. A good example may be seen in the differential responsiveness of preterm infants and infants prenatally exposed to drugs. Such biologically vulnerable infants often are overwhelmed by levels of stimulation that are quite comfortable for normal babies (Friedman & Sigman, 1996).

Surveillance

To be effective in managing children's lives, parents must keep track of the whereabouts and activities of the child. This important regulatory function performed by parents (or their proxies) we call surveillance. Most commonly, surveillance has been thought of as keeping track of the child and of the environmental conditions to which the child is exposed so as to protect the child from harm (Darling & Steinberg, 1993; U.S. Department of Health and Human Services, 1991; Lozoff, 1989; Patterson,

DeBaryshe, & Ramsey, 1989). There are concerns about sexual predators, exposure to violence on TV, risk of injury, and involvement with deviant peers, among many others (Dorr, Rabin, & Ireland, 2002; Finkelhor, Mitchell, & Wolak, 2000; Peterson, Ewigman, & Kivlahan, 1993). However, surveillance also includes observations of the child and the environment designed to determine how much the physical and social environment affords the child for productive and enjoyable engagements.

Social Integration

For anthropologists, it is accepted as axiomatic that a major goal of parenting is to effectively connect children to the social fabric of society (Weisner, 2002), for it is in connecting to important social networks and groups that children are most likely to thrive. To a large degree, Coleman's (1988) argument in behalf of the importance of social capital (resources achieved through social connections) makes much the same point. Scott-Jones (1995) discusses the value of parental efforts to help their children to become effectively engaged in school as an avenue for high achievement. She mentions that parental expectations are often a means of increasing such engagement. Nickerson (1992) presents evidence that one way parents help children forge productive connections with learning institutions is through modeling and sharing stories about their own involvement in education. Indeed, there is reason to believe that parents may help children forge productive connections to a variety of social networks and organizations through their own involvement in such networks. Pianta and Walsh (1996) use systems theory notions as a framework for elucidating how families forge productive partnerships with schools. They mention taking children to school for visits, family involvement in school activities and assisting children with homework as examples. They also include deliberate encounters with teachers and other school personnel. There is emerging evidence that parental involvement in schools increases school engagement and that school engagement increases student achievement.

Does careful attention to these six parenting tasks promote positive adaptation in children? The most straightforward answer is: The research is incomplete. However, there is suggestive evidence. For example, we conducted a study of 243 premature, low-birth weight children living in chronic poverty. The purpose was to determine whether the availability of protective factors in the home environment at age 1 and at age 3 increased the probability of resiliency. Resiliency was operationalized as being in good to excellent health, being within the normal range for growth, not being below clinically designated cutoffs for maladaptive behavior on the Child Behavior Checklist, and having an IQ of 85 or greater. Six home environment factors were considered potentially protective: (a) low household density, (b) the availability of a safe play area, (c) parental acceptance and lack of punitiveness, (d) parental responsivity, (e) the availability of learning materials, and (f) variety of experiences. The first two would be classified under the category, sustenance; the second two under the category, support; and the final two under the category, stimulation. Fifteen percent of the children with three or more protective factors present in the home at age 1 were classified as resilient. By contrast, only 2% of children with two or fewer protective factors were classified as resilient. Similarly, 20% of children with three or more protective factors present in the home at age 3 were classified as resilient, whereas only 6% of children with two or fewer protective factors were resilient (Bradley, Whiteside, et al., 1994).

Although research findings indicate that parents can be instrumental in moving their children along a positive developmental course, even the best parenting is no guarantee. The evidence does not show that parenting is highly deterministic of children's long-term well-being but rather that it combines with other influences in quite complex ways (Collins, Maccoby, Steinberg, Hetherington, & Bornstein, 2000).

THE PARENTING ENVIRONMENT

Closely related to the idea of parenting tasks is the idea of a place where parenting occurs. It seems useful to think of the environment for parenting as including all the social and physical phenomena within the child's home place (Wachs, 1992, 2000; Wapner, 1987; Wohlwill & Heft, 1977). However, it is probably counterproductive to confine the concept of the parenting environment to a particular place, even though the concepts of parenting and home are semantically linked. In a child's mind, or in a parent's mind, what constitutes "home" probably will not refer exclusively to those events, objects, and actions within the four walls of a particular residence (or within the property lines that define a place of residence). Home experiences may include any number of events seen as connected to home and family but not coterminous with the physical boundaries of a place. A walk around the block with Dad, a visit to the local library with Mom, or an argument between Mom and Dad in the car on the way to McDonald's all may be strongly associated with the network of acts and events that comprise a child's home life. By the same token, the concept of the home environment as fully divorced from any place of residence probably is not useful either, because the idea of home is generally associated with identifiable places. For both parent and child, many of the ideas and attitudes connected with "home" have their roots in scenes, episodes, and "scripts" that emanate from particular concrete places where family activities occur (Abelson, 1981).

The concept of the home environment might best be defined as phenomena emanating from the family setting. The boundaries become somewhat permeable and expansive, a boundary of meaning, not just bricks or fences. Such a capacious definition is consistent with the position of social anthropologists who contend that the social boundaries of household units do not necessarily coincide with the physical boundaries of their dwellings (Altman, 1977). Such an expansive definition seems more appropriate when one considers actual living conditions for some children (e.g., families living in cars or makeshift shelters). The concept of the parenting environment as not fully confined to a specific place becomes useful because the role of parent tends to shift from that of direct provider and teacher (most of which may well take place within the family residence) to that of mentor, guide, and arranger of experiences (some of which almost certainly will occur outside the four walls of the residence) (Fagot & Kavanaugh 1993; Maccoby & Martin, 1983).

The parenting environment is best understood not only on the basis of the activities and objects it contains or generates, but also on the basis of its instrumentality for child care and child rearing (Korosec-Serafty, 1985). For individual parents there is a sense of boundary to the spaces where parenting takes place, but what actually constitutes the boundary varies across parents and time depending on an array of cultural, familial, personal, and child factors (Belsky, 1984; Bronfenbrenner, 1995). In effect, what is appropriated to the idea of the home environment is the meaning of the acts, objects, and places connected to parental caregiving. Different families may utilize different geographic settings to be part of the parenting environment (e.g., the street beside the house, the backyard, a neighborhood park). The parenting environment encompasses the locations where the activities of parental caregiving take place (Rapoport, 1985).

WHAT DIFFERENCE DOES PARENTING MAKE IN THE LIVES OF CHILDREN?

Answering this question has dominated our attention for the past 30 years. To answer the question, we have relied on the Home Observation for Measurement of the Environment (HOME) HOME Inventory, perhaps the most widely used measures of the home environment in the world. HOME was created by Caldwell and her colleagues at the Syracuse Early Learning Center in the mid-1960s; and we, along with Caldwell, have continued to work with the HOME ever since. The HOME does not comprehensively cover all five of the parenting dimensions described above; nor does it fully capture the myriad aspects of home life. However, the lessons we have learned from constructing the measure, doing research with it, and addressing numerous questions from others who have used it allow us a useful perspective on the meaning of parenting.

The HOME Inventory is different from some other measures of the home environment in that the data are collected from the perspective of a particular child. It is well known that children growing up in a particular family do not always have the exact same experiences. Some get more attention than others, some receive harsher punishment than others, and some are read to more than others. The

TABLE 20.1
Subscales of the HOME Inventories

Infant Toddler	Early Childhood
1. Parental responsivity	1. Learning materials
2. Acceptance	2. Language stimulation
3. Organization of the environment	3. Physical environment
4. Learning materials	4. Parental responsivity
5. Parental involvement	5. Academic stimulation
6. Variety of experience	6. Modeling
	7. Variety of experience
	8. Acceptance

Middle Childhood	Early Adolescent
1. Parental responsivity	1. Physical environment
2. Encouragement of maturity	2. Learning materials
3. Acceptance	3. Modeling
4. Learning materials	4. Instructional activities
5. Enrichment	5. Regulatory activities
6. Family companionship	6. Variety of experience
7. Paternal involvement	7. Acceptance & responsivity

current interest in within-family differences in experience and development provides ample testimony to this belief (Dunn, 1991; Feinberg, McHale, Crouter & Cumsille, 2003; Plomin & Daniels, 1987). The HOME tries to capture these personal histories of experience and living conditions.

HOME is designed to assess the quality and quantity of stimulation and support available to children in the home environment (Caldwell & Bradley, 2003). There are four versions of the inventory: The Infant-Toddler version is designed for children from birth to age 3, the Early Childhood version for children age 3 to 6, the Middle Childhood version for children from age 6 to 10, and the Early Adolescent version for children age 10 to 14 (see Bradley, 1994, and Bradley, Corwyn, & Whiteside-Mansell, 1996, for reviews). Table 20.1 includes a list of the subscales from these four inventories.

The information needed to score the inventories is obtained through a combination of observation and semi-structured interviews done at home when both the child and the child's primary caregiver are present. Other family members also often are present during the 45- to 90-minute visit as well. The visit is designed to minimize intrusiveness and to allow family members to act as naturally as possible.

When constructing the four versions of HOME, we faced numerous technical concerns, but we also faced two substantive concerns: (a) What environmental dimensions or constructs are most salient to measure at each developmental period? (b) How does one most accurately capture the salient dimensions or constructs? An examination of the content of the four versions of HOME (see Table 20.1) makes concrete our judgment concerning what is salient at each of the four age periods we have assessed. Some of the dimensions or constructs measured for the various age periods are the same, some are different. For example, at each age period, we include items that measure parental responsivity, the amount and variety of materials for learning, whether harsh child management techniques are used (whether the parent is accepting of the child), whether a variety of enriching experiences are made available to the child, and so forth. However, at each developmental period, we also include items that seem particularly relevant for that age period. For example, during infancy, we assess whether parents encourage the development of particular developmental competencies (e.g., walking, talking). During early childhood, the focus shifts to an assessment of whether parents teach pre-academic skills like learning colors and shapes and whether parents provide conditions that facilitate the development of the kind of social skills required to function well outside the home. During middle childhood, there is, for the first time, an assessment of the overall emotional climate in the home and an assessment of whether the family does things as a unit. During early adolescence, there is a particular concern with the kinds of rules and policies established for the adolescent and the types of monitoring practices used. Clearly, as children age, the role of parent shifts gradually from that of direct provider of experiences and conditions (caretaker) to that of guide, broker, and facilitator of experiences. Things often are done at a greater distance and over a longer period of time; that is, monitoring the whereabouts of a baby and monitoring the life and times of an adolescent require quite different actions. Things more often are done in league with other adults and other institutions (e.g., church, school, youth organization).

How one views the issue of age differences (or similarities) in the parenting environment depends on one's level of analysis. As stated, we measure some dimensions (e.g., parental responsivity) at every developmental age, but the particular indicators we use to reveal those dimensions may change (responding to an infant's vocalization vs. encouraging a 10-year-old to contribute to a conversation, giving an infant a rattle vs. giving an 8-year-old a guitar, taking a 4-year-old to the park vs. arranging for an adolescent to go to a dance camp). Two things are clear. First, the particular needs that children express from moment to moment change as children age; thus, what they require from their home environments in order to do well changes accordingly. And, indeed, the home environment of a young child is quite different from the home environment of an adolescent in almost every way, including its physical arrangements (Bradley, 2002). Second, children become more competent (self-sufficient) as they grow older and they are able to fashion their environments more to meet their desires. Scarr and McCartney (1983) argued that, when children are young, their influence on the environment is mostly passive; by their actions they elicit different responses from their caregivers. That is, it is not that children are not active in trying to shape their environments, but they lack the full range of capacities needed to construct or find environments highly suited to their needs. However, as they become more competent, children seek out and construct environments that more fully meet their needs.

What have we learned from our long history with the HOME? The first thing is that the HOME seems to "work" in the sense that it provides a reasonably accurate—if limited—picture of the home environment, one that is correlated with a wide range of developmental markers in a wide range of populations. It has worked well enough so that it has been incorporated, in whole or in part, into a number of large-scale longitudinal studies, including the National Longitudinal Survey of Youth, the Panel Study of Income Dynamics, the Early Head Start national evaluation study, the Infant Health and Development Program, the Canadian National Longitudinal Study for Children and Youth, the Pacific Islands Families Study, and the Families, Children and Child Care project at the University of Oxford.

HOME AND COGNITIVE DEVELOPMENT

In a series of studies done in the late 1970s and early 1980s, we found that scores on the Infant-Toddler and Early Childhood versions of HOME consistently showed positive correlations with cognitive and language development from infancy through the early school years (Bradley & Caldwell, 1976a, 1976b, 1979b, 1980a, 1982, 1984b; Elardo, Bradley, & Caldwell, 1975, 1977). Importantly, we found that these relations obtained for boys as well as girls, Blacks as well as Whites, and poor as well as rich (Bradley & Caldwell, 1981; Bradley, Caldwell, et al., 1989). Our findings have been corroborated by dozens of other researchers in the United States and throughout the world. Correlations between the Infant-Toddler HOME and measures of infant developmental status (usually the Bayley Scales) typically do not exceed .40 during the 1st year of life (Adams, Campbell, & Ramey, 1984; Allen, Affleck, McGrade, & McQueeney, 1984; Bakeman & Brown, 1980; Carlson, Labarba, Sclafani, & Bowers, 1986; Coll, Vohr, Hoffman, & Oh, 1986; Cooney, Bell, McBride, & Carter, 1989; Elardo et al., 1975; Johnson, Breckenridge, & McGowan, 1984; Lozoff, Park, Radan, & Wolf, 1995; Pederson, Evans, Chance, Bento, & Fox, 1988; Siegel, 1982; Stevenson & Lamb, 1979; Wilson & Matheny, 1983). However, the strength of the relation increases during the 2nd year of life, with correlations generally ranging from .20 to .50 (Bergeman & Plomin, 1988; Consullo, 1992; Palti, Otrakul, Belmaker, Tamir, & Tepper, 1984). Although the upward trend in correlations may partially reflect the fact that infant tests contain a larger proportion of language-oriented items by age 2, research by Belsky, Garduque, and Hrncir (1984) has suggested that the higher correlations are not mere artifacts of the changing content of infant tests. They obtained correlations between HOME scores and children's performance (.64 to .73), competence (.51 to .63), and executive capacity (.27 to .46), during play at 12, 15, and 18 months. Exceptions to the generally upward trend for correlations during the 2nd year of life included poor Hispanics and poor African Americans (Adams et al., 1984; Johnson et al., 1984). Although these two exceptions may reflect a lack of measurement equivalence, they may instead reflect a more restricted range of scores on the HOME for Hispanics. They also may reflect chronic conditions of poverty that are prevalent in these minority groups (McLoyd, 1990).

Most studies have shown low-to-moderate correlations (.20 to .60) between HOME scores during the first 2 years of life and later tests of intelligence and achievement (Bradley & Caldwell, 1976b, 1984b; Bradley, Caldwell, & Rock, 1988; Coons, Fulker, DeFries. & Plomin, 1990; Elardo et al., 1975; Gottfried & Gottfried, 1984, 1988; Johnson, Breckenbridge, McGowan, 1984; Siegel, 1982; Stevens & Bakeman, 1985; Wilson & Matheny, 1983). However, in a study of Mexican American children (Johnson et al., 1984), correlations were negligible; for lower-middle-class Costa Ricans, they were somewhat lower than correlations observed in most other groups, but still significant. The studies may indicate that different relations obtain for Latino populations, but the differences are difficult to interpret given measures of intellectual competence originally were constructed using Hispanics (Super & Harkness, 1986). The contributions of culture, social status, and recency of immigration to the observed disparate results remain unclear. The increasing magnitude of correlation from birth to age 3 probably results from a number of factors including early biological protection and the changing content of mental tests.

However, it likely reflects the increasing stability of intellectual development and the emergence of self-regulatory competence as well. In effect, the cognitive system is less perturbed by extraneous (that is, non-fundamental factors) and becomes more aligned with environmental affordances. Specifically, even though the cognitive system will continue to be impeded by negative physical (e.g., noise) and social (e.g., family conflict) conditions, by age three it is generally better able to take advantage of the array of opportunities for learning inherent in the environment. From a technical perspective, the increasing stability of cognitive performance allows for more reliable assessment. When assessments have limited reliability, correlations between measures tend to be lower-bound estimates of the true relations.

HOME scores obtained when children were between 3 and 5 years old showed moderate correlations (.30 to .60) with contemporaneous measures of children's intellectual and academic performance (Billings, Jacobson, Jacobson, & Brumitt, 1989; Bradley & Caldwell, 1984b; Bradley, Caldwell, & Rock, 1988; Chua, Kong, Wong, & Yoong, 1989; Gottfried & Gottfried, 1988; Luster, Bates, Fitzgerald, Vandenbelt, & Peck, 2000; McMichael et al., 1988; Sahu & Devi, 1982). The more restricted the socio-economic status range, the more attenuated the correlations. However, no difference was found between farm and nonfarm children who otherwise had a similar diversity in socio-economic status (S. Jacobson, Jacobson, Brunitt, & Jones, 1987).

Correlations between Early Childhood HOME scores and later academic achievement have been generally low to moderate (Bradley & Caldwell, 1979; Caughy, Dipietro & Strobino, 1994; Gottfried, Gottfried, Bathhurst, & Guerin, 1994; Hammond, Bee, Barnard, & Eyres, 1983; Jordan, 1976). In one study involving 55 Black and 30 White children, HOME scores were correlated with Science Research Associates Achievement Test scores obtained when the children were 6 to 10 years old (Bradley & Caldwell, 1978). HOME shared about 25% of variance with each achievement domain. Moderate correlations were obtained for both Black males and Black females; but significant residual correlations remained for males only when socio-economic status and 3-year IQ were partialed out (Bradley & Caldwell, 1980a). Gottfried, Gottfried, and Bathurst (1994) found that high achieving 7- and 8-year-olds experienced more enriched home environments than classmates who had lower levels of achievement. In effect, the association between what the home environment affords and children's performance on cognitive measures more or less asymptotes by about the time children enter kindergarten. Even though the cognitive systems becomes even more stable during early childhood and self-regulatory capacities continue to improve, the potential gains in prediction from home environment measures are offset by the increased time children spend outside the home—particularly since schools directly target these systems.

Our experience with the Middle Childhood and Early Adolescent versions of HOME is more limited. In one of the first studies, we obtained low-to-moderate correlations between HOME subscale scores and school performance for 11-year-olds (Bradley, Caldwell, Rock, Hamrick, & Harris, 1988). Responsivity, learning materials, active stimulation, and physical environment showed the strongest relations. A separate analysis of 8- to 10-year-old African American students (Bradley, Caldwell, Rock, Casey, & Nelson, 1987) revealed that responsivity and emotional climate had the most consistent relations. Other researchers found that high-achieving students were living in homes characterized by more materials for learning, more active stimulation, greater family participation in enriching activities, and a higher level of parental responsivity (Gottfried et al., 1994). Information on the HOME-achievement relation indicates that children's achievement during early and middle childhood is related to the home environment (Baharudin & Luster, 1998). Results from studies by Gottfried and Gottfried (1988), Gottfried et al. (1994), Bradley and Caldwell (1981), and Jordan (1976) indicated that the relation is strong for both European Americans and African Americans. Kurtz, Borkowski, and Deshmukh (1988) also found a significant relation between HOME scores and school achievement for children in Nagpur, India. However, the sex, race, and social class differences obtained in those investigations suggest a complex relation. In an attempt to more fully delineate these complex patterns, we used data from the National Longitudinal Survey of Youth for children from 5 to 15 years of age (Bradley, Corwyn, Burchinal, McAdoo, & Garcia Coll, 2001). For each participant we had data on Learning Stimulation, Maternal Responsiveness, and Spanking at each data point. These were included, along with poverty status, ethnicity, and age in an hierarchical linear modeling (HLM) analysis of growth trajectories for math achievement, reading achievement and vocabulary attainment. For vocabulary scores, all three HOME scores were significant. For spanking there was a complex interaction with ethnicity and poverty status. Specifically, the effect for African American children was negative, but the negative effects were much stronger for non-poor than poor African Americans. By contrast, the effects were negative for poor Hispanics but positive for non-poor Hispanics. There was also suggestive evidence that relations were stronger for younger children. The findings pertaining to reading achievement were similar except that there was evidence for a complex interaction between ethnicity and family poverty involving European American and African American families. Learning stimulation and maternal responsiveness were also predictive of math achievement. In the case of maternal responsiveness, there was evidence that it makes more difference for younger children.

The total score from the Early Adolescent HOME was significantly related to the Wide Range Achievement Test-third edition (WRAT-3) in a sample of 10- to 15-year-olds (Bradley, Corwyn, Caldwell, Whiteside-Mansell, Wasserman, & Mink, 2000; Bradley, Whiteside-Mansell, & Corwyn, 1997). So, too, were all seven subscale scores. Analyses also were performed separately for four sociocultural groups (European American, African American, Hispanic American, and Asian American). Early Adolescent HOME scores were correlated with WRAT-3 scores in all four groups, but the pattern of correlations varied according to subscales. For Asian Americans, only the learning materials subscale was related to achievement test performance (.58); but, for the other three groups, achievement was related to other subscales as well (particularly, modeling). For Hispanic Americans, WRAT-3 scores were correlated with all subscales except physical environment. The total score, and all subscales except regulatory activities, were significantly related to adolescents' self-reported grades in school. Consistent with findings on younger children, the findings pertaining to adolescents suggest complex relations not only with socio-economic status (SES) and culture but also with other aspects of family context. For example, we observed that relations between HOME scores and WRAT-3 scores tended to be stronger for children who lived in households with moderate levels of conflict than in homes with very little conflict (Bradley & Corwyn, 2000).

In short, from infancy onward there is a substantial relation between what children experience in their home environments and their scores on cognitive, language, and achievement tests. Cognitive development appears to reflect both the physical (e.g., objects and materials for learning) and social (e.g., parental responsiveness and direct efforts to teach or encourage development) aspects of the home environment. It also likely reflects organizational aspects (e.g., routines, physical arrangements, use of time) as well, but the HOME does not capture these aspects in as much detail (Bradley & Caldwell, 1995). Variations in these aspects of home life appear connected with child developmental functioning above and beyond their connection with family SES and configuration. Part of the relation is genetically mediated, more and more so perhaps as children age gain capacity to select and produce their own environments (Plomin et al., 1985; Scarr & McCartney, 1983). Indeed, part of the reason that the strength of the association between home environment and cognitive performance reaches maximum during elementary school is that children not only spend less and less time at home as they age but begin to select the peer groups and activities where they spend their time.

HOME and Socio-Emotional Development

Scores on HOME are also associated with social development. A major component of social competence is the ability of a child to enter into and sustain social relations. Bakeman and Brown (1980) followed 21 preterm and 22 full-term Black low-income children from 9 months to 3 years of age. The Responsivity scale from the Infant-Toddler HOME predicted both social participation (involvement with others) and social competence (ability to navigate the social world smoothly, gaining both material and emotional goods from others in socially acceptable ways). Other studies also indicated that the quality of the home environment in general, and Responsivity in particular, are related to adaptive social competence during early and middle childhood (Jordan, 1979; Lamb et al., 1988; Tedesco, 1981). A good example is a study of behavior problems in very low-birth weight Dutch children (Weiglas-Kuperus, Koot, Baerts, Fetter, & Sauer, 1993). They found that HOME scores at ages 1 and 3½ years were correlated with clinician ratings of behavior problems. Scores on the HOME at 3½ years also were correlated with the total problems score on the Child Behavior Checklist.

Although not actually an index of social competence per se, having an internal locus of control is considered salient for good mental health and adaptive functioning (Rotter, Chance, & Phares, 1972). We reported low, but significant, correlations between the Early Childhood HOME and locus of control orientation at age 6 to 8 years (Bradley & Caldwell, 1979a). More recently we examined relations between the Early Adolescent HOME and self-efficacy beliefs for European American and African American children ages 10 to 15 (Bradley & Corwyn, 2001). We found low to moderate correlations for self-efficacy beliefs pertaining to both school and family but nonsignificant relations for self-efficacy beliefs pertaining to peers. This latter finding was not surprising in view of the fact that self-efficacy beliefs tend to reflect experiences in particular situations (in this case peer groups) (Bandura, 1997).

One of the most intensive investigations of the relation between HOME and children's social and behavioral competence was a prospective longitudinal study involving 267 high-risk mothers from Minnesota (Erickson, Stroufe, & Egeland, 1985). Securely attached infants who later showed behavior problems had mothers who provided less support and encouragement during problem solving and families that scored lower on the Learning Materials and Involvement subscales from Infant-Toddler HOME. Relatedly, anxiously attached infants who later showed no behavior problems had mothers who were more supportive, and provided clearer structure and better instruction during tasks.

Their mothers also had better social support and better relationships. Likewise, their families scored higher on the Learning Materials and Involvement subscales. From first through third grade children were rated on peer competence and emotional health by their teachers (Stroufe, Egeland, & Kreutzer, 1990). The ratings were averaged; and this mean rating was regressed on 6-year Middle Childhood HOME, 2½-year Infant-Toddler HOME, kindergarten rank, child functioning in preschool, and infant attachment classification. All variables in the model, save attachment classification, made a significant contribution. In general, the findings tend to support Bowlby's (1958) general model of development in which both the total developmental history and current circumstances are given important roles in social competence.

We analyzed data from a multi-site study of 549 low-birth weight children which illustrates some of the potential complexity of the relation between home environment and adaptive social behavior during the first 3 years of life (Bradley et al., 1995). This study, involving Infant-Toddler HOME at 1 year and Early Childhood HOME at 3 years plus three measures of adaptive social behavior at $2^{1}/_{2}$ to 3 years showed that: (a) correlations between 3-year Early Childhood HOME and social competence tended to be higher than correlations with 1-year Infant-Toddler HOME, though not uniformly so; (b) different HOME subscales were related to different aspects of adaptive social functioning; (c) there was little evidence that parental nurturance (e.g., acceptance, responsivity) during infancy was more strongly associated with 3-year adaptive social behavior than was parental nurturance around age 3, but apparently cognitive stimulation (e.g., learning materials, variety) at age 3 was more important than at age 1; and (d) social behavior was predicted better by a combination of support and stimulation factors than with either alone.

Using data on children from the National Longitudinal Survey of Youth (NLSY) ages 3 to 15 years, we examined relations between HOME scores and parent-reported behavior problems. Findings from the HLM analysis of growth trajectories of behavior problems revealed a complex set of relations. Both Learning Stimulation and Spanking were related to the level of behavior problems for all three ethnic groups studied (European American, Hispanic American, and African American) but Maternal Responsiveness was only significant for African American children. Moreover, there were several ethnicity by age interactions. In a related study of adolescents, Bradley, Whiteside-Mansell, & Corwyn (1997) found that scores on most subscales from the Early Adolescent HOME were related to parental reports of adolescent considerateness versus hostility in the home. The total score was also related to task orientation among European Americans (Bradley & Corwyn, 2001).

We also examined the relation of both Infant-Toddler HOME and Middle Childhood HOME to classroom behavior at 10 to 11 years of age as assessed with the Classroom Behavior Inventory (CBI; Bradley, Rock, Caldwell, & Brisby, 1989). A few significant correlations emerged between Infant-Toddler HOME and the three dimensions tapped by the CBI. Many more emerged between the Middle Childhood HOME and classroom behavior. Both Active Involvement and Family Participation were moderately correlated with consideration, task orientation, and school adjustment. Responsivity also was correlated with consideration and adjustment. We also used the data to examine three models of environmental action: Model I (primacy of early experience), Model II (predominance of contemporary environment), and Model III (cumulative effects in stable environments). Though all three models received some support, the strongest support was for Model II. The importance of the early environment was supported in terms of significant partial correlations between Responsivity and considerate classroom behavior, even with the intervening environment controlled. Similar results were obtained for Variety. The salience of the contemporary environment received greatest support in the case of the family participation and active involvement subscales and classroom behavior (task orientation, consideration, adjustment). The relation of involvement to considerate behavior seems largely a function of the cumulative effects of parental involvement.

Findings by Bakeman and Brown (1980); Lamb et al. (1988); Erickson, Stroufe, and Egeland (1985); Mink and Nihira (1987); Bradley, Caldwell, Rock, Barnard, Gray, et al. (1989), Caughy, DiPietro & Strobino, 1994, and Bradley and Corwyn (2000, 2001) suggested that particular parenting practices may interact with both particular child characteristics (e.g., quality of attachment, difficult temperament, self-efficacy beliefs, level of disability) and broader ecological factors (e.g., marital quality, support from extended family, participation in day care, family conflict, overall family style) to affect the course of social development. Moreover, the study by Plomin, Loehlin, and DeFries (1985) showing little relation between HOME and behavior problems in adopted children but a significant, yet small (.23), relation for nonadopted children suggests that genetic factors may play a role.

Perhaps it would be fair to characterize studies of parenting/child development relations done prior to 1980 as Generation 1 studies. Most studies done during that era were focused on simply establishing that relations obtained between particular dimensions of children's home experiences and particular components of their behavioral development. Studies done between 1980 and 2000 might similarly be described as Generation 2 studies in that many were concerned with moderators of key parenting/child development relations and issues such as genetic mediation of environmental effects. As the twenty-first century commences, there appears to be a new generation of studies emerging: those concerned with the mechanisms that account for relations between key aspects of the environment and particular child development outcomes. Illustrative of this new generation is a new study we have undertaken. In this study we examined the relation between having opportunities for productive activity (operationalized as access to objects and materials and exposure to potentially enriching activities and events) during infancy and early childhood and behavior problems during first grade. We tested the hypothesis that high levels of opportunity for productive activity early in life would reduce behavior problems downstream because it fostered self-control in children. The hypothesis derived from Bronson's (2000) argument that a child's motivation for self-regulation emerges as the child is able to manipulate objects and engage in tasks that engender a sense of control or agency. The hypothesis also follows from self-determination theory.

Ryan and Deci (2000) contend that self-regulation emerges as a by product of engaging in intrinsically motivated activities. Specifically, frequent exposure to a variety of objects, people, and situations (especially under the guidance of adults or more accomplished peers) not only helps satisfy the motives for curiosity and mastery but gradually promotes attention focusing, volitional control, and strategic planning. Using data from the National Institute of Child Health and Human Development (NICHD) Study of Early Child Care, we found evidence to support this hypothesis for both mother-reported and teacher-reported externalizing behavior, controlling for child temperament, family SES and size, and maternal responsiveness (Bradley & Corwyn, 2005).

In overview, both developmental and cultural theory stipulates that the social and physical conditions children encounter at home are implicated in their social competence and emotion regulation. Findings from our studies (and those of others) using the HOME support these propositions. Nurturant, responsive care, begun in infancy not only seems to increase the likelihood of social participation in children but also the quality of their interactions with others. There is suggestive evidence it may even launch the inter-generational transmission of nurturance (at least in the form of considerate classroom behavior during middle childhood). Not surprisingly, these social experiences also seemed to reduce the likelihood of externalizing behavior on the part of children. However, research also suggests that the precise impact of such experiences have on social behavior depends on what the child brings to the parent–child relationship. Evidence suggests there may be somewhat different effects depending on whether a child is securely or insecurely attached. Just as important, results from our studies suggest that social competence and social behavior reflect not only the quality of children's social environments but the amount of stimulation and support for learning those environments afford as well. Children living in environments rich in objects and activities tended to show fewer behavior problems both at home and at school. It appears that environments rich in opportunities for learning and enjoyment foster self-control.

THROUGH A CHILD'S EYES

Knowing what parents do is one thing, knowing how it matters in the lives of children is quite another. In his tantalizing book, *Altering Fate*, Lewis (1997) made much of the fact that it is extraordinarily difficult to predict the course of individual lives. It is not just that the measures of parenting and the measures of children's characteristics are imperfectly reliable. It is not just that developmental theory is imprecise. It is not even just that there are a myriad biological and contextual factors that impinge on development. Lewis (1997) argued that predicting the course of individual development is difficult because accidental occurrences pervade our real lives. He also argued that predicting the course of development for any given person is difficult because humans are conscious beings; thus, part of our fate is in our own hands. We make meaning of what we experience and we make choices that affect our lives.

Transactional and general systems theories of development (Ford & Lerner, 1992; Sameroff, 1983) portray development as a joint function of both what the environment affords a person by way of experiences and what the person brings to the environment by way of capabilities and behavioral tendencies. As an example, Bradley, Caldwell, Rock, Casey, and, Nelson (1987) found that, for low-birth weight infants, home environment in combination with child medical status predicted 18-month Bayley scores better than either did alone. A study of language delayed, Down's syndrome, and normally developing children by Wulbert, Inglis, Kriegsmann, and Millis (1975) offered yet another view of the transactional process. A high correlation (.76) was obtained in the combined sample, attesting to the impact extreme scores can have on correlations. The results are ambiguous with respect to direction of causality. It could result from effects of the children's low capabilities on the richness of the environment that these children are afforded, as well as from effects on the children's capabilities by an environment in which stimulation and support for development are far below average.

Developmental theory also stipulates that the meaning a child makes of any particular action on the part of parents is conditioned by the full tableaux of experiences within the family and in those other micro-contexts in which the child spends time (e.g., child care, school, peer group) (Bronfenbrenner, 1995). Family life is complexly organized and its influence on the lives of children involves a myriad of interwoven processes. At the moment when it is encountered, a specific parenting action operates at the foreground of a child's conscious awareness. That action is set against a background of other actions, objects, events and conditions occurring both in and through time. It is this background, together with the foreground, that determines the meaning a child makes of the specific action. Unfortunately, the vast majority of studies on parenting do not consider the impact of each child's background of experience when examining particular types of parenting actions, opting instead to treat all other experiences as if they somehow don't matter or balance out. Such an approach is inconsistent with both theory and research.

To illustrate how these multiple levels of the environment operate to determine the meaning of a parental action for a child, let us begin with a representative action (i.e., a specific action that operates in the foreground of a child's conscious awareness). Suppose Eddie, Jr. attempts to get Dad's attention, but that Dad is only vaguely responsive to Eddie's question because Dad is busy watching television. Eddie's experiences with Dad in the area of communication may lead Eddie to conclude that Dad is not a very responsive communicator (i.e., at a specific level of communication, the child may judge Dad to be nonresponsive). But, the meaning Eddie makes of this action probably will not only depend on how responsive Dad is in this specific domain (communication), but also on how responsive Dad is in general to Eddie's needs and interests. Eddie's reaction is likely to be conditioned by Dad's general level of responsiveness (i.e., responsiveness across subdomains such as responsivity to distress, responsiveness in play, and so forth). Most domains of the environment that directly involve the child (e.g., parental responsivity, object stimulation, the structuring of learning opportunities) appear to function both at a general (across subdomains) level and at a more specific (within subdomains) level in terms of their influence on behavior.

Minimally, to understand how a particular aspect of parenting affects child behavior or development requires that one control for other theoretically salient aspects of parenting and home context. Ideally, it requires that one look for key interactions between environmental dimensions. Recently, we have conducted several studies of children's behavior and competence that illustrate the potential importance of controlling for one aspect of parenting when examining the potential "influence" of another. As stated earlier, when we examined the potential impact of having opportunities for productive activity on problem behavior, we included maternal responsiveness in the model as well in that theory suggests that responsiveness is connected to externalizing behavior. As it turned out, having more opportunity for productive activity reduced the likelihood of behavior problems even with maternal responsiveness controlled. But the reverse was not true. Similar findings emerged when we analyzed NLSY data. Specifically, when learning stimulation, maternal responsiveness and spanking were used in an HLM model to predict behavior problems, learning stimulation and spanking were significant but not maternal responsiveness. By contrast all three were significant predictors of vocabulary attainment and reading comprehension (Bradley et al., 2001).

What a child makes of a particular parental action also reflects how the parent treats other household members in similar situations, as research on differential treatment of siblings as shown (Plomin & Daniels, 1987). That is, the child will compare his or her treatment to the treatment given others. To follow our scenario regarding Dad's low level of communicative responsiveness to Eddie, Eddie's reaction to Dad's failure to fully respond to his bid for attention will depend on the Eddie's belief about how responsive Dad is to siblings, the other parent, or whoever else lives in the house. In effect, there is an across persons level of parental action that affects how a child makes meaning of a particular parent action; that is, it generates social comparisons among family members. Moreover, as Feinberg, McHale, Crouter, and Cumsille (2003) have shown, perceived inequitable treatment affects how siblings respond to one another.

A child's reaction to a particular parent action also is a function of the overall ambiance or style (e.g., the overall amount of conflict present, the degree of optimism or cohesion in the family, a general style of interaction among family members, an overall level of organization or harmony) present in the home. As a rule, these pervading conditions are more distal than behaviors aimed directly at the child by other household members present; albeit, there are exceptions such as background noise. Ambient conditions indirectly affect children and they moderate the effect of direct exchanges between children and those persons and objects in the home environment (e.g., a high level of background noise reduces the effectiveness of parental attempts to teach the child, a high degree of parental conflict may reduce the effectiveness of parental attempts to nurture the child). Darling and Steinberg (1993) proposed, for example, that parenting style is best viewed as a context that modifies the influence of specific parenting practices. Mink and Nihira (1986) identified three types of family style and, for each family type, a different set of relationships between particular parenting behaviors and children's behavioral development emerged. Cummings, Zahn-Waxler, and Radke-Yarrow (1981) observed that toddlers exposed to frequent marital conflict reacted more intensively to later episodes of parental conflict than children who experienced less frequent conflict. We examined family conflict as a potential moderator of the relation between parental actions and developmental outcomes for children in early adolescence. For the three different ethnic groups studied (European Americans, African Americans, Chinese Americans) we found evidence that level of family conflict moderated relations between experiences at home (maternal responsiveness, learning materials, variety of stimulation) and adolescent outcomes. Although there was not complete consistency in findings across the three groups, in all cases it was children in families with higher levels of conflict that responded more to each type of experience (Bradley & Corwyn, 2000). It is not just aspects of the social environment that provide salient background for the influence of parental actions. Research on noise indicated that persistent intensive auditory stimuli has physiological consequences and may be inimical to task performance and interpersonal exchanges (World Health Organization, 1980).

As children grow older, they are increasingly able to integrate information from multiple sources (levels) within the home and to develop ideas about their meaning. Children construct a generalized set of expectancies and motivational propensities to act in accordance with the general level of responsivity, object stimulation, structured learning opportunities, and the like, that are present. Children also are aware of the specific ways that their environments are responsive or not so responsive, stimulating or not so stimulating, and so forth. They can discriminate among the various types of responsivity present, each of which may have different salience for various behavioral systems. Likewise, as children become older and they can comprehend more distal and general conditions. Accordingly, those conditions become more salient for behavioral development. Indeed, as children grow older, what they make of parental actions also increasingly reflects the features of the environment outside the home (e.g., the conditions present in the peer group, at school, or in the neighborhood, even images on TV) at even more distal levels. It is not unusual, for example, for an adolescent to judge his or her parents' actions in light of his or her perceptions regarding how friends are treated by their parents in similar situations. The adolescent may judge even a mild reprimand as being too controlling or the continuation of attentiveness as too smothering.

It might be reasonably easy for social scientists to predict human behavior and development if it weren't for four stubborn facts about human beings: (1) we are conscious, (2) we construct expectations, (3) we have the capacity to split attention when confronted with arrays of simultaneous and sequential information, and (4) there is an inextricable but complex link between cognitions and emotions. Accordingly, the road from experience (however it might be directly measured) to response (however incompletely measured) can be hard to follow, criss-crossed as it is by a myriad of personal interpretations. Wachs (2000), in his clever book *Necessary but not Sufficient*, makes this point brilliantly. Theory is perhaps a step ahead of empirical science in making the complex road from experience to response clearer. The availability of large data sets and sophisticated statistical procedures may help empirical science close the gap over the next decade or so.

HOW DOES CONTEXT AFFECT PARENTING?

In 1999 Jared Diamond was awarded the Pulitzer Prize for *Guns, Germs, and Steel* (subtitled "The Fate of Human Societies"). Few books in recent memory have had the impact of this remarkable treatment of the last 13,000 years of human history. The lesson from this convincing and exhaustive review is singular: "History followed different courses for different peoples because of differences among peoples' environments" (p. 25). Specifically, Diamond presents the case that societies became dominant because of their proximity to plants that could become arable crops and animals that could become domesticated; context was everything. Having spent over a quarter century traipsing into homes all over America and beyond and in discussions with others interested in children's home environments throughout the world, I have become acutely aware of the power of context in shaping the actions parents take in behalf of their children. One of the things we have learned from our experience with the HOME is that life is incredibly diverse within and across groups, be they social class or cultural (a point made by Bloom, 1964, over 30 years ago). One of the most memorable home visits made using the HOME involved a large Mexican American family in Los Angeles. During the visit, there were 14 persons present, at one time or another, from the large, tightly knit extended family group. The home was rich with language and personal exchanges between family members, and it was also rich with joy. The family offered a strong contrast to the family situation of a young Mexican American mother in San Diego, separated from the father of her only child and living with her father, who was separated from her mother. The young mother's discomfort with her living arrangement was readily apparent. So keen was this discomfort, she did not even bring her child's toys to her father's home.

In 1984, Belsky published a paper on parenting in which he argued that parenting is a joint function of the parent's own history, the context in which parenting occurs, and the characteristics of the child. Our experience with HOME provides ample evidence of the relevance of Belsky's parenting process model. Scores on the Inventory are correlated with nearly everything (one might say confounded with nearly everything): race, family structure, neighborhood, parental personality and competence, parental history. Many of the items on the HOME Inventory index objects and parenting practices more common to better educated, wealthier families (Bradley et al., 2001). Indeed, in our recent analyses of data from the NL SY, we found that each of four major components of socio-economic status (parental education, occupational status, family income, and family wealth) influence multiple aspects of parenting above and beyond what the other three contributes (Bradley & Corwyn, 2003). Most investigators have found low-to-moderate correlations between HOME and social status variables (Adams et al., 1984; Bradley et al., 2000; Bradley, Caldwell, Rock, et al., 1989; Bradley, Mundfrom, et al., 1994; Brummitt & Jacobson, 1989; Caldwell, 1967; Hollenbeck, 1978; Kurtz et al., 1988; Nihira, Tomiyasu, & Oshio, 1987; Noll, Zucker, Curtis, & Fitzgerald, 1989; Pascoe, Loda, Jeffries, & Earp, 1981; Rogozin, Landesman-Dwyer, & Streissguth, 1978; Sahu & Devi, 1982; Saxon & Witriol, 1976; Yeung et al., 2002). However, the strength of association sometimes can be quite modest (.24), as a study of working mothers from Italy attests (Fein, Gariboldi, & Boni, 1993). Results indicated that, in cultures with a highly defined class structure such as India, the link between social status and parenting practice is likely to be tight (Kurtz et al., 1988). By comparison, in societies with more mobility across classes and nearly universal access to education (but not employment), the association may be weaker.

Studies show that scores on HOME reflect many factors in addition to parental social status (Bradley & Caldwell, 1978), including parental personality (Allen, Affleck, McQueeney, & McGrade, 1982; Bergerson, 1989; Fein et al., 1993; Pederson et al., 1988; Reis, Barbera-Stein, & Bennett, 1986), parental substance abuse (Fried, O'Connell, & Watkinson, 1992; Noll et al., 1989; Ragozin et al., 1978), parental IQ (Longstreth et al., 1981; Plomin & Bergeman, 1991), family structure (Bradley et al., 1982, 1984), parental knowledge about child development and attitudes toward child rearing (Reis et al., 1986), social support (Bradley et al., 1987, 1989; Wandersman & Unger, 1983), psychosocial climate of the home (Bradley et al., 1987; Gottfried & Gottfried, 1984; Nihira, Mink, & Meyers, 1981; Wandersman & Unger, 1983), presence of traumatic events (Bradley et al., 1987), and a variety of other community and cultural factors. Ragozin, Landesman-Dwyer, & Streissguth (1980) also observed a birth order effect on Involvement and Variety.

HOME scores also vary as a function of maternal age (Coll et al., 1986, 1987; Field et al., 1980; Luster & Rhoades, 1989; Reis et al., 1986; Schilmoeller & Baranowski, 1985; von Windeguth & Urbano, 1989). Reis and Herz (1987) even found that younger teens (13 to 16 years old) had lower scores than older teens (16 to 19 years old). Coll and her colleagues found that, even with total child care support and stress controlled, older mothers scored higher on HOME. But, the parenting practices of young mothers are not uniformly worse than those of older mothers. We conducted a study of 193 mothers ranging in age from 15 to 24 years (Whiteside-Mansell, Pope, & Bradley, 1996). Each mother was assessed with the HOME when their infants were 12 months old and again when their children were 36 months old. A cluster analysis was performed on the HOME subscale scores for both ages. Results showed that the majority of young mothers had HOME score profiles similar to those of older mothers. However, four of the five clusters had some HOME scores that were at least one standard deviation lower than those of older mothers. These profiles were related to maternal competence and family context as well as to children's development.

Two decades ago we looked at the relationship of HOME and an array of demographic factors in a racially diverse sample (Bradley & Caldwell, 1984a). We found two things: (a) no one demographic factor accounted for much of the variance in HOME scores, and (b) all the demographic factors we used put together accounted for only about 50% of the variance. We repeated this study with a much larger and even more diverse sample (Bradley, Mundfrom, et al., 1994). We did it in response to a study that erroneously concluded that income accounted for most of the difference in HOME scores (that study totally confounded race, area of residence, and social class). In our analysis using data from the Infant Health and Development Program (1990) Study, we essentially reproduced the findings from the earlier study: No one factor accounted for more than about 20% of the variance and a substantial amount of variance was left unaccounted for (see Table 20.2).

In an effort to better understand how culture and socio-economic status operate to shape the character of parenting and the parenting environment, we have undertaken several lines of investigation. One of the most comprehensive efforts was a collaborative study involving 11 investigators from six sites in North America (Bradley et al., 1989). In this study, correlations between HOME scores and 2-year Bayley scores were higher for European Americans than for African Americans and Hispanic Americans. However, by age 3, the correlation between child IQ and the Responsivity subscale was higher for African Americans than for European Americans, and there were no other notable differences between these two groups. The pattern of correlations for Mexican Americans was different from other groups. Reminiscent of results for poor children in rural Mexico (Cravioto & DeLicardie, 1976), correlations with social status and mental test scores were very low. Also in keeping with previous studies, HOME was found to significantly predict 3-year IQ (from .30 to .47) when it was entered into a regression equation after socio-economic status. More recently we used multiple waves of data from NLSY to investigate the relation between SES, parenting, and child development (Bradley & Corwyn,

TABLE 20.2
HOME and Demographic Factors

Demographic Variable	Variance Accounted for	
	12 Months HOME	36 Months HOME
Black vs. White	8%	9%
Black vs. Hispanic	1%	1%
Income	5%	4%
Maternal education	2%	6%
Gestational age	1%	4%
Marital status	2%	3%
Maternal age	1%	1%
Parity	1%	4%
R^2	.38	.53

Note. From Bradley, R. H., Mundfrom, D. J., Whiteside, L., Caldwell B. M., Casey, P. H., Kirby, R. S. & Hansen, S. (1994). The demography of parenting: A reexamination of the association between HOME and income. Source: *Nursing Research, 43,* 260–266.

2003). We found that SES was related to HOME scores for European American, African American, and Hispanic American families for children ages 4 through 14 (mostly low to moderate relations). Moreover, aspects of the home environment such as learning stimulation and maternal responsiveness tended to mediate relations between SES and child outcomes at all ages in all groups.

According to Hui and Triandis (1985), "the continuum of universality-cultural difference of a construct closely parallels the construct's level of abstraction" (p. 134). In other words, group similarities are greatest when total scores, or subscales, are analyzed, while item-level analysis is more precise in detecting group differences. For that reason, we recently began exploring data from the NLSY to investigate item-level differences by sociocultural group and poverty status. The original NLSY sample included 6,283 women who were between the age of 14 and 21 in 1979. The sample was selected to be nationally representative; however, there was deliberate oversampling of African Americans, Hispanics, and poor European Americans. Data from this sample has been collected every 2 years. Beginning in 1986, NLSY also included a child supplement which contained short forms of the four versions of HOME. We found that what children experience day to day and week to week in the households of Hispanic Americans, European Americans and African Americans are quite different from infancy through adolescence. Overall, Hispanic American and African American home environments were somewhat less supportive and stimulating than were the home environments of European Americans and Asian Americans, even when controlling for poverty status. These differences likely reflect cultural and economic legacy as well as continued macro-level sociopolitical factors such as racism. However, poverty status almost always had a greater affect on aspects of the home environment than did ethnicity. A surprising, but perhaps the most salient finding, was that the effect of poverty status was proportional across ethnic groups for all HOME short form items. Table 20.3 displays a few examples of the pervasive differences in home experiences for poor and non-poor families.

One could argue that information based on the HOME short forms collected in connection with NLSY represents a first phase of constructing a topography of the parenting environment. Certainly, it is a small first step, but the effort is perhaps more significant than is initially obvious. Determining the significance of any aspect of parenting requires an understanding of the full context of parenting. What we know about parenting and its effects from existing surveys and anthropological accounts gives nothing like the full mapping of this context. As a complement to this empirical bit-mapping of children's home experiences, we reviewed over 70 studies conducted outside the United States that utilized HOME (Bradley, Corwyn, & Whiteside-Mansell, 1997). Although there were notable exceptions, HOME total scores were similarly correlated with family structure, family status, and child outcomes across cultures. However, ethnic group differences relating to HOME subscales were quite

TABLE 20.3
Percent of Households Affording Children Stimulation of Various Types

	European American		African American		Hispanic American	
	Nonpoor	Poor	Nonpoor	Poor	Nonpoor	Poor
Birth through 2 years						
Child has 10 or more books	63.1	41.8	33.0	19.7	36.5	16.0
Reads to child 3/week or more	66.7	44.9	43.8	31.7	41.9	25.1
Child has 7 or more cuddly toys	81.9	76.6	67.1	52.5	70.3	61.7
3 through 5 years						
Child has 10 or more books	93.4	74.6	67.8	39.9	68.1	37.9
Reads to child 3/week or more	71.4	55.4	45.0	33.3	48.7	29.8
Helps child learn numbers	95.9	93.5	92.9	86.7	93.1	86.7
Helps child learn alphabet	94.4	87.5	91.9	86.3	85.5	74.8
Helps child learn shapes/sizes	87.9	78.7	77.0	63.0	73.2	57.9
Taken to museum monthly or more	8.3	6.0	13.5	10.8	8.8	8.5
6 through 9 years						
Child has 10 or more books	94.7	80.3	75.3	47.8	75.8	43.7
Reads to child 3/week or more	45.2	35.7	30.3	28.0	34.5	20.9
Child has musical instrument	46.8	28.4	36.0	23.1	37.2	25.7
Child gets special lessons	61.0	36.5	44.7	34.6	43.2	23.9
Taken to museum monthly or more	8.2	8.6	15.1	11.6	9.8	9.0
With father outdoors 1/week or more	85.8	61.3	66.9	47.7	81.0	69.8
Discuss TV programs with child	89.6	79.1	79.0	61.7	81.5	69.6
10 through 14 years						
Child has 10 or more books	73.5	50.9	41.6	26.1	47.0	20.2
With father outdoors 1/week or more	76.3	57.0	51.0	41.0	71.2	56.7
Discuss TV programs with child	89.0	78.9	72.3	58.5	77.0	62.8
Child has musical instrument	55.3	41.8	39.1	24.8	38.1	23.1
Child gets special lessons	68.7	54.4	60.3	48.6	54.5	31.6
Taken to museum monthly or more	5.2	7.0	10.4	10.7	5.9	9.0

common; and item-level analysis was the most useful in detecting these differences. Several instances of culturally inappropriate items were found. For example, "Parent introduces interviewer to child," "Child has free access to musical instrument," and "Family member has taken the child on a trip over 50 miles from home" were considered inappropriate for Caribbean households (Dubrow, Jones, Bozoky, & Adam, 1996). Moreover, items from the Responsivity subscale were problematic in several Asian studies. Aina, Agiobu-Kemmer, Etta, Zeitlin, and Setiloane (1993) dropped the Acceptance subscale since Yoruba culture places little value on independence, and Nihira et al. (1987) found the items not reflective of the different emotional aspects of parenting in Japanese. Not surprisingly, European studies mirrored those from the United States and Canada.

It is difficult to summarize what we know about the influence of context on parenting. In one sense, it is safe to say that context (physical, social, political, historical, economic) has a pervasive influence on what parents do, how they do it, how often they do it, and what it means in the lives of their children. Yet, it is clear that no one aspect of context (the closest exceptions perhaps being certain aspects of climate and economics) has a consistent effect across all groups. That is because every aspect of context itself has context and creates context for the others. It is also, as Kitayama (2002) says, often difficult for us as social scientists to penetrate to the most essential aspects of context when examining behavior and development. Lack of access to certain critical resources clearly matters in almost every instance. Extreme environments (climatic, emotional) also tend to have fairly predictable impacts. Beyond that, contextual effects tend to vary as a function of other aspects of context; and their average effect appears modest.

FAMILY PROCESS MODELS

Bronfenbrenner's (1995) bioecological theory and Belsky's (1984) process model of parenting have provided useful frameworks for guiding research on parenting and child development. During the 1990s, several scholars have provided additional framing for those interested in more fully delineating how the resources available to families (or lack thereof) are implicated in parenting and child functioning (Conger, Wallace, Simons, McLoyd, & Brody, 2002; McLoyd, 1990). Generically, these frameworks can be organized under the rubric, family process models of parenting. They attempt to explicate how the resources available to parents affect parental mood, expectations, and mental health, which in turn affect quality of parenting (i.e., a cycle of exchanges between parent and child) and how that helps shape the course of behavioral development. In these models, very specific mechanisms linking the availability of resources to child adaptive functioning are stipulated. This has the advantage not only of offering something closer to an explanation for observed relations but also in designing interventions directed at forestalling or enhancing key processes. These models have been particularly useful in helping to explicate the relation between poverty and maladaptive behavior. An interesting recent use of family process models is a study by Yeung and colleagues (2002). These researchers found evidence for distinctly different paths linking family income to child outcomes depending on the outcome. The link to child achievement was primarily mediated by allowing the child greater access to stimulating experiences; the link to behavior problems was mediated through parental distress and negative parenting. Our analyses likewise implicate learning stimulation as a mediator of the link between family income and achievement test performance (Bradley & Corwyn, 2003). However, our analyses simultaneously controlled for and tested the effects of family financial assets (wealth), maternal education, and occupational prestige.

Learning stimulation was a significant mediator for all four types of socio-economic resources. However, its role as a significant mediator depended upon the age of the child and ethnicity. In our analyses we also simultaneously controlled for and tested the effects of maternal responsiveness as a potential mediator. When child behavior problems was used as the outcome variable, we found evidence that learning stimulation mediated relations between SES variables and behavior problems to at least as great an extent as did maternal responsiveness (typically more so). Moreover, we allowed for testing of direct effects as well; that is, effects unmediated through learning stimulation and maternal responsiveness. Our findings showed that there were often significant direct effects even when testing for these two mediators, which suggests that there are additional unmeasured mediators for both child achievement and behavior. Our findings attest to the value of examining what might be termed "full assets" models even if one's principal interest is in one type of asset (family assets tend to covary and they tend to covary in somewhat different ways depending on culture). It also attests to the value of investigating models with direct as well as indirect (mediated) effects.

WHY DO PARENTS INVEST IN THEIR CHILDREN?

In a recent paper, Tanfer and Mott (1997) argued that changes in family patterns, brought on by changes in social and economic conditions, "signal a weaker commitment of women to men and of men to women; a weaker commitment by the partners to their relationship, and very possibly a weaker commitment to their children" (p. 2). Trends from the past half century seem clear and compelling: smaller families, fewer and delayed marriages, increased divorce, delayed childbearing, advancing numbers of children growing up in single-parent households. Growth in materialism, stresses from work, and the rising cost of rearing children almost certainly conspire to reduce the value of children and adults' commitment to them. More and more, status (and fulfillment) is derived from outside the home, outside the role of parenting.

According to parental investment theory, "the responsibilities of caring for young, often unruly children would seem to require putting one's needs and desires on the back burner so that one can attend to the needs of one's offspring" (Bjorklund & Kipp, 1996, p. 181). The ability to inhibit one's own impulses to leave one's offspring to their own resorts, by extension, requires that one derive pleasure in caring for the child and that one identify one's own well-being with the well-being of the child (Marsiglio et al., 1997).

Concerns about parental investment in children span many decades and many disciplines, from evolutionary biology (Trivers, 1972) to economics (Becker, 1991) to psychology (Hertwig, Davis, & Sulloway, 2002). Each decade and each discipline has put its own stamp on the issue, but there is consensus on one belief: investing in children entails costs. As the trend toward disinvestment in family and child rearing has accelerated (Popenoe, 1993), our research has focused more intensively on parental involvement in the lives of children. We constructed a measure called Parents' Socioemotional Investment in Children (PIC; Bradley, Whiteside-Mansell, Brisby, & Caldwell, 1997). The PIC assesses four components of investment: acceptance of the parenting role, delight in the child, knowledge/sensitivity, and separation anxiety. A study done on 137 mothers of 15-month-old children revealed that PIC was related to the quality of caregiving, maternal depression, neuroticism, agreeableness, social support, the quality of the marital relationship, parenting stress, and perceived child difficultness.

Because of increased concerns about parental involvement in the lives of children, we examined factors that predicted three component scores from PIC (acceptance, delight, and knowledge/sensitivity) when children were 15 months old (Corwyn & Bradley, 1999). Predictors were chosen based on Belsky's process model of parenting (Belsky, 1984) and conceptions about fathering discussed by Doherty, Kouneski, and Erickson (1998). They consisted of income to needs, marital quality, mother's employment, mother's work strain, father's work strain, child's compliant behavior (adaptive social behavior inventory), and child's developmental competence (Bayley scores). Results were somewhat different for mothers and fathers. For fathers, the child's Bayley score, and father's work strain had negative influences on both acceptance while marital quality had a positive influence. Maternal employment and father's work strain were negatively correlated with paternal knowledge/sensitivity. Child temperament and being employed had negative impacts on maternal acceptance. Marital quality was positively associated with maternal knowledge/sensitivity and father's work strain had a positive impact on maternal delight. Overall, such findings are reminiscent of the findings of Woodworth, Belsky, and Crnic (1996).

A major reason for being concerned with parents' level of investment in their children is the belief that high levels of investment will redound to the benefit of children. However, the likelihood that parental investment matters for children at least partly depends on whether the parent's level of investment remains reasonably constant through time (Bloom, 1964). Accordingly, we were concerned with the stability of parental investment (Corwyn & Bradley, 2002a). To examine this issue, it was necessary that we first establish factorial invariance of PIC over time in that evidence for rank order stability through time would have equivocal meaning in the absence of factorial invariance. In a sample of 102 mothers who completed PIC when their children were 15 and 36 months of age, we found strong evidence for factorial invariance for both Knowledge/Sensitivity and Delight. However, we found evidence that one item from the Acceptance scale was less valid at 36 months. Given these results, we found evidence for substantial rank order stability from 15 to 36 months on all three components. To an extent, this was both good news and bad news. The good news: Because parental attitudes concerning investment tend to be stable, it is more likely that parents whose initial attitudes regarding investment are positive will persist in doing things in behalf of their children to the extent that investment attitudes shape their behavior. The bad news: It may be more difficult to change negative attitudes given that they tend to remain fixed. More recently, we have examined the stability of responses to PIC subscales for fathers as well as mothers (Corwyn & Bradley, 2002b). We investigated the stability of five constructs (i.e., protection, sensitivity, delight, proximity, and acceptance of the parenting role) of mothers' and fathers' socio-emotional investment in the child during early childhood (from 15 months of age to 36 months of age). Three types of stability were assessed: factor structure stability, mean level stability and rank order stability. All five constructs showed acceptable factor structure stability for both parents. The only significant mean level changes were decreases in proximity and protection among mothers. All constructs showed significant rank order stability for both parents with mothers consistently showing higher rank order stability than fathers.

The relation between parental attitudes and parental behavior remains murky (Holden & Buck, 2002). In an effort to more fully understand how attitudes regarding parental investment may help to shape parenting behaviors, we examined factors connected with paternal efforts to help prepare children to get ready to go to kindergarten. The participants were fathers of children in Head Start. Using Belsky's process model of parenting as a broad frame and Palkovitz's (2002) notions about generative fathering as a more specific frame, we selected the following variables to predict fathering behaviors such as reading to the child, sharing stories with the child, involving the child in daily activities, and involvement in Head Start: family conflict, family cohesion, marital quality, parenting stress, delight (from PIC), biological relationship to child, residency status, parenting efficacy, father's relationship with his parents. Although significant predictors varied as a function of what fathering behavior was used as the dependent variable, the father's sense of efficacy, the quality of his relationship with the child's mother, and his level of contact with his own mother tended to be the most consistent predictors. All and all they corroborate the assertion that situation/context plays a significant role in these relations (Holden & Buck, 2002).

TAROT CARDS, CRYSTAL BALLS, AND TEA LEAVES

For Americans, the twenty-first century began with a bang—literally. Two words conjure scorched images of life in the here and now, life as we did not realize it was: Columbine and September 11th. Both focus the mind on what family means and the awesome responsibility of parenting in an uncertain world. For those of us interested in the welfare of children, these events made immediately clear that the science of parenting has yet to equip parents with all the tools needed to assure that children thrive. In their aftermath, the American Psychological Association put out a book that addresses issues about how children respond to violence, terrorism, and natural disasters (La Greca et al., 2002). In that volume there is some useful advice, based on clinical experience, on how to help children cope with the aftermath of terrifying events. But, from the book, it is also clear that there is little in the way of science regarding what parents actually do to assist their children in such times or whether it is effective. Moreover, the book does not even address a myriad of other circumstances that may severely disrupt a child's sense of emotional security and move the child on a less adaptive personal life trajectory. Such research is a major need for the future. Parents need more than a solid scientific base for rearing children under more or less benign circumstances. They need a solid scientific base for helping their children cope with trouble, be it bullies, acts of terror, natural disasters, predators—whatever.

The most striking thing we have learned from our long years of studying parents and children, is how diverse life is "in the moment" for children. This "fact" has consumed us as we have struggled to develop measures that are useful representations of that broad phenomenon called parenting (a.k.a., the home environment). What, among the myriad acts, objects, conditions, and events that constitute the home environment, should be included in measures of parenting? What indicators are telling enough across the broad diversity of families in America and throughout the world that they capture what is most salient about parenting? With family life so bound up with history, culture, community, and place, it seems impossible that any one measure (given that it contains only a limited census of indicators) could sufficiently capture what is most salient about parenting for all groups and all situations. But, without "marker" measures or indicators, how can we construct an integrated science of parenting, a theory of environment-development relationships that is anything more than parochial? This dilemma would seem to lead to a kind of "Sophie's Choice" regarding which strategy to keep and which to leave behind; but should not. It has led us to recommend a dual strategy for studying parenting: It is what we call an inside and outside strategy with regard to marker measures of key parenting domains. The inside strategy means looking inside the measures themselves and, more specifically, looking at the issue of measurement invariance across groups. Using such techniques as confirmatory factor analysis, structural equation modeling, and multitrait-multimethod analysis, we are looking at whether the internal structure of measures is similar across groups and whether a measure links with similar constructs across groups (Whiteside-Mansell, Bradley, Owen, Randolph, & Cauce, 2003). Initial results suggest similarities in some of the behaviors commonly coded in mother–child interaction paradigms for European American and African American families, but not complete isomorphism. The outside strategy is to supplement marker measures with outside indicators that may be particularly revealing of a parenting domain in a particular group. Perhaps, the best example of the outside strategy in our own research has been our work with children with disabilities. In those studies, we added items to the Infant-Toddler, Early Childhood, and Middle Childhood versions of HOME that were designed for families having children with various types of disabilities. The thought was that these children may require additional things from their environments in order to do well. Our findings showed that the items on the HOME generally worked well in predicting how children would do on standard measures of social and cognitive functioning but, as the severity of the disability increased, the additional items became more useful in predicting the course of development (Bradley et al., 1989). When approached by researchers from other cultures, we now routinely recommend gathering information on parenting indicators of local value in addition to those found on the HOME, then analyzing data from the standard HOME and from the additional items in tandem. In addition to recommending the outside strategy with regard to the measurement of parenting, we also have begun examining the relation between parenting and children's development within cultures (e.g., our studies using the Early Adolescent HOME and our recent studies involving NLSY). There is convincing evidence for the value of within-group analyses for building a comprehensive science of human development (Garcia Coll et al., 1996).

If the past is prologue yet only dimly foreshadows what is to come, then one may wonder what the future of parenting science holds. The realities of child rearing in the twenty-first century present extraordinary obstacles to definitive research, with complexity and diversity in arrangements compounding the ordinary problems of linking particular parenting practices to the trajectory of development in highly evolved, phylogenetically advanced organisms living in rich, multilayered contexts. The challenge requires longitudinal designs with repeated measures of all the caregiving environments in which a child spends a meaningful amount of time (Friedman & Haywood, 1994). In the NICHD Study of Child Care and Youth Development, we have constantly been concerned with the combined effects of child care and home or school and home (NICHD Early Child Care Research Network, 2003). As a result we often include measures of both contexts in a single analysis aimed at understanding children's development. Constructing a useful knowledge base for parenting in the twenty-first century also requires a more integrated, holistic view of children. The evidence is compelling that children are not just people with behavior problems or people who regulate their emotions or people who possess a certain level of physical or academic competence (Zaff et al., 2003). The goals of parents and of cultures recognize the integrity of development and how developmental systems feed off one another. Yet most studies of parenting fail to take account of the dynamic interplay among these systems. Just as we have argued that one cannot usefully examine aspects of parenting in isolation from one another (children don't just experience one aspect of parenting separately from the rest), so it is important that we construct studies that do not consistently isolate one component of development from the others.

One way to find the whole child again in studies of development may be to use person-centered approaches to research to complement our current almost exclusive reliance on variable-centered approaches. The person-centered approach has made significant contributions to research on resiliency, personality and adolescent behaviors, but has not been equally utilized in parenting research. We recently used a person-centered strategy as a way of better understanding how socio economic status influences child behavior (Corwyn & Bradley, 2005). We found support for all three propositions of the person-centered approach outlined by Bergman (2000); that models likely do not apply to everyone, relations are frequently not linear and patterns of values often have more meaning than variables considered individually (Bergman, 2000).

As the future intrudes into daily life with ever increasing speed and persistence, the job of parenting will rely less on prescriptions and more on flexible problem-solving strategies aimed at finding the best fit between long-term goals for a child, the child's current needs and capabilities, and what the environment affords by way of demands and opportunities. Parenting science must move quickly to develop new theories and methodologies just to keep up.

REFERENCES

Abelson, R. (1981). Psychological status of the script concept. *American Psychologist, 36*, 715–729.

Adams, J. L., Campbell, F. A., & Ramey, C. T. (1984). Infants' home environments: A study of screening efficiency. *American Journal of Mental Deficiency, 89*, 133–139.

Aina, T. A., Agiobu-Kemmer, I., Etta, E. F., Zeitlin, M. F., & Setiloane, K. (1993). *Early child care, development and nutrition in Lagos State, Nigiria.* Produced by the Social Sciences Faculty, University of Lagos, and the Tufts University School of Nutrition Science and Policy for the United Nations Children's Fund (UNICEF), New York.

Allen, D. A., Affleck, G., McGrade, B. J., & McQueeney, M. (1984). Effects of single parent status of mothers on their high-risk infants. *Infant Behavior and Development, 7*, 341–139.

Allen, D. A., Affleck, G., McQueeney, M., & McGrade, B. J. (1982) Validation of the parent behavior progression in an early intervention program. *Mental Retardation, 20*, 159–163.

Ausubel, D. (1968). *Educational psychology: A cognitive view.* New York: Rinehart and Winston.

Bakeman, R., & Brown, J. V. (1980). Early interaction: Consequences for social and mental development at three years. *Child Development, 51*, 437–447.

Baharudin, R., & Luster, T. (1998). Factors related to the quality of the home environment and children's achievement. *Journal of Family Issues, 19*, 375–403.

Bandura, A. (1997). *Self-efficacy: The exercise of control.* New York: Freeman.

Becker, G. S. (1991). *A treatise on the family.* Cambridge: Harvard University Press

Belsky, J. (1984). The determinants of parenting: A process model. *Child Development, 55*, 83–96.

Belsky, J., Garduque, L., & Hrncir, E. (1984). Assessing performance, competence and executive capacity in infant play: Relations to home environment and security of attachment. *Developmental Psychology, 20*, 406–417.

Bergeman, C. S. & Plomin, R. (1988). Parental mediators of the genetic relationship between home environment and infant mental development. *British Journal of Developmental Psychology, 6*, 11–19.

Bergerson, S. (1989). *Personality characteristics of mothers whose infants are referred to early intervention programs.* Unpublished doctoral dissertation, University of Toronto, Canada.

Bergman, L. R. (2000). The application of a person-oriented approach: types and clusters. In Bergman, L. R., Cairns, R., Nystedt, L., & Nilsson, L. (Eds.), *Developmental science and the holistic approach.* Mahwah, NJ: Erlbaum.

Billings, R., Jacobson, S., Jacobson. J., & Brumitt, G. (1989, April). *Preschool HOME: Dimensions and predictive validity.* Paper presented at the meeting of the Society for Research in Child Development, Kansas City, MO.

Bjorklund, D. F., & Kipp, K. (1996). Parental investment theory and gender differences in the evolution of inhibition mechanisms. *Psychological Bulletin, 120*, 163–188.

Bloom, B. (1964). *Stability and chance in human characteristics.* New York: Wiley.

Bornstein, M. H. (Ed.) (2002). *Handbook of parenting.* Mahwah, NJ: Erlbaum.

Bornstein, M. H., Tamis-LeMonda, C. S., Tal, H., Ludemann, P. I., Toda, S., Rahn, C. W., Pecheux, M. Asuma, H., & Vardi, D. (1992). Maternal responsiveness to infants in three societies: The United States, France, and Japan. *Child Development, 63*, 808–821.

Bowlby, J. (1958). The nature of the child's tie to his mother. *International Journal of Psychoanalysis, 39*, 350–373.

Bradley, R. H. (2002). Environment and parenting. In M. Bornstein (Ed.), *Handbook of parenting* (Vol. 2, pp. 281–313). Hillsdale, NJ: Erlbaum.

Bradley, R. H. (1994). The HOME Inventory: Review and reflections. In H. W. Reese (Ed.), *Advances in child development and behavior* (Vol. 25, pp. 21–288). San Diego, CA: Academic Press,

Bradley, R. H., & Caldwell, B. M. (1976a). Early environment and changes in mental test performance in children from six to thirty-six months. *Developmental Psychology, 12*, 93–97.

Bradley, R. H., & Caldwell, B. M. (1976b). The relationship of infants' home environment to mental test performance at fifty-four months: A follow-up study. *Child Development, 47*, 1172–1174.

Bradley, R. H., & Caldwell, B. M. (1978). Screening the environment. *American Journal of Orthopsychiatry, 48*, 114–130.

Bradley, R. H. & Caldwell, B. M. (1979). Home observation for measurement of the environment: A revision of the preschool scale. *American Journal of Mental Deficiency, 84*, 235–244.

Bradley, R. H. & Caldwell, B. M. (1980). Home environment, cognitive competence and IQ among males and females. *Child Development, 51*, 1140–1148.

Bradley, R. H., & Caldwell, B. M. (1981). The HOME Inventory: A validation of the preschool scale for Black children. *Child Development, 52*, 708–710.

Bradley, R. H., & Caldwell, B. M. (1982). The consistency of the home environment and its relation to child development. *International Journal of Behavioral Development, 5*, 445–465.

Bradley, R. H. & Caldwell, B. M. (1984). The HOME inventory and family demographics. *Developmental Psychology, 20*, 315–320.

Bradley, R. H. & Caldwell, B. M. (1984). The relation of infants' home environments to achievement test performance in first grade: A follow-up study. *Child Development, 55*, 803–809.

Bradley, R. H., & Caldwell, B. M. (1995). Caregiving and the regulation of child growth and development: Describing proximal aspects of caregiving systems. *Developmental Review, 15,* 38–85.

Bradley, R. H., Caldwell, B. M., Rock, S. L., Hamrick, H. M., & Harris, P. T. (1988). Home observation for measurement of the environment: Development of HOME inventory for use with families having children 6 to 10 years old. *Contemporary Educational Psychology, 13,* 58–71.

Bradley, R. H., Caldwell, B. M., & Rock, S. L. (1988). Home environment and school performance: A ten-year follow-up and examination of three models of environmental action. *Child Development, 59,* 852–867.

Bradley, R. H., Caldwell, B. M., Rock, S. L.. Barnard. K. E., Gray. C., Hammond, M. A., Mitchell, S., Siegel, L., Ramey, C. T., Gottfried, A. W., & Johnson, D. L. (1989). Home environment and cognitive development in the first 3 years of life: A collaborative study involving six sites and three ethnic groups in North America. *Developmental Psychology, 28,* 217–235.

Bradley, R. H., Caldwell, B. M., Rock, S. L., Casey, P. H., & Nelson, J. (1987). The early development of low-birthweight infants: Relationship to health, family status, family context, family processes, and parenting. *International Journal of Behavioral Development, 10,* 1–18.

Bradley, R. H., & Corwyn, R. F. (i2005). Productive activity and the prevention of behavior problems. *Developmental Psychology, 41,* 89–98.

Bradley, R. H., & Corwyn, R. F. (2003). Age and ethnic variations in family process mediators of SES. In M. H. Bornstein & R. H. Bradley (Eds.), *Socioeconomic status, parenting, and child development* (pp. 161–188). Mahwah, NJ: Erlbaum.

Bradley, R. H., & Corwyn, R. F. (2003, April). *Family process mediators of SES for three ethnic groups.* Paper presented at the biennial meeting of the Society for Research in Child Development. Tampa, FL.

Bradley, R. H., & Corwyn, R. F. (2001). Home environment and behavioral development during adolescence: The mediating and moderating roles of self-efficacy beliefs. *Merrill-Palmer Quarterly, 47,* 165–187.

Bradley, R. H., & Corwyn, R. F. (2000). The moderating effect of perceived amount of family conflict on the relation between home environmental processes and the well-being of adolescents. *Journal of Family Psychology, 14,* 349–364.

Bradley, R. H., Corwyn, R. F., Caldwell, B. M., Whiteside-Mansell, L., Wasserman, G. A., & Mink, I. T. (2000). Measuring the home environments of children in early adolescence. *Journal of Research on Adolescence, 10,* 247–289.

Bradley, R. H., Corwyn, R. F., Burchinal, M., McAdoo, H. P., & Garcia Coll, C. (2001). The home environments of children in the United States. Part 2: Relations with behavioral development through age 13. *Child Development, 72,* 1868–1886.

Bradley, R. H., Corwyn, R. F., McAdoo, H. P., & Garcia Coll, C. (2001). The home environments of children in the United States Part I: Variations by age, ethnicity, and poverty status. *Child Development, 72,* 1844–1867.

Bradley, R. H., Corwyn, R. F., & Whiteside-Mansell, L. (1996). Life at home: Same time, different place: An examination of the HOME Inventory in different cultures. *Early Development and Parenting, 5,* 251–269.

Bradley, R. H., Mundfrom, D. J., Whiteside, L., Caldwell, B. M., Casey, P. H., Kirby, R. S., & Hansen, S. (1994). The demography of parenting: A re-examination of the association between HOME scores and income. *Nursing Research, 43,* 260–266.

Bradley, R. H., & Rock, S. L. (1985). The HOME Inventory: Its relation to school failure and development of an elementary-age version. In W. Frankenburg, R. Emde, & J. Sullivan (Eds.), *Early identification of children at risk: An international perspective* (pp. 159–174). New York: Plenum.

Bradley, R. H., Rock, S. L., Caldwell, B. M., Harris, P. T., & Hamrick, H. M. (1987). Home environment and school performance among Black elementary school children. *Journal of Negro Education, 56,* 499–509.

Bradley, R. H., Whiteside, L., Mundfrom, D. J., Blevins-Knabe, B., Casey, P. H., Caldwell, B. M., Kelleher, K. J., Pope, S., & Barrett, K. (1995). Home environment and adaptive social behavior among premature, low birthweight children. Alternative models of environmental action. *Journal of Pediatric Psychology, 20,* 347–362.

Bradley, R. H., Whiteside, L., Mundfrom, D. J., Casey, P. H., Kelleher, K. J., & Pope, S. K. (1994). Early indications of resilience and their relation to experiences in the home environments of low birthweight, premature children living in poverty. *Child Development, 65,* 346–360.

Bradley, R. H., Whiteside-Mansell, L., Brisby, J. A., & Caldwell, B. M. (1997). Parents' socioemotional investment in children. *Journal of Marriage and the Family, 59,* 77–90.

Bradley, R. H., Whiteside-Mansell, L., & Corwyn, R. (1997, August) *Early adolescent HOME Inventory: Its usefulness and validity for 4 racial/ethnic groups.* Paper presented at the annual meeting of the American Educational Research Association, Chicago, IL.

Bransford, J. D., Brown, A. L., & Cocking, R. R. (Eds.) (2000). *How people learn: Brain, mind, experience, and school.* Washington, DC: National Academy Press.

Bretherton, I., & Waters, E. (1985). Growing points of attachment theory and research. *Monographs of the Society for Research in Child Development, 50* (1-2, Serial No. 209).

Bronfenbrenner, U. (1995). The bioecological model from a life course perspective: Reflections of a participant observer. In P. Moen, G. H. Elder, & K. Luscher (Eds.), *Examining lives in context* (pp. 619–647). Washington, DC: American Psychological Association.

Bronfenbrenner, U. (1979). *The ecology of human development.* Cambridge: Harvard University Press.

Bronson, M. B. (2000). *Self-regulation in early childhood.* New York: Guilford.

Brumitt, G. A., & Jacobson, J. L. (1989, April). *The influences of home environment and socio-economic status on cognitive performance at 4 years.* Paper presented at the meeting of the Society for Research in Child Development, Kansas City, MO.

Caldwell, B. M. (1967). Descriptive evaluations of child development and of developmental settings. *Pediatrics, 40,* 46–54.

Caldwell, B. M. (1968). On designing supplementary environments for early child development. *BAEYC Reports, 10,* 1–11.

Caldwell, B. M.. & Bradley, R. H. (2003). *HOME inventory administration manual.* Little Rock: University of Arkansas at Little Rock.

Carlson, D. B., Labarba, R. C., Sclafani, J. D., & Bowers, C. A. (1986). Cognitive and motor development in infants of adolescent mothers: A longitudinal analysis. *International Journal of Behavioral Development, 9,* 1–13.

Caughy, M.O., Dipietro, J.A. & Strobino, D.M. (1994). Daycare participation as a protective factor in the cognitive development of low-income children. *Child Development, 65,* 457–471.

Chua, K. L., Kong, D. S., Wong, S. T., & Yoong, T. (1989). Quality of the home environment of toddlers: A validation study of the HOME Inventory. *Journal of the Singapore Pediatric Society, 31*, 38–45.

Coleman, J. S. (1988). Social capital in the creation of human capital. *American Journal of Sociology, 94*, 95–120.

Coll, C. G., Vohr, O., Hoffman, J., & Oh, W. (1986). Maternal and adolescent mothers. *Developmental and Behavioral Pediatrics, 7*, 230–236.

Collins, W. A., Maccoby, E. E., Steinberg, L., Hetherington, E. M., & Bornstein, M. H. (2000). Contemporary research on parenting. *American Psychologist, 55*, 218–232.

Conger, R. D., Wallace, L. E., Sun, Y., Simons, R. L., McLoyd, V. C., & Brody, G. H. (2002). Economic pressure in African American families: A replication and extension of the family process model. *Developmental Psychology, 38*, 179–193.

Consullo, M. (1992, May). *Relationship of early responsiveness to one-year outcomes in preterm and full-term infants.* Paper presented at the International Conference on Infancy Studies, Miami, FL.

Cooney, G. H., Bell, A., McBride, W., & Carte, C. (1989). Neurobehavioral consequences of prenatal low level exposure to lead. *Neurotoxicology and Teratology, 11*, 95–104.

Coons, H., Fulker, D. W., DeFries, J. C., & Plomin, R. (1990). Home environment and cognitive ability of 7-year-old children in the Colorado Adoption Project: Genetic and environment etimologies. *Developmental Psychology, 26*, 459–468.

Corwyn, R. F., & Bradley, R. H. (2002a). Stability of maternal socioemotional investment in young children. *Parenting: Science & Practice, 2*, 27–46.

Corwyn, R.F., & Bradley, R.H. (2002b). *Stability of maternal and paternal socio-emotional investment in young children.* Presented at the Third International Conference on Child and Adolescent Mental Health. Brisbane, Queensland Australia, June 11-15, 2002.

Corwyn, R. F., & Bradley, R. H. (1999). Determinants of paternal and maternal investment in children. *Infant Mental Health Journal, 20*, 238–256.

Corwyn, R.F. & Bradley, R.H. (2005). Socioeconomic status, poverty status and childhood externalizing behaviors: Theoretical and methodological considerations within a structural equation modeling framework. In V. Bengtson, A. Acock, K. Allen, P. Dilworth-Anderson, and D. Klein (Eds.), *Sourcebook of family theories and methods: An interactive approach* (pp. 469–483). Newbury Park, CA: Sage Publications.

Cravioto, J., & DeLicardie, E. (1976). Microenvironmental factors in severe protein-calorie malnutrition. In N. Scrimshaw & M. Behar (Eds.), *Nutrition and agricultural development* (pp. 25–35). New York: Plenum.

Cummings, E. M., Zahn-Waxler, C., & Radke-Yarrow, M. (1981). Young children's responses to expressions of anger and affection by others in the family. *Child Development, 52*, 1274–1282.

Darling, N., & Steinberg, L. (1993). Parenting style as context. An integrative model. *Psychological Bulletin, 113*, 487–496.

Diamond, J. (1997). *Guns, germs, and steel.* New York: W.W. Norton.

Doherty, W., Kouneski, E. R., & Erickson, M. F. (1998). Responsible fathering: An overview and conceptual framework. *Journal of Marriage and the Family, 60*, 277–292.

Dorr, A., Rabin, B. E., & Irlen, S. (2002). Parenting in a multimedia society. In M. H. Bornstein (Ed.), *Handbook of parenting,* (2nd ed., vol. 5, pp. 349–374). Mahwah, NJ: Erlbaum.

Dunn, J. (1991). The developmental importance of differences in siblings' experiences within the family. In K. Pillemer & K. McCartney (Eds.), *Parent-child relations throughout life* (pp. 113–124). Hillsdale, NJ: Erlbaum.

Dubrow, E., Jones, E., Bozoky, S. J., & Adam, E. (1996, August). *How well does the HOME Inventory predict Caribbean children's academic performance and behavior problems?* Poster session presented at the 14th biennial meeting of ISSBD, Quebec City, Canada.

Eisenberg, N., Cumberland, A., & Spinrad, T. L. (1998). Parental socialization of emotion. *Psychological Inquiry, 9*, 241–273.

Elardo, R., Bradley, R. H., & Caldwell, B. M. (1975). The relation of infants' home environment to mental test performance from six to thirty-six months: A longitudinal analysis. *Child Development, 45*, 71–76.

Elardo, R., Bradley, R. H., & Caldwell, B. M. (1977). A longitudinal study of the relation of infants' home environment to language development at age three. *Child Development, 48*, 595–603.

Erickson, M. F., Stroufe, L. A., & Egeland, B. (1985). The relationship between quality of attachment and behavior problems in a high risk sample. In I. Bretherton & E. Waters (Eds.), Growing points of attachment theory and research. *Monographs of the Society for Research in Child Development, 50*(1:2, Serial No. 209), 147–166.

Evans, G. W., Kliewer, W., & Martin, J. (1991). The role of the physical environment in the health and well-being of children. In H. E. Schroeder (Ed.), *New directions in health psychology assessment* (pp. 127–157). New York: Hemisphere.

Fagot, B. I., & Kavanaugh, K. (1993). Parenting during the second year: Effects of children's age, sex, and attachment classification. *Child Development, 64*, 258–271.

Fein, G. G., Gariboldi, A., & Boni, R. (1993). Antecedents of maternal separation anxiety. *Merrill-Palmer Quarterly, 39*, 481–495.

Feinberg, M. E., McHale, S. M., Crouter, A. C., & Cumsille, P. (2003). Sibling differentiation: Sibling and parent relationship trajectories in adolescence. *Child Development, 74*, 1261–1274.

Field, T. M., Widmayer, S. M., Adler, S., & DeCubas, M. (1990). Teenage parenting in different cultures, family constellations and caregiving environments: Effects on infant development. *Infant Mental Health Journal, 11*, 158–174.

Finkelhor, D., Mitchell, K. J., & Wolak, J. (2000). *On-line victimization: A report on the nation's youth.* National Center for Missing and Exploited Children.

Ford, D. M., & Lerner, R. M. (1992). *Developmental systems theory.* Newbury Park, CA: Sage.

Fried, P. A., O'Connell, C. M., & Watkinson, B. (1992). 60- and 72-month follow-up of children prenatal exposed to marijuana, cigarettes, and alcohol: Cognitive and language assessment. *Developmental and Behavioral Pediatrics, 13*, 383–391.

Friedman, S. L., & Haywood, H. C. (1994). *Developmental follow-up: Concepts, domains, and methods.* San Diego, CA: Academic Press.

Friedman, S. L., & Sigman, M. D. (1996). Past, present, and future directions in research on the development of low-birthweight children. In L. S. Friedman & M. D. Sigman (Eds.), *The psychological development of low birthweight children* (pp. 3–22). Norwood, NJ: Ablex.

Garcia-Coll, C., Lamberty, G., Jenkins, R., McAdoor, H. P., Crnic, K., Wasik, B. H., & Garcia, H. V. (1996). An integrative model for the study of developmental competencies in minority children. *Child Development, 67*, 1891–1914.

Gottfried, A. W., & Gottfried, A. E. (1984). Home environment and cognitive development in young children of middle-socioeconomic status families. In A. W. Gottfried (Ed.), *Home environment and early cognitive development* (pp. 329–342). Orlando, FL: Academic Press.

Gottfried, A. E., & Gottfried. A. W. (1988). *Maternal employment and children's development: Longitudinal research.* New York: Plenum Press.

Gottfried, A. E., & Gottfried, A. W., Bathurst, K., & Guerin, D. W. (1994). *Gifted IQ: Early developmental aspects.* New York: Plenum Press.

Grinker, R. R., Korshin, S. J., Bosowitz, H., Hamburg, D. A., Sabshin, M., Pershy, H., Chevalier, J. A., & Borad, F. A. (1956). A theoretical and experimental approach to problems of anxiety. *AMA Archives of Neurology and Psychiatry, 76,* 420–431.

Hammond, M. A., Bee, H. L., Barnard, K. E., & Eyres, S. J. (1983). *Child health assessment: Part IV followup at second grade* (No. RO1 NU 00816). Seattle: U.S. Public Health Service.

Hart, B., and Risley, T. (1995). *Meaningful differences in the everyday experience of young American children.* Baltimore, MD: Brookes.

Hertwig, R., Davis, J. N., & Sulloway, F. J. (2002). Parental investment: How an equity motive can produce inequality. *Psychological Bulletin, 128,* 728–745.

Hoff, E. (2003). Causes and consequences of SES-related differences in parent-to-child speech. In M. H. Bronstein & R. H. Bradley (Eds.), *Socioeconomic status, parenting, and child development* (pp. 145–160). Mahwah, NJ: Erlbaum

Holden, G. W., & Buck, M. J. (2002). Parental attitudes toward child rearing. In M. H. Bornstein (Ed.), *Handbook of parenting* (2nd ed., vol. 3, pp. 537–562). Mahwah, NJ: Erlbaum.

Hollenbeck, A. R. (1978). Early infant home environments: Validation of the home observation for Measurement of the Environment Inventory. *Developmental Psychology, 14,* 416–418.

Horowitz, F. D. (1987). *Exploring developmental theories: Toward a structural/behavioral model of development.* Hillsdale, NJ: Erlbaum.

Hui, C. H., & Triandis, H. C. (1985). Measurement in cross-cultural psychology. *Journal of Cross-cultural Psychology, 16,* 134–153.

Infant Health & Development Program. (1990). Enhancing outcomes of low-birth-weight, premature infants. *Journal of the American Medical Association, 263,* 3035–3042.

Jacobson, J. L., Jacobson, S. W., Padgett, R. J., Brummitt, G. A., & Billings, R. L. (1992). Effects of prenatal PCB exposure on cognitive processing efficiency and sustained attention. *Developmental Psychology, 28,* 297–306.

Jacobson, S., Jacobson, J., Brunitt, G., & Jones, P. (1987, April). *Predictability of cognitive development in farm and non-farm children.* Paper presented at the biennial meeting of the Society for Research in Child Development, Baltimore, MD.

Johnson, D. L., Breckenridge, J. N., & McGowan, R. (1984). Home environment and early cognitive development in Mexican-American children. In A. Gottfried (Ed.), *Home environment and early cognitive development* (pp. 151-196). Orlando, FL: Academic Press.

Jordan, T. E. (1976, April). *Measurement of the environment for learning and its effect on educational and cognitive attainment.* Paper presented at the meeting of the American Educational Research Association, San Francisco, CA.

Jordan, T. E. (1979). *Old man river's children.* New York: Academic Press.

Kagan, J. (1984). *The nature of the child.* New York: Basic Books.

Kitayama, S. (2002). Culture and basic psychological processes—toward a systems view of culture. Comments on Osserman et al. (2002*). Psychological Bulletin, 128,* 89–96.,

Korosec-Serfaty, P. (1985). Experience and use of the dwelling. In I. Altman & C. Werner (Eds.), *Home environments* (pp. 65–86). New York: Plenum Press.

Kurtz. B. C., Borkowski, J. G., & Deshmukh, K. (1988). Metamemory and learning in Maharashtrian children: Influences from home and school. *Journal of Genetic Psychology, 149,* 363–376.

Le Greca, A. M., Silverman, W. K., Vernberg, E. M., Roberts, M. C. (Eds.) (2002), *Helping children cope with disasters and terrorism.* Washington, DC: American Psychological Association.

Lamb, M. E., Hwang, C., Bookstein, F. L., Broberg, A., Hult, G., & Frodi, M. (1988). Determinants of social competence in Swedish preschoolers. *Developmental Psychology, 24,* 58–70.

Lewis, M. (1997). *Altering fate.* New York: Guilford Press.

Longstreth, L., Davis, B., Carter, L., Flint, D., Owen, J., Rickert, M., & Taylor, E. (1981). Separation of home intellectual environment and maternal IQ as determinants of child IQ. *Developmental Psychology, 17,* 532–541.

Lozoff, B. (1989). Nutrition and behavior. *American Psychologist, 44,* 231–236.

Lozoff, B., Park, A. M., Radan, A. E., & Wolf, A. W. (1995). Using the HOME Inventory with infants in Costa Rica. *International Journal of Behavioral Development, 18,* 227–295.

Luster, T., Bates, L., Fitzgerald, H. Vandenbelt, M., & Peck, J. (2000). Factors related to successful outcomes among preschool children born to low-income adolescent mothers. *Journal of Marriage and the Family, 62,* 133–146.

Luster, T. E., & Rhoades, K. (1989). The relation of child-rearing beliefs and the home environment in a sample of adolescent mothers. *Family Relations, 38,* 317–322.

Maccoby, E. E. (1992). The role of parents in the socialization of children: An historical overview. *Developmental Psychology, 28,* 1006–1017.

Maccoby, E. E., & Martin, J. A. (1983). Socialization in the context of the family: Parent-child interaction. In P. H. Mussen (Series Ed.) & E. M. Hetherington (Vol. Ed.), *Handbook of child psychology: Vol. 4. Socialization, personality, and social development* (4th ed., pp. 1–102). New York: Wiley.

Marsiglio, W., Day, R., Braver, S., Evans, V. J., Lamb, M., & Peters, E. (1997, March). *Social fatherhood and paternal involvement: Conceptual, data, and policymaking issues.* Presented at the National Institute for Child Health & Human Development-sponsored Conference on Fathering and Male Fertility, Bethesda, MD.

Maslow A. (1954). *Motivation and personality.* New York: Harper.

McLoyd, V. C. (1990). The impact of economic hardship on Black families and children: Psychological distress, parenting, and socioeconomic development. *Child Development, 61,* 311–346.

McMichael, A. J., Baghurst, P. A., Wigg, N. R., Vinpani, G. V., Robertson, E. F., & Robert, R. J. (1988). Port Pirie Cohort Study: Environment exposure to lead and children's abilities at the age of four years. *New England Journal of Medicine, 319,* 468–475.

Mink, I. T., & Nihira, K. (1986). Family life-styles and child behaviors: A study of directions of effect. *Developmental Psychology, 22,* 610–616.

Mink, I. T., & Nihira, K. (1987). Direction of effects: Family life styles and behavior of TMR children. *American Journal of Mental Deficiency, 92,* 57–64.

Nickerson, R. S. (1992). On the intergenerational transfer of higher-order skills. In T. Stricht, B. McDonald, & M. Beeler (eds.), *The intergenerational transfer of cognitive skills* (vol. 2, pp. 159–171). Norwood, NJ: Ablex.

NICHD Early Child Care Research Network (2003). Familes matter-Even for children in child care. *Developmental & Behavioral Pediatrics, 24,* 58–62.

Nihira, K., Mink, I. T., & Meyers, C. E. (1981). Relationship between HOME environment and school adjustment of TMR children. *American Journal of Mental Deficiency, 86,* 8–15.

Nihira, K., Tomiyasu, Y., & Oshio, C. (1987). Homes of TMR children: Comparison between American and Japanese families. *American Journal of Mental Deficiency, 91,* 486–495.

Noll, R. B., Zucker, R. A., Curtis, W. J., & Fitzgerald, H. E. (1989, April). *Young male offspring of alcoholic fathers: Early developmental and cognitive findings.* Paper presented at the meeting of the Society for Research in Child Development, Kansas City, MO.

Ondaatje, M. (2000). *Anil's ghost.* London: Bloomsbury.

Palkovitz, R. (2002). Involved fathering and child development: Advancing our understanding of good fathering. In C. Tamis-LeMonda & N. Cabrera (Eds.), *Handbook of father involvement* (pp. 119–140). Mahwah, NJ: Erlbaum.

Palti, H., Otrakul, A., Belmaker, E., Tamir, D., & Tepper, D. (1984). Children's home environments: Comparison of a group exposed to stimulation intervention program with controls. *Early Child Development and Care, 13,* 193–212.

Pascoe, J. M., Loda, F. A., Jeffries, V., & Earp, J. (1981). The association between mothers' social support and provision of stimulation to their children. *Developmental and Behavioral Pediatrics, 2,* 15–19.

Patterson, G. R., DeBaryshe, B. D., & Ramsey, E. (1989). A developmental perspective on antisocial behavior. *American Psychologist, 44,* 329–335.

Pederson, D. R., Evans, B., Chance, G. W., Bento, S., & Fox, A. M. (1988). Predictors of one-year developmental status in low birthweight infants. *Developmental and Behavioral Pediatrics, 9,* 287–292.

Peterson, L., Ewigman, B., & Kivlahan, C. (1993). Judgments regarding appropriate child supervision on prevent injury: The role of environmental risk and child age. *Child Development, 64,* 934–950.

Peterson, L., & Gable, S. (1998). Holistic injury prevention. In J. R., Lutzker (Ed.), *Handbook of child abuse research and treatment* (pp. 291–318). New York: Plenum Press.

Pianta, R. C., & Walsh, D. J. (1966). *High-risk children in schools.* New York: Routledge.

Plomin, R., & Bergeman, C. (1991). The nature of nurture: Genetic influence on 'environmental' measures. *Behavior and Brain Sciences, 14,* 373–427.

Plomin, R., & Daniels, D. (1987). Why are children in the same family so different from one another? *Behavior and Brain Sciences, 10,* 1–16.

Plomin, R., Loehlin, J., & DeFries, J. (1985). Genetic and environmental components of 'environmental' influences. *Developmental Psychology, 21,* 391–402.

Pollitt, E. (1988). A critical review of three decades of research on the effect of chronic energy malnutrition on behavioral development. In B. Schureh & M. Scrimshaw (Eds.), *Chronic energy depletion: Consequences and related issues* (pp. 77–93). Luzanne, Switzerland: Nestle Foundation.

Popenoe, D. (1993). American family decline, 1960–1990: A review and appraisal. *Journal of Marriage and the Family, 55,* 527–555.

Ragozin, A. S., Landesman-Dwyer, S., & Streissguth, A. P. (1978). The relationship between mothers' drinking habits and children's home environments. In F. Seixas (Ed.), *Currents in alcoholism: IV. Psychological, social and epidemiological studies.* New York: Grune and Stratton.

Ragozin, A. S., Landesman-Dwyer, S., & Streissguth, A. P. (1980). *The relationship between mothers' drinking habits and children's home environments* (Rep. No. 77-10). Seattle: University of Washington, Alcoholism and Drug Abuse Institute.

Rapoport, A. (1985). Thinking about home environments: A conceptual framework. In I. Altman & C. M. Werner (Eds.), *Home environments* (pp. 255–286). New York: Plenum Press.

Reis, J. S., Barbera-Stein, L., & Bennett, S. (1986). Ecological determinants of parenting. *Family Relations, 35,* 547–554.

Reis, J. S., & Herz, E. J. (1987). Correlates of adolescent parenting. *Adolescence, 22,* 599–609.

Roberts, W. L. (1986). Nonlinear models of development: An example from the socialization of competence. *Child Development, 57,* 1166–1178.

Rotter, J., Chance, J., & Phares, E. (1972). *Applications of social learning theory of personality.* New York: Holt, Rinehart, and Winston.

Ryan, R. M., & Deci, E. L. (2000). Self-determination theory and the facilitation of intrinsic motivation, social development, and well-being. *American Psychologist, 55,* 68–78.

Saegert, S., & Winkel, G. H. (1990). Environmental psychology. *Annual Review of Psychology, 41,* 441–477.

Sahu, S., & Devi, B. (1982). *Role of home environment in psycholinguistic abilities and intelligence of advantaged and disadvantaged preschool children.* Unpublished master's thesis, Utkal University, Orissa, India.

Sameroff, A. J. (1983). Developmental systems: Context and evolution. In P. H. Mussen (Series Ed.), & W. Kessen (Vol. Ed.), *Vol. I. Handbook of child psychology: History, theories, and methods* (pp. 237–294). New York: Wiley.

Saxon, S., & Witriol, E. (1976). Down's Syndrome and intellectual development. *Pediatric Psychology, l,* 45–47.

Scales, P. C., & Leffert, N. (1999). *Developmental assets.* Minneapolis, MN: Search Institute.

Scarr, S., & McCartney, K. (1983). How people make their own environments: A theory of genotype -> environment effects. *Child Development, 54,* 424–435.

Schilmoeller, G. L., & Baranowski, M. D. (1985). The effects of knowledge of child development and social-emotional maturity on adolescent attitudes toward parenting. *Adolescence, 20,* 805–822.

Shonkoff, J. P. & Phillips, D. A. (2002). *From neurons to neighborhoods.* Washington, DC: National Academy Press.

Scott-Jones, D. (1995). Parent-child interactions and school achievement. In. B. Ryan, G. Adams, T. Gullotta, R. Weissberg, & R. Hampton (Eds.), *The family-school connection* (pp. 75–107). Thousand Oaks, CA: Sage.

Siegel, L. S. (1982). Reproductive, perinatal, and environmental factors as predictors of the cognitive and language development of preterm and full term infants. *Child Development, 53,* 963–973.

Smith, R. E. (1979). *The subtle revolution.* Washington, DC: The Urban Institute.

Stevens, J. H., & Bakeman, R. (1985). A factors analytic study of the HOME scale for infants. *Developmental Psychology, 21*, 1196–1203.

Stevenson, M. B., & Lamb, M. E. (1979). Effects of infant sociability and the caretaking environment on infant cognitive performance. *Child Development, 50*, 340–344.

Stroufe, L. A., Egeland, B., & Kreutzer, T. (1990). The fate of early experience following developmental change: Longitudinal approaches to individual adaptation in childhood. *Child Development, 61*, 1363–1373.

Super, C. M., & Harkness, S. (1986). The developmental niche: A conceptualization at the interface of child and culture. *International Journal of Behavioral Development, 9*, 545–569.

Tanfer, K., & Mott, F. (1997, March). *The meaning of fatherhood for men.* Paper presented at the NICHD-sponsored Conference on Fathering and Male Fertility, Bethesda, MD.

Tedesco, L. (1981). *Early home experience, classroom social competence, and academic achievement.* Unpublished doctoral dissertation, State University of New York, Buffalo.

Tong, S. & McMichael, A. J. (1992). Maternal smoking and neuropsychological development in childhood: A review of the evidence. *Developmental Medicine and Child Neurology, 34*, 191–197.

Trivers, R. L. (1972). Parental investment and sexual selection. In B. Campbell (Eds.), *Sexual selection and the descent of man: 1871–1971* (pp. 136–179). Chicago: Aldine.

U.S. Department of Health and Human Services. (1991). *Health status of minorities and low-income groups* (3rd ed.). Washington, DC: U.S. Government Printing Office.

von Windeguth, B. J., & Urbano, R. C. (1989). Teenagers and the mothering experience. *Pediatric Nursing, 15*, 517–520.

Wachs, T. D. (2000). *Necessary but not sufficient.* Washington DC: American Psycholgical Association.

Wachs, T. D. (1992). *The nature of nurture.* Newbury Park, CA: Sage.

Wachs, T. D., Sigman, M., Bishry, Z., Moussa, W., Jerome, N., Neumann, C., Bwibo, N, & McDonald, M. A. (1992). Caregiver child interaction in two cultures in relation to nutritional intake. *International Journal of Behavioral Development, 15*, 1–18.

Wandersman. L. P., & Unger, D. G. (1983, April). *Interaction of infant difficulty and social support in adolescent mothers.* Paper presented at the biennial meeting of the Society for Research in Child Development, Detroit, MI.

Wapner, S. (1987). A holistic, developmental system-oriented environmental psychology: Some beginnings. In D. Stockols & I. Altman (Eds.), *Handbook of environmental psychology* (vol. 2, pp. 1433–1465). New York: Wiley.

Weiglas-Kuperus, N., Koot, H. M., Baerts, W., Fetter, W. P., & Sauer, P. J. (1993). Behavior problems of very low-birthweight children. *Developmental Medicine & Child Neurology, 35*, 406–416.

Weisner, T. S. (2002). Ecocultural understandings of children's developmental pathways. *Human Development, 45*, 275–281.

Whiteside-Mansell, L., Bradley, R. H., Owen, M. T., Randolph, S. M., & Cauce, A. M. (2003). Parenting and children's behavior at 36 months: Equivalence between African American and European American mother-child dyads. *Parenting: Science & Practice, 3*, 197–234.

Whiteside-Mansell, L., Pope, S., & Bradley, R. H. (1996). Patterns of parenting behavior in young mothers. *Family Relations, 45*, 273–281.

Wilson, R. S., & Matheny, A. P. (1983). Mental development: Family environment and genetic influences. *Intelligence, 7*, 195–215.

Wohlwill, J., & Heft, H. (1977). Environments fit for the developing child. In H. McGurk (Ed.), *Ecological factors in human development* (pp. 1–22). Amsterdam: North Holland.

Woodworth, S., Belsky, J., & Crnic, K. (1996). The determinants of fathering during the child's second and third years of life: A developmental analysis. *Journal of Marriage & Family, 58*, 679–692.

World Health Organization. (1980). *Noise. Environmental health criteria 12.* Geneva, Switzerland: Author.

Wulbert, M., Inglis, S., Kriegsmann, E., & Millis, B. (1975). Language delay and associated mother/child interactions. *Developmental Psychology, 2*, 61–70.

Yeung, W. J., Linver, M. R., & Brooks-Gunn, J. (2002). How money matters for young children's development: Parental investment and family processes. *Child Development, 73*, 1861–1879.

Zaff, J. F., Smith, D. C., Rogers, M. F., Leavitt, C. H., Halle, T. G., & Bornstein, M. H. (2003). Holistic well-being and the developing child. In M. H. Bornstein, L. Davidson, C. L. M. Keyes, & K. A. Moore (Eds.), *Well-being, positive development across the life course* (pp. 23–32). Mahwah, NJ: Erlbaum.

Poverty
Consequences for Children

Marika N. Ripke
Aletha C. Huston

INTRODUCTION

The United States faces a social problem of major proportions: child poverty. In 2002 approximately 12 million, or one in six children in the United States, lived in poverty (Bureau of the Census, 2003; U. S. Department of Health and Human Services, 2002). Compared to other industrialized nations, the United States has both a high percentage of children in poverty and a large disparity between incomes of the rich and poor. The poorest U.S. children are very poor indeed, and the richest are very affluent (Rainwater & Smeeding, 1996).

Child poverty is not new. In the 1960s, President Lyndon Johnson launched the War on Poverty, introducing Head Start, Medicaid, federal aid to education for low-income students, job training programs, and many other programs to address the barriers faced by low-income children and adults. By the end of the 1960s, the poverty rate for children was reduced from 27% to 14%, but it has fluctuated since that time, rising to 23% in 1993, then dropping to 16% in 2002 (Bureau of the Census, 2003). Although the 1995–2001 decrease was especially large for African American and Hispanic children, both groups continue to be disproportionately represented among the poor (Bureau of the Census, 2003).

Most analysts attribute these fluctuations to three major causes (Huston, 1991). First, economic conditions that affect wages and the availability of jobs influence the average incomes of families at the low end of the income distribution. During the 1980s and 1990s, increasing numbers of families with poverty-level incomes were "working poor"; that is, one or both parents worked but did not earn a "living wage" (Bernstein, 2003) in the jobs that were available to them. Nevertheless, their opportunities for earnings rose and fell with rates of unemployment and job availability.

Second, during the 1970s and 1980s, increasing numbers of children lived with single mothers, and poverty in single-mother families is much more prevalent than in two-parent families. African American and Hispanic families are more likely than Anglo families to be headed by single mothers; the social disadvantage suffered by these ethnic groups adds to their likelihood of being poor.

Third, public policies for families in poverty changed. From the 1970s on, welfare or cash assistance to poverty-level families was increasingly under attack and payments declined in value. This trend culminated in the 1996 welfare reform legislation (entitled the Personal Responsibility and Work Opportunity Reconciliation Act or PRWORA) that imposed work requirements and time limits on cash assistance. At the same time, the maximum payment under the Earned Income Tax Credit (EITC), a federal program providing cash benefits for low-income working adults, more than doubled from 1993 to 2000. The end result was an increase in support for low-income people who were employed, but a decrease in cash assistance for other low-income parents. As employment opportunities declined in the early 2000s, this combination led to increases in poverty for families of children.

POVERTY AND CHILD DEVELOPMENT

Children who grow up in low-income families begin life with several disadvantages, many of which continue through adulthood. Poor children are at risk for problems of health (e.g., low-birth weight, infant mortality, childhood death and injury, contagious diseases, and injuries), developmental delays in intellectual development, low levels of school achievement, and social-emotional and behavioral problems. By adolescence, these problems take the form of higher rates of juvenile crime, early pregnancy, and dropping out of school; in adulthood, individuals raised in poverty have lower average levels of intellectual functioning, educational attainment and income than do those from more affluent families (Chafel, 1993; Duncan & Brooks-Gunn, 1997a; Garbarino, 1992; Hill & Sandfort, 1995; Huston, 1991; Huston, McLoyd, & Garcia Coll, 1994; Luthar, 1999; McLoyd, 1997, 1998).

Poor children are more likely to experience problems with school readiness and academic performance, and are at least twice as likely to be kept back in school as children from higher income families (see Corcoran, 1995; Duncan & Brooks-Gunn, 1997a; Haveman & Wolfe, 1994; National Center for Children in Poverty, 1999). Material deficiencies related to poverty (e.g., malnutrition, inadequate health and child care, homelessness or unsafe housing conditions and neighborhoods, and insufficient schools) have detrimental effects on children's motivation and ability to learn, and can contribute to social and emotional difficulties, hamper learning, academic performance, and cognitive development (Korenman, Miller, & Sjaastad, 1995; Kotch & Shackelford, 1989). In adolescence, poverty or economic hardship predicts delinquency (Sampson & Laub, 1994) and depression and loneliness (Lempers, Clark-Lempers, & Simons, 1989).

Definitions of Poverty

Some conceptual muddiness stems from the complexity of "poverty" as a construct. For many purposes, poverty is defined simply by cash income. If a family receives less money in a year than the federal poverty threshold, they are officially defined as "poor" for most statistical analyses. The poverty threshold originally was calculated from the estimated cost of food multiplied by 3. It is adjusted for family size, but not for geographic region, despite the widely varying costs of living by city and state. Annual adjustments are made for changes in the Consumer Price Index.

There are several problems with the threshold. A family's income is defined by pretax rather than disposable income, and there are no adjustments for such nondiscretionary expenses as the costs of child care and transportation for employed parents. On the other hand, noncash benefits (e.g., food stamps) are not counted as income. In 1995, a National Academy of Sciences expert panel (Citro & Michael, 1995) recommended changing the definition of poverty to remedy these deficiencies, but virtually all available data are based on the flawed index. In recent reports, however, federal statistical agencies compare data based on revised poverty indices to that derived from the standard definition. The poverty threshold is an absolute dollar amount intended to index the minimum income needed for adequate living conditions, not a percentage of the median income or a percentile. Therefore, it is theoretically possible for everyone to be above the poverty threshold.

The income-to-needs ratio (the ratio of family income to the poverty threshold) provides a continuous index reflecting how far below or above the poverty threshold a family's income falls. A family with an income at the poverty threshold has an income-to-needs ratio of 1.0; at half the poverty threshold, the ratio is 0.5, and so forth. This ratio is a better and more complete predictor of many child outcomes than a dichotomy between poor or not poor because it takes into account the depth of poverty and variations in resources above the poverty threshold (e.g. Duncan, Brooks-Gunn, & Klebanov, 1994; Smith & Brooks-Gunn, 1994).

The effects of poverty depend on its depth and duration (Huston et al., 1994; McLoyd, 1998). Most definitions of poverty are based on current income, but longitudinal studies demonstrate that many people move in and out of poverty from year to year (Duncan, 1984). Families that experience "transitory poverty," lasting only a year or two, are demographically similar to the rest of the population (Duncan, 1991). Although income loss can cause considerable stress (e.g., Elder, 1974; McLoyd, 1998), such families usually do not live in conditions of serious material hardship for long periods of time.

Persistent poverty, lasting over several years, is another matter. Families experiencing persistent poverty have fewer savings and other assets to buffer the effects of low income than do those in transitory poverty (Duncan, 1991). Children experiencing persistent poverty are at elevated risk for negative health outcomes and deficits in cognitive and socio-emotional achievement (Korenman, Miller, & Sjaastad, 1995). A nationally representative study following children who were 4 years old in 1968 for 15 years revealed that one third of these children experienced poverty for at least 1 year, and another 5% experienced poverty during at least two thirds of their childhood (Duncan & Rodgers, 1998). Finally, annual income does not provide a perfect index of material goods (e.g., the amount of food, quality of housing, and supports for basic needs; Mayer & Jencks, 1989).

Economic Conditions and Welfare Policy

Economists and scholars concerned with welfare policy have been concerned primarily with how economic conditions and policies influence adults' work, income, and life choices and, secondarily, with how these aspects of parents' lives affect their children (e.g., Hauser & Sweeney, 1997; Haveman & Wolfe, 1994; see Foster 2003 for economists' approaches to child development). One question they often pose is, how important is family income per se, above and beyond the other factors associated with poverty (e.g., depression, education level)? To what extent are the correlates of poverty due to factors other than income (e.g., single mother families, low parent education)? Some argue that how children develop is based less on monetary resources and more on parenting practices and skills, role modeling, moral character, and other familial characteristics. Some believe the solution to poverty is to provide income to the poor rather than try to change their family structures, education levels, and so forth; others believe that addressing these nonmonetary issues (e.g., provide children with role models of working parents) are key.

This was one of the primary debates surrounding the passage of the 1996 PRWORA, which ended 61 years of federally guaranteed cash assistance to poor families (Aid to Families with Dependent Children or AFDC) and in its place created a time-limited program designed to increase employment (Temporary Assistance for Needy Families or TANF; see Greenberg et al., 2002 for provisions of this law). This law emphasizes rapid movement from welfare to work, and thereby greatly reduces opportunities for welfare recipients to engage in such human capital development activities as education and job training—activities that many argue are key to successfully reducing poverty. Proponents of the "work first" philosophy argued that getting parents into the workforce quickly would benefit families by providing important work experience for adults, positive role models for children, and (possibly) increased family income. Opponents worried that strong employment requirements coupled with few supports would exacerbate hardship for families already at-risk.

Although welfare reform was intended to affect parents' behavior, the majority of public assistance recipients are children (Children's Defense Fund, 2001). By age 10, over one-third of all U.S. children will have lived in a household receiving welfare. The rate is even higher for black, non-Hispanic children (Levine & Zimmerman, 2000).

During the same period that welfare reform took place, *work supports* for low-income families were increased. The largest cash program for the poor is the federal Earned Income Tax Credit or EITC, first established in 1975, which provides a refundable tax credit for earnings, but not for other income. During the 1990s, as a means of supporting for working poor families, the maximum federal benefit more than doubled and some states included similar credits on state income taxes as well. Medicaid eligibility was expanded to include all low-income children, not just those in the welfare system, and funds for child-care assistance to low-income families increased dramatically between 1991 and 2000 (Fuller, Kagan, Caspary, & Gauthier, 2002). Earnings supplements and other work supports can increase family income with public funds that reward employment and are relatively free of the stigma associated with "welfare."

Faced with new participation mandates, sanctions, and time limits, and with the incentive of the EITC and the context of a strong economy, significant numbers of welfare recipients entered the workforce during the first 5 years after PRWORA was passed. A dramatic 51% reduction in caseloads between 1994 and 2000 led many to describe welfare reform as an unmitigated "success." The percentage of children living in poverty declined by about 17% between 1996 and 1999 (Primus, Rawlings, Larin, & Porter, 1999), and the decline was particularly apparent for African American single mother families (Haskins & Primus, 2002). With the economic recession following 2000, however, the number of children in poverty increased from 11.7 million in 2001 to 12.1 million in 2002 (U.S. Census, 2003). More importantly, there has been an overall increase in the number of children living in poverty whose parents are working, including those meeting the work requirements set by welfare reform. The percentage of poor children living in working families increased from 34% in 1995 to 43% in 2000, before falling to 40% in 2001 (Wertheimer, 2001; Dalaker, 1999).

Although the changes brought about by the 1996 legislation were partly responsible for national caseload reductions and higher employment rates among former welfare recipients (Blank & Schmidt, 2002), it is not clear what these changes have meant for the daily lives of families and children. Examining time-series data pre-and post-welfare reform sheds light on how children are faring since the enactment of PRWORA. Some national indicators of child well-being have improved in the post-1996 years, and some have worsened. Although these changes cannot be attributed to welfare reform per se, these indicators are associated with economic security, and provide examples of trends in children's well being in the post-welfare reform era. For example, teen fertility rates have decreased and high school completion rates have increased (see Duncan & Chase-Lansdale, 2001); however, the percentages of low-birth weight babies and families headed by a single parent have increased post-welfare reform (Annie E. Casey Foundation, 2003).

HOW DOES POVERTY AFFECT CHILDREN?

Examining changes in policy and economic conditions in relation to children's well-being provides some information about the role of poverty in children's lives. For investigators interested primarily in understanding children's development, the primary goal is to understand and improve developmental outcomes for children (e.g., cognitive development, school achievement, social competence, and physical health). The theories that guide this work rest on the assumption that the physical and social environments of poverty are responsible for many of the developmental outcomes associated with it (see McLoyd, 1998). Many economists have a more focused goal: to understand how public policies can influence outcomes for children and families. That leads them to ask about the effects of changing conditions that are amenable to public policy (e.g., family income, medical care, and child care) as opposed to factors that are not easily shaped by public policy (e.g., parents' intellectual capabilities, mental health, and parenting practices).

How Important Is Income?

We already noted that "poverty" includes a complex set of individual, family, community, and cultural factors that are difficult to disentangle. Poor families are often headed by single mothers, so family structure may contribute to children's developmental patterns (e.g., McLanahan, 1997). Because African Americans, Hispanic Americans, and Native Americans are especially likely to be poor, some of the effects of poverty may be a result of racial discrimination and disadvantage (see Duncan & Rodgers,

1998). Many parents in poor families lack education and perform poorly on tests of intellectual ability. They are likely to be unemployed or to work in unstable jobs with irregular hours that pay low wages and lack benefits. Some groups of poor families live in violent or disorganized neighborhoods and in physical conditions that pose risks of environmental toxins and injury. Poor parents experience more life stress, depression, mental health problems, and lack of social support than do affluent parents (Duncan, 1984; Duncan & Brooks-Gunn, 1997a; Duncan & Chase-Lansdale, 2001; Edin & Lein, 1997; Mayer, 1997a; McLoyd, 1998; Scarbrough, 1993). All of these family characteristics could contribute to low educational attainment, health problems, and behavior problems for children. How much does income per se contribute to the outcomes associated with poverty, independent of these other conditions? Are the developmental risks of poverty a result of income per se, or are they are result of other factors that are associated with poverty? By implication, could policies that increase family income produce improvements in children's well-being?

Longitudinal Studies

The most frequently used method for determining "effects" of poverty or family income is multivariate analyses of surveys and longitudinal databases, controlling statistically for a large of number of variables. The National Longitudinal Survey of Youth (NLSY), the Infant Health and Development Project (IHDP), and the Panel Study of Income Dynamics (PSID) have been analyzed in several studies investigating family income "effects." In an edited book, Duncan and Brooks-Gunn (1997a) assembled 13 longitudinal investigations of individuals ranging from early childhood through late adulthood in which family incomes during childhood and developmental outcomes were measured. The investigators conducted parallel analyses to determine the unique contribution of family income, with controls for related demographic and family structure variables. A summary of the findings indicated that family income during children's early years was related to cognitive and academic development in early and middle childhood and to adult earnings and work. Family income during adolescence was less likely to predict grades, educational attainment, or adult job characteristics. These authors then performed further analyses on the PSID data comparing the relations of family income at three points in development (age 0 to 5, 6 to 10, and 11 to 15) to the number of years of completed schooling in adulthood. Income during the child's first 5 years of life was the major predictor of completed schooling (Duncan & Brooks-Gunn, 1997b). In a more recent analysis of the NICHD Study of Early Child Care, poverty during the child's first 3 years and during ages 4 through 8 had cumulative effects, with children living in families with persistent poverty showing lower academic performance at third grade than did those who had experienced less enduring poverty (NICHD ECRN, in press).

Mayer (1997a) reached different conclusions using similar methods of analysis on many of the same datasets. She argued that the effects of income on developmental outcomes are modest at best when the many potential confounding variables are taken into account. By implication, raising the income of poor families would have negligible effects on cognitive skills, school achievement, or behavior problems. For example, according to her calculations, doubling the incomes of poor families would reduce the overall high school dropout rate in the United States from 17.3% to 16.1% and would reduce the overall teen childbearing rate from 20% to 18% (pp. 144–145). One reason, she suggested, is that government policies have ensured that many poor children receive such basic necessities as food, shelter, and health care. Because noncash government benefits (e.g., Medicaid, food stamps, child-care subsidies) are not counted as "income" in most investigations, the effects of these family resources are not reflected in studies of income. In another paper, Mayer (1997b) demonstrated that cash income was not synonymous with material hardship (lacking food, housing, or medical care). For several reasons, then, cash income is not a very good or complete index of the material resources available to a family.

A basic methodological conundrum exists in all of these studies. Although large numbers of related family variables are controlled in regressions, there is always the possibility that other unmeasured family characteristics could have contributed to the "effects" of income or poverty. The method of choice for determining causal direction is, of course, a random assignment experiment in which income is manipulated, but experimental designs to evaluate the effects of changing income are rare. Two sets of investigations meet this definition, the Income Maintenance Experiments of the 1960s and 1970s and the Next Generation experiments testing welfare and employment policies in the 1990s.

Income Maintenance Experiments

In the 1960s and 1970s, the federal government funded a set of experiments to evaluate the impact of a guaranteed minimum income on poor families with one or two parents in New Jersey; Gary, Indiana; Seattle; Denver; and rural areas in North Carolina and Iowa (Haveman, 1986). People were randomly assigned to receive a guaranteed minimum income or to a control group. The size of the guaranteed minimum and the tax rate associated with earnings was varied. There were methodological imperfections in these studies (Haveman, 1986; Rossi & Lyall, 1978), but they are of interest as we attempt to understand how poverty and income affect families and children.

The most serious drawback for our purposes is that these studies paid scant attention to measuring outcomes for children or parenting, and instead focused primarily on adult work effort and earnings, and marriage and divorce. Salkind and Haskins (1982) summarized available information concerning outcomes for children, and we have expanded their summary using a few other sources (Goenveld, Tuma, & Hannan, 1980; Institute for Research on Poverty, 1976; Kershaw & Fair, 1976; Mayer, 1997a; Office of Income Security, U.S. Department of Health and Human Services, 1983).

One consistent effect of the guaranteed income was increased expenditure on housing. Families in the experimental groups were more likely than controls to buy a house or to spend additional money on rent. They also purchased such durable goods as major appliances. One could reasonably argue that improvements in housing might improve the physical conditions in which children were living as well as offering them better schools and better neighborhoods. The studies contain almost no measures of parent–child relations or children's socio-emotional development; however no effects were found on the few superficial indexes that were reported.

The effects on children's school performance and attendance are somewhat mixed. For elementary-school-age children, there is some evidence of positive effects but, for high-school-age adolescents, there is little indication of a positive effect on achievement or aspirations. Nevertheless, in two studies, children in the experimental treatments were more likely to complete high school and they had higher levels of ultimate educational attainment than did those in control families. Adolescents in experimental families also were employed less than controls, perhaps because they were spending more time in educational pursuits (Salkind & Haskins, 1982). Other literature has indicated that extensive employment among high school students can interfere with optimal development (Steinberg & Dornbusch, 1991), so this finding may also indicate a "positive" outcome.

The Income Maintenance Experiments provided some support for the conclusions from longitudinal, correlational investigations. There is a modest positive effect of family income change on elementary school-age children's academic and school-related outcomes, but little evidence of positive effects on adolescents. Given the fact that the absolute increase in income in the experimental families was relatively small, this result is particularly notable. On the other hand, no social experiment has a "pure" manipulation; the experimental effects could have been influenced by participants' awareness that they were in a time-limited experimental program and, in some studies, by additional counseling services provided to some subgroups.

The Next Generation Project

In the 1980s and 1990s, the federal Department of Health and Human Services granted several states and localities permission to experiment with rules for receiving welfare, but they required these efforts to be carried out with high quality evaluations. As a result, a large number of random assignment experiments were carried out testing variations in requirements for employment, time limits, earnings supplements, and child-care assistance policies for low-income families, almost all of which were headed by single mothers. Again, economic outcomes for parents—employment, welfare receipt, and income—were emphasized, but approximately a dozen of these studies also collected information about children's development, parent psychological well being, and family process.

The Next Generation Project was designed to synthesize the results of these studies, comparing the different policies tested. Several themes emerged. First, policies that led parents to increase employment without some form of earnings supplement (e.g., keeping part of their welfare grant, or direct wage supplements) did not increase overall family income because their increased earnings were accompanied by loss of welfare dollars (Morris, Huston, Duncan, Crosby, & Bos, 2001).

Second, policies that included earnings supplements, which increased overall family income, led to better school achievement and social behavior for elementary-school age children. Policies that increased employment without earnings supplements had no clear positive or negative effects on children's school achievement or behavior (Morris et al., 2001; Zaslow, Moore, Brooks, Morris, Tout, Redd, & Emig, 2002). For children who were adolescents when their parents entered a program, however, there were some negative effects on school achievement and involvement, regardless of variations in policies (Gennetian, Duncan, Knox, Vargas, & Clark-Kauffman, 2002; Zaslow et al., 2002). One reason appeared to be that teenagers had increased responsibility for caring for their younger siblings when their mothers increased employment time; teens also received less supervision.

The New Hope Project

This random assignment demonstration experiment was designed to test the effectiveness of an employment-based antipoverty program for families living in two inner city areas in Milwaukee, Wisconsin who were economically poor. Participants in the New Hope experiment were recruited beginning in July of 1994 and ending in December of 1995. The Child and Family Study (CFS) sample included all of the 745 sample members who had one or more children between the ages of 13 months and 10 years 11 months at the time of random assignment. Up to two children in each CFS family were identified as "focal children" for the study. The majority of families were headed by a single female parent, and most of these women were unemployed and receiving public assistance.

For adults assigned to the experimental group who worked full time (i.e., a minimum of 30 hours per week), New Hope provided job search assistance, wage supplements that raised their family income above the poverty threshold, and subsidies for health insurance and child care. Community service jobs were available for people who could not find other employment. Applicants in a control group did not receive these benefits. New Hope led to somewhat higher family income for program group families.

Surveys were administered to parents and focal children 2 and 5 years after random assignment; at the 5-year follow-up, children were between the ages of 6 and 16. A mail survey was sent to teachers of children whose parent gave permission. Teacher-reported outcomes are based on the reports of the 547 teachers who responded to our request. In-person interviews with parents and children were conducted in the family's home. Parents provided information about their children's achievement and social behavior, and children were given several standardized tests and questionnaires.

Children's academic progress was assessed by both parents and teachers. Parents rated their children's overall level of achievement on a 5-point scale ranging from poor to excellent. Based on their knowledge of recent report cards, parents evaluated their child's performance in reading, mathematics, and written work on 5-point scales ($\alpha = .87$). Teachers rated children's academic performance using the Academic Subscale of the Social Skills Rating System (Gresham and Elliot, 1990).

Children's educational expectations were also assessed. Children (ages 9 and over) were asked to indicate how sure they were that they would finish high school, go to college, and finish college using 5-point scales (1 = not at all sure, 5 = very sure) (Cook, Church, Ajanaku, Shadish, Jeong-Ran, & Cohen, 1996).

Children's positive social behavior was assessed by both parents and teachers using the Positive Behavior Scale (Quint, Bos, & Polit, 1997). Its 25 items include items about compliance/self-control (for example, "thinks before he/she acts," "usually does what I tell him/her"), social competence and sensitivity (for example, "gets along well with other children," "shows concern for other people's feelings"), and autonomy (for example, "tries to do things for him/herself," "is self-reliant"). The parent or teacher responds on a 5-point scale concerning how often the child shows the behavior described ranging from "never" to "all of the time." Items for adolescents were adapted to be age-appropriate. The alpha was .91 for parents' ratings and .96 for teachers' ratings.

Children's problem behavior as assessed by parents and teachers using the Problem Behavior Scale from the Social Skills Rating System (Gresham & Elliot, 1990). The measure has two subscales. *Externalizing* problems include aggression and lack of behavior control (for example, "is aggressive toward people or objects," "has temper tantrums") ($\alpha = .81$ for parents and .92 for teachers). *Internalizing* problems include social withdrawal and excessive fearfulness (for example, "appears lonely," "acts sad or depressed") ($\alpha = .61$ for parents and .78 for teachers).

In surveys conducted 2 year and 5 years after random assignment, children in New Hope families were making better educational progress, had higher aspirations and motivation for school, and showed more positive social behavior than those in control group families (Huston et al., 2001; Huston et al., 2003). The reasons for these positive outcomes (i.e., the processes by which the New Hope program affected children's outcomes) are discussed later in this chapter. The New Hope study also collected ethnographic and qualitative information on some families. We are in the process of conducting yet another follow up interview with the children, families, and teachers approximately 8 years after random assignment.

Welfare Receipt

If income improves children's life chances, then the source of that income should not matter. Income from welfare should be as beneficial as income from parents' earnings. Many have argued, however, that welfare receipt in and of itself has negative effects on children because it results in a "welfare culture" that places families outside the mainstream values of work and self-sufficiency. The influence of welfare per se on children (as opposed to lack of resources) is difficult to tease apart because welfare families have very low incomes and few assets (see Huston, 2002). However, studies that have examined the differences in child well-being between children living in poor families that did and did not receive welfare (as well as comparing families that were and were not poor) found that for the most part, children's achievement differed by poverty level and not welfare (AFDC) receipt (Zill, Moore, Smith, Stief, & Coiro, 1996).

This conclusion is consistent with other research. For example, Levine and Zimmerman (2000) examined the relations between children's exposure to the welfare system prior to adolescence and several developmental outcomes using data from the NLSY. Children in households headed by mothers receiving welfare, and especially those who were on welfare for much of the child's life, scored lower on tests of cognitive development and had greater behavior problems than other children. However, three methodological strategies were employed to examine whether these negative associations between living in a welfare household and poor developmental and behavioral outcomes in children was attributable to welfare receipt *per se* or other characteristics of mothers (observed or unobserved). They found no causal links between welfare receipt in and of itself and children's development, and concluded that income from welfare receipt does not affect how much mothers invest in their children.

In a review of two nationally representative datasets from pre-welfare reform periods (early 1970s and early 1990s), Duncan and Chase-Lansdale (2001) found large differences between welfare families and middle-class families on time use, mental health, and expenditures, adjusting statistically for differences in demographics such as mothers' age and education level. Often the outcomes favored middle class families (e.g., lower levels of maternal depression, lower family tension, greater involvement in youth activities); on other measures however, there were no differences between the two groups (e.g., parental attitudes regarding monitoring, parent-teacher involvement). However, as Duncan and Chase-Lansdale (2001) point out, welfare reform is unlikely to raise low-income families into the middle class, and therefore it is more fruitful to make comparisons between low-income families receiving welfare and low-income families not receiving welfare. When these comparisons are made, for the most part, there are few differences between these two populations.

Some research suggests that welfare receipt in the early or middle childhood years may have more sustained and negative effects on children's academic outcomes than later in life. Welfare receipt in early childhood is related to lower high school graduation rates, higher grade failure rates, and lower literacy scores, even after controlling for school readiness (Baydar, Brooks-Gunn, & Furstenberg, 1993; Brooks-Gunn, Guo, & Furstenberg, 1993; Guo, Brooks-Gunn, & Harris, 1996). Welfare receipt in middle childhood years (roughly ages 5–12) has been associated with more negative outcomes in adolescent years (see Duncan, Dunifon, Doran, & Yeung, 1998).

Many studies have focused on how welfare receipt in early adolescence affects later schooling and demographic behavior, particularly in late adolescence and early adulthood. For example, after controlling for personal and family characteristics, Gottschalk (1992) found that childbearing by the age of 18 was 50% higher for Whites and 100% higher for Black and Hispanic adolescents whose parents received welfare than those whose parents did not receive welfare. There is some evidence suggesting that the duration of welfare receipt may matter. In one sample, children in families receiving welfare for less than 2 years had better scores on tests of school readiness than those families receiving AFDC for more than 2 years (Zaslow, McGroder, Cave, & Mariner, 1999). On the other hand, results from some studies suggest positive impacts of welfare receipt. For instance, children whose families receive welfare are more likely to have health insurance and better health (Wertheimer, 2001).

There are other reasons why welfare income might not confer the same benefits as earnings. For instance, after controlling for background characteristics (including parental schooling, race, household composition, marital status, income, and residential location), women from poor families who received welfare as children were more likely to be on welfare themselves as adults than those from poor families who did not receive welfare (Martin, 1999). One possible reason is that adolescents whose parents receive welfare are more likely to have a child themselves by the age of 18 (Gottschalk, 1992); these teens may require more of a safety net than those not having children before the age of eighteen. Another possible reason is that children living in welfare families may be less likely to perceive any stigma associated with welfare receipt than children living in poor families not receiving welfare, and, in turn, may be more likely to turn to welfare assistance themselves during times of financial difficulty.

Because the 1996 law resulted in many families leaving the welfare roles, those who remained were likely to have more barriers to employment and self-sufficiency than those who were able to meet the requirements for employment. We analyzed longitudinal data for low-income families from 1995 through 2000, showing that children and parents receiving welfare prior to the new welfare requirements did not differ substantially from those who had similar low incomes, but who did not receive welfare. By the year 2000, however, the small number of families who continued to receive welfare were disadvantaged in many ways; they had considerably more material hardship, and their children were performing poorly on academic skills (Huston, Mistry, Bos, Shim, Branca, Dowsett, & Cummings, 2003). It appears that these families had multiple sources of disadvantage, and that the low incomes provided by welfare were not sufficient to counteract the other problems faced by these families.

Conclusions From Longitudinal and Experimental Studies

Collectively, existing data provide evidence for the "correlated disadvantages hypothesis"; that is, that other factors lead to both welfare receipt and less than optimal outcomes for children, and thus it is probably not welfare receipt in and of itself that causes negative outcomes for children. These correlated disadvantages may distinguish the population of families receiving welfare in the post-PRWORA era more than they did in earlier years because families with fewer barriers have managed to leave the welfare roles.

The overall conclusion from both longitudinal and experimental studies is that family income (regardless of its source), plays an important role in children's cognitive, academic, and social development, especially during the early years. The magnitude of the effect, relative to other family variables associated with poverty, is difficult to determine. Reported income is only a partial index of the material resources available to a family or the material hardships experienced. Moreover, the effects of income are probably are not linear. The difference between incomes at 50% versus 100% of the poverty threshold is potentially more influential than the difference between incomes at 350% versus 400% of the poverty thresholds (e.g., Dearing, McCartney, & Taylor, 2001). Most of this research has not taken into account the fact that long-term persistent poverty has different consequences than transitory poverty or income loss. For example, children in persistent poverty have lower scores on cognitive and achievement tests than those in transitory poverty (Duncan et al., 1994). For many socio-emotional outcomes, including aggression and antisocial behavior, however, income loss and transitory poverty are at least as strongly implicated as is persistent poverty (e.g., McLeod, et al., 1994).

HOW ARE EFFECTS OF POVERTY MEDIATED?

Even if we agree that family income and material resources affect child development, there are many questions about the pathways and processes by which these effects take place. What experiences occur in children's worlds as a result of poverty or affluence? And, what are some of the important individual differences in the experience of poverty that lead to better or worse outcomes for children? Two theoretical models provide hypotheses about environmental influences associated with poverty—one based on resources and one positing on socialization processes (Huston, 2002). Both emphasize the environments of poverty as links between income and child development. In the following section, we ask whether family economic resources predict the socialization environments in which children develop. If so, to what extent do these socialization environments mediate the effects of economic resources on child outcomes? We examine three socialization contexts: family, child care, and out of school activities. We begin with what we know about the family environment.

Environments of Poverty

Family Resources

In the resource model, income provides material goods and opportunities as well as a range of non-material resources including parents' time, parents' ability to teach and provide guidance, parents' emotional support, quality schools, safe and supportive neighborhoods, and community resources. These are described as human, social, and cultural capital (Becker, 1981; Haveman & Wolfe, 1994; Johnson, 1996). Poor families have more difficulty than more affluent families in providing intellectually stimulating home environments (Zill, 1992; Zill, Moore, Smith, Stief, & Coiro, 1996). The most frequently used index of home environment is the Home Observation for Measurement of the Environment (HOME) Scale, which is based on both interview and observation of the mother and child at home. It includes ratings of maternal affection and discipline, learning opportunities, the physical quality of the home, and children's opportunities for exposure to different environments outside the home (Caldwell & Bradley, 1984). Low-income families have lower HOME scores than do more affluent families, even when parent education, family structure, ethnic group, and a number of other child and family characteristics are statistically controlled (Bradley, Corwyn, Burchinal, Pipes-McAdoo, & Garcia Coll, 2001; Brooks-Gunn, Klebanov, & Liaw, 1995; Duncan et al., 1994; Klebanov, Brooks-Gunn, & Duncan, 1994; Watson, Kirby, Kelleher, & Bradley, 1996). Perhaps more interesting is the finding that changes in income from birth to age 4 predict changes in the HOME score (Garrett, Ng'andu, & Ferron, 1994).

Existing evidence suggests that family resources, particularly cognitive stimulation, are important mediators of the effects of poverty on cognitive and academic development (Bradley, Corwyn,

Burchinal, Pipes-McAdoo, & Garcia Coll, 2001; Yeung, Linver, & Brooks-Gunn, 2002). In analyses of two samples, for example, HOME scores accounted for one third to one half of the relations of family income to IQ, vocabulary, reading, and math scores in middle childhood (Duncan et al., 1994; Smith et al., 1997). On the whole, family resources appear to mediate poverty effects on cognitive and academic performance more consistently than on social and emotional development. In a review of the literature, Bradley and Corwyn (2002) concluded that access to stimulating learning materials and opportunities for exploration mediate the relation of socio-economic status to both cognitive performance and behavior problems, but others have found that stimulating learning environments account for the relation of poverty to school achievement but not to behavior problems (e.g., Yeung et al., 2002).

Parents' Socialization Practices

The socialization model posits that family income influences parents' psychological well being, parenting practices, values, aspirations, and modeling as well as other socialization environments (Conger, Ge, Elder, Lorenz, & Simons, 1994; McLoyd, 1990, 1998). Poverty and economic hardship are conceptualized as sources of psychological distress for adults, that in turn, lead to unsupportive or harsh, punitive parenting. There is strong support for this hypothesis in studies of poverty and of family income loss. Parents living in poverty report more financial stress, depression, and psychological distress than do more affluent parents. They worry about providing for basic needs like food and housing, racial and ethnic discrimination, dangerous neighborhoods, unemployment, lack of support systems, and lack of status in the society (McLoyd, 1990, 1998). The psychological stresses generated by poverty or income loss can affect interactions with children. Low family income is associated with: (a) harsh discipline and punitiveness (Conger & Elder, 1994; Dodge, Pettit, & Bates, 1994; Hashima & Amoto, 1994; McLeod et al., 1994; McLoyd, Jayaratne, Ceballo, & Borquez, 1994; Sampson & Laub, 1994); (b) low levels of warmth and support (Dodge et al., 1994; Hashima & Amoto, 1994; McLeod et al., 1994; McLoyd & Wilson, 1991); (c) for older children, low levels of supervision and monitoring (Sampson & Laub, 1994); (d) marital or cocaregiver conflict (Brody et al., 1994; Conger & Elder, 1994); and (e) repeated child abuse (Kruttschnitt, McLeod, & Dornfeld, 1994).

The hypothesis that parental psychological distress, lack of warmth, and harsh and insensitive parenting mediate some of the effects of poverty on social behavior has extensive empirical support (Eamon, 1998; Huston, McLoyd, & Garcia Coll, 1997; McLoyd, 1998; Mistry, Vandewater, Huston, & McLoyd, 2002; Yeung et al., 2002; NICHD ECRN, in press). For example, the mother/child data set of the NLSY was used to test the effects of poverty on the math and reading achievement of 1,324 youth aged 12–14. In this study, poverty was indirectly related to lower math and reading achievement through the mediation of less emotionally supportive and cognitively stimulation home environments; which in turn, predicted adolescents' behavior problems in school (Eamon, 2002). Although socialization processes account for poverty effects on academic performance, they appear to be particularly important reasons for poverty effects on children's socio-emotional development. Socialization theory implies that individual differences in parents' responses to poverty affect the likelihood that children will experience psychological distress and behavior problems. Parents who have strong social networks and social support socialize their children with less harshness and more positive interactions than do people who lack social support, suggesting that social networks can buffer the stresses associated with poverty (Brody et al., 1994; Hashima & Amoto, 1994; Leadbeater & Bishop, 1994; McLoyd et al., 1994).

Although longitudinal and correlational studies support the hypothesis that parenting practices mediate the effects of poverty, the experimental studies of welfare and employment policies show consistently that participation in these programs does not affect parenting practices (Morris, Knox, & Gennetian, 2002). My colleagues and I have conducted one of these studies of the New Hope program (see Huston, Duncan, Granger, Bos, McLoyd, Mistry, Crosby, Gibson, Magnuson, Romich, & Ventura, 2001; Huston, Miller, Richburg-Hayes, Duncan, Eldred, Weisner, Lowe, McLoyd, Crosby, Ripke, & Redcross, 2003).

We measured parents' and children's reports of parenting processes and parent–child relations. The experimental program had little effect on parenting after 2 years, but after 5 years, program parents reported that they were more effective in managing their children's behavior. It appears that this change in parenting was a result of improvements in boys' social behavior rather than a direct change produced by the program (Epps, 2004).

Family Income and Early Child Care

The effects of poverty on children may be mediated not only by parents and the home environment, but by the early care and educational environments in which many children spend time. Most American children from all income levels spend significant amounts of time in nonmaternal care during their early years. A 1999 Survey by the National Survey of America's Families shows that 73% of children under age 5 with employed parents were in nonparental child-care arrangements, primarily center-based care and care by relatives (Sonenstein, Gates, Schmidt, Bolshun, 2002).

The work requirements set forth by the 1996 welfare law dramatically increased the number of children who require care while parents are working. Whereas the AFDC-based welfare system was originally intended to allow single mothers to remain at home to care for young children, the new TANF-based system is motivated by the goal of making single mothers economically self sufficient. As a result, low-income parents, especially those of very young children, are working more than ever before (Haskins & Primus, 2002). Under the 1996 law, parents with children under 1 year of age are exempt from the federal work requirements, and states may require parents of infants as young as 3 months to participate in employment activities. As a result of PWRORA, an estimated additional one million preschool-age children entered child-care settings (Fuller & Kagan, 2000). Children's experiences in child care may be one means by which the effects of poverty are exacerbated or ameliorated. These effects depend on the quality, type, and amount of care the child receives. We summarize here what we know about child care for low-income families, using data from studies in which Huston has participated as well as other research.

Income and Child-Care Quality

Child-care quality usually encompasses: (1) the child-provider relationship and child experiences (e.g., amount of verbal and cognitive stimulation, responsiveness, stability); (2) structural and caregiver characteristics (e.g., ratios, group size, caregiver education, physical environment/materials); and, (3) health and safety provisions (Lamb, 1997; Phillips, 1995). High quality care may serve as a protective factor for low-income children, and low quality care may compound other risk factors (Shonkoff & Phillips, 2000).

In the first 3 years of life, most child care occurs in home settings, either with relatives or family child-care providers. Data are now accumulating showing that the quality of these home settings is considerable lower for children from poverty-level families than for children of more affluent families. In a widely publicized Study of Family and Relative Care, infants and toddlers cared for by relatives (primarily grandmothers) and nonrelatives were observed. Children from low-income families received poorer quality care than those from more affluent families (Galinsky, Howes, Kontos, & Shinn, 1994).

The NICHD Study of Early Child Care is a longitudinal study in which Huston is an investigator following 1,364 children from birth through adolescence, and includes observations of whatever child-care settings parents selected for their children. Participants were recruited from hospitals located at 10 sites across the United States in 1991. Interviews with parents, evaluations of children, and observations of both parent-child interaction and children's child-care or school settings were conducted when children were 6, 15, 24, 36, and 54 months old and in first grade. Measures included maternal education (in years), child's race and ethnicity, maternal depressive symptoms, parenting quality scores derived from videotaped observations of mother-child interactions, and observed home environmental quality as measured by the Home Observation for Measurement of the Environment (HOME; Caldwell & Bradley, 1984).

Information about the number of hours, stability, and type of child care was collected from parents by telephone every 3 or 4 months. Children who were in nonmaternal care for more than 10 hours a week were observed in whatever child-care setting their parents used at each of the major assessment periods (6, 15, 24, 36, 54 months). Both structural features (e.g., adult-child ratio, group size, caregiver training) and processes were assessed during an observation covering several hours at each point of assessment. Quality was measured with the Observational Record of the Caregiving Environment (ORCE; NICHD Early Child Care Research Network, 1996, 2000), an instrument that included time-sampled records of the frequency of specific caregiver behaviors and observer ratings of the quality of caregiving on several scales. The ORCE was systematically adapted to be age-appropriate. At 6, 15, and 24 months, composite quality scores were calculated as the mean of five, 4-point rating scales (sensitivity to child's nondistress signals, stimulation of child's development, positive regard toward child, detachment [reflected], and flatness of affect [reflected]) (α ranged from .87 to .89). At 36 months, these five scales plus two additional subscales, "fosters child's exploration" and "intrusive" [reflected], were included in the composite ($\alpha = .83$). At 54 months, the overall quality of caregiving composite was the mean of 4-point ratings of caregivers' sensitivity/responsivity, stimulation of cognitive development, intrusiveness [reflected], and detachment [reflected] ($\alpha = .72$).

To ensure that observers at the ten sites were making comparable ratings, all observers were certified before beginning data collection and tested for observer drift every 3–4 months. Agreement with master-coded videotapes and with other examiners in live observations was evaluated using intra-class correlations (i.e., Pearson correlations and the repeated measures ANOVA formulation) (Winer, 1971). Reliability exceeded .80 at all ages.

In the first year of life, home settings for children from low-income families were much lower in observed quality than home settings for children from nonpoor families (NICHD, 1997). Moreover, the cumulative quality of all types of child care over the first 4.5 years of life was lower for children from chronically-poor families than from children in nonpoor families or those who experienced short-term poverty (NICHD ECRN, in press).

On average, child-care centers attended by low-income children are better quality than the home settings their families use (Loeb, Fuller, Kagan, & Carrol, 2004; Votruba-Drzal, Coley, & Chase-Lansdale, 2004), and are of more-or-less comparable quality to centers attended by children from more affluent families. Most studies have not found strong relations between family income and quality (Phillips, 1995). One reason may be that children from poor families receive slightly better care than those from lower- to middle-income families. In the National Child Care Staffing Study, which investigated a large sample of centers serving infants and preschoolers, centers serving children from moderate-income families provided poorer quality care than those serving children from families with very low incomes or high incomes. High-income families can purchase quality center care and can use child-care tax credits; families with very low incomes have more access to government subsidies for care than do those just above eligibility levels (Phillips, Voran, Kisker, Howes, & Whitebook, 1994; Hofferth, 1995).

Type of Care

Poor families disproportionately use informal, home-based arrangements (Brown-Lyons, Robertson, & Layzer, 2001; Hofferth, Brayfield, Ceich, Holcomb, 1991), and this appears to be the case for most families leaving welfare as well (Schumaker & Greenberg, 1999). Parents at all income levels choose different types of child-care arrangements based on a complex combination of their preferences and the constraints they face. For low-income parents, these constraints are often substantial.

Poor families are less likely than others to use paid care, but when they do pay for care they spend about 20% of their income on care, compared to about 6% for families who are not poor (Smith, 2002). As a result, child care often represents the second or third greatest expense for low-income working families (Isaacs, 2002). Recent studies indicate that a large proportion of families turn to informal, unlicensed child care when trying to fulfill new work requirements because it offers more flexible hours and is less expensive.

Although some low-income parents prefer home-based care, others would choose center-based care if given the economic resources to pay for it (Fuller et al., 2002). The Next Generation Study is an analysis of approximately 20 experimental tests of policies designed to promote employment for single parents with low incomes. Although all parents in the studies, including those in the control groups, had access to some types of subsidies for child care, some of the programs included additional child-care assistance (e.g., reducing bureaucratic barriers, convenient resource and referral, and higher eligibility thresholds). Almost all of the programs increased parental employment and, as a result, almost all increased use of nonparental child care. However, the type of care chosen depended on child-care assistance policies. Parents in programs that provided expanded child-care assistance were more likely to place their children in center-based care; those in programs with standard types of assistance were more likely to put their children in home-based arrangements (Crosby et al., 2004). The reasons appear to be relatively straightforward. In the expanded assistance programs, parents were more likely to use subsidies, and they paid less out of their own pockets for child care. They also reported fewer child-care problems that interfered with their ability to get and keep a job (Gennetian, Crosby, Huston, & Lowe, 2004).

Availability places additional constraints on the types of care families can use. Care for infants and school-age children is often more difficult to find than for preschool-age children. Market supply conditions vary greatly across states and communities. In general, the supply of child care tends be lower in low-income neighborhoods than in higher-income neighborhoods, and is particularly scarce during nonstandard hours and for children with special needs (U.S. GAO, 1997). Only 10% of centers and 6% of family child-care homes offer care on weekends (Phillips, 1995), and fewer offer care during nighttime hours. Low-income parents, especially those that have transitioned from welfare, are much more likely than other parents to work evenings, early mornings, weekends, and rotating or inconsistent shifts, making it difficult to put together reliable, stable child-care arrangements (Hofferth, 1995; Lowe & Weisner, 2003; Mishel & Bernstein, 1994).

Amount of Care

Children in poor families spend less time in nonmaternal care than do those in affluent families because, on average, their mothers work fewer hours. For example, in the NICHD SECC, infants in poor families spent an estimated 14 hours per week less in child care than did children in affluent families; these estimates are adjusted for maternal education, ethnic group, family structure, and sex of the child. With income held constant, children who were in care for the longest hours had mothers who worked many hours and who had relatively low levels of education, but whose incomes were slightly above poverty (NICHD ECRN, 1997). Over the first 4.5 years of life, children in chronically poor families spent approximately 6 hours per week less in child care than did children in families that were never poor, but the amount of child care increased over time for those in chronically poor families as well as those in families that left poverty after the child's first 3 years of life, again suggesting that maternal work was an important means of escaping poverty (NICHD ECRN, in press).

Effects of Child-Care Quality, Type, and Quantity on Children

The primary challenge in examining the causal relationships between child-care characteristics and child outcomes is the fact that child care is selected by parents, not randomly assigned. Families who choose different types of care differ in many ways, making it difficult to disentangle the effects of care on children. Despite methodological challenges, child-care research over the last two decades has provided a fairly consistent and convincing argument that child care matters for developmental outcomes (Lamb, 1997; Vandell & Wolfe, 2000).

One major purpose of the NICHD Study of Early Child Care and Youth Development (SECC) was to understand the relations of child care to children's health and cognitive and social development. Information about overall health, illnesses, and injuries was collected from parents at regular intervals. Children's development of cognitive and language skills was measured at 24, 36, and 54 months and in first, third, and fifth grades. At 24 months, the Mental Development Index from the Bayley II (Bayley, 1993) was used to assess overall developmental status. At 36 months, the Bracken Scale of Basic Concepts (Bracken, 1984) and the Reynell Developmental Language Scales (Reynell, 1991) were administered. From 54 months onward, cognitive, language, and academic performance was assessed with reading, math, and cognitive subtests from the Woodcock-Johnson Psycho-Educational Battery–Revised (Woodcock & Johnson, 1989, 1990) and the Preschool Language Scale (PLS-3; Zimmerman, Steiner, & Pond, 1992).

Mothers' and caregivers' or teachers' reports of the children's behavior problems were obtained using the Child Behavior Checklist (CBCL), administered almost annually from 24 months on. The CBCL contains two broad-band subscales: externalizing problems (acting out, aggression) and internalizing problems (fearfulness, anxiety). A complete list of measures at each age can be found at http://www.secc.rti.org.

Quality

High quality care predicts children's academic functioning, including language, reading, and math skills (Phillips & Adams, 2001; Vandell & Wolfe, 2000; see review by Isaacs, 2002). Several longitudinal studies, including the NICHD Study, demonstrate that this relationship persists even after controlling for demographic and parenting characteristics (NICHD ECRN, 2000; 2002). The effects of child-care quality on cognitive functioning and school achievement have been linked specifically to levels of engagement between children and caregivers (Shonkoff & Phillips, 2000). Quality of care may be especially important for children from low-income families. In analyses of the NICHD study (NICHD ECRN, 2001; McCartney, 2003), quality of care predicted language and cognitive development for children from low-income families, but was less important for children from middle and upper income families.

Although quality of care is also related to positive social behavior and lowered behavior problems, the effects on social behavior are less consistent than the effects on cognitive development (e.g., NICHD ECRN, 2003). Other investigations following children over periods of time have shown relations between quality and social-emotional outcomes. For example, Howes (1988; 1990) demonstrated that quality of early care predicted children's levels of play and social competence in the child-care setting and, a few years later, when they reached school age. In the Child Care Costs and Quality Study, 826 four-year-olds were observed in child-care centers in four states. The quality of the adult-child interactions predicted vocabulary, math competence, children's perceptions of their own competence, and teacher ratings of positive behavior and sociability at age 8 (Peisner-Feinberg & Burchinal, 1997; Peisner-Feinberg, Burchinal, Clifford, Culkin, Howes, Kagan, & Yazejian, 2001). In another investigation, the observed quality of care at age 4 predicted children's social and academic adjustment in school at age 8 (Vandell & Corasaniti, 1990).

Much of the information on child-care effects is correlational in nature, so one cannot infer that child care causes outcomes. Some studies have examined changes in children's performance over time as a means of controlling for family and child differences; that is, a child's performance at one time is compared to his/her earlier performance. Two large-scale studies of children from very low-income families show that observed quality of care is associated with cognitive gains (controlling for initial levels) over the preschool years (Loeb et al., 2004; Coley et al., 2004). A similar analysis of the NICHD SECC demonstrated small, but reliable effects of child-care quality (NICHD ECRN & Duncan, 2003).

When naturally occurring child care is studied, the "effects" can be estimated only for the environments that exist, not for environments that might be optimal but rare. If most existing child care is of low quality, then examining effects of quality on child outcomes will not tell us how much good quality *could* contribute to children's development. There are, however, true experimental tests showing the efficacy of educational child care for children from low-income families during the first few years of life (Barnett, 1995; McLoyd, 1997). For instance, children who received educational child care from infancy to school age in North Carolina performed better than controls on measures of school achievement as late as age 21 (Campbell, Ramey, Pungello, Sparling, & Miller-Johnson, 2002). In the Infant Health and Development Project, low birth weight children were randomly assigned to an intervention that included educational child care from age 1 to 3 or to an untreated control group. The intervention had positive effects on IQ, vocabulary, and incidence of behavior problems at age 3 and 5 (Smith & Brooks-Gunn, 1994). However, the size and endurance of these effects is not yet clear. One meta-analysis demonstrated that well-designed interventions with experimental and control groups had lasting effects on children's school performance; children who had received the interventions were less likely to be retained in a grade or placed in special education classes (Lazar & Darlington, 1982). On the other hand, the positive effects of Head Start may not last if children go on to attend poor quality schools (Currie & Thomas, 2000).

Type of Care

We already noted that children from low-income families generally receive somewhat higher quality care in centers than they do in home settings. Even with quality controlled, however, low-income children showed more gains in cognitive development when they were in center care than when they were in home care (Loeb et al., 2004). Similarly, for children from across the income range, children who received center-based care during the preschool years showed more gains in cognitive performance than did those who did not, even when child-care quality was controlled (NICHD ECRN & Duncan, 2003). In the Next Generation studies of low-income families who participated in experimental welfare and employment programs, we used the experimental impacts of the programs to demonstrate that center-based care, in conjunction with improved family income, during the preschool years led to small improvements in children's school achievement in the first few years of school (Gennetian et al., 2004).

The effects of center-based care on children's social behavior are more mixed. In the NICHD study and in some other studies, there is evidence that children with center-care experience, particularly in infancy, show more behavior problems at ages 4.5 and kindergarten (NICHD ECRN, 2003; in press). Among low-income children, however, one observational study found no positive or negative effects of center care on problem behavior (Loeb et al., 2004). Our experimental analyses in the Next Generation study indicated that, once selection factors are controlled, children with center care experience in preschool are rated by elementary school teachers as having *fewer* behavior problems than those with other types of prior experience. It seems likely that children can learn aggressive and assertive behaviors when they spend a large amount of time with peers; on the other hand, centers can vary considerably in the ways in which social behavior and social conflicts among children are handled.

Quantity of Care

There is evidence from the NICHD study that children in high amounts of child care from infancy onward have less sensitive interactions with their mothers and, by age 4.5, are seen by teachers as having more externalizing behavior problems than children with less overall child-care experience (NICHD ECRN, 2003). As noted earlier, however, children from low-income families spend less time in child care than do children in more affluent families, so quantity of care is not likely to account for poverty effects on intellectual and social development.

Summary

In summary, children from poor families receive less nonmaternal care, and the care they do receive is more likely to be informal and home-based care of relatively low quality than is the case for other children. When they receive center-based care, it is closer in quality to that received by higher income children. Public policies, including subsidies for child care and high-quality preschool educational programs, can enable low-income parents to provide supportive environments for their children. Both center care and quality care contribute to children's cognitive development and academic preparation. Quality care also promotes positive social behavior, but the effects of center care on social behavior are more mixed.

Out of School Time

During their many out-of-school hours, school-age children need supervised and structured settings for positive, healthy development. After-school programs and activities are important avenues of socialization contributing to the differences in experience associated with family income. How children spend their out-of-school time has important implications for development; leisure activities may provide opportunities for learning and developing competencies (Bronfenbrenner, 1979; Larson & Verma, 1998; Weisner, 1987). Overall, current evidence suggests that "structured activities" (e.g., hobbies, lessons, sports) are "development-enhancing" ways for children to spend their time. Werner (1993) reports that such activities can help children to deal constructively with stressful family circumstances, including poverty and its sequelae.

A large literature shows that children and youth who participate in such structured activities as sports, lessons, clubs and youth groups have higher academic performance and are more socially competent than those who do not participate (Mahoney, Larson, & Eccles, 2005). For older children, such organized activities as sports, lessons, youth groups, and community and recreation centers provide supervision, structure, learning and practicing skills, as well as instruction. Formal after school arrangements that provide cognitive stimulation and positive adult interactions has been associated with higher academic achievement among low-income children (Pierce, Hamm, & Vandell, 1999; Posner & Vandell, 1994; 1999).

Once again, however, the direction of cause and effect is difficult to determine. Does participation lead to better developmental outcomes, or do more competent children and youth choose to engage in activities? In two studies of low-income youth, the causal direction question was partly addressed by either examining change over time (to control for individual and family characteristics) or by comparing siblings (to control for family characteristics). In both studies, children who participated in a range of structured activities, particularly organized sports, had better academic and social competencies than did those who did not participate (Morris & Kalil, in press; Ripke & Huston, in press).

By contrast, low-income children in first and third grade who spent more time on their own (i.e., in self-care) received lower academic grades as sixth graders in comparison to children who spent less time in self care (Pettit, Laird, Bates, & Dodge, 1997). Among slightly older children, time spent in unstructured and unsupervised activities (e.g., hanging out with friends) provides children and youth with opportunities to engage in delinquent or risk taking behaviors, particularly if they live in low-income families and dangerous neighborhoods (Osgood, Wilson, Bachman, O'Malley, & Johnston, 1996; Osgood et al., 1996; Pettit, Bates, Dodge, & Meece, 1999; Posner & Vandell, 1999). Even for children who are not from poverty families, time spent hanging out and playing outdoors is associated with lower school grades and more conduct problems (McHale, Crouter, & Tucker, 2001).

Despite the potential advantages of engaging in activities, children in low-income families get less experience in them than do more affluent children. For example, U.S. Census data from the Survey of Income and Program Participation (SIPP) shows that only 3% of children ages 6–14 living in poor families participated in organized sports; 26% of children in more affluent families participated in sports (Smith, 2002). In studies of time use, children from economically disadvantaged families read less, are less involved in sports, and watch more television (Larson & Verma, 1998; McHale et al., 2001; Medrich, Roizen, Rubin, & Buckley, 1982; Posner & Vandell, 1999; Timmer Eccles, & O'Brien, 1985). Children from more affluent families are more likely to be enrolled in lessons, organized sports, or clubs than are children from low-income families (Hofferth et al., 1991). Low-income parents rely more on community centers and such national youth-serving organizations as the Boys and Girls Club and the YMCA as out-of-school arrangements (Halpern, 1999; Pettit et al., 1997). Higher-income parents also are more likely to avail themselves of school-based out-of-school programs or lessons for their children's out-of-school time (Halpern, 1999; Pettit et al., 1997).

The reasons for income differences in activities include both family and community resources. Many activities involve costs for uniforms, equipment, and transportation that may be barriers to a family with little money. Moreover, many low-income communities have fewer opportunities for team sports, lessons, and other activities. In addition, parents in low-income communities often keep their children at home because of concerns about danger and about exposure to deviant peers and adults. In our surveys of low-income parents, we asked whether they thought such activities were positive or negative influences on their children; parents' opinions ran the gamut from positive to negative (Huston et al., 2003).

Do Child Care Arrangements and Structured Out of School Activities Mediate Poverty Effects?

Children from low-income families are most likely to receive home-based and low-quality child care and less likely to participate in center-based care and structured out of school activities. These patterns point to working poor and near-poor families as those whose children may be most at risk for extended exposure to poor-quality care centers and less likely to be involved in structured activities that may lead to the enrichment and development of skills and competencies.

Correlational, longitudinal, and experimental research also identifies the quality of child care and participation in organized activities as important contributors to children's intellectual and academic development and probably to social-emotional competence as well. The next step in testing a mediational model is to determine whether features of child care and the types of out of school activities account for the relations of family poverty to children's outcomes. The evidence available is somewhat conflicting.

On the one hand, high quality early intervention programs can improve cognitive and academic performance for children from impoverished families, counteracting some of the disadvantage associated with poverty (Devaney, Ellwood, & Love, 1997; McLoyd, 1997). Studies of settings in the typical range of child-care quality have, however, produced mixed results. An analysis of three studies produced no evidence that child-care quality mattered more for poor than for nonpoor children (Burchinal, Peisner-Feinberg, Bryant, & Clifford, 2000), but in earlier analyses of the NICHD SECC, child-care quality had stronger effects on cognitive performance at age 3 for children from poor families than for those from higher income families (NICHD Early Child Care Research Network, 2001). However, child-care quality did not predict positive or problem behavior differently for low-income and higher-income children at age 3 (NICHD ECCRN, 2001).

Observational and experimental data suggest, however, that the type of child care received mediates some of the early effects of poverty. A large-scale observational study of children from low-income families shows that center care experience predicts improvement in preacademic and cognitive skills (Loeb et al., 2004). In the Next Generation project, we evaluated the effects of exposure to center-based care by examining the effects of the experimental impacts on parents' use of center care. These analyses are free of possible confounding family and child factors that might influence both the type of child care chosen and the child's behavior.

We noted previously that programs that provided additional child-care assistance, beyond that available to control group families, led parents to use more center-based child care and less home-based care with relatives or family child-care providers (Crosby et al. 2004). This was particularly true in New Hope (Huston et al. 2001; 2003). Center-based care, in turn, contributed to children's later school achievement and to lower levels of behavior problems as reported by teachers (Crosby, Dowsett, Gennetian, & Huston, 2004; Gennetian et al., 2004).

Similarly, the New Hope program had strong effects on access to formal child care, extended day care in schools, and structured out-of-school activities, all of which appear to be important paths by which the New Hope impacts on children occurred (Huston et al., 2001; Huston et al., 2003). If that is correct, there are clear public policy implications. Public policy can readily increase availability of child care, after-school activities, and other opportunities for supervised, structured activities for children, which may, in turn, significantly alter developmental trajectories for young boys and girls in low-income families.

CONCLUSION

We opened this chapter with questions regarding the processes by which family poverty influences children's development. To what extent does family income or its economic conditions make a unique contribution to children's development, above and beyond the many other conditions associated with poverty (e.g., parent education, family structure)? Does the source of income (i.e., employment vs. welfare receipt) matter for children's development? What proximal conditions and experiences in the home environment and in other socialization contexts mediate the relations between family economic status and children's developmental outcomes?

The weight of the evidence shows that income makes a significant contribution to intellectual development, school achievement, and socio-emotional development that is independent of related demographic and family structure influences (see Ripke & Crosby, 2002 for a more detailed review of this topic). Although much of the available literature is fundamentally correlational, we now have both random assignment experiments and studies using statistical techniques that simulate experimental tests showing that income affects children's academic and cognitive development above and beyond the effects of unmeasured third variables (e.g., parents' levels of motivation, personality attributes). Moreover, family income is only one indicator of material well-being; impacts on children's development probably depend on the level material hardship and families' noncash resources.

Although longitudinal and correlational studies have demonstrated that parenting practices mediate the effects of poverty, experimental studies of welfare and employment policies, including the New Hope study, consistently show little or no evidence that employment and income changes affect parenting practices. Instead, these experimental studies suggest that participation in programs such as New Hope affects the type and quality of child care and out of school activities children engage in, and that these are the pathways by which policies that increase income and offer child-care resources affect children's developmental outcomes.

Poverty predicts the amount, type, and quality of nonmaternal care that children receive, and the amount and types of out of school activities in which they participate. Children from low-income families are more likely to receive home-based and low-quality child care and less likely to participate in center-based care and structured out of school activities. These features of children's experience, in turn, contribute to cognitive and social development, and they appear to play a role in mediating the effects of poverty on intellectual and social development. Although the amount of research on child care and out of school time is smaller than the volume of work on family influences, the body of data available is subject to fewer methodological problems.

The effects of poverty on children depend upon the depth and duration of poverty, as well as the age of the child. Family income (including changes in income) during children's early years is related to cognitive and academic development in early and middle childhood, and adult earnings and work. Conversely, family income during adolescence is less likely to predict grades, educational attainment, or adult job characteristics.

Although longitudinal methods are invaluable in understanding the complexities of children's development in context, experimental designs have some unique virtues for elucidating these issues. The studies in the Next Generation synthesis are exceptions. They include the New Hope Project, which suggests that a package of benefits that make modest improvements in family material resources can have positive effects on children (Huston et al., 2001, 2003). A parallel experiment, the Canadian Self-Sufficiency Project (Morris & Michalopoulos, 2000), is a test of the effects of increased income using larger income supplements than those in New Hope. Single mothers on welfare can receive wage supplements of several thousand dollars if they leave welfare to work full time. Because Canada has universal health coverage, it is not necessary to provide health benefits, but no extra supplements were given for child care. This program also led to significant improvements in children's achievement (Morris & Michalopoulos, 2003).

In conclusion, it is not only important to understand the relations between poverty and children's development, but also the processes by which the conditions of poverty influence children for both theoretical and policy reasons. Events within the family and experiences outside the family are both important. Seeking to understand these processes will provide a more sophisticated basic science of development and will inform intelligent and effective policies.

REFERENCES

Barnett, W. S. (1995). Long-term effects of early childhood programs on cognitive and school outcomes. *The Future of Children, 5*, 25–50.

Baydar, N., Brooks-Gunn, J., & Furstenberg, F. F. (1993). Early warning signs of functional literacy: Predictors in childhood and adolescence. *Child Development, 64*(3), 815–829.

Bayley, N. (1993). *Bayley scales of infant development, second edition manual.* San Antonio, TX: The Psychological Corporation.

Becker, G. S. (1981). *A treatise on the family.* Cambridge: Harvard University Press.

Bernstein, J. (2003). Describing the Landscape of the Low-wage Labor Market and Thoughts on Policies to Close the Gap between Earnings and Needs. In A. C. Crouter, & A. Booth (Eds.), *Work-family challenges for low-income parents and their children.* New York: Erlbaum.

Blank, R. M., & Schmidt, L. (2002). Work, wages and welfare. In R. M. Blank & R. Haskins (Eds.), *The new world of welfare* (pp. 70–96). Washington, DC: Brookings Institution Press.

Bracken, B. A. (1984). *Examiner's manual: Bracken basic concept scale.* San Antonio, TX: The Psychological Corporation.

Bradley, R. H., & Corwyn, R. F. (2002). Socioeconomic status and child development. *Annual Review of Psychology, 53*, 371–399.

Bradley, R. H., Corwyn, R. F., Burchinal, M., Pipes-McAdoo, H. P., & Garcia Coll, C. (2001). The home environments of children in the United States Part I: Variations by age, ethnicity, and poverty status. *Child Development, 72*, 1844–1867.

Brooks-Gunn, J., Klebanov, P. K., & Liaw, F. (1995). The learning, physical, and emotional environment of the home in the context of poverty: The infant health and development program. *Children and Youth Services Review, 17*, 251–276.

Brody, G. H., Stoneman, Z., Flor, D., McCrary, C., Hastings, L., & Conyers, O. (1994). Financial resources, parent psychological functioning, parent co-caregiving, and early adolescent competence in rural two-parent African-American families. *Child Development, 65*, 590–605.

Bronfenbrenner, U. (1979). *The ecology of human development.* Cambridge: Harvard University Press.

Bronfenbrenner, U., McClelland, P., Wethington, E., Moen, P., & Ceci, S. J. (1996). *The state of Americans: This generation and next.* New York: Free Press.

Brooks-Gunn, J., Guo, G., & Furstenberg, F. (1993). Who drops out and who continues beyond high school? A twenty-year follow-up of black urban youth. *Journal of Research on Adolescence, 3*(3), 271–294.

Brooks-Gunn, J., Klebanov, P. K., & Liaw, F. (1995). The learning, physical, and emotional environment of the home in the context of poverty: The infant health and development program. *Children and Youth Services Review, 17*, 251–276.

Brown-Lyons, M., Robertson, A., & Layzer, J. (2001). *Kith and Kin—Informal Child Care: Highlights from Recent Research.* New York: National Center for Children in Poverty, Columbia University.

Bureau of the Census (2003, September). *Poverty in the United States, 2002. Current Population Reports, Series, 60–180.* Washington, DC. Report prepared by Bernadette D. Proctor and Joseph Dalaker.

Bureau of the Census. (1995, February). *Income, poverty, and valuation of noncash benefits: 1993 Current Population Reports, Series P60-188.* Washington, DC: Author.

Bureau of the Census. (1997). *Poverty in the United States, 1977. Current Population Reports, 860–201.* Washington, DC: Author.

Caldwell, B. M., & Bradley, R. H. (1984). *Home observation for measurement of the environment.* Little Rock: University of Arkansas at Little Rock.

Campbell, F. A., Ramey, C., Pungello, E. P., Sparling, J. J., & Miller-Johnson, S. (2002). Early childhood education: Young adult outcomes from the Abecedarian Project. *Applied Developmental Science, 6*, 42–57.

Chafel, J. A. (Ed.) (1993). *Child poverty and public policy.* Washington, DC: Urban Institute Press.

Chase-Lansdale, P. L. & Brooks-Gunn, J. (1995). *Escape from poverty: What makes a difference for children.* New York: Cambridge University Press.

Children's Defense Fund. (2001). *Issue basics: Children and welfare.* Retrieved from http://www.cdfactioncouncil.org.

Citro, C. F., & Michael, R. T. (1995). *Measuring poverty: A new approach*. Washington, DC: National Academy Press.

Conger, R. D., & Elder, G. H., Jr. (1994). *Families in troubled times: Adapting to change in rural America*. New York: Aldine de Gruyter.

Conger, R. D., Ge, X., Elder, G. H., Jr., Lorenz, F. O., & Simons, R. L. (1994). Economic stress, coercive family process, and developmental problems of adolescents. *Child Development, 65*, 541–561.

Cook, T., Church, M., Ajanaku, S., Shadish, W., Kim, J., & Cohen, R. (1996).

The development of occupational aspirations and expectations among inner city boys. *Child Development, 67*, 3369–3385.

Corcoran, M. (1995). Rags to rags: Poverty and mobility in the United States. *Annual Review of Sociology, 21*, 237–267.

Crosby, D. A., Huston, A. C., Dowsett, C., & Gennetian, L. A. (2004). *The effects of center based care on the problem behavior of low-income children with working mothers*. Austin, TX: Next Generation Project.

Currie, J., & Thomas, D. (2000). School quality and the longer-term effects of Head Start. *Journal of Human Resources, 35*, 755–774.

Dalaker, J. (1999). *Poverty in the United States: 1998. Current Population Reports*. Washington, DC: U.S. Government Printing Office.

Danziger, S., & Gottschalk, P. (Eds.). (1994). *Uneven tides: Rising inequality in America*. New York: Sage.

Dearing, E., McCartney, K., & Taylor, B. A. (2001). Change in family income-to-needs matter more for children with Less. *Child Development, 72*, 1779–1793.

Devaney, B. L., Ellwood, M. R., & Love, J. M. (1997). Programs that mitigate the effects of poverty on children. *The Future of Children, 7*(2), 88–112.

Dodge, K. A., Pettit, G. S., & Bates, J. E. (1994). Socialization mediators of the relation between socioeconomic status and child conduct problems. *Child Development, 65*, 649–665.

Duncan, G. J. (1984). *Years of poverty, years of plenty*. Ann Arbor: Institute for Social Research, University of Michigan.

Duncan, G. J. (1991). The economic environment of childhood. In A. C. Huston (Ed.), *Children in poverty: Child development and public policy* (pp. 23–50). New York: Cambridge University Press.

Duncan, G. J., & Brooks-Gunn, J. (1997b). Income effects across the life span: Integration and interpretation. In G. J. Duncan & J. Brooks-Gunn (Eds.), *Consequences of growing up poor* (pp. 596–610). New York: Sage

Duncan, G. J., & Brooks-Gunn, J. (Eds.). (1997a). *Consequences of growing up poor*. New York: Sage.

Duncan, G. J., Brooks-Gunn, J., & Klebanov, P. K. (1994). Economic deprivation and early-childhood development. *Child Development, 65*, 296–318.

Duncan, G. J., & Chase-Lansdale, L. (2001). Welfare reform and children's well-being. In R. Blank & R. Haskins (Eds.), *The new world of welfare*. Washington, DC: The Brookings Institution Press.

Duncan, G. J., Dunifon, R., Doran, M. W, & Yeung, W. J. (1998). How different Are welfare and working families? And do those differences matter for children's achievements? In G. Duncan & L. Chase-Lansdale, (Eds.), *For better and for worse: Welfare reform and the well-being of children and families*. New York: Russell Sage

Duncan, G. J., & Rodgers, W. (1998). Longitudinal aspects of childhood poverty. *Journal of Marriage and the Family, 50*(4), 1007–1022.

Eamon, M. K. (1998). A structural model of the effects of poverty on the socio-emotional development of children. PhD Dissertation, The University of Wisconsin-Madison.

Eamon, M. K. (2002). Effects of poverty on mathematics and reading achievement of young adolescents. *Journal of Early Adolescence, 22*(1), 49-74.

Edin, K., & Lein, L. (1997). *Making ends meet: How single mothers survive welfare and low-wage work*. New York: Sage.

Elder, G. H., Jr. (1974). *Children of the great depression: Social change in life experience*. Chicago: University of Chicago Press.

Epps, S. R. (2004). Testing the direction of effects between authoritative parenting and child social competence. Unpublished Masters Thesis, University of Texas, Austin TX.

Foster, E. M. (2003). How economists think about family resources and child development. *Child Development, 73*, 1904–1916.

Fuller, B., Kagan, S. L., Caspary, G., & Gauthier, C. (2002). Welfare reform and child care options for low-income families. *Future of Children, 12*, 97–119.

Galinsky, E., Howes, C., Kontos, S., & Shinn, M. (1994). *The study of children in family child care and relative care*. New York: Families and Work Institute.

Garbarino, J. (1992). The meaning of poverty in the world of children. *American Behavioral Scientist, 35*, 220–237.

Garrett, P., Ng'andu, N., & Ferron, J. (1994). Poverty experiences of young children and the quality of their home environments. *Child Development, 65*, 331–345.

Gennetian, L. A., Crosby, D. A., Dowsett, C., & Huston, A. C. (2004). *Center-based care and the achievement of low-income children: Instrumental variables evidence using data from experimental employment-based programs*. New York: Manpower Demonstration Research.

Gennetian, L. A., Crosby, D. A., Huston, A. C., & Lowe, T. (2002). *How child care assistance in welfare and employment programs can support the employment of low-income families*. New York: Manpower Demonstration Research Corporation.

Gennetian, L. A., Duncan, G., Knox, V., Vargas, W. G., & Clark-Kauffman, E. (2002). *How welfare and work policies for parents affect adolescents: A synthesis of research* New York: Manpower Demonstration Research Corporation.

Goenveld, L. P., Tuma, N. B., & Hannan, M. T. (1980). The effects of negative income tax programs on marital dissolution. *Journal of Human Resources, 15*, 654–674.

Gottschalk, P. (1991). The intergenerational transmission of welfare participants: Facts and possible causes. *Journal of Policy Analysis and Management, 11*, 254–272.

Greenberg, M. T., Levin-Epstein, J., Hutson, R. Q., Ooms, T. J., Schumacher, R., Turetsky, V., & Engstrom, D. M. (2002). The 1996 welfare law: Key elements and reauthorization issues affecting children. *Future of Children, 12*, 27–57.

Guo, G., Brooks-Gunn, J., & Harris, K. (1996). Parental labor-force attachment and grade retention among urban black children. *Sociology of Education, 69*, 217–236.

Halpern, R. (1999). After-school programs for low-income children: Promises and challenges. *Future of Children 9*(3), 91–95.

Hashima, P. Y., & Amoto, P. R. (1994). Poverty, social support, and parental behavior. *Child Development, 65*, 394–403.

Haskins, R., & Primus, W. (2002). Welfare reform and poverty. In Isabel Sawhill & others (Eds.), *Welfare reform and beyond: The future of the safety net*. Washington, D.C.: The Brookings Institution.

Hauser, R. M., & Sweeney, M. M. (1997). Does poverty in adolescence affect the life chances of high school graduates? In G. J. Duncan & J. Brooks-Gunn (Eds.), *Consequences of growing up poor* (pp. 541–595). New York: Sage.

Haveman, R. H. (1986). Review of social experimentation. *Journal of Human Resources, 21,* 586–603.

Haveman, R., & Wolfe, B. (1994). *Succeeding generations: On the effects of investments in children.* New York: Sage.

Haveman, R., Wolfe, B., & Spaulding, J. (1991). Childhood events and circumstances influencing high school completion. *Demography, 28,* 153–157.

Hill, M. S., & Sandfort, J. R. (1995). Effects of childhood poverty on productivity later in life: Implications for public policy. *Children and Youth Services Review, 17,* 91–126.

Hofferth, S. (1995). Caring for children at the poverty line. *Children and Youth Services Review, 17,* 61–90.

Hofferth, S. L., Brayfield, A., Ceich, S., & Holcomb, P. (1991). *National child care survey, 1990.* Washington, DC: Urban Institute Press.

Howes, C. (1988). Relations between early child care and schooling. *Developmental Psychology, 24,* 53–57.

Howes, C. (1990). Can the age of entry into child care and the quality of child care predict adjustment in kindergarten? *Developmental Psychology, 26,* 292–303.

Huston, A. C. (Ed.). (1991). *Children in poverty: Child development and public policy.* New York: Cambridge University Press.

Huston, A. C. (1999). Effects of poverty on children. In L. Balter & C. Tamis-LeMonda (Eds.), *Child psychology: A handbook of contemporary issues* (pp. 391–411). Philadelphia: Psychology Press.

Huston, A. C., McLoyd, V. C., & Garcia Coll, C. (Eds.). (1994). Children and poverty: Issues in contemporary research. *Child Development, 65,* 275–283.

Huston, A. C., McLoyd, V. C., & Garcia Coll, C. (1997). Poverty and behavior: The case for multiple methods and multiple levels of analysis. *Developmental Review, 17,* 376–393.

Huston, A. C., Mistry, R. S., Bos, J. M., Shim, M.-S., Branca, S., Dowsett, C., & Cummings, J. (2003). *Parental employment, family income dynamics, and child well-being: The relations of earnings, earnings supplements, and welfare receipt to children's behavior* Austin TX: Report Submitted to the U.S. Department of Health and Human Services, Office of the Assistant Secretary for Planning and Evaluation.

Huston, A.C., Duncan, G. J., Granger, R., Bos, J., McLoyd, V. C., Mistry, R., Crosby, D., Gibson, C., Magnuson, K., Romich, J., & Ventura, A. (2001). Work-based anti-poverty programs for parents can enhance the school performance and social behavior of children. *Child Development, 72,* 318–336.

Huston, A. C., Miller, C., Richburg-Hayes, L., Duncan, G. J., Eldred, C. A., Weisner, T. S., Lowe, E., McLoyd, V. C., Crosby, D. A., Ripke, M. N, & Redcross, C. (2003). *Five-year results of a program to reduce poverty and reform welfare.* New York: Manpower Demonstration Research Corporation.

Institute for Research on Poverty. (1976). *The rural income maintenance experiment.* Madison: University of Wisconsin, Institute for Research on Poverty.

Isaacs, J. (2002). Mothers' work and child care. In D. J. Besharov (Ed.), *Family well-being after welfare reform.* College Park: Maryland School of Public Affairs, Welfare Reform Academy.

Johnson, J. H., Jr. (1996). The real issues for reducing poverty in America. In M. R. Darby (Ed.), *Reducing poverty in*

America: Views and approaches (pp. 337–363). Thousand Oaks, CA: Sage.

Kershaw, D., & Fair, J. (1976). *The New Jersey income maintenance experiment* (Vol. 1). New York: Academic Press.

Klebanov, P. K., Brooks-Gunn, J., & Duncan, G. J. (1994). Does neighborhood and family poverty affect mothers' parenting, mental health, and social support? *Journal of Marriage and the Family, 56,* 441–455.

Korenman, S., Miller, J., & Sjaastad, J. (1995). Long term poverty and child development in the United States: Results from the NLSY. *Children and Youth Services Review,17,* 127–155.

Kotch, J., & Shackelford, J. (1989). *The nutritional status of low-income preschool children in the United States: A review of the literature.* Prepared for the Food Research and Action Center. Washington, DC.

Kruttschnitt, C., McLeod, J. D., & Dornfeld, M. (1994). The economic environment of child abuse. *Social Problems, 41,* 299–315.

Lamb, M. E. (1997). Nonparental child care: Context, quality, correlates, and consequences. In I. Sigel & K. A. Renninger (Eds.), *Child psychology in practice* (5th ed., pp. 73–134). New York: Wiley.

Larson, R. W., & Verma, S. (1998). How children and adolescents spend time across the world: Work, play, and developmental opportunities. *Psychological Bulletin, 125,* 701–736.

Lazar, I., & Darlington, R. (1982). Lasting effects of early education. *Monographs of the Society for Research in Child Development, 47*(Serial No. 195).

Leadbeater, B. J., & Bishop, S. J. (1994). Predictors of behavior problems in preschool children of inner-city Afro-American and Puerto Rican adolescent mothers. *Child Development, 65,* 638–648.

Lempers, J. D., Clark-Lempers, D., & Simons, R. L. (1989). Economic hardship, parenting, and distress in adolescence. *Child Development, 60,* 25–39.

Levine, P., & Zimmerman, D. (2000). *Children's welfare exposure and subsequent development.* Northwestern University and University of Chicago: Joint Center for Poverty Research, Working Paper 130.

Loeb, S., Fuller, B., Kagan, S. L., & Carrol, B. (in press). Child care in poor communities: Early learning effects of type, quality, and stability. *Child Development.*

Lowe, E. D., & Weisner, T. S. (2003). "You have to push it—who's gonna raise your kids?": Situating child care and child care subsidy use in the daily routines of lower income families. *Children and Youth Services Review, 25,* 225–261.

Luthar, S. S. (1999). *Poverty and children's adjustment.* Thousand Oaks, CA: Sage.

Mahoney, J. L., Larson, R. W., & Eccles, J. S. (Eds.). (2005). *Organized activities as contexts of development: Extracurricular activities, after-school and community programs.* Mahwah, NJ: Erlbaum.

Martin, M. (1999). *The intergenerational relationship of welfare participation.* Paper presented at the August 1999 annual meeting of the American Sociologist Association, Chicago, IL.

Mayer, S. E. (1997a). Trends in the economic well-being and life chances of America's children. In G. J. Duncan & J. Brooks-Gunn (Eds.), *Consequences of growing up poor* (pp. 49–69). New York: Sage

Mayer, S. E. (1997b). *What money can't buy: Family income and children's life chances.* Cambridge: Harvard University Press.

McCartney, K., Dearing, E., & Taylor, B. A. (2003, April).

Is High-Quality Child Care an Intervention for Children From Low-Income Families? Paper presented at the Biennial Meeting of the Society for Research in Child Development (SRCD), Tampa, FL.

McHale, S. M, Crouter, A. C., & Tucker, C. J. (2001). Free time activities in middle childhood Links with adjustment in early adolescence. *Child Development, 72,* 1764–1778.

McLanahan, S. (1997). Parent absence or poverty: Which matters more? In G. Duncan & J. Brooks-Gunn (Eds.), *Consequences of growing up poor,* New York: Russell Sage.

McLeod, J. D., & Shanahan, M. J. (1993). Poverty, parenting, and children's mental health. *American Sociological Review, 58,* 351–366.

McLeod, J. D., Kruttschnitt, C., & Dornfeld, M. (1994). Does parenting explain the effects of structural conditions on children's antisocial behavior? A comparison of Blacks and Whites. *Social Forces, 73,* 575–604.

McLoyd, V. C. (1990). The impact of economic hardship on Black families and children: Psychological distress, parenting, and socioemotional development. *Child Development, 61,* 311–346.

McLoyd, V. C. (1997). Children in poverty: Development, public policy, and practice. In W. Damon, I. E. Sigel, & K. A. Renninger (Eds.), *Handbook of child psychology: Vol. 4. Child psychology in practice* (5th ed., pp. 135–210). New York: Wiley.

McLoyd, V. C. (1998). Socioeconomic disadvantage and child development. *American Psychologist, 53,* 185–204.

McLoyd, V. C., & Wilson, L. (1991). The strain of living poor: Parenting, social support, and child mental health. In A. C. Huston (Ed.), *Children in poverty: Child development and public policy* (pp. 105–135). New York: Cambridge University Press.

McLoyd, V. C., Jayaratne, T. E., Ceballo, R., & Borquez, J. (1994). Unemployment and work interruption among African American single mothers: Effects on parenting and adolescent socioemotional functioning. *Child Development, 65,* 562–589.

Medrich, E. A., Roizen, J. A., Rubin, V., & Buckley, S. (1982). *The serious business of growing up: A study of children's lives outside school.* Berkeley: University of California Press.

Mishel, L., & Bernstein, J. (1994). *The state of working America, 1994–95.* Armonk, NY: Sharpe.

Morris, P. A., & Kalil, A. (in press). Out of school time use during middle childhood in a low-income sample: Do combinations of activities affect achievement and behavior? In A. C. Huston & M. N. Ripke's (Eds.), *Developmental contexts in middle childhood: Bridges to adolescence and adulthood.* New York: Cambridge University Press.

Morris, P. A., & Michalopoulos, C. (2003). Findings from the self-sufficiency project: Effects on children adolescents of a program that increased employment and income. *Journal of Applied Developmental Psychology, 24,* 201–240.

Morris, P. A., Huston, A. C., Duncan, G. J., Crosby, D., & Bos, J. M. (2001). *How welfare and work policies affect children: A synthesis of research.* New York: Manpower Demonstration Research Corporation.

Morris, P., Knox, V., & Gennetian, L. A. (2002). *Welfare Policies Matter for Children and Youth: Lessons for TANF Reauthorization.* New York: Manpower Demonstration Research Corporation.

National Center for Children in Poverty (1999). *Young children in poverty: A statistical update.* New York: Columbia School of Public Health, National Center for Children in Poverty.

NICHD Early Child Care Research Network & Duncan, G. J. (2003). Modeling the impacts of child care quality on children's preschool cognitive development. *Child Development, 74,* 1454–1475.

NICHD Early Child Care Research Network (1997). Poverty and patterns of child care. In G. J. Duncan & J. Brooks-Gunn (Eds.), *Consequences of growing up poor* (pp. 100–131). New York: Russell Sage.

NICHD Early Child Care Research Network (2000). The relation of child care to cognitive and language development. *Child Development, 71,* 960–980.

NICHD Early Child Care Research Network (2003). Does amount of time spent in child care predict socioemotional adjustment during the transition to kindergarten? *Child Development, 74,* 976–1005.

NICHD Early Child Care Research Network (in press). Duration and developmental timing of poverty and children's cognitive and social development from birth through third grade. *Child Development.*

Office of Income Security Policy, U.S. Department of Health and Human Services (1983). *Overview of the Seattle-Denver income maintenance experiment. Final report.* Washington, DC: U.S. Government Printing Office.

Osgood, D. W., Wilson, J. K., Bachman, J. G., O'Malley, P. M., & Johnston, L. D. (1996). Routine activities and individual deviant behavior. *American Sociological Review, 61,* 935–655.

Peisner-Feinberg, E. S., & Burchinal, M. R. (1997). Relations between preschool children, child care experiences, and concurrent development: The cost, quality, and outcomes study. *Merrill-Palmer Quarterly, 43,* 451–477.

Peisner-Feinberg, E. S., Burchinal, M. R., Clifford, R. M., Culkin, M. L., Howes, C., Kagan, S. L., et al. (2001). The relation of preschool child-care quality to children's cognitive and social developmental trajectories through second grade. *Child Development, 72,* 1534–1553.

Pettit, G. S., Bates, J. E., Dodge, K. A., & Meece, D. W. (1999). The impact of after-school peer contact on early adolescent externalizing problems is moderated by parental monitoring, perceived neighborhood safety, and prior adjustment. *Child Development, 70,* 768–778.

Phillips, D. A., (1995). *Child care for low-income families: Summary of two workshops.* Washington, DC: National Academy Press.

Phillips, D. A., Voran, M., Kisker, E., Howes, C., & Whitebook, M. (1994). Child care for children in poverty: Opportunity or inequity? *Child Development, 65,* 472–492.

Primus, W., Rawlings, L., Larin, K., & Porter, K. (1999). *The initial impacts of welfare reform on the incomes of single-mother families.* Washington, DC: Center on Budget and Policy Priorities.

Quint, J., Bos, J., & Polit, D. (1997). *New chance: Final report on a comprehensive program for mothers in poverty and their children.* New York: Manpower Demonstration Research Corporation.

Rainwater, L., & Smeeding, T. M. (1996, April). *Doing poorly: The real income of American children in a comparative perspective.* Paper presented at the Workshop on Welfare and Child Development, Board on Children, Youth, and Families, National Research Council and Institute of Medicine, Washington, DC.

Reynell, J. (1991). *Reynell developmental language scales* (U.S. edition). Los Angeles: Western Psychological Service.

Ripke, M., & Crosby, D. (2002). The impact of welfare reform on the educational outcomes of parents and children. *Review of Research in Education, Vol. 26,* 181–262.

Ripke, M., & Huston, A. C. (in press). Does structured activity participation promote positive psychosocial and academic outcomes for low-income children during middle childhood and adolescence? In A. C. Huston & M. N. Ripke's (Eds.), *Developmental contexts in middle childhood: Bridges to adolescence and adulthood*. Cambridge University Press.

Rossi, P. H., & Lyall, K. C. (1978). An overview evaluation of the NIT experiment. In T. D. Cook, M. L. Del Rosario, K. M. Hennigan, M. M. Mark, & W. M. K. Trochim (Eds.), *Evaluation studies review annual* (Vol. 3). Beverly Hills, CA: Sage.

Rowe, D. C., & Rodgers, J. L. (1997). Poverty and behavior: Are environmental measures nature and nurture? *Developmental Review, 17*, 358–375.

Salkind, N. J., & Haskins, R. (1982). Negative income tax: The impact on children from low-income families. *Journal of Family Issues, 3*, 165–180.

Sampson, R. J., & Laub, J. H. (1994). Urban poverty and the family context of delinquency: A new look at structure and process in a classic study. *Child Development, 65*, 523–540.

Scarbrough, W. H. (1993). Who are the poor? A demographic perspective. In J. Chafel (Ed.), *Child poverty and public policy* (pp. 55–90). Washington, DC: Urban Institute Press.

Schumaker, R., & Greenberg, M. (1999). *Child care after leaving welfare: Early evidence from state studies*. Washington, DC: Center for Law and Social Policy.

Shonkoff, J. P. & Phillips, D. A. (2000). *From neurons to neighborhoods: The science of early childhood development*. Washington D.C., National Academies Press.

Smith, J. R., & Brooks-Gunn, J. (1994). Developmental effects of natural transition in welfare receipt. Paper presented at research briefing, Board on Children and Families, December 5–6, Teachers College, Columbia University, New York.

Smith, J. R., Brooks-Gunn, J., & Klebanov, P. K. (1997). Consequences of living in poverty for young children's cognitive and verbal ability and early school achievement. In G. J. Duncan & J. Brooks-Gunn (Eds.), *Consequences of growing up poor* (pp. 132–189). New York: Sage.

Smith, K. (2002). Who's minding the kids? Child care arrangements: Spring 1997. *Current Population Reports, P70-86*. U.S. Census Bureau, Washington, DC.

Sonenstein, F. L., Fates, G. J., Schmidt, S., & Bolshun, N. *Primary Child Care Arrangements of Employed Parents: Findings from the 1999 National Survey of America's Families*. The Urban Institute, Paper No. 59.

Steinberg, L., & Dornbusch, S. M. (1991). Negative correlates of part-time employment during adolescence: Replication and elaboration. *Developmental Psychology, 27*, 304–313.

Timmer, S. G., Eccles, J., & O'Brien, K. (1985). How children use time. In F. T. Juster & F. P. Stafford (Eds.), *Time, goods, and well-being* (pp. 353–382). Lansing, MI: Survey Research Center Institute for Social Research, The University of Michigan.

U.S. Department of Health and Human Services (2000). Dynamics of Children's Movement Among the AFDC, Medicaid, and Foster Care Programs Prior to Welfare Reform: 1995–1996. Report prepared by Chapin Hall Center for Children at the University of Chicago; Center for Social Services Research, University of California, Berkeley; School of Social Work, University of North Carolina, Chapel Hill; and American Institutes for Research, Prime Contractor. Report prepared for the U.S. Department of Health and Human Services, Office of the Assistant Secretary for Planning and Evaluation.

U.S. Department of Health and Human Services. (2002). *Trends in the well-being of America's children and youth: 2002*. Washington, DC: U.S. Government Printing Office. Available at http://aspe.hhs.gov/hsp/02trends/html.

U.S. General Accounting Office (1997). *Welfare reform: Implications of increased work participation for child care*. GAO/HEHS-97-75. Washington, DC.

Vandell, D. L., & Corasaniti, M. A. (1990). Variations in early child care: Do they predict subsequent emotional, and cognitive differences? *Early Childhood Research Quarterly, 5*, 555–572.

Votruba-Drzal, E., Coley, R. L., & Chase-Lansdale, P. L. (2004). Child care and low-income children's development: Direct and moderated effects. *Child Development, 75*, 296–312.

Watson, J. E., Kirby, R. S., Kelleher, K. J., & Bradley, R. H. (1996). Effects of poverty on home environment: An analysis of three-year outcome data for low birth weight premature infants. *Journal of Pediatric Psychology, 21*, 419–431.

Werner, E. E. (1993). Risk, resilience, and recovery: Perspectives from the Kauai Longitudinal Study. *Development and Psychopathology, 5*, 503–515.

Wertheimer, R. (2001). Working poor families with children: Leaving welfare doesn't necessarily mean leaving poverty. Child Trends Research Brief. Retrieved from http://www.childtrends.org/Files/May_2001.pdf.

Winer, B. J. (1971). *Statistical principles in experimental design*. New York: McGraw-Hill.

Woodcock R. W., & Johnson M. B. (1989). *Woodcock–Johnson Psycho-Educational Battery–Revised*. Allen, TX: Developmental Learning Materials.

Woodcock, R. W., & Johnson, M. B. (1990). *Woodcock-Johnson Psycho-Educational Battery, Revised*. Allen, TX: DLM Teaching Resources.

Zaslow, M. J., McGroder, S. M., Cave, G., & Mariner, C. L. (1999). Maternal employment and measures of children's health and development among families with some history of welfare receipt. In R. Hodson & T. L. Parcel (Eds.), *Research in the sociology of work: Vol. 7, Work and family* (pp. 233–259). Stamford CT: JAI Press.

Zaslow, M. J., Moore, K. A., Brooks, J. L., Morris, P. A., Tout, K., Redd, Z. A., et al. (2002). Experimental studies of welfare reform and children. *Future of Children, 12*, 79–98.

Zill, N. (1992). *Trends in family life and children's school performance*. Washington, DC: Child Trends (ERIC Reproduction No. ED378257).

Zill, N., Moore, K. A., Smith, E. W., Stief, T., & Coiro, M. J. (1996). The life circumstances and development of children in welfare families: A profile based on national survey data. In P. L. Chase-Lansdale & J. Brooks-Gunn's (Eds.), *Escape from poverty: What makes a difference for children?* New York: Cambridge University Press.

Zimmerman, I., Steiner, V., & Pond, R. (1992). *Preschool language scale* (3rd ed.). San Antonio, TX: The Psychological Corporation.

22

The Impact of Community Violence on Preschool Development

L. Oriana Linares
Nicole A. Morin

INTRODUCTION

Exposure to community violence was first identified in the early 1990s as a problem of epidemic proportion in the United States affecting the lives of a substantial number of children and youth (USDHHS/PHS, 1992). Although serious violent crime against youth has decreased in major U.S. cities during the past decade (Brener, Simon, Krug, & Lowry, 1999), a substantial number of families with limited resources continue to live in inner city neighborhoods characterized by high levels of violence, crime, and drug activity (Hill & Jones, 1997). In particular, children from ethnic minority backgrounds, such as African American and Latino, are disproportionately represented in neighborhoods with high levels of poverty, substance use, and local crime. They are at a considerably higher risk of developmental harm related to their socially toxic environment than children from nonethnic minority backgrounds, particularly those of higher socio-economic status (SES; Randolph, Koblinsky, & Roberts, 1996). Due to this tremendous public health burden, it is crucial to understand the impact of community violence, early in development, on ethnic minority children of low SES background. Such knowledge is necessary to inform effective and ecologically sound prevention and treatment interventions for this vulnerable population.

In this chapter we describe results from our Boston Community Violence Project (BCVP) which targeted African American and Latino mothers and their preschool children residing in high-crime neighborhoods and examine the contribution of exposure to community violence, a relatively less known psychosocial risk factor, on the problematic internalizing and externalizing behavior of 3–5-year-old children. We report results of the Parenting Study, which uses the sample in the BCVP, to test a multidimensional psychosocial model of the impact of community violence with special attention to the role of parenting behavior as observed during a mother-child interaction compliance task. To end, we discuss findings of the effects of community violence on preschool development from a prevention-intervention perspective.

PREVALENCE AND PSYCHOLOGICAL CONSEQUENCES OF EXPOSURE TO COMMUNITY VIOLENCE

Based on the community violence studies of the early 1990s, between 44–82% of school-aged children and youth are exposed to community violence, depending on definitional criteria, methodology, and sample characteristics (Overstreet, 2000; Stein, Jaycox, Kataoka, Rhodes, & Vestal, 2003). According to the early studies, by the end of elementary school, almost all children residing in high crime inner-city areas of Washington and New Orleans had heard (98%) or witnessed (90%) moderate to severe levels of violent occurrences (Richters & Martinez, 1993; Osofsky, Wewers, Hann, & Fick, 1993). School-aged children exposed to community violence are at risk for an array of problematic behavior including: lower self-competence (Farver, Ghosh, & Garcia, 2000), high levels of distress (Martinez & Richters, 1993), depression (Durant, Getts, Cadenhead, Emans, & Woods, 1995), post-traumatic stress disorder (Fitzpatrick & Boldizar, 1993; Jaycox, Stein, Kataoka, Wong, Fink, Escudero, & Zaragoza, 2002), increased aggression (Gorman-Smith & Tolan, 1998), anxiety/depression (Cooley-Quille, Boyd, Frantz, & Walsh, 2001), and antisocial behavior (Miller, Wasserman, Neugebauer, Gorman-Smith, & Kamboukos, 1999). Exposure to acts of community violence is highly predictive of aggressive cognitions and behavior among younger (Grade 1–3) and older (Grade 4–5) children (Guerra, Huesmann, & Spindler, 2003). In addition, exposure to neighborhood and school danger contribute between 5-16% of the variance in the prediction of school attendance, behavior, and grades (Bowen & Bowen, 1999). Lynch and Cicchetti (1998; 2002) found that exposure to acts of community violence, via witnessing or direct victimization, was related to lowered self-esteem, higher levels of separation anxiety, and less secured feelings of relatedness with their caregivers. Researchers have also identified mediating and moderating influences in the linkage between exposure to community violence and child development involving child-, and family-level factors. For example, Colder and associates (Colder, Mott, Levy, & Flay, 2000), found that a child's positive beliefs about aggression mediated, in part, the relationship between perceived neighborhood danger and childhood aggression. Using a structural modeling methodology, in a study of 732 predominantly African American fifth graders, Colder found direct and indirect effects in that perceived neighborhood danger was associated with positive beliefs about aggression, which in turn was associated with child aggression. There are also moderating familial influences of the impact of community violence on child behavior. For example, Miller and colleagues (Miller et al., 1999) found that family conflict moderated the effect of witnessed community violence on changes in antisocial behavior among 6–10-year-old boys. She found that in families with low levels of parent–child conflict, higher levels of witnessing community violence predicted increases in antisocial behavior over time. Family cohesion is another important moderator in the linkage between exposure to community violence and child outcome. Plybon & Kliewer (2001) showed that high levels of family support ameliorated the effects of living in a violent neighborhood, and resulted in fewer externalizing behavior problems among 8–12-year-old children. Taken together, these findings suggest that the consequences of exposure to community violence among school-aged children are far-reaching and involve an array of psychological, social, and academic problems, but can be mediated or attenuated by factors such as child positive social cognitions about violence, low level of family conflict, and high family support.

Shifting the Focus to the Preschool Years

In the preschool years, between the ages of 3–5, young children venture into the public spheres of their neighborhoods by becoming engaged in various social activities outside of their homes. Preschool children may attend a playgroup or a preschool program, play in public playgrounds, stay outdoors for longer periods of time, and visit community areas often accompanied by their mother or an older sibling. As compared to toddlers, increased mobility and higher levels of cognitive competence (Cicchetti, 1989) may afford young children a greater exposure to social events in the neighborhood, and a greater ability to explore the outside world. It is through this normative socialization process that preschool children develop a capacity to form and maintain cognitive "social maps," a concept described by Garbarino (1999) as "representations of the world" which emerge to give meaning to the social and interpersonal environment of the child, e.g., what or who is dangerous, who to turn to for protection, or who to trust in unsafe circumstances. The types of social constructions (e.g., whether maps are benign or hostile) are shaped by the child's immediate social experiences.

Consistent with their experiential world, preschool children who witness or experience routine acts of violence in chronically dangerous neighborhoods (Taylor, Zuckerman, Harik, & Groves, 1994; Farver, Natera, & Frosch, 1999) are likely to form distorted social maps, reflecting an unpredictable, unsafe, or dangerous world. Although there is no empirical research on the emergence of social maps during the preschool years, the concept is consistent with a social cognitive perspective for the emergence of aggressive behavior. According to social information processing (SIP) theory (Dodge, Pettit, Bates, & Valente, 1995), children who are exposed to aggressive models learn to anticipate a hostile world around them because they have developed 'social maps' consistent with their experiences. When trauma-exposed children encounter an interpersonal transgression (i.e., a child bumping into somebody else in the hallway; a child taking the chair of another child in the lunchroom), in which the intent of the perpetrator is unclear (intentional vs. unintentional harm), victimized children are more likely to retaliate because they read in others an intention to harm, as compared to their non-victimized counterparts. The findings from SIP theory are consistent with Garbarino's notion that victimized children are at risk of creating a hostile cognitive social map of interpersonal relation-ships based on their prior violence-related experiences; these hostile social maps lead to distorted attributions under conditions of uncertainty; which eventually result in child's aggressive behavior. Most recently Guerra and colleagues (Guerra, Huesmann, & Spindler, 2003), provided support for the mediational role of aggressive social cognitions, over time, on the relation between community violence and subsequent aggression.

Although exposure to community violence has been known to have serious psychological and behavioral consequences for school-age children (Garbarino, Dubrow, Kostelny, & Pardo, 1992), only recently has attention shifted downward to the preschool years (Lynch, 2003). This historical omission has jeopardized our understanding of the conditions under which trauma-related exposure may first appear; the processes by which exposure produces developmental harm in some preschool children but not in others; and how the presence of individual, family, and contextual factors mediate exposure on the developing child. The handful of existing studies focusing on preschool children suggest that community violence exposure rates are close in proportion to that of school-age children, dissipat-ing the notion that young children are protected from exposure due to their age. In one of the first studies with preschoolers, Taylor and colleagues (Taylor et al., 1994) interviewed 115 parents of 1- to 5-year-old children receiving pediatric care at Boston Medical Center. Mothers of these preschool children reported that 1 out of 10 children had witnessed, by the time they were 6 years old, a knifing or a shooting; 18% had witnessed shoving, kicking, or punching; and 47% had heard gunshots. In this study, however, the distinction between types of child exposure, i.e., community versus family violence, was not made so that above exposure rates may reflect exposure to one or both types.

In a more recent study of 64 preschoolers attending a Head Start program in California, Farver et al. (1999) reported that at least 50% of mothers reported hearing gunshots in their homes, and more than 60% reported witnessing drug deals, and arrests. In this study though, the children's exposure to community violence was not assessed. Additionally, in a small sample of 31 Latina mothers and their children (ages 4–5) attending a Head Start program in Los Angeles, Aisenberg (2001) reported that 26% of children were direct victims of violence and 45% witnessed violence, in their lifetime. Based on maternal reports of children's exposure to community violence, 71% heard gunshots near the home and 32% witnessed a beating. Finally, Shahinfar and colleagues (Shahinfar, Fox & Leavitt, 2000) studied 155 parents and their preschool children attending a Head Start program near Washington, DC. Using a cartoon-based self-report assessment of exposure to violence (VEX scale; Fox & Leavitt, 1995), they found that 78% of children and 67% of parents reported children's exposure (witnessing or experienc-ing) to at least one incident of violence during the summer when the evaluation took place. In this study, once again, there was no distinction between type of exposure, with rates reflecting exposure to either community or family violence. Furthermore, results may be questionable given that 53% of the children did not complete the self-report VEX scale due to test comprehension problems or an unwillingness to respond. The difficulty in obtaining self-reports from the preschoolers themselves underscores the challenge of gathering reliable exposure ratings at this developmental period.

EXPOSURE AND PRESCHOOL DEVELOPMENT

Mirroring the broad psychological consequences on the development of school-aged children exposed to acts of community violence, mothers of preschoolers report child distress-related problems in various functioning domains including internalizing behavior problems (i.e., anxiety and depression), externalizing behavior problems (i.e., aggression), and trauma-specific PTSD symptoms. In the Shahinfar et al., study (2000) of Head Start preschoolers exposed to interpersonal violence, CBCL internalizing (mean = 5.3 vs. 3.5) and externalizing (mean = 13.2 vs. 9.6) behavior symptoms were more likely in children who witnessed violence than in those who did not. These results are difficult to interpret, however, once again because of the lack of distinction between types of violence exposure (i.e., community violence and family violence). Finally, the Aisenberg study (2001) of a small sample of 31 Latina mothers and their children found that children exposed to acts of community violence obtained significantly higher T-scores for both CBCL internalizing ($m = 54$) and externalizing ($m = 55$) behavior problems, as compared with children in the normative sample ($m = 50$). Boys scored consistently higher than girls on both scales as well, suggesting male gender vulnerability for preschoolers following exposure to acts of community violence.

Preschool children are also at risk for developing symptoms related to Posttraumatic Stress Disorder (PTSD). According to the *Diagnostic and Statistical Manual of Mental Disorders, Fourth Edition* (DSM-IV, 1995), cardinal trauma-related PTSD symptoms include re-experiencing of the traumatic event, persistent avoidance of stimuli associated with the trauma, and symptoms of increased arousal (APA, 2000). In the *Boston Community Violence Project,* mothers of preschool children reported PTSD cardinal symptoms at a high frequency (Linares & Cloitre, 2004). For example, we found high rates of maternal endorsement of child PTSD symptoms for: re-experiencing (54%) new fears (82%), avoidance (53%), and hyper arousal (92%). Only re-experiencing symptoms during disregulated play, however, were related to exposure to community violence. Mothers with partial PTSD reported more re-experiencing symptoms as well as disregulated free play in their children than mothers with no PTSD ($p < .05$). These results supported the clinical use of observational methods using an alternative set of criteria for PTSD for preschool children as proposed by Scheeringa and colleagues (Scheeringa, Peebles, Cook, & Zeanah, 2001; Scheeringa, Zeanah, Myers, & Putnam, 2003). Our findings warned us against imposing a strict definition of PTSD based on DSM criteria developed for adults and older children to the diagnosis of preschool PTSD, without considering the unique developmental characteristics of this age period. For example, given that hyper arousal and transitional fears are very common during early childhood, caution is needed in interpreting symptom elevation in these domains as clinically important. Findings from our PTSD study underscore the need to attend to developmental level to differentiate clinically significant trauma-related PTSD symptoms from normative behaviors commonly seen during the preschool period.

The Boston Community Violence Project

Despite extensive research on the influence of multiple psychosocial risk factors on problem behavior (Forehand, Biggar, & Kotchick, 1998; Atzaba-Poria, Pike, & Deater-Deckard, 2004), community violence has been treated generally as an isolated risk variable, and seldom has been examined within a multidimensional, additive, fashion. It is likely that the preschooler's experience of community violence is not only determined by the levels and the characteristics of the exposure, and the child's understanding of the events, but also by contextual factors surrounding the child such as family relationships, maternal functioning, and parenting. The Boston Community Violence Project was designed to examine community violence within a larger psychosocial web of contextual influences. Little is known about whether exposure to community violence has a unique effect on child behavior problems, separately and beyond and above related risk factors. It is likely that multiple psychosocial stressors have an equal or higher detrimental impact on preschool internalizing and externalizing behavior problems among multiply disadvantaged preschoolers. The Boston Community Violence Project is a research project informed by ecological theory (Bronfenbrenner, 1979) that considers the child as a part of a larger ecological system of psychosocial influences (i.e., the mother-child system, the family, the neighborhood), and by an ecological-transactional perspective, which states that levels of the ecology interact on each other (Cicchetti & Lynch, 1993; 1995). In our multidimensional risk model of preschool problems we examined the influence of exposure to community violence after considering three sets of factors: demographic characteristics (maternal education, maternal immigrant status, and child age), exposure to family violence (partner violence to mother and to child), and maternal functioning (physical health, global distress, and the quality of parenting) In addition to focusing on the impact of exposure to community violence (e.g., frequency, type, and relationship to perpetrator) on preschool problems, by either witnessing or experiencing, we examined whether these effects were independent of other known risk factors affecting young children living in high crime neighborhoods, namely low maternal education, immigrant status, child older age, exposure to family violence, maternal distress, and quality of parenting.

Researchers who construct models of risk for child problems have stressed the need to attend to social class and ethnic background when studying minority children residing in the inner city (Gorman-Smith, Tolan, Zelli, & Huesmann, 1996). Lower maternal education, immigrant status, and older child age are selected because they may negatively impact on preschool outcomes. Lower maternal education increases the risk for child behavior problems among African American school children (Horn, Cheng, & Joseph, 2004). Immigration may be a source of stress for children and parents alike; older preschoolers are likely to have more behavior problems than younger preschoolers (even in a restricted range of ages 3–5). Earlier studies of community violence with school-aged children suggest that trauma-related symptoms vary by demographic and family characteristics. For example, Richters and Martinez (1993) found children of less educated mothers, living in unstable homes, experienced higher levels of distress than those of higher SES and more stable homes.

The Sample

Beginning in 1996, with funds from the National Institutes of Health (R01DA/MH11157), we began a series of maternal interviews with residents of selected inner city neighborhoods in Boston. We selected five urban contiguous residential zip codes with the highest crime police district rates (twice the citywide rate) for seven serious crimes (homicide, rape, robbery, simple assault, aggravated assault, burglary, and larceny) for the 5 years prior to the outset of the study (1991–1995) from which to draw a high-risk community sample of preschool children and their mothers. Residential zip codes corresponded to geographically contiguous census tracts with high concentration of ethnic minority residents, female-headed households, adolescent pregnancy, and school dropout rates, according to U.S. census data for 1990. The sampling strategy was aimed at over sampling dyads exposed to high levels of community violence; however, reported neighborhood crime varied widely due to the large geographic areas contained in zip codes demarcations (about 32,000 residents).

The original sample included 160 dyads and children were selected using a two step screening process described in detail elsewhere (Linares et al., 1999; Linares et al., 2001). Briefly, in level 1 screening, a consecutive sample of 689 children was identified from all current pediatric patients in a teaching city hospital who: (a) were between the ages of 3.0 and 5.11 years; and (b) resided in the preselected target neighborhoods. In level 2 screening, 89% of level 1 subjects were approached (via the telephone or an announced home visit) to determine willingness to participate and further assess study eligibility criteria. Due to the focus on the effects of community violence, stringent entry criteria were imposed to screen out mothers or children at high risk for adverse psychological outcomes due to other environmental or psychosocial stressors such as teenage parenting; children living in foster homes or shelters; residential instability; or medical disability. Level 2 screening resulted in a subject inclusion rate of 23%. Excluded mothers included those: (a) who were 18 years old or younger; (b) who resided in target address less than past 9/12 months; (c) who resided in shelters or other residential housing arrangement; (d) who were recipients of Social Supplement Income (SSI) due to a medical disability, such as a mental illness, mental retardation, or a chronic physical illness; and (e) who were not the child's primary caregiver. In addition, due to the linguistic limitations of the research team, mothers who did not speak English or Spanish were excluded. We excluded preschoolers with chronic medical problems, who were hospitalized for over two weeks in the last year, who had an identified developmental delay, genetic disability, prematurity (below 32 gestational weeks), serious birth complications, or who were SSI recipients. Refusal rate was 20%.

THE MULTIDIMENSIONAL ASSESSMENT OF EXPOSURE TO COMMUNITY VIOLENCE

We used a multidimensional perspective to the assessment of community violence involving exposure to particular (episodic) violent events by mother and her preschool child together (co-witnessing), as well as exposure to enduring (chronic) violence-related features that dyads routinely experience in their neighborhood. Our episodic co-witnessing measure, adapted from the work of Richters & Martinez (1993) refers to the frequency of the child co-witnessing events in the neighborhood, such as a police arrest, a serious violence-related accident, weapon possession, a threat of physical harm, physical assault, murder, or a dead body. We found that 81% of mothers and 42% of children witnessed at least one violent event in the past year; 21% of children saw three or more events, and 12% saw eight or more events. Events witnessed included a police arrest (31%), a serious accident (12%), a threat (11%), a beating (7%), or a gang chase (7%). Less than 5% of cases involved witnessing a weapon possession, a shooting, a mugging, a dead body, or a murder.

In addition to exposure to episodic co-witnessing of violent events in the neighborhood, we measured physical and structural aspects of the neighborhood that impact on the quality of life of residents. According to social disorganization theory (Shaw & McKay, 1972; Taylor, 1996; Perkins & Taylor, 1996), perceptions of social decay and disorder in the neighborhood (such as dilapidated or vacant housing, broken glass, or uncollected trash), although not violent criminal acts per se, erode the social fabric of neighborhood life. These negative characteristics decrease social order, increase fear of crime, and threaten the safety of local residents as much as violent crime events do (Taylor, 1996; Skogan, 1990; Bursik & Grasmick 1993; LaGrange, Ferraro, & Supancic, 1992, Perkins & Taylor, 1996). Maternal reports of perceived local crime, social disorder and decay, and fear of crime are a proxy of the level of fear and violence that families routinely experience in their neighborhoods. This measure, referred to as *chronic community violence* is used in the Parenting Study, the focus of this chapter. We found that the proportion of mothers who reported perceived local crime often or some of the time was 26%, ranging from hearing sounds of gunshots (39%) to witnessing a sexual assault (9%). The proportion of mothers who perceived social disorder as a big problem or somewhat of a problem was 47%, ranging from seeing broken glass or trash (70%) to seeing excessive use of police force (33%). The proportion of mothers who experienced fear of crime often or some of the time was 23%, ranging from feeling afraid for their child's safety (57%) to hiding away from others (9%).

The Contribution of Family Violence

There is also ample evidence that exposure to family violence (partner violence directed against the mother or the child) is associated with child internalizing behavior problems such as depression, posttraumatic stress symptomatology, and increased externalizing behavior problems, such as aggression and noncompliance (Fantuzzo, DePaola, Lambert, Martino, Anderson, & Sutton, 1991; Holden &

Ritchie, 1991; Osofsky et al., 1993; Jaffe, Wolfe, Wilson, & Zak, 1986; McCloskey, Figueredo, & Koss, 1995; Jouriles, Murphy, & O'Leary, 1989; Crockenberg & Covey, 1991). For example, in nonclinical samples, preschool children exposed to marital discord showed more externalizing behavior problems, including aggression and noncompliance (Crockenberg & Covey, 1991). A recent meta analysis examining 118 studies of children exposed to interparental violence indicate a low-to-moderate effect size ($d = -.29$) on child problems (Kitzmann, Gaylord, Holt, & Kenny, 2003), with greater exposure risk shown among preschoolers.

A critical methodological issue in the study of community violence is to distinguish types of violence exposure in multiply exposed dyads. Different types of victimization are often present in the same families (Margolin & Gordis, 2000). For example, 40% of mothers in our original sample reported lifetime exposure to family violence (i.e., intimate partner violence) in which the perpetrator in 80% of the cases was the partner or ex-partner (Linares, Groves, Greenberg, Bronfman, Augustyn, & Zuckerman, 1999), as measured by the Conflict Tactics Scale. In studies of community violence it is important to distinguish the effects of community violence from that of exposure to family violence because the psychological effects for children and mediating/moderating influences are similar across types of interpersonal violence. For example, family variables such as parental stress (Plybon & Kliewer, 2001) and parental attachment and monitoring (Formoso, Gonzales, & Aiken, 2000) moderate the relationship between family conflict and conduct problems. These same factors are important in community violence studies. Taking into account overlapping violence exposure, we considered exposure to family violence when examining the impact of exposure to community violence, so that we do not erroneously attribute to community violence effects that are related to family violence.

The Mediational Role of Maternal Functioning

As compared to school-age children, the maternal role may be more salient during the preschool years because of fewer competing socialization influences, e.g. teachers and peers; therefore we focused on the role of maternal functioning as a crucial mediator in the linkage between exposure to community violence and child problems (Linares, Heeren, Bronfman, Zuckerman, Augustyn, & Tronick, 2001). There is substantial evidence from the developmental and family relations literature that mothers' own histories of interpersonal victimization (e.g., community or intra-family violence) are associated with global, and stress-specific symptoms of psychological distress. For example, victimized women (mothers) suffer from poor physical health (Koss, Woodruff, & Koss, 1990), increased distress, and show a higher risk for PTSD symptoms, as compared with nonvictimized women (Breslau, Glenn, Davis, Andreski, & Peterson, 1991; North, Smith, & Spitz-Nagel, 1994; Zlotnick, Warshaw, Shea, & Keller, 1997). We examined the mediational role of maternal functioning as a psychosocial mechanism by which community violence might 'enter' the child's world during the preschool years (see Figure 22.1). Using a multivariate methodology (structural equation modeling), we showed that maternal distress mediated, to a large extent, the association between exposure to community violence and behavior problems. That is, for the preschool child, the mother's own psychological distress added a considerable extra risk to her own child's distress.

In a series of structural equation modeling model (see Figure 22.2), we show a nonsignificant direct effect of community violence on preschool problems (standardized path coefficient = .10 p NS) when maternal distress is entered into the model. In the final model, exposure to community violence (standardized path coefficient = .30 $p < .006$) and exposure to family violence (standardized path coefficient = .39 $p < .005$) impact directly on maternal distress, and in turn, maternal distress impact on preschool problems (standardized path coefficient =.66 $p < .001$).

The Contribution of Parenting

From epidemiological studies of children raised in war zones, there is evidence that maternal reports of responsive parenting moderate the effect of exposure to war events (Punamaki, Quota, & El Sarraj,

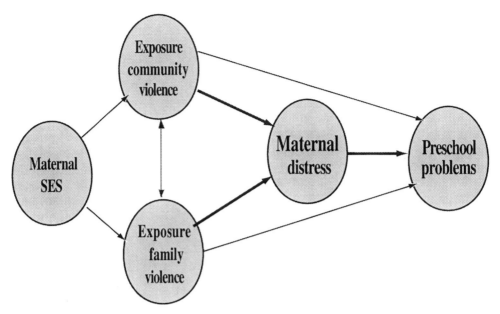

Figure 22.1 Proposed Community Violence Model.

1997). Although responsive parenting is thought to play a crucial role in the successful adaptation of children to conditions of chronic violence and dangerous neighborhoods (Garbarino, Kostelny, & Dubrow, 1991), to our knowledge, no prior study of exposure to community violence had examined, directly, the contribution of parenting behavior, i.e., mother-child interaction, on preschool problems. The parenting role is important to consider because there is substantial evidence that chronic

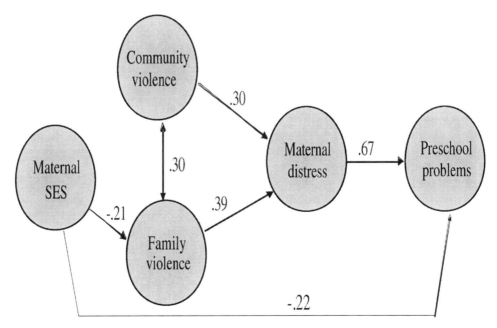

Figure 22.2 Final Community Violence Model. *Note:* Numbers represent standardized path coefficients. Depicted arrows represent significant associations using SEM methodology.

stressful life conditions are linked to adverse child outcomes by diminishing positive interactions and increasing parental coercive behavior (Patterson, 1983; Patterson, DeBaryshe, & Ramsey, 1989). Two orthogonal dimensions of parenting (positive and negative) are considered because these dimensions have been found to differentially predict child behavior. For example, harsh parenting predicted child aggression, but not social competence among dyads exposed to inner-city violence in New York City (Krenichyn, Saegert, & Evans, 2001). Based on normative parenting literature, we anticipated that positive parenting (i.e., noncontrolling, involved, warm mother-child interactions) contributes to fewer behavior problems, while negative parenting (i.e., controlling, uninvolved, angry mother-child interactions) contributes to more behavior problems. In regard to the association between exposure to community violence and parenting, we expected that mothers exposed to low levels of community violence would show more positive parenting and less negative parenting than mothers exposed to high levels of community violence.

THE PARENTING STUDY

In the Parenting Study we focused on the role of the quality of parenting as a potential contributor to child negative outcomes (internalizing and externalizing behavior problems).

Using the original sample of the Boston Community Violence Project, we analyzed, for the very first time, mother-child videotapes in the home available for 76% ($n = 121/160$ dyads) of the subjects. Videotapes were not available because of equipment problems, dyads speaking a different language than English or Spanish, or refusals. The subsample in the Parenting Study reflects the characteristics of the original sample: Families resided in a wide range of housing arrangements (such as publicly operated housing complexes, government subsidized housing apartments, or private homes), with about half residing in nongovernment subsidized homes. Subjects were predominantly from low socio-economic status and from ethnic minority background. Mothers were of African descent (71%) or Latino (22%). Sixty-three percent of the mothers who were born in the United States, while the remaining immigrated about 11 years ago from a myriad of 21 different countries reflecting the international composition of Boston residents. Mothers were in their early thirties. Close to half (42%) completed high school or a General Educational Development program (GED) while 26% had less than a high school diploma and 32% had post high school education. Mother's were employed outside of the home (52%) and some were attending school (20%); 45% received Aid to Families with Dependent Children; 40% were single head of households; and 69% were currently involved with a partner. Mothers had an average of 2.7 ($SD = 1.5$) children. The children were between 3 and 5 years of age ($M = 4.02$; $SD = .94$) and participated in a variety of day care arrangements; 48% were girls.

Assessment Procedures for the Parenting Study

For the Parenting Study, videotaped mother-child observations were gathered during the same visit in the home by one of a two-person research visiting team. The protocol was approved by the Institutional Review Board of the teaching hospital where the study took place, and was administered in either English or Spanish; it lasted about 2½ hours with a break in between. Male partner presence in the home was low (11%). The mother-child interaction videotapes, collected in the middle of the home visit, included four segments: a 10-minute segment of free play between child and mother, a 3-minute child separation episode, a 3-minute reunion episode, and a toy cleaning-up task lasting 5 minutes (or until the child finished). At the end of the 16-minutes of videotaping, while mother and child were together on the floor, the interviewer made the following request of the mother: "Please have (child's name) put the toys away in a basket." The observational mother-child interaction measure of the quality of parenting was based on this cleaning-up segment.

In addition to the observational measures, self-report measures included: (1) Exposure to chronic community violence, which included perceived local crime, social disorder, and fear of crime; (2) Exposure to family violence, which included partner violence against mother and against child; and

(3) Maternal functioning which included physical health, global distress symptoms, and positive and negative parenting. The preschool outcomes were internalizing and externalizing behavior problems. These measures are described in detail.

Exposure to Chronic Community Violence

Perceived Local Crime (8 questions). Using the Community Survey Questionnaire (CSQ; Earls, 1994), we asked mothers about the presence of certain events in the neighborhood in the past year; using a Likert scale (often, sometimes, rarely, never) such as fights with a weapon, sexual assault, robbery, burglary, and domestic violence. Across items, Perceived Local Crime was endorsed at least sometimes by one third to one half of the sample. Alpha was .85.

Social Disorder (10 questions). Using the CSQ, we assessed perceptions of local disorder, decay, drugs, anti-social activity, and business and police conflict using a Likert scale (a big problem, somewhat of a problem, not a problem). High endorsement was found for items such as drug dealings, noise, and police arrests. For example, among problems endorsed as "big" or "somewhat of a problem," mothers reported people selling or using drugs (70%), hearing police sirens (61%), or sounds of gun shots (39%). Alpha was .81.

Fear of Crime (13 questions). The Maternal Fear of Crime Scale (Linares, n.d.) was developed to assess the extent of interference related to neighborhood conditions such as mothers feeling afraid, avoiding dangerous places in the neighborhood, restricting their activities at night because of concerns about safety, or taking steps to protect their property in the past year. Mothers reported often or some of the time being afraid to let their children play outside during the day (57%), or taking longer routes for errands to avoid hot spots (30%). Alpha was .79.

A principal component analysis procedure yielded a single factor loaded positively on Perceived Local Crime ($r = .87$), Social Disorder ($r = .85$), and Fear of Crime ($r = .77$). Thus, scores in each of these measures were summed into a composite score, Chronic Community Violence, used in subsequent multivariate analyses.

Exposure to Family Violence

Partner Violence to Mother and Partner Violence to Child. The Conflict Tactics Scale-revised (CTS 2; Straus, Hamby, Boney-McCoy, & Sugarman, 1996) was used to provide an overall measure of physical violence (9 items) to mother and to child in the past thirty days. There were 21% mothers who endorsed acts of physical violence by their partners against themselves, while 5% of mothers endorsed acts of physical violence by their partners against their children. Alphas were .92 and .21 for partner violence to mother and to child, respectively.

Maternal Functioning

Physical Health. The Bodily Pain (2 items) and General Health (5 items) of the Medical Outcomes Study SF-36 (MOS SF-36; Ware, Snow, Kosinski, & Gandek, 1993) was used to assess current perceived interference due to pain and perceived general health. One item about bodily pain was rated on a 6-point scale ranging from "no pain" to "very severe pain", while the item about interference due to pain was rated on a 5-point scale ranging from "definitely true" to "definitely false." Alpha for Bodily Pain was .85 and for General Health was .58. A principal component analysis procedure indicated a single factor loaded positively on Bodily Pain ($r = .82$) and General Health ($r = .82$). Scores in each of these measures were converted to z-scores to adjust for the opposite direction in scale items; and were summed into a composite score, Physical Health, used in subsequent multivariate analyses.

Global Distress Symptoms

The SCL-90R Scale (Derogatis, 1994) was used to assess current (past 7 days) manifestations of psychological distress using a 5-point Likert scale ranging from "not at all" to "extremely". The 90-item scale yields a Global Severity Index (GSI). Alpha was .96. There were 26% of mothers who scored in the clinical range ($T > 60$) in the GSI.

Quality of Parenting

Behavioral ratings of maternal power assertion strategies, task involvement, and affective quality, were obtained from the videotapes of mother-child interaction during the toy cleaning-up task in the home. This compliance task was considered to be ecologically sound and was expected to create a moderate level of performance arousal on the part of the mother. Based on the work of Crockenberg (1987), we used an event sampling method to code interaction videotapes. Videotapes were coded by two trained coders who were blind to all interview data. Ratings of specific maternal behaviors were summed to create seven conceptually meaningful scales. Maternal scales included: power control (high, moderate, and low), task involvement (high and low), and affective quality (positive and negative). Description of the maternal scales is contained in Table 22.1. Alphas ranged from .40 to .79 across scales. Interrater agreement reached 80% on 26 randomly selected tapes. In order to create a robust behavioral measure of the quality of parenting, ratio scores of maternal power control, task involvement, and affective quality were reduced to 2 rotated factors using a principal component factor analysis procedure. The first factor (loadings of > .50), named *positive parenting,* loads on low power control, high task involvement, and positive affect. The second factor (loadings of > .50), named *negative parenting,* loads on high power control, low task involvement, and negative affect. Due to the lack of significant correlations between the negative parenting factor and child externalizing and internalizing behavior problems in the bivariate zero order analyses, the negative factor is not used in subsequent multivariate analyses. The positive parenting factor is included in subsequent multivariate analyses.

Preschool Outcomes

We examined internalizing and externalizing behavior problems separately because of prior literature suggesting that different pathways may be implicated in these types of problems (Lynch, 2003). There is evidence, for example, that levels of depression may be reduced significantly when children exposed

TABLE 22.1
Quality of Parenting During a Toy Compliance Task

Scale	Description
Power control	
Low	Frequency with which mother anticipates, encourages, bargains, or persuades to comply
Moderate	Frequency with which mother physically assists, gives directions, asks for information, or tells not to do
High	Frequency with which mother demands attention, criticizes, threatens, physically restricts, punishes, taunts, looms, or pokes at
Task involvement	
High	Frequency with which mother acknowledges, asks for attention, communicates, plays, assists with tasks
Low	Frequency with which mother ignores, moves away, or is lax
Affective quality	
Positive	Verbal or nonverbal expression of acceptance, pride, praise, or empathy
Negative	Verbal or nonverbal expression of annoyance, non empathy, sadness, anger, or tension

to violence receive maternal support (Fitzpatrick, 1993), while externalizing behavior problems may be predicted by family conflict (Fantuzzo, DePaola, Lambert, Martino, Anderson, & Sutton, 1991). To measure internalizing and externalizing behavior in the preschoolers, mothers of the 3-year-old children completed the 99-item Child Behavior Checklist for Ages 2–3 (CBC/2-3; Achenbach, Edelbrock, & Howell, 1987) while mothers for the 4-5 year olds completed the 118-item Child Behavior Checklist for Ages 4–18 years (CBCL; Achenbach, 1991). Both instruments are scored on a 3-point response scale. Internalizing and Externalizing behavior scales vary in the two versions: For the younger children, the Internalizing scale (Anxious/Depressed, Withdrawn) consists of 25 items (alpha = .83), while the Externalizing scale (Aggressive and Destructive Behavior) consists of 26 items (alpha = .89). For the older children, the Internalizing scale (Withdrawn, Somatic Complaints, Anxious/Depressed) and the Externalizing scale (Delinquent and Aggressive Behavior) consists both of 32 items (alphas .78 and .89, respectively). In this sample, child internalizing behavior scores were found elevated (T scores > 60) for 23% of the sample, while child externalizing behavior scores were found elevated for 31% of the sample, as compared with the national 10% prevalence rates in normative standardization samples.

Data Analytical Plan

First, means and SD by level of chronic community violence risk were obtained by dividing mothers (using a median split procedure) in low and high risk groups on the basis of their chronic community violence composite score to examine study predictors by level of reported chronic community violence exposure. Mean differences in preschool outcomes by level of chronic community violence risk were tested using ANCOVA methodology. Second, the bivariate correlation matrix was inspected to identify significant correlations. Only significant zero order correlations were used in subsequent multiple hierarchical regressions (MHR). The analytical plan for the MHR was as follows: Variables within the same domain were entered as a block. Less proximal (to the child) variables were entered before more proximal variables under the notion that distal variables exert presumably a lesser influence on the child's behavior than more proximal variables. In our multidimensional model, however, the exception to this analytical plan was the entering of exposure to chronic community violence last (not first) in the model. We entered chronic community violence last to provide a stringent test for its unique contribution beyond that of known factors tested in the model. In the MHR analyses, the blocks were entered according to the following steps: In Step 1 we entered the demographic block (Hollingshead maternal education category, immigrant status, and child age); in Step 2 we entered the family violence block (partner violence to mother and partner violence to child); in Step 3 we entered the maternal functioning block (physical health, global distress symptoms, and positive parenting); and in Step 4 we entered the exposure to chronic community violence composite measure.

Maternal Correlates of Community Violence Exposure

Mean Differences by Risk Levels

Means by levels of chronic community violence risk (using a median split) are presented in Table 22.2, adjusted for maternal level of education (Hollingshead education category = 1 lowest; 7 highest), and immigrant status (0 = U.S. born; 1 = foreign born). These covariates were used because they are associated with other independent variable in the study. Using maternal education and immigration status as covariates, ANCOVA analyses indicated that mothers in the high chronic community violence group reported higher partner violence to child, poorer health, higher distress, and more total internalizing and externalizing behavior problems, than those in the low chronic community violence group.

TABLE 22.2
Means by Level of Exposure Risk ($n = 121$)

Risk Factor	Low CCV	High CCV	p level
Family violence			
Partner violence to mother (CTS-R)	.95 (4.0)	3.0 (8.5)	NS
Partner violence to child (CTS-R)	.02 (.14)	.35 (1.1)	.04
Maternal functioning			
Physical health (SF-36)	.28 (1.7)	.09 (1.6)	.02
Positive parenting (factor)	63.7 (36.1)	68.6 (19.2)	.08
Preschool problems			
Total Internalizing	50.2 (10.0)	56.1 (9.3)	.001
Total Externalizing	52.0 (10.1)	57.2 (9.9)	.01

Chronic Community Violence and Psychosocial Factors

Correlational analyses (not shown here) indicated significant moderate to high correlations among chronic community violence, family violence, maternal functioning, and preschool problems. Less educated mothers reported higher child internalizing; and U.S. born mothers (as compared with foreign born) reported higher chronic community violence, global distress, internalizing and externalizing behavior problems. We found robust zero-order intercorrelations between preschool outcomes (internalizing and externalizing behaviors), control variables (partner violence to mother and child), and maternal functioning (health status, global distress, positive parenting). The correlations between internalizing and externalizing behaviors was $r = .62$. Significant zero order correlations were used in the subsequent multivariate analyses.

The Prediction of Preschool Problems

Predicting Internalizing Behavior

Blocks in the model predicted $R^2 = .43$ of the variance of internalizing (see Table 22.3). The demographic (Hollingshead maternal education, immigrant status, child age) and family violence (partner violence to mother and partner violence to child) blocks did not significantly contribute to internalizing behaviors. In contrast, the maternal functioning block contributed independently and substantially, $R^2 = .30$, to the variance of internalizing behavior problems. Within the maternal functioning block, global distress ($\beta = .60$) and positive parenting ($\beta = -.16$) yield significant standardized beta coefficients, in that mothers with higher global distress and lower positive parenting reported higher internalizing behavior problems. The exposure to chronic community violence block, entered as the last step, and after controlling for the demographic, family violence, and maternal functioning blocks contributed independently, albeit modestly, to the variance of internalizing behavior problems ($R^2 = .04$).

Predicting Externalizing Behavior

Blocks in the model predicted $R^2 = .34$ of the variance of child externalizing behavior problems (see Table 22.3). The demographic block (Hollingshead maternal education, immigrant status, child age) contributed $R^2 = .10$ to the variance of externalizing behavior. Within the demographic block, mothers with a lower educational level, born in the United States, and with older children, reported higher externalizing behavior problems. There was a tendency for the family violence block (partner violence to mother and partner violence to child) to impact on externalizing behavior ($p < .06$). The

TABLE 22.3
Hierarchical Multiple Regressions Predicting Child Problems

	CBC Internalizing			CBC Externalizing		
	Cum R^2	β	F change	Cum R^2	β	F change
Step and variable		(Step)			(Step)	
Step 1: Individual block	.04		1.85	.10		4.49*
Hollingshead Education		−.15			−.09	
Immigration status		−.12			−.27	
Child age		−.08			.09	
Step 2: Exposure to family						
violence block	.06		1.03	.15		2.97**
Partner violence to mother		−.09			.05	
Partner violence to child		.03			.20**	
Step 3:						
Maternal functioning block	.39		15.23***	.31		6.63***
Physical health		.10			.12*	
Global distress		.60***			.29**	
Positive parenting		−.16**			−.19**	
Step 4: Exposure to CCV block	.43	.20*	6.15**	.34	.19**	4.86**

*$p < .01$; **$p < .05$; ***$p < .001$

maternal functioning block contributed independently, $R^2 = .16$, to the variance of externalizing behavior problems, although to a lesser degree than to internalizing behavior problems. Within the maternal functioning block, physical health (β = .12), global distress (β = .29) and positive parenting (β = −.19) yield significant standardized beta coefficients, in that mothers with poorer physical health, higher global distress symptoms, and poorer parenting report higher externalizing behavior problems. Similar to the effects on internalizing behavior, entered as the last step and after controlling for the demographic, family violence, and maternal functioning blocks, the exposure to chronic community violence block contributed independently, albeit modestly, to the variance of externalizing behavior ($R^2 = .03$).

CONCLUSIONS

Findings of the Boston Community Violence Project highlight the importance of examining a broad picture of psychosocial factors when analyzing preschool problems. The influence of the combined sets of psychosocial variables identified in our model of community violence explained a substantial amount (43–34%) of the variance of preschool internalizing and externalizing behavior problems, respectively. The magnitude of risk accumulation as a pathogenic influence for this multi-problem sample is substantial, placing a significant burden on the ability of these young children to bounce back or to become resilient under their current circumstances of added adversity (Masten, 1994). Our results lend support for a multidimensional model for preschool problems in that multiple factors are implicated in the behavioral variation of child problems for this high risk preschool sample. Specifically, family violence and impaired maternal functioning are added risk factors for the development of child psychopathology related to community violence exposure; a finding previously found among adolescents at risk for antisocial behavior (Forehand et al., 1998).

A unique contribution of the Boston Community Violence Project is that maternal functioning plays a crucial intervening role in predicting preschool problems by diminishing or intensifying young children's behavioral reaction to violent social environments. When maternal functioning is optimum, as reflected by self-reports of good health status, low levels of global psychological distress, and observed positive parenting, children show fewer internalizing and externalizing behavior problems. Conversely, when maternal functioning is compromised, as reflected by reported poor health, high levels of global psychological distress, and low levels of observed positive parenting, children show internalizing and externalizing behavior problems, and increased risk for child psychopathology. Our findings suggest that, among the comprehensive set of psychosocial factors examined, those related to maternal adaptation to community violence are crucial to child functioning, exacerbating or buffering children's behavioral adaptation to the shared toxic social environment. Mothers who showed impaired functioning, particularly high psychological distress, but who also displayed less positive parenting behaviors, may be less equipped to buffer their children's experiences of community violence. In turn, children of better functioning mothers display fewer behavior problems.

Different psychosocial factors are implicated in child internalizing and externalizing problems. After accounting for the influence of the demographic and family violence blocks, the maternal functioning block (physical health, global distress, and positive parenting) accounted for the largest percentage of internalizing problems (33%). In contrast, although still substantial, maternal functioning accounted for a lesser percentage (half in magnitude) of child externalizing problems (16%). The distinct influence of risk stemming from the different ecological levels suggests that the trajectories of internalizing and externalizing behavioral problems may be different. Our findings suggest that factors which contribute to the presence of child internalizing behavior may not be the same ones as those for externalizing behavior problems. For example, demographic characteristics may play a role in the emergence of externalizing, but not so for internalizing behavior problems. Older children with mothers of low education level from nonimmigrant status may be more likely to show externalizing behavior problems than younger children with mothers of higher education level, and immigrant status. Likewise, we found that family violence is important for the emergence of externalizing, but less so for internalizing behavior problems. Particularly, partner violence to child is related to externalizing behavior problems, suggesting the crucial role of social learning influences in the family. Although present only in a small minority of homes, children who experienced aggression from male partners (i.e., child abuse) show externalizing behavior problems, such as aggressive and destructive behavior. The prior association between exposure to child abuse and child externalizing behavior problems (Dodge, Pettit, & Bates, 1997) is supported for the preschool children in this sample and can be understood within a social learning perspective, in which young children may reenact in their behavior the violence that they experience in their home environment.

Blind ratings of positive parenting (low power control, high involvement, and positive affective tone) contributed to fewer child internalizing and externalizing behavior problems, highlighting the crucial role of the quality of parenting. Among children exposed to family violence there is wide support for the relationship between positive parenting and fewer child problems (Margolin & John, 1997). With an improved methodology in a preschool sample, our study replicates this association, after controlling for other psychosocial correlates of positive parenting, for example, maternal education, child age, and maternal stress. On the other hand, the notion that negative parenting is a detrimental factor for preschool problems was not supported for this sample. We found that mothers rated as displaying more negative parenting (defined here as high power control; low involvement; and negative affect) during the toy cleaning up task were not more likely to report more child problems than those with less negative parenting. This is surprising given, for example, the strong association between coercive parenting and child problems (Patterson et al., 1989). It is also possible that negative parenting (particularly when it involves a power coercion component) may not have a detrimental impact for ethnic minority children (Deater-Deckard, Dodge, Bates & Pettit, 1998). From a methodological perspective, it may be that our negative parenting rating gathered in a videotaped structured task may not have detected sufficient sample variation needed for the correlational analyses. Extreme forms of negative parenting (i.e., shouting or hitting) are rarely observed when mothers know they are being videotaped. It is also possible that this brief video sequence may have not solely tapped into the quality of parenting but into other domains such as social desirability and child temperament in unknown ways.

The assumption that exposure to chronic community violence is a potent risk factor is attenuated by our new data. We had anticipated a stronger effect of exposure to chronic community violence on child problems, which did not occur. A focus of this study was to assess whether or not exposure to chronic community violence contributes to preschool problems in unique ways, different from the influence of other competing, and better known, psychosocial factors. Given the comprehensiveness of the predictor variables, by entering exposure to chronic community violence last in the model, we imposed a stringent test for associations among variables known to be highly correlated with each other. Beyond known risk factors, such as maternal education and child age, and family characteristics, we found that exposure to chronic community violence had only a minor influence on preschool problems. Maternal reports of chronic community violence contributed in the magnitude of 3–4% to the variance of internalizing behavior problems and externalizing behavior problems, respectively, after demographic variables, family violence, and maternal functioning effects were taken into consideration.

FUTURE DIRECTIONS

Our results suggest that there are important implications for future research and for prevention and intervention during the preschool years. First, the expansion to other preschool samples that experience different levels of psychosocial risk are an important topic of future research. The Boston project targeted mothers and their young children who reside in preidentified residential zip codes; studies using a different preschool population, for example, those residing in areas of higher risk for community violence (e.g., housing projects) are likely to yield different results. The task faced by mothers living in poor, high crime communities is likely to be different than that those faced by families living in neighborhoods with less violence and greater resources (Gorman-Smith & Tolan, 1998). Second, future studies should include longitudinal samples to determine with some certainty the direction of effect between violence exposure, maternal functioning, and child symptom level. It is possible, for example, that aggressive children seek out violent contexts, or that anxious children diminish maternal functioning. Under a bi-directional perspective, mother and child affect each other, so that the child's problems may impact on maternal well-being, particularly maternal distress level. Longitudinal research is needed to disentangle with some degree of certainty these competing hypotheses. Third, research should be expanded to involve a comprehensive multi-agent methodology to address the shared method variance limitation of this study as mothers are the source of data for the independent and most of the dependent variables. The use of maternal self-reports and standardized parenting ratings from videotaped mother-child interaction are important steps in the right direction. Independent behavioral observations of parenting during an ecologically meaningful task (toy cleaning compliance) are virtually non existent in research addressing the impact of parenting on preschoolers residing in high-crime neighborhoods. In future studies, direct observations of other key constructs (i.e., child behavior problems) are desirable to minimize parental bias in reporting child symptomatology (Treutler & Epkins, 2003).

The development of prevention and intervention for preschoolers exposed to community violence is a crucial area of future research. Our findings point to future intervention efforts likely to be effective for this population. To the extent that psychosocial factors may be largely malleable and subject to change, they are good targets for effective prevention interventions for this and other similar vulnerable dyads. Several macro-level approaches, such as community involvement, political action, and community policing, are geared at improving directly the quality of life in high crime neighborhoods. A safer neighborhood may ameliorate maternal distress related to perceptions of local danger and disorder experienced by mothers residing in high crime neighborhoods; and as such will eventually improve child mental health via improving maternal health. At a more micro-level, in an era of limited public resources, providing broad health services and support to increase maternal functioning (including health services, psychological treatment, and support in parenting tasks) may have a substantial benefit for both mother and child. Results suggest that helping mothers who are experiencing chronic local crime in their communities may not only ensure that their own mental health needs are met, but may indirectly, diminish the negative effects of chronic community violence on their children's behavioral adjustment. In light of the results of the Parenting Study, it may be important to add training in positive parenting skills as a focus of intervention efforts. Consistent with the salient role of mothers during the preschool years, it is likely that gains in positive parenting result in fewer child internalizing and externalizing behavior problems. The stronger link between maternal and child internalizing behavior, as compared to maternal distress and externalizing behavior problems is important for the prevention science field. For example, programs wishing to decrease problematic child internalizing behavior may target maternal distress, while programs wishing to decrease child externalizing behavior problems may need to focus at mitigating family violence. A multi-component intervention program addressing maternal distress and family violence, however, is likely to have a far reaching impact in decreasing overall child problems during the preschool years. Early childhood interventionists understand the value of addressing maternal and child health simultaneously among multi-risk young children for whom exposure to community violence remains a public health risk of considerable proportions.

ACKNOWLEDGMENT

This work was supported in part by the Category II New York University site of the National Child Traumatic Stress Network, grant SM 54254-01.

REFERENCES

Achenbach, T. M. (1991). *Program manual for the Child Behavior Checklist for 4–18 profile.* Burlington: University of Vermont Department of Psychiatry.

Achenbach, T. M., Edelbrock, C., & Howell, C. T. (1987). Empirically based assessment of the behavioral/emotional problems of 2- and 3-year-old children. *Journal of Abnormal Child Psychology, 15,* 629–650.

Aisenberg, E. (2001). The effects of exposure to community violence upon Latina mothers and preschool children. *Hispanic Journal of Behavioral Sciences, 23,* 4, 378–398.

American Psychiatric Association. (2000). *Diagnostic Statistical Manual of Mental Disorders* (4th ed.). Washington, DC: Author.

Atzaba-Poria, N., Pike, A., & Deater-Deckard, K. (2004). Do risk factors for problem behaviour act in a cumulative manner? An examination of ethnic minority and majority children through an ecological perspective. *Journal of Child Psychology and Psychiatry, 45*(4), 707–718.

Bowen, N. K. & Bowen, G. L. (1999) Effects of crime and violence in the neighborhoods and schools on the school behavior and performance of adolescents. *Journal of Adolescent Research, 14*(3), 319–342.

Brener, N. D., Simon, T. R., Krug, E. G., & Lowry, R. (1999). Recent trends in violence-related behaviors among high school students in the United States. *Journal of the American Medical Association, 282*(5), 440–446.

Breslau, N., Glenn, C., Davis, G., Andreski, P., & Peterson, E. (1991). Traumatic events and posttraumatic stress disorder in an urban population of young adults. *Archives of General Psychiatry, 48,* 216–222.

Bronfenbrenner, U. (1979). *The ecology of human development.* Cambridge: Harvard University Press.

Bursik, R. J., Jr., & Grasmick, H. G. (1993). *Neighborhoods and crime: The dimensions of effective community control.* New York: Lexington Books.

Cicchetti, D. (1989). How research on child maltreatment has informed the study of child development: perspectives from developmental psychopathology. In D. Cicchetti & V. Carlson (Eds.), *Child maltreatment. Theory and research on the causes and consequences of child abuse and neglect.* Cambridge: Cambridge University Press.

Cicchetti, D., & Lynch, M. (1993). Toward an ecological/

transactional model of community violence and child maltreatment: Consequences for children's development. Special Issue: Children and violence. *Psychiatry-Interpersonal and Biological Processes, 56*(1), 96–118.

Cicchetti, D., & Lynch, M. (1995). Failures in the expectable environment and their impact on individual development: The case of child maltreatment. In D. Cicchetti & D. J. Cohen (Eds.), *Developmental psychopathology, Volume 2: Risk, disorder, and adaptation* (pp. 32–71). New York: Wiley.

Colder, C. R., Mott, J., Levy, S., & Flay, B. (2000). The relation of perceived neighborhood danger to childhood aggression: A test of mediating mechanisms. *American Journal of Community Psychology, 28*(1), 83–103.

Cooley-Quille, M., Boyd, R. C., Frantz, E., & Walsh, J. (2001). Emotional and behavioral impact of exposure to community violence in inner-city adolescents. *Journal of Clinical Child Psychology, 30*(1), 199–206.

Crockenberg, S. (1987). Predictors and correlates of anger toward and punitive control of toddlers by adolescent mothers. *Child Development, 58,* 964–975.

Crockenberg, S., & Covey, S. L. (1991). Marital conflict and externalizing behavior in children. In D. Cicchetti & S. L. Toth (Eds.), *Rochester symposium on developmental psychopathology* (pp. 235–260). Rochester, NY: University of Rochester Press.

Deater-Deckard, K., Dodge, K. A., Bates, J. E., & Pettit, G. S. (1998). Multiple risk factors in the development of externalizing behavior problems: Group and individual differences. *Development and Psychopathology, 10,* 469–493.

Derogatis, L. R. (1994). *SCL-90R Administration, Scoring and Procedures Manual* (3rd ed.). Minneapolis, MN: Leonard R. Derogatis and National Computer Systems.

Dodge, K. A., Pettit, G. S., & Bates, J. E. (1997). How the experience of early physical abuse leads children to become chronically aggressive. In D. Cicchetti & S. L. Toth (Eds.), *Developmental perspectives on trauma: Vol. 8. Theory, research, and intervention* (pp. 263–288). Rochester, NY: University of Rochester Press.

Dodge, K. A., Pettit, G. S., Bates, J. E., & Valente, E. (1995). Social information-processing patterns partially mediate the effect of early physical abuse on later conduct problems. *Journal of Abnormal Psychology, 104*(4), 632–643.

Durant, R. H., Getts, A., Cadenhead, C., Emans, S. J., & Woods, E. R. (1995). Exposure to violence and victimization and depression, hopelessness, and purpose in life among adolescents living in and around public housing. *Developmental and Behavioral Pediatrics, 16,* 233–237.

Earls, F. (1994). *Neighborhood scales: Community survey questionnaire. The project on human development in*

Chicago neighborhoods, Cambridge, MA. (Unpublished manuscript).

Fantuzzo, J., DePaola, L., Lambert, L., Martino, T., Anderson, G., & Sutton, S. (1991). The effects of interparental violence on the psychological adjustment and competencies of young children. *Journal of Consulting and Clinical Psychology, 59,* 258–265.

Farver, J. M., Natera, L. X., & Frosch, D. L. (1999). Effects of community violence of inner-city preschoolers and their families. *Journal of Applied Developmental Psychology, 20*(1), 143–158.

Farver, J. M., Ghosh, C., & Garcia, C. (2000). Children's perceptions of their neighborhood. *Journal of Applied Developmental Psychology, 21*(2), 139–163.

Fitzpatrick, K. M. (1993). Exposure to violence and presence of depression among low-income, African-American youth. *Journal of the American Academy of Child and Adolescent Psychiatry, 61,* 528–531.

Fitzpatrick, K. M., & Boldizar, J. P. (1993). The prevalence and consequences of exposure to violence among African-American youth. *Journal of the American Academy of Child and Adolescent Psychiatry, 32,* 424–430.

Forehand, R., Biggar, H., & Kotchick, B. A. (1998). Cumulative risk across family stressors: Short- and long-term effects for adolescents. *Journal of Abnormal Child Psychology, 26*(2), 119–128.

Formoso, D., Gonzales, N. A., & Aiken, L. S. (2000). Family conflict and children's internalizing and externalizing behavior: Protective factors. *American Journal of Community Psychology, 28*(2), 175–199.

Fox, N. A., & Leavitt, L. A. (1995). *The violence exposure scale for children-VEX* (preschool version). College Park, MD: Department of Human Development, University of Maryland.

Garbarino, J. (1999). The Effects of Community Violence on Children. In L. Balter & C. S. Tamis-LeMonda (Eds.), *Child psychology: A handbook of contemporary issues* (pp. 412–428). Philadelphia: Psychology Press.

Garbarino, J., Kostelny, K., & Dubrow, N. (1991). What children can tell us about living in danger. *American Psychologist, 46*(4), 376–383.

Garbarino, J., Dubrow, N., Kostelny, K., & Pardo, C. (1992). *Children in danger: Coping with the consequences.* San Francisco: Jossey-Bass.

Gorman-Smith, D, Tolan, P. H., Zelli, A., & Huesmann, L. R. (1996). The relation of family functioning to violence among inner-city minority youths. *Journal of Family Psychology, 10*(2), 115–129.

Gorman-Smith, D., & Tolan, P. (1998). The role of exposure to community violence and developmental problems among inner-city youth. *Development and Psychopathology, 10* 101–116.

Guerra, N. G., Huesmann, L. R., & Spindler, A. (2003). Community violence exposure, social cognition, and aggression among urban elementary school children. *Child Development, 74*(5), 1561–1576.

Horn, I. B., Cheng, T. L., & Joseph, J. (2004). Discipline in the African American community: The impact of socioeconomic status on beliefs and practices. *Pediatrics, 113*(5), 1236–1241.

Hill, H. M., & Jones, L. P. (1997). Children's and parents' perceptions of children's exposure to violence in urban neighborhoods. *Journal of the National Medical Association, 89*(4), 270–276.

Holden, G. W., & Ritchie, K. L. (1991). Linking extreme marital discord, child rearing, and child behavior problems: Evidence from battered women. *Child Development, 62,* 311–327.

Jaffe, P., Wolfe, D., Wilson, S. K., & Zak, L. (1986). Family violence and child adjustment: A comparative analysis of girls' and boys' behavioral symptoms. *American Journal of Psychiatry, 143,* 74–77.

Jaycox, L. H., Stein, B. D., Kataoka, S. H., Wong, M., Fink, A., Escudero, P., & Zaragoza, C. (2002). Violence exposure, posttraumatic stress disorder, and depressive symptoms among recent immigrant schoolchildren. *Journal of the American Academy of Child and Adolescent Psychiatry, 41*(9), 1104–1110.

Jouriles, E. N., Murphy, C. M., & O'Leary, K. D. (1989). Interspousal aggression, marital discord, and child problems. *Journal of Consulting and Clinical Psychology, 57,* 453–455.

Kitzmann, K. M., Gaylord, N. K., Holt, A. R., & Kenny, E. D. (2003). Child witnesses to domestic violence: A meta-analytic review. *Journal of Consulting and Clinical Psychology, 71*(2), 339–352.

Koss, M. P., Woodruff, W. J., & Koss, P. G. (1990). Relation of criminal victimization to health perceptions among women medical patients. *Journal of Consulting and Clinical Psychology, 58,* 147–152.

Krenichyn, K., Saegert, S., & Evans, G. (2001). Parents as moderators of psychological and physiological correlates of inner-city children's exposure to violence. *Applied Developmental Psychology, 22,* 581–602.

LaGrange, R. L., Ferraro, K. F., Supancic, M. (1992). Perceived risk and fear of crime: Role of social and physical incivilities. *Journal of Research in Crime and Delinquency, 29,* 311–334.

Linares, L. O. (nd). The maternal fear of crime scale. Unpublished scale available from the author.

Linares, L. O., Groves, B., Greenberg, J., Bronfman, E., Augustyn, M., & Zuckerman, B. (1999). Restraining orders: A frequent marker of adverse maternal health. *Pediatrics, 104*(2), 249–257.

Linares, L. O., Heeren, T., Bronfman, E., Zuckerman, B., Augustyn, M., & Tronick, E. (2001). A mediational model for the impact of exposure to community violence on early child behavior problems. *Child Development, 72*(2), 639–652.

Linares, L. O., & Cloitre, M. (2004). Intergenerational links between mothers and children with PTSD spectrum illness. In R. R. Silva (Ed.), *Posttraumatic stress disorder in children and adolescents.* New York: W. W. Norton.

Lynch, M. (2003). Consequences of children's exposure to community violence. *Clinical Child and Family Psychology Review, 6*(4), 265–274.

Lynch, M., & Cicchetti, D. (1998). An ecological-transactional analysis of children and contexts: The longitudinal interplay among child maltreatment, community violence, and children's symptomatology. *Development and Psychopathology, 10,* 235–257.

Lynch, M., & Cicchetti, D. (2002). Links between community violence and the family system: Evidence from children's feelings of relatedness and perceptions of parent behavior. *Family Processes, 41,* 519–532.

Margolin, G., & John, R. S. (1997). Children exposure to marital aggression: Direct and mediated effects. In G. K. Kantor & J. L. Jasinski (Eds.), *Out of the Darkness: Contemporary Perspectives on Family Violence* (pp.90–104). Thousand Oaks, CA: Sage.

Margolin, G., & Gordis, E. 2000. The effects of family and community violence on children. *Annual Review of Psychology,* 445–479.

Martinez, P., & Richters, J. E. (1993). The NIMH community violence project: II. Children's distress symptoms associated with violence exposure. *Psychiatry, 56,* 22–35.

Masten, A. S. (1994). Resilience in individual development: Successful adaptation despite risk and adversity. In M. Wang & E. Gordon (Eds.), *Risk and resilience in inner city America: Challenges and prospects* (pp. 3–25). Hillsdale, NJ: Erlbaum.

McCloskey, L. A., Figueredo, A. J., & Koss, M. P. (1995). The effects of systemic family violence on children's mental health. *Child Development, 66,* 1239–1261.

Miller, L. S., Wasserman, G. A., Neugebauer, R., Gorman-Smith, D., & Kamboukos, D. (1999). Witnessed community violence and antisocial behavior in high-risk, urban boys. *Journal of Clinical Child Psychology, 28*(1), 2–11.

North, C. S., Smith, E. M., & Spitz-Nagel, E. L. (1994). Post-traumatic stress disorder in survivors of a mass shooting. *American Journal of Psychiatry, 151,* 82–88.

Osofsky, J. D., Wewers, S., Hann, D. M., & Fick, A. C. (1993). Chronic community violence: What is happening to our children? *Psychiatry, 56,* 36–45.

Overstreet, S. (2000). Exposure to community violence: defining the problem and understanding the consequences. *Journal of Child and Family Studies, 9*(1), 7–25.

Patterson, G. R. (1983). Stress: A change agent for family process. In N. Garmezy & M. Rutter, (Eds.), *Stress, coping and development in children* (pp. 235–264). New York: McGraw-Hill.

Patterson, G. R., DeBaryshe, B. D., & Ramsey, E. (1989). A developmental perspective on antisocial behavior. *American Psychologist, 44*(2), 329–335.

Perkins, D. D., & Taylor, R. B. (1996). Ecological assessments of community disorder: Their relationship to fear of crime and theoretical implications. *American Journal of Community Psychology, 24,* 63–107.

Plybon, L. E., & Kliewer, W. (2001). Neighborhood types and externalizing behavior in urban school-age children: Tests of direct, mediated, and moderated effects. *Journal of child and Family Studies, 10*(4), 419–437.

Punamaki, R. L., Quota, S., & El Sarraj, E. (1997). Models of traumatic experiences and children psychological adjustment: The roles of perceived parenting and the children's own resources and activity. *Child Development, 64,* 718–728.

Randolph, S. M., Koblinsky, S. A., & Roberts, D. D. (1996). Studying the role of family and school in the development of African American preschoolers in violent neighborhoods. *Journal of Negro Education, 65*(3) 282–292.

Richters, J. E., & Martinez, P. (1993). The NIMH Community Violence Project: I. Children as Victims of and Witnesses to Violence. *Psychiatry, 56,* 7–21.

Scheeringa, M. S., Peebles, C. D., Cook, C. A., & Zeanah, C. H. (2001). Toward establishing procedural, criterion, and discriminant validity for PTSD in early childhood. *Journal of the American Academy of Child and Adolescent Psychiatry, 40*(1), 52–60.

Scheeringa, M. S., Zeanah, C. H., Myers, L., & Putnam, F. W. (2003). New Findings on Alternative Criteria for PTSD in Preschool Children. *Journal of the American Academy of Child & Adolescent Psychiatry, 42*(5), 561–570.

Shahinfar, A., Fox, N. A., & Leavitt, L. A. (2000). Preschool children's exposure to violence: Relation of behavior problems to parent and child reports. *American Journal of Orthopsychiatry, 70*(1), 115–125.

Shaw, M., & McKay, H (1972). *Juvenile delinquency and urban areas* (2nd ed.). Chicago: University of Chicago Press.

Skogan, W. G. (1990). *Disorder and decline: Crime and the spiral of decay in American neighborhoods.* New York: The Free Press.

Stein, B. D., Jaycox, L. H., Kataoka, S., Rhodes, H. J., & Vestal, K. D. (2003). Prevalence of child and adolescent exposure to community violence. *Clinical Child and Family Psychology Review, 6*(4), 247–264.

Straus, M. A., Hamby, S. L., Boney-McCoy, S., & Sugarman, D. B. (1996). The revised conflict tactics scale (CTS 2): Development and preliminary psychometric data. *Journal of Family Issues, 17,* 283–316.

Taylor, R. B. (1996). Neighborhood responses to disorder and local attachments: The systemic model of attachment, social disorganization, and neighborhood use-value. *Sociological Forum, 11,* 41–74.

Taylor, L., Zuckerman, B., Harik, V., & Groves, B. (1994). Witnessing violence by young children and their mothers. *Developmental and Behavioral Pediatrics, 15,* 120–123.

Treutler, C. M., & Epkins, C. C. (2003). Are discrepancies among child, mother, and father reports on children's behavior related to parents' psychological symptoms and aspects of parent-child relationships? *Journal of Abnormal Child Psychology, 31*(1), 13–27.

U.S. Department of Health and Human Services/Public Health Services (1992). *Healthy people 2000: National health promotion and disease prevention objectives.* Boston: Jones & Bartlett.

Ware, J. E., Snow, K. K., Kosinski, M., & Gandek, B. (1993). *SF-36 Health survey manual and interpretation guide.* Boston: The Health Institute, New England Medical Center.

Zlotnick, C., Warshaw, M., Shea, M. T., & Keller, M. B. (1997). Trauma and chronic depression among patients with anxiety disorders. *Journal of Consulting and Clinical Psychology, 65,* 333–336.

23

Cultural and Maturational Influences on Long-Term Event Memory

Michelle D. Leichtman

Interviewer: Can you tell me about a memory from your childhood?
Participant: No, I have forgotten all that.
Interviewer: Can you remember any events that occurred when you were young?
Participant: Incidents mean...whom are memories for...
Interviewer: Doesn't matter. Try telling me about one or two things.
Participant: Can't remember all those things.

Excerpt from an interview with a rural Indian goatherd,
translated from the regional language, Kanada

INTRODUCTION

Over the past decade, researchers interested in memory development have pursued with exceptional vigor a variety of issues related to *real world memory for personally experienced events*. This kind of memory would appear to have high face validity; indeed, remembering the significant and daily events of one's life is exactly what many nonscientists think of as "remembering" (e.g., Stewart, 2004). Consistent with this, the study of memory development has always included some concern with how people recall and talk about the events of their lives (e.g., Stern & Stern, 1909/1999; Dudycha & Dudycha, 1933). Nonetheless, much of the contemporary history of research on memory development reflects a preoccupation with processes outside the domain of personal event memory. The large developmental literature focusing on topics such as strategy development, transfer, meta-memorial processes, recognition memory and laboratory-based episodic tasks is illustrative. Such work has led to rich insights about the ways that memory processes in general change across the course of childhood, but has been only tangentially relevant to autobiographical memory.

Researchers currently recognize that at the level of the brain what we refer to as "memory" really denotes numerous distinct, widely distributed cognitive processes (e.g., Squire, 1992). Functionally, these processes work together to support performance on tasks such as reasoning, learning, decision making and introspection. Indeed, memory is an integral and requisite component of most such higher-order cognitive tasks. At the same time, performance on many memory tasks draws on a variety of general intellectual processes, including perceptual and reasoning abilities (Ceci, 2003). The close bi-directional relationship between memory and other cognitive processes means that advances in understanding memory development are important to understanding cognitive development more generally. From this perspective, the implications of findings from the recent proliferation of studies focusing on personal event memory are relatively broad.

In part, the attention that developmental psychologists are currently paying to personal event memory reflects a trend in the field of memory research as a whole. As Pillemer (1998) argued, for the past century memory researchers trained in both mainstream cognitive and developmental psychology have tended to undervalue the importance of memories for single episodes occurring at one point in time. Traditionally, when considering memory for past experience, researchers have focused instead on semantic processes, associated with facts or world knowledge acquired over time, or on schematic memory of repeated episodes. Due in part to the nature of the processes under scrutiny, in much of this earlier literature event representations were assumed to be largely invariant across individuals and contexts. One benefit of recent examinations of specific event memories is the spotlight they have shone on individual and contextual differences. Although theorists have made a case for the importance of context specificity in numerous areas of memory development in the past two decades (e.g., Ceci & Leichtman, 1992), nowhere has there been a more powerful illustration of this than in the recent study of personal event memory. Context effects, particularly those related to cultural differences, feature prominently in the studies reviewed in this chapter. The overriding theme of the chapter is how individuals remember personally experienced events that occur early in their lives.

What are the characteristics of adults' memories of the years of infancy and childhood? This question has received renewed attention from developmental psychologists over the past 15 years. Most adults find it difficult to recall experiences from the earliest years of childhood, in particular from before age 4. This difficulty, termed *childhood amnesia*, varies extensively between individuals and populations in ways that researchers have just begun to fully document. Most American adults report having some specific childhood memories from after age 4, and some have detailed memories from even the earliest years of life. In contrast, other individuals report being unable to remember any specific experiences from childhood at all, even after extensive prompting. The opening excerpt of this chapter, taken from an interview with a rural Indian participant, provides a modal example of this latter case. In the participant's village, only a small fraction of adults reported remembering any specific event that dated from the childhood years (Leichtman, Bhogle, Sankaranarayanan, & Hobeika, 2003).

What accounts for childhood amnesia and its variations? This chapter highlights both maturational and experiential factors. Four distinct areas of developmental research on memory implicate both kinds of factors in adult recollection of childhood events.

First, studies of long-term memory during infancy and the earliest childhood years have identified characteristics of the early memory system that affect later event recall. These studies have demonstrated an ontogenetic shift from implicit to explicit event memories, and have begun to identify more precisely than ever before the timing of emergent long- term memory competencies. Conceptual strides have been made over the past few years as researchers have been able to connect such developments with underlying shifts in brain processing.

Second, research on children's event memory narratives represents a separate topic in early memory development. A significant new body of research has been directed at the issue of cultural differences in narrative, and this has resulted in a reconsideration of how culturally transmitted narrative styles affect memory. Currently, investigators are amassing much new evidence relevant to this topic. For example, researchers have begun to document the developmental trajectory of cultural differences and explore the multiple pathways through which culture may influence children's memory narratives.

Third, and closely connected with investigations of children's event memories, are direct investigations of adults' memories of childhood events. Such studies have also flourished recently and have revealed social environment and family structure variations that influence whether and in what form childhood events are remembered over the long term. Again, the cultural perspective of the most current work has been particularly fruitful.

Fourth, findings on children's suggestibility have demonstrated a pertinent relationship between source monitoring abilities and event memories. These results have suggested that frontal lobe immaturity, which appears to be related to children's source monitoring problems, also may contribute to childhood amnesia. Work in this area continues to progress, underscoring the important connections between memory and broader cognitive developments.

This chapter provides a selective review of studies in each area, with an eye toward implications for childhood amnesia and broader conceptions of long-term memory.

LONG-TERM MEMORY BEFORE AGE THREE

Current perspectives acknowledge the infant as a creature prepared from birth to begin processing and organizing incoming information in meaningful ways (e.g., Mandler, 1992; Bauer, Wiebe, Carver, Waters, & Nelson, 2003). In stark contrast, early developmental theorists perceived the capacity of infants to make sense of the environment and to meaningfully encode events as quite impoverished (James, 1950; Mandler, 1992). From this standpoint, early experiences would have little chance of enduring in memory for later conscious retrieval. Thus, most early work on infant memory development focused exclusively on short-term processes, with retention intervals under several minutes (Bornstein & Sigman, 1986; McCall, 1979; Werner & Perlmutter, 1979). Modern methodologies created for the study of infants and toddlers have revealed relatively more sophisticated cognition during these early periods, and have inspired researchers to rethink the potential for early long-term memory (e.g., Rovee-Collier & Hayne, 1987; Meltzoff, 1988, 1995).

Several diverse research paradigms have produced data indicating that infants and toddlers process and recall substantial information about specific events. Research indicates that memories are encoded earlier in life and remain accessible for retrieval longer than researchers previously thought possible (e.g., Bauer, Hertsgaard, & Dow, 1994; Meltzoff, 1995; Perris, Myers, & Clifton, 1990). As well as charting the developmental course of long-term retention, modern researchers have been interested in characterizing the nature of these early long-term memories.

Pillemer and White (1989) offered a model of long-term memory that accounts for childhood amnesia by positing two functionally distinct memory systems. In their view, the first system is concerned with social and emotional information and is present from birth. In this system, people, locations, or feelings that a child encounters may cue images, behaviors, and nonverbal expressions of emotion. Memories in this system are not connected with specific, well-delineated past events, but are apparent in feelings of familiarity in the presence of particular emotions, people, or situations. For example, a child may remember a relative she rarely sees, but may not recall any details of their earlier encounters. The second memory system consists of more socially accessible information and does not come online until the preschool years. At this point, children have the capacity to retrieve specific past experiences and items in memory, and can carry out retrieval intentionally. Children can only respond to verbal cues to remember personally experienced past events when this second system is place. In Pillemer & White's (1989) view, in the early years of life children rely only on the first memory system, while in later childhood and adulthood the two systems are in place.

The proposed emergence of two memory systems with different developmental trajectories has appeal in view of documented differences between the memories of young children and older participants. Contemporary studies of event memory have shown clear evidence of implicit memories during infancy. Implicit memories are retrieved without the awareness of remembering, as when past experience unconsciously influences present perceptions, thoughts, or actions (Schacter, 1987).

Prime evidence of implicit memory comes from research employing habituation paradigms to document recognition among infants after long delays. Such paradigms often use infants' looking behavior as an indicator of differential attention to novel and familiar stimuli. This method capitalizes on fact that infants often show decreased visual attention to stimuli they recognize as old, while they respond with renewed attention to equivalent novel or forgotten stimuli. Habituation studies have revealed delayed recognition from several days to several weeks for a variety of photographs and abstract designs in 5- to 7-month-olds (Fagan, 1971, 1979).

The mobile conjugate reinforcement paradigm that Rovee-Collier and colleagues have developed has also allowed researchers to witness recognition among infants after long delays. In this paradigm, infants learn to kick their feet to move a mobile when specific stimuli are present. When these stimuli are reinstated after a delay, infants' anticipatory foot kicking responses indicate recognition. Results using this method indicate long-term memory in 3-month-olds after an 8-day delay, and in 6-month-olds after a 21-day delay (Hartshorn & Rovee-Collier, 1997; Rovee-Collier, 1993; Rovee-Collier & Hayne, 1987).

The prelinguistic status of very young infants is a major problem for researchers interested in determining the nature of early long-term memory. When memories cannot be described verbally, it often is difficult to determine whether explicit memories exist. In contrast to implicit memories, explicit memories are accompanied by a clear sense that one is recalling the past. Such memories are apparent, for example, when individuals report narrative memories of past events, or when they recollect having encountered material in a particular past context (Schacter, 1987). Adults can often report on the experience of explicitly remembering. From this perspective, explicit memories provide the clearest evidence of "true" memory: the ability to sense the past and to recount it (Mandler, 1992). To demonstrate explicit memory requires an individual to construct a mental representation of the past, as opposed to simply showing a conditioned response upon exposure to familiar stimuli or situations (Leichtman & Ceci, 1993; Mandler, 1992; Mandler & McDonough, 1995). Conceptually, this is a prerequisite of the second memory system that Pillemer and White (1989) described, which allows children to dig purposefully into mental representations of past experience.

When the participants of interest are not in a position to provide verbal evidence of memory, how might researchers hunt for compelling evidence of explicit memory processes? Methods such as the conjugate reinforcement paradigm produce evidence of what could be explicit memory. However, it would not be judicious to conclude from an infant's foot kicking response that she is consciously behaving in response to a specific past experience. Thus, theorists have wondered what such methods reveal about the resemblance between long-term memory in infancy and at later stages in the lifecourse. Notably, demonstrations of reproductive memory come closer to providing evidence of explicit memory than recognition tasks (Mandler, 1990). These paradigms require infants to act out, or reproduce some aspect of an event, which requires some level of mental representation (Mandler, 1992).

Research directed at capturing reproductive processes has revealed long-term memory in children under 3 years of age. One approach has been to evaluate children's anticipation of events as a function of earlier experience. For example, 5-month-olds have demonstrated the ability to use event sequences, or routines for prediction, after delays of several days to weeks (Kessen & Nelson, 1978; Smith, 1984). In addition, when researchers provided children with materials cuing them to reproduce three-step action sequences, children who were 21 months at exposure did so accurately after a 6-week delay (Bauer & Shore, 1987). Further work showed that 18-month-olds could reproduce the sequences after 8 months, although 14-month-olds could not (Bauer et al., 1994). Related work has shown increased evidence of surprise in 9- to 18-month-olds when expectations established by a past event are violated (LeCompte & Gratch, 1972).

Studies of deferred imitation, which require that participants reproduce unusual behaviors that they previously either observed or acted out, offer more rigorous demonstrations of reproductive memory. Nine-month-olds have imitated the actions they witnessed after 24 hours, and 14-month-olds have imitated modeled actions after a week (Meltzoff, 1988). In a pair of studies using a large sample of 14- and 16-month-olds, Meltzoff (1995) demonstrated significant deferred imitation of experimenter-modeled actions after both 2- and 4-month intervals. These effects were present whether or not children were allowed to practice the behavior immediately after first seeing it modeled. In other words, children imitated the behaviors even when they were not allowed to contemporaneously pair the objects involved in the modeling with specific behaviors. Thus, Meltzoff concluded that the memories children displayed with their imitation after 2 to 4 months did not involve habitual or conditioned learning.

Carver & Bauer (2001) conducted a large study of deferred imitation abilities over long delay intervals in children aged 6 months- to 1 year. Their findings indicated that 9 month old infants could retrieve representations of events they experienced up to 4 months before, but not longer. In contrast, 10-month-old infants could show evidence of memory after 6 month delays. These data fit nicely with an earlier study suggesting that the delay intervals that children can endure increase significantly with age in the first 2 years. Using the deferred imitation paradigm, McDonough and Mandler (1994) provided suggestive evidence that 2-year-olds remembered and demonstrated in their behaviors a novel action that they had either observed or performed when they were 11 months old.

Using an alternative method, Perris et al. (1990) provided a striking example of early reproductive memory. Individuals who had participated in an auditory localization experiment at 6 months, requiring them to reach for a sounding object in a dark or lit room, were brought back to the original laboratory setting and reintroduced to the procedure at either 1 or 2 years of age. Children in the older group showed behavioral memory of the earlier laboratory experience by reaching out and grasping the object more than controls, and by acting less startled and more persistent in the testing situation. The younger subjects did not demonstrate similar memories, although this may have been due to very high levels of reaching by control subjects in the younger group.

Also testing after a very long delay interval, Myers, Perris, and Speaker (1994) evaluated the memories of 32-month-olds. In the original study when they were 10 months old, the participants learned to operate a toy on several occasions, and were tested 4 months later. That study indicated familiarity and fast relearning of the original toy operation by the experimental subjects, when contrasted with controls. In the follow-up, children who had been involved in only one training session at 10 months were contrasted with those who had been involved in five early sessions as well as matched controls. The results indicated that any prior experience resulted in greater interest in the target toy, more touching of the toy, and more successful responses to verbal prompts toward its operation. Notably, only children with multiple past experiences were able to operate the toy without demonstration, revealing memory for a sequence of actions they had learned 18 months earlier.

In a further study of reproductive memory processes, Leichtman (1994) presented 147 experimental participants, between 4 months and 3 years of age, with 50 minutes of interaction with a puppet, distributed over 5 consecutive days. At each session, the puppet had an edible treat hidden under one of two identical mittens. The mitten that contained the treat was removable and consistently on either the right or left hand for each child, while the other mitten was not removable. During the sessions, participants removed the mitten as many times as they desired, and it was replenished each time with a fresh treat. Participants were re-exposed to the puppet at intervals of 3 months, 6 months, or both, after the initial sessions, and their behaviors were evaluated against the behaviors of 64 controls, who had no prior exposure to the puppet.

A substantial portion of participants, as young as 6 months at exposure, demonstrated behavioral effects of prior experience with the puppet when tested after delays of 3 or 6 months. That is, starting at 6 months at exposure, indicators such as the behavior of looking inside the puppets' mittens, the amount of time taken to remove the mittens, and persistence in searching again and again for the treat were reliably affected by prior exposure to the puppet. The memories that these behaviors reflected in the children below 1 year of age were almost certainly implicit, unconscious reflections of past experience that were not accessible through language. In contrast, the youngest participants to produce spontaneous linguistic references to the past experience after 3 and 6 months were 17 to 18 months of age, respectively, at the time of exposure. This early spontaneous verbal reference was quite unusual however; only 12% of children between 1 and 2 years of age at exposure made this kind of mention after 3 months, and even fewer did so after 6 months. As would be expected, these numbers increased with age at exposure, to approximately 45% of children in the 2- to 3-year-old group at exposure, and a similar percentage who were 3 to 4 years old when they first encountered the puppet.

A few other studies have examined the possibility of verbal references to long past events before the age of 3. Myers, Clifton, and Clarkson (1987) reported that 1 child in a sample of 10 participants just under 3 years old correctly named a hidden object, apparently based on a previous experience at age 11 months. Studies by Fivush, Gray, and Fromhoff (1987) and Fivush and Hamond (1990) also documented spontaneous verbal recall by 2- to 3-year-olds of specific, salient past events more than 6 months after they occurred. Peterson and Rideout (1998) presented data that strongly support such verbal recall. Children in their sample had visited an emergency room due to having an accident sometime between 13- and 35-months of age. All children were interviewed shortly after the accident and again 6, 12, 18, or 24 months later. No child younger than 20 months at the time of the accident was able to provide a verbal account of the event after a delay of 6 months or longer, but those who were older than 20 months were often able to do so. This is striking, in that children who had been under the age of 25 months at the time of their accident did not appear to have the requisite language ability to provide verbal accounts immediately following their accident, but could do so much later, once language abilities had advanced.

In a pair of recent studies that offered a controlled examination of the verbal accessibility of early experiences, Bauer, Wenner & Kroupina (2002) exposed children three times at either 13, 16, or 20 months to multistep sequences of actions involving novel props. The researchers evaluated children for evidence of spontaneous verbal recall after delays of either 1–3 months or 9–12 months and found little evidence of such recall. However, the researchers then explicitly interviewed children about the experience when they had reached significant verbal fluency, at age three. The data indicated those children who had been 20 months old at the time of exposure, and particularly those who had relatively advanced language skills at that time, were able to offer verbal memory reports of the event.

Taken together, these studies indicated that long-term memory abilities improve significantly over the second half of the first year of life, and that a shift occurs over the first three years of life from competence on tasks requiring implicit retrieval only to competence on tasks requiring explicit retrieval. An important addition to the literature very recently has been the attempt to connect such developments directly to maturational changes at the level of the brain. As Liston and Kagan (2002) suggested, distinctive improvements in long-term memory during the latter part of the first year of life may be connected with maturation of the neocortex, in particular prefrontal cortex. Liston and Kagan supported their argument by testing 13–, 21–, and 28–month olds after a 4 month delay in a deferred imitation paradigm. Consistent with the pattern of findings from other laboratories (e.g., Bauer et al., 2002), they documented markedly better memory performance among those infants who were exposed to the target event at 17 or 24 months, rather than at 9 months.

In a more direct evaluation of the role of brain development, Bauer, Wiebe, Carver, Waters, & Nelson (2003) recorded event-related potentials (ERPs) in 9-month-old infants 1 week after exposure to a novel event, during a recognition task. The data indicated that ERP measures during this early recognition task predicted whether and how much infants recalled on a separate test of recall for the original event 1 month later. These data offered striking evidence that the maturation of storage and consolidation processes at the level of the brain have a large influence on memory competencies observed at the behavioral level. Consistent with this notion, Marshall, Drummey, Fox, & Newcombe (2002) showed significant differences in the pattern of ERPs displayed by 4-year-olds versus adults on an item recognition memory task, and linked these differences to changes in competency across development.

The body of current evidence supports the notion that biological developments in conjunction with experiential factors lead to increased competency on long-term event memory tasks across the first three years of life. With the mastery of basic language and subsequent narrative skills, children gain the capacity to recognize explicit event memories and to accurately share the details of their mental representations of the past. As Hudson & Sheffield (this volume) stress, general cognitive and meta-cognitive advances that covary with language during the first three years enable children to retrieve and express memories in response to increasingly less specific cues over time. Once they reach pre-school age, children are in a position to report some of the salient features of specific long-term event memories in response to external verbal prompts. While the content that preschool children feature in their event narratives is often different from that of adults, the essence of their reports is the same (e.g., Fivush & Hammond, 1990; Leichtman, Pillemer, Wang, Koreishi, & Han, 2000).

CHILDREN'S NARRATIVE MEMORY

Current evidence points to a compelling link between individual differences in children's memory reports and variations in the social environments in which they live. A central element of the social environment is the conversations children have with adults. Such conversations influence children's event recall in several ways that are now well documented. As Nelson (1993) noted, the process of "co-construction" of memories that takes place in conversations between children and their caregivers gives children a model for encoding and recalling events. As children make gains in language, they absorb and practice the dominant narrative structure with which those around them discuss events. In this way, children learn to discuss past events in appropriate, socially shared ways, and they also learn to accumulate and organize personal event memories that become part of their unique autobiographical history (e.g., Fivush & Hudson, 1990; Nelson, 1993; Tessler & Nelson, 1994).

Researchers attempting to document variations in the way parents—primarily mothers—talk about the past have been consistently struck by the extent of individual differences, even within relatively narrow SES and cultural groups. Two broad styles of mother-child talk have emerged across numerous studies (Fivush & Fromhoff, 1988; Reese, Haden, & Fivush, 1993; Pillemer, 1998). While various terms refer to the distinction between these styles (e.g., elaborative/high-elaborative vs. pragmatic/repetitive/low-elaborative), the findings offer a consistent picture. *High-elaborative mothers* often speak with their children about the past, provide voluminous descriptive information about past experiences, and frequently prompt children to provide embellished narratives. Even when children are unable to contribute much substantive information to conversations because of limited language, high-elaborative mothers persist in talking about the details of past experiences. In contrast, *low-elaborative mothers* talk much less about past events and provide fewer details and less prompting when they do so. Low-elaborative mothers tend to pose pointed questions with single correct and incorrect answers, rather than posing questions that call for embellished reflections on past events (Fivush & Fromhoff, 1988; Reese et al., 1993).

There is clear connection between these differences in mother's conversation styles and children's narrative development. Several studies have shown that children of high-elaborative mothers provided richer memory narratives than children of low-elaborative mothers (Haden, Haine, & Fivush, 1997; Hudson, 1990; McCabe & Peterson, 1991). Children of high-elaborative mothers tended to give longer, more detailed, and more descriptive reports about their experiences than other children, even when their mothers were not present at the interviews.

Further, discussions with adults can powerfully influence the contents of children's memory reports (Fivush, 1991; Hudson, 1990; Reese et al., 1993). For example, Tessler and Nelson (1994) tape-recorded dialogues between mothers and children as they walked through a museum together. When researchers interviewed the children 1 week later, they were able to recall exclusively those museum exhibits they had talked about with their mothers. In a larger, systematic longitudinal study, Haden, Ornstein, Eckerman, & Didow (2001) confirmed this important effect of ongoing mother-child conversations. Mother-child dyads engaged in specially constructed activities when children were 30, 36, and 42 months old, in which participants were able to converse about and handle objects. Measures of children's memories of the details of the activities were taken after 1 and 3 weeks. The data indicated that at every age, features of the activities that were handled and discussed jointly by mother and child were better remembered than features that were discussed or handled by one party alone.

These studies illustrate the effects of ongoing conversations during events; however, parents also influence the content of children's memories through their postevent conversations. In our laboratory, for example, we have documented this effect in several studies of preschool children. In one study, fifteen 4- to 5-year-old children experienced a surprise event in their preschool classroom (Leichtman et al., 2000). The children's former teacher, Martha, whom they had not seen for 3 months, came for a visit with her new baby, Maisy. A series of scripted activities occurred during the visit: Martha placed Maisy in the center of the circle of seated children, she distributed a different baby-related item to each child (e.g., diaper pin, rattle), she received and opened several gifts, and she gave out baby biscuits as a snack. Later that same day, mothers interviewed their own children individually about the event. Mothers were not present during the event and, at the beginning of the interviews, researchers told them that Martha and Maisy had visited, but gave them no other details about the visit. Researchers instructed mothers to question their children in whatever way they wished. Three weeks later, children were interviewed by a researcher who had not been present during the original event and who had no information about the content of the parent-child interviews. The researcher asked each child the same set of nine questions. She began with an open-ended question: "A few weeks ago something very special happened at school. Martha brought her baby in for a visit. I wasn't there, but I am really interested in what happened. What happened when Martha brought her baby in for a visit?" The researcher then asked eight direct questions about the event, including the following: "I heard that Mary brought a present for the baby. What was the present?" "I heard that you got to hold something. What did you get to hold?" "I heard that Martha brought other baby things for children to hold. What other things did Martha bring?" Both interviews were audiotaped and later transcribed for coding purposes.

The results of both interviews were coded on a host of variables that captured the structure and style of mother's questions and children's responses, as well as the specific content of the memories children provided. The coding of structure and style variables was adapted from previously validated schemes (Fivush & Fromhoff, 1988; Reese & Fivush, 1993). These variables included indicators of volume of speech (e.g., number of sentences spoken), number and type of questions mothers asked (e.g., memory questions such as "who" and "where" vs. yes-no questions), use of contextual statements and descriptives. Specific content variables included the number of objects, actions, time statements, and total correct details that children provided.

The results indicated that mothers' conversational style predicted the amount of information children provided during the mother-child interview. The degree to which mothers used an elaborative style of questioning their children (e.g., prompting children for details with open-ended and yes-no questions and using contextual and evaluative statements in the interviews) predicted the number of sentences children produced, the number of correct details they remembered, and the number of descriptive terms they used to explain their memories. Moreover, the mother's questioning style significantly affected children's responses during the researcher-child interview 3 weeks later. Children whose mothers gave them more elaborative-style interviews were not necessarily more talkative with the researcher than other children, but they remembered more accurate details regarding what occurred during Martha's visit. Furthermore, children's recall of the specific objects Martha distributed during the event was influenced by their conversations with their mothers. Across the sample as a whole, 83% of the items that children recalled during the researcher-child interview also had been discussed with their mothers. This general pattern of results was confirmed in a recent replication of the "Maisy" study, in which a larger sample of 44 children ranging in age from 3–5 years received a visit from a favorite teacher who had been on maternity leave (Leichtman, Pillemer, & Skowronek, 2005). Thus, revisiting the details of personally experienced events in conversation with adults appears to strengthen children's memories, increasing the likelihood that talked about aspects of their experiences will remain accessible to verbal prompting at later dates.

The powerful effects of discussion on young children's memories are readily apparent in cross-cultural studies. Parental conversational styles may vary at the cultural level as a function of larger societal norms dictating the appropriateness of extended discussions about the personal past. For example, a key dimension along which parental conversation styles vary is the independent-interdependent distinction that Markus and Kitayama (1991, 1994) proposed. According to these theorists, Western societies typically promote an independently oriented construal of self, which emphasizes the relative importance of the unique inner attributes of the individual. Eastern cultures tend to espouse an interdependently oriented construal of self, emphasizing the relative importance of others in evaluating one's own position in society. Within the social psychological literature, these divergent perspectives show extensive effects on socialization and cognition (Fiske, Kitayama, Markus, & Nisbett, 1998). The Western perspective, which encourages individuals to "stand out," consequently deems self-expression and the sharing of self-relevant autobiographical memories desirable. In contrast, Eastern cultures may discourage excessive talk about the self and, consequently, encourage less discussion of the personal past (Markus & Kitayama, 1991; Mullen, 1994).

Mullen and Yi's (1995) analysis of naturally occurring conversation between Korean or American mothers and their 40-month-old children supported this contrast. Researchers tape-recorded 1 entire day of at-home dialogue between mothers and their children in each culture. The results indicated that the Korean dyads engaged in past event talk only about one third as often, and in far less detail, than did the American dyads. The amount of children's contributions to each episode of past event talk was constant between cultures, although American mothers talked more than Korean mothers when discussing all aspects of past events except social norms. Mullen proposed that the divergent self-concepts associated with independent and interdependent cultures may influence socialization goals which, in turn, are reflected in conversations between parents and children.

Choi's (1992) study of Canadian and Korean mothers supported Mullen's suggestion that differential socialization is responsible for cultural variation in maternal communication styles. In an analysis of the types of questions Korean and Canadian mothers posed to children, Choi found that Korean mothers did not often seek information, but instead prompted children to confirm information already presented to them. Neither did Korean mothers encourage children to introduce their own ideas into the conversation. Korean mothers often made statements unrelated to children's previous utterances, and expected children to follow their leads. In contrast, Canadian mothers more often followed up and elaborated on children's utterances, encouraged children to contribute ideas, and took a partnership, rather than leadership role, in conversation. Notably, the conversational style of Korean mothers in Choi's sample resembled that of low-elaborative American mothers in other studies, while the conversational style of Canadian mothers resembled that of high-elaborative American mothers (e.g., Fivush & Fromhoff, 1988, Leichtman et al., 2000).

Several more studies in our laboratory using different research paradigms have also documented substantial differences in parent-child conversations across cultures. For example, Wang, Leichtman, & Davies (2000) studied European American and Chinese mother-child dyads in the home. Investigators asked mothers to talk with their children about two past events and a story in their usual way. When talking about both events and stories, American mothers used a high-elaborative style, asking many "wh" questions and following up on children's contributions, while Chinese mothers used a low elaborative style, often posing and repeating factual questions. In addition, the content of the conversations was different, in that American mothers prompted children for information about the child's desires, thoughts and feelings, while Chinese mothers focused on rules and discipline.

In an observational study of conversations occurring in the natural environment, we focused on 14 children living in a rural Southern Indian village and 14 children living in the suburban United States (Leichtman et al., 2003). Researchers videotaped the children at the home with their parents as they went about their daily lives and then transcribed the words that children, parents and others spoke. The data indicated that while the activities children in the two cultures engaged in were similar (e.g., dressing, playing, helping parents with chores), their narrative environments were not. American children were exposed to much more speech in general. More importantly, they were exposed to much more talk about past events, when calculated either as a percentage of speech or in absolute terms. Thus, while American children heard an average of 26 references to past events during 1 hour, rural Indian children heard an average of fewer than two. In addition, American adults' references to past events were longer, more specific and more elaborate than those of their Indian counterparts.

In view of cross-cultural variation in parental conversational styles, we have been interested in exactly how, and at what point in development children's memory narratives begin to reflect these variations. To examine this question, Han, Leichtman, and Wang (1998) conducted a comparative study of memory in upper-middle class, urban Korean, Chinese, and American 4- and 6-year-old children. The United States is a prototypically independently oriented society, while Korea and China are two interdependently oriented societies whose cultures differ enormously in other respects, including language, politics, history, and contemporary lifestyles. Researchers interviewed 50 children from each culture in their home countries and in their native languages, asking the same series of free recall questions about recent personally experienced events (e.g., questions about what the child did at bedtime the day before, a time when the child was scolded, a recent event that was fun). In addition to this autobiographical interview, researchers showed all children an identical slide show story, and gave them a story memory test after a 24-hour delay. Researchers included the story memory test in order to explore whether predicted cross-cultural differences would be unique to autobiographical reports, or whether they would extend to general narrative skill development and answers to objective questions.

The findings pertaining to children's autobiographical narratives indicated a rich array of differences between the three cultural groups, following a general pattern reflective of the independent-interdependent distinction. The volume of children's narratives, measured in terms of both the number of words and propositions they spoke, was surprising: American and Chinese children provided voluminous reports of past events, while Korean children provided only brief reports. However, the number of words per proposition told a different story. While Americans used many words per proposition, both Korean and Chinese children used far fewer. This finding indicated that American children's units of thought were comparatively long and complex, suggesting an elaborated, descriptive style of talking about the past. Qualitatively, American children generally provided rich, fleshed out descriptions of one or two single activities (e.g., a long description of taking a bath, including a detailed description of bathtub activities, objects present, and dialogue), whereas both Korean and Chinese children provided skeletal descriptions of multiple events (e.g., "watched television, took a bath, brushed my teeth, went to bed"). The major difference between autobiographical narratives of the two Asian groups was that Chinese children talked about a greater number of activities than Korean children.

Consistent with predicted contrasts between independently and interdependently oriented societies, Americans used more descriptives (i.e., adjectives, adverbs, modifiers), more terms expressing personal preferences (e.g., "I really wanted the red bag"), more personal judgments and opinions (e.g., "The game was boring") and more personal thoughts or cognitions (e.g., "I forgot about that") in talking about their experiences compared to children from both Asian countries. Furthermore, Americans provided many more memories that qualified as "specific"; that is, memories that clearly referred to a one point in time episode as opposed to routine episodes or multiple events. Finally, when the ratio of references to other people versus the self in children's narratives was calculated, the findings revealed that American children made comparatively more self references than children in either Asian culture.

Each of the above findings is consistent with the notion that independently oriented American adults encourage children to focus on themselves, their personal feelings, reactions, and thoughts during autobiographically relevant experiences, and model a relatively elaborative style of conversing about personal life events, emphasizing the unique details and social value of discussing the past. The findings also support the suggestion of an interdependently oriented Asian perspective that encourages children to focus more on others than themselves, to conform to societal norms instead of focusing on their own preferences or immediate emotions, and to avoid excessive, potentially boastful conversation about the details of their own experiences. In terms of developmental trends, children in all cultures increased their narrative volume, memorial elaboration, and discussion of personal preferences and cognitions with age. However, by age 4, the American children provided narratives that were specific and elaborative in nature, while the Korean and Chinese children spoke about their experiences in more general and unelaborated terms. By the time the Asian children were 6 years old, their narratives were characterized by a degree of specificity similar to that of the American 4-year-olds.

Children in all three cultures recalled the objective elements of the story with equal accuracy after a day-long interval. A notable difference among cultural groups arose in questions that required children to report the emotions experienced by the story's protagonist, Bear, at various points in his adventures. Researchers posed prompted questions to probe children's recollections of the story's emotional content. For example, regarding a scene in which Bear's mother told him that it was time to leave the playground while he was playing happily with his friends, researchers asked, "How did Bear feel when he had to leave the playground?" There was no single correct answer to these questions about emotions, as each required interpretation of the circumstances in which the protagonist found himself or herself.

For all such questions, the majority of U.S. children answered that Bear felt a negative emotion such as sad, scared, or bad, while the majority of children in both Asian samples answered that Bear felt a positive emotion such as good, happy, or excited. When researchers asked children to justify their answers, American children reported that Bear was upset by his mother's request that he depart from his friends. Asian children's answers showed greater acceptance of the will of authorities; they typically reported that Bear responded positively to his mother's request because he had had the opportunity to enjoy his friends. Consistent with data indicating that Japanese children are less likely than American children to express negative emotions such as anger (Zahn-Waxler, Friedman, Cole, & Mizuta, 1996), these data indicated that emotional reactions may vary between independently and interdependently oriented cultures. Children may be less likely to react to adult requests with contrary thoughts and emotions when they are raised in societies that place a premium on social harmony, personal discipline, and obedience. As the story memory task suggests, differences in emotional interpretation during events may subsequently contribute to differences in children's autobiographical narratives.

Recently, Wang (in press) has presented data illustrating that cultural differences in both children's memory reports and their self concepts emerge before the beginning of formal schooling. One hundred eighty European American and Chinese preschool children were interviewed as part of a "question and answer game" that required them to recount four autobiographical events and describe themselves in response to open-ended questions. The data indicated that consistent with other studies of autobiographical memory, in comparison with Chinese children, American children tended to provide longer, more detailed and more self-focused memory reports. In concert with this, American children provided descriptions of themselves that focused on personal attitudes, beliefs and dispositional traits, and they described themselves in a positive light. In contrast, Chinese children tended to describe themselves in terms of social roles and relationships and context-specific behaviors, and described themselves in neutral rather than positive terms. These data again emphasize the important ways in which children's memories and personalities more generally are shaped by culturally variant social norms.

In summary, from ages 4 to 6 years, the narrative system is up and running and on its way to becoming fully refined (Fivush & Hudson, 1990; Nelson, 1996). Beginning in this early period of life, children's narratives reflect the norms of discourse and the concomitant values they are exposed to daily. Cultural and sub-cultural differences in the norms of conversations with parents and in a wide variety of other social factors translate into differences in memory reports that appear early and persist throughout life.

ADULT RECOLLECTIONS OF CHILDHOOD

While contemporary research has revealed the extent of young children's event memories, for over a century it has been clear that most adults can consciously recollect few memories of early childhood (Pillemer & White, 1989; Rubin, 1982). In turn of the century Vienna, Freud noted that most adults had difficulty retrieving memories from before they were 6 to 8 years old (Freud, 1920/1953), and this "amnesia" for childhood experiences has also interested contemporary theorists (Howe & Courage, 1993; Leichtman & Ceci, 1993; Perner & Ruffman, 1995). Modern studies conducted in the United States have concluded that, on average, adults are unable to consciously recollect events experienced before the age of 3.5 years (Kihlstrom & Harackiewicz, 1982; Pillemer & White, 1989; Sheingold & Tenney, 1982). For example, Wetzler and Sweeney's (1986) analysis of Rubin's (1982) data showed disproportionate deficits in memory for events occurring before age 3 years in comparison with those occurring afterward.

The revelation that meaningful cultural differences exist in both parental conversation styles and young children's narrative reports inspires renewed consideration of cross-cultural data on adult long-term event memory. A number of studies have attested to normative cultural variations in the date of adults' earliest memories and the qualitative characteristics of their autobiographical reports. Further, several studies have been conducted in interdependently oriented cultures—some with comparative U.S. samples—and speak to the implications of the independent-interdependent distinction for memory. The studies noted below provide clues regarding the way that early socialization may influence long-term memories of childhood.

Otoya (1988) compared adult autobiographical memory across cultures, focusing on bilingual adults proficient in both Spanish and English. Half of the sample was monocultural, consisting of individuals who grew up in bilingual families in the United States, while the other half was bicultural, consisting of individuals who moved to the United States from Central or South America some time after their sixth birthdays. Participants reported the first three memories they could think of from before the age of 8, and then dated each memory. Otoya found that monocultural participants dated their earliest memories at 3.8 years of age on average, while bicultural participants dated their earliest memories at 5.1 years of age.

One interpretation of these results is that the abrupt shift that bicultural participants experienced in moving to the United States interfered with their ability to retrieve memories from before the move (Otoya, 1988; Pillemer & White, 1989). This interpretation fits with the proposal that any dramatic transition in a child's social environment will render preexisting memories more difficult to retrieve (Neisser, 1967; Schactel, 1947). Just as continuity in the retrieval environment should facilitate recall by providing a rich variety of contextual cues to earlier events, abrupt changes in a child's mindset may inhibit later memory by minimizing associations between the present and past.

While environmental transitions during childhood may indeed have contributed to the monocultural-bicultural difference Otoya recorded in the age of earliest memory, more recent international data has suggested another plausible explanation. This difference may have been due to subtle variations in the children's environments prior to the age at which the bicultural participants moved. Although parents of individuals in the two samples were raised in similar cultural milieus, for the participants themselves, growing up in the United States versus Central or South America may have introduced autobiographically relevant environmental differences. For example, while early parent–child conversations may have been similar for participants from the two samples, discussions with adults outside the family, in a larger society with less homogeneity and different values than those of the Latin American world, may have contributed to monocultural participants' ability to recall earlier memories.

The factors present early in life that might contribute to such effects on adult autobiography were highlighted by a number of studies conducted with Asian populations. As discussed earlier, living in a culture focused on interpersonal harmony and attention to others, in which attention to the self is discouraged and talk about the personal past is uncommon, appears to influence the nature of preschoolers' autobiographical reports. It follows that adults' reports of their own life experiences should reflect the normative differences in cultural orientation captured by the independent-interdependent distinction, and that memories of early life events—from the period during which normative narrative structures are first being absorbed—might be especially vulnerable to cultural differences.

Mullen's (1994) research appeared to support this connection. In a series of questionnaire studies, Mullen found that, on average, the earliest memories reported by a mixed group of Asians and Asian Americans were approximately 6 months later than those of White Americans. Subsequent comparison of the age of earliest memories of native Koreans and White Americans revealed an even larger difference of 16.7 months in the same direction (Mullen & Yi, 1995). These results relate provocatively to the pattern of findings reported in studies of Korean children: Korean parents' low-elaborative style of past event discussion and Korean children's abbreviated manner of discussing the past may indicate little early focus on the personal past and, consequently, few explicit, verbally accessible adult memories of specific early events.

In a recent study contrasting the memories of two cultural groups in New Zealand, Hayne and MacDonald (2003) were able to draw a similar connection between a global focus on the past and memory outcomes. The researchers asked Maori and Pakeha (Caucasian New Zealand) college students to provide written autobiographical accounts of their earliest memories. The researchers noted that Maori culture emphasizes richly descriptive retellings of the past in the form of stories, dances and legends, and thus predicted that Maori students might have earlier autobiographical memories than Pakeha students. The data confirmed this prediction, indicating that Maoris' earliest memories were on average dated from around 32 months of age, versus 42 months for Pakeha.

In a study of 255 Chinese adults, Wang, Leichtman, and White (1998) obtained findings that complement the foregoing data. High school and college students living in Beijing were asked to write down and date their earliest memory, and then to provide three additional childhood memories. The results indicated that, on average, Chinese adults' earliest memory dated from 3 years 9 months; several months later than typical findings among U.S. populations.

In addition, this study evaluated the influence of a number of specific factors in children's environments on adult autobiographical memories. Regression models including cohort and other factors of interest as covariates were used in analyzing the results, so that the effects reported below are independent of the historical timing of participants' births. A central question was whether the memories of participants who grew up as only children ($N = 99$) would differ from those who grew up with siblings ($N = 156$). The one-child policy, in place in China since 1979, provided a unique opportunity to evaluate the role of family structure in influencing autobiographical memory among persons from otherwise equivalent backgrounds. Significant literature has suggested that the 4-2-1 syndrome present in Chinese only child families, whereby four grandparents and two parents focus completely on one child, may create an environment that departs considerably from traditional Chinese collectivist values (Lee, 1992). Some reports have characterized Chinese only children, popularly described as "little emperors," as more self-centered, willful, and egocentric, and less disciplined, obedient, and other-oriented than children from larger families (Fan, 1994; Jiao, Ji, & Jing, 1986; Wang et al., 1983). These differences amount to a less traditionally interdependent orientation among children from only child families. A central question was how differences in the extent to which children from each type of family were encouraged to focus on themselves would be reflected in their later autobiographical memories of childhood.

To evaluate this question, all participants completed two written questionnaires in Chinese. The first, a version of Kuhn and McPartland's (1954) Twenty Statements Test eliciting self-descriptions, asked participants to fill in blanks in repeated sentences phrased "I am _____." The second asked participants to describe and date their earliest memory and to do the same for three other childhood memories. The results confirmed expectations of differences between only child and sibling child groups on both measures. Importantly, for each analysis reported below, contrasts between only-child participants and firstborns showed the same results as those reported for only child and all sibling child participants. Thus, although firstborns were only children before the births of their first sibling (for an average of 4.37 years in this sample), this early experience did not result in their resembling only children on any relevant measures.

Each answer to the Twenty Statements Test was categorized as an expression of a private, collective, or public self-description. This scoring method has been used in past studies as an index of how self-related information is differentially organized in memory across individuals (Bochner, 1994). Private self-descriptions focus on personal traits, states, or behaviors (e.g., "I am tall, intelligent, nervous."), collective self-descriptions focus on group membership (e.g., "I am a girl, a member of the Grimaldi family, a Catholic."), and public self-descriptions focus on the way in which a person interacts with or is viewed by others (e.g., "I am a person others view as kind." "I am someone who likes to help other people.") (Greenwald & Pratkanis, 1984; Triandis, 1989). Past work has indicated that participants from independent cultures typically provide overwhelmingly private self-descriptions, while participants from interdependent cultures provide more collective self-descriptions (Bochner, 1994; Trafimow,

Triandis, & Goto, 1991). Such differences presumably stem from independently oriented participants giving priority to personal values and goals, and having richly furnished, highly organized, and readily accessible sets of information about the private self in memory. In contrast, interdependently oriented persons focus significantly on the values and goals of the group and, thus, have similarly rich and accessible information regarding the collective self (Markus & Kitayama, 1991; Triandis, 1989).

This same contrast was apparent in the analysis of Chinese only and sibling child participants. Only child participants reported more private self-descriptions and fewer collective self-descriptions than sibling child participants. These findings support the notion that children from the two family structures may organize self-relevant information differently, despite the fact that they are part of the same larger cultural milieu.

In terms of autobiographical memories, only-child participants reported earliest memories dated from 39 months, while siblings reported earliest memories that were dated from 47.7 months, or almost 9 months later. The nature of the reported memories also differed between groups on a number of qualitative dimensions: only-child participants reported fewer memories focusing on social interactions, more memories focusing on personal experiences and feelings, fewer memories focusing on family, and more memories focusing solely on themselves. In addition, only-child participants reported a greater number of memories that were specific in nature (i.e., referring to one point in time events) than their sibling counterparts. Finally, only-child participants' memories contained a lower ratio of other-self mentions, indicating a differentially greater focus on their own past thoughts and activities. In addition to these between group differences, across the sample as a whole, participants' scores on the self-description questionnaire were predictive of a number of the autobiographical memory measures. Private self-description scores were positively related to memory narrative volume, mentions of the self, and the specificity of autobiographical memories, while collective self-description scores were negatively related to each. This combined evidence suggests a relationship between variables in the participants' early environments that affected the extent of focus on the self, and the degree and content of the autobiographical memories that remained accessible into adulthood.

Independent of family status, participants who attended preschool reported earliest memories that were 11 months earlier than those who did not and, the earlier preschool attendance began, the earlier was the first memory reported. Similarly, the employment status of participants' mothers during their childhood years was related to participants' autobiographical memories; a striking finding, given that all participants were top scholars enrolled in highly elite Chinese schools at the time of the study. Participants whose mothers either were professionals or urban workers had memories dating from 40 and 45 months on average, respectively, while participants whose mothers were farmers during their childhoods had memories dating from the later period of 56 months. This contrast is perhaps best conceived of as a rural-urban distinction. It is possible that socialization differences, such as farmers' children's engagement in collaborative work and the urban environment's greater emphasis on competition, self-actualization, and adaptation to modernization affected the degree to which participants focused on autobiographical events during childhood and, consequently, recalled them later.

In a study that further explored memories of childhood in rural versus urban populations, Leichtman, et al. (2003) focused on a sample of a total of 111 adults from three populations. The first group of participants lived in a remote village of goatherds in southern India. The second group lived in urban Bangalore and was of a comparable, low socio-economic status (SES). The third group was comprised of upper middle-class European Americans living in an urban region of the northeastern United States. In the Indian samples, a trained interviewer raised in the same region as the participants conducted interviews in the regional language, Kanada, while Americans were interviewed in English. The interviewer asked participants a series of scripted questions about autobiographical memory, beginning with an open-ended question asking whether they recalled any events from childhood. The interviewer asked participants to recount their childhood memories, and further prompted participants to relate any happy events and any sad events that they could recall. For each memory provided, the researcher asked participants their age at the time of the event.

In the Indian data, only 12% of participants in the rural sample and 30% of participants in the urban sample reported a specific event memory from childhood during the interview. Specific event memories were those that referred to a one point in time event (e.g., "the day my father fell into the well"), as opposed to routine or scripted activities (e.g., "going to school"). While all participants in the rural sample who reported a specific memory provided only one during the interview, 17% of participants in the urban sample provided two or more memories. Most participants in both samples did not know their own birth dates, and could not date their memories. However, of six urban participants who stated their age at the time of the events they recollected, age estimates ranged between 6 and 11 years. These data contrast dramatically with those taken from the American population, where 69% of participants reported recalling at least one specific childhood memory from childhood, and the spontaneous mention of dates of occurrence ranged between 3 and 12 years.

To examine whether there were systematic differences in the qualitative aspects of the rural and urban Indian participants' reports, 10 American raters, blind to all aspects of the study, assisted in a coding task. Raters were given a stack of 69 index cards, each with a single memory provided by a rural Indian, urban Indian, or an American control participant (one third each) in response to the same memory questions. All Indian memories that appeared on the cards were English translations, and culturally identifying information (e.g., names of Indian foods, local place references) was replaced with neutral information. (Some memories included in the rural selections were obtained from a supplementary sample of 32 rural participants who also were asked memory questions.) The memories from each group were randomly selected after eliminating all responses in which participants could not provide a memory. The number of words in each memory segment was similar, on average, for the three groups. The cards were shuffled randomly, so that memories from all three groups of participants were mixed.

Raters came to the laboratory and were told that they were to read over the cards and sort them into two approximately equal piles. They were told, "We've been interviewing people about their autobiographical memories. People differ in how vividly they remember and talk about past events. Some peoples' reports reflect very rich, vivid memories of their experiences--it seems like the events just happened yesterday and they recall every detail. Other people have fuzzier, weaker, more skeletal memories of past events, and their reports appear comparatively impoverished, lacking in vividness and richness of details." Participants were then asked to read over the cards and sort them into two approximately equal piles, placing half the cards in a box representing rich, vivid memories and the other half in a box representing relatively impoverished, skeletal reports of past events.

The cumulative results of this sorting revealed distinct patterns for memories of participants from the three populations. Sixty-three percent of those memories provided by Americans were placed in the box representing rich memories, with only 37% placed in the box representing poor memories. Similarly, 54% of memories from urban Indians were rated as rich, while 46% were rated as poor. In contrast, only 27% of rural Indian memories were rated as rich, while 73% were rated as poor. This gross rating scheme thus captured a parallel with the urban-rural difference that Wang et al. (1998) found among Chinese participants: Living in an urban area appears to increase access to early event memories, and to make reports of those memories more vivid and detailed. Notably, although there was a slight difference in years of education favoring urban participants in this study, there was no significant effect of educational status on the number or qualitative characteristics of participants' memories.

By what mechanism might urbanization influence autobiographical memory? As noted in the discussion of Wang et al.'s (1998) Chinese results, differences in general aspects of participants' social environments may have contributed to the later, more skeletal autobiographical reports documented among rural samples. In addition, the informal reactions of Indian participants provide insight into a broader explanation. A large percentage of rural Indian participants responded to questions about their autobiographical memories with an attitude of incredulity. Typically, participants said, "Why think about the past? The past is just as the future" or "It's a silly waste of time to think about the events of one's life; such thinking changes nothing."

When participants were asked directly whether, and under what circumstances they reminisced about past events, rural participants responded almost universally that they rarely did so. In contrast, urban participants seemed more comfortable reflecting on and sharing their life memories, and did not display the same attitude of indifference toward the details of specific life experiences. Even more strikingly, American participants often noted that their personal memories were an integral part of themselves, that such memories were extremely important to them, and that they commonly reflected on past experiences. This contrast in the attitudes of the two groups may reflect a difference in the need to think about the past in response to change. In rural Indian villages, lifestyles are much as they were generations ago and anticipated changes are few. In urban India or in the United States, deciding on a life course and constantly adapting to the changing demands of modern, industrialized society may increase individuals' attention to the unique aspects of their personalities and situations. This may lead to a relatively more introspective attitude toward the personal past. Further, as Wang (2003) noted, the continual novelty and change inherent in urban life provides ample material for the construal of autobiographical stories, whereas the redundancy of rural life may not. Whatever the complete explanation for their existence, urban/rural differences underscore the multiple components of the social environment that may affect the nature of autobiographical memories.

In a provocative addition to the literature on the link between early socialization and long-term personal event memories, Weigle and Bauer (2000) studied adults who had been deaf from birth, but had hearing parents, along with age and gender-matched hearing control participants. The rationale for studying these two populations was the idea that the linguistic environment of early childhood would have been relatively impoverished for the deaf participants, and language acquisition delayed until they were exposed to American Sign Language (ASL). Researchers interviewed deaf participants in ASL and hearing participants in spoken English, prompting for memories of both earliest childhood and later years (after age 10). One potential result would have been later first memories in deaf subjects, due to the importance of early language in supporting encoding and storage. In fact, the findings indicated no significant between-group differences in the timing of earliest memories. However, there were differences in the nature of the memories of the two groups in the predicted direction, in that deaf participants provided narratives that were less linguistically dense, included less visual-spatial information, and included fewer categories of information in general. The authors speculated that differences in the early environment may have prompted deaf participants to take a less linguistically dependent avenue in the retention of autobiographical events.

It is important to note that the nature and timing of childhood memories may vary as a function of the events being remembered. This point was underscored by Usher and Neisser's (1993) data on the childhood memories of American college students. In a written survey, participants were prompted to remember various episodes that occurred when they were very young. Participants were able to recall hospitalizations or the birth of siblings from the time they were between 2 and 3 years old. In contrast, they recalled deaths in the family or moves to new homes only if these events happened after age 3. Retrospective ratings of emotion and amount of postevent rehearsal were similar across events, such that these factors did not explain the differences between events. What may have been significant was the amount of preparation children received prior to the events, in discussion with parents and other significant adults. While Usher and Neisser's findings indicated group-level differences between various categories of events, the characteristics of the events driving these differences remain to be explained. It may be that as a function of socially shared meanings, for most children particular events share common features that are likely to influence their duration in long-term memory. For instance, a hospitalization may hold similar meaning, emotion, and salience for most children, despite the particular circumstances under which it occurs. Thus, although unique elements of such an event for an individual child could also influence later event memory, the particular shared cultural context in which an event occurs could be a powerful determinant of whether and how it is eventually remembered.

SUGGESTIBILITY AND LONG-TERM EVENT MEMORIES

Studies focusing on suggestibility memory have provided indirect, but pertinent insights relevant to childhood amnesia. A large contemporary literature in developmental psychology has been directed at understanding why, and under what circumstances, children's memory reports contain particular kinds of inaccuracies (Ackil & Zaragoza, 1995; Ceci & Bruck, 1993; Leichtman & Ceci, 1995, Robinson & Whitcombe, 2003). Specifically, many researchers have been interested the vulnerability of children's memories to distortion from influences external to the original memory trace.

A wealth of findings, accumulated over the two decades, attests to a decline in suggestibility with age. While adults and children of all ages are vulnerable to suggestion (Loftus, 1991; Schacter, 1995), young children are disproportionately vulnerable (Ceci & Bruck, 1993, 1995; Lepore & Sesco, 1994). Typically, children's suggestibility has been documented in misinformation paradigms in which children experience a story or event and, subsequently, receive misleading information about the details that they witnessed. For example, Ceci, Ross, and Toglia (1987) read a story about several events in the life of a protagonist to children between the age of 3 and 12. The day after the reading, a researcher interviewed the participants, asking a series of questions about the story. The researcher included subtle misinformation in his or her questions to experimental participants, while including only correct information in questions to control participants. Two days later, another researcher gave all participants two-item forced choice recognition tasks regarding the items present in the original story. The results indicated that control participants were highly accurate in recognizing the correct original items; the mean for all age groups was between 84% and 95% correct. In contrast, there was a sharp age trend in the experimental group due to younger children's incorrect selection of suggested information or "false alarms": 3- to 4-year-olds achieved a mean of 37% correct, 5- to 6-year-olds a mean of 58% correct, 7- to 9-year-olds a mean of 67% correct, and 10- to 12-year-olds a mean of 84% correct.

More naturalistic paradigms have demonstrated similar age effects. For example, Leichtman and Ceci (1995) conducted a study of 3- to 6-year-olds centering on an event staged in their preschool classrooms. The event was the unannounced visit of a man named Sam Stone. Sam Stone simply entered the children's classrooms while they were gathered in a circle, said hello, chatted, looked around the room, and left after several minutes. Researchers gave children in an experimental group a series of four misleading interviews over the course of 8 weeks. During each interview, the researchers assumed in their questioning that Sam Stone had committed clumsy acts during his visit, such as spilling and breaking things. The questions thus centered on the circumstances and details of these acts. When interviewed 10 weeks after the event, many experimental group children who participated in misleading interviews appeared convinced that Sam Stone had committed actions in line with the researchers' suggestions. In response to an open-ended question about what happened during Sam Stone's visit, 21% of 3- to 4-year-olds and 14% of 5- to 6-year-olds alleged that Sam Stone committed at least one clumsy act consistent with the suggestions. In response to direct questions regarding actions about which they had been mislead, commission error rates climbed to 53% for younger participants and 38% for older participants. In contrast, control participants of both ages, who received no misleading suggestions after Sam Stone's visit, made almost no such errors under open-ended or direct question conditions 10 weeks after the event.

The growing evidence of disproportionate vulnerability to suggestion among preschoolers has intrigued researchers, inspiring explanations on a number of different levels (e.g., Ackil & Zaragoza, 1995; Welch-Ross, Diecidue, & Miller, 1997; Principe & Ceci, 2002). Certainly, under some questioning conditions, social factors play a role in children's suggestibility. Young children, for example, may consciously bow to the suggestions of adult authority figures or mentally question the accuracy of their own recollections in the face of alternative suggestions from powerful adults (Ceci & Bruck, 1993). However, while under some conditions these social factors may give rise to or enhance children's report distortion, there is compelling evidence that fundamental cognitive elements of memory also are affected by misleading information in children's environments.

In the present discussion of factors involved in childhood amnesia, one particular explanation for the suggestibility of children's memory is of central relevance. This is the hypothesis that poor source monitoring skills cause children to make the memorial errors that distort their reports. *Source monitoring* refers to the ability to identify the origin of one's own beliefs and memories. Across a number of experimental paradigms, preschoolers show particular difficulty doing so, commonly making source misattribution errors. For example, in one paradigm, participants are asked either to perform or to imagine performing a number of actions (e.g., standing up, touching their noses). After doing so, younger children are more likely than older children to make source misattributions; they remember performing actions that they only imagined, and vice versa (e.g., Foley & Johnson, 1985; Welch-Ross, 1995a). Similarly, young children have difficulty remembering the circumstances under which they acquired new information. Taylor, Esbensen, and Bennett (1994) conducted a series of studies exploring this phenomenon. They found that, after learning novel facts, 4-year-olds incorrectly stated, and acted as though they believed, that they had always known facts they had learned just minutes earlier. Thus, across tasks requiring source monitoring, young children often are unable to specify the original context in which they encountered information, although they accurately recall the information itself.

Theorists have hypothesized that source misattributions underlie the suggestibility effects induced by misleading information (e.g., Ceci et al., 1994; Robinson & Whitcombe, 2003; Schacter, Kagan, & Leichtman, 1995). In the simplest example of how this might occur, children may confuse facts or pictures they were given after an event with those that were part of the event. In suggestibility paradigms involving only verbal questions, repeated suggestive questions may induce children to create images of suggested events while they are being interviewed. During subsequent questioning (e.g., during the fifth interview after Sam Stone's visit or after multiple visualizations in Ceci, Loftus, et al.'s, 1994, card drawing paradigm), children may call to mind the images inspired during past interviews. In doing so, children may have difficulty identifying the origins of these images; that is, they may confuse these internally generated mental pictures with the actual events they experienced. Younger participants may be particularly prone to this confusion, just as they make source misattribution errors with exaggerated frequency under other circumstances.

A set of experiments focusing on 3- to 4-year-olds illustrates the potential contribution of source monitoring to suggestibility effects. In the original study, once each week for 10 weeks, children participated in an interview in which they were asked to draw from the same group of cards. Half of the cards described real events that occurred in the children's classrooms, while the other half referenced events that never happened in the children's lives (Ceci, Huffman, Smith, & Loftus, 1994). During each one-on-one session with a researcher, the children drew one card at a time until all of the cards had been drawn. After the children drew each card, the researcher read the event described on the card aloud, and asked, "Think real hard, and tell me; did that ever happen to you?" After children answered this question with a "yes" or "no." they moved on to the next card. In the 11th and final week, a new interviewer queried children, asking a similar question for each card. In this session, however, the interviewer also asked children to elaborate. If children said that events on the cards had happened to them, the researcher asked them to tell him or her all about these events. Further, the researcher asked detailed follow-up questions after each open-ended question.

The results indicated that, by the final interview, more than one third of children reported remembering an event that never actually occurred; in most cases, events they originally denied remembering. Moreover, the children's inaccurate reports were internally consistent, full of vivid detail, and accompanied by a confident attitude. When condition-blind adult raters were asked to discriminate between the children's accurate and inaccurate memories, they were unable to do so at a level above chance.

A second study focused on the emotional nature of the imagined events, and how this might influence the children's susceptibility to incorporating the events into memory (Ceci, Loftus, Leichtman, & Bruck, 1994). Here, the manipulation was a bit more heavy handed; during the weekly sessions, researchers actively encouraged children to visualize events to which they acquiesced. The suggested events were either positive (getting a present), neutral (waiting for a bus), or negative (falling off a tricycle and cutting one leg). The results indicated that, while children were quite accurate from start to finish in reporting on the events that had actually occurred, the mean false assent rate (or rate of commission errors) rose dramatically across interviews. Three- to 4-year-olds and 5- to 6-year-olds showed similar increases in false assents across interviews, although in accordance with common development trends in suggestibility, younger children had a higher rate of baseline errors. Notably, all types of events were subject to the effects of imagining, although not equally so—negative events reflected fewer commission errors than positive. Thus, emotional content may be among the parameters that influence the difficulty of discriminating real from imagined events.

Studies of both source monitoring and suggestibility have shown substantial individual differences among children. On both types of tasks, even the performance of children in the most error-prone preschool age group varies widely; while participants on the whole make a substantial number of errors, there are individuals who consistently resist suggestions and correctly identify the origins of their past experiences. Schacter, Kagan, and Leichtman (1995) noted that children's source monitoring problems and memorial suggestibility were similar to the source amnesia and high rates of false recognition found among adults with frontal lobe damage. Given this parallel, Schacter et al. suggested that both the phenomena of suggestibility and source misattributions might be caused by immature frontal lobe development in preschoolers. Individual differences between children on both types of tasks could then be explained by differential maturity of the frontal regions.

Support for this provocative suggestion required evidence of a direct relationship between source monitoring and suggestibility performance in young children. Thus, Leichtman and Morse (1997) conducted a series of experiments to examine this relationship. In each study, the same forty-five 3- to 5-year-old children were given several traditional source monitoring tasks as well as multiple tasks measuring memorial suggestibility. In an illustrative study (Leichtman & Morse, 1997, Study 2), researchers gave children two measures of source monitoring, and two measures of suggestibility. The first source monitoring task was an adaptation of Gopnik and Graf's (1988) paradigm, in which a researcher showed children a set of six small drawers, each containing a different small object. Children learned what was inside each drawer by either being told, guessing from a clue provided them, or opening the drawer. Just after learning the drawers' contents, the researcher asked children to identify the object inside each of the closed drawers. Immediately afterward, he or she asked them to tell him or her how they learned what was inside each drawer; by seeing the object, being told about it, or guessing it with a clue.

The second source monitoring task was an adaptation of the do-imagine task designed by Foley and Johnson (1985). A researcher led children through a series of simple actions, and asked them either to actually perform or to imagine performing each one. After completing the entire list, the researcher asked the children to list all of the actions they remembered performing or imagining. Finally, she reminded the children of each of the actions, and asked whether they had performed or imagined each.

The first suggestibility task was a version of the misinformation paradigm often given to adults. Researchers showed children a narrated slide show story that included several target events. One day after they viewed the story, an interviewer asked children misleading questions about it. One week later, another interviewer gave children a forced-choice picture recognition task including the suggested detail and the original information. This forced-choice task required children to identify which was the original object they had seen in the story.

The second suggestibility task was similar to the visualization paradigm developed by Ceci and colleagues (Bruck, Ceci, & Hembrooke, 1997; Ceci, Huffman, et al., 1994; Ceci, Loftus, et al., 1994). Children were questioned once per week about the same six events; three events that they actually experienced, and three events that never happened (e.g., a boy visited school with a little puppy; a teacher found $100 under a slide). Each week, children drew the events from a hat in random order. A researcher asked children whether each occurred, and then asked them to imagine the events that they said did not occur. A final interview occurred during the 7th week, when another researcher asked children to tell whether each event occurred and then to elaborate on what they remembered about the event.

The results of this series of tasks show a compelling pattern of connection between children's source monitoring skills and their ability to resist memorial suggestion. As expected, scores indicating accurate source identification on the two source monitoring tasks (i.e., the drawer and do-imagine tasks) were highly correlated with each other ($r = .62$). Scores indicating the ability to resist suggestion on the two disparate suggestibility tasks (i.e., the traditional story misinformation paradigm and visualization task) also were significantly correlated ($r = .34$). The four critical correlations—between each of the source monitoring tasks and each of the suggestibility tasks—all were highly significant ($p < .001$), ranging between $-.75$ and $-.85$. Thus, the better children were at identifying the context in which they acquired knowledge in the source monitoring tasks, the less vulnerable they were to suggestion.

Importantly, measures indexing simple recognition of story details and recall of actions performed were not significantly related to either source monitoring skills or suggestibility. It appears that the relationship between suggestibility and source monitoring was not simply the outcome of globally better memory among some children; the two measures were more specifically related. Although this relationship is not definitive evidence of frontal lobe control of both processes, it strongly supports the theoretical possibility. Other aspects of children's cognitive development that contribute to the variance in suggestibility performance also may be either directly or indirectly related to improvements in frontal lobe functioning. For example, Welch-Ross and colleagues have provided evidence that children's understanding of conflicting mental representations in theory of mind tasks also show strong correlations with suggestibility scores (Welch-Ross et al., 1997). Whether these are an outgrowth of improvements in source monitoring skills or independent contributors to their development remains to be seen.

The cumulative literature on children's suggestibility and source monitoring has suggested that maturational processes significantly influence whether children are prone to incorporating "false memories" into their autobiographical repertoires. This literature also has provided an alternative perspective on the timing of childhood amnesia. The strict measure of autobiographical memory in adulthood is whether memories respond to explicit, verbal cueing. For example, researchers ask participants questions such as, "Tell me about an event that you remember from childhood?" "What do you remember about the birth of your younger brother?" "Remember the events of your third birthday?" These are the questions in response to which participants have a reliable dearth of memories from the first 3 to 6 years of life, and which reflect between-culture differences in terms of age boundaries.

Developmental findings pertaining to suggestibility and source monitoring inspire the following notion. The memories that children encode may not consistently respond to the kind of cues that adult autobiographical memory tasks offer until children reach a critical level of frontal lobe maturity. Young children may fail to integrate the larger context in which an experience occurs with the core facts of that experience. Ironically, when adults are asked to retrieve childhood memories, the context itself is often the cue intended to trigger personal event memories. For example, asking an adult to remember the events of her third birthday is, in some sense, akin to asking a child who has participated in Gopnik and Graf's (1988) drawer task to "remember that thing that you guessed one day with a clue." Many young children are unable to identify how they acquired information about a known object (e.g., by guessing), even minutes after doing so. Thus, it is unlikely, that being provided with the context cue (e.g., "an object you guessed") would enable these children to recall an object they had otherwise forgotten. In other words, because the associations between context and object are weak, one is unlikely to serve as an effective retrieval cue for the other over the long-term. According to this logic, the problem is not simply that adults fail to access early memories because they do not label them within useful specific contexts during childhood (e.g., "something that's happening now, while I'm 3 years old"). The problem is that the link between the context and the content of the memory is weak at encoding, and this context is exactly to cue that explicit narrative recall tasks typically provide.

This way of thinking about the cues provided in adult narrative tasks suggests a connection between disparate findings on the development of source monitoring and adult personal event narratives. Notably, adults' earliest autobiographical memories typically begin during the period from 3 to 5 years. This is the same period in which source monitoring skills dramatically improve, and in which children become significantly more accurate in discriminating real from suggested events (Welch-Ross, 1995b). Further, this period signifies the upper cusp of a developmental shift from implicit, behaviorally expressed memories to explicit, verbally accessible ones. Newcombe, Drummey, Fox, Lie, & Ottinger-Alberts (2000) noted that when a child's explicit memory trace for real events is weak, in toto, discriminating between real and imagined events becomes exceptionally difficult. Elements of the explicit trace that could support a judgment that the event was real may be missing. This is important to recognize in view of the fact that explicit event representations during the preschool years are likely to be weaker than later on in development. When coupled with data suggesting that young children may sometimes vividly imagine false events (Ceci, Loftus, Leichtman, & Bruck, 1994), the potential for error in event memory during this period becomes clear. A close, lucid, explicitly retrievable connection between context and the socially-deemed central elements of experience provides the best conditions for storage and retrieval of event representations over the long term. These conditions are unlikely to be fully met for memories encoded in the earliest years of life.

CONCLUSIONS

Perhaps the most significant fact about long-term event memory that contemporary developmental research has revealed is the sheer complexity of the web of factors that support it. Early theorists might have been surprised to learn that as evidence for a biological contribution to event memory performance has become more detailed and compelling, so has evidence for an environmental contribution.

Theory and limited empirical inquiry focusing on the influence of maturational factors on long-term event memory have brought gratifying insights in recent years. For example, recent attempts to connect a growing body of knowledge about hippocampal and frontal lobe development to developments in long-term retention have been important. They highlight the almost certain probability that changes at the level of the brain contribute substantially to specific behavioral phenomena developmentalists have long grappled with. These phenomena include, for example, the ontogenetic shift from implicit to explicit event memories and the growing ability to identify the source of memories acquired during single, one-point-in-time events. A significant challenge for the coming decades will be to map out with precision the developmental trajectory of brain functions relevant to long-term memory and the ways in which they might predict differences across individuals and across tasks at various points in development. This task is complex in and of itself, and it is made more so by the fact that memory development takes place in connection with many other dramatic cognitive shifts.

Long-term memories, most notably those carried from childhood into adulthood, are also profoundly influenced by environmental factors. In fact, it is clear that not one but many layers of the environment (Bronfenbrenner, 1993) impact upon the timing, structure, and content of memories as development unfolds. Recognition of this fact underscores the paramount importance of including a careful analysis of context in any consideration of long-term event memory, as noted in the introduction to this chapter. The cross-cultural research reviewed here has provided compelling evidence of the importance of these multiple environmental layers. The studies that we and others have conducted with populations in various countries point to differences in children's microsystems, or immediate environments, that have potency for long-term memory. Importantly, these microsystem differences are closely linked with differences at the level of the macrosystem or the more general mileu in which children live.

Work on the nature of parent–child conversations about past events provides an excellent example of this connected set of influences. Studies exploring the origin and details of differences in such conversations across cultures and individuals are ongoing. However, even in the past 5 years, we have gained clarity on the point that natural variations are more extensive than previously suspected.

Further, the implications of such variations for children's long-term memory also appear to be more extensive than previously documented. At the microsystem level, talking about the past with an adult often influences the content of children's specific memory reports, determining which details of a particular experience are strengthened and which fade. At the same time, regular exposure to a particular normative way of conversing about the past may have equally significant effects. Such differences in conversational norms are determined by macrosystem-level factors, For example, what people believe about the importance of personal event memory and about other relevant issues such as what constitutes ideal child-rearing practices or the optimal degree of self-focus are part of this broader macrosystem. Such beliefs vary normatively across cultures, and they may drive how children come to think about the meaning of personal experiences, and how children allocate attention in the face of the novel events that eventually become the subject of long-term memories.

For researchers focusing on environmental influences on long-term memory, the charge in coming years will be to continue to document the subtleties of belief, conversation, and thoughts about the personal past that differ across individuals and cultures. Equally essential, and perhaps more difficult, will be to explain with precision differences in long-term memory in connection with complex and sometimes idiosyncratic cultural value systems and practices. Eventually, advances in both the biological and environmental realms of research on long-term memory may enable us to explain the still mysterious synchrony that determines what we remember and what we forget from childhood.

REFERENCES

Ackil, J. K., & Zaragoza, M. S. (1995). Developmental differences in eyewitness suggestibility and memory for source. *Journal of Experimental Child Psychology, 60,* 57–83.

Bauer, P. J., Hertsgaard, L. A., & Dow, G. A. (1994). After 8 months have passed: Long-term recall of events by 1- to 2-year-old children. *Memory, 2,* 353–382.

Bauer, P. J., & Shore, C. M. (1987). Making a memorable event: Effects of familiarity and organization on young children's recall of action sequences. *Cognitive Development, 2,* 327–338.

Bauer, P. J., Wenner, J. A., & Kroupina, M. G. (2002). *Journal of Cognition and Development, 3*(1), 21–47.

Bauer, P. J., Wiebe, S. A., Carver, L. J., Waters, J. M., & Nelson, C. A. (2003), Developments in long-term explicit memory late in the first year of life: Behavioral and electrophysiological indices. *Psychological Science, 14, 6,* 629–635.

Bochner, S. (1994). Cross-cultural differences in the self concept. *Journal of Cross-Cultural Psychology, 25,* 273–283.

Bornstein, M. H., & Sigman, M. D. (1986). Continuity in mental development from infancy. *Child Development, 57,* 251–274.

Bronfenbrenner, U. (1993). The ecology of cognitive development: Research models and fugitive findings. In R. H. Wozniak & K. W. Fischer (Eds.), *Development in context: Acting and thinking in specific environments* (pp. 3–44). Hillsdale, NJ: Erlbaum.

Bruck, M., Ceci, S. J., & Hembrooke, H. (1997). Children's reports of pleasant and unpleasant events. In D. Read & S. Lindsay (Eds.), *Recollections of trauma: Scientific research and clinical practice* (pp. 199–219). New York: Plenum Press.

Carver, L. J., & Bauer, P. J. (2001). The dawning of the past: The emergence of long-term explicit memory in infancy. *Journal of Experimental Psychology: General, 130*(4), 726–745.

Ceci, S. J. (2003). Cast in six ponds and you'll reel in something: Looking back on 25 years of research. *American Psychologist, 58, 11,* 855–864.

Ceci, S. J., & Bruck, M. (1993). The suggestibility of the child witness: A historical review and synthesis. *Psychological Bulletin, 113,* 403–439.

Ceci, S. J., & Bruck, M. (1995). *Jeopardy in the courtroom: A scientific analysis of children's testimony.* Washington, DC: American Psychological Association.

Ceci, S. J., Huffman, M. L., & Smith, E. & Loftus, E. F. (1994). Repeatedly thinking about a non-event. *Consciousness and Cognition, 2,* 388–407.

Ceci, S. J., & Leichtman, M. D. (1992). Memory, cognition and learning: Developmental and ecological considerations. In I. Rapin & S. Segalawitz (Eds.), *Handbook of neuropsychology.* Holland: Elsevier.

Ceci, S. J., Loftus, E. F., Leichtman, M. D., & Bruck, M. (1994). The role of source misattributions in the creation of false beliefs among preschoolers. *International Journal of Clinical and Experimental Hypnosis, 42,* 304–320.

Ceci, S. J., Ross, D. F., & Toglia, M. P. (1987). Suggestibility of children's memory: Psycholegal implications. *Journal of Experimental Psychology: General, 116,* 38–49.

Choi, S. H. (1992). Communicative socialization processes: Korea and Canada. In S. Iwasaki, Y. Kashima, & K. Leung (Eds.), *Innovations in cross-cultural psychology* (pp. 103–122). Amsterdam: Swets & Zeitlinger.

Dudycha, G. J., & Dudycha, M. M. (1933). Some factors and characteristics of childhood memories. *Child Development, 4,* 265–278.

Fagan, J. F. (1971). Infants' recognition memory for a series of visual stimuli. *Journal of Experimental Child Psychology, 14,* 453–476.

Fagan, J. F. (1979). The origins of facial pattern recognition. In M. Bornstein & W. Kessen (Eds.), *Psychological development from infancy: Image to intention.* Hillsdale, NJ: Erlbaum.

Fan, C. (1994). A comparative study of personality characteristics between only and nononly children in primary schools in Xian. *Psychological Science, 17*(2), 70–74 (in Chinese)

Fiske, A. P., Kitayama, S., Markus, H. R., & Nisbett, R. E. (1998). The cultural matrix of social psychology. In D. T. Gilbert, S. T. Fiske, & G. Lindzey (Eds.), *The handbook of social psychology* (Vol. 2, 4th ed., pp. 915–981). New York: Oxford University Press.

Fivush, R. (1991). The social construction of personal narratives. *Merrill-Palmer Quarterly, 37,* 59–81.

Fivush, R., & Fromhoff, F. A. (1988). Style and structure in mother-child conversations about the past. *Discourse Processes, 11,* 337–355.

Fivush, R., Gray, J. T., & Fromhoff, F. A. (1987). Two-year-olds talk about the past. *Cognitive Development, 2,* 393–409.

Fivush, R., & Hamond, N. R. (1990). Autobiographical memory across the preschool years: Toward reconceptualizing infantile amnesia. In R. Fivush & J. A. Hudson (Eds.), *Knowing and remembering in young children.* New York: Cambridge University Press.

Fivush, R., & Hudson, J. (1990). *Knowing and remembering in young children.* New York: Cambridge University Press.

Foley, M. A., & Johnson, M. K. (1985). Confusions between memories for performed and imagined actions. *Child Development, 56,* 1145–1155.

Freud, S. (1920/1953). *A general introduction to psychoanalysis.* New York: Simon and Schuster.

Gopnik, A., & Graf, P. (1988). Knowing how you know: Young children's ability to identify and remember the sources of their beliefs. *Child Development, 59,* 1366–1371.

Greenwald, A. G., & Pratkanis, A. R. (1984). The self. In R. S. Wyer & T. K. Srull (Eds.), *Handbook of social cognition* (Vol. 3, pp. 129–178). Hillsdale, NJ: Erlbaum.

Haden, C. A., Haine, R. A., & Fivush, R. (1997). Developing narrative structure in parent-child reminiscing across the preschool years. *Developmental Psychology, 33,* 295–307.

Haden, C. A., Ornstein, P. A., Eckerman, C. O., & Didow, S. M. (2001). Mother-child conversational interactions as events unfold: linkages to subsequent remembering. *Child Development, 72, 4,* 1016–1031.

Han, J. J., Leichtman, M. D., & Wang, Q. (1998). Autobiographical memory in Korean, Chinese and American children. *Developmental Psychology, 34,* 701–703.

Hartshorn, K., & Rovee-Collier, C. (1997). Infant learning and long-term memory at 6 months: A confirming analysis. *Developmental Psychobiology, 30,* 71–85.

Hayne, H., & McDonald, S. (2003). The socialization of autobiographical memory in children and adults: The roles of culture and gender. In R. Fivush & C. Haden (Eds.), Autobiographical memory and the construction of a narrative self, 99–120.

Howe, M. L., & Courage, M. L. (1993). On resolving the enigma of infantile amnesia. *Psychological Bulletin, 113,* 305–326.

Hudson, J. (1990). The emergence of autobiographical memory in mother-child conversation. In R. Fivush & J. Hudson (Eds.), *Knowing and remembering in young children* (pp. 166–196). New York: Cambridge University Press.

James, W. (1950). *Principles in psychology.* New York: Dover.

Jiao, S., Ji, G., & Jing, Q. (1986). Comparative study of behavior qualities of only children and sibling children. *Child Development, 57,* 357–361.

Kessen, W., & Nelson, K. (1978). What the child brings to language. In B. Z. Presseisen, D. Goldstein, & M. H. Apperl (Eds.), *Topics in cognitive development* (Vol. 2). New York: Plenum Press.

Kihlstrom, J. F., & Harackiewicz, J. M. (1982). The earliest recollection: A new survey. *Journal of Personality, 50,* 134–148.

Kuhn, M. H., & McPartland, T. S. (1954). An empirical investigation of self-attitudes. *American Sociological Review, 19,* 68–76.

LeCompte, G. K., & Gratch, G. (1972). Violation of a rule as a method of diagnosing infants' level of object concept. *Child Development, 43,* 385–396.

Lee, L. C. (1992). Day care in the People's Republic of China. In M. E. Lamb & K. Sternberg (Eds.), *Child care in context: Cross cultural perspectives* (pp. 355–392). Hillsdale, NJ: Erlbaum.

Leichtman, M. D. (1994). Long term memory in infancy and early childhood. *Dissertation Abstracts International, 55,* 2024B.

Leichtman, M. D., Bhogle, S., Sankaranarayanan, A., & Hobeika, D. (2003). Autobiographical memory and children's narrative environments in Southern India and the Northern United States. Unpublished manuscript.

Leichtman, M. D., & Ceci, S. J. (1993). The problem of infantile amnesia: Lessons from fuzzy-trace theory. In M. L. Howe & R. Pasternak (Eds.), *Emerging themes in cognitive development: Vol. 1. Foundations* (pp. 195–213). New York: Springer Verlag.

Leichtman, M. D., & Ceci, S. J. (1995). The effects of stereotypes and suggestions on preschoolers' reports. *Developmental Psychology, 31,* 568–578.

Leichtman, M. D., Pillemer, D. B. & Skowronek (2005, April). Talking or not about events of the day: Effects on preschooler's long-term memories. Paper presented at the biennial meeting of the Society for Research in Child Development, Atlanta, GA.

Leichtman, M. D., Pillemer, D. B., Wang, Q., Koreishi, A., & Han, J. J. (2000). When Baby Maisy came to school: Mothers' interview styles and preschoolers' event memories. *Cognitive Development, 15,* 1–16.

Leichtman, M. D., & Morse, M. B. (1997, April). *Individual differences in preschoolers' suggestibility: Identifying the source.* Paper presented at the biennial meeting of the Society for Research in Child Development, Washington, DC.

Lepore, S. J., & Sesco, B. (1994). Distorting children's reports and interpretation of events through suggestion. *Applied Psychology, 79,* 108–120.

Liston, C., & Kagan, J. (2002). Memory enhancement in early childhood. *Nature, 419,* 896.

Loftus, E. F. (1991). Made in memory: Distortions of recollection after misleading information. In G. Bower (Ed.), *Psychology of learning and motivation* (Vol. 27, pp. 187–215). New York: Academic Press.

Mandler, J. M. (1990). Recall of events by preverbal children. In A. Diamond (Ed.), *The development and neural bases of higher cognitive functions. Annals of the New York Academy of Sciences, 608,* 485–516.

Mandler, J. M. (1992). How to build a baby II: Conceptual primitives. *Psychological Review, 99,* 587–604.

Mandler, J. M., & McDonough, L. (1995). Long-term recall of event sequences in infancy. *Journal of Experimental Child Psychology, 59,* 457–474.

Markus, H. R., & Kitayama, S. (1991). Culture and the self: Implications for cognition, emotion, and motivation. *Psychological Review, 98,* 224–253.

Markus, H. R., & Kitayama, S. (1994). The cultural construction of self and emotion: Implications for social behavior. In S. Kitayama & H. R. Markus (Eds.), *Emotion and culture: Empirical studies of mutual influence* (pp. 89–130). Washington, DC: American Psychological Association.

Marshall, D. H., Drummey, A. B., Fox, N. A., & Newcombe, N. S. (2002). *Journal of Cognition and Development, 3*(2), 201–224.

McCabe, A., & Peterson, C. (1991). Getting the story: A longitudinal study of parental styles in eliciting narratives and developing narrative skill. In A. McCabe & C. Peterson (Eds.), *Developing narrative structure* (pp. 217–253). Hillsdale, NJ: Erlbaum.

McCall, R. B. (1979). The development of intellectual functioning in infancy and prediction of later IQ. In J. D. Osofsky (Ed.), *Handbook of infant development*. New York: Wiley.

McDonough, L., & Mandler, J. M. (1994). Very long-term recall in infants: Infantile amnesia reconsidered. In R. Fivush (Ed.), *Long-term retention of infant memories: Vol. 2. Memory* (4th ed., pp. 339–352). Hove, UK: Erlbaum.

Meltzoff, A. N. (1988). Infant imitation after a 1-week delay: Long term memory for novel acts and multiple stimuli. *Developmental Psychology, 24*, 470–476.

Meltzoff, A. N. (1995). What infant memory tells us about infantile amnesia: Long-term recall and deferred imitation. *Journal of Experimental Child Psychology, 59*, 497–515.

Mullen, M. K. (1994). Earliest recollections of childhood: A demographic analysis. *Cognition, 52*, 55–79.

Mullen, M. K., & Yi, S. (1995). The cultural context of talk about the past: Implications for the development of autobiographical memory. *Cognitive Development, 10*, 407–419.

Myers, N. A., Clifton, R. K., & Clarkson, M. G. (1987). When they were very young: Almost-threes remember two years ago. *Infant Behavior and Development, 10*, 123–132.

Myers, N. A., Perris, E. E., & Speaker, C. J. (1994). Fifty months of memory: A longitudinal study in early childhood. *Memory, 2*, 383–415).

Neisser, U. (1967). Cultural and cognitive discontinuity. In T. E. Gladwin & W. Sturtevant (Eds.), *Anthropology and human behavior* (pp. 54–71). Washington, DC: Anthropological Society of Washington.

Nelson, K. (1993). Events, narrative, memory: What develops? In C. Nelson (Ed.), *Memory and affect in development: The Minnesota symposia on child psychology* (Vol. 26, pp. 1–24). Hillsdale, NJ: Erlbaum.

Nelson, K. (1996). *Language in cognitive development: Emergence of the mediated mind*. New York: Cambridge University Press.

Newcombe, N. S., Drummey, A. B., Fox, N. A., Lie, E., & Ottinger-Alberts, W. (2000). Remembering Early Childhood: How Much, How and Why (or Why Not). *Current Directions in Psychological Science, 9, 2*, 55–58.

Otoya, M. T. (1988). A study of personal memories of bilinguals: The role of culture and language in memory encoding and recall. *Dissertation Abstracts International, 48*, 2789B.

Perner, J., & Ruffman, T. (1995). Episodic memory and autonoetic consciousness: Developmental evidence and a theory of childhood amnesia. *Journal of Experimental Child Psychology, 59*, 516–548.

Perris, E. E., Myers, N. A., & Clifton, R. K. (1990). Long-term memory for a single infancy experience. *Child Development, 61*, 1796–1807.

Peterson, C., & Rideout, R. (1998). Memory for medical emergencies experienced by 1- and 2-year-olds. *Developmental Psychology, 34*, 1059–1072.

Pillemer, D. B. (1998). *Momentous events, vivid memories*. Cambridge: Harvard University Press.

Pillemer, D. B., Picariello, M. L., & Pruett, J. C. (1994). Very long-term memories of a salient preschool event. *Applied Cognitive Psychology, 8*, 95–106.

Pillemer, D. B., & White, S. H. (1989). Childhood events recalled by children and adults. In H. W. Reese (Ed.), *Advances in child development and behavior* (Vol. 21, pp. 297–340). Orlando, FL: Academic Press.

Principe, G. F. & Ceci, S. J. (2002). "I saw it with my own ears"

The effects of peer conversations on preschoolers' reports of non-experienced events. *Journal of Experimental Child Psychology, 83*, 1–25.

Reese, E., & Fivush, R. (1993). Parental styles of talking about the past. *Developmental Psychology, 29*, 596–606.

Reese, E., Haden, C., & Fivush, R. (1993). Mother-child conversations about the past: Relationships of style and memory over time. *Cognitive Development, 8*, 403–430.

Robinson, E. J., & Whitcombe, E. L. (2003). Children's suggestibility in relation to their understanding about sources of knowledge. *Child Development, 74*, 48–62.

Rovee-Collier, C. (1993). The capacity for long-term memory in infancy. *Current Directions in Psychological Science, 2*, 130–135.

Rovee-Collier, C., & Hayne, H. (1987). Reactivation of infant memory: Implications for cognitive development. In H. W. Reese (Ed.), *Advances in child development and behavior* (Vol. 20, pp.185–238). New York: Academic Press.

Rubin, D. C. (1982). On the retention function for autobiographical memory. *Journal of Verbal Learning and Verbal Behavior, 21*, 21–38.

Schachtel, E. (1947). On memory and childhood amnesia. *Psychiatry, 10*, 1–26.

Schacter, D. L. (1987). Implicit memory: History and current status. *Journal of Experimental Psychology: Learning, Memory and Cognition, 13*, 501–518.

Schacter, D. L. (1995). Memory distortion: History and current status. In D. L. Schacter (Ed.), *Memory distortion* (pp. 1–43). Cambridge: Harvard University Press.

Schacter, D. L., Kagan, J., & Leichtman, M. D. (1995). True and false memories in children and adults: A cognitive neuroscience perspective. *Psychology, Public Policy and Law, 1*, 411–428.

Sheingold, K., & Tenney, Y. J. (1982). Memory for a salient childhood event. In U. Neisser (Ed.), *Memory observed* (pp. 201–212). San Francisco: Freeman.

Smith, P. H. (1984). Five-month-old infant recall and utilization of temporal organization. *Journal of Experimental Child Psychology, 38*, 400–414.

Squire, L. R. (1992). Declarative and nondeclarative memory: Multiple brain systems supporting memory and learning. *Journal of Cognitive Neuroscience, 4*, 232–243.

Stern, W., & Stern, C. (1909/1999). *Recollection, testimony and lying in early childhood*. Translated by James P. Lamiell. Washington, DC: American Psychological Association.

Stewart, M. K. (2004). *Remembering. Martha Stewart Living, 122*, 60.

Taylor, M., Esbensen, B. M., & Bennett, R. T. (1994). Children's understanding of knowledge acquisition: The tendency for children to report they have always known what they have just learned. *Child Development, 65*, 1581–1604.

Tessler, M., & Nelson, K. (1994). Making memories: The influence of joint encoding on later recall by young children. *Consciousness and Cognition, 3*, 307–326.

Trafimow, D., Triandis, H. C., & Goto, S. G. (1991). Some tests of the distinction between the private and the collective self. *Journal of Personality and Social Psychology, 60*, 649–655.

Triandis, H. C. (1989). The self and social behavior in differing cultural contexts. *Psychological Review, 96*, 506–520.

Usher, J. A., & Neisser, U. (1993). Childhood amnesia and the beginnings of memory for four early life events. *Journal of Experimental Psychology: General, 122*, 155–165.

Wang, Z. W., Cao, D. H., Hao, Y., Cao, R. Q., Dai, W. Y., & Qu, S. Q. (1983). A preliminary study of education of only children. *Academic Journal of Shenyang Education Institute, 2,* 11–15.

Wang, Q. (in press). The emergence of cultural self-construct. *Developmental Psychology.*

Wang, Q. (2003).Infantile amnesia reconsidered: A cross-cultural analysis. *Memory, 11, 1,* 65–80.

Wang, Q., Leichtman, M. D. & Davies, K. (2000). Sharing memories and telling stories: American and Chinese mothers and their 3-year-olds. *Memory, 8, 3,* 159–177.

Wang, Q., Leichtman, M. D., & White, S. H. (1998). Childhood memory and self-description in young Chinese adults: The impact of growing up an only child. *Cognition,* 73–103.

Weigle, T. W., & Bauer, P. J. (2000). Deaf and hearing adults' recollections of childhood and beyond. *Memory, 8, 5,* 293–309.

Welch-Ross, M. K. (1995a). Developmental changes in preschoolers' ability to distinguish memories of performed, pretended and imagined actions. *Cognitive Development, 10,* 421–441.

Welch-Ross, M. K. (1995b). An integrative model of the development of autobiographical memory. *Developmental Review, 15,* 338–365.

Welch-Ross, M. K., Diecidue, K., & Miller, S. A. (1997). Young children's understanding of conflicting mental representation predicts suggestibility. *Developmental Psychology, 33,* 43–53.

Werner, J. S., & Perlmutter, M. (1979). Development of visual memory in infants. In H. W. Reese & L. P. Lipsitt (Eds.), *Advances in child development and behavior* (Vol. 14, pp. 1–55). New York: Academic Press.

Wetzler, S. E., & Sweeney, J. A. (1986). Childhood amnesia: An empirical demonstration. In D. C. Rubin (Ed.), *Autobiographical memory* (pp. 91–201). New York: Cambridge University Press.

Zahn-Waxler, C., Friedman, R. J., Cole, P. M., & Mizuta, I. (1996). Japanese and United States preschool children's responses to conflict and distress. *Child Development, 67,* 2462–2477.

24

Tuned In or Tuned Out

Parents' and Children's Interpretation of Parental Racial/Ethnic Socialization Practices

Diane Hughes
Meredith A. Bachman
Diane N. Ruble
Andrew Fuligni

INTRODUCTION

Over the past decade, developmental psychologists have become increasingly interested in how children come to understand their own and other individuals' social group memberships and the consequences of such understandings for childhood and later life outcomes (Barber, Eccles, & Stone, 2001; Downe, 2001; Kiesner, Cadinu, Poulin, & Bucci, 2001; Martin & Ruble, 2004; Ruble, Alverez, Bachman, Cameron, Fuligni, Garcia Coll, & Rhee, 2004; Ruble & Dweck, 1995; Ruble & Martin, 2002; Spencer, Fegley, & Harpalani, 2003; Swanson, Spencer, Dell'Angelo, Harpalani, & Spencer, 2002). Of particular interest has been children's developing understanding of race and ethnicity, particularly in terms of the multiple determinants of such understandings, mechanisms of change in them over time, and their developmental consequences (Nesdale, Durkin, Maas, & Griffiths, 2004; Nesdale & Flesser, 2001; Udry, Li, & Hendrikson-Smith, 2003; Yip & Fuligni, 2002). We know, for example, that even within a particular age range children and adolescents vary considerably in the salience of race and ethnicity to their sense of self (Shelton & Sellers, 2000; Sellers, Chavous, & Cooke, 1998; Umana-Taylor, 2004; Yip & Fuligni, 2002) as well as in their interpretations of racial hierarchies, systems of social stratification, and associated processes such as prejudice and discrimination (Fisher, Wallace, & Fenton, 2000; Romero & Roberts, 2003; Rosenbloom & Way, 2004; Nesdale & Flesser, 2001; Wong, Eccles, & Sameroff, 2003). Indeed, our own data has reminded us repeatedly that children make meaning of race and ethnicity in very different ways. For example, when answering the question "What does it mean to be Dominican?" a fourth-grade boy responded that it means you are "part of a Spanish country that is growing. You should be happy because the country is fun and will become famous from the people there." Answering a similar question, "What does it mean to be White?" a second-grade girl told us, "Well a lot of people are White or Black and some jobs you have to be White and some you have to be Black so you get those choices." These are potentially very different types of understandings, one emphasizing ethnic or national pride, and the other differential access to resources.

In efforts to elaborate how children come to such varied understandings, researchers have focused in part on the role that parents play in shaping children's racial knowledge (Hughes & Chen, 1999; Phinney, Romero, Nava & Huang, 2001; Quintanna & Vera, 1999). As key socializing agents, parents' values, attitudes, and behaviors transmit fundamental information to children about their own and other racial and ethnic groups. Some parents deliberately discuss racial issues with their children; others communicate that race is "taboo" by avoiding the topic. Some parents emphasize group differences and disadvantage; others emphasize similarities among all people. Although early studies showed that children's racial attitudes were unrelated to those of their parents (for reviews, see Aboud, 1988; Katz, 1982), recent research among families of color suggests that parents' race-related messages may have important consequences for children's identity formation and development (Marshall, 1995; Peters, 1985; Sanders Thompson, 1994; Spencer, 1983, 1985; Stevenson, 1994). Although studied less often, White parents obviously transmit information to their children about race, ethnicity, and intergroup relations as well (Hamm, 1999). Thus, children's orientations toward race are derived, in part, from parental practices and world views.

It seems critical to note, up front, that parents are far from the only influence on children's racial knowledge; in fact, it has not yet been established that they are the *most* important influence. As Smith and colleagues (Smith et al., in press) have noted, community members, community billboards, school textbooks, teachers, and the media all contain or communicate an abundance of racial messages to children about who is valued, smart, beautiful, dangerous, disruptive, rich, and so forth—and who is not. Moreover, children learn about race and ethnicity through a range of interactions and observations across the various contexts in which they participate. Research on youth's discrimination experiences, their awareness of stereotypes, and the like each demonstrate the power of ambient messages about race to which youth are exposed (Graham & Taylor, 2002; Graham, 2001; Hudley & Graham, 2001; Steele, 1997, 1998; Steele & Aronson, 2000).

In the present chapter, we focus on parents' racial/ethnic socialization practices, emphasizing what is known about the processes, and on some key limitations of the existing research. First, we describe our conceptualization of racial/ethnic socialization and its most salient features. Then we provide a brief review of existing research concerning the nature of racial/ethnic socialization messages parents may transmit and their potential developmental consequences. Our purpose here is simply to introduce novice travelers to current theory and empirical work in the area, since in-depth and systematic treatment of this literature is provided elsewhere (Hughes, Rodriguez, Smith, Johnson, & Stevenson, 2004). Finally, in an effort to explore in more detail some conceptual and methodological issues that are of particular concern to us, we consider the absence of knowledge about the degree of synchrony, or correspondence, between parents' and children's perceptions of parents' racial/ethnic socialization messages, and how children interpret or hear the messages that parents' believe they transmit. In doing so, we describe findings from an exploratory study in which we examined correspondence between parents' and children's views of parents' racial/ethnic socialization practices.

In closing, we consider the implications of current theoretical and empirical research in this area for future studies.

THE CONCEPT OF RACIAL/ETHNIC SOCIALIZATION

The concept of racial/ethnic socialization is based to a large extent on early scholars' efforts to identify strategies that ethnic minority parents use to rear competent and effective children in a society that is largely stratified by race. The majority of this research and theoretical writing has focused on African Americans, a group that historically has been at the bottom of the social structure in terms of access to privileges and economic resources. Consequently, current conceptualizations of racial/ethnic socialization have emphasized parents' efforts to promote racial pride in their children and to prepare them to succeed in the face of potential racial bias (Bowman & Howard, 1985; Marshall, 1995; Peters,

1985; Sanders Thompson, 1994; Stevenson, 1994, 1995; Thornton, Chatters, Taylor, & Allen, 1990). In recent years, however, both theory and empirical work has attended to racial and ethnic socialization practices in multiple ethnic groups, including various U.S. and foreign born Latino and Asian groups, adding to researchers' conceptualizations a focus on processes of cultural retention.

As in prior work (e.g., Hughes, Rodriguez, Smith, Johnson, and Stevenson, 2004; Hughes & Chen, 1999), in this chapter we use the term "racial/ethnic socialization" to refer generally to the full range of parental practices that communicate messages about race or ethnicity to children. Elsewhere, we note that the terms "ethnic" and "racial" socialization have been used interchangeably in the literature and provide guidelines for distinguishing the two (Hughes, Rodriguez, Smith, Johnson, & Stevenson, 2004). In the current chapter, however, we use term "ethnic/racial/ethnic socialization" to refer to the literature in the area. Notably, the definition we use here is both broad and limited. It is broad in the sense that it is applicable across multiple racial-ethnic groups. All parents transmit messages about race and ethnicity to their children, even if it is by way of silence on the topic. The definition is limited, however, in its exclusive focus on parents as the sole source of racial/ethnic messages to children. Moreover, it is likely to exaggerate commonalties in practices across parents of different racial-ethnic backgrounds. For instance, the behaviors that make up certain categories of racial/ethnic socialization (e.g., promoting pride in one's ethnic group; avoiding discussions about race/ethnicity) are likely to be different for different racial/ethnic groups (e.g., Hughes, 2003; Kofkin, Katz, and Downey, 1995). Thus, we recognize that although information related to ethnicity and race is transmitted in all families, the essence and specific contents of such messages, and their origins, may vary across racial and ethnic groups.

FEATURES OF PARENTS' RACIAL/ETHNIC MESSAGES TO CHILDREN

Recent efforts to delineate components of racial/ethnic socialization underscore both the subtlety and complexity of the phenomenon (e.g., Smith et al., in press; Stevenson, 1994, 1995). In this section, we highlight important features of racial/ethnic socialization that may have important conceptual and methodological implications. Specifically, we hope that this discussion will clarify the importance of assessing the degree to which various types of messages actually reach and are understood by children.

Verbal and Nonverbal Communication

Parents' communicate their values and perspectives on race and ethnicity to their children in a variety of ways—verbally, nonverbally, explicitly, and implicitly. The most commonly investigated messages are explicit verbalizations about race. For example, parents may teach their children racial attitudes or discuss race relations with them in a direct and conventional manner, just as they would teach their children rules for conduct or moral values. However, verbal communications may also contain implicit or subtle messages about race, as when parents emphasize the importance of morality, hard work, education, and self-pride in order to prepare children for potential racial bias (Peters, 1981, 1985; Richardson, 1981; Thornton et al., 1990; cf., Peters, 1985). Indeed, the later type of implicit messages are among those that parents most commonly report in studies that have coded parents' responses to open ended questions about racial/ethnic socialization (Thornton, Chatters, Taylor, & Allen, 1990).

Parents may also socialize race-related attitudes, values, and perspectives through a variety of non-verbal implicit mechanisms. Practices aimed at promoting children's racial and ethnic pride and their knowledge about their cultural history and heritage are often nonverbal and unarticulated (Boykin & Toms, 1985; Peters, 1985; Sanders Thompson, 1994; Spencer, 1983; Stevenson, 1995). Modeling racial-ethnic behaviors (e.g., cooking traditional foods, speaking in native languages), structuring children's environments (e.g., displaying culturally based art in the home, influencing children's peer choices), or selectively reinforcing children's behaviors (Hamm, 1996; Marshall, 1995; Smith, Atkins & Connell, 2003; Smith et al., in press) may each serve as nonverbal communications to children about the meaning and traditions of their racial or ethnic group. Nonverbal messages may, of course, convey negative attitudes toward other or one's own ethnic/racial groups as well as positive ones, the prototypical example being when people clutch their purse or cross the street upon seeing a group of Black or Latino teenage boys.

Proactive and Reactive Messages

Parents' racial/ethnic socialization messages may emanate from parents' preconceived values, goals, and agendas or they may occur in reaction to discrete events in parent's or children's lives. We conceive of the former type of message as being proactive and the later type of message as reactive. This distinction is important as these two types of messages are likely to have distinct properties. For example, a feature of proactive racial/ethnic socialization messages, whether explicit or implicit, is that they have internally consistent structures and are intimately linked to parents' worldviews and experiences. That is, like anticipatory socialization mechanisms (e.g., Nsamenang & Lamb, 1995), proactive racial/ethnic socialization reflects parents' views of the strengths and competencies their children will need in order to function effectively in their adult social roles. For example, research has found that many African American parents believe their children will inevitably encounter racism and discrimination (e.g., Essed, 1990; Peters, 1981) and these expectations are likely to guide discussions with children that are focused on preparing children for these events. In a similar manner, parents may value diversity and pluralism and therefore engage in proactive efforts to provide multicultural environments for their children such as diverse play groups and schools. Indeed, most parents are likely to simultaneously hold multiple ethnic/racial/ethnic socialization agendas (e.g., encouraging appreciation of diversity and preparing children for racial bias) and thus a range of proactive efforts may be observed within the same individual.

In contrast to proactive racial/ethnic socialization, we conceive of reactive racial/ethnic socialization as that which occurs inadvertently in response to race-related incidents that parents or children have experienced, or in response to children's general queries about racial issues. Whereas proactive racial/ethnic socialization messages are likely to be internally consistent, reactive messages may or may not reflect parents' intentional racial/ethnic socialization agendas because parents' discomfort with or unprepared ness for, discussions that children initiate may result in messages to children that parents did not intend. In light of this, reactive racial/ethnic socialization is characteristically ad hoc and may or may not be a part of a deliberate socialization agenda. Therein, reactive messages are less likely than are proactive messages to form a coherent entity that is consistently reproduced in interactions with children. Notably, these sorts of reactive messages pose particular methodological challenges to researchers, because parents may be unaware of, or unwilling to report, them. For instance, when parents answer survey-type items about their racial/ethnic socialization practices, it seems reasonable to assume that they will reflect on what they intend and hope to communicate to their children more so than on potentially brief exchanges that characterize the sorts of reactive racial/ethnic socialization of interest to us.

A Synergistic Process

Although scholars studying racial/ethnic socialization have focused primarily on goals initiated by parents for their children, it is important to recognize that racial/ethnic socialization is a bidirectional process shaped by parents and children. Parents' bring to the process attitudes, beliefs, values, and ideas about race and race-relations that form from their experiences. Parents also bring expectations regarding the competencies or coping skills their children will need to negotiate negative experiences that are based on their racial or ethnic group membership. However, children's developing racial knowledge and their experiences in extra-familial settings also shape the content and frequency of parents' communications to them about race. Children's experiences and questions may prompt parents to share attitudes, values, and information regarding race and intergroup relations regardless of parents' intended racial/ethnic socialization agendas.

Notably, qualitative studies have been better able to capture the dynamic, changing, and transactional qualities of racial/ethnic socialization processes than have studies based on self-report methodologies. These qualitative studies suggest that parents are quite aware of the transactional nature of their racial/ethnic socialization efforts. In a number of them, parents' narratives feature the queries and experiences children that prompt conversations about race. Thus, racial/ethnic socialization is primarily contained within nuanced microsocial exchanges between parents and children. However, studies to date have not attempted to distinguish situations in which racial/ethnic socialization is child- versus parent-initiated, or to elaborate the synergistic qualities of the process.

Deliberate and Unintended

Parents use a variety of strategies to promote children's racial pride, to teach them about their culture and history, and to prepare them for potential encounters with racial prejudice and discrimination. These emanate from parents' race-related values, their goals for their children, and their views of skills and competencies children will need to be successful in the larger society. Many messages, such as those we have described thus far, are communicated intentionally as part of a well-defined socialization agenda. Less formally recognized, and less often attended to empirically, are the ranges of "unintended messages" to children that convey parents' attitudes, values, and perspectives about race. It is not hard to imagine the range of forms such messages might take. A family is driving through an urban poor neighborhood and utters a snide remark about the (usually Black or Latino) residents' lifestyles. A Mexican parent warns his teenage son to "be careful" as he is leaving to run an errand in a White neighborhood. Children are likely to learn a great deal from these sorts of inadvertent communications about race or race relations, which may or may not be directed at them but, nevertheless, transmit information regarding their parents' attitudes, values, or views. Even parents who have clear intentions regarding the racial/ethnic attitudes, values, and orientations they wish to instill in their children racial/ethnic socialization may unwittingly transmit race-related messages to children.

Subtle and unintended messages rarely have been the focus of empirical studies, in part, because labor intensive methods such as ethnography or structured observations are required to assess them. For knowledge about racial/ethnic socialization processes to move forward, however, researchers need to grapple more so than they have with strategies for capturing these sorts of messages. Almost certainly, parents' responses to everyday occurrences sometimes contain racial messages, and such responses are quite likely to take on meaning in children's worldviews. As explained by Appelgate and colleagues (Appelgate, Burleson, & Delia, 1992) parents transmit to children an interpretive logic, or, a generalized orientation that guides children's assessment and management of situations. Boykin and Toms' (1985) also suggested that racial attitudes, values, and behaviors often are passed on to children by way of "cultural motifs" that are largely invisible to parents but are displayed to children in a "consistent, persistent, and enduring fashion" (p. 42). These cultural motifs typically are not accompanied by directives or imperatives from parents to learn but simply are absorbed by children and provide a basis for their "behavioral negotiations with the world." Thus, research that explores these elusive types of messages would be an important contribution our understanding of racial/ethnic socialization processes.

Messages Sent Versus Messages Received

In light of the complexity and subtlety of racial/ethnic socialization processes, it seems quite likely that the messages parents intend to communicate differ from the messages children actually receive (or report receiving). That is, children can miss, misinterpret, or ignore parents' communications about race, and parents can selectively remember and report only those messages that they intend to send and those messages that they would like their children to receive. In fact, in a study focused on African American families, Marshall (1995) found a great deal of incongruity between parents' and their 9- to 10-year-old children's reports of racial/ethnic socialization. However, such disparities may have multiple sources. For example, Barnes (1980) found that African American children of mothers who reported more frequent race-related socialization were less likely than other children to demonstrate pro-Black attitudes, suggesting that either parent's intended messages about racial pride may have been interpreted by children as negative messages about African Americans or that parents failed to report their own behaviors accurately. Interestingly, in Marshall's (1995) study, parents' reports of ethnic socialization were significantly correlated with children's ethnic identity stage, whereas children's reports were not. Thus, a variety of questions concerning the correspondence between parents' reports of racial/ethnic socialization and both children's reports of racial/ethnic socialization and children's outcomes (e.g., group identification, self-esteem) need to be explored. This is especially important given the overemphasis on proactive, explicit, verbal, messages among researchers studying racial/ethnic socialization to date. That is, we need to explore both how racial/ethnic socialization occurs in day to day life as well as the degree to which the messages parents willingly report actually influence children.

THE CONTENT OF PARENTS' RACIAL/ETHNIC SOCIALIZATION

The empirical literature on racial/ethnic socialization has, in part, focused on understanding the nature and content of the racial/ethnic socialization messages that parents transmit to their children. Many of these studies have utilized in-depth interviews with African American and other ethnic minority parents to identify the most prominent themes that emerge when parents are asked to consider the role of race and ethnicity in their parenting practices (e.g., Marshall, 1995; Thornton, Chatters, Taylor, & Allen, 1990). In this section, we attempt to describe more fully the different types of racial/ethnic socialization messages that parents may communicate and the consequences of such messages for children's adaptation and well being. These include: (a) emphasizing racial and ethnic pride, traditions, and history (termed "cultural socialization"); (b) promoting an awareness of racial prejudice and discrimination (termed "preparation for bias"); (c) issuing cautions and warnings about other racial and ethnic groups, or about intergroup relations (termed "promotion of mistrust"); and (d) emphasizing the need to appreciate all racial and ethnic groups (termed "egalitarianism") (Boykin & Toms, 1985; Thornton et al., 1990; Demo & Hughes, 1990; Sanders Thompson, 1994).

Although we describe these types of racial/ethnic socialization message separately, it seems likely that particular racial/ethnic socialization messages as they occur in everyday conversation are less readily distinguishable. For instance, messages emphasizing cultural pride and history (cultural socialization) also may contain messages about historical discrimination and prejudice (preparation for bias), at least among minority populations in the United States. Similarly, parents may inadvertently embed cautions or warnings about other groups (promotion of mistrust) in their efforts to prepare children for racial bias (preparation for bias). Thus, different types of messages are not mutually exclusive. Indeed, research is needed to identify how messages occur together in natural day to day exchanges.

Cultural Socialization

Cultural socialization has been used commonly to refer to parental practices that teach children about cultural heritage, ancestry, and history; that maintain and promote cultural customs and traditions; and that instill cultural, racial, and ethnic pride (Boykin & Toms, 1985; Thornton et al., 1990). Cultural socialization may be evidenced in a wide range of behaviors including: talking or reading books to children about important people in the history of their ethnic or racial group, celebrating cultural holidays, exposing children to positive role models, and so forth. Importantly, these sorts of practices have been central to many researchers' ideas about racial/ethnic socialization (Barnes, 1980; Bowman & Howard, 1985; Chen, 1998; Hughes & Chen, 1997; Knight, Bernal, Garza, Cota, & Ocampo, 1993; Ou & McAdoo, 1993; Peters, 1985; Sanders Thompson, 1994; Smith, Atkins & Connell, 2003; Spencer, 1983; Stevenson, 1994; Thornton et al., 1990).

A number of studies have found that most parents of color engage in cultural socialization practices with their children. For example, in Phinney and Chavira's (1995) study of parents with adolescent children, 88% of Mexican American, 83% of African American, and 67% of Japanese American parents described behaviors associated with cultural socialization. Spencer (1983) also found that about three quarters of southern Black mothers in her sample taught their children about Black history and famous Black leaders, although only one third of them taught their children about the civil rights movement in the United States. Hughes and Chen (1999) found that over two thirds of urban African American parents in dual-earner married families had engaged in cultural socialization practices within the previous year (e.g., reading children Black history books and storybooks, taking children to cultural events).

Scholars have consistently theorized that cultural socialization promotes children's positive racial identity development and self-esteem by preparing children to interpret and cope with prejudice, discrimination, and negative group images emanating from the outside world (e.g., Barnes, 1980). Empirical studies have suggested that cultural socialization is associated with favorable outcomes for minority youth, particularly in terms of children's ethnic identity and their knowledge and attitudes regarding their ethnic group. For example, Demo and Hughes (1990) found that Black adults who recalled that their parents had emphasized racial pride, cultural heritage, and racial tolerance reported greater feelings of closeness to other Blacks and more Afrocentric racial attitudes than did those who reported no racial/ethnic socialization. Branch and Newcombe (1986) also found that children of parents who taught them in more of a pro-Black fashion were more likely than their counterparts to have higher racial awareness, higher racial knowledge, and greater pro-Black preferences. In Knight and colleagues' (Knight et al., 1993) study, Mexican American school-age children whose mothers taught them more about Mexican culture, and those with more Mexican objects in their homes, were more likely than their peers to use racial-ethnic self-labels correctly, to engage in more racial-ethnic behaviors (e.g., language use, engagement in games from Mexican culture), and to have greater same-race/ethnic preferences. In their study of Chinese American families, Ou and McAdoo (1993) found that Chinese parents' cultural socialization was associated with greater preferences for same-race/ethnic peers among first- and second-grade girls. Notably, although it is unclear the conditions under which same-race ethnic preferences have positive or negative long-term consequences, the assumption to date has been that it is indicative of positive attitudes toward, or affiliations with, one's own ethnic group.

The consequences of cultural socialization may go beyond racial-specific child outcomes, such as ethnic identity, to reach other important aspects of children's lives (e.g., academic achievement). For instance, Smith, Atkins, & Connell (2003) found that African American parents' socialization concerning ethnic pride and racial-ethnic equality was consistently related to their children's better grades and higher test scores. Moreover, cultural socialization may have salutary influences on minority youth by way of its influence on their positive ethnic identity which, in turn, has been associated with a broad range of outcomes, such as school performance, the quality of relations with peers, and psychosocial adjustment (Phinney & Kohatsu, 1997; Porter & Washington, 1993).

Preparation for Bias

We use the term "preparation for bias" to refer to such practices as parents' efforts to promote their children's awareness of racial bias, and to prepare them to cope with prejudice and discrimination. These efforts have also been emphasized as a critical component of racial/ethnic socialization. Several scholars have suggested that enabling children to navigate around racial barriers and to negotiate potentially hostile social interactions are normative parenting tasks within ethnic minority families (Thornton et al., 1990; Fisher et al., 1998; Garcia Coll & Magnuson, 1997; Garcia Coll, Meyer, & Brillon, 1995; Kibria, 1997; Harrison, Wilson, Chan, Buriel, & Pine, 1995).

A number of the studies described in reference to cultural socialization have examined the frequency of socialization about racial prejudice and discrimination (preparation for bias). Such socialization, like cultural socialization, varies widely across samples. In some studies, a majority of African American parents report socialization related to racial barriers (Hughes & Chen, 1997; Phinney & Chavira, 1995). For example, Sanders Thompson (1994) found that 48% to 58% of African American participants recalled parental messages about racial barriers. However, in Bowman and Howard's (1985) study, only 13% of youth described parental messages about racial barriers. Similarly, only 8% of respondents in the National Survey of Black Americans reported messages to their children about racial barriers (Thornton et al., 1990). This suggests that the frequency of these types of messages needs further empirical investigation.

Parents' preparation for bias, like parents' cultural socialization, has been hypothesized to protect children from threats to their self-esteem and well being posed by the race-related stressors they encounter (Spencer, 1983; Spencer & Markstrom Adams, 1990). However, empirical studies regarding the influences of preparation for bias on youth have produced inconsistent results. A few studies have supported the view that preparation for bias serves the sorts of protective functions that scholars have proposed. (Bowman & Howard, 1985; Knight et al., 1993; Spencer, 1983). However, other studies have indicated that children are negatively affected by parental socialization regarding the existence of racial barriers (Fordham & Ogbu, 1986; Marshall, 1995; Smith, Atkins, & Connell, 2003). For instance, in a study of southern African American fourth-grade children, Smith, Atkins, and Connell (2003) found that children's perceptions of racial barriers significantly predicted lower reading and math scores on the Stanford Achievement Test. Similarly, Marshall (1995) found that African American children's reports of more parental ethnic socialization, in general, were related to lower reading grades among the 9- and 10-year-olds she studied.

In our view, inconsistencies across studies examining the influence on children of parental communications about racial barriers may be due to subtle differences in the structure or content of such communications. Specifically, messages coded as preparation for bias may in fact be what we call promotion of mistrust.

Promotion of Mistrust

We use this term to refer to parental practices that discourage children from interacting with people of other racial-ethnic groups or that foster a sense of distrust across racial-ethnic boundaries. In our view, it is distinct from preparation for bias in that it does not incorporate messages regarding strategies for coping with and overcoming prejudice and discrimination (e.g., you have to be better; you have to do more). Mistrust may be communicated in parents' warnings to children about other racial-ethnic groups or in their cautions about racial barriers to success.

Few empirical studies have distinguished promotion of mistrust from preparation for bias, perhaps because the distinction is so subtle. However, in available studies, the incidence of explicit cautions or warnings about other ethnic groups seems to be quite low. For instance, based on analysis of the National Survey of Black Americans, Thornton and colleagues' (Thornton et al., 1990) reported that in response to open ended questions about strategies parents use to teach children about race, only 2.7% of parents reported instructing their children to maintain social distance from Whites. Hughes and Chen (1997) found that about 18% of African American parents reported promotion of mistrust using survey items in which parents indicated whether or not they cautioned children about interactions with Whites or encouraged them to maintain social distance. Although these percentages are low, there are still a significant number of children receiving such messages.

Whereas preparing children for racial bias may have salutary consequences for development, socialization practices that foster intergroup mistrust and alienation from mainstream values may promote maladaptive behaviors. For example, in Ogbu's (1974) research among high school students in Stockton, California, parents' overemphasis on racial barriers and discrimination seemed to undermine children's sense of efficacy and promote distrust of and anger toward mainstream institutions. Further evidence that parental practices that promote intergroup mistrust may have negative consequences for youth comes from studies that have examined relationships between parents' attitudes (as opposed to their racial/ethnic socialization practices per se) and children's experiences, or between children's feelings of mistrust and their outcomes on a range of psychosocial indicators. Patchen (1982) found that negative parental attitudes toward other races were associated with children's increased avoidance of cross-race peers and with their reports of negative intergroup social interactions. Others have found negative consequences as well (Biafora et al., 1993; Rumbaut, 1994; Smith, Atkins, & Connell, 2003). Thus, racial/ethnic socialization messages that promote racial mistrust may prompt youth to withdraw from activities that are essential for access to opportunity and reward structures of the dominant society (Biafora et al., 1993). Moreover, they may motivate youth to engage in activities that deviate from accepted norms.

Egalitarianism

Many parents encourage their children to appreciate the values and experiences of all racial-ethnic groups or, as Spencer (1983, 1985) noted, to rear racially neutral children who notice people's individual qualities rather than their racial group membership. Theoretically, socialization that emanates from such egalitarian values may manifest itself in two distinct forms: one in which parents expose their children to the history, traditions, and current experiences of many different groups, including their own, and the other in which parents avoid any mention of race during discussions with their children.

Researchers have consistently documented that many parents either focus on promoting egalitarian views or are completely silent about race. Spencer (1983) found that over half of the southern Black parents in her sample reported that they taught their children to believe that all people are equal. In Bowman and Howard's (1985) study, 38% of African American youth reported that their parents did not transmit any information to them about Blacks or Whites, and 12% reported that their parents had emphasized equality among all people. In a study of southern Black adults (Parham & Williams, 1993), 20% of respondents reported that their parents "rarely" or "never" discussed race, racial attitudes, or both, whereas 27.8% said that their parents had emphasized egalitarian views.

Few researchers have directly investigated the influences of messages focused on the equality of all races and/or silence about race in terms of their consequences for children's development. However, scholars have emphasized that children of color socialized from an egalitarian perspective may have unrealistic expectations concerning intergroup relations and, consequently, unable to comprehend and cope with experiences involving racial bias (Smith, Fogle, & Jacobs, in press; Spencer, 1983; Stevenson, 1995). Spencer (1983) also noted that lack of direct instruction and discussion about race among parents of color means that traditional views and prevalent stereotypes remain unchallenged. Supporting this perspective, Bowman and Howard (1985) found that Black youth who were not taught anything about race had lower self-efficacy scores than did recipients of proactive racial/ethnic socialization strategies. In addition, Kofkin and colleagues (Kofkin et al., 1995) found correspondence between parents' and children's racial attitudes for only those parents who reported having race-related discussions with their children. A remaining and interesting empirical question concerns the potentially distinct consequences that may result from egalitarianism and silence about race. That is, research needs to examine whether or not overt messages concerning equality have the same consequences for children that have been observed with silence concerning race.

SUMMARY

Thus far we have outlined components of current research and theory regarding racial/ethnic socialization processes within families. First, we provided an overview of our conceptualization of racial/ethnic socialization and highlighted that such messages can be communicated through a variety of mechanisms: verbal, nonverbal, deliberate, unintended, proactive, reactive, child initiated or parent initiated or a combination of these. Importantly, we stressed that the complex synergistic nature of racial/ethnic socialization means that researchers must assess the degree to which the messages parents intend to convey to their children are actually conveyed and understood by children. We discussed the importance of assessing the substantive content of racial/ethnic socialization messages as the consequences for children's development seem to depend on the particular ideas about race and ethnicity that messages convey. For example, cultural socialization and preparation for bias appear to have salutary effects on children whereas an overemphasis on racial barriers may undermine children's efficacy and promote maladaptive behaviors.

Guided by the framework previously set out, we return now to a consideration of the extent to which children actually receive the different types of race-related messages that parents believe they are communicating. This particular issue is of concern to us, as we have noted, for a number of reasons. First, only a handful of studies regarding parents' racial or ethnic socialization processes, including those that have focused on relationships between parents' practices and children's outcomes, have included independent reports from parents and their children. Even fewer have attempted to explicitly examine relationships between children's and parents' views of racial/ethnic socialization (see Marshall, 1995 for an exception). This methodological issue, alone, severely limits our knowledge of the ways in which racial/ethnic socialization messages influence children's development and well-being. As with research in any area, relying on a single informant to report both racial/ethnic socialization and any particular outcome of interest leaves open the possibility that respondent characteristics, respondent bias, or an unmeasured third variable accounts for documented relationships. Second, there are theoretical reasons to question the extent to which children accurately hear the messages parents believe they are transmitting about ethnicity or race. It is quite likely that parents find it awkward or difficult to discuss racial issues with their children, opening the door for miscommunication. Moreover, parents are quite likely to be unaware of many of the messages they transmit, because the messages are so subtle. Thus, before we can begin to fully understand the processes of racial/ethnic socialization within families, we need to learn more about what messages parent believe they send to children, what messages parents are willing to report and how children hear and interpret messages about race and ethnicity from their parents.

AN EXPLORATION OF PARENTS' AND CHILDREN'S PERSPECTIVES ON RACIAL/ETHNIC SOCIALIZATION

Processes

In the remainder of the chapter, we present exploratory results from a larger study of ethnic identity in middle childhood which permits us to examine the degree of correspondence between parents' reports of the race-related messages they transmit and children's reports about race related messages they receive. Although far from providing definitive answers, the data permits us to raise questions and address issues that, to a large extent, remain unattended to in the available research literature. We begin by providing basic descriptive information regarding parents' and children's reports of three types of racial/ethnic socialization messages: cultural socialization, egalitarianism, and preparation for bias. Because this study utilized an abbreviated version of the measure described by Hughes and Chen (1997) that we viewed as being appropriate for young children and across multiple ethnic groups, we do not have data pertaining to promotion of mistrust. However, the dimensions of racial/ethnic socialization we include, albeit not exhaustive, have been highlighted as critically important in the available research literature. Next, using both correlational analysis and difference scores, we examine the degree of correspondence between parents' and children's reports of dimensions of racial/ethnic socialization, based on identical measures administered to parents and their children. We examine several potential racial/ethnic socialization mechanisms that would not emerge if we focused solely on parents or children's reports of racial/ethnic socialization—namely, that parents' ethnic behaviors influence children's perceptions of racial/ethnic socialization, independent of parents' racial/ethnic socialization reports; that parents' socialization influences children's ethnic identity independent of children's perceptions of parents' racial/ethnic socialization messages, and that parents' ethnic behaviors are associated with children's ethnic identity independent of racial/ethnic socialization (according to either parents' or children's reports). In addressing these issues, our primary goal is to emphasize the importance of including data from parents as well as children, and of considering the multiple ways in which sole reliance on reports from adults, adolescents, or children alone may result in mis-specified conceptual and empirical models of racial/ethnic socialization processes.

Methods

Sample

The data we discuss comes from a larger project focused on ethnic identity in middle childhood. The study involved both a cross-sectional and a longitudinal component. For the purposes of this chapter, only the first year cross-sectional data for the children whose parents also participated in the study was analyzed. Second- and fourth-grade children were recruited from New York City public schools. Children who wanted to participate took home a parent consent form which contained a description of the parent portion of the study. Researchers were able to contact and interview 151 of the 207 parents who gave consent[1]. The parent sample consisted primarily of mothers (82%), with the remainder of the sample being comprised of either fathers (12%), or grandparents (6%). The ethnic composition of the sample was diverse, with 21% third or later generation White European American children, 15% third or later generation Black American children, 25% second generation Russian children, 21% second generation Chinese children, 7% second generation Dominican children, and the remaining 11% with varied ethnic backgrounds. Thus, this research includes ethnic groups that have received little attention in the racial/ethnic socialization literature. Although we were unable to conduct detailed within group analyses due to the small number of respondents within any particular ethnic group[2], the addition of groups such as White Russian immigrants to the racial/ethnic socialization literature is an important new direction that we hope to pursue.

Procedures

Each child met individually with a trained interviewer at the child's school. At the beginning of each session children were reminded that they would be asked to answer questions about themselves and about their feelings. Children were assured that questions had no right or wrong answers and that they could discontinue participation at anytime. After completing the questionnaires children were thanked and given a small gift. Parents were contacted and interviewed by telephone. Parents were reminded that they would be asked about a variety of issues related to being a parent and that questions had no right or wrong answers. Trained interviewers administered the questionnaires in either English or in the parent's native language.

Measures

Racial/Ethnic Socialization

Parents and children each completed a measure of racial/ethnic socialization, with parents reporting how often they sent 10 different racial/ethnic socialization messages to their children and children reporting how often they received the same 10 racial/ethnic socialization messages from their parents. Both parents and children replied to each item using a 3-point Likert scale ranging from never send/receive the message to often send/receive the message.

Based on the racial/ethnic socialization measure created by Hughes and colleagues (Hughes & Chen, 1997; Hughes & Johnson, 2001; Hughes, 2003), the scale was constructed to assess dimensions of racial/ethnic socialization that have been identified in prior literature, including: an emphasis on equality of all racial/ethnic groups (egalitarianism), racial/ethnic pride (cultural socialization) and preparation for racial/ethnic related bias (preparation for bias). As noted earlier, we did not include items to assess promotion of mistrust independent of preparation for bias. Two of the original 10 items were not included in the subsequent analyses, as preliminary data exploration showed they were problematic for various reasons. One item, intended to capture an aspect of racial/ethnic pride, asked specifically how often parents emphasized the use of their native language at home. However, this item clearly was not applicable to many families in the sample and moreover appeared to reflect parents' own language skills rather than their desire to instill cultural knowledge and pride in their children. In addition, an item asking specifically about socializing children to feel American was excluded because parents seemed to interpret it in different ways, many of which did not reflect an emphasis on egalitarianism as we had intended.

The final set of items included 3 items that assess egalitarianism (e.g., "How often have you told your child/have your parents told you…People are all equal, no matter what the color of their skin or where they come from."), 2 items that assess cultural socialization (e.g., How often have you told your child/have your parents told you "You should be proud to be [insert racial/ethnic group]."), and 3 items that assess preparation for bias (e.g., How often have you told your child/have your parents told you [racial/ethnic group] people are more likely to be treated unfairly or poorly than are other people."). Several issues merit attention in this regard. First, although Egalitarianism and Cultural Socialization are conceptually distinct, they were not empirically distinct in the present sample, as revealed by a principal axes factor analysis. Notably, Hughes (2003) also found Egalitarianism and Cultural Socialization were indistinguishable empirically in a sample of urban African American and Latino adults. It seems likely that these theoretically distinct messages co-occur within individuals because the large majority of parents report each of them. Second, we had an insufficient number of items to distinguish preparation for bias from promotion of mistrust (only three items assessed discussions of unfair treatment or opportunity), which is unfortunate since misinterpretation may be most likely in this realm. Nevertheless, based on the results of principal axes factor analysis, we retained measures that assessed two dimensions of racial/ethnic socialization: egalitarianism/cultural socialization (α = .75 for parents and .74 for children) and preparation for bias (α = .72 for parents .43 for children[3]). It is important to note that for the White European American sample we were only able to analyze responses to the three items that assessed egalitarianism[4] (α = .77 for parents; 78 for children).

Ethnic Identity Evaluation and Racial/Ethnic Activity Involvement

Two additional measures were analyzed along with the measures of racial/ethnic socialization. First, we were interested in exploring the extent to which parents' reports about their racial/ethnic socialization practices were associated with children's racial/ethnic outcomes, independent of children's perceptions of those messages. Therefore, we asked children three questions intended to assess their evaluation of their own racial/ethnic identity, following the format utilized by Harter to assess other aspects of children's self concept (e.g., "Some kids are happy that they are Russian but other kids are not happy that they are Russian. Are you more like children that are happy that they are Russian or are you more like children who are not happy that they are Russian? Is this really true or sort of true?"). Items were rated on a 4-point scale (α = .73). We were also interested in exploring the extent to which parents' reports about their ethnic behaviors influenced children (in terms of both their racial/ethnic identity evaluation and in terms of their perceptions of racial/ethnic socialization messages) independent of parents' reported racial/ethnic socialization messages. Thus, we asked parents a single item about their celebration of holidays and festivals related to their countries of origin. Unfortunately, this item was not asked of the White European American sample or of the Black American sample.

Results

Mean Levels of Racial/Ethnic Socialization Reported by Parents and Children

We began by examining the mean levels of each type of racial/ethnic socialization reported by parents and their children. In line with our expectations, both parents and children reported relatively high egalitarianism (child M = 2.29; parent M = 2.58) and egalitarianism/cultural socialization (child M

TABLE 24.1
Mean Levels of Reported Racial/Ethnic Socialization Messages

Sample	Egalitarianism	Egalitarianism-pride	Prep. for Bias
Chinese parent	2.31	2.04	1.37
Dominican parent	2.88	2.65	1.42
Russian parent	2.52	2.30	1.10
Black parent	2.88	2.88	1.81
White parent	2.85	N/A	N/A
Chinese children	1.91	1.98	1.68
Dominican children	2.24	2.27	1.82
Russian children	2.42	2.35	1.58
Black children	2.50	2.53	1.91
White children	2.64	N/A	N/A

= 2.28; parent M = 2.36) and lower levels of preparation for bias (child M = 1.71; parent M = 1.32). Paired samples t-tests indicated that the difference between these means was statistically significant (parents: $t(110)$ = 21.65, p =.000; children $t(117)$ = 7.99, p = .000). In addition, paired samples t-tests showed that, for both parents and children, egalitarianism/cultural socialization was higher than preparation for bias (parents: $t(110)$ = 20.34, p = .000; children $t(117)$ = 9.41, p = .000). However, as we shall discuss in further detail, the mean value for egalitarianism was significantly higher according to parents' reports than it was according to children's reports, $t(116)$= 4.37, p = .000, indicating that parents were more likely to report Egalitarianism than were their children. Conversely, the mean value for Preparation for Bias was significantly lower according to parents' reports than according to children's reports, $t(109)$ = –6.18, p = .000, indicating that parents were less likely to report preparation for bias than were their children. Table 24.1 displays means for each ethnic group for each dimension of racial/ethnic socialization for the interested reader.[5]

Correspondence Between Parents' and Children's Reports of Racial/Ethnic Socialization Messages

Our primary and initial question concerned the extent to which parents' reports about racial/ethnic socialization messages they transmit were associated with children's reports about racial/ethnic socialization messages they receive. To examine this question, we first estimated bivariate correlations between parents and children's reports of egalitarianism/cultural socialization and preparation for bias. The relationship between parents' reports of sending messages regarding egalitarianism/cultural socialization and children's reports of receiving such messages was small, but suggestive of some communication between parents and children, r = .15, p = .124. Similarly, the relationship between parents' reports of sending preparation for bias messages and children's reports of receiving these messages suggested some degree of communication but was again quite modest, r = .13, p = .169.

Due to the fact that the White European American sample only answered questions regarding egalitarianism messages, we examined relationships between parents' and children's reports of messages regarding egalitarianism. Findings suggest that there no relationship between parents' and children's reports in this regard, r = .07, p = .413. (This correlation was even smaller when the White European American sample was excluded from the analysis, r = .03, p = .72.)

Overall, these correlations show that the correspondence between parents and children's reports about racial/ethnic socialization is much lower than one might expect. Several explanations seem plausible. For one, parents' reports of the messages they send may correspondence only minimally with their actual practices. Alternatively, parents' messages may not be understood or interpreted by children in the manner intended.

To explore the latter possibility (i.e., that children perceive parents as communicating race-related messages but misinterpret the messages that parents' intend to communicate), we examined cross-over relationships, that is, relationships between parents' reports of egalitarianism/cultural socialization and children's reports of preparation for bias, and between parents' reports of preparation for bias and children's reports of egalitarianism/cultural socialization. Interestingly, parents' reports of egalitarianism/cultural socialization were positively and significantly correlated with children's reports of preparation for bias messages, $r = .20$, $p = .039$, suggesting that the racial/ethnic messages parents intend to send may be misinterpreted by children.

Exploring the Weak Relationship Between Children's and Parents' Reports About Racial/Ethnic Socialization Messages

The relatively weak correlation between parents' and children's reports about racial socialization tells us that there is low correspondence between parents and children within a family, but provides incomplete information about the nature of that low correspondence. In an effort to unpack the relationship further, we examined patterns of agreement between parents and their children at the level of the individual item, calculating a direction of agreement score for each parent–child pair. Again, a clear pattern emerged. As we suggested earlier in our presentation of mean differences in parents and children's reports of each dimension of racial/ethnic socialization, disagreement between parents and children for each of the items assessing egalitarianism resulted from a parent reporting sending more of an egalitarianism message than a child reported receiving. These findings are depicted in detail in Table 24.2, which shows that (a) there is agreement between many parents and children in terms of egalitarianism messages that is somewhat obscured when examining simple bivariate correlations, and (b) lack of agreement can often be attributed to a pattern in which parents report greater use of egalitarianism socialization messages than children report hearing. For instance, overall 47% of parent child pairs showed correspondence in response to the item "How often have you told your child/have your parents told you 'People are all equal no matter what the color of their skin or where they are from.'" Among the 53% of pairs lacking correspondence, 39.6% were instances in which the parent reported more frequent messages than did their child whereas only 13.4% were instances in which the child reported more frequent messages than did the parent.[6] Future research will be needed to determine if this is because parents' egalitarianism messages are misinterpreted as messages about discrimination and racial bias (preparation for bias), if parents are simply reporting sending those messages that they want the researcher to believe they use, or some combination of the two.

The opposite pattern emerged upon examination of items assessing preparation for bias. In fact, for each of the three items assessing preparation for bias, parents were less likely to report sending preparation for bias messages than children were likely to report receiving preparation for bias messages. These data are also depicted in Table 24.2, and show that lack of correspondence between parent–child pairs in their response to items pertaining to preparation for bias result from a pattern in which children report receiving more frequent preparation for bias messages than parents report communicating[7]. Again, future research will be needed to determine the degree to which these findings result from miscommunication between parents and children or from biased reporting of messages.

Finally, the pattern found when looking only at the two items assessing cultural socialization was less clear, with one message having a higher parent report mean and the other message having a higher child report mean. However, upon examination of individual items, it is interesting to note that children reported hearing more messages such as, "You should be proud to be Dominican" than parents reported sending, and parents reported sending more messages such as, "It is important to know about the culture of Chinese people" than children reported hearing. Again, we are unable to determine whether parents only report sending those messages that they believe they should be sending, whether children selectively hear those messages that they most prefer, or whether children better understand some messages (e.g., those regarding cultural pride) than others (those pertaining to racial bias).

TABLE 24.2
Parent–Child Agreement (and Direction of Disagreement) for Each Racial/Socialization Item

Item	Mean agreement score	Percent with perfect parent–child agreement	Percent with parent reporting more message	Percent with parent reporting less message
Egalitarianism 1	−.40	47.0	39.6	13.4
Egalitarianism 2	−.29	51.3	34.0	14.6
Egalitarianism 3	−.15	54.1	26.4	19.6
Bias 1	+.33	45.2	18.3	36.5
Bias 2	+.32	47.9	13.7	38.5
Bias 3	+.54	44.3	9.6	46.1
Culture 1	+.56	43.1	11.2	45.7
Culture 2	−.22	43.1	33.6	23.2

Item #	Item wording
Egalitarianism 1	People are all equal, no matter what the color of their skin or where they come from.
Egalitarianism 2	It is important to get along with people no matter what the color of their skin or where they come from.
Egalitarianism 3	It is important to respect all people no matter what the color of their skin or where they come from.
Preparation for Bias 1	[Basic ethnicity] people are more likely to be treated poorly or unfairly than other people.
Preparation for Bias 2	Some people may treat you badly or unfairly because you are [basic ethnicity].
Preparation for Bias 3	It is harder to succeed in America if you are [basic ethnicity].
Cultural 1	You should be proud to be [basic ethnicity].
Cultural 2	It is important to know about the culture of [basic ethnicity] people.

Parents' Ethnic Behaviors and Children's Reported Racial/Ethnic Socialization Messages

Taking into consideration the finding that parents' messages may be misinterpreted by children, we next examined relationships between parents' actual racial/ethnic behavior (i.e., traditional holiday celebration) and children's perceptions of racial/ethnic socialization messages. We expected that "actions may speak louder than words" and thus that children might see holiday celebration as a type of racial/ethnic socialization message. However, among those who reported on ethnic holiday celebration (i.e., excluding Black American and White European American samples), parents' reports of holiday celebration were unrelated children's reports of any type of racial/ethnic socialization message.

Parents' Ethnic Behaviors and Children's Ethnic Evaluation

Although the finding that celebrating cultural holidays was unrelated to children's ethnic evaluations was somewhat surprising, in actuality holiday celebration is not a direct racial/ethnic socialization message. Thus, we did not demonstrate that holiday celebration has no impact on children but rather we found that holiday celebration was not interpreted as a type of racial/ethnic socialization message. Therefore, we next examined whether or not celebration of ethnic holidays was significantly correlated with children's racial/ethnic evaluation. Indeed, among those parents who reported on their celebration of ethnic holidays, we found that holiday celebration was actually positively correlated with children's ethnic evaluation, $r = .243$, $p = .021$.

Parents' Racial/Ethnic Socialization and Children's Ethnic Evaluation

Finally, given the finding that parents' reports of holiday celebration had a positive relationship with children's ethnic evaluation, we assessed the relationship between parents' reports of racial/ethnic socialization messages and children's reports of ethnic evaluation. In essence, because racial/ethnic socialization messages can be quite subtle, it is possible that children may not be attuned to parents' ethnic/racial socialization practices as such, but that such messages nevertheless influence children's evaluations of their ethnic group. Interestingly, we found that regardless of message type, the more parents' reported sending racial/ethnic socialization messages, the more negatively children evaluated their own ethnic identities (though the relationships were again quite modest): egalitarianism, $r = -.14$, $p = .132$; egalitarianism/cultural socialization, $r = -.15$, $p = .120$; preparation for bias, $r = -.13$, $p = .197$. Although none of these relationships were statistically significant, the consistency in direction across different indicators of racial/ethnic socialization raises important questions about how parents' discussions influence children that future studies should pursue further.

DISCUSSION

In this chapter, we focused on parents' messages to children about race and ethnicity as a central component of parenting, particularly among ethnic minority parents. After providing a brief overview of the concept of racial/ethnic socialization and the literature in this area, we focused on exploring the extent to which parents' racial/ethnic socialization messages are actually heard by children, and the conditions under which there is likely to be lack of correspondence in perceptions of, or reports about, racial/ethnic socialization among parent–child pairs. The literature, to date, has not addressed this issue, and, to a large extent, has been based on reports from a single informant—either parents or their children. Our findings, albeit exploratory, raise a number of important issues and suggest directions for future study.

We first examined relationships between parent and child reports of several dimension of racial/ethnic socialization. Our initial examination of correlations between parents' reports of messages sent and children's reports of messages received are somewhat concerning. That is, although the correlations were positive in direction they were quite modest and nonsignificant statistically, suggesting either that parents intended racial/ethnic socialization messages may be falling on "deaf ears" or that parents may be unable to verbally communicate the messages they would like to send children. Notably, several alternative explanations for the relatively weak correlations are also plausible. For one, our modest sample size probably provided insufficient statistical power to detect relationships that were small or moderate in size. Whether the correlations we reported would be statistically significant in studies based on a larger number of respondents remains to be seen. Moreover, our sample was ethnically diverse, and it is quite possible that relationships between parents' and children's reports of racial/ethnic socialization vary across ethnic groups. For instance, among groups for whom the possibility of discrimination is quite high, such as Black American or Dominican groups, relationships between parents' and children's reports of preparation for bias may be stronger than among groups for whom discrimination is not a salient issue, such as European American immigrants. Indeed, in a very exploratory set of within group analyses, it was only among Black parent–child pairs that levels of reported preparation for bias were not significantly lower for parents than they were for children. Alternatively, stronger agreement on egalitarianism/cultural socialization may be found within ethnic groups who have cultural traditions and holidays that are quite distinct from those celebrated in this country.

The finding that parents' reports of egalitarianism/cultural socialization messages were correlated with children's reports of preparation for bias messages raises the possibility that some messages from parents to children about racial or ethnic issues may be ineffectually verbalized and, thus, misinterpreted by children. This is a fascinating and potentially important finding in that it underscores the extent to which parents' messages about race must be carefully crafted to avoid misinterpretation. Findings from other qualitative interviews suggest that many parents fail to discuss racial issues with children despite their belief that is important to do so precisely because they are concerned that race-related discussion will be misinterpreted by children (e.g., Peters, 1981; 1985). Thus, future studies need to examine how children actually hear and interpret different types of messages, as well as the unintended effects of racial/ethnic socialization messages vis-à-vis a variety of child outcomes.

Despite the modest correlations we originally reported, it is important to note that a significant proportion of parent–child pairs did show agreement on individual items. This suggests that some parents send messages that children do hear, remember, and properly interpret. Thus, in the future it will be extremely important to further study those parent–child pairs who do show agreement in order (a) to identify what makes these pairs special (e.g., Are we finding parents who are simply more accurate with their reporting of messages sent or are we finding parents who have developed an effectual communication style and better understand what will make their children listen?), and (b) to determine if agreement between parent–child pairs is meaningful for other child outcomes.

Analyses that examined correspondence between parents and children on each individual item made it clear that when agreement was not found, it was most often because parents reported sending more messages pertaining to egalitarianism and fewer messages pertaining to preparation for bias than children reported hearing. Although we found this systematic source of disagreement to be quite intriguing, our current data set does not permit us to determine if the primary issue is one of biased reporting or miscommunication. Specifically, it is possible that parents believe they should be communicating messages to children about equality and that they should be promoting egalitarian principals but fail to send these messages in their day to day interactions with their children. Alternatively, parents themselves may not believe children need to hear about equality on a consistent basis but might believe that the interviewers who are asking them questions about racial/ethnic socialization think such messages are important. At the same time children who are surrounded by examples of unequal racial/ethnic treatment in the media and most likely in their day to day lives may simply believe that their parents share ideas with them concerning preparation for bias although their parents do not actually speak about such things directly. Finally, it is possible that parents may intend to convey a message about egalitarianism to children but unintentionally highlight racial or ethnic differences. In turn, children may become more aware of racial and ethnic differences and thus of the potential for biased treatment. For example, it is easy to imagine a parent showing a child history books with famous individuals from many racial and ethnic backgrounds as a way to send messages of egalitarianism, but a child might actually interpret the lesson as one suggesting that the minority individual who also made the history book was unusual. Thus, dynamic investigations of various types of racial/ethnic socialization messages as they are actually sent and actually received will be a great contribution to the literature and will answer many questions concerning the disagreement between what parents report saying and what children report hearing.

Finally, our results suggest that cultural practices influence children's evaluation of their ethnic group. Specifically, in examining the relationship between parents' practices and children's ethnic evaluation, we found celebration of cultural holiday celebration was associated with more positive ethnic evaluation, although neither parent- or child-reported racial/ethnic socialization messages were associated with children's ethnic evaluation. This suggests, that we need to look more closely at the ways in which parents report verbal messages that are intended to provide children with a positive view of themselves and with positive ways to negotiate the realities of their worlds. It may be through direct celebration of culture, race, and ethnicity that children most effectively learn to appreciate certain aspects of themselves.

NOTES

1. Unfortunately many Dominican parents who gave consent were not interviewed due to a limited number of Spanish speaking interviewers. In addition, we were unable to contact several parents due to changed phone numbers and summer vacations. In general, roughly half of the parents in each ethnic group who received consent forms agreed to be interviewed and we did not find any systematic differences in rates of participation.

2. Although within group analyses would have been fascinating and important to examine, they were not possible given the current sample. That is, we suspect that among families from certain racial/ethnic groups the socialization messages that parents intend to send children may be sent in such a way that they are clearer and have more impact on children than among other families from other racial/ethnic groups. However, the number of parent–child matches within each ethnic group in the sample was too small to obtain stable and reliable correlations, and

therefore the correspondence between parent and child reports is examined across ethnic group only.

3. We recognize that the reliability for children is extremely low, but we nevertheless retained the measure to enable us to explore parent–child congruence. Moreover, although the reliability for the preparation for bias construct was low for all children, it was particularly low for the White Russian sample ($\alpha = .16$). This again suggests that interesting within group differences in these constructs may be present and future research assessing the validity of the constructs across ethnic groups is greatly needed.

4. All White European American children were asked about receiving messages of pride and preparation for bias in regard to their "White" racial group memberships. However, many parents answered the items in regard to their European ethnic group memberships (e.g., Italian). Thus, we could not examine items related to cultural socialization or preparation for bias in a reliable manner for these parents and children.

5. Exploratory ANOVAs were conducted comparing the mean level of parent and child reported messages by ethnic group and some interesting significant findings did emerge. While these were not the focus of this chapter, it is noteworthy that both Chinese parents and Chinese children reported significantly fewer egalitarianism/cultural socialization messages than did parents and children in the other ethnic groups.

6. The same overall pattern was evident when we dichotomized each of the items assessing egalitarianism such that parents and children were coded "0" if they reported never communicating/hearing the message and "1" otherwise. Not surprisingly, the extent of agreement between parents and children was higher when items were coded in this manner (e.g., 73%, 80%, and 83% for items 1,2, and 3 respectively) but disagreement still resulted from a pattern in which parents over-report messages pertaining to egalitarianism relative to their children rather than the reverse pattern in which children over-reported egalitarianism relative to their parents (24% vs. 3%, 17% vs. 3%, and 14% vs. 4% for Egalitarianism items 1, 2, and 3 respectively).

7. Again, the same overall pattern was evident when we dichotomized each of the items assessing preparation for bias such that parents and children were coded "0" if they reported never communicating/hearing the message and "1" otherwise. The extent of agreement between parents and children was slightly higher when items were coded in this manner (e.g., 53%, 55%, 60% for items 1, 2, and 3 respectively) but disagreement l resulted from a pattern in which parents under-report messages pertaining to preparation for bias relative to their children rather than the reverse pattern in which children under-report Preparation for Bias relative to their parents (34% vs. 13%, 32% vs. 13%, and 44% vs. 7% for preparation for bias items 1, 2, and 3 respectively).

REFERENCES

Aboud, F. (1988). *Children and prejudice.* New York: Basil Blackwell.

Applegate, J. L., Burleson, B. R., & Delia, J. G. (1992). Reflection enhancing parenting as an antecedent to children's social cognitive and communicative development. In I. E. Sigel, A. V. McGuillicudy-DeLisi, & J. J. Goodnow (Eds.), *Parental belief systems: The psychological consequences for children* (2nd ed., pp. 3–40). Hillsdale, NJ: Erlbaum.

Barber, B. L., Eccles, J. S., & Stone, M. R. (2001). Whatever happened to the Jock, the Brain, and the Princess?: Young adult pathways linked to adolescent activity involvement and social identity. *Journal of Adolescent Research, 16,* 429–455.

Barnes, E. J. (1980). The black community as a source of positive self concept for black children: A theoretical perspective. In R. Jones (Ed.), *Black psychology.* New York: Harper and Row.

Biafora, F. A., Warheit, G. J., Zimmerman, R. S., Gil, A. G., Apospori, E., Taylor, D., & Vega, W. A. (1993). Racial mistrust and deviant behaviors among ethnically diverse Black adolescent boys. *Journal of Applied Social Psychology, 23,* 891–910.

Bowman, P. J., & Howard, C. (1985). Race-related socialization, motivation, and academic achievement: A study of Black youth in three-generation families. *Journal of the American Academy of Child Psychiatry, 24,* 134–141.

Boykin, A. W., & Toms, F. D. (1985). Black child socialization: A conceptual framework. In H. P. McAdoo & J. L. McAdoo (Eds.), *Black children: Social, educational, and parental environments* (pp. 33–52). Newbury Park, CA: Sage.

Branch, C. W., & Newcombe, N. (1986). Racial attitude development among young children as a function of parental attitudes: A longitudinal and cross-sectional study. *Child Development, 57,* 712–721.

Chen, L. A. (1998). A contextual examination of parental ethnic socialization and children's ethnic attitudes and knowledge among immigrant Chinese families. Unpublished doctoral dissertation, New York University.

Demo, D., & Hughes, M. (1990). Socialization and racial identity among Black Americans. *Social Psychology Quarterly, 53,* 364–374.

Downe, P. J. (2001). Playing with names: How children create identities of self in anthropological research. *Anthropologica, 43(2),* 165–177

Essed, P. (1990). *Everyday racism.* Alameda, CA: Hunter House.

Fisher, C. B., Jackson, F., & Villarruel, A. (1998). The study of African American and Latin American children and youth. In W. Damon & R. M. Lerner (Eds.), *Handbook of child psychology: Theoretical models of human development* (5th ed., pp 1145–1208). New York: Wiley.

Fisher, C. B., Wallace, S. A., & Fenton, R. E. (2000). Discrimination distress during adolescence. *Journal of Youth & Adolescence, 29(6),* 679–695.

Flanagan, C. (2003). Trust, identity, and civic hope. *Applied Developmental Science, 7(3),* 165–171.

Fordham, S., & Ogbu, J. U. (1986). Black students' school success: Coping with the "burden of acting White." *Urban Review, 18,* 176–206.

Garcia Coll, C. T., & Magnuson, K. (1997). The psychological experience of immigration: A developmental perspective. In A. Booth, A. C. Crouter, & N. Landale, (Eds.), *Immigration and the family: Research and policy on U.S. immigrants* (pp. 91–132). Mahwah, NJ: Erlbaum.

Garcia Coll, C. T., Meyer, E. C., & Brillion, L. (1995). Ethnic and minority parenting. In M. Bornstein (Ed.), *Handbook of parenting: Vol. 2. Biology and ecology of parenting* (pp. 189–209). Hillsdale, NJ: Erlbaum.

Graham, S. (2001). Inferences about responsibility and values: Implication for academic motivation. In F. Salili & C. Chiu (Eds.), *Student motivation: The culture and context of learning. Plenum series on human exceptionality* (pp. 31–59). Dordrecht, Netherlands: Kluwer Academic Publishers.

Graham, S., & Taylor, A.Z. (2002). Ethnicity, gender, and the development of achievement values. In, A. Wigfield & J. S. Eccles, (Eds.), *Development of achievement motivation. A volume in the educational psychology series* (pp. 121–146). San Diego, CA: Academic Press.

Hamm, J. V. (1996). Adolescents' cross-race peer relations as a consequence of parents' beliefs and socialization efforts (Doctoral dissertation, University of Wisconsin, Madison, 1996). *Dissertation Abstracts International,* 57(09), Z5945.

Harrison, A. O., Wilson, M. N., Pine, C. J., Chan, S. Q., & Buriel, R. (1995). Family ecologies of ethnic minority children. In N. R. Goldberger et al. (Eds.), *The culture and psychology reader* (pp. 292–320). New York: New York University Press.

Hudley, C., & Graham, S. (2001). Stereotypes of achievement striving among early adolescents. *Social Psychology of Education,* 5(2), 201–224.

Hughes, D. (2003). Correlates of African American and Latino parents' messages to children about ethnicity and race: A comparative study of racial/ethnic socialization. *American Journal of Community Psychology,* 31(1/2), 15–33.

Hughes, D., & Chen, L. A. (1997). When and what parents tell children about race: An examination of race-related socialization among African American families. *Applied Developmental Science,* 1, 198–212.

Hughes, D., & Chen, L. (1999). The nature of parents' race-related communications to children: A developmental perspective. In L. Balter & C. S. Tamis-Lemonda (Eds.), *Child psychology: A handbook of contemporary issues* (pp. 467–490). Philadelphia: Taylor and Francis.

Hughes, D., & Johnson, D. J. (2001). Correlates in children's experiences of parents' racial/ethnic socialization behaviors. *Journal of Marriage & the Family,* 63(4), 981–995.

Hughes, D., Rodriguez, J. Smith, E. P., Johnson, D. J., & Stevenson H. C. (2004). Parents' ethnic/racial/ethnic socialization practices: A review of research and directions for future study. Manuscript submitted for publication.

Katz, P. A. (1982). Development of children's racial awareness and intergroup attitudes. In L. G. Katz, C. H. Watkins, M. J. Spencer, & P. J. Wagemaker (Eds.), *Current topics in early childhood education* (Vol. 4). Norwood, NJ: Abex.

Kibria, N. (1997). The concept of "bicultural families" and its implications for research on immigrant and ethnic families. In A. Booth, A. C. Crouter, & N. Landale, (Eds.), *Immigration and the family: Research and policy on U.S. immigrants* (pp. 205–210). Mahwah, NJ: Erlbaum.

Kiesner, J., Cadinu, M. Poulin, F., & Bucci, M. (2002). Group identification in early adolescence: Its relation with peer adjustment and its moderator effect on peer influence. *Child Development,* 73(1), 196–208.

Knight, G. P., Bernal, M. E., Garza, C. A., Cota, M. K., & Ocampo, K. A. (1993). Family socialization and the ethnic identity of Mexican-American children. *Journal of Cross-Cultural Psychology,* 24, 99–114.

Kofkin, J. A., Katz, P. A., & Downey, E. P. (1995, March). Family discourse about race and the development of children's racial attitudes. Paper presented at the meeting of the Society for Research on Child Development, Indianapolis, IN.

Marshall, S. (1995). Ethnic socialization of African American children: Implications for parenting, identity development, and academic achievement. *Journal of Youth and Adolescence,* 24, 377–396.

Martin, C. L., & Ruble, D. N. (2004). Children's search for gender cues: Cognitive perspectives on gender development. *Current Directions in Psychological Science,* 13(2), 67–70.

Nesdale, D., Durkin, K., Maas, A., & Griffiths, J, (2004).

Group status, outgroup ethnicity and children's ethnic attitudes. *Journal of Applied Developmental Psychology,* 25(2), 237–251.

Nesdale, D., & Flesser, D. (2001). Social identity and the development of children's group attitudes. *Child Development,* 72(2), 506–517

Nsamenang, A. B., & Lamb, M.. E. (1995). The force of beliefs: How the parental values of the Nso of northwest Cameroon shape children's progress toward adult models. *Journal of Applied Developmental Psychology,* 16, 613–627.

Ogbu, J. U. (1974). *The next generation: An ethnography of education in an urban neighborhood.* New York: Academic Press.

Ou, Y. S., & McAdoo, H. P. (1993). Socialization of Chinese American children. In H. P. McAdoo (Ed.), *Ethnicity: Strength in diversity* (pp. 245–270). Newbury Park, CA: Sage.

Parham, T. A., & Williams, P. T. (1993). The relationship of demographic and background factors to racial identity attitudes. *Journal of Black Psychology,* 19, 7–24.

Patchen, M. (1982). Black-White contact in schools. Lafayette, IN: Purdue University Press.

Peters, M. F. (1981). Parenting in black families with young children: A historical perspective. In H. McAdoo (Ed.), *Black families.* Newbury Park, CA: Sage.

Peters, M. F. (1985). Ethnic socialization of young Black children. In H. P. McAdoo & J. L. McAdoo (Eds.), *Black children: Social, educational, and parental environments* (pp. 159–173). Newbury Park, CA: Sage.

Phinney, J. S., & Chavira, V. (1995). Parental ethnic socialization and adolescent coping with problems related to ethnicity. *Journal of Research on Adolescence,* 5, 31–54.

Phinney, J. S., & Kohatsu, E. L. (1997). Ethnic and racial identity development and mental health. In J. Schulenberg, J. L. Maggs, & K. Hurrelmann (Eds.), *Health risks and developmental transitions during adolescence* (pp. 420–443). New York: Cambridge University Press.

Phinney, J. S., Romero, I., Nava, M., & Huang, D. (2001). The role of language, parents, and peers in ethnic identity among adolescents in immigrant families. *Journal of Youth & Adolescence,* 30(2), 135–153.

Porter, J., & Washington, R. (1993). Minority identity and self-esteem. *Annual Review of Sociology,* 19, 139–161.

Quintana, S. M., & Vera, E. M. (1999). Mexican American children's ethnic identity, understanding of ethnic prejudice, and parental ethnic socialization. *Hispanic Journal of Behavioral Sciences,* 21(4), 387–404.

Richardson, B. (1981). Racism and child-rearing: A study of Black mothers. (Doctoral dissertation, Claremont Graduate School, 1981). *Dissertation Abstracts International,* 42, 125A.

Romero, A. J., & Roberts, R. E. (2003). The impact of multiple dimensions of ethnic identity on discrimination and adolescents' self-esteem. *Journal of Applied Social Psychology,* 33(11), 2288–2305.

Rosenbloom, S. R., & Way, N. (2004). Experiences of discrimination Among African American, Asian American, and Latino adolescents in an urban high school. *Youth Society,* 35(4), 420–451.

Ruble, D. N., Alverez, J., Bachman, M. A., Cameron, J., Fuligni, A., Garcia Coll, C., & Rhee, E. (2004). The development of a sense of "we": The emergence and implications of children's collective identity. In M Bennett & F. Sani (Eds.), *The development of the social self* (pp. 29–76). New York: Psychology Press.

Ruble, D. N., & Dweck, C .S. (1995). Self-perceptions, person conceptions, and their development. In N. Eisenberg (Ed.), *Social development: Review of personality and so-*

cial psychology (Vol. 15, pp. 109–139). Thousand Oaks, CA: Sage.

Ruble, D. N., & Martin, C. L. (2002). Conceptualizing, measuring, and evaluating the developmental course of gender differentiation: Compliments, queries, and quandaries: Commentary. *Monographs of the Society for Research in Child Development, 67*(2), 148–166.

Rumbaut, R. (1994). The crucible within: Ethnic identity, self-esteem, and segmented assimilation among children of immigrants. *International Migration Review, 28,* 748–794.

Sanders Thompson, V. L. (1994). Socialization to race and its relationship to racial identification among African Americans. *Journal of Black Psychology, 20,* 175–188.

Sellers, R. M., Caldwell, C. H., Schmeelk-Cone, K. H., & Zimmerman, M. A. (2003). Racial identity, racial discrimination, perceived stress, and psychological Distress among African American young adults. *Journal of Health Social Behavior, 44*(3), 302–317.

Sellers, R. M., Chavous, T. M., & Cooke, D. Y. (1998). Racial ideology and racial centrality as predictors of African American college students' academic performance. *Journal of Black Psychology, 24*(1), 8–27.

Sellers, R. M., & Shelton, N. (2003). The role of racial identity in perceived racial discrimination. *Journal of Personality & Social Psychology, 84*(5), 1079–1092.

Shelton, N., & Sellers, R. M. (2000). Situational stability and variability in African American racial identity [Special Issue]. *Journal of Black Psychology. 26*(1), 27–50.

Smith, E. P., Atkins, J., & Connell, C. M. (2003). Family, School, and Community Factors and Relationships to Racial-Ethnic Attitudes and Academic Achievement. *American Journal of Community Psychology, 32*(1-2), 159–173.

Smith, E., Fogle, V., & Jacobs, J. (in press). Assessing parental ethnic socialization: Issues and implementation. In D. Johnson (Ed.), *Racial/ethnic socialization and African American children.* Berkeley, CA: Cobb and Henry.

Spencer, M. B. (1983). Children's cultural values and parental child rearing strategies. *Developmental Review, 3,* 351–370.

Spencer, M. B. (1985). Cultural cognition and social cognition as identity correlates of Black children's personal-social development. In M. B. Spencer, G. Brookins, & W. Allen (Eds.), *Beginnings: The social and affective development of black children* (pp. 215–230). Hillsdale, NJ: Erlbaum.

Spencer, M. B., & Dornbusch, S. H. (1990). Challenges in studying minority youth. In S. Feldman & G. Elliott (Eds.), *At the threshold: The developing adolescent* (pp.123–146). Cambridge: Harvard University Press.

Spencer, M. B., Fegley, S. G., & Harpalani, V. (2003). A theoretical and empirical examination of identity as coping: Linking coping resources to the self processes of African American youth. *Applied Developmental Science, 7*(3), 181–188

Spencer, M. B., & Markstrom-Adams, C. (1990). Identity processes among racial and ethnic minority children in America. *Child Development, 61,* 290–310.

Steele, C. M. (1998). Stereotyping and its threat are real. *American Psychologist, 53,* 680–681.

Steele, C. M. (1997). A threat in the Air: How Stereotypes Shape the Intellectual Identities and Performance of Women and African Americans. *American Psychologist, 52,* 613–629.

Steele, C. M., & Aronson, J. (2000). Stereotype threat and the intellectual test performance of African Americans. In C. Stangor (Ed.), *Stereotypes and prejudice: Essential readings. Key readings in social psychology* (pp. 369–389). Philadelphia: Psychology Press.

Stevenson, H. C. (1994). Validation of the scale of racial/ethnic socialization for African American adolescents: Steps towards multidimensionality. *Journal of Black Psychology, 20,* 445–468.

Stevenson, H. C. (1995). Relationships of adolescent perceptions of racial/ethnic socialization to racial identity. *Journal of Black Psychology, 21,* 49–70.

Swanson, D. P., Spencer, M. B., Dell'Angelo, T. Harpalani, V., & Spencer T. R. (2002). Identity processes and the positive development of African Americans: An explanatory framework. In R. M. Lerner, C. S. Taylor, et al. (Eds.), *Pathways to positive development among diverse youth. New directions for youth development: Theory practice research* (pp. 73–99). San Francisco: Jossey-Bass.

Szalacha, L. A., Erkut, S., Coll, C. G., Alarcon, O., Fields, J. P., & Ceder, I. (2003). Discrimination and Puerto Rican children's and adolescents' mental health. *Cultural Diversity & Ethnic Minority Psychology, 9*(2), 141–155.

Thornton, M. C., Chatters, L. M., Taylor, R. J., & Allen, W. R. (1990). Sociodemographic and environmental correlates of racial/ethnic socialization by black parents. *Child Development, 61,* 401–409.

Udry, J. R., Li, R. M., & Hendrikson-Smith, J. (2002). Health and behavior risks of adolescents with mixed-race identity. *American Journal of Public Health, 93*(11), 1865–1870.

Umana-Taylor, A. J. (2004). Ethnic identity and self-esteem: examining the role of social context. *Journal of Adolescence, 27*(2), 139–146.

Wong, C. A., Eccles, J. S., & Sameroff, A. (2003). The influence of ethnic discrimination and ethnic identification on African American adolescents' school and socioemotional adjustment. *Journal of Personality. 71*(6), 1197–1232.

Yip, T., & Fulgni, A.J. (2002). Daily variation in ethnic identity, ethnic behaviors, and psychological well-being among American adolescents of Chinese descent. *Child Development, 73*(5), 1557–1572.

Ying, Y., & Lee, P. A. (1999). The development of ethnic identity in Asian-American adolescents: Status and outcome. *American Journal of Orthopsychiatry, 69*(2), 194–208.

25

Neighborhoods and Schools
Contexts and Consequences
for the Mental Health and
Risk Behaviors of Children and Youth

Elizabeth T. Gershoff
J. Lawrence Aber

INTRODUCTION

In the years since Bronfenbrenner (1977, 1986) outlined his ecological model, researchers have been increasingly encouraged to view development in context. Children live through and develop in multiple contexts, Bronfenbrenner argued, each with the potential to independently, or in interaction with other contexts, influence the ways in which development occurs. As places where American children spend most of their out of home time, neighborhoods and schools are two of the most important contexts for children (Duncan & Raudenbush, 1999) and thus are logical places to examine how contexts affect individual child development.

Given the ever-increasing bodies of work concerned with neighborhood (e.g., Brooks-Gunn, Duncan, & Aber, 1997a, 1997b; Leventhal & Brooks-Gunn, 2000) impacts on children and youth, and the large body of literature examining school effects on academic achievement (e.g., Mayer & Peterson, 1999), in this chapter we restrict our focus to neighborhood and school impacts on children's mental health and risk behaviors. The outcomes we consider include aggression or externalizing disorder symptoms, delinquency, depression or internalizing disorder symptoms, sexual behavior, and drug use.

HISTORICAL BACKGROUND

Identifying Neighborhoods as Contexts for Mental Health and Risk Behavior

In the last 60 years of social science research, a confluence of investigators from disparate fields, including sociology (e.g., Jencks & Mayer, 1990; Sampson, Raudenbush, & Earls, 1997; Shaw & McKay, 1942; Wilson, 1987) and psychology (Bronfenbrenner, 1977, 1986; Brooks-Gunn et al., 1997a, 1997b; Leventhal & Brooks-Gunn, 2000), has argued for and presented evidence of neighborhood context effects on children and youth.

Sociologists spearheaded investigations of neighborhood contexts as driving forces behind troubling social trends. Shaw and McKay (1942) proposed a social disorganization theory to explain neighborhood-level concentrations of crime. By mapping delinquency rates by neighborhood, they found support for their theory that economic hardship, high residential instability, and racial-ethnic heterogeneity contribute to high neighborhood crime because they undermine community social ties and community-based controls. Wilson (1987) focused attention on neighborhood-level poverty and on concern with the social isolation that accompanies concentrated poverty in urban neighborhoods. Cut off from adequate resources, opportunities, and role models, residents in such neighborhoods are drawn to antisocial and risk behaviors. Based on these and other theories, Jencks and Mayer (1990) identified five emerging theories or models of how neighborhood context influences individual behavior, namely via contagion (e.g., negative peer influence), collective socialization (e.g., role models, monitoring), institutional resources (e.g., quality and quantity of community services), competition (e.g., vying for scarce resources), and relative deprivation (e.g., residents comparing their own situation to that of their neighbors). Theoretical perspectives on neighborhood context effects are continuing to develop, such as that of collective efficacy (Sampson, Raudenbush, & Earls, 1997), an extension of the idea of collective socialization, which will be discussed below.

The search for neighborhood context explanations for individual mental health and behaviors continues, particularly among researchers concerned with children and youth. As will be demonstrated in the following sections, evidence of neighborhood influences on children and youth is mounting and providing impetus for innovative interventions designed to improve the life conditions and hence outcomes of children and youth.

Growing Interest in Schools as Contexts for Mental Health and Risk Behavior

How and why qualities of schools affect the children who attend them have been reigning questions in the field of educational research for the last several decades. Although early reports on school effects on children claimed little or no impact (Coleman et al., 1966), further research into school impacts showed clear school differences in individual achievement and social behavior (Rutter, 1980). The latter view now pervades research on schools as well as public policies and programs designed to increase student achievement through investments in poor or low-performing schools.

Given that the goal of education is to increase students' knowledge as well as their preparedness for jobs and for lives as citizens, it is not surprising that the majority of research into school impacts on children and youth focuses on learning and academic achievement (Coleman et al., 1966; Hedges, Laine, & Greenwald, 1994). Yet there is an incipient push to emphasize the fostering of mental health (Adelman & Taylor, 1998) and of social, ethical, and civic beliefs and behaviors in parallel with encouraging students to meet academic achievement goals (Battistich, Watson, Solomon, Lewis, & Schaps, 1999).

Findings that poor mental health and school misconduct co-occur with poor grades and academic failure emphasize the linked nature of academic and nonacademic outcomes in childhood and adolescence (Roeser, Eccles, & Sameroff, 2000). There is a growing body of research to support the notions that the relations among academic and mental health functioning are reciprocal (Roeser, Eccles, & Strobel, 1998) and that school contexts can impact mental health outcomes in addition to academic outcomes (Astor, 1998; Perry & Weinstein, 1998). Positive mental health has been found to predict positive academic competence beliefs and school grades a year later (Roeser et al., 2000). In addition, negative social and behavioral outcomes in adolescence such as drug use, school drop out, teenage pregnancy, and delinquency, have been predicted by early academic difficulties such as grade retention and low academic motivation (Dryfoos, 1990; Eccles, Lord, Roeser, Barber, & Jozefowicz, 1997).

Although between 5% and 8% of school-aged children in the United States experience social, emotional, or behavioral problems that can interfere with their daily functioning both in and out of school (New Freedom Commission on Mental Health, 2003), few of these children actually receive mental health services either at school or elsewhere (Kataoka, Zhang, & Wells, 2002; Knitzer, Steinberg, & Fleisch, 1991). Emotional or behavioral problems, especially those that go untreated, can inhibit children's ability to learn (Adelman & Taylor, 1998). Both children with internalizing problems (e.g., depression, anxiety) and externalizing problems (e.g., aggression) exhibit lower academic achievement (see Roeser et al., 1998). These problems have long-term consequences, with an estimated 7.2 million Americans prematurely terminating their education because of early-onset psychiatric disorders (Kessler, Foster, Saunders, & Stang, 1995).

One aspect of schools in particular, namely that of school violence, has received scrutiny over the years as a clear risk for students. From the 1950s until the present, school violence has been an increasing concern both for school administrators and the public (Warner, Weist, & Krulak, 1999). It was the Safe Schools Study, conducted by the National Institute of Education (1978) that alerted the public to the extent of violence in schools. This report spurred the addition of a School Crime Supplement to the National Crime Victimization Survey beginning in the 1988–1989 school year (Bastian & Taylor, 1991) and school violence questions present to the National Adolescent Student Health Survey (American School Health Association, 1989). As will be discussed in more detail below, school violence remains a serious problem across the country and continues to pose significant challenges to the mental health, as well as academic achievement, of American students.

THEORETICAL AND EMPIRICAL CONSIDERATIONS

Characteristics of Neighborhoods and Schools that Impact the Mental Health and Risk Behavior of Children and Youth

Through the lens of Bronfenbrenner's ecological systems theory (Bronfenbrenner, 1977, 1986), there are likely countless microsystem (directly experienced), mesosystem (cross-context), exosystem (indirectly experienced), and macrosystem (cultural) aspects of neighborhoods and schools that can affect child and youth development. Indeed, a wide variety of neighborhood and school characteristics has been linked empirically with child outcomes. The literature has yet to fully identify the dynamic processes by which neighborhood and school characteristics causally influence child and youth mental health and behavior. Neighborhoods have the potential to influence children and youth as direct, mediated, or moderated effects or through patterns that exhibit age or stage specificity (e.g., adolescents are most likely to experience neighborhoods directly, whereas young children will experience neighborhood effects as mediated through their effects on parents) (Aber, Gephart, Brooks-Gunn, & Connell, 1997). We suggest that school effects on children and youth also are likely to follow such dynamic patterns. In our reading of the literature, we found that many of the important and well-studied neighborhood and school characteristics could be grouped into three overarching categories: disadvantage, violence, and sense of community and support networks. Although we discuss them separately, we wish to emphasize that there are also reciprocal links, akin to Bronfenbrenner's mesosystem, both within categories (e.g., dangerous neighborhoods can make dangerous schools more likely: (Sheley, McGee, & Wright, 1992) and across them (e.g., levels of violence within a school affect its sense of community; Sandoval & Brock, 2002). Whenever possible, we discuss these within and between neighborhood and school influences.

It is also important to note that the vast majority of literature on neighborhood effects on children and youth refers to the neighborhoods in which children live. Clearly home neighborhoods are key environments for children, but we submit that the neighborhoods in which children attend school also have the potential to affect development.

Disadvantage

For neighborhoods in particular, the question of how contexts affect child and youth development often hinges on the extent to which the contexts are disadvantaged, with an emphasis on a lack of resources. This has resulted in a bias in the literature toward identifying negative impacts of neighborhood and school contexts on children. Although some of the literature to be reviewed looks to potential contextual buffers, the bias is reflected here in the overwhelming preponderance of negative outcomes. It should also be noted that the majority of research to be summarized was conducted in the United States; European analogs are cited when appropriate.

Disadvantaged Neighborhoods

Characterizing a neighborhood as "disadvantaged" can have one of two meanings. The first is that the neighborhood itself is bereft of crucial institutional and social resources thought to be necessary for an enhanced quality of life; such a lack resources at the neighborhood level constitutes the *neighborhood context*. The second is that the neighborhood is comprised primarily of individuals and families who themselves are low income and/or disadvantaged; the aggregation of individual-level characteristics to the neighborhood level reflects the *neighborhood composition*. These two aspects of disadvantage are often inextricably linked: disadvantaged neighborhoods are typically peopled by individuals and families who are themselves disadvantaged, and neighborhoods comprised primarily of low-income families are typically characterized by diminished community resources and restricted opportunities (Sampson, 2001).

To appreciate what it means for a neighborhood to be disadvantaged, it is helpful to consider what constitutes advantage at the neighborhood level. Leventhal and Brooks-Gunn (2003) have identified six institutional neighborhood resources that are most important for child and youth development:

1. Learning activities (such as libraries, resource centers, museums);
2. Social and recreational activities (such as parks, sports programs, art programs);
3. Child care (particularly the availability, quality, and cost of child care);
4. Schools (particularly their quality, norms, and demographics);
5. Health care services (specifically the availability, quality, and affordability of medical and social services); and
6. Employment opportunities (e.g., for adolescents, supply of and access to jobs).

A neighborhood lacking a critical number of these resources could be considered disadvantaged.

Each of these resources can affect children's social-emotional development, either directly or indirectly. Neighborhoods with adequate learning activities will attract children in off-school hours, thereby both engaging them intellectually and keeping them under adult supervision and off the streets where they would be more likely to join in antisocial activities. Similarly, social and recreational activities provide children with typically adult-monitored opportunities to structure after-school and weekend times, again diminishing opportunities to engage in antisocial activities or risk behaviors. Quality child care for preschool children and quality schools and after-school programs for school-aged children foster both social-emotional as well as cognitive development. Adequate health care services can promote social-emotional development by providing mental health counseling and preventive services regarding risk behaviors such as drug use and sexual behavior. Finally, employment opportunities will motivate adolescents to stay in school and do well if doing so will increase their ability to attain and retain good jobs (Connell & Halpern-Felsher, 1997). Part-time or full-time employment for adolescents can be important not just for their own (and often their families') financial stability but also for fostering feelings of self-esteem, self-reliance, and a positive work ethic, attributes that together will decrease the likelihood of experiencing mental health problems or engaging in risk behaviors. (Yet, see recent studies linking hours worked and type of job with lower levels of academic achievement and higher levels of stress, risk behavior, and delinquency: Staff & Uggen, 2003; Weller et al., 2003). In general, the absence of youth-serving organizations, such as boys and girls clubs, Little Leagues, and YMCAs, in disadvantaged neighborhoods leave youth without constructive, organized, attractive ways to spend their time (Connell, Aber, & Walker, 1995).

In addition to a lack of institutional resources, disadvantaged neighborhoods are also afflicted with multiple environmental stressors. Typical among environmental stressors are population density, noise, housing problems, toxins and pollution, and violence (Evans, 2004; Evans & English, 2002; Perera et al., 2003). There is some evidence that the negative associations between family poverty and children's mental health and social behaviors are at least partially mediated by exposure to the stressors present in low-income neighborhoods (Evans & English, 2002; Evans, Lercher, Meis, Ising, & Kofler, 2000). The presence of neighborhood safety hazards (e.g., drive-by shootings, gangs, drug dealing) has been associated with increases in depression and anxiety as well as in oppositional defiant disorder and conduct disorder (Aneshensel & Sucoff, 1996). Adolescents in the lowest socio-economic neighborhoods report the highest rates of stress (Allison et al., 1999).

Neighborhood disadvantage has been consistently linked with increased levels of child and youth externalizing behaviors, including criminal and antisocial behaviors and drug use (e.g., Beyers, Bates, Pettit, & Dodge, 2003; Dubow, Edwards, & Ippolito, 1997; Eamon, 2001; Loeber & Witkstrom, 1993; Simons, Johnson, Beaman, Conger, & Whitbeck, 1996). One mechanism for this link may be through social cognitive processes: perhaps through associations with violence exposure, neighborhood disadvantage has been linked with adolescents' positive beliefs about aggression and in turn with their perpetration of violence (Halliday-Boykins & Graham, 2001).

Much of the research on neighborhood effects is completely correlational in design. But findings from two uniquely powerful research designs support the notion that neighborhood disadvantage causally influences children and youth. Research with two separate samples of twins has found that neighborhood deprivation significantly increases the risk that a child will display aggression, emotional problems, inattention problems, or conduct disorder over and above genetic contributions (Caspi, Taylor, Moffitt, & Plomin, 2000; Cleveland, 2003). In addition, experimental studies, in which families are randomly assigned to move to more advantaged neighborhoods, have demonstrated that adolescents who remain in high-poverty neighborhoods are more likely to be arrested for violent crimes than their peers who moved to low-poverty neighborhoods (Leventhal & Brooks-Gunn, 2000).

Neighborhood disadvantage, indexed as having high numbers of disadvantaged families (thus an aspect of neighborhood composition), has also been linked with child and youth outcomes. There is some evidence that relatively advantaged neighborhoods (i.e., middle-class) can buffer children against the negative impact of multiple risk factors (e.g., being a minority, being poor, and having a single parent) on their levels of aggression (Kupersmidt, Griesler, DeRosier, Patterson, & Davis, 1995). Possible explanations for this finding are that aggression is relatively more adaptive in poor and stressful neighborhoods or that these children have fewer successful adult and peer role models (Kupersmidt et al., 1995). Having affluent neighbors also has been associated with decreased rates of adolescent childbearing over and above socioeconomic characteristics of individual families (Brooks-Gunn, Duncan, Klebanov, & Sealand, 1993; Ku, Sonenstein, & Pleck, 1993).

The fact that neighborhood-level disadvantage is often confounded with family-level disadvantage does suggest that family or individual characteristics might account for what is typically chalked up to a neighborhood effect. For example, one multilevel analysis found no between-neighborhood differences (with neighborhoods characterized by disadvantage, stability and collective efficacy) on adolescent prosocial behavior or behavior problems, and rather that any neighborhood-level differences could be attributed to the clustering of individual-level factors within neighborhoods (Rankin & Quane, 2002). However, other studies have confirmed neighborhood effects distinct from family disadvantage effects. Sampson et al. (1997) found that collective efficacy at the neighborhood level was associated with less perceived violence in the neighborhood, over and above individual-level demographic risk factors. A multilevel study in the Netherlands determined that levels of child behavior problems were highest when families lived in deprived neighborhoods, over and above family socioeconomic status (SES; Kalff, Kroes, Vles, Hendriksen, Feron, Steyaert, van Zeben, Jolles, & van Os., 2001). It is most likely that both neighborhoods and families have separate and combined effects on children and youth. However, it is clearly important that neighborhood- and family-level disadvantage should always be analyzed conjointly in order to determine the unique contributions of each to child development.

Disadvantaged Schools

As with neighborhoods, school-level disadvantage also can be conceptualized as having both contextual and compositional features. At the contextual level, a key determinant of school advantage or disadvantage is per-student spending. Across the country, per-student expenditures are the result of a complicated formula that combines federal, state, and local tax-based funding. As a result, the range in per-student expenditures nationally is quite large. In the 1999–2000 school year, the national median total per student expenditure by school districts was $7,463; however, individual states show great variation in spending, with the median total per student expenditure in the highest-spending state, Alaska ($14,320), being more than twice that of the median expenditure in the lowest-spending state, Arkansas ($5,624; National Center for Education Statistics, 2003). Although some differences can be attributed to differences in cost of living (i.e., Alaska is a more expensive state in which to live or operate a school than Arkansas), these discrepancies also reflect the extent of state and local commitment to school funding.

At the compositional level of disadvantage, a human marker for under-resourced schools is the percentage of the student body that qualifies for free school lunch (in other words, those students whose families earn below the poverty line). It is a sad fact of the structure of school financing in the United States that high numbers of low-income children and low per pupil spending go hand in hand. Young children whose families are poor or low income are more likely to attend schools with higher proportions of inexperienced teachers and with fewer technological resources for learning compared than are non-poor children (Mayer, Mullens, & Moore, 2000). Schools comprised predominately of children from low-income families suffer disproportionately from disrepair, forcing children to attend class in schools with such problems as inadequate plumbing, leaky roofs, or dysfunctional heating and cooling systems (National Center for Education Statistics, 2000).

These disparities in resources are reflected in student achievement: Schools with the highest percentages of students eligible for free lunch have the lowest academic achievement (Bickel, Howley, Williams, & Glascock., 2000; Wirt et al., 2003). Students attending high poverty schools are least likely to report a positive attitude toward school, and parents at high poverty schools are least likely to participate in school activities (Wirt et al., 2003). Even more troubling is the finding that students who were not themselves eligible for free lunch had lower achievement if they attended schools in which more than 50% of their peers were eligible for free lunch than if they attended schools with 25% or fewer students eligible (Wirt et al., 2003). This finding suggests that a resource-poor school environment exacts a toll even among children who are otherwise relatively advantaged.

The financial resources of a school strongly determine its human resources, the most important of which are teachers. Available funds constrain both the quality of those teachers who can be hired (with quality indexed as their education level and amount of experience) and the number of teachers who can be hired (which affects student-to-teacher ratios). Indeed, schools with high proportions of low-income students, as well as those with high proportions of minority students, have a disproportionately high share of inexperienced and academically unprepared teachers (Ingersoll, 1999; Mayer et al., 2000). Not only do children learn better from and achieve more with teachers who have strong academic training and more teaching experience (Mayer et al. , 2000), but they behave better as well. Better educated and more experienced teachers constitute a human capital resource for students to draw upon and their students tend to have fewer behavior problems in students (Parcel & Dufur, 2001).

Outside of the quality of teachers, the sheer number of teachers in a school, and their ratio to students, has important implications for individual students' social-emotional behaviors. In order to adapt to a lack of adequate financing, schools and school districts often increase the sizes of schools as well as of individual classes. This trend is likely to continue: The U.S. Department of Education has forecast fairly steady increases in the number of children enrolled in elementary and secondary schools throughout the next decade (Gerald & Hussar, 2002). Without enhanced resources, such increases in enrollment can result in overcrowded schools and classrooms, a shortage of teachers, and aging and unsafe school buildings (U.S. Department of Education, 2000).

School size is implicated in how schools are organized, the curriculum that is offered, and how school members interact (Lee, 2000), each of which can impact students' mental health and behavior. Students at large schools have a more difficult time feeling part of a school community, while administrators at large schools have a harder time monitoring potentially disruptive student behavior (Flaherty, 2001). School size has been found to be particularly important for disadvantaged students, with positive attitudes toward school and achievement decreasing among disadvantaged students who attend very large or very small schools (Flaherty, 2001; Lee & Smith, 1997). Students at small schools (less than 500 students) report higher levels of social support and caring within their schools, whereas students at large schools (more than 1,000 students) report feeling a lack of community within their school (Lee, Smerdon, Alfeld-Liro, & Brown, 2000). However, there is a caution: Students may find it difficult to respect the requests and deadlines of teachers with whom they have come to know well, suggesting that even in small schools students need direction and advocacy from adults (Lee et al., 2000). Taking such various factors into account, statistical models have suggested that schools with enrollments of 600 to 900 students have the highest levels of achievement (Lee, 2000).

The effects of having more students in a school, and thus larger class sizes, has direct impacts on individual student behavior. From an economics perspective, classrooms with large numbers of students in relation to teachers result in resource dilution (Parcel & Dufur, 2001). Overcrowding increases the difficulty teachers have in establishing meaningful relationships with their students, in offering individualized attention to students, and in monitoring and disciplining student behavior (Flaherty, 2001; Flannery, 1997). Not surprisingly, the overcrowding of classrooms and schools has been linked with an increased likelihood of school violence (Flannery, 1997).

Exposure to Violence

Children's exposure to violence in its many forms, including in neighborhoods and schools, from families, and through the media, has become an increasing concern to parents, researchers, and policymakers, and indeed to children and youth themselves, over the past few decades. Exposure to non-familial violence is typically thought of as occurring at the community, or neighborhood, level, such as that in the form of observed muggings, attacks, and murders. However, a large portion of the non-familial violence that children and youth experience both as witnesses and as victims occurs in schools. In their landmark study of Washington, D. C., children, Richters and Martinez (1993c) found that a majority of witnessed violence occurs near children's homes but a substantial minority occurs in schools (68% and 22%, respectively); in contrast, violence victimization occurred roughly equally near home (48%) or at or near school (52%). In a more recent study in New York City, youth aged 12 to 20 reported that 57% of instances of seeing someone slapped, punched, or hit occurred at or near their schools and 47% of instances in which they themselves were slapped, punched, or hit occurred at or near their schools (Gershoff & Aber, 2003). These studies and others confirm that exposure to violence in schools should be of equal importance to parents, researchers, and policymakers as exposure to violence in neighborhoods.

Family-level disadvantage and violence and neighborhood-level disadvantage and violence are often closely intertwined (Aber, 1994). At the neighborhood level, poverty has been consistently linked with violent crime (Hsieh & Pugh, 1993). Accordingly, community violence is often thought to be a problem primarily for low-income, urban adolescents, a perspective reflected in the predominance of such samples in studies of exposure to violence (Flannery, 1997). Yet, national studies have confirmed that violence witnessing and victimization are facts of life for children and adolescents throughout the country (Addington, Ruddy, Miller, & DeVoe, 2002; Barton, Coley, & Wenglisky, 1998; Boney-McCoy & Finkelhor, 1995). Sadly, although exposure is more common among adolescents, exposure to violence is common in the lives of many young children as well (Osofsky, 1995).

One of the most important characteristics of violence exposure for child and youth development is its chronicity: children in violent schools or in violent neighborhoods are often exposed to multiple repeated violent or even traumatic events. Thus, violence becomes something that children assimilate into their views of themselves and others and that they adapt to through self-protective behaviors. Such chronic violence is more likely to have pervasive effects on child development than a single event such as a natural or terrorist disaster (Kupersmidt, Shahinfar, & Voegler-Lee, 2002).

This has indeed been found relative to the events of September 11th, 2001. In our study of New York City adolescents, exposure to the single-event of the terrorist attacks had relatively few effects on their mental health and behavior problems up to 2 years later relative to their exposure to community violence. Specifically, media exposure to the event was associated with heightened symptoms of post-traumatic stress, direct exposure to the event (e.g., seeing the planes hit, the towers fall, or smelling smoke) was associated with increased social mistrust, and having a family member at, injured in, or killed in the World Trade Center was associated with increased social mistrust (Aber, Gershoff, Ware, & Kotler, 2004). In contrast, chronic witnessing and being a victim of community violence had pervasive and very strong effects. Victimization by community violence was strongly associated with adolescents' symptom levels of depression, anxiety, conduct disorder, and post-traumatic stress disorder (PTSD); witnessing community violence was associated with symptom levels of depression, conduct disorder, and PTSD as well as with increases in hostile attribution bias and social mistrust (Aber et al., 2004). We concluded from these findings that chronic violence exposure has a greater impact on urban adolescents' symptomatology and social attitudes than exposure to the single traumatic event of September 11th. Although the services directed at children and youth in the wake of the terrorist attacks were important, clearly greater efforts are needed to assist urban children and youth in dealing with chronic violence exposure (Aber et al., 2004).

Processes By Which Violence Exposure May Affect Children and Youth

There are multiple ways in which exposure to violence may affect children's mental health as well as the likelihood that they will engage in antisocial or risk behaviors. One is through the impact of exposure on mental health at the individual level. Witnessing violent events can be traumatic particularly if the victim is a friend or family member, and thus can affect children's levels of anxiety, fear, and stress. As would be expected, victimization can have more direct links to individual trauma and stress. Exposure to violent interpersonal events, such as muggings, stabbings, shootings, rapes, murder, and family violence, can have tremendous negative effects on youth's mental health if they themselves are witnesses or victims (e.g., Allen, Jones, Seidman & Aber, 1998; Farrell & Bruce, 1997; Gorman-Smith & Tolan, 1998; Horn & Trickett, 1998).

Another avenue for the impact of exposure is through social information processing. At the individual level, internal cognitive processes likely play an important role in transforming the experience of violence at the community level into behavioral differences at the individual level. Coie and Dodge (1998) suggest that context can affect aggressive behavior by altering cognitive processes, such as by making children more likely to perceive threat or experience fear, to access aggressive responses to solve problems, and to view aggression as a desirable and effective means of achieving positive consequences. By providing models of violence as an effective problem solving strategy, and thus encouraging cognitive justifications for violence, or by requiring violence as a self-protective mechanism, violent neighborhoods increase the likelihood that youth will themselves engage in violence (Attar, Guerra, & Tolan, 1994). Indeed, exposure to severe community violence (e.g., shooting, stabbing, murder) has been associated with increased levels of hostile attribution bias and approval of aggression (Guerra, Huesmann, & Spindler, 2003; Shahinfar, Kupersmidt, & Matza, 2001) and in turn with increased child aggression both directly and mediated through positive beliefs about aggression (Guerra et al., 2003; Colder, Mott, Levy, & Flay, 2000). In an interesting example of domain specificity, witnessing and victimization have been linked to aggressive behavior through distinct mediational processes: witnessing through social-cognitive biases, and victimization through emotion dysregulation (Schwartz & Proctor, 2000).

Violence in Neighborhoods

Characterizing Neighborhood Violence. Since the appearance of Richters and Martinez's (1990) exposure to violence measure, the majority of research on exposure to violence has distinguished violence that is witnessed from violence that is directly experienced as a victim. The pervasive nature of violence in many neighborhoods is such that exposure through witnessing tends to be strongly correlated with exposure through victimization (e.g., Allen et al., 1998; Schwartz & Proctor, 2000), although children are more often witnesses than victims (Richters & Martinez, 1993b). While the potentially traumatic nature of victimization is obvious, it is perhaps less understood that witnessed violence also can be quite traumatic and have mental health consequences. Indeed, witnessed violence is often referred to as "covictimization" (Shakoor & Chalmers, 1991).

The one common thread through the literature on neighborhood violence exposure in the United States is that rates of exposure among children have been and continue to be distressingly high. Homicide is the second leading cause of death for youth aged 15–24 and the fourth leading cause of death for children aged 1–14 (Minino & Smith, 2001). Nationally, 35% of children and adolescents reported being a victim of violence at some point in their lives and an additional 5% reported an attempted victimization (Boney-McCoy & Finkelhor, 1995). On Chicago's South Side in 1987–1988, 24% of 10- to 19-year-olds had witnessed a murder, 45% reported seeing more than one type of violence, between 40% and 56% of witnessed crimes involved a familiar victim, and 47% had been a victim of a violent crime in the previous year (Uehara, Chalmers, Jenkins, & Shakoor, 1996). In their study of children in Washington, D.C., Richters and Martinez (1993b) found that among first and second graders, 61% had witnessed violence and 19% had been a victim, while among fifth and sixth graders, 72% had witnessed violence and 32% had been victimized. In New Haven in 1994 and 1996, 36% of adolescents had experienced at least one type of violent act, while on average, each had witnessed nearly three different types of violence (Schwab-Stone et al., 1999).

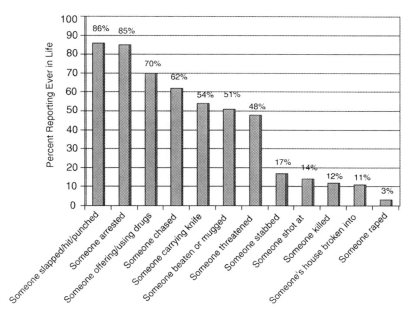

Figure 25.1 Percent of New York City youth reporting witnessed community violence (2002–2003). From Gershoff, Pedersen, Ware, and Aber (2004).

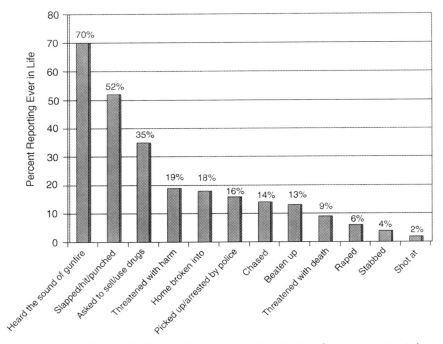

Figure 25.2 Percent of New York City youth reporting victimization by community violence (2002–2003). From Gershoff, Pedersen, Ware, and Aber (2004).

Startlingly, rates of community violence exposure do not appear to be diminishing. In our study of over 900 primarily minority, low-income New York City adolescents from 2002 to 2003, 98% reported witnessing at least one form of violence and 87% reported being a victim of at least one form of violence (Gershoff, Pedersen, Ware, & Aber, 2004). Figure 25.1 displays the rates of specific forms of witnessed violence; most youth reported seeing someone slapped, hit, or punched or seeing someone arrested, but a distressingly high 14% of youth reported seeing someone shot at and 12% reported seeing someone killed. Victimization rates are displayed in Figure 25.2; over half had been slapped, hit, or punched themselves, a third had been asked to sell, buy, or use drugs, and a fifth had been threatened with serious bodily harm. Thirteen percent had been themselves beaten up or mugged and 6% had been sexually assaulted, molested, or raped. By any measure, the rates at which youth in New York City continue to be exposed to community violence as witnesses or victims remain alarmingly high and demand increased efforts at both prevention of violence in communities and mental health service intervention to witnesses and victims.

Several demographic characteristics of children have been identified as covariates of violence exposure, although it is important to keep in mind that several of these covariates are potentially confounded with family and neighborhood socio-economic status:

- Children aged 12 to 17 years old are twice as likely to be victims of serious violent crime and three times as likely to be victims of assault than adults (Office of Juvenile Justice and Delinquency Prevention, 2000).
- Minorities are at greater risk for violence exposure than Whites (Eitle & Turner, 2002; Lauritsen, 2003; Salzinger, Feldman, Stockhammer, & Hood., 2002; Stein et al., 2003).
- The majority of violent events experienced by adolescents (53%) occur within 1 mile of their homes (Lauritsen, 2003).
- Boys tend to report more violence exposure than girls, except in the case of sexual violence (Eitle & Turner, 2002; Kuo, Mohler, Raudenbush, & Earls, 2000; Lauritsen, 2003; Myers & Thompson, 2000; Salzinger et al., 2002; Stein et al., 2003).

- The afternoon, particularly after school, hours are the most dangerous for children (Snyder & Sickmund, 1999).
- Living in urban and/or disadvantaged neighborhoods puts children at increased risk of violence exposure (Aneshensel & Succo, 1996; Lauritsen, 2003; see Salzinger et al., 2002, and Stein et al., 2003, for reviews).
- Youth living in single-parent homes are 50% more likely than youth living in two-parent homes to be victims of violence in general and 200% more likely to be victims in their neighborhoods, most likely because youth in single parent families are more likely to live in impoverished and violent neighborhoods (Lauritsen, 2003).

Identifying Impacts of Neighborhood Violence.   At the psychobiological level, a review of the literature found that some studies report hypoarousal among children exposed to violence whereas others report hyperarousal (Lynch, 2003); this inconsistency remains to be resolved but has important implications for whether internalizing or externalizing symptoms might be expected as outcomes of violence exposure. Until it is resolved, both types of outcomes might be expected.

Exposure to violence generally, and victimization and witnessing in particular, has been linked with a range of internalizing mental health problems. Foremost among these is PTSD, with several studies finding links between exposure to violence and increased PTSD symptomatology (Aber et al., 2004; Berman, Kurtines, Silverman, & Serafini, 1996; Berton & Stabb, 1996; Boney-McCoy & Finkelhor, 1995; Ceballo, Dah, Aretakis, & Ramirez, 2001; Hoven et al., 2004; Lynch, 2003; Myers & Thompson, 2000; Schwartz & Proctor, 2000). A range of other internalizing mental health problems have been linked to violence exposure, including anxiety, depressive symptoms, somatization (Aber et al., 2004; Hoven et al., 2004; Lynch, 2003; Moses, 1999; Richters & Martinez, 1993a; Schwab-Stone et al., 1999), suicidality (Elze, Stiffman, & Doré, 1999), hopelessness, and a heightened belief that they would have a violent death (Hinton-Nelson, Roberts, & Synder, 1996).

Several of these psychological reactions to violence exposure may act in combination, in other words be comorbid with each other. In particular, the associations of exposure to violence to both depressive symptoms and suicidal ideation have been found to be mediated by PTSD symptoms in children (Mazza & Reynolds, 1999), and comorbid separation anxiety symptoms and PTSD symptoms have been associated with exposure to the violent events of September 11th, 2001 (Hoven et al., 2004). Similarly, intrusive thinking has been found to partially mediate the association between victimization and internalizing (Kliewer, Lepore, Oskin, & Johnson, 1998).

The bulk of research on exposure to neighborhood violence has repeatedly found links between levels of exposure and levels of externalizing problem behaviors such as aggression or antisocial behavior (for reviews see: Overstreet, 2000; Salzinger et al, 2002; for examples see: DuRant, Cadenhead, Pendergrast, Slavens, & Linder, 1994; Eitle & Turner, 2002; Lynch, 2003; Schwab-Stone et al., 1999). In a study of youth on Chicago's South Side, 86% of youth who reported perpetrating violence were themselves witnesses and victims of violence (Uehara et al., 1996). Several studies have determined that neighborhood violence predicts externalizing problem behaviors including violence perpetration, over and above demographic and family psychosocial risks (such as parent depression and marital conflict) (Ceballo et al., 2001; Greenberg, Lengua, Coie, & Pinderhughes, 1999).

The few studies that have examined positive developmental outcomes have found that exposure to neighborhood violence tends to have a dampening effect. In the few studies that have examined competence, neighborhood violence exposure was associated with lower social competence (Cooley-Quille, Turner, & Biedel 1995; Greenberg et al., 1999; Schwartz & Proctor, 2000) and with declines in academic performance (Lynch, 2003).

Given the amount of violence in their communities and the potentially drastic effects it can have on their development, how do children cope with exposure to this violence? Youth growing up in violent neighborhoods are repeatedly exposed to challenges that are outside their control and that overwhelm their coping abilities, such that coping relying on either aggression or depression function as viable short-term tactics (Blechman, Dumas, & Prinz, 1994). In response to exposure to and fear of community violence, adolescents have reported engaging in such protective behaviors as avoiding certain parks, carrying weapons as self-defense, staying home from school, ceasing to engage in a particular activity or sport, or finding someone to protect them (Arnette & Walsleben, 1998).

Of course, it is possible that some third factor, correlated with neighborhood violence, is the causal factor in the found associations between exposure to violence and negative outcomes for children and youth. Similarly, it could be that poor and violent neighborhoods "attract" more vulnerable children and families to be residents. These issues of causality and direction of effect have plagued the neighborhood literature for decades. Only social experiments that randomly assign neighborhoods in experimental designs (e.g., the Moving to Opportunity study, discussed below: Katz, Kling, & Liebman, 2003; Ludwig, Duncan, & Ladd, 2003) or advances in the causal analysis of non-experimental data (e.g., instrumental variable analyses) hold promise in untangling various links in the causal chains. Of course, this is not simply a matter of scientific or scholarly concern. Understanding the underlying causal reality of neighborhood effects has profound implications for the design and implementation of preventions, interventions, and policy strategies.

Violence in Schools

Characterizing School Violence. The extent of violence in schools has been a persistent concern for parents, administrators, and policymakers in recent decades. The most recent data on crimes in schools (from the School Crime Supplement to the National Crime Victimization Survey) indicate that 6% of 12- to 18-year-olds reported being victims of nonfatal crimes at school during the previous 6 months (DeVoe et al., 2003). Boys, middle school students, and students at public schools were more likely to report being victims at school. Tellingly, during the period of 1992 to 2001, adolescents aged 12 to 18 were 31% more likely to be victims of theft and 300% more likely to be victims of a violent crime at or on the way to school than away from school (DeVoe et al., 2003).

One important source of violence in many schools (and neighborhoods, for that matter) is gangs. Students who report gangs at their school are almost twice as likely to experience violent or property victimization than students who do not report gangs in their school (18.4% vs. 10.8%; Addington et al., 2002), despite the fact that schools with gangs have the greatest number of security measures (Howell & Lynch, 2000). Gang presence is most likely in schools with the lowest family incomes and tends to go hand in hand with the availability of drugs in a school (Howell & Lynch, 2000).

The availability and selling of drugs at school and school violence are often co-occurring problems. As antecedents to problem behavior, the consumption of alcohol and drugs can lead to an overall harmful school environment (Fagan & Wilkinson, 1998). Twenty-nine percent of students report that someone has offered them drugs while at school (Centers for Disease Control and Prevention, 2002a). Five percent of students report drinking on school property and 5% report using marijuana at school (DeVoe et al., 2003). Another pernicious, and often overlooked, source of violence and victimization is bullying, which involves a powerful person repeatedly oppressing a less powerful person through psychological or physical means (Farrington, 1993; Olweus, 1995). Eight percent of 12- to 18-year-olds nationally reported having been bullied in the last six months; in a trend similar to that of overall victimization cited above, boys, middle school students, and public school students were most likely to be bullied (DeVoe et al., 2003). Bullying is reflective of, and contributes to, a school environment characterized by fear and intimidation (Arnette & Walsleben, 1998).

The majority of schools throughout the country have problems with violent victimization. Seventy one percent of public schools reported one or more violent incidents at their schools (DeVoe et al., 2003). Somewhat surprisingly, students at rural and suburban schools were as likely to be victims of theft or violent victimization as students in urban schools in 2001 (DeVoe et al., 2003). What does make a difference is school size: Large schools (those with 1,000 or more students) are 46% more likely to report violent incidents than schools with less than 300 students (DeVoe et al., 2003).

Of course, violence against students in schools tends to be perpetrated by other students. Eighteen percent of boys and 7% of girls in a national sample reported having been in a physical fight on school property (DeVoe et al., 2003). On average, 7% of students carried a weapon to school and 16% got into physical fights on school property (Centers for Disease Control and Prevention, 2002b). Such fights occur even when students are aware of their dangers: In a sample of middle school students, 20% reported getting into regular physical fights, despite the fact that nearly three quarters of the sample thought that fighting was a risky behavior (St. George & Thomas, 1997).

Similar to the finding that crime in neighborhoods is concentrated at certain locations, or "hotspots" (Sherman, Gartin, & Buerger, 1989), researchers have identified specific physical locations within schools that are prone to violence. School violence is often time- and place-specific. Not surprisingly, it tends to occur before or after school or during transitions between classes, and to occur in either crowded places (such as hallways, cafeterias, or playgrounds) or in unsupervised places (such as bathrooms or staircases) (Flaherty, 2001; Garofalo, Siegel, & Laub, 1987; see Astor & Meyer, 2001, for review). In addition, violence is more likely in schools that are large, are overcrowded, are poorly organized, or have poor resources (Astor & Meyer, 2001; Flannery, 1997; Warner, Weist, & Krulak, 1999). Schools characterized by fear of violence and crime will have difficulty recruiting and retaining good teachers, and the teachers who remain will be less likely to confront misbehaving students out of fear of their own safety, leading to disruptive classrooms with fewer opportunities for learning (Flannery, 1997).

Although we know that children are more likely to be exposed to violence if they live in violent and disadvantaged neighborhoods, we know little about the extent to which violence exposure depends on the characteristics of the neighborhoods in which children attend school. There is some evidence that community violence begets school violence (Sheley et al., 1992); the overlap of neighborhoods and schools, particularly with regard to exposure to violence, will be discussed further below.

Identifying Impacts of School Violence. As with community violence, exposure to school violence either as a witness or a victim can exact a toll on students' mental health. Among both elementary and high school students, violence victimization in schools has been linked with greater anxiety, depression, PTSD symptoms, and general trauma, as well as to violent behavior (Berton & Stabb, 1996; Singer, Anglin, Song, & Lunghofer, 1995). Students who report that their schools are dangerous have a decreased sense of school-based self-efficacy (Bowen, Richman, Brewster, & Bowen, 1998).

Exposure to violence in schools has often been linked with a particular form of anxiety: fear and avoidance of school. In 2001, 6% of students reported that they were fearful about their safety at school either sometimes or all of the time (DeVoe et al., 2003). Feeling that school or the neighborhood around school is unsafe led 2% of students skip school out of fear of victimization, a rate that increases to 4% among previously victimized students and 7.5% among bullied students (Addington et al., 2002). Students who report more violence and drug activity in their schools are also likely to have heightened fear of victimization and to be more vigilant about places in and around school where violence may occur (Mayer & Leone, 1999).

Sense of Community and Support Networks

The need to belong to a group or community motivates much of human activity, with acceptance by a group yielding positive emotions and experiences and rejection by a group often precipitating stress, anxiety, depression, behavioral problems, and drug abuse (Baumeister & Leary, 1995). For children and youth, two of the most salient communities to which they belong are their home neighborhoods and their schools (sports teams, school clubs, and religious organizations constitute other important communities for children and youth). The extent to which children feel a part of these communities, the level at which they feel supported by them, and the norms endemic to these communities can each impact children's mental health and the extent to which they engage in risk behaviors.

Adolescents in particular are at the stage of early development most conducive to neighborhood and school effects. Increased autonomy that comes with age as well as preparation for work and life independent from parents propel adolescents into new and varied contexts within their neighborhoods. As they age out of childhood and toward adulthood, adolescents spend less time with parents in the home and more time with peers out of the home (Connell & Halpern-Felsher, 1997); whereas when they were younger much of neighborhood effects were mediated through their parents, adolescents' exposure to their neighborhoods becomes more direct (Aber et al., 1997). We continue to discuss neighborhood and school impacts on all children, while keeping in mind that much of the literature to be reviewed focuses on adolescents.

Neighborhood as Community

We have discussed how tangible aspects of neighborhoods, such as resources and levels of violence, affect children. Now we turn to the social context of neighborhoods. Beliefs, attitudes, and norms that are held by a majority of individuals in a community can influence the developing beliefs, values, and norms held by children and youth. These, in turn, can directly affect child and youth behavior. For example, community norms regarding crime and violence, in addition to overall levels of crime and violence, determine whether youth engage in antisocial behavior (Williams, Ayers, & Arthur, 1997). Youth living in high-poverty urban neighborhoods are less likely to participate in community service, have less civic knowledge, and are less politically tolerant than youth living in low-poverty neighborhoods (Atkins & Hart, 2003), findings which suggest that adolescents in disadvantaged neighborhoods are likely to feel estranged from their neighborhoods and communities. We will focus here on two important ways in which neighborhood norms can affect children, namely through feelings of neighborhood collective efficacy and through peers' behavior and norms (Leventhal & Brooks-Gunn, 2003).

Collective efficacy is a relatively new rubric for understanding the processes by which neighborhoods affect children and families. Collective efficacy grows out of mutual trust among neighbors and their willingness to intervene and exercise social control, such as through the supervision of children and youth and the maintenance of public order (Sampson, Raudenbush, & Earls, 1997). It thus extends the notion of social capital, or relationships among persons that facilitate action (Coleman, 1988). Neighborhoods high in social capital/collective efficacy are better able to realize common values and to maintain social controls (Sampson, 2001).

Collective efficacy is distinct from, though potentially related to, the demographic characteristics of the neighborhood's population: concentrated disadvantage, immigration concentration, and residential stability have been found to account for 70% of the neighborhood variation in collective efficacy (Sampson et al., 1997). There is some evidence that the effects of neighborhood disadvantage on adolescent behavior are mediated through the levels of neighborhood-level informal control (Elliott et al., 1996). Children who live in disadvantaged neighborhoods and who report low levels of collective socialization (a similar concept to that of collective efficacy) in those neighborhoods are more likely to associate with deviant peers (Brody et al., 2001).

In the Project on Human Development in Chicago Neighborhoods, Sampson and colleagues (1997; Sampson, 2001) have found that collective efficacy was negatively associated with community violence and hypothesize that collective efficacy plays a key role in monitoring and controlling adolescent peer groups (Sampson & Groves, 1989). Adolescents in neighborhoods characterized by low collective efficacy have more unconventional friends and, in turn, are less prosocial and more likely to have behavior problems (Rankin & Quane, 2002).

By virtue of the fact that children are most likely to be interacting with peers in neighborhood contexts, peers are a main way that children and adolescents experience the "community" of a neighborhood. Peers constitute social support networks for other children; however, they are not always "supportive" of positive adjustment. Negative peer norms, or peer culture, can dispose children to engage in antisocial or delinquent behavior. Aspects of negative peer culture include the extent to which youth in one's neighborhood get in trouble with the police, use drugs or alcohol, or join a gang (Bowen & Bowen, 1999). Children's perceptions of a negative neighborhood peer culture and reports of personal threats received in neighborhoods both are associated with their trouble behavior in school (e.g., being sent out of class for behavior, having notes sent to parents about behavior, being suspended or expelled; Bowen & Bowen, 1999). When neighborhood-based institutions and norms fail to regulate peer group behavior, peer influence is exacerbated and is typically negative, increasing delinquent and problem behavior (Elliott et al., 1996; Sampson & Groves, 1989). This is sharply illustrated by the finding that in high-risk neighborhoods, peer support increases antisocial and risky behavior, whereas in low-risk neighborhoods peer support decreases such negative behaviors (Dubow et al., 1997; Gonzalez, Cauce, Friedman, & Mason, 1996).

School as Community

The major components of a school community are students' relationships with teachers as well as their relationships with fellow students (Osterman, 2002). Having a sense of belonging to a supportive school community has been associated positively with emotional well-being, intrinsic motivation, and prosocial behavior, as well as with lower levels of emotional distress and suicidal behaviors (Osterman, 2002; Resnick et al., 1997). In contrast, feelings of rejection or not "fitting in" at school are associated with behavioral problems in school, school avoidance, and school drop-out as well as with mental health problems including anxiety, distress, substance use, sexual activity, violence, and suicide (Osterman, 2002). If students perceive a mismatch between the resources and characteristics of their schools and their own needs (such as those for support or for autonomy), they may feel angry and resentful and act out as a result (Roeser, Eccles, & Strobel, 1998). Unfortunately, those students most in need of a supportive school community may be least likely to experience it; students at low-income schools are more likely to experience them as uncaring (Watson, Battistich, & Solomon, 1997).

Teachers' and administrators' attitudes and expectations about ability and achievement can affect students' performance in school as well as their mental health. Students who attend schools that have challenging curricula and that have high expectations for their students in turn have high engagement in and achievement at school (Mayer et al., 2000). When students are engaged in and value school, they will be less disposed toward disruptive and maladaptive behaviors (Dishion, Patterson, Stoolmiller, & Skinner, 1991). A classroom climate characterized by an emphasis on internal control and personal responsibility has been associated with greater individual student self-esteem (Ryan & Grolnick, 1986). School and classroom characteristics such as teachers' use of praise, a comfortable environment for students, enhanced opportunities for student responsibility and participation, and an academic emphasis together have been found to promote positive student behavior (Rutter, 1980). Absenteeism and drop-out rates are lower in schools characterized by an emphasis on academics, an orderly environment, and the presence of faculty more engaged with students (Bryk & Thum, 1989). In schools that emphasize innate ability as a determinant of academic ability, children without such ability may develop internalized feelings of low self-esteem or anxiety (Roeser et al., 1998). Middle school students who perceive that their school emphasizes competition and ability and that their teachers treat students differentially based on race or gender also report declining mental health over time (Roeser, Eccles, & Sameroff, 2000).

At the classroom level, teacher characteristics, the instructional climate, social relations within the classroom, and student aggregate characteristics are thought to affect children's adjustment (Perry & Weinstein, 1998). Teachers' levels of expectations, teachers' modeling of appropriate behavior, and teachers' reinforcement of appropriate student behavior are key to encouraging and managing appropriate student behavior, but if these norms are not consistent throughout the school or are not accepted by the students, their potential positive impact is diminished (Rutter, 1980). The social climate of a classroom, including average levels of disruptiveness, adjustment, and achievement, can affect individual behavior and achievement. Furthermore, individual students in classrooms with greater numbers of students with behavior problems are more likely to exhibit shy behaviors (Werthamer-Larsson, Kellam, & Wheeler, 1991).

General attitudes and norms of the student body can also affect individual mental health and risk behavior. Adolescents' perceptions of their school's norms regarding drug use are predictive of their use of illegal substances (Allison et al., 1999). Similarly, aggregated at the school level, students' endorsement of a subculture of violence is associated with more, and their endorsement of academic values with less, interpersonal violence, theft, and delinquency (Felson, Liska, South, & McNulty, 1994).

Neighborhoods and Schools as Opportunities for Intervention

Given the wide-ranging effects of neighborhoods and schools, and particularly the deleterious effects of certain neighborhood and school qualities on children's mental health and risk behavior, it is appropriate to consider whether and how these contexts can be enhanced to be supportive of children. Unfortunately, community-level interventions, which combine efforts at individual and environmental change across multiple settings, tend to have a "modest and mixed" record of results (Wandersman & Florin, 2003, p. 443). Those interventions that are successful in reducing adolescent risk behavior and violence perpetration, for example, tend to share nine characteristics: comprehensive, varied teaching methods, sufficient dosage, research-based/theory-driven, positive relationships, appropriately timed, socioculturally relevant, and well-trained staff (Nation et al., 2003).

A report by the National Research Council and Institute of Medicine (*Community Programs to Promote Youth Development*, Eccles, & Gootman, 2002) emphasized that children and youth experience positive development when their contexts are characterized by features such as: physical and psychological safety; emotional and moral support; opportunities to learn how to form close, supportive relationships with peers; opportunities to feel a sense of belonging and being valued; and opportunities for skill building and mastery. This range of contextual features implies that successful interventions will need to target multiple aspects of neighborhood and school communities, with a strong emphasis on interpersonal relationships.

The goal of changing a neighborhood or school context, replete with social, physical, and economic complexities, is ambitious to say the least. We describe next a select set of examples of neighborhood and school interventions aimed at improving children's lives.

Intervention Targeted at Neighborhood Disadvantage

With the knowledge that living in a disadvantaged or dangerous neighborhood places children at risk for both physical and mental harm, one logical remedy is to improve the neighborhoods themselves, an effort that often requires substantial financial commitments from local governments and agencies; such an effort would of course stand to benefit the largest number of children and families. Another remedy could be instituted at the individual family level, namely to move children and families from dangerous neighborhoods to advantaged, low-violence neighborhoods. Yet, doing so is, for the most part, infeasible; families live where they do for reasons that include economic (e.g., where relatively affordable housing is), cultural (e.g., where others with the same racial-ethnic or cultural background live), and social reasons (e.g., where their extended families live). Switching neighborhoods means changing this interplay of factors, and thus merely moving families out of one neighborhood into another may or may not on balance improve a family's overall situation.

Despite these challenges, there have been systematic attempts to move families from one neighborhood to another. Some of these efforts have been evaluated using experimental designs in order to determine whether a positive neighborhood change would have positive impacts on children and families. The largest of these, the Moving to Opportunity (MTO) study, is a demonstration project that randomly assigned families living in public housing to a low-poverty neighborhood housing voucher condition, a geographically unrestricted condition, or to a control condition. The MTO demonstration project preliminary findings vary somewhat across sites but generally indicate that providing the chance for families to relocate to low-poverty neighborhoods is associated with a range of positive outcomes, including increased academic test scores and decreased problem behaviors among young children and decreased risk of arrests and violent crime among adolescents (Katz et al., 2003; Ludwig et al., 2003). Also important is that, contrary to fears, families who changed neighborhoods did not report more social isolation than families who did not (Katz et al., 2003).

The results to date from the MTO demonstration project are encouraging in their effects but beg the question of how such opportunities might be afforded to all families living in disadvantaged or at-risk neighborhoods. One of the MTO investigators (Goering, 2003) estimates that given the number of families living in eligible project-based housing, the "take up" rate of families willing to move, and the logistic challenges involved in such moves, bringing MTO to scale could help 24,000 families nationwide move from disadvantaged to advantaged neighborhoods, a very small fraction of the families who live in disadvantaged neighborhoods. In addition, the costs of such a program are likely to be prohibitively expensive; final cost-benefit analyses of MTO are forthcoming (Goering, 2003).

Intervention Targeted at Neighborhood Violence

A board convened by the U.S. Departments of Justice and Health and Human Services recommended that preventing violence requires thinking developmentally, working from a sound knowledge based, and making adequate resources available (Jacobson, 2000). The report summarizes a variety of approaches to and examples of violence prevention initiatives. Kupersmidt et al. (2002) have identified three avenues for treatment of children exposed to community violence, specifically child-focused interventions, family-focused interventions, and community interventions including those at the school-level. We briefly describe one multi-level intervention.

A promising avenue for the prevention of and successful intervention regarding exposure to violence is community-based policing, which combines child-level, family-level, and community- (police-) level interventions. Community-based policing seeks to strengthen partnerships between the police and community members with the goal of enhancing interactions between police and children surrounding violence. One example is the Child Development and Community Policing (CD-CP) program, which trains police officers to be able to provide a sense of security and positive authority to children when instances of violence occur. There is some evidence that a growing trust in the police has fostered cooperation with the police, which in turn has related to greater crime solving and crime prevention (Marans & Schaefer, 1998). An evaluation of whether the program has positive outcomes for the children in these communities is still forthcoming (Marans & Schaefer, 1998).

Intervention Targeted at School Violence

Practical and Security Measures. Schools and school districts have tried a number of strategies to prevent violence. Primary among these are: installing metal detectors, removing lockers, creating closed campuses, minimizing the number of unlocked entrances, increasing security personnel and/or police officers presence, and creating alternative schools for particularly disruptive or violent students (Flannery, 1997; Howard, Flora, & Griffin, 1999; Kneese, Fullwood, Schroth, & Pankake, 2003). Measures that help create a "tight ship" are often advised, such as leaving classroom doors open to facilitate monitoring, responding to student rumors, monitoring previously violent students, and enforcing a zero tolerance policy by which any student bringing a weapon to school is automatically suspended (Kneese et al., 2003).

Strategies that address the specific needs of particular schools may also be appropriate. If bullying is the main issue, recommended steps to decrease bullying in schools include clear and consistent school rules against bullying, conflict resolution, activities to enhance self-esteem of all students, and cooperative classroom activities (Arnette & Walsleben, 1998). If gangs are the primary source of violence, successful strategies may include instituting dress codes or school uniforms (to eliminate gang colors), requiring life skills classes on resisting peer pressure, creating a climate of school ownership and pride among students, coordinating graffiti and vandalism cleanup campaigns, and establishing outreach to gang members (Arnette & Walsleben, 1998). Identifying the subcontexts in which violence is most likely and changing the social organizational structure of a school accordingly may be necessary to effectively prevent violence (Astor & Meyer, 2001).

However, the findings of some studies have suggested that increases in security measures (such as security guards, visitor sign-in procedures, metal detectors, and locker checks) are associated with *more*, not less, school violence and drug activity (Mayer & Leone, 1999). Although such findings may represent a reciprocal effect whereby increased security measures are in response to high levels of school violence, it is possible that such strict "tight ship" measures may have iatrogenic effects (Mayer & Leone, 1999). In contrast, the creation of a caring school climate, in which relationships among teachers and students in strengthened, has been advocated as a way to prevent violence in schools (Kneese et al., 2003).

Others have argued that having clear, publicized procedures for dealing with perpetrators of school violence may better prevent violence than restrictions on all students. Schools with greater student knowledge of school sanctions for violence and disruption have been found to have less disruption in their schools, suggesting that effective communication with students is critical in violence prevention (Mayer & Leone, 1999). Similarly, a school policy of severe punishment has been found to be the most effective means of lowering negative behaviors, as compared with other school policies such as school uniforms or a ban on gangs (Barton et al., 1998). School security procedures were associated only with fewer non-serious offenses but were not associated with drug offenses or serious offenses (Barton et al., 1998).

Given that students are often subject to violence on the way to or from school (Gershoff & Aber, 2003; Richters and Martinez, 1993c), communities have responded by instituting a variety of steps such as establishing Neighborhood Watch programs near schools and recruiting parents to provide "safe houses" along routes to school or to serve as safety watchers at school bus stops (Arnette & Walsleben, 1998).

Social-Cognitive Interventions. Schools throughout the country have also taken an individual-level approach to violence prevention by including universal violence prevention in classroom curriculum (Howard et al., 1999). These interventions typically center on enhancing children's social and cognitive processing, conflict resolution skills, and prosocial behavior. Such efforts in general have positive, although sometimes modest, success (e.g., Aber, Brown, & Jones, 2003; see Henrich, Brown, & Aber, 1999, and Samples & Aber, 1998, for reviews).

An example of child-focused, targeted intervention regarding violence exposure is Peer Coping-Skills Training, developed by Blechman and colleagues (1994) for use with early grade school children identified as being aggressive. The program focuses on information exchange as a means by which children can distinguish between controllable and uncontrollable challenges in their environment and to match their coping strategies appropriately (Blechman et al., 1994). This intervention has been found to result in improvements in prosocial coping and social skills (Prinz, Blechman, & Dumas, 1994).

Policy Interventions. Concern over students' safety within their schools has recently experienced heightened policy attention. Among the sweeping reforms of the federal No Child Left Behind Act of 2001 are (1) the acknowledgement of the problem of school safety, (2) a requirement that states report school safety information to the public, and (3) allowances for parents to exercise an "Unsafe Schools Choice Option" to transfer their children if their school is "persistently dangerous" or if the children have become victims of violent crime on school grounds (U.S. Department of Education, 2003a, 2003b). Under the legislation, all states must identify schools that are "persistently dangerous" according to their own definitions (U.S. Department of Education, 2003a).

Many schools throughout the country are now encouraged, or even required, to create school safety plans (e.g., Safe Schools Against Violence in Education (SAVE) legislation in New York: New York State Education Department, 2001). These plans are typically based on a customized violence-centered needs assessment (Stephens, 1998). The recommended main components of school safety plans concern campus access and control, administrative leadership, school climate, supervision of student behavior, staff training, student involvement, and community partnerships (Stephens, 1998).

Intervention Targeted at School Community Enhancement

An important way to enhance the sense of community within a school is to increase cooperative and supportive interactions among teachers and peers and to de-emphasize accomplishment and competition (Osterman, 2002). Some potential ways that schools can enhance both their sense of community and their safety include:

- encouraging family involvement
- developing links to the community
- emphasizing positive relations among students and staff
- discussing safety issues openly
- treating students with equal respect
- creating ways for students to safely share their concerns and feelings
- promoting good citizenship (Dwyer, Osher, & Warger,1998).

One example of a successful approach to changing the school community is the Child Development Project (Watson et al., 1997), a school-based intervention that attempts to change the environment of a school. The intervention is driven by the assumptions that children will feel connectedness with a caring school, and that for a school to be "caring" it must meet a child's needs for belonging, competence, and autonomy (Watson et al., 1997). The intervention involves literature-based reading, collaborative classroom learning, discipline that does not rely on rewards and punishments, parent involvement, and school-wide non-competitive activities (Watson et al., 1997). The intervention has been found to increase students' sense of community, which in turn predicted increases in positive student outcomes such as altruistic behavior, prosocial conflict resolution, concern for others, and prosocial behavior in class (Watson et al., 1997).

Schools as Sources of Treatment and Support for Child and Youth Mental Health

According to a recent report by the President's New Freedom Commission on Mental Health (2003), between 5% and 9% of children nationally have a serious emotional disturbance. Unfortunately, nearly 80% of children who are in need of mental health services do *not* receive services; in other words, approximately 7.5 million children have an unmet need for mental health care in the United States (Kataoka, Zhang, & Wells, 2002). Because schools play such important roles in the lives of children, they are in position to provide care and support to those children needing mental health services and interventions (Knitzer, Steinberg, & Fleisch, 1991). Although mental health services within schools remain scant, schools, sadly, remain the primary providers of mental health services to children (Burns et al., 1995). The ratio of school mental health providers to students is quite low, averaging 1 school psychologist or school social worker for 2,500 students and one school counselor for every 1,000 students (Carlson, Paavola, & Talley, 1995). As a result, other school staff without training in mental health necessarily play a role in meeting the mental health needs of students (Adelman & Taylor, 1998). In general, teachers whose students include children with identified behavioral or emotional problems receive little social support from a mental health presence in schools (Knitzer et al., 1991).

Remaining Issues in Neighborhood- and School-Level Interventions

Various ambitious efforts at changing neighborhood and school contexts to improve mental health and reduce risk behaviors in children and youth are hampered by the fact that there is a lack of verified theory of mechanisms by which neighborhood and school risks affect violent or risky behavior, as well as by the fact that there is a weak match of intervention strategies to any potential causal mechanisms. Important goals for the field will be to improve understanding of contextual influences on development as well as to more effectively design and evaluate neighborhood- and school-level interventions.

An example of such a research question is the nature of association between interventions and positive outcomes. Given that neighborhoods and schools are complex contexts, there are multiple targets for intervention: thus, it is important for those designing and evaluating interventions to determine whether they expect interventions to have effects in an additive fashion (such that for every added component of intervention a consequent increment of positive benefit is gained) or whether such effects will come only after a "tipping point" of interventions are introduced (such that effects are only seen once this point has been reached). There are, of course, many other potential patterns of associations among interventions and outcomes, but having a hypothesis about the nature of change is crucial to designing, implementing, and evaluating effective neighborhood- or school-level interventions.

The Intersection of Neighborhoods and Schools

Thus far, we have detailed the unique contributions of neighborhoods and schools to children's mental health and risk behaviors. Much of the research to date that examines joint neighborhood and school impacts often has an underlying assumption that the neighborhood is the same for both home and school. With the majority of U.S. children attending "neighborhood" public schools, this assumption is often accurate. School quality has been found to be positively correlated with neighborhood quality, and although there are large between-school differences in home neighborhood quality, source home neighborhoods of students within schools are relatively similar (Cook, Herman, Phillips, & Settersten, 2002).

A growing number of studies have examined the simultaneous effects of neighborhoods and schools on children's mental health and risk behaviors. One study found that a negative peer culture and exposure to or victimization by violence in the home neighborhood and exposure to violence in schools each independently predicted low school attendance, low trouble avoidance, and low grades (Bowen & Bowen, 1999).

As would be expected, there is some specificity in the effects: schools tend to have more impact on academic outcomes whereas neighborhoods have a greater impact on participation in activities such as volunteer work, clubs, or youth groups, in an additive rather than interactive fashion (Cook et al., 2002). This is not to say that schools do not have an impact on children's mental health and risk behaviors. Indeed, one study determined that school norms about drug use, but not neighborhood demographics and economics, predicted individual adolescent drug use (Allison et al., 1999).

Other studies that have considered school and neighborhood simultaneously have found that school environments mediate the effects of neighborhoods on adolescents. A study of Midwestern fifth and sixth graders found that school characteristics (such as safety, average drug use and availability) mediated the effects of neighborhoods on individual adolescents' alcohol and cigarette use (Ennett, Flewelling, Lindroth, & Norton 1997). A study of teens in Philadelphia found that school norms toward sexual initiation mediated the effects of neighborhoods on adolescents' sexual initiation (Teitler & Weiss, 2000). This latter study also determined that the between-school variation in the proportion of sexually active youths is greater than the between-neighborhood variation and that there was virtually no added contribution of neighborhood once the schools were accounted for.

However, the neighborhoods surrounding schools are important contexts to which children are exposed every school day; given that the children, families, and even staff of schools come from surrounding neighborhoods, schools that are centered in disorganized or violent neighborhoods are likely themselves to become disorganized and violent (Menacker, Weldon, & Hurwitz, 1990). Parents are keenly aware of this: Parents in at-risk neighborhoods report feeling that their children are unsafe walking to school (Osofsky, 1995). Characteristics of neighborhoods around the schools, along with school student body composition, have been found to be a major determinant of violence and crime within schools (Gottfredson & Gottfredson, 1985). In addition, schools in neighborhoods character-ized by poor quality housing, high population density, and population turnover have higher student suspension rates than schools in other neighborhoods (Hellman & Beaton, 1986). Few studies have examined the relations among school violence and characteristics of the communities surrounding schools (Laub & Lauritsen, 1998), but those that have conclude that community violence begets school violence; for example, gun-related violence in schools appears to be imported from dangerous neighborhoods surrounding schools (Sheley et al., 1992).

In addition to such neighborhood effects on schools, schools can also affect neighborhoods. As real estate agents across the country are well aware, high quality schools can significantly increase the value of homes in their surrounding neighborhoods. This has been confirmed quantitatively: elementary schools' academic achievement is positively associated with housing values, even after controlling for student body composition, high school characteristics, and other public services (Weimer & Wolkoff, 2001).

Yet it is only by de-linking them, such as by sending a student from a violent neighborhood to a school in a non-violent neighborhood, that home and school neighborhood influences can be distinguished (Grogger, 1997). Indeed, there is evidence that neighborhoods and schools are not in-extricably linked: some students in poor neighborhoods attend good schools and have conventional peer groups, whereas some students in affluent neighborhoods attend poorer schools and spend time with delinquent friends (Cook et al., 2002). In some cities, the busing of students from one area of a city to attend school in another is still common. Additionally, in some cities and regions, such as New York City, high school students are not limited to their local public high schools but rather can apply to any high school in any of the five boroughs of the city. When children choose to attend, as in the case of private schools, or are bused to schools outside their home neighborhood, there is the potential that characteristics of their school neighborhood will be quite different from those of their home neighborhood (Laub & Lauritsen, 1998). Identifying the distinct and combined effects of home neighborhoods and school neighborhoods on youth is an important topic for future research, and one that we are addressing in our own current research (Gershoff & Aber, 2003).

A final implication of the fact that some children attend schools in neighborhoods different from those in which they live is that their network of friends from school is not available to them in their home neighborhoods. How children growing up in disadvantaged neighborhoods without readily available peer support adapt to the multiple neighborhood risks is not fully understood and deserves further study.

The Role of Families in Enhancing or Tempering Neighborhood and School Impacts

Just as interactions between parents and children are bi-directional (Bell & Chapman, 1986; Collins, Maccoby, Steinberg, Hetherington, & Bornstein, 2000), the interactions among families and their neighborhoods and schools are expected to be bidirectional as well (Leventhal & Brooks-Gunn, 2000). Children, and adolescents in particular, can choose their peers, the neighborhoods in which they hang out, and, in cities and locales such as New York, have a role in choosing (or qualifying for) their high schools. More importantly, the decisions to live in certain neighborhoods and to attend certain schools depend on parents' background characteristics and current circumstances. For ex-ample, among a sample of incarcerated adolescents, those who reported high levels of family conflict and family socio-economic risks (e.g., family criminality, parent unemployment) were more likely to report perpetration of, witnessing of, and victimization by violence (Halliday-Boykins & Graham, 2001), likely because families with socio-economic disadvantage and forced to live in disadvantaged and dangerous neighborhoods.

These important individual- and family-level determinants of how families come to live in or remain in certain neighborhoods and of which schools children attend result in a logical and statistical problem of endogeneity (Duncan & Raudenbush, 2001), such that the process of identifying neighborhood or school impacts on individuals is clouded by the fact that individuals can choose their neighborhoods and schools. The best non-experimental solution to this problem of endogeneity is to "measure the unmeasured" (Duncan & Raudenbush, 2001) parent characteristics to reduce the endogenous membership bias. Typical family-level controls are income, education, race/ethnicity, maternal age at birth, family structure, and family size (Leventhal & Brooks-Gunn, 2000).

Beyond family socio-demographic factors that may determine the neighborhoods in which children live and the schools they attend, parents play an active role in helping children negotiate certain neighborhood challenges. Following from McLoyd's (1990) assertions that parents in dangerous neighborhoods will rely on harsh punishment of their adolescents' misbehaviors because the consequences of misbehavior are potentially grave, studies linking neighborhood characteristics to parent behavior and parenting practices abound. Parents who live in disadvantaged neighborhoods tend to show less warmth and to be more controlling of their children (Earls, McGuire, & Shay, 1994; Furstenberg, 1993; Furstenberg, Cook, Eccles, Elder, & Sameroff, 1999; Klebanov, Brooks-Gunn, & Duncan 1994; Pinderhughes, Nix, Foster, Jones, the Conduct Problems Prevention Research Group., 2001). Other neighborhood characteristics, such as dissatisfaction with public services and perceived danger, have also been linked with more harsh, inappropriate, and inconsistent discipline (Hill & Herman-Stahl, 2002; Pinderhughes et al., 2001). Neighborhood influences have been associated with parenting practices over and above family income and education (Klebanov et al., 1994).

Families formulate different strategies for raising children in high risk neighborhoods (Furstenberg, 1993; Jones, 2001) and these strategies, in turn, can either buffer or exacerbate the effects of disadvantaged neighborhoods on adolescents. For example, the success of different parent strategies in promoting adolescent autonomy has been found to depend on the level of environmental risk (Boykin McElhaney & Allen, 2001). As evidence of buffering, parents' reliance on practices high in control has been found to be beneficial for adolescents living in high-risk neighborhoods whereas low control is beneficial for adolescents in low-risk neighborhoods (Eamon, 2001; Gershoff et al., 2004; Gonzales et al., 1996; Lamborn, Dornbusch, & Steinberg, 1996). Similarly, high parental monitoring of children's activities is associated with decreased externalizing behavior problems among families who reside in neighborhoods characterized by high residential instability (Beyers, et al., 2003) or low collective efficacy (Rankin & Quane, 2002). High support from parents has been found to moderate the negative impact of disadvantaged and high risk neighborhoods on children's mental health, social competence, and intrusive thinking (Kliewer et al., 1998; Krenichyn, Saegert, & Evans, 2001; Stiffman, Hadley-Ives, Elze, Johnson, & Doré 1999). Children who reside in disadvantaged neighborhoods but whose parents are nurturant and involved are less likely to associate with deviant peers (Brody et al., 2001). In general, neighborhood social capital has been found to increase positive parenting and in turn decrease children's adjustment (Dorsey & Forehand, 2003). Consistent with Bronfenbrenner and Ceci's (1994) hypothesis that the ability of parent behavior to buffer children against negative outcomes will be greater in impoverished and unstable environments, there is indeed some evidence that parenting may play a more important role than temperament in determining children's behavior in disadvantaged neighborhoods. Specifically, violent behaviors among adolescents in advantaged neighborhoods appear to be determined more from temperament-based factors, such as hyperactivity and aggression, whereas violence among adolescents in disadvantaged neighborhoods is influenced more by quality of communication with parents (Beyers, Loeber, Wilkström, & Stouthamer-Loeber, 2001).

The extent to which parents are aware of the risks their children are exposed to can impact the quality of the parent-child relationship as well as children's mental health. When parents are more aware of and thus in agreement with children's reports of children's exposure to violence, children experience fewer PTSD symptoms (Ceballo et al., 2001). When faced with daily dangers, children who are able to discuss them with their parents, and perhaps collaboratively devise strategies for avoiding them, are likely better able to cope with such dangers as exposure to violence.

Transmission of negative neighborhood influences is also possible through increased parent stress and harsh behavior. Mothers' ratings of neighborhood danger are associated with increased maternal depression (Hill & Herman-Stahl, 2002), and levels of parents' stress have been found to mediate the effects of family socio-economic characteristics and community violence on children's behavior problems (Linares et al., 2001). Positive links between social support and parenting behavior are attenuated when parents live in primarily low-income and high-crime neighborhoods (Ceballo & McLoyd, 2002). The negative effects of community disadvantage on adolescent boys' mental health have been found to be mediated through parent behaviors such as monitoring, discipline, and communication (Simons et al., 1996).

Parents also can play a role in moderating the effects schools have on their children. Family-level resources can compensate for poor resources at school (Parcel & Dufur, 2001). For example, family social capital is more strongly associated with children's internalizing and externalizing problems than school social capital: parental monitoring, parent knowledge of child's friends, and family attendance at church have dampening effects on behavior problems, whereas teacher-student ratios, school social problems, and perceptions of teachers as caring are not significantly associated with behavior problems (Parcel & Dufur, 2001).

However, the extent to which parents, whose domain is clearly the home and neighborhood, can influence the behaviors of their children in a separate domain, that of school, is not fully understood. There is some evidence that parents' reach does not extend to the school context: Parent involvement in adolescents' school-related activities was not associated with students' levels of misbehavior at school (Otto & Atkinson, 1997). Parents' influence on their children's mental health and behavior in the context of school requires further study.

FUTURE DIRECTIONS IN THE STUDY OF NEIGHBORHOOD AND SCHOOL IMPACTS

Without appropriate datasets that include appropriate sampling strategies as well as valid and reliable measures of conceptually key constructs at both individual and context levels, it was impossible until recently to follow Bronfenbrenner's (1977, 1986) exhortation to examine development ecologically. With increasingly sophisticated analytic techniques, academic and social-emotional success have been simultaneously linked with the quality of family, peer, school, and neighborhood contexts (Cook et al., 2002). In order to model context effects, it is necessary to have data sets that sample and assess children over time and nested in complex environments. Yet such data pose challenges both in precisely conceptualizing the constructs of interest and in statistically decomposing the impacts of contextual variables on individual level outcomes. Other recent reviews have detailed the theoretical, methodological, and analytic shortcomings in the literatures on neighborhood and school impacts on child development (Duncan, & Raudenbush, 1999; Sampson, Morenoff, & Gannon-Rowley, 2002). We wish in this section to highlight two of the most important of these issues.

Operationalization of Neighborhoods

Deciding and defining what constitutes a neighborhood (or neighborhoods) of interest are key initial steps in the study of neighborhood impacts. We discuss several issues related to operationalizing neighborhoods here.

Objective Neighborhood Characteristics

Many studies of neighborhood effects rely exclusively on census-based, tract-level demographic characteristics of neighborhoods (e.g., poverty level, racial heterogeneity, residential instability) and use such characteristics as proxies for neighborhood disorganization and danger (Aber, 1994). Although the census data are important because they are comprehensive, publicly available, and include important demographic characteristics at the tract level, these characteristics are largely used by researchers as proxies for particular social characteristics of interest, including level of violence and neighborhood cohesion (Aber, 1994). Census definitions of neighborhoods as "tracts" have been criticized as not representing the ways in which the people who live in these neighborhoods define them, thus implying that meaningful measures of neighborhood boundaries must be gleaned from the perceptions of those individuals who live there (Small & Supple, 1999).

Studies using census-based sources of neighborhood characteristics typically have two main problems (Duncan & Raudenbush, 1999, 2001): (1) they use only one neighborhood characteristic (e.g., tract poverty rate) as an index of neighborhood influence, without taking into account other neighborhood dimensions that might be correlated with that one characteristic (such as crime, drug activity, collective efficacy, and school quality); and (2) they propose to test process models that are not readily testable by Census-based data. These drawbacks can be addressed in analytic steps recommended by Duncan and Aber (1997). First, descriptive associations between neighborhood characteristics and developmental outcomes should be presented. Second, these associations should be adjusted for effects of correlated family-level influences. Third, the potential for family processes to mediate neighborhood effects should be examined. Finally, developmental models should be examined within both resource-rich and resource-poor neighborhoods.

We wish to illustrate from our own work an alternative approach to using individual Census-based indicators. We have taken a multi-stage approach to characterizing the neighborhoods of the New York City youth in our study (Gershoff, Pedersen, Ware, & Aber, 2004). The 893 youth for whom we had neighborhood data resided in 369 census tracts across the city; with an average of only 2.4 participants per tract, we were more interested in the type of neighborhoods in which youth lived, rather than their physical address. Based on recommendations that factors and/or clusters of neighborhood quality will be more reliable than individual indicators (Duncan & Aber, 1997) and on previously successful efforts at using cluster analysis to characterize types of neighborhoods (Anehensel & Sucoff, 2001; Sampson et al., 1997), we thus decided to create clusters of neighborhood types within which youth would be nested. This approach entailed coding youths' home addresses into census tracts, linking tracts to socio-economic, demographic, public health and public safety data, factor analyzing the neighborhood variables, and finally clustering the factors to obtain neighborhood types.

We used socio-economic and demographic variables from the 2000 Decennial U.S. Census Neighborhood Change Database (NCDB) developed by the Urban Institute for Geolytics, Inc., and public health, public services, and public safety variables from data maintained by Community Studies of New York, Inc. (http://www.infoshare.org) and by the New York City government (http://www.nyc.gov). We submitted 17 variables to a factor analysis and obtained four factors: (1) socio-economic status, race-ethnicity, and family structure; (2) housing; (3) recreation and public safety services; and (4) danger (see Table 25.1 for specific items). We first conducted a hierarchical clustering procedure with these four factors and obtained a six cluster solution. We then conducted an iterative clustering procedure in which cases were reassigned to clusters if such reassignment would increase within-cluster homogeneity along the four factors. Through this iterative procedure we obtained a final six cluster solution (see Figure 25.3).

The six clusters that emerged from this analysis varied in size from 29 tracts to 104 tracts. Three of the clusters were comprised of low SES neighborhoods. Neighborhoods in the first cluster (Low SES/High Danger: $n = 29$) had, on average, low SES and very high danger. Neighborhoods in the second cluster (Low SES/High Danger/High Services: $n = 38$) also had, on average, low SES residents and dangerous neighborhoods but also had very high access to services. The third cluster (Low SES/Low Services: $n = 89$) also contained neighborhoods of low SES but had marginally low access to services and average levels of danger and housing density/stability. The largest cluster (Low Risk/High Density: $n = 104$) contained neighborhoods that averaged close to mean levels across most dimensions except for high housing stability/ density. Two middle income SES clusters also emerged. The first middle income SES cluster (Low Risk/High Services: $n = 43$) was comprised of neighborhoods that exhibited very high access to services and low levels of danger. Neighborhoods in the second middle income SES cluster (Low Risk/Low Services: $n = 67$) had, on average, low housing stability/density, low danger, and marginally low access to services. We thus obtained six distinct types of neighborhoods that include tracts from across the city. The next stages of our research will involve (1) replicating the factor and

TABLE 25.1
Factors and Individual Indicators of Neighborhood Quality

Factor 1: Socio-Economic Status, Race-Ethnicity, and Family Structure
- Median family income (reversed)
- Percent of adults unemployed
- Percent of people in poverty
- Percent of households receiving public assistance
- Percent of adults over 25 without high school diploma or GED
- Percent non-White
- Percent Hispanic
- Percent children under 18 years of age
- Percent female-headed households or subfamilies

Factor 2: Housing
- Residential instability
- Density (number of people per housing unit)

Factor 3: Recreation and Public Safety Services
- Recreational facilities (parks, playgrounds, libraries)
- Protective services (police station, firehouse, hospital)

Factor 4: Danger
- Rate of substantiated child maltreatment cases per number of children
- Rate of violent crime per number of residents
- Arrest rate of youth less than 20 years old
- Death rate of youth less than 20 years old

Source: Gershoff et al., 2004.

cluster analyses with all of the Census tracts in New York City so that we might place our sample of tracts within the population of tracts (Gershoff, Pedersen, & Aber, 2005); and (2) nesting youth and their families within the neighborhood clusters to see if the effects of violence exposure and received parenting on youth vary by neighborhood type.

The approach we have described here is innovative in three main ways. First, it incorporates data from multiple sources, supplementing commonly used census demographic and socio-economic

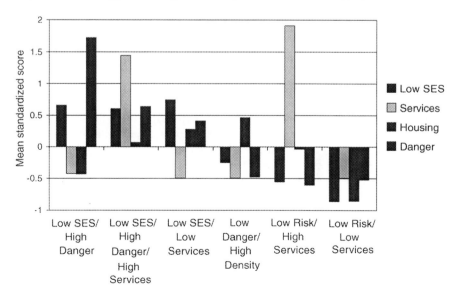

Figure 25.3   Clusters of select New York City Neighborhoods (2002–2003). From Gershoff, Pedersen, Ware, and Aber (2004).

indicators with key aspects of neighborhood service availability and danger. We were fortunate that New York City makes a supreme effort to both collect and disseminate up-to-date neighborhood quality statistics at the tract level. By including data on service availability and danger, we were able to make valuable distinctions between neighborhoods with similar income profiles but differing on factors which may prove important to youth development. Second, by combining data reduction through factor analysis with exploratory cluster analyses, we had the analytic power to include a greater number of neighborhood-level indicators than is typically included in studies that use such indicators as separate independent variables. Third, our approach compensates for not sampling at the neighborhood level by clustering participants' home tracts into neighborhood types. This method is a promising way to conduct neighborhood impact analyses that both maximize the ability of researchers to characterize neighborhoods accurately (without sampling at the neighborhood level) and to retain the ability to conduct multilevel analyses of participants nested within types of neighborhoods.

Perceived Neighborhood Characteristics

With increased interest in neighborhood constructs such as collective efficacy, researchers are interested in individuals' perceptions of their neighborhoods, rather than, or in addition to, objective characterizations of neighborhoods such as those from census data. Although neighborhood perception measures can be crucial indices of how individuals experience their neighborhoods, neighborhood data directly from adolescents or their parents is problematic because of shared error variance across reports of parenting and adolescent outcomes (Duncan & Raudenbush, 2001). This problem can be reduced if outside data sources of youth outcomes are used (e.g., test scores, attendance, arrest records). Other solutions can be achieved with the neighborhood-level data itself. One would be to get independent ratings of neighborhoods and pool them to create context-level measures (Duncan & Raudenbush, 2001); Sampson et al. (1997) did so successfully with 15–30 informants per context. A second would be to have multiple informants of perceived neighborhood characteristics, such as collective efficacy or violence. Colder et al. (2000) successfully used multiple raters of perceived neighborhood danger (child, parent) and child aggression (child, teacher, parent) in a structural equation model in order to minimize shared error variance. Unfortunately, parents tend to underreport the extent to which their children are exposed to violence (Ceballo et al., 2001; Kuo et al., 2000), which leads to an attenuation of associations between exposure and child outcomes when parent-reports or averaged parent and child reports are used (Kuo et al., 2000). Kuo et al. (2000) suggest using multiple raters in a multilevel analytic context to preserve the unique contributions of each rater.

Multiple "Neighborhoods"

Although ethnographic studies of youth have revealed that they spend their time in multiple neighborhoods and that studying just their residential neighborhood will not give a complete picture of the contexts in which they live (Burton, 2001), the empirical literature has neglected to consider neighborhood contexts other than that of the youths' home neighborhoods. In our current research, we are examining the impacts of both home and school neighborhoods on youth outcomes through cross-classified multi-level analyses (Gershoff & Aber, 2003). The vast majority of studies of which we are aware use "neighborhood" to mean the neighborhood in which youth reside; thus, we will be among the first to examine the neighborhoods surrounding youths' schools for their effects on youth development. For many children who attend neighborhood public schools, their home and school neighborhoods are the same. Yet in our New York City youth sample, the overlap of home and school neighborhoods is quite small, as high school placement in New York depends not on residence but rather on a combination of test score requirements, choice, and lottery. As a result, we will be able to identify whether the negative impacts of living in a disadvantaged neighborhood are offset by the benefits of attending school in a more advantaged neighborhood.

Impact of Neighborhood Change

With improved economies and dramatically decreased crime rates, the quality of many urban neighborhoods throughout the country is quite different now than it was 10 or 20 years ago. For example, New York City has experienced a steady decrease in crime, including a 69% drop in murder and a 66% drop in overall crime since 1993 (NYPD CompStat Unit, 2004). Very little work has been done on how the changing demographics and social characteristics of a neighborhood impact its residents. In a rigorous examination of census data over three decades, Morenoff and Sampson (1997) found that rates of homicide in a community predict rates of population loss over time, with neighborhoods characterized by violence and disadvantage tending to lose population of all race-ethnicity groups. However, how neighborhood change impacts individual child or family outcomes is a topic ripe for future research.

The Necessity of Multilevel Analyses

Research questions regarding context effects are by their nature multilevel and thus require multilevel analyses (Lee, 2000). Yet even with the advent of multilevel analyses, many key studies of neighborhood impacts (e.g., Bowen & Bowen, 1999; Colder et al., 2000; Simons et al., 1996) or school impacts (e.g., Felson et al., 1994; Mayer & Leone, 1999) on children and youth ignore the nested nature of the data. Neighborhoods and schools are well suited to multilevel modeling because they clearly exemplify Bronfenbrenner's ecological theory (1977; 1986), because they are presumed to affect youth directly and indirectly (Elliott et al., 1996), and because neighborhood and school effects are analogous to shared-family influences on siblings in that characteristics of shared-neighborhoods can influence unrelated neighborhood children (Bryk & Raudenbush, 1988; Duncan & Raudenbush, 2001).

Recent developments in multilevel modeling (Hox, 2002; Reise & Duan, 2003) and the availability of software suited to handling multilevel data (HLM: Raudenbush, Bryk, Cheong, & Congdon, 2001; Mplus: Muthén & Muthén, 2004; MLwiN: Rashbash et al., 2002) have made it possible for the structure of analyses to accurately reflect the nested nature of children in neighborhoods and children in schools (if, of course, the sampling design permits). For example, Cook et al. (2002) demonstrated through a two-level hierarchical linear model that family, peer, neighborhood, and school contexts had distinct and significant associations with an index of early adolescent academic success, mental health, and social behavior. However, they did not account for the fact that children are nested simultaneously in neighborhoods and schools. Using a three-level model of time nested in children nested in neighborhoods, Beyers et al. (2003) determined that although neighborhood socio-economic characteristics did not independently predict change in children's externalizing behaviors, they did interact with parental monitoring in predicting change in child behavior, such that parental monitoring predicted greater decreases in externalizing behavior problems when families lived in neighborhoods characterized by high residential instability. Duncan, Duncan, and Strycker (2002) tested an innovative multilevel model in a multi-group structural equation framework, finding significant between-neighborhood differences in perceptions of social cohesion and problems with youth drug use. Each of these methods is a promising example of how multi-level approaches will advance our understanding of the multiple layers of context effects.

Although for some children home and school neighborhoods are the same, as noted above, many of these neighborhoods are distinct. As Hox (2002) has observed, the case of schools and neighborhoods is a prime example of the cross-classification problem because not all students attend the school in the neighborhood in which they live, and thus pure nesting of students within schools within neighborhoods is not possible. Both the statistical understanding of cross-classification (Goldstein, 1995; Hox, 2002) and the software able to handle cross-classification (MLwiN: Rasbash et al., 2002) have become available only recently. The basic procedure for handling cross-classified data in a multilevel context is to create a dummy level for the classification with fewer categories and then to introduce dummy indicators at the first level for each of the categories of this classification (Goldstein, 1995; Hox, 2002). A rare example of school and neighborhood cross-classification is a study by Teitler and Weiss (2000) who considered students cross-classified in neighborhoods and in schools themselves (although not school neighborhoods) in multilevel prediction of onset of sexual activity. As more and more studies examine neighborhoods and schools in a multi-level fashion and tease apart the effects attributable to cross-classified contexts, our understanding of how these contexts separately and together impact children can grow exponentially.

CONCLUSION

It is clear from the literature summarized here that characteristics of the neighborhoods in which children live and the schools they attend can impact children's mental health and their likelihood of engaging in risk behaviors. Disadvantaged neighborhoods and schools leave children without adequate opportunities for positive engagement with adults and thus disposed to disruptive behavior and susceptible to negative peer influence. Violence in neighborhoods and schools can exact clear tolls on children's mental health and creates an environment in which children's own aggressive behavior is adaptive. In contrast to these negative impacts, a sense of community and cohesion in neighborhoods and schools can foster feelings of belonging and security that promote adaptive social-emotional behavior.

Aside from these conclusions, the literature summarized in this chapter suffers from two major flaws. First, the emphasis in the neighborhood literature has primarily been on negative impacts of neighborhoods on students. More research is needed that considers the positive ways in which neighborhoods can affect children and youth. Second, the school impact literature has almost exclusively been restricted to academic achievement outcomes, or at most to behavioral school-related outcomes such as drop-out. This lack of research is surprising, given growing emphases on both character development (Office of Safe and Drug-Free Schools, 2004) and violence prevention in schools (Thornton, Craft, Dahlberg, Lynch, & Baer, 2002). Additional research into how school contexts impact child mental health and risk behavior is needed in order to inform the design of learning environments and of broader school reforms whose targets are typically academic outcomes (Roeser et al., 1998).

The sheer amount of time children spend in neighborhoods and in schools establishes them as clear places of opportunity in which to promote positive mental health and to decrease the incidence of risk behaviors. We have provided examples of a very few of such interventions here, most of which are small-scale, targeted interventions. Improving neighborhoods and schools on a large scale will require significant commitments from local and national policymakers and funders. Although such interventions would be costly, their potential to enhance so many aspects of children's lives would undoubtedly make them cost-effective in the long-term.

ACKNOWLEDGMENT

Writing of this chapter was funded through grants from the Centers for Disease Control and Prevention (CCR218598), the National Institute of Mental Health (5R01MH063685), and the National Institute of Child Health and Human Development (5R01HD042144) to the authors.

REFERENCES

Aber, J. L. (1994). Poverty, violence, and child development: Untangling effects of family and community. In C. Nelson (Ed.), *Threats to optimal development: Integrating biological, psychological, and social risk factors. The Minnesota Symposium on Child Psychology* (Vol. 27, pp. 229–272). Mahwah, NJ: Erlbaum.

Aber, J. L., Brown, J. L., & Jones, S. M. (2003). Developmental trajectories toward violence in middle childhood: Course, demographic differences, and response to school-based intervention. *Developmental Psychology, 39,* 324–348.

Aber, J. L., Gephart, M. A., Brooks-Gunn, J., & Connell, J. P. (1997). Development in context: Implications for studying neighborhood effects. In J. Brooks-Gunn, G. J. Duncan, & J. L. Aber (Eds.), *Neighborhood poverty: Context and consequences for children,* (Vol. 1, pp. 44–78). New York: Russell Sage.

Aber, J. L., Gershoff, E. T., Ware, A., & Kotler, J. A. (2004). Estimating the effects of September 11th and other forms of violence on the mental health and social development of New York City's youth: A matter of context. *Applied Developmental Science, 8*(3), 111–129.

Addington, L. A., Ruddy, S. A., Miller, A. K., & DeVoe, J. F. (2002). *Are America's schools safe? Students speak out: 1999 school crime supplement* (NCES 2002-331). Washington, DC: National Center for Education Statistics, U.S. Department of Education. Retrieved January 7, 2004, from http://nces.ed.gov/pubs2002/2002331_1.pdf

Adelman, H. S., & Taylor, L. (1998) Reframing mental health

in schools and expanding school reform. *Educational Psychologist, 33*, 135–152.

Allen, L., Jones, S. M., Seidman, E., & Aber, J. L. (1998). The organization of exposure to violence among urban adolescents: Clinical, prevention, and research implications. In Flannery, D. J. & Huff, C. R. (Eds.), *Youth violence: Prevention, intervention, and social policy* (pp. 119–141). Washington, DC: American Psychiatric Press.

Allison, K. W., Burton, L., Marshall, S., Perez-Febles, A., Yarrington, J., Kirsh, L. B., & Merriwether-DeVries, C. (1999). Life experiences among urban adolescents: Examining the role of context. *Child Development, 70*, 1017–1029.

Allison, K. W., Crawford, I., Leone, P. E., Trickett, E., Perez-Febles, A., Burton, L. M., & Le Blanc, R. (1999). Adolescent substance use: Preliminary examinations of school and neighborhood context. *American Journal of Community Psychology, 27*, 111–141.

American School Health Association. (1989). *The national adolescent student health survey: A report on the health of America's youth*. Oakland, CA: Society for Public Health Education.

Aneshensel, C. S., & Sucoff, C. A. (1996). The neighborhood context of adolescent mental health. *Journal of Health and Social Behavior, 37*, 293–310.

Arnette, J. L., & Walsleben, M. C. (1998). *Combating fear and restoring safety in schools*. Washington, DC: U. S. Department of Justice, Office of Justice Programs, Office of Juvenile Justice and Delinquency Prevention. Retrieved January 16, 2004, from http://www.ncjrs.org/pdffiles/167888.pdf.

Astor, R. A. (1998). Moral reasoning about school violence. *Educational Psychologist, 33*, 207–221.

Astor, R. A., & Meyer, H. A. (2001). The conceptualization of violence-prone school subcontexts: Is the sum of the parts greater than the whole? *Urban Education, 36*, 374–399.

Atkins, R., & Hart, D. (2003). Neighborhoods, adults, and the development of civic identity in urban youth. *Applied Developmental Science, 7*, 156–164.

Attar, B. K., Guerra, N. G., Tolan, P. H. (1994). Neighborhood disadvantage, stressful life events, and adjustment in urban elementary-school children. *Journal of Clinical Child Psychology, 23*, 391–400.

Barton, P. E., Coley, R. J., & Wenglisky, H. (1998). *Order in the classroom: Violence, discipline, and student achievement*. Princeton, NJ: Policy Information Center, Educational Testing Service.

Bastian, L., & Taylor, B. (1991). *School crime: A national crime victimization survey report* (NCJ-131645) Washington, DC: U.S. Department of Justice, Bureau of Justice Statistics.

Battistich, V., Watson, M., Solomon, D., Lewis, C., & Schaps, E. (1999). Beyond the three R's: A broader agenda for school reform. *The Elementary School Journal, 99*, 415–432.

Baumeister, R. F., & Leary, M. R. (1995). The need to belong: Desire for interpersonal attachments as a fundamental human motivation. *Psychological Bulletin, 117*, 497–529.

Bell, R. Q., & Chapman, M. (1986). Child effects in studies using experimental or brief longitudinal approaches to socialization. *Developmental Psychology, 22*, 595–603.

Berman, S. L., Kurtines, W. M., Silverman, W. K., & Serafini, L. T. (1996). The impact of exposure to violence on urban youth. *American Journal of Orthopsychiatry, 66*, 329–336.

Berton, M. W., & Stabb, S. D. (1996). Exposure to violence and post-traumatic stress disorder in urban adolescents. *Adolescence, 31*, 489–498.

Beyers, J. M., Bates, J. E., Pettit, G. S., & Dodge, K. A. (2003). Neighborhood structure, parenting processes, and the development of youths' externalizing behaviors: A multilevel analysis. *American Journal of Community Psychology, 31*, 35–53.

Beyers, J. M., Loeber, R., Wilkström, P. H., & Stouthamer-Loeber, M. (2001). What predicts adolescent violence in better-off neighborhoods? *Journal of Abnormal Child Psychology, 29*, 369–381.

Bickel, R., Howley, C., Williams, T., & Glascock, C. (2001). High school size, achievement equity, and cost: Robust interaction effects and tentative results. *Education Policy Analysis Archives, 9*(40). Retrieved January 6, 2004, from http://epaa.asu.edu/epaa/v9n40.html.

Blechman, E. A., Dumas, J. E., & Prinz, R. J. (1994). Prosocial coping by youth exposed to violence. *Journal of Child and Adolescent Group Therapy, 4*, 205–227.

Boney-McCoy, S., & Finkelhor, D. (1995). Psychosocial sequelae of violent victimization in a national youth sample. *Journal of Consulting and Clinical Psychology, 63*, 726–736.

Bowen, N. K., & Bowen, G. L. (1999). Effects of crime and violence in neighborhoods and schools on the school behavior and performance of adolescents. *Journal of Adolescent Research, 14*, 319–342.

Bowen, G. L., Richman, J. M., Brewster, A., & Bowen, N. (1998). Sense of school coherence, perceptions of danger at school, and teacher support among youth at risk of school failure. *Child and Adolescent Social Work Journal, 15*, 273–286.

Boykin McElhaney, K., & Allen, J. P. (2001). Autonomy and adolescent social functioning: The moderating effect of risk. *Child Development, 72*, 220–235.

Brody, G. H., Ge, X., Conger, R., Gibbons, F. X., Murry, V. M., Gerrard, M., & Simons, R. L. (2001). The influence of neighborhood disadvantage, collective socialization, and parenting on African American children's affiliation with deviant peers. *Child Development, 72*, 1231–1246.

Bronfenbrenner, U., & Ceci, S. J. (1994). Nature-nurture reconceptualized in developmental perspective: A biological model. *Psychological Review, 101*, 568–586.

Brooks-Gunn, J., Duncan, G. J., & Aber, J. L. (Eds.) (1997a). *Neighborhood poverty: Context and consequences for children, Volume 1*. New York: Russell Sage.

Brooks-Gunn, J., Duncan, G. J., & Aber, J. L. (Eds.) (1997b). *Neighborhood poverty: Context and consequences for children, Volume 2*. New York: Russell Sage.

Brooks-Gunn, J., Duncan, G. J., Klebanov, P. K., & Sealand, N. (1993). Do neighborhoods influence child and adolescent development? *American Journal of Sociology, 99*, 353–395.

Bronfenbrenner, U. (1977). Toward an experimental ecology of human development. *American Psychologist, 32*, 513–531.

Bronfenbrenner, U. (1986). Ecology of the family as a context for human development: Research perspectives. *Developmental Psychology, 22*, 723–742.

Bryk, A. S., & Raudenbush, S. W. (1988). Toward a more appropriate conceptualization of research on school effects: A three-level hierarchical linear model. *American Journal of Education, 97*, 65–108.

Bryk, A. S., & Thum, Y. M. (1989). The effects of high school organization on dropping out: An exploratory investigation. *American Educational Research Journal, 26*, 353–383.

Burns, B. J., Costello, E. J., Angold, A., Tweed, D., Stangl, D., Farmer, E., & Erkanli, A. (1995). Children's mental health service use across service sectors. *Health Affairs, 14*, 147–159.

Burton, L. (2001). One step forward and two steps back: Neighborhoods, adolescent development, and unmeasured variables In A. Booth & A. C. Crouter (Eds.), *Does it take a village? Community effects on children, adolescents, and families* (pp. 149–159). Mahwah, NJ: Erlbaum.

Carlson, C., Paavola, J. & Talley, R. (1995). Historical, current, and future models of schools as health care delivery settings. *School Psychology Quarterly, 10*, 184–202.

Caspi, A., Taylor, A., Moffitt, T. E., & Plomin, R. (2000). Neighborhood deprivation affects children's mental health: Environmental risks identified in a genetic design. *Psychological Science, 11*, 338–342.

Ceballo, R., Dahl, T. A., Aretakis, M. T., & Ramirez, C. (2001). Inner-city children's exposure to community violence: How much do parents know? *Journal of Marriage and the Family, 63*, 927–940.

Ceballo, R., & McLoyd, V. C. (2002). Social support and parenting in poor, dangerous neighborhoods. *Child Development, 73*, 1310–1321.

Centers for Disease Control and Prevention. (2002a). Youth risk behavior surveillance—United States, 2001. *Morbidity and Mortality Weekly Report, 51* (SS-04), 1–64. Retrieved January 2, 2003, from http://www.cdc.gov/mmwr/preview/mmwrhtml/ss5104a1.htm

Centers for Disease Control and Prevention. (2002b). *YRBSS: 2001 Information and Results. Youth 2001 Online*. Atlanta, GA: Author. Retrieved Jamuary 2, 2003, from http://www.cdc.gov/nccdphp/dash/yrbs/2001/youth01online.htm.

Cleveland, H. H. (2003). Disadvantaged neighborhoods and adolescent aggression: Behavioral genetic evidence of contextual effects. *Journal of Research on Adolescence, 13*, 211–238.

Coie, J. D., & Dodge, K. A. (1998). Aggression and antisocial behavior. In N. Eisenberg (Ed.), W. Damon (Series Ed.), *Handbook of child psychology (5th ed.), Vol. 3: Social, emotional, and personality development* (pp. 779–862). New York: Wiley.

Colder, C. R., Mott, J., Levy, S., & Flay, B. (2000). The relation of perceived neighborhood danger to childhood aggression: A test of mediating mechanisms. *American Journal of Community Psychology, 28*, 83–103.

Coleman, J. S. (1988). Social capital in the creation of human capital. *American Journal of Sociology, 94*, S95–S120.

Coleman, J. S., Campbell, E. Q., Hobson, C. J., McPartland, J., Mood, A. M., Weinfeld, F. D., & York, R. L. (1966). *Equality of educational opportunity*. Washington, DC: U. S. Government Printing Office.

Collins, W. A., Maccoby, E. E., Steinberg, L., Hetherington, E. M., & Bornstein, M. H. (2000). Contemporary research on parenting: the case for nature and nurture. *American Psychologist, 55*, 218–232.

Connell, J. P., Aber, J. L., & Walker, G. (1995). How do urban communities affect youth? Using social science research to inform the design and evaluation of comprehensive community initiatives. In J. P. Connell, A. Kubisch, L. Schorr, & C. Weiss (Eds.), *New approaches to evaluating comprehensive community initiatives: Concepts, methods and contexts* (pp. 93–125). Roundtable on Comprehensive Community Initiatives for Children and Families. Queenstown, MD: The Aspen Institute.

Connell, J. P., & Halpern-Felsher, B. (1997). How neighborhoods affect educational outcomes in middle childhood and adolescence: Conceptual issues and an empirical example. In G. Duncan, J. Brooks-Gunn & J. L. Aber (Eds.), *Neighborhood poverty: Context and consequences for children, Vol. 1* (pp. 174–199). New York: Russell Sage.

Cook, T. D., Herman, M. R., Phillips, M., & Settersten, Jr., R. A. (2002). Some ways in which neighborhoods, nuclear families, friendship groups, and schools jointly affect changes in early adolescent development. *Child Development, 73*, 1283–1309.

Cooley-Quille, M. R., Turner, S. M., & Biedel, D. C. (1995). Emotional impact of children's exposure to community violence: A preliminary study. *Journal of the American Academy of Child and Adolescent Psychiatry, 34*, 1362–1368.

DeVoe, J. F., Peter, K., Kaufman, P., Ruddy, S. A., Miller, A. K., Planty, M., Snyder, T. D., & Rand, M. R. (2003). *Indicators of school crime and safety: 2003*. (NCES 2004-004/NCJ 201257). Washington, DC: U. S. Departments of Education and Justice.

Dishion, T. J., Patterson, G. R., Stoolmiller, M., & Skinner, M. L. (1991). Family, school, and behavioral antecedents to early adolescent involvement with antisocial peers. *Developmental Psychology, 27*, 172–180.

Dorsey, S., & Forehand, R. (2003). The relation of social capital to child psychosocial adjustment difficulties: The role of positive parenting and neighborhood dangerousness. *Journal of Psychopathology and Behavioral Assessment, 25*, 11–23.

Dryfoos, J. G. (1990). *Adolescents at risk: Prevalence and prevention*. New York: Oxford University Press.

Dubow, E. F., Edwards, S., & Ippolito, M. F. (1997). Life stressors, neighborhood disadvantages, and resources: A focus on inner-city children's adjustment. *Journal of Clinical and Child Psychology, 26*, 130–144.

Duncan, G., & Aber, J. L. (1997). Neighborhood models and measures. In G. Duncan, J. Brooks-Gunn & J. L. Aber (Eds.), *Neighborhood poverty: Context and consequences for children, Vol. 1* (pp. 44–61). New York: Russell Sage.

Duncan, G. J., & Raudenbush, S. W. (1999). Assessing the effects of context in studies of child and youth development. *Educational Psychologist, 34*, 29–41.

Duncan, G. J., & Raudenbush, S. W. (2001). Neighborhoods and adolescent development: How can we determine the links? In A. Booth & A. C. Crouter (Eds.), *Does it take a village? Community effects on children, adolescents, and families* (pp. 105–136). Mahwah, NJ: Erlbaum.

Duncan, S. C., Duncan, T. E., & Strycker, L. A. (2002). A multilevel analysis of neighborhood context and youth alcohol and drug problems. *Prevention Science, 3*, 125–133.

DuRant, R. H., Cadenhead, C., Pendergrast, R. A., Slavens, G., & Linder, C. W. (1994). Factors associated with the use of violence among urban Black adolescents. *American Journal of Public Health, 84*, 612–617.

Dwyer, K. Osher, D., & Warger, C. (1998). *Early warning, timely response: A guide to safe schools*. Washington, DC: U. S. Department of Education. Retrieved January 13, 2004, from http://cecp.air.org/guide/guide.pdf

Eamon, M. K. (2001). Poverty, parenting, peer, and neighborhood influences on young adolescent antisocial behavior. *Journal of Social Service Research, 28*, 1–23.

Earls, F., McGuire, J., & Shay, S. (1994). Evaluating a community intervention to reduce the risk of child abuse: Methodological strategies in conducting neighborhood surveys. *Child Abuse and Neglect, 18*, 473–.

Eccles, J., & Gootman, J. A. (Eds.). (2002). *Community programs to promote youth development*. National Research Council and Institute of Medicine, Committee on Community-Level Programs for Youth, Board on Children, Youth, and Families, Division of Behavioral and Social Sciences and Education. Washington, DC: National Academy Press.

Eccles, J. S., Lord, S. E., Roeser, R. W., Barber, B. L., & Jo-szefowicz, D. M. H. (1997). The association of school transitions in early adolescence with developmental trajectories through high school. In J. Schulenberg, J. Maggs, & K. Hurrelmann (Eds.), *Health risks and developmental transitions during adolescence* (pp. 283–320). New York: Cambridge University Press.

Eitle, D., & Turner, R. J. (2002). Exposure to community violence and young adult crime: The effects of witnessing violence, traumatic victimization, and other stressful life events. *Journal of Research in Crime and Delinquency, 39*, 214–237.

Elliot, D. S., Wilson, W. J., Huizinga, D., Sampson, R. J., Elliott, A., & Rankin, B. (1996). The effects of neighborhood disadvantage on adolescent development. *Journal of Research in Crime and Delinquency, 33*, 389–426.

Elze, D. E., Stiffman, A. R., & Doré, P. (1999). The association between types of violence exposure and youths' metal health problems. *International Journal of Adolescent Medicine and Health, 11*, 221–255.

Ennett, S. T., Flewelling, R. L., Lindrooth, R. C., & Norton, E. C. (1997). School and neighborhood characteristics associated with school rates of alcohol, cigarette, and marijuana use. *Journal of Health and Social Behavior, 38*, 55–71.

Evans, G. W. (2004). The environment of childhood poverty. *American Psychologist, 59*, 77–92.

Evans, G. W., & English, K. (2002). The environment of poverty: Multiple stressor exposure, psychophysiological stress, and socioemotional adjustment. *Child Development, 73*, 1238–1248.

Evans, G. W., Lercher, P., Meis, M., Ising, H., & Kofler, W. W. (2000). Community noise exposure and stress in children. *Journal of the Acoustical Society of America, 109*, 1023–1027.

Fagan, J., & Wilkinson, D. (1998). Social contexts and functions of adolescent violence. In D. S. Elliott, B. A. Hamburg, & R. Williams (Eds.), *Violence in American schools: A new perspective* (pp. 55–93). New York: Cambridge University Press.

Farrell, A. D., & Bruce, S. E. (1997). Impact of exposure to community violence on violent behavior and emotional distress among urban adolescents. *Journal of Clinical Child Psychology, 26*, 2–14.

Farrington, D.P. (1993). Understanding and preventing bullying. *Crime and Justice, 17*, 381–458.

Felson, R. B., Lika, A. E., South, S. J., & McNulty, T. L. (1994). The subculture of violence and delinquency: Individual vs. school context effects. *Social Forces, 73*, 155–173.

Flaherty, L. T. (2001). School violence and the school environment. In M. Shafii and S. L. Shafii (Eds.), *School violence: Assessment, management, prevention* (pp. 25–51). Washington, DC: American Psychiatric Press.

Flannery, D. J. (1997). School violence: Risk, preventive intervention, and policy. *Urban Diversity Series No. 109.* New York: ERIC Clearinghouse on Urban Education.

Furstenberg, F. F. (1993). How families manage risk and opportunity in dangerous neighborhoods. In W. J. Wilson (Ed.), *Sociology and the public agenda* (pp. 231–238). Newbury Park, CA: Sage.

Furstenberg, F. F., Jr., Cook, T. D., Eccles, J., Elder, G. H., Jr., & Sameroff, A. (1999). *Managing to make it: Urban families and adolescent success.* Chicago: University of Chicago Press.

Garofalo, J., Siegel, L., & Laub, J. (1987). School-related victimizations among adolescents: An analysis of National Crime Survey (NCS) narratives. *Journal of Quantitative Criminology, 3*, 321–38.

Gerald, D. E., & Hussar, W. J. (2002). *Projections of education statistics to 2012* (NCES 2002-030). Washington, DC: National Center for Education Statistics, U.S. Department of Education.

Gershoff, E. T., & Aber, J. L. (2003). Youth violence in multilevel neighborhood context. Unpublished data, grant proposal funded by the Centers for Disease Control and Prevention.

Gershoff, E. T., Pedersen, S., Jones, & Aber, J. L. (2005). *Creating neighborhood types for hierarchical analyses through the use of factor and cluster analyses for reduction of GIS-based data.* Manuscript submitted for publication.

Gershoff, E. T., Pedersen, S., Ware, A., & Aber, J. L. (2004, March). Violence exposure and parenting impacts on behavior problems and risk behaviors in multilevel neighborhood context. In E. Gershoff (Chair), *Advances in Measurement, Trajectory, and Multilevel Analyses of Violence Exposure and Adolescent Problem Behaviors and Achievement.* Paper presented at the biennial meetings of the Society for Research in Adolescence, Baltimore, MD.

Goering, J. (2003). Comments on future research and housing policy. In J. Goering & J. D. Feins (Eds.), *Choosing a better life?: Evaluating the moving to opportunity social experiment* (pp. 383–407). Washington, DC: The Urban Institute.

Goldstein, H. (1995). *Multilevel statistical models* (2nd ed.). New York: Halstead.

Gonzales, N. A., Cauce, A., Friedman, R. J., & Mason, C. A. (1996). Family, peer, and neighborhood influence on academic achievement among African American adolescents: One-year prospective effects. *American Journal of Community Psychology, 24*, 365–387.

Gorman-Smith, D., & Tolan, P. (1998). The role of exposure to community violence and developmental problems among inner-city youth. *Development & Psychopathology, 10*, 101–116.

Gottfredson, G., & Gottfredson, D. (1985). *Victimization in schools.* New York: Plenum.

Greenberg, M. T., Lengua, L. J., Coie, J. D., & Pinderhughes, E. E. (1999). Predicting developmental outcomes at school entry using a multiple-risk model: Four American communities. *Developmental Psychology, 35*, 403–417.

Grogger, J. (1997). Local violence and educational attainment. *The Journal of Human Resources, 32*, 659–682.

Guerra, N. G., Huesmann, R., & Spindler, A. (2003). Community violence exposure, social cognition, and aggression among urban elementary school children. *Child Development, 74*, 1561–1576.

Halliday-Boykins, C. A., & Graham, S. (2001). At both ends of the gun: Testing the relationship between community violence exposure and youth violent behavior. *Journal of Abnormal Child Psychology, 29*, 383–402.

Hedges, L. V., Laine, R. D., & Greenwald, R. (1994). Does money matter? A meta-analysis of studies of the effects of differential school inputs on student outcomes. *Educational Researcher, 23*, 5–14.

Hellman, D., & Beaton, S. (1986). The pattern of violence in urban public schools: The influence of school and community. *Journal of Research in Crime and Delinquency, 23*, 102–127.

Henrich, C. C., Brown, J. L., & Aber, J. L. (1999). Evaluating the effectiveness of school-based violence prevention: Developmental approaches. *SRCD Social Policy Report, 13*, 1–17.

Hill, N. E., & Herman-Stahl, M. A. (2002). Neighborhood safety and social involvement: Associations with parenting behaviors and depressive symptoms among

African American and Euro-American mothers. *Journal of Family Psychology, 16,* 209–219.

Hinton-Nelson, M. D., Roberts, M. C., & Synder, C. R. (1996). Early adolescents exposed to violence: Hope and vulnerability to victimization. *American Journal of Orthopsychiatry, 66,* 346–353.

Horn, J. L., & Trickett, P. K. (1998). Community violence and child development: A review of research. In P. K. Trickett & C. J. Schellenbach (Eds.), *Violence against children in the family and community* (pp. 103–138). Washington, DC: American Psychological Association.

Hoven, C. W., Duarte, C. S., Lucas, C. p., Wu, P., Mandell, D. J., Goodwin, R. D., Cohen, M., Balaban, V., Woodruff, B. A., Bin, F., Mei, L., Cantor, P. A., Aber, J. L., Cohen, P., & Susser, E. (2004). The broad reach of September 11: Psychopathology among New York City public school children six months later. Unpublished manuscript, Columbia University.

Howard, K. A., Flora, J., & Griffin, M. (1999). Violence-prevention programs in schools: State of the science and implications for future research. *Applied and Preventive Psychology, 8,* 197–215.

Howell, J. C., & Lynch, J. P. (2000). *Youth gangs in schools.* Washington, DC: U.S. Department of Justice, Office of Justice Programs, Office of Juvenile Justice and Delinquency Prevention. Retrieved January 16, 2004, from http://www.ncjrs.org/pdffiles1/ojjdp/183015.pdf

Hox, J. J. (2002). *Multilevel analysis. Techniques and applications.* Mahwah, NJ: Erlbaum.

Hsieh, C., & Pugh, M. D. (1993). Poverty, income inequality, and violent crime: A meta-analysis of recent aggregate data studies. *Criminal Justice Review, 18,* 182–202.

Ingersoll, R. M. (1999). The problem of underqualified teachers in American secondary schools. *Educational Researcher, 28,* 26–37.

Jacobson, W. B. (2000). *Safe from the start: Taking action on children exposed to violence.* Washington, DC: Office of Juvenile Justice and Delinquency Prevention, U.S. Department of Justice.

Jencks, C., & Mayer, S. (1990). The social consequences of growing up in a poor neighborhood. In L. Lynn & Mc-Geary (Eds.), *Inner-city poverty in the United States* (pp. 111–186). Washington, DC: National Academy Press.

Jones, S. M. (2001). Youth exposure to community violence: Neighborhood and familial risk. Unpublished predissertation, Yale University.

Kalff, A. C., Kroes, M., Vles, J. S. H., Hendriksen, J. G. M., Feron, F. J. M., Steyaert, J., van Zeben, T. M. C. B., Jolles, J., & van Os, J. (2001). Neighbourhood level and individual level SES effects on child problem behaviour: A multilevel analysis. *Journal of Epidemiological Community Health, 55,* 246–250.

Kataoka, S. H., Zhang, L, & Wells, K. B. (2002). Unmet need for mental health care among U.S. children: Variation by ethnicity and insurance status. *American Journal of Psychiatry, 159,* 1548–1555.

Katz, L. F., Kling, J. R., & Liebman, J. B. (2003). Boston site findings: The early impacts of Moving to Opportunity. In J. Goering & J. D. Feins (Eds.), *Choosing a better life?: Evaluating the Moving to Opportunity social experiment* (pp. 177–211). Washington, DC: The Urban Institute.

Kessler, R. C., Foster, C. L., Saunders, W. B., & Stang, P. E. (1995). Social consequences of psychiatric disorders, I: Educational attainment. *American Journal of Psychiatry, 152,* 1026–1032.

Klebanov, P. K., Brooks-Gunn, J., & Duncan, G. J. (1994). Does neighborhood and family poverty affect mothers' parenting, mental health, and social support? *Journal of Marriage and the Family, 56,* 441–455.

Kliewer, W., Lepore, S. J., Oskin, D., & Johnson, P. D. (1998). The role of social and cognitive processes in children's adjustment to community violence. *Journal of Consulting and Clinical Psychology, 66,* 199–209.

Kneese, C., Fullwood, H., Schroth, G., & Pankake, A. (2003). Decreasing school violence: A research synthesis. In M. S. E. Fishbaugh, T. R. Berkeley, & G. Schroth (Eds.), *Ensuring safe school environments: Exploring issues—Seeking solutions* (pp. 39–57). Mahwah, NJ: Erlbaum.

Knitzer, J., Steinberg, Z., & Fleisch, B. (1991). Schools, children's mental health, and the advocacy challenge. *Journal of Clinical Child Psychology, 20,* 102–111.

Krenichyn, K., Saegert, S., & Evans, G. W. (2001). Parents as moderators of psychological and physiological correlates of inner-city children's exposure to violence. *Applied Developmental Psychology, 22,* 581–602.

Ku, L., Sonenstein, F. L., & Pleck, J. H. (1993). Neighborhood, family, and work: Influences on the premarital behaviors of adolescent males. *Social Forces, 72,* 479–503.

Kuo, M., Mohler, B., Raudenbush, S. L., & Earls, F. J. (2000). Assessing exposure to violence using multiple informants: Application of hierarchical linear model. *Journal of Child Psychology and Psychiatry, 41,* 1049–1056.

Kupersmidt, J. B., Griesler, P. C., DeRosier, M. E., Patterson, C. J., & Davis, P. W. (1995). Childhood aggression and peer relations in the context of family and neighborhood. *Child Development, 66,* 360–375.

Kupersmidt, J. B., Shahinfar, A., & Voegler-Lee, M. E. (2002). Children's exposure to community violence. In A. M. La Greca, W. K. Silverman, E. M. Vernberg, & M. C. Roberts (Eds.), *Helping children cope with disasters and terrorism* (pp. 381–401). Washington, DC: American Psychological Association.

Lamborn, S. D., Dornbusch, S. M., & Steinberg, L. (1996). Ethnicity and community context as moderators of the relations between family decision making and adolescent development. *Child Development, 67,* 283–301.

Laub, J. H., & Lauritsen, J. L. (1998). The interdependence of school violence with neighborhood and family conditions. In D. S. Elliott, B. A. Hamburg, & R. Williams (Eds.), *Violence in American schools: A new perspective* (pp. 127–155). New York: Cambridge University Press.

Lauritsen, J. L. (2003, November). How families and communities influence youth victimization. *Juvenile Justice Bulletin.* Washington, DC: Office of Juvenile Justice and Delinquency Prevention, Office of Justice Programs, U.S. Department of Justice.

Lee, V. E. (2000). Using hierarchical linear modeling to study social contexts: The case of school effects. *Educational Psychologist, 35,* 125–141.

Lee, V. E., Smerdon, B. A., Alfeld-Liro, C., & Brown, S. L. (2000). Inside large and small high schools: Curriculum and social relations. *Educational Evaluation and Policy Analysis, 22,* 147–171.

Lee & Smith (1997). High school size: Which works best and for whom? *Educational Evaluation and Policy Analysis, 19,* 205–227.

Leventhal, T., & Brooks-Gunn, J. (2000). The neighborhoods they live in: The effects of neighborhood residence on child and adolescent outcomes. *Psychological Bulletin, 126,* 309–337.

Leventhal, T., & Brooks-Gunn, J. (2003). Moving on up: Neighborhood effects on children and families. In M. H. Bornstein & R. H. Bradley (Eds.), *Socioeconomic status, parenting, and child development* (pp. 209–230). Mahwah, NJ: Erlbaum.

Linares, L. O., Heeren, T., Bronfman, E., Zuckerman, B., Augustyn, M., & Tronick, E., (2001). A mediational model for the impact of exposure to community violence on early child behavior problems. *Child Development, 72,* 639–652.

Loeber, R., & Witkstrom, P. H. (1993). Individual pathways to crime in different types of neighborhoods. In D. P. Farrington, R. J. Sampson, & P. O. H. Wikström (Eds.), *Integrating individual and ecological aspects of crime* (pp. 169–204). Stockholm: National Council for Crime Prevention.

Ludwig, J., Duncan, G. J., & Ladd, H. F. (2003). The effects of MTO on children and parents in Baltimore. In J. Goering & J. D. Feins (Eds.), *Choosing a better life?: Evaluating the moving to opportunity social experiment* (pp. 153–175). Washington, DC: The Urban Institute.

Lynch, M. (2003). Consequences of children's exposure to community violence. *Clinical Child and Family Psychology Review, 6,* 265–274.

Marans, S., & Schaefer, M. (1998). Community policing, schools, and mental health: The challenge of collaboration. In D. S. Elliott, B. A. Hamburg, & R. Williams (Eds.), *Violence in American schools: A new perspective* (pp. 312–347). New York: Cambridge University Press.

Mayer, D. P., Mullens, J. E., & Moore, M. T. (2000). *Monitoring school quality: An indicators report* (NCES 2001-030). Washington, DC: U.S. Department of Education.

Mayer, M. J., & Leone, P. E. (1999). A structural analysis of school violence and disruption: Implications for creating safer schools. *Education and Treatment of Children, 22,* 333–356.

Mayer, S. E., & Peterson, P. E. (Eds.). (1999). *Earning and learning: How schools matter.* Washington, DC: Russell Sage.

Mazza, J. J., & Reynolds, W. M. (1999). Exposure to violence in young inner-city adolescents: Relationships with suicidal ideation, depression, and PTSD symptomatology. *Journal of Abnormal Child Psychology, 27,* 203–213.

McLoyd, V. C. (1990). The impact of economic hardship on black families and children: Psychological distress, parenting, and socioemotional development. *Child Development, 61,* 311–346.

Menacker, J., Weldon, W., & Hurwitz, E. (1990). Community influences on school crime and violence. *Urban Education, 25,* 68–80.

Minino, A. M., & Smith, B. L. (2001). Deaths: Preliminary data for 2000. *National Vital Statistics Reports, 49*(12). Washington, DC: National Vital Statistics Program, National Center for Health Statistics, Centers for Disease Control and Prevention.

Morenoff, J. D., & Sampson, R. J. (1997). Violent crime and the spatial dynamics of neighborhood transition: Chicago, 1970–990. *Social Forces, 76,* 31–64.

Moses, A. (1999). Exposure to violence, depression, and hostility in a sample of inner city high school youth. *Journal of Adolescence, 22,* 21–32.

Muthén, L. K., & Muthén, B. O. (2004). *Mplus User's Guide* (3rd ed.). Los Angeles, CA: Muthén & Muthén.

Myers, M. A., & Thompson, V. L. S. (2000). The impact of violence exposure on African American youth in context. *Youth and Society, 32,* 253–267.

Nation, M., Crusto, C., Wandersman, A., Kumpfer, K. L., Seyboldt, D., Morrissey-Kane, E., & Davino, D. (2003). What works in prevention: Principles of effective prevention programs. *American Psychologist, 58,* 449–456.

National Center for Education Statistics. (2000). *Condition of America's public school facilities: 1999* (NCES 2000-032). Washington, DC: U.S. Department of Education.

National Center for Education Statistics. (2003). *Revenues and expenditures by public school districts: School year 1999–2000* (NCES 2003-407). Washington, DC: U.S. Department of Education, Institute of Education Sciences.

National Institute of Education. (1978). *Violent schools-safe schools: The Safe Schools Study report to Congress.* Washington, DC: U.S. Department of Education.

New Freedom Commission on Mental Health. (2003). *Achieving the promise: Transforming mental health care in America.* Final Report (Pub. No. SMA-03-3832). Rockville, MD: Department of Health and Human Services.

New York Police Department CompStat Unit. (2004). Citywide: Report covering the week of 1/12/2004 through 1/18/2004. *Compstat, 11*(3). Retrieved February 5, 2004, from http://www.nyc.gov/html/nypd/pdf/chfdept/csc-ity.pdf

New York State Education Department. (2001, April). *Project SAVE (safe schools against violence in education): Guidance document for school safety plans.* Albany, NY: University of the State of New York, State Education Department.

Office of Juvenile Justice and Delinquency Prevention. (2000). *Children as victims. 1999 National report series.* Washington, DC: Office of Justice Programs, U.S. Department of Justice.

Office of Safe and Drug-Free Schools, Department of Education. (2004). Partnerships in Character Education: Notice inviting applications for new awards for fiscal year (FY) 2004. Federal Register Doc. 04-3989, file 2-23-04.

Olweus, D. (1995). Bullying or peer abuse at school: Facts and interventions. *Current Directions in Psychological Science, 4,* 196–200.

Osofksy, J. (1995). The effects of exposure to violence on young children. *American Psychologist, 50,* 782–788.

Osterman, K. (2002). Schools as communities for students. In G. Furman (Ed.), *School as community: From promise to practice* (pp. 167–195). Albany, NY: State University of New York Press.

Otto, L. B., & Atkinson, M. P. (1997). Parental involvement and adolescent development. *Journal of Adolescent Research, 12,* 68–89.

Overstreet, S. (2000). Exposure to community violence: Defining the problem and understanding the consequences. *Journal of Child and Family Studies, 9,* 7–25.

Parcel, T. L., & Dufur, M. J. (2001). Capital at home and at school: Effects on child social adjustment. *Journal of Marriage and the Family, 63,* 32–47.

Perera, F. P., Rauh, V., Tsai, W. Y., Kinney, P. L., Camann, D. E., Barr, D. B., Garfinkel, R., Tu, Y-H., Diaz, D., Dietrich, J., & Whyatt, R. M. (2003). Effects of transplacental exposure to environmental pollutants on birth outcomes in a multi-ethnic population. *Environmental Health Perspectives, 111,* 201–05.

Perez-Smith, A., Spirito, A., & Boergers, J. (2002). Neighborhood predictors of hopelessness among adolescent suicide attempters: Preliminary investigation. *Suicide and Life-Threatening Behavior, 32,* 139–145.

Perry, K. E., & Weinstein, R. S. (1998). The social context of early schooling and children's school adjustment. *Educational Psychologist, 33,* 177–194.

Pinderhughes, E. E., Nix, R., Foster, M., Jones, D., & The Conduct Problems Prevention Research Group. (2001). Parenting in context: Impact of neighborhood poverty, residential instability, public services, social networks, and danger on parental behaviors. *Journal of Marriage and the Family, 63,* 941–953.

Prinz, R. J., Blechman, E. A., & Dumas, J. E. (1994). An evaluation of peer coping-skills training for childhood aggression. *Journal of Clinical Child Psychology, 23,*

193–203.

Rankin, B. H., & Quane, J. M. (2002). Social contexts and urban adolescent outcomes: The interrelated effects of neighborhoods, families, and peers on African-American youth. *Social Problems, 49*, 79–100.

Rasbash, J., Browne, W., Goldstein, H., Yang, M., Plewis, I., Healy, M., Woodhouse, G., Draper, D., Langford, I., & Lewis, T. (2002). *A user's guide to MLwiN.* London: Multilevel Models Project, University of London.

Raudenbush, S. W., Bryk, A. S., Cheong, Y. F., & Congdon, R. (2001). *HLM 5: Hierarchical Linear and Nonlinear Modeling* (2nd ed.). Lincolnwood, IL: Scientific Software International.

Reise, S. P., & Duan, N. (Eds.). (2003). *Multilevel modeling: Methodological advances, issues, and applications.* Mahwah, NJ: Erlbaum.

Resnick, M. D., Bearman, P. S., Blum, R. W., Bauman, K. E., Harris, K. M., Jones, J., Tabor, J., Beuhring, T., Sieving, R. E., Shew, M., Ireland, M., Bearinger, L. H., & Udry, J. R. (1997). Protecting adolescents from harm. Findings from the National Longitudinal Study on Adolescent Health. *Journal of the American Medical Association, 278*, 823–832.

Richters, J. E., & Martinez, P. E. (1990). *Things I have seen and heard: An interview for young children about exposure to violence.* Rockville, MD: Child and Adolescent Disorders Research Branch, Division of Clinical Research, National Institute of Mental Health.

Richters, J. E., & Martinez, P. E. (1993a). Children as victims of and witnesses to violence in a Washington, D. C. neighborhood. In L. A. Leavitt & N. A. Fox (Eds.), *The psychological effects of war and violence on children* (pp. 281–301). Mahwah, NJ: Erlbaum.

Richters, J. E., & Martinez, P. E. (1993b). The NIMH Community Violence Project: I. Children as victims of and witnesses to violence. *Psychiatry, 56*, 7–21.

Richters, J. E., & Martinez, P. E. (1993c). Violent communities, family choices, and children's chances: An algorithm for improving the odds. *Development and Psychopathology, 5*, 609–627.

Roeser, R. W., Eccles, J. S., & Sameroff, A. J. (2000). School as context of early adolescents' academic and social-emotional development: A summary of research findings. *The Elementary School Journal, 100*, 443–471.

Roeser, R. W., Eccles, J. S., & Strobel, K. R. (1998). Linking the study of schooling and mental health: Selected issues and empirical illustrations at the level of the individual. *Educational Psychologist, 33*, 153–176.

Rutter, M. (1980). School influences on children's behavior and development: The 1979 Kenneth Blackfan Lecture, Children's Hospital Medical Center, Boston. *Pediatrics, 65*, 208–220.

Ryan, R. M., & Grolnick, W. S. (1986) Origins and pawns in the classroom: Self-report and projective assessments of individual differences in children's perceptions. *Journal of Personality and Social Psychology, 50*, 550–558.

St. George, D. M. M., & Thomas, S. B. (1997). Perceived risk of fighting and actual fighting behavior among middle school students. *Journal of School Health, 67*, 178–181.

Salzinger, S., Feldman, R. S., Stockhammer, T., & Hood, J. (2002). An ecological framework for understanding risk for exposure to community violence and the effects of exposure on children and adolescents. *Aggression and Violent Behavior, 7*, 423–451.

Samples, F., & Aber, L. (1998). Evaluations of school-based violence prevention programs. In D. S. Elliott, B. A. Hamburg, & . R. Williams (Eds.), *Violence in American schools: A new perspective* (pp. 217–252). New York: Cambridge

University Press.

Sampson, R. J. (2001). How do communities undergird or undermine human development? Relevant contexts and social mechanisms. In A. Booth & A. C. Crouter (Eds.), *Does it take a village? Community effects on children, adolescents, and families* (pp. 3–30). Mahwah, NJ: Erlbaum.

Sampson, R. J., & Groves, W. B. (1989). Community structure and crime: Testing social-disorganization theory. *American Journal of Sociology, 94*, 774–780.

Sampson, R. J., Morenoff, J. D., & Gannon-Rowley, T. (2002). Assessing "neighborhood effects": Social processes and new directions in research. *Annual Review of Sociology, 28*, 443–478.

Sampson, R. J., Raudenbush, S. W., & Earls, F. (1997). Neighborhoods and violent crime: A multilevel study of collective efficacy. *Science, 277*, 918–924.

Sandoval, J., & Brock, S. E. (2002). School violence and disasters. In J. Sandoval (Ed.), *Handbook of crisis counseling, intervention, and prevention in the schools* (2nd ed., pp. 249–270). Mahwah, NJ: Erlbaum.

Schwab-Stone, M., Chen, C., Greenberger, E., Silver, D., Lichtman, J., & Voyce, C. (1999). No safe haven II: The effects of violence exposure on urban youth. *Journal of the American Academy of Child and Adolescent Psychiatry, 38*, 359–367.

Schwartz, D., & Proctor, L. J. (2000). Community violence exposure and children's social adjustment in the school peer group: The mediating roles of emotion regulation and social cognition. *Journal of Consulting and Clinical Psychology, 68*, 670–683.

Shahinfar, A., Kupersmidt, J. B., & Matza, L. S. (2001). The relation between exposure to violence and social information processing among incarcerated adolescents. *Journal of Abnormal Psychology, 110*, 136–141.

Shakoor, B. H., & Chalmers, D. (1991). Covictimization of African American children who witness violence: Effects on cognitive, emotional, and behavioral development. *Journal of the National Medical Association, 83*, 233–238.

Shaw, C., & McKay, H. D. (1942). *Juvenile delinquency and urban areas.* Chicago: University of Chicago Press.

Sheley, J. F., McGee, Z. T., & Wright, J. D. (1992). Gun-related violence in and around inner-city schools. *American Journal of Diseases of Children, 146*, 677–682.

Sherman, L. W., Gartin, P. R., & Buerger, M. E. (1989). Hot spots of predatory crime: Routine activities and the criminology of place. *Criminology, 27*, 27–56.

Simons, R. I., Johnson, C., Beaman, J. J., Conger, R. D., & Whitbeck, L. B. (1996). Parents and peer group as mediators of the effect of community structure on adolescent behavior. *American Journal of Community Psychology, 24*, 145–171.

Singer, M. I., Anglin, T. M., Song, L. Y., & Lunghofer, L. (1995). Adolescents' exposure to violence and associated symptoms of psychological trauma. *Journal of the American Medical Association, 273*, 477–482.

Small, S., & Supple, A. (2001). Communities as systems: Is a community more than the sum of its parts? In A. Booth & A. C. Crouter (Eds.), *Does it take a village? Community effects on children, adolescents, and families* (pp. 161–174). Mahwah, NJ: Erlbaum.

Snyder, H. N., & Sickmund, M. (1999). Violence after school. *Juvenile Justice Bulletin (NCJ 178992)* (pp. 1–8). Washington, DC: Office of Juvenile Justice and Delinquency Prevention, U.S. Department of Justice.

Staff, J., & Uggen, C. (2003). The fruits of good work: Early work experiences and adolescent deviance. *Journal of Research in Crime and Delinquency, 40*, 263–290.

Stein, B. D., Jaycox, L. H., Kataoka, S., Rhodes, H. J., & Vestal,

K. D. (2003). Prevalence of child and adolescent exposure to community violence. *Clinical Child and Family Psychology Review, 6*, 247–264.

Stephens, R. D. (1998). Safe school planning. In D. S. Elliott, B. A. Hamburg, & . R. Williams (Eds.), *Violence in American schools: A new perspective* (pp. 253–289). New York: Cambridge University Press.

Stiffman, A. R., Hadley-Ives, E., Elze, E., Johnson, S., & Doré, P. (1999). Impact of environment on adolescent mental health and behavior: Structural equation modeling. *American Journal of Orthopsychiatry, 69*, 73–6.

Teitler, J. O., & Weiss, C. C. (2000). Effects of neighborhood and school environments on transitions to first sexual intercourse. *Sociology of Education, 73*, 112–132.

Thornton, T. N., Craft, C. A., Dahlberg, L. L., Lynch, B. S., & Baer, K. (2002). *Best practices of youth violence prevention: A sourcebook for community action* (rev.). Atlanta, GA: Centers for Disease Control and Prevention, National Center for Injury Prevention and Control.

Uehara, E. S., Chalmers, D., Jenkins, E. J., & Shakoor, B. H. (1996). African American youth encounters with violence: Results from the community mental health council violence screening project. *Journal of Black Studies, 26*, 768–781.

U.S. Department of Education. (2000). *A back to school special report on the baby boom echo: Growing pains.* Washington, DC: Author. Retrieved January 5, 2004, from http://www.ed.gov/pubs/bbecho00/index.html.

U.S. Department of Education. (2003a, February). Choice Provisions in_*No Child Left Behind.* National Title I Directors' Conference. Washington, DC: No Child Left Behind, U. S. Department of Education. Retrieved from January 2, 2004, from http://www.ed.gov/admins/comm/parents/choice03/edlite-index.html

U.S. Department of Education. (2003b). *The facts about... School safety.* Washington, DC: No Child Left Behind, U. S. Department of Education. Retrieved January 2, 2003, from http://www.ed.gov/nclb/freedom/safety/keepingkids.html.

Wandersman, A., & Florin, P. (2003). Community interventions and effective prevention. *American Psychologist, 58*, 441–448.

Warner, B. S., Weist, M. D., & Krulak, A. (1999). Risk factors for school violence. *Urban Education, 34*, 52–68.

Watson, M. S., Battistich, V., & Solomon, S. (1997). Enhancing students' social and ethical development in schools: An intervention program and its effects. *International Journal of Educational Research, 27*, 571–586.

Weimer, D. L., & Wolkoff, M. J. (2001). School performance and housing values: Using non-contiguous district and incorporation boundaries to identify school effects. *National Tax Journal, 54*, 231–253.

Weller, N. F., Kelder, S. H., Cooper, S. P., Basen-Engquist, K., & Tortolero, S. R. (2003). School-year employment among high school students: Effects on academic, social, and physical functioning. *Adolescence, 38*, 441–458.

Werthamer-Larsson, L., Kellam, S., & Wheeler, L. (1991). Effect of first-grade classroom environment on shy behavior, aggressive behavior, and concentration problems. *American Journal of Community Psychology, 19*, 585–602.

Williams, J. H., Ayers, C. D., & Arthur, M. W. (1997). Risk and protective factors in the development of delinquency and conduct disorder. In M. W. Fraser (Ed.), *Risk and resilience in childhood: An ecological perspective* (pp. 140–170). Washington, DC: NASW Press.

Wilson, W. J. (1987). *The truly disadvantaged: The inner city, the underclass, and public policy.* Chicago: University of Chicago Press.

Wirt, J., Choy, S., Provasnik, S., Rooney, P., Sen, A., Tobin, R., Kridl, B., & Livingston, A. (2003). *The condition of education: 2003* (NCES 2003-067). Washington, DC: National Center for Education Statistics, Institute of Education Sciences, U.S. Department of Education. Retrieved January 5, 2003, from http://nces.ed.gov/pubs2003/2003067.pdf.

Author Index

Subject Index

Printed in the United States
100424LV00001BA/11-28/A

9 781841 694153